African American National Biography

African American National Biography

SECOND EDITION

HENRY LOUIS GATES JR.

EVELYN BROOKS HIGGINBOTHAM

Editors in Chief

VOLUME 2: BLAKE, EUBIE – CHAMBERS, PAUL

OXFORD

UNIVERSITY PRESS

OXFORD
UNIVERSITY PRESS

Oxford University Press is a department of the University of Oxford.
It furthers the University's objective of excellence in research, scholarship,
and education by publishing worldwide.

Oxford   New York
Auckland   Cape Town   Dar es Salaam   Hong Kong   Karachi
Kuala Lumpur   Madrid   Melbourne   Mexico City   Nairobi
New Delhi   Shanghai   Taipei   Toronto

With offices in
Argentina   Austria   Brazil   Chile   Czech Republic   France   Greece
Guatemala   Hungary   Italy   Japan   Poland   Portugal   Singapore
South Korea   Switzerland   Thailand   Turkey   Ukraine   Vietnam

Oxford is a registered trademark of Oxford University Press in the UK and certain other countries.

Published in the United States of America by
Oxford University Press
198 Madison Avenue, New York, NY 10016

Library of Congress Cataloging-in-Publication Data
African American national biography / editors in chief Henry Louis Gates Jr., Evelyn Brooks Higginbotham. – 2nd ed.
p. cm.
Includes bibliographical references and index.
ISBN 978-0-19-999036-8 (volume 1; hdbk.); ISBN 978-0-19-999037-5 (volume 2; hdbk.); ISBN 978-0-19-999038-2 (volume 3; hdbk.);
ISBN 978-0-19-999039-9 (volume 4; hdbk.); ISBN 978-0-19-999040-5 (volume 5; hdbk.); ISBN 978-0-19-999041-2 (volume 6; hdbk.);
ISBN 978-0-19-999042-9 (volume 7; hdbk.); ISBN 978-0-19-999043-6 (volume 8; hdbk.); ISBN 978-0-19-999044-3 (volume 9; hdbk.);
ISBN 978-0-19-999045-0 (volume 10; hdbk.); ISBN 978-0-19-999046-7 (volume 11; hdbk.); ISBN 978-0-19-999047-4 (volume 12;
hdbk.); ISBN 978-0-19-992077-8 (12-volume set; hdbk.)
1. African Americans – Biography – Encyclopedias.   2. African Americans – History – Encyclopedias.
I. Gates, Henry Louis.   II. Higginbotham, Evelyn Brooks, 1945-
E185.96.A4466 2012
920'.009296073 – dc23
[B]
2011043281

1 3 5 7 9 8 6 4 2
Printed in the United States of America
on acid-free paper

African American National Biography

B CONTINUED

Blake, Eubie (7 Feb. 1883–12 Feb. 1983), composer and pianist, was born James Hubert Blake in Baltimore, Maryland, the son of John Sumner Blake, a stevedore, and Emily Johnston, a launderer. His father was a Civil War veteran, and both parents were former slaves. While the young Blake was a mediocre student during several years of public schooling, he showed early signs of musical interest and talent, picking out tunes on an organ in a department store at about age six. As a result, his parents rented an organ for twenty-five cents a week, and he soon began basic keyboard lessons with Margaret Marshall, a neighbor and church organist. At about age twelve he learned cornet and buck dancing and was earning pocket change singing with friends on the street. When he was thirteen, he received encouragement from the ragtime pianist Jesse Pickett, whom he had watched through the window of a bawdy house in order to learn his fingering. By 1898 he had steady work as a piano player in Aggie Shelton's sporting house, a job that necessitated the lad's sneaking out of his home at night, after his parents went to bed. The objections of his deeply religious mother when she learned of his new career were overcome only by the pragmatism of his sporadically employed father, once he discovered how much his son was making in tips.

In 1899 (the year SCOTT JOPLIN's famous "Maple Leaf Rag" appeared), Blake wrote his first rag, "Charleston Rag" (although he would not be able to notate it until some years later). In 1902 he performed as a buck dancer in the traveling minstrel show *In Old Kentucky*, playing briefly in New York City. In 1907, after playing in several clubs in Baltimore, he became a pianist at the Goldfield Hotel, built by his friend and the new world lightweight boxing champion JOE GANS. The elegant Goldfield was one of the first establishments in Baltimore where blacks and whites mixed, and there Blake acquired a personal grace and polish that would impress his admirers for the rest of his life. Already an excellent player, he learned from watching the conservatory-trained "One-Leg Willie" Joseph, whom he often cited as the best piano player he had ever heard. While at the Goldfield, Blake studied composition with the Baltimore musician Llewellyn Wilson, and at about the same time he began playing summers in Atlantic City, where he met such keyboard luminaries as WILLIE "THE LION" SMITH, LUCKEY ROBERTS, and JAMES P. JOHNSON. In July 1910 he married Avis Lee, the daughter of a black society family in Baltimore and a classically trained pianist.

In 1915 Blake met the singer and lyricist NOBLE SISSLE, and they quickly began a songwriting collaboration that would last for decades. One of their songs of that year, "It's All Your Fault," achieved success when it was introduced by Sophie Tucker. Sissle and Blake also performed in New York with JAMES REESE EUROPE's Society Orchestra. While Sissle and Europe were in the service during World War I, Blake performed in vaudeville with Henry "Broadway" Jones. After the war Sissle and Blake formed a vaudeville act called the Dixie Duo, which became quite successful. In an era when blacks were expected to shuffle and speak in dialect, they dressed elegantly in tuxedos, and they were one of the first black acts to perform before

Eubie Blake, veteran jazz pianist performs during his surprise birthday party, New York's Waldorf Astoria Hotel, 7 February 1976. (AP Images.)

white audiences without burnt cork. By 1917 Blake also had begun recording on both disks and piano rolls. In 1920 Sissle and Blake met the successful comedy and dance team of Flournoy Miller and Aubrey Lyles, who suggested combining forces to produce a show. The result was the all-black *Shuffle Along*, which opened on Broadway in 1921 and for which Blake was composer and conductor. The score included what would become one of his best-known songs, "I'm Just Wild about Harry." Mounted on a shoestring budget, the musical met with critical acclaim and popular success, running for 504 performances in New York, followed by an extensive three-company tour of the United States. The show had a tremendous effect on musical theater, stirring interest in jazz dance, fostering faster paced shows with more syncopated rhythms, and paving the way in general for more black musicals and black performers. *Shuffle Along* was a springboard for the careers of several of its cast members, including JOSEPHINE BAKER, ADELAIDE HALL, FLORENCE MILLS, and PAUL ROBESON.

Sissle and Blake worked for ten years as songwriters for the prestigious Witmark publishing firm. In 1922, through Julius Witmark, they were able to join ASCAP (American Society of Composers, Authors, and Publishers), which did not at that time include many blacks. They also appeared in an early sound film in 1923, *Sissle and Blake's Snappy Songs*, produced by the electronics pioneer Lee De Forest. In 1924 they created an ambitious new show, *The Chocolate Dandies*. Unable to match the success of *Shuffle Along*, the lavish production lost money, but Blake was proud of its score and considered it his best.

The team returned to vaudeville, ending their long collaboration with a successful eight-month tour of Great Britain in 1925–1926. The two broke up when Sissle, attracted by opportunities in Europe, returned to work there; Blake, delighted to be back home in New York, refused to accompany him. Over the next few years Blake collaborated with Harry Creamer to produce a few songs and shows; reunited with "Broadway" Jones to perform the shortened "tab show" *Shuffle Along Jr.* in vaudeville (1928–1929); and teamed with the lyricist ANDY RAZAF to write songs for *Lew Leslie's Blackbirds of 1930*, including "Memories of You," later popularized by Benny Goodman. After Lyles's death in 1932, Sissle and Blake reunited with Miller to create *Shuffle Along of 1933*, but the show failed, in part because of the Depression. The remainder of the decade saw Blake collaborating with the lyricist Milton Reddie on a series of shows, including the Works Progress Administration–produced *Swing It* in 1937, and with Razaf on several floor shows and "industrials" (promotional shows). Blake's wife died of tuberculosis in 1939, but despite his grief he managed to complete, with Razaf, the show *Tan Manhattan*.

During World War II, Blake toured with United Service Organizations shows and worked with other collaborators. In 1945 he married Marion Gant Tyler, a business executive and former showgirl in several black musicals. She took over management of his financial affairs and saw to the raising of his ASCAP rating to an appropriate level, enhancing their financial security considerably.

After the war, at the age of sixty-three, Blake took the opportunity to attend New York University, where he studied the Schillinger system of composition. He graduated with a degree in music in 1950. Meanwhile, the presidential race of 1948 stirred renewed interest in "I'm Just Wild about Harry" when Harry Truman adopted it as a campaign song. This resulted in a reuniting of Sissle and Blake and in a revival in 1952 of *Shuffle Along*. Unfortunately, the producers' attempts to completely rewrite the show had the effect of eviscerating it, and the restaging closed after only four performances.

Following a few years of relative retirement, during which Blake wrote out some of his earlier pieces, a resurgence of popular interest in ragtime in the 1950s and again in the 1970s thrust him back into the spotlight for the last decades of his life. Several commemorative recordings appeared, most notably, *The Eighty-six Years of Eubie Blake*, a two-record retrospective with Noble Sissle for Columbia in 1969. In 1972 he started Eubie Blake Music, a record company featuring his own music. He was much in demand as a speaker and performer, impressing audiences with his still considerable pianistic technique as well as his energy, audience rapport, and charm as a raconteur. Appearances included the St. Louis Ragfest, the Newport Jazz Festival, the *Tonight Show*, a solo concert at Town Hall in New York City, and a concert in his honor by Arthur Fiedler and the Boston Pops in 1973, with Blake as soloist. In 1974 Jean-Cristophe Averty produced a four-hour documentary film on Blake's life and music for French television. The musical revue *Eubie!*, featuring twenty-three of his numbers, opened on Broadway in 1978 and ran for a year. Blake was awarded the Presidential Medal of Freedom at the White House in 1981.

Blake's wife, Marion, died in June 1982; he left no children by either of his marriages. A few months after his wife's death, his hundredth birthday was feted with performances of his music, but he was ill with pneumonia and unable to attend. He died five days later in New York City.

Over a long career as pianist, composer, and conductor, Blake left a legacy of more than two thousand compositions in various styles. His earliest pieces were piano rags, often of such extreme difficulty that they were simplified for publication. As a ragtime composer and player, he, along with such figures as Luckey Roberts and James P. Johnson, was a key influence on the Harlem stride-piano school of the 1930s. In the field of show music, Blake moved beyond the confines of ragtime, producing songs that combined rhythmic energy with an appealing lyricism. Particularly notable was his involvement with the successful *Shuffle Along*, which put blacks back on the Broadway stage after an absence of more than ten years. Over his lifetime he displayed a marked openness to musical growth, learning from "all music, particularly the music of Mozart, Chopin, Tchaikovsky, Victor Herbert, Gershwin, Debussy, and Strauss," and, indeed, some of his less well known pieces show these influences. Finally, his role in later years as an energetic "elder statesman of ragtime" provided a historical link to a time long gone as well as inspiration to many younger fans.

FURTHER READING

Blake's papers are at the Maryland Historical Society in Baltimore.

Jasen, David A., and Trebor Jay Tichenor. *Rags and Ragtime: A Musical History* (1978).

Kimball, Robert, and William Bolcom. *Reminiscing with Sissle and Blake* (1973).

Rose, Al. *Eubie Blake* (1979).

Southern, Eileen. *The Music of Black Americans: A History* (1971; 2d ed., 1983).

This entry is taken from the *American National Biography* and is published here with the permission of the American Council of Learned Societies.

WILLIAM G. ELLIOTT

Blake, Margaret Jane (c. 1811–10 Mar. 1880), slave and later servant, was born in Baltimore, Maryland, to Perry Blake, a free African American, and his wife Charlotte, a slave in the household of a prominent merchant, Jesse Levering. The couple had several other children. In 1897 Jesse's daughter Sarah R. Levering published a booklet about Margaret Jane Blake's life through the Press of Innes & Son in Philadelphia. As of 2011, other sources concerning Blake's life were unknown. Thus we should read this account with care, recognizing that it provides only one perspective on Blake's life, and that it comes from a member of the family who once owned her. It nonetheless offers several insights on the life of an urban African American woman in slavery and freedom. Levering designated the proceeds from the booklet's sale to a Presbyterian-affiliated "manual labor school for the benefit of the Afro-American citizens, as they prefer being called" (Levering, pp. v–vi).

Perry Blake served as a U.S. Navy marine during the War of 1812. When the British attacked Baltimore, the men in the Levering household took up arms. Charlotte Blake supplied them with food. For her "unremitting and cheerful service during this anxious time" (Levering, pp. 7–8), Jesse Levering manumitted her. Sarah Levering states that Charlotte Blake tried unsuccessfully to return to slavery, then arranged for her children to remain in bonds.

Margaret Jane Blake cleaned the house and tended Sarah R. Levering, born in 1825. It is unclear whether Blake ever learned to read. Levering does note that Blake resisted male attentions and offers of marriage because she did not want to create new slaves. Blake never wed or had biological children. At the same time, Levering presents her as critical of abolitionists.

Blake injured herself in a fall as a young woman. She suffered severe pain and periods of inactivity the rest of her life. After Jesse's death in 1832, the Leverings' wealth diminished. They hired Blake out to work in other households. When the Leverings moved outside Baltimore, "Blake … was allowed to remain there. From that time she went and came as suited her, and never was with us but as an invalid to be nursed or as a visitor to be entertained." The Leverings agreed "to allow Blake to buy herself … [B]efore Blake was old, she had her free papers" (Levering, p. 18).

She then worked as a household servant for the Baltimore railroad magnate Walter Booth Brooks, caring for his children, including his daughter Eleanor. On 23 October 1873, at Baltimore's Brown Memorial Presbyterian Church, Eleanor Brooks married William Grigsby McCormick. The groom came from Chicago's wealthy McCormick family, who started the company eventually called International Harvester. Levering writes:

"Mammy Blake [brought] up the rear of the bridal procession … the crowning indulgence of the life of the affectionate servant" (Levering, p. 20). Blake then moved to Chicago with the couple and cared for their children.

At about age sixty-nine, while on a visit back to her hometown, Margaret Jane Blake died in the Baltimore Infirmary from erysipelas, a virulent skin infection. She was buried in Laurel Cemetery under a headstone that Eleanor Brooks McCormick had inscribed "Faithful unto Death." Sarah Levering comments that "fidelity was the keynote of [Blake's] life… he served her masters well … [and] held her faith … in childlike simplicity" (Levering, 21).

Because the biography is replete with such statements, late twentieth- and early twenty-first-century scholars categorize Levering's biography among the many "unreliable" slave narratives. White authors or editors have burdened these stories so much with their own ideologies and biases, "there is little room for the testimony" of the slaves themselves and "few of the details of slave life are revealed" (Blassingame, xxviiii). Thus Levering's narrative leaves a legacy of important questions. Did Charlotte Blake really want to return herself to slavery and keep her children there? If so, why? What actually were Margaret Jane Blake's views of abolitionists?

Considering Blake's own decisions about marriage and motherhood for herself, what did it mean to her from her own perspective to participate in the Brooks-McCormick wedding party and help raise three generations of prosperous white children? Levering describes Blake as happy in these activities. Yet she also describes Blake as "unwilling to breed slaves for any master." Levering further comments: "If all the bondwomen had been of the same mind, how soon the institution would have vanished from the earth, and all the misery belonging to it been lifted from the hearts of the holders and the slaves!" (Levering, p. 13). This part of Levering's narrative most contradicts or complicates her stereotypical portrayals of Blake as a "Mammy" in ever-loyal service to ever-benevolent slavemasters and employers. Yet Levering's account still leaves unanswered the many questions it raises about Blake's own vantage points on the institutions of slavery and domestic service.

FURTHER READING

Blassingame, John W. *Slave Testimony: Two Centuries of Letters, Speeches, Interviews, and Autobiographies* (1977).

Davis, Charles Twitchell, and Henry Louis Gates Jr.,
eds., *The Slave's Narrative* (1991).

Giddings, Paula. *Where and When I Enter: The Impact of Black Women on Race and Sex in America* (2001).

Levering, Sarah R. *Memoirs of Margaret Jane Blake of Baltimore, Md.: And Selections in Prose and Verse* (1897).

MARY KRANE DERR

Blake, Robert (c. 1836–?), Medal of Honor winner, was born into slavery in Santee, South Carolina. When war came he was a slave on the Arthur Blake Plantation on the South Santee River, McClellanville, South Carolina, possibly the same plantation on which he was born. The Blake Plantation, one of many rice plantations in the area, was no small affair; according to the 1860 census it had 538 enslaved men and women and was the twelfth largest plantation in the country. When the Union navy invaded the coastal areas of South Carolina, it not only created widespread panic among slave-holders but also influenced many of those who were enslaved to emancipate themselves and flee to freedom. In May 1862, with the Union navy off the coast of South Carolina, Robert Blake and four others, Prince, Michael, Jack, and Captain Blake, fled the Blake Plantation. All were picked up by the Union navy's *Gem of the Sea* off Georgetown, South Carolina, and would soon thereafter enlist in the Union navy as "contrabands."

The importance of contraband sailors to the manning of the Union navy during the Civil War was considerable. Of the estimated eighteen thousand African Americans that served in the Union navy during the war, only four thousand (of those whose native state is known) were born in free states. The remainder, over eleven thousand, including men such as Robert Blake and ROBERT SMALLS, were born in slave states, with the likelihood that only a fraction of this number was born free. Over one thousand former slaves alone enlisted in the South Atlantic Blockade Squadron from South Carolina, Georgia, and Florida.

African American sailors who entered the Union navy from slave states were called "contrabands" because they were legally considered part of the property seizures made against belligerents of the United States (that is, any slave owner), an idea conceived early in the war by General Benjamin Butler. Legally, the status of these individuals was ambiguous until they were formally made free through Abraham Lincoln's Emancipation Proclamation on 1 January 1863. Prior to this time those formerly enslaved individuals that were either "captured" or were "self-emancipated" and sought refuge with Union forces were often set up in temporary camps and employed by the government, or enlisted to serve in the military.

Robert Blake would choose the later of the options listed above and immediately joined the Union navy, enlisting as a "First Class Boy" on 15 June 1862 aboard the *Gem of the Sea*. He listed his birthplace as Santee, South Carolina, his age twenty-six, and his height at five feet six inches. Enlisting along with Robert were the other men that escaped from the Blake Plantation. One of them, Captain Blake, was called "a good pilot of all the inland creeks and rivers from the South Santee to Savannah" (King, 5). Because all slaves from the plantation carried the last name of their master, it is unknown if Robert and Captain Blake were related. Even lacking a family connection, it may be that Robert learned a bit about sailoring from Blake and, as events would later prove, turned out to be a fine addition to the Union navy.

Upon joining, Robert Blake served on the *Gem of the Sea* until 1 October 1862, at which time he was transferred for duty on the steamer *Norwich*. He would continue on this vessel for the next year, taking part in the ship's actions as part of the South Atlantic Blockade Squadron. Every indication is that Robert Blake was a diligent sailor, enjoying his newfound freedom by practicing his duties faithfully. He would experience his first fighting on 10 March 1863 when the *Norwich* escorted Union transports up the St. John's River and shelled Confederate positions near Jacksonville, Florida. Among the fellow contrabands serving with Blake at this time was Frederick Gardiner, a Jacksonville river pilot.

On 1 October 1863 Robert Blake was temporarily assigned for duty on board the *Marblehead*. The transfer may have been occasioned by the ship's pending operations off the coast of South Carolina, an area familiar to Blake. Whatever the reason, Blake's transfer would soon prove prophetic. Several months later, on Christmas day, the *Marblehead* was in operation on the Stono River off Legareville, South Carolina, and engaged Confederate positions on John's Island. The action was heavy and the *Marblehead* was hit twenty times by Confederate artillery. The ship's commander, Richard W. Meade Jr., however, could not help but notice the actions of the contraband Robert Blake. He would later report that Blake "excited my admiration by the cool and brave manner in which he served the rifle gun" (Quarles, 231). In the end, the men of the *Marblehead* prevailed and the Confederates retreated from the island, leaving their munitions behind. For his action on 25 December 1863 Robert Blake was awarded the Medal of Honor, the first African American sailor to be so honored.

Following this historic achievement Robert Blake continued in the Union navy, and was later advanced in rate from "boy" to seaman. Just six days after the action on the Stono River he returned to duty aboard the *Norwich*; here he would serve until his naval service ended on 31 March 1865. Blake was mustered out of the service aboard the bark *Gem of the Sea*, the ship on which he had first gained his freedom. After the war the exact fate of Robert Blake is uncertain. It is unknown whether he kept the last name of Blake or, like so many newly freed slaves, shed the name of his former master and took on a new identity. Perhaps he is the same Robert Blake that lived in King William County, Acquinton Township, Virginia, after the war and married, had a family, and worked as a farmer into the 1880s. Whatever his final fate Robert Blake, who transformed himself from a slave to a sailor defending his newfound freedom and that of countless others, will always have an honored place in America's hall of heroes.

FURTHER READING

King, Lisa Y. "They Called Us Bluejackets," *International Journal of Naval History* 1.1 (Apr. 2002).

Quarles, Benjamin. *The Negro in the Civil War* (1953).

Reidy, Joseph P. "Black Men in Navy Blue during the Civil War," *Prologue Magazine* 33.3 (Fall 2001).

United States Navy. *Medal of Honor, 1861–1949: The Navy* (1950).

GLENN ALLEN KNOBLOCK

Blakeley, Adeline (10 July 1850?–?), former slave from Fayetteville, Arkansas, was born on 10 July 1850 in Hickman County, Tennessee. She was aged eighty-seven years in 1937, when she was interviewed as part of the New Deal Works Progress Administration's Slave Narrative project. She was interviewed by Mary D. Hudgins, a grand-niece of the woman for whom Blakeley had worked in Fayetteville, Arkansas. Thus, as with other WPA narratives, Blakeley's testimony should be interpreted within the context of the unequal relationships between blacks and whites under slavery and in the Jim Crow South. According to her interviewer, she had become quite assimilated into white society

and spoke with no discernable dialect. She also occupied a relatively high position within the inner social circle of the woman for whom she worked as a servant, as the friends and acquaintances of her deceased employer, Mrs. Hudgins, regularly came to visit Blakeley, whom they considered an old friend. Blakeley even pointed out that she had cared for five generations of the interviewer's family. This close relationship between Blakeley and the family of Ms. Hudgins includes some inherent biases. The vast majority of former slaves in the segregated south did not maintain such high status within white society, and the close familial bonds between Blakeley, her former masters, and the interviewer obviously make this an exceptional case. Despite the limitations of using this single narrative as the only source, Adeline Blakeley's experiences nonetheless bequeath for posterity some valuable insights into the life of a domestic slave living on the front lines of the Civil War in the Old Southwest.

According to the narrative, while a slave, Blakeley had initially belonged to a Mr. John P. Parks, a Tennessee slaveowner, who had purchased her mother as a child. Parks moved Blakeley and her mother to Arkansas when Adeline was just a year old, and they lived near what was called Hog Eye and then Hillingsley but eventually became known as Prairie Grove, located near the state's western border. A domestic slave in the Parks home, Blakeley credited the Parks family with treating her "like a plaything." They "spoiled me-rotten" she claimed (quoted in Rawick, 180). At age five, Blakeley was given to the Parks's daughter on the occasion of her marriage; young Adeline joined the Blakeley family and adopted their surname.

Blakeley mistakenly believed that laws existed in Arkansas prohibited slaves from being educated, perhaps because those laws existed in many other southern states. Blakeley noted her desire to learn as a young girl but that she feared that it would be discovered, and she recalled the story of how hard things were made for a slave woman she knew who had dared to be literate. After the war, she recalled that folks tried to educate her but she regrettably resisted their overtures—"it sounds funny, but if I had a million dollars, I would give it gladly to be able to read and write letters to my friends" (in Rawick, 183).

Adeline Blakeley's owners, like a minority of Arkansas slaveholders, were seemingly of the Unionist persuasion. Mr. Blakeley was not well enough to fight in the war, while Mr. Parks, who opposed secession as long as he felt it was safe to do so, had two sons and a son-in-law fight in the Civil War—one was killed at Gettysburg. Adeline remembered the little Blakeley boy playing outside with an American flag, but soon his mother forced him to bring it inside to avoid the harassment from Confederate supporters. During the war, Blakeley's town changed hands quite often, though the Union Army controlled the region. The federal soldiers built barracks and camped all over the surrounding area, and Blakeley remembered dead men's feet sticking out of the windows of the makeshift hospital they created across the street. She was even paid to cook for the troops. Adeline Blakeley claimed that the Blakeley family were good cooks, so the northern troops asked them to prepare their rations, which she believed was critical in sustaining them and getting them through the tough war years. In fact, sometimes the only food the Blakeley family had consisted of leftovers from what they helped prepare for the federal soldiers.

From Blakeley's point of view, northerners and southerners often worked together. For example, during a bombardment of the town, she and her master's family welcomed a northern officer's wife into their cellar. Blakeley's mistress even slapped her when she laughed at the woman's fat legs, which was one of the only times Mrs. Blakeley ever struck Adeline. After the war was over, Adeline decided to remain with her white former masters. When the federal troops accused the Blakeley's of keeping Adeline against her will, she assured them that she had stayed on her own accord. Whites let her be, but her fellow African Americans objected to her decision, calling her names and even picking fights with her. Blakeley claimed that the years after the war remained quite difficult. Eventually, things gradually improved—Nora Blakeley ultimately married Harvey M. Hudgins and opened up a hotel, and Adeline listed attending the Barnum & Bailey's Circus as an especially memorable highlight of her postwar days. In summation of her life, Adeline Blakeley could not decide which juncture of her life had been the best or "whether it's a better world now or then" (in Rawick, 193).

FURTHER READING

Rawick, George P., ed. *The American Slave: A Composite Autobiography* (1972). See volume 8, part 1, pp. 180–193.

Taylor, Orville W. *Negro Slavery in Arkansas* (1958).

JOHN FRENCH

Blakely, Allison (31 Mar. 1940–), historian, author, and university professor, was born in Clinton,

Alabama, to Ed Walton and Alice Blakely, sharecroppers. When Blakely was young his mother moved north to secure better employment, and he was raised by a great aunt in the coal-mining town of Preco, near Birmingham. In 1946 his mother returned to Alabama and moved him and his older sister to Oregon, where Alice Blakely had worked as a seamstress and in the Portland shipyards during World War II.

An avid reader since his early years, Blakely particularly enjoyed Russian literature and studied the Russian language in both high school and college. His interest in revolutions and popular democracy further stimulated his interest in Russian history. He received a B.A. from the University of Oregon in 1962, where he majored in history and was elected to Phi Beta Kappa. He also graduated as a Distinguished Military Graduate in the Army Reserve Officers Training Corps (ROTC). Blakely then pursued graduate studies in Russian and modern European history at the University of California at Berkeley, where he received his M.A. and Ph.D. in 1964 and 1971, respectively. These studies, however, were interrupted by his fulfillment of a two-year military service ROTC obligation. He served as an army intelligence officer and attained the rank of captain during the Vietnam War. Wounded in combat, Blakely was awarded both a Bronze Star and a Purple Heart in 1968. That same year, he married Shirley Ann Reynolds, a nutritional scientist. They had two children.

A recipient of the Woodrow Wilson Fellowship that encouraged fellows to consider teaching at historically black colleges and universities (HBCUs), Blakely was recruited to teach Russian history at Howard University in 1971, after having taught one year as an instructor in the Western civilization program at Stanford University. During three decades at Howard, Blakely rose in the academic ranks, becoming a full professor and also serving in various high academic and administrative posts that included associate dean of the College of Arts and Sciences and director of the honors program. As a professor of European history at Howard University he developed a particular interest in the interconnections between European history and the African diaspora. Professor Blakely's scholarly interests were also stimulated by both his own personal background—an African American who lived mostly in predominantly white areas since leaving his native Alabama at the age of six—and his interest in comparative history, revolutionary change, and the evolution of color prejudice.

His first book, *Russia and the Negro: Blacks in Russian History and Thought* (1986), was widely and generally positively reviewed in both general and Russian historical journals and was awarded the American Book Award from the Before Columbus Foundation in 1988. This unique work examines the historical Russian attitudes toward Africans, the black diaspora, native Russians of African descent (for example, Alexander Pushkin), and the experiences of numerous African American writers and political activists who either lived in Russia or were active in the international communist movement.

His interest in comparative history and revolution further spurred him to do research at the International Institute for Social History in Amsterdam. While in the Netherlands, Blakely became acutely aware of the racism directed against recent immigrants from the former Dutch colony of Surinam who had moved to Holland after their country became independent. Since the Dutch strongly perceived themselves as both liberal and tolerant, Blakely thought it would be a "fascinating case study" to examine their historical attitudes toward blacks. In 1988 he authored *Blacks in the Dutch World: The Evolution of Racial Imagery in a Modern Society*, an extensive survey of the depiction of blacks in Dutch folklore, painting, literature, and religion since the fifteenth century. This pathbreaking work received much praise—although not without criticism—from African, Dutch, and other European historians. Writing in the *Journal of Interdisciplinary History*, a reviewer described the book as "provocative and exceptionally well written—a significant contribution to the history of Dutch overseas expansion," while a University of Utrecht professor observed in the *Journal of African History* that "Blakely detects facts about Dutch culture and society which somehow elude many Dutch historians."

Blakely's writings influenced a generation of African diaspora scholars. In the last decades of the twentieth century and the first years of the twenty-first century his seminal studies have been acknowledged in works written by scholars in Japan, England, Holland, and other European countries, as well as the United States. The editor of the *Russian Review* noted that one of Blakely's articles published in that influential publication was a "landmark" in redefining the issues in the American historiography of Russia. Fluent in Dutch and Russian and working also extensively with French and German sources, Blakely complemented his books through the publication of numerous journal articles, book chapters

and conference papers. In 2001 Boston University recruited Blakely for a joint appointment as professor of European and comparative history and professor of African American studies. In 2003 he was designated as the first incumbent of the newly endowed George and Joyce Wein Professorship in African American studies. His teaching career included visiting professorships at Spelman College and the École des Hautes Études en Sciences Sociales in Paris and affiliations with Johns Hopkins University and the University of Leiden in the Netherlands. Blakely received many academic fellowships, grants, and honors, including the Ford Foundation Postdoctoral Fellowship, the Fulbright-Hays Research Fellowship, the National Defense Foreign Language Fellowship, the National Endowment for the Humanities Traveling Fellowship, and the Mellon Fellowship at the Aspen Institute. An elected senator of the Phi Beta Kappa Society, he also served on the editorial board of its quarterly journal, the *American Scholar*. In 2006 he became the president of this prestigious academic honor society.

Blakely's career was inspired by a number of influences, but especially that of his mother Alice, a deeply religious woman who valued education, though she herself only reached the sixth grade. She instilled in him pride in his background and taught him not to "hate people although you may hate the bad things people do." In 1997 Allison Blakely endowed the Alice Blakely Brink Memorial Scholarship to help needy students attend the University of Oregon.

FURTHER READING

Blakely, Allison. "American Influences on Russian Reformist Thought in the Era of the French Revolution," *Russian Review* 52 (Oct. 1993).

Jordan, Winthrop. "Allison Blakely. "*Blacks in the Dutch World: The Evolution of Racial Imagery in a Modern Society*," *American Historical Review*, vol. 99, no. 4 (1994).

Kuitenbrouwer, Maarten. "*Blacks in the Dutch World: The Evolution of Racial Imagery in a Modern Society* by Allison Blakely," *Journal of African History*, vol. 36, no. 3 (1995).

Postma, Johannes. "*Blacks in the Dutch World: The Evolution of Racial Imagery in a Modern Society* by Allison Blakely," *Journal of Interdisciplinary History*, vol. 26, no. 4 (1996).

DONALD ALTSCHILLER

Blakely, Nora Brooks (8 Sept. 1951–), teacher, poet, playwright, and artistic director of a theater company, was born Nora Brooks Blakely in Chicago, one of two children of poet GWENDOLYN BROOKS and Henry Blakely, a poet, auto mechanic, and insurance adjuster. Blakely's mother was a leading figure in the Black Arts Movement, the poet laureate of Illinois, and the first African American to receive the Pulitzer Prize, which she did in 1950, just a year before Nora's birth. Nora's father was the author of *A Windy Place*, a 1974 collection of poetry, and he later founded the Perspectivists, a group of black Chicago writers. As a child, Nora displayed a natural ability and love for reading and writing, no doubt cultivated by her parents' passion for the same.

A propensity for teaching emerged early as well; at the age of three Blakely rounded up the children of her South Side Chicago neighborhood and taught lessons in the pretend classroom in her backyard. Her parents emphasized learning and knowledge, and they taught their daughter the importance of understanding and being able to articulate her beliefs. For instance, Blakely remembers once announcing that she supported John F. Kennedy for president, a preference in line with the rest of her family's views, but her parents would not accept this as justification; they pressed her to explain her inclination with solid reasons and logic (Kent, 148).

Blakely was educated at Hirsch High School in Chicago and graduated in 1968. After a short tour of France and England, she enrolled at the University of Illinois. While in college she had the opportunity to further her foreign travels, studying briefly at the University of Dar es Salaam in Tanzania. Blakely received her B.A. in Education from the University of Illinois at the age of twenty and, in her own words, "assumed that I was going to be teaching until they rolled me out of the classroom in a wheelchair" (Whitaker, 122). After receiving her degree she taught in the Chicago public school systems for eight years, but she eventually became frustrated with a lack of administrative support and failed attempts at reaching some of the more apathetic, undisciplined students.

When the negatives began to eclipse the rewards of teaching, Blakely turned to an alternative venue through which she knew she could have an impact on young people: the theater. In 1982 she founded the Chocolate Chips Theatre Company of Chicago. Her training and previous performance experience at such prestigious groups as Chicago's Kuumba Theatre and the Muntu Dance Theatre of Chicago had prepared Blakely for directing her own theater company. Chocolate Chips first consisted of

a traveling troupe of teen performers, but it soon progressed to a professional adult company with a scheduled season. Making stops around the Midwest, but mostly performing in the Chicago area, the company dedicated itself to bringing the vibrancy of African American culture alive on stage for children, teenagers, and adults. Their productions celebrated African American folklore and history and explored the contemporary experiences of blacks, in both national and local contexts; the company strove to use theater as a forum to encourage young people to read and write as well. Blakely kept her mother's legacy alive through her mother's work, with Chocolate Chips frequently performing *A Day in Bronzeville: Black Life through the Eyes of Gwendolyn Brooks*. This production was a stage adaptation of her mother's first volume of poetry, *A Street in Bronzeville* (1945), and featured song and poetry as dialogue for children aged three through twelve. Gwendolyn Brooks passed away on 3 December 2000 at the age of eighty-three, and Blakely is said to have placed a pen in her hand as she died (*Chicago Tribune*, 4 Dec. 2000).

From that time Blakely continued her mother's role as an active citizen of the city of Chicago, both through her own work and in carrying on her mother's legacy. She served as an Illinois Arts Council artist-in-residence, read her own work throughout the city, taught writing, and conducted creative-performance workshops to students of all ages, from preschool to adult. Active in many of the state of Illinois's efforts to honor their late poet laureate, Blakely unveiled the plaque at the 2003 ceremony commemorating the naming of the Illinois state library after the poet and speaking at scholarly conferences on her mother's work. She served as managing artistic director of Chocolate Chips and wrote many of their productions, including *Brother, Man*, a play for teenagers and adults that identifies and counteracts negative stereotypes of black men, and *Moyenda and the Golden Heart*, which details the quest of an African man in a fictional African village. Her poetry appeared in the collection *The Woman That I Am: The Literature and Culture of Contemporary Women of Color* (1994). Blakely once said of her mother:

Gwendolyn Brooks introduced and shared experiences … entrances to the lives of people you might, otherwise, never know. Gwendolyn, whether as manic parent, literary midwife, or life mapper, opened places for people—new doorways and mindpaths. And, after all, isn't that what a mother is supposed to do? (Madhubuti)

Blakely also continued her mother's tradition of opening new "mindpaths," using theater as her forum to introduce the young people of Chicago to the lives of people such as Moyenda and those characters of her mother's *Bronzeville*. Blakely's work at Chocolate Chips helped children and adults alike celebrate African American culture through song, movement, and literacy.

FURTHER READING

Brooks, Gwendolyn. *Report from Part One* (1972).
Brooks, Gwendolyn. *Report from Part Two* (1996).
Kent, George E. *A Life of Gwendolyn Brooks* (1990).
Madhubuti, Haki. *Chicken Bones: A Journal* (2003). This online journal is found at http://www. nathanielturner. com/gweninmontgomery.htm.
Whitaker, Charles. "The Disappearing Black Teacher: Blacks Leaving Careers in Education," *Ebony* (Jan. 1989).

CASEY KAYSER

Blakey, Art (11 Oct. 1919–16 Oct. 1990), jazz drummer and bandleader, was born Art William Blakey in Pittsburgh, Pennsylvania, the son of Burtrum Blakey, a barber, and Marie Roddericker. His father left home shortly after Blakey was born, and his mother died the next year. Consequently, he was raised by a cousin, Sarah Oliver Parran, who worked at the Jones and Laughlin Steel Mill in Pittsburgh. He moved out of the home at age thirteen to work in the steel mills and in 1938 married Clarice Stuart, the first of three wives. His other wives were Diana Bates and Ann Arnold. Blakey had at least ten children (the exact number is unknown), the last of whom was born in 1986.

As a teenager Blakey taught himself to play the piano and performed in local dance bands, but he later switched to drums. Like many of his contemporaries, Blakey initially adapted the stylistic drumming techniques of well-known swing era drummers, including CHICK WEBB, SID CATLETT, and Ray Bauduc, to whom he frequently paid tribute. As a result, his earliest playing experiences away from Pittsburgh centered around ensembles fronted by well-known, big-band leaders.

Although some sources indicate Blakey first worked with the FLETCHER HENDERSON Orchestra in 1939, it seems unlikely. The drummer Pete Suggs joined the Henderson band in June 1937 and remained with him until the group disbanded two years later, when Henderson became an arranger and pianist for the Benny Goodman band. However, Blakey did join a newly formed

Art Blakey, percussionist of The Jazz Messengers, 30 November 1955. (AP Images.)

Henderson band in the spring of 1943 after playing with MARY LOU WILLIAMS's twelve-piece band and briefly leading his own group at a small Boston nightclub in 1942. During the early 1940s Blakey was assimilating the innovative bop drumming styles of KENNY CLARKE and MAX ROACH, as evidenced by his selection as drummer for the BILLY ECKSTINE big band organized in 1944. This group (with the trumpeter DIZZY GILLESPIE as musical director) started at the Club Plantation in St. Louis and was among the first big bands to play bebop-influenced arrangements. Although somewhat unsuccessful as a commercial venture, the band rehearsed and recorded from 1944 to 1947. Blakey's playing with this ensemble indicates that regardless of the bebop bent of the repertoire, he played mainly late, swing-style drums. But it was during his tenure with Eckstine that Blakey came in contact with several major bop luminaries, including Gillespie, CHARLIE PARKER, MILES DAVIS, DEXTER GORDON, and Kenny Dorham. His association with these musicians placed him firmly in the bop camp, where he remained throughout his career. After the dissolution of Eckstine's band, Blakey joined THELONIOUS MONK for the pianist's first Blue Note recordings in 1947; theirs was a complementary collaboration that continued off and on for the next decade. That same year Blakey organized a rehearsal band, the Seventeen Messengers, and in December made several recordings for Blue Note with his octet, Art Blakey's Jazz Messengers, which included Dorham on trumpet. This group was the first to bear the name through which Blakey would later become famous.

In 1948 Blakey made a brief, nonmusical trip to Africa, at which time he converted to the Islamic religion, changing his name to Abdullah Ibn Buhaina. By mid-1948 he had returned to the United States, recording once again with Monk that July and with the saxophonist James Moody in October. The next year he joined LUCKY MILLINDER's R&B-based band and recorded with him in February. Although Blakey never recorded under his Muslim name, several of his children share this name with him, and later he was known to his musical friends as "Bu."

During the early 1950s Blakey solidified his bop drumming style by playing with well-known bop musicians such as Parker, Davis, Buddy DeFranco, CLIFFORD BROWN, Percy Heath, and HORACE SILVER. In the mid-1950s Blakey and Silver formed the first of the acclaimed Jazz Messengers ensembles that initially included Dorham, HANK MOBLEY, and Doug Watkins. When Silver left in 1956, Blakey retained leadership of the group that with constantly changing personnel became an important conduit through which many young, talented jazz musicians would pass. For the next twenty-odd years the Jazz Messengers' alumni comprised a list of virtual "who's who" in modern jazz, including Donald Byrd, Bill Hardman, JACKIE McLEAN, Junior Mance, LEE MORGAN, Benny Golson, BOBBY TIMMONS, Mobley, WAYNE SHORTER, Curtis Fuller, Freddie Hubbard, Cedar Walton, Reggie Workman, Keith Jarrett, Chuck Mangione, McCOY TYNER, WOODY SHAW, Joanne Brackeen, Steve Turré, WYNTON MARSALIS, and Branford Marsalis.

Despite impaired hearing, which ultimately left him deaf, Blakey continued to perform with the Jazz Messengers until shortly before his death in New York City. Throughout his dynamic and influential career he worked with nearly every major bop figure of the last half of the twentieth century, and his Jazz Messengers ensembles provided a training ground for dozens more. He was inducted into the *Down Beat* Jazz Hall of Fame in 1981, and the Jazz Messengers received a Grammy Award for Best Jazz Instrumental Group Performance in 1984. The group recorded several film soundtracks (mainly overseas) from 1959 to 1972, and a documentary film, *Art*

Blakey: The Jazz Messenger (Rhapsody Films), containing interviews with Blakey and other musicians as well as performances by the Jazz Messengers, was released in 1988. Blakey also appears in a jazz video series produced by Sony called *Art Blakey and the Jazz Messengers: Jazz at the Smithsonian* (1982).

Blakey's recorded legacy spans forty years and documents his prodigious and prolific career as drummer and leader. His earliest big-band recordings with Eckstine (De Luxe 2001, 1944) demonstrate an advanced swing style comparable to the best of the late swing era drummers. Although his early Monk recordings (*The Complete Blue Note Recordings of Thelonious Monk*, Mosaic, MR4-101) are clearly bop-oriented, he retains some of his earlier swing characteristics. By the beginning of the 1950s, however, several of Blakey's well-defined playing characteristics emerge, including his heavy and constant high-hat rhythm and effective use of both bass drum and high-hat as additional independent rhythmic resources, which identify him as a progressive and influential bop drummer.

The Jazz Messengers' recordings are numerous and contain performances of varying degrees of success; however, Blakey's playing remains somewhat consistent, regardless of whom he is accompanying. The most impressive of the Messengers' playing is in a collection of recordings the group made in 1960 (*The Complete Blue Note Recordings of the 1960 Jazz Messengers*, Mosaic, MD6-141). Here, the group, consisting of Lee Morgan, Wayne Shorter, Bobby Timmons, Jymie Merritt, and Blakey, demonstrates exceptional talent and produces some of the Messengers' most memorable numbers, including Blakey's signature tune, "Night in Tunisia," composed by Gillespie. Later Messenger recordings with such notables as Jarrett and Mangione (*The Best of Art Blakey*, EmArcy 848245-2 CD, 1979) and the Marsalis brothers (*Keystone 3*, Concord CJ 196/CCD 4196, 1980), provide excellent examples of the continued influence Blakey's leadership had on the growth of jazz in the last quarter of the twentieth century.

The harshest criticism of Blakey's playing was directed at his loud, often overpowering drumming style, which developed in the 1950s and may have contributed to his early hearing loss. Nevertheless, he could also be a sensitive and unobtrusive drummer, as many of his ballad accompaniments demonstrate. Furthermore, his frequently recorded, unaccompanied, improvised drum solo pieces provide numerous examples of his imaginative and flashy, but somewhat musically misdirected, solo ability.

FURTHER READING

Goldberg, Joe. *Jazz Masters of the Fifties* (1965).

Harricks, Raymond, et al. *These Jazzmen of Our Times* (1959).

Stewart, Zan. "Art Blakey in His Prime," *Down Beat* (July 1985).

Taylor, Arthur. *Notes and Tones: Musician to Musician Interviews* (1977).

Obituary: *New York Times*, 17 Oct. 1990.

DISCOGRAPHY

The Best of Art Blakey (EmArcy 848245-2 CD, 1979).

The Complete Blue Note Recordings of the 1960 Jazz Messengers (Mosaic, MD6-141, 1960).

This entry is taken from the *American National Biography* and is published here with the permission of the American Council of Learned Societies.

T. DENNIS BROWN

Blakey, Theodore Robert (31 Aug. 1925–14 Oct. 2004), historian of African Americans in South Dakota, civic leader, entrepreneur, and philanthropist, was born in Yankton, South Dakota, the youngest of eleven children of Henry and Mary (Fristoe) Blakey. The large, extended Blakey clan began migrating from Missouri to South Dakota in 1904, where they acquired land and built a profitable and respected truck gardening business. Young Blakey completed eighth grade in country school and worked in the family business. Beginning in the mid-1960s Blakey returned to school at Springfield State College (which later closed), where he obtained his GED and completed advanced training in building maintenance and pest control. On 22 October 1948 he married Dorothy Edwards in Athabaska, Alberta, Canada; the couple had three children.

Blakey was an ambitious, self-taught businessman with a keen interest in civic activities and public service. Of his three successful businesses, Blakey's Janitorial Services, established in 1956, provided jobs for both blacks and whites and led to leadership in the South Dakota Custodians' Association, which he reorganized and improved. In 1968 he added a pest control business, and in 1975 he established Ted Blakey's Bail Bonds.

Active in public service, Blakey joined the Jaycees and became the first African American to be named to the post of international senator. He was one of two blacks elected president of state Kiwanis organizations. He earned highest rank as a thirty-third-degree Prince Hall Mason, and was also an active Republican, serving as delegate to three national and eleven state Republican conventions, where he was well known and widely respected. In 1963 the South Dakota governor Archie Gubbrud appointed him commissioner of the state Emancipation Proclamation Committee, dedicated to passage of a constitutional amendment to eliminate the poll tax. Blakey mobilized black leaders in the state who helped bring the issue to a successful state vote. South Dakota approved the Twenty-fourth Amendment to the constitution, which was ratified in 1964. Moving into the civil rights struggle, Blakey led statewide efforts to ease removal of local Jim Crow customs, which had since become illegal with the passage of civil rights legislation.

Blakey remained active in Yankton's Allen Chapel, the state's oldest black church, which was built in 1885 by former slaves, proudly serving a devoted congregation of African Methodist Episcopalians (AME). When the congregation dwindled and the building fell into disrepair, Blakey began a statewide effort to preserve the building and the history of African Americans in the upper Midwest. Through his efforts the building was saved and deeded to a local preservation organization. In 1981 Dorothy Blakey passed away, and ten years later he married Chessie Wheeler, who preceded him in death. In 1996 Governor William Janklow named Blakey South Dakota black historian, an honor he held until his death.

In 1997 Blakey became the second African American inducted into the South Dakota Hall of Fame, a prestigious statewide organization with a museum and organizational headquarters in Chamberlain, dedicated to honoring prominent South Dakotans. The first African American inducted was Leonard (Bud) Williams the previous year. (Williams, who retired as a lieutenant colonel after a distinguished career in World War II and Korea, also served as mayor in his hometown of Mitchell.) Also in 1997, Blakey was honored by his fellow Yanktonians in a citywide celebration as Citizen of the Year. In 1998 he was named grand master of the South Dakota IOOF, the first African American to lead a state lodge.

Blakey died at the age of seventy-nine, much beloved by his town and his many friends in the state.

FURTHER READING

Blakey, Theodore Robert. "Early Black Residents," and "Blakey, Ted," in *Yankton County History* (1986).

Blakey, Theodore Robert, with Mary Lovey Kinney Blakey. Interview by Sara Bernson, 1 June 1976. Transcription of tape-recorded interview #1718, 171, University of South Dakota.

Erdman, Patricia A. "Dakota Images: Theodore R. (Ted) Blakey," *South Dakota History*, vol. 34, no. 4 (Winter 2004).

BETTI CAROL VANEPPS-TAYLOR

Blanchard, Terence (13 Mar. 1962–), composer and jazz musician was born Terence Oliver Blanchard in New Orleans, Louisiana, the only child of Wilhelmina and Joseph Oliver Blanchard. His father was an insurance salesman who was a part-time opera singer in the 1930s and 1940s. Blanchard, encouraged by his father to become a musician, had learned to play the piano by age five. Three years later he had taken interest in the trumpet and began playing alongside his childhood friend, WYNTON MARSALIS, at summer music camps. In the 1970s Blanchard was a member of the marching band at St. Augustine, a black Catholic high school; however, disenchanted with the music program there he decided to enroll in public school and explore his options. He began attending extra-curricular courses at the New Orleans Center for Creative Arts (NOCCA) under the tutelage of the jazz musicians Roger Dickerson and Ellis Marsalis, the father of Wynton Marsalis and his brother Bradford. During this period Blanchard also played Dixieland on Sunday afternoons and performed with the New Orleans Civic Orchestra. In 1980 he enrolled at Rutgers University in New Jersey to study classical music and during his tenure received instruction from the trumpeter Bill Fielder and the saxophonist Paul Jeffrey. While a student he toured with the jazz musician and composer LIONEL HAMPTON. In 1982 Wynton Marsalis recommended Blanchard as his replacement with ART BLAKEY and the Jazz Messengers; Blanchard accepted the offer and left Rutgers.

Blanchard toured with Blakey until 1986, emerging from the band with the rich experience of a lead soloist and musical director. In 1984 the band had won a Grammy Award for Best Instrumental Performance Group. From 1984 to 1988 he was the coleader of a popular quintet with the saxophonist Donald Harrison; together they recorded five albums for the Concord and Columbia labels. In 1990 Blanchard made another evolution in his career after an embouchure change and left the Blanchard/Harrison Group to emerge as a soloist. He performed on the soundtracks for the SPIKE LEE films, *Do the Right Thing* (1989) and *Mo' Better Blues* (1990); he also recorded his first album as a solo artist, *Terence Blanchard*, released on Columbia in 1991. In 1991 Spike Lee invited Blanchard to write the score for his film *Malcolm X*; intimidated by the magnitude of such a project, Blanchard assumed the task reluctantly, He was, however, acclaimed for his work on that film and has since scored subsequent Lee films, including *Crooklyn* (1994) and *4 Little Girls* (1997), Lee's documentary about the 1963 Birmingham church bombing that killed ADDIE MAE COLLINS, DENISE MCNAIR, CAROLE ROBERTSON, and CYNTHIA WESLEY.

Following his association with Lee, Blanchard became a much sought after composer in Hollywood. In all, by 2010 he had written over forty scores, including *Eve's Bayou* (1997), *Cadillac Records* (2008), and (again with Lee) *25th Hour* (2002), for which he was given the award for best score by the Central Ohio Film Critics Association. Between his solo debut in 1991 and 2009 Blanchard also produced thirteen albums on Columbia, Sony Classical, Blue Note, and Concord, among them *In My Solitude: The Billie Holiday Songbook* (1994); *Let's Get Lost* (2001), with performances from Dianne Reeves and Cassandra Wilson; *Bounce* (2003); and *Flow* (2005), produced by the jazz pianist HERBIE HANCOCK. In 2007 Blanchard produced the powerful and moving *A Tale of God's Will (A Requiem for Katrina)*, for which he won the Emmy Award for Best Large Jazz Ensemble. On 10 February 2008 he won his first Grammy Award as a bandleader. Blanchard also wrote the score for Lee's documentary for HBO about Hurricane Katrina, *When the Levees Broke: A Requiem in Four Acts*. In the film he returns to New Orleans with his mother to find his childhood home obliterated.

Blanchard earned twelve Grammy nominations through 2010 and won five Grammy Awards, including the award for best jazz instrumental solo in 2008 for the track "Be-Bop" on the album *Live at the 2007 Monterey Jazz Festival* and again in 2009 for "Dancin' for Chicken" on the album *Watts*. In 2000 Blanchard was named the artistic director of the Thelonius Monk Institute of Jazz at the University of Southern California. After the Hurricane Katrina disaster in New Orleans, Blanchard announced in April 2007 that he would relocate the institute to Loyola University in New Orleans, in order assist the preservation of the city's musical heritage. In 2009 Disney introduced its first African American princess in the animated film *The Princess and The Frog*. The story takes place in New Orleans, and Blanchard was there to play the trumpet for Louis the alligator; he also performed the voice of Earl, the bandleader in the band on the riverboat.

FURTHER READING

Magro, Anthony. *Contemporary Cat: Terence Blanchard with Special Guests*, Scarecrow Press (2002).

Yanow, Scott. *Trumpet Kings: The Players Who Shaped the Sound of Jazz Trumpet* (2002).

SAFIYA DALILAH HOSKINS

Bland, Bobby "Blue" (27 Jan. 1930–), rhythm and blues vocalist, was born Robert Calvin Brooks in Rosemark, Tennessee, son of May Lee and I. J. Brooks. He grew up in the rural town listening to white country singers and gospel music. At age six his mother married Leroy Bridgeworth, also known as Leroy Bland; Bland adopted his stepfather's surname in his teens. At age seventeen, Bland moved with his mother and stepfather to Memphis, Tennessee. He worked in a garage but his love for music continued to flourish. He sang gospel in church and with secular street groups, joining the Miniatures in 1949. By 1950 Bland was working as a chauffeur for blues singer and musician B. B. KING and occasional valet to the singer Roscoe Gordon in order to be near blues music. It was his affinity for blues that earned him his nickname. Bland's persistence paid off and in 1951 he became a member of the Beale Streeters, a group named for the lively urban street known for blues, which included JOHNNY ACE, Junior Parker, B. B. King, and Roscoe Gordon.

Bland was twenty-one years old when he signed with D. J. James Mattis's Duke's Recordings in 1951. Already he had released three recordings on three different labels: Chess, Modern, and Duke. Bland's Modern release was produced by the rock and roll musician IKE TURNER and Sam Phillips produced his Chess single. Bland was drafted into the U.S. Army in 1952, suddenly halting his career but not his love for singing. Bland was performing with Special Services by the end of his tour, covering NAT KING COLE and Charles Brown tunes. When he returned to Memphis in 1955 his cohorts were enjoying considerable success and his recording label had been sold to the Houston entrepreneur Don Robey. Robey immediately paired Bland with Bill Harvey's Orchestra to begin recording for the label. Bland's unique style had evolved into a rapid vibrato and mixture of gospel, rhythm and blues, and blues that would inspire the new soul-blues sound along with the likes of RAY CHARLES, Little Milton, SAM COOKE, and Jimmy McCracklin. Later, his revolutionary sound would be accented by a guttural growl, crying, and snorting sound that became his signature. His first release on Duke was "It's My Life Baby" (1955) and by 1957 Bland

had a number one hit on the rhythm and blues charts, "Farther up the Road. Little Boy Blue" (1958), ascended the U.S. Rhythm and Blues Top Ten and in 1961 he had another number one hit on the rhythm and blues charts with "I Pity the Fool." "Turn Your Love Light On" (1958) reached number two and Bland's 1963 release "That's the Way Love Is" became his third number one hit. Bland toured with Junior Parker and the Blue Flames from 1957 to 1961. In 1958 he married Grace Towles. Bland reached the height of his popularity after going solo in 1961 and began working with the bandleader Joe Scott and guitarist Wayne Bennett. He experienced success on the Top Forty pop charts with "Turn on Your Lovelight" (1962), "Call on Me" (1963), "That's the Way Love Is" (1963), and "Ain't Nothing You Can Do" (1964). His album *Call on Me/That's the Way Love Is* (1963) charted for six months on the Top Forty. Between 1958 and 1968 Bland executed three hundred performances per year. He earned gold records and received critical acclaim. The trio disbanded in 1968 due to financial pressures and Bland's alcoholism. In 1971 Bland married a college student named Marty, with whom he had five children, and stopped drinking after eighteen years of alcoholism. Duke Records had been purchased by ABC-Dunhill in 1972 from Robey who had pocketed royalties from Bland's songs under the pseudonym Deadric Malone. The new label had aspirations of taking Bland mainstream and paired him with producer Steve Barri and bandleader Ernie Fields Jr. and subsequently released his first pop chart albums in a decade, *His California Album* in 1973 and *Dreamer* in 1974. "Ain't No Heart in the City" from his *Dreamer* album was a huge rhythm and blues success. It was later covered by a Scottish progressive rock band Café Jacques in 1977 and U.S. hard rock band Whitesnake in 1978 and sampled by hip-hop artist Jay-Z in 2001 on his album *The Blueprint*. Bland performed two live albums for the label with B. B. King; the first, *Together for the First Time* (1974), went gold. Subsequently, Bland experimented with disco music before returning to rhythm and blues to perform a Joe Scott tribute album, *Sweet Vibrations* (1980). In 1985 Bland signed to Malaco Records, an independent rhythm and blues label in Jackson, Mississippi. Despite age-related health challenges Bland continued to perform occasional tours with King and dates at festivals worldwide. Bland experienced crossover success but primarily sold on the rhythm and blues market. He had twenty-three Top Ten hits on the Billboard rhythm and blues charts.

Bland married his third wife, Willie Mae Martin, in 1983; together they had a son named Roderick who sometimes played the drums for his father while on tour. In 1989 Bland received a Grammy Award nomination for *Get Your Money Where You Spend Your Time*. He was inducted into the Blues Foundation's Hall of Fame in 1981. In 1992 Bland was inducted into the Rock & Roll Hall of Fame and received the R&B Foundation's Pioneer Award. Bobby "Blue" Bland received the Grammy Lifetime Achievement Award in 1997.

FURTHER READING

Pareless, John, and Patricia Romanowski. *Rolling Stone Encyclopedia of Rock & Roll* (1983).

Rees, Dafydd, and Luke Crampton. *Rock Movers and Shakers* (1991).

Scott, Frank. *The Down Home Guide to the Blues* (1991).

SAFIYA DALILAH HOSKINS

Bland, James Allen (22 Oct. 1854–5 May 1911), minstrel performer and composer, was born in Flushing, Long Island, New York, the son of Allen M. Bland, an incipient lawyer, and Lidia Ann Cromwell of Brandywine, Delaware, of an emancipated family. Bland's father, whose family had been free for several generations, attended law school at Howard University in Washington, D.C., and in 1867 became the first black to be appointed an examiner in the U.S. Patent Office.

James Bland entered Howard University as a prelaw student in 1870 at the urging of his father, but the subject and the life associated with it did not appeal to him. Instead he was attracted to the minstrel show that was approaching its peak during the 1870s. He played the guitar, danced the steps, sang the minstrel songs, and, most important, composed songs for the shows. A free black man who attended college for two years, Bland had to learn from the workers at Howard University, mostly former slaves, something of the actions and the speech of plantation blacks. He was a good actor and a sweet singer and projected himself successfully into the minstrel milieu. In 1875 he left home to tour as a professional minstrel with the Black Diamond troupe of Boston; later he joined the Bohee Brothers, Sprague's Georgia Minstrels, and Haverly's Genuine Colored Minstrels.

It was with Haverly's group that Bland traveled in 1881 to London, where they played with great success at Her Majesty's Theatre. After a highly profitable year the Haverly troupe returned to the United States, but Bland and several others remained and enjoyed great success as music hall performers in England and Scotland. It was said that the Prince of Wales (Edward VII) showed special favor to Bland and once presented the actor with a gold-headed ebony cane. With these successes the performer-composer was able to indulge in lavish living (which sadly did not provide for his comforts in later life). Bland's career continued flourishing throughout the 1880s and part of the 1890s.

By 1901, however, Bland was back in the United States. He toured with W. S. Cleveland's Colossal Colored Carnival Minstrels, where he was billed as "the eccentric original James Bland." He and Tom McIntosh were called "the two greatest comedians of their race." In 1898 he appeared briefly with Black Patti's Troubadours. The minstrel show days were over, however, replaced in the public's affection by the musical comedy.

Bland made one try at writing a musical show, *The Sporting Girl*, but it was not a success. He had referred to himself as "the best Ethiopian song writer in the world," a knack that did not carry over into the new musical comedy. Many had called him "the Negro Stephen Foster," yet in the early 1900s even Foster himself was not a great success. By 1911 Bland was in Philadelphia—out of fame, out of work, and out of money. He died there of pneumonia and was buried in an unmarked grave in the Merion graveyard for blacks. Only in 1939 did James Francis Cooke, editor of the magazine *The Etude*, find his grave (with the help of Bland's sister) and arrange for a proper gravestone, which was erected in 1946. Bland never married, so far as is known.

James Bland's name has been kept alive by his music. The number of his compositions—minstrel songs, a few marching songs, a campaign song or two (for example, "The Missouri Hound Dog")—has been estimated at seven hundred, but this seems a considerable overestimate. The number of Bland's copyright deposits in the Library of Congress has been counted at only thirty-eight. (No doubt, of course, many songs and pieces were tossed off for particular occasions and did not always get published or even copyrighted.)

In 1875 Bland had written his best-known song, "Carry Me Back to Old Virginny," which as "Carry Me Back to Old Virginia" became the official state song of Virginia in 1940. Among his other best-known songs were "In the Evening by the Moonlight" (followed by "In the Morning by the Bright Light"), "Oh, Dem Golden Slippers" (which he sang with a special dance routine), "Dancing on de Kitchen Floor," "The Colored Hop," and "Dandy Black Brigade." Many of Bland's songs were sung not only by him and other members of his troupe but also by members of other troupes. His songs had a combination of sentiment and lyric appeal that exemplified the spirit of the black minstrel show, which ironically was forwarded primarily by white performers in blackface makeup.

FURTHER READING

Materials relating to Bland are in the Jesse E. Moorland Collection at Howard University.

Daly, John J. *A Song in His Heart* (1951).

Haywood, Charles. "James A. Bland, Prince of the Colored Songwriters." Published by the Flushing Historical Society as *A Discourse Delivered before the Flushing Historical Society* (1944).

Hughes, Langston. "James A. Bland: Minstrel Composer, 1854–1911," in *Famous Negro Music Makers* (1955).

Miller, Kelly. "The Negro 'Stephen Foster': The First Published Biography of James A. Bland," *Etude* (July 1939).

Southern, Eileen. *The Music of Black Americans: A History* (1971; rev. eds., 1983, 1997).

This entry is taken from the *American National Biography* and is published here with the permission of the American Council of Learned Societies.

WILLIAM LICHTENWANGER

Blanks, Birleanna (18 Feb. 1889–12 Aug. 1968), vaudeville entertainer and singer, was born in Iowa but grew up in East St. Louis, Illinois. Her mother, Amanda Billups, was a Native American, and her father, Addison Blanks, was an African American.

After her studies were complete, Blanks first taught school in her hometown; however, she soon spread her wings as a professional entertainer, performing around the country and appearing in shows in Chicago and New York City. She began her career in a touring vaudeville act, dancing and singing with her sister, Arsceola Blanks, in the late 1910s. Her sister married Leonard Harper and formed Harper & Blanks, another vaudeville act; Birleanna married the baseball player Chesley Cunningham (the date of the marriage is unknown).

In 1919 Blanks made her debut in Harlem at the Lafayette Theatre, where she sang in *Over the Top*. This musical comedy was the first Billy King show in which she performed for the Harlem theater. That same year she appeared in a few more of the company's shows, including *They're Off* and *Exploits in Africa*. In 1921 she appeared in King's *New Americans: A Trip Round the World* and *Derby Day in Dixie*.

The Lafayette Theatre was a landmark in its time for being one of the first theaters to allow integrated seating. In addition it was known for its acting troupe, the Lafayette Players, which presented dramatic plays to black audiences. These dramatic plays starred black actors, an uncommon choice in casting at a time when blacks were known primarily for their singing and dancing in comedies. Anita Bush, the founder of the Lafayette Players, wanted to prove that black people were capable of acting in serious as well as in comedic roles. The Lafayette Theatre also catered to new playwrights in the 1910s and 1920s by producing new plays. One of the playwrights that benefited from this opportunity was Billy King, the playwright whose shows Birleanna Blanks performed in at the Lafayette.

In her mid-thirties, having made a name for herself with the Billy King Stock Company, Blanks went on to sing in other production companies such as the Panama Amusement Company in Chicago, Illinois, and the Harlem Producing Company. Around 1923 she became a member of the Three Dixie Songbirds, singing with AMANDA RANDOLPH and Hilda Perlina in Chicago nightclubs. She then performed with this group in the 1925–1926 run of *Lucky Sambo* with Mae Barnes. During this time Blanks recorded "Mason Dixon Blues" and other songs with Paramount, singing with the FLETCHER HENDERSON Orchestra.

For unknown reasons Blanks left the music industry to seek other job opportunities and did not perform in any shows or record any songs after 1928. As in the experiences of many actors and singers, the Depression possibly was a factor in her absence from the theater and music scene. At the age of seventy-nine Birleanna Blanks died of cancer in New York City at the Florence Nightingale Nursing Home. She was buried at the Woodlawn Cemetery in the Bronx.

Half Native American and half African American, Blanks was a singer who led the way for mixed-race women in the entertainment business. With her vaudeville acts, musical comedy roles, and Paramount recordings, she served as a model of success for women of future generations.

FURTHER READING

Harris, Sheldon. "Birleanna Blanks," in *Blues Who's Who: A Biographical Dictionary of Blues Singers* (1979).

Kellner, Bruce. "Birleanna Blanks," in *The Harlem Renaissance: A Historical Dictionary* (1984).

Peterson, Bernard L., Jr. *The African American Theatre Directory, 1816-1960: A Comprehensive Guide to*

Early Black Theatre Organizations, Companies, Theatres, and Performing Groups (1997).

Southern, Eileen. *The Music of Black Americans: A History* (1997).

ALLISON KELLAR

Blanton, Jimmy (18 Nov. 1918–30 July 1942), bass player, was born James Blanton in Chattanooga, Tennessee. Little is known about his parents except that his mother was a pianist and bandleader. Blanton is widely regarded as the most outstanding bass player of the late 1930s and early 1940s, almost single-handedly revolutionizing jazz bass playing both technically and conceptually. As a child Blanton studied violin, making his first public appearance at age eight. Showing exceptional talent and a serious interest in music, he learned music theory from an uncle and later switched to string bass while studying at Tennessee State College (1934–1937). Precociously gifted on this instrument, Blanton was soon playing with local bands. In 1937 he moved to St. Louis to play with the Jeter-Pillars Orchestra and FATE MARABLE's Mississippi riverboat bands.

In late 1939 Blanton was heard by DUKE ELLINGTON, who immediately asked him to join the famous Ellington orchestra. Along with the tenor saxophonist BEN WEBSTER, Blanton contributed significantly to a revitalization of the Ellington orchestra, particularly with regard to its deep, rich sound and its strong sense of swing. Blanton recorded prolifically during his relatively brief tenure with the band, including a remarkable series of six bass and piano duets with Ellington, a format unprecedented in the early 1940s and hardly ever tried again since then. Within a short time Blanton came to be regarded as the leading bass player in jazz. His influence is to a large extent attributable to the happy circumstance that his playing was superbly recorded by new microphone and recording techniques, giving the bass a distinctive prominence on recordings. During his years with Ellington, Blanton also frequently played at Minton's Playhouse in Harlem in informal jam sessions that were crucial in the development of the bop style.

In late 1941 signs of the illness—later diagnosed as tuberculosis—that caused Blanton's death began to show, forcing him to leave the Ellington orchestra and retire to a sanatorium in Los Angeles, California, where he died within a few months. He was never married.

Blanton's contribution to the development of jazz, particularly with regard to the full emancipation of the rhythm section, is immeasurable. He expanded jazz bass techniques by considerably extending the upper range of the bass; by developing greater agility in his solos and "walking" bass lines, both in his right-hand pizzicato dexterity and in his left-hand nimbleness; by approaching improvisation more as a horn (brass or saxophone) player would; and by creating more harmonically explorative and wide-ranging (not just scalar) bass lines. In these ways Blanton contributed significantly to the greater musical independence of the rhythm section, thereby freeing him to make substantial contributions melodically, harmonically, contrapuntally, and texturally.

As the first major soloist on the bass, Blanton elevated the instrument to a new and higher status. His strong, well-focused sound and his highly original walking bass lines, often exploring the uppermost range of the instrument, profoundly influenced all subsequent important jazz bass players long after his death—especially Ray Brown, George Duvivier, OSCAR PETTIFORD, Milt Hinton, Eddie Safranski, Chubby Jackson, and CHARLES MINGUS, among others.

FURTHER READING

Carrère, Claude. *Pitter Panther Patter: Les bassistes de Duke Ellington* (1975).

Ellington, Duke. *Music Is My Mistress* (1973).

Schuller, Gunther. *Swing Era* (1989).

This entry is taken from the *American National Biography* and is published here with the permission of the American Council of Learned Societies.

GUNTHER SCHULLER

Blanton, John W. (25 Jan. 1922–7 May 2003), mechanical engineer and rocket scientist, was born in Louisville, Kentucky, the son of John O. and Carolyn Blanton.

Blanton attended Purdue University in Indiana, graduating with a bachelor's degree in Mechanical Engineering in 1943. He began his career at Bell Aircraft Corporation in Buffalo, New York, where he worked from 1943 to 1945 and from 1950 through 1956. Initially involved in the research and development of gas and rocket engines, Blanton helped develop the X-1, which on 14 October 1947 became the first aircraft to break the sound barrier in a human-operated, level flight.

Two years after marrying Corinne Jones of Mississippi in 1943, Blanton was named the chief engineer of thermo and fluid dynamics at Frederick Flader Incorporated, in Buffalo, New York, where he worked for five years. In 1956 he joined General

Electric in Evendale, Ohio, and continued to make significant advances in transonic and supersonic compressor technology. Blanton's career evolved to include more management and marketing opportunities after he was named general manager of General Electric's Aircraft Engine Field Programs in 1974, and he eventually became responsible for all of General Electric's propulsion products, working mostly with jet engines. For two years, before he retired in 1982, he served as general manager of commercial advanced engines and technical programs.

Blanton is also distinguished by the significant contributions he made to his local community, where he served on several public and private boards, including the Cincinnati Zoo, the Ohio Governor's Coordinating Council on Drug Abuse, and the Community Chest. Leadership positions he held include chair of the Cincinnati-Dayton Section of the American Institute of Aeronautics and Astronautics, president of the Urban League Board of Greater Cincinnati, and vice president of the Dan Beard Council of the Boy Scouts of America. As one of the founding members of the Southwest Ohio Regional Transit Authority, and as its president from 1973 to 1979, Blanton was actively involved in preserving and maintaining the Queen City Metro System at a critical juncture in its history as it faced several financial crises. Blanton continued to receive notable recognition throughout his life by two principal institutions, Purdue University and General Electric. In 1968 his alma mater inducted Blanton into its Old Masters Program, conferred upon him the Distinguished Engineering Alumnus Award in 1973, and elected him a member of the Engineering Dean's Visiting Committee from 1976 to 1979. For his public service, General Electric presented Blanton with the Gerald L. Phillippe Award in 1981 and inducted him into its Aircraft Engine's Propulsion Hall of Fame in 1991.

Survived by his wife and one child, Dr. John W. Blanton Jr., a onetime assistant clinical professor of pediatrics at Yale University, John Blanton Sr. was buried in Cincinnati, Ohio. Blanton was an instrumental figure as both an engineer and marketing director in the early stages of jet engines and rocket science.

FURTHER READING

Sammons, Vivian. *Blacks in Science and Medicine* (1989).

Obituary: *Cincinnati Enquirer*, 11 May 2003.

WILLIAM A. MORGAN

Blassingame, John (23 Mar. 1940–13 Feb. 2000), historian, was born in Covington, Georgia, to Grady and Odessa Blassingame. He grew up within the confines of rural Jim Crow in the nearby town of Social Circle. Like so many African Americans of his generation, he was blessed with great teachers and parents, despite the state-sanctioned inequities by race in educational resources. His own good fortune in that regard was also the reason that, when he became a professor, the mentoring of African American students and faculty members was always one of his priorities. Among those influenced and mentored by Blassingame was the literary scholar, HENRY LOUIS GATES JR. Thanks in part to his own hard-working and unsung professors at Fort Valley College, an all-black public institution in central Georgia, Blassingame excelled at history and earned a bachelor of arts degree in that discipline there in 1960. He then went on to get his master's degree in History in 1961 at Howard University in Washington, D.C., which was one of only a handful of graduate programs in the country at that time with any emphasis on African American history.

As a result of several U.S. Supreme Court's decisions culminating in the 1954 Brown decision, as well as the civil rights movement, institutions of higher education began to desegregate, slowly, in the 1960s. Young and talented scholars like Blassingame who happened to be black benefited from these gradual steps. Unlike previous generations of scholars, he was able to teach at first-rate history programs in historically black colleges (such as Howard, where he began his career) and also in predominately white schools, such as Carnegie-Mellon University in Pittsburgh, and the University of Maryland, College Park. In the late 1960s, he was accepted into one of the most elite doctoral programs in the discipline at Yale University in New Haven, Connecticut. His dissertation adviser was C. Vann Woodward, a white liberal southerner, whose 1954 study, *The Strange Career of Jim Crow*, was recognized by many as the "bible of the civil rights movement" for, among other things, highlighting the remarkable degree of black agency and political success between Reconstruction and the 1890s.

Blassingame was first appointed a lecturer at Yale in 1970. His impeccable training and credentials made him a stickler for the historical profession's traditions, which emphasized the importance of primary sources. Staying at Yale the rest of his career and chairing the African American Studies department there in the 1980s, he was determined to use what had been considered the methods of conventional history to expose and reject the destructive myths of inherent white supremacy and its obverse, natural black dependency. Accordingly, immediately after earning his Ph.D. from Yale in 1971, Blassingame applied the then-fashionable concept of doing history "from the bottom up" to key topics in African American history such as slavery and Reconstruction. In contrast, most academic works on slavery and Reconstruction to that point in the twentieth century had centered on whites and their attitudes toward slaves and freedmen and not vice versa. Before World War II, Ulrich B. Phillips, a white professor of history at Columbia University, then the nation's leading history department, and his followers had lent their professional credibility to the popular misconception of slavery being a benign institution for an inferior people. In this narrative, which became entrenched, slaves liked slavery, and slaveholders civilized slaves, who had no culture of their own. Selectively using only records that buttressed their prejudice, these historians dominated the intellectual landscape and were consulted on famous iconic films such as *Gone with the Wind*. This pro-slavery consensus among historians in white elite schools was challenged after World War II by Kenneth Stampp in *The Peculiar Institution: Slavery in the Antebellum South* (1956), which documented the savagery of slavery, and Stanley Elkins in *Slavery: A Problem in American Institutional and Intellectual Life* (1959). Elkins portrayed blacks as passive and damaged victims of slavery; he agreed with Stampp that American slavery was oppressive, but linked that oppression in ways that merely confirmed Phillips's depiction of overly deferential slaves.

In the 1960s the Black Power movement challenged the very notion of any whites such as Stampp or Elkins having any scholarly authority to write on black history, but it was the respectable and well-researched work of the black historian John Blassingame from Yale that did the greatest damage to the once-familiar trope of slaves as nameless or helpless props in their own history. In this regard Blassingame was one of the first using the historical method, though it should be noted that the anthropologist Melville J. Herskovitz had argued for the persistence of African survivals in African American folklore, language, music, and family structure in his classic 1941 study *The Myth of the Negro Past*.

A remarkable burst of early productivity helped quickly to establish Blassingame in history's top tier of scholars. In 1971, the year he received his doctorate, Blassingame edited an influential anthology of articles, *New Perspectives on Black Studies*; the very next year, he published his signature masterpiece, *The Slave Community: Plantation Life in the Antebellum South*. This title itself beckoned a refreshing departure from previous studies with "community" and "life" being mentioned as well as the institution of slavery. Most significantly, his book was the first widely regarded historical monograph to use black autobiographies, songs, and folklore to expose vibrant African-inspired cultures that had shaped the making of mainstream American society and ideas. To Blassingame, slavery not only built America from an purely economic standpoint, but the slaves themselves from a wide variety of West African cultures influenced the most intimate and personal routines of their masters. Like Stampp, Blassingame stressed the resistance of many, if not most, slaves to slavery, but he also underscored the diversity, complexity, and, thus, humanity of his subjects. In his research, not every slave was either a strangely content "Sambo" or a dangerous NAT TURNER, the two extremes of white literature and history that, as Blassingame repeatedly pointed out, told more about the desires and fears of whites than they did of actual bondspeople. Blassingame used this same assumption of black individuality and community in his detailed *Black New Orleans, 1860–1880* (1973), a reworking of his doctoral dissertation, in which he explored African American sources, figures, and institutions in depth. It was one of the first civil rights era histories of Reconstruction to build on W. E. B. DuBois's earlier *Black Reconstruction* (1941), which viewed that period as a time of thwarted black agency, rather than as an era of corruption and chaos, as had been argued by the racist Dunning school of Reconstruction studies. (William Dunning had been Ulrich Phillips's mentor at Columbia.)

Blassingame was so concerned with recovering the black voices in American history that he devoted the lion's share of his professional life to finding and annotating those precious primary sources that had for so long been overlooked or forgotten. Most important was his publication of *Slave Testimony* (1977) and his meticulous editing of six volumes of the papers of the abolitionist FREDERICK DOUGLASS between 1979 and 1999. He also coauthored with the legal scholar and historian Mary Frances Berry, *Long Memory: The Black Experience in America* (1982), one of the first and most enduring general histories of the African American experience. A topical, interdisciplinary synthesis, the volume delivered on its authors' promise to reject "the view of Afro-Americans as an atomized, rootless people who begin each generation without any sense of what preceded them" (*Long Memory*, x). A vital oral tradition in music, folklore, and family networks, Blassingame and Berry argued, provided African Americans with a "long memory," a vital and usable past.

Blassingame was married to Teasie Blassingame and had two children, John Jr. and Tia. He died at home in New Haven at the young age of fifty-nine.

FURTHER READING

Harris, Robert L., Jr. "John W. Blassingame: March 23, 1940–February 13, 2000." *Journal of Negro History* 86, no. 3 (Summer 2001): 422–423.

Huff, Christopher Allen. "John Blassingame (1940–2000)." In *The New Georgia Encyclopedia* (2007).

Novick, Peter. *The "Objectivity Question" and the American Historical Profession* (1988).

Obituary: "John Blassingame, 59, Historian; Led Yale Black Studies Program." *New York Times*, 29 Feb. 2000.

CHARLES H. FORD

Blayton, Jesse Bee (6 Dec. 1897–13 Sept. 1977), business leader and educator, born in rural Fallis, Oklahoma territory, to Lester Blayton, a Baptist preacher and Mattie E. Carter, a schoolteacher. Despite having only a fourth-grade education Mattie Blayton was a schoolteacher who continually underscored the importance of academic achievement. Blayton's father, the mixed-race, illiterate son of a Creek Indian, was a shaman before becoming a preacher. Blayton attended federally funded elementary and high schools for Native Americans in Meridian, Oklahoma. Later in life he reported that he had been unaware of the poverty of his childhood, though he noted that the only job he had ever hated was when his parents rented him and the family mule out by the day to work in the fields.

With his parents' encouragement Blayton attended Langston University, working menial jobs to cover his costs. His education was interrupted when he volunteered for the U.S. Army during World War I; he served in France from 1918 to 1919 and reached the rank of sergeant major. During his service he learned about the accounting field, and after graduating from Langston he attended the Walton School of Commerce in Chicago, from which he graduated in 1923. While in school he married Willa Mae Daniels on 27 December 1920; they had two children. After finishing his second degree Blayton moved to Atlanta, where he worked as an accountant and auditor for several black-owned insurance companies, including the Standard Life Insurance Company, where he worked for the prominent Atlanta entrepreneur HERMAN PERRY.

Blayton became a certified public accountant in 1928 after passing the challenging CPA examination. He was forced to do so in Illinois because the test sites in Georgia would not accommodate an African American. He was only the fourth African American in the country to earn a CPA, and the first in the Deep South. He soon opened his own accounting firm, Blayton and Company CPAs, where he was known as "Chief" by the many employees, both men and women, whom he trained to follow in his professional footsteps.

He began his career as a professor two years later when he joined the faculty of Morehouse College in Atlanta. Soon thereafter, JOHN HOPE, the president of Morehouse, led the creation of Atlanta University, the first institution in the South to provide graduate education to African Americans. Blayton joined Atlanta University as the Carnegie Professor of Business Administration, and he soon became a key figure in the cadre of Atlanta University professors who actively encouraged African Americans to enter business. The African American historian E. FRANKLIN FRAZIER severely criticized their efforts as illusory, insignificant, and counterproductive to racial progress (Frazier, 154–155). But Blayton was a firm believer in the premise that only black-owned business would create solid opportunities for well-educated black Americans, and he published articles and gave speeches on the importance of black-owned business throughout his career. Because of Blayton's influence, Atlanta University offered more accounting courses than any other black college or university, and many promising African American students were drawn to Atlanta to study with him. He provided education and training to many of the first African American CPAs across the United States, becoming known as the "Dean of Negro Accountants."

Blayton practiced what he preached: he was a successful entrepreneur. In 1925 he and fourteen friends contributed one hundred dollars each to form the Mutual Federal Savings and Loan Association of Atlanta. This association, which grew to over 10 million dollars in assets by 1959, played a major role in enabling African American Atlantans to own their own homes. With his wife, he formed the Blayton Accounting Laboratories in 1927 to provide education to bookkeepers and accountants working in small black-owned businesses.

Blayton formed a partnership known as Blamiya, Inc., with two of his closest business colleagues, Lorimer D. Milton and Clayton A. Yates. Their several ventures included purchasing Citizens Trust Company in 1933, which soon became one of the largest black-owned banks in the United States. In addition to providing loans to small black-owned businesses that often found their access to capital quite limited, Citizens Trust helped develop new neighborhoods, including Hunter Hills and Collier Heights, for Atlanta's growing black elite. When the Federal Housing Administration and Works Progress Administration built new homes for the growing black middle class in Atlanta in the early 1940s, Citizens Trust provided the loans.

In 1938 Blayton became part owner of the first black-owned night club in Atlanta, the Top Hat, which lured the top black acts of the mid-century. The club admitted only white patrons on Saturday nights but was open to African Americans the rest of the week. Blayton achieved another first in 1949 when he bought Atlanta radio station WERD, making it the first black-owned and operated radio station in the United States. His business acumen was widely recognized; in 1956 he was featured in an article on African American business in *Fortune* magazine.

Even as he expanded his business holdings and teaching, Blayton continued his own education, attending the Graduate School of Business at the University of Chicago in the summers of 1933 through 1935 and earning an LLB from the American Extension School of Law in 1936. He was also active in the civic arena: he was a trustee of the Ebenezer Baptist Church, president of the Atlanta Negro Chamber of Commerce, and chairman of the Atlanta Urban League from 1956 to 1967. In 1964 he became the first African American to serve on the Atlanta Housing Authority board.

The advent of the civil rights movement had an effect on Blayton's CPA firm, whose clients grew to include the Montgomery Improvement Association and the Southern Christian Leadership Conference. When the Alabama authorities charged MARTIN LUTHER KING JR. with felony tax evasion, Blayton unraveled the young minister's tangled finances and provided testimony that helped get him acquitted. The movement also contracted his business. Most of his firm's major clients in the 1930s through

the 1960s were small black colleges, but during the Johnson Administration more federal funding was provided to these schools and, simultaneously, state funding increased as states tried to preserve the illusion of equality in order to maintain their justification for segregation. As these schools grew, white influence on their leadership increased, and many new board members insisted that the schools hire major white-owned firms to conduct their audits.

After his retirement from teaching in 1969 Blayton remained active in his business undertakings until he died of a heart attack in an Atlanta barbershop where he often socialized. Because of his prominence, several obituaries mistakenly identified him as the first black CPA in the United States. He was eulogized by BENJAMIN E. MAYS, president of Morehouse, who recognized Blayton's many firsts, and by the Reverend MARTIN LUTHER KING SR.

FURTHER READING

Branch, Taylor. *Parting the Waters: America in the King Years 1954–63* (1988).

Frazier, E. Franklin. *Black Bourgeoisie* (1957).

Hammond, Theresa. *A White-Collar Profession: African American Certified Public Accountants since 1921* (2002).

Hughes, Emmet John. "The Negro's New Economic Life," *Fortune* (Sept. 1956).

Seder, John, and Berkeley Burrell. *Getting It Together: Black Businessmen in America* (1971).

Obituaries: *Atlanta Journal-Constitution*, 16 Sept. 1977; *Atlanta Daily World*, 15 Sept. 1977; *Jet*, 29 Sept. 1977.

THERESA A. HAMMOND

Bledsoe, Jules (29 Dec. 1897–14 July 1943), baritone, was born Julius Lorenzo Cobb Bledsoe in Waco, Texas, the son of Henry L. Bledsoe and Jessie Cobb, occupations unknown. Following his parents' separation in 1899, Jules lived with his maternal grandmother, a midwife and nurse, who encouraged him to appreciate music. After graduating magna cum laude in 1918 from Bishop College in Marshall, Texas, Bledsoe began graduate medical studies at Columbia University, withdrawing after the death of his mother in 1920 to dedicate himself to singing. In 1924 he presented his debut recital at Aeolian Hall in New York.

Bledsoe's first major stage role was as Tizan in the racially mixed opera *Deep River* by Frank

Harling and Laurence Stalling in 1926. That same year he performed in the premiere of Louis Gruenberg's *The Creation* (conducted by Serge Koussevitzky in New York) and worked as an actor at the Provincetown Playhouse. Bledsoe is best known for creating the role of Joe in 1927 in Jerome Kern's *Show Boat*, which ran for two years at the Ziegfeld Theater. (Bledsoe later estimated that he had sung "Old Man River" twenty thousand times.) In 1929 Bledsoe recorded "Lonesome Road" and "Old Man River" to be added to the soundtrack of the 1929 silent film of *Show Boat*. On screen he was represented by the black actor and comedian STEPIN FETCHIT. In 1925 he appeared at the Gallo Theater in New York as Amonasro in the third act of Verdi's *Aida*, performing with members of the New York Philharmonic. In that year he also began a two-year tour of *Show Boat*, followed by a Carnegie Hall recital and concerts in Europe.

In 1932 Bledsoe sang in the Cleveland performance of *Tom-Tom*, an opera by SHIRLEY GRAHAM [DuBois], later the wife of W. E. B. DuBois. He then returned to the role of Amonasro in Cleveland and New York, with occasional vaudeville and radio engagements. He performed the *Aida* role in Amsterdam the next season and toured Europe in *The Emperor Jones*. Beginning in 1934, Bledsoe performed in New York, adding to his repertoire the major baritone roles of *Carmen*, *Faust*, and *Boris Godunov*. His recitals and radio broadcasts, however, included spirituals and even blues.

In 1935 Bledsoe participated in charity events in New York, helping to raise money for the Metropolitan Opera—though because of his race he was not even considered for employment by that company—for out-of-work actors, and for pacifist causes. He also returned to Europe to work in musicals. By 1936 he composed and performed his own song cycle, *African Suite*, with Amsterdam's Concertgebouw Orchestra, conducted by Willem Mengelberg.

Bledsoe's plans to leave his home in Roxbury, New York, to return to Europe were thwarted by the outbreak of war in 1939. He spent the remainder of his career largely in recitals to benefit patriotic or humanitarian causes, although he did appear in several films: *Safari* (1940), *Santa Fe Trail* (1940), *Western Union* (1941), and *Drums of the Congo* (1942). He died of a cerebral hemorrhage in Hollywood, where he had been promoting the sale of war bonds. His funeral was held the next week at his boyhood church, New Hope Baptist, in Waco, Texas. He never married.

Although cast in opera for several "race" roles in the United States, Bledsoe was also successful in European productions in roles that were not race-based. Reviews indicate that he was a major vocal talent with an outstanding ability to communicate. One New York critic observed in 1926, "He has a baritone voice of truly exceptional quality. He is a singer who can pick the heart right out of your body—if you don't look out. And in the second act [of *Deep River*] he showed last night that he is a very fine actor as well." A Parisian critic, praising Bledsoe in 1931, said, "If he remained absolutely what he is, he would be unique in the history of song."

Among Bledsoe's compositions, in addition to the *African Suite*, are arrangements of spirituals for voice and piano, *Ode to America* for baritone and chorus—dedicated to Franklin Roosevelt and first performed in a 1941 broadcast hosted by Eleanor Roosevelt—and the opera *Bondage*, after Harriet Beecher Stowe's *Uncle Tom's Cabin* (never produced).

Bledsoe's career was distinguished by his opera performances, particularly in Europe. American performance opportunities sometimes allied him with figures of the Harlem Renaissance and of vaudeville. Few other black concert artists during this period were able to sustain careers, the major exceptions being ROLAND HAYES, MARIAN ANDERSON, and PAUL ROBESON (who followed Bledsoe as Joe in *Show Boat*).

In 1939 Bledsoe wrote to a former classmate, "I have to be very careful not to injure my prestige. I have had to refuse lesser offers already this year. Most people don't understand that an artist is like a piece of merchandise, which has to be maintained and kept around a certain value, or else ... the downward grade is begun."

FURTHER READING

The Jules Bledsoe Papers are in the Texas Collection of Baylor University Library, Waco, Texas. The vertical file of the Schomburg Research Center at the New York Public Library contains newspaper clippings.

Geary, Lynnette G. "Jules Bledsoe: The Original 'Ol' Man River,'" *Black Perspective in Music* 17, no. 1/2 (1989): 27–54.

Obituary: *Waco Tribune*, 21 July 1943.

This entry is taken from the *American National Biography* and is published here with the permission of the American Council of Learned Societies.

DOMINIQUE-RENÉ DE LERMA

Blind Boone (17 Mar. 1864 or 17 May 1864–4 Oct. 1927), pianist and composer, was born John William Boone in a Union army camp in Miami, Missouri, to Rachel Boone, an army cook and former slave to descendants of Daniel Boone, and to a white bugler for the Seventh Missouri State Militia, Company I, suggested by the historian Mike Shaw to have been Private William S. Belcher (Shaw, 2005). Although Boone's early biographer, Melissa Fuell, referred to Boone as having had five brothers—Ricely, Edward, Sam, Tom, and Harry (Fuell, 137)—according to Shaw it is likely that, except for a half brother, Edward (alternately referred to in census records as both Wyatt and Edward), all were step siblings via Rachel Boone's 17 May 1871 marriage to James Harrison Hendrick (aka Harrison Hendrix).

"Little Willie," as the newborn John William was called, and his mother soon moved to Warrensburg, Missouri, where at the age of six months the infant developed "brain fever," variously diagnosed in sources as encephalitis, meningitis, or *Opthalmia neonatorum* (Batterson, 23–24), a condition that required his eyes to be removed and his eyelids sewed shut. The resulting loss of sight, rather than undermining the boy's happiness and self-esteem, only fueled an upbeat sense of purpose that was to become a hallmark of Boone's adult character and onstage persona.

Little Willie's penchant for music first manifested itself in his vocal imitations of the sounds of animals and nature, his rhythmic beating on a tin pan to accompany his singing, and his early facility on the tin whistle and harmonica, both of which he played in a seven-piece street band he formed with friends by the age of five. The group's local popularity exposed Boone's talent to the same members of Warrensburg white society for whom his mother was a domestic servant, and who in 1873 contributed money to send him, as a nine-year-old, to the St. Louis School for the Blind (known in Boone's day as the Missouri Institute for the Education of the Blind).

There Boone proved an inattentive student. As punishment he was demoted to the school's trade department, where he made brooms, and soon became fascinated by a nearby piano and the students studying it. One of them, Enoch Donley, became his first piano teacher. So fast was Boone's progress under Donley that within a year he was asked to perform regularly for the school superintendent. He further expanded his repertoire during summers, playing at church services and socials.

In Boone's second year at the school, however, a policy of racial segregation was instituted by a new administration that left the boy both despondent and ostracized from the white student body that, up to then, had so readily embraced him. Stripped of his sense of belonging, the budding musician began to take frequent all-night excursions to hear ragtime in St. Louis, a behavior that led to his expulsion from the school after only two and a half years.

Too ashamed to confront his family in Warrensburg, Boone remained in St. Louis, panhandling on Franklin Avenue and Morgan Street in the heart of the city's tenderloin district. Soon, however, he was returned to his mother by his stepfather, Harrison Hendrix, and to the police after Mark Cromwell, a local gambler, attempted to offer the boy as barter in a card game.

Back in Warrensburg, Little Willie's wanderlust won out again. In exchange for travel fare he began singing and playing harmonica on trains traversing the Midwest. Between Glasgow and Mexico, Missouri, he formed a trio with fellow itinerant musicians Tom Johnson, a Sedalia banjo player, and Ben Franklin, a tea cup artist. Boone also played in the black churches of Glasgow and Fayette.

A turning point in Boone's career was his appearance on an 1879 Christmas concert at the Second Baptist Church in Columbia, Missouri, where he met John Lange Jr., a former slave who, as a building contractor and philanthropist, had amassed considerable wealth constructing roads, public schools, and churches, providing, in the process, much-needed jobs for the local African American community. So impressed was Lange with Boone's pianism that he offered to become the young musician's agent. The subsequent agreement between the parties, guaranteeing Boone's mother $10 per month until her son reached twenty-one and the pianist equal partnership thereafter, was the beginning of a long relationship between musician and manager.

Aware of his client's need for further artistic development, Lange initially kept Boone out of the limelight, arranging first for him to study with a professor (probably Anna Heuermann) at Christian College in Columbia, who introduced the boy to the music of Bach, Beethoven, and Brahms, and later with Mrs. M. R. Samson of the Iowa State Teachers' College. Boone's official coming-out party did not occur until 3 March 1880, the date of an impromptu play-off that Lange was able to orchestrate at Garth Hall in Columbia between his protégé and the celebrated Georgia pianist and former slave Thomas Wiggins, known more popularly as BLIND TOM. After the local favorite purportedly matched Wiggins note for note, it was reported that a humiliated Blind Tom "disappeared backstage. He left town the next day and never again crossed Boone's path" (*Kansas City Times*, 6 Feb. 1950).

Wiggins's influence on Boone's career, however, was profound. Boone's programs, like his predecessor's, not only featured performances of his own compositions, transcriptions of well-known operas, and mainstream classical works by Beethoven, Chopin, Liszt, Thalberg, and the New Orleans pianist LOUIS MOREAU GOTTSCHALK (the first person to compose concert music influenced by African American culture), but also several of Blind Tom's signature stunts—for example imitating various musical instruments and mechanical devices on the keyboard; rendering three songs at once, one in the right hand, another in the left, and the third vocally, each in a different key; and playing back clusters of random notes and an original piece performed moments earlier by a local pianist onstage. *Marshfield Tornado*, a musical recreation of the catastrophic storm that struck Marshfield, Missouri, on 18 April 1880, and Boone's most popular work (unfortunately never recorded or published), was, no doubt, inspired by *Battle of Manassas*, one of several Blind Tom selections in Boone's repertoire. Even "Blind John," an early stage name Boone adopted but later abandoned, was an homage to Wiggins.

However, the Boone Concert Company, officially established in 1880, also departed significantly from the Blind Tom model. Its motto, "Merit, Not Sympathy, Wins" discouraged the kind of sordid attention to the star's infirmity that had served as such an effective drawing card in Wiggins's career. An activist impulse, in fact, lay at the core of the Boone Company mission. By exposing both blacks and whites in the audience to African American–inspired music, Boone and Lange sought to break down those racial barriers that had been so zealously exploited by Blind Tom's handlers. In what Boone liked to characterize as "putting cookies on the lower shelf so that everyone can get at them" (Batterson, 55), the Missourian played camp meeting tunes, coon songs, negro spirituals, and ragtime on every program. The first instrumentalist to bring such fare into the concert hall (preceded only by the Fisk Jubilee Singers), Boone was an important link between nineteenth-century rural black folk music and the more urban jazz and popular music that would emerge in the twentieth. And by incorporating a violinist, a banjo player, and a well-trained singer (Melissa Fuell among them) into each performance, the Blind Boone Concert Company could be

viewed, along with the minstrel show, as a precursor of the traveling "revues" that would become a staple of black music in the post–World War II era. Even the jewel-encrusted pocket watch, numerous gold rings, and diamond-studded cross the pianist always wore alongside a dazzling array of secret society pins (proudly displayed military-style on his vest in order to draw attention to the many fraternal organizations of which he was a member) anticipated the sartorial splendor of show business to come.

Further distinguishing Boone from Blind Tom is the greater extent to which the Missourian's own music drew upon black culture. Among Boone's seventeen published solo piano works (including four waltzes, a polka, a serenade, a spinning song, as well as four character pieces), six—his *Southern Rag Medley Nos. 1 and 2*; *Caprice de Concert: Melodies de Negres Nos. 1 and 2*; *Danse des Negres: Caprice de Concert*; and *Theme and Variations on Stephen Foster's "Old Folks at Home"*—are direct outgrowths of African American music. The same is true of six of his eight published songs—"Dat Mornin' In De Sky," "Dinah's Barbecue," "When I Meet Dat Coon Tonight," "Whar Shill We Go When de Great Day Comes?," "Melons Cool and Green," and "Geo'gia Melon." And, if Edward A. Berlin's suggestion is correct that the "Alabama Bound" section of *Southern Rag Melody No. 2* (1909) may have been the first published boogie-woogie (Berlin, 155), Boone, in turn, could be credited as the first to draw the connection, in print, between ragtime and the blues.

Following its inaugural concert in 1880 at the Columbia courthouse, the Boone Company's early tours were marred by a shortage of funds, three fires, two train wrecks, and racial segregation of the Jim Crow era. In some cities Lange had to organize two concerts, one for whites, the second for blacks. But Boone's assumption of full partnership in 1885 and his 1889 marriage to Lange's sister, Eugenia, coincided with the company's peak period. Between 1885 and 1916 Boone and Lange toured the Western and Midwestern United States, Canada, and Mexico virtually non-stop, traveling ten months out of the year, giving six concerts a week, and, between them, taking in $150 to $600 a night. The signing in 1912 of a contract with the QRS Company allowed Boone to become the first African American to make piano rolls and one of the first musicians of any color to make "hand-played" rolls, directly recorded, using the latest technology, from actual performances by the artist.

Lange's death at the age of seventy-five, which came on 23 July 1916 of a cerebral hemorrhage and shock arising from an automobile accident (Shaw, pers. comm.) was an emotional and commercial blow from which Boone never recovered. Although the pianist, as sole owner of the company, hired John and Marguerite Day and then Wayne B. Allen as managerial assistants, competition over the next decade from movies, radio, and other emerging forms of entertainment made bookings increasingly difficult to secure. By the 1920s Boone's nightly net income had plummeted to between $50 and $70. Other than a tour of the East in the 1919–1920 season, during which the pianist performed at Harvard and Yale as well as in Boston, New York, and Washington, D.C., engagements during this final period were mostly limited to smaller towns in the Midwest. Contemplating retirement and convalescing in Warrensburg from a case of "dropsy," Boone suffered a heart attack and died in the backyard of his stepbrother Sam Hendrix's home. He was buried at Columbia Cemetery in a grave that remained unmarked until 1971.

Preceded by Louis Moreau Gottschalk and later Blind Tom, Blind Boone will be remembered as the last of a trio of overlapping nineteenth-century classical pianist/composers, each a musical descendent of his immediate predecessor. All three were influenced by African American culture, and were seminal figures in the development of twentieth-century popular music in the United States.

FURTHER READING

Batterson, Jack A. *Blind Boone: Missouri's Ragtime Pioneer* (1998).

Berlin, Edward A. *Ragtime: A Musical and Cultural History* (1980).

Fuell, Miss Melissa. *Blind Boone: His Early Life and His Achievements* (1915).

Shaw, Mike. *Compass*, Newsletter of the Boone Society, Inc. (July 2005).

Obituary: *New York Times*, 5 Oct. 1927.

DISCOGRAPHY

Marshfield Tornado: John Davis Plays Blind Boone (Newport Classic Ltd., NPD 85678).

Merit, Not Sympathy Wins: Blind Boone's Strains from the Flat Branch (The Blind Boone Renovation Group).

JOHN DAVIS

Blind Tom (25 May 1849–13 June 1908), pianist and composer, was born Thomas Greene Wiggins to Domingo Wiggins and Charity Greene, field slaves on the Wiley Jones Plantation in Harris County, Georgia. In 1850 Tom, his parents, and two brothers were auctioned off to General James Neil Bethune, a prominent attorney and antiabolitionist newspaper publisher from Columbus, Georgia. The discovery two years later of the toddler, newly renamed Thomas Greene Bethune, blind from birth, possibly mentally impaired, and unusually captivated by random sounds, playing one of the general's daughter's piano pieces "totally 'stonished us,'" according to Charity (*New York Times*, 27 Nov. 1886).

The general, however, viewed Tom's unforeseen musical ability as an opportunity. Eulogized in 1895 as "almost the pioneer free trader in this country" and "the first editor in the south to openly advocate secession" (*New York Times*, 21 Jan. 1895), Bethune saw the potential for this helpless, prodigiously talented boy to become a symbol of what Bethune would argue were "sufficient reasons why we should keep our slaves as they are … a class of laborers … incapable of taking care of themselves, and controlled by individuals who are not only capable of taking care of them but interested in doing it" (*Corner Stone*, 3 Feb. 1859). Soon Tom would be even more valuable to him as a cash cow.

Ensuring Tom's musical success became Bethune's top priority. Otherwise uneducated, Tom began his piano studies under Mary, the eldest Bethune daughter. Her expertise was soon eclipsed, and more professionally recognized teachers were engaged. Tom's acute ear, phenomenal auditory memory, and natural keyboard facility allowed him to assimilate the repertoire they favored so quickly that in 1857 Bethune produced a debut for the eight-year-old at Columbus's Temperance Hall that led to numerous other concerts around the state of Georgia. But the death in May 1858 of Bethune's wife, Frances, and the increasingly active role the Georgia attorney was assuming in the emerging debate over states' rights made it impossible for the general to stay on as Tom's manager. So, in 1859, he leased Tom out for three years to the Savannah impresario Perry Oliver, whose savvy promotion of the pianist paid dividends well in excess of the fifteen thousand dollars Bethune received in return. Trading on long-standing racial stereotypes and on the public's fascination with the freak show during this period, Oliver advertised Tom as "The Wonder Negro Child … whose feats at the piano baffle the most scientific and learned men in the land" (*New Orleans Times Picayune*, 5 Feb. 1861). Further fueling the carnival atmosphere was the incorporation of an onstage master of ceremonies, a by-request format, and a series of sensational pianistic and extramusical stunts designed to shift attention away from the legitimate aspects of the boy's talent. Still guaranteed were concert performances rendered "with all the taste, expression, and feeling of the most distinguished artist" (*New Orleans Times Picayune*, 5 Feb. 1861) of compositions by Bach, Beethoven, Chopin, Gottschalk, Liszt, Mendelssohn, Meyerbeer, Rossini, Thalberg, Verdi, and even Wiggins himself, chosen by members of the audience off a list of eighty-two items drawn from the pianist's purported repertoire of seven thousand established works. But these mainstream pieces increasingly gave way to a series of sensational pianistic and extra-musical stunts. Among these stunts were Tom's flawless re-creations of original compositions played moments earlier by a local pianist onstage; performances of complicated classical works with his back to the piano; on-the-spot improvisations of an accompaniment to any piece presented, even one he had never heard before; and simultaneous renderings of three different songs, one using the right hand, another using the left, and the third sung, each in a different key. Other program innovations were Tom's recitations of texts in foreign languages he could not even speak and famous political speeches of the era in the same rhythm and pitch pattern in which they were originally uttered. A final otherworldly touch was the verbal introduction by Tom of each of his own compositions in the third person.

Significant in this era before recordings was the deal Oliver cut in 1860 with Horace Waters in New York and Oliver Ditson in Boston to publish "Oliver Galop" and "Virginia Polka," the first of nineteen solo piano pieces by Wiggins to make it into print. On the surface, most of Tom's keyboard works come off as run-of-the-mill rehashings of nineteenth-century European dance and concert music—waltzes, gallops, a mazurka, a polka, a theme and variations, and a nocturne. A deeper probing, however, reveals in them sophisticated compositional materials and evocative imagery that offer a window onto Wiggins's unique and insular world. "The Rainstorm" (composed when Wiggins was just five years old), "Cyclone Galop," "Voice of the Waves," "Water in the Moonlight," and "Daylight" all grew out of Tom's documented fascination with sounds of nature. The hypnotic ostinato of mechanical devices, yet another of Tom's obsessions, was realized musically by him in both "Sewing Song: Imitation of a Sewing Machine" and "Battle of Manassas," Wiggins's signature piece. Based on a firsthand account by one of Bethune's

sons of that important Confederate victory, "Manassas" employed tone clusters and mouthed effects, materials not adopted again by composers until the twentieth century.

Leading up to the Civil War, the annual revenue from Wiggins's concerts and the sale of his sheet music reached $100,000, equivalent today to $1.5 million per year, making Blind Tom undoubtedly the nineteenth century's most highly compensated pianist. Wiggins, of course, saw almost none of this money, as it was deposited directly into the Bethune bank account. So widespread had the pianist's reputation become under Oliver that in 1860 he gave a command performance for the president at the White House, the first African American to do so.

Traveling became so difficult after the beginning of the Civil War that in 1861 Oliver and Bethune were forced to void the final year of their contract. Wiggins, however, continued to give concerts south of the Mason-Dixon Line, ironically often arranged by Bethune for the benefit of the Confederate war machine. In response to Abraham Lincoln's 1863 Emancipation Proclamation, the general persuaded Wiggins's parents to sign an indenture agreement in 1864. This arrangement bound their son to his former owner for the next five years in exchange for "a good home and subsistence and $500 a year" for the parents and "$20 per month and two percent of the net proceeds" for Tom (*Cincinnati Daily Commercial*, 20 June 1865). It was at this time that "Blind Tom," the stage name assigned to Wiggins, first appeared in broadsides and newspapers advertising his concerts.

The Confederate surrender in 1865, however, opened the door for Bethune's guardianship to be challenged. That year, in fact, a habeas corpus petition was filed against Bethune in a Cincinnati court, not by Tom's parents but by Tabbs Gross, a former slave turned show business promoter, known publicly as "the Barnum of the African Race." The six-day trial, covered nationally in the press, culminated on 26 June 1865 in a controversial verdict leaving Wiggins in the care of General Bethune.

Blind Tom's only tour of France and England, the following year, earned his handlers an additional $100,000 and written testimonials by Ignaz Moscheles and Charles Hallé, the first praise of Tom's ability from pianists of international repute. That year, too, the French physician and educator Edouard Seguin included a profile of Blind Tom's behavior in his seminal work on autism, *Idiocy and Its Treatment by the Physiological Method* (1866).

Whether Wiggins had a mental disorder is a question that may never be fully answered.

Increasingly dependent on income from Tom's concerts after the war, Bethune decided in 1868 to move his immediate family and Tom to a more centrally located base of operations in Warrenton, Virginia, just forty miles southwest of Washington, D.C. The general's indenture contract with Wiggins's parents was soon to expire, but with Domingo recently dead and Charity still living in Georgia, no one was present to object when, in 1870, Bethune had a Virginia probate judge declare Tom mentally incompetent and name Bethune's son John as Wiggins's new legal guardian.

In 1875 John Bethune, acting as Wiggins's manager, moved with Tom to New York City, where in 1882 John married Eliza Stutzbach, owner of the boardinghouse he and the pianist shared in Greenwich Village. The bloom was soon off the rose, and in 1884 annulment proceedings were initiated against the bride, characterized in John's will as "a heartless adventuress who sought to absorb my estate" (*New York Times*, 23 Mar. 1884). Before any resolution could be worked out, John Bethune was accidentally killed while attempting to board a moving train in Wilmington, Delaware.

The repercussions for Wiggins were enormous. Eliza Bethune, finding that she had been frozen out of her deceased husband's will, persuaded Tom's mother to file a second habeas corpus petition in 1885 against General Bethune, with the understanding that, should Charity prevail, guardianship of Tom would be turned over to Eliza herself. Exactly that improbable scenario played out when, on 30 July 1887, Judge Hugh L. Bond, a federal judge in Baltimore, extricated Thomas Wiggins from the thirty-eight-year custody of Bethune and his immediate family.

Reports that Wiggins lapsed into a self-imposed semiretirement for the last twenty years of his life, as a silent protest against his forced separation from his former owner, appear exaggerated. Clearly, he was distraught over the new arrangement, but he continued to give concerts, albeit not at the same tireless pace as before, and to compose new pieces for publication, their copyright now assigned to Eliza Bethune. Wiggins's occasional absence from the stage, however, did spawn both rumors of his death, most notably in the 1889 flood of Johnstown, Pennsylvania, and the appearance of various Blind Tom impersonators on the nascent vaudeville circuit. Retired in 1908 and well on his way to musical obscurity, Wiggins suffered a stroke and died at age fifty-nine in Hoboken, New Jersey, where he had moved from Manhattan with Eliza in 1903. His body was taken to the Evergreens Cemetery in Brooklyn for burial in a grave that remained unmarked until 1 July 2002. Blind Tom may have been the first in a long line of black musicians, including many of the bluesmen that followed him, to have been canonized and exploited in life and marginalized and all but forgotten in death.

FURTHER READING

Jay, Ricky. *Learned Pigs and Fireproof Women* (1986).

Riis, Thomas L. "The Legacy of a Prodigy Lost in Mystery," *New York Times*, 5 Mar. 2000.

Southall, Geneva Handy. *Blind Tom, the Black Pianist-Composer, Continually Enslaved* (1999).

Obituary: *New York Times*, 16 June 1908.

DISCOGRAPHY

John Davis Plays Blind Tom (Newport Classic Ltd. NPD 85660).

JOHN DAVIS

Block, Samuel (17 July 1939–13 Apr. 2000), civil rights activist, was born in Cleveland, Mississippi, the son of Sam Block, a cotton compress laborer, and Alma Shacklefoot Block, a domestic worker. After graduating from high school, Block enlisted in the Air Force but was discharged for medical reasons. He attended Marlboro College in Vermont for two years, then returned to Mississippi and enrolled at Mississippi Vocational College (later Mississippi Valley State University). When he was expelled for civil rights activities, the veteran National Association for the Advancement of Colored People (NAACP) activist AMZIE MOORE encouraged Block to set up citizenship education classes around Cleveland. ROBERT MOSES, leader of Mississippi voter registration efforts, then recruited Block to work for the Student Nonviolent Coordinating Committee (SNCC).

On 17 June 1962 Block arrived alone in Greenwood, a stronghold of the segregationist White Citizens' Council. In an interview with Joe Sinsheimer in *Southern Exposure*, Block described his first efforts at community organizing:

I would go canvassing, just talking to people in the community about voter education and registration, sort of testing the pulse of the people. Hanging out in the pool halls, wherever people were, the laundromat, run around the grocery stores, meeting people.

Fifteen people showed up for his first meeting at the Elks Hall. Whites soon discovered what Block was up to and pressured his hosts. The Elks withdrew the use of their hall and his landlady evicted him. For a week Block slept in an abandoned car in a junkyard. Despite these setbacks, he slowly gained support in the community. The Reverend Aaron Johnson allowed a meeting in his First Christian Church where Block led the singing of freedom songs. He told Sinsheimer that the next day people "asked me when we were going to have another meeting and sing those songs. And I began to see the music itself as an important organizing tool." After a second meeting Block led a group of twenty-one people to the courthouse. Their presence prompted Leflore County registrar Martha Lamb to summon the sheriff, who confronted Block. JAMES FORMAN recounted their exchange in *The Making of Black Revolutionaries*: "I don't want to see you in town any more…. Pack your clothes and get out and don't never come back," the sheriff demanded. Block boldly replied, "Sheriff, if you don't want to see me here … the best thing for you to do is to pack *your* clothes and leave, get out of town, 'cause I'm here to stay." That night Block noticed a gang of armed white men in the street outside the SNCC office. He and two companions escaped out of a second story window. When they returned the next morning they found the door broken and the office vandalized.

In October county commissioners stopped the distribution of federal surplus food in reprisal for black voter registration activities. SNCC organizers appealed to northern supporters, who delivered truckloads of food and clothing. Block and WAZIR PEACOCK coordinated the distribution of goods to poverty-stricken families. Although the amount collected was not nearly enough to feed those in need, it was a powerful stimulus for voter registration.

Block endured constant harassment and assaults. Shortly after arriving in Greenwood he was beaten by three white men. On 20 February 1963 four buildings near the SNCC office were burned. Block told a reporter the fire was in retaliation for voter registration activities. Two days later he was arrested and charged with making a false statement—his seventh arrest in eight months. On 28 February a car without license plates fired into a carload of SNCC workers, critically wounding Jimmy Travis. On 6 March a shotgun blast struck the car in which Block, Peacock, and two young women were sitting. No one was seriously injured.

Despite this violence, voter registration activities increased. In the first three weeks of March more than 250 blacks attempted to register. In *I've Got the Light of Freedom*, Charles M. Payne attributed the growth of the Greenwood movement, in large part, to "the sheer courage and persistence of the young organizers." Sam Block, he observed, "had patiently earned the respect and admiration of a great many people."

Following Greenwood, Block continued voter registration work in Holmes and Humphreys counties. By early 1964, however, Block was showing symptoms of "battle fatigue." The historian John Dittmer wrote in *Local People*, "Eighteen months of beatings and jailings, along with disagreements with other staff members, had taken their toll." One area of conflict was the recruitment of outside volunteers for the Freedom Summer project. Block argued that the presence of inexperienced northern students would undermine the indigenous movement he had helped build. In June 1964 he was brutally beaten by a state trooper in Columbus, Mississippi, suffering permanent damage to one eye.

Block left Mississippi and settled in California where he launched business ventures to manufacture a sealant for flat tires and nutritional supplements. From 1984 to 1988 he served time in federal prison following a conviction on wire fraud charges. His marriage to Peggy Marye ended in divorce. They had one daughter. He remained active in civil rights causes in Los Angeles until his death due to complications from diabetes.

The largely unsung work of young organizers like Sam Block built the grass roots movement that toppled Jim Crow. They faced the entrenched power of segregationists and risked their lives daily to bring basic civil rights to African Americans in the Deep South.

FURTHER READING

Dittmer, John. *Local People: The Struggle for Civil Rights in Mississippi* (1994).

Forman, James. *The Making of Black Revolutionaries* (1972).

Payne, Charles M. *I've Got the Light of Freedom: The Organizing Tradition and the Mississippi Freedom Struggle* (1995).

Sinsheimer, Joe. "Never Turn Back: An Interview with Sam Block," *Southern Exposure* (Summer 1987) 37–50.

Obituary: *New York Times*, 22 April 2000.

PAUL T. MURRAY

Blocker, Sarah (27 Oct. 1857–15 Apr. 1944), educator, was born Sarah Ann Blocker in Edgefield, South Carolina, one of the five children of Sarah A. Stewart of Delaware and Isaiah Blocker of Edgefield, South Carolina. Nothing is known about her early childhood. Blocker briefly attended Atlanta University and enrolled in teacher education classes. At the age of twenty-two, Sarah Blocker moved to Live Oak, Florida, where she taught at the Florida Baptist Institute, a school established by African American Christian ministers of the First Bethlehem Baptist Association of West Florida in 1879.

Resistance and hostility toward African Americans in Live Oak resulted in escalating violence. Blocker herself was almost wounded in a shooting incident in 1892. Blocker's determination remained steadfast, however. In 1892 she cofounded the Florida Baptist Academy, an elementary and secondary educational institution for African American girls and boys. She was assisted in this project by the Reverends Matthew W. Gilbert and J. T. Brown of the Bethel Institutional Baptist Church in Jacksonville, Florida, who helped her secured financial assistance from the American Home Mission Society.

The academy, which began operation in the basement of the Bethel Baptist Church, relocated to east Jacksonville's Campbell Addition, an African American community, in 1894, where the institution purchased a large three-story building in December. Blocker's fund-raising, administrative, and management skills substantially contributed to the growth and economic prosperity of the institution, including its recognition as the site where JOHN ROSAMOND JOHNSON and JAMES WELDON JOHNSON composed the song "Lift Every Voice and Sing," which was first performed by the school's students in 1902. She served as assistant to the president of the academy, as secretary to the institute, and as principal of the normal department. She also served as dean of women, and she chaired all of the institution's committees. Blocker recommended the selection of NATHAN WHITE COLLIER as Florida Baptist Academy president, a post in which he served from 1896 until 1941. Collier's leadership transformed the institution and earned him recognition as one of the most revered African American educators in the state of Florida. Blocker mobilized women in Jacksonville to endorse a fund-raising venture for the institution, eventually raising two thousand dollars.

The institution briefly adopted the name of Florida Baptist College in the early 1900s but reclaimed its original name of Florida Baptist Academy until 1918. Blocker participated in educational conferences and was an active member of the Florida Teachers Association. In 1918 the academy relocated to St. Augustine, Florida, where Blocker remained in leadership positions at the school, serving as ex officio chair of all committees, orchestrating faculty activities, and counseling the students. In 1918 the Florida Baptist Academy changed its name to the Florida Normal and Industrial Institute. In 1931 the school received accreditation as a junior college from the Southern Association of Colleges and Secondary Schools and the Florida State Department of Education. Blocker continued to train African American teachers who then taught at local schools throughout the state. Two of her best-known students include the writer ZORA NEALE HURSTON and the social worker EARTHA MARY MAGDALENE WHITE. Blocker worked for the YWCA and the War Camp Community Agency at Newport News, Virginia, during World War II, assisting in providing housing and basic services to local communities.

In April 1941 Blocker terminated her appointment with the War Camp Community Agency and returned to the Florida Normal and Industrial Institute as dean of women. Her timely return was crucial to the institution following President Collier's death several months before. The institution experienced mounting debts, which accumulated as Collier's illness prevented him from engaging in fund-raising activities. Blocker's leadership at this pivotal time was instrumental in the merger of Live Oak's Florida Baptist Institute, which changed its name to Florida Memorial College in 1918, and the Florida Baptist Academy to form the Florida Normal and Industrial Memorial Institute in 1941. The merger brought increased financial support from Baptist organizations and national recognition for the institution. Blocker became the vice president of Florida Normal and Industrial Institute. Despite her ailing health, which played a role in her release from official administrative duties in 1942, Blocker continued to provide valuable assistance to the school's newly elected president, WILLIAM HERBERT GRAY JR. Parents sought her supervision of their daughters and her intervention on financial and academic matters. Blocker's commitment and dedication to the institution were duly noted when she was honored at the fifteenth anniversary of the Florida Normal and Industrial Institute, at which she was presented with the institution's Loving Cup of Appreciation award for her help in developing the institution. She was honored again in 1943, on the occasion of the school's fifty-first anniversary.

Blocker remained very active in the Woman's American Baptist Home Mission Society, which honored her posthumously in 1957. Throughout her life she was affiliated with the First Baptist Church. Blocker was buried on the Florida Normal and Industrial Institute campus when she died in 1944. Her grave was moved to Woodlawn Cemetery in West Augustine, Florida, when the college moved to Miami in 1967. After several name changes, the institution became known as the Florida Memorial College. The only historically black college in Miami, Florida Memorial College honored Blocker with a posthumous honorary doctorate and by naming its classroom building the Sarah A. Blocker Hall. Each year the school issues one of its female students its highest honor, the Sarah Blocker Meritorious Service Award. In 2004 Sarah Blocker was inducted into the Florida Women's Hall of Fame.

FURTHER READING

Colburn, David R. *Racial Change and Community Crisis: St. Augustine, Florida, 1877–1980* (1985).

McKinney, George Patterson, and Richard I. McKinney. *History of the Black Baptists of Florida, 1850-1985* (1987).

ROSE C. THEVENIN

Blockson, Charles L. (16 Dec. 1933–), African American history scholar, was born in Norristown, Pennsylvania, to Charles E. Blockson and Annie Parker, who preached the importance of learning African American history to him from his earliest youth. Blockson's interest in African American history was sparked when he took umbrage at the racist comments of his fourth-grade teacher. When his teacher said to him, "Negroes have no history; they are meant only to serve white people," Blockson vowed to learn as much as possible about black history and to educate both blacks and whites on the effect that people of African descent had on America (Sinnette, Coates, and Battle, 119). His family encouraged him in this pursuit, and he began collecting items connected to black history at the age of ten.

Blockson attended Pennsylvania State University, where he was recognized for his outstanding athletic performance in football and track and field. He set records for Penn State in shot put and discus, and his performance as a fullback on the football team earned him the nickname Blockbuster Blockson.

He graduated from Penn State in 1956. He declined a chance to play for the New York Giants, and after briefly serving in the military, Blockson began a teaching career in Pennsylvania's Norristown Area School District, focusing on American history and multicultural and diversity education, particularly African American studies. Blockson was married to Elizabeth Parker, but the union, which produced a daughter, Noelle, ended in divorce.

Blockson went on to become recognized as one of America's foremost scholars on the Underground Railroad, which indeed had played a significant role in Blockson's family history: his great-grandfather had been liberated from slavery and guided to Canada by the Railroad. Charles L. Blockson's poem, "The Ballad of the Underground Railroad," published in *Jump Up and Say! A Collection of Black Storytelling* in 1995, describes the various participants in and effect of the Railroad. The poem describes the diversity of the Railroad's participants and praises their courage in a metered, rhymed structure. Blockson took his interest in the Railroad to the political sphere, campaigning successfully for passage of the National Underground Railroad Network to Freedom Act in 1998. The act led to further legislation, eventually resulting in the National Park Service's increased involvement in preserving historical sites connected to the Underground Railroad.

Blockson also pioneered the study of African Americans in Pennsylvania. He wrote numerous books and essays on the subject, including *Pennsylvania's Black History* (1975), one of the first books to provide an in-depth look at the history of African Americans in a northern state. This book not only described the leading black intellectuals, artists, and activists in Pennsylvania's history but it also provided information on the major landmarks connected to the black experience, such as meeting houses for abolitionists and stops on the Underground Railroad. In 1977 he published *Black Genealogy* in collaboration with Ron Fry, in response to the widespread problems encountered by many African Americans in discovering their family history before their ancestors were transported to the United States as slaves. *Black Genealogy* discussed information sources ranging from public records connected to the slave trade to the analysis of facial characteristics to estimate the locations of one's African ancestors, all in an attempt to make genealogy accessible to the average person.

Blockson was most widely known for his work as an antiquarian of African American artifacts, and earned a reputation for being a leading force in bringing black history to a wider audience. Throughout his life he added to his eclectic collection of items connected to the African American experience. Most of the items in the collection were printed materials—books, musical compositions, newspapers, posters, prints, and photographs—but the collection also included artwork, sports memorabilia, and other rare and unique items such as busts and statues of prominent African Americans and handcrafted Bibles. Some notable pieces included first editions by W. E. B. DuBois and Phillis Wheatley, and letters by the Haitian revolutionaries Toussaint L'Overture and Henri Christophe.

One of the most represented subjects in the collection was Paul Robeson, the performer, athlete, and activist whom Blockson considered to be one of his heroes. More than 3,000 items in the collection pertain to Robeson, including programs from his plays, autographed books, and voice recordings. Robeson himself was a collector of artifacts connected to black history. When Blockson met Robeson in the late 1960s Robeson inspired Blockson to follow his example and continue to safeguard African American history.

In 1984 Blockson donated his collection to Temple University in Philadelphia and became curator of the collection. At that point the collection contained more than 150,000 items, needed five large rooms to house it, and expanded outside of American history to cover black history across the world. Some items were four centuries old. Blockson declared that he sincerely hoped that making the collection accessible to the wider public would "help eliminate ignorance, because in many ways it is the worst form of slavery" (*Temple News*, 21 Feb. 2002). He retired from his position as curator on 31 December 2006.

Blockson received numerous accolades for his work, including several honorary degrees and the Before Columbus Foundation's Lifetime Achievement Award. He served as president of the Pennsylvania Abolition Society and was a member of the American Antiquarian Society, the Historical Society of Pennsylvania, and the NAACP. Blockson also was a driving force in a project to celebrate the history of African Americans in Philadelphia during the late twentieth and early twenty-first centuries by installing historical markers honoring notable people, places, and events around the city. Some of the honorees were Underground Railroad sites and the homes of prominent abolitionists. His

memoir *Damn Rare: The Memoirs of an African-American Bibliophile* was published in 1998.

FURTHER READING
Goss, Linda, and Clay Goss, eds. *Jump Up and Say! A Collection of Black Storytelling* (1995).
Sinnette, Elinor Des Verney, W. Paul Coates, and Thomas C. Battle, eds. *Black Bibliophiles and Collectors: Preservers of Black History* (1990).
Stewart, Jeffrey C. *Paul Robeson: Artist and Citizen* (1998).

CHRIS CHAN

Blount, Mel (10 Apr. 1948–) football player, was born Melvin Carnell Blount in Vidalia, Georgia. Blount was the youngest of eleven children who grew up in rural Georgia in extreme poverty, often going barefoot and living in a home with no indoor plumbing. Blount's father, a deeply religious man, instilled values in his children through hard work and high expectations, and Blount recalled that some of the most satisfying moments of his childhood came from doing chores for his father and earning his praise. Blount learned football from his seven older brothers, who played a rough brand of football in which Blount excelled at an early age. In high school Blount proved that he was a gifted athlete on the football field and beyond. He was a multiple-sports star, running track as well as playing baseball, basketball, and football. Blount made such an impression in high school that by the time he graduated in 1966 he was offered a football scholarship to Southern University in Baton Rouge, Louisiana.

Blount had a tremendous college career playing for Southern's football team. In the late 1960s he was twice named to the Southwestern Athletic Conference's first team, and in 1968 he was named the conference's Most Valuable Player. Blount was versatile and could play both safety and cornerback so well that he was named to the Pro Scouts' All-American team to play both positions. Blount graduated with a B.A. in Physical Education in 1970.

It was also in 1970 that Blount got a chance to prove himself on football's biggest stage: the National Football League (NFL). Based on his solid career at Southern, Blount was drafted in the third round of the 1970 NFL draft, the fifty-third pick overall by the Pittsburgh Steelers. Throughout the 1970s and early 1980s, Blount was instrumental in turning the Steelers from a perennially losing team into play-off regulars and four-time Super Bowl champions. Blount started nine games for the

Steelers in his rookie year. He realized even more playing time in his second year, and by his third year was a full-time starter at cornerback for the Steelers, adept at playing both man-to-man and zone coverages. Blount never used blazing speed to achieve NFL success, but he was able to break up passes and make interceptions through impeccable positioning and fierce intimidation. Perhaps the best bump-and-run corner of all time, he developed both a keen understanding of offensive patterns and a punishing style that forced receivers to work for every catch. Blount was known as the prototype cornerback of his era, and his strong defensive style, which he employed so skillfully to break up passes and intimidate receivers, was partly responsible for eventual NFL rule changes that prevented much of the contact between receivers and cornerbacks. These rule changes served the goal of player safety, but they were also meant to help receivers who had a difficult time getting open against physical cornerbacks such as Blount.

Blount earned a series of accolades throughout his career. In 1975, he led the league in interceptions with eleven, and he was named the National Football League's Most Valuable Player. He was named All-Pro in 1975, 1977, and 1981, and he played in five Pro Bowls in 1976, 1977, 1979, 1980, and 1982. Blount played in six American Football Conference Championship Games, winning four of them. He was also on all four Pittsburgh Steelers Super Bowl winning teams, in 1974, 1975, 1978, and 1979. His key interception in the 1974 Super Bowl helped the Steelers to their first championship. Finally, Blount had fifty-seven career interceptions, the most in Steelers history.

Blount retired from the NFL in 1983, but his career was not soon forgotten. He was enshrined in the NFL Hall of Fame in his first year of eligibility, 1989. Also in 1989 Blount was inducted into the Louisiana Sports Hall of Fame, and one year later, in 1990, he was inducted into the Georgia Sports Hall of Fame. From 1983 to 1990, the NFL employed him as the director of player relations.

Although Blount remained active in football following his retirement, he was not content to simply fade into NFL lore, and he pursued other interests and goals. Even during his glory years Blount recognized that football would only be a part of his life and that he needed to find some other outlet to be his "life's work." Blount and his brother Clinton looked to their childhood to find a way to give back, and they decided to open up two licensed youth homes. One was located in Blount's hometown of Vidalia,

and the other was to be located in Taylorstown, Pennsylvania. Unfortunately, the plans for the Mel Blount Youth Home in Taylorstown met with some racist resistance because many Taylorstown residents claimed that the home would be a harm to the community. However, in 1989, at a meeting called to debate the merits of awarding Blount the permit to build his youth home, he received some support from the community and was finally able to open it. In 1993, Blount published an account of the harrowing experience in a book titled *The Cross Burns Brightly: A Hall of Famer Tackles Racism and Adversity to Help Troubled Boys*.

Following his retirement from the NFL, Blount won numerous awards for his commitment to bettering the community. In 1990 he won an NAACP Human Rights Award, a Service Award from the Boy Scouts of America, and a Peoplehood Award from the National Conference of Christians and Jews. In 1996 he won a Martin Luther King Jr. Humanitarian Award, and in 1997 he was inducted into the World Sports Humanitarian Hall of Fame. In 2002, Blount was awarded the prestigious NFL Alumni Order of the Leather Helmet and Community Service Award. The recognition by so many varied sources reaffirms Blount's commitment to community service and to giving back. Throughout his career Blount proved that with a strong work ethic anything is possible, and after his retirement, he has taught that philosophy to young people in need.

FURTHER READING

Blount, Roy, Jr. *About Three Bricks Shy—and the Load Filled Up: The Story of the Greatest Football Team Ever* (2004).

Chastain, Bill. *Steel Dynasty: The Team that Changed the NFL* (2005).

Mendelson, Abby. *The Pittsburgh Steelers: The Official Team History* (2006).

Sahadi, Lou. *Super Steelers: The Making of a Dynasty* (1980).

Wexell, Jim. *Tales from Behind the Steel Curtain* (2004).

DANIEL A. DALRYMPLE

Blue, Carroll (23 Aug. 1943–), a still photographer and documentary filmmaker, was born in Houston, Texas, the second child and only daughter of the schoolteacher Mollie Carroll Parrott and the dentist Frederick Douglas Parrott Sr. At least one grandparent had been born a slave. Both parents were the first in their respective families to obtain advanced college degrees, but racism kept the family poor. The Parrotts lived in the Third Ward, one of Houston's African American neighborhoods, and Blue attended a segregated grade school. As she wrote in her memoir, *The Dawn at My Back*, the challenges of growing up poor and black in a racist, classist society put a shadow over her life.

Blue did not intend to pursue a career in the visual arts. She enrolled as an English literature student, specializing in the sixteenth- and seventeenth-century English Renaissance period, at Boston University in 1960 with the goal of becoming a writer. Upon graduating in 1964, Blue moved to Los Angeles and became a probation officer. While working this job, she kept wondering how to do something creative with her life. Blue decided to go into still photography. She requested a demotion to night attendant at Central Juvenile Hall and, from nine to five, attended the Los Angeles Trade-Technical College as a still photography major. From 1967 to the late 1970s, Blue photographed all sorts of public happenings—rock concerts, Black Panther rallies, anti–Vietnam War demonstrations, and civil rights actions. The photographers ROY DECARAVA, Leonard Taylor, and Robert Nakamura were among her major influences. Nakamura encouraged her to go into film by blending still photography and film.

Meanwhile, Blue had obtained a darkroom technician job at the California Institute of Technology's Solar Astronomy Laboratory. She printed and processed both 16-mm and 35-mm images of the sun, giving her a chance to see how film worked at a technical level. Encouraged by Nakamura, Blue enrolled at the University of California at Los Angeles (UCLA) Film School in 1976. Before graduating in 1980, Blue met a number of African American student filmmakers including JULIE DASH, Larry Clark, and Charles Burnett, who were also part of the Ethno Communications program that had been established in 1968. She cites them among her influences, as well as Topper Carew's *Say Brother*, Elliz Haizlip's *Soul!*, and William Greaves's *Black Journal*. The Ethno Communications program taught students to try to find leaders in their communities and make films about them. Much of Blue's work reflects this influence. Her mentors from UCLA included the African American independent film pioneers Carlton Moss and Frances Williams. Blue built on the foundation established by black and Asian American pioneer filmmakers. She worked on Nakamura's *Hilo Hata*, the first Asian American feature film.

In her art, Blue tells stories through archival photos. *Two Women* (1976), her first film, a Super-8, contrasted the approach to life of a young woman and an elderly woman. While the older woman discussed her focus on the spiritual, the young adult used her own will. The film took second prize in the 1976 Virgin Islands Film Festival and first place in the 1977 Los Angeles International Film Festival. Blue used it as a portfolio piece to win an American Film Institute grant to make her next film, *Varnette's World: A Study of a Young Artist* (1979). This second film won the top award at the 1979 Chicago International Film Festival. With funding from the Corporation for Public Broadcasting, Blue produced her most acclaimed work, *Conversations with Roy DeCarava* (1980), which aired on PBS's *Non-Fiction Television*. She spent the remainder of the early 1980s working for Jane Fonda on three feature films—*Rollover*, *On Golden Pond*, and *Nine to Five*. Blue then worked as a producer on *Eyes on the Prize, Part II*, on the segments on Malcolm X and Harold Washington. After experiencing Hollywood, Blue made a conscious decision to make personal films out of documentaries, a trend among filmmakers that has continued into the twenty-first century. Blue has not been as prolific as other black artists, undoubtedly because her output has been slowed by her need to earn a living by working in the juvenile justice system. Blue's 2003 autobiography is a blend of text, still photographs, and newspaper clippings that serves as capstone to her artistic career.

FURTHER READING

Blue, Carroll Parrott. *The Dawn at My Back: Memoir of a Black Texas Upbringing* (2003).

CARYN E. NEUMANN

Blue, Daniel T., Jr. (18 Apr. 1949–), lawyer and the first black Speaker of the North Carolina House of Representatives, was born in Lumberton, Robeson County, North Carolina, to Daniel T. Blue Sr. and Allene Morris. Blue excelled in school and later attended North Carolina Central University in Durham, North Carolina, where he earned a B.S. degree in Mathematics. There he emerged not only as a leader in academics but also in campus politics. Blue furthered his career by receiving his J.D. degree in Law from Duke University School of Law, where again he distinguished himself and graduated in 1973. He held the certification of the National Institute for Trial Advocacy and served four times as a faculty member of that institute.

When Blue was hired by the firm of Sanford, Adams, McCullough & Beard, he became one of the first blacks to integrate a major North Carolina law firm. However, a desire to own his own practice inspired him to form a firm with several associates in 1976. He was later motivated to run for public office, and in 1980 Blue was elected to the Twenty-first Representative District (Wake County) in the North Carolina House of Representatives. He went on to be elected to ten terms and held several leadership posts in the house, including chair of the Judiciary and Appropriations Committee. From 1983 to 1985 Blue chaired the North Carolina Criminal Code Revision Study Committee. He also served as chair of the Law and Justice Committee of the National Conference of State Legislators. Among his greatest achievements was his term as chair of the Legislative Black Caucus (1984 to 1989), where he advocated for racial equality and inclusiveness for African Americans in the political process.

On 30 January 1991 Blue was elected the first African American speaker of the North Carolina House of Representatives, and he was elected to this office in January 1993. He served the state of North Carolina with distinction as speaker of the house until January 1995. In 2002 he ran unsuccessfully as a candidate for the U.S. Senate seat formerly held by the U.S. senator Jesse Helms from North Carolina. He later returned to serve as a managing partner of the firm Thigpen, Blue, Stephens & Fellers in Raleigh, North Carolina, and was a visiting instructor at the Terry Sanford Institute of Public Policy at Duke University. In November 2006 Blue was appointed by the governor of North Carolina to fill the unexpired term of Representative Bernard Allen and was able to use his votes and eventually took his seat to serve a full term in January 2007.

Blue was consistently recognized by his peers in the state and country as one of America's outstanding and politically gifted leaders. He was actively involved in the national political scene and was a member of the State Democratic Executive Committee. He served on the executive committees of the Southern Legislative Conference, the State and Local Legal Center in Washington, D.C., and as president of the National Conference of State Legislatures (NCSL). In 1984 he was a coordinator of the Mondale–Ferraro campaign in North Carolina. He was chair of the JESSE JACKSON campaign in North Carolina in 1988, and after the Democratic National Convention he served as co-chair of the Dukakis–Bentsen campaign in the state. He served twice as chair of the Clinton–Gore campaign for North Carolina.

Blue was a member of the Executive Council for the Association of Governing Boards for Colleges and Universities in Washington, D.C., the NCSL Board of Directors of the Foundation for State Legislatures, and the Democratic National Committee. Blue was also a member of the board of trustees of Duke University.

During his distinguished career Blue received numerous awards, including, in 1985, the Outstanding Legislator Award of the North Carolina Association of Trial Lawyers and the Outstanding Community Service Award of the North Carolina Association of Black Lawyers. In 1991 he received the Adam Clayton Powell Leadership Award by the Congressional Black Caucus, and in 1993 he received the Leadership Award by the National Association for Equal Opportunity in Higher Education. He also received numerous honorary doctorate degrees. Blue was recognized by many organizations, churches, and civic groups for his various contributions to the community, state, and nation.

Blue was a member of the American Bar Association, the North Carolina Association of Black Lawyers, the North Carolina Bar Association, Alpha Phi Alpha Fraternity, Inc., the Raleigh Wake Citizens Association, and the Kiwanis Club. In January 1995 North Carolina Central University received a gift from the C.D. Spangler Foundation, which fully endowed the Daniel T. Blue Jr. Chair in Political Science in Blue's honor. Blue lived in Raleigh and was married to Edna Earle Smith; the couple had three children.

FURTHER READING

Crow, Jeffrey J., Paul D. Escott, and Flora J. Hatley. *A History of African Americans in North Carolina* (2002).

ANDRE D. VANN

Blue, Thomas Fountain (8 Mar. 1866–10 Nov. 1935), the first African American to manage a public library, founded a widely acclaimed program to train African Americans as library assistants in Louisville, Kentucky, where he supervised the first library department established for African Americans in an era of Jim Crow exclusion. Blue was the first person of African descent to appear in an American Library Association conference program (1922) and a founder of the Conference of Colored Librarians in 1927.

Blue was born in Farmville, Virginia, the second child of Noah and Henri Ann Crowly Blue, who had previously been enslaved. By 1870, Noah Blue was listed in the U.S. Census as a carpenter; he may have been the twelve-year-old male listed in the 1850 slave census as the property of Thomas Blue, District No. 24, Hampshire County, Virginia (now West Virginia). The family included a six-year-old daughter, Alice, and a two-year-old, recorded only as C. S. Ten years later, Noah had a wife named Julia, and while his fourteen-year-old son was still alive, there was no record of the daughters (Census). It seems possible that the family had been struck by an epidemic or other fatal illness during the intervening years.

Graduating from Hampton Normal and Agricultural Institute in 1888, Thomas F. Blue graduated from a three-year summer program "for the benefit of the colored teachers of the public schools of this State" at Virginia Collegiate and Normal Institute in 1893 and received a bachelor of divinity degree in 1898 from Richmond Theological Seminary. In 1896 Blue was an incorporator with several others of McDaniel and Farmville Academy (*Acts of the General Assembly of Virginia 1895–1896*, 689). He served as YMCA army secretary attached to the Sixth Virginia Regiment of Volunteers during the Spanish–American War.

Blue supervised the "colored branch" of the Louisville, Kentucky, YMCA as secretary from 1899 to 1905. In 1900 he was boarding with the family of Edward and Florence Walker, at 729 W. Walnut Street (Census). In 1905 the Louisville Free Public Library opened the first of ten branches, supplementing a central library constructed with a grant from Andrew Carnegie in 1902 (Wright). Access to the central library and most branches was limited to people classified as "white." Two branches were intended for "colored" residents of the city. Blue accepted a position as manager of the Western Branch Library, which opened 23 September 1905, staffed by Blue and two assistants he had trained. Starting with a collection of 4,000 books, within three months it was visited by 4,000 people. By 1914 it held 10,046 volumes and subscribed to 91 magazines and journals, with 7,132 registered borrowers and attendance in eight years of 330,715 (*Southern Workman* 43, 537).

Blue initiated a training class, which he later called a "child of necessity." Because a public library for colored people was something "new under the sun," the need to train assistants resembled wartime mobilization. The course of study he devised required four to six months on library methods and practical work. Four years later he was nationally recognized for the only apprenticeship program training African Americans aspiring to be librarians in the South. By 1922 Blue and his staff had trained eleven young women from Houston, Birmingham, Atlanta, Evansville, Memphis, Knoxville, Nashville, and Chattanooga (*Southern Workman* 51, 437). Not until 1925 was Hampton to open a library school, modeled on Blue's work.

On 28 October 1908 the Western Branch library moved out of cramped quarters in a former residence into its own newly constructed building, also funded by a Carnegie grant. Blue wrote that "the opening of its doors was regarded as an epoch in the development of the race, for it was the first institution of its kind in existence" (*Special Libraries* 11, 145). Never before had a brand new building been constructed specifically for a colored library. A second building, the Eastern Branch Colored Library, also in a new building funded by Carnegie, opened in January 1914, with Blue's duties expanded to manage both branches, while senior assistants took charge of each. Louisville formally designated a Colored Department, headed by Blue, within the Free Public Library.

In 1920 Blue was lodging with the family of Frank W. Clayborn and his wife Leanna at 1723 Chestnut Street, a few blocks from the Western Branch library (Census). He was still living at this address when he died in 1935. Sometime in his last fifteen years, Blue married Cornelia Phillip Johnson, oldest sister of Lyman T. Johnson, who moved to Louisville at his sister's invitation, later heading the Louisville NAACP and initiating a lawsuit that desegregated the University of Kentucky in 1949. The Johnsons were from Maury County, Tennessee, where their father taught and then served as principal of a high school for "colored" students, while the family also owned and worked a farm.

In March 1927 Blue presented a paper on "The Library as a Community Center" to twenty-five librarians from across the South at the Hampton Institute, where the Conference of Colored Librarians was formed, 15–18 March 1927. Two years later, in 1929, it was considered a bold innovation that Blue, a delegate to the ALA conference in Washington, D.C., and the writer Edward C. Williams, the only other delegate with a dark complexion, were included in the picture of conference members with President Herbert Hoover.

A 1930 survey by Louis B. Shores recognized Louisville's colored libraries for having over twice the number of books found in other colored libraries, receiving double the appropriations, employing more African American librarians, and coming in third (to Atlanta and Birmingham) in the number of registered library card holders (Jones, p. 55). Blue died after an acute illness in 1935, remaining at his post in the library system until the end.

FURTHER READING

Blue, Thomas F. "Work with the Negro Round Table." *Southern Workman* 51, p. 437.

Blue, Thomas F. "Colored Branches of the Louisville Free Public Library." *Special Libraries* 11 (1920): 145–147.

Jones, Reinette F. *Library Service to African Americans in Kentucky, from the Reconstruction Era to the 1960s* (2002).

Wright, L. T. *Thomas Fountain Blue, Pioneer Librarian, 1866–1935* (1955).

CHARLES ROSENBERG

Blue, Vida (28 July 1949–), baseball player, was born Vida Rochelle Blue Jr., the eldest of six children in Mansfield, Louisiana, to Vida Blue Sr., a foundry hand, and Sallie, a homemaker. Blue was particularly athletically inclined, and during his time attending local schools he played both football and baseball, excelling at both. During his senior year at De Soto high school, he tossed thirty-five touchdown passes and scrambled for more than 1,600 yards. That same year, as pitcher for the school's baseball team, he hurled a no-hitter. Offers from colleges began rolling in, but before Blue could decide where to attend, his father died unexpectedly. Determined to make money to help his family—his mother briefly took work at a local shirt factory, but found keeping up with a job and such a large family surpassingly difficult—he bypassed college and instead chose to go pro. In 1967 he entered the amateur draft and was taken in the second round by baseball's Oakland Athletics.

Blue spent his first two years with the Oaks, the Athletics' farm team in Iowa. In July 1969 he was called up to pitch for Oakland. He quickly showed himself to be a player of considerable skill and power. That fall, he threw a one-hitter and a no-hitter (with a walk) inside of ten days. Despite his performance Blue returned to the Oaks, remaining there until 1971.

Called back to the majors, in 1971 Blue went 24–8 and ended the season with an extraordinary 1.82 ERA. He was chosen as an All-Star, seized the

Cy Young Award, and was named league MVP, one of only a few players to accomplish all three in a single season. Additionally, Blue's outstanding performance helped propel the A's to the postseason for the first time since 1931. His fame was such that he graced the covers of both *Time* and *Sports Illustrated*. In remarkably short order, Blue had gone from a farm leaguer to one of the most recognizable stars in all of pro sports.

It was in part because of that fame that his next season, 1972, was disrupted by a contract holdout. A's owner Charles Finley refused to renegotiate Blue's salary, and Blue missed much of the '72 season, pitching inconsistently when he did take the mound. Still, Blue did pitch in that year's World Series against the Cincinnati Reds, the first of his three world championships.

The following year, 1973, Blue settled his dispute with the A's organization and enjoyed another outstanding year. He went 20–9 with a 3.28 ERA, and was again part of a World Series–winning team. In all, from Blue's entrance into the league in 1971, the Oakland franchise won five consecutive American League Western Division titles and won the World Series three straight years. Soon after, however, the

Vida Blue, 21-year-old Oakland Athletics' southpaw, eyes the batter as he kicks out in a pitch to the plate in a game with the Kansas City Royals on 14 May 1971. (AP Images.)

A's entered a rebuilding phase, and in 1978 Blue was traded to the San Francisco Giants. He played respectably there for three seasons before being traded again to the Kansas City Royals. Before long he was back with the Giants, where he ended his career in 1986. After leaving the Athletics, he never won more than fourteen games. In 1989 Blue married Peggy Shannon.

Throughout his career, Blue struggled with both alcohol and cocaine abuse. He was repeatedly cited for drunk driving (1999, 2003, and 2005), and in 1983 pled guilty to purchasing cocaine. Two years later, he joined a group of his fellow Major Leaguers to testify (with immunity) about the rampant drug abuse and cocaine trade taking place within the league. The hearings before a Pittsburgh grand jury came to be called the Pittsburgh drug trials. The results of the trial were prison sentences, player suspensions, fines, and orders to take part in community service. Since that time, Blue has taken part in various community projects and donated his time to teaching baseball to young people in urban areas and inner cities. In 1995 he was inducted into the Bay Area Hall of Fame.

FURTHER READING

Rielly, Edward J. *Baseball and American Culture: Across the Diamond* (2003).

Skirboll, Aaron. *The Pittsburgh Cocaine Seven: How a Ragtag Group of Fans Took the Fall for Major League Baseball* (2010).

JASON PHILIP MILLER

Bluford, Guion (Guy) Stewart, Jr. (22 Nov. 1942–), engineer, astronaut, and the first African American in space, was born in Philadelphia, Pennsylvania, the eldest son of Lolita Bluford, a public school special educator, and Guion Bluford Sr., a mechanical engineer. Guion Jr. was raised in a middle class, racially mixed neighborhood in West Philadelphia. Both parents instilled strong values and a powerful work ethic in him and his two younger brothers, Eugene and Kenneth. The boys were encouraged to never allow skin color to deter them from obtaining a successful career.

Throughout his youth the introverted Bluford, though well spoken, was quiet and often struggled with schoolwork. Many teachers did not see much potential in him, and indeed one school counselor went so far as to notify his parents that their son was not college potential and advised him to choose a different avenue after his graduation

from Overbrook High School. Yet behind his quiet demeanor was an active and intelligent mind. Bluford was interested in math and science, and enjoyed playing chess and building model planes. He was active in the Boy Scouts and achieved the rank of Eagle Scout, but more than anything he was interested in flight. Influenced by his father's work as an engineer Bluford was so intrigued with the process of flight that he decided to become an aerospace engineer.

Thanks to the development of the National Aeronautics and Space Administration (NASA) during Bluford's youth in the 1950s and 1960s, space exploration had become a viable career field. Upon graduation from high school in 1960 Bluford enrolled at Penn State University, majoring in aerospace engineering; he was the only African American in the engineering school. Bluford immersed himself in subjects like calculus, statistics, and physics, actively overcoming the scholastic struggles of his youth. He was an active member of the Air Force ROTC program, and earned the Phi Delta Kappa leadership award in 1962. When he completed his studies at Penn State in 1964 he

Guion Steward Bluford Jr., the first African American to travel into space, speaking at the University of Cincinnati on 17 May 1984. (AP Images.)

enlisted in the air force and was sent to Williams Air Force Base in Arizona to train as a pilot. Bluford's entry into the air force led to two new beginnings. In addition to his training as a certified F-4C pilot he also became a husband and father. After marrying Linda Tull, whom he had met at Penn State during his senior year, Bluford's two sons, Guion III and James Trevor, were born in 1964 and 1965, respectively. Bluford was called for combat duty in Vietnam in 1967 to join the 557th Tactical Fighter Squadron stationed in Cah Ranh Bay. As a member of the 557th Bluford flew 144 combat missions from 1967 until 1972. He was awarded ten air force Air Medals, including the Vietnam Cross of Gallantry, as well as Vietnam Campaign and Service medals. When his combat duty was complete he moved on to Sheppard Air Force Base in Texas to teach aspiring pilots how to fly.

Bluford also continued his academic pursuits, enrolling in the Air Force Institute of Technology, where he earned an M.S. in Aerospace Engineering in 1974 and a Ph.D. in Aerospace Engineering with a minor in Laser Physics in 1978. That same year Bluford decided to apply to the NASA program with hope of getting back in the air and possibly seeing outer space. Over 8,800 applications were submitted to NASA, and only 35 people were chosen to become new members of the space program. The quiet boy from West Philadelphia who had grown into an established pilot and engineer was one of the 35 people chosen from the highly competitive process. His training as a mission specialist began in 1979, studying topics like advanced engineering mechanics, navigation, geology, and oceanography. In early 1982 he learned he would be part of a space mission the following year. As a mission specialist of a five-member crew, Bluford would become the first African American in space.

To Bluford, the prospect of going into space was a fulfillment of a lifelong dream and a testament to the hard work he endured from his days as a youth. He never sought the spotlight of being the "first." But as news spread Bluford became a point of interest for the entire country, especially the African American community. Nearly 250 prominent African Americans from various professions attended the launch, including Dr. DOROTHY HEIGHT (the president of the National Council of Negro Women), BILL COSBY (the actor and entertainer), WILT CHAMBERLAIN (the professional basketball star and fellow graduate of Overbrook High School), and C. ALFRED ANDERSON (the "father of black aviation" who trained the Tuskegee Airmen). Bluford's flight was also significant because it was the first space launch and landing to take place at night. The crew made successful liftoff on 30 August 1983 at 2:32 A.M. from Kennedy Space Center. Among Bluford's responsibilities on the weeklong mission were to launch a $45 million communications satellite that belonged to India and conduct experiments on the separation of body cells and fluids in space. The STS-8 *Challenger* shuttle landed successfully in California on 5 September 1983.

Bluford would go on to make three successive flights into space on 30 October 1985, 28 April 1991, and 2 December 1992. Over his four missions Bluford compiled 688 total hours in space. He subsequently retired from NASA in 1993 to become vice president and general manager of the Engineering Services Division of NYMA Inc. of Greenbelt, Maryland. Throughout the late 1990s Bluford was employed in numerous executive positions in the aerospace, engineering, and information technology fields. As of 2006 he was serving as president of the Aerospace Technology Group in Cleveland, Ohio. Bluford was recognized by many organizations for his accomplishments throughout his professional career. Among his numerous awards and recognitions were the *Ebony* Black Achievement Award and NAACP Image Award, 1983; Black Engineer of the Year, 1991; Induction into the International Space Hall of Fame, 1997; and over ten honorary doctoral degrees.

FURTHER READING

Gilbert, Betty Kaplan, Miriam Sawyer, and Carolina M. Fannon. *Distinguished African Americans in Aviation and Space* (2002).

Jeffrey, Laura S. *Guion Bluford: A Space Biography* (1998).

Phelps, J. Alfred. *They Had a Dream: The Story of African American Astronauts* (1994).

Schraff, Anne. *American Heroes of Exploration and Flight* (1996).

JOHN BRYAN GARTRELL

Blunden, Jeraldyne (10 Dec. 1940–22 Nov. 1999), dancer and choreographer, was born Jeraldyne Kilborn in Dayton, Ohio, the daughter of Elijah Kilborn, an insurance agent, and Winifred Keith, who worked at Wright Patterson Air Force Base. Her mother played the piano, and her father had an artistic nature, which included writing poetry and soft shoe dancing. Although Dayton was geographically divided along racial lines at the time,

Jeraldyne attended Irving Public School, which was not segregated, and Roosevelt High, which was all white when she entered and fully integrated by the time she graduated. Segregation had never been the official policy of Dayton, and African Americans freely shopped in department stores, although there were no black employees except for cleaning help. Jeraldyne's grandmother was one of the first blacks to build her own home.

Beginning at the age of eight, Blunden trained in classical ballet with Josephine Schwartz, who, with her sister Hermene, was considered the premier dance teacher in Dayton. Their company, the Dayton Ballet, was one of the first regional ballet companies in the United States. A group of mothers had previously invited "Miss Jo" to teach at Linden House, a black community center, where she conducted classes three days a week, thereby breaking racial boundaries. Schwartz and her sister were to become Blunden's role models and greatest supporters. Choreography, improvisation, and modern dance were part of the training given by the Schwartz sisters, and Blunden actually started to create dances while still in elementary school. Eventually the Schwartzes helped Blunden obtain scholarships to study dance outside of Ohio. When Schwartz formed the Linden Dance Company, Blunden was one of ten girls in the group, which rehearsed in a church on Saturday mornings. The ballet company rehearsed at the same time and place.

At thirteen Blunden was a well-trained and obviously talented dancer, and she went to the Schwartz sisters' main studio, where, although she was African American, she was accepted by the other students because of her abilities. Even before *Lincoln's Portrait*, a racially integrated production of the sisters, she danced with the Dayton Ballet Company, but always as a guest and never with a partner. For several years she went to New York City to take the annual Christmas course at the School of American Ballet. At fifteen she danced and briefly toured with Karamu, a black company from Cleveland. Blunden enrolled at Connecticut College, choosing it because of its dance program, but returned home after three weeks. She attended Central State College for two years, planning to major in elementary education, but did not graduate. In 1959 she married Charles Blunden; they had two children. She spent the summers of 1958 and 1959 at the American Dance Festival in Connecticut on a scholarship. There she was exposed to the Horton, Graham, Cunningham, and Limón modern dance techniques, saw the three

latter companies perform, and learned repertoire from Helen Tamiris. The first year she was the only black student; the second year there was one other. During this time she also went to New York City on weekends to study ballet with Karel Shook.

While still in college, Blunden taught dance classes at the Linden Center. In 1963 she was asked to direct the program. This formed the basis for her own school, Dayton Contemporary Dance, which she modeled on that of her mentors. She sent her young students to study on scholarship at the American Dance Festival, the ALVIN AILEY American Dance Center, and ARTHUR MITCHELL's Dance Theatre of Harlem. The small performing group, which was started as an outlet for these students, turned professional in 1968. When the company performed Blunden's ballet *Flite* at the Northeast Regional Ballet Association in 1973, the Dayton Contemporary Dance Company became the first African American troupe to gain membership in that organization.

Blunden's company performed works by the invited artists Eleo Pomare, TALLEY BEATTY, Donald McKayle, ULYSSES DOVE, and Lynn Taylor Corbett, among others, with an emphasis on preserving works that were in danger of being lost, particularly those by black choreographers. Hers was the first predominantly black company in the nation to acquire a dance by Merce Cunningham. The company performed throughout the United States, receiving recognition for its vitality and varied repertoire.

Blunden, who gave up performing to devote herself to teaching, felt that ballet was the basis for all dance. When she taught, however, it was a modern class based on the Horton technique, borrowing from Graham, Limón, and others.

Blunden died in Dayton. She was honored with a MacArthur Foundation grant (1994), the *Dance Magazine* Award (1998), a Lifetime Achievement Award from the National Black Arts Festival (1998), and a Dance USA Honors Award (1999). These accolades were for her energy, her warm humor, and her fierce determination to showcase the contributions of black choreographers and performers to American modern dance. Jennifer Dunning noted that Blunden had mixed feelings about that role, quoting Blunden: "What I do is from a black perspective. But people who are sure of themselves don't bother with that." Before her death Blunden arranged for her daughter, Debbie Blunden-Diggs, and Kevin Ward to take over as codirectors of the Dayton Contemporary Dance Company.

FURTHER READING

Blunden, Jeraldyne. "Board Spotlight," *Dance/USA Journal* 2, no. 1 (Summer 1994).

Blunden, Jeraldyne. "Remembering the Membership Evaluation," *Dance Magazine* (Oct. 1944).

Hering, Doris. "The Future of Dance Is in Dayton?" *Dance Magazine* (Dec. 1993).

Obituary: *New York Times*, 24 Nov. 1999.

This entry is taken from the *American National Biography* and is published here with the permission of the American Council of Learned Societies.

DAWN LILLE

Blyden, Edward Wilmot (3 Aug. 1832–12 Feb. 1912), educator, diplomat, and advocate of Pan-Africanism, was born on the island of St. Thomas, part of the present-day Virgin Islands, the son of Romeo Blyden, a tailor, and Judith (maiden name unknown), a schoolteacher. The family lived in a predominantly Jewish, English-speaking community in the capital, Charlotte Amalie. Blyden went to the local primary school but also received private tutoring from his father. In 1842 the Blydens left St. Thomas for Porto Bello, Venezuela, where Blyden showed his–facility for learning foreign languages. By 1844 the family had returned home to St. Thomas. Blyden attended school only in the morning, and in the afternoons he served a five-year apprenticeship as a tailor. In 1845 the Blyden family met the Reverend John P. Knox, a famous white American minister who had assumed pastorship of the Dutch Reformed Church in St. Thomas, where the Blydens were members. Knox quickly became Blyden's mentor and encouraged his academic studies and oratorical skills. Because of Knox's influence, Blyden decided to become a clergyman, an aspiration his parents supported.

In May 1850 Blyden accompanied Mrs. John Knox to the United States and attempted to enroll in Rutgers Theological College, which was Reverend Knox's alma mater, but was refused admission because he was black. Blyden's attempts to gain admission to other theological colleges also failed. During this time he met important white Presbyterian clergymen, such as John B. Pinney, Walter Lowrie, and William Coppinger, who became his lifelong supporters. All three men were involved with the American Colonization Society. They convinced Blyden to go to Liberia, which had become an independent nation in 1847.

Blyden left the United States for Liberia on 21 December 1850 and arrived at Monrovia on 26 January 1851. Initially, he worked as a part-time clerk for a merchant and resumed his studies at Alexander High School, a new Presbyterian institution headed by the Reverend D. A. Wilson, a graduate of Princeton Theological Seminary. Blyden's intellectual abilities impressed Wilson, who then persuaded Knox to support Blyden as a full-time student. By 1853 Blyden was a lay preacher, and by 1854 he was a tutor at his high school and acted as principal during Wilson's frequent absences due to illness. Blyden published one of the first of his many provocative pamphlets on African affairs, *A Voice from Bleeding Africa*, in 1856, the year he married Sarah Yates, the mixed-race niece of B. P. Yates, the vice president of Liberia. Their marriage was an unhappy one, though they had two children. Blyden blamed his marital troubles on his wife's loyalty to what he termed the "mulatto clique" that dominated Liberian politics. However, other important reasons for the marriage's collapse were financial problems due to Blyden's insufficient income and his wife's

Edward Wilmot Blyden, Liberian intellectual, nationalist, and advocate of Pan-Africanism, who tried to convince blacks throughout the diaspora to repatriate, c. 1855. (Library of Congress, American Colonization Society Records, 1972–1964.)

lack of interest in her husband's intellectual pursuits. In 1858 he was ordained a Presbyterian minister, succeeding Wilson as principal of Alexander High School. Throughout the 1860s and 1870s Blyden became intensely involved in the educational and political affairs of Liberia. In 1861 he was appointed Liberian educational commissioner and traveled to the United States and Britain on a lecture and fund-raising tour. He encouraged African Americans to immigrate to Liberia, "back home to the Fatherland," where he contended they could live free from slavery and racial inequality. From 1860 to 1871 he taught classics at Liberia College; he was also the Liberian secretary of state (1864–1866). In 1871 Blyden was forced to leave Liberia temporarily for Sierra Leone after a coup d'état against the EDWARD ROYE administration (1870–1871) endangered his life. He returned to Liberia in 1872 to become principal of Alexander High School again, a post he held until 1878. As the Liberian ambassador to the Court of St. James's in Britain from 1877 to 1879, Blyden unsuccessfully tried to win financial support for Liberia from Britain. He then served as president of Liberia College (1880–1884) and was minister of the interior (1880–1882). In 1885 he ran unsuccessfully for president of Liberia, though he had left the country to live in Sierra Leone.

From the late 1880s to the early 1900s Blyden wrote his most important work on Pan-Africanism, *Christianity, Islam, and the Negro Race* (1887), and maintained his diplomatic and educational commitments. The Liberian government again appointed him ambassador to the Court of St. James's in 1892, and he served as a special envoy to London and Paris in 1905. From 1901 to 1906 he was director of Mohammedan education in Sierra Leone. Poor and frail, he underwent an operation for an aneurysm in the knee at the Royal Southern Hospital in Liverpool, England, in 1909. His friends in the Colonial Office in London helped secure a small pension for him in 1910. He died in Sierra Leone two years later. His funeral service represented the unity he tried to forge among Africans during his lifetime: it was a Christian service in which Muslim men bore his coffin from his residence. His long career as an educator, diplomat, and proponent of Pan-Africanism attracted scholarly attention from African, Caribbean, and African American historians, biographers, and political scientists.

FURTHER READING

Cole, Julius Ojo. *Edward Wilmot Blyden: An Interpretation* (1935).
Esedebe, P. *Pan Africanism: The Idea and the Movement, 1776–1963* (1982).
Lynch, Hollis. *Edward Wilmot Blyden: Pan-Negro Patriot* (1967).
Moses, Wilson. *The Golden Age of Black Nationalism, 1850–1925* (1978).
This entry is taken from the *American National Biography* and is published here with the permission of the American Council of Learned Societies.

KIMBERLY WELCH

Blythe, Arthur (7 May 1940–), composer, alto saxophonist, bandleader, and teacher, was born Arthur Murray Blythe in Los Angeles, California, the son of Charles Blythe, an auto mechanic, and Nancy Blythe. Blythe's first musical inspiration was the rhythm and blues music he heard on local jukeboxes. His mother's passion for the music of JOHNNY HODGES, EARL BOSTIC, and Tab Smith led her to purchase an alto saxophone for Blythe, despite his desire to play trombone. Upon receiving his first saxophone at the age of nine, Blythe began to play in school bands, and at the age of thirteen he was performing in a local blues band. Blythe's early experience with rhythm and blues had a strong influence on his powerful, penetrating alto sound and on his composition's tendencies to utilize ostinatos and dance rhythms. As a teenager, Blythe studied alto saxophone with Daniel Jackson, a former RAY CHARLES sideman, and Kirtland Bradford, a former lead alto saxophonist with JIMMIE LUNCEFORD's orchestra. At the age of sixteen, Blythe was exposed to the music of THELONIOUS MONK, an experience that inaugurated his career in jazz.

After attending high school in San Diego and splitting time between family there and in Los Angeles, Blythe returned full time to Los Angeles in 1960. There he met the like-minded pianist HORACE TAPSCOTT, and the two of them formed a working musical partnership that would last a decade and a half. In 1961, Blythe and Tapscott founded the Underground Musicians Association (UMGA, also known as the UGMAA—the Union of God's Musicians and Artists Ascension), an organization dedicated to furthering the aesthetic and economic aims of creative musicians and to keeping alive the history and performance of music within the black community. Part of a nationwide trend toward greater artistic independence for African American artists and the forging of closer ties between art and the social and political goals of African American communities, the UMGA was the West Coast version of organizations like New York's Black Arts Movement, Chicago's Association for the Advancement of Creative Musicians (AACM), and St. Louis's Black Artist's Group (BAG). In his work with Horace Tapscott and the UMGA, and in his teaching of jazz workshops at the Malcolm X Center (1961–1963), Blythe was at the center of the progressive wing of the Los Angeles jazz community in the sixties and early seventies.

In 1969 Blythe made his recording debut on a Horace Tapscott album titled *The Giant is Awakened*. The album was well received, but it failed to gain wide notice and did little to further Blythe's career. Tiring of the Los Angeles music world and its limited opportunities for his style of performance, Blythe moved to New York in 1974 and soon became a central figure in the vibrant downtown loft scene that served as a hothouse for the jazz avant-garde of the period. His playing attracted much attention, and he quickly found himself playing in Chico Hamilton's band (1974–1977), and recording with Gil Evans, Hamilton, and JULIUS HEMPHILL. In 1977 Blythe made his first recordings as a bandleader, taking a six-piece ensemble (including tuba and cello) into the studio to record *The Grip* and *Metamorphosis* for India Navigation, a small independent label known for promoting adventurous jazz. Blythe soon attracted the attention of the major labels, and in 1979, he signed with Columbia Records.

The first album that Blythe recorded for Columbia, *In the Tradition* (1978), received widespread critical acclaim and marked Blythe as a major figure in the jazz scene. Recorded at a time when the aggressively avant-garde jazz of the 1970s seemed to be running out of steam, *In the Tradition* signaled a new willingness in the jazz community to turn to the music's less recent past for inspiration. It included performances of compositions by DUKE ELLINGTON, FATS WALLER, and JOHN COLTRANE as well as originals by Blythe. The album and the live performances of the band, which came to be known as In the Tradition, were instrumental in inaugurating a movement in jazz that placed emphasis on the music's roots and historical continuity. This movement had its conservative revivalist elements, exemplified by the music and attitudes of WYNTON MARSALIS, but Blythe was always more eclectic and more open-minded in his utilization of the jazz tradition than Marsalis and the other younger figures whose popularity

and acclaim overshadowed Blythe's in the second half of the 1980s.

Throughout the 1980s, Blythe played and recorded both with In the Tradition and in a decidedly less traditional quintet made up of tuba, cello, electric guitar, drums, and his own alto. This ability to create innovative and vibrantly moving music in a wide variety of contexts was a hallmark of Blythe's career and of his approach to jazz. Blythe ended his association with Columbia in 1988. His departure led to his commercial decline, but not to a slackening of his seemingly ceaseless creativity. During the 1990s and into the first decade of the twenty-first century, Blythe continued to lead his own ensembles and to work in a variety of contexts, fostering musical interchanges with virtually all of the significant jazz artists of the period; he made recordings with David Murray, the World Saxophone Quartet, Jack DeJohnette, LESTER BOWIE, Chico Freeman, James Newton, Joey Baron and BILLY HART.

Blythe is an important figure in the history of jazz. Ranking with CHARLIE PARKER, Johnny Hodges, and CANNONBALL ADDERLEY as one of the tradition's major alto saxophone stylists, Blythe's work as a composer and bandleader is no less important. His constant exploration of the possibilities of group counterpoint and nontraditional instrumentation has expanded the vocabulary of jazz. An eloquent synthesis of innovation and tradition, Blythe's body of recordings is remarkable for its diversity, exuberant emotional intelligence, and consistently high level of musicianship. Perhaps the most eloquent testimony to Blythe's significance is the lengthy poem that AMIRI BARAKA dedicated to him in 1980: "In the Tradition: For Black Arthur Blythe."

FURTHER READING

Baraka, Amiri, "In the Tradition: For Black Arthur Blythe," in *Transbluency: The Selected Poems of Amiri Baraka/LeRoi Jones (1961–1995)* (1995).

Francis Davis. "Apples, Oranges, and Arthur Blythe," in *In the Moment: Jazz in the 1980s* (1996).

Kernfeld, Barry, ed. "Blythe, Arthur," in *The New Grove Dictionary of Jazz* (2002).

Levenson, Jeff. "Arthur Blythe's Creative Challenge," *Downbeat* (October 1987).

DISCOGRAPHY

In the Tradition (Columbia, 1978).
Lenox Avenue Breakdown (Columbia, 1979).
Retroflection (Enja, 1994).

BRUCE BARNHART

Blythe, Jimmy (20 May 1901–21 June 1931), jazz pianist, composer, and bandleader, was born James Louis Blythe in Keene, Kentucky, about twelve miles southwest of Lexington, the youngest of five children of Richard Blythe and Rena (or Arena) (Stovall) Blythe. When Jimmy was around ten, the family moved to Lexington, where his father worked at different times as a laborer, houseman, and janitor. Jimmy left home about 1918 and moved to Chicago's South Side, staying at first with his older sister Effie. The South Side—the cultural heart of Chicago's black community—was to remain Blythe's base for the rest of his life. Soon after the move Blythe went to study with Clarence M. Jones, a classically trained black pianist who had set up a music studio in the South Side. The musically versatile Jones, who was a skilled jazz, blues, classical performer, as well as a successful composer, seems to have been a strong influence on Blythe. Other than his study with Jones, nothing is known of Blythe's musical activities before 1922.

Blythe's reputation rests almost entirely on his recordings. His career is unique for an African American musician of the era, with roughly 500 recordings squeezed into a ten-year period (even more celebrated performers like DUKE ELLINGTON and LOUIS ARMSTRONG were not so intensively recorded at this time). Beginning in 1922 with piano-roll recordings for the Columbia Music Roll Company of Chicago, Blythe recorded extensively for this medium. Although the total number of rolls recorded will never be known (as roll recordings were not always attributed), they probably reached 300. He recorded both for the home market and also for coin-operated "nickelodeons" that were popular in bars and similar public establishments. Piano rolls are often denigrated by critics and historians for their seemingly mechanical quality (the particular system that Blythe recorded on removed dynamics, pedaling, and nuances of rhythm from his performances). Despite this, many of Blythe's rolls transcend their limitations and at their best are as exciting as any recorded jazz of the 1920s. An example is the 1923 roll of "Barney Google" (Columbia 607), a light popular song of the day. After playing through the song once he unexpectedly inserted a hot blues chorus, which, though entirely unrelated to the earlier material, enormously builds up tension.

In April 1924 Blythe began making phonograph records, initially for the Paramount label. Paramount had recently entered the booming race record market (records marketed to blacks) and actively acquired a stable of jazz and blues performers. Blythe operated as a house pianist for the company, recording a total of 105 sides. At first he mainly worked as an accompanist for female vaudeville blues singers in the Paramount roster, such as GERTRUDE "MA" RAINEY, Priscilla Stewart, and Sodarisa Miller. Around November 1924 he also began to record small-band jazz with a series of trio performances featuring the clarinetist Jimmy O'Bryant. As his reputation as a jazz performer spread Blythe began recording for some of the other leading companies of the era: Vocalion beginning in 1926, and Okeh and Gennett in 1927. With his group the State Street Ramblers, which included some of the leading jazz instrumentalists of the period, he recorded on Gennett between 1927 and 1931 what are probably his most famous issues. There are, however, dozens of other recordings, less well known but just as rewarding. An example is "Bow to Your Papa" (Champion 16451), a piano duet played with his nephew Charlie Clark (the same performers also recorded the work on piano roll under the title "Regal Stomp," Capitol A-roll 2360). Made in Blythe's last recording session less than two months before his death, "Bow to Your Papa" is an idiosyncratic yet remarkably integrated performance for an unusual medium.

Blythe performed actively in the 1920s, though this part of his career is poorly documented. Some have reported him playing at Mamie Ponce's, a tavern a few doors south of the better-known Dreamland Café, and he probably represented a number of successful jazz pianists playing regularly in entertainment venues on Chicago's South Side. An important associate seems to have been the singer Alex (also known as Bob) Robinson, the husband of Paramount employee Aletha Dickerson, with whom Blythe recorded and composed. A 1926 article in the *Chicago Defender* newspaper mentioned the duo giving twice-weekly radio broadcasts on Chicago's KYW station.

Blythe, a fluent and able composer, created dozens of songs and instrumental numbers for recording and performing. His most enduring song was probably "Mecca Flat Blues," co-composed with Robinson, which was recorded by the boogie-woogie pianist ALBERT AMMONS in the 1930s and which appeared in the *Paramount Book of the Blues* in 1927. Blythe's only other works published in his lifetime appeared through the agency of Axel Christensen, a Chicago-based white piano pedagogue with whom he owned a chain of piano-teaching schools. Christensen published Blythe's boogie-woogie composition "Chicago Stomps" in 1927 under the name "Walking Blues," and included it in his jazz teaching method (in the 1930s, when boogie-woogie caught on, he changed the title to "Boogie Woogie Blues"). Christensen also published a series of five piano *Syncophonics* claiming himself as the composer; the evidence, however, indicates that at least two of the set (numbers four and five) were Blythe material. An earlier Christensen publication, "Pomeranian Blues" (1924), was probably also by Blythe.

Little personal information is available about Blythe. His friend Lathair Stevens, who was to be one of his pallbearers, apparently remembered him as slight and stout, a description borne out by Blythe's only known photograph, which first appeared in an advertisement in a 1926 *Defender*. Blythe was married by 1924 but nothing is known of his wife Janice, and they had no children.

Blythe's sudden death from meningitis cut short the career of an important popular composer and musician: he had just turned thirty. Yet his achievement within his short career was remarkable. Not only was he the most prolific African American recording artist of the 1920s but he was also one of the most creative. His style is a highly individual blend of the most important genres of the day: jazz, blues, and novelty piano, often underpinned by a strong barrelhouse feel. Always superbly crafted, his compositions anticipated the stride piano style of EARL HINES and FATS WALLER that would become standard in the 1930s. His "Chicago Stomps," recorded for Paramount in 1924 and on piano roll (and published by Christensen), is the earliest known boogie-woogie composition (that is, using left-hand riffs throughout the entire piece), and the intermittent use of left-handed boogie-woogie riffs is a recurring feature of his style. Perhaps his greatest gift was his ability as an accompanist and bandleader to put his fellow musicians at ease, allowing them to play at their most relaxed and creative. For this reason Blythe was responsible for some of the most exhilarating jazz recordings of the 1920s. Despite his enormous talent Blythe has been little recognized or appreciated by jazz historians. A modest man, he did little in the way of self-promotion. The drummer BABY DODDS described him as "a very quiet fellow, not the boisterous type at all." He was a consummate studio musician deserving a central place in the canon of jazz history.

FURTHER READING

Dodds, Baby. *The Baby Dodds Story as Told to Larry Gara* (rev. ed., 1992).

Montgomery, Michael. Liner notes for *Jimmy Blythe in Chronological Order, 1924–1931* (1994).

Silvester, Peter. *A Left Hand like God: The Story of Boogie-Woogie* (1988).

PETER MUIR

Boatner, Edward Hammond (13 Nov. 1898–16 June 1981), composer, educator, choral conductor, music professor, singer, and author, was born to Dr. Daniel Webster Boatner, former slave, and Sophie Stuart, in New Orleans, Louisiana. Dr. Daniel Webster Boatner was born in South Carolina and was nine years old when Abraham Lincoln signed the Emancipation Proclamation in 1863. Edward Boatner's grandmother was a slave who was determined that her son, Daniel, would receive a good education. She worked very hard scrubbing floors, washing, cooking, and nursing children of wealthy whites to send him to school. Dr. Boatner attended Fisk University in Nashville, Tennessee, and graduated from New Orleans University where he received his bachelor's and master's degrees. After earning his doctorate from Gammon Theological Seminary at Atlanta, Georgia, he served on the faculty of Philander-Smith College (a Methodist School) in Little Rock, Arkansas, where he taught Hebrew, Latin, Greek, German, French, Italian, and Spanish. His intellectual ability made him capable of being an instructor in all college subjects and he gained the reputation of being an all-around versatile professor.

Edward Boatner's great-grandmother, Carrie Adams, and his aunt, Belle Lawry, were former slaves. His two sisters were Mamie and Louise. Edward Boatner's father wanted him to follow in his footsteps and become a preacher. However, against his father's wishes, Edward Boatner became interested in music at an early age, especially the spirituals, after hearing them being sung by the congregations in the churches where his father preached. Edward began collecting spirituals during his early years and also became interested in singing. His father refused to pay for lessons for Edward but did pay for voice lessons for his sister, Mamie.

Boatner's education began in the public schools of St. Louis, Missouri, and Kansas City, Missouri, and despite his father's wishes, he chose to study music. During his early years, he was self-trained. In spite of his talent, he was denied admission to the University of Missouri because of his race. In 1916, he entered Western University in Quindaro, Kansas, where he studied voice and piano. Boatner was encouraged to move to Boston to further his studies by the famous tenor, ROLAND HAYES, who heard him sing at a recital. The famous African American composer, NATHANIEL DETT, also encouraged Boatner to go to Boston to audition for a scholarship. Boatner worked two years to earn his money to travel to Boston by teaching piano lessons. Shortly after arriving in that city in 1918, Boatner recorded three of HARRY T. BURLEIGH's spirituals, including "Sometimes I Feel Like a Motherless Child," for Broome Phonograph Records, an African American—owned label in Medford, Massachusetts. He also continued his musical studies at the New England Conservatory of Music and in 1920 published his first spiritual setting of "Give Me Jesus." He was put behind a screen to audition at The Boston Conservatory. He sang, "Vision Fugitive" by Massenet for baritone and won a one-year scholarship to Boston Conservatory of Music in 1921. While there, he studied German, French, and Italian vocal literature. R. NATHANIEL DETT heard Boatner sing in a concert at Hampton University, became a mentor to him, and asked Boatner to accompany him in a tour across New England.

In 1925 Boatner moved to Chicago and served as Director of Music for the National Baptist Convention from 1927–1932. In 1927 he published *Spirituals Triumphant Old And New* with Willa A. Townsend. After earning a bachelor's degree from the Chicago College of Music in 1932, Boatner served on the faculty of two historically Texas black colleges, Samuel Houston, in Austin, and Wiley College, in Marshall, where he was Dean of Music and was known as "Professor Boatner" by the students. His years on the faculty of Wiley in the 1930s coincided with that of the college's celebrated debate team, led by Professor Melvin B. Tolson. In the late 1930s, Boatner moved back to New York, where he opened a vocal studio.

Boatner's spiritual arrangements for voice and piano have been sung by such outstanding singers as ROLAND HAYES, PAUL ROBESON, MARIAN ANDERSON, ELLA BELLE-DAVIS, CAROLE BRICE, LEONTYNE PRICE, GEORGE SHIRLEY, and Nelson Eddie. He taught such famous artists as JOSEPHINE BAKER, Robert Guillaume, LOLA FALANA, ESTHER ROLLE, Lonnie Satin, and many others.

During his career, Boatner wrote and arranged more than three hundred spirituals, which were published by Galaxy, Colombo, Presser, Schirmer, McAfee Music, and his own music publishing company, Hammond Music. Some of Boatner's spiritual arrangements are: "On Ma Journey" (1928), "Trampin" (1930), "I Want Jesus to Walk with

Me" (1939), "Oh, What a Beautiful City" (1940), "Don't Feel No Ways Tired" (1952), and "He's Got The Whole World in His Hands" (1968). In 1941 he wrote four gospel songs: "Happy In Jesus," "I Am Satisfied," "I Will Answer When He Calls Me" (words by Francis Hunter), and "My Lord Offers Peace." His other works include music textbooks, humorous short stories, musical plays, and operas dealing with African American life. His Freedom Suite in three movements for full orchestra, chorus and narration, was presented in Washington, D.C., at Constitution Hall and dedicated to President Lyndon B. Johnson in 1967.

Boatner was married three times and had four children. Edward Boatner, Jr., better known as SONNY STITT, was considered to be one of the leading jazz saxophonists in America. Clifford Boatner, pianist, mathematician, and innovator, developed "musicimatics," a fusion of music and mathematics. Adelaide Boatner was an opera singer who sang with symphony orchestras and performed in Broadway productions. Sarah Boatner is also a singer. Boatner maintained his vocal studio and taught until the day he died, 16 June 1981.

FURTHER READING

The Edward Hammond Boatner Papers 1941–1980, are housed in the Schomburg Center for Research in Black Culture, New York Public Library, New York, NY. There is also a website, Afrocentric Voices in Classical Music, created by Randye Jones, available at www.afrovoices.com/boatner.html.

Boatner, Edward. *The Story of the Spiritual: 30 Spirituals and Their Origins* (1973).

Vinton, John. "Freedom Suite Premiered Here," *Evening Star*, 4 April 1967.

Wiegers, Mary. "Suite Was His Song," *Washington Post*, 4 April 1967.

Discography

Bellamy, Lois, (Soprano) in *A Tribute to Edward H. Boatner Contemporaries and Friends*, St. Ambrose Episcopal Church, Bellami Productions/Smedley Studios (2008).

Holder, Robert Laurence. *The Man from Nazareth* (2006).

LOIS BELLAMY

Bo Diddley. *See* Diddley, Bo.

Boen, William (c. 1735–12 June 1824), a Quaker, was born a slave near Rancocas, New Jersey, and was sometimes known as William Bowen or "Heston."

His owner treated him well, and Boen was allowed to learn to read and write. As a boy, Boen was afraid of dying during an Indian attack because of all of the stories circulating among the neighbors about others that were killed by Indians. Whenever he worked in the woods alone, he was on constant guard for Indian arrows. He felt he was not yet ready to die until he accepted what was within him that made him do good and reject evil, as the Quakers he was growing up around had done. The Society of Friends is a Christian sect founded by George Fox in 1660 that rejects formal sacraments, a formal creed, priesthood, and violence. They are also known as Quakers and are recognized by their plain speech, dress, pacifism, opposition to slavery, and philanthropy. Boen decided to follow this path of good, honest, and just living. From that time onward he felt he had two masters, one, God, and the other, the man who owned him. This realization affected every aspect of his life from that point onward, including his everyday work.

One day while out chopping down trees as requested by his master, he felt God telling him not to chop down a particular tree. He decided not to chop it down, leaving the one tree standing and chopping down the rest as requested. His master never asked why he did this; he just chopped that one tree down himself. Boen took this as a sign that God would take care of him if he followed God's path and devoted himself to a life of good. While still a young man, he made the acquaintance of John Woolman, who was a Quaker and member of the Society of Friends. Boen became interested in the Friends and began attending their meetings and studying their demeanor. Before long, he was a Quaker in most respects—except he was still not an official member of the Society of Friends.

Offered his freedom at the age of twenty-eight by his master, Boen accepted and became a freeman by the age of thirty. It was felt that his master's decision was influenced by John Woolman, who spoke out against slavery and encouraged all Quakers to free their slaves. He and many other Quakers felt that slavery and slave owning went against the very heart of the Quaker way of life and beliefs. Two years later Boen married Dinah (Dido), a servant in the house of Joseph Burr. They were married in a Society of Friends ceremony on 3 May 1763 arranged by John Woolman at Burr's house, even though neither was officially a member of the Society of Friends. The marriage certificate was signed by both Quaker and African American witnesses. Shortly after their wedding, Boen applied for membership in the Society of Friends but was denied because of his race. He was encouraged to stay true to his faith and was invited to continue attending meetings. He continued his studies and also preached to other African Americans.

Boen worked hard enough to acquire a home and property where his family lived comfortably in or around Mount Holly. Dinah is reported to have died in 1811 while they were living in Philadelphia, Pennsylvania. No mention is made of when or why they moved to that particular city. After Dinah's death, Boen returned to the area where he grew up. In 1814 he finally was made a member of the Society of Friends. He was seen as a pious, hardworking, honest, and pleasant man. He exhibited these and other Quaker qualities through his words and actions. Throughout his life he refused to wear any clothes or use any articles that were produced through slave labor. He was particular about not using plural language instead of *thou* and *thee* in the name of social equality, as was the custom of Quakers of that time. As a Quaker, he was opposed to war and greed and spoke against both.

As he grew older, his hair and long beard became white. He did not wear dyed clothing bleached of natural color, which contrasted with his dark skin. He lived his adult life relatively free of sickness. At the age of eighty-six, he was still able to recount his life in detail. His health began to fail at the age of eighty-seven, but his mental faculties stayed sharp until his death. He died quietly at the age of ninety on 12 June 1824. His death was marked by a memorial meeting given by the Mount Holly monthly meeting of Friends, and the memorial speech was read at the Yearly Meeting of Friends in Philadelphia in 1829.

FURTHER READING

Boen, William. *Anecdotes and Memoirs of William Boen, a Colored Man, Who Lived and Died Near Mount Holly, New Jersey. To Which Is Added, the Testimony of Friends of Mount Holly Monthly Meeting Concerning Him* (1834).

Cadbury, Henry. "Negro Membership in the Society of Friends (1)," *Journal of Negro History* (1936).

Child, Lydia Maria. *The Freedman's Book* (1866).

Griscom, Lloyd E. *The Historic County of Burlington* (1973 [cited 2 Apr. 2007]).

Ives, Kenneth. *Black Quakers: Brief Biographies* (1991).

Woolman, John. *The Journals of John Woolman* (1922).

DARSHELL SILVA

BOGAN, LUCILLE (BESSIE JACKSON) 47

Bogan, Lucille (Bessie Jackson) (1 Apr. 1897–10 Aug. 1948), blues singer, was born Lucille Anderson in Amory, Mississippi. Although little is known of her early life, she was raised in Birmingham, Alabama, where her family moved early on in search of work in the numerous steel and coal mills. She was married to Nazareth Lee Bogan Sr., a locomotive fireman, in about 1914 and had a son, Nazareth Lee Bogan Jr., in 1916 and a stepdaughter, Ira Betty Bogan, in 1911. In addition, she was the aunt of trumpeter and pianist Thomas "Big Music" Anderson.

Bogan began her recording career in 1923 with a session for Okeh Records in New York City. Pianist Henry Callens accompanied her. The tracks she recorded were more vaudeville oriented than they were blues, and they reflect the major influence of BESSIE SMITH, IDA COX, and other vaudeville artists. Bogan's style is distinct, however. Like the other classic blues vocalists, her vocal approach and lyrical subject matter reflect her own unique positioning in larger social and political currents. She addresses and responds to current events, economic realities, and romantic and sexual relationships in ways that reflect her standpoint as a black woman. Unlike Cox, whose early musical training was in an African Methodist choir, or even Smith, who toured on the Theater Owners' Booking Association vaudeville circuit early in her career, Bogan apparently had strong ties to Alabama's black criminal underworld, and trained in brothels, barrelhouses, and juke joints. The sexually candid and earthy style she honed in these contexts becomes particularly apparent with the Brunswick recordings of the 1930s (around the time she adopted the name Bessie Jackson).

Shortly after her 1923 session in New York, Bogan again recorded for Okeh, this time in Atlanta. Eddie Heywood Sr. accompanied her on more vaudeville-inspired blues sides. While these did not sell well, they are notable as the first "territory" recordings (i.e., recorded outside of New York or Chicago) made by an African American blues artist. In 1927, she ventured to record again in Chicago for the Paramount label. Will Ezell accompanied her on most of these sides, except for "Sweet Petunia," which featured Alex Channey on piano. This song, in which the female protagonist expresses her love for a "big fat man" nicknamed Tunie, was a modest hit. In 1928 and 1930, Bogan returned to Chicago to record for Brunswick. These sides featured TAMPA RED and COW COW DAVENPORT in supporting

roles. Several of the sides she recorded on these sessions were reissued as inexpensive singles by the American Record Corporation (later subsumed by Columbia) during the Depression. Bogan first adopted the name Bessie Jackson on these 1932 reissues. They became popular, and several were remade by other artists. LEROY CARR, Bumble Bee Slim, SONNY BOY WILLIAMSON, and others recorded "Sloppy Drunk Blues." Georgia White took up "Alley Boogie," and Tampa Red and B. B. KING redid "Black Angel Blues."

The success of her "Bessie Jackson" reissues was an important juncture in Bogan's professional life. Her ARC reissues released under the name Bessie Jackson sold better than any of her previous recordings. This may have been the result of their affordability and the sexually themed material. Because of the success, Bogan continued to record under that name, and she continued to explore explicit sexuality in her lyrics. She recorded exclusively as Bessie Jackson between 1933 and 1935. Her approach was fresh, frank, and intelligent, and her thinly veiled euphemisms and double entendres were original. As a result, her lyrics are shocking, even by contemporary standards, but they also document a range of issues that affected black women's lives. Finally, Walter Roland joined her on piano. While Roland was not as technically skilled as some of her past accompanists were, Roland's rolling barrelhouse and boogie-woogie–inflected style was the perfect accompaniment to Bogan's blossoming southern, down-home style.

The success of their partnership resulted in several recording sessions and well-known sides. They collaborated in July 1933, July and August 1934, and March 1935 (blues singer and guitarist JOSH WHITE is also featured on this session). "Groceries on the Shelf," "Down in Boogie Alley," "B.D. Woman's Blues," and "Shave 'Em Dry" (infamous for its unambiguous lyrics: "I got nipples on my titties / big as the end of my thumb. / I got somethin' 'tween my legs / would make a dead man come") are some of the tracks they produced together.

"Groceries on the Shelf," recorded in 1933, is a good example of the ways in which Bogan's songs could provide commentary on multiple levels. On one level, food euphemisms abound as stand-ins for sex and sexual activity. Piggly Wiggly, the first self-service grocery store, was founded in 1916 and quickly grew in popularity with chains opening across the South throughout the 1920s. Here, Bogan uses the store (and its business model) as a metaphor for sexual transactions:

My name is Piggly Wiggly, and I swear you can help yourself,
My name is Piggly Wiggly and I swear you can help yourself,
And you've got to have your greenback, and it don't take nothin' else.

The metaphor is artfully extended throughout the song in a way that makes clear the protagonist's terms but that also expresses ambivalence over the rapid takeover of the stores and the threat they posed to smaller local stores:

You can go to your five, you can go to your ten-cent store,
You can go to your five, you can go to your ten-cent store,
But if you come to my Piggly Wiggly, you won't go back there no more.

Bogan stopped recording in 1935 and moved back to Birmingham. While there, she managed the group in which her son played bass, Bogan's Birmingham Busters. She and her husband divorced in 1941, and she moved to Los Angeles shortly thereafter and remained active as a songwriter until her death in 1948 of coronary sclerosis. She is buried at the Lincoln Memorial Park Cemetery in Los Angeles.

While not as well known as Bessie Smith or Ida Cox, Bogan ranks with these artists as a major performer and songwriter in the classic blues style of the 1920s and 1930s. As her recording career extended from 1923 to 1935, she was one of the last of the great vaudeville-inspired, big-voiced blues vocalists to be recorded.

FURTHER READING

Bourgeois, Ann Stong. *Blueswomen: Profiles and Lyrics, 1920–1945* (1996).

Harris, Sheldon. *The Blues Who's Who: A Biographical Dictionary of Blues Singers* (1979).

Harrison, Daphne. *Black Pearls: Blues Queens of the 1920s* (1990).

Komara, Edward, ed. *Encyclopedia of the Blues* (2006).

Spottswood, Dick. Liner notes, *Shave 'Em Dry: The Best of Lucille Bogan* (2002).

MONICA HAIRSTON

Boggs, James (28 May 1919–22 July 1993), autoworker, Black Power militant, and community activist, was born in Marion Junction, Alabama, a small town near Selma in the highly segregated Dallas County. James was the youngest of four children born to Ernest Boggs, a blacksmith and iron ore worker who died when James was eight, and Leila Boggs, a domestic worker and cook. He attended elementary school in Marion Junction and throughout his life proudly retained his "Alabamese" diction. After graduating in 1937 from Dunbar High School in Bessemer, near Birmingham, he hopped a freight train to Detroit, pursuing his brothers William and Jesse, and hoping to find a job like his uncle's at Budd Wheel. When no work materialized, Boggs rode the rails to the Pacific Northwest before returning South in 1938 to marry his childhood sweetheart Annie McKinley, with whom he fathered seven children. That year he returned permanently to Detroit, securing road-building Works Projects Administration (WPA) relief work and then entering the George Washington Trade School. As production accelerated with the approach of World War II he secured industrial employment in 1940 as a template maker at Chrysler's Jefferson plant, where he remained until he retired twenty-eight years later.

Participation in the United Auto Workers (UAW) labor union, Boggs said, gave him his "real organizing skills—in strikes, wildcats, picketing, goon squads, stuff like that" (Moon, 153). Union activism also introduced him to the political left. Boggs sometimes claimed to have joined the Communist Party, which he may have done during the war, when he supported the UAW faction led by George Addes and R. J. Thomas. By the mid-1940s, however, he was searching for something more radical, and he became associated with anti-Stalinist leftists in the Socialist Workers Party (SWP) and the Industrial Workers of the World. In the late 1940s Boggs served on a fair employment practices committee created to challenge racial discrimination in and near the plant. The committee pushed for seniority as the criterion for admission to skilled trades and, beginning in 1949, joined with the Detroit branch of the National Association for the Advancement of Colored People (NAACP) to launch direct-action protests against restaurants on Woodward Avenue that were violating a state law prohibiting discrimination in public accommodations.

By the early 1950s Boggs had grown close to Correspondence, a small group that had recently left the SWP, where it had been called the Johnson-Forest Tendency after the party names of its leaders, C. L. R. JAMES ("Johnson") and Raya Dunayevskaya ("Forest"). In 1952 Correspondence opened a Third Layer School in New York City that reflected its passion for the primacy of working people. The school was premised on Lenin's observation that a revolutionary party contains three layers: a first of Marxist theoreticians, a second of experienced labor activists, and a third of raw workers and peasants. Johnson-Forest worried that these strata would crystallize, reproducing the division between manual and intellectual labor and opening the door to a "state capitalist" bureaucracy rather than socialism. To prevent that, the leadership needed to listen attentively to the rank-and-file-workers—to be tutored, as it were, by the untutored. Boggs was invited to the Third Layer School to explain shop-floor realities while the group's intellectuals took notes with what Dunayevskaya termed a "full fountain pen." This was a microcosm of the role Boggs later performed for the American left throughout the 1960s. At the school, he met Grace Lee, whom he married in 1954.

Lee (b. 1915), the daughter of a prominent New York Chinese American restaurateur, held degrees in philosophy from Barnard (B.A., 1935) and Bryn Mawr (M.A., 1937; Ph.D., 1940). Her political commitments fueled her desire "to become a movement activist in the black community" (Grace Lee Boggs, 89). In June 1953 she moved to Detroit, where Correspondence had its headquarters. Boggs's first marriage had ended in divorce in 1953, and he proposed to Lee after dinner at her house, on their first date. From the moment they were married by a justice of the peace in Toledo, Ohio, the Boggses were an indomitable team. They coauthored numerous publications, especially in the heightened feminist atmosphere of the 1970s, but even work published under James Boggs's name suggested Grace Lee Boggs's involvement. Their marriage, she reveals, challenged them both:

> I did follow Jimmy at first, consciously and openly, because he was so rooted in reality and in his community and knew so many things about politics that you can't get out of books. After about ten years I began to struggle more with him because I had begun to feel more rooted myself and also because I was concerned that the young people around us would get the wrong idea about how women should relate to men. Then we began arguing so vigorously that people around us often had to switch their eyes from one side to the other as if at a tennis or Ping-Pong match. (Grace Lee Boggs, 79–80)

Throughout the 1950s, while working two jobs, as janitor and autoworker, to meet his child support payments, Boggs remained a dedicated labor activist. He participated in a rank-and-file caucus critical of the UAW leadership and was elected to his local's steering committee but resigned in protest over its closed meetings. By 1962 disaffection with the union and enthusiasm about the civil rights upturn led the Boggses to break with C. L. R. James's Marxism. Their conclusions that automation was making labor superfluous and that unions were being absorbed into the capitalist system (a widely shared idea among 1960s leftists) informed Boggs's first book, *The American Revolution: Pages from a Negro Worker's Notebook* (1963). Published first as an issue of *Monthly Review*, whose editor Paul M. Sweezy suggested its title, *The American Revolution* maintained that black Americans, together with countries like Cuba and China, not unions, were the new catalysts of change. Especially because it bore the imprimatur of a black worker, the book was embraced by new-left students already dismissive of the labor movement, a disdain many would reconsider by the 1970s.

Boggs was an early Black Power advocate, collaborating with the Reverend ALBERT BUFORD CLEAGE JR., Max Stanford, and other Detroit militants, and organizing the Detroit meeting where MALCOLM X gave his "Message to the grass roots" speech in 1963. Boggs favored black-only organizations but opposed nostalgia for Africa: "Our destiny is right in this country," he declared. Against the fantasy of a separate nation within the United States, the Boggses in 1965 raised the slogan, "The city is the black man's land." They held that inner cities were colonies dominated by an absentee white power structure of landlords, merchants, school administrators, and police, and that urban dwellers should fight for self-determination. The 1967 Detroit uprising, however, prompted them to distinguish between rebellion and revolution. *Manifesto for a Black Revolutionary Party* (1969) and *Racism and the Class Struggle* (1970) portrayed the black proletariat, particularly street youth, as the dynamic revolutionary force, depicted white workers as racist, roundly criticized "black capitalism," and called for a black vanguard party.

By the mid-1970s the Boggses had concluded that black militancy, like labor before it, had sold out to self-interested careerism and reformist politics. In a 1983 article in *Monthly Review* Boggs reflected that the black liberation movement of the 1960s had been blind to reality in "the United States, where blacks are only a section of the population and where therefore blackness cannot be the basis for a total struggle for power." In *Revolution and Evolution in the Twentieth Century*

(1974) and *Conversations in Maine* (1978), the Boggses espoused a multicultural revolutionary humanism attuned to American conditions and informed by a dialectical view of reality as constantly changing. The collapse of radicalism in the black community, they argued, gave wider play to violence, drug abuse, and vandalism, requiring a reassertion of such values as trust, respect, and discipline. The Boggs pamphlet *But What about the Workers?* (1973), coauthored with the black autoworker James Hocker, argued that the United States is technologically and materially advanced but politically and socially backward, so that radicals who raised economic demands alone, such as welfare or wages, merely fostered the selfishness of capitalism.

Such thinking inspired the creation of a small interracial group, the National Organization for an American Revolution, that the Boggses led from 1978 to 1987. However, conditions in Detroit's black community drew most of their attention. From their home on Field Street, they objected to developers' gentrification projects, which included plans to construct a stadium building and introduce casino gambling to the city. Instead, the Boggses posed alternative solutions to disinvestment in the age of multinational capitalism. For example, in 1992 they initiated "Detroit Summer" to bring out-of-town and local youths together to rehabilitate houses, plant gardens, paint murals, and march against crack dealers. A lively vernacular speaker, Boggs emulated Malcolm X's chiding, denying that oppression was an excuse for irresponsibility, urging blacks not to see themselves as victims, and rejecting "biological" thinking that places skin color above beliefs. He championed self-reliance, perseverance, and pride in creative work. To the end, James Boggs remained deeply committed to the struggle for black liberation. Even as he battled the cancer that would take his life, he rewrote the final line of the civil rights anthem by insisting, "We shall overcome *today*."

FURTHER READING

The James and Grace Lee Boggs Collection is housed in the Archives of Labor and Urban Affairs in the Walter P. Reuther Library at Wayne State University in Detroit, Michigan.

Boggs, Grace Lee. *Living for Change* (1998).

Moon, Elaine Latzman. *Untold Tales, Unsung Heroes: An Oral History of Detroit's African American Community, 1918–1967* (1994).

Mullens, Bill. *Afro-Orientalism* (2004).

Nicholas, Xavier. *Questions of the American Revolution: Conversations with James Boggs* (1976).

Obituary: *Detroit Free Press*, 24 July 1993.

CHRISTOPHER PHELPS

Bogle, Donald E. (13 July 1944–), film and television historian, was born in Philadelphia to Roslyn, a homemaker and arts advocate, and John Dudley Bogle, vice president and advertising director of the *Philadelphia Tribune*, the oldest continually published black newspaper in the country. Bogle's father was educated at the Virginia Theological Seminary where his maternal grandfather, Robert Clisson Woods, had also been president. His father had studied history and was a charismatic speaker on behalf of African Americans' civil rights. Bogle's mother decided against college and eloped with John Bogle when she was a teenager. Because of her upbringing in a highly educated family, however, she had developed a deep knowledge and appreciation for the arts and culture, which she passed on to her children.

While Bogle was still an infant, his large family moved to a suburb of Philadelphia, and he grew up in a predominately white, middle-class community. Bogle's father died when he was still young, but his mother raised the family on her own.

As a child, Bogle suffered from asthma, which frequently limited his physical activities. As a result, he read books in his family's library and watched a lot of television. He was particularly fascinated with films featuring black actors, some of whom his parents spoke about at the family dinner table. In the preface to his first book, *Toms, Coons, Mulattos, Mammies & Bucks*, Bogle wrote about the first movie he had ever seen with an all-black cast, "I decided one gloomy rainy afternoon to run away from home and go to live at the movies. By chance, the movie I went to 'live at' was something called *Carmen Jones*. In no conceivable way has my life been the same since."

After graduating from a mostly white high school, Bogle acceded to his mother's wishes and attended the historically black Lincoln University. There he studied literature under professors H. Alfred Farrell, Lou Putnam, and Edward Groff, who had a vast knowledge of movie history and encouraged Bogle's cinema interests. After graduating with honors, Bogle briefly pursued a master's degree in Creative Writing at Indiana University, but he left the program after one year. He moved to New York City where he took graduate courses at

Columbia University. Before completing a degree, he left again, this time to take a job as a story editor for Otto Preminger, the acclaimed director of *Carmen Jones* and *Porgy and Bess*. Through Preminger, Bogle heard firsthand accounts and assessments about black Hollywood, particularly about the actress DOROTHY DANDRIDGE. In addition to having directed the Oscar-nominated actress in two of his most memorable films, Preminger had been romantically involved with Dandridge before her death from an accidental suicide in 1965. By this time, Bogle was already formulating an idea to write about the history and contributions of African Americans in Hollywood cinema. He was influenced by the writings of several cultural critics, particularly AMIRI BARAKA's (Leroi Jones) *Blues People*, ALBERT MURRAY's *Stomping the Blues*, and by the film criticism of Pauline Kael. He was also influenced by the cultural criticism of STERLING BROWN and L. D. REDDICK.

After nine months of working for Preminger, Bogle moved to Chicago where he worked as a journalist for *Ebony* magazine. Bantam Books offered Bogle a contract to write what later became *Toms, Coons, Mulattos, Mammies & Bucks: An Interpretive History of Blacks in American Films* (1973). He spent four years researching the book, tracking down rare films, such as a 1934 edition of John Stahl's *Imitation of Life*, and also interviewing dozens of black film stars, including several who had worked for the independent black director OSCAR MICHEAUX. He also spoke with other industry notables, such as King Vidor, who made one of the first Hollywood sound movies with an African American cast, *Hallelujah!*, which starred NINA MAE MCKINNEY. Bogle's aim with the book had been not only to catalog and analyze common portrayals of blacks in American films but also to decode the ways in which some black performers subverted the narrow, sometimes demeaning roles offered to them in Hollywood and how African American audiences responded. It was one of the first books by an American writer to document and analyze the experience and contributions of black actors and filmmakers in the twentieth-century development of the Hollywood film industry, and the study quickly became a classic.

Buoyed by the book's success, Bogle taught briefly at his alma mater, Lincoln University, and also lectured around the country for several years. Bogle's second book, published in 1980, was *Brown Sugar: Eighty Years of America's Black Female Superstars*. That survey was later reproduced as a four-part, four-hour television documentary for PBS by German Educational Television for which Bogle wrote the scripts and served as executive producer. The documentary series won an award from the American Women in Radio & Television. Immediately on the heels of the documentary, Bogle wrote a 510-page encyclopedia, *Blacks in American Films and Television*, which was published in 1988.

Throughout his career, Bogle was hampered by debilitating migraine headaches that sometimes left him immobile for days at a time. He became known as an intensely reclusive person who, although he interviewed others for a living, rarely felt comfortable discussing his own life. Occasionally, he had difficulty getting publishers interested in his book ideas that typically centered around black Hollywood. He said, for example, that several publishers passed on his idea to write a biography of Dandridge, who had been largely forgotten by mainstream America at that point, until a black-owned house, Amistad Press, took the project on. The resulting 613-page book, *Dorothy Dandridge: A Biography*, brought the actor's life and career to the attention of a new generation of film enthusiasts.

Bogle went on to publish a history of blacks in television, *Primetime Blues* (2001), and another on black Hollywood, *Bright Boulevards, Bold Dreams* (2005), which garnered excellent reviews and earned Bogle the 2006 Hurston-Wright Legacy Finalist Award in Non-Fiction.

Between writing projects, Bogle appeared as a commentator in numerous documentaries about film and television, including the RICHARD PRYOR–executive-produced *Mo' Funny (A History of Black Humor)*, SPIKE LEE's *Jim Brown: All-American*, and the American Movie Classics channel's *Small Steps ... Big Strides*. He also hosted Turner Classic Movies' groundbreaking 38-film series *Race and Hollywood*, which won the cable industry's Vision Award in 2007. Bogle has served on the board of the Film Forum in New York City and taught film history at Rutgers University, the University of Pennsylvania, and New York University. He has also curated a major retrospective on the career of SIDNEY POITIER at the American Museum of the Moving Image and another on the career of Lee, who has referred to him as "our most noted black cinema historian."

FURTHER READING
Bogle, Donald. *Toms, Coons, Mulattoes, Mammies & Bucks: An Interpretive History of Blacks in American Films* (1973).

Jackson, Ronald L., II, and Sonja M. Brown Givens. *Black Pioneers in Communication Research* (2006).

JODY BENJAMIN

Bohannon, Horace (22 Aug. 1922–14 May 2003), pilot, Tuskegee Airman, civil servant, teacher, and juvenile probation officer, was born in Atlanta, Georgia, the youngest child of Georgia Crane and Earl Bohannon, occupations unknown. Bohannon was the youngest of ten children, although only his oldest sister and a brother were alive when Bohannon was born. One of his greatest influences growing up was his mother, who taught him the importance of principles, hard work, and honesty.

Bohannon began working at eight years of age in a hardware store. His next job was working on a laundry truck. It was the laundry job that ultimately led Bohannon to his dream of becoming an aviator. Bohannon stopped twice a week at Atlanta's Candler Field (later William B. Hartsfield Airport). While picking up the aviators' laundry he listened to the pilots discussing their flights, the difficulties of flying in adverse weather conditions, and other matters that inspired him to become a pilot. From the start people were negative about his aspiration. One white Georgia pilot told Bohannon, "Horace, I know you like that stuff, but I think you are wasting your time. There is no chance in the world that you could work around them [airplanes] or be one of the pilots" (Moye, 58–71). Bohannon would not let the prevailing racial attitude stop him from his dream of becoming a pilot.

Bohannon graduated from Booker T. Washington High School in 1939, at that time the only high school for blacks in Atlanta. He attended Lincoln University in Chester County, Pennsylvania, where he studied to become a teacher from 1939 to 1942. It was at Lincoln that he got his first opportunity to train as a pilot. However, at the end of Bohannon's junior year he was forced to return to Atlanta to work and earn money for his senior year.

Upon returning to Atlanta, Bohannon was recommended for a job as a carpenter's helper in Alabama where the Tuskegee Air Base was being built. While helping to build the airbase he learned that the United States Army was testing for instructor pilots in Atlanta at the Butler Street YMCA. Over 200 men of all races took the test, but only Bohannon and one other man passed.

Unfortunately delays and interruptions forced Bohannon to find other jobs to fill in gaps in the training. He worked as a timekeeper at Tuskegee's airfield, recording the time each plane took off and when it returned so the pilots were credited with the correct number of flight hours. Eventually he became frustrated with the interruptions in training and living hand-to-mouth and returned to Atlanta, where he became a cab driver for the company Harlem Cab. Bohannon was able to average about $70 working three days a week. It was a tremendous sum of money for a black man at that time, especially in comparison to a black porter who made only $11 every two weeks.

In the summer of 1943 Bohannon met Ora Jean Whyte, who became his wife in November 1943. The couple had a son and two daughters. It was Whyte's influence that led Bohannon back to Lincoln University, where much to his surprise he received a draft notice. Bohannon was drafted in to army air corps on 15 October 1943. He attended primary flight training at Moton Field in Tuskegee, Alabama, which was the only army air corps primary flight training facility for black pilots during World War II.

After finishing primary flight training Bohannon moved on to Tuskegee Army Air Field, the base at which Bohannon worked as a carpenter. Bohannon graduated on 20 December 1944 in Class SE-44-J, SE standing for "single engine plane," 44 indicating the year the class graduated, and J, the tenth letter of the alphabet, indicating that it was the tenth graduating class of the year. After graduation Bohannon was sent to Godman Field in Walterboro, South Carolina, for training on how to fly the P-40. He was scheduled to deploy to Europe, but when the fighting ended Bohannon began training to fly in the South Pacific against Japan. However, the war ended before Bohannon got the chance to fly in combat.

Bohannon was discharged from the army air corps not long after in 1945. Like many other black veterans Bohannon returned to the civilian world with the hopes that the situation of black people would improve. Finding few opportunities for work, he went back to driving cabs.

Because blacks were not allowed to join the American Legion as full-fledged members, Bohannon helped set up the Georgia Veterans League (GVL). The GVL eventually became affiliated with the American Veteran's Committee, which accepted members regardless of race. In 1946 or 1947 Bohannon began working for the Southern Regional Council (SRC), an Atlanta-based civil rights organization. It was while working for the SRC that Bohannon met Dr. George Mitchell, director of the Veterans Education Program for the Southern Regional Council. Mitchell wanted to use blacks as contact officers and representatives for the Veterans Administration. Bohannon spent the next year and a half working for the Veterans Education Program.

Bohannon returned to Lincoln University in January 1948 and graduated with a degree in teaching on 8 June 1948. He worked as a teacher for two years at Atlanta's John Hope School and the English Avenue School. During the summer Bohannon supplemented his family's income by working for the post office. Teaching proved to be unable to hold Bohannon's interest and he quickly became frustrated with the post office's blatant discrimination against blacks.

In 1952 Bohannon took an examination to become a probation officer for the Fulton County Juvenile Court. Bohannon worked for the Fulton County Juvenile Court until 1961, when he began looking for another job after refusing to attend a segregated Christmas party given by one of the Fulton County Juvenile Court judges.

Bohannon interviewed for a job at the post office and became a training officer for the states of North Carolina, South Carolina, and Florida. From there he moved on to other civil service positions, including contract compliance position with the United States Navy and finally to the Department of Health, Education, and Welfare (HEW).

While at HEW, Bohannon assisted six states, including Mississippi, to comply with federal desegregation laws. Despite the high quality of his work and the mandate of the agency for which he worked, Bohannon regularly faced discrimination from within the organization and from other government employees. In Charleston, South Carolina, during the early 1960s Bohannon worked with the Medical University of South Carolina (MUSC) to establish a plan and set the dates for desegregating MUSC's offices; however, when it was time to implement the plan South Carolina Senator Strom Thurmond told the hospital they did not have to implement the agreement.

Frustrated with the situation, Bohannon accepted a job offered by his former boss from his navy contract compliance position. Bohannon was made manager of Special Projects for the Maritime Administration. He worked there until he retired in 1981.

Even after retiring Bohannon was much in demand as a speaker during Black History Month.

He remained active in the Atlanta community, raising money for various groups and organizations. Bohannon died of congestive heart failure at age eighty in Atlanta.

FURTHER READING

Brooks, Jennifer E. "Winning the Peace: Georgia Veterans and the Struggle to Define the Political Legacy of World War II," *Journal of Southern History* 66 (Aug. 2000).

Moye, J. Todd. "I Never Quit Dreaming about It; Horace Bohannon, the Tuskegee Airmen, and the Dream of Flight," *Atlanta History* 47½ (2005).

Onkst, David H. "First a Negro ... Incidentally a Veteran: Black World War Two Veterans and the G.I. Bill of Rights in the Deep South, 1944–1948," *Journal of Social History* (Spring 1998).

Obituary: *Atlanta Journal-Constitution*, 19 May 2003.

ANNE K. DRISCOLL

Bojangles. *See* Robinson, Bill.

Bol, Manute (16 Oct. 1962–19 June 2010), professional basketball player and humanitarian activist, was born in Gogrial, Sudan. Born to Madut and Okwok Bol, his father was a herder in the Sudan. Legend has it that Bol, who shared this task, once killed a lion with a spear while tending the family's cattle. Members of the Dinka tribe, noteworthy for their height, Bol's parents were tall—his mother was 6 feet 10 inches. Bol grew to an extraordinary 7 feet 7 inches. When he was a teenager with such height, a cousin suggested he take up basketball. Playing for a team in the larger city of Wau and later in the Sudanese capital of Khartoum, Bol was discovered by Don Feeley, a coach from Fairleigh Dickinson University in New Jersey. He came to the United States in 1983, and although he weighed only 180 pounds and lacked athleticism, Bol was drafted by the then San Diego Clippers in the fifth round of the 1983 National Basketball Association (NBA) draft. When the league ruled him ineligible for the draft, his selection was voided. Knowing almost no English, Bol landed in Cleveland at the invitation of Cleveland State basketball coach Kevin Mackey. He attended English classes, but after Cleveland State was placed on NCAA probation for providing improper benefits to Bol and two other recruits from Africa, Bol never played there. In 1984 he enrolled at the University of Bridgeport (CT), where he played one season of college basketball, averaging twenty-two points, thirteen rebounds, and seven blocked shots a

Manute Bol, in this 1985 photo, is shown during his three-times-a-week fitness program at the University of Maryland in College Park to build up his slender body. (AP Images.)

game, once again drawing interest from professionals scouts.

After only one season he left Bridgeport to play with the Rhode Island Gulls of the United States Basketball League, where pro scouts flocked to see his shot blocking ability. Most teams were hesitant about Bol—he was tall but terribly thin and had few basketball skills. In 1985 the Washington Bullets decided to take a chance and drafted him in the second round. Over the next ten seasons, Bol played for four teams and established himself as a legitimate shot blocker and a fan favorite.

Despite his remarkable height, Bol was never an NBA star. He was too frail and possessed few basketball skills. In his first year with Washington (1985–86), Bol played in eighty games, starting a career high sixty, and established a rookie record with 397 blocks (a figure that also led the league overall), but he averaged under four points and six rebounds a game. These were his high marks for Washington,

and despite his wild popularity among fans, he was traded to the Golden State Warriors after the 1987–88 season. In two seasons with the Warriors he started eight games but played in almost all his team's games—Bol once again led the NBA in blocked shots in 1988–89, but his scoring was virtually nonexistent. In August 1990 he was traded once again, this time to the Philadelphia 76ers, where he played a full three seasons. The 76ers released Bol in the summer of 1993, and he played with three teams the next year—Miami, Washington, and again with Philadelphia. He ended his NBA career with Golden State after five games in the 1994–95 season. For his ten year career Bol averaged 2.6 points, 4.2 rebounds, and 3.3 blocks. He is the only player in NBA history to have more blocked shots (2,086) than points (1,599). Additionally, in the 1995/96 season Bol played twenty-two games for the Florida Beach Dogs of the Continental Basketball Association (CBA).

Bol was a fan favorite and later in his career he often took an unorthodox three-point shot that resembled an inbounds soccer throw; when he scored the fans responded with enthusiasm. Popular among NBA players as a practical joker, his highest earnings for any one season was $1.65 million with Philadelphia in 1992–93, but it was what he did with his money that drew the most attention.

Bol was an advocate of Sudanese freedom and donated much of his NBA earnings to Sudanese refugees and victims of religious oppression. A Christian, Bol worked for human rights organizations in the Sudan and worldwide such as Sudan Sunrise, the Ring True Foundation, and the Sudan Relief and Redemption Association, and was once prohibited from leaving Sudan because of his political beliefs. After the NBA, Bol participated in a number of charitable events—a boxing match with the gigantic football player William "The Refrigerator" Perry, a one-day contract with a minor league hockey team, and even a stunt as a jockey—but what he earned went to support relief work in his native Sudan, much of it through Sudan Sunrise, a nonprofit aimed at charitable causes in the Sudan.

On a trip to the Sudan in early 2010, Bol became ill with a kidney ailment. Although treated there, he was hospitalized at the University of Virginia Medical Center (Charlottesville) in June with kidney failure and Stevens-Johnson Syndrome, a skin disease. Bol died at age forty-seven, almost destitute due to his support of Sudanese causes.

FURTHER READING

"Manute Bol's Radical Christianity," *Wall Street Journal*, 25 June 2010.

Manute Bol, Basketball-Reference.com, http://www. basketball-reference.com/players/b/bolma01.html

Manute Bol: Basketball Warrior. Documentary, available through NBA.com. 2004.

Obituary: *Washington Post*, 20 June 2010.

BOYD CHILDRESS

Bolden, Buddy (6 Sept. 1877–4 Nov. 1931), jazz musician, was born Charles Joseph Bolden in New Orleans, Louisiana, the son of Westmore Bolden, a drayman, and Alice Harrison. Although Bolden is one of the earliest known figures in the development of jazz in New Orleans, there was little factual information about him until the publication in 1978 of Donald M. Marquis's *In Search of Buddy Bolden.* In this admirable piece of investigative research, Marquis dispels much of the rumor that had grown around Bolden's life in New Orleans and establishes him as an important member of the founding generation of jazz musicians. Marquis confirms that Bolden was not a barber and did not own a barbershop, as popularly believed, although he apparently spent considerable time at barbershops, which served as musicians' meeting places, where information on jobs could be exchanged. Nor did he edit a "scandal sheet" called the *Cricket*. He did drink a lot, played a loud cornet, and was eventually committed to an asylum for erratic behavior resulting from chronic alcoholism.

Like most other New Orleans musicians of that period, Bolden pursued a part-time career performing jazz (then called ragtime). Not until 1902 did city directories begin listing him as a "musician." Before that year he was identified as a "plasterer" and resided in his family's uptown home on First Street in New Orleans. Sufficient documentation and testimony exist to verify that in about 1895 Bolden became active as a cornetist and bandleader at various indoor and outdoor locations in New Orleans. These venues included Lincoln and Johnson parks, Longshoreman's Hall, and Tulane University in the uptown area; the Milneburg and West End resorts on Lake Pontchartrain; the Masonic Hall in Algiers; the Fairgrounds Race Track; and a number of "social clubs" whose halls lined the Perdido–South Rampart Street area. The period from 1897 to 1906 marked the prime of Bolden's tenure as a jazz musician—a time when he enjoyed a sort of preeminence among other players for his boldness and audacity and the barrelhouse nature of his music.

Essentially an "uptown" musician, Bolden had limited contact with the more learned downtown musicians and performed primarily for black audiences. As an untutored musician with little if any formal education, and as one who played mostly by ear, he made music of the "rough blues" variety used to accompany the "slow drag" and other enticing dances of prostitutes. The downtown Creoles called it "honky tonk" music, and Bolden's repertoire was reputed to be particularly coarse. According to Marquis, it appealed "especially to a liberated, post–Civil War generation of young blacks." One number in particular, "Buddy Bolden's Blues," also known as "Funky Butt," was popular enough to cause Union Sons Hall (a location where Bolden's band frequently played) to be commonly referred to as Funky Butt Hall in his honor.

The principal difficulty in assessing the musical contributions of Bolden stems from the total absence of audio recordings. Although he was active during a period when early recordings were being made, no cylinders or records of his playing are known to exist. The search for a cylinder allegedly made by Bolden and his band in the late 1890s, and first reported by one of Bolden's sidemen, Willie Cornish, to the *Jazzmen* editor Charles Edward Smith in 1939, proved fruitless. The only photograph (the original now lost) of Bolden shows him with a six-piece ensemble that included cornet, trombone, two clarinets, guitar, and string bass. Nonetheless, legendary accounts abound of his playing and bandleading and even his lifestyle.

As his celebrity as a cornetist and bandleader grew, so did his appetite for high living. Even as early as 1895 he had become a "ladies' man," known to have consorted with the sporting crowd and prostitutes, one of whom, Hattie Oliver, gave birth to his illegitimate son. Their common-law marriage lasted only a few years, and in 1902 Bolden met Nora Bass and entered into a second common-law marriage that produced his only daughter. The Boldens' domestic environment was anything but tranquil, as contemporary police records and testimony from family members attest. Early in 1906 Bolden began suffering severe headaches, fits of depression, and episodes of violent behavior—all apparently related to his excessive drinking. An attack on his mother-in-law on 27 March, during which he struck her in the head with a water pitcher, led to his arrest and detainment by police, initiating the only apparent newspaper coverage he was to receive during his lifetime. Continued episodes of depression and violent behavior left him in a deranged state that placed him in conflict with many of his former musical cohorts as well as members of his family. Finally, in April 1907, having been confined to the house of detention, Bolden was moved to the state hospital for the insane in Jackson, Louisiana. There he lived out the remaining twenty-four years of his life, separated from his family and largely forgotten for the role he had played as one of the earliest identifiable jazz pioneers.

FURTHER READING

Marquis, Donald M. *In Search of Buddy Bolden* (1978). This entry is taken from the *American National Biography* and is published here with the permission of the American Council of Learned Societies.

CHARLES BLANCQ

Bolden, Charles F., Jr. (19 Aug. 1946–), astronaut, test pilot, military and NASA administrator, was born in Columbia, South Carolina, to Charles Frank Bolden Sr. and Ethel M. Bolden, both teachers. A child during the early years of the civil rights movement, Bolden was encouraged by his parents and teachers to pursue his dream of becoming a pilot, despite the fact that there were few opportunities at the time for African Americans to fly.

After graduating with honors from C. A. Johnson High School in Columbia in 1964, Bolden entered the U.S. Naval Academy at Annapolis, Maryland; he graduated with a B.S. in Electrical Science in 1968. Following graduation he married Alexis (Jackie) Walker. The couple would later have a son Anthony, born in 1971 and a daughter, Kelly, born in 1976.

In 1968 Bolden accepted a commission in the Marine Corps. Quickly rising to the rank of second lieutenant, Bolden, who had completed two years of military flight training, became a naval aviator in 1970. He served as a fighter pilot during the Vietnam War, carrying out more than one hundred missions in 1972 and 1973, flying an A-6A Intruder, an attack plane that carries a pilot and a bombardier-navigator.

After the war, Bolden served as a marine recruiting officer in California for two years (1973–1975), and then completed three years of other assignments at the Marine Corps Air Station El Toro; during this time he earned his M.A. in Systems Management from the University of Southern California in 1977. Bolden had toyed with the idea of applying to NASA to be an astronaut, but he felt he lacked the test-pilot experience necessary to be accepted into the program. In an effort to gain more flying experience, he enrolled in the U.S. Naval Test Pilot School at Patuxent River, Maryland. By the time he graduated in 1979, Bolden had logged more than 6,000 hours of flight time, and was assigned to the Systems Engineering and Strike Aircraft Test Directorates of the Naval Air Test Center, also at Patuxent River.

In 1980 Bolden was accepted into NASA's space shuttle program (STS). On 12 January 1986 he became the second African American to pilot a space shuttle (Frederick Drew Gregory had been NASA's first African American pilot in 1978), when he manned the controls of the shuttle *Columbia* on STS-61C. This was a science-oriented mission in which various astrophysics experiments were performed and a communications satellite was launched. Only ten days after *Columbia* had landed, on 28 January 1986, the *Challenger* space shuttle exploded soon after liftoff. Bolden led the investigative team that would determine the cause of the disaster: faulty O-ring seals in a solid-rocket booster.

Shuttle flights resumed in 1988. Bolden's next space shuttle flight was a historic one: On 24 April 1990 he piloted the *Discovery* on mission STS-31, which deployed the Hubble Space Telescope. This mission also set a record for the highest orbit—400 miles above the Earth—captured with IMAX cameras that offered the public a glimpse of life on a space shuttle.

Bolden commanded and piloted his next shuttle mission on 24 March 1992 aboard the *Atlantis*. An international science mission, with astronauts from NASA, the European Space Agency, and Japan, STS-45 carried out experiments on Earth's atmosphere, land masses, and oceans.

By 1992, however, NASA was confronted with a damaged public image and severe budget cutbacks. Charges of mismanagement led to the hiring of a new director, Daniel Goldin. Impressed with Bolden's work in the aftermath of the *Challenger* explosion, Goldin appointed Bolden to be NASA's assistant deputy administrator. Bolden was responsible for reporting to Congress on efficiency—or the lack thereof—within NASA. After this appointment, Bolden made his final shuttle flight as commander aboard the *Discovery*, on science mission STS-60, which launched on 3 February 1994.

After the mission had returned safely to Earth, Bolden left NASA, having logged more than 680 hours in space, and in June 1994 he returned to active duty in the U.S. Marine Corps, where he finished out the year as deputy commandant of the U.S. Naval Academy. For the next two years, Bolden served as the Assistant Wing Commander, Third Marine Aircraft Wing in Miramar, California, and in July 1997 was assigned to Japan to be Deputy Commanding General, I MEF (1st Marine Expeditionary Force), in the Pacific.

In 1998 President Bill Clinton was concerned that Saddam Hussein was violating the American- and British-mandated no-fly zone in northern Iraq; as a result, Bolden was called back from Japan. From February to June 1998 he served as Commanding General, I MEF (FWD) (Marine Expeditionary Force, Forward), in support of Operation Desert Thunder in Kuwait.

In July 1998 Bolden was promoted to the rank of major general and resumed his previous duties as the deputy commander of the U.S. forces in Japan. In August 2000 he became commanding general of the Third Marine Aircraft Wing.

On 31 January 2002 President George W. Bush nominated Bolden to be deputy administrator of NASA, but Bolden turned down the post. He retired from the marine corps in August 2002 after thirty-four years of service, and he also received a certificate of appreciation from President Bush and a Distinguished Service Medal. Bolden became a director of the Marathon Oil Corporation in 2003.

After nomination by President Barack Obama and subsequent confirmation by the U.S. Senate, Bolden became the 12th Administrator of NASA on 17 July 2009.

In addition to his Distinguished Service Medal, Bolden's awards include three NASA Exceptional Service Medals for 1988, 1989, and 1991, the NASA Outstanding Leadership Medal in 1992, and such military awards as the Defense Superior Service Medal, the Defense Meritorious Service Medal, the Distinguished Flying Cross, the Air Medal, and the Strike/Flight Medal. He was honored with the University of Southern California Alumni Award of Merit for 1989 and received honorary degrees from the University of South Carolina, Winthrop College, Johnson C. Smith University, and San Diego State University.

FURTHER READING

Bigelow, Barbara Carlisle, ed. *Contemporary Black Biography* (1994).

Burns, Khephra, and William Miles. *Black Stars in Orbit: NASA's African-American Astronauts* (1995).

Phelps, J. Alfred. *They Had a Dream: The Story of African-American Astronauts* (1994).

Spangenburg, Ray, and Kit Moser. "Bolden, Charles," in *African Americans in Science, Math, and Invention, A to Z of African Americans* (2003).

Wellford, Alison. "Charles F. Bolden, Jr.," in *Notable Black American Scientists* (1990).

JOSEPHA SHERMAN

Bolden, Ethel Martin (14 Dec. 1918–20 Oct. 2002), teacher, librarian, and community leader, was born Ethel Evangeline Veronica Martin in Charleston, South Carolina, the only girl of four children born to Thomas Jerry Martin, a laborer, and Ethel Sinkler Martin, a schoolteacher. Martin's youth was spent in constant transition because of family loss. Her father relocated to Chicago in search of employment and died in a streetcar accident. In 1927 her mother died of natural causes while working at the Fairwold School for Colored Girls in Columbia, South Carolina. Having lost both parents by the age of six, Martin was initially reared by her paternal grandmother, Sara Martin, who was an educator at Saint Simon Episcopal Mission in Peak, South Carolina. Ethel Martin later lived with her aunt, Dora Dillard, a seamstress in Columbia, South Carolina. Both women had a lasting influence on Martin. Her grandmother exposed her to books and PAUL LAURENCE DUNBAR's poetry. Growing up in her aunt's interracial neighborhood of Edgewood near downtown Columbia left Martin with a belief that blacks and whites could live and interact in a peaceable manner.

Martin attended the all-black Booker T. Washington High School in the Wheeler Hill section of Columbia. She graduated in 1936 and continued her education at Barber Scotia Junior College, a historically black institution in Concord, North Carolina. Working at her first job under the tutelage of the librarian Robbie L. Goodloe, Martin became enamored with the library environment and set her sights on joining the profession. Upon her graduation in 1938, she matriculated at Johnson C. Smith College in Charlotte, North Carolina, graduating in 1940 with a B.A. in English. Martin returned to Columbia to teach fourth grade at Waverly Elementary School. In 1941 she married her childhood sweetheart, Charles Frank Bolden. The couple had two sons, Charles Jr. and Warren.

Ethel Bolden's dream of becoming a librarian came true through an opportunity provided by

John Whiteman, a Waverly Elementary administrator, who expressed interest in establishing a school library. This motivated Bolden to take library courses at neighboring Allen University and Benedict College. With her acquired knowledge, she established the first elementary library in an all-black Richland School District One public school in 1946. Within a twelve-year span, Bolden created libraries at two more African American schools, Carver Elementary and C. A. Johnson High School. Despite her accomplishments, she felt the need to acquire a master's degree in library science. The major obstacle was that the nearest accredited library school that admitted blacks was Atlanta University in Georgia. With the cooperation of her husband, who agreed to take care of their sons, Bolden was able to attend the college beginning in 1954. Mentored by VIRGINIA LACY JONES, the library school's dean, Bolden finished her course work in Atlanta in 1957. She returned home the following year to write her thesis on another pioneer librarian, Sara Dart Butler, who established Dart Hall Branch Library in Charleston. Bolden earned her M.A. in Library Service in 1959 and soon became the head librarian at Columbia's W.A. Perry Junior High School.

When Columbia dismantled its segregated school system in 1968, Bolden was hired at the formerly all-white Dreher High School. She became the first African American head librarian in a desegregated Richland District One school.

In addition to pursuing a career as a librarian, Bolden was determined to improve the social conditions of Columbia residents. Throughout the Jim Crow era, Bolden was instrumental in providing religious and cultural programs for African American youth. She did this by creating programs through her church, Northminster United Presbyterian, and her membership with the Gamma Nu (Beta Zeta) Omega Chapter of the Alpha Kappa Alpha Sorority, the Columbia chapters of the Pan-Hellenic Council, and Jack and Jill of America. Professionally Bolden chaired the librarian section of the Palmetto State Teachers' Association (PSTA), the South Carolina African American teachers' organization, in 1964. She was also an integral force for interracial cooperation in the Columbia branch of the South Carolina Council on Human Relations, a private, biracial, and interfaith association established in 1954. One of Bolden's proudest affiliations was with Columbia's Community Relations Council, established by Mayor Lester Bates during the 1960s to prevent violent racial unrest and rioting that prevailed throughout other cities in the Southeast. Bolden was among one hundred black and white business and professional leaders on the council who utilized methods of community dialogue for the city's peaceful integration.

Bolden was actively involved in integrating numerous institutional and civic organizations. She often was the only African American to serve on community boards during the 1950s through the 1970s. She was one of fifteen members, and the only African American woman, who served on the Richland County Public Library Board of Trustee's (RCPL) in 1977. Within a fifteen-year period, Bolden oversaw relocation plans for three branches and new construction plans for the main branch in downtown Columbia. She was also in constant demand as a motivational speaker, as she fondly spoke to youths about the virtues of reading, African American history, and obtaining an education. She also talked about her son, who had become a NASA astronaut in 1980. Bolden retired from Dreher High in 1982, having served a thirty-eight-year tenure as teacher and librarian.

During her lifetime Bolden served on over thirty institutional, civic, and religious boards. She also received numerous awards for her civil rights involvement and volunteerism. In 2002 she was honored with the Order of the Palmetto, the state's highest award, given for lifetime achievement and service.

FURTHER READING
Ethel Bolden's papers are at the South Carolina Library, Manuscripts Division, University of South Carolina, Columbia.
Mayo, Georgette. "'A Voice in the Wilderness': Ethel Evangeline Martin Bolden; Pioneer Librarian," master's thesis, University of South Carolina, Columbia (2005).
Williams, Robert V. "Interview with Ethel Bolden," in *Speaking of History: The Words of South Carolina Librarians* (1988).

GEORGETTE MAYO

Bolden, Frank E. (24 Dec. 1912–28 Aug. 2003), journalist and historian, was born Franklin Eugene Bolden Jr. in Washington County, Pennsylvania, the eldest of three sons of Franklin Eugene Bolden Sr., the first black mail carrier in the city of Washington, Pennsylvania, and Mary Woods Bolden. Frank Bolden's parents instilled in him the importance of education and achievement at an early age. His father often told him, "When you're average, you are just as far from the bottom as you are from the top" (Rouvalis, *Post-Gazette*). With that mentality, Bolden's life was anything but average.

Bolden attended the Washington public school system and graduated from high school in 1930. He went on to attend the University of Pittsburgh, where he was the first African American to play in the university's varsity marching and concert bands. He said in a documentary film about his life that his audition for the band was twice as hard as what was required of white members. While in college, Bolden also became one of the first three black students to perform in the Cap and Gown drama club. He joined Alpha Phi Alpha national fraternity in 1931. Bolden graduated in 1934, earning a B.S. with honors in Education. Bolden intended to enroll in the university's medical school, but racism kept him out. Upon visiting the school's dean, Bolden was told that his transcript was impeccable and he would be admitted that day if only he were white. At the time, the university refused to admit blacks to the medical school. Bolden instead chose to pursue his doctorate in biological studies. He was inducted into Phi Sigma, an honorary biology society, and was a member of the Pennsylvania Academy of Science, with publications in 1936 and 1938. Bolden, who was also the first black graduate assistant to teach in Pitt's biology department, had a teaching certificate and tried to apply for a teaching position with the Pittsburgh public schools. He was again denied entry because the system did not hire black teachers.

Bolden had no formal training in journalism, but around 1935 a friend who worked for the *Pittsburgh Courier*, one of the most renowned black newspapers in the country, asked him if he wanted to work part-time as a sportswriter. He primarily covered the Pittsburgh Crawfords and Homestead Grays, both Negro League baseball teams, and boxing. His talent attracted the attention of editors at the paper as well as its publisher, ROBERT L. VANN. As his career grew, Bolden would become well known for what were later coined "Bolden-isms," phrases he used to describe his subjects. For instance, he referred to black soldiers serving in World War II as "Tan Yanks" because he said he was tired of calling them "Negro Soldiers" in his articles. He called numbers runners "digitarians," and prostitutes were members of the "nocturnal sisterhood." Bolden's career at the *Courier* spanned twenty-seven years and included positions as columnist, feature writer, copy desk editor, and eventually city editor, a post he held from 1956 to 1962. In between his work at the *Courier*, around 1940, Bolden worked late afternoons and evenings as a bacteriologist for the county's Department of Public Health.

Pittsburgh's Hill District, which was one of the most famous African American neighborhoods in the country between the 1930s and 1950s, was Bolden's beat. He covered the neighborhood's nightlife, political, social, and cultural events. He was especially interested in stories of everyday people and their good works. This idea of spotlighting unsung heroes would continue through Bolden's tenure as city editor at the *Courier*. His articles would also speak out against discriminatory practices and ill treatment against blacks. He was an outspoken critic of Pittsburgh's urban renewal plans that destroyed the Hill District in the late 1950s.

During World War II Bolden was eager to unearth stories of the black troops fighting for freedom abroad. In 1942 he became one of the first two blacks accredited by the War Department as a war correspondent. His first assignments were to cover the mobilization of black troops including the Ninety-second and Ninety-third Infantry Divisions at Fort Huachuca, Arizona (which included the Buffalo Soldiers), and aviation training at the Tuskegee Institute in Alabama. He went overseas to cover the China-Burma-India theater of operations for the National Negro Publishers Association (later called the National Newspaper Publishers Association). His goal was to counter reports in the white press that painted black soldiers as cowards who would retreat in combat. Instead, Bolden's stories showed black troops who fought with dignity and courage. He also documented the exploits of the black engineering troops who built the Ledo Road (later Stilwell Road) in Burma. The National Negro Publishers Association distributed his articles to the *Courier* and to other black publications around the country.

In the course of one year, beginning with the Tehran Conference in 1943, Bolden landed a bevy of interviews with several twentieth-century world leaders. At the conference, he interviewed President Franklin Delano Roosevelt, Premier Joseph Stalin, and Prime Minister Winston Churchill. The conference was held to strengthen the cooperation of the United States, Great Britain, and the Soviet Union in World War II. Later, Bolden traveled to India to interview Muhammad Ali Jinnah, the founder of Pakistan, and the Indian leaders Mohandas K. Gandhi and Jawaharlal Nehru. Bolden was invited to stay in the homes of both Gandhi and Nehru; he stayed fifteen days with Gandhi and twelve days with Nehru. Bolden also interviewed General and Madame Chiang Kai-Shek in China. Bolden was the first African American journalist to set foot in India, Burma, and China.

Bolden's war reporting was cited by the War Department for Distinguished Reporting during World War II. When he returned from overseas, he was offered jobs at *Life* and the *New York Times*, but he settled back into the *Courier*. Bolden said he did not think he would have had as much of an influence on civil rights working at a white publication. Upon his return to the *Courier*, he produced an impressive series of articles that traced the complete histories of eight prominent African American families in the Pittsburgh region. In 1960 he married Nancy Travis, and the two were married forty-three years until Bolden's death. They had no children.

Bolden left the *Courier* in 1962 after the paper's financial failure left him and fellow employees without pensions. He went on to work briefly at the *New York Times*, the *Christian Science Monitor*, and at NBC News on the *Huntley-Brinkley Report*. By 1963 he had returned to Pittsburgh to accept a job with the Pittsburgh Board of Education as associate director of information services and community relations. His main task was to promote the board's desegregation policy. He took a leave of absence from the board in 1964 to cover the Democratic and Republican conventions for NBC News. At the Republican National Convention he scooped other national news outlets by scoring an exclusive interview with the Republican presidential candidate Barry Goldwater. Bolden retired from the board of education in 1978 with a pension after seventeen years of service.

While in retirement, Bolden raised prizewinning African violets and orchids and bred champion show dogs. He coauthored a book, *Legacy in Bricks and Mortar: African-American Landmarks in Allegheny County* (1995), and continued to work as a lecturer, historian, consultant, and senior archivist for the Honorable K. LEROY IRVIS, Speaker of the House of Representatives, Commonwealth of Pennsylvania. Bolden was also deeply concerned with the education and welfare of young people and devoted much of his time to boards and organizations serving their needs. He received numerous honors and awards, including the prestigious George Polk Career Award in Journalism, the Legacy Award from the National Association of Black Journalists, and the Heritage Award from the Tuskegee Airmen. Bolden died in Pittsburgh at the age of ninety. The following year, in 2004, he was honored posthumously with a Pennsylvania State Historical Marker erected on the former site of the *Courier* office in Pittsburgh's Hill District.

FURTHER READING
Rosenwald, Mike. "The Bold(en) Story," *Pitt Magazine*, vol. 14, no. 3. (Sept. 2001): 31–35.
Obituary: Rouvalis, Christina. "Reporter, Raconteur Frank Bolden Dies at 90," *Pittsburgh Post-Gazette*, 29 Aug. 2003.

MICHELLE K. MASSIE

Bolden, Melvin R. (28 Jan. 1919–29 Jan. 2000), artist and political activist, was born in Baltimore, Maryland. In 1937 Bolden received a four-year scholarship to the Philadelphia Museum School of Art, where he majored in illustration and advertising design. Upon his graduation he became an artist and layout designer for a top advertising agency in Philadelphia. His duties included prep work for original work by Norman Rockwell. In fact Bolden and Rockwell became close friends, and it was Rockwell who "encouraged Bolden to use neighbors and local townspeople as models for his art," according to a New Hampshire Circle of Friends flyer.

After World War II Bolden moved to New York and became a full-time illustrator, working first for black newspapers, then for such general magazines as *Fortune*, *Saturday Review*, *Colliers*, *Saturday Evening Post*, *Boy's Life*, as well as for major newspapers like the *New York Times* and the *New York Herald Tribune*. In 1949 Bolden married the actress Gwendolyn Claire Hale, and the two spent their honeymoon in New Hampshire. Falling in love with the New Hampshire countryside, the Boldens moved to the state in 1954, residing near the state capital of Concord.

Once in New Hampshire, Bolden continued his successful artistic career, but also took up an active interest in New Hampshire and local politics and community affairs. As chairman of the Merrimack County Democratic Party in the 1960s, he was the first black chairman ever in the state, and possibly in the nation. Bolden's interest in politics was also expressed in artistic form; in 1983 he co-wrote and illustrated a book of political cartoons entitled *The New Hampshire Presidential Primary Rulebook* with David Wysocki and Charles Russell. Because his political achievements came in a predominantly white state, they are seldom remembered today but are nonetheless significant and mirrored locally what was going on nationally during the civil rights era.

Mel Bolden's interest in community activism was also far reaching; he was a founding member of the New Hampshire Circle of Friends, a group devoted to celebrating racial diversity in a state whose black population has been historically low, and also became an educator, teaching at New England College in Henniker and the New Hampshire Art Institute in Manchester.

Bolden, however, will probably be best remembered for his outstanding artistic career, during which he gained the title of "dean" of African American illustrators. Among his best known works, in addition to his magazine illustrations, are President Jimmy Carter's 1973 White House Christmas card, a portrait of Dr. MARTIN LUTHER KING JR. that would be displayed in the Portsmouth, New Hampshire, city hall, his series on jazz and big band musicians, and his moving portrait of Christa McAuliffe, the New Hampshire teacher-astronaut lost in the explosion of the space-shuttle *Challenger* in 1986, which became part of the Smithsonian Air and Space Museum's permanent collection. Even after his death Bolden's works gained critical acclaim; in 2004 his dramatic paintings of combat in World War II, including the Tuskegee Airmen of the 99th Pursuit Squadron and their air battles over Europe, were displayed at the newly opened National World War II Memorial in Washington, D.C.

FURTHER READING
Wysocki, David, with Mel Bolden and Charles Russell. *New Hampshire Presidential Primary Rulebook* (1983).

GLENN ALLEN KNOBLOCK

Bolin, Jane Matilda (11 Apr. 1908–8 Jan. 2007), attorney and jurist, was born in Poughkeepsie, New York, the youngest daughter of Matilda Emery and Gaius C. Bolin, an attorney and the first black graduate of Williams College. Bolin's mother died when she was eight years old, leaving her father solely responsible for her upbringing. Consequently, she spent a good deal of time in his office around the law books as he worked, absorbing a feel for the law. She later commented that "those leather bound books just intrigued me"(Margolick). Even as a child she was aware of events in the larger world. In 1919, when she was eleven years old, a series of antiblack race riots swept across the nation during what became known as the "red summer." Two years later, the

black population of Tulsa, Oklahoma, was driven from the city and the community burned. Apart from the Tulsa race riot more than 120 blacks were lynched during 1921 and 1922, and in 1923 the black community in Rosewood, Florida, was burned and its population scattered. Bolin regularly read the *Crisis*, the journal of the NAACP, as a child and was well aware of the nation's tormented racial scene. Looking back on that period years later, she would comment, "It is easy to imagine how a young, protected child who sees portrayals of brutality is forever scarred and becomes determined to contribute in her own small way to social justice" (*New York Times* 10 Jan. 2007).

Graduating from Poughkeepsie High School in 1924, she entered Wellesley College in Massachusetts, one of only two black freshmen in her class. Her experiences at Wellesley shaped her later sensibilities. The racial isolation was profound. Years later she would recall that she did develop some genuine friendships at Wellesley, but that her time there was largely a lonely experience, in which she was ignored outside the classroom. Despite the isolation and the lack of encouragement from her professors, she graduated in 1928 as a "Wellesley Scholar," one of the top twenty students in her class. Her adviser tried to discourage her from pursuing an interest in law, indicating that there was no future for a black woman in the legal profession. Nevertheless, she applied to Yale Law School and was accepted. Upon learning of her interest in law, her father also sought to dissuade her from pursuing a legal career. He wanted Bolin to go into teaching, a profession he saw as less likely to expose her to the brutal and ugly side of life; but when she persisted, he relented.

In the fall of 1928 she entered Yale Law School, one of only three women (and the only black woman) in her class. She graduated three years later as the first black woman to receive a law degree from Yale. Decades after graduation she commented on rudeness directed at her by some of the southerners in her class.

Upon graduating from Yale, she joined her brother and father in their Poughkeepsie, New York, law firm. Her older brother, Gaius Jr., had graduated from New York University Law School in 1927. In 1933 Bolin married fellow attorney Ralph Mizzell and moved to New York City, believing that she had a better chance of achieving her lifelong goals there than in Poughkeepsie.

Bolin was a Republican, and like many blacks of her era, her loyalty to the GOP was tied to that party's actions during the Civil War and Reconstruction eras. In 1937 she ran on the Republican ticket for the New York State Assembly, and even though she lost she came to the attention of New York's popular mayor, Fiorello LaGuardia, who appointed her to the city law department as an assistant corporation council. Two years later, on 22 July 1939 LaGuardia appointed her to fill an unexpired term on the city's domestic relations court (renamed the family court in 1962), making her the fist black woman in the United States to serve as a judge. Within a few years of the appointment, twin events occurred that tested her capacity to survive the intense and often hostile scrutiny her position brought.

A son, Yorke Mizzell, was born to Bolin and her husband in 1941, but shortly thereafter Ralph Mizzell died, leaving her a widow and a thirty-five-year-old single mother with a demanding, high-profile job. Years later, she commented, "I don't think I shortchanged anybody but myself—I didn't get all the sleep I needed and I didn't get to travel as much as I would have liked, but I felt my first obligation was to my child" (*New York Times*, 8 Dec. 1978).

Despite her personal challenges, she set in motion major changes in how the court did business. Her comment on one of those changes was succinct, "When I came in the one or two black probation officers handled only black families—I had that changed"(*New York Times*, 8 Dec. 1978). Probation officers were assigned without regard to race or religion. In addition, she commented, "They used to put N or PR on the front of every petition to indicate if the family was black or Puerto Rican … because the agencies that the families were referred to were segregated"(*New York Times*, 8 Dec. 1978). Along with two other judges, she lobbied successfully for change. Any private agency receiving public funds had to accept children without regard to race or ethnicity.

During a career spanning forty years, Judge Bolin presided over cases involving major crimes committed by juveniles such as robbery and murder; she also handled child neglect and abandonment cases, spouse abuse cases, and adoptions. She despaired of ever fully understanding the parade of violent youngsters coming before her, but drew comfort from those instances where she knew that her decisions had helped a particular person who might have otherwise ended up in worse trouble. "There are no easy answers," she observed, when asked about the violent young people coming

before her day after day, "I get distressed and dismayed when I hear psychiatrists and social workers handing out easy answers, saying its because of the wars children have seen, or the violent programs on television, or its because violence is as American as apple pie. Those answers are just too facile, and I can't accept any of them"(*New York Times*, 8 Dec. 1978).

She remained vigilant about issues of equity in her workplace, even after almost four decades on the job. A colleague recalled that in the 1970s when legal assistants were first assigned to family court judges, Judge Bolin ensured that some of the first assistants were African American.

Community service was vitally important to Bolin. She served on the board of directors of a number of organizations, including the Child Welfare League of America, the Neighborhood Children's Center, and the Wiltwyck School for Boys. She was also an active member of the NAACP.

In December of 1978 Judge Bolin reluctantly retired, having reached the mandatory retirement age of seventy. Thereafter she worked as a volunteer in the New York City school system and served on the State Board of Regents. Jane Bolin died on 8 January 2007 in Queens, New York, at the age of ninety-eight.

FURTHER READING

Klemesrud, Judy. "A Remarkable Judge, a Reluctant Retirement," *New York Times*, 8 Dec. 1978.

Margolick, David. "At the Bar," *New York Times*, 14 May 1993.

Obituary: *New York Times*, 10 Jan. 2007.

JOHN R. HOWARD

Bolivar, William Carl (18 Apr. 1844–12 Nov. 1914), book collector, historian, and journalist, was born in Philadelphia to George Bolivar, and Elizabeth LeCount Proctor Bolivar. There is some uncertainty about his precise year of birth, with historians suggesting 1844 (Silcox) or 1849 (Welborn), while census data inclines toward an 1847 date. His father was employed as a sailmaker by JAMES FORTEN, a local businessman and founder of the Philadelphia Library Company of Colored Persons.

The family numbered themselves among the "O.P."—Old Philadelphians—of the African American community. George Bolivar had been born in Philadelphia, to a Pennsylvania-born mother and a father from North Carolina. Elizabeth Bolivar was born in Pennsylvania to parents born in Maryland (1850 census). In 1850 George Bolivar owned real estate valued at $8,000, while a North Carolina–born cousin, Nicholas Bolivar, lived with the family, working as a tailor. Throughout Bolivar's life, there were relatives or boarders wherever he lived.

Bolivar received his primary education at the Lombard Street School, Philadelphia's only "school for Negroes," commonly known as "the Bird school" for its principal, a man with melanin-deficient skin named James Bird. Whatever his color, parents adored him, because he was a competent, caring teacher, while most "white" teachers in "colored" schools were people who couldn't hold onto a job anywhere else. Bolivar later recalled running to school over hard packed snow crossing hostile territory near South Street, not only because of the cold, but the threat of "the idle volunteer fireman."

He later attended the Institute for Colored Youth, a secondary school located at Bainbridge and 9th Street in Philadelphia. At the end of the century, the school moved to Cheney Station, Pennsylvania, and became Cheney College. Bolivar worked for a time as a clerk at the U.S. Treasury Department, but returned to Philadelphia in 1866, contributing his first column to the Philadelphia *Tribune* that year. He supported himself for the rest of his life as a clerk, mostly at the John Ashhurst and Co. bank, while pursuing his passion for collecting books and manuscripts documenting the history and communities formed by Americans of African descent.

By 1870, his father appears to have died; William Bolivar and his younger brother George lived with their mother, who kept house, while William worked as a courthouse clerk, and George, age nineteen, as an "errand boy" (1870 census). There is no record that either brother ever married. The family of Eugene Lindsay, a carpenter born in South Carolina, and his wife Lydia, Pennsylvania-born to parents from Delaware and Maryland, had joined the household. A fifty-six-year-old janitor and his wife, a dressmaker, also boarded at the house. William Bolivar was the only one with sufficient personal property to have its value recorded in the census, at $400.

In 1892 he began writing a column called "Pencil Pusher" for the Philadelphia *Tribune*, the city's leading black newspaper. An active member of St. Thomas Episcopal Church, sometimes known as the African Episcopal Church of St. Thomas, Bolivar regularly featured the church's history, dating to 1794, in his column. He displayed a detailed familiarity with local history back to the early nineteenth century. An 18 October 1913 column recalled: "The first break away from lined out singing in Bethel Church was in 1840, when a quartette was organized consisting of Mrs. Margaret Jones, Miss Elizabeth Clark and Mssrs. Hans Shadd and John Johnstone" (Abbott, Lynn and Doug Seroff, *Out of Sight: The Rise of African American Popular Music, 1889–1895*, 2002, 103). He also extensively covered Negro League baseball.

Shared interest in history cemented a close friendship with Arturo Schomburg, whose collection of books, documents, manuscripts, and photographs became the initial core of what is now the Schomburg Center for Research in Black Culture in New York. They frequently visited New York and Philadelphia bookstores together, Bolivar serving as Schomburg's guide whenever he visited "Quakertown." Schomburg, often referred to him as "Uncle Billy," as did many who knew him in Philadelphia. Another fellow collector was Bolivar's cousin, Daniel Alexander Payne Murray, assistant to the Librarian of Congress.

In 1897 Bolivar was a charter member of the American Negro Historical Society, with Robert M Adger, Jacob C. White, William H. Dorsey. By 1904 membership was opened to women, including Frances Ellen Watkins Harper, who first protested their exclusion, and Gertrude Bustill Mossell, who often wrote as Mrs. N. F. Mossell. The same year he became a member of the American Negro Academy, founded by Reverend Alexander Crummell in Washington, D.C. He was inducted in 1912 as a member of the Negro Society for Historical Research, cofounded by Schomburg.

Bolivar's collection came to include over three thousand books, pamphlets, prints, and manuscripts dealing with the antislavery movement, including an original copy of Phyllis Wheatley's poems, dated 1773; reports of ant-slavery conventions from 1831–1836; and bound volumes of *American Moral Reform Magazine*, one of the earliest periodicals written by and for Americans of African descent. It was all contained in his ten- by twelve-foot room on the third floor of 761 South 15th Street. The 1910 census lists Bolivar at that address as one of four boarders, another being fifty-nine-year-old George Bolivar, living with Julius and Adence Forbes, their two sons, and one daughter, ages nineteen to twelve. Another boarder was Lydia Lindsay, who had been, off and on, part of the Bolivar household for forty years. The census taker may have been confused about status and relations, but it was a large and diverse household.

During the last year of his life, Bolivar was elected professor of racial history at Downingtown University, Downingtown, Pennsylvania. Six months before he died, friends and family surprised Bolivar with 250 printed copies of a catalog, *The Library of William C. Bolivar*, listing more than eight hundred of the items in his collection. After his death in 1914, at least part of his collection was acquired by HENRY PROCTOR SLAUGHTER, whose library was acquired by Atlanta University in 1946.

FURTHER READING

Silcox, Harry C. "William Carl Bolivar: Philadelphia Black Historian 1844–1914." Manuscript, Balch Institute for Ethnic Studies, Philadelphia.

Sinette, Elinor Des Verney. *Arthur Alfonso Schomburg, Black Bibliophile and Collector: A Biography* (1989).

Welburn, William C. "To 'Keep the Past in Lively Memory': William Carl Bolivar's Efforts to Preserve African American Cultural Heritage," *Libraries and the Cultural Record* 42, no. 2 (2007).

CHARLES ROSENBERG

Bond, Horace Mann (8 Nov. 1904–21 Dec. 1972), college professor and administrator, was born in Nashville, Tennessee, the son of James Bond, a Congregationalist minister, and Jane Alice Browne, a graduate of Oberlin College and a schoolteacher. Horace Bond's paternal grandmother, Jane Arthur Bond, was a slave who raised two sons by herself. These two sons, Bond's father and his uncle, Henry, both earned college degrees and embarked on professional careers. Three of Bond's four siblings earned college degrees, and his cousins on his father's side also distinguished themselves academically. This family achievement was important to Horace Bond, because it exemplified the way in which numerous scholars of his generation were nurtured within the African American community. He published a book on the family origins of African American scholars near the end of his life, *Black American Scholars: A Study of Their Beginnings* (1972).

Bond was an intellectually precocious child. He was educated at schools attached to colleges and universities in towns where his father served as a minister—Talladega, Alabama, and Atlanta, Georgia. He finished high school at the age of fourteen at the Lincoln Institute in Shelbyville, Kentucky. He then attended Lincoln University (Pennsylvania) and graduated at the age of eighteen in the class of 1923. He stayed on at Lincoln for a year as a teaching assistant, attended graduate school for a summer at Pennsylvania State College (later Pennsylvania State University), and earned master's (1926) and doctoral (1936) degrees from the University of Chicago. Bond married Julia Washington in 1929; they had three children. Their second child, JULIAN BOND, became famous as a member of the student civil rights movement in the 1960s and served as a Georgia state legislator. Bond's major field was education, and he specialized in both the history of education and the sociology of education in his graduate studies. He served on the faculties of Langston University in Oklahoma, Alabama State College in Montgomery, Fisk University in Nashville, and Dillard University in New Orleans between 1926 and 1935. He also was chairman of the education department at Fisk and the founding academic dean at Dillard. In the first two decades of his academic career he was closely associated with the Julius Rosenwald Fund and its president, Edwin Embree. In part because of this relationship, he was chosen as president of Fort Valley (Georgia) State College in 1939. He served in that position until 1945, when he became president of his alma mater, Lincoln University. Bond remained as president of Lincoln until 1957, when he resigned amid controversy over a plan to increase the number of white students at the institution; his relations with older, white faculty, many of whom had taught him as an undergraduate and had difficulty seeing their former student as their superior; and his frequent trips away from campus. He then moved to Atlanta University, where he served as dean of the School of Education for five years and then as director of its Bureau of Educational and Social Research. He retired in 1971 and died in Atlanta one year later.

Bond was the author of six books and numerous articles. In the 1920s he published articles critical of the racial bias in tests assessing intelligence quotient (IQ). His two most enduring books were published in the 1930s, *The Education of the Negro in the American Social Order* (1934), a study of the inferior conditions in black schools and colleges, and *Negro Education in Alabama: A Study in Cotton and Steel* (1939), an economic interpretation of educational conditions for blacks in Alabama. His articles from the 1930s until the end of his life were published in both academic and popular journals, and he made numerous speeches to black church and civic groups in his later years. His scholarly output was a lifelong concern for Bond, but it diminished in the 1940s and 1950s as he took on the duties of a

Horace Mann Bond (right) with W. E. B. DuBois (left); E. Franklin Frazier; his daughter, Jane Marguerite; and his son, Julian Bond. (Courtesy of Julian Bond.)

college president. Bond worked as a historian for the National Association for the Advancement of Colored People as it prepared a legal brief answering historical questions asked by the U.S. Supreme Court in deliberating the famous *Brown v. Board of Education* (1954) school desegregation case.

Bond became particularly interested in Africa and Africans in the late 1940s, and he took nearly twenty trips to that continent in the 1940s and 1950s. He was a founder of the American Society for African Culture and was active in numerous groups that advocated cooperation between Africans and African Americans. He developed the Institute for African Studies at Lincoln University and made sure that African students were welcome at Lincoln and were supported financially whenever possible. In this regard he built on a long-standing commitment of Lincoln to Africa and Africans. Bond was especially interested in Liberia, Nigeria, and Ghana. During Bond's university presidency, the Gold Coast (later called Ghana) political leader and Lincoln alumnus Kwame Nkrumah was awarded an honorary doctorate from Lincoln.

During his career Bond carefully balanced concern for personal survival and professional advancement with a pursuit of social and political activism on behalf of his race that often risked reprisals. He was a representative of the middle generation of African American intellectuals that followed the generation of W. E. B. DuBois and BOOKER T. WASHINGTON of the early twentieth century and preceded the civil rights activists of the 1960s. He was one of the first of his race to be recognized for his professional academic accomplishments and also was one of the first to head an institution of higher learning.

FURTHER READING

Bond's papers are in the Archives and Manuscripts Division, University of Massachusetts (Amherst) Library.

Urban, Wayne J. *Black Scholar: Horace Mann Bond, 1904–1972* (1992).

Urban, Wayne J. "The Black Scholar and Intelligence Testing: The Case of Horace Mann Bond," *Journal of the History of the Behavioral Sciences* 25 (1989): 323–334.

Urban, Wayne J. "Philanthropy and the Black Scholar: The Case of Horace Mann Bond," *Journal of Negro Education* 58 (1989): 478–493.

Williams, Roger. *The Bonds: An American Family* (1971).

This entry is taken from the *American National Biography* and is published here with the permission of the American Council of Learned Societies.

WAYNE J. URBAN

Bond, John Robert (May 1846–Jun. 1905), sailor, Civil War veteran, and laborer, was born in Liverpool, England, to James Bond, a carter in that city's dockland, and Eliza Kelly. As one of the British Empire's major port cities, Liverpool was home to many migrants. James Bond was of African descent, though it is unclear how long he and his family had lived in England. Kelly was an immigrant from Ireland, probably of the Roman Catholic faith, but the child was baptized as an Anglican, the established state church in England, which was perhaps also James Bond's faith.

Though we know few details of his early life, it is probable that Bond witnessed discrimination and violence against both black and Irish immigrants. Shortly after Bond's birth the family moved to the Toxteth section of Liverpool, then as now the city's most ethnically diverse and desperately poor neighborhood. It is not known whether he attended school, but he was unable to read and write. Like most of his contemporaries in Toxteth, the teenaged Bond had few economic opportunities other than to find a job at sea or on the docks like his father had done. By 1862 those opportunities appear to have narrowed even further, in part because of the U.S. Navy's blockade of cotton grown in the Confederate States of America. That year, with work hard to find on the Liverpool docks and in the nearby Lancashire cotton mills, sixteen-year-old John Bond signed on as an apprentice seaman on the *Pactolus*, a steamer engaged in the salt codfish trade. Probably during his voyage across the Atlantic, Bond lost his right index finger and part of his right middle finger, though it is uncertain as to whether this was the result of a shipboard accident or as punishment.

The *Pactolus* arrived in New Bedford, Massachusetts, then the world's busiest whaling center, in September 1862. Bond remained there for nine months, most likely working as a dockland laborer, before enlisting for one year in the U.S. Navy. Britain was neutral in the American Civil War, but Bond, though born in Britain, could not be. Although he had just arrived in the United States, Bond family folklore has it that Bond joined the Union forces to further the abolitionist cause of black folk in his new home. Claiming that he was twenty-two years of age, he served on the *Ohio*, an elderly vessel that had earlier been used to suppress the illegal international slave trade. The vessel had an interracial, international, and non-segregated crew. As on other U.S. Navy ships, blacks and whites of the same rank received the same pay. Bond and his fellow black sailors—none of whom were officers—nonetheless faced racist treatment and attacks on board ship.

In July 1863 Bond disembarked at Boston Harbor and transferred from the *Ohio* to the *Cambridge*, a much faster, recently built gunboat famed for its exploits in capturing Confederate blockade runners. The *Cambridge* patrolled the coast of New England and traveled as far south as the North Carolina port of Beaufort, which was then in Union hands. Much of Bond's early service, however, was spent in port. Given the high rates of disease and violence among the bored and restless seamen while in port, the ship's enforced stay in the Union-controlled port of Portsmouth, Virginia, was almost as dangerous for the crew as were its infrequent cruises along the Atlantic coast.

In January 1864 the *Cambridge* set out to patrol the waters off Wilmington, North Carolina, the Confederacy's best-protected Atlantic port. In February of that year John Bond was part of a small detachment of sailors sent by the *Cambridge*'s captain, William Spicer, to investigate Confederate blockade runners who had run aground near barrier islands off the Wilmington coast. The occupants of two U.S. Navy dinghies sent from the *Cambridge*, which included Bond, were fired on by Confederate snipers hidden behind sand dunes on one of the barrier islands. As the Union sailors scrambled to return to the safety of the *Cambridge*, one of the snipers fired a rifle ball at Bond. The ball hit the young sailor in his right chest and shoulder, narrowly missing his heart and other vital organs, but smashing his shoulder blade and piercing one of his lungs. Bond bled heavily. None of the men on the USS *Cambridge*, including Bond, were rewarded with medals for their actions on that day.

For John Bond, as for most other soldiers and sailors wounded in the Civil War, the period immediately following his injury proved crucial. Only one-third of those who suffered similar wounds survived; most died as a result of infection, which was often caused by the incompetence of military surgeons and extremely poor hygiene in battle conditions. Perhaps because he was young and healthy, Bond was one of the more fortunate casualties, even though he remained on board the *Cambridge* in the chilly and choppy February waters of the North Atlantic. The ship's physician had few medicines other than whiskey, but that, and vigorous cleansing of Bond's wounds, proved enough to save him. After ten days aboard the *Cambridge*, Bond was taken to Hammond Hospital, a Union-run facility in Beaufort, North Carolina, where many of the patients suffered from highly contagious diseases like typhoid and smallpox. Bond survived, however, and left Hammond Hospital in May 1864, embarking on a perilous coastal journey past the barrier islands of Cape Hatteras and into the Great Dismal Swamp Canal, stopping finally at Portsmouth, Virginia, where he was admitted to the Union hospital. Bond's injuries were such that his right arm no longer functioned properly, but again he survived the poorly sanitized, under-equipped, and overcrowded conditions.

Bond's recuperation was undoubtedly aided by the help of a local woman, Emma Thomas, who was born into slavery near the James River in Isle of Wight, Virginia, in 1846, the same year as Bond's birth. In 1863 Thomas had joined the vast exodus of Virginia slaves who had sought freedom in Union-controlled cities, first in Norfolk, and then in Portsmouth, where she brought fruit to recovering Union troops and met John Bond. Thomas continued to look after Bond in Norfolk following his honorable discharge in June 1864, and the couple began courting. They married on 21 June 1865 at Norfolk's Bute Street Baptist Church, where Emma Thomas was a member. The Bonds had four children. John Percy, known as Percy, was born in 1868, and John Robert, known as Bob, eight years later. Daughters Lena Emma and Mary Ellen, known as Tooty, were born in 1879 and 1887, respectively. Another child survived only two days.

Finding himself again in a seaport, John Bond probably found work in the docks at Portsmouth or Norfolk. Although he also received a Union pension of eight dollars per month, Bond's job prospects were limited by his war wounds and by the narrowing opportunities for blacks in Virginia after 1870. That year the Bonds left Virginia for Worcester, Massachusetts, where John found a job, working a six-day, sixty-hour week as a fireman in the boiler room of the Bay State House, one of the state's finest and most fashionable hotels. There was little fine or fashionable about the Bonds's cramped quarters, a couple of miles away in the working-class southern section of Worcester. Bond's job required him to spend many nights away from his family, which settled rather uneasily in a town with relatively few black people. Bond never converted to his wife's Baptist faith and remained an Anglican, attending both the well-heeled All Saints Episcopal Church and St. Matthews Episcopal Church, whose congregants included many recent working-class English immigrants to Worcester but numbered few blacks.

Following the 1873 depression, the family moved to Hyde Park, Massachusetts, a community nine miles south of Boston that, unlike Worcester, but like John's native Liverpool and Emma's Norfolk, was close to the sea. During the Civil War, Hyde Park had also been home to the famed colored infantry regiments, the Fifty-fourth and Fifty-fifth Massachusetts. A sizeable number of black Civil War veterans also made Hyde Park a more congenial home to John Bond than had Worcester. Bond befriended several neighbors who had served in black regiments, and he became active in the Grand Army of the Republic (GAR), the leading Union veterans' organization. Although the GAR was an interracial body dominated by whites, it flourished in Massachusetts in part because of the leadership of black veterans like Amos Webber of Worcester and JAMES TROTTER of Hyde Park. By 1880, probably with the assistance of the GAR, Bond found work as a janitor at the Damon Grammar School, a short distance from his home in Hyde Park. Combined with John's increased Navy pension, the Bonds gradually moved from poverty to a relatively comfortable working-class existence by the 1890s. John Bond had also learned to read and write by the time he began working as a janitor, again, perhaps through the efforts of the GAR.

By 1884, at any rate, Bond had acquired sufficient writing skills to apply for American citizenship. Once granted he began to pay the state's two-dollar-a-year poll tax and was eligible to vote and serve on local juries. He later found work as Hyde Park's town constable, responsible for lighting and dousing streetlamps, and again as a janitor. Throughout the 1890s Bond was active in the local and statewide activities of the GAR, as well as an all-black group, the Massachusetts Colored Veterans Assembly. Bond was also active in the Oddfellows and Prince Hall Masons and in the Episcopal church. In June 1905 he died of rectal cancer at his Hyde Park home. Although Bond had been a faithful congregant at the smaller and more humble Episcopal Church of the Good Shepherd in Dedham, his funeral was held at Hyde Park's more prestigious Episcopal Christ Church, so as to accommodate the many mourners and the honor guard of Bond's fellow veterans and Masons.

FURTHER READING

Alexander, Adele Logan. *Homelands and Waterways: The–American Journey of the Bond Family, 1846–1926* (1999).

STEVEN J. NIVEN

Bond, Julian (14 Jan. 1940–), activist and politician, was born Horace Julian Bond in Nashville, Tennessee, the second of three children of Julia Washington, a librarian, and HORACE MANN BOND. He grew up in the relatively insulated environment of the black college campus, a crossroads for leading black intellectuals and artists during the segregation era. Horace Mann Bond, a prominent scholar and educator, was president of Fort Valley State College in Georgia at the time of Julian's birth. In 1945 he became the first African American president of Lincoln University, outside of Philadelphia. When Julian was a child, his father and W. E. B. DuBois had a mock ceremony dedicating him to a life of scholarship. His life took a different course, but reflected the influence of both men.

In 1957 Horace Mann Bond became dean of the Atlanta University School of Education, and the family moved to Georgia. Bond's first real introduction to life under segregation in the Deep South coincided with the courageous efforts of nine students in Little Rock to integrate Central High School, an episode that, Bond later recalled, "set a high standard of bravery and behavior" for him and his contemporaries. Bond was in his junior year at Morehouse College in Atlanta, Georgia, in February 1960 when four college students in Greensboro took seats at the lunch counter in the local Woolworth's in defiance of segregation laws, sparking a wave of similar protests across the South. Bond and his classmate Lonnie King organized students in Atlanta, and initiated their protest with a full-page ad in the city newspapers. "An Appeal for Human Rights," coauthored by

Julian Bond, testifying at a legislative hearing before a Special Committee in Atlanta, Georgia, 10 January 1966. (AP Images.)

Bond, put a stark spotlight on the racial segregation and discrimination that confined black lives and opportunities. It was followed by a campaign of direct action targeting segregation in public places. Bond was among the protesters arrested. In April he attended a meeting with fellow student activists in Raleigh, North Carolina, and founded the Student Nonviolent Coordinating Committee (SNCC). In the spring of 1961 Bond dropped out of Morehouse College, became communications director for SNCC, and married Alice Clopton, a student at Spelman College in Atlanta. Operating out of a sparse office on Auburn Avenue, Bond had a WATS line that provided continuous telephone contact with SNCC field workers across the South, often as events unfolded. Short but frequent visits to areas of SNCC activity also exposed him to the texture and range of movement activism. He churned out press releases documenting the battles being waged in cities and rural areas, which black newspapers around the country routinely printed. The reach of Bond's network, along with his talent as a writer and his cool yet engaging demeanor ensured his success as the propagandist for the movement. White journalists were drawn to him as a source. He also edited the *Student Voice*, SNCC's newspaper, and was a founder and managing editor of the *Atlanta Inquirer*, established in 1961 as an alternative to the conservative black publication *Atlanta Daily World*. In 1964 Bond took his first trip to Africa. Bond, along with fellow SNCC activists John Lewis and ROBERT P. MOSES, went as guests of the entertainer HARRY BELAFONTE. It was an extraordinary personal experience. Treated like visiting dignitaries in Guinea, they gained an appreciation of the broader significance of the civil rights movement in the American South.

The Civil Rights Acts of 1964 and 1965 dismantled state-mandated segregation and provided for federal enforcement of voting rights, removing the underpinnings of the South's caste system. In the aftermath of these legislative victories, Bond concentrated his efforts on expanding black political participation through voter registration, electing black candidates to office, and securing black representation in the state's Democratic Party. He ran a grassroots campaign for the Georgia House of Representatives from a poor district in Atlanta, winning with what was proportionately the highest voter turnout in the state. Five other black men and one black woman were also elected to the Georgia state legislature in November 1965, becoming the first blacks to serve in that body since 1907. Georgia's House of Representatives, however, refused to seat Bond because of his public opposition to the Vietnam War, as expressed in an SNCC policy statement. After a yearlong legal fight, a unanimous decision by the U.S. Supreme Court upheld Bond's right to free speech and compelled the Georgia House to seat him. Bond went on to serve in the Georgia legislature for the next twenty years, with four terms in the House and six in the Georgia Senate.

In 1968 Bond cochaired the Georgia Loyal National delegation to the Democratic convention in Chicago. His group challenged the regular delegation for virtually excluding black participation in the selection of delegates, in violation of rules set by the Democratic Party in the aftermath of the 1964 challenge by the Mississippi Freedom Democratic Party. They succeeded in securing half of the seats assigned to the Georgia delegation, causing most of the regular delegates to walk out. In a convention where Mayor William Daley came to rival the worst southern demagogues and police battled protesters in the streets, Julian Bond captured the hopes of many. He was, noted one observer, "the most charismatic figure at the convention" and a symbol of the civil rights movement. Shouts of "We want Julian" erupted from the floor of the convention as his name was placed in nomination for vice president, the first time either major party had nominated an African American. Bond requested that his name be withdrawn since, at age twenty-eight, he was seven years shy of the legal age. Chicago secured Bond's standing as one of the best-known figures of the civil rights movement. In constant demand as a speaker, particularly on college campuses, he traveled around the country, addressing the persistent problems of racial inequality and economic injustice. He promoted the enduring lesson of the movement; that it was individuals working steadily in their communities who changed the South and the nation.

Bond's own efforts remained anchored in Georgia and in the South at large. During the 1970s, while John Lewis was head of the Voter Education Project, the two men took weeklong tours to towns and rural areas around the region, promoting voter registration. Bond authored a pamphlet highlighting the campaign experiences of black elected officials for the Southern Regional Council, which served as a "how to" guide on running for local office. He cofounded the Southern Election Fund to raise and distribute money to rural black candidates. Bond considered running in the presidential primaries in 1976 as a way to get more black delegates elected to the Democratic convention. In 1978 Bond was elected president of the Atlanta branch of the National Association for the Advancement of Colored People and served in that post for more than a decade. In 1986 he resigned from the Georgia Senate to run for Congress from Atlanta. In a four-way race, he won with 47 percent of the vote and faced his longtime friend John Lewis in a runoff. Bond carried the majority of black voters in the hotly contested race, but white precincts gave Lewis the edge, and he won the election. That year Bond and his wife Alice separated; they divorced three years later. In 1990 Bond moved to Washington, D.C., and married Pamela Horowitz.

Through lectures, radio and television commentary, and occasional essays, Bond maintained a high profile as a serious and cogent commentator on issues of race and their impact on society. From 1980 to 1997 he was host of the syndicated television program *America's Black Forum*. Sometimes referred to as the "voice" of the civil rights movement, he served as narrator for countless documentaries, most notably the public television series *Eyes on the Prize*, which aired in 1987 and 1990 and became the standard film-documentary history of the civil rights movement. Well-known for his sense of humor, Bond turned up as guest host on *Saturday Night Live* in the late seventies.

As he neared fifty, Bond took a path that his father and DuBois had imagined for him decades earlier. After a series of visiting appointments at several colleges, including Harvard University and the University of Pennsylvania, he secured permanent positions on the faculties of the University of Virginia and American University, teaching courses on a variety of topics concerning the civil rights movement, black politics, and the African American experience. In 1998 he was elected chairman of the national board of the NAACP, the organization founded by DuBois nearly a century earlier. In a telephone interview on 22 May 2007. Bond commented, "After the 1960s, the NAACP was the only soldier standing" in terms of civil rights organizations. He attributed this in part to its grassroots apparatus, and the continuing relevance of its mission to fight racial discrimination and advance social justice. The position provided Bond with a national platform for raising issues, holding political leaders of both major parties to account, and supporting the efforts of people around the country in the ongoing struggle to realize the promise of the civil rights movement.

In 2009 Bond was awarded the NAACP's Spingarn Medal.

FURTHER READING

Neary, John. *Julian Bond: Black Rebel* (1971).
Tuck, Stephen. *Beyond Atlanta: The Struggle for Racial Equality in Georgia, 1940–1980* (2001).
Williams, Roger M. *The Bonds: An American Family* (1971).

PATRICIA SULLIVAN

Bond, Scott (1852–?), farmer and entrepreneur, was born near Canton, Mississippi, the only child of Wesley Rutledge and Anne Maben. Rutledge was the nephew of William H. Goodlow, the owner of the estate where Anne Maben was a house slave. Wesley worked as the manager of the house for his aunt and uncle. At birth Bond was given the surname Winfield, and at the age of eighteen months he was sent with his mother to Collierville, Tennessee, where they lived until he was five years old. Subsequently, they were sent to work on the Bond farm in Cross County, Arkansas. In Arkansas Anne Maben met and married William Bond, who gave Scott Bond his surname.

The family remained on the Bond farm until the conclusion of the Civil War, when, only months after gaining her freedom, Anne Maben died, leaving Bond in the care of his stepfather. Bond, his stepfather, and half brothers remained as sharecroppers on the Bond farm until 1872 when they moved to Madison, Arkansas, where William Bond purchased a small farm. Scott Bond remained there with his family, working as a sharecropper until 1874. In 1875 he moved eighteen miles away to become an independent sharecropper on the Allen farm, which he selected for its particularly fertile soil.

In his first year at the Allen farm, he rented twelve acres. Bond cultivated this land by himself and was able to make a small profit; this profit enabled him to rent thirty-five acres and hire a farmhand in 1876. After a second successful year the widow Allen insisted that Bond rent and cultivate the entire 2,200-acre farm. The farm was in a state of disrepair and heavily populated by squatters. Mrs. Allen recognized this and, trusting Bond, decided to do everything possible to get the entire farm under his control. She loaned him money to buy seeds and tools and allowed Bond to pay his rent after the harvest season. Bond secured the farm, rid it of squatters, and built a fence around the entire 2,200 acres. At the end of his first year Bond had made a profit of $2,500.

In addition to his farming success, Scott Bond met and married Maggie Nash of Forrest City, Arkansas, in 1877, with whom he had eleven children, all boys. When his seventh child was born, Bond decided that, after living on the Allen farm for eleven years, it was time to buy his own farm and work for himself. Bond bought a 320-acre farm in Madison, Arkansas, for two dollars an acre and moved back to Madison, where he farmed successfully for two years. In contrast, the Allen farm saw two crop failures and was inundated with silt from repeated flooding; some thought the farm ruined. Remembering Bond's success and having collected no rent for two years, Mrs. Allen decided to offer the Allen farm for sale to Bond.

Bond purchased the farm with his partner T. O. Fitzpatrick, a prominent white businessman, for five thousand dollars. Bond continued to improve his own farm in Madison while renting out his interest in the Allen farm to Fitzpatrick. After five years Bond sold his share of the farm to Fitzpatrick. In the same year that he had bought the Allen farm, Bond had also purchased the Madison Mercantile Company, with which he established a profitable retail business, selling supplies to area farms.

Bond took the money from the sale of the Allen farm and bought seven farms that adjoined his Madison property. These farms became available when a group of about three hundred African Americans from the Madison area joined the back-to-Africa movement and left the country. While the fate of most of these emigrants remains unknown, several eventually returned to Madison destitute but determined to recapture their past prosperity. One such man was Taylor Swift, whom Scott Bond helped to reestablish by giving him a mule and land to rent at a reduced rate. By 1893 Scott Bond owned approximately twelve hundred acres of farmland, much of which bordered the Rock Island Railroad, making it easy for him to ship goods to and from his farms. In the years that followed, Bond not only employed laborers to expand the amount of land he cultivated, he also diversified his business ventures. The most profitable of these new ventures were ginning cotton and selling gravel.

Before building his first cotton gin, Bond approached Ed Berry of Madison, who already owned a small gin. Bond offered to buy out a half interest in Berry's gin if they could agree to put it out of service and build a modern, steam-powered one as partners. Berry refused to partner with Bond and vowed to do everything in his power to prevent him from being able to build a gin. Bond decided that he would simply build the gin himself. He contacted three companies that sold steam powered gins and arranged for their agents to have a joint meeting to discuss price. Bond played each company against the others, so he was able to purchase a gin from the Continental Gin Company at a steep discount. Ed Berry did not stand in the way of Bond buying or building the gin machinery and structure, but he did seek an injunction to prevent Bond from building a railroad platform to load his cotton. Bond anticipated this and had the contractor lay out all the materials for the 150-foot platform so that it could be assembled in two hours. In this way the platform was built before Berry could have Bond served with injunction papers from the court. Once built, the gin was a huge success, pumping money into all aspects of the local economy and allowing local farmers to see an increase in their profits.

Seeing how this cotton gin had invigorated and improved the lives of the African American farmers in Madison, Bond decided to build a gin in another town. He picked Edmondson, Arkansas, an African American town that had only two non-steam-powered cotton gins. On arriving in the town, he addressed a town meeting with his business proposition. He let the residents vote on whether they should become stockholders or whether Bond should undertake this venture himself. The town voted to let Bond be the sole owner of the gin. Bond's second gin ran so successfully that after two years the Richmond Cotton Oil Company approached him about leasing its gin in Widener, Arkansas. Bond accepted this lease and subsequently operated three gins at peak capacity.

The second major venture that Bond undertook was to set up business selling gravel to the local railroad. Bond was given the idea for this venture when he was approached by a Memphis businessman about purchasing gravel from his land. Bond was interested and agreed to sign a contract for two dollars per carload. Unfortunately, when the man from Memphis found out that there would be a five-dollar-per-car charge to use the railroad bridge to get to Memphis, his interest was withdrawn. However, the Rock Island Railroad, whose tracks ran near the bed, was expanding, and the railroad owners expressed an interest in obtaining the gravel. Unfortunately for Bond, he was only able to obtain a price of fifty cents per car. He agreed but retained the right to cancel the contract at any time. Using the possible cancellation of the contract as leverage, he was eventually able to raise the price per car to ninety cents. In addition, he renegotiated with the railroad for a twenty-thousand-dollar contract paid in advance, which allowed him to build a steam-powered excavator and loader that would load a rail car in seven minutes.

Word of Scott Bond's success reached BOOKER T. WASHINGTON, who requested that Bond speak at the Tuskegee Institute about farming. Bond accepted this invitation. The next year, 1911, Washington requested that Bond speak to the National Negro Business League. Bond agreed, and in return Washington spoke in Madison the same year.

Bond's success was a result of his agricultural skill, which allowed him to form the capital necessary to take on additional business ventures. His skill was formally recognized in 1917 when he was awarded a Tuskegee Institute certificate for his agricultural knowledge. Bond began his life as a slave, became free after the Civil War, and through hard work and sound investments was able to preside over property that was valued at $250,000 when he died in 1933. At their height his farms totaled more than twelve hundred acres and employed around eight hundred people who also lived on the land.

FURTHER READING

Rudd, Dan A., and Theo Bond. *From Slavery to Wealth, the Life of Scott Bond: The Rewards of Honesty, Industry, Economy, and Perseverance* (1917).

JACOB ANDREW FREEDMAN

Bonds, Barry Lamar (24 July 1964–), baseball player, was born in Riverside, California, the first of four children born to Patricia and Bobby Bonds, a baseball player. In 1968 Bobby Bonds was called up to join the San Francisco Giants. The Bonds family moved to the San Francisco Bay Area city of San Carlos. By the time Bonds was five, he was spending his leisure time in the Giants' Candlestick Park locker room with some of the greatest baseball players of the time, among them WILLIE MAYS, who adopted him as his godson.

Though an outstanding hitter and base stealer, Bobby Bonds was traded frequently in his career, and had a tense relationship with the press. Young Bonds was deeply affected by his father's treatment at the hands of apparently unsympathetic sports reporters, something that would greatly shape his

Barry Bonds, hitting his 73rd home run of the season against the Los Angeles Dodgers at Pacific Bell Park in San Francisco, 7 October 2007. (AP Images.)

own relationship with reporters in years to come. Although his father played for teams around the country, Bonds's family stayed in San Mateo, California. Perhaps owing to his father's long periods away from home, Bonds later recalled being much closer to his mother than to his father as a child.

Bonds excelled in athletics while growing up and eventually starred in football, basketball, and baseball at Junipero Serra High School in San Mateo. As a baseball player he showed considerable talent and was drafted out of high school by the San Francisco Giants in 1982 but decided instead to accept a baseball scholarship to Arizona State University, where he helped lead the Sun Devils to the College World Series in 1983 and 1984.

After Bonds's junior season at Arizona State, he elected to enter the baseball draft once more. This time he was picked by the Pittsburgh Pirates in 1985. He signed with the Pirates shortly thereafter and was sent to the team's single-A franchise in Prince William of the Carolina League in 1985 and later to its AAA franchise in Hawaii in 1986. Bonds played less than two months in Hawaii before being called up to play for the Pirates. Pittsburgh had been struggling and hoped to rebuild the team around a talented group of rookies, at the center of which was Bonds. His career in Pittsburgh began slowly. Manager Jim Leyland decided to take advantage of Bonds's speed and assign him to the position of leadoff hitter, but Bonds had difficulty fitting into this role and it was not until 1988 that he was able to finish a season with a batting average over .280. That same year Bonds married his first wife, Susann "Sun" Branco, in Montreal. They would eventually have two children, son Nikolai and daughter Shikari.

The 1990 season was Bonds's first big year. Hitting .311 with thirty-four home runs and 103 runs batted in, he led the Pirates to the play-offs and won the first of six National League Most Valuable Player awards. Yet during the play-offs that year Bonds performed poorly. Sportswriters started to tag him as a player who folded in clutch situations. Bonds also became the target of media scorn the following February when he became involved in a public shouting match with Leyland during spring training. Leyland had grown impatient when Bonds acted irritably toward the press and the coaching staff. Although Bonds greatly admired Leyland, the incident was one of the first to establish a public image of Bonds as a player with a petulant attitude.

During the 1991 and 1992 seasons Bonds led the Pirates to consecutive playoff appearances, and each time his team came up just short of victory. In 1993 his contract with Pittsburgh expired, and Bonds entered the free agent market, signing with the San Francisco Giants under the management of longtime family friend Dusty Baker. Although he enjoyed a spectacular first year with San Francisco, Bonds became a symbol of arrogance for many fans. Often short tempered with reporters, Bonds came to be portrayed by many writers as a symbol of what many fans and critics perceived as the widespread greed and insensitivity of Major League Baseball players. In 1994 Bonds separated from his wife, Sun. Earlier in the year, she had called the Atherton, California, police to their home and had told authorities that Bonds had thrown her against a car, grabbed her around the neck, and thrown her partway down a set of stairs. Charges were later dropped owing to lack of evidence and the unwillingness of Sun Bonds to cooperate. The incident received widespread media attention over the next year. In 1998 Bonds married Liz Watson and together they had a daughter, Aisha Lynn. Two years later Bonds helped lead his team to the playoffs, and in 2001 he exploded for seventy-three home runs, breaking a single season record set by Mark McGwire of the St. Louis Cardinals only three years earlier. In 2002 Bonds shed his reputation as a poor postseason performer, leading his team to game seven of the World Series. The Giants lost the series to the California Angels four games to three, but Bonds was the team's top performer, batting .471 and hitting four home runs. At the beginning of the 2004 season Bonds hit his 661st home run, passing his godfather Willie Mays. On 28 May 2006 Bonds hit his 715th career home run, moving him ahead of Babe Ruth and placing him second only to HANK AARON, who hit 755 home runs while playing in the major leagues.

In 2004 four people affiliated with a drug lab called the Bay Area Laboratory Co-operative, or BALCO, were indicted for illegally producing and distributing steroids and human growth hormones. The indicted included Bonds's longtime friend and personal trainer Greg Anderson, along with BALCO founder Victor Conte Jr., vice president James J. Valente, and the track coach Remi Korchemny. Leaked grand jury testimony revealed that Bonds had used rubs that contained steroids. He said that he did not know that these items were illegal performance-enhancing drugs. Nevertheless, he yet again became a symbol in the game, this time

of an era in baseball marked by widespread steroid use and doping scandals.

When, on 7 August 2007, in the fifth inning of a home game against the Washington Nationals, Bonds hit his record-breaking 756th home run, Bonds's alleged involvement with steroids served for many fans and baseball pundits to taint that record. At a press conference following the game, however, Bonds was adamant. "This record is not tainted at all, at all. Period," he told journalists (Jack Curry, "Bonds Hits No. 756 to Break Aaron's Record," *New York Times*, 8 Aug. 2007). In a prerecorded video broadcast, Hank Aaron congratulated the new home run leader for his "skill, longevity, and determination." However, not even Aaron's blessing could silence Bonds's critics or put the steroid issue to rest, and on 15 November 2007 a federal grand jury indicted Bonds on four counts of perjury and one count of obstruction of justice. In December 2011 Bonds was sentenced to 30 days of house arrest, two years of probation, and 250 hours of community service, and fined $4,000.

FURTHER READING

Bloom, John. *Barry Bonds: A Biography* (2004).

Fainaru-Wada, Marc, and Lance Williams. *Game of Shadows: Barry Bonds, BALCO, and the Steroids Scandal That Rocked Professional Sports* (2006).

Grann, David. "Baseball Without Metaphor," *New York Times Magazine*, 1 Sep. 2002.

Pearlman, Jeff. *Love Me, Hate Me: Barry Bonds and the Making of an Antihero* (2006).

Suchon, Josh. *This Gracious Season: Barry Bonds and the Greatest Year in Baseball* (2002).

JOHN BLOOM

Bonds, Margaret Jeannette Allison (3 Mar. 1913–26 Apr. 1972), composer, pianist, and teacher, was born in Chicago, Illinois, the daughter of Dr. Monroe Alpheus Majors, a pioneering black physician, medical researcher, and author, and Estelle C. Bonds, a music teacher and organist. Although legally born Majors, she used her mother's maiden name (Bonds) in her youth and throughout her professional life. She grew up in intellectually stimulating surroundings; her mother held Sunday afternoon salons at which young black Chicago musicians, writers, and artists gathered and where visiting musicians and artists were always welcomed. Bonds first displayed musical talent in her piano composition "Marquette Street Blues," written at the age of five. She then began studying piano with local teachers, and by the time

Margaret Bonds, composer and pianist who fused European musical Romanticism with the varied strands of her African American heritage to form a distinctive musical corpus, October 1956. (Library of Congress/Carl Van Vechten.)

she was in high school she was taking lessons in piano and composition with FLORENCE B. PRICE and WILLIAM LEVI DAWSON, two of the first black American symphonic composers, both of whom were professionally active in Chicago. Bonds later remarked that through her mother's circle she had "actual contact with all the living composers of African descent." As a young girl she served as the pianist at the Berean Baptist Church, where her mother was organist. One of several black Chicago churches that fostered performances of classical music, Berean Baptist was the home of a black community orchestra led by Harrison Farrell.

When Bonds was a teenager, the singer Abbie Mitchell introduced her to the European art song and to songs by American black composers, especially those of HENRY T. BURLEIGH. At about the same time Bonds ran across the first published poem of LANGSTON HUGHES, "The Negro Speaks of Rivers," which made a great impact on her and which she later set to music. Bonds set many of Hughes's texts and also collaborated with him

in theater works, such as *Shakespeare in Harlem* (1959).

Bonds studied with Emily Boettscher Bogue at Northwestern University, where she received bachelor of music and master of music degrees (1933, 1934). While still a student, she received the Wanamaker Foundation Prize for her song "Sea Ghost" (1932). In 1933 she became the first black American soloist to perform with the Chicago Symphony, playing John Alden Carpenter's *Concertino*. Bonds was also the soloist in a performance of Florence Price's piano concerto at the 1933 World's Fair. During the 1930s Bonds performed frequently in the United States and Canada, and she also founded and taught at the Allied Arts Academy in Chicago, an institution devoted to the teaching of ballet and music to black children.

In 1939 Bonds moved to New York City, where she became more active as a composer and arranger and where she served as an editor in the CLARENCE WILLIAMS music publishing firm. For a time she composed pop music; her most famous hits were collaborations—with ANDY RAZAFAR for "Peachtree Street" (1939) and with Hal Dickinson for "Spring Will Be So Sad" (1940). Her popular songs were recorded by Glenn Miller, Charley Spivak, and Woody Herman. In New York she studied both piano (with Djane Herz) and composition (with Robert Starer) at the Juilliard School of Music. She also studied composition with Roy Harris. She made her Town Hall debut as a pianist in 1952. Bonds taught at the American Music Wing in New York and was music director for such theaters as the East Side Settlement House, the White Barn Theater, and the Stage of Youth. She promoted the works of black American musicians and composers by organizing a chamber music society and establishing a sight-singing program at Harlem's Mount Calvary Baptist Church. She married Lawrence Richardson in 1940, and the couple had one child. In 1968 she moved to Los Angeles, where she taught at the Inner City Institute and Repertory Theater and worked as an arranger for the Los Angeles Jubilee Singers.

John Lovell Jr., in *Black Song: The Forge and the Flame* (1972), described Bonds as one of the most significant twentieth-century arrangers of traditional spirituals, along with Burleigh and WILL MARION COOK, all of whose arrangements cultivated widespread appreciation of the repertoire. Bonds arranged spirituals throughout her career, many for solo voice and piano, and some as choral pieces; the singer LEONTYNE PRICE commissioned and recorded Bonds's arrangement of "He's Got the Whole World in His Hands." Other compositions of Bonds's, such as the piano piece *Troubled Water* (1967, also set later for cello and piano), were often strongly steeped in the spiritual idiom.

Bonds's forty-two art songs include "The Pasture" (1958) and "Stopping by the Woods on a Snowy Evening" (1963)—both set to texts of Robert Frost—and "Three Dream Portraits" (1959) and "To a Brown Girl, Dead" (1956), perhaps her best-known songs, both settings of Hughes poems. Bonds's major choral works include the *Ballad of the Brown King* (1954, to text by Hughes), which has been performed annually in many black churches, and a Mass in D Minor for chorus and orchestra or organ (1959). The *Montgomery Variations*, dedicated to MARTIN LUTHER KING JR. and composed at the time of the march on Montgomery in 1965, was her most successful orchestral piece. Bonds's last work, "Credo," for baritone, chorus, and orchestra (text by W. E. B. DuBois), was performed the month after her death by the Los Angeles Philharmonic, conducted by Zubin Mehta. Bonds died in Los Angeles.

Bonds was recognized during her lifetime with many commissions and awards, including a Distinguished Alumna Award from Northwestern University (1967). Although much of her music is still in manuscript, there is a renewed interest in making the music more available for performance, especially her piano music and songs. Some of Bonds's most significant works were her modern Shakespearean musical theater works (*Shakespeare in Harlem* and *Romey and Julie*), as well as other dramatic musicals and ballets, which brought her music to a broad audience. These important works were not published, however, and the manuscripts remain in the hands of the family.

Bonds's close friendship and collaboration with Langston Hughes, as well as her many settings of his poems (from "The Negro Speaks of Rivers" to the 1964 choral work "Fields of Wonder"), resulted in a significant body of work that exemplifies the close mutual interaction of poet and composer in expressing African American ethnic identity. Bonds's many programmatic works for piano and for orchestra also speak of the black experience through their use of spiritual materials, jazz harmonies and rhythms, and social themes. Her music fuses European romanticism with the varied strands of her African American heritage to form a distinctive musical corpus, although access to her most extended works has been limited since her death.

FURTHER READING

Bonds's papers and manuscripts are owned and held by her daughter, Djane Richardson, in New York.

Bonds, Margaret. "A Reminiscence," in *The Negro in Music and Art*, ed. Lindsay Patterson (1967).

Walker-Hill, Helen, ed. *Black Women Composers: A Century of Piano Music (1893–1990)* (1992).

Obituaries: *New York Times*, 29 Apr. 1972; *Variety*, 10 May 1972; *Jet*, 18 May 1972; *Chicago Defender*, 13 Jan. 1973.

DISCOGRAPHY

Hitchcock, H. Wiley, and Stanley Sadie, eds. *New Grove Dictionary of American Music* (1986).

Tischler, Alice. *Fifteen Black American Composers with a Bibliography of Their Works* (1981).

This entry is taken from the *American National Biography* and is published here with the permission of the American Council of Learned Societies.

BARBARA G. JACKSON

Bonner, Marita Odette (16 June 1898–6 Dec. 1971), educator and author, was born in Boston, Massachusetts, the daughter of Joseph Bonner, a machinist and laborer, and Mary A. Nowell. Educated in the Brookline, Massachusetts, public schools, Bonner applied to Radcliffe College at the urging of her high school adviser and was one of the few African American students accepted for admission. She majored in English and comparative literature and founded the Radcliffe chapter of Delta Sigma Theta, a black sorority. A gifted pianist and student of musical composition, Bonner won the Radcliffe song competition in 1918 and 1922. Bonner also studied German, a language in which she became fluent. During her last year in college she taught English at a Cambridge high school. After graduating with a B.A. in 1922, she taught at the Bluefield Colored Institute in Bluefield, Virginia, until 1924 and at Armstrong High School in Washington, D.C., from 1924 to 1930, when she married William Almy Occomy, a Brown graduate. The couple moved to Chicago, where they raised three children.

Bonner began writing in high school, contributing pieces to the student magazine, the *Sagamore*. At Radcliffe she was selected to study writing under Charles Townsend Copeland. Copeland, who encouraged her to write fiction, advised Bonner not to be "bitter"—advice that she thought clichéd and consequently ignored. During her literary career she published short stories, essays, and plays, most of which examined the debilitating effects of economic, racial, and sexual prejudice on black Americans. Bonner's first publication, a short story called "The Hands," was published in *Opportunity* in August 1925, and her award-winning essay "On Being Young—A Woman—and Colored" was published in December of that year in *Crisis*; these two magazines continued to publish her work. In the essay, Bonner examines the triple jeopardy facing black women writers and answers Copeland when she addresses "white friends who have never had to draw breath in a Jim-Crow train. Who never had petty putrid insult[s] dragged over them."

She continues these themes in her other writings. In her 1928 essay "The Young Blood Hungers," a haunting refrain captures the anger and despair of a generation facing economic slavery and brutal racism. In her short story "Nothing New" she introduces Frye Street, a fictional neighborhood in Chicago that she describes as running "from freckled-face tow heads to yellow Orientals; from broad Italy to broad Georgia; from hooked noses to square black noses…. Like muddy water in a brook" (*Crisis*, 1926). She later returned to this neighborhood for many of her stories. Although multiethnic, black Frye Street does not have the same opportunities as white Frye Street.

While living in Washington, D.C., Bonner wrote and published several works that won awards from *Crisis*, including "Drab Rambles" (1927) and "The Young Blood Hungers" (1928). She was also an active member of the S Street literary salon of black writers established by the poet and playwright Georgia Douglas Johnson. During this time Bonner wrote and published three plays: *The Pot-Maker: A Play to Be Read* (1927), *The Purple Flower* (1928), and *Exit an Illusion* (1929); the latter two also won *Crisis* awards. In her introduction to *Nine Plays by Black Women* (1986), Margaret Wilkerson calls Bonner's *The Purple Flower* a black quest for freedom and happiness in a racist society and "perhaps the most provocative play" of the first half of the twentieth century.

After her marriage and subsequent move to Chicago, Bonner took a three-year break from publishing, and when she returned she devoted herself exclusively to fiction, publishing her stories under her married name. These stories offer a vivid portrait of black Chicago and its strained interactions with other minorities and with a racist white society. Her first work was a three-part narrative titled "A Possible Triad on Black Notes," published in the July, August, and September 1933 issues of *Opportunity*. "Tin Can," a two-part narrative, won the 1933 *Opportunity* literary prize for fiction and was published in the July and August 1934 issues of that magazine. These stories and the eight that followed all show the destructiveness of the urban environment on a people suffering from economic slavery and enforced poverty. All set on Frye Street in Chicago, these stories work together, as critics have noted, much the same way that James Joyce's *Dubliners* stories work; Bonner may have intended this, as shown by the heading to her story "Corner Store": "Three Tales of Living: From 'The Black Map' (A Book Entirely Unwritten)" (*Opportunity*, 1933).

Bonner's literary career ended in 1941, the year in which she and her husband joined the First Church of Christ, Scientist. Although the church tenets did not conflict with her writing, Bonner nonetheless devoted her intellectual energy to the church rather than to a literary career. After her children were all in school, Bonner resumed teaching. The Chicago Board of Education, dismissing both her Radcliffe degree and her prior teaching experience, required that she take education classes that she passed easily. She taught at Phillips High School from 1944 to 1949 and at the Dolittle School from 1950 to 1963, where she taught mentally and educationally disadvantaged students. Bonner's daughter, Joyce Occomy Stricklin, remembers her mother—a woman who approached everything she did "with every fiber of her being"—frequently spending her evenings calling students' parents to offer encouragement and advice: "She believed in her students and was convinced that lack of love and attention were the most serious handicaps they faced" (Flynn and Stricklin, ix).

Bonner died of complications after a fire in her Chicago apartment. She left behind a notebook containing six completed but unpublished stories. All her works have since been collected in one volume, *Frye Street and Environs: The Collected Works of Marita Bonner* (1987), by Joyce Flynn and Joyce Occomy Stricklin. In her introduction Flynn writes, "Bonner's works offer the perspective of an educated black female consciousness on a rapidly changing America between the world wars." Bonner was a thematic associate of Jessie Faust, Nella Larsen, and Zora Neale Hurston and the literary foremother of many black writers, including Richard Wright, Alice Walker, and Toni Morrison.

FURTHER READING

A notebook of previously unpublished stories and Bonner's letters are in the Arthur and Elizabeth Schlesinger Library at Radcliffe College.

Flynn, Joyce, and Joyce Occomy Stricklin, eds. *Frye Street and Environs: The Collected Works of Marita Bonner* (1987).

Peterson, Bernard L., Jr. *Early Black American Playwrights and Dramatic Writers* (1990).

Roses, Lorraine Elena, and Ruth Elizabeth Randolph. "Marita Bonner: In Search of Other Mothers' Gardens," *Black American Literature Forum* 21 (Spring–Summer 1987): 165–183.

This entry is taken from the *American National Biography* and is published here with the permission of the American Council of Learned Societies.

ALTHEA E. RHODES

Bontemps, Arna Wendell (13 Oct. 1902–4 June 1973), writer, was born in Alexandria, Louisiana, the son of Paul Bismark Bontemps, a bricklayer, and Maria Carolina Pembroke, a schoolteacher. He was reared in Los Angeles, where his family moved when he was three. He graduated from Pacific Union College in Angwin, California, in 1923. Bontemps then moved to Harlem, New York, where the Harlem Renaissance had already attracted the attention of West Coast intellectuals. He found a teaching job at the Harlem Academy in 1924 and began to publish poetry. He won the Alexander Pushkin Prize from *Opportunity*, a journal published by the National Urban League, in 1926 and 1927 and the *Crisis* (official journal of the NAACP) Poetry Prize in 1926. His career soon intersected that of the poet LANGSTON HUGHES, with whom he became a close friend and sometime collaborator. In Harlem, Bontemps also came to know COUNTÉE CULLEN, W. E. B. DUBOIS, ZORA NEALE HURSTON, JAMES WELDON JOHNSON, CLAUDE MCKAY, and JEAN TOOMER.

In 1926 Bontemps married Alberta Johnson; they had six children. In 1931, as the Depression deepened, Bontemps left the Harlem Academy and moved to Huntsville, Alabama, where he taught for three years at Oakwood Junior College. By the early 1930s Bontemps had begun to publish fiction as well as poetry. His first novel, *God Sends Sunday*, was published in 1931, and an early short story, "A Summer Tragedy," won the *Opportunity* Short Story Prize in 1932. *God Sends Sunday* is typical of the Harlem Renaissance. Little Augie, a black jockey, earns money easily and spends it recklessly. When his luck as a jockey runs out, he drifts through the black sporting world. Slight in plot, the novel is most appreciated for its poetic style, its recreation of the black idiom, and the depth of its characterization. While most reviewers praised it, DuBois found it "sordid" and compared it with other "decadent" books of the Harlem Renaissance, such as Carl Van Vechten's *Nigger Heaven* (1926) and McKay's *Home to Harlem* (1928). But Bontemps thought enough of the basic story to collaborate with Cullen on *St. Louis Woman* (1946), a dramatic adaptation of the book.

Bontemps's next novel would be on a much more serious theme, but he first attempted another genre. In collaboration with Hughes, he wrote *Popo and Fifina* (1932), the first of his many children's books. A travel book for children, it introduced readers to Haitian life by describing the lives of a boy named Popo and his sister Fifina. Bontemps followed his initial success in the new field with *You Can't Pet a Possum* (1934), a story of a boy and his dog in rural Alabama.

Northern Alabama in the early 1930s proved inhospitable to an African American writer and

Arna Bontemps, poet, novelist, historian, and librarian who played a major role in shaping modern African American literature, 15 August 1939. (Library of Congress/Carl Van Vechten.)

intellectual. The SCOTTSBORO BOYS were being tried in Decatur, just thirty miles from Huntsville. Friends visited Bontemps on their way to protest the trial, and the combination of his out-of-state visitors and the fact that he was ordering books by mail worried the administration of the school. Bontemps claimed in later years that he was ordered to demonstrate his break with the world of radical politics by burning a number of books from his private library—works by Johnson, DuBois, and FREDERICK DOUGLASS. Bontemps refused. Instead, he resigned and moved back to California, where he and his family moved in with his parents.

In 1936 Bontemps published *Black Thunder*, his finest work in any genre. Based on historical research, *Black Thunder* tells the story of GABRIEL PROSSER's rebellion near Richmond, Virginia, in 1800. Prosser, an uneducated fieldworker and coachman, planned to lead a slave army equipped with makeshift weapons on a raid against the armory in Richmond. Once armed with real muskets, the rebels would defend themselves against all attackers. Betrayed by another slave and hampered by a freak storm, the rebels were crushed, and Prosser was hanged. But in Bontemps's version of the affair, whites won a Pyrrhic victory; they were forced to recognize the human potential of slaves.

Although *Black Thunder* was well reviewed by both black and mainstream journals, such as the *Saturday Review of Literature*, the royalties were not sufficient to support Bontemps's family in Chicago, where they had moved just before publication. Bontemps taught briefly in Chicago at the Shiloh Academy and then accepted a job with the WPA Illinois Writers' Project. In 1938, after publishing another children's book, *Sad-Faced Boy* (1937), he received a Rosenwald Fellowship to work on what became his last novel, *Drums at Dusk* (1939), based on the Haitian rebellion led by Toussaint-Louverture. Although the book was more widely reviewed than his previous novels, the critics were divided, some seeing it as suffering from a sensational and melodramatic plot, others praising its characterizations.

The disappointing reception of the book and the poor royalties it earned convinced Bontemps that "it was fruitless for a Negro in the United States to address serious writing to my generation, and … to consider the alternative of trying to reach young readers not yet hardened or grown insensitive to man's inhumanity to man" ("Introduction," x). Henceforth Bontemps addressed most of his books to youthful audiences. He wrote *The Fast Sooner Hound* (1942) in collaboration with Jack Conroy, whom he had met through the Illinois Writers' Project.

In 1943 Bontemps earned his master's degree in Library Science from the University of Chicago. The necessity of earning a living then took him to Fisk University, where he became head librarian, a post he held until 1964. Thereafter he returned to Fisk from time to time. He also accepted positions at the Chicago Circle campus of the University of Illinois and at Yale University, where he served as curator of the James Weldon Johnson Collection of Negro Arts and Letters.

During these years Bontemps produced an astonishing variety and number of books. His children's books include *Slappy Hooper* (1946) and *Sam Patch* (1951), which he wrote in collaboration with Conroy, *Lonesome Boy* (1955), and *Mr. Kelso's Lion* (1970). At the same time he wrote biographies of Douglass, GEORGE WASHINGTON CARVER, and BOOKER T. WASHINGTON for teenage readers; *Golden Slippers* (1941), an anthology of poetry for young readers; *Famous Negro Athletes* (1964); *Chariot in the Sky* (1951), the story of the Fisk Jubilee Singers; and *The Story of the Negro* (1948).

For adults Bontemps and Hughes edited *The Poetry of the Negro* (1949) and *The Book of Negro Folklore* (1958). With Conroy, Bontemps wrote *They Seek a City* (1945), a history of African American migration in the United States, which they revised and published in 1966 as *Anyplace but Here*. Bontemps's historical interests also led him to write *One Hundred Years of Negro Freedom* (1961) and to edit *Great Slave Narratives* (1969) and *The Harlem Renaissance Remembered* (1972). He also edited a popular anthology, *American Negro Poetry* (1963), just in time for the black reawakening of the 1960s.

Bontemps had been forced by the reception of his work to put his more creative writing on hold after 1939, but the 1960s encouraged him to return to it. He collected his poetry in a slim volume, *Personals* (1963), and wrote an introduction for *Black Thunder* when it was republished in 1968 in a paperback edition. At the time of his death, he was completing the collection of his short fiction in *The Old South* (1973). Bontemps died at his home in Nashville.

Bontemps excelled in no single literary genre. A noteworthy poet, he published only one volume of his verse. As a writer of fiction, he is best known for a single novel, written in midcareer and rediscovered in his old age. Yet the impact of his work as poet, novelist, historian, children's writer, editor, and librarian is far greater than the sum of its parts. He played a major role in shaping modern African American literature and had a wide-ranging influence on African American culture of the latter half of the twentieth century.

FURTHER READING

The major collections of Bontemps's papers are at Fisk University; the George Arents Research Library, Syracuse University; and the James Weldon Johnson Collection, Beinecke Rare Book Room and Manuscript Library, Yale University.

Bontemps, Arna. "Introduction," in *Black Thunder* (1968).

Bontemps, Arna. "Preface," in *Personals* (1963).

Bontemps, Arna. "Why I Returned," in *The Old South* (1973).

Fleming, Robert E. *James Weldon Johnson and Arna Wendell Bontemps: A Reference Guide* (1978).

Gwin, Minrose C. "Arna Bontemps," in *American Poets, 1880–1945*, ed. Peter Quartermain (1986).

Jones, Kirkland C. "Arna Bontemps," in *Afro-American Writers from the Harlem Renaissance to 1940*, ed. Trudier Harris (1987).

O'Brien, John. *Interviews with Black Writers* (1973).

This entry is taken from the *American National Biography* and is published here with the permission of the American Council of Learned Societies.

ROBERT E. FLEMING

Booker, Cory A. (27 Apr. 1969–), mayor of Newark, New Jersey, was born Cory Anthony Booker in Washington, D.C., the younger of two sons of Carolyn and Cary Booker, executives at IBM. Booker graduated from North Valley Regional High School at Old Tappan, after which he entered Stanford University in Palo Alto, California. At Stanford Booker studied political science and was active in student politics, serving in student government as senior class president. He played football and was awarded for his talent. Upon graduating with a B.A. in 1991, Booker decided to stay at Stanford for another year. In 1992, Booker received his M in Sociology and was awarded one of the highly coveted Rhodes Scholarships. In Great Britain, he continued his studies at The Queen's College of Oxford University. In 1994 Booker received a degree in modern history with honors. After completing his studies in England, Booker enrolled at Yale Law School. Building on his earlier experiences with community outreach and helping others, Booker worked at legal clinics that provided pro bono legal assistance to those in and around New Haven, Connecticut. In addition, he was a mentor to young African Americans lacking guidance and direction. Following his law school graduation in 1997, Booker left the comfortable confines of New England and returned to New Jersey. There Booker embarked upon his political career.

While working with the Urban Justice Center of New York in 1996, Booker met a woman who urged him to run for political office. Booker worked with her and others to demand better services from city government and more cooperation from local apartment owners. He subsequently moved into a public housing project and was elected to the city council of Newark. Booker was just twenty-eight years old. It was an odd twist for a young man from the upper class with Ivy League degrees. He could have made six figures in the private sector or taken a prestigious clerkship; however, he chose public service as a way to improve others' lives.

Once in office, Booker worked to build relationships with both the elite and those forgotten by society. Ambitious to move up and take on more leadership and power, Booker made a play for the mayor's office in 2002. He faced stiff opposition from not only Mayor Sharpe James but also those suspicious of his pedigree. The Reverend AL SHARPTON campaigned against Booker as too young, too disrespectful, and unacquainted with the daily experiences of the average African American. Booker garnered only 47 percent of the vote; however, his success helped set up another run for mayor four years later.

Booker basically campaigned for the next four years in Newark. He solidified his contacts, expanded his network, and became better grounded in the nuances of the city. In 2006, Booker was ready for a rematch. This time Mayor James bowed out to concentrate on his political future in the New Jersey State Senate. Booker raised millions of dollars for the 2006 race and succeeded in besting Deputy Mayor Ronald Rice in May with 72 percent of the vote. Once in office Booker moved to fulfill his campaign pledges to get tough on crime, put more police on the streets, and revitalize Newark into a productive, family-friendly city. His tenure, however, has not been without its difficulties. Mayor Booker was forced to take on added security when credible death threats were directed at him from local members of the Bloods street gang. The mayor has also been criticized for increasing city workers' wages and cracking down on corruption and political and professional malfeasance.

Cory A. Booker, mayor of Newark, greets Shirley Little, left, outside a polling place on election day in Newark, New Jersey, 9 May 2006. (AP Images.)

Mayor Booker's leadership has drawn praise for his hands-on approach and turning a once dreary city into a promising urban area with a bright future ahead of it. This is evidenced by the growing financial commitments from philanthropic organizations and Booker's rising star within the Democratic Party.

In 2008 Cory Booker supported the seemingly quixotic presidential candidacy of BARACK OBAMA. After Obama was elected, Booker was offered the position of head of the White House Office of Urban Affairs but decided to remain mayor. Booker has been somewhat controversial within the African American community because of his new and innovative approaches to governing and politics. At the end of the first decade of the twentieth century Booker was considered one of the best young politicians, Republican or Democrat, in the country. Like Obama, his political appeal lay in his ability to build multiracial, multiethnic and cross-class coalitions that transcend traditional black politics.

Booker was reelected mayor of Newark in 2010, a testament to his success in dramatically cutting violent crime in what had been one of America's most notoriously violent cities. As Booker began his second term, homicides were at their lowest rate in the city since before World War II.

FURTHER READING

Cave, Damie. "Newark Feature: A New Political Era." *New York Times*, 10 May 2006.

Curry, Marshall. *Street Fight*. Documentary film on the 2002 Booker vs. James mayoral campaign, 2005.

Gillespie, Andra. *Whose Black Politics? Cases in Post-Racial Black Leadership* (2009).

Gregory, Sean. "Why Cory Booker Likes Being Mayor of Newark." *Time*, 27 July 2009.

Ifill, Gwen. *The Breakthrough: Politics and Race in the Age of Obama* (2009).

Malanga, Steven. "Cory Booker's Battle for Newark." *City Journal*, Spring 2007.

DARYL A. CARTER

Booker, James Carroll, III (17 Dec. 1939–8 Nov. 1983), classical, jazz, and rhythm and blues pianist, was born in New Orleans, Louisiana, to James Carroll Booker Jr., a minister, and Ora Champagne Booker, a hairdresser. A child prodigy on the piano, Booker professed to have played the instrument as an infant. As a result of his father's ill health, his family moved to nearby Bay St. Louis, Mississippi, in the early 1940s. At the age of seven, while at a Catholic grade school, Booker took his first formal piano lessons. Following his father's death in 1953, Booker returned to New Orleans, entering high school in the fall of that year. He made an immediate impression on fellow classmates (including a young Aaron Neville), and began playing in local bands. Booker made his first appearance on a professional recording at the age of fifteen, performing on DAVE BARTHOLOMEW's 1954 "Hambone" for the Chess label.

In 1957 Booker graduated from high school and performed in clubs as a backing musician for artists such as JOE TEX, Huey Smith, and Shirley Lee. He also made regular appearances as "Little" Booker at the notorious Dew Drop Inn, where he gained notice for his lightning-fast runs across the piano keys. In 1959 he entered Southern University, which he attended for more than a year, until offers to play piano lured him onto the road as a touring musician for LITTLE RICHARD and FATS DOMINO.

In 1960 Booker recorded "Gonzo," a blistering instrumental that sold more than one hundred thousand records, establishing him as a distinctive and skillful stylist. The record's B-side, "Cool Turkey," signaled an emerging trait of Booker's music—sly drug references that eventually would dominate his work. During the late 1950s he had started using heroin, a habit he picked up from the clientele that frequented the Dew Drop Inn. While the success of "Gonzo," which reached number forty-three on the *Billboard* pop charts, garnered Booker increasing attention from other musicians, Booker remained throughout his career largely unknown to audiences outside of New Orleans.

In 1962–1963 he toured successively with LIONEL LEO HAMPTON, Little Richard, and Earl King. After his mother died in late 1965, Booker composed "Ora," a soulful elegy that became a mainstay of his repertoire. The following year his sister Betty Jean died of breast cancer. Booker left New Orleans for New York City in 1967, joining the Neville Brothers and other Crescent City transplants in the vibrant downtown Manhattan music scene. He worked as a session player on albums by ARETHA FRANKLIN and RAY CHARLES, and toured in support of saxophonist KING CURTIS. He also appeared on Fats Domino's *Fats Is Back*, which featured Booker's stellar organ and piano accompaniment.

Booker returned to New Orleans in early 1970, but he was arrested for possession of cocaine and sentenced to two years at the state penitentiary in Angola. During his incarceration he worked in the prison library, taught fellow inmates how to read, studied Eastern philosophy, began to practice yoga, and played in the prison's rhythm and blues band. He also began to exhibit early signs of psychological problems, primarily paranoid delusions, that would plague him for the rest of his life.

After serving almost a year of his sentence, Booker gained release and moved to Los Angeles, where he renewed his career as a session musician. His obscure recordings with his fellow New Orleans performer Dr. John later became legendary among aficionados, but it was his work with rock and roll stars the Doobie Brothers, Jerry Garcia of the Grateful Dead, and the former Beatle Ringo Starr that provided him with financial, if not personal, stability. During a recording session with Starr, Booker got involved in a dispute over drugs, which led to a physically violent encounter resulting in the loss of his left eye. Convinced that Starr had ordered the assault on him, Booker began wearing an eye patch emblazoned with a large blue star. Still addicted to heroin and drinking heavily, Booker returned to New Orleans in 1975 and began performing at local night spots: Rosy's, the Maple Leaf, and the Toulouse Theatre.

In late 1975, with the help of his manager John Parsons, Booker attempted to get control of his finances as well as his drug and alcohol problems. He volunteered at local halfway houses and youth centers, yet his behavior grew increasingly bizarre. His stage shows became wildly unpredictable, with moments of brilliance and clarity—in which he seamlessly blended classical music with jazz and boogie-woogie—giving way to extreme mood swings and paranoid outbursts. His career, however, continued to progress. An acclaimed performance at the 1975 New Orleans Jazz and Heritage Festival drew the interest of a German promoter who arranged for Booker to play, in 1976, his first solo European tour. Foreign audiences greeted him with enormous accolades, dubbing him the "piano prince" of New Orleans. Combining mournful ballads with freewheeling rave-ups, Booker created music in a stream-of-consciousness manner, playing any tune that occurred to him—often improvising new arrangements on the spot. A typical performance might include a medley that comprised one of his signature songs, "On the Sunny Side of the Street," followed by elements of Tchaikovsky, the Beatles, and ragtime. His virtuosity thrilled European audiences and led to the release of his first long-playing album, *Junco Partner*, released in 1976, on Island Records.

After performing in front of large, appreciative European audiences throughout the late 1970s, Booker returned to New Orleans and took a regular gig as the lobby entertainment at the Toulouse Theatre. His mental health continued to decline, and by 1980 his performances had become rife with psychological turmoil. He incorporated into songs his long-standing belief that the CIA was following him, openly criticized local drug enforcement, and failed to fulfill recording obligations. Booker also periodically checked himself into a local hospital mental ward, where he played piano for the doctors on duty.

In 1983 Booker cut his final album, *Classified*, for Rounder Records. His drug and alcohol addictions intensified, and, attempting to remove himself from the influences of nightclubs, he took a job as a file clerk for the New Orleans Department of Economic Analysis. His drug abuse continued, however, and after one year he was fired. In November of that year, Booker died of heart failure in the waiting room of Charity Hospital in New Orleans.

James Carroll Booker's unparalleled skill at the piano drew acclaim from critics and fans around the world. Many notable New Orleans musicians—the Neville Brothers, the Marsalis family, ALLEN TOUSSAINT, and Dr. John—cited his enormous influence. Booker's dexterity and imaginative approach to his instrument made him unique, as did his ability to cross genres with ease. Largely unknown outside of jazz aficionado circles, James Carroll Booker's influence on the New Orleans piano sound nevertheless remained a timeless tribute to his artistry.

FURTHER READING

Berry, Jason, Tad Jones, and Jonathan Foose. *Up from the Cradle of Jazz: New Orleans Music since World War II* (1992).

Booker, James Carroll, III. *The James Booker Collection* (2000).

Johnson, Pableaux. *Legends of New Orleans* (2001).

DISCOGRAPHY

Classified (Rounder 612036).

Gonzo: More Than All the 45's (Night Train International 7084).

Junco Partner (Hannibal 1359).

Resurrection of the Bayou Maharajah (Rounder 612118).

BRENTON E. RIFFEL

Booker, Joseph Albert (26 Dec. 1859–9 Sept. 1925), college president, minister, journalist, and agriculturalist, was born a slave in Portland, Arkansas, to Albert Clark Book and Mary Punsard. Booker was orphaned at three years of age; his mother died when he was one year old and his father was whipped to death two years later, having been found guilty of teaching others how to read. At the end of the Civil War Booker's grandmother sent him to a school established to educate freed slaves.

Booker excelled in school. By the time he was seventeen he had earned the right to open his own subscription school; subscription schools were established during a time before the wide availability of public schools. Parents paid a monthly fee for their children to attend these institutions. Booker saved his money from teaching in order to attend college. He attended Branch Normal School (later the University of Arkansas at Pine Bluff) in Pine Bluff, Arkansas, from 1878 to 1881.

Booker transferred to Roger Williams College in Nashville, Tennessee, and graduated in 1886. While studying at Roger Williams, Booker supported himself by washing dishes, chopping wood, and starting the fires at college. He managed to excel at mathematics and in Latin and upon his graduation was asked to lead Arkansas Baptist College.

At the time Booker became president in 1887, Arkansas Baptist College had only fifteen students and its classes were scattered throughout various local churches. By 1902 the school had its own campus on High Street in Little Rock, Arkansas, its own farm (the Griggs Industrial Farm), and employed nine teachers.

During his thirty-two-year tenure Booker served as editor of a church newspaper, as a missionary preacher traveling through many southern states, and on local and national Baptist organizations.

On 28 June 1887 Booker married Mary Jane Caver, a teacher, of Helena, Arkansas. Together the couple had eight children. It was said that, in spite of all of his activities, Booker enjoyed spending as much time as possible with his family. One of his daughters became an accomplished musician and taught at Arkansas Baptist College. Other children entered various professions such as law and education.

Booker received his A.M. degree in 1889 and his doctorate from State University at Louisville, Kentucky, in 1901. In his later years he served on many state and national boards and traveled throughout the United States and Europe. Booker remained a loyal member of the Republican Party, was a member of the Negro National Life Insurance Company, the Southern Sociological Congress, Searchlight, Owl, and Lotus. Additionally, as did so many other men of his social class, he joined several fraternal orders, such as the International Order of Twelves, Knights of Pythias, Freemasons, and Mosaic Templars. Booker died on 9 September 1926, from a heart attack, while attending the National Baptist Convention in Fort Worth, Texas.

FURTHER READING

Bacote, Samuel William. *Who's Who among Colored Baptists of the United States*, vol. 1 (1913).

Gibson, John W., and William H. Crogman. *The Colored American from Slavery to Honorable Citizenship* (1902).

Hartshorn, William Newton. *An Era of Progress and Promise, 1863–1910* (1910).

Penn, Irvine Garland. *The Afro American Press and Its Editors* (1891).

Peques, A. W. *Our Baptist Ministers and Schools* (1892).

Pipken, J. J. *The Story of a Rising Race: The Negro in Revelation, in History, and in Citizenship* (1902).

Richardson, Clement. *The National Cyclopedia of the Colored Race* (1919).

Richings, George F. *An Album of Negro Educators* (1900).

Richings, George F. *Evidences of Progress among Colored People* (1896).

KECIA BROWN

Booker, Kinney Ibis (21 Mar. 1913–1 Mar. 2006), survivor of the 1921 Tulsa, Oklahoma, riot, was one of five children born to Hood Booker, a chauffeur and mechanic, and his wife. Kinney Booker graduated from the segregated Booker T. Washington High School in Tulsa and from Xavier University in New Orleans. Though he was only seven years old when the Tulsa riot broke out on the evening of 31 May 1921, his recollections of the event were central to the Tulsa Race Riot Commission's discussions in the late 1990s and early 2000s. He was quoted extensively in media sources about it, from the *New York Times* to the *Los Angeles Times* to *Nightline* to National Public Radio.

The Tulsa riot began after rumors of an impending lynching of a young African American man circulated in both white and black communities in Tulsa. When some African American veterans of World War I appeared at the Tulsa Courthouse to prevent the lynching, there was a confrontation with police officers and the riot ensued. Before it ended about noon the next day, most of the

African American section of Tulsa was burned to the ground.

Booker recalled being awakened by his parents in the early morning hours of 1 June 1921 and hiding in the attic of his parents' house with his mother and sister. He heard men searching their house. Presumably they were the special deputies and members of the mob that were going house to house to arrest everyone they could in Greenwood, the African American section of Tulsa, and bring them to detention centers in the city. When the riot began, the Tulsa police department hastily deputized hundreds of men to help put down the riot. Booker also remembered bullets—perhaps fired by airplanes or, perhaps more likely, by people on neighboring Standpipe Hill—hitting the roof of their house. He recalled hearing his father beg the men not to burn the house to no avail. Booker's house, along with about thirty-five blocks of Greenwood, burned that morning. Booker, his sister, and mother escaped the house shortly after it was set on fire. In a *60 Minutes* television interview in 1999, Booker remembered that his sister asked, "Kinney, is the world on fire?" to which he replied, "I don't know, but we in trouble, deep trouble." They were taken into custody and brought to the Tulsa Convention Center (later the Brady Theater) on the edge of Greenwood.

In the aftermath of the riot Greenwood residents were released from custody only when they could present a white employer or friend to vouch for them. They were then issued green tags that had their name and their employer's name printed on them. Shortly after the riot ended the Booker family was released into the custody of a Tulsa oilman named Homer F. Wilcox, who employed Hood Booker as a chauffeur and mechanic. The Bookers lived in the Wilcox's basement for a time.

The Bookers also lived temporarily in a tent in Greenwood. Shortly after the riot ended the city passed a fire code ordinance, which required the use of fireproof material for rebuilding in the burned area. Toward the end of the summer of 1921, as it became apparent that the use of fireproof materials was prohibitively expensive, Greenwood residents won a lawsuit in the Tulsa County Court that allowed them to rebuild using whatever materials they wanted.

After graduating from Xavier University in New Orleans, Booker played in jazz bands and worked for sixteen years for the U.S. Postal Service as a railroad clerk in Oklahoma and California. For thirty years he taught music in the Los Angeles school system, before retiring to Tulsa where he was a constant presence at meetings of the Tulsa Riot Commission, established in 1997 upon the recommendation of the state representative Don Ross, who grew up in Greenwood after the riot.

As the riot commission gained increasing national attention Booker spoke frequently to the media. He was quoted in 1999 as saying that he had been angry for many years about the riot and even refused to tell his children about it. Eventually, however, Booker overcame his anger. He realized the importance of the memory of the riot as a reminder of the continuing presence of racism and as a warning to future generations. He spoke frequently in favor of reparations being paid to survivors of the riot, though he expressed doubts that it would ever happen. Nevertheless he continued to speak about the riot and, according to many people who knew him, Booker's dignified resolution and his warm personality helped to keep the issue of reparations alive and to make sure that the riot received the attention it deserved in American memory.

In 2003, after it became apparent that neither the city nor the state would pay reparations, Booker was a plaintiff in a lawsuit filed by a distinguished team of lawyers, including Harvard Law School professor Charles Ogletree and Los Angeles lawyer Johnnie Cochran, and with assistance from a distinguished group of expert witnesses, including history professor Leon Litwack of the University of California, Berkeley. The suit, *Alexander v. Oklahoma*, sought financial compensation for the actions of Tulsa and Oklahoma officials in the riot. A key part of the lawsuit was the desire to remember the riot and to get an official acknowledgment of the long-forgotten role of the Tulsa police and their special deputies in the riot, thus affirming that it was not just a white mob that destroyed Greenwood, but a mob working with and supported by the authorities. Booker told *People* magazine in 2003, "No one has ever taken responsibility for what happened, but because of the lawsuit people are going to have to face it now."

The lawsuit was dismissed on technical grounds in 2004 by the federal district court in Tulsa, in an opinion that acknowledged the culpability and negligence of Tulsa officials. The lower court's decision was affirmed by the U.S. Court of Appeals, and the U.S. Supreme Court refused to hear the case.

Booker died in Tulsa. His sister, Dorothy Boulding, survived him, as did one daughter, Darlene Miller, of Savannah, Georgia.

FURTHER READING

Brophy, Alfred L. *Reconstructing the Dreamland: The Tulsa Riot of 1921—Race, Reparations, Reconciliation* (2002).

Brophy, Alfred L. "The Tulsa Race Riot Commission, Apology, and Reparation: Understanding the Functions and Limitations of a Historical Truth Commission," in *Taking Wrongs Seriously: Apology and Reconciliation*, eds. Elazar Barkan and Alexander Karn (2006).

ALFRED L. BROPHY

Boone, Clinton Caldwell, Sr. (c. 1878–3 July 1939), minister, author, physician, dentist, and missionary, was born in Winton, North Carolina. His father, Lemuel Washington Boone (1827–1878), was a prominent minister and politician, and one of the original trustees of Shaw University.

Boone received his early education at Waters Normal and Industrial Institute in Winton. From 1896 to 1899 he attended Richmond Theological Seminary in Richmond, Virginia. In 1899, when the seminary merged with Wayland Seminary College of Meridian Hill in Washington, D.C., to form Virginia Union University and moved to its new Richmond campus at North Lombardy Street, Boone finished his senior year and became part of the university's first graduating class in 1900; he received the bachelor's of divinity degree.

During his final year at Virginia Union, Boone met Eva Roberta Coles from Charlottesville, Virginia, who studied at the neighboring African American women's institution, Hartshorn Memorial College, from which she graduated in 1899. Eva Coles taught school in Charlottesville while Boone completed his studies, and they were engaged to be married. Clinton Boone was the first missionary named by the newly established Lott Carey Baptist Mission Convention, in partnership with the Missionary Union of Boston and the American Baptist Foreign Mission Society, under the auspices of the Northern Baptist Convention. He was assigned to the station at Palaballa (sometimes called Mpalaballa) in what was then the Congo Free State, now the Republic of the Congo.

On 16 January 1901 Boone and Eva Coles were married and soon took up residence at the Palaballa mission, some three hundred miles inland from the Atlantic Ocean. Though EVA ROBERTA BOONE and Clinton Boone proved to be an extraordinarily committed and hardworking team, their eighteen months together at Palaballa were touched by tragedy. Their infant son died, and on 8 December

1902 Eva herself succumbed to what seems to have been the effects of a poisonous insect or snake bite. Widowed and isolated from familiar surroundings, Boone continued the work alone, often trekking through hundreds of miles of dangerous territory to baptize, officiate, and minister to the local population, until his service in the Congo came to an end in 1906.

Boone then returned to the United States to take medical courses at the Leonard Medical School of Shaw University. He earned his M.D., and immediately upon graduation in 1912 he journeyed to Liberia as a qualified medical missionary. There he served for nearly a year on an interim basis as secretary to the U.S. diplomatic staff in the capital at Monrovia. In 1918 he became pastor of the oldest Baptist church in Liberia, Providence Baptist Church in Monrovia, founded by Lott Carey in 1822.

In 1919 Boone took a leave of absence and returned to the United States in order to study at the Bodee Dental School in New York City, with the purpose of fulfilling what he perceived as a dire need of his parishioners. The only dentist in Liberia had died the previous year in the great influenza epidemic. Back in Richmond, Boone met Rachel A. Tharps, who had graduated from Hartshorn Memorial College in 1911 and was teaching in the Richmond public schools. She became his second wife and in 1920 traveled with him to Liberia, where he continued his pastoral duties at Providence Baptist Church. He served on the Board of Managers of the Liberia Missionary and Educational Convention, and his wife ran the Mission School, which had an enrollment of ninety-one students. The couple had two children, both born in Monrovia. Their son, Dr. Clinton Caldwell Boone Jr., was born on 23 February 1922 and served as pastor at the Union Baptist Church in Hempstead, New York, from 1957 to 2003 and as commissioner of the Department of Occupational Resources for the town of Hempstead. Their daughter, Dr. Rachel Hannah Celestine Boone Keith, born on 30 May 1924, became a noted medical practitioner in Detroit and the wife of Judge DAMON J. KEITH of the United States Court of Appeals for the Sixth Circuit.

Returning once more to Richmond in 1926, the Boone family settled in the old Navy Hill neighborhood on the city's north side. Mrs. Boone resumed teaching, and Dr. Boone ministered to congregations in Richmond and Petersburg and also published two autobiographical accounts of his missionary career: *Congo as I Saw It* and *Liberia as I Know It*, in 1927 and 1929, respectively. The first was dedicated to Eva, and the second was dedicated to Rachel, who died of tuberculosis in 1938.

On 3 July 1939, while swimming in the James River at the Elder Solomon Michaux's Beach near Jamestown, Virginia, Boone was pulled away by a strong tidal current and drowned. He had been a pillar of support for the missionary movement, and his two published books, with their notable tone of humanity, their meticulous descriptions of the Congo's geography, natural history, and society, and their account of Liberia's history, were instrumental in arousing increased interest in ongoing evangelizing efforts and providing a valuable primary insight into early twentieth-century Baptist missions to Africa.

FURTHER READING

Boone, Clinton Caldwell, Sr. *Congo as I Saw It* (1927).

Boone, Clinton Caldwell, Sr. *Liberia as I Know It* (1929).

Fisher, Miles Mark. *Virginia Union University and Some of Her Achievements* (1924).

Freeman, Edward A. *The Epoch of the Baptists and the Foreign Mission Board, National Baptist Convention, USA, Inc.* (1954).

Jacobs, Sylvia M., ed. *Black Americans and the Missionary Movement in Africa* (1982).

Whitted, J. A. *The Reformed Reader: A History of the Negro Baptists of North Carolina* (1908).

Obituaries: *Richmond Afro-American*, 8 July 1939 and 15 July 1939.

RAYMOND PIERRE HYLTON

Boone, Eva Roberta (or Mae) Coles (8 Jan. 1880– 8 Dec. 1902), teacher and missionary, was born Eva Coles in Charlottesville, Virginia. Nothing is known about her parents or her early years. She is sometimes confused with Elizabeth Coles, and her parents are often erroneously listed as John J. Coles and Lucy A. Henry Coles, who married in 1886 and went to Liberia as missionaries in 1887.

Eva Coles was one of the first young women to attend Hartshorn Memorial College in Richmond, Virginia. This institution had been established in 1883 by northern white Baptists as the world's first college for African American females (Spelman College in Atlanta did not become a college until 1924, and Bennett College in North Carolina was coeducational until 1926). Hartshorn was established by the American Baptist Home Mission

Society (ABHMS) through the donation of Joseph C. Hartshorn of Rhode Island as a memorial to his late wife. The first classes at Hartshorn were held in 1883 in the basement of Ebenezer Baptist Church. Then the college moved its campus to the northwest corner of Leigh and Lombardy streets. After its relocation, Hartshorn took both day and boarding students and offered its young women a solid academic curriculum based on that of Wellesley College. A close-knit family atmosphere stressed Christian life and values and community service. In 1892 Hartshorn gave the first bachelor's degrees ever conferred at an African American female college, and Coles graduated in May 1899.

It is likely that Coles met her future husband, CLINTON CALDWELL BOONE SR., in Richmond. On 11 February 1899, Coles joined others in the groundbreaking ceremony of the newly founded all-male Virginia Union University in Richmond. The ABHMS proposed a National Theological Institute to provide education and training so that recently freed black men could enter the Baptist ministry. Separate branches of the National Theological Institute were set up in Washington, D.C., and Richmond, Virginia. Classes began at both National Theological Institutes in 1867. In Washington, the school became known as Wayland Seminary, named in commemoration of Francis Wayland, former president of Brown University and a leader in the antislavery struggle. The first and only president of Wayland was George Mellen Prentiss King, who administered the school for thirty years, from 1867 to 1897. In Richmond, efforts at establishing a theological school for black men were more difficult, but classes at Colver Institute in Richmond also began in 1867. In 1899 the Richmond Theological Institute (formerly Colver Institute) joined with Wayland Seminary of Washington, D.C., to form Virginia Union University (VUU) at Richmond.

Clinton Boone completed Waters Normal Institute in Winton, North Carolina, and graduated from the theological seminary at Richmond's Virginia Union University with a BD degree on 21 May 1900. After his graduation, Clinton Boone served as a traveling agent for the Foreign Mission Board of North Carolina of the National Baptist Convention (NBC) and the LOTT CAREY Baptist Foreign Mission Convention. After graduating from Hartshorn, Eva Coles taught for a year and a half at a school (probably on an elementary level) in her hometown of Charlottesville. On 16 January 1901 Clinton Boone and Eva Coles were married.

In its early years the Lott Carey Convention (LCC) cooperated with other black Baptist boards that were engaged in foreign mission work. On 31 August 1900 the Women's Auxiliary to the LCC was founded. Surprisingly, though, considering the attitude of the founders concerning cooperation with whites, in 1900 the LCC agreed to join the white American Baptist Missionary Union to mutually support Clinton and Eva Boone. On 8 April 1901 Clinton Boone was appointed a missionary to Africa, and he and his wife sailed from New York on 13 April 1901 to the Congo Free State (later known as the Belgian Congo, as of this writing known as Democratic Republic of the Congo) under the auspices of the American Baptist Missionary Union (later known as the American Baptist Churches U.S.A.) in cooperation with the Lott Carey Baptist Foreign Mission Convention. The couple was stationed at Palabala, the oldest station in Africa for the American Baptist Missionary Union.

Eva Boone's husband preached and taught the Congolese people in their own language. Boone was stationed at Palabala for a little more than a year and a half before her death. During her first year at the station, Eva Boone took charge of the infant classes held at the day school. Through the teaching methods that she probably had learned in Charlottesville she conducted the kindergarten classes. She convinced thirty to forty young children to attend school daily, many of whom did not understand or see the value of this Western education. Boone was also one of the first missionaries in the Congo to advance the idea of a sewing school for women. Despite the fact that most African women saw sewing as men's work, she was able to enroll more than forty in a sewing class. Since missionary women also were expected to do some medical work with women and children, she was sometimes put in charge of administering medical treatment to women and children at the mission station.

Boone made many friends among the Congolese people as a result of her kind words and loving disposition. The villagers respected her and the work that she was doing. They affectionately called her Mama Bunu, a nickname that probably referred to her efforts in getting the women to sew. (For the Bunu Yoruba people of central Nigeria, cloth is a symbol of continuing social relations and identities, and the Bunu mark every critical juncture in an individual's life—from birthing ceremonies to funeral celebrations—with handwoven cloth).

Although the Boones won the respect of many Congolese, fate was unkind to them. The couple endured heartrending hardships and sorrow, which tragically included the loss of their own baby. Boone herself then fell gravely ill from a poisonous bite from a worm or snake. The village women held a vigil around her house during her illness, but after several weeks of sickness Boone died on the morning of 8 December 1902, one month shy of her twenty-third birthday, and she was buried at Palabala Station. Boone's contributions continue to be cherished and honored at Virginia Union University.

FURTHER READING

Boone, Clinton Caldwell, Sr. *Congo as I Saw It* (1927).

Freeman, Edward A. *The Epoch of Negro Baptists and the Foreign Mission Board* (1953).

SYLVIA M. JACOBS

Boone, Sarah (fl. 1890s), inventor, lived in New Haven, Connecticut, in the early 1890s. Little is known of her early life; it is not known who her parents were or where she was born. She was, however, one of the first African American women to receive a patent from the U.S. Patent Office in the nineteenth century. On 26 April 1892 Sarah Boone received her patent for an improved ironing board. As a result, Boone became the fourth African American woman to apply for and receive a patent for a new invention and the first person to receive a patent for an ironing board design.

Those who have written about Boone and her improved ironing board note that her invention was a significant improvement over existing devices. According to James Brodie, before Boone's "ironing board, this task normally required taking a plank and placing it between two chairs or simply using the dining table" (Brodie, 70). Women would place clothes across the plank and press them with an iron heated on the hearth. Biographers have also noted improvements to earlier ironing technologies found in Boone's design, including a narrow part for ironing sleeves, collapsible leg supports, and a padded cover.

Boone's patent application describes a complex design intended for a specific purpose. "My invention relates to an improvement in ironing-boards, the object being to produce a cheap, simple, convenient, and highly effective device, particularly adapted to be used in ironing the sleeves and bodies of ladies' garments" (U.S. Patent 473,653). Not only was Boone's ironing board particularly useful

for ironing sleeves, it was also specifically designed for ironing the curved sleeves and waistlines of nineteenth-century dresses.

According to her patent specifications, Boone's ironing board consisted of a narrow board with its edges curved so that the outside and inside seams of a sleeve could be fitted around it and more easily pressed. The curved edges of the ironing board were "most pronounced … at the 'elbow-point' … of the sleeve." In addition to the curved surface, Boone's ironing board was supported at one end by a fixed stand and "at its opposite end with a movable support attached to it by a hinge and arranged in line with the board." While the fixed stand provided support, the hinged support allowed the board to be easily adjusted for ironing the various seams of the same garment. This allowed one to efficiently and skillfully, iron the inner and outer curved seams of a garment's sleeves or waistline. Boone described the function of the adjustable support: "When the board is to be used for pressing inside seams, the movable support is turned down … and then co-operates with the transverse support in maintaining the board in this position. For ironing or pressing outside seams the board is reversed."

Boone's application also considered possible variations on its design and the flexibility of its usefulness. She recognized that the design intended to ease pressing of the seams of sleeves would be useful in working with curved seams wherever they occurred. By including alternative uses and variations on her design in the patent application, Boone protected herself against future patent infringements. Further reinforcing the breadth of her patent design, Boone notes in her application, "I would have it understood that I do not limit myself to the exact form herein shown and described, but hold myself at liberty to make such changes and alterations as fairly fall within the spirit and scope of my invention."

Through her invention and patenting of an improved ironing board, Sarah Boone made a historic contribution to American society and culture. While women's inventions over the centuries have ranged from household items to heating furnaces to missile guidance systems, many, like Sarah Boone's ironing board, fell within the range of domestic tasks often performed by women in their own homes or in the homes of an employer. Women, Boone among them, found creative ways to improve the efficiency and quality of their workdays when they invented new technologies or improved on existing ones.

FURTHER READING

Boone, Sarah. Letter of Application and Letter Patent No. 473,653 (26 Apr. 1892).

Baker, H. R. "The Negro Inventor," in *Twentieth Century Negro Literature*, ed. Daniel Wallace Culp (1902).

Brodie, James Michael. *Created Equal: The Lives and Ideas of Black American Innovators* (1993).

Sluby, Patricia C. "Black Women and Invention," *Sage: A Scholarly Journal on Black Women*, vol. 6, no. 2 (Fall 1989): 33–35.

Vare, Ethlie Ann, and Greg Ptacek. *Patently Female: From AZT to TV Dinners, Stories of Women Inventors and Their Breakthrough Ideas* (2002).

PAMELA C. EDWARDS

Boothe, Charles Octavius (13 June 1845–1924), Baptist minister, missionary, and author, was born in Mobile County, Alabama, to a Georgia-born slave woman belonging to and carried west by the slave owner Nathan Howard Sr. Little is known of Boothe's Georgian parents, but he proudly claimed that his great-grandmother and stepgrandfather were Africans. Boothe's description of his ancestors reflects his lifelong pride in his African heritage, but he was equally effusive about the spiritual influence that these Christian elders had on his life. His earliest recollections included his stepgrandfather's prayer life and singing of hymns and "the saintly face and pure life of my grandmother, to whom white and black went for prayer and for comfort in the times of their sorrows." These early familial Christian influences were further reinforced by attending a "Baptist church in the forest, where white and colored people sat together to commune and to wash each other's feet" (Boothe, 9).

An intelligent and precocious child, Boothe learned the alphabet at age three by studying imprinted letters on a tin plate. Later he gained literacy under the tutelage of teachers boarding in the home of Nathan Howard Jr., thus beginning a love affair with the written word, particularly the Bible. As a teenage slave, Boothe worked as an office boy in the Clark County, Mississippi, law office of Colonel James S. Terrel, an experience that afforded him even greater access to books. Clearly, Boothe encountered greater leniency from whites during slavery than most African Americans did; of James Terrel he could even write, "I think I can say that the Colonel and I really loved each other." However, Boothe was still a slave, and he was therefore exposed to "life's sterner facts," such as the apparent absence of a father and the separation from his remaining family upon moving to the home of Nathan Howard Jr. (Boothe, 10). Still, his early positive experiences with many educated whites and Christianity shaped the remainder of his life.

By 1860 a childhood filled with prayer and "refreshing seasons of love and joy" led Boothe to "an experience of grace which so strengthened me as to fix me on the side of the people of God" (Boothe, 10). Boothe followed his conversion with formal baptism in March 1866 and was ordained as a Baptist minister at the Saint Louis Street Church of Mobile, Alabama, in December 1868. Already engaged in educating his fellow African Americans as a teacher for the Freedmen's Bureau in 1867, Boothe's ordination cemented his course on a lifelong journey of ministry and public service. In 1877 Boothe served as the first pastor for the now-legendary Dexter Avenue Church of Montgomery, Alabama, turning a former slave trader's pen into a house of God. He was an early and active participant in the Colored Baptist Convention of Alabama, serving at various times as convention clerk, editorial assistant to the convention newspaper the *Baptist Pioneer*, instructor of ministers' and deacons' institutes, president of the denomination's Selma University, and state missionary.

At some point between 1877 and 1882 Boothe attended Meharry College in Nashville, Tennessee, where he studied medicine and most likely met and married Mattie Alice Roach, a Baptist minister's daughter and graduate of Roger Williams University of the same city. The thirty-five-year marriage complemented Boothe's ministry because Mattie was also an educator and served as the first president of the Colored Women's Christian Temperance Union of Alabama. The couple had eight children, of whom only four lived to maturity. Later Boothe served as pastor for the First Colored Baptist Church, Meridian, Mississippi, until he resigned in 1892.

Throughout his ministry Boothe urged African Americans to develop a "ripened manhood, out of which shall [grow] great enterprises, manned by unity, wisdom, wealth and righteousness" (Boothe, 267). Although Boothe described slavery as harmful and "dark times" (Boothe, 13), he also believed that God used whites to elevate African Americans into Christian civilization and unabashedly praised the achievements of white society as goals worthy of emulation. Accordingly, Boothe did not hesitate to build relationships across the color line and worked closely with the white Alabama Baptist Convention and the American Baptist Home Missionary Society at various times from the 1880s until 1917. In fact, Boothe dedicated his 1890 theological primer, *Plain Theology for Plain People*, to the memory of a dear white friend and fellow Christian laborer, the Reverend Harry Woodsmall of Indiana. In return, whites praised Boothe, describing him as "a graceful speaker, a gifted preacher" whose "services have been of distinguished value" (Cathcart, 114–115). Boothe's appeal to whites in part reflected his willingness openly to criticize African Americans for behavior that he deemed unchristian or counterproductive, a trait that he shared with BOOKER T. WASHINGTON. Indeed, he embraced Washington's philosophy of racial progress begetting civic inclusion and worked closely with Washington as a teacher at Tuskegee Institute's Phelps Hall Bible Training School beginning in 1893.

Although Boothe grossly misjudged white willingness to accept African Americans as equals, he believed that he sought the best for his race. Boothe saw his chastisement of blacks as a wake-up call, and he fashioned himself as a teacher who demanded much from his most promising pupils. Calling for greater race pride, his *Cyclopedia of the Colored Baptists of Alabama: Their Leaders and Their Work* (1895) reflects this tone in declaring, "Because we made it to the top of one mountain, we could therefore make it to the top of another" (Boothe, 54). Self-criticism aside, Boothe also challenged white Alabamians' bigotry and denial of African American opportunities. In 1901 he joined Washington in challenging the Alabama Constitutional Convention's intention to disfranchise African American voters, and in 1913 he investigated the treatment of black prisoners in state camps and mines. He also served his community as a practicing physician in Birmingham and as a teacher at Alabama A&M University. For these reasons he remained a valued, multitalented member of his community until his death in Detroit.

FURTHER READING

Boothe, Charles Octavius. *The Cyclopedia of the Colored Baptists of Alabama: Their Leaders and Their Work* (1895).

Cathcart, William, ed. "Boothe, Rev. C. O.," in *The Baptist Encyclopedia: A Dictionary of the Doctrines, Ordinances, Usages, Confessions of Faith, Sufferings, Labors, and Successes, and of the General History of the Baptist Denomination in all Lands, with Numerous Biographical Sketches of Distinguished American and Foreign Baptists, and a Supplement* (1883).

Crowther, Edward R. "Charles Octavius Boothe: An Alabama Apostle of 'Uplift,'" *Journal of Negro History* 78, no. 2 (Spring 1993): 110–116.

Crowther, Edward R. "Interracial Cooperative Missions among Blacks by Alabama Baptists, 1868–1882," *Journal of Negro History* 80, no. 3 (Summer 1995): 131–139.

DANIEL L. FOUNTAIN

Borde, Percival (31 Dec. 1922–31 Aug. 1979), Afro-Caribbean dancer and choreographer, was born Percival Sebastian Borde in Port of Spain, Trinidad, the son of George Paul Borde, a veterinarian, and Augustine Francis Lambie. Borde grew up in Trinidad, where he finished secondary schooling at Queens Royal College and took an appointment with the Trinidad Railway Company. Around 1942 he began formal research on Afro-Caribbean dance and performed with the Little Carib Dance Theatre. In 1949 he married Joyce Guppy, with whom he had one child. The year of their divorce is unknown.

Borde took easily to dancing and the study of dance as a function of Caribbean culture. In the early 1950s he acted as director of the Little Carib Theatre in Trinidad. In 1953 he met the noted American anthropologist and dancer PEARL PRIMUS, who was conducting field research in Caribbean folklore. Primus convinced Borde to immigrate to the United States as a dancer and teacher of West Indian dance at her New York City school. Borde developed courses in traditional Caribbean dance forms for the Pearl Primus School and began performing with the Pearl Primus Dance Company. Shortly thereafter he and Primus were married (date unknown). The couple had one child.

Performing success with Primus's modern dance company brought Borde appearances on television and the popular stage. He appeared on Broadway as the African Chief in Joyce Cary's 1956 play *Mr. Johnson*. In 1956 and 1957 he toured with the Primus dance company throughout Europe. Borde brought his own self-named dance troupe to the St. Marks Playhouse in New York City on 23 September 1958. He performed his own works and dances created for him by Primus, who acted as the artistic director of the company. John Martin, dance critic for the *New York Times* and a longtime supporter of Primus's dance anthropology, called the concert an "unusually well unified and atmospheric presentation, unpretentious in manner but with a wealth of knowledge behind it." Raves also came from the

African American press, and Borde's arrival as a leading male figure in Afro-dance was confirmed. In 1959 the separate Borde and Primus companies combined to form the Pearl Primus and Percival Borde Dance Company.

Borde's performances always included ethnographic dance characterizations of several African American archetypes. For instance, his four-part 1958 program titled *Earth Magician* included portrayals of an Aztec warrior, a giant Watusi, a Yoruba chief, and a Shango priest. Borde performed sections of this program throughout his career, honing the authenticity of his dance movements through research and study. His performance style was consistently described as dynamic yet elegant, his strong physicality offset by his striking good looks. Martin described him as "light and easy of movement, with strength, admirable control and authority."

In 1959 Borde and Primus toured Africa and performed in Ethiopia, Ghana, Mali, Kenya, Nigeria, and Liberia, which held special import for the couple. It was in Liberia that Borde was named Jangbanolima, or "a man who lives to dance," by Chief Sondifu Sonni during an official adoption ritual. Also in 1959 Borde and Primus became the directors of the Performing Arts Center of Monrovia, Liberia. They remained in Liberia until November 1961. During this time Borde wrote articles for the *Liberian Age* and was active in the Liberian Chamber of Commerce. He was awarded the Gold Medal of Liberia for his work in the dance of the African diaspora.

After returning to the United States, Borde produced *Talking Drums of Africa*, an education-in-the-schools program sponsored by the New York State Department of Education. He was active in the Congress on Research in Dance, a dance scholars' organization, and served on its board of directors. He also continued to work in the theater, serving as the resident choreographer for the Negro Ensemble Company's 1969 season.

Borde completed a bachelor's degree (1975) and coursework toward a master's degree at the School of the Arts at New York University. He taught movement courses there, at Columbia University Teachers College, and at the State University of New York at Binghamton, where he was an associate professor of theater arts and black studies. Borde's highly popular courses offered participatory, dance-based studies of Afro-Caribbean culture, which emphasized the connections between dance, ritual, and everyday life. He often reminded

his students, "Just as one should prepare oneself to enter a temple, one should prepare to dance" (*Wichita Eagle*, 20 Aug. 1969).

Borde died of a heart attack backstage at the Perry Street Theater in New York City immediately after performing "Impinyuza," the strutting Watusi solo he had danced for more than two decades.

Borde's masculine stage presence and dynamic performance style helped widen interest in concert African American dance forms. His work continued the efforts of the dancer-choreographers Primus and KATHERINE DUNHAM in the insertion of ceremonial, anthropologically researched dance on the concert stage. After his death, Primus characterized Borde as "the outstanding exponent of African influences on Caribbean culture."

FURTHER READING
The Dance Collection of the New York Library for the Performing Arts at Lincoln Center holds a file of newspaper reviews of Borde's performances. The New York Public Library's Schomburg Center for Research in Black Culture holds listings of materials from the Black Press.
Obituary: *New York Times*, 5 Sept. 1979.
This entry is taken from the *American National Biography* and is published here with the permission of the American Council of Learned Societies.

THOMAS F. DEFRANTZ

Bostic, Earl (25 Apr. 1913–28 Oct. 1965), alto saxophonist, was born in Tulsa, Oklahoma. Details about his parents are unknown. Bostic played clarinet in school and saxophone with the local Boy Scouts. By 1930 or 1931 when he left Tulsa to tour with Terrence Holder's Twelve Clouds of Joy, Bostic was already a saxophone virtuoso. Fellow saxophonist Buddy Tate recalls that Bostic was asked to join the band because of his dexterity and maturity as a soloist. Holder's band members then informally tested Bostic's ability to read difficult music: skipping the opportunity to rehearse, Bostic counted off an impossibly fast tempo and played the piece on first sight with such skill that only he and the drummer made it through to the end. "We let him alone after that," Tate said.

Sometime in the early 1930s Bostic spent a year at Creighton University in Omaha, Nebraska, playing by day in an ROTC band and by night with jazz groups. He was briefly a member of BENNIE

MOTEN's band early in 1933. Later that year he enrolled at Xavier University in New Orleans to study music theory, harmony, and various instruments; again he played with military bands at school and jazz groups in the city. One year later he left to work mainly with lesser-known bands, although in 1935–1936 he played and arranged for a band led by Charlie Creath and FATE MARABLE.

After moving to New York at the beginning of 1938, Bostic joined DON REDMAN's band in April, played briefly with Edgar Hayes's orchestra, and then led his own band at Small's Paradise in Harlem intermittently from 1939 to the early 1940s. In this group he occasionally played trumpet, guitar, or baritone sax in addition to his alto sax. During these years he also contributed his best-known composition and arrangement, "Let Me Off Uptown," to Gene Krupa's big band, which recorded it in 1941, and he was a member of HOT LIPS PAGE's group in 1941 and again around 1943. From June 1943 to August 1944 Bostic played and wrote for LIONEL HAMPTON's big band. He left to resume leading a group at Small's. In September 1944 he recorded several sides with Page, including "Good for Stompin'" and "Fish for Supper." His solos on these recordings reveal an alto saxophonist with a full-bodied tone, a precise articulation of notes, and considerable technique, but an uncertain sense of melodic architecture, with the result that sometimes he relied on stiff, étude-like figurations. Ironically, in light of what was to come, the worst of these solos was in a blues piece, "You Need Coachin'," which finds Bostic so busy with technique that he sounds out of touch with characteristic blues timbres, melodies, and emotions.

For the remainder of his career Bostic led bands. In the mid- to late 1940s he changed his stylistic orientation by adopting a ferocious, gritty, vocalized tone; by playing simple, singable melodies—although many tunes still left room for improvising; by using the catchy dance rhythms of contemporary rhythm and blues; and by basing the group's sound on a twangy electric guitar and smooth-toned vibraphone—the vibes perhaps inspired by his year with Hampton, but used in a less aggressive style. Early recordings in this vein were done for the Gotham label, including "That's the Groovy Thing" (1946), "8:45 Stomp," and "Temptation" (probably late 1947). After signing with the King label (which reissued these titles) in 1949, the new approach came to fruition with a recording of "Flamingo," which held the top position on the rhythm and blues popularity chart for twenty weeks in 1951. Other hit records included "Sleep" (also 1951), "Moonglow" and "Ain't Misbehavin'" (both 1952), and "Blue Skies" (1954); incidentally, the 1952 sides included a young JOHN COLTRANE in the band.

Bostic toured the country, and it is a testimony to his unusually high level of success in rhythm and blues and jazz that for several years he was able to take six-week vacations. In 1956 he suffered a serious heart attack that, apart from recordings, rendered him inactive. He resumed touring in 1959, but he soon became ill again. After years of semiretirement, he began an engagement in October 1965 in Rochester, New York, only to die there two days after suffering another heart attack.

Tate summarized Bostic's career: "Oh man, he could read.... He was a virtuoso.... He could play … way out, progressive, but he made it big, just playing the melody. That's what people wanted to hear." It might be added that, in pursuing this path, Bostic discovered a musicality that had sometimes been lacking in the earlier part of his career. By the mid-1980s Bostic was felt to be a "forgotten" man (Schonfield), but with the reissue in the late 1980s and 1990s of much of his work for the King label, it is possible for new generations of listeners to discover his best music.

FURTHER READING

Cage, Ruth. "Rhythm & Blues Notes," *Down Beat*, 29 Dec. 1954.

Chilton, John. *Who's Who of Jazz: Storyville to Swing Street*, 4th ed. (1985).

Schonfield, Victor. "The Forgotten Ones: Earl Bostic," *Jazz Journal International* 37 (Nov. 1984): 10–11.

Obituary: *Down Beat*, 2 Dec. 1965.

This entry is taken from the *American National Biography* and is published here with the permission of the American Council of Learned Societies.

BARRY KERNFELD

Boston, Absalom (1785–6 June 1855), prosperous businessman, whaling captain, and community leader, whose court case against Nantucket led to the integration of the public schools, was a member of one of the largest and most influential black families on the island. His father was Seneca Boston, a manumitted slave, who was a self-employed weaver. His mother was a Wampanoag Indian named Thankful Micah. They had four sons and one daughter. Absalom Boston, the third-born, went to sea, as did many of Nantucket's young men, signing onto the whale ship *Thomas* in 1809 when he was twenty-four. Little is known about his early education. Anna Gardner, in her memoir *Harvest Gleanings*, mentions him visiting her family and hints that it may have been her mother, Hannah Macy Gardner, who taught the young man to read.

Shortly before he went to sea, Boston married his first wife, Mary Spywood, about whom little is known. He returned to land because of the deaths of his father and his eldest brother, Freeborn; he was left the sole supporter of the family, which included his mother, Thankful; his brother's widow, Mary; and her two young children. Boston's wife died in 1813, leaving him with four-year-old Charles. In 1814 he married a widow, Phebe Spriggins, née Williams, in the South Congregational Church (later Unitarian), as there were no separate black churches on the island at that time. Their union produced three more children: an unnamed baby who died at birth, Henry, and Caroline.

Two years later he returned to the sea. This time he went as Captain Boston, the captain and master of the whale ship *Industry* with an all-black crew. This was a rare event in maritime history. The landmark voyage became the subject of a song that included the lyrics: "AF Boston was commander and him we will obey.... " It ends with the promise that, should Boston ever captain another ship, the crew would sign up again (Nantucket Historical Association Archives). Whaling was a risky business, however, and the *Industry*'s voyage proved a financial failure, forcing Boston to auction his ship upon returning to Nantucket. He remained on land for the rest of his life, although he continued to invest in whaling ventures.

The failure of the *Industry* was only a temporary setback for the enterprising Boston, who continued to prosper on Nantucket and became a successful businessman and entrepreneur. By 1812 town records show him venturing into real estate, a business in which he was active throughout his life, successfully buying and selling properties in the segregated community of New Guinea, sometimes known as Newtown, where most of the African Americans of Nantucket lived. He also made mortgage loans to others in the New Guinea community, and when he turned thirty-five, he was granted a license for a public house and inn in New Guinea. His inn was frequented by transient sailors passing through the island. His wealth enabled him to contribute to the improvement of life for the African American community on the

island. Around 1825 he helped found the island's first black church, which still stands on the corner of York and Pleasant streets. The African Meeting House, as it is now called, was also used as a one-room school for black children, and the trustees rented the building to the town to use a primary school until 1838.

Absalom's second wife died in 1826 at thirty-two years of age, leaving him once again with motherless children. He remarried within a year, this time to Hannah Cook of Dartmouth, Massachusetts, and together they had five more children, Phebe Ann, Absalom Jr., Oliver, Thomas, and Sarah.

Boston continued to prosper. In 1827 he paid for an ad in the local newspaper offering a reward for the recovery of a French-made silver watch, and in 1833 the local newspaper reported that a "gang of foreign vagabonds" had burgled his house and taken forty to fifty dollars in silver coins; few of the island's blacks would have such money readily at hand. His influence in the community grew with his affluence; a notice in the local paper in 1840 listed him as "attorney" for the executor of a will and in 1844 he served as the executor for the will of an Abel Norcross, a mariner. When the whale ship *Loper*, with an all-black crew under the command of a white captain, Obed Starbuck, returned from a particularly successful voyage in the Pacific in 1830, Boston led a triumphant parade through the main streets of Nantucket. He also became increasingly active in reform and politics. In 1826, he placed a notice in the local paper that Jacob Perry, at the time a minister and a teacher at the African School, would deliver a "discourse against slavery" at the Meeting House. In 1839 Boston became the first African American on Nantucket to run for public office, one of thirty to run for the five-member board of selectmen. He also ran to be a fire warden, but he failed to win either position.

An eight-year battle began in 1838 to integrate the public schools after seventeen-year-old EUNICE Ross qualified to attend the all-white high school but was denied entrance. There were frequent but unsuccessful attempts at the annual town meetings during the time period to integrate the public schools. The trustees of the African Meeting House refused to let the town continue to use their facility as a primary school, protesting the exclusion of black children from the town's upper-level schools. This forced the school committee to build a new primary school in New Guinea. (It was during this time that Boston made his unsuccessful bid for the board of selectmen.) During the controversy, the library closed its doors to blacks and to abolition meetings. In 1842 the New Guinea community wrote an address to the town, which was printed in the local newspapers, as well as in the *Liberator*, complaining "that for a mere accident, the difference of complexion, we are denied the right of privilege of education in common with our fellow citizens; we must pronounce it to be *unkind, unjust.*" That summer, emotions connected with school integration resulted in an explosive anti-slavery convention that culminated in riots, necessitating visiting abolitionist speakers, including William Lloyd Garrison and CHARLES LENOX REMOND, to leave the island.

That same year, Nantucket voted to build a third grammar school not far from the New Guinea neighborhood, and controversy intensified as to whether black children, including Boston's daughter Phebe Ann, would be admitted to the new school. Boston put his name up for the school committee that year with nine other black Nantucketers, none of whom was elected. He continued to seek public office almost every year during the school integration controversy. He ran for assessor in 1843, for the school committee again in 1844, for highway surveyor in 1845, and for fire warden again in 1846. He won none of these elections.

In 1843 abolitionists were elected to the school committee, and they integrated the public schools despite a vote at the annual town meeting directing maintenance of the status quo in the schools. Anecdotal evidence suggests that Phebe Ann Boston and others were admitted to integrated grammar schools. The integration was short-lived, however, as the abolitionists lost their positions on the school committee at the next annual town meeting. That newly elected school committee forcibly expelled black students from all the schools, except the one that had been built on York Street. The students were humiliated, called to the front of the class and made to leave in the middle of the school day. With Absalom Boston as one of their leaders, the New Guinea community began a two-year boycott of the public schools. There is some evidence that a classroom was set up during that time by local abolitionists, who pressed for school integration at the next annual town meeting. Failing there, the integrationists turned to the state legislature for redress. Boston, along with his wife and oldest daughter, signed one of the petitions that eventually led to the passage of a law in 1845, stating that any student unlawfully excluded from a public school had the right to recover damages in court.

Boston, on behalf of Phebe Ann, now seventeen, began legal procedures against the town based on the new legislation. She had applied to one of the town's upper-level schools—it is unclear whether grammar school or high school—in June 1845 and had been refused admittance. A special town meeting was convened in September 1845, according to the Nantucket town records, "to see what order the town will take, in relation to an action brought by Phebe Ann Boston, by her Father … for depriving her of the advantage of Public School Instruction." The case went from the Court of Common Pleas to the Supreme Judicial Court, which caused a delay of almost a year.

In the meantime, the Great Fire of 1846 destroyed much of the downtown of Nantucket, devastating the economy of the island, as the wharves and most of Main Street went up in smoke. Luckily for the New Guinea community, the fire did not make it as far as their neighborhood, although several black businesses were destroyed in the center of town. The fire may have changed the voters' attitude regarding school integration on Nantucket. At the next annual town meeting, they rejected the segregationist town officers and voted in a solid abolitionist school committee. Their first act was to reintegrate the schools. Boston dropped his lawsuit, and Phebe Ann was admitted to an integrated school. Unfortunately, in 1849, not long after completing her education, she died at age twenty-one from dysentery.

Her father retired from public activities. He had lost seven of his ten children and two of his three wives. One son, Oliver, a mariner, enlisted in the navy during the Civil War. Another son, Thomas, lived in Boston and Washington, D.C., supporting himself in a variety of ways, from giving music lessons to banking. At the age of sixty-nine, Absalom Boston died in Nantucket in 1855, the year the commonwealth legally integrated public education. He left a large estate valued at more than one thousand dollars, including several houses, a shop, and an inn.

FURTHER READING

Karttunen, Francis. *The Other Islanders: People Who Pulled Nantucket's Oars* (2005).

Nantucket Historical Association Archives.

White, Barbara. *The African School: The African School and the Integration of Nantucket Public Schools, 1825–1847* (1978).

BARBARA A. WHITE

Bottoms, Lawrence Wendell (9 Apr. 1908–1 Sept. 1994), pastor, theologian, and churchman, was born in Selma, Alabama, the son of Wilbur McDonald Bottoms, a teacher, and Gussie Adolphus Shivers. While his mother's family had been Methodists, his father was a Reformed Presbyterian who graduated from Wilberforce College in Ohio and answered a call to teach at the Knox Academy in Selma. This school was operated by the Reformed Presbyterian Church of Selma, and it was upon taking this post that Wilbur Bottoms met and married Shivers. Lawrence was raised in a highly unusual situation, for neither the school nor the church was segregated. Whites who taught at the school also lived on the school property and attended the church as members alongside African American teachers and other members in the congregation. At times the church had a white pastor, and at other times the pastor was African American.

Lawrence continued his education in Pennsylvania, first at Geneva College from 1929 to 1931 and then at the Reformed Presbyterian Theological Seminary in Pittsburgh from 1932 to 1935. During his college years, Bottoms came to believe that the key to racial reconciliation lay in a strong sense of personhood with a firm identity that began inwardly, that rose above culture, and that was not imposed by others. During his time as a seminary student, Bottoms married Elizabeth Loutisha Stallworth, a schoolteacher from Selma, in September 1933. Reverend Bottoms was licensed to preach in May 1934, and even before graduation from the seminary in 1935 he often returned to Selma to fill the Reformed Presbyterian pulpit there. He was ordained in November 1936. Bottoms left the Selma church and the Reformed Presbyterian denomination in 1938 and became pastor of Grace Presbyterian Church in Louisville, Kentucky. Bottoms's new pulpit had the distinction of being the only African American church in the Louisville Presbytery, a regional division of the Presbyterian Church, U.S. (PCUS), denomination, more commonly known as the Southern Presbyterian Church, which remained crippled by the legacy of segregation. Bottoms was pastor of Grace Presbyterian until 1949. During these years, he and his wife raised their four children.

For many years Bottoms worked for change within the denomination. From 1953 to 1964 he was secretary of the Department of Negro Work for the PCUS. He was the first African American moderator of the Presbytery of Louisville and the first African American moderator of the Synod of Kentucky, serving in 1963 and 1964. He served as assistant secretary of the Division of Home Mission, Board of Church Extension (PCUS), from 1964 to 1966. From 1966 to 1969 he served as associate secretary of the Division of Education and Research, Board of Church Extension (PCUS), and from 1969 to 1973 he was coordinator of the Support Services, Board of National Ministries (PCUS). As pastor of the Oakhurst Presbyterian Church in Decatur, Georgia, from 1973 to 1975, Bottoms became the first African American to serve as moderator of the General Assembly of the Southern Presbyterian Church. Elected on the first ballot in a three-way race for the denomination's top leadership position, he won that election by an overwhelming majority. As a young commissioner to the assembly, he was not allowed to eat in the dining hall because of his race; however, some thirty-five years later he was widely received as one of the church's key leaders.

In his final years, Bottoms served as president of the Christian Council of Metropolitan Atlanta (1980) and as associate pastor of the Morningside Presbyterian Church. Bottoms received the 1960 Distinguished Service Award from Geneva College, honorary doctor of divinity degrees from Davis and Elkins College, Stillman College, and Oglethorpe University, the doctor of humane letters from Tarkio College, and the doctor of laws degree from Geneva College. During his ministry Bottoms helped to plant African American congregations throughout the South. By 1993 he was listed as honorably retired, and he died in 1994 while residing in the Atlanta area.

FURTHER READING

Brackenridge, R. Douglas. "Lawrence W. Bottoms: The Church, Black Presbyterians and Personhood," *Journal of Presbyterian History* (Spring 1978).

Presbyterian Church (U.S.A.). *All-Black Governing Bodies: The History and Contributions of All-Black Governing Bodies in the Predecessor Denominations of the Presbyterian Church (U.S.A.)* (1996).

WAYNE SPARKMAN

Bouchet, Edward Alexander (15 Sept. 1852–28 Oct. 1918), educator and scientist, was born in New Haven, Connecticut, the youngest of four children of William Francis Bouchet, a janitor, and Susan Cooley. Part of New Haven's black community, the Bouchets were active members of the Temple Street Congregational Church, which was a stopping point for fugitive slaves along the Underground Railroad. During the 1850s and 1860s New Haven had only three schools that black children could attend. Edward was enrolled in the Artisan Street Colored School, a small (only thirty seats), ungraded school with one teacher, Sarah Wilson, who played a crucial role in nurturing Bouchet's academic abilities and his desire to learn.

In 1868 Bouchet was accepted into Hopkins Grammar School, a private institution that prepared young men for the classical and scientific departments at Yale College. He graduated first in his class at Hopkins and four years later, when he graduated from Yale in 1874, he ranked sixth in a class of 124. On the basis of this exceptional performance, Bouchet became the first black student in the nation to be nominated to Phi Beta Kappa. In the fall of 1874 he returned to Yale with the encouragement and financial support of Alfred Cope, a Philadelphia philanthropist. In 1876 Bouchet successfully completed his dissertation on the new subject of geometrical optics, becoming the first black person to earn a Ph.D. from an American university as well as the sixth American of any race to earn a Ph.D. in Physics.

In 1876 Bouchet moved to Philadelphia to teach at the Institute for Colored Youth (ICY), the city's only high school for black students. ICY had been founded by the Society of Friends because African Americans had historically been denied admittance to Philadelphia's white high schools. Members of the ICY board of managers like Cope, Bouchet's Yale benefactor, believed firmly in the value of a classical education and were convinced that blacks were capable of unlimited educational achievement. In 1874 Cope had provided forty thousand dollars to establish a new science program at ICY, and soon thereafter recruited Bouchet to teach and administer the program.

Although Philadelphia was as segregated as any southern city, it offered a supportive environment for a man of Bouchet's abilities. The city's black population, the largest in the North, had made considerable progress in education during the decades preceding his arrival. As early as 1849 half the city's black population was active in one or more of the many literary societies established by the black community. After the Civil War the ICY played an important role in training the thousands of black teachers that were needed throughout the country to provide freedmen with the education they sought.

Bouchet joined St. Thomas's Church, the oldest black Episcopal church in the country, served on the vestry, and was church secretary for many years. The bishop also appointed Bouchet to be a lay reader, which gave Bouchet the opportunity to take a more active part in church services. Bouchet took his scientific interests and abilities beyond the ICY into the broader black community, giving public lectures on various scientific topics. He was also a member of the Franklin Institute, a foundation for the promotion of the mechanic arts, chartered in 1824. Bouchet maintained his ties with Yale through the local chapter of the Yale Alumni Association, attending all meetings and annual dinners.

By the turn of the century, a new set of ICY managers emerged, more receptive to the industrial education philosophy of BOOKER T. WASHINGTON than to academic education for blacks. In their efforts to redirect the school's programs, the all-white board fired all the teachers, including Bouchet, in 1902 and replaced them with instructors committed to industrial education.

Over the next fourteen years Bouchet held five or six positions in different parts of the country. Until November 1903 he taught math and physics in St. Louis at Sumner High School, the first high school for blacks west of the Mississippi. He then spent seven months as the business manager for the Provident Hospital in St. Louis (November 1903–May 1904), followed by a term as a United States inspector of customs at the Louisiana Purchase Exposition held in St. Louis (June 1904–October 1906). In October 1906 Bouchet secured a teaching and administrative position at St. Paul's Normal and Industrial School in Lawrenceville, Virginia. In 1908 he became principal of Lincoln High School of Gallipolis, Ohio, where he remained until 1913, when an attack of arteriosclerosis compelled him to resign and return to New Haven. Undocumented information has Bouchet returning to teaching at Bishop College in Marshall, Texas, but illness once again forced him to retire in 1916. He returned to New Haven, where he died in his boyhood home at 94 Bradley Street. He had never married or had children.

Bouchet had the misfortune of being a talented and educated black man who lived in a segregated society that refused to recognize his particular genius and thus hindered him from conducting scientific research and achieving professional recognition. Segregation produced isolation as Bouchet spent his career in high schools with limited resources and poorly equipped labs. Even with Bouchet's superior qualifications, no white college would have considered him for a position on its faculty. Completely excluded from any means of utilizing his education and talent, Bouchet languished in obscurity. The ascendance of industrial education also served to limit his opportunities, since his academic training in the natural sciences made him unattractive as a candidate at the increasing number of black institutions that adopted a vocational curriculum.

The absurdity of the claims made by some proponents of vocational education concerning the innate inability of blacks to undertake an academic education could not have been more obvious to Bouchet. From his own accomplishments and those of his students, it never occurred to Bouchet that blacks could not master the fields of classical education or excel in science. In the face of personal setbacks and a changing public mood on black education, Bouchet maintained his standards and never altered his educational ideals.

FURTHER READING
Some of Bouchet's writings and those of his classmates are available in the Yale University Manuscripts and Archives, Sterling Memorial Library.
"Edward A. Bouchet, Ph.D." *Negro History Bulletin* 31 (Dec. 1968).
Mickens, Ronald E. "Edward A. Bouchet: The First Black Ph.D." *Black Collegian* 8, no. 4 (Mar.–Apr. 1978).
Perkins, Linda M. *Fanny Jackson Coppin and the Institute for Colored Youth, 1865–1902* (1987).
Obituary: *Bulletin of Yale University, Obituary Record of Yale Graduates, 1918–1919*, no. 11 (1919).
This entry is taken from the *American National Biography* and is published here with the permission of the American Council of Learned Societies.

H. KENNETH BECHTEL

Bouey, Harrison N. (4 Aug. 1849–1909), educator, clergyman, missionary, and community leader, was born in Columbia County, Georgia, the son of Lewis Bouey, a carpenter, and Maria, a cook. The couple had no other children. Bouey spent his early life in Augusta, Georgia, where he was apprenticed to learn the painter's trade and attended night school. He passed the examination to become licensed as a teacher and taught in the public schools of Augusta for two years. From 1870 to 1873 he attended the Baptist Theological School in Augusta, an institution that later moved to Atlanta and in 1913 was renamed Morehouse College. Upon graduation he moved to Ridge Springs, South Carolina, where he became principal of a school and taught there for two years.

Bouey's work as an educational and community leader brought him into politics in 1874. He was elected to a two-year term as probate judge in Edgefield County, South Carolina. He moved from Ridge Springs to the county seat, Edgefield Court House, where he took a call as minister to the Macedonia Baptist Church.

In 1876 white Democrats in South Carolina determined to take back control of local and state offices from black and white Republicans. Edgefield County in particular served as a model for radical extralegal actions by former Confederates to defeat the county's black majority. An all-out battle between black militiamen and members of white rifle clubs in Hamburg, on the Georgia border of Edgefield County, in early July 1876 left eight men dead, seven of whom were black, and launched a frenzy of legal and political activity to prepare for the fall elections. More than seven hundred armed and mounted Democrats wearing red shirts rode through the streets of Edgefield County to intimidate black voters before the election, despite the presence of two companies of federal troops. On voting day, 7 November, hundreds of black voters were turned away from the polls, and when votes were counted, there were two thousand more ballots than eligible voters in the county.

Bouey claimed he was elected as county sheriff but was counted out through election fraud. The Republican Party contested the elections in Edgefield and neighboring Barnwell and Laurens counties. Tension and confusion followed the corrupt elections until April 1877 when President Rutherford B. Hayes withdrew federal troops, finally ending Reconstruction in the state. Black Republicans felt betrayed by the federal government for leaving them at the mercies of white Democrats. Given this situation, it is no surprise that some black leaders, such as Bouey, began talk of leaving not just South Carolina or the South, but the United States.

Claiming to speak for a large number of black families in Edgefield County who wished to immigrate to Liberia, on 23 May 1877 Bouey wrote to the American Colonization Society office in Washington, D.C., and to Bishop HENRY MCNEAL TURNER in Atlanta, the black leader most associated with the back-to-Africa movement. The American Colonization Society had founded

Liberia to receive black American expatriates. Black South Carolinians in several other counties also began to organize for an exodus to Liberia. Later in the spring Bouey traveled to Charleston to serve as a juror in the United States District Court, and there he linked up with other black leaders interested in African migration, including B. F. Porter, the pastor of Morris Brown African Methodist Episcopal (AME) Church. In July they formed the Liberian Exodus Joint Stock Steamship Company, selling stock at ten dollars a share to raise money for the expedition. Porter was named the president and Bouey the secretary of the company. By early 1878 the company had raised six thousand dollars and in February purchased a sailing ship, the bark *Azor*. The ship was consecrated at a ceremony in March in Charleston attended by five thousand people, including black dignitaries such as MARTIN ROBISON DELANY and Bishop Turner.

On 21 April the *Azor* sailed from Charleston, carrying Harrison Bouey and 274 other emigrants. The largest number hailed from Edgefield, Barnwell, and Clarendon counties, with several others from Charleston and east central Georgia. By most standards the expedition was a failure. The ship was quickly overloaded, so 175 passengers were left on the dock to await a second voyage, which never materialized. The officers had stored insufficient food and water for the monthlong voyage, and poor diet and cramped quarters took a toll; twenty-three passengers died and were buried at sea, and six more died soon after their arrival in Africa. After leaving the emigrants in the capital, Monrovia, the *Azor* returned to Charleston empty of freight but with plenty of debt. The company never made another voyage, and the *Azor* was sold in November 1879 to pay the company's remaining debts. In the next month eighteen of the emigrants returned to South Carolina, bringing stories of extreme poverty of the emigrants who remained in Liberia to add to the bad publicity for the endeavor. Several of the *Azor* passengers settled in Royesville, to the north of Monrovia, and some prospered in Liberia.

Bouey labored as a Baptist minister in Monrovia, traveled throughout the country to organize the National Baptist Convention, and did some missionary work in the western part of Liberia among the Gola people. He returned to the United States in 1881 and served as the agent of the Liberian Baptist Convention, working to promote missions to Africa among the black Baptist churches.

In April 1882 he married Laura P. Logan, of Charleston, South Carolina, and the couple lived in Selma, Alabama, where Bouey worked as a Sunday School missionary, financial agent of Selma University, and then corresponding secretary for the Alabama Baptist Mission Board. He later served as associate editor and business manager of the *Baptist Pioneer*, published in Selma. He also served on the board for the national Baptist Foreign Mission Convention. He returned to Liberia as a missionary sometime shortly after 1902 and died there in 1909.

FURTHER READING

Foner, Eric. *Freedom's Lawmakers: A Directory of Black Officeholders during Reconstruction* (1993).

Tindall, George Brown. *South Carolina Negroes, 1877–1900* (1952).

Williams, Walter L. *Black Americans and the Evangelization of Africa, 1877–1900* (1982).

KENNETH C. BARNES

Bousfield, Midian Othello (22 Aug. 1885–16 Feb. 1948), physician, was born in Tipton, Missouri, the son of Willard Hayman Bousfield, a barber, and Cornelia Catherine Gilbert. From the start Bousfield exemplified what W. E. B. DuBois meant by the term "talented tenth." Awarded a bachelor's degree from the University of Kansas in 1907, Bousfield earned his M.D. two years later from Northwestern University in Chicago and did an internship at Howard University's Freedmen's Hospital in 1910. He was lured back to Kansas City for his initial medical practice following an unlikely adventure in Brazil, where, when medical prospects dimmed, he took up prospecting for gold. Bousfield soon felt a need for a larger stage, and in 1914, with his new bride, Maudelle Tanner Brown, he shifted his base to Chicago. There he embarked on a career of astounding breadth that took him to leadership positions in the business, health, medical, philanthropic, educational, and military worlds of Chicago and beyond. He and his wife had one child.

Bousfield's first success was in the black business sphere. Perhaps perceiving the larger influence of a corporate career, in 1919 he gave up an affiliation with a fledgling black railroad union and helped found the Liberty Life Insurance Company, remaining on as medical director and vice president. A decade later, as president, he guided the company through a merger and a reorganization as the Supreme Liberty Life Insurance Company. For the next four years he led the new firm as both medical director and chair of its executive committee.

But the worlds of health, medicine, and philanthropy absorbed most of Bousfield's energy, and his primary interests there lay in improving the opportunities and quality of black physicians and the health care of black citizens, especially the underserved majority in the South. His great chance to promote those interests came in 1934, when the Chicago-based Julius Rosenwald Fund named him its director of Negro health.

Although the appointment was due mostly to Bousfield's stature as a business leader, the post itself was largely one he created by cultivating the Rosenwald medical director, Michael M. Davis, and convincing him of the need and possibilities for Rosenwald involvement in black health issues. Largely at Bousfield's initiative, the fund (both before and after 1934) launched projects aimed at improving black hospitals and nurses' training and creating openings for black doctors within southern health agencies, in part by using the lure of Rosenwald money for their initial salaries. By 1942, when the fund ceased operations, the color line in southern public medicine had been substantially breeched and the black profession greatly strengthened.

For Bousfield 1933–1934 proved a take-off year apart from the Rosenwald post. It also brought him the presidency of the all-black National Medical Association, making him for a time the leading spokesman of black medicine. Moreover the year provided him an influential, inside forum from which to exert that prestige to good ends through the annual meeting of the American Public Health Association (APHA), where Bousfield became its first black speaker. He did not mince words. It was simply "inconceivable," Bousfield said, that anything but racism could account for the fact that health officers could "so complacently review, year after year, the unfavorable vital statistical reports of one-tenth of the population and make no special effort to correct them" (210). Members must shed their racist blinders and start solving blacks' health problems, using black professionals as partners. For the first time the APHA got the African American perspective and learned to its surprise that "darky" dialect stories and racial disdain raised barriers to black community participation in vital health work. Thanks in part to Bousfield, a new racial sensitivity among health professionals had begun.

Despite such bluntness, Bousfield never lost his ties to white leadership. Whether this was due to his reputation in business or his visibility as an Episcopal layman (surely a mark of acceptability to whites), Bousfield nonetheless continued to enjoy opportunities to serve the African American community from the upper reaches of the white establishment. In 1939 the Democratic boss Edward J. Kelly named Bousfield the first black member on Chicago's board of education, a move black Chicago had been urging for twenty-five years. In 1942 Bousfield got a national call: to take charge of the U.S. Army hospital at Fort Huachuca, Arizona. The army's first all-black hospital, it would also be under the direction of the medical corp's first black colonel. Not only did his leadership give black physicians new opportunities, but the quality of their care was so patently good that neighboring whites sought out Fort Huachuca in preference to their own white facility.

One final creative venture remained. In 1946 Bousfield helped organize the Provident Medical Associates, a group of well-heeled (but progressive) Chicago black doctors, whose purpose was to fund the education of aspiring medical specialists and in the process break another racial barrier in American medicine. Upon Bousfield's death in Chicago, a momentum was building that in little more than a decade and a half would demolish the structure of medical segregation, thanks substantially to his efforts. Ironically, it was Bousfield's separate but (truly) equal strategy that helped bring on integration, for his approach helped ensure the quality the black medical profession needed to convince white physicians that integration was an acceptable next step.

Bousfield's career is significant for two reasons apart from his own professional contributions. It demonstrated that African Americans—North and South—were making large strides toward equality well before the civil rights movement, even before World War II. It further showed that a conservative approach to social change, that is, stressing gradualism and reliance on the white power structure for help, did bring some results. Bousfield did associate publicly and early on with black unionism through work with the Railway Men's International Association, and he was a key leader in the National Urban League. Perhaps most importantly, he spoke bluntly to white professionals when straight talk seemed a surer course than tact and cajolery.

FURTHER READING
Bousfield, Midian Othello. "Reaching the Negro Community," *American Journal of Public Health* 24 (Mar. 1934).

Beardsley, Edward H. *A History of Neglect: Health Care for Blacks and Mill Workers in the Twentieth-Century South* (1987).

Obituaries: *Chicago Daily News*, 17 Feb. 1948; *Journal of the National Medical Association* 40 (May 1948).

This entry is taken from the *American National Biography* and is published here with the permission of the American Council of Learned Societies.

E. H. BEARDSLEY

Boutelle, Frazier Augustus (12 Sept. 1840–12 Feb. 1924), military officer and conservationist, was born in Troy, New York, the son of James Boutelle of Fitchburg, Massachusetts, and Emeline Lamb Boutelle. Little is known of his childhood and adolescent years. However, at age twenty-one, possibly passing as white, Boutelle began his ascent through the ranks of the military to become a highly decorated officer, including earning the rank of adjutant general.

On 15 August 1861 Boutelle enlisted in the Fifth New York Calvary Regiment. On 4 November 1862 he was promoted from quartermaster sergeant to second lieutenant. Boutelle and his regiment were then assigned to Pennsylvania to battle against Robert E. Lee's Confederate forces. During the Gettysburg campaign Boutelle was injured when he fell from his horse during a charge on Hanover on 30 June 1863. Because of his injuries Boutelle was assigned to the First Brigade, Third Calvary Division on 17 January 1864 as an ambulance driver. During his stint as an ambulance driver, Boutelle's former commanding officer, Captain Theodore A. Boice, was captured, resulting in Boutelle's being recruited as the replacement to lead the Fifth New York Calvary Regiment. Boutelle remained with the regiment until 10 July 1865.

After the dissolution of New York Calvary, Boutelle enlisted in the regular U.S. Army. Upon enlisting, Boutelle lost his rank from a volunteer regiment and was deemed a private on 12 February 1866. However, he received the commission of sergeant major followed by the rank of second lieutenant on 8 May 1869. After being transferred to Fort Klamath, Oregon, Boutelle and his regiment were instructed to escort the Modoc tribe to a reservation as was outlined in a Senate treaty approved on 14 October 1864. Upon contact between the regiment and the Modoc tribe, a gunfight erupted between Boutelle and Scarface Charley of the Modoc tribe. As a result of the skirmish, the war between the Modoc tribe and the United States began. For his participation in what became known as the Modoc War, Boutelle was cited for his bravery in the Lost River engagement at Lava Beds, Oregon.

On 30 May 1888 Boutelle was promoted to the rank of captain and the following year was named head of Yellowstone National Park. Boutelle began his tenure, replacing Captain Moses Harris, at Yellowstone National Park on 1 June 1889. As head of the park Boutelle sought to reduce the number of forest fires, protect the Snake and Missouri rivers, and stock the park with various types of fish. He also devised procedures that limited the number of parasites in the park's waters. Boutelle garnered mass support with his measures to protect the bison herds throughout the Northwest. He urged Congress to pass and enact laws protecting the bison from slaughter, ordered the elimination of animals in the park that preyed on bison, deer, and elk, and provided the National Zoological Park in Washington, D.C., with animals that were captured in Yellowstone.

Although he was recommended for promotion to brevet major on 1 July 1830, Boutelle chose to retire from the U.S. Army, but he was not mustered out of service until 27 August 1895. Before retirement Boutelle accepted the post of brigadier general of Washington State. As brigadier general he streamlined the National Guard and its procedures. Before his four-year term had expired, Boutelle was removed from his position by Governor John R. Rogers. It has been suggested that Boutelle was forced out of his post once news of his African American genealogy reached the governor. He ended his tenure in Washington State on 13 January 1897. During the ensuing years Boutelle remained active by serving as an army recruiter from 1 August 1905 to 20 September 1918. During his retirement Boutelle was once again promoted, earning the rank of colonel.

Boutelle married Mary Adolphine Augusto Haydon on 12 October 1873. They had one son, Henry Moss Boutelle, born 17 June 1875. Henry Boutelle was killed in action in Manila, the Philippines, on 2 November 1899. Colonel Frazier A. Boutelle died on 12 February 1924 in Seattle. He was survived by his wife. As a soldier Boutelle displayed qualities that led to his ascension through the ranks of the U.S. Army, assured by his willingness to hide his African American ancestry. As a conservationist Boutelle helped to establish laws that protected and enriched the splendor of Yellowstone National Forest.

FURTHER READING

Johnson, Charles, Jr. "Frazier A. Boutelle: Military Career of a Black Soldier," *Journal of the Afro-American Historical and Genealogical Society* 3 (1982).

Quinn, Arthur. *Hell with the Fire Out: A History of the Modoc War* (1997).

MICHAEL J. RISTICH

Bowden, Artemisia (1879–18 Aug. 1969), Texas school administrator and civic leader, was born in Albany, Georgia, the eldest of five children of Milas and Mary Bowden, former slaves. When Bowden was sixteen years old her mother died, and her father sent her to St. Augustine's Normal, Industrial, and Collegiate School (later St. Augustine's College) in Raleigh, North Carolina, where she graduated in 1900. There Bowden came into contact with educated African American Episcopalian role models.

Having gained two years of teaching experience in North Carolina, Bowden moved to San Antonio, Texas, to accept the position of chief administrator and primary teacher of St. Philip's Normal and Industrial School. St. Philip's had been founded in 1898 for the Episcopalian Church by Bishop James Steptoe Johnston, the son of a Mississippi plantation owner. Initially operating as a day school, St. Philip's consisted of two classrooms where sewing was taught to African American girls. For the next fifty-two years Bowden dedicated her life to providing the educational and cultural and economic needs of the African American community in San Antonio. As principal her first charge was to organize the school into three departments, primary, grammar, and industrial. Later she increased the staff of instructors and expanded the course work in each department. Boarding facilities were added, a normal and a music department were added, and an off-campus kindergarten was organized. By 1908 the school's enrollment had reached a high of 117 students. However, in 1913 the enrollment fell to eighty-five, and the school continued to be underfunded by the diocese and was on the brink of financial ruin.

Retaining a vision of the school as a great institution of learning, Bowden took on the responsibility for fund-raising, in addition to her teaching and administrative duties. Not afraid to ask anyone she thought would give her a donation, she raised funds to make an initial payment to buy approximately four acres, including a two-story brick house and two frame buildings in east San Antonio. In 1918 the school occupied its new location, and by 1921 St. Philip's began receiving approximately two thousand dollars annually from the American Church Institute for Negroes, an Episcopal organization. With financial security in place, Bowden set a new goal: to establish St. Philip's as a junior college. In 1927, with the support of the mayor, the Chamber of Commerce, and a number of African American organizations and business people, St. Philip's Junior College and Industrial School became a reality. Bowden's title changed from principal to president of the newly established junior college.

The Great Depression brought new challenges for Bowden and her beloved St. Philip's Junior College. By 1940 the Episcopal Church relinquished all ties to the college, leaving it again at the brink of financial ruin. Bowden refused to allow the school to die and began a campaign to have the San Antonio Board of Education assume responsibility for the school. Since 1926 the board had operated a publicly funded junior college for whites only. Although African Americans living in San Antonio helped support the college through taxes they paid, none was allowed admission. Reluctantly, in 1942, the San Antonio Board of Education incorporated St. Philip's into the municipal junior college system, operating it as a branch of San Antonio Junior College. The president of San Antonio Junior College also administered the St. Philip's branch, and Bowden became the school's dean.

Bowden did graduate work during the summers at Columbia University, Pennsylvania's Cheyney State Teachers College, the New York School of Social Work, and the University of Colorado. In 1952 she received an honorary doctorate from Tillotson College in Austin, Texas. Bowden held memberships in the National Association of College Women's Clubs and several state and national associations for professional educators. In 1947 she was named to the Texas Commission on Interracial Relations. The National Council of Negro Women cited Bowden as one of the ten most outstanding women educators in the country. A member of Delta Sigma Theta Sorority, Inc., Bowden was recognized by a number of local organizations for her lifetime of service, including Zeta Phi Beta Sorority, Inc., which in 1955 named her Woman of the Year. An elementary school in San Antonio and the San Antonio chapter of the Business and Professional Women, Inc., were named in her honor. St. Philip's College honored her with an endowed scholarship in her name and with the Bowden Administration Building located on campus.

Bowden devoted her time not only to St. Philip's but also to civic projects benefiting African Americans in greater San Antonio. She is given primary credit for securing Lindberg Park for African American residents, establishing the East End Settlement House, and the introduction of an African American nursing unit in Robert B. Green Hospital. She was a member of the Southern Conference of Christians and Jews and of St. Philip's Episcopal Church in San Antonio. At the time of her retirement in 1954 Bowden was given the title dean emeritus. Although Bowden never married and had no children, her life touched many and continued to assure that generations would obtain a valuable education in San Antonio. St. Philip's College would grow into a multi-campus institution of the Alamo Community College District, joining three other colleges: San Antonio College, Palo Alto College, and Northwest Vista College. It became one of the fastest growing colleges in the southwest. With a student population per semester that exceeded eight thousand, it ranked as one of the largest of the 160 historically black colleges and universities. Bowden died in San Antonio.

FURTHER READING

Eckerman, Jo. "Artemisia Bowden: Dedicated Dreamer," *Texas Passages* (Winter 1987).

St. Philip's College, available online at http://www.accd. edu/spc/main/history.aspx.

LINDA EVERETT MOYÉ

Bowe, Riddick (10 Aug. 1967–), boxer and activist, was born Riddick Lamont Bowe in the Brownsville neighborhood of Brooklyn, New York, the twelfth of thirteen children of Dorothy Bowe, a factory worker. Little is known of Bowe's father, whose first name is believed to have been Jake, as he left the family when Bowe was very young. Brownsville was notable for its high crime rate and poverty, forces that affected Bowe directly. Several of his brothers spent time in prison, and his sister Brenda was assaulted and robbed of a welfare check, dying of injuries sustained in the incident. Bowe stayed clear of such troubles, and as a teenager began training at the New Bedford-Stuyvesant Boxing Club. He married Judith (her maiden name is unknown) in 1986 and shortly afterward she gave birth to the first of their five children (Riddick Jr., Riddicia, Brenda, Julius, and Diamond). He graduated from Thomas Jefferson High School that same year.

Success in the ring came early for Bowe. As an amateur he won four New York Golden Gloves titles in addition to a gold medal as a light heavyweight in the 1985 World Junior Championships. It was not until the 1988 Olympics in Seoul, South Korea, that Bowe experienced his first setback as a boxer, losing the gold-medal bout in the super heavyweight division to the Canadian boxer Lennox Lewis.

Bowe turned professional following the 1988 Olympics. He hired veteran trainer Eddie Futch, who had helped many boxers realize their potential and win titles. Under Futch's tutelage, Bowe accumulated an impressive record, going 21-0 in his first two years as a professional fighter.

In November 1992 Bowe fought the undisputed World Heavyweight Champion EVANDER HOLYFIELD. This dramatic fight, won in the eleventh round by Bowe, became an instant classic and revived the public's previously dwindling interest in boxing. With the victory Bowe became the sport's unified champion, his status acknowledged by all three of boxing's major governing bodies: the World Boxing Council (WBC), the World Boxing Association (WBA), and the International Boxing Federation (IBF). Charismatic and politically active, Bowe met with world leaders such as Pope John Paul II, Nelson Mandela, and President Bill Clinton. He supported a wide range of causes, including the anti-apartheid movement, ending world hunger, and raising awareness of the perils of drug addiction. Despite all the philanthropy he was participating in, some sportswriters believed his passion and ambition had waned upon achieving boxing's ultimate distinction as undisputed world heavyweight champion.

Because of a breakdown in negotiations between Bowe's management and that of Lennox Lewis's, Bowe lost his WBC title belt after failing to fight the top-ranked challenger; Lewis became the WBC heavyweight champion by default. The seemingly unflappable Bowe discarded his WBC championship belt into a trash can at a London press conference, one of many controversial actions that would take place during his career. His championship reign was also marred by a lack of quality title defenses. He lost his IBF and WBA belts in a rematch with Holyfield in November 1993. The fight was a close one, despite the fact that Bowe had not prepared as thoroughly as he had for their first bout and was noticeably overweight. Bowe would have problems with his weight throughout his career. His dislike of training and his love of food proved to be an unfortunate combination; between fights his weight would rise significantly, leaving him either flabby

Riddick Bowe reacts after defeating opponent Marcus Rhode at Fire Lake Casino in Shawnee, Oklahoma, 25 September 2004. (AP Images.)

or, in those instances where he lost the extra weight on a crash diet, weakened.

Bowe's career was marked by several strange and controversial moments. In a bout with Buster Mathis Jr. in August 1994, Bowe struck his opponent with an unsportsmanlike blow as Mathis was on one knee, regrouping from a knockdown. The fight was ruled a no-contest by the New Jersey Boxing Commission. Violence would occasionally erupt outside of the ring as well, as Bowe engaged in violent altercations with other boxers at prefight press conferences and weigh-ins. Prior to these events, Bowe had been known for being good-natured with a sense of humor, characteristics that sportswriters and commentators frequently contrasted with fellow Brownsville native and prizefighter MICHAEL GERARD TYSON.

Bowe fought Holyfield a third time, in November 1995, winning the fight in the eighth round, despite being knocked down for the first time in his career. Despite all his successes, he did not figure prominently in the title picture after losing his belts. He did win the belt of a smaller organization, the World Boxing Organization, by defeating Herbie Hide in March 1995, making him a champion again; but the major belts remained beyond his grasp. Bowe's inability to get into the ring with key contenders for the major boxing titles may have been out of retribution for the cutthroat negotiating style of his manager and promoter, Eugene Roderick "Rock" Newman.

In July 1996 Bowe would once again see controversy in the ring and violence outside it with a bout at Madison Square Garden. Following a bloody fight in which Bowe's opponent, Andrew Golota, had been disqualified for punching below the belt, the arena erupted into violence and a riot ensued. This was blamed largely on Bowe's rowdy corner crew and Newman's inability to control them. The boxers had a rematch in December of 1996, and once again the fight ended in a disqualification for Golota. Between the two bouts Bowe's longtime trainer, Eddie Futch, quit. Bowe had been overweight and underprepared for his first fight with Golota, and Futch had grown tired of the fighter's lack of discipline. Bowe himself retired in May 1997.

In February 1997 Bowe joined the U.S. Marine Corps. He lasted a total of eleven days, completing just three days of basic training. It was also in 1997 that his marriage broke up; his wife and their five children moved to Cornelius, North Carolina. A year later Bowe, attempting to reunite his family, abducted Judy Bowe and their children at knifepoint from their home. Bowe was apprehended and forced to go through a mental health evaluation and serve eighteen months in jail. The relative leniency of the sentence was due in part to a plea deal, and in part to the testimony of several doctors that Bowe had sustained brain damage as a boxer. Bowe had initially received an even lighter thirty-day sentence for kidnapping from North Carolina; assault charges in Maryland (where Bowe lived) were set aside. The North Carolina sentence was twice rejected by an appeals court; in 2003 Bowe was sentenced to eighteen months in prison. Bowe and his wife divorced in 1998.

In 2000 Riddick married Terri Blakney. He was arrested on a domestic violence charge of second-degree assault against his wife in 2003, shortly before he was to start serving the North Carolina prison term.

He staged a boxing comeback in September 2004 with a victory over Marcus Rhode and had a narrow victory over Billy Zumbrum in April 2005. He filed for bankruptcy in October 2005.

FURTHER READING

Myler, Thomas. *The Sweet Science Goes Sour: How Scandal Brought Boxing to Its Knees* (2006).

Sugar, Bert Randolph. *Boxing's Greatest Fighters* (2006).

THOMAS EDWARD GUASTELLO

Bowen, John Wesley Edward (3 Dec. 1855– 20 July 1933), Methodist educator and theologian, was born in New Orleans, Louisiana, the son of Edward Bowen and Rose Simon. John's father was a carpenter from Maryland who was enslaved when he moved to New Orleans. After purchasing his own freedom, Edward Bowen bought that of his wife and son in 1858 and served in the Union army during the Civil War. After the war, young J. W. E. Bowen studied at the Union Normal School in New Orleans and at New Orleans University, which was founded by the Methodist Episcopal Church for the education of freedmen. Bowen received a bachelor's degree with the university's first graduating class in 1878. Eight years later, New Orleans University awarded him a master's degree. From 1878 to 1882 Bowen taught mathematics and ancient languages at Central Tennessee College in Nashville.

In 1882 Bowen began theological studies at Boston University. While he was a theological student he was also the pastor of Revere Street Methodist Episcopal Church in Boston. Bowen earned a bachelor of sacred theology degree in 1885, and soon after he became pastor of Saint John's Methodist Episcopal Church in Newark, New Jersey. He continued graduate study in theology, and he married Ariel Serena Hedges of Baltimore, Maryland, in 1886; they had four children. Bowen was the second African American to earn a Ph.D. in the United States when Boston University conferred the degree on him in 1887. After leaving Saint John's in 1888, Bowen went on to serve as pastor of Centennial Methodist Episcopal Church in Baltimore and of Asbury Methodist Episcopal Church in Washington, D.C.

At Centennial Church he conducted a notable revival in which more than seven hundred people claimed conversion. He also served as professor of church history and systematic theology at Baltimore's Morgan College from 1888 to 1892 and as professor of Hebrew at Howard University in Washington, D.C., from 1890 to 1891. From 1889 to 1893 Bowen was also a member and examiner for the American Institute of Sacred Literature. In 1892 he published *What Shall the Harvest Be? A National Sermon; or, A Series of Plain Talks to the Colored People of America, on Their Problems*. He represented the Methodist Episcopal Church at conferences of world Methodism in Washington, D.C., in 1891 and in London in 1901.

In 1892, after leaving his posts at Centennial and Asbury, Bowen became a field secretary for the Freedmen's Aid Society of the Methodist Episcopal Church. He left the Freedmen's Aid Society in 1893, however, to become professor of historical theology at Gammon Theological Seminary in Atlanta, Georgia. As the first African American professor

at the school—founded in 1883 by the Methodist Episcopal Church for the preparation of African American clergymen—Bowen was awarded an honorary doctor of divinity degree by Gammon in 1893. As secretary of the seminary's Stewart Missionary Foundation for Africa, he also edited its periodical, the *Stewart Missionary Magazine*.

In October 1895, after praising BOOKER T. WASHINGTON's emphasis on industrial education and the work ethic in Washington's address to Atlanta's Cotton States' Exposition a month earlier, Bowen delivered his own address, "An appeal to the king," on "Negro Day" at the exposition. In December 1895 Bowen organized an important three-day conference on Africa that was held in conjunction with the exposition; he published its proceedings as *Africa and the American Negro: Addresses and Proceedings of the Congress on Africa … in Connection with the Cotton States … Exposition, Dec. 13–15, 1895* (1896). Subsequently, however, Bowen distanced himself from Washington by defending liberal arts education for leadership and joined W. E. B. DuBOIS in protesting state legislation to segregate railroad transportation and limit funds for black public schools to taxes paid by black people.

In 1896 Bowen was elected a delegate to the quadrennial general conference of the Methodist Episcopal Church, a position that he retained until 1912. As the most distinguished African American clergyman in the Methodist Episcopal Church, Bowen received many votes for the episcopacy at the general conferences in 1896, 1900, and 1904. As a member of the Board of Control of the Methodist Episcopal Church's Epworth League, he organized a national conference in Atlanta on the Christian education of African American youth. With I. GARLAND PENN, Bowen also edited and published its proceedings, *The United Negro, … Addresses and Proceedings: The Negro Young People's Christian and Educational Congress, Held August 6–11, 1902* (1902).

In January 1904 Bowen and JESSE MAX BARBER launched the *Voice of the Negro*, a literary journal addressed to a national audience of African Americans. In September 1905 they endorsed the Niagara Movement, which was organized by DuBois and others to protest African Americans' loss of civil rights; months later they promoted the organization of the Georgia Equal Rights League, which had similar objectives. At the peak of its circulation in 1906 the *Voice of the Negro* claimed twelve to fifteen thousand subscribers.

After the death of his first wife in 1904, Bowen married Irene L. Smallwood in 1906. They had no children. That same year Bowen became the president of Gammon Theological Seminary. In September, however, his inaugural year was shadowed by a severe race riot in which white rioters brutally attacked black people in Atlanta. Bowen opened the seminary to shelter black refugees from the riot. Three days after the rioting began Bowen himself was beaten and arrested by Atlanta's white police. Barber fled the city, taking the *Voice of the Negro* with him to Chicago, where he continued its publication as the *Voice* for a year without Bowen's assistance.

Bowen survived the Atlanta race riot and served as president of Gammon until 1910, when its administration was merged with that of Clark University. He became vice president of the merged institution and continued as professor of historical theology. A lecturer on the Chautauqua circuit, Bowen was an active member of the American Historical Association, the American Negro Academy, and the National Association for the Advancement of Colored People. The frustration of African American hopes for leadership in the church eventually led to Bowen's publication of *An Appeal for Negro Bishops, but No Separation* in 1912. When the Methodist Episcopal Church finally determined to elect its first two African American bishops in 1920, however, it chose younger men, Robert Elijah Jones and Matthew Wesley Clair. Bowen retired as head of the church history department at Gammon in 1926 but continued to teach until 1932, when he became an emeritus professor. He died in Atlanta. Throughout a distinguished career Bowen was an eloquent example of an African American Christian intellectual.

FURTHER READING

The J. W. E. Bowen Papers are in the Gammon Theological Seminary Archives at the Atlanta University Center's Woodruff Library.

Harlan, Louis R. "Booker T. Washington and the *Voice of the Negro*, 1904–1907," *Journal of Southern History* 45 (Feb. 1979): 45–62.

Luker, Ralph E. *The Social Gospel in Black and White: American Racial Reform, 1885–1912* (1991).

Meier, August. *Negro Thought in America 1880–1915: Racial Ideologies in the Age of Booker T. Washington* (1963).

Moss, Alfred A., Jr. *The American Negro Academy: Voice of the Talented Tenth* (1981).

Obituaries: *Atlanta Constitution*, 21 July 1933; J. R. Van Pelt, "John Wesley Edward Bowen," *Journal of Negro History* 14 (Apr. 1934): 217–221.

This entry is taken from the *American National Biography* and is published here with the permission of the American Council of Learned Societies.

RALPH E. LUKER

Bowen, Ruth Jean (1924–24 Apr. 2009), business owner and entertainment promoter, was born in Danville, Virginia, to Claude Carlton and Marion Baskerville, about whom little is known. Ruth attended the Westmoreland Elementary School and Langston High School in Danville. Ruth's family moved to New York City when she was a teenager, and she graduated from Girls High School in Brooklyn. After attending New York University for two years, she met and fell in love with Wallace "Billy" Bowen, a member of the popular Ink Spots, one of the few entertainment groups in the 1940s and 1950s to break the race barrier and perform for white audiences across the United States. Bowen left school and she and Billy were married until his death in 1982.

Bowen managed the daily office responsibilities of her husband's business. She also traveled the United States with the Ink Spots during their concert tours. During the 1940s the Bowens and the members of the Ink Spots often experienced the sting of segregation when they were denied hotel rooms or forced to lodge in special back rooms designated for "coloreds only." While on tour in Pittsburgh, Bowen's husband introduced her to the legendary blues singer DINAH WASHINGTON. The two women quickly became friends and eventually Bowen became Washington's publicist.

Bowen's endeavors as a publicist were successful, and she soon also became Washington's manager., Washington's booking agent taught Bowen everything about the entertainment industry—from how to handle correspondence to how to book acts. After Bowen noticed that the earning potential of black entertainers was limited because of the social restrictions placed on where they could perform in the United States, she began to book Washington for European concerts, a successful stroke that solidified her reputation as an entertainment booking agent.

In 1959 Bowen and Washington became business partners, opening the Queen Artists booking agency. After Washington won a Grammy

Award that same year for "What a Difference a Day Makes," Bowen had to hire office staff so that she could personally manage Washington's growing career. While the two were on the road for concert venues, Washington often referred new acts to Bowen, including popular groups like the Dells and the dancer LOLA FALANA.

Queen Booking grew quickly and Bowen found that she had to train her office staff to become talent-booking agents. The agency was responsible for booking acts in big theaters like the Apollo in Harlem and the Regal in Chicago, and many popular jazz clubs across the United States. Bowen trained her staff—which was both black and white—in the art of entertainment booking. Queen Booking handled the publicity and bookings for popular acts like EARL BOSTIC, KENNY BURRELL, and the Basin Street East Nightclub. When Washington died in 1963, the Queen Booking agency employed thirty workers and managed more than 100 acts. The company name was soon changed to Queen Booking Corporation (QBC). Within five years the company had become the largest black-owned entertainment agency in the United States. Its client base had expanded beyond music groups to include other acts like comedians, gospel choirs, and rock bands. Bowen was able to demand and receive top venues and pay for her clients—even from nightclubs that had developed reputations for discrimination against African Americans.

Despite the fact that Bowen had excelled in a traditionally male industry, she found that occasionally she still had to prove herself. Club owners were sometimes not as accommodating to her as they were to male counterparts. For example, sometimes she would only be given one chance to successfully book an act before losing all other booking opportunities. With the growth in popularity of rock and roll and rhythm and blues, QBC began to handle both black and white artists. Bowen had a reputation as a tough negotiator for all of her acts—black and white. Her philosophy was that if the same money was being paid, then the same respect and comforts should be provided, and she did not compromise. Despite the obstacles Bowen faced, she was able to build QBC into an industry powerhouse with a net worth of $3 million. She received further recognition in 1973 when the Manhattan borough president PERCY SUTTON issued a proclamation and declared it "Ruth Bowen Day." Among the top entertainers managed by QBC were ARETHA FRANKLIN, PATTI LaBELLE,

the O'Jays, SMOKEY ROBINSON, STEVIE WONDER, MARVIN GAYE, IKE TURNER and TINA TURNER, the Ohio Players, AL GREEN, RAY CHARLES, SHIRLEY CAESAR, the Mighty Clouds of Joy, and RICHARD PRYOR. Bowen died at age 85 in New York City, her home and career base for some seventy-odd years.

FURTHER READING

Cohodas, Nadine. *Queen: The Life and Music of Dinah Washington* (2004).

Hine, Darlene Clark, ed. *Black Women in America: An Historical Encyclopedia* (1993).

Who's Who among Black Americans, 1994/95, 8th edition (1993).

Obituary: *New York Daily News*, 24 Apr. 2009.

ANGELA BLACK

Bowen, Uvelia Atkins (23 Apr. 1922–21 May 2010), educator and community activist, was born Uvelia Atkins in Middlesex County, Virginia. She attended public elementary schools in Middlesex County, and in 1940 she graduated from the Rappahannock Industrial Academy, a private high school in Essex County. Atkins graduated in 1945 from Virginia Union University, in Richmond, where she majored in English and was vice president of the YWCA, secretary of Kappa Gamma Chi, and a member of the NAACP. She married the Reverend Walter Duncan Bowen, a Presbyterian pastor, in Philadelphia, Pennsylvania, in 1954. The couple did not have any children, and throughout their lives they worked with inner-city young people. She received a master's in Social Service from Bryn Mawr College in 1957.

From 1951 to 1965 Bowen worked in Philadelphia for the United Neighbors Association, a multiprogram agency that provided services to city residents; she was the association's first woman assistant director from 1959 through 1965. During the years 1961 through 1964, she served as the national chair of the United Presbyterian Women's Target: Youth in a Troubled World. Often considered a forerunner to the federal government's War on Poverty program of the late 1960s, it established tutoring and mentoring programs as well as employment and housing initiatives.

In 1967 Bowen founded HEART—the Household Employment Association for Reevaluation and Training in Philadelphia—at a time when household employment was the third largest occupation for women and usually the only employment women of color could obtain. It also was the poorest paid. HEART worked to establish policies to upgrade the status of household employment, including the education of employers about fair work practices. The association's goal as stated in its literature involved training both the employer and the employee so that "equity and dignity in the home existed for employees and employer." HEART aimed at developing a work relationship between employer and employee characterized by communication and professionalism. In addition, HEART opened a licensed, private trade school for community education, job development, and placement counseling. The school selected, trained, and placed workers as professional technicians in households, and by 1971 had become a national training center for people interested in establishing programs to upgrade the service occupations.

Bowen also wrote *What Is a Day's Work?*, published by HEART in 1970, which argued that greater respect should be accorded to household work and that the relationship between household employee and employer should be redressed. She wrote about specific new policies for the employee–employer household work relationship regarding work hours, wages, sick leave, vacations, and work assignments. She detailed twenty-two employment categories, from cleaning technician with light laundry, geriatrics assistant, foods technician, and party aide. She changed the name of caretakers of the elderly to "geriatrics assistants," housekeeper to "cleaning technician," cook to "foods technician," and party waitress to "party aide." Other aspects of the book included the rights and responsibilities of both the employee and employer with a focus on policies that create a balanced employer-employee relationship. Employees' needs are also discussed in the book, including neighborhood-based day care for employees' children. The final chapter examined the role of the employer as a supervisor and suggested guidelines for determining what should be considered a realistic "day's work." Bowen's second book, *Thursday's People on the Move!*, was published by HEART in 1971 and is a teaching tool for organizations interested in upgrading work policies in the service occupations. The first section outlined HEART's policies and procedures for recruiting, training, and counseling household employees. The second section discussed job development, placement counseling, and community education. Instructive case histories were included along with open-ended discussion questions.

In 1974 Bowen founded the International Congress of Virginia Union University Women Graduates. The goals of the congress were to create a registry of female graduates from the university and to provide a resource to help new graduates. Also in 1974 she founded Personnel Resources Inc., a private trade school that trained students in household employment. Despite politically motivated criticism as reported in the *Philadelphia Inquirer* in 1988 when the Philadelphia Housing Authority was instructed by HUD to investigate documentation of a grant to Personnel Resources Inc., Bowen continued her work in upgrading policies for employees in the service occupations. She was named an Outstanding Professional in Human Services in 1974 and 1975 by the American Academy of Human Services. From 1977 through 1981 she served as a member of the Board of Trustees at Temple University in Philadelphia. She also established the Youth Assistance Endowment in memory of her husband when he died in 1997.

In 2000 Bowen received the Presidential Award for Exemplary Service from the National Association of Social Workers, which was presented to her for "exemplary service and excellence in social work education." She died in Williamsburg, Virginia, at the age of eighty-eight.

FURTHER READING

The papers of Uvelia Atkins Bowen are at the Archives and Special Collections Library, L. Douglas Wilder Library, Virginia Union University in Richmond, Virginia.

"Bad Housekeeping PHA Is Squandering More Than Money," *Philadelphia Inquirer*, 25 Oct. 1988.

Loeb, Vernon. "HUD Wants to See Data on City Housekeeping Course," *Philadelphia Inquirer*, 21 Oct. 1988.

National Association of Social Workers, Inc. NASW News, available online at http://www.socialworkers.org/pubs/news.

LINDA SPENCER

Bowens, Beverly Elizabeth Dodge (2 Sept. 1934–1 July 2006), nursing administrator, who as a teenager in 1952 caused racial integration of a Washington, D.C., public accommodation, was born in Portland, Maine, the daughter of Emory C. Dodge Sr. and Irene Isabel Eastman. Her father, a native of Kenosha, Wisconsin, served in the Canadian Army and the U.S. Navy before settling in Portland, Maine, where he was employed in local hotels and at the Maine Medical Center. Emory Sr. married Irene Eastman, a member of a long-established black Maine family, on 18 October 1928. They raised two children on Anderson Street in Portland's ethnically mixed Munjoy Hill neighborhood. As a young woman Beverly took a particular interest in family history, especially through a cousin Mary E. Barnett, who had preserved letters and documents that would eventually lead Beverly back to the family's origins in Demerara (Guyana) and the Netherlands during the 1700s. Further, more serious research into family history had to be put off because of school and other pressing events.

Beverly excelled in school and as a senior at Portland High School won the "Good Citizenship Award" from the Daughters of the American Revolution in 1952. The class planned a trip to Washington, DC, but she was soon notified that she would be unable to go "because of the segregated accommodations in Washington, DC." As she recalled, "I had no thought of embarrassing my school: I simply joined the Washington Club and wasn't discouraged from doing so by school officials nor, surprisingly, by my parents." An English teacher, Barbara Johnson, asked Beverly if she would mind if she spoke to the press; "I replied 'No.' It briefly occurred to me that perhaps I should have discussed this with my parents, but the commitment was already made so I put it out of my mind" (Bowens, p. 302). When she told her parents she could not go with the class they were "uneasy" but "not angry," and she made plans for an alternate trip. However the next day, 20 March 1952, her story made the front page of the *Portland Press Herald*. "Embarrassed and mortified" she went to school in a daze but soon found resounding support from classmates, who proposed a boycott of the Capital, and public advocacy from Maine's governor Frederick G. Payne and its redoubtable U.S. Senator Margaret Chase Smith. Direct pressure from these sources broke the will of the Columbia Hotel Association, and the owners of the Lafayette Hotel opened their doors to all the Portland High School visitors. Senator Smith remained in communication with Miss Dodge, following her professional career with interest.

Portland at the time had some 340 "Negro" citizens in a population of about 77,634, but the Washington hotel desegregation incident was a positive learning experience for the community. As Beverly summed it up, "It was a significant victory for my school and for the State of Maine, even though at the time I considered it a nuisance situation, ordinary rather than extraordinary. In truth it was like a raindrop falling into an ocean of change. As the 1950s and 1960s progressed, there would be storms of raindrops larger than mine, falling into

the ocean of civil rights changes." On a personal level, "It was a significant victory for myself and my family, including my brother who was stationed in Morocco with the United States Air Force, not yet fully exempt from Washington's segregation laws" (Bowens, 304).

Beverly worked for many years at Mercy Hospital in Portland, all through high school and while she attended its School of Nursing, graduating in 1955. She moved to New York City, where she earned her B.S. in nursing and two masters (nursing service administration and nursing education) from Teachers College at Columbia University. She became certified as a Nurse Administrator Advanced (CNAA), working at St. Luke's Hospital and Lenox Hill Hospital in New York City before being appointed special assistant to the director of the Department of Nursing Services of the American Nurse's Association in 1971. She was married to Dr. Oliver L. Bowens of New Bedford, Massachusetts, with whom she had a daughter, Alison Bowens-Bailey of California.

"Beverly Bowen's knowledge, courage and caring spirit gave me inspiration and passion to become a professional nurse," expressed BARBARA WARE NICHOLS (in a 2011 e-mail, included among Bowens's materials at the Maine Historical Society). Barbara graduated from Portland High School four years after Beverly. "She was my role model," said Nichols, who became the first African American to be elected president of the American Nurses' Association.

Upon retiring in 1993 from the nursing profession, Beverly Dodge Bowens returned to Portland, where she became involved in history and family research, picking up where she had left off years earlier and assembling a formidable collection of materials and helping other African American researchers to untangle their roots. Always generous with her research, she was a key participant, along with GERALD TALBOT, BOB GREENE, RANDOLPH STAKEMAN, and others in the June 1997 "African Americans in Maine" Roundtable, held at the Maine Historical Society. In 2002 she was honored for her part in the African American community and her activism by the City of Portland and the University of Southern Maine. Beverly was also an important contributor to *Maine's Visible Black History: The First Chronicle of Its People* (2006), where she helped with editing the book and contributed essays about her 1952 high school trip to Washington, DC, and her mother's family origins. Her early death, in California, was not only a misfortune to friends and family but to scholars and students of African American history.

FURTHER READING
Materials about Beverly Dodge Bowens can be found in the Maine Historical Society, Portland, Maine. These include copies of City of Portland & University of Maine, Presentation Certificate, "Home Is Where You Find It": African American Community and Activism in Greater Portland, Maine 7 Nov. 2002; and Pat Garassic, "American Nurses Association," 19 Nov. 1971.

Bowens, Beverly Dodge. "Mary Ann Barnett (Marianna de Remila), 1780–1872" and "A Senior Class Trip to Washington, D.C., 1952." In H. H. Price and Gerald E. Talbot, *Maine's Visible Black History: The First Chronicle of Its People* (2006).

"Capital Hotels' Color Line Bars PHS 'Best Citizen.'" *Portland Press Herald*, 20 Mar. 1952.

"1952 PHS Seniors May Shun Country's Color-Conscious Capital." *Portland Press Herald*, 21 Mar. 1952.

WILLIAM DAVID BARRY

Bowers, Thomas J. (1826–4 Oct. 1885), tenor, was born in Philadelphia, Pennsylvania, the son of John Bowers, a prominent member of Philadelphia's black elite and vestryman at St. Thomas's African Episcopal Church, and Henrietta Bowers (c. 1795–1868). Widowed in October 1844, his mother was a member of St. Thomas's congregation for more than fifty years. The 1860 federal census listed her occupation as cook. Bowers learned to play pianoforte and organ from his elder brother, John C. Bowers, and at the age of eighteen became organist at St. Thomas's. Although his parents encouraged their children's musical abilities at home and in church, they looked unfavorably on public performances of music. As a consequence, Bowers declined an offer to join the popular Philadelphia band led by FRANCIS JOHNSON.

Despite his parents' objections, however, in 1854 Bowers made his first public performance as a vocalist at Sansom Street Hall in Philadelphia. He appeared as the student of ELIZABETH TAYLOR GREENFIELD, a well-known singer with an extraordinary range who had been given the sobriquet "Black Swan." During her career Greenfield sang in the United States, Canada, and Great Britain, where she made a command performance for Queen Victoria. Bowers received high praise for the Sansom Street Hall performance and other concerts in Philadelphia, and subsequently he and Greenfield embarked on a tour of New York State and Canada, where they garnered excellent reviews. While on tour in Hamilton, Ontario, Bowers successfully defied that city's segregationist policy, refusing to perform unless six black ticket holders were permitted to take their seats. Bowers's opposition to performing before segregated audiences continued throughout the tour as well as during the remainder of his career. Politically active in Philadelphia, he was a supporter of the anticolonization movement, which opposed the emigration of free blacks and slaves from the United States to Africa, and was later elected a delegate to the National Convention of Colored Men in 1865.

Because of his remarkable singing abilities, Bowers was dubbed the "colored Mario" or "American Mario" after the famous Italian opera singer of the nineteenth century, Mario (Giovanni Matteo, Cavaliere de Candia). In response he adopted the stage name Mareo. Bowers performed in a number of states during his career. Continuing to sing publicly on occasion into middle age, he sang "The Star-spangled Banner" upon request at the opening of the first grammar school for African American children in Philadelphia in 1876. His repertoire included ballads as well as many of the popular solos for tenors from the operas and oratorios of the period. He hoped that his performances would prove to whites that black musicians were not minstrels—popular entertainers, both black and white, who performed a caricatured version of African American songs and dances while made up in blackface—but were capable of performing music from the classical repertoire as well as white musicians. Along with his sister, Sarah Sedgewick Bowers, who was also a professional singer known as the "Colored Nightingale," Bowers was an outstanding example of the gifted black classical performers of the nineteenth century. In addition to his musical performances, Bowers worked as a tailor, and then became a prosperous coal merchant. Around 1850 he married Lucenia (Serenia?) Bowers, and they had one daughter, Adelia (Alice?). He died in Philadelphia in 1885.

FURTHER READING
Southern, Eileen. *The Music of Black Americans: A History* (1971, 3d ed. 1997).
Trotter, James Monroe. *Music and Some Highly Musical People* (1881, repr. 1968).
Obituary: *New York Times*, 5 Oct. 1885.

WILLIAM S. WALKER

Bowie, Lester (11 Oct. 1941–8 Nov. 1999), jazz trumpeter, composer, and cofounder of the Art Ensemble of Chicago, was born William Lester Bowie Jr. in Frederick, Maryland, and raised in St. Louis, Missouri, the eldest son of the cornetist W. Lester Bowie Sr. and Earxie Lee Willingham, who worked for the Social Security Administration. Bowie came from a musical family; in 1911 in Bartonsville, Maryland, his grandfather founded the Bartonsville Cornet Band, which included several uncles; his father directed school bands in Little Rock, Arkansas, and St. Louis; and his brothers Byron and Joseph became professional musicians. As a baby Bowie played with his father's cornet mouthpiece, at five he started playing the trumpet, and as a teenager he joined the musicians' union and worked regularly with St. Louis R&B musicians like ALBERT KING and IKE TURNER.

In spite of his early musical success, Bowie did not expect to make music his life, and after graduating from high school in 1958 he enlisted in the air force for four years. He served with the military police, performing in his spare time. During his military service he learned that he preferred playing music to being a soldier, so after he was discharged, he studied music first at Lincoln University in Missouri, and then a year later at North Texas State. After a year in Texas he returned to St. Louis, where he began performing full time with blues and R&B musicians and touring occasionally with circus bands.

Bowie developed a workmanlike philosophy. Reflecting on the diversity of his musical experiences, he told his interviewer Bob Bernotas: "You have to learn how to feed yourself with the instrument, period. And that entails playing everything you can" (Bernotas, 23). At the same time his love of jazz continued to grow. He was influenced by bebop and post-bop musicians, but even stronger was the influence of earlier trumpeters like BUBBER MILEY, COOTIE WILLIAMS, and especially LOUIS ARMSTRONG; these players spoke directly to his sense of playful exploration and showmanship. Bowie was well versed in the jazz tradition, but he was not content to reproduce the music of the past. He thought of jazz as a way of life that embraced innovation and exploration, one that sought to move beyond the classic performers and composers of the past while honoring their accomplishments. This philosophy led him to develop his own unique and highly personal musical voice. He experimented with other young, avant-garde musicians including Oliver Lake and JULIUS HEMPHILL,

who later helped found the Black Artists' Group in St. Louis.

In 1965 Bowie moved to Chicago, where he became music director for R&B singer Fontella Bass. They married and had four children together. Chicago was home to many great blues and R&B musicians such as JERRY BUTLER and JACKIE WILSON and influential recording studios such as Chess Records, so Bowie was able to earn a good living in the city. Chicago's growing free jazz scene also drew him. In 1966 Bowie began performing with a group led by Roscoe Mitchell and he joined Chicago's black avant-garde collective, the Association for the Advancement of Creative Musicians (AACM), becoming the organization's second president. The AACM embraced free improvisation, African musical practices, and aspects of ritual and theater. At times AACM members seemed to reject standard jazz characteristics like popular song forms, functional harmony, swing rhythm, and a clear distinction between a soloist and the rhythm section. Many condemned their music as the end of jazz. On the 1966 Roscoe Mitchell Art Ensemble recording, *Congliptious*, Bowie addressed this issue. His piece "Jazz Death?" opens with the question, "Isn't jazz, as we know it, dead yet?" His answer is an unaccompanied improvisation in which he plays his way through the history of jazz trumpet styles, incorporating them into the avant-garde performance practices of the AACM. At the end of the piece Bowie says, "Well, I guess that depends on what you know," presenting the music of the AACM and the Art Ensemble of the Chicago not as the end of jazz but as a legitimate continuation of jazz's spirit of innovation.

In 1969 Bowie, saxophonist Roscoe Mitchell, bassist Malachi Favors Maghostut, and saxophonist Joseph Jarman moved to Paris, where they were later joined by their fellow AACM member and percussionist Famoudou Don Moye. Previously, in Chicago, the group had rehearsed constantly but performed infrequently; in Europe, where they became known as the Art Ensemble of Chicago (AEC), they found themselves in constant demand. Their groundbreaking improvisations included brass band–flavored melodies, African-inspired percussion work, and "little instruments" like whistles, bells, and toys, as well as aspects of performance art. The musicians wore face paint, African robes, and costumes, heightening the ritual aspects of their performance. In the spirit of experimentation and irony, Bowie frequently appeared in a white lab coat, his long goatee waxed into two devilish points.

Having established himself as a leading voice in experimental jazz, Bowie returned to the United States in 1971. He moved to Jamaica in 1975 and returned to the United States in 1976. He and Bass divorced, and he married photographer Deborah Neeley in 1979. Though Bowie and Neeley settled in the Bronx, he maintained close ties with Chicago musicians. He continued to play with the AEC until his death, but he became involved in many other projects; in 1978 he joined drummer Jack DeJohnette's quartet New Directions; in 1979 he organized the fifty-nine-piece Sho'Nuff Orchestra; and in 1982 he formed the New York Hot Trumpet Repertory Company, which included Olu Dara and WYNTON MARSALIS. (Bowie and Marsalis parted ways, and Marsalis would go on to represent a very different approach to the jazz tradition.) In 1983 he renamed the Hot Trumpets Lester Bowie's Brass Fantasy. The group played original compositions as well as songs by the Spice Girls, Marilyn Manson, and Puccini, offering succinct expressions of Bowie's iconoclastic yet all-embracing philosophy of music in album titles such as *Avant Pop* (1986) and *Serious Fun* (1989). In the 1980s Bowie also led From the Root to the Source, a quintet plus three gospel singers (including Fontella Bass), which blended jazz, pop, and gospel; in the 1990s Bowie formed the New York Organ Ensemble.

In describing his music, Bowie said: "People ask me, 'What kind of music do you play?' I tell them free jazz—free to play whatever I feel like" (Green, 86). Indeed, he drew inspiration from a broad range of African American musical expressions that included not only early and mainstream jazz but also sources as diverse as doo-wop, soul, the *Howdy Doody* theme song, and African musical traditions. He was among the first avant-garde trumpeters to use and expand upon the wails, growls, and sneers of early trumpeters like Bubber Miley and Cootie Williams, adapting those techniques to the performance of free jazz and bringing to the trumpet the kind of sonic flexibility that came so readily to avant-garde saxophonists. Some, like Wynton Marsalis, trumpeter and artistic director of Jazz at Lincoln Center, and Ken Burns, director of the epic documentary *Jazz*, seek to understand jazz as a collection of canonical composers, compositions, and practices. Lester Bowie's eclecticism and his humorous, ironic, and unorthodox improvisations suggest alternative, more open-ended

histories of jazz that, in the twenty-first century, continue to inspire new generations of jazz musicians, including trumpet players such as Dave Douglas and Corey Wilkes, who replaced Bowie in the AEC after his death.

FURTHER READING
Bernotas, Bob. "Lester Bowie," *Jazz Player* (Oct.–Nov. 1995).
Green, Tony. "Profile: Lester Bowie," *Jazziz Magazine* (Mar. 1996).
Jordan, Phillippa, and Rafi Zabor. "Lester Bowie: Roots, Research, and the Carnival Chef," in *The Jazz Musician*, eds. Mark Rowland and Tony Scherman (1994).
Livingston, Tim. "Interview: Lester Bowie," *Cadence* (Jan. 2001).
Obituaries: *New York Times*, Arts section, 11 Nov. 1999; *Village Voice*, 8–14 Dec. 1999.

JOHN HARRIS-BEHLING

Bowles, Charles (1761–16 Mar. 1843), soldier and evangelist, was born in Boston, Massachusetts. His father was an African servant and his mother was the daughter of Colonel Morgan, an officer in the rifle corps during the American Revolutionary War. As an infant Bowles remained with his father but dwelled with a foster parent in Lunenburg, Massachusetts, until age twelve. After the death of his foster parent, he lived with a Tory family until fourteen, when he joined the Colonial artillery as a waiter to an officer. Two years later he enlisted in the American army and served until the war concluded.

The war over, Bowles traveled to New Hampshire and married Mary Corliss, his cousin and the granddaughter of Colonel Morgan. Soon after marriage, he was baptized and joined the Calvinist Baptist Church in Wentworth, New Hampshire. Finding the Calvinist denomination too inflexible, he later converted to the Free Will Baptist, embracing its fostering of religious pragmatism. Though he felt called to pastor, his lack of formal education initially discouraged him.

As Bowles struggled with finding his place and purpose in life, he worked as a cook on a ship out of Boston for three years. The ribald lifestyle of his shipmates aboard ship troubled him deeply. Thus he left the ship to pursue an inner call to preach. Although his wife did not support him, he accepted an invitation to preach at a revival, after which he left home to pursue the ministry with complete determination. After the Free Will Baptist

Conference licensed him to minister, he pastored for a while in Vermont.

From 1808 to 1817 Elder Bowles labored in Ashburn, Massachusetts, with "good success" before leaving for Gloucester, Rhode Island, to pastor with Elder Colby. However, in Rhode Island, as elsewhere, there was resistance to the ministry. Bowles recalled occasional encounters with "mob violence" and "irreligious" men who celebrated the "orgies of Bacchus" (Lewis, 3–19). He returned to New Hampshire momentarily but moved to Williamstown, Vermont, in 1816, delivering his first sermon in Huntington, Vermont, on July 24. Shortly thereafter he purchased a farm in Huntington and moved three of his children to live with him there. On 26 November 1816, the Free Will Baptist Order ordained him "to the work of the Gospel Ministry" (19). Again he triumphed over bigotry, hate, and belligerence with conviction and devoutness. He also preached successfully in Richmond, Duxbury, Waterbury, Stowe, and Middlesex, his style always simple and practical.

From 1817–1826 Bowles preached to Free Will Baptists throughout New England and Canada, organizing churches and quarterly meetings, converting disbelievers, baptizing, leading revivals, and confronting racism. He became so respected in Vermont, which identified with the confederacy at the time, that his powerful sermons and demeanor won support for the abolitionists, especially when he teamed with abolitionist Jeffrey Brace, who was kidnapped from Africa as a small boy. Bowles also found time to labor on his farm with his children. Bowles lived with his daughter Eunice and his grandchildren in Huntingdon for about twenty years. On 22 May 1834 he moved with them to Rutland, Vermont. In 1835 and 1836 he focused on evangelical work and committed significant effort to Corinth, Wheelock, and Enosburg Quarterly Meetings.

During the latter part of 1837 Rev. Charles Bowles II, Bowles's son, visited his father in Vermont. Much impressed by his father's work, the son invited his father to his church in Hopkinton, New York, to conduct evangelist work. Not only did the father accept his son's invitation, but he also ministered so effectively that he founded the First Free Will Baptist Church in Lawrence, New York, in 1837. In 1839 at the September Lawrence Quarterly Meeting, the elders changed the name to the First Free Will Baptist Church in Dickinson, the real location of the church.

Though partially blind at this time, Elder Charles Bowles continued his effective ministry and made converts of whites unaccustomed to black elders. He labored in local churches until relieved by Elder N. W. Bixby from Vermont. He returned to a small place in Dickinson, giving up his farm in Hopkinton. Still losing his eyesight, he persisted in organizing churches and preaching, having memorized the Bible.

In October 1842 at the yearly meeting in Lawrenceville, Elder Bowles's ancient age and feeble health became apparent. Yet he relished laboring with the brethren, ministering, and saving souls. By the winter of 1843 his attendance at meetings and visitations had diminished dramatically. During the latter part of January he succumbed to erysipelas in the feet, which quickly grew malignant and spread throughout his body. He lingered until 16 March 1843. His life and death serves as a testament to transcendence of patriotism, religion, and service over racism, class, and ignorance.

FURTHER READING

Dearing, Rev. Arthur. *Essay on the Fugitive Law of the U.S. Congress of 1850* (1852). Available online at http://docsouth.unc.edu/neh/lewisjw/menu.html.

Knoblock, Glenn A. *Strong and Brave Fellows: New Hampshire's Black Soldiers and Sailors of the American Revolution, 1775–1784* (2003).

Lewis, John W., ed. *The Life, Labors, and Travels of Elder Charles Bowles, of the Free Will Baptist Denomination.* Available online at http://docsouth.unc.edu/neh/lewisjw/menu.html.

Lewis, John W., ed. *Essay on the Character and Condition of the African Race.* Available online at http://docsouth.unc.edu/neh/lewisjw/menu.html.

FLOYD OGBURN, JR.

Bowles, Eva Del Vakia (24 Jan. 1875–14 June 1943), organization leader, was born in Albany, Athens County, Ohio, the daughter of John Hawkes Bowles and Mary Jane Porter. Unlike most African Americans born during the Reconstruction era, Bowles grew up in comfortable circumstances. Her grandfather John R. Bowles served as a chaplain for the all-black Fifty-fifth Massachusetts Infantry and later became the first black teacher hired by the Ohio Public School Fund. Her father was the first black postal clerk in Columbus, Ohio.

Bowles was educated in Columbus at a business college and attended summer courses at Ohio State University. After a short teaching career in Kentucky, North Carolina, and Virginia, she was recruited in 1905 to work in New York City as secretary of the Colored Young Women's Christian

Association (later affiliated with the New York City YWCA as the 137th Street branch in Harlem). This position made her the "first employed Negro YWCA Secretary in the country." In 1908 she received training in social work at Columbia University School of Philanthropy.

In 1913, after a brief return to Columbus, where she worked as a caseworker, Bowles returned to New York as secretary of the newly formed Subcommittee for Colored Work of the YWCA national board. The position had been created in recognition of the fast-growing interest in association work among urban black women. Among Bowles's responsibilities was helping the organization accommodate its black membership without jeopardizing the support of whites. At a time when many whites supported race separation, this was no easy task.

At the time of Bowles's appointment, the national board had fourteen local "colored" affiliates. For the most part, these associations were organized by black club women to provide services similar to those offered by white YWCAs—namely, lodging and club activities for young single women who moved into cities to work. Black women were routinely excluded from white facilities. Furthermore, although local black and white associations were affiliated with the national board, there was often little communication between the local organizations. Bowles's solution was to create a structure whereby there would be only one YWCA in each city. Because the black associations were usually smaller and less financially stable, they became branches of the larger, white organization.

Although this arrangement made black women accountable to white women, Bowles insisted that the volunteers and staff of the black branches be in charge of day-to-day operations and fund-raising. In addition she regularly scheduled skills and leadership training opportunities for black volunteers and staff. Bowles believed that integration was inevitable. She felt that this structure would provide a way for the two races to become accustomed to working together and that black women would have the opportunity to prove their administrative and decision-making abilities.

World War I offered a unique opportunity for the YWCA when the national board was granted $4 million by the U.S. War Department Commission on Training Camp Activities to work with women and girls on the home front. The War Work Council of the YWCA set aside $200,000 for projects with African Americans, and Bowles was made secretary in charge of expanding services to black women. Under this mandate, the association was able to open recreation centers, industrial work centers, and fifteen hostess houses (facilities that provided entertainment for soldiers and sometimes lodging for their families) near army installations. By the end of the war, black women were being served in forty-five cities, and the association had over thirty-nine thousand black members. Most notable was the use of funds leftover from the war effort to build a much-needed association facility in Washington, D.C., to accommodate the city's growing black population. Bowles's accomplishments during the war so impressed former president Theodore Roosevelt that he designated $4,000 of his Nobel Peace Prize to be dispersed according to her directions.

To accomplish this expansion of work during the war, Bowles sought the support of the network of prominent black club women in the National Association of Colored Women. She later used the influence of this group to press the national board for more equitable representation for black women on local and national committees and boards. This move resulted in significant steps toward more biracial cooperation in student and community associations. Furthermore black women gained their first representative on the national board in 1924.

After the war, Bowles concentrated on the improvement of race relations within the national association. As secretary of the Council on Colored Work, she increased the number of black staff employed by the national board to nine at headquarters and three in the field. Under her leadership, the board led other organizations in negotiations to hold nationally sponsored conventions and meetings only in cities that would guarantee that all members, regardless of race, could be accommodated. She also worked tirelessly as an advocate of the international work of the association, especially in Africa and the Caribbean. She became disillusioned with the YWCA, however, and resigned in 1932, charging that a recent reorganization would "diminish participation of Negroes in the policy making of the Association" by dispersing black staff in a way that she felt decreased their effectiveness in behalf of the specific needs of black women.

Bowles did not confine her interest in race work to the YWCA. She was an active volunteer in such important organizations as the Urban League, the National Interracial Conference, the American

Interracial Peace Committee, the National Association for the Advancement of Colored People, the National League of Women Voters, the Commission of Church and Race Relations of the Federal Council of Churches, and her denominational Episcopalian Women's Interracial Council.

After her resignation from the YWCA, Bowles worked briefly as an executive of the National Colored Merchants Association, sponsored by the National Business League. Then, after returning to her native Ohio, she served for a brief time as acting secretary of the West End branch of the YWCA of Cincinnati. During the 1940 presidential campaign, she became the Harlem organizer for the Wendell Willkie Republican organization. She died in Richmond, Virginia.

FURTHER READING

Information on Bowles's work is on microfilm in the national board YWCA archives under Colored Work, Interracial Work, and War Work Council.

Olcott, Jane, ed. *The Work of Colored Women* (1919).

Obituaries: *Norfolk Journal and Guide*, 19 June 1943; *Woman's Press*, Sept. 1943.

This entry is taken from the *American National Biography* and is published here with the permission of the American Council of Learned Societies.

ADRIENNE LASH JONES

Bowling, Frank (29 Feb. 1936–), a modernist painter, was born in Guyana. Bowling shaped his art to insert a black cultural sensibility into forms such as abstract painting, generally viewed as "Western," insisting that art should not be stereotyped by race or national identity. Working on both sides of the Atlantic, his solo exhibits since 1962 number well over eighty.

Little has been written about Bowling's childhood. His mother owned a variety store in Bartica, Guyana, which he looked after when it was being built. At age fifteen, he was sent to England, where he joined the British Library to research Guyana's history and culture. He enrolled in 1957–1959 at Regent Street Polytechnic, Chelsea School of Art, and in 1959–1962 at the Slade School of Fine Art, University College London, and the Royal College of Art. During this period he was a founder of the Young Commonwealth Artists Group, working with Billy Apple, Jonathan Kingdon, and Neil Stocker.

Bowling graduated from the Royal College with a Master of Fine Arts degree in 1962, receiving a silver medal with a traveling scholarship. Rather than study in a destination like Rome, he spent it on a return to his homeland, focusing his art on his birthplace and the confluence of the Essequipo and Mazaruni rivers. The following year, he was commissioned to paint three canvases for the Shakespeare Quarto-Centenary in Stratford-on-Avon and in 1966 won the Senegal Grand Prize for Contemporary Art at the First World Festival of Negro Art, in Dakar. He joined the London Group of artists in 1962 and served as vice president in 1965.

Bowling moved to New York in 1966, as the beginning of a successful career in London was overshadowed by his work being left out of significant shows, including an exhibit at Whitechapel Gallery in 1964. Bowling was informed, "England is not yet ready for a gifted artist of colour." He and his contemporaries at the college were experimenting with painting from newspaper cuttings, photographs, and films, but he chose different subject matter. Concluding that he didn't fit the accepted notion of "pop art" he reminisced later, "I chose my own themes, such as the death of Patrice Lumumba, because this was where my feeling was. ... I did not paint Marilyn Monroe because she did not interest me. [Ron] Kitaj did not paint Marilyn Monroe either. He painted *The Murder of* [German Marxist] *Rosa Luxemburg*."

Bowling deftly avoided being stereotyped as a "black artist," writing that "there is something which is very distinctly Black—as there is something very distinctly Jewish, or Scots/Irish. But there is no Black Art. I believe that the Black soul, if there can be such a thing, belongs in Modernism. Black people are a new and original people." In New York he adopted a more abstract style, supported and influenced by the art critic Clement Greenberg, who confirmed Bowling's understanding that "modernism belonged to me also." Bowling developed a method of laying canvases on a thirty-foot-wide platform, mixing colors in jars, and then pouring out the paint in a thick liquid state to spread and bleed. "I would readjust the painting according to the geometry" he explained, "or to [mathematician] Fibonacci and Jay Hambidge [an artist known for his emphasis on symmetry], or something like that, but sometimes chance played its part."

He received a Guggenheim Memorial fellowship in 1967 and again in 1973, holding positions as artist in residence and in a visiting artist program for the New York State Council of the

Arts, 1968–1972. During this period he taught at Columbia University, Rutgers University, Massachusetts College of Art, Rhode Island School of Design, and the School of Visual Arts in New York.

In 1970 Bowling produced *Middle Passage*, which he described as autobiographical, observing that "I am a product of the middle passage." The same year, he participated in the controversial exhibition *Some American History*, sponsored by the Houston Institute for the Arts, Rice University, in Texas. Curator Larry Rivers was both praised and criticized for being a "white" artist who chose to focus on the black experience in American life, inviting Bowling and five other artists of African descent to work with him. Bowling contributed a series of articles on black art to *Arts Magazine* in 1969–1971, including "Is Black about Color?" and "Silence: People Die Crying When They Should Love."

Bowling alternated between work in Britain and the United States, winning a painting prize at the Edinburgh Open 100 in Scotland in 1967. Since the mid-1960s, he has maintained studios in both New York and London. He was recognized in the 1970s as a leading painter in what became known as the Colour Field style and began referring to his work as "poured paintings." During the 1980s he experimented with rectangular slabs of gel to create new patterns and served as Artist in Residence for 1984 at the Skowhegan School of Painting and Sculpture in Maine. In the late twentieth century Bowling became known for large-scale, multicolored, textured acrylic paintings, including *Bamboudan* (1983), *Fishes, Wishes and Uncle Jack* (1989), and *Silver Birch* (1985). Bowling observed that he chose titles for his paintings that are "private jokes," intentionally "ironic and evocative. An awful lot is personal and in riddles."

At the dawn of the twenty-first century, Bowling's paintings were featured in many permanent collections, including the Tate Museum in London and the Metropolitan Museum of Art in New York. He was elected to the Royal Academy of Arts, London, 26 May 2005, the first black British artist to have the honorific "RA" placed after his name. A solo show at the Royal Academy followed in 2006, as well as exhibitions at the Serpentine Gallery and the Whitney Museum of Modern Art, New York. In 2007 he received an honorary doctorate from the University of Wolverhampton, England; in 2008 he was awarded the Order of the British Empire for services to art.

FURTHER READING

Bowling, Frank, and Eddie Chambers. *Frank Bowling: Bowling on through the Century; A Major Touring Exhibition of Recent Paintings* (1996).

Bowling, Frank, Dorothy Désir, and Spencer Richards. *Bending the Grid: Black Identity and Resistance in the Art of Frank Bowling* (2003).

Doy, Gen. *Black Visual Culture: Modernity and Postmodernity* (2000).

Heyd, Milly. *Mutual Reflections: Jews and Blacks in American Art* (1999).

Oguibe, Olu. *The Culture Game* (2004).

Riggs, Thomas. *St. James Guide to Black Artists* (1997).

CHARLES ROSENBERG

Bowman, Euday Louis (9 Nov. 1887–26 May 1949), American ragtime and blues composer and pianist, was born in Tarrant County, Texas, to A. Bowman and Marguerite Olivia Estee Landin Bowman. His grandfather, Gatewood Bowman, cared for him and his older sister and brother where they lived, on a farm close to Mansfield, Texas. Bowman attended the public schools in the area and frequently visited Kansas City, Missouri, as a youngster.

In 1905 Bowman's parents divorced. Along with his mother he moved in with his sister, Mary M. Bowman, who lived in Fort Worth. His sister was not only a teacher in the school system but also a piano instructor and is credited with teaching Bowman to play the piano. The tall and thinly built Bowman became an itinerant ragtime pianist performing at local homes, at parties, and night clubs in Forth Worth through the 1920s. It is alleged that a train accident contributed to the amputation of one of his legs. He frequently visited Kansas City to publicize and sell his music. Bowman played at the bordellos in Kansas City and other nearby states and also arranged music for local musicians and orchestras. Bowman's fair complexion and features made it easy for him to pass as white. But his permanent home was in the black section of Fort Worth.

In 1914 Bowman self-published his "Twelfth Street Rag." Some ragtime researchers believed that it represented his experience in Kansas City and commemorated a street in this locale, while others stated that it paid tribute to a street in Fort Worth, Texas. The unique and exceptional feature of this rag was its thirty-two-bar theme and variations form, three-note motif or secondary rag, syncopated rhythms, and duple meter. It had an improvisatory character, was not difficult to play, and was quite captivating to many. Bowman sold the publishing rights to the rag to J.W. Jenkins' Sons Music Publishers in Kansas City for between fifty to one-hundred dollars. It became very popular over the years that they published it, but Bowman earned little of the royalties. In 1919 it was later arranged and published with a fox trot dotted rhythm and titled, "Fox Trot Arrangement." The fox trot was gaining popularity during this time.

Records indicate that Bowman served in the draft in 1918. Bowman's marriage to Geneva Morris lasted a few months, after which she abandoned him. They divorced in 1926. By 1937 the rights of "Twelfth Street Rag" were transferred back to Bowman, and he made several arrangements of the work, even adding words to it. So popular and influential was this rag that over 120 early recorded versions of it existed, including some by many of the top bands from the swing era: LOUIS ARMSTRONG and his Hot Seven (1927), the BENNIE MOTEN and his band (1927), DUKE ELLINGTON with Benny Payne (1931), FLETCHER HENDERSON (1931), FATS WALLER (1935), COUNT BASIE with LESTER YOUNG (1939), LIONEL HAMPTON (1939), ANDY KIRK and his Twelve Clouds of Joy with MARY LOU WILLIAMS (1940), SIDNEY BECHET and his New Orleans Feetwarmers (1941), and Teddy Buckner and his Dixieland Band (1955). White musicians, including the country and western star Bob Wills (1946), and the jazz guitarist Al Caiola (1958) also recorded the track. Unissued recordings were also made by Bowman for Gennett (1924) and ARC (1938).

During the 1940s there was a decline in interest in the big band sound and a revival in ragtime, largely aided by the record industry. Jazz artists and bands were also performing ragtime music and even the jazz journals now published articles on ragtime. Shapiro-Bernstein Music Publishers of New York City bought the publishing rights to "Twelfth Street Rag" from Bowman, and published it from 1941. "Twelfth Street Rag" became legendary through the acclaimed recording by Walter "Pee Wee" Hunt and Orchestra in 1948 on Capital 15105. This version of the work contained several jazz and swing styles. The disc jockeys played the recording on the radio, and the listeners loved what they heard. It sold three million copies and Bowman earned revenue from the recording.

By 1949 Bowman's health was deteriorating and his finances were in ruins. On 6 February 1949 he married Ruth Emma Thompson, but he filed for divorce one month later on grounds of cruelty inflicted by his wife. By the time Bowman received his royalties from "Pee Wee" Hunt's recording of "Twelfth Street Rag," he was already $2,000 in debt with doctors' bills. Most of the funds were used to cover his medical expenses. He collected and sold junk as a means of income. Bowman had moved back with his sister sometime in 1947 and the two shared an old, dilapidated house at 818 South Jennings Street in Fort Worth. It was noted that she wrote some of the music to the "Twelfth Street Rag" and shared in the royalties with her brother. Bowman had his own record company and later recorded "Twelfth Street Rag" on the piano. Shortly after moving to New York City to publicize his new recording of the rag and negotiate royalties, Bowman died there of pneumonia on 26 May 1949. He was buried in Oakwood Cemetery located in Tarrant County, Fort Worth, Texas. Royalties from "Twelfth Street Rag" were transferred to his sister along with his old car.

According to Campbell (1951), most of Bowman's and his sister's personal possessions were sold at public auction on 14 August 1950 to settle his estate. Included were Bowman's piano that he had purchased in Hartford, Connecticut, in 1895, which was sold to his friend Myrtle Steward for forty-six dollars; his accordion; six hundred unopened records of "Twelfth Street Rag"; his large collection of sheet music; and the original manuscript of the "Twelfth Street Rag." As Bowman's possessions were being sold, his "Twelfth Street Rag" was performed by his friend, Ed Lally, as they bid adieu to the composer. Along with his furniture, dishes, and other household items, the auction fetched three-thousand dollars to Bowman's estate. But there were no heirs.

In summary, Bowman composed other rags, some in honor of streets in Kansas City: "Petticoat Lane Rag" (1915), "Eleventh Street Rag" (1917), and "Thirteenth Street Rag." Works commemorating streets in Fort Worth's famous bordello district included "Sixth Street Rag" (1914) and "Tenth Street Rag" (1914). Other works by Bowman were "Shamrock Rag" (1916), "Chromatic Chords" (1926), "White Lily Dreams," and "Old Glory on Its Way." These unpublished rags displayed technically challenging bass passages. Works influenced by the midwestern style blues and lyricism included the rag "Petticoat Lane" (1915), along with "Colorado Blues," "Fort Worth Blues," "Kansas City Blues," "Tipperary Blues," and "Jubilee Ball" (1934). With lyrics by Edward Payne, Bowman composed the music for songs in 1934: "My Love Dream of You," "Forgotten Rose (How I Miss You—No One Knows)," "Yesterday's Joys (You're Cherished but for a Day)," and "There's a Rainbow Down in Texas." But it is "Twelfth Street Rag" that left its imprint and remained one of the favorite rags throughout history. It had a profound influence on many jazz composers and performers from the 1920s onward and was instrumental in the evolution of Kansas City jazz. Some of Bowman's original notated music is housed at the Pate Museum of Transportation in Fort Worth, Texas.

FURTHER READING

Campbell, S. Brun. "Euday Bowman and the 12th Street Rag." *Jazz Journal*, 1951.

Jasen, David A., and Trebor Jay Tichenor. *Rags and Ragtime: A Musical History* (1978).

Oliphant, Dave. *Texan Jazz* (1996).

Simon, Cheryl L. "Bowman, Euday Louis." Texas Historical Association Handbook of Texas Online.

Waldo, Terry. *This Is Ragtime* (1976).

BARBARA BONOUS-SMIT

Bowman, James E., Jr. (5 Feb. 1923–), pathologist and geneticist, was born in Washington, D.C., the oldest of six children born to James E. Bowman, a dentist, and Peterson Bowman, a homemaker. Bowman completed his undergraduate and medical school education in Washington, receiving a B.S. in 1943 and an M.D. in 1946, both from Howard University. After completing an internship at the Freedman's Hospital in Washington, D.C. (1946–1947), Bowman moved to St. Luke's Hospital in Chicago for a residency in pathology (1947–1950). It was during his residency that he met his future wife, Barbara Taylor, a Chicago native who was then completing her undergraduate degree at Sarah Lawrence College in Bronxville, New York. The couple married in 1950, the same year that Bowman was made chairman of the department of pathology at Chicago's Provident Hospital, a primarily African American institution (1950–1953).

From 1953 until 1955 Bowman served as a captain in the U.S. Army Medical Corps with an appointment as chief of the pathology branch of the Medical Nutrition Laboratory at Fitzsimmons Army Hospital in Denver, Colorado. Bowman's career then took a turn pioneered by many other black doctors and scientists before him: he went abroad in search of further opportunities. He and he wife spent the next six years in Iran, where Bowman held appointments at Namazaee Hospital (chairman, department of pathology, 1955–1961) and Pahlavi University (associate professor and professor of pathology, 1957–1961), both in Shiraz,

Iran. Bowman's exposure to the particular set of diseases, mainly favism, experienced by Iranian patients stimulated his growing interest in population genetics, particularly the distribution of inherited metabolic and blood disorders. After leaving Iran in 1961 Bowman spent the following year as a special research fellow in biometry and genetics at the University of London's Galton Laboratory, a leading research center for the study of what was then known as inborn errors of metabolism.

Bowman published several papers in the early 1960s on the origins of favism, an inherited disease in which patients lack glucose-6-phosphate dehydrogenase, an enzyme necessary for the normal functioning of hemoglobin. The enzyme deficiency can cause a sudden destruction of red blood cells after eating certain legumes—particularly fava beans, a staple of the Iranian diet. Bowman's research in genetic blood disorders was taking place during a revolution in biochemistry and genetic medicine. In 1948 Linus Pauling had demonstrated that sickle cell anemia is caused by a protein abnormality in hemoglobin. Proteins are the molecules that carry out most of the biological processes within the cell. The structure of a protein is determined by its sequence of amino acids, which in turn is specified by the DNA sequence that codes for the specific protein. Because proteins' functions are tied so closely to their structure, a single point change in the DNA sequence (a mutation) can have a dramatic effect on cellular function. In 1956 a new era of molecular medicine was born when researchers located the point mutation that caused sickle cell anemia. These findings explained that any number of inherited blood diseases had specific genetic origins; for Bowman they established a research agenda for the rest of his career.

In 1962 Bowman and his wife returned to Chicago to accept an appointment as medical director of the Blood Bank (1962–1972) and assistant professor of medicine and pathology at the University of Chicago. He became associate professor in 1967 and full professor in 1972. Bowman occupied a number of leadership positions at the University of Chicago, including director of laboratories (1971–1981), director of the Comprehensive Sickle Cell Center (1973–1974), and liaison officer for International Activities (1969–1971), the Committee on Appointment Inequities (1971–1975), and University Senate (1971–1974).

As head of one of the country's leading sickle cell treatment centers Bowman soon became involved in debates within both the black and scientific communities about the benefits and limits of genetic screening programs. As genetic screening tests became available for diseases such as sickle cell anemia, PKU, and Tay-Sachs, some states began making these tests mandatory for marriage and admission to public schools. Although many physicians, including Bowman, were enthusiastic about the possibilities of this research for human health, some in the black community pointed a skeptical finger at the long association of genetics with scientific racism and eugenics. In the late 1970s, for example, the Du Pont Company required genetic screening as a preemployment test and refused to hire workers with sickle cell. These debates only intensified with the launch of the Human Genome Project—a massive effort to sequence the entire human genome—in 1990. Throughout the 1980s and 1990s Bowman served on a number of national committees and policy boards on genetics, including, most visibly, the National Institutes of Health's (NIH) Working Group on Ethical, Legal, and Social Issues (1995–1998). With Robert F. Murray, a professor of pediatrics and medicine at Howard University, Bowman authored what would become the standard textbook on genetic variation in persons of African heritage, *Genetic Variation and Disorders in Peoples of African Origin* (1990).

Bowman's interest in international population genetics and scientific issues continued throughout his career, with over ninety publications on genetic variation in populations in Iran, Turkey, Taiwan, the United States, Ghana, Nigeria, Cameroon, Uganda, Ethiopia, Mexico, and South Vietnam. Bowman was a fellow of the College of American Pathologists, the American Society of Clinical Pathologists, the Royal Society of Tropical Medicine and Hygiene, and the Hastings Center. He held memberships in thirteen scientific societies in pathology, hematology, genetics, ethics, anthropology, clinical research, and ethics. He retired in 1993 and was named professor emeritus in the departments of pathology and medicine at the University of Chicago. In 2006 his daughter, Valerie Jarrett, was named chair of the University of Chicago Medical Center Board.

FURTHER READING

Much of the information for this entry was gathered through personal correspondence with its subject, 16 Feb. 2007.

Bowman, James E., and Robert F. Murray Jr. *Genetic Variation and Disorders in Peoples of African Origin* (1990).

American Men and Women of Science, 22d ed. (2005).

Harris, Ron. "Tampering with Genes: A New Threat to Blacks?" *Ebony* (Sept. 1980).

AUDRA J. WOLFE

Bowman, Laura (3 Oct. 1881–29 Mar. 1957), actor and singer, was born Laura Bradford in Quincy, Illinois, the daughter of a Dutch mother and a father with mixed black and white parentage. She grew up in Cincinnati, where she sang in church choirs. Her early family life was difficult, and her father arranged her marriage at sixteen to Henry Ward Bowman, a railroad porter. The unhappy marriage lasted only two years. In 1902 Bowman's dream of a singing career began with her professional debut as a member of the chorus in the Midwest tour of the Williams and Walker Company's production of *In Dahomey*. The show went on to New York and in 1903 toured England, where it also played at Buckingham Palace for the ninth birthday of the Prince of Wales, Edward VIII.

During the tour of *In Dahomey* Bowman fell in love with PETE HAMPTON, another performer in the show. Soon after arriving in England the original company broke up, and Bowman and Hampton decided not to join the new one. Instead, they formed the Darktown Entertainers quartet with singers WILL GARLAND and Fred Douglas. Performing everything from grand opera to lullabies, the Darktown Entertainers appeared on stage in Germany, Hungary, Austria, France, Switzerland, and Russia. When increasing political unrest forced the group to leave Russia, they returned to London and disbanded. Bowman and Hampton, now in a common-law marriage, returned to the United States, where Bowman appeared in the chorus of *The Southerns* during its thirty-two-week run in New York. Then the couple returned to London to join the second company of *In Dahomey*, this time with Bowman as one of the show's principal actors. After the show closed, Bowman and Hampton worked as a duet throughout Europe and purchased a house in England in 1910. But with war approaching, the British government ordered all foreigners to leave the country. Extremely ill on the voyage home, Hampton died shortly after their arrival.

In 1916, just weeks after Hampton's death, Bowman joined the Lafayette Players, the well-known stock acting troupe from Harlem, New York. She appeared in numerous dramatic and musical productions, often receiving positive reviews from critics. There she also met and fell in love with actor Sidney Kirkpatrick. Because the Lafayette Players management did not want married couples in the company, Bowman and Kirkpatrick eventually left. They married and formed a duo that performed in Boston, Philadelphia, and Washington, D.C. Settling for a time in Indianapolis, Kirkpatrick's hometown, the light-skinned couple circumvented racial prejudice that prohibited African Americans from performing in many of the town's venues by billing themselves as the Hawaiian Duet. During this time Bowman also made her screen debut in the African American independent filmmaker OSCAR MICHEAUX's *The Brute* (1920), an association that would continue into the early 1940s.

In 1923 Bowman and Kirkpatrick moved to New York, where they became involved with the Ethiopian Art Players. Bowman took on the role of Aunt Nancy in the Broadway production of *The Chip Woman's Fortune* by the black playwright WILLIS RICHARDSON. She also played Herodias to Kirkpatrick's Herod in Oscar Wilde's *Salome*, as well as the role of Aemilia in a jazz version of Shakespeare's *Comedy of Errors*. After the company disbanded, Bowman and Kirkpatrick performed in Indianapolis shortly before rejoining the Lafayette Players. By this time, the couple's popularity convinced the troupe's management to put aside the stipulation against married actors. Bowman's role, in 1928, was as the wife of the lead character in thirty-two performances of *Meek Mose*, written by actor and playwright FRANK H. WILSON. Although the production received fairly negative reviews, Bowman was uniformly praised for her part.

While in New York, Bowman established the National Art School, which taught drama to aspiring African American actors and staged performances at churches, schools, and social events. When the Lafayette Players moved to Los Angeles in August 1928, Bowman and Kirkpatrick followed. The company, after good attendance and reviews at the outset, soon struggled to fill seats and in January 1932 disbanded. Joining the JUANITA HALL Singers, Bowman and Kirkpatrick sang in several films, including *Dixie Anna* and *Check and Double Check*.

The couple moved back to New York City, where Bowman appeared in *Sentinels* in 1931 and *The Tree* in 1932 on Broadway. As had happened earlier in her career, the shows received bad reviews, but Bowman's performances were applauded. Although her roles were based on the black mammy stereotype, by the early thirties she had established herself as a legitimate actor on the stage.

Bowman and Kirkpatrick traveled to Los Angeles briefly to join the revived Lafayette Players in 1932. The troupe lasted only three weeks, but she remained in Los Angeles for several months. There she made *Ten Minutes to Live* (1932), with Micheaux, and had a role in the film *Drums of Voodoo* (released 1934). By the end of 1932 Bowman and Kirkpatrick were back in New York performing their duo act. Soon after their return Kirkpatrick died suddenly from a heart attack, leaving Bowman widowed for the second time.

Despite her personal tragedy Bowman continued to work, and just weeks after her husband's death played Auntie Hagar in the all-black cast of *Louisiana*. She also began to drink heavily, and while at a Harlem bar frequented by black performers, she met her next husband, LeRoi Antoine, a Haitian immigrant twenty-three years younger than Bowman, with aspirations to become an opera singer. Bowman and Antoine married soon after they met in 1933.

During the remainder of the 1930s Bowman appeared in stage, screen, and radio productions. After *Drums of Voodoo* was released, the original Broadway cast restaged a production of *Louisiana*, with Bowman once again as Auntie Hagar. She also appeared in the short-lived *Yesterday's Orchid* (1934). She played Edgar Allan Poe's housekeeper in *Plumes in the Dust*, which opened in Washington, D.C., in 1936 before moving to New York's Forty-sixth Street Theatre. Critics singled out Bowman for her well-executed role as Parthenia, the *Conjur* woman in 1938's Conjur, which featured an all-black cast. The following year she once again played the stereotypical role of domestic servant, this time in a short-lived production of *Please, Mrs. Garibaldi*.

As a radio actor, Bowman could be heard on numerous shows, including *Southernaires, Personal Column on the Air*, and *Pores and Drums* as well as radio soap operas such as *Stella Dallas* and *Pretty Kitty Kelly*. Indeed, her radio performances became a steady source of income during the 1930s. In 1938 she had a role in Micheaux's film *God's Stepchildren*. Bowman and Antoine decided to move to Los Angeles to help his career as an actor, and in 1940 Bowman played the leading role of Dr. Helen Jackson in the movie *Son of Ingagi*, notable as the first all-black horror film. In the same year she also appeared in *The Notorious Elinor Lee*, another independent film by Micheaux.

An amateur theater group Bowman created during the early 1940s landed her work on radio, and the group's show—often featuring biblical stories—became widely popular. The venture paid little but kept Bowman busy until the mid-1940s, when she began acting again. Her role in the Hollywood production of *Decision* led to a role in a new postwar drama, *Jeb*, in New York. She played the mother of a black World War II hero who struggles with racial prejudice after returning to the South at the end of the war. Opening on 7 February 1946 at the Locust Street Theatre in Philadelphia, it enjoyed a short run on Broadway. Afterward Bowman was invited to perform with a company touring with *Anna Lucasta*. With more than nine hundred performances, the play was an overwhelming success, and the company took it to Europe. Bowman remained in the United States and continued with the play on the "subway circuit"—the Bronx, Brooklyn, Atlantic City, and other nearby locations. After four years as Theresa in *Anna Lucasta*, she returned to Los Angeles when the show finally closed. The role of Theresa was her last.

In 1951, shortly after arriving in Los Angeles, Bowman, by then weighing more than two hundred pounds, suffered a stroke that confined her to a wheelchair for the rest of her life. Although she had made a significant amount of money during her career, she had no savings during her last years. For the next six years Antoine attended dutifully to his bedridden wife. Bowman died at her home in Los Angeles at the age of seventy-six. In her obituary the *New York Times* noted, "It was said of Miss Bowman that she played in about every country that had a theatre." In 1961 Antoine published her biography, *Achievement: The Life of Laura Bowman*, "as told by Laura Bowman to her husband."

FURTHER READING

Sampson, Henry T. *Blacks in Black and White: A Source Book on Black Films* (1977).

Tanner, Jo A. *Dusky Maidens: The Odyssey of the Early Black Dramatic Actress* (1992).

MARY ANNE BOELCSKEVY

Bowman, Thea (29 Dec. 1937–30 Mar. 1990), Roman Catholic religious leader, sacred music performer, and social justice activist, was born Bertha J. Bowman in Yazoo City, Mississippi, the granddaughter of slaves and only child of physician Theon Edward Bowman and high school music teacher Mary Esther Coleman. Baptized an Episcopalian, Bertha attended Methodist services. Growing up in segregated, impoverished Canton, Mississippi, she absorbed the spirituality and music of black

community elders and her parents' own deep commitments to lives of service. At age ten, she chose to be baptized as a Roman Catholic because she admired the work of the Franciscan Sisters of Perpetual Adoration (FSPA) in Canton. In the face of public uproar, white nuns from this order taught black students at Holy Child Jesus Catholic School. Unable to read after five years of poor quality education in segregated public schools, Bertha finally became literate after transferring to this school in 1949. That same year, Bertha decided to become an FSPA nun herself, despite her priest's counsel to join a historically black order instead.

In 1953, Bertha moved to Wisconsin to enter the novitiate (preparation for joining a Catholic religious order) at the FSPA mother house in La Crosse, Wisconsin. Her entry was delayed by a year in a tuberculosis sanitarium. Out of respect for her father, she took the name "Thea" upon her religious vows. In 1961, she returned to Canton to teach English and music at Holy Child Jesus School. In 1965, Bowman achieved a bachelor's degree in English with a minor in speech and drama from FSPA-run Viterbo College (now University) in La Crosse. She cofounded the National Black Sisters Conference in 1968. In 1969 she earned a master's degree in English from the Catholic University, Washington, D.C., and in 1972 a doctorate in the same field at the same institution. During her stay in Washington, D.C., Bowman's reimmersion in black churches revived and deepened her appreciation of the spirituality and sacred songs she learned from her elders in Canton. She longed to reconnect black Catholics with the heritage they so often had not been permitted to express in worship.

The reforms of Vatican II, women's liberation, and the civil rights struggle, including the Black Power and Black Arts movements, paved the way for the work to which Bowman dedicated the rest of her life. Beginning in 1972, when she joined the Viterbo faculty, Bowman became known as a talented gospel singer, inspirational preacher, and advocate of racial and gender justice within and outside the Catholic Church. At a time when many nuns sought to adopt more modern, culturally appropriate garb than their traditional habits, Bowman donned a head wrap and dashiki. She travelled widely in the United States and in Africa to give presentations and workshops. Sister Thea Bowman moved back to Canton in 1978 to take care of her frail, elderly mother and father. Even as she took on these family responsibilities, she worked for the Diocese of Jackson, Mississippi, as an intercultural awareness consultant, calling attention to her home state's Native American and African American heritages. In 1980 Bowman cofounded the Institute for Black Catholic Studies at New Orleans' Xavier University, the only historically black college or university affiliated with the Catholic Church. She taught black theology and arts there until 1989.

In 1984, the same year she lost both her parents, Bowman was diagnosed with breast cancer. Even as the cancer metastasized to her lymph system and bones, and she went through debilitating but ultimately unsuccessful chemotherapy, she prayed "to live until I die" (quoted on FSPA website, http://www.fspa.org) and continued to travel, preach, sing, teach, and organize. In 1985 she travelled to Nairobi, Kenya, for the International Eucharistic Congress. In 1987 she contributed to the groundbreaking *Lead Me Guide Me: The African American Catholic Hymnal*, cofounded the National Black Catholic Congress, and appeared on the popular CBS TV program "Sixty Minutes." The interviewer, veteran journalist Mike Wallace, called her the most inspiring person he ever met. In 1988 Bowman received the American Cancer Society's Courage Award and recorded *Sister Thea: Songs of My People*, an album of spirituals. She shared her wisdom about illness and caregiving in the 1989 videotape *Almost Home*. On June 17, 1989, she addressed the National Conference of Catholic Bishops. After challenging them to leave behind institutionalized racism and treat individuals and communities of color as genuine equals, she brought the bishops to their feet in a tearful, joyous rendition of "We Shall Overcome." The same year, *US Catholic Magazine* recognized Bowman's advocacy for women's rights. Like many feminists of color, Bowman stressed the interconnectedness of women's liberation with the liberation of all people.

In Canton, Mississippi, Sister Thea Bowman died at age fifty-two. In accord with her wishes, these words of nineteenth century feminist SOJOURNER TRUTH were proclaimed at her funeral: "I'm not going to die. I'm going home like a shooting star" (quoted in *National Catholic Reporter*, 24Mar.2000). Bowman was buried near her mother and father in Elmwood Cemetery, Memphis, Tennessee. The University of Notre Dame posthumously awarded her its Laetare Medal. The Sister Thea Bowman Educational Foundation was established to provide scholarships to African American students, including single mothers. The Franciscan Sisters of Perpetual Adoration established their Thea Bowman Legacy Office. A number of service organizations across the United States were named after Bowman, including schools (both Catholic and public) in Jackson, Mississippi; East St. Louis, Illinois; Gary, Indiana; and Washington, D.C.; the women's center at Siena College; the social justice center at John Carroll University; and community health centers in Detroit, Michigan, and Cleveland, Ohio. Even after her death, Thea Bowman's life and work encouraged many of the nation's over two million African American Catholics to believe that they genuinely had an equal home among the diverse groups making up their church. To lasting effect, Bowman taught people of different races, genders, classes, and religions that "God's Glory is revealed because we love one another across the barriers and boundaries" (quoted on the Bowman Foundation website, http://www.cermusa.francis.edu/sistertheabowmanfoundation/).

FURTHER READING
The Roman Catholic Diocese of Jackson, Mississippi, and the Franciscan Sisters of Perpetual Adoration, La Crosse, Wisconsin, maintain archives on Thea Bowman.

Bowman, Thea, and Margaret Walker. *God Touched My Life: The Inspiring Autobiography of the Nun Who Brought Song, Celebration, and Soul to the World* (1992).

Bowman, Thea. *Families—Black and Catholic, Catholic and Black: Readings, Resources, and Family Activities* (1985).

Bowman, Thea. "The Gift of African American Sacred Song," in Gia Publications, *Lead Me Guide Me: The African American Catholic Hymnal* (1987).

Cepress, Celestine, ed. *Sister Thea Bowman, Shooting Star: Selected Writings and Speeches* (1993).

Koontz, Christian, ed. *Thea Bowman: Handing on Her Legacy* (1991).

McGrath, Michael O'Neill. *This Little Light: Lessons in Living from Sister Thea Bowman* (2008).

Obituary: *New York Times*, 1 Apr. 1990.

MARY KRANE DERR

Bowser, David Bustill (1820–30 June 1900), commercial painter, artist, and activist, was born in Philadelphia, Pennsylvania, the only known child of Jeremiah Bowser from Maryland and Rachel Bustill, daughter of the prosperous black abolitionist and educator Cyrus Bustill. The intermarriage among the region's free black Quaker families headed by Cyrus Bustill, Robert Douglass Sr., Jeremiah Bowser, and David Mapps created a dynamic force that benefited all African Americans and particularly spurred David's personal growth and accomplishments. Jeremiah, a member of the Benezet Philosophical Society, served as a steward on the Liverpool lines and, later, it seems he was the proprietor of an oyster house near the intersection of 4th and Cherry Streets, where David Bowser first hung up his sign as a commercial painter. Later, the Bowser family moved to the Northern Liberties section of Philadelphia, into a house at 481 North 4th Street where Bowser remained for the rest of his life. Many members of the Bustill, Douglass, and Bowser families lived and worked within or near Northern Liberties and attended local meetings of the Society of Friends (Quakers).

Bowser was taught by Cyrus's granddaughter SARAH MAPPS DOUGLASS (his cousin), who was herself a well-known artist and activist. Having demonstrated a talent for painting, David was apprenticed at the age of eleven to Sarah's younger brother, Robert Douglass Jr. Robert began his professional life as a barber, like his father, but having been instructed in art both in Philadelphia and London, he later earned his living in Philadelphia as a sign painter and artist. Bowser also learned hairdressing in the lucrative family business, and he made his way across America for several years plying the trade. When he returned to Philadelphia, Bowser was perhaps emboldened in pursuing a painting career by the Register of Trade of the Colored People (1838), a measure initiated by the Pennsylvania Abolition Society to encourage the employment of black artisans. He accepted commissions during the 1840s, 1850s, and 1860s to design banners, signs, and paraphernalia for various institutions, including volunteer fire companies and fire insurance businesses.

Some of his early ornamental works and his marine and landscape paintings were displayed in various exhibitions at the Philadelphia Museum, the Franklin Institute, and the Colored American Institute. Pictorial banners were his specialty, and his commissions during the Civil War included flags for all eleven units of the United States Colored Troops. These banners depicted black soldiers engaged in battle, usually in an allegorical setting. The abolitionist activism preceding the Civil War and the northern support for slave emancipation encouraged Bowser to turn his hand to portraits of cultural heroes. He had entertained the revolutionary abolitionist John Brown at his home, and he painted a portrait of Brown from life in 1858. Yet another Brown portrait, which he painted after

1860, commemorated the raid on Harpers Ferry. In addition Bowser received commissions for more than twenty portraits of Abraham Lincoln: two well-known examples are a hand-painted photograph for the black Philadelphia businessman and abolitionist ROBERT PURVIS, and an oil painting showing Lincoln freeing a kneeling female slave (1863?).

In addition to conceptualizing African American social empowerment and military achievement and bolstering the authority of white abolitionists, Bowser was directly involved in several causes. He aided in the escape of slaves; he was instrumental in helping to abolish Philadelphia's segregated streetcars; and he belonged to several African American reform groups. In 1853 he attended the thirtieth meeting of the American Moral Reform Society, which was held in Rochester, New York. This organization had been founded in Philadelphia in 1837 under the auspices of JAMES FORTEN and WILLIAM WHIPPER for the promotion of African American education, temperance, economy, and universal liberty. Its mandate to integrate all Americans under the banner of universal Christian love evidently guided Bowser's subsequent activism and explains his profound distrust of the colonization movement. Bowser was also a member of the Philadelphia delegation to the Pennsylvania Equal Rights League in 1865. Although he was probably married twice, it seems that only his second wife, a dressmaker by trade, named Elizabeth H. S. (1833–1908) bore children: these were Raphield Bowser, born in 1858, an artist, and Ida E. Bowser, born in 1869, the first woman to graduate with a degree in music from the University of Pennsylvania.

Black fraternal and social orders serving to create community bonds and to ensure the provision of mutual aid became popular during his lifetime. Bowser may well have joined the black Freemasons, but his primary commitment was to the Grand Order of Odd Fellows (an African American offshoot of the British fraternal society of Odd Fellows) to which he was initiated in 1844. His cousin Joseph Cassey Bustill, who is thought to have helped frame the Fifteenth Amendment to the Constitution, belonged to the same lodge. After 1871, when the volunteer fire companies lost their professional standing, the Odd Fellows became Bowser's primary market for banners and regalia. He held several high-ranking offices during his membership, including grand master, deputy grand master, grand director, and grand secretary. His motivations for this lifelong involvement in fraternal activity doubtless included family ties, a devotion to the welfare of African Americans, a love of ritual, a need for egalitarian religious fellowship, and the development of business contacts. His fraternal contacts assured him of a secure, if not an exceptionally profitable, niche in Philadelphia society despite the building pressure of nineteenth-century racism, which ignited several antiblack riots.

Bowser died in Philadelphia at his home, his obituary appearing in several major newspapers. Little remains of his substantial commercial output, but some portraits, photographs of his banners and flags, and a number of painted hats, which all attest to his talent, can still be seen in various museums. In an era of increasing racism, job discrimination, and, for many years, black disenfranchisement, Bowser held firm to his faith in African Americans' achievement and in their right to be integrated into mainstream American society, which seemed determined to exclude even the most gifted.

FURTHER READING

Details about Bowser and his extended family can be researched in the Dorsey Collection, Cheyney University, Cheyney, Pennsylvania, and in the Bustill-Bowser-Asbury Collection, Moorland-Spingarn Research Center, Howard University, Washington, DC.

Jones, Steven Loring. "A Keen Sense of the Artistic: African American Material Culture in 19th-Century Philadelphia," *International Review of African Art*, vol. 12 (1995): 4–29, esp. 16–22.

SUSAN B. IWANISZIW

Bowser, Mary Elizabeth (1839?–?), Union spy during the Civil War, was born a slave on the Richmond, Virginia, plantation of John Van Lew, a wealthy hardware merchant. Very little is known about her early life. Upon Van Lew's death in 1843 or 1851, his wife and daughter, Elizabeth, manumitted his slaves and bought and freed a number of their family members, Mary among them. Like most of their former slaves, Mary remained a servant in the Van Lew household, staying with the family until the late 1850s. Noting her intellectual talent, Elizabeth, a staunch abolitionist and Quaker, sent Mary to the Quaker School for Negroes in Philadelphia to be educated.

Mary returned from Philadelphia after graduating to marry Wilson Bowser, a free black man. The ceremony was held on 16 April 1861, just days after the Civil War began. What made the ceremony so unusual was that the parishioners of the church were primarily white. The couple settled outside Richmond. There is no record of any children. Even after her marriage, Bowser was in close contact with the Van Lew family, clearly sharing their political goals. As a result, their wartime record was very much intertwined, and information about Bowser can be gleaned through the records of Elizabeth Van Lew.

Despite her abolitionist sentiments, Elizabeth Van Lew was a prominent figure in Richmond. Shunned by many before the war began, her loyalty to the Union during the war earned her further enmity. Unlike other spies, Van Lew used this enmity as a cover for her serious efforts on behalf of the Union. Adopting a distracted, muttering personae, she was dubbed "Crazy Bet." During the war, Van Lew helped manage a spy system in the Confederate capitol, went regularly to the Libby Prison with food and medicine, and helped escapees of all kinds, hiding them in a secret room in her mansion.

Perhaps Van Lew's most trusted and successful source of information was Mary Bowser. Like Van Lew, Bowser had considerable acting skills. In order to get access to top-secret information, Bowser became "Ellen Bond," a slow-thinking, but able, servant. Van Lew urged a friend to take Bowser along to help out at functions held by Varina Davis, the wife of the Confederate president, Jefferson Davis. Bowser was eventually hired fulltime, and worked in the Davis household until just before the end of the war.

At the Davis's house, Mary worked as a servant, cleaning and serving meals. Given the racial prejudice of the day, and the way in which servants were trained to act and seem invisible, Mary was able to glean considerable information simply by doing her work. That she was literate, and could thus read the documents she had access to—and, in that way, better interpret the conversations she was hearing—could only have been a bonus. Jefferson Davis, apparently, came to know that there was a leak in his house, but until late in the war no suspicion fell on Mary.

Richmond's formal spymaster was Thomas McNiven, a baker whose business was located on North Eighth Street. Given his profession, he was a hub for information. His bakery was an unexceptional destination for his agents, and McNiven was regularly out and about town, driving through Richmond making deliveries. When he came to the Davis household, Mary could daily—without suspicion—greet him at his wagon and talk briefly. In 1904, just before he died, McNiven reported his wartime activities to his daughter, Jeannette B. McNiven, and her nephew, Robert W. Waitt Jr., chronicled them in 1952. According to McNiven, Bowser was the source of the most crucial information available, "as she was working right in the Davis home and had a photographic mind. Everything she saw on the rebel president's desk, she could repeat word for word. Unlike most slaves, she could read and write. She made a point of always coming out to my wagon when I made deliveries at the Davis' home to drop information" (quoted in Waitt, Thomas McNiven Papers).

By the last days of the Confederacy, suspicion did fall on Mary—it is not known how or why—and she chose to flee in January 1865. Her last act as a Union spy and sympathizer was an attempt to burn down the Confederate White House, but this was not successful.

After the war ended, the federal government, in an attempt to protect the postwar lives of its Southern spies, destroyed the records—including those of McNiven's and Van Lew's activities—that could more precisely detail the information Bowser passed on to General Ulysses S. Grant throughout 1863 and 1864. The journal that Bowser later wrote chronicling her wartime work was also lost when family members inadvertently discarded it in 1952. The Bowser family rarely discussed her work, given Richmond's political climate and the continuing attitudes toward Union sympathizers. There is no record of Bowser's postwar life, and no date for her death.

Bowser is among a number of African American women spies who worked on the Union side during the Civil War. Given the nature of the profession, we may never know how many women engaged in undercover spy operations, both planned and unplanned. Harriet Tubman is the most well known, especially for her scouting expeditions in South Carolina and Florida that resulted in the freedom of hundreds of slaves. In 1995 the U.S. government honored Mary Elizabeth Bowser for her work in the Civil War with an induction into the Military Intelligence Corps Hall of Fame in Fort Huachuca, Arizona.

FURTHER READING

Coleman, Penny. *Spies! Women in the Civil War* (1992).

Forbes, Ella. *African American Women during the Civil War* (1998).

Kane, Harnett T. *Spies for the Blue and Gray* (1954).

Lebsock, Suzanne. *A Share of Honor: Virginia Women 1600–1945* (1984).

Van Lew, Elizabeth. *A Yankee Spy in Richmond: The Civil War Diary of "Crazy Bet" Van Lew*, ed. David D. Ryan (2001).

Varon, Elizabeth. *Southern Lady, Yankee Spy: the True Story of Elizabeth Van Lew, a Union Agent in the Heart of the Confederacy* (2003).

LYDE CULLEN SIZER

Bowser, Rosa (7 Jan. 1855–7 Feb. 1931), educator and community leader, was born in Amelia County, Virginia, probably a slave, to Henry Dixon, a carpenter, and Augusta Hawkins Dixon, a domestic servant. After emancipation she moved with her family to Richmond, where they were active in the First African Baptist Church and where she would teach Sunday school for the next half century. Bowser completed her education at Richmond Colored Normal School, where she was taught by the school's founder, Rabza Morse Manly, a noted educator throughout the South.

In 1872 Bowser began her teaching career at Richmond's Navy Hill School. She became the first black woman appointed to teach in Richmond public schools and continued to teach until her marriage to James Herndon Bowser on 4 September 1878. Their only child, Oswald Barrington Herndon Bowser, who became a well-known physician in Richmond, was born two years later. Her husband died in 1881, and in 1883 Bowser returned to the Navy Hill School. The following year she began teaching at Baker Street School, where she would remain until her retirement in 1923.

Bowser is believed to have organized Richmond's first night school for black men in 1896. In the nineteenth century former slaves lobbied for universal education and the creation of black schools, aware that schooling for blacks was the primary vehicle to achieve economic independence. The night school Bowser created allowed men to work and still receive basic literacy instruction during evening hours.

Outside the classroom, Bowser participated in several church and civic organizations. From 1890 to 1892 she served as president of the Virginia State Teachers Association, an organization of professional African American educators who lobbied for equal salaries and better facilities. In August 1895 she helped to found the Richmond Women's League at a time when black women had launched a national campaign to denounce lynching. As the first president of the organization, Bowser oversaw a campaign that generated more than five hundred dollars for the defense of three black Lunenburg women charged with murder. She also worked in collaboration with national figures such as MARY ELIZA CHURCH TERRELL and MAGGIE LENA WALKER in support of the treatment of tuberculosis and the creation of kindergartens for African American children. She participated in the founding of the National Association of Colored Women (NACW) in 1896 and was once nominated—though not elected—to be president of the organization. Bowser also helped to found the Virginia State Federation of Colored Women's Clubs in 1908 and became the first chairperson of the Women's Missionary and Educational Society of Virginia.

Working in these civic organizations, Bowser bore witness to the community consciousness and black agency that afforded blacks a sense of dignity in the face of social and political repression. In the Jim Crow South, black educational institutions, when they existed at all, were extremely underfunded and neglected. Black citizens paid property taxes to finance schools but, because of insufficient aid from public school authorities, they were forced to raise more money among themselves. Bowser's service exemplified black commitment to provide schooling to as many people as possible.

As an active member of the NACW, whose motto was "Lifting as We Climb," Bowser worked to improve the conditions of black homes. She believed that improving black homes and families would foster the advancement of the entire black community. NACW women held classes on housekeeping and childrearing and advocated temperance. The NACW also supported passage of the Nineteenth Amendment, which guaranteed women the right to vote and helped make the 1920s antilynching campaign an issue of national prominence. The organization remains an integral part of the black community and, among other things, awards annual college scholarships to young black students.

In recognition of Bowser's lifelong commitment to the people of Richmond, the first branch of the Richmond Public Library system for African American patrons was named in her honor on 2 December 1925. Six years later Bowser died of complications from diabetes at her home in Richmond. In 1976 the National Biscuit Company (now Nabisco) awarded Bowser posthumous national recognition by including her in its Bicentennial Salute to Twenty-Four Outstanding Black Educators.

FURTHER READING
Lebsock, Suzanne. *Murder in Virginia: Southern Justice on Trial* (2003).
Lee, Lauranett. "More Than an Image: Black Women Reformers in Richmond, Virginia, 1910–1928," master's thesis, Virginia State University (1993).
"Rosa D. Bowser: Talent to Spare, Talent to Share," *Richmond Literature and History Quarterly* (Fall 1978).

CRYSTAL RENÉE SANDERS

Boyce, Mildred L. (17 Mar. 1942–), educator and administrator, was born in the borough of Manhattan, New York, New York, Her parents' names are unknown. Raised in Brooklyn, New York, Mildred L. Boyce received all of her education in Brooklyn, attending public schools 44 and 181, junior high school 246, and then Erasmus Hall High School in the Flatbush section of Brooklyn. She then attended Brooklyn College, where she received her associates degree in 1963, a Bachelor of Arts in Humanities in 1965, her Master of Science degree in Education in 1972, and an advanced certificate in administration and supervision in 1975.

Boyce had a great interest in education since the age of seven, when she conducted her own school by making paper dolls as students. She really enjoyed the idea that she was helping all of her students to learn. This sparked her desire to choose education as a career. Boyce began her career in education as a sixth grade teacher at P.S. 106, in 1965. From 1965 to 1977 she taught at P.S. 106. Here, she worked in various positions such as teacher, master teacher, teacher of common branches, and interim acting assistant principal. In 1977 Ms. Boyce began working at Philippa Schuyler Middle School for the Gifted and Talented, a new and special school that had just been created for black and Latino children. The school was named after the child musical prodigy PHILIPPA DUKE SCHUYLER. Boyce taught AP English. Boyce continued as a teacher until 1984, when she became assistant principal of the intermediate school.

When the school's founding principal, Ms. Loretta U. Boyce (no relation) retired in 1989, Mildred Boyce was promoted to the position of principal of the school, which also known as Intermediate School 383 (I.S. 383). She held that position for the next decade. Under her leadership, the school's achievements in reading consistently ranked it among the top schools in New York City. She has stated that her greatest joy is having her students come back after many years to say, "You have made a difference in my life."

In addition to her duties as a school principal she has as a member and advisor to the President of the Council for Supervisors and Administrators as well as an elected delegate from District 32. She also served on the executive board of District 32's supervisors.

In 1991, because she played a key role in increasing the growth and improvement of the New York City public education system, she was honored by the United States House of Representatives. In his tribute, Representative EDOLPHUS TOWNS stated, "It is individuals like Mildred Boyce who have chosen careers in education that benefit the entire Nation." Ms. Boyce has been the recipient of many awards including the NAACP Educator's Award and the Black Professional Business Women's Educator Award. Additionally, New York's 54th Democratic Club honored Ms. Boyce for her contributions in the field of education. In 1999 Boyce was honored by the office of Brooklyn District Attorney Charles Hynes in celebration of Women's History Month.

In 2001 Ms. Boyce was recognized for the second time by the United States House of Representatives for her contribution to the education of New York's children. After retiring from Philippa Schuyler, she became the assistant director of field services for the Council of School Supervisors and Administrators, where she has long served as a key player in ensuring that the school administrators' labor union contracts are enforced as well as providing support to members when issues arise. Ms. Boyce has been an active member of the St. Laurence Catholic Church in Brooklyn, New York, serving as a lector, and a member of the baptismal team.

FURTHER READING

Einhorn, Erin. "Fear Hard Lessons in New Tutor Plan." *New York Daily News*, 7 Dec. 2005.

"Five Borough Women Leaders Were Honored." *New York Daily News*, 25 Mar. 1999.

Library of Congress, Congressional Record 102nd Congress, *Mildred L. Boyce*—Hon. Edolphus Towns (Extension of Remarks—February 28, 1991), p. E695.

Library of Congress, Congressional Record 107th Congress, *A Tribute to Mildred L. Boyce*—Hon. Edolphus Towns, March 7, 2001; p. P305.

ALEXANDER J. CHENAULT

Boyd, Gerald M. (3 Oct. 1950–23 Nov. 2006), journalist, was born in St. Louis, Missouri, the second of three children of Odessa and Rufus Boyd. Boyd's

Gerald Boyd, walking to a meeting with fellow *New York Times* editor Howell Raines in New York, 14 May 2003. (AP Images.)

mother died from sickle cell anemia when he was a small child, so he and his older brother, Gary, were raised by their paternal grandmother, Evie, while maternal relatives in California raised Boyd's sister, Ruth. Boyd attended Soldan High School in St. Louis, playing clarinet and writing for the school paper. He supplemented his grandmother's pension by bagging groceries at Cooper's, a neighborhood mom-and-pop store. As a high school student Boyd became interested in journalism while attending Upward Bound, a program that helped prepare him for college, doing layout and writing editorials on a paper produced at Webster College in suburban St. Louis.

Boyd attended the University of Missouri at Columbia from 1969 to 1973 on a journalism scholarship. There Boyd and fellow student Sheila Rule founded *Blackout*, a minority-run paper. Boyd's scholarship guaranteed him a job at the *St. Louis Post-Dispatch* upon graduation, and Boyd joined the paper as a copy clerk while still a college student. While at the *Post-Dispatch*, Boyd and George Curry, a *Post-Dispatch* reporter, cofounded the Greater St. Louis Association of Black Journalists in 1977 and created seven-week journalism workshops for black high school students. Boyd also taught journalism at Howard University and was an instructor at the University of Missouri's journalism workshop for minority students. In 1977 he was named Sigma Delta Chi's journalist of the year, and in 1979 he became a Nieman Fellow at Harvard—the youngest journalist so chosen.

While in St. Louis, Boyd reported on city hall and wrote on housing and consumer affairs. In 1978 he was assigned to the paper's Washington bureau, which gave him the opportunity to cover Congress, the 1980 presidential campaign, and the early years of the Ronald Reagan White House. Few minorities covered the White House in the early 1980s, something Boyd believed helped him to receive an inordinate amount of attention from the president. Boyd joined the *New York Times*'s Washington bureau in 1983, covering then vice president George H. W. Bush during the 1984 presidential campaign. Boyd was promoted to White House correspondent following Reagan's reelection, and he covered the Iran-contra affair and the subsequent shake-up in the administration, including Chief of Staff Donald Regan's resignation. Boyd reported on George H. W. Bush's presidential nomination, campaign, and election in 1988, and he produced numerous articles on Bush's appointees and the administration's plans.

In 1991 Boyd was named special assistant to the managing editor of the *Times*, then worked as chief editor in the Washington bureau and on the national and metropolitan news desks. As metropolitan editor Boyd oversaw a significant expansion and reorganization of that department, directing coverage of the 1993 World Trade Center bombing, for which the Times earned a Pulitzer Prize in 1994 for spot news reporting. Boyd was promoted to assistant managing editor in 1993 and to deputy managing editor in 1997. In the latter role he supervised the *Times*'s reporting on metropolitan, Washington, national, and foreign news, and he oversaw the layout of the front page. Boyd was co-senior editor of the Times's 2001 series "How Race Is Lived in America," for which the paper won the Pulitzer for national reporting. The National Association of Black Journalists honored Boyd as Journalist of the Year in 2001.

Executive editor Howell Raines named Boyd managing editor—the second highest position at the *New York Times*—in 2001, and Boyd took over less than a week before the 11 September terrorist attacks. The *Times* won six Pulitzers for its coverage of 9/11 and its aftermath, and Boyd pointed to helping lead the *Times* newsroom during that tragedy as his proudest moment as a journalist.

Boyd's tenure as managing editor was short-lived: in June 2003 he and Raines resigned after Jayson Blair, a twenty-seven-year-old *Times* reporter, was revealed to have fabricated stories and plagiarized. Following his resignation from the *Times*, Boyd wrote a syndicated column for Universal Press Syndicate, worked briefly as a consultant to Columbia University's Graduate School of Journalism, and wrote his memoir.

Boyd was married to Sheila Rule, a St. Louis neighbor and colleague at the *Times*. That marriage ended in divorce, as did his marriage to the newscaster Jacqueline Adams. Boyd and the journalist Robin Stone married in 1996, and they had a son, Zachary. Boyd died from complications of lung cancer.

FURTHER READING

Boyd, Gerald. "My Story," in *Reaching Generation Next*, ed. Lisa Frazier Page (2003).

Poniewozik, James. "Mutiny at the *Times*," *Time* (16 June 2003).

Obituaries: *New York Times*, 24 Nov. 2006, 1 Dec. 2006.

DAVID SCHROEDER

Boyd, Henry Allen (15 Apr. 1876–28 May 1959), publisher, entrepreneur, and banker, was born to RICHARD HENRY BOYD, a publisher, and the former Harriet Moore in Grimes County, Texas, one of nine children. Henry Allen went to public school in Palestine, Texas, and attended the West Union Baptist Church. The Boyd family later moved to San Antonio and Henry found work at the local postal office. He became the first black to be hired as a postal clerk in San Antonio. He married Lula M. Smith, who bore him a daughter, Katherine. Lula did not live long after her daughter's birth. In 1908 he married again, this time to Georgia Ann Bradford. Around the early 1900s Henry Allen moved to Nashville, Tennessee, at the request of his father who had preceded him there. R. H. Boyd was making a name for himself in Nashville as founder and secretary-treasurer of the National Baptist Publishing Board (NBPB), a publisher of Sunday school literature, hymnals, and Christian education materials for black Baptists. Until 1896 nearly all black Baptists had bought their materials from the white American Baptist Publication Society (ABPS). After the creation of the National Baptist Convention (NBC) in 1895, black ministers asked the ABPS to hire black writers. The ABPS failed to comply, and the result was the NBPB, a reflection of the growing efforts of post-Emancipation blacks to gain respect from whites while affirming their own self-reliance.

About 1905, to generate a steady flow of sales, R. H. Boyd created the Sunday School Congress, an annual convention to train Sunday school workers. Through it the NBPB made itself indispensable to the churches affiliated with the NBC. When Boyd arrived in Nashville, his father made him assistant secretary-treasurer and secretary of the Sunday School Congress. He quickly immersed himself in the operation of what would become the largest black publishing enterprise in America. Boyd, who became an ordained minister in 1904, became involved in all his father's business activities. In addition to the NBPB, R. H. Boyd had opened and ran several moneymaking enterprises: the Citizens Savings Trust and Bank Company (1904); the *Globe*, a weekly secular newspaper, and its parent company, the Globe Publishing Company (1905); the National Negro Doll Company; and the National Baptist Church Supply Company. Boyd's father also published two other papers, the *Clarion* and the *National Baptist-Union Review*.

Both Boyds addressed social issues and in 1907 they led a protest when President Theodore Roosevelt visited Nashville but ignored the black community. The *Globe*, the official paper of the Republican Party in the county, supported the successful campaign of William H. Taft for president in 1908. The next year father and son successfully lobbied the state legislature for the creation of a school for black teachers, which became the Tennessee Agricultural and Industrial State Normal School for Negroes (later Tennessee State University). In 1910 Boyd used his influence as editor of the *Globe* to help raise funds for a new building for the local black YMCA.

In 1915 a major controversy split the black Baptist community. The NBC incorporated and tried to take control of the NBPB by pursuing its legal case all the way to the Tennessee Supreme Court. Right before founding the publishing house, R. H. Boyd had been elected corresponding secretary of the NBC's Home Mission Board (HMB) and it was as such that he encouraged the denomination to authorize the creation of the NBPB, which printed and sold Christian literature to churches affiliated with the NBC. He served on the HMB until he resigned in 1914. Because Boyd did not share his publishing profits with the NBC, many NBC leaders thought that he was manipulating the denomination for personal gain. The NBC lost the case, however, because Boyd's father had incorporated as a private, nonprofit corporation that was independent of the NBC. As a result the pro-NBPB faction seceded from the NBC and founded the National Baptist Convention of America (NBCA). The Sunday School Congress survived the split and continued to serve as a promotion outlet for the NBPB.

Boyd supported the U.S. entrance into World War I through the *Globe*. Many African Americans supported the war out of patriotism and thought that black participation in the war effort would force the government to grant civil rights to the black minority at home. Boyd visited Camp Meade, an army camp in Maryland that trained black soldiers, and published articles and photographs about black trainees and black units fighting the war abroad. When Boyd's father died in 1922 the NBPB through its board of directors elected Boyd as secretary-treasurer. He inherited all of his father's leadership positions and remained active in social work. During the twenties he protested black lynching in Texas and Alabama. He was elected president of the local Lincoln-Douglass Voters' League that recruited voters for the Republican Party. As a seasoned political observer and activist he used the *Globe* to attract thousands of new black voters for the Republican Party.

The NBPB's stature increased when in 1925 the NBCA signed a joint agreement with the Lott Carey Baptist Foreign Mission Convention (LCBFMC), a black Baptist organization founded in 1897 to support missionary work in Africa. This agreement meant that the publishing house would be able to sell materials to LCFMC workers. A shrewd manager, Boyd in 1930 added correspondence theological courses to extend his client base. To further increase business he traveled widely so that by 1934 he was supplying materials to 20,000 Sunday schools and 8,000 churches. Boyd also contributed to the outstanding growth of the Citizens Bank that was managing $300,000 in deposits by 1940. During World War II Henry Allen led a successful campaign that landed 1 million dollars' worth of deposits in the Citizens Bank's coffers.

After World War II the NBPB hired and trained veterans to work as art preservationists and printers, a practice in keeping with the Boyd family's interest in the social uplift of the black race. By the 1950s both the doll company and church supply subsidiaries had closed. Higher prices led the NBPB to connect with the Protestant-Church Owned Publishers of America to buy paper at lower rates.

Boyd's second wife died in 1952. As Boyd grew older he relinquished his duties to his nephew, Theophilus Bartholomew Boyd Jr., who was made assistant secretary-treasurer and who would replace Henry Allen upon his demise. At the time of Henry Allen's death the NBPB's assets were worth nearly $900,000. In 1960 the *Globe* ceased publication. Henry Allen's funeral was held at Tennessee State University upon request of the school's president. His greatest accomplishment is to have kept the NBPB and the Citizens Bank in operation through the years. Through these two institutions Henry Allen significantly affected black America both during and after his association with his father.

FURTHER READING

Lovett, Bobby L. *A Black Man's Dream: The First 100 Years, Richard Henry Boyd and the National Baptist Publishing Board* (1993).

DAVID MICHEL

Boyd, Richard Henry (15 Mar. 1843–23 Aug. 1922), Baptist minister, was born Dick Gray in Noxubee County, Mississippi, the son of Indiana, a slave woman; nothing is known of his father's identity, but the surname Gray is the same as the owner of the plantation. When the master died, Boyd accompanied members of the Gray family to Washington County in western Texas. During the Civil War he served his new master in the Confederate camps until he was sent back to Texas, where he was given responsibility for managing the Gray plantation. After the war he left the plantation and took on several occupations in Texas, including that of cattleman. Having had no formal education in his early years, it was not until the mid-1860s that he learned to read and write.

In 1867 he changed his name to Richard Henry Boyd, and two years later he enrolled at Bishop College in Marshall, Texas. Although he did not complete his studies, he was ordained a Baptist minister. In 1868 Boyd married Laura Thomas, who died shortly thereafter. In 1871 he married Harriett "Hattie" Albertine Moore. At least five children resulted from the two marriages.

During the 1870s and 1880s Boyd became a leader of the black Baptist community in Texas. He formed and led congregations throughout the state, aided in organizing the Texas Negro Baptist Convention (TNBC), and became the convention's education secretary.

Boyd's influential role in American religious history is best understood against the background of racial conflict among the major Baptist denominations in the late nineteenth century. At the 1892 meeting of the TNBC, Boyd opposed a plan that would have allowed the northern and predominantly white American Baptist Home Mission Society (ABHMS) to consolidate schools for black freedmen; the plan would have given oversight of the publication and dissemination of Baptist school literature to the American Baptist Publication Society (ABPS), which declined to publish the writings of black ministers. Some black Baptists viewed Boyd's opposition as escalating the issue of race. Boyd's vision of a publishing house that served black educational needs eventually led him and his supporters to separate from the TNBC in 1893 and form the General Missionary Baptist Convention (GMBC), with Boyd serving as superintendent for the new convention's missions program.

Resigning his pastorate of Mount Zion Church in San Antonio, Texas, Boyd worked to create a central repository from which to disseminate Sunday school materials to black churches in the GMBC. He achieved this aim by skillfully negotiating with the Southern Baptist Convention's Sunday School Board for the delivery of materials. Boyd's efforts lessened the dependency of black Baptist Sunday schools on the ABPS's literature and distribution network and eventually decreased the influence of white northern Baptists in the affairs of southern black Baptists. He was criticized by some black Baptists, who believed he had diminished the prospect for cooperation and undermined the Fortress Monroe Agreement, a cooperative pact between the Southern Baptist Convention and the ABHMS.

Throughout 1895 Boyd strengthened his position. He prompted a convening of Sunday school teachers and superintendents in Grimes County, Texas, where he convinced church officials to direct their requests for Sunday school materials to his newly established repository. He also received the endorsement of the Palestine Baptist Association of Texas and was able to convince many at a Palestine Sunday school convention of the importance of having a black publishing house.

Boyd's influence grew when he represented the Texas delegation from the GMBC at the predominantly black National Baptist Convention, U.S.A. (NBC-U.S.A.) in St. Louis, Missouri, in 1896. His proposal to establish a publishing board capable of producing materials on a national scale for the black Baptist population was initially rejected by supporters of the ABPS and by people within the TNBC who opposed his efforts. However, the TNBC's Home Mission Board, to which Boyd had been elected corresponding secretary, accepted Boyd's idea to establish a committee in charge of printing Sunday school materials. On Boyd's recommendation, the committee was granted board status by the convention and was named the National Baptist Publishing Board (NBPB). Boyd became the new board's corresponding secretary and treasurer.

In October 1896 Boyd resigned his position as the GMBC's superintendent of missions and proceeded to establish the operations of the NBPB in Nashville, Tennessee. By 1897 the board had begun printing Sunday school materials copyrighted in Boyd's name. In 1898 he obtained a state charter and incorporated the NBPB in Tennessee.

Although Boyd resigned his position as corresponding secretary of the NBC-U.S.A's Home Mission Board in 1914, his chartering of the NBPB had heated up a long-simmering conflict over the control and legal ownership of the publishing board's operations and copyrights that culminated at a meeting of the National Baptist Convention, U.S.A., in Chicago in 1915. The courts of Tennessee ruled in Boyd's favor, the NBC-U.S.A. having failed to support its legal claims over the publishing board. The conflict, however, led Boyd and his supporters to organize an "unincorporated" faction of the National Baptist Convention in 1915, now known as the National Baptist Convention of America (NBCA). In 1916 the NBCA declared that the NBPB was an independent legal entity and hence was not owned by or subject to the control of any convention.

From its inception in 1896 to 1922 Boyd served as secretary and treasurer for the NBPB. From 1905 the NBPB held annual congresses of Sunday school leaders and teachers, and by 1909 it had established service training for Baptist teachers.

Boyd also became a successful businessman in Nashville. He founded the National Negro Doll Company in 1911 to manufacture dolls with African American features; he helped establish and was president (1904–1922) of Nashville's One Cent Savings Bank, a savings and loan bank for African Americans; he helped organize and became the president in 1906 of the Globe Publishing Company, which produced the *Globe* newspaper primarily for African American readers; and he served as a national vice president of the National Negro Business League. Boyd died in Nashville.

FURTHER READING

Boyd, Richard Henry. *A Story of the National Baptist Publishing Board: The Why, How, When, Where, and by Whom It Was Established* (1915).
Lovett, Bobby L. *A Black Man's Dream: The First One Hundred Years* (1993).
Montgomery, William E. *Under Their Own Vine and Fig Tree: The African-American Church in the South, 1865–1900* (1993).
Tyms, James D. *The Rise of Religious Education among Negro Baptists* (1979).
Washington, James Melvin. *Frustrated Fellowship: The Black Baptist Quest for Social Power* (1986).
Obituary: *Nashville Banner*, 24 Aug. 1922.

This entry is taken from the *American National Biography* and is published here with the permission of the American Council of Learned Societies.

ZIPPORAH G. GLASS

Boyer, Frances (1871–1949), teacher, farmer, and entrepreneur, was born Frances Marion Boyer in Pelham, Georgia, the son of Henry Boyer, a former slave and onetime teamster for the U.S. Army. Nothing is known of Boyer's mother. In 1846 the elder Boyer passed through the Pecos Valley region of New Mexico. Impressed by the spaces the elder Boyer returned to his home in Georgia and reportedly spoke regularly about returning to New Mexico with his family and friends. Henry Boyer was never able to realize his dream, but his youn son Frank, one of eight children, probably went well beyond anything his father had thought of doing when he later founded Blackdom, one of the first towns in New Mexico, albeit one of the last founded in America. Frank Boyer was educated at the Atlanta Baptist Seminary, and later received his bachelor's degree in teacher's education from More College, Atlanta. He also took advanced classes at Fisk College, Nashville.

Pelham, Georgia, was home for the Boyer family and also the place from which Frances Boyer began his long walk with a in-law, Daniel Keyes. By means of the Homestead Act of 1863, which allowed a person to homestead up to 160 acres, Frank and his wife, Ella, whom he had met in 1892 while at a summer teaching session at Atlanta University, had discussed using this as an opportunity. This, combined with his father's love of the land he had traveled during his army days, apparently convinced Boyer that it might be possible to begin a utopian community for blacks in the wide-spaces of New Mexico. Boyer and Keyes left Georgia in January 1900, walking and working their way west until October of the same year. Odd jobs covered part of their expenses, but it is also reported that they danced for drunken cowboys or other travelers they met. Upon their arrival in New Mexico, which was a territory until 1912, Boyer and Keyes were able to find work with ranchers in the area around Roswell and Dexter, in the southeastern part of the state. Boyer also worked as a bellhop in a Roswell hotel for a time.

Ella and the Boyer children came to New Mexico in 1901, which was also the time that Frank Boyer and Daniel Keyes were visiting surrounding states to promote their idea of Blackdom to other black citizens. One of Boyer's employers was successful in drilling a well that hit artesian water at six hundred feet, nearly ten times deeper than other drillers had gone. This discovery turned the Roswell area into a temporary boomtown, since it helped make Roswell, at least for a while, a garden area. It was also in 1901 that Boyer was able to secure a loan and drill for water in the area chosen for Blackdom. An artesian well was soon operating, and Blackdom was on its way to becoming a dream fulfilled.

Things went well for Boyer at first, with crops of hay and apples plentiful. Other black homesteaders began to arrive, many of whom stayed with the Boyers until they could establish themselves. Blackdom began to grow, and in 1903 Boyer and Keyes, along with several other residents, signed the articles of incorporation for the Blackdom town site. It was not until 1920, however, that the actual town site was dedicated, ironically not long before Blackdom itself ceased to exist. The town site comprised about 40 acres, with 166 lots, each 35 x 100 feet. All of the home sites were set around a public square and park, and most streets were apparently named after noted African Americans of the era. The actual Blackdom settlement, which grew up around the Boyer homestead, entailed 15,000 acres and was home to black and white families that settled there under the various land laws of the time. A store, post office (from at least 1913 to 1920), hotel, school, and two churches soon sprang up. A one-sheet newspaper was also printed for a short time. Population estimates vary from three hundred to five hundred at Blackdom's high point.

Historical texts do not note any major problems between black and white residents, and it was noted that both races celebrated Juneteenth, the annual commemoration of the abolition of slavery in Texas. However, the town failed when the apple crops proved unreliable and the wells, overdrilled for the aquifer, ran dry.

Francis and Ella Boyer, who eventually had ten children, finally left Blackdom in 1921, and relocated briefly in Pacheco, New Mexico. Here again they were probably the first black settlers in the area, and one more move to what would later become Vado, New Mexico, just south of Las Cruces, brought the Boyer's and their eventual ten children to their last stop. They were also successful in helping approximately fifty other black families settle in the area. Both Frank and Ella became involved in education in the area, starting the Paul L. Dunbar School. Their farm was also the first to grow cotton successfully in New Mexico, where it remains a major crop for southern New Mexico farmers. Frank and Ella both died in Vado. Blackdom itself lasted until 1925. The site is now noted on a state historical marker, located about eighteen miles south of present-day Roswell.

FURTHER READING

Baton, Maisha, and Henry Walt. *A History of Blackdom, N.M., in the Context of the African American Post Civil War Colonization Movement* (1996).

Fleming, Elvis. "Lillian Westfield Collins Blackdom, N.M., Interview for the Chaves County Historical Society," in *Roundup on the Pecos* (1985).

JEFF BERG

Boykin, Keith (28 Aug. 1965–), civil rights and gay rights advocate, was born in St. Louis, Missouri, to Bill Boykin, a bus driver and salesman, and Shirley, a federal employee. Shortly after the birth of his sister Krystal in 1966, the family moved from inner-city St. Louis to the predominantly white suburb of Florissant, Missouri. As he grew up, Boykin displayed an interest in politics, becoming student body president in the fifth grade and dreaming of the White House.

Boykin's parents separated when he was in elementary school, and both left the St. Louis area in 1980. Boykin moved with his father and sister to Clearwater, Florida, where his father opened a black beauty-supply business. Boykin attended Countryside High School, where as a senior he was elected student government president, and graduated in 1983. He enrolled in Dartmouth College in Hanover, New Hampshire, that fall, and joined the track team and in his junior year was editor in chief of the campus newspaper, the *Dartmouth*. He graduated with a degree in Government in 1987 and subsequently moved to Boston to work on the Michael Dukakis presidential campaign until

Keith Boykin, author and commentator on issues of race and sexual orientation, near his home in Harlem, New York, 2 March 2004. (AP Images.)

November 1988, after which he joined his father at his new home in Atlanta, Georgia, and worked as a high school teacher while applying to law school. Boykin enrolled in Harvard Law School in 1989, where he served as general editor of the *Harvard Civil Rights–Civil Liberties Law Review*, and graduated in 1992. As a law student, he was also one of eleven plaintiffs in a 1990 suit against Harvard Law School protesting its lack of minority and female faculty hiring, even arguing a portion of the case in court. The case was dismissed on appeal by the Massachusetts Supreme Judicial Court in 1992. Boykin came out as gay in 1991, and as he gave up a lucrative job with a San Francisco law firm to work on Bill Clinton's presidential campaign after law school, he gradually intensified his commitment to gay and lesbian as well as African American civil rights issues. After Clinton's election, Boykin was hired in January 1993 as a special assistant and was later promoted to director of specialty press, a position in which he coordinated communications between the administration and minority publications. The highest-ranked openly gay official in the White House, Boykin helped organize a historic April 1993 meeting between President Clinton and gay and lesbian community leaders.

In the course of his work, Boykin became frustrated by what he considered the inaccurate portrayal of race and sexuality in the media, and he left his position in 1995 to work on his first book, *One More River to Cross: Black and Gay in America* (1996). Based on Boykin's own experience and dozens of interviews across the country, the book revealed the alienation often felt by black gays and lesbians, given racism within the gay community and denial or antigay harassment in the black community and the black church. Boykin asserted that despite these tensions and despite the differences in the civil rights goals of African Americans and gays, both groups share a common struggle for equality.

From 1995 to 1998 Boykin was executive director of the National Black Lesbian and Gay Leadership Forum in Los Angeles, California. His second book, *Respecting the Soul: Daily Reflections for Black Lesbians and Gays*, was published in 1999 and won the 1999 Lambda Literary Award for Spirituality. He was an adjunct professor of political science at American University in Washington, D.C., from 1999 to 2001, winning the School of Public Affairs award for outstanding adjunct professor in 2000. In 2001 Boykin moved to New York City where he founded the National Black Justice Coalition, an antiracism and antihomophobia advocacy group for black gays, lesbians, bisexuals, and transgendered men and women and their supporters. He later became president of its board of directors.

Boykin's advocacy work included challenging negative images of black gays and lesbians in the media. In August 2004 he was featured on the Showtime television network reality series *American Candidate*, in which ten contestants organized mock presidential campaigns. He also published his third book, *Beyond the Down Low: Sex, Lies, and Denial in Black America* (2005), which became a *New York Times* best-seller. The book was written in response to the phenomenon of the "down low," widely publicized in books such as J. L. King's *On the Down Low: A Journey into the Lives of "Straight" Black Men Who Sleep with Men* (2004), in which African American men in heterosexual relationships engage in clandestine, often risky, homosexual encounters. Boykin criticized the implications that the down low occurs only among African Americans and that black men are to blame for rising rates of HIV infection among black women. Boykin urged a more honest account of the means by which HIV spreads in the African American community and public policy initiatives to provide better prevention and treatment.

Born on the second anniversary of the 1963 March on Washington and MARTIN LUTHER KING JR.'s call for a racially integrated America in his "I have a dream" speech, Boykin used his work to reflect both the continuation and the expansion of the goals of the civil rights movement since the 1960s. Gays and lesbians joined African Americans, Latinos, Native Americans, and women in applying the language and techniques of that movement to their own demands for equality. Boykin suggested that the dream is incomplete without a society that confers the same rights to all people, regardless of their sexual orientation.

FURTHER READING

Boykin, Keith. *One More River to Cross: Black and Gay in America* (1996).

Graham, Chad. "The Other Presidential Race," *Advocate*, 17 Aug. 2004.

Strong, Lester. "Fighting Demons," *A&U Magazine* (Jan. 2005).

FRANCESCA GAMBER

Boyne, Thomas (c. 1846–21 Apr. 1896), Civil War and Indian Wars soldier and Medal of Honor recipient, was born in Prince George County, Maryland. Nothing is known of his early life; he was likely born enslaved, but if so, the circumstances in which he gained his freedom are unknown. His military service began when he enlisted in the Union Army from St. Mary's County, Maryland, on 5 February 1864. Boyne served in Battery C of the 2nd U.S. Colored Light Artillery and saw action in and around Richmond, Virginia, during the last year of the Civil War at Wilson's Wharf and City Point. Boyne and his regiment were subsequently sent westward, and he ended the war stationed in Texas. In March 1866 Thomas Boyne was discharged from the army at Brownsville, Texas, as his regiment, like all other volunteer regiments that served in the Civil War, black and white, was disbanded when the army reverted to peacetime status. In February 1867 Boyne reenlisted in the army under the name Thomas Bowen (though he soon reverted to his old surname) and initially served with the 40th Infantry Regiment.

The service of soldiers such as Thomas Boyne, Thomas Shaw, and JOHN DENNY was important not just because they were decorated for valor, but also because they were among the first African American soldiers allowed to serve in the U.S. Army as career soldiers while the service was on a regular peacetime footing. This service was authorized by Congress in 1866, resulting in the formation of six all-black army units, the 38th, 39th, 40th, and 41st infantry regiments and the 9th and 10th cavalry regiments. Soon thereafter, the four infantry regiments were consolidated into two regiments and were redesignated as the 24th and 25th infantry regiments, while the 9th and 10th cavalry regiments remained unchanged. These all-black units comprised nearly ten percent of the army's overall strength, while the cavalry regiments comprised some twenty percent of the cavalry force. As a group, these men soon gained the nickname "Buffalo Soldiers" from the enemies with whom they fought, the Native American tribes struggling to retain their land in the west. Often referred to in more derogatory and racist terms by white soldiers in other regiments, the Buffalo Soldiers heartily adopted the new name as a badge of honor. While the Buffalo Soldiers are best known for the skirmishes collectively known as the Indian Wars, which they fought with Native Americans from 1866 to 1890, they actually performed a wide range of duties that enabled the opening of the American west, including building roads, protecting new settlements from outlaws, and transporting supplies.

In 1875 Thomas Boyne left the infantry after a period of service in Texas and Kansas and reenlisted in the 9th Cavalry Regiment as part of Company C. By 1879 Boyne, now a sergeant, was serving with his regiment in New Mexico, and that year saw a great deal of action while fighting the warriors of the Apache tribe, led by the famed chief Victorio. The first action of note involving Boyne came on 29 May, when the troopers of C and I companies were employed preventing the Apaches from leaving the barren San Carlos reservation and escaping to Mexico. During the action that ensued in the Mimbres Mountains, Sergeant Boyne noticed that Lieutenant Henry Wright and several men escorting a wounded soldier were cut off and surrounded; he subsequently gathered several of his men and came to their rescue. Four months later, on 27 September 1879, Boyne and the men of the 9th Cavalry were again fighting Victorio and his warriors, this time near Ojo Caliente. In a battle that lasted several days, a wounded Thomas Boyne killed one warrior and single-handedly captured most of the opponents' horses. Sergeant Thomas Boyne, who eventually took part in eight of his regiment's fourteen battles with the Apaches, subsequently applied for a Certificate of Merit in 1881 for his actions and was warmly endorsed by Lieutenant Wright, the officer he had previously saved, as well as by Major Albert Morrow, under whom he had served in the action of September 1879. In speaking of Boyne, Morrow wrote, "I have seen him repeatedly in action and in every instance he distinguished himself. ... I cannot speak too highly of his conduct. ... If ever a soldier deserves a Certificate of Merit or a Medal of Honor Sergeant Boyne does" (Hanna, 59). Thomas Boyne was subsequently awarded the Medal of Honor on 6 January 1882.

Following his service in New Mexico, Thomas Boyne would see further service with the 9th Cavalry in the Indian Territory of Oklahoma, where he suffered a severe case of frostbite in 1884–1885, and at Fort Missoula, Montana, where he was injured while supervising a wood-gathering detail. Worn out by his twenty-four years of military service, Thomas Boyne was discharged from the army in January 1889 and soon thereafter went to live the remainder of his days at the U.S. Soldier's Home in Washington, D.C. Upon his death from consumption, Boyne was interred in the Soldier's Home National Cemetery, the final resting place of many Medal of Honor recipients, including several of his fellow Buffalo Soldiers.

FURTHER READING

Hanna, Charles W. *African American Recipients of the Medal of Honor* (2002).

Schubert, Frank N. *Black Valor: Buffalo Soldiers and the Medal of Honor, 1870–1898* (1997).

GLENN ALLEN KNOBLOCK

Boynton Robinson, Amelia (18 Aug. 1911–), civil rights and voting rights activist, was born in Savannah, Georgia, the seventh of ten children born to Anna Eliza Hicks and George Platts, the latter of whom owned and operated a wood supply business for years before moving to Philadelphia, Pennsylvania, and engaging in real estate.

Amelia Platt's childhood was idyllic; she was raised in Savannah and its outskirts in an affectionate middle-class family and community that encouraged her aspirations. She graduated from Tuskegee Institute (later Tuskegee University) in 1927, later adding course work from colleges in Tennessee, Virginia, and Georgia. She briefly taught school in Georgia before being named home demonstration agent for the Dallas County, Alabama, Cooperative Extension Service. In the early 1930s she served alongside Samuel William "Bill" Boynton, who was the county agent for Dallas County. The Cooperative Extension Service at that time was segregated by both race and gender in the South, with black home demonstration agents teaching farm women ways to improve their lives, and black county agents instructing farm men in agricultural improvements. Although the work was intended to assist farmers in improving their economic lot, the combination of the entrenched poverty brought on by tenant

farming and the racial caste system hindered the efforts of extension agents. Platts was shocked by the racial and economic oppression in Dallas County, a startling contrast to her own middle-class background.

In 1936 Platts left home demonstration work to marry Boynton, who worked in real estate and insurance after retiring from the extension service in 1949. The Boyntons had two sons, William and Bruce. William Boynton worked for the postal service, and later in real estate. Bruce Boynton, as a college student, was arrested in 1958 for challenging segregation in a restaurant. *Boynton v. Virginia* was decided by the Supreme Court in 1960 in Boynton's favor. He later became a lawyer.

Both Boyntons were registered voters in the 1930s, and both were strong advocates for voter registration. Bill Boynton served openly in the Fourth Congressional District for Registration and Voting for nearly twenty years, and was president of the Dallas County Voters League, coaching many African Americans in preparation for registration. He also served as NAACP president for Selma in the 1950s. He used his expertise gained as a county agent to press for improved economic conditions for black farmers, assisting individuals in finding loans for land purchases. Keenly aware and frustrated with the roadblocks to economic and political advancement for blacks, Boynton testified before Congress in 1955 about the hindrances to the enjoyment of civil rights.

By the early 1960s both Boyntons were assisting the Justice Department by supplying evidence of voter intimidation, and they assisted Bernard Lafayette of the Student Nonviolent Coordinating Committee (SNCC) in encouraging voter registration. The Dallas County Voters League found it difficult to overcome local black fears of recrimination should they register to vote, but Lafayette chipped away at such fears by enlisting youth from Selma schools to attend meetings and marches. The first of these mass meetings was held as a memorial service for Bill Boynton on his death in 1963, and proved an effective means through which to raise local interest in voter registration.

As more SNCC volunteers arrived in Selma, and as mass meetings were followed by marches and arrests, in July 1964 Circuit Judge James A. Hare reacted by slapping an injunction on civil rights leaders and participants, prohibiting more than three of them from gathering in public meetings. Prior to the injunction, Amelia Boynton ran for office on the Democratic ticket in the race for

Amelia Boynton Robinson listens with high school student Natalie Ortiz to speakers during an American Civil Rights Education Services tour at the Martin Luther King Jr. National Historic Site, 26 August 2003 in Atlanta.

the Fourth Congressional District. She lost in the primary but heightened her visibility in both the black and white communities. Although prohibited from attending public meetings by the injunction, Boynton continued working for voter registration.

In response to the shutdown in free expression brought about by Judge Hare's order, Boynton wrote to MARTIN LUTHER KING JR, and the Southern Christian Leadership Conference (SCLC), asking them to come to Selma. King agreed, established a headquarters in Boynton's office, and set about turning Selma's local resistance to voter registration into a nationally recognized problem. The injunction was quashed in early 1965, and demonstrations resumed. In January 1965, while assisting African Americans who waited in long lines to register to vote, Boynton was accosted and arrested by Sheriff Jim Clark. The photographs of Clark's rough handling of Boynton made national press. Tensions in Selma grew as King was arrested in February 1965 and briefly held in jail.

White response to the heightened civil rights activities often included acts of violence, one instance of which was the killing of JIMMIE LEE JACKSON during a civil rights march in nearby Marion. To protest Jackson's death, SNCC leaders decided to walk to Montgomery, about fifty miles from Selma, to carry their grievances to Governor George Wallace. On Sunday, 7 March 1965, Boynton and about six hundred other protesters began peacefully walking out of Selma, heading across the Edmund Pettus Bridge at the end of town. At the base of the bridge the marchers were confronted by state and local police, some on horseback, who ordered them to turn around and head back into Selma. Barely waiting for a response, police charged the crowd, clubbing and tear-gassing many individuals, including Boynton, who was struck unconscious. News coverage of the "Bloody Sunday" attack prompted President Lyndon Johnson's decision to ask Congress to pass the 1965 Voting Rights Act. This law transcended local efforts by ensuring federal intervention in districts where there was significant evidence of voting rights fraud.

In 1968 Amelia Boynton worked with the ill-fated Poor People's Campaign and Resurrection City in Washington, D.C., which was an attempt by King to draw attention to poverty. She later joined the Schiller Institute, founded by Lyndon LaRouche, to attack injustice on a national and international level.

FURTHER READING

Robinson, Amelia Boynton. *Bridge across Jordan* (1979, rev. 1991).

Branch, Taylor. *Parting the Waters: America in the King Years, 1954–1963* (1989).

Branch, Taylor. *Pillar of Fire: America in the King Years, 1963–1965* (1999).

Chestnut, J. L., Jr., and Julia Cass. *Black in Selma: The Uncommon Life of J. L. Chestnut, Jr.* (1990).

MARY A. WAALKES

Bozeman, Sylvia Trimble (1 Aug. 1947–), mathematician, was born Sylvia Trimble in Camp Hill, Alabama, the daughter of Horace Edward Trimble Sr., an insurance agent, and Robbie Jones Trimble. She had four siblings, three brothers and one sister. She attended the segregated public schools in her rural hometown, and was motivated by the standards and values instilled in her by her parents. Early in her education, Bozeman's parents helped her develop confidence that she was capable of accomplishing her goals. Though her father worked with numerical calculations in his career, it was her mother who encouraged Bozeman to pursue her interest in mathematics. Her enthusiasm for the subject grew into advanced mathematical knowledge when her high school mathematics teacher, Frank Holley, returned after school to teach trigonometry to a small group of students because the course was not part of the school's curriculum. Her excellence in mathematics and other subjects led to Bozeman's honor as class valedictorian upon graduating from Edward Bell High School in 1964.

Following graduation, Bozeman entered the historically black Alabama Agricultural and Mechanical University in Huntsville, where she majored in mathematics. Encouraged by Howard Foster, the head of the department of math and physics, she contributed to a computer research project sponsored by the National Aeronautics and Space Administration (NASA). Additionally, Trimble participated in a summer research program

at Harvard University, where she learned the early computer programming language FORTRAN. In 1968, after serving as student government vice president, Trimble graduated second in her class from Alabama A&M University with a bachelor of science degree in Mathematics.

Several weeks after graduating, Sylvia Trimble married Robert Bozeman, a fellow mathematics student whom she met during her freshman year in college. The newlyweds moved to Nashville, Tennessee, where they both enrolled in graduate school at Vanderbilt University to study mathematics. In 1970 Sylvia Bozeman graduated from Vanderbilt with her master of science degree in Mathematics. While her husband pursued his doctorate at Vanderbilt, Bozeman worked at Vanderbilt as an instructor of mathematics for two years. In 1972 she served as an Upward Bound math instructor at Tennessee State University. A year later the Bozeman family, which had expanded to include two young children, moved to Atlanta, Georgia, when Bozeman's husband earned his Ph.D. With her husband as a newly appointed professor at historically black, all-male Morehouse College, Sylvia Bozeman was hired by Spelman College, its female counterpart.

As an instructor of math at Spelman, Bozeman recognized the need to earn a doctorate degree to further her career. With the support of mentors, including ETTA ZUBER FALCONER, head of the math department at Spelman, Bozeman took a leave of absence to enroll in a doctoral program at Emory University in Atlanta. She studied functional analysis, an area of mathematics that merges algebra and topological geometry. Under the tutelage of her academic adviser, Luis Kramarz, Sylvia Bozeman earned her Ph.D. in 1980. Her dissertation was titled "Representations of Generalized Inverses of Fredholm Operators." Immediately following graduation, Bozeman returned to Spelman College as an assistant professor of mathematics. In 1982 she became the head of the mathematics department and held that post for eleven years. She was promoted to associate professor in 1984 and full professor in 1991. In 1998 Bozeman was promoted to associate provost for science and mathematics at Spelman College.

From 1980 to 1984 the National Science Foundation and the U.S. Office of Army Research funded Bozeman's continued research on functional analysis. In 1986 Bozeman received a grant from NASA to study a computer-based subject, image processing. Because of her strong work in this area, Bozeman was awarded the White House Initiative Faculty Award for Excellence in Science and Technology in 1988. That same year Bozeman was granted the Tenneco United Negro College Fund's Excellence in Teaching Award. Her recognition for distinction continued with her election to Phi Beta Kappa, an academic honor society, and to Pi Mu Epsilon, the honorary national mathematics society.

In addition to her academic achievements, Bozeman participated in professional organizations. She served as the vice president of the National Association of Mathematicians from 1984 to 1988. In 1989 Bozeman became the first African American to be elected to the board of governors of the Mathematics Association of America, the largest mathematics organization of college and university professors. In 1993 Bozeman was appointed project director for the Center for Scientific Applications of Mathematics, Spelman College's initiative to increase African American participation in the sciences. This project also affected high school mathematics by exposing high school math teachers to innovations in mathematics and mathematics instruction.

In the mid-1990s Lee Lorch, the eminent mathematician and human rights activist, introduced Sylvia Bozeman to Rhonda Hughes. Hughes was a mathematics professor at Bryn Mawr College in Pennsylvania. Sharing common circumstances—both were mathematicians at small liberal arts, historically female colleges, and both recognized a need to increase the participation of women in mathematics—Bozeman and Hughes collaborated to develop the Enhancing Diversity in Graduate Education (EDGE) program. In 1998 EDGE was created to improve opportunities for women who wished to earn graduate degrees in the mathematical sciences.

FURTHER READING

Hine, Darlene Clark. *Black Women in America: An Historical Encyclopedia* (1993).

Morrow, Charlene, and Teri Peri, eds. *Notable Women in Mathematics: A Biographical Dictionary* (1998).

Proffitt, Pamela. *Notable Women Scientists* (1999).

COURTNEY A. HOWARD

Brace, Jeffrey (1742?–1827), slave, sailor, soldier, and farmer, was born Boyrereau Brinch, the seventh of eight children (four boys and four girls) born to Whryn Brinch, the son of Yarrah Brinch, and of Whryn Douden Wrogan, the daughter of Grassee

Youghgon. He lived in the city of Deauyah in the kingdom of Bow-woo, which was probably situated in the Niger River basin, in the area that would later become Mali. In 1758, when he was around the age of sixteen, Boyrereau was abducted by slave traders, transported to Barbados, and sold to Captain Isaac Mills of New Haven, Connecticut, who trained him for British naval service. Like thousands of other slaves and freed Africans in the Caribbean, Brace (as he would come to be called years later, after his manumission. This may have been an anglicized version of Brinch) was forced to labor aboard ship during the Seven Years' War. He remained at sea for two years, and Mills renamed him Jeffrey after the British commander Sir Jeffrey Amherst, in recognition of his bravery but lack of prudence in battle.

Though he was wounded in a skirmish, Brace continued on voyages to Ireland, Georgia, Nova Scotia, New York, Rhode Island, and Boston. In the fall of 1763 Mills sold him to John Burrell, a sadistic Puritan from Milford, Connecticut. For the next five years Brace passed from one cruel Yankee owner to another until he was purchased by an elderly widow, Mary Stiles, around 1768. A devout grandmother from Woodbury, Connecticut, Stiles taught Brace how to read and write. Upon her death he passed into the hands of her son, Benjamin Stiles, a prominent lawyer and politician.

In 1777 Brace enlisted in the Revolutionary army in hopes of gaining his manumission. He fought for more than five years and was honorably discharged with a badge of merit in 1783. A year later, under community pressure, Stiles consented to Brace's manumission. Brace went to Vermont, which through its 1777 constitution became the first state to abolish adult slavery. The Vermont constitution also established universal male suffrage.

Arriving in Poultney in 1784, Brace found southern Vermont rich in both promise and disappointment. Initially, he said, "I enjoyed the pleasures of a freeman; my food was sweet, my labor pleasure: and one bright gleam of life seemed to shine upon me" (Brace, 166–167). He worked hard and earned more than a subsistence, but periodically he found himself cheated out of promised wages and victimized by broken contracts. Eventually he bought land in Poultney and then went to the neighboring town of Dorset to attempt to earn enough money to farm his land. While working in John Manley's tavern in Dorset, Brace met and married Susannah (or Susan) Dublin, whom he described as "a native African female, who possessed a reciprocal abhorrence to slavery." As a couple, Jeffrey and Susan contributed to a growing New England patchwork of abolitionist Africans who remembered and valued their cultural origins.

Through hard work and persistence, the Braces achieved moderate success, but the peace and material comfort they deserved were never fully realized. The most painful problem they encountered stemmed from Vermont's pervasive racism and its entrenched practice of exploiting children, especially black children. Susan had two children from her first marriage, a twelve-year-old boy, whose name is not known, and a young girl named Bersheba. Coveting these children as servants, two powerful white citizens, Elizabeth Powell of Manchester and Archibald Dixon of Poultney, forced the Brace children into indenture.

The couple also had children of their own. Although the exact number is uncertain, the 1790 U.S. census lists five free people of color in the Poultney household of "Jeffrey Bran," which suggests that they had three children by 1790. They may have had more later on. Around 1795 they returned to Poultney to clear their land, which was rocky and full of trees. Compounding their hardships was a jealous, spiteful neighbor who harassed them relentlessly for seven years, finally threatening to "bind out" (that is, force into indenture) their children. Faced with this threat Brace decided to sell his farm and move to northern Vermont. After attempting to settle in other villages, Jeffrey and his son-in-law eventually purchased land in a small village named Georgia, on the fertile shores of Lake Champlain. Here they cleared a farm and prospered for a while. In 1804 a grandson, most likely his first, was born in the neighboring town of Saint Albans. On 19 March 1807 Susan Brace died.

In 1810 Jeffrey Brace, who became blind in his late sixties, narrated his life story to Benjamin Prentiss, a white lawyer who, despite his education, was poor and obscure. Published under the title *The Blind African Slave, or Memoirs of Boyrereau Brinch, Nicknamed Jeffrey Brace*, the memoir elicited almost no recorded reader or critical responses. In an 1852 biography of an African preacher from Vermont named Charles Bowles, the biographer John Lewis provided a rare glimpse into a racially mixed abolitionist community in Vermont. Lewis suggested that through storytelling and moral suasion, "Brother Jeffrey Brace" helped shape the political climate of Vermont, which by the mid-nineteenth century was the most antislavery state in America.

On 18 March 1818 the U.S. Congress passed an act to provide pensions for eligible Revolutionary War veterans. On 4 April Jeffrey Brace filed a pension application, which was rejected on the grounds that the War Department could not find his service record. He had forgotten that he had enlisted under the name of Stiles. The Franklin County judge of probate, Seth Wetmore, became his impassioned advocate, but it was three years before Brace, on 11 July 1821, received a pension of $8 a month, plus arrears totaling $328.23. This money was most likely sufficient to make his final six years of life materially comfortable.

Jeffrey Brace died in Georgia, Vermont, and was memorialized in Poultney, where the 9 May 1827 *Northern Spectator* published an unusually long, laudatory obituary, saying in part: DIED In Georgia, Vt., Jeffrey Brace, an African, well known by the appellation of "Old Jeff," supposed to be nearly 100 years old. … He had for many years been totally blind, yet his mental powers appeared to be hardly impaired. The powers of his memory were frequently tested by repeating whole chapters of the scriptures nearly verbatim. He was formerly a resident of this town. Despite his accomplishments and regional reputation, Brace and his memoir virtually vanished from history until the dawn of the twenty-first century.

FURTHER READING

Brace, Jeffrey. *The Blind African Slave, or Memoirs of Boyrereau Brinch, Nicknamed Jeffrey Brace*, ed. Benjamin F. Prentiss (1810; 2004).

Obituary: *Northern Spectator*, 9 May 1827.

KARI J. WINTER

Bradford, Alex (23 Jan. 1927–15 Feb. 1978), composer, singer, and choir director, was born in Bessemer, Alabama, a town with a rich musical tradition of blues, gospel, and male quartets. His mother, Olivia Bradford Spann, worked as a hairdresser, among other occupations, and his father, Alex Bradford Sr., was an ore miner. Bradford exhibited early musical talent, performing on stage at the age of four. This experience, reinforced by his brief attendance at a church that embraced more exuberant displays of emotion and livelier music than did the Baptist church of his mother (who put a halt to her son's foray), initiated his lifelong love for theater. He soaked up the performance styles of local showmen like Prophet Jones, and national gospel stars like ARIZONA DRANES, MAHALIA JACKSON (whom he later accompanied on piano), and Queen C.

Anderson, who traveled to Bessemer during the town's annual gospel event. Spann sent her teenaged son to school in New York for one year and then to an African American private school in Alabama, where he led other students in the performance of blues and gospel and acquired the title "Professor" because he taught as a student.

After graduating from high school and serving in the army during World War II, Bradford moved to Chicago in 1947, where he proceeded to perform both blues and gospel. His first big break came a few years later when Willie Web invited him to join his gospel group and soon after recorded Bradford's arrangement of the hymn "Every Day and Every Hour." The encouraging reception of this song inspired him to form his own vocal group, the all-male Bradford Specials. Their first release, "Too Close to Heaven" (1953), was written by Bradford and sold over a million copies. During the 1950s Bradford performed and recorded with luminaries like SALLIE MARTIN, ROBERTA MARTIN, DELOIS BARRETT CAMPBELL, Maceo Woods, and CLARA WARD. While Chicago was the epicenter of gospel during this time, Bradford moved to New York City to escape the inhibiting control exerted over the sacred music scene by the city's most established performers.

Like older gospel legend SISTER ROSETTA SHARPE, Bradford disrupted boundaries by performing sacred music in decidedly non-religious settings. In his mid-twenties he performed at Chicago's famous Regal Theater in a midnight show, along with other blues and gospel performers, in what one newspaper labeled as "flesh entertainment" because it included nearly nude female dancers (*Chicago Defender*, 28 Nov. 1953). He later claimed to have appeared at Harlem's Apollo Theater more than any other gospel singer. His unparalleled flamboyancy and theatricality, which he accentuated through colorful robes and stoles, made some people question whether his primary motivation was religious faith or self-aggrandizement. The gospel historian Anthony Heilbut asserted that Bradford was "a born star, the cynosure of all eyes" (*Gospel Sound*, 146). Attesting to his penchant for publicity, his first marriage took place in February 1956 in the Bronx funeral home owned by his bride, Susan Cannon, and attracted hundreds of onlookers.

Bradford's second vocal group, the Men of Song, helped to popularize gospel among white audiences by appearing at the 1959 Newport Jazz Festival, the Indiana Jazz Festival, and on the Mike Wallace

television show. The *Chicago Defender* noted that he was "widely regarded as America's leading male gospel singer" (18 Sept. 1961). In addition to the sacred compositions for his own group he wrote popular songs for RAY CHARLES and LAVERN BAKER, and the National Baptist Convention awarded him a trophy as "America's Top Gospel Writer." His distinctive baritone voice, known for its gravelly timbre and wide range, influenced the vocal styling of other well-known singers like SAM COOKE.

In 1961 Bradford performed in and wrote music for *The Black Nativity*, the first of several gospel plays in which he participated. Based on poetry by LANGSTON HUGHES and directed by VINNETTE CARROLL, the play opened in New York and was a smash hit on its European, Asian, and Australian tours. Along with that of the gospel legend MARION WILLIAMS, Bradford's performance in the play helped to popularize gospel music outside the African American community. According to his second wife, Alberta Carter Bradford, who served as musical conductor and pianist for the play and with whom he had two daughters, the cast performed for the Dutch, Danish, and British royal families and for many celebrities, like DUKE ELLINGTON and the Beatles. When asked about the appropriateness of bringing religious expression into the commercial theater, Bradford, who had become an ordained minister, responded, "The church was in fact the first theater, and theater is an extension of the pulpit. The play came from the church and it was from the church that Satan took the dance. These are the Biblical facts" (*New York Times*, 11 Sept. 1977).

Although typically not outspoken on social issues Bradford did protest certain personal experiences with racism. As a teenager in Bessemer he refused to be disrespected at work by a belligerent white man, which prompted his mother to send him away to New York for safety. In 1958, on a delayed cross-country airline trip, Bradford and his vocal group were denied accommodations at a motel in Chicago. He responded by suing the airline and motel for fifty thousand dollars and taking his story to the *Chicago Defender*. Over the years he performed at various benefits and church-sponsored events. For some his extravagant musical style symbolized black pride. Months before he died he formed the Creative Movement Repertory Company in Newark, New Jersey, which, similar to the WILLA SAUNDERS JONES Passion play in Chicago, offered young African Americans an opportunity to develop their dancing, music, and theatrical skills.

Bradford remained active in theater until the time of his death. In 1972 he received an Obie Award for his performance in the gospel musical *Don't Bother Me, I Can't Cope* and wrote many of the songs for Vinnette Carroll's *Your Arms Too Short To Box with God* (1976). His own gospel musical, *Don't Cry, Mary*, opened shortly before he suffered a stroke, dying two weeks later in New York's Beth Israel Hospital. Professor Alex Bradford will be remembered as a remarkably versatile showman who helped to popularize gospel music by packaging his extraordinary musical talents in the flashiest and most audacious displays of religious fervor.

FURTHER READING

Boyer, Horace. *The Golden Age of Gospel* (2000).

Dunning, Jennifer. "His Music Celebrates the Gospel Truth," *New York Times*, 11 Sept. 1977.

Heilbut, Anthony. *The Gospel Sound: Good News and Bad Times* (2004).

"Prof. Bradford Set for 'Jubilee Showcase,'" *Chicago Defender*, 8 Feb. 1964.

"Singers to Sue Motel, TWA for $50,000, Charge Bias," *Chicago Defender*, 25 Mar. 1958.

Obituary: *New York Times*, 16 Feb. 1978.

BRIAN HALLSTOOS

Bradford, Mark (2 Apr. 1961–), a multimedia artist who incorporates found material from his urban environment to depict African American life, was born in Los Angeles. As a hairdresser in his mother's beauty shop, Bradford developed his artistic sensibility. He did not seriously examine painting until college. He earned a B.A. in 1995 and an M.A. in 1997, both from the California Institute of Arts.

His studio, once his mother's beauty shop, sits in the Leimert Park neighborhood of South Central Los Angeles. The studio is symbolic of Bradford's close connection to the community that fueled and continues to drive much of his work. Although Bradford refers to his works as paintings, he does not paint in the traditional sense with brushes or supplies from an art store. Much of his paint consists of found material and his palette is the range of colors that occur in the materials—primarily paper—that he gathers from a narrow radius surrounding his studio. Bradford also does not engage in preparatory drawing but rather builds intricate networks of lines using thick- and thin-gauge twine as the first gesture in a multistep process. Rather than prepare his canvases for the application of other media, Bradford conceals the surface with layers of deep black paper. He then tears away and sands down his surfaces,

quickly adding and subtracting. Bradford attributes his frenetic style to his past as a hairdresser. Looking in the mirror at the head he was working on, Bradford would shape and reshape, working fast in short bursts to locate the correct form.

Stylistically, Bradford seems inspired yet uniquely his own artist. Jean Dubuffet coined the phrase "Art Brut" (raw art), and his outsider art paved a passageway to today's brilliant, visionary artists like Bradford. Bradford's use of raw media dances across his large-scale canvases as he utilizes supplies from Home Depot more often than an art supply store. When Andre Breton and Dubuffet started a nonprofit group in 1948 to collect outsider art evoking dreamscapes associated with the Surrealist movement, they aggressively hunted for the likes of Bradford. His art exposes the most intimate emotions of the human subconscious, naked and raw for the viewer.

Bradford might be found using sandpaper after he has added billboard paper, carbon paper, and layered pigment, which provide his works with

Mark Bradford attends the Annual MOCA Gala, An Artists Life Manifesto featuring Artistic Direction by Marina Abramovic, held at MOCA Grand Avenue in Los Angeles, California, Saturday, 12 November 2011. (AP Images.)

aesthetically pleasing and dynamic texture for the viewer. Like Dubuffet's use of kitchen utensils and objects in the next room, Bradford has used salon materials such as foil and hair dye, which are reminiscent of his childhood. He credits this found and active approach to "building" his works, as he says, to his mother and grandmother, whom he calls "creators." He pools creative juices and applies them to visuals as an active doer, not an observer or member of the crowd. Moreover, rather than observing, he is more likely to be found teaching the crowd with his credentials and past supporters, such as the Andy Warhol Foundation for the Visual Arts Resource interactive. His art has hung in top American museums such as the Whitney Museum of American Art and the Studio Museum in Harlem, New York.

On 21 September 2009, the *Los Angeles Times* wrote an article about Bradford's peak achievement of receiving the 2009 MacArthur Fellowship. In the article they explain, "His subjects are small, like daily life in an urban neighborhood, recorded in hand-bills and homemade fliers posted on fences and telephone poles; and they're also monumental, like the 2005 Hurricane Katrina and the trauma of an entire city." Like the inspiring "pro-human" works of JACOB LAWRENCE, Bradford's images show you a reality, but not anger or fear, just reality. The use of such an unbiased yet poignant approach shows the mastery of Bradford's skills and heart. This emotion is also exposing the hearts of others, all of the others in that neighborhood.

One of his more brilliant artworks is a post-Katrina 64-foot-long ark he built in a vacant lot. The viewer can hear telephones ring and people chatting as they live day to day, absorbing the imagery on his ark. It glides and sails through any urban neighborhood as a reminder of human existence combined with bold reminders of what divides us—race, gender, and class. Bradford's works call out to all, connecting us like a single strand of human DNA. We twist and bend around on canvas or boats as part of the action, like Pollock yelling at a canvas and willing life to come out. We are in his lines.

In *Scorched Earth* (2006), giant spears stab the sky with a feeling of triumph, as though people are standing up for some sort of change, that life conquers heat itself. Behind the enormous spears exist the masses. These people are going about their business, making life count for something. As previously stated, like Lawrence, there seems to be a unity, the feeling that all humans are simply humans. Any of us can be the superheroes, the spears, leading the front lines. His use of Abstract Expressionist shape, biomorphic dynamism, and motion further add to the unity—his art's most obvious gift.

Bradford has been recognized with awards such as the Louis Comfort Tiffany Foundation Award in 2003 and the Bucksbaum Award from the Whitney Museum of American Art in 2006. He has exhibited at the Wexner Center for the Arts in Columbus, the Chicago Museum of Contemporary Art, and the San Francisco Museum of Modern Art among others.

FURTHER READING
Bedford, Christopher, et al. *Mark Bradford* (2010).
STARLA ALEXANDER-EVILSIZOR
CARYN E. NEUMANN

Bradford, Perry (14 Feb. 1895–20 Apr. 1970), blues and vaudeville songwriter, publisher, and musical director, was born John Henry Perry Bradford in Montgomery, Alabama, the son of Adam Bradford, a bricklayer and tile setter, and Bella (maiden name unknown), a cook. Standard reference books give his year of birth as 1893, but Bradford's autobiography gives 1895. Early in his youth Bradford learned to play piano by ear. In 1901 his family moved to Atlanta, where his mother cooked meals for prisoners in the adjacent Fulton Street jail. There he was exposed to the inmates' blues and folk singing. Bradford attended Molly Pope School through the sixth grade and claimed to have attended Atlanta University for three years, there being no local high school. This is chronologically inconsistent, however, with his claim to have joined Allen's New Orleans Minstrels in the fall of 1907, traveling to New Orleans for Mardi Gras performances in February 1908 and then moving on to Oklahoma.

After working as a pianist in Chicago, Bradford toured widely from about 1909 to 1918 with Jeanette Taylor in a song-and-dance act billed as Bradford and Jeanette. His nickname "Mule" came from his being featured in a piano and vocal vaudeville song titled "Whoa, Mule," although the jazz dance historians Marshall and Jean Stearns point out that the name also fit Bradford's personality. Bradford learned countless dances from local performers as he toured. When appropriate he memorialized the best dances in lyrics to songs such as "The Bullfrog Hop" (c. 1909) and "Rules and Regulations" (printed in 1911). A shrewd entrepreneur, he initially published his songs as sheet music to be sold after performances. This informal method of distribution was caused in part by the racist structure of the publishing industry, which put roadblocks in the paths of aspiring African American songwriters. (Compare the experiences of the lyricist and composer ANDY RAZAF.) Bradford's financial situation improved slightly with the commercial publication of "Scratchin' the Gravel" (1917) and "The Original Black Bottom Dance" (1919). During these final years of the decade he produced and performed in the musical revues *Sergeant Ham of the 13th District* (1917 and 1919), *Made in Harlem* (at the Lincoln Theatre in New York, 1918)—for which he wrote "Harlem Blues"—and *Darktown after Dark* (1919). Around 1918 Bradford married his first wife, Marion Dickerson, who took Taylor's place in the revues; details of his subsequent marriage or marriages are unknown.

In 1920 Bradford initiated a revolution in popular music. After several companies had turned him down, Bradford convinced Fred Hager of Okeh records to take a chance in spite of racist warnings "not to have any truck with colored girls in the recording field" (Bradford, 118). In February the African American singer MAMIE SMITH recorded for Okeh Bradford's songs "That Thing Called Love" and "You Can't Keep a Good Man Down," accompanied by a white band; these were not immediately released, owing to an industry-wide patent dispute that was still half a year from settlement. In August, with an African American band, the Jazz Hounds, that was put together hastily, Smith recorded "It's Right Here for You" and "Crazy Blues." "Crazy Blues" became a huge hit, selling perhaps more than a million copies. It initiated the 1920s craze for female blues singers and more broadly opened up the field of recording to African Americans, not only in general markets but also in a newly created market: race records.

In 1921 Bradford organized tours for Smith, directed further recording sessions, and established his own publishing company. He quickly made five-figure sums in royalties, and when a Columbia Records lawyer, unaware of the immediate success of "Crazy Blues," offered to make the song a big hit if Bradford would waive his rights to royalties, Bradford made the classic reply, "The only thing Perry Bradford waives is the American flag" (Bradford, 155). Also in 1921 the singer ETHEL WATERS featured Bradford's song "Messin' Around" on the Theater Owners' Booking Association circuit, and Bradford himself performed in the show *Put and Take* (1921). But all did not go smoothly in this year. Bradford reached an out-of-court settlement for having previously sold "Crazy Blues" (a retitled version of "Harlem Blues") to other publishers

under the alternative titles "The Broken Hearted Blues" and "Wicked Blues." Also, a series of financial and touring disputes with Smith's husband and her boyfriend led Bradford to switch from Okeh to Columbia to promote the singer EDITH WILSON, who recorded Bradford's "Evil Blues" in 1922. The same year he was sued for publishing a song owned by another publisher, was convicted of this charge and also of having witnesses commit perjury while testifying on his behalf, and was sentenced to four months in prison.

Among his achievements in the 1920s Bradford claimed to have taught the Black Bottom dance to Ethel Ridley, who introduced it in Irvin C. Miller's show *Dinah* (1923). From this point on his star descended quickly. He assembled great musicians such as LOUIS ARMSTRONG, JAMES P. JOHNSON, and BUSTER BAILEY for undistinguished recordings made from 1923 to 1927 under the name of Perry Bradford's Jazz Phools, and in 1927 he introduced his song "All I Had Is Gone." He also wrote lyrics to the musical revue *Messin' Around* (1929). He seems to have made no further impact, however, apart from a hit song recorded by LOUIS JORDAN's new band in 1939, "Keep a Knockin' (But You Can't Come In)." The singer and songwriter NOBLE SISSLE asserts: "The industry, especially some of the publishers, finally had Perry's terrific catalog of 1,400 songs blackballed from being recorded because he would not sell out to them. They practically broke him. His only brother Negro publisher, CLARENCE WILLIAMS, offered him the same fate. He had to sell out to a white publisher" (Bradford, 10). Bradford lived on relief and worked in New York as a mailman at Queens General Hospital, where he died after having spent his last years in ill health and confined to a nursing home.

As a musician Bradford was no match for the pianist and composer JELLY ROLL MORTON, but they resembled one another in crucial ways. Both were aggressive, perceptive self-promoters who backed up brash claims with documented achievements. Touring the country during the developmental years of blues and jazz, they absorbed and disseminated what they heard, thus helping to create an international music from scattered rural and urban folkways. Both were inflexibly hardheaded and after a period of great success—Bradford's financial and sociocultural, Morton's artistic—found themselves left behind as they stuck doggedly to musical styles that had fallen out of fashion.

Bradford's autobiography is a sustained outburst against his having been left out of early histories of blues and jazz and also against what was in his (probably incorrect) opinion an overestimation of the significance of New Orleans jazzmen in comparison to African American jazz musicians in other places. Although he distorts history as much as he repairs it, his essential arguments have been taken into account in most subsequent studies, and the great significance of his personal contribution to the music's flowering is now widely acknowledged.

FURTHER READING

Bradford, Perry. *Born with the Blues: Perry Bradford's Own Story, The True Story of the Pioneering Blues Singers and Musicians in the Early Days of Jazz* (1965).

Charters, Samuel B., and Leonard Kunstadt. *Jazz: A History of the New York Scene* (1962; rpt. 1981, 1984).

Stearns, Marshall, and Jean Stearns. *Jazz Dance: The Story of American Vernacular Dance* (1968).

This entry is taken from the *American National Biography* and is published here with the permission of the American Council of Learned Societies.

BARRY KERNFELD

Bradley, Aaron Alpeora (1815?–Oct. 1882), Reconstruction politician, was born in Edgefield District, South Carolina, the son of unknown slaves on the plantation of Francis Pickens, a prominent politician. Little is known of Bradley's youth and early manhood other than that he was a shoemaker for a time in Augusta, Georgia, and that he escaped slavery and made his way to the North, apparently during the 1830s. He lived for a time in New York and in Boston. In Boston he not only met abolitionists but also studied the law and eventually became a practicing attorney.

The Civil War opened new horizons. Bradley returned south late in 1865 and settled in Savannah, Georgia, intending, it seems, to open a law practice and a school. Drawn inexorably to the public arena, he began to champion the cause of freed people who were resisting President Andrew Johnson's policy of restoring plantation land to its antebellum owners. Bradley's advocacy took the form of leading mass public demonstrations as well as petitioning authorities in Washington. Military officials in Georgia deemed his spirited criticism of government policies seditious, convicted him of the charge of sedition before a military tribunal, and permitted him to leave the state in lieu of a year's imprisonment. When he returned to Savannah from Boston late in 1866, he resumed his role as champion of the freed people with the same militancy that he had earlier displayed. He immediately

took up the cause of rice-plantation laborers, who were locked in a dispute with both the antebellum plantation owners and the Freedmen's Bureau over rights to the land; both sides threatened to use armed force to gain their objectives.

Despite his ambivalent relationship with military authorities, Bradley had no doubt that federal power—military as well as executive, legislative, and judicial—was essential for revolutionizing the South. Accordingly, he appealed to federal officials both broadly to protect freed people in what he termed the "free enjoyment of Equal Rights and Immunities" and narrowly to redress an assortment of pressing grievances. One representative campaign aimed to remove from office the mayor of Savannah, a former Confederate colonel who treated former slaves with undisguised contempt. Although often unpolished and by turns brazen and elliptical, Bradley's numerous petitions articulated the political aspirations of his constituents in the language of constitutional rights.

For Bradley and like-minded political activists throughout the South, the Reconstruction acts of March 1867 marked a milestone in the struggle to revolutionize the political system. The acts granted suffrage to black men and required elections for delegates to write new constitutions for the former Confederate states. Bradley put his name forward as a candidate, won the hearty support of the voters in his black-majority district, and assumed his seat in the constitutional convention that met in Atlanta from December 1867 to February 1868. By downplaying his constituents' demands to press for a redistribution of plantation land and by supporting the package of debtor relief and homestead-exemption measures tailored to the needs of white yeoman farmers, Bradley aligned himself behind the state's Republican leadership. He seemed to defer to the Republican strategy of appealing to potential white voters (although he never said so directly). At the same time his black constituency grew broader—including urban laborers who showed less interest in land grants than plantation laborers had shown—and he surely began to see more realistically how slim the prospects of legislating land reform at the state level were. Despite his loyalty, Republicans raised neither hand nor voice in his defense when Democratic delegates maneuvered to expel him from the convention on grounds of a past criminal conviction on a morals charge in New York City in 1851. Unfazed, his constituents promptly elected him to the state senate, only to see him, together with every other black senator, driven from that body as well. Bradley ran unsuccessfully for Congress in 1868 and 1870 but reclaimed his state senate seat in January 1870, when federal authorities initiated Georgia's third postwar reconstruction.

For the next two years Bradley labored on behalf of his working-class constituents, introducing various bills to lower taxes, shorten the workday for urban workers, and guarantee civil and political rights. Increasingly convinced that state officials cared more about preserving the trappings of office than about satisfying the freed people's needs, Bradley castigated the Republican governor Rufus B. Bullock and party regulars in Savannah, who were backpedaling before a Democratic onslaught. At the same time Bradley petitioned Washington officials to grant him a sinecure. Appointed a special customs inspector in 1872, he soon politicked his way out of favor and out of his position.

When Georgia Democrats assumed full control over the state government in 1872, Bradley grew increasingly disenchanted. In his search to realize Reconstruction ideals, he advocated a strategy of migration to Florida in the mid-1870s and to Kansas at the end of the decade. Frustrated by his inability to garner support for the Kansas exodus among black Georgians, he headed west on his own in 1882, making it to St. Louis, where he died without any known descendants. Whether he ever married is unknown.

Assessing Bradley's role in Reconstruction requires an appreciation of his role as a leader in a mass movement for radical social change. He consistently identified his political agenda with that of ordinary former slaves, especially the field laborers on coastal rice plantations and the semiskilled and unskilled workers in Savannah. Their collective demand that constitutional rights be extended to all citizens regardless of color or former condition of servitude was frustrated at the time, but it resurfaced with unstoppable force in the twentieth-century civil rights movement.

FURTHER READING
Reidy, Joseph P. "Aaron A. Bradley: Voice of Black Labor in the Georgia Lowcountry," in *Southern Black Leaders of the Reconstruction Era*, ed. Howard N. Rabinowitz (1982).
Obituary: *Savannah Morning News*, 25 Oct. 1882.
This entry is taken from the *American National Biography* and is published here with the permission of the American Council of Learned Societies.

JOSEPH P. REIDY

Bradley, Buddy (1908–1972), choreographer and jazz tap dancer, was born Clarence Bradley in Harrisburg, Pennsylvania. His parents' names and occupations are unknown. His father died when he was quite young, and his religious mother brought him up strictly. After seeing the tap dancers Jack Wiggins and Clarence "Dancing" Dotson at a local theater, Bradley learned to do the time step on one foot by age eight. He taught himself the Charleston, the strut, the drag, the shuffle, and a vast assortment of African American vernacular dances.

After his mother died when he was fourteen, Bradley went to live with a brother-in-law in Utica, New York, and worked as a hotel busboy. A few months later he ran away to New York City and lived at a Harlem boardinghouse inhabited by many show people, especially dancers. With a group of other youngsters that included Derby Wilson, who became a well-known tap dancer, Bradley learned how to tap dance in a blind alley next to Connie's Inn in Harlem and picked up flash and acrobatic steps as a chorus boy both at the downtown Kentucky Club and at Connie's Inn. In 1926 he made his stage debut as a dancer in a FLORENCE MILLS revue at the Lincoln Square Theatre.

Around 1928, at the Billy Pierce Dance Studios off Broadway, Bradley found himself tailoring routines for specific dancers—from gangsters' molls to Broadway stars—for $250 a routine. His dance formula was radically new: he simplified rhythms for the feet while sculpting the body into shapes from African American social dance, blending easy tap dance and jazz dance into routines that rose to a climax and finished gracefully. Well paid but known only in show-business circles, Bradley created dozens of dance routines for white stars of Broadway musicals—stars such as Adele Astaire, Ruby Keeler, and Eleanor Powell—although his name never appeared on any program. It was the custom that so long as the dance director, who grouped scenes and coached the stars, got his pay, there was no need for program credit. Bradley coached Tom Patricola, Ann Pennington, and Francis Williams in the Black Bottom musical numbers in George White's *Scandals* (1926). In 1928 he rechoreographed the entire production of *Greenwich Village Follies*, even though Busby Berkeley's name remained as choreographer on the program. Bradley created routines and sometimes staged complete scenes for Mae West, Gilda Gray, Irene Delroy, Jack Donahue, and Paul Draper in shows such as *Ziegfeld Follies* (1929) and Erroll Carroll's *Vanities* (1924). The "High Yaller" routine from the "Moanin' Low" number in *The Little Show* (1929), which established Clifton Webb as one of the hottest dancers since EARL "SNAKE HIPS" TUCKER, was choreographed by Bradley.

Inspired by the music of the day, Bradley ignored the melody and translated the accents of improvising jazz-musician soloists into dance patterns that were new to Broadway. Bradley received the first full choreographic credit in his career in 1930 in London with *Evergreen*, a new Rodgers and Hart musical at the Adelphi Theatre. His choreography for C. B. Cochran's 1931 revue catapulted him into English musical theater. In the 1930s alone, Bradley choreographed more than thirty musical productions in London, including *Revels in Rhythm* (1931), *Words and Music* (1932), *Mother of Pearl* (1933), *Tulip Time* (1935), Cochran's 1936 revue *Follow the Sun*, and Lew Leslie's *Blackbirds of 1936*. *Evergreen*, which was made into a film in 1934, launched him into the emerging English film industry.

In simplifying dance steps, Bradley used the body to express rather than to accompany the music; and although he simplified rhythms, he never sacrificed the distinctive accents of rhythm tap. Bradley collaborated with Frederick Ashton in creating the first English jazz ballet, *High Yellow* (1932), which featured Alicia Markova. He also created a cabaret act for the ballet dancers Vera Zorina and Anton Dolin, and he collaborated with Agnes de Mille on *Words and Music* (1934), with Antony Tudor on *Lights Up!* (1940), and with George Balanchine on Cochran's 1930 revue.

Bradley lived in London for thirty-eight years, working in Europe as a teacher, choreographer, and producer of musical revues, films, and television shows. By 1950 the Buddy Bradley Dance School in London had more than five hundred students. It remained in operation until 1968, when he returned to New York, where he died. He was survived by his wife Dorothy (maiden name unknown).

Bradley was a key figure in the transplantation of African American jazz and tap dance onto the American and English musical theater stage. "His dance ideas were well ahead of his time, and knowing performers of the musical comedy stage flocked to him," Bradley's obituary in *Variety* (26 July 1972) stated. "He was personally popular in the profession, together with respect given to his creative choreography."

FURTHER READING

"Buddy Bradley: Nimble Ex-Harlemite Runs Most Successful School in England," *Ebony* (July 1950).

Hill, Constance Valis. "Buddy Bradley: The 'Invisible' Man of Broadway Brings Jazz Tap to London," *Proceedings of Society of Dance History Scholars* (14–15 Feb. 1992).

Stearns, Marshall, and Jean Stearns. *Jazz Dance: The Story of American Vernacular Dance* (1968).

Obituary: *Variety*, 26 July 1972.

This entry is taken from the *American National Biography* and is published here with the permission of the American Council of Learned Societies.

CONSTANCE VALIS HILL

Bradley, David (7 Sept. 1950–), writer and educator, was born David Henry Bradley Jr. in Bedford, Pennsylvania, the only son of Reverend David Henry Bradley Sr. and Harriette M. (Jackson) Bradley. His family has been closely involved with the black church for three generations, as he told an interviewer in 1992: "I'm a super preacher's kid. My great-grandfather was a preacher, my grandfather and granduncle were preachers, my father was a preacher. This is the first generation of my family since we liberated ourselves from slavery where there hasn't been a preacher" (Bonetti, 69). This familiarity with the black church and with preachers would influence his work and inspire his characters.

After he graduated from Bedford Area High School in 1968, Bradley entered the University of Pennsylvania. He graduated in 1972 with a bachelor of arts, summa cum laude, in Creative Writing, and was awarded a Thouron British-American Exchange Scholarship for King's College at the University of London, where he received his master of arts in 1974 in Area Studies, particularly nineteenth-century American history. This interest in history was apparent in Bradley's novel *The Chaneysville Incident* (1981), which was inspired by his mother's discovery of thirteen unmarked graves near Chaneysville while she was researching local history for Bedford County's 1969 bicentennial. After his return from England, Bradley spent a short period in editing and teaching, after which he settled at Temple University in Philadelphia, Pennsylvania, where he taught from 1976 to 1996.

Bradley's first novel, *South Street* (1975), drew on the African American oral tradition, celebrating the vernacular culture of Bradley's unemployed working-class characters. The novel was set in the 1970s in South Street, close to central Philadelphia. Taking place in a black bar, a black church, and a hotel lobby, it was structured around a series of vignettes exploring the lives of black ghetto dwellers, ranging from unemployed prostitutes, hustlers, and henchmen to bartenders, preachers, janitors, and winos. The protagonist was Adlai Stevenson Brown, a black, middle-class, educated poet, who temporarily moved to South Street in order to live with the prolctariat and to experience the conditions of the black poor. An outsider to South Street, he was viewed with suspicion. His interaction with South Street's working classes revealed his feelings of inadequacy and alienation. Through this class dynamic the novel played on identity politics and shed light on class hierarchy and racial divisions.

While *South Street* received little critical attention, Bradley's second novel, *The Chaneysville Incident*, established him as an important voice in African American fiction. The novel won the 1982 PEN/Faulkner Award and an Academy Award from the American Academy and Institute of Arts and Letters and prompted comparisons to the works of RALPH ELLISON, JAMES BALDWIN, and TONI MORRISON.

The novel told the story of John Washington, a successful African American historian, and his attempt to resolve the mystery of his father's death, which was linked to the deaths of a group of runaway slaves. The novel fashioned a continuous dialogue with the past that was informed by the present, constantly moving between rural Pennsylvania in the 1970s where John was currently investigating the death of his father, Moses Washington, and nineteenth-century America, to which John traced his family's history. His family's past, which intersected with and illuminated significant aspects of African American history, became the impetus for John's self-exploration and formation of a new cultural and racial identity.

There was a tendency among critics to focus on the novel's treatment of African American history, and to fail to emphasize the novel's cultural implications. Although Bradley's narrative was shaped by storytelling, and the oral tradition was privileged in the novel, the role of written history and narrative was never displaced or dismissed. John Washington's quest for personal and cultural identity was further complicated by his relationship with Judith, the white girlfriend whom John initially kept at a distance and refused to trust. A shift occurred toward the close of the narrative; racial and gender relationships became reconfigured as Judith moved to the center of Bradley's narrative. She entered John's world imaginatively, becoming both his audience and a contributor to his story.

In addition to his fictional work, Bradley also contributed essays, book reviews and interviews to a diverse range of scholarly periodicals, magazines, and newspapers, including *The Village Voice*, *Savvy*, *Signature*, the *Washington Post*, *Book World*, *Esquire*, *Callaloo*, *The New Yorker*, *Time Magazine*, *Philadelphia Magazine*, *New York Arts Journal*, the *New York Times Book Review*, *Southern Review*, and the *Los Angeles Times Book Review*. He was also awarded a Guggenheim Fellowship for fiction in 1989, and a National Endowment for the Arts Literature Fellowship for creative non-fiction. In 2003 Bradley became director of the creative writing program at the University of Oregon.

FURTHER READING

Blake, Susan L., and James A. Miller. "The Business of Writing: An Interview With David Bradley," *Callaloo* 21 (1984).

Bonetti, Kay. "An Interview with David Bradley," *Missouri Review* 15 (1992).

Brigham, Cathy. "Identity, Masculinity, and Desire in David Bradley's Fiction," *Contemporary Literature* 36 (1995).

Ensslen, Claus. "Fictionalizing History: David Bradley's *The Chaneysville Incident*," *Callaloo* 35 (1988).

Hogue, W. Laurence. "Problematizing History," *College Language Association Journal* 38 (1995).

Wilson, Matthew. "The African American Historian: David Bradley's *The Chaneysville Incident*," *African American Review* 29 (1995).

MAHA MAROUAN

Bradley, Edward (22 June 1941–9 Nov. 2006), journalist, was born Edward Rudolph Bradley Jr. in Philadelphia, Pennsylvania, to Edward Bradley Sr., a businessman, and Gladys Bradley. After his parents divorced, Bradley, an only child, lived in Philadelphia with his mother during the school year and with his father in Detroit during the summer. He graduated from Cheyney State College in 1964 with an education degree and taught elementary school in Philadelphia while working as an unpaid jazz disc jockey at the radio station WDAS. Bradley's career break as a reporter came during the race riots in the summer of 1965.

After leaving a club in the early morning, Bradley heard reports that rioting had broken out in the northernmost part of the city, but WDAS did not have reporters to cover the events. Bradley took the initiative, picked up a tape recorder and a station engineer, and headed out to cover the rioting himself. He took a job as a full-time news reporter for New York's WCBS radio in 1967 and remained at the station through 1971. He next took his savings and went to Paris to live as an author, but when his savings ran out, Bradley found part-time work late in 1971 as a stringer for CBS News. He moved to the network's Saigon bureau full time in 1972 and was wounded while on assignment in 1973. Bradley was reassigned to the Washington bureau in 1974, but asked to return to Southeast Asia in 1975 to cover the fall of Saigon at the end of the Vietnam War. His coverage of Cambodian refugees was given a George Polk Award for Foreign Television Reporting, one of the most respected awards given to print and broadcast journalists.

Bradley was hired to report on Jimmy Carter's campaign and went on to become the first black White House correspondent, covering the Carter administration from 1976 to 1978. He took over the evening anchor position on the *CBS Sunday Evening News* from 1976 to 1981 and became a principal correspondent for *CBS Reports* in 1978. It was on the latter assignment that he famously reported on Indochinese political refugees escaping from their homelands by boat. Bradley also received honors for his report on the state of integration in public schools mandated by the U.S. Supreme Court in *Brown v. The Topeka Board of*

Ed Bradley, at the Republican National Convention in the Joe Louis Arena in Detroit, July 1980. (AP Images.)

Education in the special *Blacks in America: With All Deliberate Speed. CBS News* executive Don Hewitt lured Bradley away from the nightly news to work on *60 Minutes*, the news magazine show that featured Harry Reasoner, Mike Wallace, and Morley Safer. During the following years his reporting was marked by prestigious industry awards, including the Robert F. Kennedy Journalism Award in 1995, the George Foster Peabody Award in 1997, the 2000 Paul White Award given by the Radio/News Directors Association, and the Denver Press Club's Damon Runyon Award for career journalistic excellence in 2003. Bradley marked a milestone in the 2005–2006 television season, celebrating his twenty-fifth year as a correspondent on *60 Minutes*. He won several Alfred I. duPont Columbia University awards as well as nineteen Emmys given by the National Academy of Television Arts and Sciences, including an Emmy for lifetime achievement. Bradley also received Peabody, Overseas Press Club (the Edward R. Murrow Award), Capital Press Club National Media, and Ohio State awards for his broadcasting work. His hour-long features covered controversial topics, and he gained interviews with people who rarely spoke to reporters. Bradley reported on the AIDS crisis in Africa before it was widely covered, the shockingly high level of violence in American cities, and manufacturing defects that led to the recall of a quarter of a million Audi automobiles.

Bradley's biographical pieces showed his appreciation of the human condition, and his personal interview style successfully illuminated personalities ranging from cultural stars to ordinary people who had overcome physical challenges. He was an ardent jazz and gospel music fan and enjoyed attending concerts and interviewing singers and instrumental musicians. His report on the singer LENA HORNE, for which Bradley earned an Emmy, remained his lifelong favorite. His weekly broadcasts *Jazz at Lincoln Center Radio with Ed Bradley* were heard on 240 public radio stations. The Oklahoma City bomber Timothy McVeigh gave Bradley his only televised interview in 2000, and the convicted killer and book author Jack Henry Abbott agreed to an interview that Bradley later said was his most difficult.

Bradley's legacy includes mentoring a new generation of black newscasters, including CHARLAYNE HUNTER-GAULT, former journalist for the *New York Times, the McNeil/Lehrer News Hour*, and National Public Radio. One of the first black correspondents to maintain a high-profile presence on network news, Bradley was given a National Association for the Advancement of Colored People Anniversary Award.

Bradley was married three times but had no children. His first marriage to Diane Jefferson ended in divorce, as did his second marriage to singer Priscilla Coolidge in 1984. Bradley married his companion of several years, Patricia Blanchet, in 2004.

Years before his third marriage Bradley contracted lymphocytic leukemia. He hid his condition from colleagues and friends and continued to work. He underwent quintuple bypass heart surgery in 2003 but resumed work at a breakneck pace, turning out more reports than any other *60 Minutes* correspondent.

Despite a sudden downturn in his condition in October 2006 when his illness became unmanageable by medication, he was able to complete a final assignment for *60 Minutes* before entering a New York hospital.

FURTHER READING

Campbell, Richard. *"60 Minutes" and the News: A Mythology for Middle America* (1991).

Coffey, Frank. *"60 Minutes": 35 Years of Television's Finest Hour* (1993).

Hewitt, Don. *Minute by Minute* (1985).

Madsen, Axel. *"60 Minutes": The Power and the Politics of America's Most Popular TV News Show* (1984).

Obituary: *Washington Post,* 9 Nov. 2006.

PAMELA LEE GRAY

Bradley, Thomas (29 Dec. 1917–29 Sep. 1998), mayor of Los Angeles, was born in a log cabin on a cotton plantation near Calvert, in Robertson County, Texas, the son of Lee Thomas Bradley and Crenner Hawkins, sharecroppers. Calvert had thrived in the late nineteenth century, buoyed by the cottonseed industry and the Southern Pacific Railroad, but its economy had declined by the time of Thomas's birth. Life for sharecroppers like the Bradleys was precarious—little better, in fact, than it had been for Lee's father, a slave in the Carolinas. They knew the certainty of picking cotton for eighteen hours a day and the annual uncertainty of the price of that cotton. Heavily indebted to white landlords, Lee and Crenner struggled to provide their family with vital necessities, such as food and health care; five of their children died in infancy. Like many southern blacks in the 1920s, the Bradley family saw only one answer to the restrictions of Jim Crow: migration, first to Dallas; then briefly to Arizona,

where even the six-year-old Tom picked cotton for a while; and, finally, in 1924, to Los Angeles.

The Bradleys struggled in their new home. Unable to find steady employment in Los Angeles, Lee served as a crewman on Pacific Coast ocean liners. Crenner found work as a maid, and Tom's elder brother dropped out of school to work on farms in Orange County. Even so, as a boyhood friend of Tom's recalled, the Bradleys "were poorer than a lot of folks were poor" (Sonenshine, 59). His parents' enforced absences left Tom as the de facto head of the household. As a teenager, he had to balance the family budget, negotiate sibling rivalries, and take care of his handicapped younger brother, experiences that he would later draw upon as a politician. Although Crenner relied heavily on Tom, she was also determined that her son, a studious child, should take advantage of the educational opportunities available to him in the Los Angeles school system. A combination of academic success and prowess on the track brought him to Polytechnic High School, one of the best schools in the city. As one of the few black students at Poly, and one of the poorest, Tom faced discrimination, but he quickly earned a reputation as a mediator, often called on by the administration to ease tensions among the diverse student body. Those skills and his high profile as the captain of the track team and as a star football player helped Tom win his first political campaign, as president of the Poly Boys' League. They also helped him win a full athletic scholarship to the University of California, Los Angeles (UCLA) in 1937.

Bradley thrived at UCLA. He continued to star on the track and also played football on a team that included the future baseball legend JACKIE ROBINSON. Fraternity politics occupied much of Bradley's time in college; his membership in Kappa Alpha Psi helped him create a network of black professionals who would later back his political ambitions. Bradley continued to help his family in the summertime by shoveling scrap iron, gardening, and working as a photographer for the comedian Jimmy Durante. That connection to Hollywood would later prove invaluable in Los Angeles politics. In 1940, his junior year, Bradley took the Los Angeles Police Department (LAPD) entrance exam, placed near the top, and decided to leave UCLA to join the police force. With a steady income of $170 a month, Bradley felt secure enough to propose marriage to Ethel Arnold, a fellow member of the New Hope Baptist Church; they married in May 1941. Tragically, their first child died the day she was born, the Bradleys' first wedding anniversary. Two daughters were born later.

Although Bradley had broken racial barriers at UCLA with ease, the LAPD presented a far greater challenge. Only three of his seventy-one colleagues at the police academy and one hundred of the four thousand members of the force were black, a situation that changed little in Bradley's twenty years on the force. By the time he resigned in 1961, Bradley had risen to lieutenant, the highest rank held by an African American on the force at that time. Bradley did much to improve race relations, most notably in his role as head of the LAPD's community-relations detail. Bradley's superiors, however, resisted his efforts to bolster the image of the force in nonwhite neighborhoods. In 1960 Police Chief William Parker vetoed Bradley's unilateral decision to integrate the radio cars in his division. That reversal undermined the lieutenant's authority and also suggested that reform of the LAPD—and the city's other racist institutions—would have to come from outside.

After Bradley resigned from the police force, he became increasingly active in the Democratic Party, and in 1961 he was elected city councilman for Los Angeles's ethnically diverse Tenth District, defeating his white opponent by a 2-to-1 margin. The Tenth District did not include Watts, but when that neighborhood rebelled against police brutality, overcrowding, and high unemployment in August 1965, Bradley emerged as the leader of all Angelenos opposed to the policies of Mayor Sam Yorty and Chief Parker. Parker inflamed black opinion by blaming the riots on "monkeys in a zoo." Yorty was less offensive, but equally inaccurate, in reproaching "Communists for agitating Negroes with propaganda over past police brutality" (Payne and Ratzan, 73).

Bradley knew from his own experience on the force that police brutality was no myth, and over the next four years he became the most visible critic of the LAPD excesses and the most vocal proponent of increased federal and local efforts to improve equal economic opportunity. In 1969

Tom Bradley, campaigning in Los Angeles, 1973. (AP Images.)

Bradley challenged Yorty for the position of mayor. The election was racially divisive, though most of the mud was flung by Yorty, who disingenuously, but successfully, linked the moderate Bradley to militants such as the Black Panther ELDRIDGE CLEAVER. Bradley chose not to respond in kind, a stance that some commentators viewed as a tactical error. In a rematch in 1973 Bradley won easily. Yorty again tried to paint his opponent as an extremist, but this time Bradley responded with a television campaign that highlighted his police experience and charming, far-from-militant demeanor. Bradley energized his base of African American voters, made gains among Asians and Latinos, and won over significant sections of the city's white business community, most notably in Hollywood. Yorty had misread the electoral dynamics of an increasingly diverse Los Angeles.

Over the next twenty years Bradley tried to govern the city as inclusively as he had run his campaign; this was no easy task, given the city's rapid growth and the increasing diversity of its population. In his first term in office Bradley attempted to redevelop the crumbling downtown of Los Angeles. He skillfully deployed state and federal funds to bring jobs to depressed neighborhoods, but the antitax crusade of the late 1970s wreaked havoc with any meaningful effort to use government to solve the city's problems. In 1978 Californians approved Proposition Thirteen, a referendum measure that cut property taxes and drastically reduced the revenues available to local governments. Given that Bradley had already cut property taxes in 1976, the revenue loss proved devastating to those impoverished Angelenos most dependent on government services. Downtown business leaders, however, were delighted by what they saw as Bradley's fiscal rectitude and worked closely with him in the late 1970s and 1980s on his three flagship projects: revitalization of the downtown business district, expansion of the Los Angeles International Airport, and bringing the Olympic Games to the city in 1984. The latter undertaking was particularly rewarding to Bradley, the UCLA track star who, as a child, had read avidly about the ancient games and who, as a teenager, had peered through the L.A. Coliseum fence to catch a glimpse of the 1932 Olympians. Despite a Soviet boycott, the Los Angeles Olympics, the first privately funded games, proved to be a resounding commercial success. That year Bradley was the recipient of the NAACP's Spingarn Medal. Bradley succeeded in diversifying the city workforce, but the deep-rooted racism of the LAPD proved intractable. After 1978 he faced a formidable foe in Daryl Gates, the new police chief. In the 1980s a rash of police shootings and beatings of minorities provoked anger in the black community, not only at Gates but also at Bradley for failing to fire him. Constitutionally, however, the mayor did not have the power to do so. The 1991 police beating of a black motorist, RODNEY KING, videotaped by a bystander and later relayed worldwide on television, however, was the final straw for Bradley, who worked behind the scenes to remove Gates. The acquittal of King's attackers in 1992 was an "outrage," Bradley told a news conference.

Many of the citizens of South Central, Los Angeles, agreed. Within hours of the acquittal, the city experienced its greatest civil unrest since the Watts riot. More than fifty people were killed, four hundred were injured, and seventeen thousand were arrested. Property damage amounted to $1 billion. In his last year in office, Bradley worked hard to bring the city's fractious communities together. Although all races had participated in the riots, relations between African Americans and Korean Americans were particularly fraught, since many of the black rioters had targeted Korean shopkeepers. While Bradley had his share of political disappointments, notably his defeat in two gubernatorial campaigns in 1982 and 1986 and a 1989 financial disclosure scandal, the South Central riots would remain the low point of his career. Bradley had earned a law degree at Southwestern University while still a policeman, and on leaving office in 1993 he practiced law until he suffered a heart attack and a stroke in 1996. He died of a heart attack two years later in Los Angeles.

Mourners at Bradley's funeral recalled his electoral victories and losses and agreed upon his warmth, courtliness, and charm. Bradley's abiding legacy, however, was an ability to craft and to maintain for two decades a broad, multiracial, and ideologically diverse political coalition in one of the world's most fragmented cities.

FURTHER READING

The Mayor Tom Bradley Administrative Papers (1973–1993) at the Department of Special Collections of the UCLA Library provide the most comprehensive introduction to his five terms as mayor and include some materials on his earlier career. The UCLA Oral History Program, also at the Department of Special Collections of the UCLA Library, has interviews with Bradley and many of his contemporaries in Los Angeles and California politics.

Davis, Mike. *City of Quartz: Excavating the Future in Los Angeles* (1992).

Payne, J. Gregory, and Scott C. Ratzan. *Tom Bradley: The Impossible Dream* (1986).

Sonenshine, Raphael J. *Politics in Black and White: Race and Power in Los Angeles* (1993).

Obituaries: *New York Times* and *Los Angeles Times*, 30 Sept. 1998.

STEVEN J. NIVEN

Bradley, Wallace "Gator" (7 Feb. 1952–), former gang enforcer and social and political activist, was born Wallace Bradley in Chicago, Illinois, the third of eleven children of Wallace Sr. and Eddie Mae Bradley. His father was a general labor foreman, and his mother was a homemaker. Bradley grew up in the Racine Courts housing project on Chicago's Southside in the Morgan Park community made famous by Lorraine Hansberry in her play, *A Raisin in the Sun*. He earned the moniker "Gator" from close friends and family, after the cartoon character "Wally Gator," a name he preferred to Wallace. Bradley attended John D. Shoop Elementary School (now John D. Shoop Academy of Math, Science, and Technology) and had early aspirations of becoming an attorney. Upon graduating from Shoop he enrolled at Morgan Park High School, but was expelled in 1968 when, after the assassination of civil rights leader Dr. Martin Luther King Jr., he threw a fellow student from the third-floor balcony in the high school's hallway. Subsequently, Bradley moved with his mother to the city's "low end," in the famed Bronzeville neighborhood on the Southside, first settled in 1779 by Jean Baptiste Point DuSable, founder of the city of Chicago, and later home to a bustling community of African American entrepreneurs, leaders, and artists such as ANDREW "RUBE" FOSTER and RICHARD WRIGHT. He enrolled at Calumet High School but dropped out in 1969.

Already a seasoned member of Chicago's largest street gang, the "Gangster Disciples" (GDs) founded by his childhood friend Larry Hoover, Bradley rapidly ascended the ranks, becoming an enforcer. Bradley was respected throughout the Southside of Chicago. However, in 1975, he was convicted of armed robbery and sentenced to serve time at Stateville Penitentiary in Joliet, Illinois. At Stateville, Bradley joined Hoover, also at Stateville serving a 150- to 200-year sentence for a 1973 murder of William Young, who allegedly stole drugs and money from the GDs. Having already experienced a change of heart in the short time he had served, Hoover convinced Bradley of the need for political

involvement, and the value of life beyond prison bars without the illusion of riches earned via criminal activity. To these ends, the two decided to change the GDs into a community service organization. During his tenure in prison, Bradley set his mind toward a different way of life and took the opportunity to earn his GED and study the law (Interview with author, 2010). On 5 January 1980, Governor James Thompson of Illinois issued Bradley a pardon for his work with Chicago's inner-city youth. Bradley committed himself to political activism, community service, and the eradication of gang violence. In 1981, with a vision of building an economic base through politics and business, Hoover officially changed the name Gangster Disciples to Growth and Development, with the new mission to effect positive change in the African American community through initiatives to encourage youth to stay in school, stop gang violence, and enhance employability skills.

In 1985, Bradley established LeGator productions, a public relations firm, on the Southside of Chicago. Primarily, his firm promoted bowling leagues and performers, including the former lead singer for The Impressions and Rock and Roll Hall of Fame inductee, JERRY "ICEMAN" BUTLER. When Butler ran for Cook County 3rd District Commissioner, Bradley took on the task of campaign manager. A victorious Butler was impressed with Bradley's work ethic and hired him as an assistant, a position that he retained until 1992.

In 1991, representing for the 21st Century V.O.T.E. (Voices of Total Empowerment), the political brain trust of Hoover, Bradley announced his candidacy for 3rd Ward alderman against the incumbent, Dorothy Tillman. The 21st Century V.O.T.E. was a political organization founded by Hoover, Bradley, and members of the Gangster Disciples that served to direct the energy of disenfranchised youth as a positive impetus behind growth and development on Chicago's Southside. Bradley was an unlikely candidate against Tillman due to his emergence from the underclass and nontraditional political foundations. While he found support for his candidacy, it also stirred up an air of controversy throughout the city. He garnered 375 votes, finishing third of nine candidates, but his crusade for political office had earned him national attention. Two years later, in October 1993, Bradley was brought into the national spotlight as one the chief organizers of the Chicago Gang Peace Summit Meeting, which took place at the Congress Hotel in the city's South Loop. In association with the 21st

Century V.O.T.E., Bradley led workshops and discussion groups to audiences of rival gang members belonging to twelve "gang nations" or affiliations, ultimately motivating a citywide truce. In addition to media attention, Bradley had gained the support and participation of the Nation of Islam minister LOUIS FARRAKHAN, the former NAACP president Dr. BENJAMIN CHAVIS-MUHAMMAD, and the first African American candidate for president of the United States, Reverend JESSE JACKSON. The same year, Hoover took the stage to reaffirm his earlier avowal that the Gangster Disciples would now be known as Growth and Development and no longer involved in criminal activity.

In January 1994, Bradley was part of a delegation handpicked by Jackson to visit President William Jefferson Clinton at the White House to deliver a briefing on violence in African American communities, on the day before the president's State of the Union Address and ratification of the Senate's Crime Bill. Bradley spoke passionately about the need for training, job placement, and alternative education for at-risk youth. On 4 April 1995 Bradley publicly announced that he no longer subscribed to the Gangster Disciple doctrine but in alliance with Hoover and his mission to effect positive change in African American communities, stood for the guiding principles of Growth and Development. During the 1996 Democratic National Convention, Bradley led two youth protests against corrupt law officials.

In 2006, Attorney Frank Avila hired Bradley to serve as an "urban translator" for his client, Aaron Patterson, a former death row inmate in a case involving his torture by Chicago Police. Bradley was tasked with interpreting and communicating on behalf of Patterson for the courtroom; additionally Avila sought assistance from Bradley in controlling his client's unpredictable outbursts of rage. Patterson won the case, but Bradley had to sue both Patterson and Avila for what amounted to over $350,000 owed to him. Thanks to his work as an urban translator, Bradley established a specialization for which he serves otherwise misrepresented individuals in court for a nominal fee. Subsequently, the term "Ebonics linguist" has emerged as a professional designation for which Bradley has yet to receive recognition from the American Bar Association.

In 2007, Bradley raised eyebrows when Cook County Judge Michael B. Hyman hired him to perform community relations for his campaign. Despite the controversy, Bradley established himself as a political activist nationally since his prison release by maintaining close ties with Chicago politicians, including regular meetings with Mayor Richard M. Daley of Chicago, and he was among the first city organizers to work with PRESIDENT BARACK OBAMA when he was a community organizer at a Southside church. He has worked with the Reverend AL SHARPTON and the National Action Network, Illinois Congressman BOBBY L. RUSH, and the Congressional Black Caucus.

Bradley has been recognized for his work by Mayor Daley of Chicago; Mayor James Maloof of Peoria, Illinois; Mayor Kurt L. Schmoke of Baltimore, Maryland; and the South African consul general Erica A. Broekhuysen. He has received the 1989 United Negro College Fund Meritorious Service Award; the 1992 No Dope Express Foundation Outstanding and Dedicated Service Award; the 1994 God's Gifted Production Humanitarian Award; and the 1997 Center for Community Change Certificate of Achievement Award. He is a member of United in Peace, the NAACP Economic Development Committee, Northstar Masonic Organization, Target Hope Crime and Violence Committee, and the Coalition for the Remembrance of ELIJAH MUHAMMAD. Bradley maintains a close relationship with Hoover, whom he maintains is a political prisoner unlawfully incarcerated in violation of his constitutional rights.

Bradley and wife Terri have one daughter, Afrika, and three sons, Waitari, Hahdmiel, and Leviticus. Also, they have three grandchildren, DeWayne Jr., Porsche, and Alexandria.

FURTHER READING

Braun, Stephen. "'Gator' Bradley Is Chicago's Pied Piper of Street Gangs," *LA Times*, 18 Feb. 1995.

Johnson, Dirk. "In Chicago, a Gang Tries to Show Political Muscle," *New York Times*, 28 Feb. 1995.

Main, Frank. "'Gator' Sues over Urban Translating," *Chicago Sun-Times*, 23 Apr. 2009.

Pollack, Neal. "The Gang That Could Go Straight," *Chicago Reader*, 26 Jan. 1995.

SAFIYA DALILAH HOSKINS

Bradshaw, Tiny (23 Sept. 1905–26 Nov. 1958), singer, drummer, and bandleader, was born Myron Carlton Bradshaw in Youngstown, Ohio. His parents' names are unknown. He played the drums from the age of ten and soon after was performing professionally as a drummer and vocalist. Early in his career he served as the drummer of the Jump Johnson Band in Buffalo, New York. He attended Wilberforce University in Wilberforce, Ohio, and majored in psychology. Before forming his own

Tiny Bradshaw, singer, drummer, and bandleader, March 1942. (Library of Congress/Carl Van Vechten.)

big band in 1934, he sang with Horace Henderson's Collegians, and in New York he either drummed or sang with Marion Hardy's Alabamians, the Savoy Bearcats, Mills Blue Rhythm Band (1932–1933), and LUIS RUSSELL (1933–1934).

Bradshaw's own band enjoyed long engagements in the ballrooms and nightclubs of Harlem (notably the Savoy and the Apollo), Philadelphia, and Chicago and toured throughout the United States and Europe, making its reputation with powerful, blues-based jazz. His band was introduced to the public at the Renaissance Ballroom in New York City in 1934. That same year it landed a recording contract with Decca and earned nationwide recognition. The performances and recordings of this ensemble typically featured the highly energized singing of its leader—a combination of blues belting, scat improvisations, and patter reminiscent of CAB CALLOWAY, whom Bradshaw was known to greatly admire. In 1935 the teenage ELLA FITZGERALD won an amateur contest at the Harlem Opera House, earning her a week of performances with the newly popular Bradshaw band. These performances with Bradshaw at the Harlem Opera House resulted in her first mention in the press and her introduction to the bandleader CHICK WEBB, with whom she catapulted to national fame. A high rate of turnover in band membership suggests the continual financial and artistic challenges that Bradshaw faced over a fifteen-year period. Such constant changes in personnel, however, also reveal Bradshaw's uncanny ability to identify talent, especially among alto saxophonists. At one time or another his lineup included RUSSELL PROCOPE, BILL JOHNSON, George Dorsey, Bobby Plater, SONNY STITT, and GIGI GRYCE. With Plater and Edward Johnson, Bradshaw composed the evergreen riff song "Jersey Bounce" (1942), which was popularized initially by Glenn Miller and later by Benny Goodman. During World War II, with the rank of major, Bradshaw led a large military show band that performed for the troops both at home and overseas. In 1945 he made a USO-sponsored tour of Japan and in the same year made his last big band recordings. After World War II Bradshaw downsized his ensemble and shifted its emphasis to the rhythm and blues idiom, in which he achieved great popularity during the 1950s. Between 1949 and 1958 he was affiliated with the King label as leader, piano soloist, and accompanist. In the "jump" tradition he issued approximately sixty recordings and scored several hits, including "Big Town" with rhythm and blues vocalist Roy Brown and "Soft" (1953). Bradshaw's hard-driving instrumental pieces and novelty songs were among the models imitated by early rock and roll singers. Toward the end of his life, Bradshaw settled in Chicago, where he worked regularly until two strokes brought his thirty-five-year entertainment career to a close. He died in Cincinnati, Ohio.

In his assessment of Bradshaw's early work, Gunther Schuller praised the bandleader's own jazz-oriented singing and the consistent quality of the solos of the trumpeter Shad Collins and the alto saxophonist Procope as well as the effective integration of improvised solos into arrangements. Yet Schuller faulted the formulaic nature of the arrangements themselves. Putting Bradshaw's big band in the context of its era, Schuller wrote, "Bradshaw and his band were a rhythmically exciting, hard-swinging group, perhaps not exactly ahead of its time in that respect, but certainly undeviatingly committed to a strong propulsive swing as the essence of jazz—at a time when so many bands could not swing at all or reserved it only for special up-tempo instrumental numbers" (423–424). Summarizing Bradshaw's achievements, Schuller continued, "With jazz and the blues always at his side, he was swinging long *before* swing arrived in full force and long *after* it had disappeared" (425).

FURTHER READING
McCarthy, Albert. *Big Band Jazz* (1974).
Schuller, Gunther. *The Swing Era: The Development of Jazz, 1930–1945* (1989).

DISCOGRAPHY
Garrod, Charles. *Tiny Bradshaw and His Orchestra* (1994).
Mohr, Kurt. *Discography of Tiny Bradshaw* (1961).
This entry is taken from the *American National Biography* and is published here with the permission of the American Council of Learned Societies.

MICHAEL J. BUDDS

Brady, St. Elmo (22 Dec. 1884–25 Dec. 1966), chemist and educator, was born in Louisville, Kentucky, the eldest son of Thomas Brady, a tobacco factory laborer, and Celester Brady, both of whom were born free around the time of the Civil War. Brady's father, himself illiterate, made sure that all of his children attended school. St. Elmo Brady graduated from high school with honors before enrolling at Fisk University in Nashville, Tennessee, in 1904. At Fisk, he studied with Thomas W. Talley, who was regarded as one of the best chemistry teachers in the black college system.

After graduating from Fisk in 1908 Brady accepted a teaching position at the Tuskegee Institute in Alabama. He quickly became friends with both BOOKER T. WASHINGTON, the institute's first president and leading advocate, and GEORGE WASHINGTON CARVER, the scientist famous for his agricultural research on peanuts, soybeans, sweet potatoes, and pecans. Brady was deeply impressed with both men and strived thereafter to emulate their dedication to education, service, and improving opportunities for their race. It was at Tuskegee that Brady also met his wife, Myrtle Travis.

In 1913 Brady broke new ground when he left Tuskegee to pursue a graduate degree at the University of Illinois. In 1916 he became the first African American to receive a Ph.D. in Chemistry and one of only a very few African Americans to hold a Ph.D. in any scientific field. Brady's research on the divalent oxygen atom was completed under the supervision of Clarence G. Derick in the prestigious Noyes Laboratory. The Noyes Lab was the site of a number of chemical achievements, including the development of nuclear magnetic resonance spectroscopy, the invention of high-intensity X-ray

tubes, and the birth of the polymer industry. Brady broke additional barriers at Illinois, becoming the first African American to join Phi Lambda Upsilon, the chemistry honor society, and one of the first African Americans to be accepted into Sigma Xi, the science honor society.

Partially because of connections established during his time at Illinois, Brady was offered a position in industry after he completed his degree; however, he was also offered a new position at Tuskegee. As Brady would later recount to SAMUEL PROCTOR MASSIE JR., another pathbreaking African American chemist, he faced a choice between financial success and duty: "Here I was, an ambitious young man, who had all of the advantages of a great university, contact with great minds, and the use of all modern equipment. Was I willing to forget these and go back to a school in the heart of Alabama, where I wouldn't even have a Bunsen burner?" (Massie). In the end he returned to Tuskegee in 1916 as head of the division of science.

After four years at Tuskegee, Brady left to become the head of the chemistry department at Howard University in Washington, D.C. Brady's experience at Howard (1920–1927) set the pattern for his appointment at Fisk University (1927–1952). Brady developed a strong undergraduate curriculum, strengthened the faculty, and laid plans for new buildings and laboratories. At Howard and Fisk, Brady also established graduate degree programs.

The bulk of Brady's career was spent at Fisk, his alma mater. The chemistry building he built, later named the Talley-Brady Building, was the first modern laboratory at a black college devoted entirely to chemistry. A strong believer in the importance of research, Brady established an infrared spectroscopy program at Fisk, open to faculty from all colleges and universities, and ensured that his faculty's labs were stocked with modern equipment and instrumentation.

Although Brady thrived at Fisk, his personal life suffered. His wife, Myrtle, was unable to find employment in Nashville. A teacher, she preferred to live and work in Washington, D.C., where she raised their only son, St. Elmo Jr. Having spent much of the previous twenty-five years shuttling back and forth between Washington and Nashville in the segregated South, Brady moved back to Washington upon his retirement from Fisk in 1952. He had planned to stay there, but he found it difficult to refuse a request for help from the president of Tougaloo College in Mississippi and accepted a position there from approximately 1956 to 1961. As he had at Howard and Fisk, Brady established a fully functioning chemistry department at Tougaloo, where none had existed before.

In a career that spanned more than forty years, Brady personally supervised the work of hundreds of young African American chemists. Primarily remembered as an administrator and teacher, he also maintained a modest research program on the chemical characteristics of native southern plants in the model of his mentor, George Washington Carver. Brady died on Christmas Day at his home in Washington, D.C., at the age of eighty-two.

FURTHER READING

Information about St. Elmo Brady's family was reconstructed from records in the 1860, 1870, 1880, 1900, 1910, and 1920 federal census.

Feldman, Martin R. "St. Elmo Brady, 1884–1966: American Chemist," in *Notable Twentieth-century Scientists*, ed. Emily J. McMurray (1995).

Massie, Samuel Proctor, Jr. "St. Elmo Brady: The Lengthened Shadow," *Chemistry* 43 (1970).

AUDRA J. WOLFE

Brady, Xernona Clayton (30 Aug. 1930–), broadcaster and civil rights leader, was born in Muskogee, Oklahoma, one of a pair of twins (her sister was Xenobia) to James Brewster, a Baptist minister, and Lillie Elliott Brewster. In addition to helping her husband run the church, Lillie Brewster administered Indian Affairs in the Muskogee area. For her part, Brady began to play piano in the church but one Sunday chose to skip services (and playing) to instead socialize with friends. She would later credit the resulting lecture from her father for fostering in her a respect for the importance of honoring whatever role she was playing and the faith that others would place in her. Brady attended local schools, and planned for a career in education. She matriculated at Tennessee State Agricultural and Industrial College (later Tennessee State University) and graduated with honors in 1952. She then relocated to Chicago, Illinois, and the University of Chicago, where she pursued graduate studies before becoming involved with the Urban League.

Brady and her twin sister (who had moved to the city with her) were enlisted by the Urban League as part of its newly mounted effort to root out employment discrimination through undercover investigations. The sisters were tasked with applying for work with a local liquor distributor suspected of refusing to hire African Americans. They did this during the summer and between classes, and it was then that Brady's zeal for civil rights began to form. In 1957 Brady married Ed Clayton, a journalist. The couple would remain together until the time of Clayton's death in 1966. They had no children.

In 1965 she relocated to Atlanta, Georgia, leaving behind a brief teaching stint in Chicago when offered a position with the Southern Christian Leadership Council (SCLC). It was then and there that she got to know MARTIN LUTHER KING JR. and to develop a lasting friendship with his wife CORETTA SCOTT KING. In 1966 Brady was instrumental in organizing Atlanta's African American doctors to push for the desegregation of the city's hospitals. The effort was successful, and its model was subsequently adopted in other cities. Shortly thereafter, she began writing for the *Atlanta Voice*, the African American newspaper formed in 1966 in response to the refusal of white newspapers in the area to report stories of interest of blacks or to hire black reporters. Such was Brady's growing local renown that when in 1968 the Grand Dragon of the state Ku Klux Klan disavowed his own racism as well as his allegiance to the racial terrorist organization, he named Brady as one of his inspirations. The resulting publicity brought Brady and her work to the attention of a wider community.

In that same year, 1968, Brady became the first black woman in the South to host a prime-time talk show, *Themes and Variations*. Such was her success that the show would soon become the *Xernona Clayton Show*. That stint lasted until 1975. A year earlier, in 1974, she married Paul Brady, a federal judge. Brady brought with him two children from a previous marriage. When Ted Turner created the Turner Broadcast System (TBS) in Atlanta, Brady left her show on WAGA-TV and went to work in programming at the larger network. In 1981 she took up a seat on the public affairs program *Open Up*, and around that same time was named vice president of public affairs for the network. In 1987 she produced a documentary about juveniles in the justice system that was awarded a local Emmy. In 1988 she was elevated to the position of assistant corporate vice president for urban affairs and was instrumental in crafting TBS's Black History Month programming. Her "Moments in History" shorts—which featured prominent African Americans talking about the historical achievements of black activists, inventors, leaders, and educators—became especially popular and were soon seen on networks all across the country. In 1991 she published an autobiography, *I've Been Marching All the Time*. Two years later she created the Trumpet Awards to honor the achievements of blacks who had overcome significant obstacles to their achievement. The event was originally aired on TBS but soon had grown its own foundation. In 1997 she retired from her work with TBS but remained active in a host of activities too long to enumerate here. Among them, however, Brady has served as president of the National Association of Media Women (1982–1990). She was on the board of directors of the National Urban League. In 2004 the SCLC bestowed on her the Drum Major for Justice Award for her pioneering role in bringing the stories of black Americans to a broader audience.

FURTHER READING

Bogle, Donald. *Primetime Blues: African Americans on Network Television* (2001).

Brady, Xernona Clayton. *I've Been Marching All the Time: An Autobiography* (1991).

Fairclough, Adam. *To Redeem the Soul of America: The Southern Christian Leadership Conference and Martin Luther King, Jr.* (1987).

JASON PHILIP MILLER

Bragg, George Freeman, Jr. (25 Jan. 1863–12 Mar. 1940), Episcopal clergyman, was born in Warrenton, North Carolina, the son of George Freeman Bragg Sr. and Mary Bragg (maiden name unknown). He was two years old when the family moved to Petersburg, Virginia, where he studied at the elementary school and at St. Stephen's Parish and Normal School. His family helped found St. Stephen's Church for Negroes in 1867. At age six he was employed as a valet by John Hampden Chamberlayne, editor of the *Petersburg Index*. In 1879 he entered a school founded by Major Giles B. Cooke, a former chaplain on Robert E. Lee's staff; the school had become a branch of Virginia Theological Seminary. The next year he was suspended for not being "humble" but was appointed a page in the Virginia legislature by the Readjuster Party. After a severe case of typhoid fever and a period of teaching school in 1885, he returned to his theological studies at Cooke's school, renamed the Bishop Paine Divinity and Industrial School. He was ordained deacon on 12 January 1887 and priest on 19 December 1888 by Bishop Francis M. Whittle. He married Nellie Hill in 1887; they had four children.

Bragg's parish ministry began in 1887 at St. Luke's Church in Norfolk, Virginia, where within four years he built a new church and rectory, renovated a school, organized the Holy Innocents (which became Grace Church), and founded the Industrial School for Colored Girls. After becoming rector of St. James First African Church in Baltimore, Maryland, in 1891, he opened St. James Mission in Portsmouth, Virginia. Under his leadership, St. James Church became self-supporting, purchased a rectory, and built a new church. By 1931 there were five hundred communicants, and the church made annual charitable contributions of a thousand dollars. At least four young men entered the priesthood under Bragg's guidance. In addition, he established the Maryland Home for Friendless Colored Children and was associated with St. Mary's Home for Boys and St. Katharine's Home for Little Girls. For thirty-five years he was general secretary of the Conference of Church Workers among Colored People and a special chaplain to the bishop of the diocese of Maryland. Beyond his service within his denomination, Bragg performed many duties. In 1884 he was honorary commissioner to the New Orleans Exposition. Virginia's governor Fitzhugh Lee appointed him a curator to the Hampton Normal and Agriculture Institute in 1887. He also served as chaplain to the second battalion of Virginia Colored Militia. In Maryland he was on the board of managers for the House of Reformation for Colored Boys and a member of the State Inter-Racial Commission.

George Freeman Bragg Jr. (seated) with two of his sons, also clergymen, in an undated photograph. (Courtesy of Documenting the American South, University of North Carolina at Chapel Hill Libraries Rare Book Collection.)

He started the Committee of Twelve, a group of black leaders, including BOOKER T. WASHINGTON and W. E. B. DuBOIS, that campaigned against the Poe Amendment, designed to disfranchise blacks in Maryland. He led the fight to have Negro teachers assigned to Negro schools in Baltimore. In 1905 he joined the Niagara Movement, a forerunner of the NAACP, and became a supporter of DuBois, its founder.

Bragg's early association with the *Petersburg Index* had generated a lifelong interest in journalism. At age nineteen he had begun publishing the *Virginia Lancet*, a pro-Republican paper involved in Virginia politics. In 1886 he founded a new paper, the *Afro-American Churchman*, published, he said, in the interests of the Colored Episcopal church. Also that year he founded the *Afro-American Ledger*, which he later merged with the *Baltimore Afro-American*. The *Church Advocate* served for many years as the unofficial organ of the Conference of Church Workers among Colored People and was filled with biographical sketches of clergy, histories of local black Episcopal churches, and commentary on the continuing struggles of blacks in the Episcopal Church. In later years it served as a parish paper for Bragg's church. The *Maryland Home* was a monthly, published to promote the Maryland Home for Friendless Colored Children.

Some of his published works, all of which contain biographical data, are *The Colored Harvest in the Old Virginia Diocese* (1901), *Afro-American Church Work and Workers* (1904), *The Story of Old St. Stephen's, Petersburg, Va.* (1906), *The First Negro Priest on Southern Soil* (1909), *Bond Slave of Christ* (1912), *Men of Maryland* (rev. ed., 1925), *The Pathfinder Absalom Jones* (1929), and *Heroes of the Eastern Shore* (1939). A major work still of prime importance is *History of the Afro-American Group of the Episcopal Church* (1922). Many of these volumes were printed on Bragg's own printing press, under the imprint of the Church Advocate Press.

Race relations would be improved, Bragg believed, by morally sensitive, educated people of both races, and he did not hesitate to denounce racial discrimination within his own denomination. Petitions for his selection to the episcopate were made in 1911 and 1917, but he was not elected. He died in Baltimore.

FURTHER READING

Bragg's papers are in the Schomburg Center for Research in Black Culture of the New York Public Library; the Moorland-Spingarn Research Center, Howard University, Washington, D.C.; and Virginia State University, Petersburg.

Brydon, George M. *The Episcopal Church among the Negroes of Virginia* (1937).

Burkett, Randall K., et al., eds. *Black Biography, 1790–1950: A Cumulative Index* (3 vols., 1991).

Suggs, Henry L., ed. *The Black Press in the South* (1983).

This entry is taken from the *American National Biography* and is published here with the permission of the American Council of Learned Societies.

FREDERICK V. MILLS

Bragg, Janet (24 Mar. 1907–11 Apr. 1993), aviator, nurse, and nursing home proprietor, was born Janet Harmon in Griffin, Georgia, the daughter of Cordia Batts and Samuel Harmon, a brick contractor. The Batts family had long been established in Griffin. Janet's maternal grandfather was a freed slave of Spanish descent, and her maternal grandmother was a Cherokee. Janet's grandfather had built the house in which she and her siblings were born; her mother had been born in the same house. The youngest of seven children, Janet had a happy childhood, enjoying sports and games and excelling at school. In an interview conducted at the University of Arizona as part of a project called "African Americans in Aviation in Arizona," Bragg reminisced: "We were a very happy family. We were not a rich family, only rich in love."

Independence was encouraged in the Harmon household. The children were allowed to attend any church they chose. They were also encouraged to work up to their potential academically, regardless of gender. In her autobiography, *Soaring above Setbacks* (1996), Bragg recalled her father saying, "If Jack can do it, so can Jill." This statement bolstered Bragg's courage, leading her to believe, "I could do anything I set my sights on." She transferred from public elementary school to St. Stephen's Episcopal School, which provided a better education in those days of strict segregation. She chose to attend an Episcopal boarding school, Fort Valley Episcopal High School, in Fort Valley, Georgia, where she did well in math, science, and sports.

Bragg next attended Spelman Seminary (later Spelman College), a historically black women's college in Atlanta, Georgia, where she majored in nursing. Her training took place at MacVicar Hospital on the Spelman campus. MacVicar's nursing program was selective and demanding, and Bragg was but one of two out of an entering class of twelve who survived the probationary period. The hospital had no interns, so nursing students assisted in operations and performed other procedures customarily handled by interns. As a result they received first-rate training. Bragg received her registered nurse degree in 1929.

After her graduation from Spelman, Bragg worked as a nurse in the segregated department of a hospital in her hometown, but she left after a month because of the inferior care offered to black patients. She moved to Rockford, Illinois, to live with a sister. While there, she passed the Illinois nurses' license test. Unable to find professional employment in Rockford, she moved to Chicago, where she became a nurse at Wilson Hospital. About 1931, while working at Wilson, she met and married Evans Waterford; they had no children. The marriage lasted only a few years (five, according to one source), but she kept the name Waterford until she married again.

In 1933 Bragg's father died. Bragg took on the support of her mother and two nieces, who moved into her Chicago home. She left the hospital for a better-paying nursing job in a medical office. Graduate work in pediatric nursing at the Cook County School of Nursing and a graduate certificate in public health administration from Loyola University led to a more lucrative position as health inspector for the Metropolitan Burial Insurance Company. She could now afford to pursue her dream of learning to fly.

Bragg wrote in her autobiography: "I saw a billboard with a bird ... nurturing her young fledglings into the flying world. It read, 'Birds Learn to Fly. Why Can't You?' ... It was so beautiful." In 1933 she enrolled in the Aeronautical University ground school. The black aviation pioneers JOHN ROBINSON and CORNELIUS COFFEY instructed her in meteorology, aeronautics, aircraft maintenance, and aircraft mechanics. Because the school owned no airplanes, it offered no actual flight instruction. Such instruction cost $15 an hour, so Bragg decided that it made more sense financially to purchase her own plane, which she could then rent to others. The plane, which cost $600, was the first of three she would own.

Finding an airfield where she and other aspiring black flyers would be permitted to learn to fly proved impossible. Black pilots were not allowed to fly out of airports used by whites. If they truly wanted to fly, they needed to build their own airfields. The class at the ground school, with the aid of Robinson and Coffey, formed the Challenger Aero Club. The group purchased land and built an airfield with their own hands in the small all-black town of Robbins, Illinois. In the spring of 1934, in her own plane and from the airfield that she had helped build, Bragg learned to fly. After thirty-five solo hours, she passed the test for the private pilot's license. In addition to her other activities, in the 1930s Bragg wrote a weekly column, "Negro Aviation," in the *Chicago Defender* under the byline Janet Waterford.

In 1939 the federal government announced the Civilian Pilot Training Program (CPTP) for whites only. Black pilots, civil rights organizations, and prominent politicians lobbied successfully to have the race restriction removed. African Americans would be trained, but separate from whites and in different facilities.

In 1943, during World War II, Bragg and several other black women applied for appointments with the Women's Auxiliary Service Pilots (WASPS). The interviewer rejected Bragg outright, and her appeal was unsuccessful. She then applied to the military nurse corps but was informed that the quota for black nurses was filled.

Unable to join the war effort, Bragg went to the CPTP school at Tuskegee, Alabama, to obtain her commercial pilot's license. After successfully completing her written work, she took and passed her flight test, but a bigoted instructor refused to issue her license. Bragg returned to Chicago, where she passed the test with ease, the first black woman to do so.

Flying was a hobby, and Bragg continued to work as a health inspector until an opportunity arose to start her own business. Bragg and her brother had arranged to purchase a property, but her brother backed out. A friend suggested that she turn the property into a health-care facility for patients on welfare. With the aid of cousins from Georgia, Bragg's venture grew into a nursing home business that eventually housed sixty patients. She married Sumner Bragg late in 1951, and he joined her in running the business. They operated several nursing homes successfully until their joint retirement in 1972. They had no children.

Bragg befriended several Ethiopian students studying in the United States, traveling with them and showing them around. For her helpfulness she was invited to Ethiopia to meet the emperor, Haile Selassie, in 1955. In the 1970s she traveled widely in Africa, leading tour groups. In 1986, after the death of Sumner Bragg, she moved permanently to Arizona, where the Braggs had been spending their winters.

Bragg's achievements were recognized during her later years. Invited to appear at aviation events around the country, she received many awards and honors. She was also active in such civic organizations as the Tucson, Arizona, Urban League, Habitat for Humanity, and the Adopt-a-Scholar Program at Pima College in Tucson. She died in Blue Island, Illinois, a suburb of Chicago. She wrote in her autobiography, "I think I've had a wonderful life."

FURTHER READING
Bragg, Janet. *Soaring above Setbacks* (1996).
Hine, Darlene Clark. *Black Women in America* (1993).
Obituaries: *Jet*, 5 May 1993; *Chicago Defender*, 15 April 1993.

This entry is taken from the *American National Biography* and is published here with the permission of the American Council of Learned Societies.

MIRIAM SAWYER

Braithwaite, William Stanley Beaumont (6 Dec. 1878–8 June 1962), poet, critic, and anthologist, was born in Boston, Massachusetts, the son of William Smith Braithwaite and Emma DeWolfe. Of his two avocations—American poetry and the status of the American Negro—the second clearly had its origins in an unusual cultural heritage. The Braithwaite family, of mixed black and white descent, was wealthy and held prominent positions in British Guiana. Braithwaite's father studied medicine in London but quit because of apparent mental strain and moved to Boston, where he married DeWolfe, whose family had been in slavery. His father remained aloof from neighbors, educating his children at home. Braithwaite's autobiography mentions no employment held by his father, whose death, when his son was eight years old, left the family destitute. Braithwaite's mother was forced into menial employment, and at the age of twelve, so was Braithwaite. After showing interest in reading, he was given a job as a typesetter, where exposure to the poetry of John Keats fixed the course of his life: "Keats had created in me an aspiration that became the most passionate urgency in my life, and Wordsworth and Burns nourished it into an ambition that developed into a fanatical determination" (Butcher, 174). Braithwaite read widely and completed a volume of poetry before he was twenty-one, but a series of disappointments made him aware of the tremendous racial barriers he would have to overcome as an African American in order to make a living in the literary field. He became determined to prove that a black poet could be successful despite the fact that he was black—without being forced into a special category as a Negro writer. With this resolve he developed a

Keatsian theory of poetry: "It is not the feeling of contemplative anxiety aroused by the philosophic or moral imagination that gives to poetry its highest value, but the agitated wonder awakened in the spirit of the reader by the sudden evocation of magic" (Butcher, 29–30). Braithwaite's attempted evocations of sheer beauty show virtually no awareness of his racial heritage or of the social problems confronting black Americans, and as a result he has often been criticized or dismissed by those concerned with black literature. It should be remembered, however, that Braithwaite frequently championed black writers, offered his guidance to writers of the Harlem Renaissance, and analyzed the position of black writers in essays such as "The Negro in American Literature."

In "The Negro in American Literature" he traces the treatment of black people in American literature by both black and white writers from *Uncle Tom's Cabin* through the mid-1920s. He does not praise authors whose work shows no signs of race but whose work transcends the racial. Of JAMES WELDON JOHNSON he says, "Mr. Johnson's work is based upon a broader contemplation of life, life

William Stanley Braithwaite, poet, critic, and anthologist, c. 1915. (Library of Congress, National Association for the Advancement of Colored People Records.)

that is not wholly confined within any racial experience, but through the racial he made articulate that universality of the emotions felt by all mankind" (Butcher, 77). Of JEAN TOOMER's *Cane* he writes: "So objective is it, that we feel that it is a mere accident that birth or association has thrown him into contact with the life he has written about. He would write just as well ... about the peasants of Russia, or the peasants of Ireland" (83). Although Braithwaite's poetry is not a reflection of his black heritage, he admired writers whose work went beyond their black heritage to universal human experience.

In 1903, with his career still before him, he married Emma Kelly; the couple had seven children. A few months after his marriage, he dedicated himself full time to literature. His first volume, *Lyrics of Life and Love* (1904), was published by subscription. In 1906 he began writing reviews and criticism for the staid but influential *Boston Evening Transcript*. The collections of the year's best poetry that he published there developed into an annual anthology of magazine verse that appeared from 1913 until 1929.

Braithwaite was an important guiding force during the emergence of modern poetry in the United States. He recognized the genius of Edwin Arlington Robinson before the turn of the century and became a close friend. Among the others whose careers he advanced was Robert Frost, whom he first praised in 1915. He was receptive to imagism, although he did not share the American poet and editor Harriet Monroe's enthusiasm for Ezra Pound.

In spite of his influence, Braithwaite was hampered by financial difficulties. He published his yearbooks at his own expense, and he was unable to publish a projected anthology of Negro poetry. His *Poetry Journal*, begun only months after Monroe's *Poetry*, failed after a few issues. It was not until 1935, when he accepted a professorship at Atlanta University, that he enjoyed financial security. He taught ten years before retiring to Harlem, where he produced *Selected Poems* (1948) and *The Bewitched Parsonage: The Story of the Brontës* (1950). He died at his home in New York City.

It is doubtful that Braithwaite will be remembered as a poet. His *Selected Poems* is a very slim volume, and the poetry is fragile and overly delicate. Between this volume and his first appeared only one other, *The House of Falling Leaves* (1908). His work rarely appears in anthologies. Philip Butcher, editor of *The William Stanley Braithwaite Reader*, predicts that "William Stanley Braithwaite's stature is sure to grow as scholars give attention to the records of his life and work" (7). If Braithwaite is remembered, it will be as an important critical voice of the early twentieth century.

FURTHER READING

Forty libraries have papers relating to Braithwaite. The major collections are at Harvard University and Syracuse University.

Bardolph, Richard. *The Negro Vanguard* (1971).

Butcher, Philip, ed. *The William Stanley Braithwaite Reader* (1972).

Redding, J. Saunders. *To Make a Poet Black* (1939).

Obituary: *New York Times*, 9 June 1962.

This entry is taken from the *American National Biography* and is published here with the permission of the American Council of Learned Societies.

DALTON GROSS AND
MARYJEAN GROSS

Branch, Frederick Clinton

Branch, Frederick Clinton (1923–10 Apr. 2005), first black marine officer and distinguished educator, was born in Hamlet, North Carolina, the son of a Methodist minister. Little is known of his parents or his early education, but he was educated in New York state public schools and attended Temple University in Philadelphia, Pennsylvania, until he was drafted into the U.S. Marine Corps in 1943. Branch completed basic training at the segregated Marine Corp Recruit Depot for black recruits known as Montford Point, located on a desolate portion of Camp Lejeune in North Carolina. Following basic training, Branch served overseas as part of the Fifty-first Defense Battalion, a supply unit stationed on a Pacific island near the International Dateline. While in the Pacific, Branch applied to the navy's V-12 commissioning program for college draftees and was accepted. After participating in the V-12 program he attended the Sixteenth Platoon Leaders Class at the Marine Corps Officer Candidate School in Quantico, Virginia.

On 10 November 1945, the 170th birthday of the U.S. Marine Corps, Branch became the first African American officer in marine corps history. Following his commissioning he commanded an all-black reserve unit in Philadelphia. During the Korean War, Branch commanded an integrated anti-aircraft training platoon at Camp Pendleton in California. He married Camilla "Peggy" Robinson around 1950. Although he was promoted to captain in 1955 he resigned his commission in order to begin a career in education.

After earning a degree in Physics from Temple University Branch began a thirty-five-year career in the Philadelphia school system. During his tenure he was awarded a geology fellowship at Princeton University and a Shell Oil Merit Fellowship to Cornell University to study chemistry. In addition Branch served as a curriculum writer for the school system. More than merely a groundbreaking figure in the marine corps, Branch was also a consummate professional educator.

On 7 July 1997 the marine corps dedicated a building in honor of Branch at its Officer Candidate School in Quantico, Virginia, in recognition of his achievements as a U.S. marine and professional educator. Frederick Clinton Branch died in 2005 and was buried at Quantico National Cemetery with full military honors. Shortly after his death in North Carolina the senators Elizabeth Dole and Richard Burr sponsored a U.S. Senate resolution commemorating Branch's life and achievements.

FURTHER READING

Some of the information for this article was found in the Marine Corps Files, courtesy of the History and Museums Division, U.S. Marine Corps.

Danelo, David. "Branching Out," *U.S. Naval Institute's Proceedings* (June 2005).

Davis, Mark. "How a Philadelphia Man Reshaped the History of the Marine Corps," *Philadelphia Inquirer*, 1 Aug. 1997.

Gilliam, Gregory. "Standing Alone," *Marines Magazine* (Sept. 1997).

CHARLES EDWARD WILES, IV

Branch, Mary Elizabeth (20 May 1881–6 July 1944), educator, was born in Farmville, Virginia, the daughter of Tazewell Branch, a former slave who served in the Virginia legislature and worked as a shoemaker and tax collector, and Harriett Lacey, a domestic worker. Although she learned to read at home, Branch began her quest for formal education when she was thirteen. Because her mother did laundry for students and teachers at State College in Farmville, Branch often made trips to the school to pick up or deliver clothes; in time she herself became a maid in the college library. Exposed for the first time to a wide variety of books and knowledge, she was determined to obtain her own education. Within a few years she had earned a high school diploma from the normal school of Virginia State College, a land-grant college for black students in Petersburg, where she also took teacher education classes.

Eager to share her knowledge, Branch accepted a position as an English teacher at an elementary school in Blackstone, Virginia, soon after completing her secondary education. After a few years she returned to Virginia State, where she taught English for twenty years and also served as housing director for both men's and women's dormitories. While at Virginia State, Branch spent her summers continuing her own education. She studied at the University of Pennsylvania and at Columbia University, as well as at the University of Chicago, where she earned a bachelor's degree in Philosophy in 1922 and a master's degree in English in 1925. She also began, but did not complete, a doctorate in Education.

In the late 1920s Branch moved to Kansas City, Kansas, to teach social studies at Sumner Junior College. After one year she moved to St. Louis to serve as dean of girls at Vashon High School, then the largest school in the United States for black girls. Working at Vashon—located in a poor urban neighborhood—was challenging, but it paid well and provided Branch with a prominent position within black education circles. By 1930 the American Missionary Association (AMA) had noted her work and invited her to become president of its Tillotson College in Austin, Texas. Branch initially declined two offers from the association, but she accepted after the third request. Noting that many white teachers had gone to the South after the Civil War to help newly freed slaves, Branch determined that accepting the presidency of Tillotson could be no more difficult than that. In taking her new position in 1930 she became the first black woman to serve as a college president in Texas.

The task ahead of her was a formidable one. Chartered by the AMA in 1877 and opened in 1881, Tillotson College was declining when Branch was hired to lead it. Originally established as one of several AMA schools for former slaves throughout the South, the school had prospered for many years; it provided industrial and traditional education at the elementary and secondary levels and then achieved collegiate status in 1909. By 1930, however, black migration out of Texas and poor administrative leadership had deeply hurt the school. It was reduced to a junior college in 1925, and in 1926 it converted to a women's college; its enrollment at that time dropped below 150 students.

Branch arrived at Tillotson on 1 July 1930 and found a few run-down buildings on a physically unkempt campus. She appreciated the challenge that awaited her and took advantage of the AMA's promise to let her run the school with minimal interference. Branch quickly established a five-year plan for Tillotson, with immediate goals to improve the physical plant and increase enrollment. Radical and activist in her approach, Branch directed her attention to every aspect of the campus. She was responsible for vastly expanding the library's holdings—often shopping at used bookstores to acquire volumes—renovating several old buildings, and adding numerous others. She solicited donations and initiated a long-term fund-raising program for the physical plant. The campus was landscaped, the high school program was dropped, the faculty was doubled, and the minimum requirement for faculty was raised to a master's degree. To attract more students, Branch sent teachers throughout the Southwest, added scholarships, and invited high school girls to special events on the campus. In 1935 she returned Tillotson to its coeducational status. By this time enrollment had increased to more than two hundred students, and it topped five hundred students by the time of her death.

Branch understood the importance of outside recognition for her college. She secured Tillotson's senior college ranking by the Texas Board of Education in 1931, gained its membership in the American Association of Colleges in 1936, and garnered an "A" rating for it from the Southern Association of Colleges and Secondary Schools in 1943. Branch was an early supporter of the United Negro College Fund, founded in 1944, and made Tillotson one of its first affiliates.

At the same time that she rejuvenated Tillotson and ensured its survival, Branch took a prominent role in the Austin community. She served in 1943 as president of the Austin chapter of the National Association for the Advancement of Colored People, was a member of the state's Commission on Interracial Cooperation, and served on the state's Negro Advisory Board for the National Youth Administration from 1935. In this capacity she worked closely with Lyndon Johnson, then the state's Youth Administration director, and established two freshmen college centers under the auspices of Tillotson to encourage unemployed black youth to further their education. Such efforts, she wrote to Johnson, "bolstered up the self-respect of those young folks" (Winegarten, 183). She participated in a local book club and women's club and was a regular walker on Tillotson's twenty-three-acre campus.

Branch's efforts garnered nationwide attention. For her work at Tillotson, Virginia State College gave her an honorary doctorate of pedagogy, and Howard University presented her with an honorary doctor of laws degree. Never one to be satisfied

with past accomplishments, Branch continued to push for needed improvements at Tillotson. She initiated shared faculty and speakers programs with Samuel Huston College, a black Methodist Episcopal college also located in Austin. These arrangements ultimately led to the merger of the two schools into Huston-Tillotson College in 1952. Branch had died in Camden, New Jersey, eight years earlier.

Mary Elizabeth Branch gave singular attention to Tillotson College and moved the college from almost certain failure to exemplary success. Described by those who knew her as frank and at times even brusque, she was also recognized as one who loved her institution and loved those who shared its life with her. Her interest in the welfare of her students was extensive and included her adoption of one female pupil as her own daughter. She never married. One of only a few black women college presidents in the United States in the 1930s and 1940s, Branch was an inspiring leader for her students, a talented and successful college administrator, and a visionary for the direction of black education in the South.

FURTHER READING
Branch's papers are in the archives of the Downs-Jones Library at Huston-Tillotson College in Austin, Texas.
Brown, Olive D., and Michael R. Heintze. "Mary Branch: Private College Educator," in *Black Leaders: Texans for Their Times*, ed. Alwyn Barr and Robert A. Calvert (1981).
Winegarten, Ruthe. *Black Texas Women: 150 Years of Trial and Triumph* (1995).
This entry is taken from the *American National Biography* and is published here with the permission of the American Council of Learned Societies.

DEBBIE MAULDIN COTTRELL

Branch, Wallace (29 Oct. 1945–6 Sept. 2004), historian, collector, archivist, photographer, and entrepreneur, was born Wallace Michael Branch in Brooklyn, New York, one of two sons of Byrd Branch, an entrepreneur who operated a cleaning and tailoring business in New York City and held down a thirty-five-year job at the weekly newspaper *Irish Echo* to support his family, and Vera Barbour Branch. In Brooklyn, Branch and his family lived a solid middle-class lifestyle, making their home in a four-floor brownstone home that they owned.

Branch was born with sickle cell anemia, a hereditary, incurable, chronic disorder with which patients suffer severe pain and tissue and organ damage as a result of oxygen and nutrient deficiencies. At the time of Branch's birth, information about and treatment of the disease were limited. According to his family, doctors who treated Branch as a child never gave him much hope for survival. At fourteen Branch became so ill that he had to have a bone marrow transplant. In 1983, in an effort to help others with the disease, Branch's mother, Vera, founded the Connecticut chapter of the Sickle Cell Disease Association of America, a nonprofit organization providing support and education for sickle cell patients and their families. The family took regular recreational excursions together. It was on one of these trips, to Atlantic City, New Jersey, that the family was blindsided by tragedy. Sixteen-year-old Calvin, Branch's brother, died in a drowning accident. After years of mentally preparing for Wallace to die prematurely, he and his parents were not equipped to handle the death of his healthy, vibrant brother.

Wallace Branch attended grammar and high school in Brooklyn before enrolling at Monroe College, where he earned an associate's degree. After graduating from the Germain School of Photography in New York City, Branch began a career as a professional photographer. In 1977 he received a job offer from a CBS affiliate, WFSB-TV Channel 3. He accepted the position and moved to Hartford, Connecticut, where he spent the next fifteen years as a news photographer for the station, capturing local and regional news events and social activities. Branch was married for a short time in the early 1980s to Gladys Adams. The couple had no children and the union ended in divorce.

In 1992 Branch left Channel 3 and started his own business, Empire Photo and Video Studios, in Hartford, Connecticut, and New York. He specialized in portrait photography as well as business and special-event photography. He took many photos of politicians and entertainers, and was a photographer for events sponsored by the Essence Awards and Black Entertainment Television.

When not taking pictures Branch was collecting them. A self-proclaimed historian, he accumulated photos, news and magazine articles, and other items of historical significance. He was particularly interested in black memorabilia and was an advocate of the importance of chronicling cultural history. Branch amassed a huge collection of items and co-founded the Black Historians, in Hartford which maintained a mobile historical exhibit that it displayed at public venues. He gave speeches about the collection and black history in general. He co-organized a Black Historian exhibit at the Hartford Public Library called *Upon Reflection: A Half-Century of African American Cultural Highlights*, which was displayed in the summer of 2003. Branch held membership in the Photographers Association of America and the Charter Oak Photographic Society and was a founding member of the Russwurm Wells Society, a local black history group for enthusiasts.

In 1991 Branch traveled to Caux, Switzerland, to videotape performers at a peace conference of international ambassadors and heads of state. In 1996 he traveled to China, documenting his trip with an impressive collection of photos.

Defying longevity odds dictated by a devastating incurable disease (sickle cell patients generally live approximately forty years with the disease), Branch so rarely complained about the pain he endured that many friends and associates never knew he was sick until the years just before his death. Those years were the most difficult for him, yet he still managed to care for his ailing father, who died mere months before he did. Wallace Branch died from complications of sickle cell disease at the age of fifty-eight.

FURTHER READING

Icon Health Publications. *The Official Patient's Sourcebook on Sickle Cell Anemia* (Jan. 2005).

Obituaries: *Hartford Courant*, 9 Sept. 2004; *Hartford Inquirer*, 15 Sept. 2004.

NANCY T. ROBINSON

Branche, George Clayton (10 Jan. 1896–10 Sept. 1956), physician, was born in Louisburg, North Carolina, the son of the Reverend Joel Branche and Hanna Shaw. He attended the Mary Potter Academy in Oxford, North Carolina. The Branche home was located near this Presbyterian school; George Branche enjoyed playing on the campus, and he acquired his early education there.

After his high school graduation in 1913, Branche enrolled at Lincoln University in Pennsylvania, where he participated as an athlete. He graduated in 1917 and served in World War I as a master sergeant. After the armistice he focused on medicine as a career. Branche graduated from the Boston University Medical School in 1923, and he was an intern at the Boston Psychopathic Hospital.

While Branche was in medical school, federal officials sought a site to establish a hospital for black veterans. African American World War I veterans suffered from treatment at inferior hospitals or were neglected. Health care for many black Americans was poor, and few black physicians were available to serve the vast population. Government leaders sought a southern town in which to build a black veteran's hospital, but only black citizens from Tuskegee, Alabama, expressed interest in the project.

The Tuskegee Veterans Administration (VA) Hospital was approved in 1921 and initially had a white staff. White area residents opposed black physicians' securing control of the facility and threatened violence if they did so. Black medical professionals were disappointed that promises made by government officials to place black physicians in leadership positions at the hospital were not kept. General Frank T. Hines, director of the Veterans Bureau, and leaders of the National Medical Association had selected promising physicians to replace the white physicians at the hospital. After it was announced in 1923 that six black physicians, including Branche, would soon arrive, some local whites responded by burning crosses.

Branche moved to Tuskegee in November 1923 as a junior medical officer at the hospital. He served on rotations and treated patients in general medicine, neuropsychiatry, and tuberculosis wards. In 1927 he was accepted for postgraduate study in neuropsychiatry in New York City, and later he returned to be chief of Neuropsychiatric Service at the Tuskegee VA Hospital.

Perhaps Branche's most significant work involved the development of new treatments for neurosyphilis occurring in blacks. He had experimented unsatisfactorily from 1928 with the tertian strain of malaria to treat neurosyphilis. In November 1932 he inoculated seven patients with the quartan strain of malaria as a possible treatment for neurosyphilis. Branche considered the results favorable. He first discussed his work at the 1934 American Psychiatric Association meeting. After inoculating thirty-six patients with the quartan strain, he had experienced a 91 percent success rate as compared to a 14 percent rate with the tertian strain injected into twenty-two patients. Psychiatric professionals considered his quartan treatment as some of the most outstanding research performed at Tuskegee.

Branche read his paper "Therapeutic Quartan Malaria in the Treatment of Neurosyphilis among Negroes" at the 1939 American Psychiatric Association meeting in Chicago. During panel discussion his peers agreed that his work was a "real contribution." Dr. Walter L. Bruetsch of Indianapolis, Indiana, remarked that "the work of Dr. Branche and his associates in Tuskegee represents an admirable contribution and has an important practical application. It also comes at the right moment" because most hospitals at that time were dealing with treatment of malaria. "I believe it is one of the best contributions which have been made in recent years in the treatment of neurosyphilis," Bruetsch concluded (*Journal of the National Medical Association* [1941]: 84–85).

Physicians traveled to Tuskegee to learn Branche's method, and the treatment was quickly adopted. Branche explained that treatment with the tertian type of malaria had failed in blacks because he believed that they had acquired immunity because of the "entrenched endemic nature of tertian malaria in the South." Dr. TOUSSAINT TOURGEE TILDON, the African American manager of the Tuskegee VA Hospital, said that "Dr. Branche's greatest single attainment was the contribution he made when he gave to the medical profession and to the world an improved method of treating neurosyphilis by means of quartan malaria" (*Journal of the National Medical Association* [1958]: 140).

Branche's work took place during the same period as what came to be known as the Tuskegee Syphilis Experiment, in which the Public Health Service allowed African American men with syphilis to remain untreated so that the effects of the disease could be studied. In the years since the experiment came to light in 1970, scholars have grappled with questions over the culpability of the black medical professionals who collaborated with the PHS, which used Tuskegee facilities for much of its work.

World War II interrupted Branche's work. Serving as assistant clinical director from 1941, he embarked on a tour of duty as a lieutenant colonel in the U.S. Army Medical Corps in February 1944. When he was discharged in May 1946, Branche returned to Tuskegee as director of Professional Services.

Branche was a fellow of the American Psychiatric Association and a diplomate of the American Board of Psychiatry and Neurology. He was a member of the American Board of Neuropsychiatry, the National Medical Association, the American Association for the Advancement of Science, and the Association of Military Surgeons of the United States. Branche earned many honors, including the 1944 E. S. Jones Award for research in medical science from the John A. Andrews Clinical Society at Tuskegee Institute. He was named "Omega Man of the Year" in 1954 by Iota Omega Chapter of Omega Psi Phi fraternity.

Branche had married Lillian V. Davidson in 1924; they had two sons, who both became doctors, and a daughter. Branche was active in civic organizations and helped to establish the Presbyterian church at Tuskegee, as well as establish athletic teams, including baseball, basketball, and tennis, at the Tuskegee Institute. After a year's illness, Branche died at the Tuskegee VA Hospital, where he had devoted thirty-three years on staff. He was buried at Arlington National Cemetery.

FURTHER READING

Barker, Prince P. "Psychiatry at the Tuskegee VA Hospital in Retrospect," *Journal of the National Medical Association* 54 (Mar. 1962): 152–153.

Daniel, Pete. "Black Power in the 1920s: The Case of Tuskegee Veterans Hospital," *Journal of Southern History* 36 (1970): 368–388.

This entry is taken from the *American National Biography* and is published here with the permission of the American Council of Learned Societies.

ELIZABETH D. SCHAFER

Brandon, Barbara (1960–), cartoonist, was born in Brooklyn, New York, the youngest of three children of BRUMSIC BRANDON JR., a pioneering black cartoonist and creator of the long-running comic strip *Luther*, which debuted in the late 1960s and was syndicated by the Los Angeles Times Syndicate in 1971.

As a young girl growing up in New Cassel, Long Island, Brandon often assisted her father with his work. Later she studied illustration in the College of Visual and Performing Arts at Syracuse University but left six credits short of completing her degree. At age twenty-four Brandon created her own comic strip called *Where I'm Coming From*, which featured the faces of a diverse group of nine African American women friends.

Although her characters' perspectives were quintessentially African American, the cartoonist stressed that the voices were universal reflections on life and love. The characters were talking heads without bodies. Women are "too often summed up by our body parts," she said. "I'm saying 'We have opinions,' and 'Look me in the eye and talk to me'" (*New York Times*, 19 July 1992).

Although the strip was originally created for and sold to a fledgling black women's magazine called *Elan* in 1982, the publication folded before Brandon's work ever appeared. Moving back to Brooklyn in 1983, Brandon next approached *Essence* magazine. While her strip was not accepted for publication, she was offered a job as a beauty and fashion writer, which she accepted. She went on to work at the magazine for more than five years.

In 1988 Brumsic Brandon referred his daughter to the *Detroit Free Press*, where editors were looking for African American cartoonists. As *Free Press* editor Marty Claus noted in explaining her motives, "My community happens to be largely black, and we know young readers turn to the comic pages." *Where I'm Coming From* first ran in the *Free Press* in 1989 and continued to make regular Sunday appearances. Then in September of 1991 it appeared for the first time as an acquisition of the Universal Press Syndicate, making Brandon the first black female syndicated cartoonist—and only the eighth black cartoonist of either gender—to be published in the mainstream American press (in the 1930s JACKIE ORME's strip *Torchy Brown* had appeared in the African American press, making her the first black woman cartoonist to have her work syndicated).

Encouraged by Universal Press Syndicate to feature political and racial themes in her strip, Brandon incorporated musings about the MARTIN LUTHER KING JR. holiday, CLARENCE THOMAS's appointment to the U.S. Supreme Court in 1991, and the RODNEY KING verdict and subsequent uprisings in Los Angeles in 1992. Brandon also made use of culturally specific references to black hair care, music, and history, saying that she thought it was more important to be "thought-provoking than funny" (*New York Times*, 19 July 1992). Brandon added that she was primarily concerned "with recording the experiences black women are having in this country and how some of us are feeling about them."

In the early 1990s it appeared that Brandon was "poised for wide recognition," as the *New York Times* (19 July 1992) put it. There were plans for marketing her characters on greeting cards, coffee mugs, and T-shirts, and in 1993 a collection of her strips, *Where I'm Coming From*, was published in book form by Andrews & McMeel. A second collection, *Where I'm Still Coming From*, appeared in 1994.

Yet there were still challenges facing professional black cartoon artists, who in the early 1990s still numbered fewer than a 100. As Brandon remarked, as late as the 1960s, illustrations of African Americans were still mostly caricatures drawn by white people, images of "big lips and pickanniny heads" (*New York Times*, 19 July 1992). In 1996 such tensions came to a head when *The New Yorker* magazine commissioned but failed to publish a number of works by black cartoonists for its special double issue, "Black in America" (29 April/6 May 1996). Although illustrations were solicited from as many as nine black artists for the special issue, including Brandon, all but one of the African American–oriented images chosen were created by white artists. The magazine's editors reportedly felt nervous about some of the submissions, fearing that they might be controversial. Brandon handled the rejection with the even-tempered grace that seemed to define her public persona over the years, saying that she was proud to be among those whose work they considered too difficult.

In May 1997 Brandon married the musician Monte Croft and became Barbara Brandon-Croft. Their son, Chase, was born in October 1998.

In 1999 the cartoon landscape took a dramatic turn when twenty-four-year-old African American cartoonist AARON MCGRUDER made his debut with *The Boondocks*, a highly politicized comic strip featuring a young, would-be black nationalist named Huey (after the Black Panther HUEY P. NEWTON). The strip, acquired by the Universal Press Syndicate, enjoyed major success in hundreds of mainstream newspapers across the country, and again it looked as though the fortunes for black cartoonists might be improving.

Meanwhile Brandon-Croft accepted work as a freelance researcher and fact-checker for magazines to make ends meet, as her comic strip work did not earn more than $30,000 a year. In 2002, after living in Brooklyn for nearly two decades, she relocated with her family to Queens, New York. Then, in March 2005, Brandon-Croft announced that she would end her comic strip after sixteen years of publication as her client list had declined dramatically. That same year, however, the cartoonist signed a development deal with Universal Press Syndicate to design a daily comic strip.

FURTHER READING

Adell, Sandra, ed. *Dictionary of Twentieth-Century Culture* (1996).

"Barbara Brandon Is First Black Female Cartoonist Nationally Syndicated," *Jet* (26 Aug. 1991).

"Crusaders with Pen and Ink—African Americans Cartoonists," *Ebony* (Jan. 1993).

Hine, Darlene Clark, ed. *Black Women in America* (1993).

Lindin, Amy. "A Comic Strip for Us," *Essence* (Mar. 1990).

Rule, Sheila. "The 'Girls' Talking with a Black Perspective," *New York Times*, 19 July 1992.

KRISTAL BRENT ZOOK

Brandon, Brumsic, Jr. (10 Apr. 1927–), artist and creator of *Luther*, one of the first comic strips with African American characters to be widely published in U.S. newspapers, was born in Washington, D.C., two blocks north of Union Station, then the national capital's major transportation center. Brumsic Brandon Sr. worked there as a railway porter. Brandon Jr.'s mother, the former Pearl Brooks, was a stock clerk and maid at the Kann's Department Store.

At Charles Young Platoon Elementary School, Brandon was a high achiever who loved to draw, which inspired him to pursue art as a career. In 1942, when he entered Armstrong Technical High School, he took nearly every painting, sketching, and sculpture course. Also, at the urging of teachers, he added courses in drafting, which later made him more employable. Brandon graduated in February 1945, intent on becoming a comic strip artist, but instead he became one of the first African Americans recommended for an appointment to the United States Naval Academy in Annapolis, Maryland.

The Reverend ADAM CLAYTON POWELL JR., a freshman Democratic congressman from New York's Twenty-Second District in Harlem who made a political career knocking down racial barriers, was responsible for nominating Brandon and WESLEY A. BROWN, a Maryland native, for academy enrollment. Powell told the young men they might be rejected, but the navy would have to answer some tough questions if they passed the admissions test. Brown passed, becoming Annapolis's first African American graduate. Brandon, however, flunked, largely because his passion was art. In fall 1945 he entered the art program at New York University.

An honor student, Brandon made extra money with sales of gag cartoons to pulp magazines such as *Pack o' Fun*. After less than a year he left school to be a full-time cartoonist. Around 1947 the price of paper shot up because of post–World War II shortages, contributing to the demise of the pulp magazine industry. Comics were the first sections dropped, so Brandon went home to Washington, D.C.

He took a job as a mail sorter on the night shift in the U.S. Post Office. As the U.S. Army bulked its ranks for the Korean conflict, Brandon was drafted in 1950. He was a sergeant in the all-black 594th Field Artillery battalion, part of the U.S. occupation forces in postwar Germany. After he was discharged, Brandon went back to his wife, Rita Broughton, a Howard University graduate, who worked for the government, whom he had married in 1950 in Washington. They raised two daughters, Linda, an entertainment attorney, and BARBARA BRANDON, who gained prominence as a cartoonist, and a son, Brumsic III, who taught in Westbury, Long Island, New York.

Cartoons were in Brandon's heart and mind, but he was unable to pay his bills as a cartoonist. He worked through a swift series of jobs, as an IBM machine operator, a statistical draftsman, and a technical illustrator for John R. O'Brien and Associates Incorporated, a professional services company. He drew exploded views of diesel and aircraft engine parts. In 1957 Brandon, with his wife, eldest daughter, and son, moved to New York City again for a full-time job with Bray Studios. The job gave him a chance to learn the basics of animation from Max Fleischer, a pioneer and innovator in animation who brought Betty Boop, Popeye, and Superman to the silver screen. Brandon worked at Bray Studios until 1970, when his now famous comic strip *Luther* rose to prominence.

While employed at Bray, Brandon continued to draw cartoons on his own time. He experimented with a variety of characters. Some of his worst efforts included early strips that featured an abstract figure and an inventor. The early strips matured into gag cartoons that took on issues of race. In 1963 Brandon became a regular contributor to *Freedomways*, a black-run quarterly magazine that showcased works by the best human rights advocates, thinkers, and artists of the sixties, seventies, and eighties. He stayed on as a contributing editor until the publication's demise in 1986.

In 1968 his cartoons in *Freedomways* drew the attention of editors at Newsday Specials, the syndication service of Long Island's daily newspaper, which asked Brandon to develop a comic strip. That year, on the evening of 4 April, on a hotel balcony in Memphis, the Reverend MARTIN LUTHER KING JR. was assassinated. Riots broke out throughout the nation. *Luther* was born; Brandon named the strip and its main character to honor the late civil rights leader. Still, the comic strip's success did not come easily. Newsday Specials' editors changed their minds.

Brandon continued to develop the idea, nonetheless. Luther, a boy who lived in a black, working-class neighborhood, strove to understand the world around him. By 1960s' standards the cartoons were edgy. Brandon's cast of children included Hardcore, a militant outsider; Oreo, whose white mind-set was only thinly disguised by black skin; and their white teacher, Miss Backlash, who represented a faceless, oppressive power structure. The strip debuted in 1968 in the *Manhattan Tribune*, a weekly newspaper owned by William F. Haddad and distributed on New York City's Upper West Side. Soon the Los Angeles Times Syndicate picked up *Luther* and distributed the comic until 1986.

Offers flowed in, and suddenly *Luther* seemed to blossom. Between 1969 and 1976 publisher Paul S. Eriksson released six volumes of *Luther* comic strips—*Luther, from Inner City* (1969); *Luther Tells It* (1970); *Luther Raps* (1971); *Right On, Luther!* (1971); *Outta Sight, Luther!* (1972); and *Luther's Got Class* (1976). At the same time, Joya Sherrill, a former jazz singer and host of *Time for Joya* (later renamed *Joya's Fun School*), a New York children's television show, called on him to draw pictures for the stories and various art projects. Known as "Mr. BB," he was on the show until 1982. Richard Nixon's White House called, too. The insightfulness of *Luther* earned him a place at the White House Conference on Children in 1970.

Brandon's television work expanded during the mid-1970s. He wrote and illustrated several *Luther* segments for *Vegetable Soup*, a children's show produced by the New York State Department of Education. African American publishers wooed him as well. In 1974 Brandon developed *Black Cat's Bebop Fables* as a newspaper strip distributed to 125 black newspapers throughout the country through Black Media. Brandon stayed with the distributor, later called Black Resources, until 1999. He also showcased a television version of the cartoons on *Vegetable Soup*. The jazz icon DIZZY GILLESPIE narrated the stories. In 1995 thirty-two of his pen and ink drawings were added to the Library of Congress's permanent collection African American Odyssey: A Quest for Full Citizenship. He considered the inclusion to be his highest honor, although many of his cartoons are in Pelican Books' Best Editorial Cartoons of the Year from 1996 to 2003.

FURTHER READING

Robinson, Matt. *The Six Button Dragon* (1971).
Strömberg, Frederik. *Black Images in the Comics: A Visual History* (2003).

VINCENT F. A. GOLPHIN

Branson, Herman Russell (14 Aug. 1914–7 June 1995), physicist, educator, and academic administrator, was born in Pocahontas, Virginia, the son of Harry P. Branson, a coal miner, and Gertrude Brown. In 1928, after several years at his local elementary school, Herman enrolled at Dunbar High School in Washington, D.C., one of the nation's preeminent black secondary schools. He was encouraged in this move by a young black physician, William Henry Welch, who practiced in Pocahontas and who rented lodgings from young Branson's grandmother.

At Dunbar, Branson was introduced to studies in Latin, advanced mathematics, and other disciplines to which he would not have been exposed in his local high school. After graduating as valedictorian in 1932, he enrolled at the University of Pittsburgh with a view to studying medicine, partly because his great-uncle had been trained as a physician there. Branson completed the premedical program in two years and still found time to immerse himself in a wide range of science courses. "Physics could answer more questions than any other science," he later recalled, "so I decided physics was what I'd go into—but I really liked biology and chemistry, so as an undergraduate I took almost enough for a major in four fields: biology, chemistry, math, and physics" (Manning interview).

When the University of Pittsburgh turned down his application to the medical school in 1934—they had no intention of admitting blacks at the time, he was convinced—he transferred to all-black Virginia State College, where he majored in physics, graduating summa cum laude in 1936. His eclectic mix of scientific interests as an undergraduate foreshadowed the versatile, interdisciplinary character of his later research.

In 1936 Branson enrolled as a doctoral student in physics at the University of Cincinnati. He chose Cincinnati in part because he had relatives with whom he could live in the city, but also because the university had an excellent physics department, including the faculty member Boris Podolsky, known for his work in quantum mechanics. Podolsky was a primary mentor, but Branson—still intent on shaping his program in multidisciplinary ways—took courses in other fields as well, for example with Harris Hancock, a mathematician specializing in the theory of elliptic functions. Branson earned a Ph.D. in Physics in 1939, and that year he married Corolynne Gray of Cincinnati; they had two children, Corolynne Gertrude and Herman Edward, both physicians.

His first academic appointment was at Dillard University, where he served as instructor in mathematics and physics from 1939 to 1941. Part of that period was spent as a Rosenwald Fellow in physics at the University of Chicago; the Rosenwald fellowships had been established by the Julius Rosenwald Fund in 1936 to support advanced study for "Negroes of unusual talents and abilities in any field of work." In 1941 Branson was appointed assistant professor of physics and chemistry at Howard University; he was assistant professor of physics, 1942–1944, professor of physics, 1944–1968, and department head, 1955–1968.

At Howard, Branson embarked on a lifelong commitment to improving science education for African Americans. He developed a physics undergraduate major and a graduate program there in the 1940s, when physics in black colleges and universities was thought of primarily as a service course for premedical majors, rather than as a discipline in its own right. In 1942 and 1943 he published several articles on blacks in science and technology, particularly addressing issues relating to research, education, and the war effort, as in "The Role of the Negro College in the Preparation of Technical Personnel for the War Effort" (*Journal of Negro Education* 11 [July 1942]); "Physics Training for the Negro Student" (*American Journal of Physics* 10 [Aug. 1942]); and "Contribution of Natural Sciences to the Development of Attitudes" (*Quarterly Review of Higher Education Among Negroes* 11 [Jan. 1943]). After the war he continued to address the role of blacks in the sciences and published two notable articles: "The Negro in Scientific Research" (*Negro History Bulletin* 15 [Apr. 1952]), and "The Negro Scientist" (in *The Negro in Science*, ed. Julius H. Taylor [1955]).

The next decade was a time of remarkable productivity in Branson's scientific research as well. He pioneered the use of integral equations in describing processes in biological systems, published as "A Mathematical Description of Metabolizing Systems" (*Bulletin of Mathematical Biophysics* 8 [1946]; 9 [1947]). He was also among the first to use radioactive phosphorus ($32P$), mathematical methods, and electron microscopy in the study of sickle cell anemia blood cells (*Science* 115 [25 Jan. 1952]). Another innovative line of research brought him to the intersection between biology and information theory. He calculated, for example, the information content of several protein molecules in "Information Theory and the Structure of Proteins" (in *Information Theory in Biology*, ed. Henry Quastler [1953]).

Most important of all, and least recognized, is his contribution to early discoveries about the structure of proteins. In the late 1940s, working as a National Research Council senior fellow with Linus Pauling and others at the California Institute of Technology, Branson helped discover the "alpha-helix," the first clear vision of three-dimensional order in proteins. He established and solved the relevant spatial equations and demonstrated the hydrogen-bonded helical structure of certain amino acids. The "alpha helix," announced in a paper coauthored by Branson, Pauling, and Robert B. Corey, "The Structure of Proteins: Two Hydrogen-Bonded Helical Configurations of the Polypeptide Chain" (*Proceedings of the National Academy of Sciences* 37 [1951]), ranks as one of the most important discoveries in the history of biology in the twentieth century, anticipating the helical structure of DNA. Pauling was awarded the Nobel Prize in Chemistry for the achievement in 1954, while Branson's role has been all but forgotten.

After nearly three decades at Howard University, Branson served as president of Central State University, Wilberforce, Ohio, from 1968 to 1970, and of Lincoln University, from 1970 to 1985. His leadership at these two historically black institutions reflected his ongoing commitment to educational opportunity for African Americans. In the spring of 1970 he led a group of fifteen black college and university presidents to a White House meeting with President Richard Nixon, laying out the frustration felt by blacks nationwide toward the administration's policies; Nixon responded with a 30 percent increase in federal aid for historically black educational institutions.

Following his retirement as president of Lincoln University in 1985, Branson directed the Pre-College Science and Mathematics Program at Howard University, bringing high school seniors into mentoring relationships with professional scientists. He worked hard throughout his career to raise public awareness about the role and potential of scientific careers for blacks. "The civil rights struggle is quite a recent thing," he said in a 1966 interview, "and until we provide Negroes with suitable opportunity from the time they are born, we are not going to have as many Negro physicists as numerically we should." An early critic of "black studies" as a discrete academic discipline, he feared that such programs would emphasize emotion at the expense of intellectual rigor and distract attention from more practical goals.

In 1969 Branson became a cofounder of the National Association for Equal Opportunity in Higher Education and from 1970 to 1973 he served as its president. He was elected to membership in the Institute of Medicine, National Academy of Sciences in 1975. His stellar accomplishments over a life of service distinguished him as both a scholar and administrator.

FURTHER READING

Important archival sources for Branson's career may be found in the Moorland-Spingarn Research Center at Howard University, the Julius Rosenwald Fund Archives in the Fisk University Library Special Collections, Nashville, Tennessee, and in the Lincoln University Archives, Lincoln University, Pennsylvania. Oral histories conducted by Kenneth R. Manning in 1976 are held at the Massachusetts Institute of Technology. There is no published biography.

Hodes, Bernard. "The Negro in Physics—An Interview with Herman Branson," *Physics Today* 19 (Sept. 1966): 72–73.

Obituaries: *New York Times*, 13 June 1995; *Jet*, 26 June 1995.

PHILIP ALEXANDER

Branton, Wiley Austin (13 Dec. 1923–15 Dec. 1988), lawyer and civil rights activist, was born in Pine Bluff, Arkansas, to Pauline Wiley and Leo Branton, who operated a taxicab company. The family was of mixed race on both sides, and Wiley Branton attended segregated public schools through the twelfth grade, benefiting from the fact that Pine Bluff was one of the few Arkansas towns offering a high school education to African Americans.

The Wiley and Branton families were prominent in the Pine Bluff African American community and were respected in the white community. Wiley's maternal grandfather was a charter member of Pine Bluff's chapter of the NAACP. His grandmother, Effa Wiley, was a community activist who had a great influence on Wiley's early development. He accompanied her on neighborhood visits to troubled homes and to meetings and conferences of black groups where problems of segregation and unequal treatment were discussed. From her, Wiley learned compassion for others and absorbed a sense of duty and obligation to his community.

Branton was drafted into the segregated U.S. Army in 1943 for service in World War II. At that time, military leaders discounted, and even objected, to the participation of black soldiers in fighting units. African Americans usually found themselves performing the most menial jobs in the camps under the supervision of white officers. Branton scored well on the Army General Classification Test used to determine the working ability of new soldiers. He was sent for special training in drafting and then was assigned to the segregated 1894th Engineering Aviation Battalion at MacDill Field, Florida. By the end of 1943 Wiley had been promoted to sergeant. Three months later he received training as an intelligence specialist and was made an operations NCO. By mid-April 1944, however, Branton was being investigated for disaffection by the army. He and another soldier had sent a letter condemning the treatment of black soldiers to President Franklin D. Roosevelt, the War Department, and to a number of African American publications. The investigation was extensive but apparently came to nothing as his service record contains no mention of it. Branton's unit was sent to Okinawa, Japan, in March 1945, arriving after the Battle of Okinawa was officially over. He spent a year on Okinawa Island, engaged in surveying and serving as a construction foreman and technician in building airfields in preparation for the invasion of Japan. Branton left Okinawa in February 1946 and was honorably discharged at Camp Chaffee, Arkansas, as a master sergeant on 17 March 1946.

Branton returned from service determined to work against segregation. He took up management of his family's taxicab company and also became active in the Pine Bluff NAACP, particularly with regard to issues of voter education and registration work, which he believed were the key to changing southern society. Branton married Lucille McKee of Memphis, Tennessee, in January 1948. The couple delayed their honeymoon so that Branton could accompany a classmate whom he had convinced to test the University of Arkansas' claim that its law school would accept qualified African Americans if they tried to register. The friend, Silas H. Hunt, was admitted to the law school in January 1948.

In the summer of 1948 Branton's civil rights work led to his arrest and conviction for violating an Arkansas law, when he used a copy of a voting ballot to teach people how to mark their ballots when they voted. In 1950, having earned sufficient academic credits from Arkansas Agricultural, Mechanical & Normal College at Pine Bluff (later the University of Arkansas at Pine Bluff), Branton entered law school. Three years later he received a law degree from the University of Arkansas at Fayetteville. During law school he continued to manage the taxicab company, the proceeds of which supported his family, which included his four children.

Within three years of admission to the bar, Branton was representing black clients in civil rights matters. The case that brought him to national prominence was the suit against the school board of Little Rock, Arkansas, on behalf of African American parents and children seeking to integrate the city's schools following the U.S. Supreme Court's 1954 decision in *Brown v. Board of Education*. Branton served as lead attorney, although he worked with lawyers, including THURGOOD MARSHALL, from both the NAACP and the NAACP Legal Defense and Education Fund. During the court battles, and the publicity and segregationist defiance that accompanied them, Branton and Marshall became fast friends.

In 1962 Branton was asked to become executive director of the Voter Education Project (VEP), a foundation-funded entity created to distribute grants to local and national Negro organizations that would educate and register Southern African Americans to vote. His family, which now included six children, moved with him to Atlanta, Georgia. Two and a half years later VEP had registered more than six hundred thousand new black voters, despite having its workers beaten, jailed, and otherwise punished by white segregationists. Branton was called upon many times to use his legal and advocacy skills in their defense.

In 1965 Branton's reputation led Vice President Hubert H. Humphrey to ask Branton to work with him on the President's Council on Equal Opportunity, which was created to coordinate the federal government's implementation of the 1964 Civil Rights Act. When President Lyndon B. Johnson abolished the council in September 1965, he asked Branton to become his representative within the Department of Justice to work on achieving the goals of the 1965 Voting Rights Act. Branton spent two years acting as liaison between the government and civil rights groups.

In 1967 Branton left the Department of Justice to become executive director of the United Planning Organization, Washington, D.C.'s, antipoverty program. For two years he used his skills and contacts to provide education, job training, and other social services to the district's poorest residents. When President Richard M. Nixon slashed antipoverty funding, Branton accepted the invitation of labor leader and president of the United

Automobile Workers Union, Walter Reuther, to begin the Alliance for Labor Action (ALA) in July 1969. The ALA was to be an anti-poverty program funded by union dues to improve the lives of workers. It was a unique idea, but its progress was cut short by Reuther's death in an airplane accident in 1970.

Branton then went into private practice with a black law firm in Washington, D.C., and he stepped up his involvement in professional activities and groups. He served on the Washington, D.C., Home Rule Committee, which made efforts to allow D.C. residents to govern themselves. Historically, D.C. was governed by congressional committees and had no voting rights as to the people who administered the city. As a member of the Lawyers' Committee for Civil Rights Under Law, he helped to defeat the nomination of Robert Bork to the U.S. Supreme Court in 1987. He served as the grand sire archon (an office equivalent to president) of Sigma Phi Pi, a black fraternity of professional men.

In 1977 Branton was named dean of Howard University School of Law. Supreme Court Justice Thurgood Marshall delivered the address at Branton's investiture. Branton hoped to return the school to its glory days, when it was a beacon of legal training for civil rights lawyers. While his six-year effort improved the school's standing among other law schools, its former prominence in civil rights could not be regained. During this period Branton was a member of the Judicial Nomination Commission of the District of Columbia and was on the Council of Legal Education for the American Bar Association.

In 1983 he left Howard Law School to join the Washington, D.C., office of the Chicago firm Sidley & Austin, where he maintained a general practice not too different from those of prior years, except that he also worked on cases involving major firm clients, such as AT&T. He represented CORETTA SCOTT KING when the U.S. senator Jesse Helms tried to open FBI files on MARTIN LUTHER KING JR. in 1983. After only one year as an associate, Branton was made a partner with the firm. It was during this period of his life that he began receiving honors from his peers for the length and breadth of his civil rights work.

In an interview nine months before his death, Branton said, "If I had to do it all over again, I would do exactly what I did." As advice for young people, Branton stated, "You've got to work damn hard. You've got to be better than the next guy, white or black. Your words have to mean something. You've got to be honest in your dealings. … And you have to enjoy what you're doing. I genuinely enjoy what I do. In addition to it being a profession, it has become a hobby. I'm always dabbling in law or reading law. I love it" (Adelman, 114).

FURTHER READING

Branton's papers are on deposit at the Moorland-Spingarn Research Center, Howard University, Washington, D.C.

Adelman, Ken. "You Can Change Their Hearts," *Washingtonian* (Mar. 1988).

Kilpatrick, Judith. "Wiley Austin Branton, A Role Model for All Times," *Howard University Law Journal* (2005).

Kilpatrick, Judith. "Wiley Austin Branton and the Voting Rights Struggle," *UALR Law Review* 26.641 (Summer 2004).

Obituary: *New York Times*, 17 Dec. 1988.

JUDITH KILPATRICK

Brashear, Carl Maxie (19 Jan. 1931–25 July 2006), U.S. Navy diver, was born in Tonieville, Larue County, Kentucky, the son of McDonald and Gonzell Brashear, sharecroppers. He attended the Tonieville Elementary School until he reached the seventh grade, in 1946, when he decided to quit school and go to work as an attendant at a filling station. He was dissatisfied with that job, however, and began to explore other areas of interest. In 1948, at the age of seventeen, Carl Brashear joined the U.S. Navy. His enlistment coincided with President Harry Truman's executive order to desegregate all branches of the armed forces. Brashear felt comfortable in his new position, and, being a proud member of the U.S. Navy, went on to complete the education he had abandoned in elementary school by earning his GED in 1960. His first marriage, to Junette Wilcoxson in 1952, ended in divorce in 1972.

Upon enlisting in the navy in 1948, Brashear entered the Naval Training Center Beach Master Unit at Great Lakes, Illinois. He completed the course of training for salvage diver in 1951 with the intention of becoming a boatswain's mate. He possessed the physical ability and stamina needed by a diver and did well academically. In 1954 he graduated from diving school, becoming a U.S. Navy diver. Brashear was promoted to senior chief boatswain's mate (E-7) in 1960 and was assigned to the aircraft carrier *Tripoli*. There he learned to dive from the carrier's deck by observing navy divers. So impressed

Carl Maxie Brashear, the U.S. Navy's first African American master diver, posing with Cuba Gooding Jr., the actor who portrayed him in the 2000 film *Men of Honor*. (Library of Congress.)

was Brashear by these maneuvers that he decided that he would attempt to become the first African American navy deep-sea diver. Brashear applied to diving school several times before he was accepted. Once admitted, he was forced to endure many racial obstacles and comments. Upon his arrival at the Deep Sea Diving Program in Bayonne, New Jersey, the training instructor mistook him for the cook and directed him to the mess hall. On another occasion one officer commented that the navy did not have any "colored" deep-sea divers, to which Brashear politely responded that the navy was about to have one. Ignoring the racist remarks, Brashear concentrated on his training and, as a result, earned his way from salvage diver to first- and second-class diver to saturation diver and finally, in October 1979, to the pinnacle of success, master diver. Brashear was the first African American to attend and graduate from the U.S. Navy Diving and Salvage School. His second marriage, to Hattie R. Elam in 1980, ended

in 1983. In 1966 Brashear was involved in what is known as the Curv accident (Curv was an acronym for Cable-controlled Underwater Recovery Vehicle). In January of that year a hydrogen bomb was lost off the coast of Palomares, Spain, as a result of a collision between two U.S. Air Force planes; one plane was a B-2 and the other was a KC-139 (tanker). The navy was called in to find and recover the bomb, and Brashear, onboard the carrier *Hoist*, was assigned this critical mission. On 23 March, during the recovery process, a towing cable broke, causing a mechanical device to strike Brashear in his left leg just below the knee, almost severing his leg. Brashear was sent to the Naval Hospital in Portsmouth, Virginia, where doctors, after trying to save his leg, were forced to amputate. Despite his terrible injury, Brashear accepted the loss as a challenge and immediately started therapy. He remained at the Navy Regional Medical Center in Virginia from May 1966 to March 1967, during which time he began the strenuous rehabilitation process. In March 1967 Brashear was released from the hospital and then set out to convince the navy that he could continue with his diving career. He was assigned to the Harbor Clearance Unit Two, Diving School, to begin training to return to full active duty as a navy diver. In April 1968 Brashear became the first amputee to be certified as a diver, and in 1970 he became the first African American U.S. Navy master diver, eventually achieving the rank of master chief boatswain's mate in 1971. Brashear's final marriage was to Jeannette A. Burndage in 1985, ending two years later. He was the father of four children. In 2000 a movie, *Men of Honor*, starring Cuba Gooding Jr. as Brashear, was made about his life.

Carl Brashear received many citations, decorations, and medals for his dedicated service in the navy. He was awarded the Navy and Marine Corps Medal for Heroism in Saving Lives, the Good Conduct medals (eight awards), the Navy Commendation Medal, the Navy Achievement Medal, the National Defense Medal, the China Services Medal, and the Korean Service Medal. He retired from the U.S. Navy in 1979 as a master chief petty officer (E9) and master diver. Brashear died of respiratory and heart failure at the Portsmouth Naval Medical Center.

FURTHER READING

Stillwell, Paul. *The Reminiscences of Master Chief Boatswain's Mate Carl Brashear* (1998).
U.S. Naval Institute's Oral History of Carl Brashear (interview).

Obituaries: *Virginian Pilot*, 26 July 2006; *Navy Newsstand*, 30 July 2006.

AGNES KANE CALLUM

Brashear, Donald (7 Jan. 1972–), hockey player, was born in Bedford, Indiana, the youngest of three children of the Canadian Nicole Gauthier and the American Johnny Brashear. His great uncle, CARL MAXIE BRASHEAR, made history in 1970 as the first African American to rise to the ranks of master diver for the United States Navy. Brashear grew up in a household marked by domestic violence and his father's struggle with alcohol addiction, and was repeatedly the victim of physical assaults starting when he was just an infant. Even after his parents' separation, Brashear remained with his father and when he was six years old was reunited with the rest of his family, which by then included a stepbrother, Danny Roy. Brashear's new home in Loretteville, Quebec, wasn't any safer as he was particularly targeted by his stepfather, Gerard Roy, who emotionally and physically abused him. His mother eventually placed Brashear in foster care, where he at last found stability in the household of Raymond and Jean-Marie St. Pierre.

The move to Val Bélair, Quebec, where the St. Pierres lived posed new challenges. The eight-year-old Brashear, who spoke only English, had to learn French and to cope with racially motivated teasing and taunting from his predominantly white peers. Hockey provided the perfect venue for Brashear to excel at something he was passionate about; at the same time, it was also an outlet for his physicality and aggression. Once Brashear realized that he was unlikely to succeed as an offensive player, he began focusing on other parts of the game like body checking and on honing his fighting skills. He played junior hockey for the Longueuil Collège-Français and the Verdun Collège Français between 1989 and 1992, where he averaged nearly two hundred penalty minutes per season.

Brashear signed his first professional contract with the Montreal Canadians in 1992 and spent the next four years as part of that organization before being traded to the Vancouver Canucks prior to the 1996–97 season. It was as a member of the Canucks that Brashear made headlines when on 21 February 2000 he was struck on the head with a hockey stick by Boston Bruin forward Marty McSorley during the latter stages of the game, rendered unconscious, and subsequently diagnosed with a grade three concussion. Although McSorley was immediately suspended by the National Hockey League, the public outrage from fans and media outlets, particularly in Canada, resulted in a criminal investigation of the on-ice events. On 6 October 2000, McSorley was found guilty of assault with a weapon in a trial that turned out to be a referendum on hockey violence and its place in the sport. There was a certain irony that the criticism leveled at the role of instigators and enforcers focused on the very aspect of hockey that allowed players like Brashear to gain and maintain a place on an NHL roster.

After making a full recovery following the McSorley incident, Brashear resumed his career, solidifying his status as one of the toughest individuals in the game, as evidenced by his league-leading 249 penalty minutes in the 2002–2003 season as a member of the Philadelphia Flyers. During the 2004–2005 NHL work stoppage, Brashear kept busy doing double duty as a boxer in a number of Coors Light events, as well as playing hockey in the Ligue Nord-Américaine de Hockey for the semiprofessional team Radio X. Brashear was suspended twelve games by the LNAH following a brawl on 7 December 2004, in which he continued to hit his opponent, Glen Kjernisted, after Kjernisted had fallen to the ice.

In 2006 Brashear signed a contract with his fourth professional team, the Washington Capitals, where he continued to rack up penalty minutes as the team's top enforcer. Brashear was once again immersed in controversy when he was suspended for severely injuring the New York Ranger's Blair Betts on 6 April 2009 during a playoff game between the Rangers and the Capitals. Unable to reach financial terms with the Capitals, Brashear signed with the New York Rangers in the off-season, and appeared in his 1000th game on 12 November 2009. His stint with the Rangers proved to be less than successful, as he played only thirty-six games with the team.

After sixteen seasons in the NHL Brashear was not yet ready to retire, and on 30 September 2010 he was welcomed back to the Ligue Nord-Américaine de Hockey, signing with Sorel-Tracy GCI. Since 2007, he has been the co-owner of DEC Construction based in Quebec City and devotes much of his off-season to that business endeavor. Brashear has two sons, Jordan and Jackson with his former partner, Gabrielle Desgagne.

FURTHER READING

Farber, Michael. "Brashear's Road to NHL Rocky, Implausible," *Gazette (Montreal)*, 21 Nov. 1993.
Fay, Dave. "Winning the Fight: Enforcer Role Opened Doors for Brashear," *Washington Times*, 12 Oct. 2006.

Wise, Mike. "For Capitals' Brashear, Fighting Is a Way of Life," *Washington Post*, 2 May 2009.

DÁLIA LEONARDO

Braud, Wellman (25 Jan. 1891–29 Oct. 1966), jazz bassist, was born Wellman Breaux in Saint James Parish, Louisiana. Nothing is known of his parents except that they were of Creole heritage, and it is not known when he anglicized his name. Braud began playing violin at age seven and later took up guitar. His earliest work was with string trios playing on the streets of New Orleans. During the 1910s he worked regularly at Tom Anderson's cabaret, probably playing guitar in a group with the violinist ARMAND J. PIRON while also playing drums and trombone in various ad hoc brass bands.

In 1917 Braud moved to Chicago, where he began playing bass and toured with John Wickliffe's band, later joining the Original Creole Band (or Orchestra) at the Pekin Café as a replacement for Ed Garland. When Braud joined the band the other members included the cornetist "Sugar" Johnny Smith, the clarinetist Lawrence Duhé, the trombonist Roy Palmer, the guitarist Louis Keppard, and the drummer Tubby Hall. In 1918 the clarinetist SIDNEY BECHET was added to the group, which during Braud's stay also worked at the Dreamland and De Luxe cafés. From 1920 to 1922 Braud was with Charlie Elgar's orchestra, most likely at the Dreamland, and from March to May 1923 he doubled on trombone and bass with WILL VODERY's orchestra in the *Plantation Revue* in London.

Later in 1923 he moved to New York, where he worked with the vaudevillian clarinetist and bandleader Wilbur Sweatman. In early 1925 Braud and Bechet joined the ten-piece orchestra of the *Seven-Eleven* revue, with which they played in vaudeville and burlesque houses in Newark, Baltimore, Washington, D.C., Boston, and Providence, before opening at New York's Columbia Theater. After leaving *Seven-Eleven*, Braud joined the *Lucky Sambo* revue and remained with it through early 1927.

In mid-1927 Braud joined DUKE ELLINGTON's Kentucky Club orchestra and made his first recordings with the band in October. Among the many titles that he recorded with Ellington over the next few years, those most revealing of his prominently featured capabilities are, from 1927, "Washington Wobble"—his debut solo performance, which may be the first example of the "walking bass" style, with its four beats to the bar; from 1928, "Diga Diga Doo," "Move Over," "Hot and Bothered," and "Bandanna Babies"; and from 1930, "Flaming

Youth," "Saturday Night Function," "High Life," "Hot Feet," "Stevedore Stomp," "Saratoga Swing," "Freeze and Melt," "Cotton Club Stomp," "Ring Dem Bells," and "Old Man Blues."

Although Braud's technically advanced style of alternately picking and slapping the strings of his bass provided an undeniably powerful lift to the sound of Ellington's late 1920s "jungle-style" band, particularly on fast stomp tempos, by the early 1930s Ellington wanted to cultivate a smoother, more sophisticated sound and rhythm. Braud's inability to read music proved no impediment, for he could play any of Ellington's arrangements by ear. But his seemingly dated, New Orleans–style rhythmic conception was no longer what Ellington wanted. Not wishing to fire the mild-mannered older man, Ellington devised a scheme by which Braud would leave the band of his own will, his pride intact. In November 1934 Ellington added the younger, more modern-thinking bassist Billy Taylor to the fold, and the following March Braud quit, probably never realizing how he had been eased out. Ellington, though, must have seen the potential in having two bassists in the band, because in May 1935 he hired the equally young Hayes Alvis as an adjunct to Taylor.

In mid-1935 Braud worked briefly at the Vodvil Club in Harlem in a band that he had formed with the New Orleans clarinetist Jimmie Noone, and when that ended he spent some time working with the drummer Kaiser Marshall at a club in New Jersey. Later in the year he joined the Spirits of Rhythm, a novelty vocal and instrumental group, as both bassist and manager, but he also worked sporadically with his own trios through 1937. In March 1938 he recorded with the trumpeter HOT LIPS PAGE and may have played engagements with Page's band as well.

Either during or after his stay with pianist Edgar Hayes's orchestra in 1939, Braud participated in two important recording dates with JELLY ROLL MORTON's New Orleans Jazzmen in September. In these sessions he was reunited with old hometown friends such as the clarinetist ALBERT NICHOLAS, the drummer ZUTTY SINGLETON, and, most significantly, Sidney Bechet, the most formidable soprano saxophonist alive. In January 1940 Braud recorded three more dates with Morton, once again with Nicholas and Singleton but now also with the New Orleans trumpeter HENRY "RED" ALLEN.

The next few months were even more fruitful. In March and April 1940 Braud recorded with the Bechet-Spanier Big Four, which produced one of the most perfectly realized jazz recording groups of all time, and in May he participated in the reunion of Bechet and LOUIS ARMSTRONG for Decca's *New Orleans Jazz* album. As a more or less regular member of Bechet's working bands, Braud was present in three of Bechet's dates for Victor between June 1940 and September 1941. Meanwhile he continued playing engagements with his quartet at Nick's in Greenwich Village, at the Log Cabin in Fonda, New York, and at BILL "BOJANGLES" ROBINSON's Mimo Club in Harlem.

In 1943 and 1944 Braud worked in the swing bands of the saxophonists Al Sears and Garvin Bushell, but in 1944 he also began operating a poolroom and a meat-marketing business in New York, playing music only on weekends. In January 1947 Braud and Bechet appeared at a Town Hall concert produced by the clarinetist Mezz Mezzrow to promote his autobiography *Really the Blues*, and in September Braud replaced the bassist POPS FOSTER in a recording date with the Mezzrow-Bechet Quintet for the clarinetist and author's King Jazz label.

Braud was also the New Orleans trumpeter BUNK JOHNSON's choice for three recording dates in December that ultimately appeared on a Columbia album called *The Last Testament*. In early 1956 Braud joined the equally venerable New Orleans trombonist KID ORY's band in California and toured Europe with the band later in the year. In 1958 Braud settled in Los Angeles, where in 1960 he worked in the clarinetist Joe Darensbourg's band. After recovering from a mild heart attack in the summer of 1961, Braud sat in with the Ellington band in the fall and later worked with the traditional jazz singer Barbara Dane. Braud worked only infrequently after that, including a tour in Oregon in the fall of 1966. He died in Los Angeles.

FURTHER READING

Schuller, Gunther. *Early Jazz: Its Roots and Musical Development* (1968).
Schuller, Gunther. *The Swing Era: The Development of Jazz, 1930–1945* (1989).
Stewart, Rex. *Jazz Masters of the Thirties* (1972).

DISCOGRAPHY

Bruyninckx, Walter. *Traditional Jazz Discography, 1897–1988* (5 vols., 1989).

This entry is taken from the *American National Biography* and is published here with the permission of the American Council of Learned Societies.

JACK SOHMER

Braun, Carol Moseley. *See* Moseley Braun, Carol.

Brawley, Benjamin (22 Apr. 1882–1 Feb. 1939), educator and author, was born Benjamin Griffith Brawley in Columbia, South Carolina, the son of Margaret Saphronia Dickerson and EDWARD MCKNIGHT BRAWLEY, a prosperous Baptist minister and president of a small Alabama college. Brawley was an exceptionally bright boy, and the family's frequent moves never interfered with his learning. Up until the third grade he was tutored at home by his mother, but he also attended schools in Nashville, Tennessee, and Petersburg, Virginia. During summers, when he was not studying the classics, Latin, and Greek at home, he earned money by doing odd jobs, working on a tobacco farm in Connecticut or in a printing office. One summer he drove a buggy for a white doctor—and studied Greek while the doctor was out. At age twelve he was sent to Virginia to be tutored in Greek and he also studied the language with his father.

By age thirteen Brawley had excelled so much in his studies that he was sent to the preparatory program at Atlanta Baptist College (later Morehouse College). He was surprised and disappointed on his arrival to note that most of the older students there knew nothing of classical literature, much less Greek or Latin. His classmates were equally surprised to find such a young man in their midst, but they soon discovered just how valuable an asset he was. Aware of his intellectual and grammatical prowess, they brought their compositions to him before passing them on to their instructors. Brawley excelled outside the classroom as well. He played football, managed the baseball team, and cofounded the school newspaper, the *Athenaeum* (later the *Maroon Tiger*), for which he wrote numerous articles and poems. Brawley is also said to have initiated the first debate among African American colleges when his Morehouse team challenged another group from Talladega College.

In 1901 Brawley graduated with honors from Atlanta Baptist College and immediately took a teaching position, for five months at thirty-five dollars a month, in a one-room school in Georgetown, Florida, but then, in 1902, he took a teaching job at his alma mater, where he stayed until 1910. During his years at Atlanta Baptist College, he also earned his B.A. (1906) from the University of Chicago and his M.A. (1908) from Harvard by taking mostly summer courses. Then he accepted a professorship at Howard University and while teaching there met Hilda Damaris Prowd, who became his wife in

1912. They had no children. After only two years at Howard, he returned to Atlanta Baptist, where, in addition to teaching, he became the college's first dean and where his teaching techniques became legendary.

Brawley considered teaching to be a divine profession that should be used to bring students "into the knowledge of truth," the success of which depended as much upon the efforts of the teacher as on those of the student. He expected of his students the same high academic and moral standards that he had learned as a child, and he stressed that teaching should take into account the whole student—his or her physical, emotional, economic, and moral background. Brawley would commonly make students memorize long passages from classical literature, and he returned any compositions with even the slightest degree of sloppiness or imprecision, marking them with terse comments like "Too carelessly written to be carefully read" (Parker, *Phylon* [1949], 18). A traditionalist first, last, and always, Brawley was also dissatisfied with the state of education in the country, which emphasized materialism and innovation rather than rote learning.

Although Brawley still earned his primary living as a teacher, he also began to turn seriously toward another profession. He had written articles for his school paper and other publications for several years, but from 1921 on he produced at least ten books and about one hundred newspaper and magazine articles, book reviews, editorials, and other efforts. Whether he was writing about African American life and culture, as in *A Social History of the American Negro* (1921), or more literary topics, as in *A New Survey of English Literature* (1925), Brawley stressed two major themes: first, that literature must rest on a sound artistic and moral basis, and second, that it should present not just the struggles of individuals and races, but "a mirror of our hopes and dreams" as well (*The Negro Genius* [1937], 196). He was particularly saddened that most novels and short stories about African Americans that came out of Harlem and other places in the 1920s depicted characters as comic or appealed to readers' lower natures. "We are simply asking," he wrote in *The Negro Genius*, "that those writers of fiction who deal with the Negro shall be thoroughly honest with themselves" (206). Only by strict adherence to these high ideals, Brawley believed, could the lot of his own race be improved and race relations be dealt with honestly.

In 1920, after many years at Morehouse, Brawley went to the African Republic of Liberia to conduct an educational survey. Shortly after his return in early 1921, he followed in his father's footsteps and became an ordained Baptist minister at the Messiah Congregation in Brockton, Massachusetts. After only a year, however, he found the congregation's type of Christianity not to his liking and resigned. Brawley returned to teaching, first at Shaw University in North Carolina, where his father, by then in failing health, taught theology, and then, in 1931, at Howard, where he stayed until the end of his life. In 1936 he published PAUL LAURENCE DUNBAR: *Poet of His People*. He died at his home in Washington, D.C., from complications following a stroke.

Brawley's impeccable academic credentials and high standards earned him the respect of almost all his students, although that respect was shown in unusual ways. One story goes that a student came to class carrying under his arm a bundle wrapped in newspaper, which everyone assumed was laundry. Instead, the student had carefully wrapped his essay in the bundle to be sure that it met Brawley's exacting standards. Brawley's techniques, coupled with his difficulty in abiding by any standards other than his own, earned him his share of criticism, but far more often than not they achieved desirable results.

FURTHER READING
The Brawley papers are at the Moorland-Spingarn Research Center at Howard University.
A complete bibliography of Brawley's published works appears in *North Carolina Historical Review* 34 (Apr. 1957): 165–175.
Parker, John W. "Benjamin Brawley and the American Cultural Tradition." *Phylon* 16 (1955): 183–194.
Phylon Profile XIX. "Benjamin Brawley—Teacher and Scholar." *Phylon* 10 (1949): 15–24.
Price, Charlotte S. *Richard Le Gallienne as Collected by Benjamin Griffith Brawley* (1973).
Obituaries: *New York Times*, 7 Feb. 1939; *Crisis* 46 (1939).
This entry is taken from the *American National Biography* and is published here with the permission of the American Council of Learned Societies.

ROGER A. SCHUPPERT

Brawley, Edward McKnight (18 Mar. 1851–13 Jan. 1923), Baptist minister, educator, and editor, was born in Charleston, South Carolina, the son of free African American parents, Ann L. (maiden name unknown) and James M. Brawley. Brawley's parents took a keen interest in the education and professional development of their son, providing him private schooling in Charleston, sending him at the age of ten to Philadelphia to attend grammar school and the Institute for Colored Youth, and apprenticing him to a shoemaker in Charleston from 1866 to 1869. He enrolled as the first theological student at Howard University for a few months in 1870 but then transferred to Bucknell University in Lewisburg, Pennsylvania, in January 1871. The first African American student at Bucknell, Brawley completed his education with the encouragement and financial support of a white couple named Griffith and with his own work teaching vocal music and preaching during school vacations. The white Baptist church in Lewisburg with which he had affiliated ordained him to the ministry the day after his graduation, 1 July 1875; he was examined by a board composed largely of professors and other learned individuals. In 1878 he received an AM from Bucknell and, in 1885, an honorary doctor of divinity degree from the State University in Louisville, Kentucky.

Brawley's first marriage in 1877 lasted only a year; his wife, Mary W. Warrick, and their baby both died. His second marriage, to Margaret Dickerson in 1879, produced four children; one of them, BENJAMIN BRAWLEY, became a renowned historian and author.

Immediately after Brawley left Bucknell, the predominantly white, northern-based American Baptist Publication Society (ABPS) appointed him as a Sunday school missionary, or agent, for his home state of South Carolina. There he found little organization among the black Baptists. He set about establishing new Baptist associations and reorganizing existing ones, as well as encouraging the founding of Sunday school conventions at the state Baptist regional or associational levels. After two years the first statewide Sunday school convention among African American Baptists was held, with Brawley serving as corresponding secretary and financial agent. Brawley also helped black Baptists organize African missions, and South Carolina sent its first missionary, HARRISON N. BOUEY, to Africa in the late 1870s. Not only did Brawley strengthen denominational structures in the state but he also raised considerable funds for Benedict College in South Carolina.

Eight years of strenuous work in South Carolina took their toll on Brawley's health. Following his doctor's advice despite the ABPS's strong desire that he continue his duties, in 1883 Brawley traveled to Alabama to assume the presidency of Alabama Baptist Normal and Theological School (later Selma University), a position that he had declined several times before. Once again Brawley's service was successful. He upgraded the school's standards and collegiate rank, and the first class graduated in May 1884. Fiercely committed to education, Brawley, like many other early educators both black and white, gave as much as half of his income to needy students.

With his wife's health in decline, Brawley returned to South Carolina after two years to preside over a school that he had helped to establish, Morris College. In 1912 he assumed the pastorship of White Rock Baptist Church in Durham, North Carolina. Around 1920 he became professor of biblical history and evangelism at Baptist-supported Shaw University in Raleigh, North Carolina, serving there until his death.

Brawley was highly valued as a speaker and lecturer. He was also an accomplished writer and editor. At different points in his career he edited the *Baptist Pioneer* in South Carolina, the weekly *Baptist Tribune*, and the monthly *Evangel*. Ever concerned about raising the educational standards of both ministers and the laity, he wrote *Sin and Salvation*, which focused on evangelism, and his most significant work, *The Negro Baptist Pulpit: A Collection of Sermons and Papers* (1890; repr. 1971). Of the twenty-eight sermons and addresses in the latter work, Brawley authored four. Throughout his career he also published numerous sermons, speeches, and addresses.

In addition to his church, educational, and publishing work, Brawley left a theological and philosophical legacy of one committed to uplifting the African American race by moral and spiritual education. Furthermore, Brawley passionately supported cooperation with sympathetic whites as a way to advance the race, believing that all racial sentiments should be subordinate to the greater principle of building up American Christianity. That position often placed him at odds with African American leaders who were increasingly restless with the racial parochialism and paternalism of their white benefactors. Whereas some African American Christians, including Brawley, emphasized the necessity of continued white financial assistance, the more independent complained of the stifling effect that these whites had on the development of racial responsibility and self-respect. Nonetheless, Brawley's contributions to denominational organization, church leadership, education, and publishing left an impressive mark on American religious history.

FURTHER READING

Brawley, Edward McKnight. *The Negro Baptist Pulpit: A Collection of Sermons and Papers* (1890; repr. 1971).

Pegues, Albert W. *Our Baptist Ministers and Schools* (1892).

Simmons, William J. *Men of Mark: Eminent, Progressive, and Rising* (1887; repr. 1968).

Washington, James M. *Frustrated Fellowship: The Black Baptist Quest for Social Power* (1986).

This entry is taken from the *American National Biography* and is published here with the permission of the American Council of Learned Societies.

SANDY DWAYNE MARTIN

Brawley, James P. (26 Sept. 1894–3 Dec. 1986), college president and lay Methodist Church leader, was born James Phillip Brawley in Lockhart, Texas, the son of Thomas H. Brawley and Emma Storey. Despite being born in the Jim Crow era, Brawley received a college education, graduating from Samuel Houston College in 1920. He did graduate work at the University of Chicago and Northwestern University, where he received his M.A. in Religious Education in 1925 and his Ph.D. in Education in 1941.

Brawley took his first teaching position in 1922 at Rust College in Holly Springs, Mississippi, a school founded by the Methodist Episcopal Church's Freedmen's Aid Society following the Civil War. He moved from Rust College to Clark College in Atlanta, Georgia, in 1925, where he taught education and religious education. Clark College was another Freedmen's Aid Society school that had traditionally emphasized the training of ministers and teachers. Brawley became the college academic dean there in 1926 and also served as registrar. One of his first accomplishments was to regularize the recording of student grades, determine whether all graduate requirements were fulfilled, and create transcripts, which was a vital step for students to receive Georgia teacher certification. Brawley married Georgia L. Williams, an English teacher, on 20 June 1929, and the marriage lasted until his death; they had no children.

During the Great Depression, Clark College, like other historically black colleges in the South, struggled to keep its doors open. However, the college strengthened its curriculum and eliminated pre-collegiate programs to increase its academic standing. This period in the college's history culminated with a coalition of philanthropic support by the Methodist General Education Board

(successor to the Freedmen's Aid Society) and private gifts, making it possible for Clark to move from its location just south of Atlanta to a new site adjacent to Atlanta University and its affiliated institutions, Morehouse and Spelman colleges (and later Morris Brown). The new facility opened in 1941, the year Brawley became president of Clark College.

A committed Methodist layman, Brawley was a delegate, in 1939, to the Uniting Conference of the Northern Methodist Episcopal Church; the Methodist Episcopal Church, South; and the Methodist Protestant Church. The purpose of this conference was to create a new Methodist Church to heal the division between Northern and Southern Methodists that began over slavery in 1844. Although most African American Methodists were members of the African Methodist Episcopal Church (AME), the African Methodist Episcopal Zion Church, or the Colored Methodist Episcopal Church (after 1954, the Christian Methodist Episcopal Church), for black Methodists who were members of the Northern Methodist Episcopal Church, the Uniting Conference was a humiliating experience, because the newly created Methodist Church put all black Methodists into a separate jurisdictional conference called the Central Jurisdiction. For the first time, these black Methodists were able to elect their own bishops and had representation on church councils and agencies, but the Central Jurisdiction was a bitter reminder that white Methodists still did not accept African American members as equals, or even as members of the same denomination.

Brawley served as a lay delegate to the Methodist General Conferences in 1948, 1952, 1956, 1960, and 1964. In the Central Jurisdiction, he chaired self-studies in 1952 and 1956 that assessed the problems of the jurisdiction and the prospects for racial change within the Methodist Church. He also wrote numerous articles for the Central Jurisdiction's newspaper advocating racial inclusiveness.

In 1956 the Methodist Church General Conference established an interjurisdictional commission of seventy members to review church race relations. Brawley served as the chair of the Central Jurisdiction representatives on that commission, which held hearings in all regions of the country. It recommended to the 1960 General Conference that desegregation proceed using Amendment IX to the church constitution, which had been ratified by Methodist annual conferences in 1958. Amendment IX provided a way to abolish the Central Jurisdiction by transferring black Methodist church and annual conferences out of the Central Jurisdiction into overlapping regional annual and jurisdictional conferences. Brawley supported desegregation, but in the commission's deliberations he opposed establishing a target date for the abolition of the Central Jurisdiction. Brawley, while anxious to see desegregation begin, wanted the church to make a greater commitment to change in order to prevent token desegregation.

Desegregation also presented new challenges to historically black colleges, which found themselves being judged by the standards of white institutions, whether they had comparable financial resources or not. Clark College was among the first fifteen African American colleges accredited by the Southern Association of Schools and Colleges when it began receiving these institutions into full membership in 1957. During the 1960 student sit-ins, Brawley joined with other black college presidents in Atlanta to support the students. While he was very concerned about the safety of the protesting students and refused to cancel classes, he urged faculty members to make allowances for student participants. When white business leaders urged him to discipline student demonstrators, Brawley instead praised the students' courage and condemned further segregation by the businesses.

Between 1960 and 1964 Brawley served as vice chair of another Methodist commission regarding race, the Commission of Thirty-six. The purpose of this commission was to speed the use of Amendment IX, but its first plan to accomplish this encountered black Methodist opposition. At a special meeting of Central Jurisdiction's leaders in March 1962 held in Cincinnati, Ohio, Brawley gave the keynote speech. He stressed that white Methodists were trying to speed the use of Amendment IX in other parts of the country while there was no plan to ensure eventual desegregation in the South. Moreover, the church had not convinced its African Americans that it was committed to abolish all areas of segregation, including church-related institutions. In 1963 Brawley wrote a memorandum to the entire Commission of Thirty-Six outlining why the Central Jurisdiction still held back from using Amendment IX. At the 1964 General Conference held in Pittsburgh, Pennsylvania, the Methodist Church took actions to answer many of the concerns outlined by Brawley. The Central Jurisdiction met for the last time in 1967.

After his retirement as president of Clark College in 1965, Brawley wrote two books about African American higher education. *Two Centuries of Methodist Concern: Bondage, Freedom, and Education of Black People* (1974) chronicled the Methodists' work in higher education for African Americans. In 1977 he completed *The Clark College Legacy: An Interpretive History of Relevant Education, 1869–1975*. Brawley died on 3 December 1985 in Atlanta, Georgia. In September 1984 the Atlanta City Council honored him by renaming Chestnut Street, a major street that runs adjacent to Clark College and Atlanta University, James P. Brawley Drive.

As a college dean and president in the early and mid-twentieth century, Brawley was part of a small group of influential African American educational leaders. Although Brawley was not as well known as other African American college presidents such as JOHN HOPE, he was remarkably adept at moving a small and relatively weak institution into a position of strength.

Brawley's leadership guided Clark College through difficult times to make it a strong African American educational institution. His successful stewardship of resources and his recruitment of talented faculty, such as the young sociologist CHARLES ERIC LINCOLN, eventually contributed to the merger of Clark College and Atlanta University in 1987 that created Clark Atlanta University. More than any other African American lay Methodist, Brawley worked to develop a policy of racial inclusiveness that reached through all levels of the church. Born and educated in the Jim Crow South, he prepared more than a generation of African American leaders for the day when civil rights would create new opportunities in American society and in Methodism. He was a model of industry and moral rectitude, and he never wavered in his faith in a desegregated society or in his belief that education was the key to African American success.

FURTHER READING

An extensive collection of Brawley's papers is available at the Atlanta University Center Archives. These papers cover his career as an educator, a Methodist layman, and a resident of Atlanta, Georgia.

Murray, Peter C. *Methodists and the Crucible of Race, 1930-1975* (2004).

PETER C. MURRAY

Braxton, Anthony (Delano) (4 June 1945–), composer and multi-instrumentalist specializing in alto saxophone and contrabass clarinet, was born in Chicago to Clarence Dunbar Braxton Sr., a railroad worker, and Julia Samuels Braxton. Braxton experienced a rich childhood centered in Chicago's Washington Park neighborhood. His parents and his stepfather, Lawrence Fouche, imbued Braxton and his siblings with values of tolerance and perseverance. Exposed to a wide range of popular media, Braxton developed an early interest in rock and roll, particularly CHUCK BERRY and FRANKIE LYMON, and he sang in his Baptist church's choir. He had begun to play clarinet at about the age of eleven, and in high school became interested in jazz and the alto sax. In 1959 he entered the Chicago Vocational High School, in part because of his interest in technology.

Through his teens, Braxton studied both jazz and European classical music at the Chicago School of Music of Roosevelt University. In 1963 he graduated from high school and enrolled in Wilson Junior College, where he met musicians like Jack DeJohnette, Henry Threadgill, Joseph Jarman, and Roscoe Mitchell. He was drafted into the U.S. military in 1963 and became a member of the army band, stationed at Fort Sheridan in Highland Park, Illinois. He returned to Chicago regularly to continue his musical pursuits, practicing up to six hours a day, and intermittently taking courses in music history and theory at Roosevelt from 1964 to 1968.

Early on Braxton nurtured an interest in free jazz and musicians like JOHN COLTRANE. In 1965–1966, while stationed in Korea, he discovered the music of Arnold Schoenberg, which emphasized line and rhythm, qualities he saw as central to the African American musical heritage. Returning to Chicago in the fall of 1966, he joined the Association for Advancement of Creative Musicians (AACM) under the sponsorship of Roscoe Mitchell, a core member of the group. MUHAL RICHARD ABRAMS, the organization's key figure, became an important mentor and influence. Braxton also extended his study of European composers like Schoenberg, Edgar Varese, Anton Webern, and particularly John Cage. He became politically active, joining the Congress of Racial Equality (CORE) and reading widely in philosophy, religion, and radical political literature, sources that helped shape his musical style. Philosophically, he accentuated the spiritual basis of modernist jazz language, a "sacred-sonic linkage" (Radano, 69) between the spiritual and the world of sound. He also came under the influence of musicians like JACKIE MCLEAN, Lee Konitz, Warne

Marsh, and Paul Desmond. In 1966 Braxton made his first appearance on record, on Abrams's *Levels and Degrees of Light*. In 1967 he formed his own group, Creative Construction Company, a trio with violinist Leroy Jenkins and trumpeter Leo Smith. In 1968 he released his first album under his own name, *3 Compositions for New Jazz*, with Jenkins, Smith, and Abrams on piano. Considered one of the more innovative recordings of the period, it overturned some of the most basic assumptions of jazz practice.

Nevertheless, Braxton received little critical attention and less work. He was forced to take jobs at a Pepsi-Cola bottling plant and at the Roosevelt University library. In 1969 he and several other members of the AACM moved to Paris, where he enjoyed some public success and critical acclaim, although on the whole neither listeners nor critics understood or appreciated his music. In 1970 he returned to New York, where he briefly joined Musica Elettronica Viva, an Italian improvisational ensemble. He also joined Circle, the avant-garde group that included pianist Chick Corea, bassist Dave Holland, and drummer Jack DeJohnette. In appearances and recordings with the group, Braxton pursued a black-based modernism that extended the association of art and the sacred, honoring the tradition, yet testing its boundaries. While performing with Circle in London in 1971, he also recorded some of his own compositions on *The Complete Braxton*, a recording that reflected the integration of improvisation and modernist compositional material.

In 1968 Braxton recorded *For Alto*, a double-record set that was the first-ever recording of solo alto saxophone improvisations. The album is filled with instrumental shouts and screeches and other experiments in sound, phrasing that revealed the influence of Coltrane, and a lyricism that affirmed the legacy of Desmond. A critical success, the recording also brought a measure of financial stability, allowing Braxton to devote more time to composition. Throughout the 1970s he maintained a working quartet with drummer Barry Altschul, bassist Holland, and either trombonist GEORGE LEWIS or trumpeter Kenny Wheeler; this group appeared on the Arista albums recorded in the mid-1970s that confirmed Braxton's status as the leading avant-garde figure of his day. By 1974 Braxton had married Nickie Singer, who became his creative partner, copying scores, doing the photography for some of his albums, and creating costumes for projects like the Trillium operas.

Though Braxton would record for the Arista label at least in part to gain financial independence and support his family (the couple would have three children, and Braxton had another from an earlier relationship), his albums *New York, Fall 1974* (1974), *Five Pieces* (1975), and *Creative Orchestra Music* (1976) were creative gems. *New York, Fall 1974*, a collection of six- and seven-minute compositions that ranged from boppish improvisations to modernist sound experiments, sold more than twenty thousand copies, and *Creative Orchestra Music* won *Down Beat* magazine's Best Album Award for 1977, highlighted by its parodic, celebratory parade march.

The success of these albums allowed Braxton to record more of his own concert music, though mostly at his own expense. And the resultant albums for Arista, *For Trio* (1977), *For Four Orchestras* (1978), and *For Two Pianos* (1980), though aesthetically triumphant, were much less successful both commercially and critically. Braxton viewed jazz as only part of what he did; *Four Orchestras*, for instance, was the first of a projected series for six, eight, and up to one hundred orchestras playing in different cities, linked by satellite. Other recordings from the period emanated from the jazz tradition. These included recordings for HatHut with MAX ROACH, *Birth and Rebirth* and *Two in One* (both 1979); a second solo recording, *Alto Saxophone Improvisations* (1979, Arista); and *Performance 9-1-79* (HatArt) with a new group of the trombonist Ray Anderson, the violinist John Lindberg, and the bassist Thurman Barker. Braxton also played with a variety of European avant-garde groups, including Company and the Globe Unity Orchestra, and he made the first of a series of recordings with synthesizer player and composer Richard Teitelbaum.

Braxton lived and worked in New Haven from 1983 to 1985, joined the faculty at Mills College in 1986, and was appointed to a tenured position at Wesleyan University in 1990. From 1985 to 1994 he led a quartet with Marilyn Crispell on piano, Gerry Hemingway on drums and percussion, and Mark Dresser on bass. The group toured and recorded extensively. Their most notable recordings are a series of concerts in England at Coventry, London, and Birmingham, and at Willisau in Germany, which showcased musicians with a seemingly telepathic anticipation of each other's musical direction. This was avant-garde music both virtuosic and accessible even to the mildly adventurous. He continued his interest in large-scale ensembles with 1989's *Eugene*, perhaps his most approachable large

piece, and he recorded albums with British avant-garde saxophonist Evan Parker and trombonist Paul Rutherford.

Braxton also continued to explore the African American tradition in a "stylist" fashion, taking the music of past masters and reimagining it, on long series of recordings: 1985's *Seven Standards*, a tribute to CHARLIE PARKER, MILES DAVIS, and THELONIOUS MONK; *Six Monk Compositions*, a 1987 tribute; a 1989 album of Lennie Tristano compositions, recorded as a tribute to Tristano's student Warne Marsh; the 1993 sextet recording of the *Charlie Parker Project*; and the quartet album *Nine Standards* (1993), a profound statement on the music of John Coltrane. Most unusual, perhaps, is *14 Compositions* (1996), consisting of fourteen tunes from the first half of the century, including "Rosetta" and "Stardust."

In 1994 Braxton was awarded a MacArthur Grant; he used a portion of the award to establish the New York–based, nonprofit Tri-Centric Foundation. He also began to play the piano in concerts and on a series of small-group recordings, and in 1995 he recorded a solo piano album. Also in 1995 Braxton began to compose his "Ghost Trance Music," a style that involved interaction between notated and improvised materials and sought to bring together Native American and Eastern ritual, often creating a dream-like, meditative atmosphere. In 1997 he founded his own label, Braxton House, on which he released recordings of ensembles of varied sizes, often with Wesleyan students, and pieces that embraced his fondness for multimedia experiments, such as "Composition No. 102 for Orchestra and Puppet Theatre." During these years he also composed a two-act musical, and he embarked on a projected series of thirty-six operas, *Trillium*. These works were satirical portrayals of a Western culture undermined by materialism, contrasted with African American and world group cultures that remain rooted in spiritual values. He continued to record prolifically during the first years of the twenty-first century.

As an improviser, performer, and composer, Braxton explored the widest possible range of musical styles, from the earliest days of jazz to Schoenberg and the aleatory music of John Cage, and moved beyond them to create his own restructuralist music that drew new musical maps for the future. He wrote music for seemingly every possible performance combination, from solo instruments to huge ensembles, and he explored the integration of music with puppetry, theater, video, and cinema. Intellectually and in practice, he completely rejected the validity and constraint of traditional musical categories. His work was rooted in the African American musical tradition, in the conception of black music as the embodiment of the African American collective memory. For Braxton, music was far more than a duplication or extension of the past. Music was a force for social change, a creator of alternative universes.

FURTHER READING

Lock, Graham. *Blutopia: Visions of the Future and Revisions of the Past in the Works of Sun Ra, Duke Ellington, and Anthony Braxton* (1999).

Lock, Graham. *Forces in Motion: The Music and Thoughts of Anthony Braxton* (1998).

Radano, Ronald. *New Musical Figurations: Anthony Braxton's Cultural Critique* (1994).

RONALD DUFOUR

Brazier, Arthur (22 July 1921–22 Oct. 2010), community organizer and Pentecostal bishop, was born in a Hyde Park apartment on Chicago's South Side. His parents were among the waves of African Americans who migrated from the South to the North in pursuit of greater economic opportunity and social mobility during the Great Migration. His mother, Geneva, was a household domestic and lay Pentecostal preacher, eventually leading the Universal Church of Christ in Chicago. His father, Robert, was a maintenance man at the Hyde Park Laundry Company from 1921 to 1940. One of five children, Brazier grew up in a highly segregated black community, since restrictive covenants bound blacks to certain areas of the city.

From his early teenage years, Brazier worked whenever he wasn't in school, first as a milkman's helper for the Bowman Dairy Company and later as a parking attendant at the Chicago World's Fair in 1933 and 1934. During the Depression, Brazier was forced to drop out of Wendell Phillips High School after only one year to work at the laundry with his father and to take a job as a delivery boy for a drugstore. When he was drafted into the army in 1942, he saw it as an opportunity to see the world and escape the poverty of his urban environment.

His experience in the army (1942–1945) was transformative. While stationed with an all-black unit (the 2033d Quarter Master Unit attached to the Fifty-Second Air Service Group) in Ripley, Tennessee, Brazier had his first encounter with southern-style Jim Crow. Although clear racial borders demarcated Chicago, Brazier was struck by the difference between the socially accepted segregation in the North and the legally enforced segregation he found in the South. However, when Brazier toured in Burma and India with the army, he was shocked to find even more extreme levels of poverty and social stratification. "India gave me my first glimpse of what life must have been like during the time of Christ," Brazier explained (Dortch, 29). Brazier's experiences in South Asia not only cultivated his appreciation for American opportunity but also made him more acutely aware of oppression and class divisions in other countries.

After he left the army, Brazier worked as a welder, a molder's helper at Western Electric, and a postal carrier. Throughout this fifteen-year period, Brazier also cultivated his professional profile as a minister. In 1947 he was baptized at the Apostolic Pentecostal Church of Morgan Park. That same year he met his wife, Esther Isabel Holmes, with whom he had four children: Lola, Byrson, Janice, and Rosalyn. In 1960 he left the United States Postal Service to enter the ministry full time. Although Brazier believed in the driving theological principles of Pentecostalism, he was constantly at war with his parents' conservative Pentecostalism, which emphasized external behavior and constructed elaborate prohibitions against smoking, certain types of clothing, makeup, and dancing. Brazier disdained such exclusionary regulations and developed his own progressive Pentecostalism after attending evening classes at the Moody Bible Institute from 1955 to 1961, where he gained a critical understanding of the Bible. Unlike most Pentecostals, who tend to eschew involvement with worldly matters, Brazier believed that those bent on personal salvation could not ignore the problems of the world. "The soul cannot be dealt with as a separate entity divorced from the body," Brazier wrote (*Black Self-Determination*, 133). He pointed to Jesus's concern for the poor to argue that if an individual needed food or housing or clothing, he or she could not be expected to work toward salvation (*Black Self-Determination*, 130).

Brazier also decided to enter political life against the counsel of his own tradition because he believed that Jesus modeled a theology that demanded spiritual salvation combined with worldly restoration. Upon graduation from Moody Bible Institute, Brazier began the aggressive implementation of his spiritual mission. He took a position at the Apostolic Church of God in the Woodlawn area of town. Located near the University of Chicago, Woodlawn was on a steady decline, experiencing increased levels of crime, poverty, and unemployment. Without a vigorous community response, Woodlawn would become a major slum. Saul Alinsky, the famed community organizer and founder of the Industrial Areas Foundation (IAF), had targeted Woodlawn as the next cite for IAF mobilization. IAF provided technical services to community residents who wanted to organize themselves. During a chance encounter at the Apostolic Church of God, one of Alinsky's operatives saw Brazier at work among his congregants and subsequently introduced the two men. Brazier began working with a local IAF-backed group, the Temporary Woodlawn Organization (TWO) and soon became the official spokesman for TWO. TWO functioned as an operational center for several community institutions and social welfare organizations. During the early 1960s TWO focused on three issues: preventing the University of Chicago from land development in Woodlawn; squelching the growing gang wars between the Blackstone Rangers and the East Side Disciples; and protesting school and housing segregation. TWO attracted national acclaim and was described by one journalist as "the most impressive experiment affecting the Negro anywhere in the U.S." (*Fortune* [Mar. 1962], 140).

According to Brazier, the people of Woodlawn did not need to fight for political power; they simply needed to claim the power that was already theirs. "Nobody, including the government, has the right to make plans and dictate arrangements for whole populations," he announced in a 1961 TWO press release. "We are not asking for our rights. We are asking them to respect our rights, and we are telling them that if they do not respect our rights we will defend ourselves against them." This combination of political pragmatism and righteous rage won Brazier a large following in his own community and respect from the city's political leaders. As spokesman and eventually president of TWO, Brazier never demanded anything beyond the scope of the law. He focused on bringing desegregation and economic opportunity to one small community. This focus brought grassroots success, but little national recognition to Brazier. When MARTIN LUTHER KING JR. came to lead the Chicago Freedom Movement (CFM) in the summer of 1966, Brazier and TWO participated in his marches, yet continued to protect their relationship with Mayor Daley and their local accomplishments. King's disappointment with the CFM is usefully contrasted with Brazier's persistent local success. Whereas King arrived in Chicago without much northern denominational familiarity or sensitivity to the urban political machine, Brazier was a rapacious precinct worker, respected in the dominating evangelical black churches as well as in city hall.

In 1969 Brazier authored a study of TWO and outlined his faith in black self-determination. "America cannot keep down thirty million people who are moving up, without destroying the entire nation in the process," he concluded (*Black Self-determination*, 147). Throughout the 1970s and 1980s Brazier continued to fight for better conditions in the Woodlawn community. He chaired the Woodlawn Preservation and Investment Corporation and the Fund for Community Redevelopment and Revitalization. Later he was vice president of the Center for Community Change, a Washington, D.C., think tank that provided technical assistance through the Community Development Corporation on large-scale housing and commercial projects throughout the country. However, Brazier never forgot his Chicago congregation. Founded on Easter Sunday 1963 the Apostolic Church of God grew to more than eighteen thousand parishioners by 2004. With his emphasis on spiritual salvation and material ministry, Brazier was pivotal in the church's growth and continued development. Named bishop of the Pentecostal Assemblies of the World in 1976, Brazier established himself as a key figure in the rapid growth of African American Pentecostalism. He died in Chicago at the age of eighty-nine.

FURTHER READING

Brazier, Arthur. *Black Self-determination: The Story of the Woodlawn Organization* (1969).

Brazier, Arthur. *From Milk to Meat: A Primer for Christian Living* (1996).

Anderson, Alan B., and George W. Pickering. *Confronting the Color Line: The Broken Promise of the Civil Rights Movement in Chicago* (1986).

Dortch, Sammie M. *When God Calls: A Biography of Bishop Arthur Brazier* (1996).

Fish, John. *Black Power/White Control: The Struggle of the Woodlawn Organization in Chicago* (1973).

Ralph, James, Jr. *Northern Protest: Martin Luther King Jr., Chicago, and the Civil Rights Movement* (1993).

KATHRYN LOFTON

Breedlove, Sarah. *See* Walker, Madam C. J.

Brent, Linda. *See* Jacobs, Harriet.

Brewer, John Mason (24 Mar. 1896–24 Jan. 1975), teacher, historian, and folklorist, was born in Goliad, Texas, one of five children of John Henry Brewer, a cattle drover, and Minnie Tate Brewer, a teacher. John Mason grew up with his three sisters, Jewel, Marguerite, Gladys, and his brother Claude in a household that provided a fertile environment for his imagination. His father told exciting stories about his adventures on the cattle drives from the Media Luna Ranch in Texas to the cattle market in Kansas. His mother, a teacher in Texas for over forty years, read the poetry of PAUL LAURENCE DUNBAR to John Mason during his early childhood. As an adult poet, Dr. Brewer would write dialect verse in the manner of Dunbar. Dr. Brewer's love for the oral tradition in African American culture was also nurtured by his grandfathers, Joe Brewer and Pinckney Mitchell, who told him folktales. John Mason developed a strong interest in folklore and devoted more than forty years of his life to gathering, collecting, and preserving folklore in Texas and elsewhere in the South.

When Brewer was seven years old, his family moved to Austin, Texas, to take advantage of the schools and to pursue better job opportunities. He graduated from Austin's black high school and enrolled at Wiley College in Marshall, Texas. He received a bachelor of arts degree in 1917 and taught school in Austin for a year. Then in 1918 he joined the American Expeditionary Forces and was sent to France with the rank of corporal. Fluent in French, Spanish, and Italian, Brewer served as an interpreter for his brigade officers. After the war, he accepted a principalship in Fort Worth, Texas, but he left that post in 1924 to take a job with an oil company in Denver, Colorado, where he wrote for the company's trade journal. However, he soon lost interest in that job and returned to teaching, serving briefly as a principal in Shreveport, Louisiana.

Brewer devoted over fifty years of his life to teaching, mostly at the college level. In the 1920s and 1930s he taught creating writing at Tillotson College in Austin, and Romance languages at Samuel Huston College, also in Austin; the two institutions would later merge to become Huston-Tillotson University. Brewer taught one year (1942) at Claflin College in Orangeburg, South Carolina, and then returned to Austin. From 1943 to 1959 he served as chair of the Department of English at Huston-Tillotson College (later University); from 1959 to 1969 he taught English at Livingston College in Salisbury, North Carolina. From 1969 until his death in 1975 Brewer served as distinguished visiting professor of English at East Texas State University (later Texas A&M University at Commerce). His students from the East Texas State period remembered him as a brilliant, entertaining

lecturer. Brewer and his wife, Ruth Helen, frequently invited students to their home near campus for socials and weekend parties. He was one of the most popular professors at East Texas State, and his classes were always fully enrolled.

Brewer's engagement with folklore as an academic discipline began in 1932 when he sought advice from J. Frank Dobie. A noted professor and author, Dobie was also secretary of the Texas Folklore Society. After reading Brewer's shoebox full of folktales, Dobie arranged to have the tales published in the Texas Folklore Society's annual yearbook. Brewer joined the Texas Folklore Society, launching his long and distinguished career as a folklorist. He published his work in four of the Texas Folklore Society's yearbooks. Brewer's professional affiliations also included membership in the American Folklore Society, which elected him second vice president.

In 1933 he began his formal study of folklore under Dr. Stith Thompson at the University of Indiana, where he earned his master of arts degree in 1950. Brewer's master's thesis, entitled "Negro Preacher Tales of the Brazos Bottoms," was published by the University of Texas Press in 1953 (and republished, in an expanded version, in 1976). Paul Quinn College in Waco, Texas, awarded Brewer an honorary Doctor of Literature at its August Convocation in 1951. As an expression of his appreciation, Brewer established the Minnie Tate Brewer Creative Writing and Oral Literature Prize at Paul Quinn College.

Although Brewer never learned to drive an automobile, beginning in 1925 he managed to collect folklore in Texas as well as in the Carolinas and throughout the South. He also pursued an interest in African American history, and he enjoyed writing poetry. His 1936 book, *The Negro in Texas*, remains a classic in Texas history. *Negrito: Negro Dialect Poems*, published in 1932, reflected his early exposure to the dialect poetry of Paul Laurence Dunbar. In 1945 Brewer published *Humorous Folktales of the South Carolina Negro*. But his best-known collection, *The Word on the Brazos: Negro Preacher Tales from the Brazos Bottoms of Texas*, illustrated by JOHN BIGGERS, was published by the University of Texas Press in 1953. In the Brazos Bottoms, the Holy Bible was known as "the Word." J. Frank Dobie, Brewer's friend and mentor, praised the collection for the humanity that informs the characters. In his brief introduction to the collection, Brewer compared the preacher tales to medieval exempla, narratives that illustrated or confirmed a moral or lesson. The tales also revealed the humorous side of the Brazos Bottom Negroes, especially in the comic anecdotes that poked fun at preachers who craved status and control over the folk.

The fifty-six tales in *The Word on the Brazos* covered a variety of themes, touching on cultural history, the trickster figure, and values. The tales stood as a testament to the survival of blacks in the Brazos Bottoms and celebrated the richness of their culture. Like ZORA NEALE HURSTON, Brewer developed an excellent ear for a variety of African American dialects. He captured the nuances of the oral performance in tales such as "A Sermon, a Cat, and a Churn." In that tale, the speaker recalled the harsh working conditions that prevailed on the plantations after Emancipation. Brewer's transcription went beyond the quaint spellings that characterized black dialect recorded by less able folklorists. Brewer's rendering of the dialect not only recorded the sounds of the speech but also conveyed a sense of the speech rhythms typical of the blacks in the Brazos Bottoms. In another tale, entitled "Mulatto Boys and the Religious Test," light-skinned black men passed for white in order to get better jobs. The trickster figure was highlighted in "The Preacher who Walked on Water," a satirical tale about a preacher who devised a scheme to make his parishioners believe he could walk on water. However, the preacher's trick was exposed when pranksters removed his submerged platform, causing him to sink when he stepped into the water. The tales in *The Word on the Brazos* were entertaining, to be sure, but they also documented the social and cultural history of the African Americans who lived in the Brazos Bottoms in the early twentieth century.

In 1958 Brewer published another major collection of tales titled *Dog Ghosts and Other Texas Negro Tales.* Illustrated again by Brewer's friend, Dr. John Biggers, an art professor at Texas Southern University, *Dog Ghosts* featured tales on a variety of subjects, including slavery, animals, ranch life, religion, and dog ghosts and spirits. There were sixty-three tales in the collection, but only eighteen tales dealt specifically with dog ghosts. Like *The Word on the Brazos*, the *Dog Ghosts* collection was a repository of cultural history, social history, and values. The dog ghost tales usually concerned deceased family members who came back from the dead in the form of a dog to assist the living. For example, in "The Oak Cliff Dog Ghost" a man's dead wife returned every year on the day she died and brought him a ten-dollar bill. Although *Dog Ghosts and Other Stories* explored serious topics such as slavery, the humorous tone made the tales a pleasure to read.

Brewer published several books of folklore in addition to *The Word on the Brazos* and *Dog Ghosts and Other Stories.* These included the delightful *Aunt Dicy Tales* (1956), *Worser Days and Better Times* (1964), and an anthology, *American Negro Folklore* (1968), for which he received the Chicago Book Fair Award, and he was among the Texas writers who received the Twenty-First Annual Writers Roundup award in 1969. Brewer also published many scholarly essays and newspaper articles. Dr. J. Mason Brewer left an impressive body of work that deserves further study. He died in Fort Worth.

FURTHER READING

Byrd, James W. *J. Mason Brewer: Negro Folklorist.* Southwestern Writers Series, no. 12. (1967).

Byrd, James W. "In Memory of John Mason Brewer (1896–1975)," *CLA Journal* 18 (June 1975).

Thomas, Lorenzo. "The African-American Folktale and J. Mason Brewer," in *Juneteenth Texas: Essays in African American Folklore*, ed. Francis E. Abernethy, et al. (1996).

Turner, Darwin T. "J. Mason Brewer: Vignettes," *CLA Journal* 18 (June 1975).

ELVIN HOLT

Brewster, William Herbert (2 July 1897?–15 Oct. 1987), gospel composer and pastor, was born into a family of sharecroppers in Somerville, Tennessee. Although Brewster stemmed from a humble background, he managed to study a wide variety of subjects, including theology, law, and Hebrew. After graduating from Roger Williams College in 1922 he moved to Memphis, Tennessee. By 1930 Brewster had begun a lifelong tenure as pastor of the East Trigg Baptist Church. A major aspect of Brewster's early ministry centered on the founding of theology schools, and these centers of learning helped to establish his voice as one of moral authority and spiritual guidance in religious circles.

By the time Brewster began seriously publishing his songs in the 1940s, he had gained over a decade of experience in his pastoral role. This experience provided a wellspring of material for songs that often relayed Old Testament stories and were enjoyed by African American congregations across the United States. Drawing on the gospel blues style of Thomas Dorsey, Brewster composed "I'm Leaning and Depending on the Lord" in 1939 and published it two years later. During this time, he made it a priority to write scripts and songs for pageants and biblical dramas, genres to which he had been exposed through attendance at National Baptist Conventions. His best-known biblical drama, a historical piece titled *From Auction Block to Glory*, was written in 1941. This play represented a move away from a primary reliance on Negro spirituals and toward the use of modern gospel music in African American religious dramas. Brewster was the first to compose gospel songs specifically for biblical plays that appeared before a racially mixed, national audience. His success in writing music and scripts for black religious pageants would have a profound impact on American writers such as LANGSTON HUGHES, OSSIE DAVIS, and Micki Grant.

Brewster refined many compositional devices that distinguished his gospel songs from those of his predecessors. By creatively manipulating the rhythm of a melodic line, changing tempos from one section of a piece to another, and occasionally employing a waltz time feel—as he did in "Surely God Is Able"—Brewster was able to maximize the emotional effect his songs had on listeners. His most often cited compositional contribution is the use of a repetitive section, known as the "vamp" or "drive," which provided a relatively stable harmonic texture on which singers could improvise mini-sermons as a song grew in intensity. Such vamp sections were particularly popular among the many Holiness congregations within the Memphis-based African American Pentecostal organization, the Church of God in Christ.

By 1943 several vocal ensembles began to embrace Brewster's compositions and incorporate them into their repertoires. Brewster himself also put together vocal groups to perform his songs, and he often showcased a talented young singer named "Queen" Candace Anderson, who would influence legendary singers such as CLARA WARD and MAHALIA JACKSON. The Brewsteraires, featuring Anderson, were heard regularly on African American radio stations such as WDIA, which also ran Brewster's program, *Camp Meeting in the Air*. Singers such as Dorothy Love Coates, the Soul Stirrers, and Elvis Presley also credited Brewster's radio programs with influencing their musical and professional development. The gospel singer Mahalia Jackson became an immediate sensation after recording Brewster's "Move on up a Little Higher" in 1948. Eventually, the song sold 2 million copies, becoming the first million-selling recording

in the history of gospel music. The following year, Brewster's prosperity continued, as Clara Ward's rendition of "Surely God Is Able" also sold over 1 million copies. Throughout the subsequent decade and a half, Clara Ward and the Ward Sisters built their career on Brewster's compositions. Their versions of pieces such as "God's Amazing Love," "The Old Landmark," and "How I Got Over" were enormous hits with African American audiences.

The 1940s and 1950s were Brewster's most fruitful decades, and he composed several songs that would eventually become gospel classics. He achieved unprecedented fame and became the most prolific and influential gospel songwriter of the post–World War II era. Along with LUCIE CAMPBELL, Brewster was also a pivotal figure who facilitated a stylistic transition from the jubilee style of quartet singing to the modern brand of sacred song that flourished during gospel's golden age from 1940 to 1960. He became one of the first gospel superstars, influencing generations of audiences and performers through songs that provided expressive vehicles for both amateur and professional gospel performers.

Often hailed as the greatest American gospel songwriter, Brewster was admired by both his contemporaries and successors, who sometimes referred to him affectionately as "Old Man" Brewster. His songs are appreciated for their lyrical and musical content, as well as their implicit social and political messages, which predated the civil rights movement of the 1960s. Indeed, songs such as "I'm Climbing Higher and Higher" speak to the need for social uplift and justice while resonating with Christian aspirations to reach heaven. For his many contributions to the musical and social landscapes of American society, Brewster was honored by the Smithsonian in 1982. He continued to work as pastor of East Trigg Baptist Church and as musical mentor to countless others until his death.

FURTHER READING

Boyer, Horace Clarence. *How Sweet the Sound: The Golden Age of Gospel* (1995).

Cusic, Don. *The Sound of Light: A History of Gospel Music* (1990).

Darden, Robert. *People Get Ready!: A New History of Black Gospel Music* (2004).

Heilbut, Anthony. *The Gospel Sound: Good News and Bad Times* (1971).

Lornell, Kip. *Happy in the Service of the Lord: African-American Sacred Vocal Harmony Quartets in Memphis* (1995).

Reagan, Bernice Johnson, ed. *We'll Understand It Better By and By: Pioneering African American Gospel Composers* (1992).

MELVIN L. BUTLER

Brice, Carol Lovette (16 Apr. 1918–15 Feb. 1985), contralto concert singer, recording artist, and professor, was born in Indianapolis, Indiana, the youngest of four children born to the Reverend Dr. John Brice, a 1904 graduate of Knoxville College who served as a chaplain during World War I. He was a Congregationalist minister and served as vice president and religious director at Palmer Memorial Institute for thirty years, retiring in 1950. Her mother, Ella Hawkins, also of Knoxville College, was an educator and musician who taught history and pursued a career as a singer. She spent so much time on the road that Brice and her siblings were taken by her father when she was only eighteen months old to Sedalia, North Carolina, and placed in the custody of her first cousin, Dr. CHARLOTTE HAWKINS BROWN, whom Brice called "Aunt." Dr. Brown was the founder and president of Palmer Memorial Institute. The institute was the only finishing school for blacks in the United States. By the age of three Brice's singing voice was exceptional, and as an early student at Palmer she toured the country with the Sedalia Singers.

In 1930, at the age of thirteen, Brice won a cup for the best contralto voice at a North Carolina music festival. The following year she appeared with the Sedalia Singers at Town Hall in New York City and later performed in such places as Symphony Hall in Boston and the White House. The group served as the major fund-raising arm of Palmer Memorial Institute and it performed traditional Negro spirituals.

Brice graduated from the high school department of the institute in 1933 and completed Palmer Memorial Institute Junior College in 1935. There she became acquainted with numerous luminaries who visited the school, including W. E. B. DuBois, MARY McLeod Bethune, MARIAN ANDERSON, and First Lady Eleanor Roosevelt. With the aid of a Palmer Memorial Institute supporter and benefactress, Carrie L. Stone, Brice journeyed to Talladega College in Alabama, where she majored in music, studied under the noted voice teacher Frank G. Harrison, gave numerous concerts, joined the Alpha Kappa Alpha sorority, and received a bachelor of music degree. Upon graduation from Talladega she went to New York City, where her mother, who was now divorced, and her brother Jonathan were residing. She was a fellowship recipient to the Juilliard School of Music in New York (from 1939 to 1943), where she came under the tutelage of Francis Rogers.

In the summer of 1939 Brice received wide acclaim when she performed with BILL "BOJANGLES" ROBINSON in the musical *The Hot Mikado* at the New York World's Fair. There she met her future husband, Cornelius Wiley "Neil" Scott, a baritone in the chorus; they had two children before his death in 1967.

In the 1940s, as a versatile contralto Brice was able to attain recognition that was not as readily available to other black musicians at that time. Her voice was often compared to that of Marion Anderson and other giants of her day, and as an African American singer she succeeded in many firsts. She had the pleasure in January 1941 to sing at the third inauguration of President Franklin D. Roosevelt, which was one of the first times an African American performed at an inauguration. She was the first black singer to earn the prestigious Naumberg Foundation Award for young performers in 1943, a prize that included a recital at Town Hall in New York City on 13 March 1945. From here her career blossomed as she began to receive wide acclaim, not only as a contralto but also on stage. After the Town Hall concert, she performed with the Pittsburg Orchestra in 1945, with the Boston Symphony in 1946, and with the San Francisco Symphony in 1948. During the summer of 1950 she toured in South and Central America, singing in Puerto Rico, Curaçau, Venezuela, Brazil, Argentina, Ecuador, Chile, and Panama. From 1944 until 1977 she sang in recitals across the United States, most often accompanied on the piano by her brother, Jonathan.

In 1958 Brice formed a trio with her brothers Eugene, also a graduate of Juilliard, who performed in numerous Broadway productions, and Jonathan, who sang with the Robert Shaw Chorale and the New York City Opera. They called themselves the Brice Trio, and in 1958 they performed at Town Hall.

Brice's Broadway career included the roles of Addie in *Regina* (1959), Maude in *Finian's Rainbow* (1960), Queenie in *Showboat* (1961), HARRIET TUBMAN in *Gentlemen, Be Seated* (1963), and Maria in *Porgy and Bess* (1961, 1976). She was a member of the Vienna Volksoper from 1967 until 1971. Brice made a number of outstanding and much-praised recordings, as she was among the first black classical artists to record extensively in the United States. Her most noted recordings include Gustav Mahler's "Songs of a Wayfarer," with Fritz Reiner and the Pittsburg Orchestra; Falla's *El Amor Brujo*; *The Grass Harp* by Claibe Richardson; and her Grammy-winning recording of *Porgy and Bess* in 1976.

In 1968 Brice met the baritone Thomas Carey during a tour for the U.S. State Department in France. They were married the following year and together performed in *Porgy and Bess* throughout the world. Brice received numerous awards for her pioneering spirit and commitment to singing. In 1948 she was honored as the outstanding "Negro woman musician" by the National Council of Negro Women; in 1954 she was chosen one of Long Island, New York's, "Women of the Year." In 1955 her alma mater, Talladega College, awarded her with an honorary doctor of humane letters; in 1963 she was presented the Emancipation Proclamation Award by the National Association of Negro Musicians; and in 1965 she and her two brothers were honored at the Fifth Annual Founder's Day Program of the National Association of Negro Musicians, Eastern Region.

In 1973 Brice was appointed associate professor of music at the University of Oklahoma. In 1974 she and her husband founded the Cimarron Circuit Opera Company, which prospered under their leadership. In 1977 both Brice and Carey were named Oklahoma Musicians of the Year. Carol Brice died of cancer.

FURTHER READING

The Carol Brice Papers are at the Amistad Research Center at Tulane University in New Orleans, Louisiana. Also, a significant vertical file has been maintained at the Charlotte Hawkins Brown Museum at Historic Palmer Memorial Institute in Sedalia, North Carolina.

Burns-Vann, Tracey, and Andre D. Vann. *Sedalia and the Palmer Memorial Institute*, Black America Series (2004).

Marteena, Constance H. *The Lengthening Shadow of a Woman: A Biography of Charlotte Hawkins Brown* (1977).

Nettles, Darryl G. *African American Concert Singers before 1950* (2003).

Wadelington, Charles W., and Richard K. Knapp. *Charlotte Hawkins Brown and Palmer Memorial Institute: What One Young African American Woman Could Do* (1999).

ANDRE D. VANN

Bricktop (14 Aug. 1894–31 Jan. 1984), entertainer and nightclub operator, was born in Alderson, West Virginia, the daughter of Thomas Smith, a barber, and Hattie E. (maiden name unknown), a domestic worker. Christened Ada Beatrice Queen Victoria Louise Virginia, because her parents did not wish to disappoint the various neighbors and friends who offered suggestions for naming her, Bricktop received her nickname because of her red hair when she was in her late twenties from Barron Wilkins, owner of a nightclub called Barron's Exclusive Club in Prohibition-era Harlem.

Bricktop's father died when she was four, and her mother moved with the children to Chicago to be near relatives. Hattie Smith worked as a domestic in Chicago, and her children attended school. Bricktop showed early musical talent and interest in performing. She made her stage debut as a preschooler, playing the part of Eliza's son Harry in a production of *Uncle Tom's Cabin* at the Haymarket Theatre. As an adolescent, she had the opportunity to perform onstage again when she was hired as part of the chorus for a show at the Pekin Theatre. She quit school at age sixteen to pursue a career as an entertainer, first touring with (Flournoy) Miller and (Aubrey) Lyles, a well-known black comedy team. After the Miller and Lyles show folded, Bricktop toured with a variety of black vaudeville acts across the northern half of the United States. In the early 1920s she returned to Chicago and worked as a saloon performer at Roy Jones's and the Cafe Champ, owned by heavyweight champion JACK JOHNSON. In 1922 she went to Harlem, where

Bricktop, expatriate who ran nightclubs in Paris and Rome frequented by American celebrities, June 1934. (Library of Congress/Carl Van Vechten.)

she worked in Connie's Inn, among other night-clubs, and received her nickname. In 1924 she was invited to work in Paris at Le Grand Duc, a tiny club in Montmartre managed by EUGÈNE BULLARD, an African American pilot who had distinguished himself during World War I in the French Foreign Legion and the Lafayette Escadrille.

Never a great song stylist, Bricktop attracted the attention of white Americans in Paris because of her charming personality and her ability to make them feel at home. T. S. Eliot wrote a poem for her. F. Scott Fitzgerald liked to say, "My greatest claim to fame is that I discovered Bricktop before Cole Porter." But it was her discovery by Porter, who later wrote the song "Miss Otis Regrets" for her, that put the imprimatur of acceptance upon her. Under Porter's aegis, Bricktop became a darling of the American celebrity set in Paris. By the fall of 1926, Bricktop had opened the first Bricktop's nightclub in Paris, catering to such American luminaries as Fitzgerald, Elsa Maxwell, Tallulah Bankhead, Ernest Hemingway, and Barbara Hutton, and to international celebrities like the Aga Khan. "Everybody belonged, or else they didn't bother coming to Bricktop's more than once," she wrote in her autobiography.

A succession of Bricktop's nightclubs followed, both in Paris and, in the summertime, at Biarritz, where Bricktop claimed to have cradled the romance of the Duke of Windsor and the American divorcée Wallis Simpson. Among the careers she nurtured was that of the British-born black singer MABEL MERCER.

The stock market crash in the United States in October 1929 had no effect, at first, on the "gay" life in Paris. In December 1929 Bricktop married Peter Ducongé, an African American saxophonist from New Orleans, and the two purchased a country home in Bougival, outside Paris. Childless, each led an independent life, as well as sharing a life together. Some years after their marriage, however, Peter had an affair with a young African American singer whom Bricktop had taken under her wing in Paris. On learning of her husband's infidelity, Bricktop refused to sleep with him again, although she never divorced him. He died in 1967.

In 1939, as war in Europe and the invasion of France seemed imminent, the Duchess of Windsor (the former Wallis Simpson) and Lady Mendl (Elsie de Wolfe) helped Bricktop escape from Paris to New York, where her friend Mabel Mercer had already relocated. Mercer managed to find a niche as a singer in New York cabarets, but Bricktop's special talents as a self-described "saloonkeeper par excellence" went unappreciated. Bankrolled by the tobacco heiress Doris Duke, she relocated to Mexico City, where she successfully ran clubs until the war in Europe was over. In 1943 she converted to Catholicism and remained a devout Catholic for the rest of her life.

Returning to Paris in 1950, she found her old stomping grounds much changed, as was the clientele. After trying and failing to revive the prewar atmosphere, Bricktop removed to Rome, where on the Via Veneto from 1951 to 1965 she recreated the feeling of the old Bricktop's for a new celebrity crowd, primarily American film stars. The romance of Richard Burton and Elizabeth Taylor first made the gossip columns when they were seen together at the Rome Bricktop's during the filming of *Cleopatra*. To Bricktop, her career in Rome was secondary to the golden years in Paris, and she never fully accepted the Hollywood film stars as the nouveau royalty.

When Bricktop's older sister Blonzetta became ill in 1965, Bricktop returned to Chicago to nurse her and, after her death, went back to straighten out her affairs. Blonzetta left Bricktop a substantial inheritance. In her early seventies, Bricktop moved to Los Angeles, returned briefly to Europe, and then in 1970 settled in New York City. She made a recording of "So Long, Baby" with Cy Coleman, briefly ran a club owned by Huntington Hartford and then one called Soerabaja, and appeared from time to time at clubs in Chicago, at the Playboy Club in London, and at "21" in New York. Ill health caused her to cease working in 1979.

In August 1983 Bricktop published her autobiography, *Bricktop*, written with Jim Haskins. Five months later she died in New York City. To the end she was a lady of the dawn who drank only champagne and expected a rose from every male visitor.

FURTHER READING

Bricktop's papers are in the collection of the Schomburg Center for Research in Black Culture of the New York Public Library.

Boyle, Kay, and Robert Altman. *Being Geniuses Together, 1920–1930* (1968).

Haskins, Jim. *Mabel Mercer: A Life* (1968).

Obituary: *Rolling Stone*, 29 Mar. 1984.

This entry is taken from the *American National Biography* and is published here with the permission of the American Council of Learned Societies.

JIM HASKINS

Bridgewater, Cecil (10 Oct. 1942–), jazz trumpeter, composer, arranger, and educator, was born Cecil Vernon Bridgewater in Urbana, Illinois, into a family of musicians. His mother, Erma Pauline Scott Bridgewater, was the daughter of Ramon Mack Scott, who sang, played saxophone, piano, and drums, and led a band called Mack Scott and the Foot Warmers, in which Erma played piano for a time. Bridgewater's father, Cecil Bernard Bridgewater, played trumpet in the U.S. Navy band during World War II, and he was stationed at Great Lakes Naval Base with other African American musicians such as CLARK TERRY, Marshall Royal, Jerome Richardson, and others. Bridgewater's grandfather, Preston Bridgewater, played trumpet and cornet professionally with the circus.

When Cecil Bridgewater was a student at Marquette Grade School in Champaign, Illinois, the school's band director noticed his potential and encouraged his parents to find a private trumpet teacher for their son. Haskell Sexton, then head of the trumpet section at the University of Illinois School of Music, became Bridgewater's musical mentor from the time Bridgewater was thirteen years old through his high school and college years. Sexton took Bridgewater through the European classical tradition for trumpet and symphony orchestra, and even though Sexton admitted that he did not know much about the jazz tradition, he taught Bridgewater how to practice.

Bridgewater enlisted in the U.S. Army in 1964 and was accepted into the 25th Infantry Army Band. Eventually, Bridgewater ended up in Vietnam, stationed at Cu Chi, home of some of the famous network of hidden tunnels built by the North Vietnamese northwest of Saigon. He completed his stint in the army band in 1966. From 1968 to 1970 Bridgewater toured the Soviet Union and Europe with the University of Illinois band. In 1969 he formed the Bridgewater Brothers Band with his brother, the saxophonist Ronald Scott Bridgewater. They played and recorded together on and off until about 1989. Among these recordings was "Lightning and Thunder" (Denon, 1977) and "Bridgewater Brothers Generation Suite" (Denon, 1978).

In 1970 Bridgewater married Denise Eileen Garrett, a jazz singer who became known as DEE DEE BRIDGEWATER, and moved to New York City, where he joined the THAD JONES/Mel Lewis Jazz Orchestra, which he played in until 1976. This move put Bridgewater right in the middle of the "Loft Jazz" scene, where musicians were finding new places to create and play jazz outside of the mainstream venues. The Collective Black Artists (CBA) were renting out halls, publicizing their artistic goals, and creating a space for new jazz artists with the help of established musicians. Bridgewater's first daughter, Tulani Adenike Bridgewater, was born in 1972. Having divorced his first wife in 1975, Bridgewater married again, this time in 1977 to Mattie Bowman, with whom he would have a second daughter, Chelsea Amber Bridgewater.

Over the years, Bridgewater worked with many of the great musicians of the time: HORACE SILVER (in 1970), MAX ROACH (from 1971), ART BLAKEY (in 1972), JIMMY HEATH (from 1974 to 1976), LENA HORNE (from 1982 to 1983), Mercer Ellington (from 1985 to 1986), Grover Mitchell, Richard Davis, and the Count Basie Orchestra with Frank Foster. In 1970 Bridgewater recorded with the pianist Horace Silver for the Blue Note label on Silver's album *Total Response*, and in 1973 he played with the pianist McCOY TYNER on his *Song of the New World* and *Inner Voices*. Bridgewater's extensive recorded work with the drummer Max Roach includes *Cecil Bridgewater Nonet Plus* (1992) and *I Love Your Smile* (1993) for Mesa Blue Moon, *To The Max!* (1992) for Enja, and *Max Roach with the New Orchestra of Boston and the So What Brass Quintet* (1993) for Blue Note. In 1997 Bridgewater received a Grammy nomination for his arrangement of the song "Undecided" on Dee Dee Bridgewater's Grammy Award–winning album *Dear Ella*. Bridgewater joined the faculty of the Manhattan School of Music in 1991, and he also received commissions from the Cleveland Chamber Symphony, the Atlanta Arts Festival, the Jazzmobile, and Meet the Composers, which produced the *Cannonball Adderley Suite*, performed in Los Angles in 1994 and in Washington, D.C., in 1998. A consummate educator, Bridgewater's advice to aspiring jazz musicians was that there are two parts to taking care of business if they wanted to play. Part one is being "curious about every aspect of what [you] … do so [you] don't make the same mistakes that [your] elders made … don't overlook something out of ignorance." Part two of taking care of business was to "create places where the creative process can take place."

FURTHER READING
Joyce, Mike. "Cecil Bridgewater: Brassman's Holiday," *Washington Post*, 25 June 1993.
Joyce, Mike. "Trumpeter Bridgewater, Unmuted," *Washington Post*, 22 Mar. 2000.

Mathieson, Kenny. *Giant Steps: Bebop and the Creators of Modern Jazz 1945–65* (1999).

SUZANNE CLOUD

Bridgewater, Dee Dee (27 May 1950–), jazz singer, was born Denise Eileen Garrett in Memphis, Tennessee. Her father, Matthew Turner Garrett, was a jazz trumpeter and a teacher at Manassas High School in Memphis. He taught music to BOOKER LITTLE, CHARLES LLOYD, and George Coleman and during summers played with DINAH WASHINGTON's band. Her mother, Marion Hale Holiday, born in Flint, Michigan, was one of the first African Americans hired at the Flint unemployment office; she also worked as a legal secretary. When her parents divorced, Bridgewater's mother returned to Flint and raised her along with her sister, Rhonda Garrett Whiters.

During her early years in Flint, Bridgewater went to Southwestern High School, and at sixteen she joined an all-girl trio, modeled after the

Dee Dee Bridgewater, performing at London's Barbican Theatre in "Billie and Me," a Billie Holiday tribute concert 5 April 2004. (AP Images.)

Marvelettes, called the Iridescents and sang in local clubs in Flint. In 1968, when she was eighteen years old, the singer attended Michigan State University in East Lansing and sang in saxophonist Andy Courtridge's group. Bridgewater transferred to the University of Illinois at Urbana-Champaign at the urging of the university's band director. It was there that she met the trumpeter CECIL BRIDGEWATER, who was also a student. In 1969 they toured the Soviet Union and Eastern Europe with the University of Illinois Concert Jazz Band, and in 1970 they moved to New York City when he got a gig with HORACE SILVER's quintet. They married the same year. In 1971, when her husband joined the THAD JONES/Mel Lewis Jazz Orchestra, Dee Dee Bridgewater became its lead vocalist. In 1972 the Bridgewaters had a daughter, Tulani Adenike Bridgewater. Dee Dee Bridgewater's career took off after her debut with the famed New York jazz orchestra, and she began to perform with some of the legends of the 1940s, 1950s, and 1960s: SONNY ROLLINS, DIZZY GILLESPIE, DEXTER GORDON, and MAX ROACH. In 1974 Bridgewater recorded her classic first album, *Afro Blue*, with Cecil Bridgewater, Ron Bridgewater, George Mraz, and Roland Hanna. The twenty-four-year-old singer was not ready to be pigeon-holed by the jazz community, however, so she auditioned for the original Broadway production of *The Wiz* (an adaptation of the *Wizard of Oz*) and landed the role of Glinda the Good Witch. Her performance earned her the 1975 Tony Award for Best Featured Actress in a Musical.

Bridgewater divorced Cecil Bridgewater that year, and in 1976 she married the film and television director Gilbert Moses. She had a second daughter, China Nicole Moses, in 1978. Dee Dee Bridgewater toured the United States and France from 1983 to 1984 in the Broadway musical *Sophisticated Ladies* and then moved to Paris in 1986. The same year saw her starring in *Lady Day* as Billie Holiday, a role that garnered her a nomination for the Laurence Olivier Award. In 1989 Bridgewater divorced Gilbert Moses.

She returned to jazz in 1990, when she performed at the Montreux Jazz Festival. In 1991 she married the French concert promoter Jean-Marie Durand, and they had a son, Gabriel Morgan Durand, in 1992. In 1994 Bridgewater collaborated with the jazz composer/pianist Horace Silver and released the album *Love and Peace: A Tribute to Horace Silver* in 1995. Her tribute to ELLA FITZGERALD, *Dear Ella*, won Bridgewater a 1998 Grammy Award for best jazz vocal album, and another nomination followed for *Live at Yoshi's* in 2000. She also reconceptualized the music of Kurt Weill on her 2002 album for Verve called *This is New* and recorded a project of French classics called *J'ai Deux Amours* in 2005. She was the host of *JazzSet* for National Public Radio beginning in 2001 and also was one of the United Nations's (U.N.) first ambassadors for the Food and Agriculture Organization (FAO), a movement that grew out of the World Food Summit in 1996 and which pledged to end world hunger by 2015. Dee Dee became an ambassador in 1999 and visited food projects in Senegal. In 2002 she gave the greeting message on the occasion of World Food Day at the U.N. for the FAO. In 2007 Bridgewater released *Red Earth*, which she recorded in Barnako for the Emarcy Label.

FURTHER READING

Byrnes, Sholto. "Dreadlock Diva; Dee Dee Bridgewater Is a Force to be Reckoned With," *(London, England) Independent*, 10 May 2002.

Hunter, Al. "Don't Stick Her with 'Jazz' Label," *Philadelphia Daily News*, 13 Feb. 2004.

MacNeil, Jason. "Dee Dee Bridgewater: *J'ai Deux Amours*," *PopMatters* (21 Oct. 2005).

Ouellette, Dan "Six Questions with Dee Dee Bridgewater," *Billboard* (24 Sept. 2005).

Schudel, Matt. "Brilliance at Both Ends of the Jazz Universe," *Washington Post*, 7 May 2006.

Thomas, Jo. "Arts in America: A Singer Is Returning to a Stage Where It All Began," *New York Times*, 22 Sept. 1998.

SUZANNE CLOUD

Briggs, Bunny (22 Feb. 1922–), dancer, was born in Harlem, New York, to Alma Briggs and Bubba Jones. Born out of wedlock, "Baby" Briggs received no first name; however, his grandmother Abrella delighted in the toddler's quickness and nicknamed him "Bunny." The Briggs family gravitated toward entertainment. His mother, Alma, and her brothers held various jobs at Harlem hot spots, and her sister, Gladys, became a dancer (she was sometimes known as Gerry Wiley). The home was frequented by musicians and dancers, who used the space for socializing and rehearsing. The musicians JAMES P. JOHNSON and Kid Lippy practiced on the family's piano and played their rent parties, an important part of African American urban economy and social life, providing an evening of entertainment for a small admission. The Cotton Club performers Mordecai, Wells, and Taylor rehearsed there, exposing Briggs to the rhythms and footwork of

tap. Steeped in this atmosphere he became a natural performer, entertaining guests with his delivery of popular dances like the Charleston, Shimmy, Mess Around, and Truckin'. When he was five years old Briggs saw BILL "BOJANGLES" ROBINSON at the Lincoln Theatre. Robinson's charisma and style captivated the child. Backstage, Gladys Briggs, a prominent "end-dancer" in the chorus line, had her nephew perform his rent-party repertoire for Robinson. Charmed, he asked Alma's permission to bring Briggs into his act, but she declined the offer, reluctant to let her five-year-old go on the road. Regardless, this was a life-changing experience for Briggs, who determined to become a tap dancer.

Like most performers of his time, Briggs learned informally, by seeing and doing. While performing on the sidewalk for small change, he was spotted around 1928 by a dancer named Porkchops, who developed an act called Porkchops, Navy, Rice, and Beans with Briggs and two other boys, Juney Miller and Paul White. Briggs started school, attending St. Mark the Evangelist. He was baptized into the Catholic faith as Bernard Morris, after his mother's marriage to Clifton Morris. Neither the marriage nor the name change lasted, but Briggs's devotion to Catholicism would. Performing frequently interfered with school, a problem that would continue until he turned sixteen, the legal age to join the workforce.

In 1932 Briggs came to the attention of the stride pianist and composer LUCKEY ROBERTS. Roberts's Society Entertainers, a premiere society orchestra, was popular with New York's elite. Mentored by Roberts, Briggs began earning an income, and he developed social graces and performance dynamics, learning how to play to an audience to suit the occasion.

In adolescence Briggs began to shape his personal style. Around age fourteen he danced with the jazz trumpeter ERSKINE HAWKINS and his band at the Ubangi Club, where he was partnered with another teen, BABY LAURENCE. Laurence was developing a musicality and rhythmic complexity similar to innovations in jazz drumming. Briggs's concept of tap was completely changed by this musical approach and departure from the trick steps common in tap. Their partnership was cut short when Briggs was discovered to be underage and truant, but the friendship endured. Around age sixteen, working at Small's Paradise and under the guidance of the dancer Brother Ford, Briggs learned to develop material from the steps he knew and to make use of the stage. Briggs never set routines, instead improvising like a jazz soloist from a repertoire of steps. And like jazz musicians, tap dancers had their own cutting contest, where dancers would compete with each other, demonstrating their virtuosity. Briggs became known as one to beat.

The 1940s brought Briggs into the world of the big bands. His work with EARL "FATHA" HINES, COUNT BASIE, JIMMIE LUNCEFORD, and the Dorsey Brothers furthered his relationship with jazz and jazz musicians, especially his interplay with drummers. From 1945 to 1949 Briggs performed with Charlie Barnet as vocalist as well as tap dancer. His numerous recordings with Barnet included the hit "East Side West Side," also featured in the 1949 film *Charlie Barnet and His Orchestra*. Briggs's years with Barnet honed his professional skills and familiarized him with the music of DUKE ELLINGTON, Barnet's idol.

The 1950s saw a decline in the popularity and commercial viability of tap as theaters closed, jazz venues grew smaller, and television kept audiences at home. Briggs found work in the remaining clubs, theaters, Catskills resorts, television, and occasional appearances with, among others, LOUIS ARMSTRONG and Count Basie. In 1960 Briggs appeared at the Apollo with the Duke Ellington Orchestra. Ellington, who continued to employ dancers, was taken with Briggs's gliding intricacies, dramatic accents, and rapport with his audience. For the next fourteen years Ellington provided an inspiring environment and consistent employment for Briggs, often of historic importance. At the 1962 Newport Jazz Festival, for example, Briggs participated in a presentation titled "The History of the Tap Dance and Its Relationship to Jazz," bringing to life the "lost art," followed by a stunning performance with BABY LAURENCE and backed by Ellington. In 1963 he performed in *My People*, Ellington's contribution to the centennial celebration of the Emancipation Proclamation, *A Century of Negro Progress Exposition*, at Chicago's McCormick Place. Here Briggs first performed "David Danced before the Lord," an up-tempo arrangement of Ellington's "Come Sunday," inspired by the biblical story of King David. In 1965 he reprised "David Danced" for the finale of Ellington's triumphant First Sacred Concert.

After Ellington's death in 1974 Briggs worked cruise ships and stage shows with the luminaries PEARL BAILEY, Tony Bennett, Jerry Lewis, and SAMMY DAVIS JR. He was featured in the 1979 documentary *No Maps on My Taps*. In 1982 Briggs married the jazz harpist Olivette Miller, the daughter of Flournoy Miller, who coauthored the 1921 musical *Shuffle Along*. The couple moved to Las Vegas, and Briggs continued to perform as a solo act and with Miller.

In the 1980s tap began to experience a revival, creating new opportunities for Briggs, including two 1988 projects with GREGORY HINES: the Emmy-winning *Gregory Hines, Tap Dance in America* and the film *Tap*. From 1989 to 1991 Briggs costarred in the Broadway review *Black and Blue*, receiving a Tony nomination. A founding member of the International Tap Association, Briggs received an honorary doctorate from the University of Oklahoma, along with eight other tap masters in 2002. That same year Miller died and Briggs settled into retirement. In 2006 he received the International Tap Dance Hall of Fame Award from the American Tap Dance Foundation. During his long career Briggs had contact with virtually every notable entertainer and jazz musician of the twentieth century. He remained active in the tap community, sharing his colorful history and coaching dancers in the fine art of performance.

FURTHER READING
Frank, Rusty. *Tap!: The Greatest Tap Dance Stars and Their Stories, 1900–1955* (1994).
Radecki, Allana. "Bunny Briggs, A Quality of Heart," *On Tap* 15.2–3 (2004).
Stearns, Marshall, and Jean Stearns. *Jazz Dance: The Story of American Vernacular Dance* (1968).
ALLANA RADECKI

Briggs, Cyril Valentine (28 May 1888–18 Oct. 1966), journalist and activist, was born on the Caribbean island of Nevis, the son of Marian M. Huggins, a woman of color, a plantation worker and Louis E. Briggs, a white native of Trinidad and plantation overseer. From childhood Briggs had a stutter that made verbal communication difficult, but he more than compensated through the power of his pen. Butting heads with colonial school administrators, he was dismissed from two primary schools before settling at Ebenezer Wesleyan on the island of St. Kitts; he graduated from this school in 1904. In his autobiographical writings Briggs indicated that despite its challenges, colonial education shaped his later career by introducing him to radical thinkers like the freethinking agnostic Robert Green Ingersoll. After his graduation Briggs embarked on his lifelong career in journalism by becoming a reporter for the *St. Kitts Daily Express* and the *St. Christopher Advertiser*.

Briggs immigrated to the United States on 4 July 1905 and joined a growing West Indian activist community in Harlem. Little is known about his first years in the United States except that he became engaged to Bertha Florence Johnson in Norfolk, Virginia. Johnson moved to New York in 1912, and the couple married on 7 January 1914. In 1912 Briggs became a society reporter for the *New York Amsterdam News*, an African American newspaper founded in 1909. He rose through the ranks at the *Amsterdam News* as sporting editor and editorial writer for three years before he resigned to join the staff of the *Colored American Review*, a black business magazine. He returned to the *Amsterdam News* almost immediately, but his work with the *Colored American Review* launched his career as a radical nationalist journalist. From 1915 to 1919 Briggs published hard-hitting editorials urging African Americans to have race pride and to seek self-determination, notably through the creation of a separate black state. When President Woodrow Wilson argued that post–World War I peace in Europe should rest not on governments but on the rights of European peoples, Briggs published an editorial calling for a separate state within the geographical borders of the United States where the rights of African Americans would be respected.

When the United States entered World War I, Briggs registered for military service, joining the many African Americans who believed that wartime service could counteract white racism. His hopes were dashed with the 2 July 1917 antiblack race riot in East St. Louis, and he became an outspoken opponent of U.S. participation in the war. Southern mobs lynched at least sixteen African American World War I veterans between 1918 and 1920, and summertime race riots were so violent in 1919 that JAMES WELDON JOHNSON, writer and later executive secretary of the NAACP, termed it "Red Summer." Briggs is perhaps best known for organizing the African Blood Brotherhood for African Liberation and Redemption (ABB) in response to this turmoil. The nationalist fraternity recruited men willing to arm themselves against racial violence, fostered pride in African ancestry, and promoted African American participation in a global anticapitalist struggle.

Briggs launched his own paper, the *Crusader*, in September 1918. The mission of the *Crusader* was to advance a movement to "help make the world safe for the Negro" (*Crusader*, Sept. 1918). In choosing these words, Briggs noted the irony of President Wilson calling World War I a war to make the world

"safe for democracy" while African Americans still faced oppression on the home front. In early issues Briggs advocated self-pride and armed resistance, and after Red Summer he expressed increasingly anticapitalist and anti-imperialist opinions. His radical views led to a break with the *Amsterdam News* in 1919. From 1919 until the Tulsa race riot of 1921 the *Crusader* acted as the official organ of the Hamitic League of the World, a nationalist organization of which Briggs was a member. In the June 1921 issue he praised black residents who fought back against the white mobs, declared the *Crusader* the official organ of the ABB, and introduced the latter as an above-ground organization.

Dissatisfied with the platforms of mainstream politics, Briggs allied with the Communist Party. He saw communism as a means of ending racial oppression and in an October 1919 editorial wrote, "If to fight for one's rights is to be Bolshevist, then we are Bolshevists and let them make the most of it!" ("Bolshevist!!!" *Crusader*, Oct. 1919). Briggs's allegiance to racial nationalism and class-based communist revolution put him at odds with both African American and Communist Party leaders. His relationship with MARCUS GARVEY, founder of the United Negro Improvement Association, was particularly problematic. Briggs originally sought an alliance with Garvey as a fellow West Indian immigrant in favor of racial self-determination, but a conflict over Garvey's strict anticommunism and a feud over adherents left the men estranged.

The *Crusader* folded due to decreased funding and government anticommunist pressure in 1922, and the ABB disbanded in 1925. Undeterred, Briggs was at the forefront of African American and communist cooperation in the 1920s and helped spur increasing black membership in the Communist Party into the late 1930s. Nevertheless, he maintained his black nationalist views and in 1942 was expelled from the party for holding this line. Briggs is also significant as one of a cadre of West Indian immigrants who took leading roles in an era of post–World War I radicalism and were sometimes referred to as the New Negro movement. Perhaps due to his own international experience, he was a global thinker who garnered inspiration from such disparate sources as his Caribbean upbringing, African history, the Irish independence movement, and Soviet Communism.

Briggs migrated to California and worked as editor of the *California Eagle* from 1945 to 1949. He remained an outspoken radical and in 1958 was called before the House Un-American Activities

Committee, where he angered representatives by refusing to offer any information about communism. Instead, he took the opportunity to criticize the slow pace of school desegregation efforts in the South. Briggs died in Los Angeles.

FURTHER READING

Blake, Gene. "Integration Issue Raised by Witness at Red Quiz," *Los Angeles Times*, 4 Sept. 1958.

Hill, Robert A., and Cyril V. Briggs. *The Crusader* (1987).

James, Winston. *Holding Aloft the Banner of Ethiopia: Caribbean Radicalism in Early Twentieth-Century America* (1998).

Kornweibel, Theodore, Jr. *"Seeing Red": Federal Campaigns against Black Militancy, 1919–1925* (1998).

Makalani, Minkah. "For the Liberation of Black People Everywhere: The African Blood Brotherhood, Black Radicalism, and Pan-African Liberation in the New Negro Movement, 1917–1936," Ph.D. diss., University of Illinois at Urbana-Champaign (2004).

Solomon, Mark. *The Cry Was Unity: Communists and African Americans, 1919–1936* (1998).

AMBER MOULTON-WISEMAN

Briggs, Martha Bailey (21 Mar. 1838–28 Mar. 1889), educator and public school administrator, was born in New Bedford, Massachusetts, the only child of Fannie Bassett of Vineyard Haven, Martha's Vineyard, Massachusetts, and John Briggs of Tiverton, Rhode Island. Her parents were married in 1831. Brigg's mother died when she was a young girl, and as a result, she was raised by her father, with the help of an aunt, Mrs. Bailey. John had grown up poor, in a rural area where he was allowed to attend school only in the winter. At about age twelve, he came to the city of New Bedford to work for George Howland, a Quaker and a whaling ship agent. John stayed employed by the Howland family until his death, more than fifty years later. When his daughter was still an infant, John was fitting Howland's whaling ships, the *Java* and *Golconda*, and he developed a friendship with another of Howland's workers, an escaped slaved and abolitionist named FREDERICK DOUGLASS. Though his own access to formal schooling was limited, he was known to be a well-read man of high intelligence. His commitment to education and to uplifting members of his race were traits that he passed on to his daughter.

After several years of private tutoring, when she was twelve-and-a-half years old (slightly younger than the required age thirteen), Martha began her studies at New Bedford High School in 1850. She finished with honors and is believed to be the first African American to graduate from the school. Shortly thereafter, she opened a private school for ten or twelve pupils at her father's home on Allen Street in New Bedford. She also offered evening lessons in reading and writing for fugitive and former slaves.

Briggs attended Boston Medical College from 1857 to 1859, with aspirations of becoming a nurse, but she later decided that she preferred teaching. She returned to teaching at private schools in southeastern Massachusetts, including one in Christiantown, Martha's Vineyard, as well as at public schools in Newport, Rhode Island. It is here that she served as governess to the children of GEORGE T. DOWNING, a wealthy African American restaurateur and hotel proprietor whose home was frequented by Frederick Douglass and other notable persons. Downing, an abolitionist and advocate for school desegregation, loaned a building in which Briggs and two other teachers taught school. While teaching in Newport, Briggs was recruited in 1859 by Myrtilla Miner, a white American educator, to teach at her Miner School, also known as the School for Colored Girls, in Washington, D.C. Briggs turned the offer down, reportedly because of her father's concern that with tensions increasing between the North and the South over slavery, Washington, D.C., would not be a safe place for his daughter.

By 1867 Briggs accepted a teaching position in Easton, Maryland, and two years later she applied to teach in the "colored" schools of Georgetown and Washington, D.C. She received an offer to teach in the public schools of Washington, D.C., and served as principal of Anthony Bowen during 1869–1873. She then accepted a position to teach at Howard University, which she did for six years, serving as head of the Normal Department, a department she helped to create during 1873–1879. (Normal schools, often the predecessors to modern-day teacher's colleges or schools of education, were institutions for training teachers and establishing teaching standards or norms.) Briggs left Howard University in 1879 to return to public schools as principal of the Miner Normal School, the same school for which Miner had tried to recruit her some twenty years earlier, and where Douglass served as a board member. She continued her work at the Miner Normal School for four years, graduating some eighty teachers (more than any teacher trainer at the time). Many of her graduates went on to teach for District of Columbia public schools.

Briggs left the Miner Normal School to return to Howard University in 1883, where she served as head of the Normal School until the time of her death. In addition to her administrative roles, Briggs taught French and mathematics, as was noted in Howard University's school catalogues and the Modern Language Association of America's annual conference in 1884–1985. She had been elected president of the Industrial Institute Association of Washington, D.C., an educational organization, and was a member of the Monday Night Literary Club.

Briggs died in Washington, D.C. The District of Columbia Certificate of Death cites the cause of death as a tumor. A memorial service was held on 14 May 1889 by the Bethel Historical and Literary Society, during which she was eulogized as an outstanding educator. Another memorial service was held at Howard University's Andrew Rankin Chapel, in which a tributary marble tablet was inserted into the wall. The tablet is inscribed, "Her works do follow her." She was returned to New Bedford for her burial.

Following her death, the District of Columbia Board of Education named two elementary school buildings in Washington, D.C., in her honor, most notably the Martha B. Briggs Building of the Briggs-Montgomery School. Both school buildings have since been demolished. The Martha Briggs Educational Club, Inc., a member of the National Association of Colored Women's Clubs, Inc., was founded in New Bedford in 1920, and Miner Teachers College (a predecessor of the University of the District of Columbia) celebrated Briggs's service as the third principal of Miner Normal School during its March 1934 Founder's Day program. Briggs is considered a pioneer in the field of teacher education and is regarded as a founder of both the Teachers College of Howard University and Miner Teachers College in Washington, D.C.

FURTHER READING

Cooke, Paul P. "Martha B. Briggs," in *Black Women in America: An Historical Encyclopedia*, ed. Darlene Clark Hine, Elsa Barkley Brown, and Rosalyn Terborg-Penn (1993).

Gregory, J. Francis. "Martha Bailey Briggs," *Journal of Negro History*, vol. 20, no. 2. (April 1935).

Iturralde, Lucilla Hiomara, and Adrienne Lash Jones. "Martha Bailey Briggs," in *Notable Black American Women, Book II*, ed. Jessie Carney Smith (1996).

Scruggs, Lawson Andrew. *Women of Distinction: Remarkable in Works and Invincible in Character* (1893).

Turner, Geneva C. "For Whom Is Your School Named?" *Negro History Bulletin* 22 (April 1959).

SIMONE MONIQUE BARNES

Brimmer, Andrew Felton (13 Sept. 1926–), economist and educator, was born in Newelton, Louisiana, the fourth of five children of Andrew Brimmer Sr., a sharecropper and warehouse worker, and Vellar (Davis) Brimmer. The family abandoned farming when they found it impossible to make a decent living under the crop lien system, an economic arrangement in which farmers borrowed money at high interest rates to work land that they did not own in hopes of sharing profits that rarely materialized. His parents' efforts to escape debt and poverty were young Andrew's first exposure to economic forces and monetary policy.

As a child Andrew was bright and serious. In 1944 he graduated from Tensa Parish Training School, a segregated high school in St. Joseph, Louisiana. Brimmer joined the U.S. Army and served from May 1945 to November 1946, becoming a staff sergeant in the 645th Ordinance Ammunition Company in Hawaii. After the war, he took advantage of the G.I. Bill to enroll at the University of Washington in Seattle. Initially, he was interested in journalism and became an assistant editor of the *Seattle Dispatch* before a professor persuaded him that he might have a more promising career studying the role of money in society. Brimmer switched his major to economics, and when he earned his B.A. in 1950 he was awarded a John Hay Whitney Foundation fellowship. While continuing his graduate studies at the University of Washington he won a Fulbright Fellowship, which allowed him to study in India at the Delhi School of Economics at the University of Bombay.

After receiving his master's degree in 1951 Brimmer worked for the Wage Stabilization Board in Seattle before entering Harvard University in the fall of 1952. The following year he married Doris Millicent Scott, a graduate student at Radcliffe College. Eventually they would have one child, Esther Diane. From 1953 to 1954 Brimmer worked as a research assistant at the Center for International Studies at the Massachusetts Institute of Technology before getting a job at the Federal Reserve Bank of New York City. While there he took part in a fact-finding mission to the Sudan to determine the feasibility of establishing a central bank in that developing African nation. Brimmer was especially interested in the economic forces that affect poor communities in the United States and in the Third World—particularly the role that banks and insurance companies play in promoting or retarding growth. This became the focus of his dissertation, which earned him a Ph.D. in 1957, and was the basis of several scholarly articles and a book, *Life Insurance Companies in the Capital Market* (1962).

Brimmer held his first academic post at Michigan State University, where he served as an assistant professor from 1958 to 1961. He then joined the Wharton School of Finance at the University of Pennsylvania from 1961 to 1963. In addition to his teaching responsibilities he was a consultant for the Securities Exchange Commission from 1962 to 1963. Brimmer joined the Kennedy Administration in 1963 as deputy assistant secretary to Richard Holton in the Department of Commerce in Washington, D.C. When the U.S. Supreme Court unanimously upheld the constitutionality of the 1964 Civil Rights Act, it cited Brimmer's testimony in its decision. The following year he was promoted to Assistant Secretary for Economic Affairs, and President Lyndon Johnson appointed him to a panel charged with investigating the 1965 Watts riots in Los Angeles, California.

Brimmer became the first African American to serve as a governor on the Federal Reserve Board in 1966, when President Johnson appointed him to a fourteen-year term. To ensure that Brimmer would be confirmed by the Senate, President Johnson invited Senator Russell Long of Louisiana, chair of the Senate Finance Committee, to the White House. Senator Long had been trying to get someone from Louisiana onto the Federal Reserve Board for some time, but when Johnson showed Long a picture of Brimmer, the senator responded, "When they all jump on me because I couldn't get one Louisianan on the FRB, I can say I did get one—a nigger" (Goodwin, Doris Kearns, *Lyndon Johnson and the American Dream* [1991], 186).

As one of the seven governors of the Federal Reserve Board, which exists to ensure the stability of the nation's monetary system, Brimmer supported moderately raising long-term interest rates in order to reduce the liquidity of capital and thereby act as a check on inflation, which had become a major fiscal concern of the 1960s and 1970s. In 1974 Brimmer resigned from the Federal Reserve Board to join the Harvard University Graduate School of Business Administration as the Thomas Henry Carroll Ford Foundation Visiting Professor. From this post Brimmer advised President Ford in 1974, that the best way for him to stimulate the economy

and bring the nation out of recession was to cut personal income taxes by 10 percent. Congress implemented many of his recommendations as part of its $22.8 billion tax reduction plan in 1975.

In 1976 Brimmer returned to Washington, D.C., to establish his own economic consulting firm, Brimmer & Co., Inc. While in private practice he continued to write on public policy issues, including the oil crisis of the late 1970s and the looming problem of Third World debt, which often forced poor countries to choose between paying the interest on their loans to the International Monetary Fund or feeding and educating their people. In addition Brimmer maintained his membership in such professional organizations as the American Academy of Arts and Sciences, the Association for the Study of Afro-American Life and History (serving as president from 1970–1973 and again from 1989–1990), the Council of Foreign Relations, Tuskegee University Board of Trustees, the Brookings Institute, the Ford Foundation, the National Urban League, and the Chamber of Commerce of the United States

When EARL GRAVES invited him to join the economic board of *Black Enterprise*, the nation's largest black business magazine, Brimmer began to write a series of articles that assessed the economic health of black America, made strategic recommendations, and tracked investment in Africa. His columns were penetrating and hard-hitting, excoriating the often poor business skills of black businessmen in impoverished neighborhoods, imploring blacks to take better advantage of opportunities to improve their education and skills, and expressing little faith in most government programs. However, Brimmer's essays also exposed patterns of racial bias in banking that made it harder for black people to acquire credit and buy homes. He found that "even when blacks' incomes were well above average … they still had the highest rejection rate," causing him to conclude that "a major reason for the lending gap appears to be discrimination" (Brimmer, "The Cost of Bank Bias," *Black Enterprise* 12 [July 1992]: 43).

In 1986 Brimmer published *International Banking and Domestic Economic Policies: Perspectives in Debt and Development* (1986). His reputation for sound business advice had grown, and when the District of Columbia found itself facing bankruptcy and suffering a crisis in confidence under the leadership of Mayor MARION SHEPILOV BARRY JR., President Bill Clinton appointed Brimmer to lead a five-member control board to put the district's finances in order. This was the most controversial job of Brimmer's career. Instead of achieving statehood, which the district had demanded for years, district residents found that Congress had suspended their limited home rule until fiscal responsibility was restored. Although the board was empowered to approve all contracts and budgets, this placed it at odds with Mayor Barry and other elected officials in the district who felt that their authority was being usurped. Moreover, Brimmer was forced to institute painful austerity measures that involved thousands of proposed job cuts in order to reach a balanced budget.

Even ELEANOR HOLMES NORTON, who had initially celebrated Brimmer's appointment, found the board to be too secretive; others described Brimmer's management style as autocratic. By late 1995 Brimmer's relationship with Barry could only be described as poor. Nevertheless, when Brimmer informed FRANKLIN DELANO RAINES, President Clinton's budget director, of his decision to leave the control board in 1998, the district had accrued a surplus of $185 million and was projecting a $300 million surplus by the end of the fiscal year.

Brimmer spent the twilight of his illustrious and pathbreaking career consulting on economic matters, serving on charitable boards, and receiving over twenty-two honorary degrees. Though not autobiographical, Brimmer's published works are nevertheless the best presentation of his economic philosophy. They include: *International Banking and Domestic Economic Policies: Perspectives in Debt and Development* (1986), *Trends, Prospects, and Strategies for Black Economic Progress* (1985), and *Capital Shortage: Real or Imagined?* (1976).

FURTHER READING

Brimmer's personal papers have not yet been made available to the public. However, periodic reference to his public service can be found among various presidential papers: the Gerald R. Ford Library, Ann Arbor, Michigan; "Stanley S. Scott" collection contains a few speeches by Brimmer; the Lyndon B. Johnson Library and Museum, at the University of Texas in Austin, Texas, holds papers relating to his appointment to the Federal Reserve Board and information on his role on the commission that investigated the Watts riots; and the William Jefferson Clinton Presidential Library, Little Rock Arkansas, has material on Brimmer's chairmanship of the D.C. control board.

Henneberger, Melinda. "Andrew Brimmer: Prideful Economist Is Capital's Local Power Center," *New York Times*, 20 Aug. 1997.

SHOLOMO B. LEVY

Briscoe, Marlin (10 Sept. 1945–), professional football player, was born in Oakland, California, to Geneva Moore and a father he would never get to know. His parents split when he was three years old, and his mother relocated the family to Omaha, Nebraska, where she had relatives and where she was able to get work at a local packinghouse. From a cousin, a youth sports coach, Briscoe learned a love of sports and athletics that would last the rest of his life.

Briscoe attended local schools, including South Omaha High, where he was both a football and basketball standout. He graduated in 1962 and accepted a scholarship to the University of Nebraska, Omaha. Black quarterbacks were at the time still a rarity, but Briscoe had occasionally played the position at South Omaha High and he wanted to continue in college. His new coach, Al Caniglia, recognized his talent and offered him the quarterback spot. His junior year, he threw for 1,668 and was a threat with his feet as well. His combined offense of 2,181 set a UNO record. What was to be his senior year, however, was lost to a fractured vertebra. Briscoe sat out the rest of the year and was drafted by the U.S. Army, though he received a medical deferment. Amazingly, he healed enough that his doctors cleared him for the play the following year, and he was back under center with UNO. In that year, he combined for 2,639 and threw for twenty-five touchdowns. He was drafted by the American Football League's (AFL) Denver Broncos in the fourteenth round of the 1968 draft. The Broncos didn't want him as quarterback, however, instead signing him as a defensive back.

By the beginning of the season, however, the Broncos had lost a number of quarterbacks. Briscoe had made it clear to his coaches that he wanted the job, and when Steve Tensi went down with a broken collarbone, he was finally offered it, making him the first black quarterback in professional football history. Throughout the remainder of that season, Briscoe posted 1,589 passing yards, a Broncos rookie record, and added 308 rushing yards.

The following year, 1969, Briscoe returned to school and finished a degree in architecture. Upon his return to Broncos training camp, his coaches informed him that his days under center were over; he wasn't even allowed to compete for the job. Aggrieved, Briscoe demanded his head coach Lou Saban let him go, and soon he was on his way to Buffalo to join the Bills. Like the Broncos, the Bills had no interest in a black quarterback, and

Briscoe was placed instead as a wide receiver, a position he had never played. In his first season as a Bill, Briscoe scored five touchdowns and became the first 1,000-yard receiver in franchise history. His next year (which was the first in the newly formed National Football League [NFL]) he racked up 1,036 yards, averaged 18.2 yards per catch, and hauled in eight touchdowns. As a result, he was selected to that year's Pro Bowl. His tenure with the Bills ended in 1972, however, when Buffalo hired Briscoe's former coach, Lou Saban, who still carried a grudge against Briscoe and traded him to the Miami Dolphins.

In response, Briscoe and a number of other players filed suit against League commissioner Pete Rozelle to overturn the so-called Rozelle Rule, which restricted the free agency rights of players in favor of team owners. The players eventually won the suit, in 1975, but the damage to their reputations would lead to difficulties down the line.

After joining the Dolphins, Briscoe enjoyed what is still the NFL's only perfect season: zero regular-season losses and a Super Bowl victory. In 1973 the Dolphins were again crowned NFL champions. All of a sudden, Briscoe was a two-time Super Bowl winner. The following year, however, he suffered repeated injuries and his career quickly began to unravel. Over the next few seasons Briscoe spent time with the San Diego, Detroit, and Boston franchises, but played only minor roles. Labeled a troublemaker for his role in the Rozelle suit, he found it difficult to attract interest from teams. He retired in 1977.

This was the beginning of a bad time for Briscoe. He moved to Los Angeles with his wife and family and managed to establish himself as a successful stockbroker, but he soon began to use drugs. He became addicted to cocaine and crack, and his wife divorced him. He was briefly jailed for drug possession in San Diego County. He put up his Super Bowl rings as collateral on a loan and lost them both when he defaulted.

In 1992 he began to recover. He quit using drugs and began doing community work with local youth. Unable to recover his lost Super Bowl rings, he asked for (and received) permission from the Miami Dolphins to commission duplicate-replacements.

Despite his difficulties, Briscoe is remembered today as a trailblazer for black quarterbacks in the National Football League and as a versatile athlete whose gifts were not always fully recognized during his playing days.

FURTHER READING

Biga, Leo Adam. "Prodigal Son, Marlin Briscoe Takes the Long Road Home." In *Out to Win: The Roots of Greatness* (2010).

Briscoe, Marlin, and Bob Schaller. *The First Black Quarterback: Marlin Briscoe's Journey to Break the Color Barrier and Start in the NFL* (2002).

JASON PHILIP MILLER

Briscoe, Neliska Ann "Baby" (7 Apr. 1914–25 Aug. 1994), dancer, jazz bandleader, and businesswoman, was born in New Orleans, Louisiana, the daughter of Eddie Briscoe, a meatpacker, and Neliska Thomas, a cook and housekeeper born in Mexico. She had two half brothers and a sister who died young. Briscoe's career as an entertainer began early, at about the age of nine, when she performed in a club where her uncle, Escaliere Thomas, was employed part time in the evenings. Soon thereafter Briscoe acquired the nickname "Baby" (sometimes "Babe"), a moniker she retained in her entertainment career even as an adult.

Briscoe performed in New Orleans at the St. Bernard Alley Cabaret, known for its talented jazz band, as an acrobatic dancer in a floor show in which she was the sole child performer, accompanied there in the evenings by her mother after work. A natural on the stage, Briscoe continued to perform as a popular acrobatic dancer and singer in such New Orleans cabarets as the Astoria, Entertainers, and the Owl throughout her early teenage years, often mentioned in newspaper articles as a cabaret's main draw.

The development of jazz music and its historic roots in New Orleans has been well documented. However, the historian Sherrie Tucker noted that while "the musicians credited with bearing, rocking, and nurturing early New Orleans jazz are invariably men[,] … women *did* contribute … in many and significant ways. … They were instrumentalists, vocalists, dancers, and bandleaders" (Tucker, 68). Many of these women and the contributions they made to this uniquely American style of music have been forgotten or "miscast as *precursors* to jazz rather than essential participants in the birth of music" (Tucker, 68). Indeed there were opportunities enough for talented women of color in the many cabarets and nightclubs in New Orleans, and while the life of a performer was often difficult, the performance industry offered an exciting option to women who were otherwise usually limited to employment as a domestic, as was Briscoe's mother.

In February 1931, at age seventeen, the talented Briscoe moved to New York City to pursue a career as a dancer. She was employed at two clubs in the city, one of them Small's Paradise Club. Her time in New York may have ended prematurely when in late November 1931 she was one of two "coloured girls" caught in a gang shootout in a club and suffered a gunshot wound in the arm (*Louisiana Weekly*, 14 Dec. 1931). She was out of work for at least several weeks during her recovery period, and her subsequent activities until 1933 are unknown. In 1933 she returned to her native New Orleans to rise to such renown in the local jazz scene that she later gained the title "the Sweetheart of New Orleans."

In 1933 the pianist Joe Robichaux hired Briscoe to front his band, Robichaux's New Orleans Rhythm Boys, a group consisting at various times of up to fifteen members, including three women: Briscoe, Joan Lunceford, and Ann Cooper. Dressed in what became her trademark tuxedo, Briscoe worked as a tap dancer, entertaining the crowd in front of Robichaux's band during and between musical sets.

Briscoe worked with Robichaux for nearly five years before joining another group, the Harlem Playgirls, in early 1938. Based out of Minneapolis, Minnesota, this African American all-woman band toured the country to popular and critical acclaim, dubbed in club circles variously as "the World's Greatest Sepia Women's Orchestra" and "the American Woman's Foremost Expression in Music." From 1938 to 1940 Briscoe, in her tuxedo, fronted the band as it toured the country, playing at the famed Apollo Theater in New York on Thanksgiving Day in 1938 as well as at smaller venues in such locales as Frederick, Maryland; Cleveland, Ohio; Youngstown, Ohio; and Jackson, Tennessee. The Harlem Playgirls also made numerous appearances at the Tick Tock Tavern in New Orleans. By this time Briscoe was not just a "front" for the band but a true bandleader.

Following her two-year tour with the Harlem Playgirls, Briscoe returned to New Orleans, where she met a merchant mariner named David "Val" Mouton. At the peak of her success Briscoe left her career in show business to marry Mouton in 1942. They had two daughters, Avon ("Vonnie") and Debra. Brisco, an energetic advocate for the right to vote, became a registered voter in New Orleans in 1948, unusual at the time for an African American woman. Briscoe divorced her husband in 1950 after enduring physical abuse and even gun threats at his hands.

After Briscoe's divorce she and her daughters lived with her mother on North Tonti Street in New Orleans, and Briscoe became a successful businesswoman. She became a cosmetologist, operated a gift boutique named Avon and Debra's Gift Shop after her daughters, owned a small restaurant, and worked as a seamstress, making ball gowns for Mardi Gras. The same energy that Briscoe applied to her stage show she applied to whatever she did in her private life.

In 1957 Briscoe married Clarence Casimire, whom she had known from her youth. The marriage ceremony was performed by Briscoe's half brother Joseph Mitchell at the Christian Mission Baptist Church he had cofounded in New Orleans. Shortly after their marriage the couple moved to Cleveland with Briscoe's daughters and Casimire's daughter from a previous marriage. Together they had one son. Despite her retirement from the stage, Briscoe never abandoned performing entirely. She took up the saxophone in her sixties, did splits on her seventy-fifth birthday, and danced on her eightieth birthday.

In 1994 Briscoe was hospitalized with bone cancer at St. Alexis Hospital. A nun at the hospital told one of Briscoe's daughters that Briscoe "had talked of being a famous dancer, … about wearing a satin tuxedo and conducting an orchestra. The nun added quickly that it was surely the morphine" (Mouton, 27).

Though she was undiscovered for many years, Briscoe's legacy has been reexamined, and through the research efforts of the historian and author Sherrie Tucker and the national park ranger Margie Ortiz, she has gained her rightful place among America's early jazz pioneers. In 2004 Briscoe was included in a feature exhibition celebrating the Women of Jazz at the National Historic Jazz Park in New Orleans.

FURTHER READING

The Hogan Jazz Archive Collection at Tulane University in New Orleans has information about Briscoe and her only known contemporary recording, singing "When the Sun Goes Down" with Robichaux's band at the Rhythm Club in New Orleans on 20 Mar. 1936. Although recorded by Decca (Master #60838), it was one of four Robichaux songs that were never released in record form to the public. Seventy years later, in 2006, Briscoe's version (a recording of this song with male vocals had been previously released) was made publicly available for the first time on the video

New Orleans Piano Players by the Jazzology label of New Orleans.

Barker, Danny. *A Life in Jazz*, ed. Alyn Shipton (1986).

Mouton, Debra. "Baby Briscoe Plays the Majestic," *Northern Ohio Live* (Apr. 2004).

Tucker, Sherrie. "Rocking the Cradle of Jazz: These Are the Women Who Changed the Face of Music," *Ms.* (Winter 2004–2005).

GLENN ALLEN KNOBLOCK

Bristol, Johnny (3 Feb. 1939–21 Mar. 2004), singer, songwriter, producer, and arranger, was born John William Bristol in Morganton, North Carolina, the son of James and Mary Bristol. While in high school, Bristol was named to the All-State Football Team, and he formed a singing group known as the Jackets. After graduating from high school he enlisted in the United States Air Force and was stationed at Fort Custer, in Battle Creek, Michigan. Bristol and Robert "Jackey" Beavers formed part of the group the High Fives, though soon left to form the duo Johnny and Jackey. In 1959 Gwen Gordy and Billy Davis signed the two young men to their Anna Records label, and Johnny and Jackey recorded two 45s before Gordy and HARVEY FUQUA established Tri-Phi Records in 1961. Johnny and Jackey recorded four 45s. The duo's songs garnered a modicum of success in the Midwest, but failed to attract national attention. After Tri-Phi's dissolution in 1963, a number of the label's artists—including Bristol—signed with Motown Records, the company founded by Gwen's brother, BERRY GORDY.

At Motown, Bristol began as a staff writer before ultimately becoming one of the company's top writers and producers. He cowrote and produced such hits as GLADYS KNIGHT and the Pips' "Daddy Could Swear, I Declare" (1970) and "I Don't Want to Do Wrong" (1971) as well as SMOKEY ROBINSON and the Miracles' "We've Come Too Far to End It Now" (1971), yet he is best known during his Motown years for his songwriting and producing collaboration with Fuqua. Among the hit songs written and produced by Bristol and Fuqua are MARVIN GAYE and Tammi Terrell's "If I Could Build My Whole World around You" (1967), David Ruffin's "My Whole World Ended (The Moment You Left Me)" (1969), Junior Walker and the All Stars' "What Does It Take (To Win Your Love)" (1969), and Edwin Starr's "Twenty-Five Miles" (1969). Bristol and Fuqua also produced additional hits such as Junior Walker and the All Stars' "How Sweet It Is" (1966), as well as "Pucker Up Buttercup" (1966);

and Gaye and Terrell's "Ain't No Mountain High Enough" (1967), "Your Precious Love" (1967), and "If This World Were Mine" (1967). In 1969 Bristol produced "Someday We'll Be Together," a Diana Ross hit recorded originally by Johnny and Jackey eight years earlier. Written by Bristol, Beavers, and Fuqua, the single also featured Bristol singing background, and was the last number one record for DIANA ROSS and the Supremes. He also wrote and/or produced songs for a variety of other Motown acts, including the Jackson Five and the Four Tops.

In 1973 Bristol left Motown Records. During the rest of the decade and the 1980s, he continued to work as a songwriter and/or producer for a variety of artists including JOHNNY MATHIS, Tom Jones, Tavares, JERRY BUTLER, Buddy Miles, O. C. Smith, and Boz Scaggs. Bristol resumed his recording career in 1974. That same year *Hang on in There Baby*, Bristol's debut album and first recording as a solo artist, was released. The title song, which was the album's first single, ranked eight on Billboard's Top 100 chart and second on Billboard's R&B chart. The single generated two Grammy nominations for Bristol in 1975: Best New Artist as well as Best R&B Vocal Performance—Male. The album's follow-up single, "You and I," also became a hit. Bristol's second album, *Feeling the Magic* (1975) contains the song about his hometown, "Morganton, North Carolina," and the hit single, "Go On and Dream." The next album, *Bristol's Crème* (1976), features the hit singles, "Do It to My Mind" and "You Turn Me On to Love." Bristol's subsequent albums are *Strangers* (1978), *Free to Be Me* (1981), *Come to Me* (1995), and the two compilation releases: *Best of Johnny Bristol* (1978) and *Johnny Bristol: The MGM Years* (2004). Each album contains songs written and produced by Bristol.

On 21 March 2004 Bristol died at his home, near Howell, Michigan, from natural causes. He was sixty-five. At the time of his death, Bristol was working on a gospel album and finalizing plans to tour England. He is survived by a son and daughter from his marriage to Maude Bristol Perry, who would later become the first African American female to be elected mayor of Battle Creek, Michigan. Bristol is also survived by a daughter from his marriage to Iris Gordy, Berry Gordy's niece. Both marriages ended in divorce.

FURTHER READING

Dahl, Bill. *Motown: The Golden Years* (2001).

Henderson, Andrea, ed. "Johnny Bristol," in *Contemporary Musicians*, vol. 62 (2008).

Obituaries: *Washington Post*, 23 March 2004; *Independent*, 25 March 2004.

LINDA M. CARTER

Bristow, Lonnie Robert (6 Apr. 1930–), physician and organization president, was born in New York City, the son of Lonnie Harlis Bristow, a Baptist minister, and Vivian Wines, a nurse. At age ten Bristow was exposed to the medical profession by his mother, who was an emergency room nurse at Harlem's now defunct Sydenham Hospital. Bristow would observe the hospital staff from a distance while waiting to escort his mother to their apartment. She introduced him to the hospital's African American doctors, who became his role models as he came to believe that a career in medicine was something he could attain. Bristow graduated from the High School of Commerce in Manhattan and entered Morehouse College in Atlanta, Georgia, in 1947. There he became acquainted with fellow student MARTIN LUTHER KING JR.

Two years later Bristow signed up with the U.S. Navy and was on active duty until 1950. He enrolled at the City College of New York, where he gained notoriety as the football team's quarterback. He graduated with a bachelor of science degree in 1953 and then went on to the New York University College of Medicine where he was awarded an M.D. in 1957. Bristow's first marriage to Margaret Jeter in 1957 ended in divorce. The couple had one daughter, Mary. In 1961 he married his office manager, Marilyn Hingslage, a union that produced a son, Robert, also a prominent physician, and a second daughter, Elizabeth.

Upon completing an internship at San Francisco City and County Hospital, Bristow was a resident in internal medicine at the U.S. Veterans Administration Hospital in San Francisco, from 1958 to 1960. He held corresponding positions at Francis Delafield Hospital (affiliated with Columbia University) in New York City in 1960 and the U.S. Veterans Administration Hospital in the Bronx in 1961. He returned to northern California to establish his private practice in 1964 and had staff privileges at Brookside Hospital in San Pablo. In 1969 he was elected president of the East Bay Society of Internal Medicine. That same year he managed the political campaigns of three pro-school busing candidates for the Richmond, California, school board. By the mid 1970s he was a fellow of the American College of Physicians and was on the Federated Council of Internal Medicine. In 1976 he headed the California Society of Internal Medicine. From 1979 to 1981 Bristow was a resident in occupational medicine at the University of California at San Francisco School of Medicine. After serving on a number of health and professional committees and commissions, in 1981 he ascended to the presidency of the American Society of Internal Medicine, the most important professional group related to his medical specialty.

Aside from his formidable personal attributes, commitment, and competence, Bristow's success in these predominantly white medical organizations was facilitated, in large part, by the agitation of black doctors pushing for their inclusion as respected, full-fledged members with something to contribute. Exclusion from the white-controlled medical profession and its organizational groups, particularly in the South, led African Americans to form their own groups starting in the late 1880s, most notably the National Medical Association, which was founded in 1895 as a result of the segregationist policy of the American Medical Association (AMA). The country's largest physicians' advocacy group, the AMA was founded in 1847 but only began (officially) accepting African American members in 1948. The AMA was also slow in adopting policies that would boost its black membership or amend its constitution to end racial discrimination in its constituent groups. From 1963 until 1968, when the AMA finally banned such discrimination, its annual meetings were picketed by protesters who were unable to join the national AMA because their regional and state AMA-affiliated organizations remained segregated.

Bristow had joined the AMA in 1957. His climb to the top of the AMA bureaucracy began when he was voted an alternate delegate to the AMA's House of Delegates in 1978. The following year he was placed on the AMA's Council of Medical Services, which he chaired from 1983 to 1985. From 1988 to 1990 he was president of the AMA's Education and Research Foundation. In 1985 he was elected to the fourteen-member Board of Trustees of the American Medical Association, becoming its first-ever African American member. From 1993 to 1994 he served as the board's chair. While on the board he was well known for backing the AMA's health-care reform proposal called Health Access America. Capitalizing on his national exposure and contacts, Bristow ran unopposed to become the AMA president-elect in 1994, representing 295,000 physicians.

As the AMA's first African American president, Bristow became the subject of numerous press stories, including a segment on the popular CBS television news show *60 Minutes*. Bristow downplayed his personal achievements and insisted that the fact that he was black and presiding over the nation's largest and most prestigious medical association should not be the defining legacy of his term in office on the House of Delegates. During his tenure as president he helped to refashion the AMA's public image by emphasizing its role as an agent for the common good. He refused to shy away from controversial positions and confronted the powerful tobacco industry and heath maintenance organizations (HMOs). He challenged the federal government to enact universal health care and advocated measures to expand health education and increase the production of minority race doctors and nurses.

Among the many honors Bristow received were the 1977 Award of Excellence from the California Committee for Political Action, the 1989 Contra Costa Humanitarian of the Year award, California Society of Internal Medicine Most Distinguished Internist award in 1990, and honorary doctorates from Morehouse College, City University of New York, and Wayne State University.

Bristow's speeches and articles on medical ethics and health-care reform were published in popular and scholarly periodicals, including *The Internist*, the *Journal of the American Medical Association*, and the *Annals of the New York Academy of Sciences*. Aside from his AMA duties, Bristow was actively involved in committee work and projects of the Center for Disease Control, the California Department of Prisons, the California Department for Health, the University of California at Berkeley, the Institute of Medicine, the National Council on Health Care Technology, and the Health Care Financing Administration.

In 1998 Bristow officially retired from private medical practice and continued to live in his home in Walnut Creek, California. In 2002 he was selected to chair the Institute of Medicine's Committee on Institutional and Policy-Level Strategies for Increasing the Diversity of the U.S. Health Care Workforce, for which he issued the report "In The Nation's Compelling Interest: Ensuring Diversity in the Health-Care Workforce," published in February 2004 by the National Academic Press.

FURTHER READING

Jones, Lisa C. "New American Medical Association President, Lonnie R. Bristow," *Ebony* (Aug. 1995).

Libman, Gary. "First Black on AMA Board Makes His Mark," *Los Angeles Times*, 12 Aug. 1985.

Sammons, Vivian O. *Blacks in Science and Medicine* (1990).

ROBERT FIKES JR.

Broadnax, Wesley Jerome (17 Feb. 1970–), music educator and musician, was born in Marshall, Texas, the son of Maude Irene Jernigan, a home health-care provider, and Leon Broadnax Sr., a truck driver. Wesley Broadnax is the sixth of seven children, having five sisters and one brother. Broadnax began his musical pursuits at age twelve when he took his first trombone lesson. Throughout his middle school and high school years in the Marshall public schools he participated in every band-related program, including marching band (drum major), concert band, jazz band, and various small ensembles. Between 1983 and 1988 he was selected to the All-Area Bands and Orchestras and the All-Region Bands and Orchestras (for Region IV), and he received first division ("superior") medals in the Texas University Interscholastic League Solo and Ensemble Contests. In 1988 he was chosen as bass trombonist for the Texas All-State Symphony Orchestra. Later that year he graduated from Marshall High School, where he won the John Philip Sousa Award for Best Bandsman.

In fall 1988 Broadnax entered Stephen F. Austin State University (SFASU) in Nacogdoches, Texas, where he studied conducting with John L. Whitwell and trombone with William Young, J. Mark Thompson, and Nathaniel Brickens, a leading figure in trombone performance and pedagogy and a past president of the International Trombone Association. Broadnax was awarded the Mel Montgomery Band Scholarship all five years that he attended SFASU, and in 1990 he was selected to Pi Kappa Lambda, a national honorary fraternity for academic and musical achievement. In 1993 he earned a bachelor of music education degree and graduated with honors (magna cum laude).

In August 1993 Broadnax began his professional teaching career, serving for two years as band director for both Wylie Middle School (Wylie, Texas) and Paris High School (Paris, Texas). In fall 1995 he returned to college to pursue advanced studies in conducting at Michigan State University (MSU) in Lansing, where he resumed his work with Whitwell, who left SFASU in 1993 to become director of bands at MSU and who later received a Distinguished Faculty Award there for outstanding teaching. In addition Broadnax studied bass trombone with Curtis Olson and euphonium with Philip Sinder. Throughout his master's degree studies at MSU, Broadnax received the Leonard Falcone Scholarship. In spring 1997 he completed a master of music degree in Wind Conducting. The following fall he began doctoral coursework at MSU and was awarded the Kenneth G. Bloomquist Scholarship for graduate wind conducting. From 1998 to 2000 he was the recipient of a King/Parks/Chavez Future Fellowship. In spring 2000 he completed his dissertation, "The Chamber Music of Joseph Schwantner: How Text Influences Instrumental Music," and he was awarded a doctor of musical arts degree in Wind Conducting.

Shortly after graduation Broadnax became assistant director of bands at MSU, where he led the symphony band, concert band, chamber winds, and Musique 21 (a new music ensemble) and taught undergraduate and graduate courses in conducting and wind literature. He received numerous honors. In spring 2001 he was selected by Pierre Boulez to participate in his symposium on twentieth-century music at Carnegie Hall in New York City, in summer 2002 he was a conducting fellow under the mentorship of Frank Battisti at the world-renowned Tanglewood Music Festival, and in summer 2003 he was a minority scholar fellow at Indiana State University.

As an acclaimed advocate for new music, Broadnax conducted the premieres of works by many notable contemporary composers, including Paul Barsom, Jere Hutcheson, David Maslanka, Joel Puckett, Stephen Rush, Lawrence Singer, Michael Weinstein, Dana Wilson, and Davide Zannoni. He was a guest conductor and presented conducting seminars throughout the United States and a frequent adjudicator and clinician for various state and national band and orchestra festivals. His scholarly work focused on a published analysis of Dana Wilson's "The Avatar: Concerto for Bassoon and Chamber Orchestra" (*Journal of Band Research*, 2007) and in expanding his dissertation research into a book on the influence of text on the instrumental music of Joseph Schwantner.

In addition to his teaching responsibilities at MSU, Broadnax maintained an active performance schedule on bass trombone and euphonium with the West Shore Symphony (Muskegon, Michigan) as well as various appearances throughout Michigan with orchestras in Grand Rapids, Greater Lansing, Jackson, Kalamazoo, and Midland and chamber performances with the West Shore Symphony Brass Trio and the Capitol Brass Quintet (Lansing).

In August 2007 Broadnax left MSU to become an assistant professor of instrumental music education and director of bands at California State University at East Bay in Hayward, California.

DANIEL CHRISTOPHER JACOBSON

Brock, Lou (18 June 1939–), baseball player, was born Louis Clark Brock in El Dorado, Arkansas, the son of a sharecropping family. When Lou was a child, his mother relocated to Collinston, Louisiana, where he grew up on a cotton plantation. A quiet and shy youth, Brock attended Union High School in Mer Rouge. Upon graduation he accepted an academic scholarship to Southern University in Baton Rouge. He chose to major in math for one simple reason: he had seen his family "duped" by plantation owners year in and year out, leaving the family deep in debt (Halberstam, 151). Despite hard work Brock lost his academic scholarship and turned to sports to stay in school, making the baseball team as a walk-on. He earned an athletic scholarship on the spot when he was given five practice swings in a batting session, three of which went for home runs.

Brock's career in baseball started slowly at Southern University. He broke out in his sophomore year when he hit .545 and sparked Southern

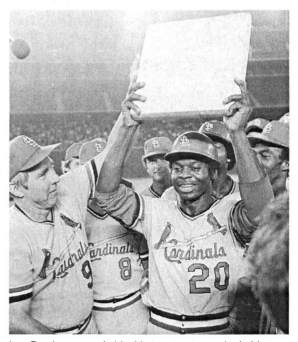

Lou Brock, surrounded by his teammates as he holds second base plate after breaking Ty Cobb's record of 892 stolen bases in San Diego, California, 29 August 1977. (AP Images.)

to a victory in the National Association of Intercollegiate Athletics (NAIA) World Series, the first black school to win the title. Although major league scouts had paid Brock some attention, one scout in particular maintained a close relationship with him, the Chicago Cubs's JOHN "BUCK" O'NEIL. A renowned Negro League player and a great baseball mind, O'Neil saw in Brock the same skills that had made his friend JAMES "COOL PAPA" BELL one of the greatest players in the Negro Leagues. O'Neil also saw in Brock the same hunger for success as his earlier Cubs protégé, ERNIE BANKS. In 1960 Brock flew to St. Louis with the belief that he was scheduled for a meeting and tryout with the Cardinals organization. However, the meeting never materialized and Brock, low on money, took a bus to Chicago to stay with a friend. There Brock earned a living washing floors while trying to get a tryout with the two Chicago franchises, the White Sox and the Cubs. In 1961, after two workouts, the Chicago Cubs signed Lou Brock to a contract for $12,000 and paid him a $5,000 bonus. Brock played one season of minor league ball for the Cubs before being brought up late in the 1961 season. However, his play the next two years at the big league level inspired little confidence among Cubs management. His inexperience and Chicago's unusual coaching system of revolving managers, each with his own ideas as to what Brock should or should not be doing, led to his slow development. By mid-1964, with a journeyman's average and just fifty stolen bases to his credit, the Cubs traded him to the St. Louis Cardinals for the pitcher Ernie Broglio, an eighteen-game winner in 1963. The "Brock for Broglio" deal then seemed like a steal for the Cubs, but has since gone down as one of the most lopsided trades in baseball history; while Broglio won just seven more games in his career, Lou Brock blossomed into a Hall of Famer.

Brock made his debut with the Cardinals on 15 June 1964 and ignited the team. When he joined the Cards they were in fourth place, but they ended the season by winning the National League pennant and subsequently defeating the New York Yankees to win the World Series. One of the keys to Brock's early success in St. Louis was the relaxed attitude of the Cardinals's clubhouse. More importantly, manager Johnny Keane recognized Brock's amazing speed and let him put it to good use. Early on, in a team meeting, Keane told Brock, "I want you to keep running. If I don't tell you to stop running, then no one else on this team does [sic] either, and if someone tries to stop you, then you can tell them where to go" (Halberstam, 141). Indeed, Brock's base-stealing abilities not only helped the Cardinals to win but also revolutionized baseball. His aggressive style of base-running often forced the opposition to make errors. Brock also popularized the "pop-up" style of stealing a base; not only did he go into a base cleats first and deal punishment to fielders but he was also up and on his feet in a hurry, ever-ready to take the next base if the opportunity arose. Brock's steals did not happen just by chance. He was an early proponent of using game film of opposing pitchers, studying their moves and tendencies from 8-mm game film shot from the Cardinals dugout. Brock's base-stealing became legendary, and he led the league in stolen bases from 1966 to 1969 and 1971 to 1974. In 1974 he shattered the single season record for stolen bases set by Maury Wills, stealing 118 bases. When he retired after the 1979 season Brock held the record for steals with 938. Though this record was eclipsed by RICKY HENDERSON in 1982, Brock remains second all-time in this category.

Not to be forgotten is Lou Brock's hitting ability. He batted over .300 in nine seasons and in 1967 became the first player ever to hit twenty-one home runs and steal over fifty bases in a season. In 1962 Brock hit one of only three home runs that ever went over the center-field wall at New York's Polo Grounds. His stellar career notwithstanding, Brock had his critics in the baseball world. Not a typical lead-off man, Brock struck out often and at his retirement was the career leader with 1,730 strikeouts. However, it was not with his bat and power that Lou Brock made history, but with his legs and his intelligence. He helped his team win the World Series in 1964 and 1968 and was a six-time All Star who was enshrined into the Baseball Hall of Fame in 1985, his first year of eligibility. Brock was also voted as one of the twentieth century's top one hundred players by Major League Baseball.

Following his retirement after the 1979 season Brock remained active both with the St. Louis Cardinals and with the local community. Operating a successful florist business and acting as spring training instructor for the Cardinals, Brock and his wife, Jacqueline, were also both ordained ministers and elders at the Abundant Life Fellowship Church and were well-known for their scholarship programs and their work with disadvantaged young people in the St. Louis area.

FURTHER READING
Brock, Lou. *Biography*. Available online at http://www.loubrock.com.

Brock, Lou. *Stealing Is My Game* (1976).

Bucek, Jeanine, ed. *The Baseball Encyclopedia* (1996).

Halberstam, David. *October 1964* (1994).

GLENN ALLEN KNOBLOCK

Brock, Ralph Elwood (15 February 1883–9 December 1959), conservationist, landscaper, and the first African American forester in the United States, was born in Pottsville, Pennsylvania, the fifth of six children born to Alcinda (Dickson) a homemaker, and the Reverend John Calvin Brock, an educator and minister in the African Methodist Episcopal (AME) Church. Reverend Brock was a veteran of the Civil War, serving as quartermaster sergeant of Company F of the 43rd Pennsylvania Regiment. The Brock family moved throughout south central and south eastern Pennsylvania, settling in West Chester, Pennsylvania, around 1890. Four of the six Brock children (including Ralph) were known to be college educated and active in the community. Maria L. (8 May 1879–1968) taught in the West Chester School District for over thirty years; she was the English and Elocution teacher of the civil rights campaigner, BAYARD RUSTIN, and bequeathed the family home to the Charles A. Melton Arts & Education Center. John Robert Paul (31 October 1880–22 November 1922) was, at the time of his death, superintendent of the colored school in Atlantic City, New Jersey, and Dr. Howard F. (23 July 1889–?) was a physician in Westfield, New Jersey. Ralph received most of his education in the West Chester public schools; however, he graduated with the Class of 1900 from Howard High School in nearby Wilmington, Delaware.

The Brock family was an integral part of the African American community in West Chester. A catalyst to Ralph's success was Rev. Brock's relationship with Addison Jones, the Superintendent of West Chester Schools from 1889 until 1924. When Rev. Brock passed away in August 1901, Jones began to mentor Ralph and advocated for his employment with Pennsylvania Department of Forestry. Jones wrote a letter to Dr. Joseph Rothrock, the first commissioner of the Pennsylvania Department of Forestry. In his letter, Jones sought "a place" for Ralph in the Department of Forestry. Rothrock and Brock began corresponding in 1902. In April of that year, Pennsylvania Governor William Stone appointed Brock the Student Assistant Forester at Mont Alto State Forest Reserve. Immediately following his appointment, Brock and George Wirt, a forester of the Pennsylvania Department of Forestry, arrived at Mont Alto State Forest Reserve

to initiate the formation of a forestry school. In May 1903, an Act of the Pennsylvania Legislature created the Mont Alto Forest Academy. This was the third school of forestry established in the United States after the Biltmore Forest School (1898) and the Yale school of Forestry (1901).

In September 1903, thirteen men enrolled in the Mont Alto State Forest Academy; only six graduated with B.S. degrees in Forestry. Ralph Brock was the only African American. Brock excelled in essential areas of study, in such classes as Business Law, Constables Manuals & Laws, Political Geography, Forestry, Political Economy, French, Forest Finance, Forest Economics & Policy, Chemistry, and Forest Management & Working Plans. These classes would later prove to be the foundation for his success in landscaping. His commitment to education garnered him many accolades including being appointed student superintendent of the nursery and class salutatorian.

In May 1903, while still a student at the Forest Academy, Brock initiated a trip to Tuskegee, Alabama, to study the work being done with forests. In a letter to Dr. Rothrock, Brock expressed his desire to "learn first handed the work done in the pineries and turpentine forests." It is speculated that he chose Tuskegee Institute because he was African American and thus few places would accept him as a visiting student. However, he may have chosen Tuskegee because a friend of his father, Bishop Turner, was affiliated with Tuskegee Institute and willing to assist young Brock in his educational endeavors.

Following graduation in 1906, he was appointed the superintendent of the nursery at Mont Alto Forest Academy. He was also an educator. His lecture notes demonstrate an extensive knowledge of plants and trees including care, treatment, and conservation. Correspondence indicates that Brock had created his own solutions and compounds to treat diseased trees and seedlings.

In 1908, Brock married Pauline Wethers of West Chester, Pennsylvania. The couple had one son, Russell T. Brock. Little is known of Brock's personal life beyond his lifelong commitment to serving West Chester's African American community. This was often documented in the local newspaper, the *Daily Local News*.

At Mont Alto, Brock encountered many problems, including issues of race. There was the appearance of poor personal finance management; however, it is evident through his correspondence that his personal bills were submitted to the Forest Academy. Whether the bills were submitted to the Forest Academy erroneously or intentionally, they were a source of frustration for Brock. This issue, initially addressed in December 1908, plagued Brock throughout his employment with the Pennsylvania Department of Forestry. In Brock's curt and direct correspondence his anger is palpable. Brock resigned from the Pennsylvania Department of Forestry's Mont Alto Forest Academy on 1 March 1911. During his tenure at Mont Alto Forest Academy, Brock was responsible for over one million seedlings or trees planted throughout the Commonwealth of Pennsylvania.

After leaving the Department of Forestry, he established a landscaping business servicing urban and suburban estates in New York City, West Chester, and Philadelphia, Pennsylvania. His gardening and landscaping skills were recognized by John D. Rockefeller, Jr. and in 1928 he was hired as gardener at the Paul Laurence Dunbar Apartments in Harlem. Later, his responsibilities were expanded to supervisor of gardens for the New York City Riverside Park, Radio City Gardens in Rockefeller Center, and the Harlem River House. Harlem River House was a nine acre complex built as a part of President Franklin Roosevelt's New Deal. The complex was built in 1937 using federal funding. It was the first public housing project and was designed specifically for African Americans. Brock retired in 1957 due to failing health and moved, with his wife Pauline, to Westfield, New Jersey, to be closer to his brother. Ralph Elwood Brock died on 9 December 1959. He is buried in historic Chestnut Grove Cemetery in West Chester, Pennsylvania.

FURTHER READING

The Brock Papers including correspondence and lecture notes are located in Record Group 65 ACCN. 4817 of the Pennsylvania State Archives in Harrisburg, Pennsylvania.

Hocking, Joan M., ed. *Centennial Voices: The Story of Mont Alto—A Continuing Story, 1903–2003* (2003).

RACHEL L. JONES WILLIAMS

Brodhead, John Henry (21 Apr. 1898–1951), teacher and educational psychologist, was born in Washington, New Jersey, the son of Robert and Elizabeth Brodhead. His father, born in New York, was an assistant chef on a railroad cafe car, and his mother, born in Pennsylvania, a laundress at a hotel. He had one older brother, Frank E., and an older sister, Annie. Their father died prior to 1910.

Brodhead graduated from West Chester State Normal School, Pennsylvania, in 1919 and began teaching in the West Chester public schools, boarding with W. J. Williams, his wife, Mary, and infant son, William Jr. During the early 1920s he moved to Philadelphia, beginning a lifelong career in the city's public school system. He married Fleta Marie Jones, a native of Philadelphia, around 1924. Their only child, a daughter named for her mother, was born 12 August 1928.

While teaching, Brodhead pursued his own higher education, earning a bachelor of science degree from Temple University in 1927. By 1930 he was a principal in Philadelphia, where Fleta Brodhead was a nurse. The same year, he completed a masters degree in Education, also from Temple. In 1937 Brodhead received a doctor of education degree in Educational Psychology at Temple, after completing the dissertation "Educational Achievement and Its Relationship to the Socio-Economic Status of the Negro in the High Schools of Philadelphia."

A lifelong Republican, and member of the African Methodist Episcopal (AME) church, Brodhead was a charter member of the Philadelphia branch of the Committee on Participation of Negroes in National Defense, organized beginning in 1938 at the initiative of the *Pittsburgh Courier* newspaper, published by Robert L. Vann. Along with his professional workload and involvement in community affairs, Brodhead completed an LL from Wilberforce University in 1942. There is no record that he practiced law afterward. He served on the board of a local YMCA, and was a member of the Alpha Phi Alpha fraternity.

Brodhead chaired a citizens' committee to integrate the nursing profession in Philadelphia. The city's public General Hospital had no doctors of African descent until 1937, and had no students of African descent in its prestigious nursing school program. His role in this field undoubtedly owed much to Fleta Brodhead, a charter member of the Theta Chapter, Chi Eta Phi Sorority, formed by graduates of Philadelphia nursing schools, including those trained at Douglass Memorial Hospital, founded specifically to serve the city's African American population. She served as Basileus of the chapter, 1950–1952.

Records of the schools led by Brodhead are sparse. In 1942 he was principal of the Pratt-Arnold School on West Dauphin Street in the northern part of the city. Later in the 1940s, he was assigned as principal of General John F. Reynolds School, serving 2,400 students, a position he still held in 1950, and most likely until very close to the time he died. Pennsylvania law by this time declared that it was unlawful for a school district to make any distinction on account of the color or race of any pupil or scholar. However, an article by Reid E. Jackson in the *Journal of Negro Education*, which acknowledged Brodhead as its primary source of information on Philadelphia schools, reported in 1947 that "there has been a tendency to assign Negro teachers primarily to schools located in neighborhoods that are primarily Negro" (vol. 16, summer 1947, 301, 309).

Brodhead was an active member and officer of the American Teachers Association (ATA), originally founded as the National Association of Teachers in Colored Schools. He was an ATA representative to the First National Conference on the United Nations Educational, Scientific, and Cultural Organization (UNESCO) in Philadelphia, 24–26 March 1947. Serving as ATA vice president that year, he signed the historian Carter G. Woodson's certificate of life membership in the association in December. He was elected president of American Teachers Association for two successive one-year terms, at the 1948 convention in Atlantic City, and the 1949 convention in Wilberforce, Ohio. Brodhead had previously served as president of the Association of Pennsylvania Teachers, organized April 1916, the state affiliate of the ATA.

Although the founding documents of the National Teachers Association, a forerunner of the National Education Association (NEA), did not mention race, the existence of rigidly dual school systems in the southern states, and schools designated for "colored children" in many other states, had resulted in the NEA being overwhelmingly composed of teachers classified as "white." The two organizations had worked together since 1926 to secure accreditation for segregated "colored" schools—lack of accreditation being a major obstacle to college admission for students of African descent. Brodhead frequently served on joint committees appointed by the two organizations. Fifteen years after Brodhead's death, the ATA merged with the NEA.

The cause of Brodhead's death at the age of fifty-three is not documented. He was survived by his wife, and by their daughter, who graduated from West Chester State College in 1949 with a major in Elementary Education, and in 1951 married Elliot Drexel Waters Sr.

FURTHER READING

Guthrie, Robert V. *Even the Rat Was White: A Historical View of Psychology* (2004). (Details appearing in this source should be corroborated when possible).

CHARLES ROSENBERG

Bronson, James H. (ca. 1838–16 Mar. 1884), Civil War soldier and Medal of Honor recipient, was born in Burrell Township, Pennsylvania. Little is known about Bronson's life before the war except that he was a barber. Perhaps enthusiastic about getting a chance to fight for the Union cause, he journeyed from Pennsylvania to Delaware, Ohio, to enlist in the 127th Ohio Regiment on 4 July 1863. When he joined, James Bronson was in the vanguard of black service in the army; less than two months prior, the War Department had created the Bureau of Colored Troops. This military agency was created to aid in the establishment of black regiments and the enlistment of both black troops and the white officers who would command them. In some cases these regiments were raised entirely under the bureau's guidance. However, as was the case with Bronson's 127th Ohio Regiment, some were raised by individual states and were later incorporated into the Union army. Thus it was that the 127th Ohio would be redesignated in 1863 as the Fifth United States Colored Troop (USCT).

Most of the men in James Bronson's regiment came from Ohio and the surrounding states. Because Ohio was a major link in the Underground Railroad, a number of black soldiers in the 127th Ohio were former slaves, or the children of former slaves, and they made Ohio their home. Camp for the new recruits of the 127th Ohio was established at Delaware, near Columbus, and Colonel James Conine was chosen as its leader. His second in command was Lieutenant Colonel Giles Shurtleff, a graduate of Oberlin College who was sympathetic to the abolitionist movement. Because Conine would not join the regiment until it was sent southward, Shurtleff trained the new recruits, and he chose his company sergeants, including Bronson, MILTON MURRAY HOLLAND, ROBERT PINN, and POWHATTAN BEATTY. These men originally enlisted as privates but were likely promoted based on their aptitude and the respect they commanded among their fellow soldiers; sometimes company sergeants were chosen by vote among the soldiers they would lead. Bronson was not just a soldier; he also served as a musician in the regimental band.

The Fifth USCT departed for the war on 18 November 1863 and first served in Virginia, where Colonel Conine assumed command upon the regiment's arrival in Norfolk. In December the regiment was assigned to duty in North Carolina, where it remained until January 1864, when it returned to Virginia. The Fifth USCT saw little action until it was assigned to the Army of the James, an element of Grant's Union army operating in the James River area of Virginia in May 1864. Bronson and the men of the Fifth USCT saw their first combat during the siege of Petersburg, losing fourteen men during the Battle of the Crater on 30 July 1864. Afterward, the Fifth USCT continued with the Army of the James, stationed opposite the Confederate fortifications around Richmond near New Market Heights. In late September 1864 the Union general Ulysses S. Grant concocted a plan to take four key Confederate forts in the Richmond line by launching simultaneous attacks on both sides of the James River. The attacks would be conducted by a number of USCT units, including the Fifth Regiment. Perhaps fortuitously, the Fifth USCT underwent a command change on the eve of battle. With Colonel Conine injured, Lieutenant Colonel Shurtleff, the man responsible for training the men of the original 127th Ohio, now took command. While awaiting orders to attack, Shurtleff visited with his men and told them, "If you are brave the stigma of diminished pay must be removed and the greater stigma of denying you full and equal rights of citizenship shall also be swept away" (Mercer, 23). That was all the men of the Fifth USCT needed to hear.

The Battle of New Market Heights commenced in the early morning hours of 29 September 1864 and lasted two days. The outcome of the battle was a stalemate, and only one of the objectives was taken. It cost the Union 5,000 casualties, and out of 550 men, the Fifth USCT counted 85 dead and 257 wounded. However, the battle was one of historic proportions, for black soldiers fought with such valor and distinction that they achieved the only success of the battle. They captured Fort Harrison against overwhelming odds. The fighting was so fierce that many white officers, Shurtleff included, were shot down while storming Confederate fortifications, and the outcome of the fighting fell on the shoulders of sergeants who were now in positions of leadership. And lead they did, men like James Bronson, EDWARD RATCLIFF, CHRISTIAN ABRAHAM FLEETWOOD, SAMUEL GILCHRIST, and three of Bronson's fellow regimental sergeants, Pinn, Holland, and Beatty. Indeed, the actions of USCT soldiers at New Market Heights were so inspired that sixteen men earned the Medal of Honor in the fighting. Two weeks following the battle, Major General Benjamin Butler was inspired to comment that "All these gallant colored soldiers were left in command, all their company officers being killed or wounded, and led them gallantly and meritoriously through the day. For these services they have

most honorable mention, and the commanding general will cause a special metal to be struck in honor of these gallant colored soldiers" (Official Records, 168). In addition to receiving the Medal of Honor, Bronson and a number of other men also received the Butler Medal, specifically created by General Butler after this battle to honor those black soldiers who fought bravely and heroically at New Market Heights.

Following this battle, Sergeant James Bronson continued with the Fifth USCT, but with one change; perhaps tired of fighting, he asked that he be allowed to relinquish his rank of sergeant and return to his position in the regimental band. Bronson's request was granted, and he later served in 1864 at the Battle of Fair Oaks, the expeditions to capture Fort Fisher in December 1864–January 1865, and the capture of Wilmington, North Carolina, in 1865. It was possibly while stationed in North Carolina that James Bronson met and married his wife, Ellen, a native of that state. When he was discharged from the Fifth USCT on 20 September 1865 at Carolina City, North Carolina, Bronson's rank was listed as musician.

James Bronson would live for less than twenty years after the Civil War; he resided with his wife and worked as a barber in Salem Boro, Columbiana County, Ohio, for a time before moving back to his native Pennsylvania. At the time of his death at the approximate age of forty-five, Bronson was living near Pittsburgh in Carnegie, Pennsylvania, and he is buried in Chartiers Cemetery in that town.

FURTHER READING

Mercer, John. "Giles Waldo Shurtleff: Leadership in the Cause of Freedom," available online at http://www.oberlin.edu/external/EOG/shurtleffBio-Mercer.htm.
United States Government Printing Office. *The War of the Rebellion: A Compilation of the Official Records of the Union and Confederate Armies*, vol. 42, series I, part III (1893).

GLENN ALLEN KNOBLOCK

Brooke, Edward (26 Oct. 1919–), lawyer and U.S. senator, was born Edward William Brooke III in Washington, D.C., to Edward Brooke Jr., an attorney for the Veterans Administration, and Helen Seldon. Growing up in an integrated middle-class neighborhood, Brooke readily absorbed his mother's instruction to respect others and treat all people equally. The Brookes lived relatively free from much of the racism endured by other African Americans. "We never felt hated," his mother recalled (Cutler,

Edward Brooke, at his office in Boston, Massachusetts, 22 January 1964. (AP Images.)

14). Brooke attended Dunbar High School, an elite public school with many middle- and upper-class African American students and then went on to Howard University, where he became president of the school's chapter of the Alpha Phi Alpha fraternity and earned his bachelor's degree in 1941. Following the bombing of Pearl Harbor later that year, Brooke was drafted into an all-black combat unit in the army. He served in many roles, including as a defender of those who had been court-martialed. His tour of duty during World War II took him to Africa and to Italy, and he earned a Bronze Star for leading an attack on a military battery. While in Italy he met his wife, Remigia Ferrair-Scacco, who had served in the underground resistance against the Nazis. The couple married in 1947 and later had two daughters.

Brooke enrolled in law school at Boston University in 1946. He became editor of the law review during his final year of school and went on to earn LLB and LLM degrees. Brooke then practiced law in the Roxbury area of Boston, where he witnessed firsthand the problems African Americans faced regarding housing, education, employment, and health care. At the same time, he worked as legal counsel for the local chapter of the NAACP and served on the board of directors of the Greater Boston Urban League. He lobbied the state legislature for the elimination of segregation in the state's National Guard units and worked on an appeal to the U.S. Supreme Court to outlaw segregation in

railroad dining cars. Brooke was also very active in the AMVETS, an organization for World War II veterans, and in 1956 he served as the National Judge Advocate for the group.

In 1950 Brooke's friends persuaded him to run for the state legislature. A Republican in a heavily Democratic state, he lost the election and vowed never to run for office again, in part because his wife was upset over campaign talk about their mixed marriage. He nonetheless ran for the legislature two years later but lost again. Brooke narrowly lost another election in 1960, this time for secretary of state for Massachusetts. Although he had failed in his quest for political office, Brooke won the respect of numerous leaders in the state's Republican Party and soon accepted an appointment to the Boston Finance Commission. He quickly earned a reputation as a tough crime fighter as he exposed corruption in several city agencies, including the police department. In 1962 Brooke was elected as Massachusetts attorney general, becoming the first African American ever to win such a statewide position. He first won a difficult primary battle, overcoming strong objections from Republican leaders concerning his liberalism and inexperience, and then went on to win the general election by appealing to white voters on the strength of his personal charm and his record with the Boston Finance Commission. As would be the case throughout his career, Brooke resisted attempts to label him a "black" politician. He commented, "I'm the lawyer for the five million citizens of Massachusetts, not for its … Negroes" (Cutler, 117). He did not ignore racial matters, however. While in office Brooke filed a brief in support of a fair housing law and helped draft legislation to forbid employment discrimination by businesses and unions. A firm believer in gradual change through legal means, he clashed with civil rights leaders over their plans to have students boycott school for a day, which would have violated the state's truancy laws, to protest de facto segregation in Boston.

Brooke's triumph as an African American in an overwhelmingly white state propelled him into national Republican debates in 1964. Like other liberal Republicans, Brooke grew alarmed at the conservative movement's efforts to nominate the Arizona senator Barry Goldwater, who had voted against the 1964 Civil Rights Act, as the party's presidential candidate that year. Attending the Republican convention in San Francisco, Brooke urged the party to adopt a strong civil rights plank and seconded the nomination of Governor

William Scranton of Pennsylvania, a more moderate candidate on race and other issues, for president. Goldwater withstood the Scranton challenge, and Brooke, like several other northeastern liberals, refused to support the Arizonan that fall. Although Goldwater suffered a crushing defeat in November, Brooke was overwhelmingly reelected as Massachusetts attorney general.

Two years later Brooke won election to the U.S. Senate. The victory marked him as the first black senator since Reconstruction and as the first African American to win a Senate seat by popular vote. As conservatives gained influence within the Republican Party nationally, Brooke continued to support many of President Lyndon Johnson's social-welfare Great Society programs. Brooke even attacked Johnson on occasion for doing too little to combat poverty, and in 1966 he published his views on racial and economic problems facing black Americans in *The Challenge of Change*. He also became deeply involved in debates over the future of the Republican Party. Although he once again refused to make his race an issue, Brooke urged the party to broaden its appeal beyond white, middle-class suburbanites by reaching out to African Americans and other minorities. Many political pundits saw him as a leader who could bring at least some of the black vote back to the party of Abraham Lincoln. Soon after his election, there was speculation among some Republicans, as well as in the media, that Brooke would make an excellent choice for the Republican vice-presidential nomination in 1968.

Brooke was at the center of debates over the racial violence of the mid- and late 1960s. Following enormously destructive riots in the summer of 1967 in Newark, New Jersey, and Detroit, Michigan, President Johnson chose Brooke to serve on his Advisory Commission on Civil Disorders (also known as the Kerner Commission). Brooke toured several riot-torn areas and firmly rejected conservative claims that the riots were the result of communist influence or a conspiracy among radical black leaders. Instead, he insisted that the riots stemmed from social and economic problems related to jobs, housing, education, and health care. At the same time, Brooke held to his beliefs in integration and peaceful change. He worried that the media gave too much attention to more radical black leaders, such as STOKELY CARMICHAEL, and he rejected Black Power, calling it "a turn in the wrong direction" (Cutler, 197). In 1968 Brooke worked closely with Senator Walter Mondale of Minnesota, a liberal Democrat, on behalf of the Fair Housing Act.

During the late 1960s and early 1970s Brooke regularly criticized Richard Nixon's civil rights policies. He blasted the president for his early approach to school desegregation in the South and for not following through on his promise to promote economic development in the inner cities through "black capitalism." Worried that Nixon was too eager to appeal to white southerners and suburbanites, Brooke played a prominent role in successful efforts to defeat Nixon's nominations of the conservatives Clement Haynsworth and G. Harrold Carswell to the Supreme Court. He also opposed the nomination of William H. Rehnquist out of concern about his right-wing views on civil rights, though the Senate confirmed Rehnquist.

Brooke won reelection in 1972 but lost six years later, in part because of press revelations that he had lied about his personal finances in a deposition related to his divorce that year from his wife. Brooke was never charged with any crime, however, and the Senate Ethics Committee absolved him of any wrongdoing. In 1979 he became head of the National Low-Income Housing Coalition, resumed practicing law in Virginia, and married Anne Fleming. The couple had one son, Edward W. Brooke IV. In 2002 Brooke underwent successful surgery for breast cancer, and subsequently launched an effort to alert men to the dangers of this relatively rare disease among men. A recipient of the NAACP's Spingarn Medal for black achievement in 1967, and the Presidental Medal of Freedom in 2004, Brooke symbolizes the post–World War II rise of African Americans to prominent political positions, as well as his generation's faith in integration and working through established political and legal channels to achieve change. In 2009 Brooke was awarded the Congressional Gold Medal.

FURTHER READING

Edward Brooke's papers are in the Library of Congress, Washington, D.C.

Brooke, Edward. *Bridging the Divide: My Life* (2006).

Cutler, John. *Ed Brooke: Biography of a Senator* (1972).

TIMOTHY N. THURBER

Brooks, Avery (2 Oct. 1948–), actor and performer, was born in Evansville, Indiana, to Sam Brooks, a choir singer and tool and die worker active in local unions, and Eva Crawford Lydia, a music teacher and one of the first African American women to graduate from Northwestern University. The family relocated to Gary when Avery was eight years old. There he attended the local schools before matriculating at Indiana University and Oberlin College, though he left both schools before taking a degree.

Soon, Brooks enrolled at Rutgers University, and it was from there that he received a B.A. in 1974 and an MFA in 1976. He was the first African American at that institution to accomplish the latter. That same year, he married Vicki Lenora, a dean at the school. The couple went on to have three children.

After graduation, Brooks stayed on at Rutgers as a drama teacher and acting coach in the theater department. He also began to sing and act professionally. In 1979 he landed a role in a play at the Public/Anspache Theater in New York, and it was from that stage that he began to be noticed by a larger audience. In 1982, he appeared as PAUL ROBESON in a one-man play in theaters in Los Angeles, New York, and Washington, D.C. Two years later, Brooks made the leap to television, appearing on PBS's *American Playhouse* series.

It was in 1985, though, that Brooks became a much more widely recognized performer. That year, he appeared as the savvy, streetwise Hawk in ABC's private-eye series *Spenser: For Hire* (based on the best-selling novel series by Robert B. Parker). A year later, he played the title character in the Showtime cable channel's mounting of *Uncle Tom's Cabin*, a performance for which he was critically lauded (and nominated for a cable ACE Award) and which helped him to secure a part in 1988's *Roots* sequel, *Roots: The Gift*. In 1989, Brooks's Hawk character had become so popular that the network developed a spin-off, *A Man Called Hawk*, in which Brooks played the lead. The show was poorly received, however, and was canceled after just one season.

In 1993, Brooks won his most popular and most widely recognized role. Gene Roddenberry's *Star Trek* series had been revived some years earlier with the popular *Star Trek: The Next Generation*, and the show's producers were ready to expand the franchise with a new hour-long series. Brooks tried out and was offered the role of Benjamin Sisko, commander of an interstellar outpost in *Star Trek: Deep Space Nine*. He was the first African American actor to head a *Star Trek* series or film (interestingly, and as was not the case with other iterations of the franchise, both former and later, Brooks's character began as a Commander and not a Captain. This was remedied some seasons later, when the Sisko character was promoted). In 1998, Brooks directed an episode of the series, "Far

beyond the Stars," in which he played an alternate-reality version of himself, Benny Russell, a pulp sci-fi magazine stringer in 1950s New York. The civil rights–themed installment (Benny struggles to sell stories featuring African American heroes) is widely regarded as one of the best in all of the franchise's long history. *Star Trek: Deep Space Nine* ran for seven seasons and, if not as widely popular as *Star Trek: The Next Generation*, it nevertheless had a dedicated core of fans and was critically lauded for its novelistic approach to storytelling (then far less common on television) and emotionally complex character depictions.

Brooks also appeared in a number of motion pictures, though usually in relatively small, supporting roles. In 1998, he appeared in *American History X* and *The Big Hit*. In 2001, he had a small role in the Robert De Niro vehicle *15 Minutes*. He lent his distinctively growly voice to a number of projects, including animated series, audio books, video games, and documentaries. Among the latter, Brooks lent his voice talents to works for PBS's *Nova* series and to cable's *Discovery Channel*, among numerous other projects.

After *Star Trek*, Brooks focused mostly on the stage, however, both as actor and as director. In 2005, Brooks joined the Shakespeare Theatre Company to play the title role of *Othello*. Two years later, he again collaborated with the Shakespeare Theatre Company for its production of Christopher Marlowe's *Tamburlaine*, again playing the lead.

Avery Brooks has the unusual distinction of being both a highly regarded dramatic actor and performer and an instantly recognizable and much-loved figure to fans of two long-running television series from around the world.

FURTHER READING

Guerrero, Ed. *Framing Blackness: The African American Image in Film* (1993).

Hill, Errol G., and James V. Hatch. *A History of African American Theatre* (2003).

MacDonald, J. Fred. *Blacks and White TV: African Americans in Television since 1948* (1992).

JASON PHILIP MILLER

Brooks, Carolyn Branch (8 July 1946–), academic dean and scientist, was born Carolyn Daphne Branch in Richmond, Virginia, the second of two daughters born to Shirley Marian Booker Branch and Charles Walker Branch, owners of a grocery store. Shirley Branch earlier held a job at an antique store, while Charles Branch's early job was as a truck driver. Shirley later worked for the Virginia Department of Motor Vehicles. Carolyn's sister Delores was born in 1942, and both children attended segregated public schools in Richmond, Virginia, where Carolyn graduated from Maggie Walker High School as salutatorian. Branch excelled in academics and was encouraged to pursue a college education. With the aid of her teachers, she sought college scholarships because her supportive parents were unable to afford college tuition. Branch, a first-generation college student, chose Tuskegee University after being offered a choice of six scholarships to attend a historically black college or university (HBCU).

Her freshman year, she met her husband, Henry M. Brooks, a senior at Tuskegee, and they married in 1965 during her sophomore year. Brooks had one son, Charles, during her junior year, and another, Marcellus, during her senior year. Despite her busy family life, Brooks completed her B.S. in Biology in four years, graduating in 1968. Brooks also earned an M.S. in Biology in 1971 from Tuskegee, where she was mentored by Dr. Howard P. Carter and worked as an undergraduate research assistant and a graduate teaching assistant. Brooks gave birth to a daughter, Alexis, while working on her M.S. During this time Brooks developed a keen interest in teaching and research and decided to pursue a Ph.D. and become a college professor.

During her doctoral studies at Ohio State University, she found the social climate much different from that at Tuskegee. While her mentor, Dr. Julius Kreier, was strongly supportive, at an institution with very few African American students, she had to overcome hurdles related to racism. She became an activist to increase minority recruitment and retention in science, and she became a dedicated mentor of students. She persisted in her work with the support and encouragement of her husband. It was during this time that Brooks gave birth to Toni, her second daughter. She received a Ph.D. in Microbiology in 1977, and later in her career she took continuing education courses in molecular biology at Indiana University, University of Minnesota, University of Maryland (Center of Agricultural Biotechnology of MBI), and University of Wisconsin (La Crosse campus).

After she completed her Ph.D., Brooks pursued her career at HBCUs and advanced steadily upward through the academic ranks. Brooks began as a principal investigator and progressed to acting program director at Kentucky State University (1977–1981). From 1981 to 2007 she worked at the University of Maryland Eastern Shore (UMES). At UMES she began as research assistant professor on USDA-funded research projects. Brooks progressed in various administrative roles until 1995 when she became dean of the School of Agricultural and Natural Sciences, and she subsequently became the research director. In 1997 she was named executive assistant to both the president and the chief of staff at UMES while still holding the positions of dean and research director.

Brooks gained a reputation for her work at HBCUs and the black land grant colleges. At UMES she won recognition for her work in increasing minority participation in the sciences, especially microbiology. She significantly improved the experiences of minority students in the sciences through winning external and university grants, establishing a state-of-the-art research lab, recruiting high school students, working with high school counselors, creating precollege summer programs and the Scientific Enrichment Program for Minority Students, and instituting a graduate education bridge program.

Brooks's three-decade career in higher education was marked with accomplishment in teaching, research, administration, and service. Not only did she become a full professor but she became dean of the School of Agricultural and Natural Sciences at the University of Maryland Eastern Shore and research director of land grant programs. She increased science participation by African American students at Kentucky State University and at the University of Maryland Eastern Shore, and she directed the United States Department of Education–funded Scientific Enrichment Program. In 1998 she became the program codirector of the LOUIS STOKES Alliance for Minority Participation in the Sciences grant, funded by the National Science Foundation, and she remained a passionate mentor. Awards related to her work with students include the Outstanding Educator Award from the Maryland Association for Higher Education (1990), student awards for her dedication and devotion (1989 and 1996), and Advisor of the Year (1995).

Brooks's list of honors and awards includes the 2007 William A. Hinton Research Training Award from the American Society for Microbiology. She was also named one of the 2007 recipients of Maryland's Top 100 Women awards and was a recipient of the first annual White House Initiative for Historically Black Colleges and Universities Faculty Award for Excellence in Science and Technology (1988).

FURTHER READING

American Academy of Microbiology of the American Society for Microbiology. "William A. Hinton Research Training Award," *Microbe* 2, no. 2 (Feb. 2007).

Kessler, James H., et al. *Distinguished African American Scientists of the 20th Century* (1996).

Maryland's Business and Legal News since 1888, vol. 118, 127 (2 Mar. 2007).

TERRI L. NORRIS

Brooks, Elizabeth Carter (1867–1951), educator, social activist, and clubwoman, was born in New Bedford, Massachusetts. She was the daughter of a freed slave, Martha D. Webb, who had been sent north to be educated. Her father is unknown.

Elizabeth Carter began her formal education in the New Bedford public school system, where she attended New Bedford High School, the Swain School of Design, and, later, the Harrington Normal Training School. While attending the Harrington Normal Training School for Teachers, Carter started planning a home for the aged. In 1897, true to her convictions as a social activist, she opened the New Bedford Home for the Aged under her direction and financial support. The home welcomed anyone, regardless of race. Carter continued supporting the institution throughout her life, dedicating her time and experience and providing financial support.

Carter was a diligent, committed, and compassionate student, destined to leadership. After finishing high school, Carter journeyed to Brooklyn, New York, where in the 1880s she accepted a teaching position at the Howard Colored Orphanage. During this period she became involved in civic and club activities, which would play an integral role in formulating her perception of the social injustices suffered by African Americans, particularly African American women and girls, and her desire to achieve social equality.

While at the Howard Colored Orphanage, Carter became active in club work. She acquired a wealth of knowledge about administrative functions which helped propel her into leadership positions in several social activist clubs that were designed to improve the lives of African American women, both married and single, while eventually extending assistance to young African American girls.

These social clubs sought to demonstrate that African American women were intelligent and responsible, and that they should be allowed to fill social leadership roles and exercise all the rights and privileges of citizenship. Many educated, middle-class African American women felt it was part of their civic duty to elevate the "uneducated, less fortunate female members of her race"(Davis). Carter joined an elite group of her contemporaries, such as MARY ELIZA CHURCH TERRELL, JOSEPHINE SILONE YATES, MARGARET MURRAY WASHINGTON, IDA B. WELLS-BARNETT, Lucy Thurman, and MARY MCLEOD BETHUNE, all of whom sought to expand the realm of activities for African American women.

While working as a teacher in Brooklyn, Carter became the first recording secretary for the National Federation of Afro-American Women, which had been formed as a direct result of the First National Conference of Colored Women of America held in Boston in 1895. Through her club work and activities, Carter was instrumental in forming and co-founding the Northeastern Federation of Colored Women's Clubs, later serving as recording secretary and president. Her experience especially in this latter role would prove most beneficial in improving the administrative functions of the National Association of Colored Women and its affiliates across the country. From 1899 to 1904, she served as a recording secretary for the National Association of Colored Women and from 1904 to 1906 she served as its first recording secretary. In 1906 Carter was appointed vice president-at-large, relinquishing this post only when elected as the association's fourth president, holding the office from 1908 to 1912.

During her tenure as president of the National Association of Colored Women, Carter traveled to affiliate clubs across the nation, reviewing and helping to improve their organizational structures. Her diligence and skill resulted in standard organizational procedures for all associate clubs, improvements in financial recording, and the creation of an annual scholarship program for one extraordinary young black female to attend the Educational and Industrial Training School in Daytona, Florida (later Bethune-Cookman College).

After completing her training as a teacher at the Harrington Normal Training School, she became the first African American to graduate from this institution and be appointed to a teaching position in the New Bedford public school system. However, with the outbreak of World War I, the War Work Council summoned her to plan and supervise the erection of the new Phillis Wheatley Building at Rhode Island Avenue and Ninth

Streets, N.W., Washington, D.C. After completing this building project Carter returned to teaching until her retirement from the New Bedford public school system, after twenty-nine years of dedicated service.

In 1930 Carter married W. Simpson Brooks, bishop of the African Methodist Episcopal (AME) Church in Texas. The couple returned to Texas, where they built a thriving ministry until his death in 1934. On 14 June 1934 Elizabeth Brooks received an honorary law degree from Wilberforce University in Ohio. Returning to New Bedford, she remained active in missionary and civil rights work. In 1951 she was stricken with a cerebral hemorrhage and taken to St. Luke's Hospital, where she died. For her dedication to advancing education for African Americans, her commitment to caring for the elderly, and her steadfast fight for social equality and justice, the city of New Bedford named an elementary school in her honor, the Elizabeth Carter Brooks School.

FURTHER READING

Afro-American (Baltimore), 14 Apr. 1926.

Dannett, Sylvia G. L. *Profiles of Negro Womanhood*, vol. 1 (1964).

Davis, Elizabeth Lindsay. *Lifting as They Climb* (1933).

"Elizabeth Carter Brooks," in *Notable Black American Women*, book 1 (1992).

New Bedford Standard Times, 20 June 1948; 13 July 1951.

JANET E. MOORMAN

Brooks, Gwendolyn (7 June 1917–3 Dec. 2000), poet and novelist, was born Gwendolyn Elizabeth Brooks at her grandmother's home in Topeka, Kansas, the daughter of David Anderson Brooks, a janitor, and Keziah Wims Brooks. When she was two months old, the family settled in Chicago, where she would live the rest of her life. Brooks and her brother had a sheltered upbringing in a cheerful, orderly household. (She would later draw on memories of those years for her poem "a song in the front yard" [1945].) At Forrestville Elementary School, where she learned that light skin and fine hair were valued, this shy child with dark skin and coarse hair felt socially isolated. Her mother, however, encouraged her interest in writing, and Brooks published her first poem in *American Childhood* magazine in 1930.

Later, to escape further isolation at a mostly white high school, she transferred to an all-black school; finally, at the somewhat more integrated Englewood High School, she found a peer group

and teachers who encouraged her writing. From then on, she was constantly publishing—in national periodicals and regularly in Chicago's African American newspaper, the *Defender*. With her mother's encouragement, she showed her work to the poets JAMES WELDON JOHNSON, whom she found cold and distant, and LANGSTON HUGHES, with whom she established a long friendship.

Her family struggled financially during the Great Depression, but the year she finished high school Wilson Junior College opened with a low tuition that made it possible for her to earn an associate's degree. After college Brooks endured a series of dead-end jobs, including a humiliating position as a domestic; she later fictionalized that experience in her poem "Bronzeville Woman in a Red Hat" and in a chapter of her novel *Maud Martha*. She also worked several months for a charlatan spiritual healer operating out of the Mecca Building, a once fashionable apartment building that had decayed into a tenement; her experiences therein would later become the basis of her long narrative poem "In the Mecca." Active in the Youth Council of the NAACP, she cofounded a club for young black artists and writers. Through the NAACP, she met fellow poet Henry Blakely, whom she married in 1939; they had two children. Blakely died in 1996. Brooks's mature style developed after 1941, when she and her husband joined a South Side poetry workshop run by the white socialite Inez Cunningham Stark. Brooks credited Stark with introducing her to the artistic possibilities available in poetic form and forcing her to submit her work to more rigorous aesthetic judgment. She began winning poetry contests, and book publishers encouraged her to develop more poems about African American life. The title of her first book, *A Street in Bronzeville* (1945), refers to the *Defender's* name for the African American section of Chicago. The book includes some of her most admired poems, such as "The Sundays of Satin-Legs Smith," a portrait of a Bronzeville dandy; "The Mother," a bold and compassionate poem about abortion; and two poems that present African American perspectives on World War II, "Negro Hero" and "Gay Chaps at the Bar."

Working on poetry, fiction, and book reviews while her son attended school, Brooks wrote *Annie Allen* (1949), which loosely follows the life of the title character, an intelligent, sensitive African American woman. The centerpiece is the poem "The Anniad"; the title alludes to Virgil's ancient epic the *Aeneid*, and the language strives for Virgilian complexity, suggesting the extraordinary

Brooks's next collection, *The Bean Eaters* (1960), took an explicitly political turn with such poems as "The Ballad of Rudolph Reed," about the tragic result of a black family's move into a white neighborhood. Her most popular and most often reprinted poem, "We Real Cool," in eight short, infectiously rhythmic lines, introduces seven dropouts bragging about their wild lives despite their expectation of early death. She came to consider this poem her most successful combination of artistry with popular appeal, since, with its clarity and catchiness as well as its frequent inclusion in anthologies, it has spoken to an unusually broad audience.

In 1963 Brooks was offered a teaching position at Chicago's Columbia College. Throughout the 1960s and 1970s she would go on to teach also at Elmhurst College, Northeastern Illinois University, and the University of Wisconsin at Madison, among other schools. Brooks identified 1967 as the turning point in her career. Attending a Black Writers Conference at Fisk University, she was impressed by the contrast between the formal respect for her and the enthusiasm for the more radical AMIRI BARAKA. That striking contrast indicated to her a shift in African American culture from liberal integrationism toward a more militant black nationalism. Returning home, she was asked by the writer and community organizer Walter Bradford to lead a workshop for some members of the Blackstone Rangers street gang who were interested in writing. Although she eventually turned that workshop over to Bradford, she started meeting with black college students (including Don L. Lee [later Haki R. Madhubuti] and Carolyn Rodgers) for workshops in her home. Both these groups resisted Brooks's attempts to teach traditional poetic forms and high cultural aesthetics, insisting rather on a populist aesthetic in tune with their radical politics.

Also in 1967 Brooks read at the dedication of a mural depicting African American cultural heroes, including herself. Afterward, some of her workshop students led her into a local bar, where they gave an impromptu poetry reading, much to the appreciation of the patrons. The literary ambitions of the gang members and the warm reception of the tavern customers opened Brooks's eyes to an audience she had neglected. The events of that year initiated her commitment to the Black Power movement and black cultural nationalism, as well as to the Black Arts Movement, which in the late 1960s and early 1970s encouraged black artists and writers to reject European-derived aesthetics and the production of works for white audiences in favor of

Gwendolyn Brooks, sitting in the Poet Room of the Library of Congress in Washington, D.C., March 1986. (AP Images.)

heroism and ingenuity it takes to get through an ordinary life. For that book she became the first African American to receive a Pulitzer Prize.

Ironically, as Brooks was receiving high literary honors, her family was having trouble finding suitable housing. The tiny apartments they lived in are described in many of her poems. Housing for African Americans in Chicago was then limited to one area on the South Side; it had expanded very little over the decades, while its population had increased, nearly doubling in the 1940s. Part of her motivation for writing a novel, therefore, was to earn enough of an advance to be able to put a down payment on a house. The resulting autobiographical novel, *Maud Martha* (1953), is now considered a classic of African American literature, with its intimate, affectionate, and sometimes infuriated view of urban African American life in mid-century, before the rise of the civil rights movement. It portrays, through a series of lyrical scenes and frequent linguistic play, the childhood and young adulthood of an African American woman in Chicago.

African and African American themes and forms for a specifically African American audience.

In 1968 she succeeded Carl Sandburg as poet laureate of Illinois, and, using her own funds, she established an award for young writers in the state. That same year Harper and Row, Brooks's publisher since 1945, brought out the collection *In the Mecca*, which includes her narrative poem set in the Mecca Building, as a tribute to martyred heroes such as MALCOLM X and MEDGAR EVERS, and a sequence of poems about the Blackstone Rangers. Starting with *Riot* (1969), she published new work only with black presses. DUDLEY RANDALL's small but influential Broadside Press in Detroit began publishing chapbooks of her new poetry, two anthologies she edited, and her unconventional autobiography *Report from Part One* (1972). Rather than providing a straightforward narrative of her life, the latter volume offers a collage of anecdotes, comments on her own and others' writing, interviews, photographs, and commentary on her work by other writers. She would publish other chapbooks and the collection *To Disembark* (1981) through Madhubuti's Third World Press and her own imprints.

In 1969 she and her husband separated, and she felt a renewed sense of freedom. She traveled on her own to East Africa, an experience that influenced her sense of American blacks as Africans in the New World. It was during this period that she wrote the first volume of her autobiography and began editing an annual periodical, *The Black Position* (1971–1974). Her mother, however, encouraged Brooks and her husband to reconcile, which they did in 1973; in part to celebrate that reunion, they traveled together to Ghana.

In 1976 Brooks became the first black woman elected to the National Institute of Arts and Letters. She was appointed poetry consultant to the Library of Congress in 1985. By this point, however, much of her early work, except for *Selected Poems* (1963), was out of print, so she self-published her collected works, *Blacks* (1987). Over the years, she received numerous awards, including over fifty honorary doctorates. She died in Chicago.

With passion, clarity, and rich literary craft, Brooks's writings present and comment on urban African American life in the mid- to late twentieth century. As the struggle for racial justice heated up, she became a more overtly political public figure. She was the most prestigious African American poet of her generation, so her conversion in the late 1960s to a radical black politics was an important endorsement of that position. Her decision to publish only with black presses restricted the audience for her later work, but it made concrete her commitment to African American readers and cultural institutions. She successfully married political engagement with the highest quality of artistry and in the latter part of her career sought to present poetry as a cultural practice available to everyone, not just the literary elite. A major figure in American poetry, she used her personal prestige to support and inspire young black writers and to establish publishing institutions that would serve the specific cultural interests of African Americans.

FURTHER READING

Brooks's papers are at the Bancroft Library, University of California, Berkeley.

Brooks, Gwendolyn. *Report from Part One* (1972).

Brooks, Gwendolyn. *Report from Part Two* (1996).

Bodlen, B. J. *Urban Rage in Bronzeville: Social Commentary in the Poetry of Gwendolyn Brooks* (1998).

Kent, George E. *A Life of Gwendolyn Brooks* (1990).

Melhem, D. H. *Gwendolyn Brooks: Poetry and the Heroic Voice* (1987).

Mootry, Maria K., and Gary Smith, eds. *A Life Distilled: Gwendolyn Brooks, Her Poetry and Fiction* (1987).

Wright, Stephen Caldwell, ed. *On Gwendolyn Brooks: Reliant Contemplation* (1996).

Obituary: *New York Times*, 4 Dec. 2000.

This entry is taken from the *American National Biography* and is published here with the permission of the American Council of Learned Societies.

JAMES D. SULLIVAN

Brooks, Hallie Beachem (9 Oct. 1907–10 Oct. 1985), educator and librarian, was born Hallie Mae Beachem in West Baden, Indiana, the youngest daughter of Mary Lucy and Hal Beachem, a businessman. Brooks's love of libraries developed when she was nine years old, and the family moved to Indianapolis allowing her to visit the well-stocked neighborhood branch every two weeks with her siblings.

Brooks began her career in librarianship as a tenth grader at Shortridge High School when she received a scholarship to attend the Indiana State Public Library Training Course. At the end of the program, Brooks received a certificate and an appointment as an assistant librarian, attending high school classes in the morning and working forty-two hours a week at the public library in the afternoon. After graduating from high school, Brooks received a bachelor of arts degree from

Butler University in Indianapolis in 1934. Two years later she married Frederic Victor Brooks, an insurance company employee.

In 1930, while working as a public librarian in Indianapolis, Brooks met JOHN HOPE, the president of Atlanta University, who recruited her to head the library of the university's newly established laboratory school for students in kindergarten through the twelfth grade. Brooks ensured that the library bought engaging, thought-provoking books that would inspire a love of reading and learning in children of all ages. A fierce advocate for quality children's literature, Brooks protested publishers associations for publishing children's books that contained demeaning depictions of African Americans. As a northerner, Brooks was appalled by the scarcity of library services for African Americans in segregated Atlanta. She operated the laboratory school library on the model of a public library in order to include services for the black community in general.

Brooks received her bachelor of Library Science at Columbia University in 1940. The Atlanta University Laboratory School closed in 1941, and the following year Brooks joined the Atlanta University School of Library Service as a part-time faculty member. From 1940 to 1942, Brooks served as a consultant librarian for the Association of College and Secondary Schools for Negroes, visiting the sixteen member schools to help them upgrade their educational programs by improving library services. Brooks's work came to the attention of the General Education Board, a philanthropy focused on the education of blacks, which asked her to devise a set of recommendations for improving all Negro school libraries in the South. As a result, Brooks developed and directed the Field Service Program at Atlanta University with funding from the Carnegie Corporation of New York. From 1942 through 1945, Brooks and her program assistant, VIRGINIA LACY JONES, traveled to southern urban and rural communities, often enduring hardships and danger, to assist black schools in organizing their library services and preparing bibliographies for library purchases.

In 1946 Brooks was granted leave from Atlanta University to earn her master of arts in Library Science from the University of Chicago. From 1948 to 1949 Brooks completed additional coursework toward a Ph in Library Science at the University of Chicago. In 1948 Brooks was promoted to assistant professor at Atlanta University, and rose through the ranks until she attained a full professorship in 1969. Her academic specialties included book arts, children's literature, the history of books, literature of the humanities, mass communications, and publishing. One of Brooks's class projects, *A Panoramic Chart of the Manuscript Period in Bookmaking, Fifth to Fifteenth Centuries* (1949), was published to wide acclaim and was used by library schools for decades to teach book arts courses. To enrich her teaching, Brooks spent her 1955 sabbatical touring major European libraries such as France's Bibliothèque Nationale and the Laurentian Library in Italy. In addition to teaching technical knowledge, Brooks prepared her students to face any situation, including the challenges of providing a variety of rich services to underresourced black communities.

In 1965 Brooks's husband Frederic, then an executive with the Atlanta Life Insurance Company, died. Brooks retired in 1977 after forty-seven years at Atlanta University. In 1983 the Atlanta University Trustees awarded Brooks the status of professor emerita in recognition of her outstanding contributions to the university, the School of Library Service, the profession of librarianship, and the community in general. Brooks was a member of Beta Phi Mu and Phi Lamda Theta, international honor societies for librarians and educators, respectively.

Brooks died in Atlanta. As a leader in librarianship and an educator of generations of black librarians, Brooks had a vast impact on improving the provision of library services to African Americans.

FURTHER READING

Miller, Rosalind. "One Georgia Librarian, Hallie Beachem Brooks, Remembers, 1930 to 1977," *Georgia Librarian* 14 (1977).

Woodson, Almeta Gould. "Fifty Years of Service: A Chronological History of the School Library Service, Atlanta University," *Georgia Librarian* 28 (1991).

KRYSTAL APPIAH

Brooks, Lucy Goode (13 Sept. 1818–7 Oct. 1900), community activist and founder of the Friends Association for Children, was born a slave in Richmond, Virginia, to Judith Goode and an unidentified white male. Born Lucy Goode, she learned to read while a slave by listening secretly to the lessons taught to her master's children.

Lucy Goode learnt one of slavery's harshest lessons early in life. With few formal legal rights, slaves' lives were largely controlled by their masters, as was the fate of their families. A master could dictate the rules of any attempt at intimacy, marriage, or reproduction between slaves, so the forming of durable love and relationships became one of the greatest challenges facing slaves. Even if a family bond could be created under such circumstances, mothers and fathers lived in fear of the not uncommon possibility that their children would be sold away from them. This was another horror that Lucy had to face when she was raped by her master's son. Not only had she been violated and become pregnant with her rapist's child, but she was forced to give up her newborn son, who was sent away, never to be seen by Lucy again.

During the 1830s, Lucy began a courtship with Albert Royal Brooks, also a slave in Richmond. Her literacy allowed this relationship to flourish, as she taught Albert how to read and write so that he could forge passes to enable his visits to her. In 1839, Lucy and Albert gained permission to marry and reside in Albert's house, where they had twelve children, three of whom died in infancy. The household was strictly Christian with a strong sense of family values. But this semblance of a normal family life was destroyed in 1858 when, with seven living children, Lucy and her three youngest were sold to another slaveholder, Daniel Von Groning.

Albert was a successful black businessman by the standards of the day—a slave who operated a livery stable and eating house and was able to keep some of his wages. After many years, he was able to use this money to buy his own freedom. Then, over the course of four years, he paid eight hundred dollars in installments for the freedom of his wife and their three children, Lucy, Alberta, and Robert. On 21 October 1862, Daniel Von Groning signed their manumission papers, declaring the four slaves "and the increase in future of the females" free.

Concerned to keep her family together, but with four children still in bondage and Albert unable to afford their freedom, Lucy took up the cause of maintaining her family unit. With a burning determination never to be separated from her kin, and with the desperate heartache of a powerless mother, she persuaded three local Richmond businessmen to buy the enslaved children so that they would remain in Virginia. Yet, as often happened in such cases, the man who purchased Lucy's eldest daughter, Margaret Ann, broke his promise to keep her in Richmond and sold her to a buyer in Tennessee. It is there that Margaret Ann died in 1862, reportedly because of her "dangerous" ability to read and write. The Brooks' other three sons remained in Richmond until freed by the Union army in 1865. One of these sons, WALTER HENDERSON BROOKS,

went on to become a prominent Baptist leader, poet, and a leading light in the Association for the Study of Negro Life and History.

After the Civil War and emancipation, thousands of African Americans flocked to Richmond, many of them former slaves searching for work and searching for lost family. Lucy Brooks was deeply touched by the plight of these displaced people with no loved ones or community support. Since her own son and daughter had been sent away from her, she felt keenly their loss. In particular she was concerned for the plight of children without parents, probably touched by thoughts of her own children who had been cruelly separated from her. Lucy was convinced that an orphanage was needed to take care of these children, and persuaded the Ladies Sewing Circle for Charitable Work, of which she was leader, to support her. The Sewing Circle sought endorsement and financial support from the local Cedar Creek Society of Friends, potentially because some of the ladies in the Circle knew of Quakers' humanitarian traditions and support for black education in other communities. Lucy also won the support of several black churches, and in 1867 Richmond City Council deeded a lot for the orphanage in Richmond's Jackson Ward neighborhood. The building was completed in 1871 at the corner of Saint Paul and Charity Streets, and was incorporated by the Virginia General Assembly in March 1872 as the Friends' Asylum for Colored Orphans.

Lucy Goode Brooks died 7 October 1900, but the legacy of her commitment to the importance of family remains. In 1932, her orphanage was turned into a child-placement agency, and has since become a large, multi-service family support center renamed the Friends Association for Children. It now consists of three family support centers, focusing on youth enrichment, child care, leadership and career advancement, one of which remains on the site of the original orphanage building of 1871. It is here, at the corner of Saint Paul and Charity Streets, that a historical marker was dedicated to Lucy Goode Brooks in March 2008, to honor her love of and dedication to caring for children and families, despite the horrors she suffered in her own life.

In 1984, the Lucy Brooks Foundation was created to raise funds for the Association. One of the fundraising ideas was "The Lucy Bracelet." Inscribed with the maxim "Isn't it amazing what one woman and her friends can do?" the bracelet is another way of remembering, according to the

Friends' Association, "the power of the human spirit to respond in love despite surviving the cruelest indignities."

FURTHER READING
The manumission papers of Lucy Goode Brooks and her children are available from the Library of Virginia and can be viewed online through its Virginia Women in History 2008 website.

Brooks, Charlotte K., Joseph K. Brooks, and Walter H. Brooks III. *A Brooks Chronicle: The Lives and Times of an African American Family* (1989).

VERITY J. HARDING

Brooks, Owen (18 Nov. 1928–), civil rights activist, was born Owen Herman Brooks in New York City to West Indian immigrant parents, but was raised by an aunt and uncle in Boston, Massachusetts. His family was conscious of its West Indian identity, and as the civil rights movement developed Brooks also became conscious of his blackness. He joined Boston's NAACP Youth Council in 1942. Attracted to left-wing politics, he became involved in the Progressive Party and Henry Wallace's unsuccessful presidential campaign in 1948. In September 1948 Brooks picketed a Selective Service office in protest against registration for conscription. Drafted into the army in March 1951, he served in the Korean War and spent a year in Savannah, Georgia, witnessing the South's racial problems firsthand.

After leaving the army Brooks returned to Boston, where he earned a degree in electrical engineering from Northeastern University. He met MARTIN LUTHER KING JR., then a doctoral student at Boston University, and also heard MALCOLM X speak in Boston. Though a number of his friends were members of the Nation of Islam, he remained an Episcopalian, like his parents, and an associate in the church. A serious car accident in 1962 put Brooks in the hospital for several months just as the direct-action phase of the civil rights movement was gaining momentum. After his recovery Brooks participated in the March on Washington in August 1963. He also helped organize support for the Student Nonviolent Coordinating Committee (SNCC) in Boston and met FANNIE LOU HAMER, an SNCC worker from the Mississippi Delta, when she came north on an SNCC fund-raising tour.

Brooks's white former pastor, Warren McKenna, spent the summer of 1964 in Mississippi as resident director of the National Council of Churches' (NCC) minister orientation program, which trained clergy volunteers to assist the Mississippi Summer Project. After the project ended McKenna stayed in Mississippi to work for the NCC's Delta Ministry (DM), which in September 1964 began a ten-year program of relief, literacy, voter registration, economic development, and community mobilization primarily in the Delta but with other projects in Hattiesburg and McComb. McKenna tried to recruit Brooks for the DM, which at first had only one African American staff member, but work commitments prevented him from joining until May 1965. In June 1965 Brooks became the DM's project director for Bolivar County, where he worked in voter registration and with the fledgling Mississippi Freedom Labor Union (MFLU), which organized low-paid agricultural workers in an unsuccessful Delta strike for higher wages and union recognition.

In January 1966 Brooks participated in the occupation of the unused Greenville Air Force Base by one hundred civil rights activists, MFLU members, and other displaced plantation workers in an attempt to pressure the state and federal governments to address the Delta poor's economic problems. Although 150 air police forcibly evicted the group and the occupation had no long-term effect, it did help to break logjams in implementing an emergency federal surplus food program in Mississippi and re-funding a federal Head Start program run by the Child Development Group of Mississippi. In June 1966 Brooks helped plan the strategy of the Meredith March, which the leaders of the Southern Christian Leadership Conference, the Congress of Racial Equality, and SNCC undertook to complete after JAMES HOWARD MEREDITH, who had begun a lone "March against Fear" from Memphis to Jackson, Mississippi, was shot and temporarily hospitalized on the second day of his march. Brooks successfully encouraged the civil rights leaders to route the Meredith March through the Delta and also to create a voter registration program in adjoining counties.

Brooks became the DM's acting director in September 1966 and director two years later. He inherited and maintained a DM commitment to create a model agricultural and industrial cooperative for unemployed agricultural families at Wayside, Washington County, called Freedom City. Although its residents built twenty of the projected fifty houses, the experimental community failed to become self-sustaining and consumed much of the DM's staff time and budget. Brooks concentrated his efforts on raising federal loans and foundation and church grants to try to create jobs and modernize the infrastructure of Mound Bayou, an all–African American town in Bolivar County. While some improvements occurred, they were insufficient to attract industry or stem black migration north.

A drastic budget cut by the cash-strapped NCC forced Brooks to release all but three of the DM's staff in 1971 and end its county projects. The remaining staff focused the organization's efforts on assisting Mound Bayou; aiding ROBERT CLARK, the state's only African American legislator; and providing technical assistance to community organizers and citizenship education groups. The terminated staff, who had run the county projects and objected to Brooks's domineering management style and his growing emphasis on developing independent black economic and political power, complained unsuccessfully to the NCC. Brooks worked closely with Hamer and the Mississippi Freedom Democratic Party, but the party withered as the state's moderate blacks and whites coalesced in the Loyal Democrats of Mississippi, which the national Democratic Party recognized in preference to the regular, segregationist Mississippi Democratic Party.

Brooks enjoyed some success. His efforts helped keep the Delta Community and Health Center in Mound Bayou funded for another ten years after it faced closure in the early 1970s. However, the hospital, like the DM, eventually succumbed to lack of funding. By 1977 the DM was little more than the office Brooks maintained in Greenville, which he kept through much of the 1990s, remaining active in community organizing. Brooks became an aide to MICHAEL ALPHONSO ESPY, Mississippi's first African American congressperson since Reconstruction, and to Espy's successor, BENNIE G. THOMPSON, with whom the DM had worked when he was mayor of Bolton. In the mid-1990s Brooks worked with Greenville youth, trying to combat drug culture. He became an oral historian, assisting Kim Lacy Rogers in interviewing African American community leaders in the Delta for her book *Life and Death in the Delta: African American Narratives of Violence, Resilience, and Social Change* (2006). Brooks also served on the board of the Mississippi ACLU.

Although little known outside Mississippi and only briefly mentioned in accounts of the state's civil rights movement and its aftermath, Brooks was involved in many facets of the struggle for racial equality in Mississippi.

FURTHER READING

Owen Brooks's interview with Robert Wright, from 18 September 1968, is available in the Ralph J. Bunche Oral History Collection, Oral History Department, Moorland-Spingarn Research Center, Howard University, Washington D.C. An interview by Tom Dent, from 18 August 1978, is available in the Mississippi Oral History Collection, L. Zenobia Coleman Library, Tougaloo College, Tougaloo, Mississippi.

Newman, Mark. *Divine Agitators: The Delta Ministry and Civil Rights in Mississippi* (2004).

MARK NEWMAN

Brooks, Shelton (4 May 1886–6 Sept. 1975), songwriter, was born Shelton Leroy Brooks in Amesburg, Ontario, near Detroit, to Potter, a Methodist minister, and Laura Brooks. Both of his parents sang and played the organ, and they kept a harmonium (pump organ) in the home. Shelton began experimenting on this while still a small child. Because Shelton was too small to reach the foot pedals, however, an older brother operated them while he played the keyboard. The family moved to the United States while Shelton was a boy, and he began his career in Detroit and Cleveland, honing the performing skills that would later make him a popular entertainer. He migrated to Chicago, the unrivaled hub of African American entertainment in the Midwest, sometime before 1909.

Brooks's first known song, "You Ain't Talking to Me," was published in 1909 by Will Rossiter of Chicago, and Brooks stuck with this firm for most of his publications. The second of these, "Some of These Days," became an enormous hit. Brooks personally persuaded the vaudeville star Sophie Tucker to feature the song in her act at Chicago's Orpheum Theatre; it became a sensation and became Tucker's theme song for the remainder of her long career. Each of her four varying recordings of the song (1911, 1926, 1927, and 1929) became a hit, and a short feature film named for the song was released with Tucker as its star. Brooks followed this song with a number of lesser efforts, including "The Cosey Rag" and "Jean" (1911), "All Night Long" (1912), "At an Old-Time Ball" (1913), and "Rufe Johnson's Harmony Band" (1914). His best and most successful song during these years was "I Wonder Where My Easy Rider's Gone" (1913), which cleverly combined horse racing and romantic subject matter with blues touches. It in turn helped inspire W. C. HANDY's 1914 hit "Yellow Dog Blues," which serves as an answer to Brooks's song and even readapts the chorus of the Brooks song for the verse of Handy's.

Brooks was reputed to be a gifted improviser, and like many vaudevillians, he chose not to write down much of his material. Thus he may well have created numerous songs that did not survive his stage acts. He almost always composed alone, writing both music and lyrics, but occasionally he collaborated with others. For the 1912 "Oh You Georgia Rose," his co-authors were the little-known Johnnie Watters and W. R. Williams. Most of Brooks's songs were published by the major white firms of the day, initially all by Rossiter of Chicago and after 1913 also by some of the New York firms. His "You Ain't No Place but Down South" (1912) was published in Dallas by his African American songwriting peer Chris Smith. Sometime around 1912 Brooks married a woman named Lina; they had one son.

Brooks had his second hit in 1916 with the dance song "Walking the Dog," which lived on as a title and as a concept beyond Brooks's actual piece. GERTRUDE "MA" RAINEY probably used Brooks's music in a dog-walking number that she performed in vaudeville around 1920. Brooks's piece may also have given George Gershwin the idea for an instrumental number of the same name that he wrote some years later. Another Brooks dance hit of the World War I years was "I Want to Shimmie" (1919), which capitalized on a shoulder-shaking dance featured by Gilda Gray and other leading vaudevillians of the period.

It was in 1917 that Brooks had his second universally popular smash hit with "The Darktown Strutters' Ball." Whereas most of Brooks's songs, even the best of them, feature rather weak verses leading to a payoff in the chorus, this one is strong throughout. In both its overall structural integrity and its theme, "The Darktown Strutters' Ball" may have owed something to Irving Berlin's 1911 hit "Alexander's Ragtime Band." An invitation is issued to a potential dancer or audience member to join one or more persons at a musical event, whether as passive listeners or (preferably, in the dance-mad era in which these songs were issued) as dancers, participants. The verse slides smoothly into the infectious chorus, which supplies the rhythmic and harmonic payoff for what preceded it. Among the innumerable jazz and vaudeville artists who recorded "The Darktown Strutters' Ball" were LOUIS ARMSTRONG, CAB CALLOWAY, COLEMAN HAWKINS, FLETCHER HENDERSON, Benny Goodman, ETHEL WATERS, Benny Carter, Artie Shaw, the Quintet of the Hot Club of Paris (featuring Django Reinhardt), the Original Dixieland Jazz Band, Red Nichols, VALAIDA SNOW, and the Original Indiana Five. Brooks himself recorded some duets with the blues singer Sara Martin in 1923 and served in 1926 as an accompanist on some Ethel Waters sides featuring his songs.

By 1920 Brooks's best years as a songwriter were behind him. In 1920 he contributed songs to two shows, *Canary Cottage* and *Miss Nobody from Starland* (neither was a notable success). In 1922 his career got a second wind when he was hired by the producer Lew Leslie to appear in *Plantation Revue*, one of many shows mounted to cash in on the runaway success of the 1921 EUBIE BLAKE-NOBLE SISSLE show *Shuffle Along*. Leslie's shows, which ran at his own Plantation Club, became a major success after he discovered a scintillating young singer-dancer named FLORENCE MILLS. Mills was teamed up with Brooks in the show *From Dover Street to Dixie*, which combined British and African American material. This became a sensation in London, and Mills and Brooks gave a highly successful command performance before King George V, Queen Mary, and the royal family of England.

Although his inspiration was winding down, Brooks remained active through the 1930s. He appeared in a short film for Vitaphone in 1929 and was on radio regularly in the period around 1930. He made cameo appearances in stage productions, including *Brown Buddies* in 1930. His friend W. C. Handy, ever willing to take a chance on African American talent, published Brooks's "Swing That Thing" in 1933 and "After All These Years" in 1936. Neither song was particularly successful. Brooks appeared in a film entitled *Double Deal* in 1939, and he continued to make stage appearances, including one at the Apollo Theater in 1942. In the same year he was recognized as one of the grand old men of American music at an ASCAP tribute, alongside Irving Berlin, W. C. Handy, and Harold Arlen. By this time he had moved to Los Angeles, where he died at the age of eighty-nine, largely forgotten despite his importance as the creator of popular music standards. The musical style he pioneered had receded several generations into the past.

FURTHER READING

Jasen, David A., and Gene Jones. *Spreadin' Rhythm Around* (1998).
Morgan, Thomas L., and William Barlow. *From Cakewalks to Concert Halls* (1992).

ELLIOTT S. HURWITT

Brooks, Tyrone (10 Oct. 1945–), Georgia state legislator and civil rights activist, was born in the back seat of a car rushing from his parents' home in Warrenton, Georgia, to the "colored ward" of the hospital in neighboring Wilkes County. He was the second of three children born to Mose Brooks, a Pullman car porter, and Ruby Cody Brooks, who worked as a clerk in two white-owned Warrenton stores.

Rural Warren County in east-central Georgia was removed from the influence of Atlanta and psychologically distant even from the nearby city of Augusta. Although its population was nearly two-thirds African American at the time of Brooks's birth, black residents experienced all the disadvantages of southern apartheid in the 1940s: political powerlessness, segregated public accommodations, and an unequal share of poverty, to name a few. Brooks recalled that from an early age he was aware of the outside world and the social struggle going on around him. At the home of his maternal grandmother, the younger Brooks read *Ebony*, *Jet*, the *Atlanta Daily World*, the *Pittsburgh Courier*, and *Muhammad Speaks*. "We were being exposed to the world from this little town," Brooks said years later. The combined influences of his father and grandmother, he said, "motivated me to take a keener interest in the civil rights revolution" (interview with Tyrone Brooks, 22 Sept. 2005).

At age fifteen, inspired by the 1960 sit-ins in Greensboro, North Carolina, Brooks and some of his friends decided to take direct action in their hometown. They targeted the segregated school system and the Knox Theatre in downtown Warrenton, where black moviegoers had to view the films from the balcony. "When we started our little campaign in Warrenton to desegregate the school system and the theater and the businesses, we really didn't know what we were doing," Brooks recalled. Their sit-in downstairs at the Knox brought the manager with his flashlight, but no ejection or police action. Brooks said their demonstration outside the county board of education did provoke a response. The police chief brought them to the jail, where their parents picked them up. After creating a stir with his activism, Brooks was sent to Boggs Academy, a long-established black boarding school in nearby Keysville, to finish his high school education (interview with Brooks).

The Warren County children's crusade came to the attention of civil rights leaders in Atlanta. Two staff members from the Southern Christian Leadership Conference (SCLC), Carl Farris and Willie Bolden, were assigned to Warren County. Farris and Bolden became Brooks's mentors, bringing him along to demonstrations in Albany, Georgia; Birmingham, Alabama; St. Augustine, Florida; and elsewhere. They also introduced Brooks to the Reverend MARTIN LUTHER KING JR., who stopped in Warrenton one day on his way to South Carolina. Brooks and his friends served lemonade to King and his associates, got over their surprise that King was not a tall man, and beamed under his benediction. By 1967 Brooks had joined the SCLC's staff.

"I was just one of those who were caught up in the movement," Brooks said. "You couldn't say no. It was an overwhelming desire to make a contribution to defeating Jim Crow and also to changing the course of our nation. For some of us it became our life." Brooks intended to remain on the SCLC staff only two years. But King's assassination in 1968 sealed his commitment to the movement. Summoned from Georgia to Memphis with the rest of the SCLC staff, Brooks heard the Reverend RALPH ABERNATHY's exhortation to "stay on the team." He remained on the SCLC staff and became a close associate of HOSEA WILLIAMS. When Williams was forced out in 1979 during a struggle for control of the organization, Brooks went with him.

Brooks was soon approached by a group of Atlanta ministers who asked him to run for a seat in the Georgia General Assembly. Brooks considered himself too much of a street radical to be a viable candidate. But he agreed to run, and he won the 1980 election. During his tenure, Brooks pressed for an increase in the number of black judges on Georgia's superior courts, supported the "black max" redistricting plan that increased the number of majority-black election districts in 1992, and led the Georgia Association of Black Elected Officials (GABEO) from obscurity to become an outspoken voice in Georgia's political debates.

Brooks is best known for his nearly two-decade struggle to remove the Confederate battle cross from Georgia's state flag. The Dixie symbol had been placed there by the 1956 general assembly in a symbolic gesture of disdain for integration following the 1954 *Brown v. Board of Education* decision. Brooks drew little support until 1992 when the then governor Zell Miller—looking to clean up Georgia's image in advance of the 1996 Atlanta summer Olympic Games—called for its removal. Miller not only failed but also nearly lost the 1994 election as a result. Miller's successor, Roy Barnes, succeeded in removing the Dixie cross in 2001. Brooks was at the center of the negotiations that led to the successful legislation. Barnes's 2002 election defeat was partly attributed to white discontent over the flag amendment. Barnes's successor, Sonny Perdue, got rid of the flag that Barnes and Brooks created but did not bring back the Dixie emblem.

From his platform as a lawmaker and as president of GABEO, Brooks became involved in human rights cases throughout Georgia. He spearheaded efforts to reopen the investigation of the mass lynching at Moore's Ford in Walton County, which federal agents failed to solve in 1946. Arrested at least sixty-five times for his civil rights work, Tyrone Brooks stayed true to his roots even while helping to bring about significant changes in his native state.

DON SCHANCHE JR.

Brooks, Walter Henderson (30 Aug. 1851–6 July 1945), clergyman, temperance leader, and poet, was born in Richmond, Virginia, the son of Albert Royal Brooks and Lucy Goode, slaves. Brooks's father, an enterprising slave, owned his own "snack house" and a livery business that brought him into contact with some of Virginia's wealthiest citizens, including his wife's owner, the German consul Daniel Von Groning. Albert Brooks purchased his wife's freedom in 1862 for eight hundred dollars. Still a slave, Walter Brooks at age seven was sold to the Turpin & Yarborough tobacco firm. He woefully recalled his time there, writing: "It was all I could do to perform the task assigned to my little hands. What I do remember is that I stood in mortal fear of 'the consequences' of failing to do what was required of me." When the Richmond manufacturer fell victim to wartime economic decline, Brooks was allowed to reside with his mother and began working in hotels, boardinghouses, and restaurants. In his youth he acquired the doctrines that served as the foundation for his life's work. He learned temperance from his pastor, the Reverend Robert Ryland, who taught songs at Christmas to curb the consumption of "egg-nog and the drinking of wine in countless homes," and Brooks's parents instilled "lessons of uprightness and sobriety."

After the Union victory in the Civil War, Brooks worked to make a place for himself in the world. In 1866 he entered the preparatory program at Lincoln University, a Presbyterian school founded for African Americans in Pennsylvania. He obtained his college degree in 1872 and one year later earned his theological degree. He joined the Ashmun Presbyterian Church in Lincoln in 1868. When he returned to Richmond after graduation, he changed denominations and was baptized into the First African Baptist Church. In 1874 he married the pastor's daughter, Eva Holmes; they had ten children.

Between 1874 and 1876 Brooks worked with the American Baptist Publication Society as a Sunday school missionary in Virginia. He gained national attention for his views on temperance when he addressed the society at its anniversary meeting in Philadelphia in 1875. His speech, entitled "Facts from the Field," sparked controversy when he "drew a picture of the drinking habits of preachers" in an effort to illustrate the critical need for temperance. That same year Brooks became the chaplain of the Anti-Saloon League of the District of Columbia. He retained this position until 1882.

Brooks's greatest legacy came from his work as a Baptist minister. In 1876 he was formally ordained into the ministry and a year later became pastor of the Second African Baptist Church of Richmond. In 1880 he briefly returned to his missionary work, but by 1882 he had accepted the pastorate of the Nineteenth Street Baptist Church in Washington, D.C. Over the next sixty-three years Brooks established a national reputation. He assisted John W. Cromwell in creating the Virginia Historical and Literary Society and for a time served as vice president in the Bethel Literary and Historical Association in Washington, D.C. Brooks was a trustee of NANNIE BURROUGHS's National Training School for Women and Girls and the Virginia Theological Seminary and College in Lynchburg, Virginia. He supported the black women's club movement, and in 1896 his church was the site of the foundational meeting of the National Association of Colored Women.

Brooks played an important role in efforts to build and maintain a national black Baptist convention. He was chairman of the American National Baptist Convention's Bureau of Education, a black organization founded in 1886, and he continually mediated relationships with national white Baptist conventions. In 1889 the American Baptist Publication Society, in an effort to increase black participation, agreed to accept literary contributions from Brooks and two of his colleagues for its regular publication. The society, however, reneged on its offer when its southern white contingency voiced opposition. The society opted instead to create a special publication for black clergymen, the *Negro Baptist Pulpit*. Although Brooks authored an article for that volume, he and his colleagues were infuriated by this palliative act and predicted that it would typify future relations. Further difficulties led eventually to the formation of a black-controlled denominational body, the National Baptist Convention, U.S.A., in 1895.

Brooks's intellectual capabilities and dedication earned him recognition as an exceptional scholar. He wrote a number of essays on the history and development of black Baptist organizations and their relationships with white Baptists. For the *Journal of Negro History* he wrote "The Evolution of the Negro Baptist Church" (Jan. 1922) and "The Priority of the Silver Bluff Church and Its Promoters" (Apr. 1922). For *The Crisis* he wrote "Unification and Division among Colored Baptists" (May 1925). In his work with the Bethel Literary and Historical Association, he offered a "severe but eloquent criticism" of FREDERICK DOUGLASS's lecture "The Philosophy and History of Reform" that "occasioned a battle royal between him and Mr. Douglass, in which 'Greek met Greek' with vigorous onslaught and heroic defence [*sic*]." Brooks was a member of the American Negro Academy and a lifelong member of the Association for the Study of Negro Life and History, where he worked closely with CARTER G. WOODSON.

Brooks's first wife died in 1912, and three years later he married Florence H. Swann. Following Florence's death, he married Viola Washington in 1933. Late in his life Brooks established himself as a poet. Two books of his poetry were published, *Original Poems* (1932) and the *Pastor's Voice* (1945). His poems thematically reflect his lifelong concerns for temperance, faith in God, and racial progress.

Brooks, like many black clergy of his time, used the church and his role as pastor for purposes that extended beyond the sacred. He was uncompromising in his struggle to promote education and the use of Christian morals as means to improve the quality of life for black Americans. As racial segregation gained legal precedent and race-related violence reached new heights, Brooks fought for equality and clung to a faith in the American creed that was second only to his faith in God.

FURTHER READING

Brooks's granddaughter Evelyn Brooks Higginbotham, Harvard University, possesses some of his papers, including a 1935 autobiographical piece, "Memories of a Life Time," some untitled autobiographical notes, and a genealogical "History of the Brooks Family."

Higginbotham, Evelyn Brooks. *Righteous Discontent: The Women's Movement in the Black Baptist Church, 1880–1920* (1993).

Moss, Alfred A. *The American Negro Academy* (1981).

Washington, James Melvin. *Frustrated Fellowship: A Black Baptist Quest for Social Power* (1986).

Woodson, Carter G. "Introduction to Walter Brooks," *Pastor's Voice* (1945).

Obituaries: *Journal of Negro History*, 30 Oct. 1945; Washington, D.C., *Evening Star*, 8 July 1945.

This entry is taken from the *American National Biography* and is published here with the permission of the American Council of Learned Societies.

ADAM BIGGS

Broonzy, Big Bill (26 June 1893?–15 Aug. 1958), blues singer and guitarist, was born William Lee Conley Broonzy in Scott, Bolivar County, Mississippi, the son of Frank Broonzy and Nettie (or Mittie) Belcher, former slaves who became sharecroppers. One of at least sixteen children, including a twin sister, he lived in Mississippi until age eight, when his family moved to Arkansas, near Pine Bluff, to try sharecropping there. As a youngster he made violins out of cornstalks, learning music from an uncle, Jerry Belcher, and a local musician known as See See Rider. He and a friend began playing homemade instruments to entertain local children, though always out of sight of his parents—stern Baptists who frowned on secular music. The parental disapproval eased, however, when he graduated to a real instrument (supposedly bought for him by a white patron) and began earning money as a musician. When he was twelve, the family moved to Scotts Crossing, Arkansas, where he continued to play, mainly for white dances. In 1912, however, he joined the Baptist Church, briefly putting music aside to try his hand at preaching. In 1914 (some accounts say 1916) he married a fellow church member, seventeen-year-old Guitrue (or Gertrude) Embria, who allowed him to take up music again, he said later, because it paid more than preaching. In 1918 he was drafted, serving with an army supply company in France. Returning to Arkansas, he grew dissatisfied with life in the South. In early 1920 he left his wife and went to Chicago, where he eventually found work as a Pullman railroad sleeping-car porter. He took guitar lessons from Papa Charlie Jackson, a recording artist who introduced him to the

Paramount Records executive J. Mayo Williams. After an unproductive session for Paramount in 1926, Broonzy and the guitarist John Thomas cut four sides in late 1927 and early 1928, launching Broonzy on one of the most prolific recording careers in blues history.

Through the 1930s and 1940s he recorded hundreds of sides for a dozen labels, including the most important blues labels of that era: Bluebird, Columbia, Okeh, and Vocalion. He recorded both as a solo artist and in small-combo formats. He became active on Chicago's house-party circuit and then the tavern and club scene as it developed in the late 1930s and 1940s, working with such artists as MEMPHIS MINNIE and John Lee "SONNY BOY" WILLIAMSON.

As early as 1938 he began making inroads on a new market, participating in John Hammond's *From Spirituals to Swing* programs at Carnegie Hall in New York City—possibly the first appearance of a Mississippi-born blues musician in concert format. He also worked New York's Cafe Society nightclub in 1939 and 1940. In 1941 and 1942 he toured with a Mississippi protégé, the vocalist Lil Green, until she started singing with big rhythm-and-blues bands. On tour in Houston, Texas, Broonzy married a "Creole woman," Rosie Syphen, who returned with him to Chicago, where he plunged back into a steady schedule of club work. They had five children.

Although World War II interrupted his recording career, the interruption apparently did not cause a major financial blow. Partly because he recorded under contract to the music publisher Lester Melrose, not to any specific labels, Broonzy received little more than session fees as a recording artist. He once claimed that he earned a total of only two thousand dollars for the hundreds of songs he had recorded. As a result, even during his tenure as the nominal king of Chicago blues, he always worked nonmusical jobs on the side.

Broonzy returned to the recording studio in 1945, working in a new band format as he tried, with diminishing success, to keep pace with the postwar rhythm-and-blues sound. In 1947 the folklorist Alan Lomax brought Broonzy to New York, along with MEMPHIS SLIM and Sonny Boy Williamson, for a Town Hall concert. The next day, Lomax supervised a recording session at which the three blues artists, identified by pseudonyms (Broonzy's was "Natchez"), played music and talked candidly about life in the South. That session, like the *From Spirituals to Swing* concert, marked another stage in Broonzy's shift from racial/ethnic recording star to interpreter of blues for white audiences.

By the 1950s African American popular musical tastes had passed Broonzy by, and his recordings were more of a documentary or folk music nature. In 1950 and 1951 he briefly left the Chicago blues scene and took a job as a janitor at Iowa State University, where he learned to read and write. Returning to music, Broonzy looked more and more to the predominantly white folk revival audiences for work—for example, touring with the Chicago critic and oral historian Studs Terkel's program *I Come for to Sing*. He also looked to overseas markets and was one of the first artists to bring traditional American blues to British, European, Australian, African, and South American audiences in the 1950s. He appeared in several films and, with his newly acquired literacy, became the first Delta artist to be credited with an autobiography, *Big Bill Blues* (1964), a compilation of anecdotes, tall tales, and recollections originally written as letters to the Belgian enthusiast Yannick Bruynoghe. On tour in England in 1957, Broonzy was forced by health problems to return to Chicago, where he was diagnosed with lung cancer. He died in Chicago.

Big Bill Broonzy's performing career spanned five decades, taking him from the Deep South to Chicago and on to Europe, where he became one of the first and most effective ambassadors for American blues. As a recording artist, he recorded over 250 songs—many of them his own—prior to World War II and hundreds more in the postwar era. He also played as a sideman at countless sessions for other artists. As an instrumentalist, he could handle down-home finger picking or single-string electric styles, and, even late in his career, he could flash techniques that dazzled the guitar-oriented folk-music audience. Although he ended his career singing protest songs and other folk material in coffeehouses and cabarets, Broonzy was the central character in the first generation of Chicago blues musicians and spent most of his adult life performing blues, ragtime, hokum, and pop material for the so-called race market. Because he was one of the first blues artists to work successfully for white audiences, though, Broonzy helped shape the way several generations thought about the blues. Perhaps his most enduring musical influence was on a host of young, white British blues aficionados, notably John Mavall, Eric Clapton, and Jimmy Page, who in the 1960s sparked a blues-inspired "British invasion" of America. Broonzy was elected to the Blues Foundation Hall of Fame in Memphis, Tennessee, in 1980.

FURTHER READING

Broonzy, Bill. *Big Bill Blues: Big Bill Broonzy's Story as Told to Yannick Bruynoghe* (1964).

Harris, Sheldon. *Blues Who's Who: A Biographical Dictionary of Blues Singers* (1989).

Lomax, Alan. *The Land Where Blues Began* (1993).

DISCOGRAPHY

Dixon, Robert M. W., and John Godrich. *Blues and Gospel Records: 1902–1943*, 3d ed. (1982).

Leadbitter, Mike, and Neil Slaven. *Blues Records 1943–1970: A Selective Discography*, vol. 1 (1987).

Oliver, Paul, ed. *The Blackwell Guide to Blues Records* (1989).

This entry is taken from the *American National Biography* and is published here with the permission of the American Council of Learned Societies.

BILL MCCULLOCH AND
BARRY LEE PEARSON

Broteer (Venture Smith) (1729?–1805), slave, entrepreneur, and autobiographer, was born in Guinea, Africa, to Saungm Furro, a West African prince with three wives. Broteer was the eldest son of the first wife. When he was six years old an "army supplied by whites" captured him and marched him to the coast (Smith, 544). During the capture Broteer had seen his father tortured and killed, a haunting memory that stayed with him for the rest of his life. After being imprisoned for two years Broteer was one of 260 Africans sold into slavery to a Rhode Island slaver named Robertson Mumford, who purchased Broteer for four gallons of rum and a piece of calico cloth. It was Mumford who gave Broteer his American name, Venture, a result, as Broteer recalled in his memoir, of his master "having purchased me with his own private venture" (Smith, 545).

With new slaves in tow Mumford's first stop was Barbados. En route, however, a quarter of his cargo died, having been afflicted with smallpox during the Middle Passage. The remaining slaves were sold to planters there, except for Venture and three others who continued on to Rhode Island. During his time in bondage he lived with various slaveowners along the Atlantic seaboard. He spent a dozen years with Mumford in Rhode Island and on Fischer's Island near Long Island, New York, and at least a dozen more with another master, Thomas Stanton of Stonington Point, Connecticut. His third and final master was Colonel Oliver Smith of Long Island, New York, whose surname he kept after his emancipation. Smith spent his adolescent years working as both a household servant and field hand. In his teenage years he began to resent those who exerted control over him, particularly his master's son James Mumford, who, on one occasion, charged Smith with a pitchfork only to be sent home in tears after Smith got the best of him. As punishment for this act of self-defense Smith was beaten, whipped, and hung on a butcher's gallows for an hour.

Smith survived the gallows and went on to make a life for himself in slavery. He married and had a family. He also saved a considerable sum of money, hiring out his labor as a fisherman, woodsman, and farmer. Because of his work ethic he acquired the reputation as a tireless laborer who could paddle a canoe several miles across the river and back and then cut nine cords of wood—all in a single day. Known also for his size, Smith weighed over three hundred pounds, stood just over six feet tall, and measured six feet around the waist. In his memoir he reported that he "was pretty large and stout," which played to his advantage against his whip-cracking masters (Smith, 544). Once he snatched a whip away from his master and on another occasion he beat his master and his master's brother after they viciously attacked him.

Nearly three decades after his capture in Africa, Smith had saved enough money to buy his freedom. In 1765, at age thirty-six, he paid his enslaver Colonel Oliver Smith seventy-one pounds and two shillings, a sum roughly the cost of four thousand acres of land. At last a free man again he supported himself by whaling, fishing, chopping wood, and hunting. With the money from his labors he saved enough to buy his family's freedom as well. He also purchased three other slaves from their masters and freed them. In 1776 Smith moved his family to East Haddam, Connecticut, where he built a home and employed two black indentured servants. Soon thereafter he acquired more than a hundred acres of land and bought three homes. He supported these endeavors by buying and selling land, running a shipping business, and acting as a creditor by loaning money to both blacks and whites. Of this last pursuit he once complained that he had "been cheated out of considerable money by people" who took "advantage of my ignorance of numbers" (Smith, 556).

In 1798, in his sixty-ninth year, Smith published his memoir, *A Narrative of the Life and Adventures* of *Venture, a Native of Africa*, a twenty-page account that was republished at least four times in the two centuries after his death. The *Narrative* begins with a preface by the Connecticut schoolteacher and antislavery activist Elisha Niles, the man to whom Smith dictated the memoir and who encouraged Smith to write the account. Accompanying the publication of Smith's memoir was a December advertisement in the *New London Bee* describing Smith as "a negro remarkable for size, strength, industry, fidelity, and well known in the state of Rhode Island, Long Island, and in Stonington, East Haddam, and several other parts" of Connecticut. Among the earliest examples of its kind in the Americas Smith's memoir offers a clear and concise account of his rise from slavery to that of a self-made man. It spans the years just prior to the outbreak of the American Revolution and concludes in 1798. The memoir was, in Niles's words, "a pattern of honesty, prudence and industry to people of his own color"—a true rages-to-riches story that could inspire slaves to revolt (Smith, 539).

Smith died in East Haddam, Connecticut, at the age of seventy-seven. His tombstone reads: "Sacred to the Memory of Venture Smith, African. Though the son of a King, he was kidnapped and sold as a slave, but by his industry he acquired money to purchase his freedom."

FURTHER READING

Smith, Venture. *A Narrative of the Life and Adventures of Venture, a Native of Africa*. Reprinted in *Early Negro Writing, 1760–1837*, ed. Dorothy Porter (1798; repr. 1971).

Andrews, William L. *To Tell a Free Story: The First Century of Afro-American Autobiography, 1760–1865* (1986).

Caretta, Vince, and Phillip Gould. *Genius and Bondage: Literature of the Early Black Atlantic* (2001).

Kaplan, Sidney. *The Black Presence in the Era of the American Revolution, 1770–1800* (1973).

MATTHEW L. HARRIS

Broughton, Virginia E. Walker (1856–21 Sept. 1934), one of the first four graduates from Fisk University, school teacher, missionary, founder of the Tennessee and National Baptist Women's Convention, was born free in Nashville, Tennessee, to Nelson and Eliza Smart Walker. Her father had been enslaved in Virginia, but was allowed to hire his time, earning enough money to purchase both his own freedom and that of his wife. Moving to Tennessee, by 1870 he had accumulated $1,200 in real property working as a barber, while Eliza Walker worked as a dressmaker, supporting three daughters and three sons (1870 Census). Virginia was named for the state of her father's nativity, "which he never ceased to praise" (Broughton, 7).

At an early age she enrolled at a private school in Nashville, opened in the 1850s by Daniel Watkins, later pastor of the First Colored Christian Church. When Fisk School convened 9 January 1866, Walker enrolled, continuing her studies at Fisk University (incorporated 22 August 1867) and receiving her B in May 1875. She may have been the first woman in the South to attain a bachelor's degree, observing that "The prevailing custom in the South at that time regarding the education of woman made it possible for this Negro girl to have such a distinction" (Broughton, 8). She received a master's degree from Fisk in 1879.

Moving to Memphis, she passed the exam for teaching in public schools and taught for twelve years, later becoming principal of the North Memphis School. About 1876 she married Julius A. O. Broughton, a clerk (mistakenly listed as Junius in the 1880 Census but correctly as Julius Broughton in 1910 and 1920), in the county register's office, who later owned a barber shop (Census, 1910, 1920). Although some published accounts describe him as having served in the state legislature, there is no Tennessee legislator by that name. It is not clear whether he was at some point an attorney. Broughton is listed as a native of Atlanta, Georgia, and a student in the 1869–1870 Atlanta University directory. Several of his classmates achieved prominence, including William Sanders Scarborough, the esteemed classical scholar, William H. Finch, who served on the Atlanta city council; Henry O. Flipper, the first black West Point graduate; and his brother Joseph Flipper, later an AME bishop. The couple had five children and lost their third daughter, Selena, in childhood.

About 1882, influenced by Joanna P. Moore, a white missionary popular among African Americans, Broughton joined a Bible band—a women's group engaged in daily Bible study. The teaching and discipline of the movement were morally conservative, denouncing "intemperance in beer drinking, tobacco using, excessive eating and dressing, and the desecrating custom of using church houses for fairs, festivals and other worldly amusements" (Broughton, 34).

In 1885 Broughton was passed over for the position of head teacher (the equivalent of assistant principal) at Kortrecht Grammar School, the most advanced public school in Memphis admitting students classified as "colored." A man who shared Broughton's color, with less experience in teaching, was initially appointed. After filing a complaint, with the support and assistance of her husband, Broughton eventually secured the appointment.

In 1887 the Midwestern Auxiliary of the American Baptist Home Mission Society opened a permanent missionary station in Memphis, relying heavily on Broughton's leadership. Still teaching school full time, she spent weekends traveling in rural districts, in ox-drawn wagons, on small boats up the Mississippi River, and on horseback. That year, recovering from the traumatic death of her mother and her own serious illness, she heard a call from God to enter missionary work full time.

In 1888 she began work with Emma King Jones, organizing a women's district association that raised money for the Bible and Normal Institute, later the Howe Institute. In September of that year, the first organizational meeting of black Baptist women convened at Mt. Zion Baptist Church in Stanton, Tennessee. For the next decade, the group continued annual meetings, amid growing controversy. Broughton's work brought her into direct conflict with male Baptist clergy who opposed a proselytizing role for women. In her memoirs, Broughton recalled a number of ministers determined to destroy her work, who changed their minds after hearing her speak. One made a confession and pledged "to do all in my power to forward this branch of God's work as jealously as I had determined to oppose it," (Broughton, p. 36) so that she later affirmed, "our woman's work has no better friend among the able ministers of the race than that brother."

Responding to common citation of Paul's admonition that women should be silent in church, Broughton insisted that "Woman according to the flesh is made for the glory of man; but when recreated in Christ or born of the Spirit, she is recreated for such spiritual service as God may appoint through the examples given in his Word." Still, she insisted that women were not called to serve as clergy, because she found no female precedent for this in the Bible. Throughout the 1890s she taught missionary training and Bible studies at the Bible and Normal Institute, particularly serving women from rural areas. In his *History of the Negro Baptists of Tennessee* (1936), THOMAS O. FULLER notes that "Sister Broughton, while well educated,

felt perfectly at home among the masses. She loved them and they loved her" (83).

In 1892 she received formal appointment as a missionary from the Women's Baptist Home Mission Society. By 1894, the society had organized fifty-seven Bible bands in Tennessee and ran twenty industrial schools. After an 1895 meeting of the mission society in Saratoga, New York, Broughton embarked on a multistate speaking tour in the north, receiving commendations everywhere she went. One of her most often-quoted statements, responding to her husband's protest over long absences from home, was "I belong to God first, and you next; you two must settle it." In her memoirs, she added that her husband, "after a desperate struggle with the world, the flesh and the devil, yielded to God" and "has ever since been helpful" in his wife's missionary work (Broughton, 46–47).

Following the 1895 founding of National Baptist Convention, U.S.A., Broughton was a leading voice in launching a Woman's National Baptist Convention (NBC), which she served as recording secretary. Although the separate women's organization was formally disbanded by the following NBC convention, Broughton was one of four women chosen by a meeting of Baptist women in 1900 to seek support for their own distinct organization. This brought her into both cooperation and competition with a dynamic new women's voice, NANNIE HELEN BURROUGHS, who served as corresponding secretary of the revived women's convention.

In 1899 the Broughton family moved to Nashville. She associated there with the Fireside School program, organized by Joanna P. Moore to evade "white" opposition to schools for "colored" children. Moore promoted study groups around the fireside at home, with connection to local churches, improvement of home life, daily prayer, and home Bible study, promoting temperance and industry, while providing good books to homes to stimulate reading. Broughton served as assistant editor of *Hope*, a monthly magazine published by the Fireside School program.

In 1906 Broughton was appointed lecturer for the woman's department of the John C. Martin Bible movement, organizing women's unions in Tennessee, Arkansas, Alabama, Georgia, Mississippi, North Carolina, South Carolina, Kentucky, and Illinois. She spent the remainder of 1906 and 1907 teaching at the A&M College in Normal, Alabama, and then was sent as a delegate of the Women's NBC to the World's International

Sunday school convention. Sometime before 1910, the Broughtons returned to Memphis (Census, 1910). In 1912 she was the first African American ever appointed by the Associated Charities of Memphis to assist in flood relief. The last two decades of her life are obscure, recorded neither by her own autobiography nor by others. Broughton was widowed, and Secretary of the Women's Auxilliary of the NBC at the time of her death from diabetes, 21 September 1934. She was survived by her children, Emma O. Broughton, Elizabeth Branson, and Julius A. Broughton, of Memphis, and Virginia Cameron of Los Angeles, as well as her brothers Robert and Rufus Walker, of Nashville.

FURTHER READING

Broughton, V.W. *Twenty Year's Experience of a Missionary* (1907).

DeCosta-Willis, Miriam. *Notable Black Memphians* (2008).

Higginbotham, Evelyn Brooks. *Righteous Discontent: The Women's Movement in the Black Baptist Church, 1880–1920* (1997).

Smith, Jessie Carney, and Shirelle Phelps. *Notable Black American Women* (1992–2003).

CHARLES ROSENBERG

Brown, Ada (1 May 1890–31 Mar. 1950), singer and actor, was born Ada Scott in Kansas City, Kansas, the daughter of H. W. and Anna Morris Scott. (Some scholars list her as being born on 1 May 1889 in Junction City, Kansas.) Nothing is known about her education, except that she began piano lessons at an early age. She also started singing in the local church choir, developing the voice that the historian Bruce Kellner calls "full, rich, and mellow" (Kellner, 55). Indeed, musical ability ran in Brown's family: Her cousin was renowned ragtime pianist and composer JAMES SYLVESTER SCOTT.

Brown's professional life began in 1910, when she became a performer at Bob Mott's Pekin Theater in Chicago. Barely out of her teens, Brown also performed in clubs in Paris, France, and Berlin, Germany. In the early 1920s Brown joined BENNIE MOTEN's band, which was considered the Midwest's preeminent band. During the 1920s and 1930s Brown sang the blues on both the West Coast and the East Coast, as well as in recording studios in Chicago and St. Louis. She recorded "Evil Mama Blues," "Ill Natured Blues," and "Break o' Day Blues" with Moten's band in September 1923 for the Okeh label. By the end of the 1920s, however, Brown had left the band for the East Coast's vaudeville theater circuit. There she became a popular attraction. She toured with the shows *Step on It* (1922) and *Struttin' Time* (1924), both musical revues written by the African American team of Flournoy Miller and Aubrey Lyle. By 1928, when Brown made her second record, including "Panama Limited Blues" and "Tia Juana Man," critics and audiences alike applauded her sweet voice. Such popularity not only earned her the title the "Queen of the Blues" but also brought her to the stage. Brown's stage appearances at Harlem's Lafayette Theatre included *Plantation Days* (1927), *Bandannaland* (1928), and *Tan Town Tamales* (1930). She also played at the Liberty Theater with BILL "BOJANGLES" ROBINSON in *Brown Buddies* (1930), a musical comedy about African American soldiers in France during World War I. The show had a thin plotline but featured plenty of song and dance.

In 1936 Brown moved to Chicago, where she sang with the Fletcher Henderson Orchestra at the Grand Terrace Café. That same year, along with actor Leigh Whipper and actress FREDI WASHINGTON, Brown helped found the Negro Actors Guild of America in New York City, a benevolent welfare organization for African American performers composed of six committees: finance, administrative, membership, entertainment, sickness, and welfare. Brown's first and only film appearance came in 1943, when she played herself in *Stormy Weather*, the thinly disguised life of Bill "Bojangles" Robinson ("Bill Williamson"). Critics now consider this film, a cinematic survey of African American entertainment from 1918 to 1943, an unusual opportunity for audiences to see African American entertainers prominent in the 1940s. Even into the twenty-first century, Brown's performance in the film was still winning critical accolades. In his 2001 book *Toms, Coons, Mulattoes, Mammies, and Bucks*, DONALD BOGLE writes: "FATS WALLER and Ada Brown provided spicy renditions of 'Ain't Misbehavin' and 'That Ain't Right'"(131).

Before her sudden and unexplained retirement from music in 1945, Brown teamed up with Robinson once again, this time at the Broadway Theater in New York City in *Memphis Bound*. After the show closed, she returned to Kansas City, Kansas (some sources give Kansas City, Missouri, as the location). Brown died at home of kidney disease on 31 March 1950. She is buried in the Westlawn Cemetery in Kansas City, Kansas. Ada Brown belonged to the first generation of African American blues singers.

Along with MA RAINEY, BESSIE SMITH, and many others, she helped to make the female blues singer an icon in American culture.

FURTHER READING
Bogle, Donald. *Toms, Coons, Mulattoes, Mammies, and Bucks: An Interpretive History of Blacks in American Films* (2001).
Kellner, Bruce. *The Harlem Renaissance: A Historical Dictionary for the Era* (1987).
Stewart-Baxter, Derrick. *Ma Rainey and the Classic Blues Singers* (1970).

MARY ANNE BOELCSKEVY

Brown, Addie (21 Dec. 1841–7 January 1870), a literate domestic servant, grew up in Philadelphia and in New York City with her family. While her parents' names remain unknown, in one of her 1859 letters, she revealed that her father owned a restaurant. Brown severed ties with her family after her father's death in October 1862. In her letters to Rebecca Primus, her beloved friend, she discussed how her mother had remarried a man whom Addie described as often present in her nightmares.

Brown is known today primarily because of her relationship to REBECCA PRIMUS of Hartford, Connecticut. Primus was the only African American among the five teachers selected by the Freedman's Society in 1865 to head to the south and start schools for freed blacks. She relocated to Royal, Maryland, and founded a school there, working until 1869. She was an inspirational figure and a close friend to Addie Brown and seems to have become her lover. Brown's correspondence with Primus, beginning in 1865, is valuable for the insight into the African American community of nineteenth-century Hartford, including the activities of the Talcott Street Congregational Church, where Primus's father, HOLDRIDGE PRIMUS, served as deacon.

The Brown letters are the subject of Farah Griffin's book, *Beloved Sisters and Loving Friends: Letters from Rebecca Primus of Royal Maryland and Addie Brown of Hartford Connecticut, 1854–1868*, which highlights the significance of the same-sex relationship of the women as voiced by themselves and viewed by their families. They were so close and intimately linked that Primus's mother, Mehitable Jacobs, said that "if either Addie or Rebecca were a gent then they would marry." Three months later, Addie wrote to Rebecca informing her she would be happy to address her as "my husband." In addition to calling her "my husband,"

Addie affectionately called Rebecca "Stella" and signed her own letters "Perthena." While the letters suggest that Addie, at least, had other lovers of both sexes, she reminded Rebecca in a letter, "No kisses is like yours" (Hansen, 153–182).

Addie Brown made her living by sewing, mending, and cleaning, and was employed at various places, including Miss Porter's School in Farmington. In 1868 in New Haven, Brown married Joseph Tines, a waiter on the *Granite State*, a steamship that traveled from New York City to Hartford three times a week. They did not have any children. Two years later, Brown died. Her death was recorded by Rebecca on Addie's last letter: "Addie died at her residence Phila. 7, Jan 1870 at 11 o'clock am." Addie Brown's correspondence with Rebecca Primus is of historical significance on several counts: it is a loving exchange between two African American women a domestic in New England and an early Reconstruction educator, a rarely documented nineteenth-century same-sex relationship. In addition, Brown's letters illustrate the vibrant social fabric of Hartford's African American community and churches, while Primus's letters document the struggles of a young teacher starting a school all alone in the South in the years immediately following the Civil War.

FURTHER READING
Beeching, Barbara J. "The Primus Papers: An Introduction to Hartford's Nineteenth Century Black Community." Master's thesis, Trinity College, Hartford, CT, 1995.
Griffin, Farah Jasmine. *Beloved Sisters and Loving Friends: Letters from Rebecca Primus of Royal Maryland, and Addie Brown of Hartford Connecticut 1854–1868* (1999).
Hansen, Karen. "'No Kisses Is Like Youres,': An Erotic Friendship between Two African-American Women during the Mid-Nineteenth Century," *Gender and History* 7, no. 2 (1995): 153–182.

YASMINE ALI

Brown, Anne (9 Aug. 1912–13 March 2009), concert opera singer and teacher, was the oldest of four girls born to Dr. Harry F. Brown and Mamie Wiggins in Baltimore, Maryland. Her mother was her first music teacher, and mother and daughters would frequently sing around the piano. Anne grew up listening to the recordings of Caruso, Melba, and Schumann-Heink. Toward the end of World War I, when Anne was six years old, she made her concert debut with her younger sister Henrietta singing for returning African American soldiers at Camp Meade in Baltimore. At age twelve Anne began attending Frederick Douglass Senior High School, then the city's only public high school open to blacks. During her high school years, she attended a wider range of concerts including performances by MARIAN ANDERSON and ROLAND HAYES at Baltimore's Lyric Theatre. After graduation from high school Anne hoped to continue her education at the Peabody Conservatory. Her audition was so impressive garnering positive comments until her mother mentioned the fact that Anne and she were black. Because of Anne's light complexion she was naturally assumed to be white. Positive feedback was soon followed by a flat refusal to admit her because of her race. The Peabody Conservatory rectified this mistake in 1998 by honoring Anne Brown with an award for lifetime achievement in music.

The young singer benefited from the intervention of Constance Black, wife of the *Baltimore Sun* newspaper chairman Harry C. Black. She had heard about Anne from her chauffeur, who was a patient of Dr. Harry Brown. His glowing reports of how beautiful his doctor's daughter sang prompted Mrs. Black to request that Anne be driven out to the house to meet her. Anne sang songs from the German classics accompanied by her mother. Black was impressed by the young singer and invited her back on several occasions to perform in her home. Black also encouraged Anne to audition for the Institute of Musical Art of the Juilliard School in New York. Anne's father was initially opposed to his daughter's leaving Baltimore, believing that New York was full of the devil's spawn and did not believe that she would succeed in entering that school. Only after her mother threatened to leave her husband did the father relent. Mother and daughter packed their bags and headed to New York. Anne sang for Frank Damrosch, head of the school, and at the age of sixteen was accepted as a pupil. Entering Juilliard in 1928 Brown studied musical technique for three years. From 1931 to 1934 she won the coveted Margaret McGill three-year tuition scholarship to study opera and singing technique under the musical tutelage of Lucia Dunham. During the first two years of study, she was the only black student. Ruby Elzy, another African American singer, was shortly to gain admittance. Later she would gain prominence playing Serena in *Porgy and Bess* with Brown. Though a soprano, Brown developed her lower range, developing a mezzo-like quality with Dunham's training. In New York Brown felt a freedom from the South's strict racial codes, but in the 1930s the opportunities for a black classically trained singer were limited. Brown did not expect the way to be easy for an African American performer to have a serious musical career. Although ROLAND HAYES, PAUL ROBESON, MARIAN ANDERSON, and Dorothy Maynor had shown it possible to achieve success with a concert career, the world of opera still held its color line. Brown was determined to face this racial stricture and beat it. She received her diploma in voice in 1932 and artist's diploma in 1934.

A couple of years before graduation, she read in a newspaper article that George Gershwin was going to write an opera about black people in North Carolina named *Porgy and Bess*. Brown called Gershwin's secretary and requested an audition. Brown's initial audition with Gershwin was so successful that a long series of meetings with other members of the production team including Gershwin's brother Ira, the director Rouben Mamoulian, and the librettist Dubose Heyward was immediately put into motion. Prior to being offered the role of Bess in *Porgy and Bess*, she took a two-month job singing in London in the chorus of a musical titled *Blackbirds*.

Porgy and Bess premiered in Boston in September 1935, and opened on Broadway at the Alvin Theatre on 10 October 1935. The show opened to mixed reviews and played for 124 times on Broadway before embarking on a three-month tour. In March 1936 Brown refused to perform at the National Theatre in Washington, D.C., unless the theater's racially segregated house policy was abolished. With the help of MARY MCLEOD BETHUNE and RALPH BUNCHE the National Theatre was desegregated. After *Porgy and Bess* moved on, the policy of segregated seating policy was immediately restored.

Throughout the 1940s and 1950s, Brown commanded a European concert repertoire of French and Italian opera arias. After World War II, Todd Duncan and Brown reprised their roles of Porgy and Bess for the Royal Opera in Copenhagen. She toured nationally and internationally, and in 1948 married the Norwegian ski jump champion Thorleif Schelderup. Her performances on the Norwegian stage include *Dido and Aeneas, Member of the Wedding*, and *Amal*. From 1953 to 1955 she lived in Italy, where she studied the vocal technique of bel canto. In the 1960s Brown began teaching at the National Theatre School of Norway. It was during this time that she directed a production of *Porgy and Bess* in France with Avon

Long as Sportin' Life. The principals were African American and the chorus was made up of white French singers. In Norway, she continued private coaching. Her students included the Norwegian opera singer Elizabeth Norberg-Schultz and the actress Liv Ullmann. In 1990 Brown was awarded the Oslo Kultur Prisen (Oslo Culture Prize) for her artistic achievements. Among her other awards are Honorary Citizen of New Orleans (1991) and a special plaque from Frederick Douglass Senior High School in Baltimore, Maryland, for superior contributions in the performing arts and bel canto (1998). Brown retired to Norway in the mid-1960s and lived there until her death in 2009.

FURTHER READING

Brown, Anne. I Gave Up My Country for Love, *Ebony* (Nov. 1953).

Hine Darlene, Clark. "Anne Brown" in *Black Women in American Music* (1997).

Obituary: *CBC News*, 18 March 2009.

BARON KELLY

Brown, Arthur McKimmon (9 Nov. 1867–4 Dec. 1939), physician, was born in Raleigh, North Carolina. Little is known about his family or upbringing. Some sources suggest that Brown briefly attended Shaw University, the Baptist-affiliated postsecondary school for blacks founded in Raleigh in 1865; contemporary accounts indicate that Brown graduated from Cleveland High School in Cleveland, Ohio. Brown pursued undergraduate studies at Lincoln University in Pennsylvania, earning a B.A. in June 1888. That fall, Brown enrolled in the medical school of the University of Michigan at Ann Arbor. He earned his M.D. with a special qualification in surgery in 1891. At his graduation, friends from Ann Arbor's Second Baptist Church presented him with a new medical case, as a token of recognition and thanks for his active involvement in the church's choir and social activities during his student days in Ann Arbor.

Brown soon moved to Jefferson County, Alabama, where a local examining board certified him to practice medicine. He initially practiced for three years in Bessemer, located a few miles southwest of Birmingham; but in 1894 he moved his practice to Birmingham proper. Brown quickly became an important figure in that city's black community. He helped establish the Children's Home Hospital, Birmingham's first medical facility specifically for the treatment of African Americans.

In 1898 Brown volunteered for military service in the Spanish-American War. After being ignored in the initial call-ups, apparently because of his race, Brown served as an assistant surgeon to the U.S. Cavalry's Tenth Regiment, an all-black unit created under Congressional authorization in 1866 and popularly known as the "buffalo soldiers" for the unit's exploits in the American West. Brown reported for duty in Cuba in early August 1898 as an assistant surgeon at the rank of first lieutenant, thereby becoming one of the first African Americans to serve as a commissioned medical officer in the U.S. armed forces. He worked briefly at the regimental hospital before returning with his unit to the United States at the end of August 1898. He transferred with much of the Tenth Regiment to Alabama, where he had, in his words, "the privilege to go back to civil life." He was discharged from the U.S. Army in March of 1899.

Brown's activities as a civilian were varied. With Herschel V. Cashin and others, he helped to write a history of the U.S. Army's Tenth Regiment and its exploits during the Spanish-American War; the book, titled *Under Fire*, was published in 1899. He also worked on numerous inventions, including innovations to deep-shaft mining cars, and he operated a drug store in addition to his continuing medical practice. In February 1902 Brown was acknowledged by the state of Alabama as one of only seventy-six African American men who satisfied the highly restrictive criteria established in the state's new constitution and were thus issued official certificates permitting them to legally cast ballots in Alabama elections.

In 1903 Brown moved to Chicago, Illinois, where he lived part time until at least 1907. Meanwhile, he maintained connections, business activities, and his medical practices in Birmingham and also in Cleveland, Ohio. His broad experience and contacts in the medical profession resulted in his being elected, in 1914, president of the National Medical Association, the principal professional association for African American physicians. After a long career Brown died in Birmingham, Alabama, at the age of seventy-two from complications associated with diabetes. His home in Birmingham, designed by noted local African American architect Wallace A. Rayfield, is still maintained as a community center by the Birmingham Arts Club.

FURTHER READING

Cashin, Herschel V., et al. *Under Fire with the Tenth U.S. Cavalry* (1899).

Savitt, Todd L. "Entering a White Profession: Black Physicians in the New South, 1880–1920," *Bulletin of the History of Medicine* (Spring 2005).

LAURA M. CALKINS

Brown, Benjamin (1859–5 Sept. 1910), a soldier and Medal of Honor recipient, was a veteran of the Indian Wars and the Spanish-American War. Brown was born in Spotsylvania, Virginia, but nothing is known about his early life. He was in Harrisburg, Pennsylvania, by 1880, when he enlisted in the U.S. Army with the 24th Infantry Regiment.

The 24th Infantry Regiment in which Benjamin Brown enlisted in 1880 was one of four black units in the U.S. Army at this time, which, along with the 25th Infantry and 9th and 10th Cavalry regiments, were collectively known as the "Buffalo Soldiers." These units, consolidated from the original six that were authorized by Congress as part of the regular army in 1869, were originally manned by black Civil War veterans, as well as freed slaves and free blacks, and led by white officers. These units would subsequently prove their worth many times over in the western campaigns against Native Americans, known as the Indian Wars, from 1866 to 1890. The service of the Buffalo Soldiers in the west was varied and arduous, its men employed not just in fighting, but also in scouting duties, surveying, and road building, as well as protecting emerging settlements and travelers from outlaws. By 1880 the Buffalo Soldier units, which constituted approximately 10 percent of the army's overall strength, were staffed by a mixture of hard-fought career soldiers and a new generation of young black recruits. Among these new soldiers were men such as Brown, ISAIAH MAYS, and WILLIAM McBRYAR, who would subsequently earn their country's highest decoration for military valor.

By 1889 Benjamin Brown had served in the army for over eight years and had risen to the rank of sergeant. Now the senior man in Lieutenant Cartwright's Company C of the 24th Infantry, he had seen service in the Oklahoma Territory at Fort Sill and, since the summer of 1888, had been stationed at Fort Grant in the Arizona Department, where his reputation as a "fine shot" (Schubert, 93) would soon come into play. On 11 May 1889 Sergeant Brown and Corporal Isaiah Mays were the senior soldiers of an eleven-man detail assigned to escort the payroll wagon of Major Joseph Wham, loaded with more than $28,000 in gold coins intended for the garrison at Fort Grant. Near Cedar Springs, where the road passed through cliffs and rocky hills, the payroll wagon and its escort were ambushed by a group of outlaws, consisting of at least ten men and possibly as many as twenty. At the head of the train, Sergeant Brown and two privates were caught in the open and subject to intense gunfire, while Wham and the rest of the escort took cover in a nearby creek bed. In a fight that lasted over thirty minutes, Sergeant Benjamin Brown, though wounded in the abdomen and both arms, maintained a steady fire, first with his pistol and then with the carbine rifle from a wounded soldier. Despite the vigorous defense of Brown and his fellow soldiers, the outlaws succeeded in their efforts and the payroll was lost. However, Major Wham, a veteran of sixteen Civil War battles, recognized his men for their valiant efforts, later stating that he had "never witnessed better courage or better fighting than shown by these colored soldiers" (Hanna, 61), and recommended Benjamin Brown for the Medal of Honor. This award was subsequently issued on 19 February 1880.

Following his award for gallantry, Benjamin Brown remained in the army for most of the remainder of his life. When he reenlisted in the 24th Infantry at Huachuca, Arizona, in March 1898 he was a sergeant-major and described as an excellent soldier. He would subsequently serve with his unit at Santiago, Cuba, during the Spanish-American War and at San Isidro and Luzon during the Philippine Insurrection, reenlisting yet again in 1901. Brown was serving at Fort Assinniboine, Montana, when he suffered a stroke, no doubt due to his years of arduous service. He subsequently received a disability discharge from the army on 3 June 1905 while hospitalized in Washington, D.C., and resided at the Soldier's Home there until his death. He was buried at the Soldier's Home National Cemetery in Washington, D.C.

FURTHER READING

Hanna, Charles W. *African American Recipients of the Medal of Honor* (2002).
Schubert, Frank N. *Black Valor: Buffalo Soldiers and the Medal of Honor, 1870–1898* (1997).

GLENN ALLEN KNOBLOCK

Brown, Buster (17 May 1913–7 May 2002), American tap dancer and choreographer, was born James Richard Brown in Baltimore, Maryland, to William Brown and Marie Ella Otho-Brown. The only boy, he had seven sisters.

Dance played an important part in Brown's life beginning in elementary school. Inspired by BILL "BOJANGLES" ROBINSON while at the Douglas High

School, Brown developed a serious interest in tap dancing and tapped in his high school annual production, *Autumn Follies*. He was not given dance instruction but picked up a bebop jazz style of dance from the streets and from performances he attended at the Royal Theatre in Maryland. Brown and his friends imitated and further developed steps they saw at theaters and they also taught each other any new steps they picked up. At the Royal Theatre in 1929 Brown saw an inspiring performance of the celebrated WHITMAN SISTERS and their nephew, Pops Whitman. They would have a great influence on Brown to the extent that he changed his mind on becoming a doctor and was hooked on tap dancing.

Brown soon formed a dance group, the Three Aces, with two of his high school friends. Their sensational style was characterized by breathtaking and dazzling speedy quick steps and meticulous dancing. He made his professional debut with this troupe, and during the 1930s the Three Aces toured for the first time throughout the United States and Canada. They later changed their name to the Three Speed Kings. By the time Brown was eighteen in 1931, he was already dancing with the female trio, the Brown Skin Models. He continued touring and playing at vaudeville theaters for many years in the United States and Canada, appearing with Beige & Brown, SARAH VAUGHAN, and on the Rudy Vallee Show.

By the time Brown moved to New York during the 1940s, the bebop tap dancing style was in full swing and was well accepted by him. A favorite hangout of Brown was at the back of Harlem's Apollo Theatre, where he competed and improvised with friends, each attempting to out-tap the other. Brown's career soared nationally and internationally during this decade, and he appeared with Don Ameche in the 1943 Hollywood musical film *Something to Shout About*.

Shortly after the death of BILL "BOJANGLES" ROBINSON in 1949, Brown created the famous tap dance troupe the Copasetics in order to perpetuate this dance form. Brown performed numerous times with this group and also danced and toured internationally with such icons as COUNT BASIE, DIZZY GILLESPIE, CAB CALLOWAY, and DUKE ELLINGTON. It was Ellington who further opened doors for Brown by asking him to join his national and international tours, and this honor Brown never forgot.

During the early 1950s, tap dancing was on the decline. There were few or no tap dancing jobs for Brown, and no one would book him. Brown endured many hardships in order to make it and support his family in Baltimore—his wife, mother, and two children. He did menial jobs, working as a hotel clerk and janitor and cleaning offices.

Tap dancing was still on the decline in the United States in the 1960s, but Duke Ellington again came to Brown's aid and featured him in his *Sacred Concert*, where Brown played the role of David. In 1966, Brown toured with the Harlem Uptown All Star Dancers performing at various locations in Europe and at various jazz festivals. The Harlem Uptown All Star Dancers later became the famous dance troupe, the Hoofers. Besides Brown, its members included CHUCK GREEN, Baby Lawrence, and Jimmy Slyde.

One of the highlights in Brown's life came in 1967 when, accompanied by the Duke Ellington Orchestra, he gave a command tap performance for Ethiopia's Emperor Haile Selassie. Selassie awarded the highest honors to him, the Lion of Judah Coin. Two years later, in 1969, the U.S. State Department sponsored and commissioned Brown's *Back to Africa* tour, where he performed in African countries such as Senegal and Ethiopia.

By the 1970s, there was a revival in tap dancing, and Brown welcomed the opportunity to dance in *No, No Nanette* (1971) and *Bubblin' Brown Sugar* (1976). Brown was finally gaining the recognition he deserved. He appeared on the Dick Cavett Show in 1979. By the 1980s with popular interest in tap dancing, Brown appeared in *Black and Blue* (1989). He was also featured with GREGORY HINES in the films *The Cotton Club* (1984), directed by Francis Ford Coppola, and *Tap* (1989). Brown was also featured on PBS's *Great Performances*, "Tap Dance in America," the "Gershwin Gala," and "Great Feats of Feet." In 1989 he performed at the Village Gate and also appeared in 1989 on PBS *Frontline*'s "Talented, Black and Blue," where he was part of a discussion on the racial atmosphere during his early touring and performance days including problems he encountered with segregation and racism.

In 1990 Brown received the Flo-Bert award. More young black tap dancers were entering the field, including SAVION GLOVER. Mentored by Brown, Glover honored him with a special tribute in the Broadway show he produced, *Bring in 'Da Noise, Bring in 'Da Funk* (1995), and Glover's *Footnotes*. In an article in the *New York Times*, the tap dancer Jane Goldberg, who was mentored by Brown, stated: "He had no mean words to say about anyone. And no one had mean words to say about him. He was a role model ... Buster just let dancers go, so they developed their own style … He didn't criticize. He was always encouraging."

In 1997, Brown started a weekly Sunday tap jam at the Swing 46 Super Jazz Club located at 349 West 46th Street in New York City. Performers included friends from Brown's early vaudeville dancing years, children, and others. He hosted this event until shortly before his death. In 1997, he also performed in a Tap Extravaganza at Town Hall.

Another high point in Brown's life and one of his biggest honors was serving as faculty of dance at Harvard and New York University. He also gave dance master classes and workshops in the United States and Europe, including at various dance festivals. Much to his surprise and amazement, in February 2002 Brown was the recipient of an honorary doctorate degree from Oklahoma City University's School of American Dance and Arts.

During the final three years of his life, tap dancers who were inspired, coached, assisted, and touched by Brown often brought his meals to him. He spent his final years in Manhattan, where he died in his sleep on 7 May 2002 at Columbia Presbyterian Hospital at age eighty-nine. He was later honored by the Harlem Jazz Dance Festival. Brown left his mark on this art form, influencing many. His style of precision and speed influenced many including SAMMY DAVIS JR. and GREGORY HINES. Brown brought tap dancing back after decades in decline. Audiences were fascinated by Brown's intricate tap dancing, and he has been a big inspiration and influence not only to tap dancers but also in rap music.

FURTHER READING

Information is available on the Dr. James Buster Brown website, http://www.drbusterbrown.com.

Andrews, Laura. "Tapping at 86, Buster Brown Brings in the Funk," *New York Amsterdam News*, 7 May 1999.

Sanchez, Brenna. "Brown, James 'Buster,'" in Jessie Carney Smith, ed., *Notable Black American Men* (2007).

Obituaries: *New York Times*, 9 May 2002; *Guardian* [London, England], 9 May 2002.

BARBARA BONOUS-SMIT

Brown, Cecil (3 July 1943–), novelist, playwright, screenwriter, memoirist, folklorist, and educator, was born in Bolton, North Carolina, to Dorothy and Cecil Culphert Brown. His father was in prison until Brown was thirteen, so he and his brother Donald Ray were raised until then by his Uncle Lofton, who recognized and nurtured young Cecil's talent for academics and his facility with words. Brown describes this part of his life as a kind of idyll haunted by the mysterious but terrible situation of his father.

When he was fourteen years old Brown reluctantly moved with his brother and father to Green Swamp, North Carolina, to grow tobacco. Considerably less supportive of Cecil's bookishness, Culphert Brown beat him for reading when he should have been plowing. It was around this time that Brown first encountered the Stagger Lee story, which would be the focus of much of his scholarly research. Friends of his father would sing a version of the ballad, and then tell young Cecil that his father was a bad man like the murderous Stagger Lee (also known as STAGOLEE, Stack Lee, and other variants). It was around this time, too, that Brown at last learned the truth behind his father's imprisonment: he had murdered a man in a fight over a card game. It was also while living in Green Swamp, however, that, having been thrilled by a magic show at school, Brown became a magician himself. An able hypnotist, the young man captivated crowds of peers and adults, and saw a career in magic as a way out of the sharecropping life he hated.

Brown's deliverance came in a different form, however: with a scholarship to Agricultural and Technical State University at Greensboro in 1961. Unsatisfied with the library at Greensboro A&T, Brown transferred to Columbia University, where in 1966 he earned a B.A. in Comparative Literature. Upon graduating from Columbia he completed a master's degree in English and American Literature at the University of Chicago. The mastery of the traditional, Eurocentric Western canon was an important part of his intellectual and artistic development. Also important were the connections he made there with his fellow writers, like LEROI JONES (later AMIRI BARAKA), ISHMAEL REED, and ELDRIDGE CLEAVER. Together they were at the forefront of a new, politically engaged black art.

In the spring of 1968 Brown was impressed with a speech delivered by Eldridge Cleaver, whose *Soul on Ice* (1967) he admired, at a political rally. The two became close friends and moved to California together. They shared an interest in the oral tradition in black culture and a conviction that the writer was an essential actor in the struggle for equality. Brown was an important part of a vital new school of writers who expanded the purview of American literature to include black voices. The political aspect of this literature was important, but so was its stylistic innovation. In 1968 Brown began to publish his criticism, essays, and interviews in such journals such as the *Negro Digest, Kenyon Review*, and *Evergreen Review*. At this time he was also working on his own novel and teaching at the University of Illinois.

In 1969 Brown published his first novel, *The Lives and Loves of Mr. Jiveass Nigger*, a work that bespoke the mixture of density, political relevance, and aesthetic novelty that would mark all of Brown's work. Linguistically and stylistically playful, with voices vernacular and formal, Brown told the story of a character called George Washington. A black American abroad, Washington made his living catering to the sexual wishes of white European women, retaining a dubious freedom from penury and menial labor. He philosophized about race and literature throughout. In the end, a ghostly narrator counseled him against hopelessness and suicide, warning that if he were not vigilant in representing himself, white sociologists and "experts" would attempt to destroy that which he had brought to light. The book received mixed reviews and gained Brown some notoriety.

Having befriended the comedian RICHARD PRYOR in 1971, Brown began to work in Hollywood as a screenwriter, collaborating with Pryor on the controversial comedy *Which Way Is Up?* From 1977 to 1979 he was engaged as a screenwriter by Warner Brothers and Universal Studios. He drew on his experiences in Hollywood to write his 1982 novel, *Days without Weather*, a Hollywood satire about the attempts of a black screenwriter to bring a historical film about a slave riot to the screen. His project was continually corrupted and foiled by producers and studios. *Days Without Weather* won the Before Columbus Foundation American Book Award in 1984.

In 1990 Brown returned to academia and to Stagger Lee. He obtained his Ph.D. in African American Literature, Folklore, and Theory of Narrative in 1993 from the University of California at Berkeley. His dissertation was published by Harvard University Press in 2003 as *Stagolee Shot Billy*. In this work Brown wrote elliptically, interspersing various versions of the song with historical facts and historical conjecture. He used the myth of Stagger Lee as a repository of buried historical fact, a folktale that could instruct about race relations, pimps, and politics in turn-of-the-century St. Louis. At the same time, the story in all of its many versions conferred upon Stagger Lee the status of archetype. Brown

sorted out what this archetype might represent for black men in America in the age of hip-hop.

Brown was a professor at a number of universities. He pioneered courses on orality, hip hop, and popular culture. He continued writing as well, taking another approach to the Lee mythos in his historical novel *I, Stagolee* in 2005. In 2007 he published a book of academic rabble-rousing called *Dude, Where's My Black Studies Department?*, the extension of a controversial 2004 essay in the *Eastbay Express* that strongly criticized his employer at the time, the University of California, Berkeley. In this work Brown argued that black studies departments had shifted their focus, both in content and hiring practices, to Pan-African and Caribbean studies, and called for a black studies that was engaged more specifically with African American life and employed more African American professors.

FURTHER READING
Brown, Cecil. *Coming Up Down Home: A Memoir of a Southern Childhood* (1993).
"Cecil Brown," in *Dictionary of Literary Biography, Volume 33: Afro-American Fiction Writers after 1955*, eds. Thadious M. Davis and Trudier Harris (1984).

ANN MCCARTHY

Brown, Charles (13 Sept. 1922–21 Jan. 1999), blues songwriter, singer, and pianist, was born in Texas City on the Gulf Coast of Texas. His mother, Mattie, died when he was six months old, and his father, Mose, a cotton picker, ignored the boy. Brown was raised by his maternal grandparents, Swanee and Conquest Simpson. Mose Brown, planning to reclaim his son, was struck and killed by a train in 1928.

Brown's grandmother arranged for him to begin piano lessons when he was six so that he could play for the Barbous Chapel Baptist Church. He began singing in the church choir, and an uncle taught him to play the guitar and sing the blues. Knowing his grandmother would disapprove, he practiced singing and playing the blues when she was out of the house.

When he was around thirteen Brown created the style of blues he called "Walkin' and Driftin'" to express the alienation and loneliness he felt, while continuing to study classical music. Although he gave one recital, Brown lacked the necessary devotion to the more respectable form of music.

After graduating from high school with honors, Brown went to Prairie View College in Hempstead, Texas. He majored in chemistry and mathematics with a minor in education, planning to realize his grandmother's dream and become a teacher.

In 1942 he became a chemistry teacher at George Washington Carver High School in Baytown, Texas. Dissatisfied with his $22-a-week salary, Brown took a Civil Service examination, which led to a junior chemist position at a military arsenal in Pine Bluff, Arkansas. After a few months he decided to abandon this post because of the racial prejudice he experienced. He was drafted but was classified 4-F because of asthma. Brown moved to Los Angeles and worked in menial jobs while planning his professional music career.

Winning an amateur contest led to his becoming part of the Three Blazers, with the guitarist Johnny Moore and bassist Eddie Williams, performing pop songs in Los Angeles clubs. In 1945 the trio recorded Brown's "Driftin' Blues," which sold 350,000 records and eventually became his signature tune. This success led to bookings at Harlem's Apollo Theatre. Around the same time Brown wrote his other best-known song, "Merry Christmas, Baby," which soon became both a holiday and blues standard. Moore forced him to share writing credit for these and other songs. Columbia Records offered Brown a contract, but he lacked the confidence to leave Moore's trio. After a disagreement over money, Brown finally broke with Moore in 1949. He signed with Aladdin Records and immediately had a hit with "Get Yourself Another Fool." He was soon touring as a headliner, with such performers as RUTH BROWN and RAY CHARLES opening for him.

Brown had a string of rhythm and blues hits from 1946 through 1952 but only one more afterward, "Please Come Home for Christmas" in 1960. He sued Aladdin Records for unpaid royalties, was awarded only $8,000, and then was punished by not being promoted by the company, which would not release him from his contract. His leisurely style also seemed old-fashioned with the advent of rock and roll. After years of sporadic performing and recording, Brown was working in the used furniture business by the late 1960s. Brown alternated between menial jobs and performing low-paying engagements through the 1970s.

Brown's comeback began in 1979, when he was booked at Tramps, a New York blues club. In 1982 Stephen Holden of *The New York Times* gave Brown's performances a rave review, calling him the missing link between the gentility of NAT "KING" COLE and the gospel-based blues of Ray Charles. Brown began recording again in 1987 to enthusiastic notices, and his comeback continued with bookings at New York's legendary Blue Note and acclaim from such fellow performers as Elvis

Costello, Dr. John, and Bonnie Raitt, who invited Brown to open for her on her 1990 national tour. Raitt told *Rolling Stone* that Brown was "the greatest living piano player." Brown plays both piano and organ, with guest appearances by Ruth Brown and Dr. John, on *All My Life* (1990), considered his greatest album by many.

Brown suffered from numerous health problems in the 1990s, and a benefit was held for him in San Francisco in December 1998 featuring Dr. John, JOHN LEE HOOKER, Maria Muldaur, and Bonnie Raitt. Brown, who was married and divorced twice, died in Oakland of heart failure on 21 January 1999, and the singer SOLOMON BURKE presided at his funeral. Brown was inducted into the Rock and Roll Hall of Fame the following April.

FURTHER READING

Deffa, Chip. *Blue Rhythms: Six Lives in Rhythm and Blues* (1996).

di Perna, Alan. "Jazzin' the Blues with Charles Brown," *Musician*, April 1991.

Harris, Sheldon. *Blues Who's Who: A Biographical Dictionary of Blues Singers* (1991).

Morris, Chris. "Charles Brown, 76, Dies," *Billboard*, 6 Feb. 1999.

Obituary: *New York Times*, 25 Jan. 1999.

MICHAEL ADAMS

Brown, Charlotte Eugenia Hawkins (11 June 1883– 11 Jan. 1961), educator, was born Lottie Hawkins in Henderson, North Carolina, the daughter of Edmund H. Hight, a brick mason, and Caroline Frances Hawkins. Accounts vary as to whether her father and mother separated before or after her birth, and it is also unclear whether her parents ever married. After her mother married Nelson Willis, Lottie (as she was called until she changed her name to Charlotte Eugenia in high school) relocated with nineteen members of her extended family to Massachusetts in 1888. By joining the widespread migration of African Americans, the family hoped to enjoy greater economic opportunities and a better life. After settling in Cambridge, her stepfather worked odd jobs to support the family, while her mother boarded African American Harvard students, operated a laundry, and babysat. Hawkins began her elementary education at the Allston School in Cambridge, where she befriended two of Henry Wadsworth Longfellow's daughters and excelled in her studies. She also attended Baptist Sunday school, where at the age of twelve she organized a kindergarten department.

Hawkins then attended Cambridge English High and Latin School. During her senior year she met and made a favorable impression upon the former president of Wellesley College, Alice Freeman Palmer. Although Hawkins wanted to attend Radcliffe in order to gain the best possible preparation for a teaching career, her mother urged her to enter teaching immediately. As a compromise, Hawkins entered the Salem Normal School (later Salem State College) in 1900. Having spotted Palmer's name in the school catalog, Hawkins wrote to her in search of advice; her inquiry gained her a letter of recommendation and an offer of financial assistance from Palmer.

A second chance encounter at the beginning of Hawkins's second year at Salem determined the course of her life. After meeting a representative of the American Missionary Association on a train between Salem and Cambridge, she decided to accept an offer to return to her native state and operate a school for the association. Leaving Salem before graduating (she later received credit for her work in the South and was awarded a diploma), she traveled south by train and arrived in McLeansville, North Carolina. After walking four miles to the community of Sedalia, she boarded with a local minister and on 12 October 1901 welcomed fifteen children to the poorly maintained one-room shack that was the Bethany Institute. Although Hawkins was accepted by the community and encouraged by her accomplishments during the five-month school term, her future in Sedalia looked bleak when the association moved to close all its smaller schools at the end of the school year. Undaunted and determined to complete her work in the community, Hawkins rejected an offer from the association to teach elsewhere and returned north with the goal of raising sufficient funds to open her own school.

Upon returning to Cambridge, she approached Palmer for assistance, only to find her benefactress in poor health and bereft of her fortune. Palmer did, however, provide her with the names of several possible financial contributors. After soliciting funds from these people, Hawkins traveled to the resort community of Gloucester, Massachusetts, where she gave dramatic recitations and musical performances to raise money. She returned to Sedalia with less than four hundred dollars and, with that money and a donation of fifteen acres of land and an old blacksmith shop, she opened the school on 10 October 1902.

The school, which was named the Palmer Memorial Institute the following summer in honor of her recently deceased mentor, soon became a success story. Inspired by and patterned after BOOKER T. WASHINGTON's Tuskegee Institute, Palmer in its early years emphasized basic instruction and manual training. Students were responsible for daily chores and farm work as well as academics. The school filled a dire need in a state in which educational opportunities for African Americans were few. (No teacher-training institutions existed until the 1930s, and there was no public schooling in the Sedalia area until 1937.) Fund-raising was a constant concern; fortunately, wealthy northerners, such as Charles W. Eliot (who also served as the president of the first board of trustees), Seth Low, and Galen S. Stone, were generous in their support. The American Missionary Association added its resources in 1924, and Hawkins's own fund-raising efforts resulted in a permanent endowment of $250,000.

Despite her many commitments, Hawkins did not neglect her own intellectual development. She took summer and regular courses at Simmons College, Temple University, and Harvard University. It was at the latter that she met Edward S. Brown, whom she married in June 1911. Although he initially returned with Hawkins to Sedalia and taught at Palmer, he left after five years to teach at a similar school in South Carolina, and the marriage ended in divorce. Charlotte Hawkins Brown, though childless, raised several nieces and nephews at her on-campus home, the Canary Cottage. One of her nieces, Maria Hawkins Ellington, became a singer and later married NAT KING COLE.

The Palmer Institute eventually grew to three hundred acres in size and shifted its academic emphasis; in its latter years it became a preparatory school with a focus on high school and junior college–level instruction. While Brown's students remained central in her life, she also engaged in professional activities and social activism. She helped found the North Carolina State Federation of Negro Women's Clubs in 1909 and also served as its president (1915–1936). While she was president, the federation purchased and maintained the Efland Home for Wayward Girls in Orange County, North Carolina; it was the only institution of its type for African American women in the state.

Charlotte Hawkins Brown's interest in interracial harmony led to her work in founding the Commission on Interracial Cooperation in 1919. That same year she published *Mammy: An Appeal to the Heart of the South*, a fictional indictment of the treatment of African Americans during slavery. Fully supportive of civil rights, Brown chafed under the restrictive racial atmosphere of her day and frequently challenged established Jim Crow standards. She refused to ride in segregated elevators and was sometimes ejected from "whites only" Pullman berths. Nonviolent in outlook, she occasionally resorted to lawsuits in order to challenge the discriminatory practices that she encountered during her travels. Despite her outspoken nature, Brown was a firm believer in the social graces. She constantly sought to inculcate manners as well as education into her students and published *The Correct Thing to Do, to Say, and to Wear* in 1941 as a guidebook in this area.

Brown remained busy throughout her life. She was named in 1940 to the North Carolina Council of Defense—one of the first African Americans so nominated—and also served as a member of the Executive Committee of the Home Nursing Council of the American Red Cross during World War II. Although she retired as president of Palmer in October 1952, she retained the post of director of finance until 1955. She died in Greensboro, North Carolina, after a lingering illness.

Charlotte Hawkins Brown is remembered for her pioneering efforts at Palmer Memorial Institute. Given early advantages of education and upbringing, she returned to her native state to provide educational opportunities for her fellow African Americans at a time when those opportunities were not readily available. She succeeded against often overwhelming odds in creating a preparatory school that provided hundreds of students with opportunities for a better life. Although Palmer Institute closed because of financial problems in 1971, its graduates are Brown's greatest legacy.

FURTHER READING

The papers of Charlotte Eugenia Hawkins Brown are held at the Schlesinger Library of Women in America at Radcliffe College, Cambridge, Massachusetts. Additional material on Brown and on Palmer Institute is available at the Charlotte Hawkins Brown Museum and Historic Site in Sedalia in the W. C. Jackson Library at the University of North Carolina at Greensboro and in the North Carolina Historical Room at the Greensboro Public Library.

Marteena, Constance Hill. *The Lengthening Shadow of a Woman: A Biography of Charlotte Hawkins Brown* (1977).

Wadelington, Charles W., and Richard F. Knapp. *Charlotte Hawkins Brown and Palmer Institute: What One Young African American Woman Could Do* (1999).

Obituary: *New York Times*, 12 Jan. 1961.
This entry is taken from the *American National Biography* and is published here with the permission of the American Council of Learned Societies.

EDWARD L. LACH JR.

Brown, Chuck (31 Aug. 1934–16 May 2012), music pioneer, musician, and singer, was born Charles L. Brown in Charlotte, North Carolina; his parents were migrant farmers about whom little information is available. In 1942 Chuck moved with his parents to Fairmont Heights in Prince George's County, Maryland, a small suburban neighborhood just outside of Northeast Washington, D.C. As a boy Chuck worked odd jobs to assist his parents financially. He sold newspapers, cut logs, shined shoes, laid bricks, and could be heard singing "watermelon, watermelon" for the horse-drawn watermelon cart. Chuck's love for music began as a boy in North Carolina, replaying the piano and rhythms he heard in church of the bass drum, cymbals, and the snare over and again in his head. In Fairmont Heights at Mount Zion Holiness Church he played piano while his mother accompanied him on harmonica. Chuck studied piano with Sister Louise Murray, who exposed him to church-music conventions. His inclination toward music was innate.

After sparring with a prizefighter for thirty dollars, Chuck began working with boxers Harold Smith and Bobby Foster who would become a light-heavyweight champion and International Boxing Hall of Famer, respectively. In 1948 at the age of fourteen Chuck left home. When work was slow he played pool, cards, and craps for money. A few years later he joined the Marines but was dismissed for lying about his age. Soon thereafter Chuck began a brief career as an armed robber and by age seventeen he had landed himself in jail. He served time in several penitentiaries along the East Coast before finally arriving at Lorton Penitentiary in Virginia for assault with a deadly weapon. The assault charge was elevated to murder when six months later the man he shot in self-defense died. The four years Chuck spent at Lorton would prove to be a turning point in his life. He earned his high school diploma (GED), worked in the tailor shop, and began learning to play guitar on an instrument made by a man in the carpentry shop. Later he got his first guitar in exchange for five packs of cigarettes. Chuck listened to singer SISTER ROSETTA THARPE and learned to play guitar like CHARLIE CHRISTIAN, soon becoming a popular entertainer at Lorton.

In 1962 Chuck was released from prison and turned away from a life of crime. Having set his sights on becoming a musician, his ensuing career progressed naturally. Chuck's first gigs were playing with Top 40 cover bands in Washington, D.C., such as Jerry Butler, the Earls of Rhythm, and Los Latinos. He could play all of the radio hits and took work wherever he could—at school gymnasiums, recreation centers, hotels, and backyard cookouts. Chuck found steady work with Los Latinos performing three and four shows a night sometimes attended by headliners from Washington D.C.'s popular Howard Theater, such as GENE CHANDLER, SAMMY DAVIS JR., and ISAAC HAYES. Soon he became lead singer of Los Latinos.

In 1966 Chuck left Los Latinos to start his own band, the Soul Searchers. The Soul Searchers became regulars at the Ebony Inn in Fairmont Heights playing Top 40 hits. Chuck Brown began formulating his unprecedented sound in 1966, a unique combination of rhythms inspired by the church and Afro-Latin percussions he became acquainted with as a member of Los Latinos. In the 1970s disco music saturated the clubs and any cover band wanting to survive would need to satisfy a dance crowd demanding the latest tunes. Although Chuck grew tired of playing disco he was ever dedicated to pleasing his audience. Offering his unique brand of music as a soulful alternative to the rapid tempo in disco, Chuck spliced the disco beat in half for a funky groove played over his signature percussions. Chuck even developed a unique way of engaging the crowd. As evidence of influence from the African American church, in Chuck's performance he engaged the crowd in call and response with the audience responding to the beckoning of his bass voice. These call and response routines became regular chants like fans pleading the musician to "Wind Me Up Chuck." Chuck maintained a report with his crowd by conversing with them casually over the music and announcing messages or "shout outs" from scraps of paper handed up onto the stage from the crowd.

When Chuck heard the song "Mister Magic" by saxophonist GROVER WASHINGTON JR., he recognized some of the same rhythmic influences he most admired. The groove from "Mister Magic" was added to his already signature style to create an entirely new genre of music. The Soul Searchers played this signature style, conga, cow bells, bongo, and drums between songs for a continuous Afro-Latin rhythm and an uninterrupted party; Chuck Brown named this brand of music "go-go" because it never stopped. His performances are a collage of jazz, R&B, and classical compositions all performed to the rhythm of Chuck's distinctly D.C. go-go sound. Soon to follow were a number of go-go bands in the Washington, D.C., area such as Trouble Funk, E.U., and Rare Essence, all inheritors of Chuck Brown's sound earning him the exclusive title, Godfather of Go-Go. The Soul Searchers playing Chuck's go-go music grew rapidly in popularity.

In the early 70s he was approached by Daniel Clayton, a longtime D.C. music entrepreneur known as Breeze, who offered the Soul Searchers a generous wage to perform at the popular Pitts Red Carpet Lounge in northwest Washington, D.C. Pitts was frequented by members of the Black Arts and Black Power Movement. People like MARION BARRY who would become Washington, D.C.'s, first African American mayor and his Pride, Inc. organization hung out to discuss politics and music. At Pitts, Chuck met a number of influential individuals who helped to get the Soul Searchers shows all over the D.C. metropolitan area. By the time Chuck Brown and the Soul Searchers appeared on the local television show, Teenorama, he was already exceedingly popular among area youth.

The Soul Searchers's first hit was "We the People" in 1972 followed by "Blow Your Whistle" in 1974. Chuck achieved national acclaim with his 1979 gold album and hit single "Bustin' Loose" spending four weeks at the top of the R&B singles chart and peaking at thirty-four on the Billboard Hot 100 singles chart. The Washington Nationals baseball team adopted "Bustin' Loose" as their official homerun song in 2005. In 1986 "Go-Go Swing" was released internationally, changing the face of go-go and garnering a cult following for the Godfather of Go-Go including Europe and Japan. Chuck Brown has released a wealth of go-go classics, among them, "Run Joe," "Day-O," and "We Need Some Money." Chuck Brown has produced over twenty albums including a Christmas album and collaboration with jazz artist Eva Cassidy.

In 2007 he released "We're about the Business," featuring his rapper daughter KK and a go-go version of the "Love Theme" from Francis Ford Copolla's classic film The Godfather. Chuck Brown appeared in the 1986 film about go-go music entitled "Good to Go." In 2000 he was featured in the Smithsonian Folklife Festival and presented with the District of Columbia's Mayor's Arts Award. In 2003 Chuck received the National Academy of the Recording Arts & Sciences Board of Governors Award. The National Endowment for the Arts awarded Chuck with a Lifetime Heritage Fellowship Award September 2005. Chuck also appeared in television commercials for the *Washington Post* and D.C. Lottery. Chuck wrote and performed the songs for National Geographic's shows "Caesar's Way" and the "Dog Whisperer." In 2008 a bobble head doll was created in Chuck's image. In the District of Columbia Chuck Brown, the Godfather of Go-Go, was also lovingly referred to as a "national treasure."

In 2012, Chuck died of complications from a sepsis infection at Johns Hopkins Hospital in Baltimore.

FURTHER READING

Chang, Jeff. "Wind Me Up, Chuck!" *San Francisco Bay Guardian*, June 2001.

Lornell, Kip, and Charles C. Stephenson, Jr. *The Beat: Go-Go's Fusion of Funk and Hip-Hop* (2001).

Pareles, John. "Still Soulful, Still Swinging, Still Ready to Bust Loose," *New York Times*, 21 April 2007.

Wartofsky, Alona. "What Go-Goes Around," *Washington Post*, 3 June 2001.

OBITUARY: *WASHINGTON POST*, 16 MAY 2012.

SAFIYA DALILAH HOSKINS

Brown, Clara(Aunt Clara) (1803?–26 Oct. 1885), former slave, western pioneer, church founder, businesswoman, and philanthropist, was born in Gallatin, Tennessee—some sources offer a birth date of 1800—and at the age of three was sold with her mother to a planter in Virginia. There, at the age of eighteen, she married a slave named Richard and had several children. When her owner, Ambrose Smith, died in 1835 Clara and her children were auctioned off to different slaveholders. Her daughter Margaret was sold to a slaveholder in Kentucky and reportedly died a few years later. Clara lost contact with her son Richard, who was sold repeatedly. Another daughter, Eliza Jane, was sold to a James Covington, also in Kentucky. Clara was sold again at auction, this time to a Kentucky slaveholder named George Brown, a merchant, and for the next two decades served the Brown family as a house slave. During this time Clara took on the Brown surname and became known as "Aunt" Clara Brown, a name that followed her for the rest of her life. In 1857 George Brown died, and Clara Brown's life shifted dramatically. She received three hundred dollars from the Brown estate and bought her freedom, which was

Aunt Clara Brown, a freed slave who built a successful laundry business catering to the mining community of Central City, Colorado, in an undated photograph. (AP Images.)

allowed by Brown's will. She left Kentucky immediately (state law mandated that freed slaves had to migrate) for St. Louis, Missouri. Brown may have done some laundry work in St. Louis, but not for long. She moved on to Fort Leavenworth, in the Kansas Territory, right in the midst of a civil war that had exploded over the future of slavery in the western territories.

In the spring of 1859 Brown left Kansas with a wagon train headed west, agreeing to cook and launder in exchange for passage. She arrived in the Denver area in June after eight weeks of grueling travel, thus becoming one of the first black women—and certainly the oldest—free or enslaved, to arrive in the Colorado Territory. Her washtubs in tow, Brown now set about making money to enable her to search for her family. She remained in the area less than a year before moving closer to the mining camps in the Cherry Creek area. It proved to be a wise decision. By 1860 she had become a landowner, "paying $50.00 for a lot in Mountain City. Gilpin County records show that in 1868 she sold that same lot for $500.00, after building a house on the property"

(Baker, 32). Brown's assets grew rapidly. Her booming laundry business in Central City, coupled with land and mining investments in several Colorado counties, plus the occasional payment from the county for the board or care of an indigent person, brought her fortune to an estimated ten thousand dollars by 1864. Although Brown belonged to the Central City Presbyterian Church, she used her wealth to support a variety of local congregations. She provided more than one hundred dollars toward the building of the Congregational church and contributed money to the founding of the St. James Methodist Church and even opened her home to its religious services until construction was complete. Five years after her arrival in Colorado, Brown was one of the wealthiest women in the West. Her success remains an astonishing achievement.

In 1865, at the age of sixty-two and with financial security, Brown returned to Kentucky to find her daughter, Eliza Jane. Her search proved fruitless and keenly disappointing. Kentucky and Tennessee were in chaos after the Civil War, and thousands of African Americans were free yet jobless, hungry, and often without homes. Brown gathered a group of emancipated black families and paid for them to travel with her back to Colorado. The twenty to thirty people who traveled by rail to Leavenworth and then by wagon train to Colorado likely cost her more than five thousand dollars. The payoff for Central City did not occur overnight, but in time, as Brown helped find homes and jobs for these families, the contributions of the African American community grew and continued for generations. Brown was the heart of this community.

Brown then shifted her focus to her own business concerns and for the next fourteen years bought and sold land and homes. She signed at least one quitclaim deed to provide land for one of the people she brought from Kentucky. She dealt with claim jumpers and in at least one case went to court to settle a land dispute. Brown's tax records indicate a considerable valuation of property, reaching a high of $2,500 in 1869. By 1872, however, her property valuation had dropped to $1,500. She fell behind in property taxes in 1869, 1870, and 1871, although those taxes were paid in 1874. Yet at the same time, Brown was sending money to several young female students at Oberlin College in Ohio. She continued opening her door to those in need, giving shelter, food, or medical care when asked. Disaster struck in 1873 and again in 1874 when fires swept large areas of Central City. Brown lost a number of rental properties and possessed no insurance to cover her losses.

In 1879, at the age of seventy-six, Clara Brown was called upon again to help people in need. The governor of Colorado suggested that Brown travel to Kansas to survey the dire situation of the so-called Exodusters, the free southern African Americans who were moving into Kansas in huge numbers. She carried a letter of introduction from the governor, authorizing her to ask for aid from the governor of Kansas. It may be that Brown thought that if some of the stranded blacks would be an asset to Colorado they could be brought back to work and live there; however, she returned to Colorado with little fanfare and brought back no one. Existing records indicate that little money donated from anywhere in Colorado went to the Exodusters relief efforts, and the purpose of the mission remains baffling.

By 1882 Brown had moved from her beloved Central City back to Denver. At age seventy-nine and ailing, she lost most if not all of her remaining properties to fraud, failure to pay taxes, and natural disasters. She took up residence in a home of an old friend who charged her no rent. For those who believe in miracles, there was one left for Brown. She was contacted by a stranger who told her that her daughter, Eliza Jane, might be living in Council Bluffs, Iowa. Brown went there in February 1882 and found not only her daughter but also a grandchild. Eliza Jane Brewer, probably in her mid- to late fifties, was widowed and had at least one child, although records are uncertain as to the precise number of her children. The reunion was widely reported in newspapers in Colorado and throughout the Midwest. Her daughter and grandchild returned with Brown to live with her in Denver. But the next three years proved difficult. Brown's health began to fail, and she fell on hard financial times. As word circulated about her poverty, many of those whom Brown had assisted over the many years offered contributions. In January 1884 the pioneer society in Central City invited Brown to its annual banquet. That September the Colorado Society of Pioneers made Brown its first female and first African American member. Although terribly ill, Brown put in an appearance at the September 1885 annual reunion. Brown died at home in Denver, and her funeral service on 29 October was an ecumenical event, held at the Central Presbyterian Church. Hundreds attended the services, including the governor of Colorado, the mayor of Denver, many old pioneers, and most of the Central City African American community. On 10 January 1896 Brown's body was removed to another burial site, a plot owned by Harriet Mason, one of the original members of the group of African Americans Brown brought back from her trip to Kentucky. Posthumous awards and honors preserve the memory of Brown's life, including induction into the Colorado Women's Hall of Fame in 1989 and installation of a stained glass window of Brown's image at the Colorado State Capitol.

FURTHER READING

Baker, Roger. *Clara: An Ex-slave in Gold Rush Colorado* (2003).

Obituaries: Denver *Republican*, 27, 30 Oct. 1885.

MARIAELENA RAYMOND

Brown, Clarence "Gatemouth" (18 Apr. 1924–10 Sept. 2005), blues singer, songwriter, guitarist, and fiddle player, was born in Vinton, Louisiana, and moved across the Sabine River with his family to Orange, Texas, when he was a few weeks old. He began playing the fiddle when he was five, learning the instrument from his father, Clarence Brown Sr.—

a railroad worker who played and sang everything from traditional French songs to German polkas—and taught himself to play the guitar when he was ten. Brown's mother, Jenny, played the piano.

As a boy Brown would hang outside the local jazz clubs, and once when he was listening to DUKE ELLINGTON practice, the musician invited him to sit with him on the piano bench. Brown claimed he acquired his nickname when a high school teacher said he had a voice like a gate, though he long promised to reveal the true account of how he became Gatemouth. He served in the army during World War II and made his professional debut as a drummer in San Antonio in 1945.

Brown's big break came in 1947 when the guitarist T-BONE WALKER left a performance at the Peacock Club in Houston because of an ulcer and Brown leaped onto the stage and improvised "Gatemouth Boogie." The club owner, Don Robey, was impressed enough to become the young musician's manager, surrounding him with a twenty-three-piece orchestra. Robey started Peacock Records in 1949 with Brown as his first artist. Brown's brother, James "Widemouth" Brown, was also a blues guitarist and began recording in the early 1950s.

Clarence "Gatemouth" Brown plays at the Juneteenth blues festival in Houston, Texas, on 10 June 1987. (AP Images.)

Brown had regional hits during the 1950s with such songs as "Boogie Rambler," "Dirty Work at the Crossroads," "Okie Dokie Stomp," and "Rock My Blues Away." In 1966 he became bandleader for *The Beat*, a syndicated rhythm-and-blues television show originating in Dallas. Brown toured Europe and Africa in the 1970s as a musical ambassador for the U.S. State Department. He performed at Switzerland's Montreux Jazz Festival in 1973 and appeared on Professor Longhair's 1974 album *Rock 'n' Roll Gumbo*. After appearing several times on the country-music television program *Hee Haw*, Brown recorded an album, *Makin' Music* (1979), with one of its stars, the guitarist Roy Clark.

Brown signed with the Chicago blues label Rounder in 1981 and made the album *Alright Again!* which won a Grammy as best traditional blues album. His subsequent recordings for Alligator and Verve emphasized the swing and jump blues styles he had grown up with.

In addition to his Grammy, Brown was an eight-time winner of the W.C. Handy Award given by the Blues Foundation. He was inducted into that organization's hall of fame in 1999 and received the Pioneer Award from the Rhythm & Blues Foundation in 1997. His participation in a 2003 all-star blues concert at New York's Radio City Music Hall is captured in the documentary *Lightning in a Bottle* (2004). Married and divorced three times, Brown was the father of three daughters and a son.

Brown is notable for exploring and merging several types of music, performing blues, rhythm and blues, jazz, swing, country, Cajun music, and even calypso, often making the genres overlap, sometimes switching from guitar or fiddle to mandolin, viola, or harmonica. He eschewed the label "blues," which he associated with sad songs about being mistreated by women, and created arrangements in the big-band traditions of COUNT BASIE and DUKE ELLINGTON, whose "Take the A Train" he frequently performed. Brown's love for the spirited vitality of Cajun music is demonstrated on *Back to Bogalusa* (2001).

Brown referred to his music simply as "American music, Texas-style," also the title of his 1999 album, and always wore a Western shirt and cowboy hat onstage. Although he began by emulating the technique of T-Bone Walker, Brown's guitar playing is harsher and more forceful. His influence can be heard in such musicians as Lonnie Brooks, Eric Clapton, ALBERT COLLINS, Ry Cooder, Johnny Copeland, Joe Louis Walker, and JOHNNY "GUITAR"

WATSON. Frank Zappa frequently called Brown his favorite guitarist.

Brown left his home in Slidell, Louisiana, on Lake Pontchartrain, on 28 August 2005, shortly before Hurricane Katrina hit, and retreated to his hometown of Orange, Texas. He died there on 10 September of a combination of lung cancer, emphysema, and heart disease. Brown's cancer had been diagnosed a year earlier, but he continued to tour and issued his last album, *Timeless*, in March 2005. With the help of an oxygen tank, he performed at the New Orleans Jazz Festival that April.

FURTHER READING

Russell, Tony. *The Blues: From Robert Johnson to Robert Cray* (1997).

Obituary: *New York Times*, 12 Sept. 2005.

MICHAEL ADAMS

Brown, Claude (23 Feb. 1937–2 Feb. 2002), writer, was born in Harlem, New York, the eldest of four children of Henry Lee, a railroad worker, and Ossie Brock, a domestic. Both parents had moved in 1935 from South Carolina to New York, seeking a better life in the North. Brown characterized his father as a man who worked hard, drank too much, enjoyed gospel music (especially when under the influence of alcohol), and whose parenting skills were limited to corporal punishment, which he meted out with great frequency. Brown's mother attended to the material needs of her children and attempted to save their souls by occasionally bringing them to an evangelical preacher who ran a makeshift church in her apartment. Growing up in a household with two working parents, Brown got much of his upbringing on the streets and thus developed a tough attitude. He recalls that around the age of four he was hit by a bus in some kind of accident in which he was only slightly injured. His father attempted to benefit financially from the incident, but his submissive behavior around the white judge and lawyers in court transformed him in his son's eyes from a "bad nigger" (i.e., a black man who commands respect by being or acting tough), into a "simple-actin' nigger." Brown decided that unlike his posturing father, he was going to be a "bad nigger" all the time.

At the age of five, Brown started school and by December of his first year, had become a truant almost a third of the time. The following year he started stealing—not because he was hungry or destitute but because it was fun. At the age of six he felt deprived for not being allowed to participate in

Claude Brown, standing on the corner of 125th Street in Harlem, New York, on 2 March 1986, the 20th anniversary of the publication of his book *Manchild in the Promised Land.* (AP Images.)

the Harlem riot of 1943. By the age of eight he was staying out all night and had seen a man killed for urinating in the hallway of his building.

Neither his father's beatings nor his mother's pleadings could sway Brown from his early road to perdition. Out of desperation his parents had him admitted to Bellevue Hospital for psychiatric observation to determine if there was any medical explanation for his apparent incorrigibility; none was found. However, each incident of antisocial behavior enhanced Brown's reputation among older juvenile delinquents, and at the age of nine he became one of the youngest members of the Forty Thieves, an apprentice division of the Buccaneers street gang.

In 1948 Brown was sent to the Wiltwyck School in rural Ulster County, New York, an institution for troubled boys. Already having learned to roll reefers and make homemade zip guns, Brown's criminal education continued at Wiltwyck to

include the art of picking pockets, as taught by the older boys. But there he also came under the countervailing influence of the school's new director, Ernest Papenek. Papenek's innovative techniques for working with disturbed youth in Austria were soon to earn him great acclaim in the United States through the later achievements of Wiltwyck's most famous alums, Brown and the boxer FLOYD PATTERSON; however, at that crossroads in Brown's life Papenek was just the "smartest and the deepest cat" he had ever met, "the best thing that could ever happen to any boy who got into trouble" (Brown, *Manchild*, 85).

In spite of these positive influences, Brown could not resist the attractions of a life of crime during his adolescence. After leaving Wiltwyck, at the age of thirteen, Brown was shot in the stomach during a burglary, and he subsequently divided his time between mischief-making in Harlem and three trips to Warwick, a reform school for hardened teenagers where "we all came out ... better criminals" (Brown, *Manchild*, 146). If he were not killed first, Brown expected to advance from reform school and serve time with his mentors at Sing Sing or Attica prison. But at Warwick he was encouraged by Mrs. Cohen, the wife of the superintendent, to read the autobiographies of MARY MCLEOD BETHUNE, Albert Einstein, JACKIE ROBINSON, Albert Schweitzer, and others.

When he left Warwick for the last time in July 1953, an epidemic of heroin use, which Brown described as a plague of biblical proportion, was beginning to ravage Harlem. Brown's first experiment with the drug resulted in a physical reaction that was so violent and unpleasant that he never tried it again—though he liberally used cocaine and marijuana. His hustle on the streets consisted of a series of con games perpetrated against the naive and the greedy. At seventeen Brown felt as if he had lived a full and successful career as an outlaw, and in his weariness he wondered if it was not time to "retire." Conventional occupations did not appeal to him; he could never see himself working for "Mr. Charlie" or "Goldburg" (euphemisms for gentile or Jewish businesses) for any length of time. Yet, while attending Washington Irving High School at night, he worked as a watch-crystal fitter, shipping clerk, cosmetics salesman, and at various other odd jobs.

Around 1954 Brown moved from Harlem into an apartment in New York City's Greenwich Village, immersing himself in its bohemian, interracial environment. He became a jazz enthusiast, decided to become a pianist in the bebop tradition of THELONIOUS MONK, and began practicing up to eight hours each day until he played well enough to join a local band. While he had had numerous sexual encounters with black women, who were in his opinion mostly "bitches," he entered into his first serious romantic relationship with a white Jewish woman who played classical piano. He did not think that she was particularly attractive, but "compared with her, most of the colored chicks I'd known seemed crude and hard. They were chicks who you couldn't be but so sweet to, because they weren't sweet themselves. Her voice and manner were warm. She seemed to be more feminine than most of the women I knew, and more of everything a woman was supposed to be" (Brown, *Manchild*, 356). They discussed marriage, but when her parents learned of her relationship with Brown, she was whisked out of the state.

Brown received his high school diploma at the age of twenty-one and then moved back to Harlem in search of a personal sense of community. A friend from his old gang had turned his life around through religion and introduced Brown to the Coptic faith. Brown was intrigued by this black nationalist theology, with its veneration of the Ethiopian emperor Haile Selassie and its interest in mysticism and ancient history. Brown also found himself drawn to the more militant teachings of the Nation of Islam, which seemed to be the only organization in Harlem that was trying to replace the stigma of being black with the confidence of black pride. Brown attended meetings but never formally joined either organization; however, his association with them helped build a bridge to a new way of life.

By the late 1950s Brown knew that he wanted to extricate himself from the conditions that had trapped his brother in a cycle of crime and drug addiction. He hoped to go to college, but without a scholarship that seemed impossible. Brown began to confide in the Reverend William M. James of the Metropolitan Community Methodist Church. James was so impressed with Brown that he secured enough financial assistance to send him to Howard University. There Brown studied with TONI MORRISON, then a little-known writing instructor, and he prepared for a career in the law. During Brown's senior year, Dr. Papenek recommended that Brown could best fulfill a request from *Dissent* magazine for an article about inner-city youth. Bram Cavin, an editor at Crowell-Collier and Macmillan, was so taken with the resulting article that he offered Brown a two thousand dollar advance for a book. Brown wrote frantically, mostly out of a stream of consciousness, and in the fall of 1963 he submitted a fifteen-hundred-page manuscript. The draft languished for six months, until Alan Rinzler discovered it and helped Brown shape and condense it into *Manchild in the Promised Land* (1965). Brown related the brutal truth of his life in Harlem in this straightforward and uncompromising autobiographical novel. *Manchild in the Promised Land* is both a coming-of-age narrative and a eulogy for a generation of young black men perishing in America's ghettos.

Although RICHARD WRIGHT, RALPH ELLISON, ANN PETRY, JAMES BALDWIN, and others had been writing powerfully about the black urban experience for years, reviewers welcomed Brown into this exalted circle. Black magazines and newspapers were disturbed by the often true but negative depictions of black life, and most critics praised Brown's work for its plain, authentic, candid, and uncompromising presentation. Some, however, such as ALBERT MURRAY, scoffed at its lack of sophistication. Perhaps no one was less prepared for the book's success than was Brown. He had married Helen Jones, a telephone operator, while still at Howard, and after graduating in 1965, he was in his first year at Stanford University Law School when he suddenly became famous. He transferred to Rutgers Law School to accommodate frequent invitations to New York book parties; but by 1968, the dream of becoming a lawyer could no longer compete with the reality of being a writer earning sixty thousand dollars a year lecturing about his book.

Brown initially thought of using his popularity to run for the Harlem congressional seat held by ADAM CLAYTON POWELL JR. He never became a formal candidate and eventually felt the need or desire return to writing. *The Children of Ham* (1976) continues in the same tone and style that had won Brown such acclaim ten years earlier, as it recounts the struggles of thirteen Harlemites against poverty, drugs, and crime. But times and literary tastes had changed, reviews were harsh (with the notable exception of one by ARNOLD RAMPERSAD), and sales were disappointing. Brown never completed his third book, though he did write many articles and essays. His marriage ended in divorce, and he moved to New Jersey, where he devoted much of his time to working with troubled youth and prison inmates until he was overcome by lung cancer.

Manchild in the Promised Land was undoubtedly Brown's most enduring work. It sold more than four million copies in fourteen languages and earned a place in the literary canon as a period piece if not as a classic of African American autobiographical writing.

FURTHER READING
Hartshorne, Thomas L. "Horatio Alger in Harlem: Manchild in the Promised Land," *Journal of American Studies*, vol. 24, no 2 (Aug. 1990): 243–9.
Madhubuti, Haki R. "In Memoriam," *Black Issues in Higher Education Magazine*, vol. 19.1 (Feb. 2002): 26.
Obituaries: *New York Times*, 6 Feb. 2002; *Boston Globe* and *New York Amsterdam News*, 7 Feb. 2002.

SHOLOMO B. LEVY

Brown, Cleo (8 Dec. 1907–15 Apr. 1995), jazz pianist and singer, was born in Meridian, Mississippi, the daughter of a Baptist minister. The names of her parents are unknown. Some sources set her birth in 1909, while others suggest that she may have been five or more years older than that; the year 1907 is based on Social Security records, where her name is listed as Cleo Patra Brown. Her surname is sometimes spelled Browne.

Cleo began taking piano lessons as early as age four, and she was soon accompanying the choir in her father's church. The family moved to Chicago when Brown was ten years old. Though her father came to disapprove of his daughter's playing, she continued studying piano and, when only fourteen years old, she found a job with a traveling orchestra and went on the road. She worked in South Side Chicago's Three Deuces Club, leading her own group in that club and in other places in Chicago and New York from the late 1920s to perhaps as late as the 1950s. For a time she broadcast her own show on WABC in New York.

Chicago in the 1930s was known for its blues stars, and Brown became part of the crowd that made blues and boogie-woogie the rage at the time. Through her brother, Everett, she got to know and was influenced by the barrelhouse pianist Pinetop Smith, who died in 1929. In March 1935 she recorded a version of "Pinetop's Boogie-Woogie" for Decca that made her a star in Chicago. She also recorded during that same session four songs with a quartet that included the drummer Gene Krupa, and later that year she recorded another side with the Decca All Star Revue, including Victor Young and the Scottish-born singer Ella Logan. In her recording sessions through the thirties and forties, Brown performed with other notable musicians, both white and black, including ZUTTY SINGLETON.

Though her recordings spread her influence as a singer and especially a jazz pianist in the 1930s and 1940s, Brown remained a virtual secret from the mainstream jazz world for most of her long life, largely because she retired early from the national scene. It may be that life on the road was too difficult for her, causing her to fall ill from the strain. It was especially difficult for African American women to find places to sleep and eat or simply to exist comfortably on the road. Women players were frequently harassed by audiences and often were forced to sleep in the vehicles they had traveled to their jobs in. That is probably why Brown, at least for a time, chose Los Angeles as her headquarters. The city was becoming a lively mecca for jazz, and many well-known musicians settled in the area. There Brown recorded for the California-based Hot Shot label and then for Capitol Records in 1949. By the late 1940s a string of hits by NAT KING COLE had already done much to establish Capitol's reputation.

In the early 1950s Brown became a Seventh-day Adventist, stopped performing in public, and found work as a nurse. At some point Brown left California; in 1973 she surfaced in Denver, Colorado, where she played and taught piano under the name of C. Patra Brown and then Cleopatra, a name she had always favored for herself. She had become a member of the Seventh-day Adventist Church and played primarily church music—gospel and hymns. In 1987, at age seventy-eight, she played and sang church music, including some of her original compositions, on McPartland's Peabody Prize–winning radio show, *Piano Jazz*. That same year the National Endowment for the Arts awarded her an NEA Jazz Masters fellowship.

A number of women pianists have acknowledged their debt to Brown. According to the singer and pianist NELLIE LUTCHER, such tunes as Brown's "It's a Heavenly Thing" fostered a trend for women to emphasize "a sly, coy, or somewhat risqué humor backed by boogie-woogie piano." In the 1980s the British-born pianist Marian McPartland recalled that Brown's distinctive boogie-woogie style was one of her earliest influences back in the 1930s and 1940s, when she was looking for role models to develop her skills and tastes. McPartland went so far as to say that Brown was one of the few pianists who actually convinced her to make a career for herself in jazz.

A year after Brown's death Audiophile Records released *Living in the Afterglow*, a set of mostly religious songs that she performed with McPartland. The jazz pianist Dave Brubeck, who wrote a tribute to Brown, "Sweet Cleo Brown," in 1957, called her "one of the greatest women pianists," and he noted in a later interview, "When FATS WALLER died, the musicians in that band wanted her to take over, that's how great she was."

FURTHER READING

Dahl, Linda. *Stormy Weather: The Music and Lives of a Century of Jazzwomen* (1984).

DISCOGRAPHY

Lord, Tom. *The Jazz Discography* (1992).
Cleo Brown, 1935–1951 (Melody Jazz Classics, 2002).
The Legendary Cleo Brown (President, 2003).
Living in the Afterglow (Audiophile, 1996).

LESLIE GOURSE

Brown, Clifford (30 Oct. 1930–26 June 1956), trumpeter, was born in Wilmington, Delaware. Brown's parents' names are unknown. Brown's father was a self-taught musician who played the trumpet, violin, and piano for his own amusement. He kept several instruments around the house. Young Clifford eventually picked up the bugle and demonstrated an aptitude for it. At age twelve Clifford was taken by his father to study with the renowned Wilmington teacher and bandleader Robert Lowery. Clifford spent three years with Lowery, studying jazz harmony, theory, trumpet, piano, vibraphone, and bass and playing in Lowery's big band.

Brown's father bought Brown a trumpet in 1943, the year he entered high school. He studied the trumpet with his high school band director, Harry Andrews, who had done advanced brass study at the University of Michigan. Brown became an outstanding trumpet player under Andrews's tutelage. He perfected octave jumps, developed a beautiful range, and ornamented melodies with little grace notes. These grace notes became a hallmark of his jazz trumpet style. Brown also began writing arrangements for his high school band. He left a lasting impression on Andrews with his brilliant "Carnival of Venice" graduation solo.

Brown showed a DIZZY GILLESPIE bebop trumpet influence all the way through high school. He graduated from high school and enrolled at Delaware State College in 1949. The school did not have a music department, so he studied mathematics. The following year Brown transferred to Maryland State College on a music scholarship. This school had a good fifteen-piece band, which gave Brown playing and arranging experience. While at Maryland State, Brown played a couple of times a month as a member of a Philadelphia house band for jazz concerts. He played with innovators such as the trombonist J. J. JOHNSON, the drummer MAX ROACH, the alto saxophonist ERNIE HENRY, and the trumpeters MILES DAVIS and FATS NAVARRO.

Navarro encouraged Brown and became his major stylistic influence. Navarro's trumpet roots were in the Cuban trumpet tradition and the American bebop style. He was known for his clear articulation, melodic inventiveness, and ringing, bell-like tone. Brown's own melodic inventiveness, clear articulation, and fat, bell-like tone can be traced to Navarro's influence. Gillespie's big band played a date in Wilmington one night in 1949. Benny Harris, one of Gillespie's trumpet players, was late, so Brown got the opportunity to replace Harris for forty-five minutes. Gillespie was impressed and encouraged the youngster to pursue a jazz career.

Brown was seriously injured in a 1950 car crash and was hospitalized from June 1950 to May 1951. Gillespie visited him during this period and encouraged him to resume his trumpet career. Brown left the hospital and played successful gigs on the piano until he was able to resume his trumpet playing. One of his trumpet gigs was with the alto saxophonist CHARLIE "BIRD" PARKER. Brown said of this gig, "Benny Harris was the cause of that one, too. He left Bird shortly after the engagement began so I worked in his place for a week. Bird helped my morale a great deal. One night he took me into a corner and said, 'I don't believe it. I hear what you're saying, but I don't believe it'" (Hentoff, "Clifford Brown").

Brown toured with Chris Powell's rhythm and blues band for a year and a half during 1952 and 1953. He played both trumpet and piano with this group. Brown made his first modern jazz recordings during this period, playing on a Blue Note recording for the alto saxophonist Lou Donaldson. Brown played with the composer-pianist TADD DAMERON in Atlantic City, New Jersey, in 1953 and recorded for Prestige Records with Dameron. During the summer of 1953 the arranger-trumpeter QUINCY JONES was working with the Lionel Hampton Band in Wildwood, New Jersey. Jones begged Hampton to hire three musicians from Dameron's band, which was nearing the end of its Atlantic City engagement: alto saxophonist

GIGI GRYCE, tenor saxophonist Benny Golson, and trumpeter Brown. Hampton listened to them and hired all three. Brown stayed with Hampton from July until November 1953. During the band's European tour, Brown recorded several albums with Swedish, French, and American musicians, including Gryce.

Brown freelanced in New York City in 1953 and 1954. He recorded with the drummer ART BLAKEY and the pianist Horace Silver in the band that subsequently became the Jazz Messengers. Brown won the 1954 *Down Beat* magazine Critic's Poll as the new star of the year on trumpet. Late in March 1954 Brown joined MAX ROACH in California to form and colead a new quintet. During this time he met and married a University of California music student named LaRue Watson; they had one child.

The Clifford Brown–Max Roach Quintet became one of the most important jazz combos in history. The quintet's 1954–1955 personnel consisted of Brown on trumpet, Harold Land on tenor saxophone, Richard Powell on piano, George Morrow on bass, and Roach on drums. In January 1956 the tenor saxophonist SONNY ROLLINS replaced Land.

The Brown-Roach quintet established new standards of quality and balance between combo arrangements and improvisations. Roach commented that they desired the quintet "to be interesting musically and emotionally at the same time" (Hentoff, "Roach & Brown, Inc."). The quintet's 1955 and 1956 Em Arcy recordings are masterpieces of artistry and creativity. Brown's solos are unequaled in their melodic beauty and emphatic clarity.

Brown introduced a new trumpet style. The nebop trumpeter Gillespie said that "Brown was gifted. And he established a new style, a way of playing the trumpet that was a little different from what we were doing before" (West, 30). Brown's career was short, but it was long enough to influence virtually every major trumpeter that followed him. Brown, Richard Powell, and Powell's wife died in an auto accident on the Pennsylvania Turnpike.

FURTHER READING

Catalano, Nick. *Clifford Brown: The Life and Art of the Legendary Jazz Trumpeter* (2000).

Hentoff, Nat. "Clifford Brown: The New Dizzy," *Down Beat* (7 Apr. 1954).

Hentoff, Nat. "Roach & Brown, Inc.: Dealers in Jazz," *Down Beat* (4 May 1955).

West, Hollie. "Clifford Brown: Trumpeter's Training," *Down Beat* (July 1980).

This entry is taken from the *American National Biography* and is published here with the permission of the American Council of Learned Societies.

MILTON STEWART

Brown, Cora (16 Apr. 1914–17 Dec. 1972), state legislator, attorney, police officer, and social worker, was born Cora Mae Brown in Bessemer, Alabama, the only child of Richard and Alice Brown. Her father and mother were employed as a tailor and cook respectively. In 1922 the family moved to Detroit when Brown was seven years old. After graduating from Cass Technical High School in 1931, Brown attended Fisk University and received a degree in sociology in 1935.

Brown returned to Detroit, and until 1941, she was employed as a social worker. After working for the Children's Aid Bureau, Old Age Assistance Bureau, and the Works Progress Administration, Brown, as a policewoman in the Women's Division of the Detroit Police Department from 1941 to 1946, prepared legal cases. In 1946 Brown enrolled in Wayne State University's School of Law; she received her LLB degree in 1948 and passed the Michigan bar examination several weeks after her graduation. She then became a partner in the firm of Morris and Brown and practiced general law.

In 1950 Brown launched her campaign to become the state senator from Detroit's Second District and lost by six hundred votes. One year later a special election was held to replace State Senator A. J. Wilkowski, and Brown campaigned unsuccessfully for the office. In 1952 a persistent Brown campaigned for the same office, defeated eight Democratic opponents in the primary, and won the general election on 4 November. Brown, at the age of thirty-eight, was sworn in as senator in January 1953, which marked the 118th anniversary of the Michigan Senate as well as thirty-one years after Eva McCall Hamilton, Michigan's first female senator, left office after one term. Brown was the first African American woman elected to the Michigan State Senate and the first African American woman elected to a state senate in the United States. (CRYSTAL BIRD FAUSET was the first African American woman elected to a state legislature, the Pennsylvania House of Representatives, in 1938.) Brown served two terms in the senate; from 1953 through 1954 she represented Detroit's Second District, and from 1955 through 1956 she represented Detroit's Third District. During her tenure as a Michigan legislator, Brown was the only woman among the thirty-plus senators. She focused on civil rights, education, health, and community issues. Brown was named "Woman of the Year" by the Zeta Phi Beta sorority in 1954 and by the National Council of Negro Women in 1955 as well as "Outstanding Woman Legislator" in 1956. One of Brown's greatest accomplishments in the Michigan Senate occurred in February 1956 when an anti-discrimination bill, cosponsored by Brown, was passed by her fellow legislators with a seven-vote margin. The bill called for suspending or revoking all Michigan state and local licenses for businesses that practiced racial discrimination. The *Detroit Free Press*, in its 25 February 1956 edition, hailed Brown as a "champion of the underprivileged."

Also in February 1956 Brown, after accusing Congressman Thaddeus Machrowicz of exhibiting preferential treatment to his Polish constituents and neglecting the black residents of his district, entered the race for the Democratic nomination for the United States House of Representatives from Michigan's First Congressional District. She was defeated in the August primary election. In October 1956, after a White House meeting with President Dwight Eisenhower, Brown urged Michigan voters to reelect the Republican president and to elect Democratic state and local candidates

One year later, on 15 August 1957, Brown was appointed the special associate general counsel of the United States Post Office; she was the first African American female appointee to the post office's legal staff. Three years later, Brown moved to Los Angeles and established a law practice. After returning to Detroit in the early 1970s, Brown was the Michigan Employment Security Commission's first African American female referee in thirty-five years. In October 1972, illness forced Brown to take a leave of absence from the MESC, and on 17 December 1972, Brown died at Grace Central Hospital. She was survived by her mother and her stepfather, Clifton Todd.

Two days after Brown's death, she was remembered in the 19 December 1972 edition of the *Detroit Free Press*, as a "pioneering legislator ... [who was a] perennial thorn in the conscience" of Michigan's Democratic party. In 1992 she was posthumously inducted into the Michigan Women's Hall of Fame.

FURTHER READING

Cora M. Brown's papers are housed in the Burton Historical Collection, Detroit Public Library in Detroit, Michigan.

Carter, Linda M. "Cora M. Brown." *Notable Black American Women, Book II*, ed. Jessie Carney Smith (1996).

Clayton, Edward T. *The Negro Politician: His Success and Failure* (1964).

"Cora M. Brown." In *Contemporary Black Biography*, Vol. 33, ed. Ashyia Henderson (2002).

LINDA M. CARTER

Brown, Corrine (11 Nov. 1942–), U.S. congresswoman, was born in Jacksonville, Florida, where she lived from childhood through her high school years. Brown has not made much information about her early years, her parents, or her personal life known. In 1965 she gave birth to her only daughter, Shantrel, the same year she began college. Brown received a B.S. in 1969 and a master's degree in Education in 1971 from Florida A&M University. She earned an education specialist degree from the University of Florida in 1974. From 1977 to 1982 Brown worked as a faculty member and guidance counselor at Florida Community College in Jacksonville. As a member of Sigma Gamma Rho Sorority Inc. at Florida A&M, Brown became close friends with her sorority sister Gwendolyn Sawyer-Cherry, who was the first African American woman to serve in the Florida state legislature. Sawyer-Cherry influenced Brown to enter politics, and after Brown lost

Corrine Brown, voicing her opposition to Governor Jeb Bush's order to end affirmative action and minority set-asides in Florida at a news conference in Orlando on 15 November 1999. Listening (left) is Orlando City Commissioner Daisy Lynum. (AP Images.)

her first race for a seat in the Florida state legislature in 1980, Sawyer-Cherry encouraged her to try again. Brown followed her advice and remained an active member of the political scene, supporting the Jacksonville Democratic Party. In 1980 she joined the Duval County Democratic Executive Committee. In 1982 Brown was elected as the Seventeenth District Florida state representative in the Florida legislature, a position that she held for ten years.

Following the 1990 U.S. Census, Florida was one of many states influenced by the U.S. Department of Justice to redraw its voting districts. The new crookedly shaped districts were designed to give minority groups majority representation, but they immediately came under criticism as being unconstitutional. The Florida districts would be redrawn two additional times following the 1992 election to comply with a federal court ruling that deemed them unconstitutional. In 1992 Brown campaigned for the U.S. House of Representatives to represent the new black-majority Third District. She endured a tough Democratic primary, facing charges of ethical misconduct from her opponents, but she won in a runoff with 64 percent of the vote. After winning the primary, Brown proclaimed, "This is the year of the woman, so get out of the way, men" (*CQ Weekly*, Jan. 1993). She secured her seat in Congress with 59 percent of the vote in the general election against Republican Don Weidner. Brown was successful in winning each of her bids for reelection thereafter.

Brown's congressional activities focused on improving the lives of Floridians. She sought an assignment on the Transportation and Infrastructure Committee to address the problems of highway congestion and road flooding in eastern Florida. She also used her seat to bring new jobs into Florida. When federal transportation programs were redesigned in 1998, Brown was instrumental in making sure Florida received a 57 percent increase in federal funding. She also worked on the Veteran Affairs and Government Operations Committee to advocate for the interest of military installations around her district and the growing number of military veterans in the Jacksonville area. She maintained memberships in the Congressional Black Caucus, Women's Caucus, Human Rights Caucus, and Progressive Caucus, advocating on behalf of the underprivileged, the unemployed, and the undereducated citizens of her state and the nation. A vocal liberal, Brown consistently supported social programs such as affirmative action and advocated for improved health care for minorities, children, and the elderly.

Brown's advocacy for the poor and disadvantaged, as well as her consistent representation of the interests of Floridians, has at times been overshadowed by her outspoken nature and repeated allegations of ethics violations. After just one hundred days in office, she became the subject of state and federal probes into her staff spending and campaign finance. In 1998 the *St. Petersburg Times* reported that Brown received a ten-thousand-dollar gift from the Reverend Henry Lyons, president of the National Baptist Convention; Brown denied all charges of misconduct. Later that year, the *Times* reported that Brown's daughter, Shantrel, a government lawyer in Washington, had received a luxury car from a West African businessman for whom Brown had lobbied to keep him out of federal prison. Brown again denied the allegations, but further attention to the issue was encouraged by Republicans, and the House Ethics Committee launched its own investigation. After fifteen months, the committee found no evidence of ethical misconduct, but expressed that Brown likely exercised "poor judgment" (Foerstel, *CQ Weekly*, Sept. 2000).

In 2000 Brown became an outspoken advocate for voters' rights, as the United States faced one of the most controversial presidential elections in history. Many Florida voters in 2000, and many minority and senior voters, of particular concern to Brown, were turned away at the polls, and thousands of ballots were miscounted or miscast. As late as 2004 Brown spoke out against the injustice she believed had occurred in Florida in 2000. Her sharp words on the floor of Congress resulted in her speaking privileges being revoked for a day because she violated protocols of decorum. "I come from Florida, where you and others participated in what I call the United States coup d'etat," Brown said. "Over and over again, after the election when you stole the election, you came back here and said, 'Get over it'" (Allen, *CQ Weekly*, July 2004). Brown remained unapologetic, saying, "If they're going to take my words down for telling the truth, that's OK" (Allen, *CQ Weekly*, July 2004). Brown backed a 2002 measure to heighten election standards and continued to push for election reform.

Brown was reelected for an eighth term in the U.S. House of Representatives in November 2006. As a senior House member, she was selected as chair of the Transportation Subcommittee on Railroads, Pipelines, and Hazardous Materials. This position allowed Brown to continue to secure federal funding for the improvement of the Jacksonville and Orlando road and transit projects. Additionally, Brown was selected as the first vice chairwoman of the Congressional Black Caucus. Following her reelection she remained an outspoken critic of the Republican Party, particularly of the Bush administration's economic and foreign policies.

FURTHER READING

Allen, Jonathan. "Florida on Her Mind: Rep. Brown Invokes 2000, Ignores Decorum," *CQ Weekly* (July 2004).

Anonymous. "Special Report: 103rd Congress House Freshman Profiles Florida—3rd District: Corrine Brown," *CQ Weekly* (Jan. 1993).

Foerstel, Karen. "No Ethics Violations Found in Brown Probe," *CQ Weekly* (Sept. 2000).

Gill, LaVerne McCain. *African American Women in Congress: Forming and Transforming History* (1997).

MONIKA R. ALSTON

Brown, Dorothy Lavinia (7 Jan. 1919–13 June 2004), surgeon and Tennessee legislator, was born to a single mother, Edna Brown, in Philadelphia, Pennsylvania. When she was five months old, her mother placed her in the Troy Orphanage. In 1932 Brown's mother reclaimed her daughter, but the two clashed and Brown ran away from home. She was subsequently taken in by Samuel Wesley and Lola Redmon. Brown obtained a job as a mother's helper in the W.F. Jarrett Home and graduated from high school, possibly Troy High School, about 1937.

Several factors inspired Brown to become a surgeon. As a child, she entered the hospital for the removal of her tonsils and adenoids. She loved the special attention that she received and wanted to duplicate that experience for other patients. Later, in her teens, she attended a performance by the African American opera star MARIAN ANDERSON. Impressed by Anderson's greatness and graciousness, Brown resolved to do something to make other African Americans proud of her. To achieve this dream, she had to overcome the double burden of discrimination based on race and gender.

Brown graduated from Bennett College, a historically black college for women, in Greensboro, North Carolina, in 1941. While in college, she joined the Delta Sigma Theta sorority, with which she remained affiliated throughout her life. Upon graduation she spent two years working in the Rochester (New York) Army Ordnance Department. Brown entered Meharry Medical College, a historically black medical school, in Nashville in 1944. In the

Dorothy Lavinia Brown, addressing supporters for her mayorial campaign at a news conference in Chicago, 31 August 2006. (AP Images.)

1940s no white southern medical school would accept an African American student despite the black community's strong need for medical professionals. Graduating in the top third of her class, she earned her M.D. in 1948. Although Brown served her internship at the historically black Harlem Hospital in New York City, she was denied a residency there because she was a woman. Brown returned to Nashville in 1949 to become a resident at the George W. Hubbard Hospital on the Meharry campus. She completed her residency in 1954. Brown spent the remainder of her medical career in Nashville. One of the first black female surgeons in the country, she became clinical professor of surgery at Meharry Medical College in 1954, chief of surgery at Riverside Hospital in 1957, and an attending physician at several other hospitals in the city. At the time that Brown became a fellow of the American College of Surgeons in the mid-1960s, only two other African American women were fellows.

As a physician in the South in the age of Jim Crow, Brown was well acquainted with the effect of racism on health care for African Americans. Blacks were less healthy than whites and died earlier. They did not receive the quality of medical care provided to whites because of a lack of monetary resources, a lack of trust between blacks and white medical professionals, a refusal on the part of some whites to treat black patients, and a lack of access to quality hospital care. A desire to improve the lives of African Americans may have prompted Brown to enter politics. In 1966 she became the first African American woman to be elected to the Tennessee State Legislature. A Democrat, she was elected to one term in the house of representatives in 1967.

Brown took the politically risky step of attempting to liberalize Tennessee abortion laws. A number of states had begun to reform their abortion laws in the 1960s; Tennessee never joined them. Tennessee law permitted abortions only in cases where the mother's life was in danger. Brown's 1967 bill would have legalized abortions caused by rape or incest. The bill fell two votes short of passage. Brown had better success in pushing through an African American history bill. The legislation required all Tennessee public schools to conduct special programs during Black History Week to recognize accomplishments made by African Americans. Brown ran for a seat in the Tennessee Senate in 1968 but lost. She left the legislature when her house term expired at the end of 1968.

African American women of Brown's generation were taught that they had an obligation to help uplift the black race. Brown's life reflected this teaching. She became the first single woman in Tennessee to adopt a child, doing so in 1956, and she named the child Lola Denise in honor of her foster mother. Brown also served as a member of the board of trustees of Bennett College and remained active in the United Methodist Church. In 1959 she became only the third woman to become a fellow of the American College of Surgeons. In her lifetime, she received honorary degrees from Bennett College and Cumberland University.

FURTHER READING

Alpha Kappa Alpha Sorority. *Women in Medicine* (1971).

Neumann, Caryn E. "Status Seekers: Long-Established Women's Organizations and the Women's Movement in the United States, 1945–1970s," Ph.D. diss., Ohio State University (2006).

CARYN E. NEUMANN

Brown, Earl (24 July 1903–13 Apr. 1980), politician, journalist, and Negro League professional baseball pitcher, was born in Charlottesville, Virginia, one of four children. His father was a Baptist minister and his mother was a nurse. His mother wanted him to pursue medicine, but Brown was interested in sports and studying social problems. After preparing at Howard Academy in Washington, D.C., Brown went to Harvard.

Brown majored in economics but also played baseball, lettering as a left-handed pitcher. He worked his way through Harvard as a janitor and waiter. During summer breaks he was a Red Cap at Grand Central Station in New York, and also played in the Negro Leagues. In 1923 and 1924 he pitched for the New York Lincoln Giants. Interestingly Harvard, usually aggressive about enforcing early NCAA rules barring athletes from playing professional sports, apparently did not punish Brown when he played in the professional ranks before returning to the Harvard baseball team for his senior year.

Brown suffered discrimination on the baseball team. In April of his senior year Harvard hosted the University of Georgia, which objected to playing against African Americans. Harvard obliged and barred Brown from playing in the two-game series. He did go on to win four games that season, including an impressive twelve strikeout victory over Amherst. After graduating in 1924 Brown went into real estate and continued to play baseball, appearing with the Lincoln Giants and the Harrisburg Giants in 1924 and the Baltimore Black Sox in 1925, before finishing up with the Lincoln Giants in 1926.

Brown taught economics, first at Union University in Virginia, then at Louisville Municipal College, before going into journalism. He married Emma Moseley in 1931. They had no children. He became a reporter for the *New York Herald Tribune* then took a managing editor position at the *Amsterdam News*. While at the *Amsterdam News* Brown wrote an unflattering profile of the boxing great JOE LOUIS for *Life* magazine. The resulting furor got him fired, but he was hired by *Life* and worked there as an editor for many years.

Brown's political career started when he was named a delegate to the 1944 Democratic National Convention. In 1949 the Republican, Democratic, and Liberal parties united to nominate him for the Harlem City Council seat held by BENJAMIN JEFFERSON DAVIS, a Communist then just a year away from being imprisoned for his political beliefs. In this era of growing red-baiting, Brown won easily. During his time in the City Council he took the lead on securing passage for numerous laws fighting discrimination, including the Sharkey-Brown-Isaacs Housing Law, which banned discrimination in private rental housing. This law served as a model for similar ordinances in cities throughout the United States.

In 1958 he was recruited by the Democratic Party to oppose incumbent ADAM CLAYTON POWELL JR. for the Sixteenth Congressional Seat in Harlem. Powell was an extremely popular Congressman who had angered Democratic regulars by openly supporting the Republican Dwight Eisenhower for president in 1956, and Powell was also under federal indictment for income tax evasion. Even with these impediments, Powell was viewed as an overwhelming favorite. The campaign was ugly. Brown accused Powell of "racist tendencies" and "treason to the Democratic Party" for supporting Eisenhower. Powell labeled Brown's charges ridiculous and in turn accused him of "playing Uncle Tom's game" for not protesting southern democrat hostility to civil rights.

As expected, Brown was soundly beaten, but that wasn't the only fallout from that bitter election. A dying Tammany Hall, New York's longtime Democratic political machine, was behind Brown's challenge to Powell, who in turn attacked Brown as a "hand-picked Uncle Tom selected by the Tammany plantation bosses to work against his own people." Brown retaliated by claiming that Powell hurt Harlem by refusing to work with Tammany Hall, pointing out Tammany's help in getting a housing discrimination bill passed.

Powell said votes for him were votes "to defeat Tammany," and the New York Times agreed, declaring that "the attitude of Negro voters toward Tammany Hall … is sure to be tested when those voters go to the polls." Brown's defeat surely hastened Tammany Hall's demise and left him politically damaged. In 1961 he left the city council to join New York's Housing and Redevelopment Board. In 1963 he was named a deputy Manhattan Borough President, with the expectation that he would become Borough President in 1965.

But it was not to be. In addition to acquiring Adam Clayton Powell as a political enemy Brown also angered Councilman J. Raymond Jones by opposing his reelection. When Brown came up for appointment Jones vehemently opposed it, announcing that Brown as Borough President would be "personally obnoxious" to him. Powell also opposed it. They prevailed, and Mayor Robert Wagner chose CONSTANCE BAKER MOTLEY instead of Brown. He took the appointment with good grace, appearing at Motley's swearing-in and joking that if his enemies were successful in forcing him out of politics he could always "get a job with the Mets." Brown was appointed head of New York's Commission on Human Rights but soon retired due to poor health. He suffered from emphysema and died in New York.

Earl Brown was called a political maverick, which is curious. He did take on powerful personages: everyone from Joe Louis at the height of his fame, to Adam Clayton Powell and J. Raymond

Jones. But he opposed Powell at the behest of Tammany Hall, and Tammany leader Carmine De Sapio supported him for Borough President. It is hard to call someone who worked with Tammany Hall a maverick.

Brown also made a poor choice politically in aligning himself with Tammany Hall, which was clearly a dying institution during Brown's time. The New York Times observed that Brown had weak political skills, describing him as "diffident, not very good at handling a crowd, weak at oratory," with a reputation for snobbishness, derided as "look-down Brown." Although he lacked innate political skills, Brown had considerable political influence, passing seminal civil rights legislation in such an influential locale as New York City.

FURTHER READING

"City's New Rights Chief: Earl Louis Brown," New York Times, 27 May 1965.

Egan, Leo. "Mayor and De Sapio Favor Brown for Borough Post," New York Times, 2 Jan. 1961.

Knowles, Clayton. "Dudley Studied for State Court," New York Times, 2 Jan. 1961.

Knowles, Clayton. "Mrs. Motley Gets Mayor's Backing as Borough Head," New York Times, 17 Feb. 1965.

"Rivals in Harlem Trade Hot Words," New York Times, 4 Aug. 1958.

Robinson, Layhmond. "House Campaign Arouses Harlem," New York Times, 4 Aug. 1958.

Obituary: New York Times, 15 Apr. 1980.

STEPHEN ESCHENBACH

Brown, E. C. (Edward Cooper) (1877–28 Jan. 1928), businessman and banker, was born in Philadelphia, Pennsylvania, to Robert Brown, a turnkey in the local jail, and Anne Brown, a homemaker. Brown was the eldest of three children. He attended the public schools in Philadelphia and after his high school graduation worked for three years as a mail clerk at the financial firm of Bradstreet Mercantile. He took stenography and typewriting classes at the Spencerian Business College in Philadelphia and subsequently worked as a stenographer for the National Railway Company but was soon laid off. Brown then became secretary to a Frank Thompson, who ran a catering business in Florida in the late 1890s. Around 1901 Brown left Thompson and started a real estate business in Newport News, Virginia. By 1908 he was renting more than 300 houses and had more than 800 tenants. On 27 June 1908 he opened the Crown Savings Bank, a private bank catering to African Americans in Newport

News, while still holding onto his real estate business. In 1909 Brown founded another private bank for African Americans, the Brown Savings Bank in Norfolk, Virginia. The success of both banks made Brown nationally known within African American business circles. Later it would be discovered that both banks were financially unsound and that Brown was using depositors' funds to finance his real estate deals.

Brown was active in BOOKER T. WASHINGTON's National Negro Business League, which was founded in 1900 and provided a forum for black businesspeople to discuss their successes and problems in business operations. At the league's 1908 meeting Brown described his career in real estate, endorsing Washington's philosophy of black self-help. At that time Brown was treasurer of the Colored Bankers Association, and a member of the National Negro Bankers' Association, which was dissolved around 1916. At the 1919 National Negro Business League meeting Brown cited his success in Virginia as an example of why southern blacks should support black businesses. He also said that he was still the president and a stockholder in the Brown Savings Bank of Norfolk. Despite his popularity among black businessmen and -women, Brown lost a bid to become president of the National Negro Business League in 1921.

Brown's lasting accomplishments, however, were made in the North. In 1913, for reasons that are unclear, he returned to Philadelphia to open a real estate office. About this time Brown formed a business partnership with the Philadelphia politician Andrew Steven Jr. In January 1916 they opened a private bank in Philadelphia known as Brown and Stevens. Its advertisements in the *Philadelphia Tribune* beckoned African Americans recently arrived in Philadelphia during the Great Migration. Migrants found the Brown and Stevens Bank attractive because it welcomed small savings accounts and encouraged clients to invest in real estate and black business. In 1917 Brown and other black entrepreneurs established the Payton Apartments Corporation to manage the Payton Apartments—considered a desirable address for members of the black middle class—in Harlem. Around this time Brown married Estelle Smith, although the exact year of the marriage is unclear. The Browns raised Estelle's daughter Suzie.

In July 1918 Brown and Stevens founded the Dunbar Amusement Company to finance a new theater in Philadelphia and in 1919 bought the Quality Amusement Company from Robert Levey of New York City. That company controlled the Lafayette Players Stock Company and the Lafayette Theatre in Harlem. Under Brown the company later acquired the Howard Theatre in Washington, D.C., the Avenue Theatre in Chicago, and the Douglass Theatre in Baltimore. As head of the Quality Amusement Company, Brown featured weekly performances by the Lafayette Players in Philadelphia. They starred in the show *Within the Law*, a comedy-drama, at the grand opening of the Dunbar Theatre in Philadelphia on 29 December 1919. The Dunbar Theatre also featured motion pictures for black audiences such as OSCAR MICHEAUX's *The Symbol of the Unconquered*, released in 1920, vaudeville acts such as the blues singer MAMIE SMITH, and musicals like EUBIE BLAKE and NOBLE SISSLE's *Shuffle Along*.

In 1920 Brown lost his bid to become president of the National Negro Business League. Meanwhile yet more serious setbacks loomed in his financial matters. In July of that year Brown sold his stock in the Quality Amusement Company, which controlled the Lafayette Theatre in New York. Then, citing a $2,000 weekly deficit, in August 1921 Brown persuaded stockholders in the Dunbar Amusement Company to sell the Dunbar Theatre in Philadelphia to JOHN TRUSTY GIBSON. This was the first time the public became aware of Brown's financial problems. In 1925 there was a run on the Brown and Stevens Bank, forcing it to file for involuntary bankruptcy. As a private bank Brown and Stevens was not subject to oversight by the state banking department that could have identified problems early on. An auditing of the bank's books revealed evidence of inadequate record keeping and fraud. The state auditor alleged that Brown and Stevens used their companies for their own financial gain. Because of the bankruptcy, hundreds of African Americans lost their savings. Brown moved to New York City and set up a real estate business. He remained in the city until his death. An ambitious man with questionable business practices, his business empire collapsed as rapidly as it had risen. Yet Brown's lasting legacy was his promotion of the Lafayette Players and black theaters during the Harlem Renaissance.

FURTHER READING
Hamilton, Kenneth M., ed. *Records of the National Negro Business League* (c. 1994).
Harris, Abram Lincoln, Jr. *The Negro as Capitalist: A Study of Banking and Business among American Negroes* (1969).

Kellner, Bruce. "E.C. Brown," in *The Harlem Renaissance: A Historical Dictionary for the Era*, ed. Bruce Kellner (1987).

Richardson, Clement, ed. *The National Cyclopedia of the Colored Race*, vol. 1 (1919).

Sampson, Henry T. *Blacks in Blackface: A Source Book on Early Black Musical Shows* (1980).

Obituary: *New York Age*, 28 Jan. 1928.

ERIC LEDELL SMITH

Brown, Elaine (2 Mar. 1943–), activist and author, was born in Philadelphia, Pennsylvania, the only child of Dorothy Clark, a factory worker, and Dr. Horace Scott, a neurosurgeon who never publicly acknowledged his daughter's existence. As a result Elaine was raised by a single mother.

Elaine Brown grew up in poverty in a row house on York Street in North Philadelphia. Hoping for a better life for her daughter, Dorothy Clark enrolled Elaine in an experimental elementary school, Thaddeus Stevens School of Practice. There she was exposed to the lives of her often privileged, white Jewish classmates, and from an early age she learned to assimilate their habits. She learned to adopt their speech patterns and cadence of voice using words such as "these" instead of "dese" or "he'll be going" instead of "he be goin'." Thus Brown lived in two worlds in which she was able to act "white" while at school and "black" when she was with the girls from her neighborhood. Brown's mother provided her with opportunities not widely available to other children in her neighborhood, such as private piano lessons and ballet classes. Throughout her adolescence Brown played the piano and composed original songs. In 1957 she was admitted to the prestigious Philadelphia High School for Girls on the basis of her high IQ score. She excelled in Latin and English and graduated in 1961. Brown entered Temple University in Philadelphia but she did not take her course of study seriously, and withdrew in 1962, later taking a job as a service representative at the Philadelphia Electric Company.

In 1965, at age twenty-two, Brown moved to Los Angeles to be a professional songwriter. She began as a waitress at the Pink Pussycat nightclub, where she met the writer Jay Kennedy, with whom she had an affair. It was through her relationship with Kennedy that she became aware of social and political movements of the1960s. When their relationship ended in 1967 Brown began giving piano lessons to girls living in the Jordan Downs Housing Project in the Watts section of Los Angeles as a part of a tutorial program organized by her friend Beverlee Bruce. It was through her teaching that she became aware of the circumstances of African Americans and realized the need to create conditions for fundamental change in their lives. Bruce introduced her to people in the Black Power movement and she became a member of the Black Congress and was involved with producing the organization's newspaper, *Harambee*. The Black Congress was founded in Los Angeles after the 1965 Watts riots as an umbrella group that represented many of the African American organizations in the area. It consisted of an executive committee on which each member served as a representative from a different organization. The Black Congress served to meet the concerns and interests of African Americans in Southern California. Brown also served on the Executive Committee to the Black Student Alliance, which was a vision of Harry Truly, a professor of sociology at California State University, Los Angeles, who wished to form a union of all-black student unions in the United States to act as a base of power in the black student movement.

In 1967 at a Black Congress Executive Committee meeting she met Earl Anthony, a Central Committee member of the Black Panther Party for Self-defense, working for the HUEY P. NEWTON Legal Defense Fund. The Black Panther Party for Self-defense was formed in 1966 in Oakland, California, by Newton and BOBBY SEALE to further the aims of the civil rights movement to bring equality to African Americans. In April of 1968 Brown joined the Southern California Chapter of the Black Panther Party (BPP). Brown rose through the ranks, learning the Panthers' rhetoric, selling Panther newspapers, and learning to handle firearms. She attended UCLA as part of the High Potential Program for disadvantaged students with a high potential for success, a program organized by Beverlee Bruce. During this time she worked with the party to expand its platform of community Survival Programs in Los Angeles. These Survival Programs, such as the Breakfast Program, which provided free breakfasts to school-age children, and free clinics that provided medical care, were designed to benefit the lives of the black community. Brown assisted in organizing rallies against police brutality and organized financial support among Hollywood personalities such as movie producer Bert Schneider.

An accomplished songwriter, Brown released her first album of original music dedicated to the

BPP, *Seize the Time*, in 1969. That year she was appointed deputy minister of information for the chapter. In March 1970 Brown gave birth to her daughter, Ericka Brown, with Masai (Raymond) Hewitt. In June of that year she accompanied the BPP minister of information ELDRIDGE CLEAVER to North Korea to announce the establishment of an International Section of the party. When she returned from the trip she met the chairman of the party, Huey P. Newton, and began a personal and professional relationship that lasted during most of the 1970s. She moved to Oakland in 1971 and assumed duties as editor of the BPP newspaper, the *Black Panther*. Newton appointed her minister of information, filling the vacancy of the expelled Eldridge Cleaver, who felt that the party should put more emphasis on guerrilla activity and less on community programs and spoke out publicly against the party leadership, causing a fracture within the general membership. In assuming that role Brown became the first woman elected to the Central Committee of the party. In 1972 she began recording a second album of original music, *Until We're Free*. To expand the reach of the BPP, Brown ran unsuccessfully in 1972 for a seat on the Oakland City Council.

In 1974, after the 1973 expulsion of Bobby Seale by Newton, Brown was named chairman of the Black Panther Party. In 1974 the already fragmented party was further strained by the arrest and subsequent self-imposed exile to Cuba of Newton. In his absence Newton charged Brown with leadership of the BPP. Brown had inherited an organization weakened by internal rivalries and years of police subversion; surveillance by the FBI and various local police departments became constant, and BPP offices were raided frequently. She also faced great opposition from the members of the party who objected to a woman in a leadership role. As chairman of the Black Panther Party, Brown expanded community Survival Programs in the areas of health care and education, establishing the Intercommunal Youth Institute, a school for children in Oakland. She also ran, again unsuccessfully, for Oakland City Council in 1975. She began installing women for the first time in key administrative positions in the party. In 1977 Newton returned from Cuba to face trial and reassume co-leadership of the BPP. Brown faced the reality of a changed party. Many members questioned the legitimacy of her power since the return of Newton. Newton's drug use increased, and so did his violent temper. After witnessing the result of a particularly brutal discipline of a female member, Brown decided to leave the party and Oakland to move to Los Angeles.

Brown went on to explore a variety of personal and professional interests, including law school. In 1992 she published her autobiography, *A Taste of Power*, chronicling her life in the BPP. In 1996, after living seven years in France, she moved to Atlanta and established the nonprofit organization Fields of Flowers to build an education center for African American and poor children. Brown continued to advocate community concerns and cofounded Mothers Advocating Juvenile Justice in 1997. She also cofounded and became a board member of the National Alliance for Radical Prison Reform, one of the many nonprofit and activist organizations she founded beginning in the mid-1990s. In 2002 she wrote *The Condemnation of Little B*, highlighting the case of Michael Lewis, who was arrested at age thirteen for murder in Atlanta.

Brown entered politics again in 2005 and moved to the poor, predominantly black city of Brunswick, Georgia, to run for mayor. She was later disqualified on a residency requirement. Brown lectured at colleges and universities, in addition to writing and pursuing social activism.

FURTHER READING

The papers of Elaine Brown are housed at the Manuscript, Archives, and Rare Book Library at Emory University.

Brown, Elaine. *A Taste of Power: A Black Woman's Story* (1992).

Bray, Rosemary L. "A Black Panther's Long Journey," *New York Times Magazine* (31 Jan. 1993).

Steinfeld, Dave, et. al. "What Ever Happened to …," *Essence* 36 1 (May 2005).

WENDY PFLUG

Brown, Emma V. (c. 1843–Oct. 1902), educator, was born Emmeline Victoria Brown in Georgetown, District of Columbia, the daughter of JOHN MIFFLIN BROWN, a bishop of the African Methodist Episcopal Church, and Emmeline (maiden name unknown), a dressmaker. Emma Brown and her siblings were born and raised in what the racial climate of the period called a "better class of colored." When Brown was still a young girl her father died, and her mother worked to support the family. Brown attended Miss Myrtilla Miner's School for Colored Girls, which opened in 1851 with the goal of training teachers for public schools in the Washington, D.C., area. Brown soon distinguished herself as an outstanding student. When illness forced Miner to take a leave of absence, Brown was recruited to stay on and assist Emily Howland, who had moved from New York to be Miner's replacement. In 1858 Brown ran the school during Howland's temporary absence, and by the summer of 1859 Brown was ready and able to open her own small school (twelve students) in Georgetown. At the insistence and encouragement of Miner and Howland, Brown chose to continue her education and enhance her teaching skills at Oberlin College.

Located in Oberlin, Ohio, Oberlin College was the institution of choice for many African American women. Founded by abolitionists, Oberlin was the first coeducational and interracial college in the country. Accompanied by a friend, Matilda A. Jones, Brown arrived in February 1860 for the spring term and enrolled as a literary degree candidate. Her matriculation at Oberlin was cut short because of long-standing health problems that included a humor in her blood, severe headaches, insomnia, and stress. So determined was Brown to continue her studies, however, that she consented to the drastic treatment of having her head completely shaved in an effort to combat her debilitating headaches. But the combination of complaints proved to be too much for Brown, and she was forced to leave Oberlin in June 1861.

On returning to Washington, D.C., Brown's health gradually improved to the point that, in 1862, she was able to start her own modest school. Armed with a new spirit of abolition and reform Brown became one of a new class of "black schoolmarms" dedicated to educating and improving the lives of newly freed slaves. During the 1860s and 1870s Washington attracted many educators and reformers because it was the first southern city to offer blacks a free, tax-supported school system. On 1 March 1864 the Board of Trustees of Public Schools in Washington opened a black school in Ebenezer Church on Capitol Hill and offered Brown the first teaching position. Brown began with an annual salary of four hundred dollars and forty students. By summer, enrollment reached 130. Brown continued at the school until 1869, when recurring health problems forced her to abandon teaching and secure less stressful work as a clerk in Washington's Pension Office.

During 1870 Brown lived and worked among the black social elite of Charleston, South Carolina, where she taught school, and in Jackson, Mississippi, where she copied the acts of the legislature. Her health renewed, Brown returned to Washington and became the principal of the John F. Cook School on Capitol Hill. Brown received a prestigious appointment in the Washington school district in 1872, when she was named principal of the new Sumner School. The school, named for Senator Charles Sumner, was very modern and had ten classrooms, offices, playrooms, and an auditorium. With a starting annual salary of nine hundred dollars, the appointment was the pinnacle of Brown's teaching career.

In 1879 Emma Brown married Henry P. Montgomery, a former slave from Mississippi, a former Union army soldier, and principal at the John F. Cook School. Because married women were banned from teaching, Brown's career in Washington's school system ended. Her educational interests remained strong, however, and she worked as a corresponding secretary for the Manassas Industrial School in Virginia. Suffering from declining health, Brown died at the age of fifty-eight. Her last known address was Washington, D.C.

Brown was a pioneer and a crusader in the mid- to late-nineteenth-century movement directed toward educating and improving the lives of freedmen. Whether the subject was astronomy or algebra or botany, Brown taught adults and children to have self-respect and to use education as their chief tool for personal and social betterment.

FURTHER READING

Lawson, Ellen N., and Marlene Merrill. "Antebellum Black Coeds at Oberlin College," *Oberlin Alumni Magazine* (Jan.–Feb. 1980).
Sterling, Dorothy, ed. *We Are Your Sisters: Black Women in the Nineteenth Century* (1984).
This entry is taken from the *American National Biography* and is published here with the permission of the American Council of Learned Societies.

THEA GALLO BECKER

Brown, Ernest "Brownie" (25 Apr. 1916–21 Aug. 2009), tap dancer, was born in Chicago, Illinois. Raised in Chicago's South Side neighborhood, where his father worked as a barber, Brown was the youngest of nine children. By the age of twelve Brown was already a professional dancer with a vaudeville act, Sarah Venable's "Mammy and Her Picks." There he met Charles Cook, and the two formed an act originally called "Garbage and His Two Cans," but later simplified to "Cook and Brown," which would become one of the most successful comedy dance acts of the twentieth century.

Cook and Brown performed consistently for several decades from the 1930s through the 1960s.

They combined rhythm tap with acrobatics, slapstick, and eccentric dance and exploited the physical contrast between the tall and lanky Cook and the diminutive Brown, whose disputed height is generally placed between four feet eight inches and five feet. Brown would perform taxing physical stunts such as sliding across the stage in a full split and taking pratfalls while Cook played the straight man. In the 1930s and 1940s they became a headline act in the United States and Europe, performing with top musicians including DUKE ELLINGTON and ELLA FITZGERALD at venues such as the Cotton Club and Radio City Music Hall in New York, the Latin Casino in Paris, and the Palladium in London. In 1948 they appeared on Broadway in the musical *Kiss Me Kate*.

In 1949 Brown was among the twenty-one founding members of the Copasetics, a collective of dancers and musicians seeking to honor and preserve the memory of the recently deceased master tap dancer BILL "BOJANGLES" ROBINSON; other members of the Copasetics included the jazz composer BILLY STRAYHORN and the trumpeter Milt Larkin as well as the headlining tap dancers CHARLES "HONI" COLES, the future Motown choreographer Charles "Cholly" Atkins, and the one-legged CLAYTON "PEG LEG" BATES. The group's tap dancers often performed together yet prominently featured their own individual and idiosyncratic styles through improvised simulations of the competitive backroom "cutting contests," in which their generation of dancers pushed each other to develop new and innovative steps. When the Copasetics performed, Brown was often given the honor of closing the show. The Copasetics are widely credited with keeping tap dancing alive during the "lean years" of the 1950s and 1960s when public interest in the art form waned.

In 1963 Brown was among several prominent tap dancers who participated in the "Old Time Hoofers" lecture demonstration at the Newport Jazz Festival. This exhibition, put together by the jazz historian and Hunter College English professor Marshall Stearns, is credited with catalyzing the strong revival of interest in tap dancing in the 1970s and 1980s. However, failing to find sufficient employment as a dancer in the later 1960s, Brown took a job in New York as a messenger for Manufacturer's Hanover Bank, where he remained for fourteen years. In the late 1970s Brown appeared in two significant experimental shows organized by the dancer and historian Jane Goldberg, *It's about Time* in 1978 and *Shoot Me while I'm Happy* in 1979. These performances, in a loft studio in New York City's SoHo neighborhood, led to the founding of the Changing Times Tap Dance Company, which sought to present a fusion of old and new styles and provide a platform for interracial and intergenerational collaboration. In 1980 Brown participated in *By Word of Foot*, a week-long workshop where older masters of tap taught intensive classes for younger dancers.

Around the time of Cook's death in 1991, Brown began teaching Reginald "Regio the Hoofer" McLaughlin, who became his protégé and dance partner. The two performed and taught together until 2008, when they gave their final performance at the Tap City festival in New York. They also appeared in the Emmy-nominated documentary "JUBA—Masters of Tap and Percussive Dance," produced by the Chicago Human Rhythm Project. In 2004 Brown received the Hoofer's Award from the American Tap Dance Foundation, and in 2008 the team of Cook and Brown was inducted into the foundation's hall of fame. Brown died in Burbank, Illinois, in 2009 of prostate cancer and was the last surviving member of the original Copasetics. Brown's first marriage to Hazel Coates Brown, with whom he had his daughter Barbara, ended in divorce, and his second wife, Patricia Brown, died in 1989. While his career as an international headliner is itself noteworthy, Brown's most significant contribution is arguably his vital role in the American tap revival that began in the 1970s, which revitalized a distinctly American art form once on the brink of obscurity.

FURTHER READING

Stearns, Marshall Winslow, and Jean Stearns. *Jazz Dance: The Story of American Vernacular Dance* (1964, reprinted 1994).

Valis-Hill, Constance. *Tap Dancing America: A Cultural History* (2010).

Obituaries: *New York*, 25 Aug. 2009, *Washington Post*, 28 Aug. 2009.

CHRISTOPHER J. WELLS

Brown, Everett (1 Jan. 1902–25 Oct. 1953), actor, was born in Texas. Little is known of his early life or how he came to film. He played, often uncredited, a series of African or South Seas characters in mainstream adventure movies such as *King Kong* and *Tarzan*. He is best remembered for his role as Big Sam in the 1939 movie *Gone with the Wind* and is an example of an actor making the most of what was available to him in a period of segregation and extreme stereotyping in movies.

Brown's first credited movie role was as Nahalo, an island "native" in the 1923 silent movie *South Sea Love*. He continued with roles of this ilk, playing natives or Africans in *Danger Island* (1931), *Hell's Headquarters* (1932), and *Kongo* (1932). That same year he had a small part in *I Am a Fugitive from a Chain Gang*, where he played an American, Sebastian T. Yale, who helps the star, Paul Muni, escape. His next role, in *Nagana* (1933), gave him the chance to play something different: an educated man, willing to sacrifice his life in the pursuit of science. He received a one-line credit in the *New York Times* review of that movie: "Everett Brown makes the most of the role of Nogu" (16 Feb. 1933). In his next role in *King Kong*, in 1933, however, he returned to his demeaning (and often uncredited) characters when he appeared simply as "native in ape costume." Such roles continued in three *Tarzan* films: the 1933 *Tarzan the Fearless*, 1934's *Tarzan and His Mate*, and *Tarzan Escapes*, from 1936. Interspersed throughout his roles as slaves and natives were a few others, such as the Iron Man in *Under Pressure* (1935), a movie about an underwater tunnel project, and then as a convict in the 1935 *Les Misérables*.

At about this time, Brown looked to the race-film industry to expand his choices of roles. Race films were made by all-black or mixed-race production companies. They were specifically geared toward African American audiences, and they offered performers and entertainers a wider range of roles than those being offered by Hollywood at the time. With the "black Clark Gable," Ralph Cooper, Brown played in the all-black cast gangster film *Dark Manhattan* (1937). In 1938 he again acted with Cooper in *The Duke Is Tops* (alternate title: *Bronze Venus*), also LENA HORNE's first feature movie. That same year he also appeared with NINA MAE MCKINNEY in *Gang Smashes*, directed by Cooper.

During this time Brown continued to work in Hollywood films. For example, in 1937 he appeared as "a darky" (uncredited) in *Boys Town* with Spencer Tracy. In 1939 he was in five movies, including the one for which he is best known, *Gone with the Wind*, where he played Big Sam, the foreman of the plantation Tara. While the success of the film gave many African American actors hope that Hollywood would open up for more black talent, such was not the case, and Brown continued landing roles of slaves and natives, including *Congo Maisie* (1940) and *Zanzibar* (1940).

After *Zanzibar*, Brown disappeared from films for eight years, and little is known of his activities from this time. He returned to film in 1949 in *Rope of Sand*, where he again played a native chief (again uncredited). That same year, he was in a Three Stooges film, *Malice in the Palace*, and a movie about a racing horse, *The Great Dan Patch*. Both roles were uncredited. His last role was in 1953, as the Babuka King in *The White Witch Doctor* with Robert Mitchum.

Brown died in Los Angeles and is buried in the Evergreen Cemetery. While he enjoyed a long career in Hollywood, his legacy has gone largely unnoticed by film historians, yet it provides a perfect example of the film industry's inability to see African American performers outside certain roles.

FURTHER READING

Bogle, Donald. *Bright Boulevards, Bold Dreams: The Story of Black Hollywood* (2005).

Bogle, Donald. *Toms, Coons, Mulattoes, Mammies, and Bucks: An Interpretive History of Blacks in American Films*, 4th ed. (2001).

Cripps, Thomas. *Slow Fade to Black: The Negro in American Film, 1900-1942* (1977).

Sampson, Henry T. *Blacks in Black and White: A Source Book on Black Films*, 2d ed. (1995).

ROBIN JONES

Brown, Frank London (7 Oct. 1927–12 Mar. 1962), writer, musician, journalist, and civil rights activist, was born in Kansas City, Missouri, to Myra Myrtle and Frank London Brown Sr., the eldest of their three children. In 1939, when Brown was twelve years old, the family relocated to the South Side of Chicago in hopes of better economic opportunities. Brown attended Colman Elementary School and went on to DuSable High School. His adolescence in Chicago's "Black Belt" during the 1940s, which Sterling Stuckey referred to as a "dark nether-world of crime" and "shattered idealism," deeply influenced his artistic and writing career. In the streets of the South Side's slums he learned how to sing and soon discovered a deep passion for music, especially for jazz and blues. Brown is credited with being the first person to recite short stories (as opposed to poetry) to a jazz music accompaniment.

After graduating from high school in 1945, Brown attended Wilberforce University in Ohio; he left without receiving a degree and joined the U.S. Army, serving from 1946 to 1948 and singing baritone in an army band. He married Evelyn Marie Jones on 30 November 1947. The couple had three daughters and a son who died shortly after birth. Brown attended Roosevelt University on the GI Bill and received his B.A. in Political Science in 1951. He then enrolled at Kent College of Law in Chicago, but decided later to go to the University of Chicago. In 1960 he graduated with a master's degree in Social Science, and followed his doctoral studies in political science as a fellow of the prestigious University of Chicago's Committee on Social Thought. He did not complete his Ph.D. because of his early death in 1962.

While in school and writing, Brown also worked many jobs to feed his family, including stints as a jazz singer, bartender, loan interviewer, machinist, and, most significantly, organizer for the United Packinghouse Workers and other labor unions. After earning his master's degree, Brown was appointed director of the University of Chicago's Union Research Center. Apart from his own objectives in life, one of his major concerns was standing up for the rights of the underprivileged. His leftist social activism during the McCarthy and cold war era testifies to his courage. Some of Brown's actions as a social activist included helping a black man escape from Mississippi after the lynching of EMMETT LOUIS TILL in 1955, which Brown had covered as a journalist. He also actively demonstrated against segregation on Chicago beaches and protested against discrimination in apartment buildings owned by the University of Chicago.

Brown's literary career began while he was still an undergraduate. He contributed several articles and short stories to such publications as the *Chicago Review, Down Beat, Ebony,* and *Negro Digest.* Brown also authored a short play, *Short Ribs,* and short stories like "A Matter of Time," "McDougal," and "The Ancient Book." Meanwhile, he cultivated his interest in music by not only performing with modern jazz ensembles but also writing about music. He published an interview with jazz musician THELONIOUS MONK, as well as an article on poet GWENDOLYN BROOKS. In 1959 he was made associate editor of *Ebony.* Brown kept actively involved in the literary scene of his time and was friends with such writers as WILLARD FRANCIS MOTLEY. Literati like Gwendolyn Brooks were partially influenced by Brown's style of writing.

His first public success was his award-winning novel *Trumbull Park,* published in 1959. It garnered immediate critical acclaim and brought him recognition as an author and social activist. In the first chapter of *Trumbull Park,* the death of a neighbor girl due to a broken banister prompts Louis "Buggy"

Martin and his family to choose to either stay in their dilapidated and rat-infested ghetto building or move to an outlying white area of Chicago. They become one of the first black families to move into Trumbull Park, the first integrated housing project in Chicago during the 1950s. The Martins, like all black tenants, face massive protest, violence, intimidation, and humiliation by their white neighbors. They are forced to live imprisoned under police protection and are only able to leave the building in a patrol wagon, while white people stone their windows and bombs are going off around them.

Trumbull Park is a semiautobiographical work for which Brown drew upon his own experience with race-related violence. Brown, his wife, and children were one of the first black families in "white" Trumbull Park, where they lived from 1954 to 1957 in a constant state of fear. The story of an everyday struggle for better housing conditions can be directly transplanted into the larger context of the civil rights movement, wherein African Americans proudly stood up for their rights. Brown successfully depicted the conditions, daily terrors, and struggles for a better life faced by African Americans during the 1950s, a time when laws were changing in their favor, but law enforcement still favored the white majority. Most reviews praised Brown's vivid characters and psychological insight and cited him as an auspicious author.

In his second novel, *The Myth Maker,* Brown delves into the fatal psychological effects of racism on the individual's mind. In this story racism leads to a deeply felt self-loathing of the protagonist, a drug addict named Ernest Day, who is both an offender and victim. His aggressiveness and longing for self-annihilation, caused by a hostile and racist environment in an indifferent universe, lead him to murder an innocent old man. Day is punished twice, first with a body subject to worldly penalty, and second with the pangs of his own conscience. *The Myth Maker* was often compared to Fyodor Dostoevsky's *Crime and Punishment* for its underlying themes of sin and redemption, crime and punishment. Brown could not find a publisher for this novel in his lifetime.

In 1961 Brown discovered that he suffered from a terminal case of leukemia. His body quickly degenerated while his mind remained vibrant and his creativity undiminished. Brown died at the age of thirty-four at the University of Illinois Educational Research Hospital in Chicago. His second novel, *The Myth Maker,* was published posthumously in

1969, as was a collection of his short stories, *Short Stories of Frank London Brown*, published privately in 1965.

Brown wrote first and foremost about the African American experience in everyday life and consistently demonstrated an insight into the human heart and the needs of black American people. He also wrote and spoke in favor of social protest. Although *Trumbull Park* found public acclaim during Brown's lifetime, his complete works have not yet been fully credited as among the important literary works of the 1950s and early 1960s.

FURTHER READING

Brooks, Gwendolyn. "Of Frank London Brown: A Tenant of the World," *Negro Digest* 18 (1962).

Hall, James C. "Frank London Brown," in *Oxford Companion to African American Literature*, eds. William Andrews et al. (1997).

Hauke, Kathleen A. "Frank London Brown," in *Dictionary of Literary Biography: Afro-American Writers, 1940-1955*, ed. Trudier Harris (1988).

Stuckey, Sterling. "Frank London Brown," in *Black Voices*, ed. Abraham Chapman (1968).

Tita, Charles. "Frank London Brown," in *Contemporary African American Novelists*, ed. Emmanuel S. Nelson (1999).

Obituary: *New York Times*, 13 Mar. 1962.

BÄRBEL R. BROUWERS

Brown, Fredi Sears (4 Nov. 1923–), museum cofounder, college equity officer, educator, and community volunteer, was born Fredi Mae Sears in Bradenton, Florida. She was the only daughter of three children born to Mary Miller, a laundress, and Oscar C. Sears Sr., a laborer at a trailer park operated by the local Kiwanis Club. She grew up in a deeply religious community that valued family, friends, and the church, and her father was a deacon and a founding member of St. Mary Baptist Church. Such lived experiences prepared Sears for a life of service.

In 1939 she graduated as valedictorian of her class at Lincoln High School in Bradenton. Upon graduation, she enrolled at Florida A&M College (later University) in Tallahassee, Florida, where in 1944 she earned a bachelor of science degree in Home Economics with minors in Science and English. While at Florida A&M, Sears wrote for the student newspaper, and her extracurricular activities in college would prove to be rewarding, both professionally and personally. Upon graduating in

1944 she moved to Kansas City, Missouri, where she landed the post of assistant advertising manager with the black-owned newspaper *Kansas City Call*. It was at the *Call* that Fredi Sears met Ernest Leroy Brown, the paper's sports editor. During her brief stay in Kansas City, Sears also volunteered as an essay contest editor for the National Negro Newspaper Publishers Association.

Fredi Sears and Ernest Brown were married in 1946, and they eventually had four children. The couple relocated to Detroit, Michigan, where Ernest Brown became the manager of urban affairs with Detroit's Urban League. This new position began for both of the Browns a life of engagement within the city's black communities. Sharing her life-partner's passion for service, Fredi Brown touched many lives. From 1964 to 1974 she counseled teenaged substance abusers and prepared them for the GED test at the Salvation Army's Harbor Light House, established a library for a community center in one of the city's housing developments, organized parents of elementary school children to become more actively involved in the education of their children, taught English to incarcerated women at Louise Groom's Business College, and taught preschoolers at the Unity Church.

It was during their years in Detroit that the Browns were drawn into the world of collecting black memorabilia and materials. Though she did not consider herself a collector, Brown soon found herself accumulating books, posters, artifacts, and other ephemera relating to black life and history, some of which was gathered during her husband's work trips for the Urban League and the Equal Opportunity Commission. These would become the nucleus of the collection housed at the Family Heritage House, an African American Gallery and Resource Center located on the campus of Manatee Community College in Bradenton, Florida. Included in the collection were artifacts, newspaper clippings of the civil rights movement in Detroit, the 1872 edition of William Still's *Underground Railroad*, West African masks, the sixtieth anniversary publication of the *Crisis* magazine, and the 1994 South African presidential election ballot.

Upon Ernest's retirement in 1974, the Browns moved to Bradenton. There Brown became an instructor and Equal Access/Equal Opportunity coordinator at Manatee Community College. Remembering the segregated system that during her youth had barred blacks from attending the school, Brown accepted the opportunity to help bridge the gap between the African American community and the college. While employed at the college, Brown continued her education at the University of South Florida, Sarasota Campus. She earned a master of science in Education in 1981.

Initiatives implemented under Brown's leadership included establishing Future Unlimited Scholarships for minority students, inviting black artists to the community, and providing networking and mentoring opportunities between students and local professionals through the Talking and Touching dialogues. Brown also created community-based study centers. While she was employed at Manatee Junior College, Brown displayed items from her collection of black memorabilia in her office and shared them with students. By the time of her retirement in 1989, Brown had built a sturdy bridge that connected the community with the college.

Reluctant to store their collection in boxes, the Browns sought another space for the books, newspaper clippings, photographs, and audiocassettes on the local, state, and national figures that they had collected over the years. As a result, in 1990, the Family Heritage House was founded in a trailer belonging to the Bradenton Head Start program. By 1999, however, the Browns began to seek another home for their museum, especially as the collection became an important community resource. As a result the Browns once again gained a presence at Manatee Community College, which welcomed the idea of housing the collection because it would serve as a magnet in the college's continued efforts to reach out to the African American community. Local businesses, organizations, and residents demonstrated their support for the Browns when they raised $370,000 for a 2,085-square-foot wing, which would be the new location for the Family Heritage House museum, to be built on to the college's Sara Scott Harlee Library. The doors of the Family Heritage House museum officially opened on 20 September 2000. Ernest Brown died on 26 December 2001, but Fredi Brown continued their work with the collection.

The Family Heritage House indeed became a magnet for the community college. An array of excellent programming activities, which included lectures, jazz concerts, and other performances, and permanent and traveling exhibitions enriched the lives of the county residents. Listed on the Florida Black Heritage Trail and included on the National Park Service Network to Freedom, the Family Heritage House attracted visitors from across the nation.

Brown was the recipient of numerous awards in honor of her influence on the community, including the 2001 Distinguished Alumni Award from the University of South Florida, Sarasota Campus; the 1999 Service to Youth and Community Education awarded by the Links, Inc.; and the 1998 Passing the Torch award, given by Delta Sigma Theta sorority. The Family Heritage House serves as a living monument to the life and service of Fredi Mae Sears Brown.

FURTHER READING

Some of the information for this entry was gathered during a telephone interview with Brown on 28 Dec. 2006.

Ayres, Annette. "Funding Raised for New MCC Museum," *Bradenton Herald*, 10 Sept. 1999.

Ayres, Annette. "Museum to Get New Home," *Bradenton Herald*, 18 Feb. 1999.

Reddick, Tracie. "Heritage House Opens Doors," *Bradenton Herald*, 21 Sept. 2000.

DOROTHY A. WASHINGTON

Brown, George S. (25 July 1801–10 April 1886), Methodist Episcopal minister, missionary to Liberia, and expert stone mason, was born on Newport Island, Rhode Island, the son of Amos Brown, an elder in the Baptist Church. When George S. Brown was two years old, he moved with his family to Windham, Connecticut, and two years later to Ashford, Connecticut, where he grew up. According to his *Journal* (8) Brown finally found himself in Kingsbury, New York, in order to recover from the effects of many years of carousing. He earned his living by building stonewalls, charging $1/day and a night's room and lodging for every rod (16.5 feet).

In 1828 Brown was converted by some Baptist friends but soon came under the influence of the Reverend William Ryder, whom he describes in his *Journal* (19) as a "Holy Ghost man, an exhorter in the Methodist Episcopal Church …" He finally was led to join the "Episcopal Methodists" and preach the word of God. In April 1831 Brown was granted an exhorter's license and two years later was approved for a license to preach, the first such license granted to an African American in the Troy Annual Conference of the Methodist Episcopal Church (MEC). Brown was a powerful preacher and often gathered large crowds when he preached.

During these years Brown experienced a call from God to go as a missionary to Liberia. He was originally sent to Liberia in 1836 as a schoolteacher but was unable to resist the call to preach, as well. He was received as a probationary member of the Liberia Conference (MEC) in January 1838 and elected to both deacon's and elder's orders. He then sailed back to America, and at the New York Annual Conference of the MEC, held on March 25–26, 1838, Brown was ordained as a deacon one day and as an elder the next day. Upon returning to Liberia he was admitted as a full member of the Liberian Annual Conference on 14 February 1839. At this time African Americans in the Methodist Episcopal Church were not allowed to become full members of an annual conference except in missionary conferences. It would not be until 1864 that African Americans in the MEC would be granted full clergy rights.

George S. Brown was married to Nancy Wilson, the daughter of one of the other black preachers in Liberia, on March 14, 1838. Nancy's health was poor and she died seven months later. Brown married a second time, this time to Harriet Ann Harper on 30 January 1841; they had a daughter also named Harriet Ann, who died of whooping cough in May 1843.

For the first few years that Brown was in Liberia he was a very successful missionary to the native Africans. Eunjin Park in *White Americans in Black Africa* (142) describes Brown as "the missionary who was more devoted to African evangelization than anyone else." In 1840, however, the white Superintendent of the Liberia Mission of the MEC, Reverend John Seys, became embroiled in a struggle with the Liberian government over custom duties owed on goods brought into Liberia from the United States. Seys attempted to persuade all of his pastors to support him in this political battle. Brown, who firmly believed that he had only been called to Africa to save souls, refused to become involved. As a result he was eventually suspended from all of his duties in 1843 and was expelled from the Liberia Conference on 1 January 1844. Shortly thereafter he sailed to America, leaving his wife behind, assuming that he would be able to resolve his problems with the MEC Missionary Board in a timely manner and then return to Africa. This took much longer than anticipated, however, and Brown never was able to return.

After finally resolving his issues with the Missionary Board, Brown attempted to have his preaching credentials reinstated by the Troy Annual Conference. This process took many years due primarily to the opposition of a few individuals. In order to clear his name Brown sued Reverend John Seys in New York Civil Court and won his case in 1848. It would still be another five years before Brown's preaching credentials were finally restored at the 1853 Troy Annual Conference session. By this time he was living in northern Vermont.

In 1855 Brown moved to the small village of Wolcott in north central Vermont and began gathering Methodist classes there. The following year under his direction the Wolcott Methodist Episcopal Church was built and is still in use in the present day. Brown kept a detailed record of the work on the church; the last entry was dated September 23, 1856.

During the following winter Brown became ill with "bleeding at the lungs" and was near death. He did manage to recover, however, and in 1863 he took the train from Fort Edward, New York, along with a number of men he had hired to assist him in building a stone wall on the farm of Dwight Merriman in Jackson, Michigan. Merriman had learned of Brown's stone walls from his father-in-law who lived in Glens Falls, New York. The wall took about two years to build and was about a half a mile long. In 1869 the Michigan Agricultural Society cited the wall for its artistic and engineering design. Much of the wall still stands today and can be seen on the property of what is now the Ella Sharpe Museum in Jackson.

Brown returned to the Glens Falls, New York, area and lived there until his death. He died as a result of complications following a fall on the ice. Despite his many trials with the Methodist Episcopal Church Brown never left to join one of the African Methodist Episcopal denominations. He states in his *Journal* (258), "I call heaven to witness that I truly love the M.E. Church with all my soul. I love her nonetheless for what a few individuals have mangled me."

FURTHER READING

Brown, Geo. S. *Brown's Abridged Journal, Containing a Brief Account of the Life, Trials and Travels of Geo. S. Brown, Six Years a Missionary in Liberia, West Africa: A Miracle of God's Grace* (1849).

Child, Hamilton. *Gazetteer and Business Directory of Lamoille and Orleans Counties, VT, for 1883–84* (1883).

Park, Eunjin. *White Americans in Black Africa* (2001).

PATRICIA J. THOMPSON

Brown, Grafton Tyler (22 Feb. 1841–2 Mar. 1918), draftsman, lithographer, painter, and entrepreneur, was born free in Harrisburg, Pennsylvania, to Thomas Brown and Wilhelmina (maiden name unknown). Nothing is known about Brown's family or childhood. It appears that in the mid-1850s, Brown moved to San Francisco on the heels of the gold rush. While black fur traders, including EDWARD ROSE and JIM BECKWOURTH, had already explored the West by the mid-1850s, few African Americans were living in California before this time. By 1860, though, close to five thousand blacks had moved to California, including MARY ELLEN PLEASANT and EDMOND WYSINGER. Just what precipitated Brown's decision to move to San Francisco is unknown, but records show that by 1861 he was employed as a draftsman for the commercial lithography firm of Kuchel and Dressel. While his skill is evidenced by the quality work he produced for the firm, Brown must also have been considered a competent businessman, because following the 1866 death of Charles Kuchel he assumed management of the firm. A year later the twenty-six-year-old opened his own business, G.T. Brown and Company, at 520 Clay Street in San Francisco. Brown was a prolific lithographer, known for his keen drafting skills, exactness, and attention to detail.

Brown was exceedingly busy throughout the 1860s and 1870s, producing a host of topographical and street maps, stock certificates, sheet music, letter- and billheads, and advertising materials for banks, municipalities, mining companies, and California companies. Brown's clients included Levi Strauss Co., Ghirardelli Chocolate & Spice, and the California Fertilizing Company, for whom he designed stock certificates. The image of a stagecoach he designed for Wells Fargo Mining Co. remains the company's logo today. A major component of Brown's business was the production of aerial-view maps of western cities and towns, including Santa Rosa and Oakland, California, and Fort Churchill, Nevada, which he would visit to sketch their major buildings and structures. Brown's 1861 map of Virginia City, Nevada, features individual renderings of thirty of the town's buildings in a border surrounding a bird's-eye view of the city nestled into the hills of Nevada Territory. Brown's hand-tinted lithograph of San Francisco from around 1876 became a standard source, and in 1878 he completed his largest commission, *The Illustrated History of San Mateo County*, which consisted of seventy-two views of ranches and towns in San Mateo County.

The discovery of gold in 1848 and the subsequent Gold Rush transformed California, especially San Francisco. By 1854, 300,000 people from across the United States, Asia, Mexico, South America, and Europe had arrived in California, increasing the state's population from around 13,000 residents in 1848. San Francisco, home to 600 people in 1848, quickly and abruptly grew into a major, racially diverse, boomtown with a population of 50,000 by 1856. Nearly a half-billion dollars' worth of gold passed through the city in the 1850s. A plot of San Francisco real estate that cost $16 in 1847, for instance, sold for $45,000 just eighteen months later. In less than two years the city burned to the ground—and was rebuilt—six times. By 1856, even after the major mining companies had wrested control of the area's mining profits, many gold rushers remained in California, opening banks, shops, saloons, and other businesses that catered to the new population. Lithography, in the years before the universal adoption of photography, was an integral part of this boom, benefiting from and contributing to the settling and commercialization of California and the West. Brown's lithographs, including an 1878 commission scrip for five dollars, an 1879 bank note for the Pioneer Woolen Factory Bank, an 1870s billhead for J.A. Folger & Co., and an 1869 sheet music frontispiece for "Under the Snow," reveal a great deal about the growth, manner, and priorities of California's new businesses.

Brown's work documented the rapid growth of California's cities, ranches, and businesses, as well as other changing conditions. City views, which were used by local businesses on their letterhead and correspondence, also served a broader purpose, advertising the new West as a concrete, solid, and stable environment for entrepreneurial investment. The clarity and meticulousness of Brown's city views articulated the philosophy of westward expansionism and Manifest Destiny. In his 1875 view of the Iron Clad Mine in Nevada County, the indigenous forest has been neatly cleared, replaced by the orderly geometry of main streets and abutting houses, all built by human imagination and hard work.

In 1879 Brown left San Francisco and traveled through the Pacific Northwest, apparently joining an 1882 geological survey of the Cariboo gold mines in British Columbia, Canada, led by Amos Bowman. By 1883 he had settled in Victoria, British Columbia, and was advertising himself in the *Williams British Columbia Directory* as a landscape painter. That same year he held his first, and only documented, exhibition of paintings. While living in British Columbia, he painted many tender and intimate views of Victoria locales, including *Goldstream Falls, B.C.* (1882) and *View of Lake Okanogan, B.C.* (1883). Trips to Washington and Oregon in 1884 and 1885, respectively, yielded paintings of the area's rivers and mountains, including Puget Sound, Mount Hood, Mount Tacoma, and Cascade Cliffs. Brown's new dedication to painting, indicated by his prolific output and his efforts in advertising his work, marked a career shift from commercial lithography to landscape painting. His paintings—pure landscapes devoid of figures or manmade elements—may also reflect a shift in his attitudes toward expansionism. Celebrations of the area's untouched wilderness, particularly the Yellowstone area, which was designated the country's first national park in 1872 partly as a result of the paintings of Thomas Moran, indicate that Brown may have supported the growing conservation movement. In 1886 Brown relocated to Portland, Oregon, where he became an active member of the Portland Art Club. He continued painting, producing larger works, including many of the Grand Canyon.

Around 1892 Brown made yet another dramatic career shift. Settling in St. Paul, Minnesota, he returned to work as a draftsman, first for the U.S. Army Corps of Engineers (from 1892 to 1897) and then the St. Paul Civil Engineering Department (from 1897 to 1910). Whether or not he continued to paint is unknown, since no canvases have survived. Brown died of pneumonia and arteriosclerosis.

In 1972 the Oakland Museum of California mounted an exhibit of Brown's work, focusing primarily on his lithographs. In 2004 Grafton Tyler Brown: Visualizing California and the Pacific Northwest, a traveling exhibition organized by the California African American Museum, included the first serious exhibition of his paintings. Brown's work is held in a number of collections, including the British Archives, Victoria, British Columbia, and the National Museum of American Art, Washington, D.C.

FURTHER READING
Grafton Tyler Brown: Nineteenth Century American Artist. The Evans-Tibbs Collection (exhibition pamphlet, Spring 1988).
Lewis, Jo Ann. "A Painting Pioneer," *Washington Post,* 2 May 2004.

LISA E. RIVO

Brown, H. Rap (4 Oct. 1943–), militant political activist and religious leader, was born Hubert Geroid Brown in Baton Rouge, Louisiana, the youngest child and second son of Eddie C. Brown, a laborer for Esso Standard Oil, and Thelma Warren, a teacher. According to his own account, Brown was a rebel from the earliest days against the color biases of his community as well as the authoritarianism and Eurocentric curricula of the schools in Baton Rouge. He identified with youth street culture and its heroes, whose verbal and physical jousting he extolled in his 1970 memoir *Die Nigger Die!* His facility at signifying or "playing the dozens" earned Brown the "Rap" sobriquet that he was to carry throughout the first phase of his public career. Brown attended Southern University in Baton Rouge from 1961 to 1963 but dropped out to pursue his growing interest in the civil rights movement. Following his brother Ed, whose social

H. Rap Brown, answering a question at a Student Nonviolent Coordinating Committee news conference, 27 July 1967. (Library of Congress.)

activism was also lifelong, he moved to Washington, D.C., and became active in the Nonviolent Action Group (NAG), an affiliate of the Student Nonviolent Coordinating Committee (SNCC), composed largely of Howard University students. Although Brown never enrolled at Howard, he participated increasingly in the group's meetings and demonstrations and became deeply involved in SNCC activities. He worked with the Mississippi Summer Project and in 1966 was appointed director of the Greene County Project in Alabama, part of the group's campaign to organize black voters and elect black candidates.

Brown was elected chairman of SNCC in 1967, succeeding STOKELY CARMICHAEL at a time when the organization's community-organizing programs were on the wane and as the mainstream media had begun to denounce SNCC's turn to Black Power. Brown's incendiary rhetoric—"They're scared of me with this .45, wait till I get my atomic bomb!" (from the film *King: From Montgomery to Memphis*, 1970)—alienated many of SNCC's former liberal allies, but his denunciations of government racism and corruption struck a chord with disillusioned young African Americans. So, too, did Brown's approving remarks about the July 1967 Detroit riots, in which he urged blacks to stop "trying to love that honky to death … shoot him to death, brother. Cause that's what he's out to do to you" (Sitkoff, *Struggle for Black Equality*, 217).

Many commentators, especially whites, understood the "burn, baby, burn" refrain of one of Brown's speeches as an unqualified call to violence. However, his political philosophy was less nihilistic than that phrase might suggest. In fact, Brown stated in that speech in Cambridge, Maryland, that "if America don't come around, we going to burn it down, brother. We going to burn it down, brother, if we don't get our share of it." America, then, could prevent violence by radically redistributing wealth and resources. Yet if violence were to come, Brown reminded his audience—and the journalists and politicians who denounced him for his militancy—that "violence is as American as cherry pie."

Brown's tenure as SNCC chairman was hampered by numerous arrests and indictments on a variety of charges. His effectiveness was severely undermined by constant litigation. The most consequential of these legal troubles arose out of an uprising in Cambridge, Maryland, where authorities charged him with incitement following his speech there in July 1967. The federal government also charged Brown with unlawful interstate flight

to avoid prosecution, violation of the National Firearms Act, arson, and violation of the terms of his bond. Although many of these charges would ultimately be dropped, Brown spent much of his twelve-month tenure as SNCC chairman behind bars. Brown was also appointed the Black Panther Party's minister of justice in 1968, though, with his own legal troubles and SNCC duties, this was largely a titular office. Brown went underground in 1970 rather than stand trial for the incitement to riot charges, and little is known of his activities at that time. He resurfaced in October 1971, when he was captured along with three others in the aftermath of an armed holdup of a New York City nightclub. Although it was not part of the legal defense, supporters claimed that this robbery was directed at drug dealers, whose illegal and immoral profits from exploiting the black community were to be used for the movement. If true, such actions were in line with those of the Black Liberation Army, whose members engaged in similar activities, often with equally unsuccessful results. In any case, Brown, who converted to Islam while imprisoned in the Tombs and changed his name to Jamil Abdullah al-Amin, was convicted of armed robbery and assault with a deadly weapon and sentenced to five to fifteen years in prison. He was paroled in 1976 and moved south, where he lived quietly as the owner of a small neighborhood store in Atlanta's West End. Al-Amin eventually became the imam of a small Muslim community in Atlanta, and in 1993 he published a book of sermons entitled *Revolution by the Book: The Rap Is Live*. His community earned a reputation as a positive force in lowering the incidence of street crime in the neighborhood. However, the group, and al-Amin in particular, seemed to be targets of numerous investigations by police agencies over the years. (During his later murder trial, Atlanta police would accuse them in the press of involvement in a dozen unsolved murders in the neighborhood.) Perhaps the most bizarre episode was a 1995 charge of attempted murder, in which the police alleged that al-Amin shot at a man walking down the street for no apparent reason. This well-publicized case was later dropped when the supposed victim denied that al-Amin was his attacker and later joined the *masjid*, or mosque. Federal authorities also tried to tie members of the *masjid* to the 1993 World Trade Center bombing in New York City, with much press attention. Eventually two *masjid* members were convicted of gunrunning.

On 16 March 2000 two Atlanta police officers, who stated that they were seeking to arrest al-Amin on charges of driving a stolen car and impersonating a police officer, approached his house at ten thirty at night. Both were shot; one was killed. The survivor claimed to have shot his assailant, and a blood trail seemed to confirm his story. Al-Amin was the prime suspect. He fled to Alabama, where he was captured several days later, uninjured and proclaiming his innocence. There were sensational headlines across the country about the bloodthirsty former Black Panther cop killer, while an international campaign supporting al-Amin's right to a fair trial was mounted. Nonetheless, an all-black Fulton County jury found him guilty of murder in March 2002 and sentenced him to life without parole.

Al-Amin's story is unsettling, bizarre, and tragic. He is painted by opponents of social change as a violent murderer with a history of involvement in active violence. His supporters cite a legacy of FBI repression of black activists leading to his ultimate fate as a prisoner for life. Yet al-Amin's SNCC activities, as well as his later leadership of a religious community, clearly display a commitment to humanistic concerns at odds with his status as a convicted murderer.

FURTHER READING

Al-Amin, Jamil Abdullah. *Die Nigger Die!: A Political Autobiography* (1970, 2d ed. 2002).

Carson, Clayborne. *In Struggle: SNCC and the Black Awakening of the 1960s* (1981).

W. S. TKWEME

Brown, Hallie Quinn (10 Mar. 1845?–16 Sept. 1949), elocutionist, educator, women's and civil rights leader, and writer, was born in Pittsburgh, Pennsylvania, the daughter of Thomas Arthur Brown, a riverboat steward and express agent, and Frances Jane Scroggins, an educated woman who served as an unofficial adviser to the students of Wilberforce University. Thomas Brown was born into slavery in Frederick County, Maryland, the son of a Scottish woman plantation owner and her black overseer. Brown purchased his freedom and that of his sister, brother, and father. By the time of the Civil War, he had amassed a sizable amount of real estate. Hallie's mother, Frances, was also born a slave, the child of her white owner. She was eventually freed by her white grandfather, a former officer in the American Revolution.

Both of Hallie's parents became active in the Underground Railroad. Around 1864, the Browns and their six children moved to Chatham, Ontario, where Thomas worked as a farmer and Hallie began to show a talent for public speaking and performance. The Browns returned to the United States around 1870, settling in Wilberforce, Ohio, where Hallie and her youngest brother enrolled in Wilberforce University, an African Methodist Episcopal (AME) liberal arts school and the first four-year college owned and operated by African Americans in the United States. Wilberforce was at that time under the direction of the AME bishop DANIEL ALEXANDER PAYNE, America's first black college president and a Brown family friend. Brown graduated with a B.S. from Wilberforce University in 1873. (The university later gave Brown two honorary degrees, an M.S. in 1890 and a doctorate in Law in 1936.) Shortly after graduation Brown moved to the South, beginning what would become a lifelong commitment to education and to the advancement of disenfranchised women and African Americans. For more than a decade, in plantations and public schools from Yazoo, Mississippi, to Columbia, South Carolina, Brown taught literacy skills to black children and adults denied education during slavery.

Attracted to its combination of education with entertainment, Brown had joined the Lyceum movement in 1874. The Lyceum, a nineteenth-century movement that fostered adult education in the arts, sciences, history, and public affairs through traveling programs of lectures and concerts, brought Brown's eloquent lectures to a wide audience in the South and Midwest. By the early 1880s Brown was touring with the Lyceum full time. She continued her elocution training at the Chautauqua Lecture School from which, in 1886, she graduated at the top of her class, having completed several summer sessions.

As Brown's eminence and reputation grew, so did her job prospects. From 1885 to 1887 she served as dean of Allen University in Columbia, South Carolina, the first black college in South Carolina, founded in 1870. In 1887 Brown returned to Ohio, where for the next five years she taught in the Dayton public schools and at a night school she founded for migrant African American adults recently relocated from the South. The Tuskegee Normal and Industrial Institute brought Brown to Alabama from 1892 to 1893 to serve as lady principal, or dean of women, under the direction of BOOKER T. WASHINGTON.

Brown's lasting dedication to Wilberforce University began in 1893, when she was hired by her alma mater as professor of elocution. Brown would remain a part of the Wilberforce community, as an English and elocution teacher, trustee, and fund-raiser, until her death. Shortly after her appointment, however, Brown suspended her classroom teaching duties in favor of a series of extensive lecture tours of Europe.

Brown left for Europe in 1894 and remained on tour for much of the next five years. She quickly became an internationally lauded lecturer and performer, speaking on the themes of African American culture, temperance, and women's suffrage. Enamored audiences flocked to experience Brown's lectures on topics like "Negro Folklore and Folksong" and her recitations of the works of PAUL LAURENCE DUNBAR and other African American authors. Brown was a featured speaker in London at the Third Biennial Convention of the World's Woman's Christian Temperance Union in 1895 and a representative to the International Congress of Women held in London in 1899. Having been introduced to the royal family via letter by FREDERICK DOUGLASS in 1894, Brown performed for Queen Victoria on several occasions, even joining the monarch for tea at Windsor Castle and as a guest during the Jubilee Celebration in 1899. Brown was made a member of the exclusive Royal Geographical Society in Edinburgh, and in 1895 she helped form the first British Chautauqua, a Lyceum-style touring educational program, in North Wales.

Brown returned to teaching full time at Wilberforce around the turn of the century but visited Europe once again in 1910 as a representative to the Woman's Missionary Society of the AME Conference held in Edinburgh. For Brown, this trip marked the culmination of over ten years of work with the AME Church and validated her role in the church outside of her association with Wilberforce University. In 1900 Brown had campaigned for the job of AME secretary of education. Although she failed to get the appointment, she remained committed to expanding the role of women in the church. Brown remained in Britain for seven months, raising enough money for Wilberforce to build a new dormitory. Still popular as a lecturer, Brown gave a command performance for King George and Queen Mary and was a dinner guest of the Princess of Wales.

While Brown is remembered for her achievements as an elocutionist, it is her vision of a nationally organized African American women's community that has secured her place in history. Brown was a pioneering force in the formation of the black women's club movement, the development of which saw the establishment of schools, scholarships, museums, elder-care facilities, and political institutions.

Concerned that the achievements of African Americans would be omitted from the exhibitions at the 1893 World's Fair and Columbian Exposition in Chicago, Brown petitioned for a seat on the Board of Lady Managers, the planning committee presiding over the U.S. exhibits. "For two hundred and fifty years the Negro woman of America was bought and sold as chattel," Brown argued. "Twenty-five years of progress find the Afro-American woman advanced beyond the most sanguine expectations. Her development from the darkest slavery and grossest ignorance into light and liberty is one of the marvels of the age. … What more is needed? Time and equal chance in the race of life" (*The World's Congress of Representative Women*, May Wright Sewall, ed., 1894). The Board denied Brown's request, explaining that only individuals representing organizations could participate. Provoked by her exclusion and motivated to set up a national organization devoted to and run by black women, Brown cofounded the Colored Women's League of Washington, D.C. Two years later Brown's organization merged with JOSEPHINE ST. PIERRE RUFFIN's Boston Women's Era Club, becoming the National Federation of Afro-American Women, which was later renamed the National Association of Colored Women (NACW).

Brown served as national president of the NACW from 1920 to 1924 and as honorary president until her death. During her tenure at the NACW, Brown took a leadership role in two projects: the creation and maintenance of a memorial at the former home of Frederick Douglass in Washington, D.C., and the establishment of the Hallie Q. Brown Scholarship Loan Fund for the education of black women, a national program open to college students and postgraduate women, that allots generous loans to be repaid with no interest.

In addition to her work with the NACW, Brown played major roles in several other African American and women's organizations. She served as president of the Ohio State Federation of Colored Women's Clubs from 1905 to 1912 and worked as an organizer for the Women's Christian Temperance Union. Brown lent her support and oratorical skill to a variety of issues. In 1922 she lobbied President Warren Harding and several key U.S. senators in support of a federal antilynching law and worked with the NAACP in its efforts to defeat a national bill outlawing interracial marriages. On another occasion, in an incident reported in the *New York Times*, Brown arrived in Washington, D.C., for the 1925 All-American Musical Festival of the International Council of Women and found the auditorium segregated. In a biting speech condemning the council's racist policy, Brown threatened a boycott by the festival's black performers if segregation continued. When her demands were not met, many of the audience members joined the two hundred black performers in a boycott of the program.

Brown was also engaged in mainstream political organizations. An ardent Republican, she spoke in support of local, state, and national candidates in Ohio, Pennsylvania, Illinois, and Missouri. Brown's Republican activities increased in the 1920s and 1930s, during which time she labored on behalf of the National League of Women Voters and as vice president of the Ohio Council of Republican Women. In 1924 Brown emerged on the national stage, addressing the Republican National Convention in Cleveland. Speaking in support of Warren Harding's nomination, Brown took the opportunity to discuss issues of significance to African Americans. After the convention, Brown directed the Colored Women's Activities at the Republican national campaign headquarters in Chicago and the new National League of Republican Colored Women, which adopted the slogan "We are in politics to stay and we shall be a stay in politics."

Concurrent with her teaching, lecturing, and organizing, Brown worked as a writer, essayist, and anthologist. She published several collections of speeches and prose, including *Bits and Odds: A Choice Selection of Recitations* (1880), *Elocution and Physical Culture* (1910), *First Lessons in Public Speaking* (1920), *The Beautiful: A True Story of Slavery* (1924), *Our Women: Past, Present and Future* (1925), and *Tales My Father Told* (1925). She often wrote of the power and complexity of black America's relationship to language, frequently using black vernacular speech in her writing, and of the importance of African American heritage, family history, and culture. In 1926, when Brown was in her seventies, she published her best-known book, *Homespun Heroines and Other Women of Distinction*, a collection of sixty biographies of black women born in North America between 1740 and 1900.

"Miss Hallie," as Brown was known at Wilberforce, remained active until her death in 1949, near age one hundred. Her legacy continues through the scholarship fund that bears her name; the good works of the Hallie Quinn Brown Community House in St. Paul, Minnesota; and the Hallie Q. Brown Memorial Library at Wilberforce University, a facility that includes a collection of books by and about African Americans.

FURTHER READING

Brown's unpublished papers are held at the Hallie Q. Brown Memorial Library at Wilberforce University in Wilberforce, Ohio.

Davis, Elizabeth Lindsay, ed. *Lifting as They Climb* (1933, 1996).

Majors, M. A. *Noted Negro Women: Their Triumphs and Activities* (1893).

LISA E. RIVO

Brown, Henry "Box" (1815?–?), escaped slave, was born on a plantation in Louisa County, Virginia, to unknown parents. As a youth, Brown lived with his parents, four sisters, and three brothers until the family was separated and his master hired him out at age fifteen to work in a tobacco factory in Richmond, Virginia. Brown's autobiography illuminates the vicissitudes of slave life but does not recount any further major events in his own life other than his marriage around 1836 to Nancy, the slave of a bank clerk, with whom he had three children. In August 1848 Nancy's owner sold her and her three children (Brown's children) to a slave trader who took them South. Brown begged his own master to purchase them, but he refused. Brown later wrote in his autobiography: "I went to my *Christian* master ... but he shoved me away." According to his autobiography, Brown actually saw his wife and children being marched out of town, but they did not see him. Angry over the loss of his family and his master's callous refusal to buy his wife and children, the formerly mild-mannered Brown resolved to liberate himself from "the bloody dealers in the bodies and souls of men."

In response to Brown's prayerful search for a way to freedom, "an idea," he reported, "suddenly flashed across my mind." Brown's revelation was that he have himself nailed into a wooden box and "conveyed as dry goods" via the Adams Express Company from slavery in Richmond to freedom in Philadelphia (Brown, 57–58). This plan was carried out with the assistance of two friends, a white abolitionist, Dr. Samuel A. Smith, and James Caesar Anthony Smith, a free black. Brown had met Dr. Smith while singing in an integrated church choir. J. C. A. Smith helped Brown obtain a wooden box—complete with baize lining, air holes, a container of water, and hickory straps—that was constructed by a carpenter, who

THE RESURRECTION OF HENRY BOX BROWN AT PHILADELPHIA.
Who escaped from Richmond Va in a Box 3 feet long 2½ ft deep and 2 ft wide

Henry "Box" Brown, emerging from his box in the office of the Pennsylvania Anti-Slavery Society, in a nineteenth-century broadside published in Boston. (Library of Congress, Broadside Collection.)

measured it precisely to hold Brown's five-feet eight-inch, two-hundred-pound body. The crate was addressed to Dr. Smith's friend, William Johnson, an abolitionist on Arch Street in Philadelphia and marked "this side up with care." On 29 March 1849, at four o'clock in the morning, the box was loaded onto a wagon and delivered to the depot, and Brown began his historic, twenty-seven-hour, 350-mile odyssey, some of it upside down and all of it in danger. The box with its human content eventually found its way to the Anti-Slavery Committee's office on North Fifth Street in Philadelphia. A small, nervous group, including WILLIAM STILL, the African American conductor of Philadelphia's Underground Railroad, pried open the lid to reveal, in "my resurrection from the grave of slavery," the disheveled and battered Henry Brown, who arose and promptly fainted (Brown, 62). Revived by a glass of water, he proceeded to sing Psalm 40, which includes the line "Be pleased, O Lord, to deliver me" (Psalms 40:13). Discovering a flair for the dramatic, he immediately took the name "Box" to celebrate his new identity as well as his escape.

Brown became an instant celebrity. The novelty of his escape caught the attention of abolitionists around the country. Two months after his escape he sang his psalm before an antislavery convention in Boston. Within months a narrative of his life and escape appeared (mostly written by the abolitionist Charles Stearns). Woodcuts of Brown emerging from his box were printed and reprinted; his story appeared in a children's book that year as well. Brown quickly began a career as an abolitionist speaker and entertainer. He traveled in the North telling his story with his friend J. C. A. Smith, who had left Virginia, selling copies of the 1849 edition of his narrative, and singing not only psalms, but lyrics of his own creation. He cleverly adapted to his own purposes a popular song of the day, Stephen Foster's 1848 ballad "Uncle Ned." The original text begins:

Dere was an old Nigga, dey called him Uncle Ned—
He's dead long ago, long ago! He had no wool on de top ob his head—
De place where de wool ought to grow.
Chorus: Den lay down de shubble and de hoe,
Hang up de fiddle and de bow;
No more hard work for poor old Ned—

He is gone whar de good Niggas go.

Brown's version begins:

Here you see a man by the name of Henry Brown,
Ran away from the South to the North,
Which he would not have done but they stole all
    his rights,
But they'll never do the like again.
Chorus: Brown laid down the shovel and the hoe,
Down in the box he did go; No more slave work
    for Henry Box Brown,
In the box by *Express* he did go.

Brown later published this parody of "Old Ned" as a broadside which he sold along with his narrative. Not only is Brown's revision witty and entertaining, it also is a window into his mind. He used a song everyone knew, a song with racist lyrics, stereotypical images, and a condescending attitude, all set in a sentimentalized South. Brown subverted the norms and values of a white supremacist society, turning Uncle Ned upside down, as it were, by replacing negative representations with positive ones.

Another way the imaginative and entrepreneurial Brown broadened the appeal and effect of his performance was through the addition of a large didactic panorama, "The Mirror of Liberty," which consisted of thousands of feet of canvas, divided into scores of panels painted with scenes depicting the history of slavery. Josiah Wolcott, a white Massachusetts artist, designed and painted it, perhaps with the assistance of other artists. Brown recruited Benjamin F. Roberts, an African American activist from Boston, to write an accompanying lecture, "The Condition of the Colored People in the United States." To dramatize its message, the panorama showed alternating scenes, one a traditional and romanticized American view and the next an image of the cruelty of slavery—a whipping post, for instance—in the same place. Just as Brown's version of "Uncle Ned" turned a popular ballad into a protest song, so the "Mirror of Liberty" transformed idealized American myths into the realities of a slave society.

It is not known whether Box Brown solicited an author to tell his story or whether he was approached by abolitionists; in either event, Brown submitted his life to Charles Stearns for presentation to the world. A nephew of Brook Farm's Utopian founder, George Ripley, Stearns was a militant antislavery activist. Though earlier a pacifist, he had participated so ardently in the violent struggle between proslavery and antislavery factions in

Kansas during the late 1850s known as "Bleeding Kansas" that he lost his pacifism. In Boston in 1849 Stearns published his *Narrative of Henry Box Brown Who Escaped from Slavery Enclosed in a Box 3 Feet Long and 2 Wide Written from a Statement of Facts Made by Himself. With Remarks upon the Remedy for Slavery. By Charles Stearns.* The book's problem was Stearns's "Remarks." As well as appearing in a separate essay, they permeated the entire text with Stearns's dogmatic ideology and arrogant and opinionated style. Brown's personal response was to edit or, more likely, to have the book heavily edited at the first opportunity. Most of Stearns's overblown rhetoric was simply excised.

Brown was forced to leave the United States, even the free North, before he could find his own voice. With the passage of a stronger fugitive slave law in 1850, the North was legally obliged to participate in the recapture and return of escaped slaves. Skirting the threat of arrest in Providence, Rhode Island, Brown immediately left for England. A second edition of his autobiography, with a Manchester 1851 imprint, appeared with a new title: *Narrative of the Life of Henry Box Brown Written by Himself.*

At this point he fell out with J. C. A. Smith, who reported to abolitionists in the United States that Brown had begun to lead a dissolute life, engaging in drinking, swearing, smoking, and "many other things too Bad" to name. By this time, Brown had fully escaped from his life as a slave, and remade himself as a freeman, living under the protection of Queen Victoria. In fact, Brown had become a successful entertainer in England, where he married an English woman, rather than attempting to use his earnings to buy his wife and children out of slavery.

For the rest of the decade Brown toured the British Isles, lecturing on the history of slavery as well as acting and singing. He used a large moving panorama to depict the history of blacks in Africa and America, as he lectured on "African and American Slavery." He often appeared as an "African Prince" as he melded antislavery sentiments and propaganda, popular history, and entertaining theatrical production. In 1862 he developed a new lecture and panorama called the "Grand Moving Mirror of the American War." However, by this time his career as a political speaker was beginning to play itself out, and he moved into other forms of entertainment.

By 1864 he was billed as "Mr. H. Box Brown, the King of all Mesmerisers," although he continued to perform his "Panorama of African and American Slavery." In 1875 the sixty-year-old Brown returned to the United States with his wife and daughter Annie, performing as the magician and mesmerist Prof. H. Box Brown; he toured New England in the mid- and late 1870s with a show called the *African Prince's Drawing-Room Entertainment*. He still advertised himself as the man "whose escape from slavery in 1849 in a box 3 feet 1 inch long, 2 feet wide, 2 feet six inches high, caused such a sensation in the New England States, he having traveled from Richmond, Va., to Philadelphia, a journey of 350 miles, packed as luggage in a box." There is no record of Brown's life after 1878.

Brown's narrative was a dramatic moment in the antislavery movement. His escape was brave and striking; he emerged from the "box" of slavery to become an icon of those who loved liberty. However, there was also a darker side to Brown's story. After Brown's successful escape Samuel Smith tried to help another slave to escape in the same way. But Richmond authorities were now well aware of how Brown had escaped, and Smith was arrested. He would spend six years in the penitentiary. Dr. Smith was feted in the North after his release but soon disappeared from view. It is striking that while Brown was entertaining audiences in Britain, and living the life of a celebrity, the man who literally sent him on to freedom was himself in prison. FREDERICK DOUGLASS was somewhat disdainful of Brown for exposing the way he escaped. In his own *Narrative*, Douglass was careful not to reveal his method, lest someone else be unable to use it, or because it might imperil those who helped him (as happened with Samuel Smith). However, it was hardly Brown's fault that his escape became famous. Abolitionists were thrilled with its novelty and audacity. It was not only Brown himself, but the abolitionists who supported him, who turned the fugitive Henry Brown into "Box" Brown.

Douglass and other abolitionists were also probably disappointed that Brown chose the life of the entertainer instead of the life of the reformer and advocate. However, his career as an entertainer, his marriage to an English woman, and his later return to the United States as a "mesmeriser" also suggest another way of understanding him. While he traded in on the dramatic circumstances of his escape, he refused to be defined in later life as a runaway slave, or even a black person. A talented singer and showman, Brown used freedom to freely recreate himself in a white world as an entertainer/entrepreneur. He made himself free to be who he wanted to be, and not who society or the abolitionist movement expected him to be. He is remembered for his escape, but his later life illustrates the power of freedom for someone once held in bondage.

FURTHER READING

Brown, Henry Box. *Narrative of the Life of Henry Box Brown Written by Himself* (1851, repr. 2002 with an Introduction by Richard Newman).

Ruggles, Jeffrey. *The Unboxing of Henry Brown* (2003).

PAUL FINKELMAN
RICHARD NEWMAN

Brown, Homer S. (23 Sept. 1896–22 May 1977), attorney, judge, and civil rights activist, was born in Huntington, West Virginia, to the Reverend William Roderick Brown and Maria Wiggins Rowlett Brown. He attended Virginia Union University in Richmond and in 1923 earned a law degree from the University of Pittsburgh, graduating third in a class of twenty-two students.

Following his graduation in October 1923, Brown joined the Allegheny County Bar Association and became active in his community to reduce crime and improve the quality of life for youth. He married Wilhelmina Byrd in 1927, and the couple had one son, Byrd Rowlett Brown, who also became a well-known attorney and civil rights activist in Pittsburgh. During the 1930s, when there was an increase in crime as a result of the Great Depression, Brown chaired the Friendly Service Bureau, a committee established to help reduce crime in Pittsburgh. Along with the help of the mayor of Pittsburgh, the committee successfully reduced crime and improved the quality of life for youth within the district—a major feat for that era.

From 1934 to 1950 Brown served in the Pennsylvania House of Representatives. In 1937 he began to pay attention to the Pittsburgh Board of Education's hiring practices, noting that since desegregation rulings, Pittsburgh had refused to hire black teachers. Brown subsequently paved the way for a major lawsuit, and facilitated the hiring of the first black music instructor in a Pittsburgh school. He was voted the most able member of the House in 1943 by the Capital News Correspondents' Association and also named the most outstanding legislator.

In 1945 Brown faced an important struggle to secure human rights for working class residents of Pennsylvania. After conducting extensive research into the hiring practices of Pennsylvania businesses, Brown concluded that the majority of them practiced racial and religious discrimination. As a result of his research, Brown authored Pennsylvania's Fair Employment Practices Act, gaining him notoriety and a victory for the working class citizens of Pennsylvania.

Brown also served as founder and first president of the Pittsburgh chapter of the National Association for the Advancement of Colored People (NAACP) for twenty-four years, and was also the first African American to be appointed to the Board of Education. In 1949 he was elected the first African American Allegheny County Judge, a role that empowered him to facilitate numerous positive changes for the community. In 1956 he was elected to the Court of Common Pleas, and held that position until illness forced him to retire in 1975, two years before his death.

During his years as an attorney and judge, Brown handed down several significant rulings that were subsequently upheld by the Supreme Court of Pennsylvania. For example, in 1968 he decided that the city's "sick tax" on hospitals was unconstitutional, and in 1973 he ruled that prayer should be allowed during graduation ceremonies. Brown became well known and highly respected in his community, often entertaining luminaries such as U.S. Supreme Court Justice THURGOOD MARSHALL It was within this environment that Homer and Wilhelmina nurtured their son, Byrd, to carry on their legacy of civil and political activism in Pittsburgh.

In 1969 the Homer S. Brown Law Association was founded in Brown's honor. The Association represents over 200 African American attorneys. A membership group that supports minority lawyers and tracks hiring progress in Pittsburgh, the association assists local law students and increases legal knowledge within the community. Still quite active in the community, the association continues to monitor hiring practices and support minorities in Pittsburgh.

Besides his work in the Pittsburgh community, Brown was also the member of a number of other organizations. He was a member of the Pennsylvania Governor's Committee on Education in 1960, chaired the Board of Directors of the YMCA, and was a member of the White House Commission on Education in 1955. He was also on the advisory board of the United Nations Educational, Scientific, and Cultural Organization. Brown received honorary Doctor of Law degrees from several universities, including Virginia State College, Lincoln University (Pennsylvania), Virginia Union University, and the University of Pittsburgh.

Homer Brown died at home following a long illness. Both before and following his death, Brown's son, Byrd, complemented his father's important work in the Pittsburgh community, particularly gaining respect for his courage during the civil rights movement. Brown's widow, Wilhelmina Byrd Brown, also a well-known civil and political rights activist, collected and compiled twenty-three volumes of material belonging to her late husband. These volumes are on deposit at Virginia Union University in Richmond.

FURTHER READING
Who Was Who in America, 1977–1981, vol. 7 (1981).
CHERYL DUDLEY

Brown, James (c. 1795–Aug. 1857), a sailor during the War of 1812, served with Commodore Oliver Hazard Perry in the Battle of Lake Erie. A native of Maryland, Brown was a free man and resident of Somerset, Pennsylvania, when he married his wife Elizabeth, also from Maryland, in April 1812. Although details are lacking, Brown may have served in a local militia unit in 1812–1813 before being sent to serve in Perry's newly formed Lake Erie squadron in the spring of 1813. When Perry arrived at Erie, Pennsylvania, to finalize the construction of the twenty-gun brigs *Lawrence* and *Niagara*, the mainstays of his fleet, he found that he was severely lacking in manpower and requested more men from his superior, Commodore Isaac Chauncey. After some dispute and delay, a disappointed Perry finally received 150 men, commenting that "The men that came … are a motley set, blacks, Soldiers, and boys" (Altoff, 36). In defense of his actions, Chauncey responded, in part, that "I have yet to learn that the colour of the skin, or cut and trimmings of the coat, can effect a man's usefulness. I have nearly 50 Blacks on board of this ship [the *General Pike*], and many of them are amongst my best men" (Altoff, 37). Although historians continue to debate the issue as to whether Chauncey sent Perry the dregs of his fleet and kept his best men, African Americans included, in his own fleet on Lake Ontario, subsequent events would prove that the black soldiers and sailors in Perry's Lake Erie squadron, men such as James Brown, Jesse Williams, and ANTHONY WILLIAMS, would conduct themselves in battle with skill and valor.

The action in which Brown took part unfolded on 10 September 1813 in the waters of western Lake Erie, off Put-In-Bay. On that morning, a fleet of nine American ships, led by Perry in his flagship *Lawrence*, sallied forth to meet a fleet of six British ships; the outcome of this battle would decide which side controlled the lake and the area surrounding it in Ohio, the Michigan Territory, and parts of upper Canada. We know not which ship James Brown may have served on that day, just the general statement that he served with Perry during the battle according to a pension application filed by his wife Elizabeth in 1871. Interestingly, her pension claim was denied because she had lost her marriage certificate and could not prove she was his wife.

After the war, James and Elizabeth Brown moved to Erie, living in that city's ninth ward along with at least one other black sailor who fought on Lake Erie. Here Brown lived for the rest of his life. The 1850 Federal Census lists Brown and his wife, he employed as a laborer, she a domestic, without any children. The lone additional member of the household, whether a relative or boarder, was a young sailor named Harmon Lee.

FURTHER READING

Altoff, Gerard T. *Amongst My Best Men: African-Americans and the War of 1812* (1996).

GLENN ALLEN KNOBLOCK

Brown, James (3 May 1933–25 Dec. 2006), rhythm-and-blues singer, was born James Joe Brown Jr. in a country shack just outside Barnwell, South Carolina, to Joe Gardner and Susan Behlings. His father did various jobs, while nothing is known about his mother's occupation. Brown was raised in extreme poverty, and his parents separated when he was four; two years later he went to live with his great-aunt, Minnie Walker, in Augusta, Georgia.

Brown's father often sang blues songs in the evening, and when Brown was four, his father gave him a ten-cent harmonica. His earliest years were spent tap dancing in the street for spare change. He claimed that his formidable sense of rhythm stemmed from such humble beginnings. A self-taught musician, Brown began to play organ at the age of eight and later acquired a rudimentary knowledge of bass, guitar, saxophone, and trumpet. At eleven Brown won his first talent contest as a singer, and a year later he formed a group he called the Cremona Trio. In those same years Brown was involved in petty crime, shoplifting and stealing car batteries and hubcaps to obtain money for school clothes and food. In 1948, at the age of fifteen, he was caught stealing cars for the second time and was sentenced to eight to sixteen years in the Georgia Juvenile Training Institute in Rome, Georgia, thus ending his formal schooling at the seventh grade. Nicknamed Music Box, Brown formed a gospel quartet in prison. In 1952, Brown was paroled and went to live in Toccoa, Georgia. There he joined a group formed by Bobby Byrd, whom Brown had met during a baseball game while he was still in prison. Byrd's group originally sang gospel and was known as the Gospel Starlighters. Just before being joined by Brown, they had switched to singing rhythm and blues and consequently had changed their name to the Avons. They would soon be known as the Flames and eventually as James Brown and the Famous Flames. As word of the group's incredibly intense live shows spread throughout the South, they were summoned to Macon, Georgia, by LITTLE RICHARD's manager, Clint Bradley, after Richard became a national star in 1955.

A year later Ralph Bass signed Brown and the Famous Flames to Cincinnati-based King Records, their releases appearing on the subsidiary Federal label. Legend has it that upon hearing the demo recording of "Please Please Please," King's owner, Syd Nathan, fired Bass. Nathan could not believe that anyone would want to buy a record that consisted of six straight eight-bar verses, each of which was made up solely of one bar after one bar call-and-response patterns between Brown and the Flames. What Nathan did not understand, Brown knew from playing the song night after night in concert. Audiences would go crazy over the heightened emotion Brown conveyed, using numerous gospel-derived vocal devices. It took several months, but eventually "Please Please Please" reached the number-six position on *Billboard*'s R&B charts. Brown's debut effort and later singles, such as 1958's "Try Me" and 1960's "Think," were, along with early efforts by RAY CHARLES and SAM COOKE, the first examples of what would become known as soul music.

In 1962 Brown suggested that he wanted to record a live album at the Apollo Theater in New York. Long billed as "The Hardest Working Man in Show Business," Brown was positive that a recorded version of his legendary show would sell in significant numbers. When Nathan refused to finance the recording, Brown paid for it himself. Upon its release in 1963, *Live at the Apollo* climbed all the way to number two on *Billboard*'s LP charts. Such success was pretty well unprecedented for black artists and totally unheard of for live albums.

As the 1960s unfolded and Brown enjoyed a string of successes, American society underwent momentous changes. The civil rights movement had successfully brought about legal desegregation, but as the end of the decade approached most African Americans still found themselves the last

James Brown, who became "The Godfather of Soul," performing with the Famous Flames in 1964. (Library of Congress.)

hired and first fired, being paid less money than white workers for the same labor, living in inferior housing and sending their children to substandard schools.

As this reality slowly made itself manifest, the mood of black America began to change. In 1966 during the JAMES MEREDITH march in Mississippi, STOKELY CARMICHAEL popularized the phrase "Black Power." A year earlier the predominantly black neighborhood of Watts in Los Angeles had burned in the first of the modern-day race rebellions. In 1967 Newark, New Jersey, and Detroit, Michigan, would also burn. This new militancy no longer asked for equality, nor did it seek to achieve such equality by adopting mainstream (i.e., "white middle class") standards of deportment. Rather, black Americans were encouraged to celebrate and embrace everything black and to assume and demand equality. Inspired by the belief that "black is beautiful," many African Americans began to explore their historical and psychological connections to their African motherland. While some blacks adopted African names and wore African garb, many more began to sport an "Afro" or "natural" haircut.

This re-Africanization of black culture was also reflected in popular music, most radically in the development of funk by James Brown. In the simplest terms, Brown, beginning in 1967 with "Cold Sweat," de-emphasized melody and harmony (for example, by having whole sections of a song with no chord changes and by delivering the lyrics in a voice closer to speaking than singing) while privileging rhythm (by employing more complex syncopated figures and using several different rhythmic patterns simultaneously, creating interlocking grooves). This reconstruction of Brown's music could be interpreted as de-emphasizing parameters favored by white American society while highlighting sub-Saharan African characteristics; this was, in effect, re-Africanizing the music, thus paralleling the re-Africanization of African American society at large at the time.

Brown could be a temperamental and demanding bandleader—his trombonist Fred Wesley once noted that "James was bossy and paranoid." But when it came to performance, Brown was often able to submerge his ego in pursuit of a more democratic, communal sound. Notions of community and solidarity are connoted in "Cold Sweat" in a number of ways. Throughout the performance Brown utters any number of vocables judiciously placed within the rhythmic matrix. In doing so, he projects himself as part of the band rather than as a separate, somehow special, more important front man. Similarly, he can be heard during the performance calling out such things as "Maceo, Maceo," "Give the drummer some," and "Bernard, come on and help him out; play that thing." In this way, Brown conveys a sense of community. He explicitly *names* those who are contributing, recognizing their intrinsic value as individuals and the equality implicit in *collectively* unleashing the spiritual magic of the performance. "Cold Sweat" ends after seven and a half minutes with an extraordinary section in which Brown seems to be shredding his larynx while singing, "I can't, I can't, I can't, I can't stop, I can't stop, I can't stop singing." The effect is cathartic. Brown thus demonstrates an exceptional level of commitment that is not lost on his audience. It is as if he has no choice in the matter.

Within a year Brown had connected funk lyrically to the newly emergent black consciousness, specifically with the song "Say It Loud, I'm Black and I'm Proud." Around that time he made clear that he was "totally committed to black power, the kind that is achieved not through the muzzle of a rifle but through education and economic leverage." Brown believed in the bootstraps philosophy of BOOKER T. WASHINGTON, and like the 1960s civil rights activists JAMES FORMAN and FLOYD MCKISSICK, in 1972 he supported Richard Nixon, whose presidential platform advocated "black capitalism," in the form of federal loans to small black businesses.

Significantly, "Black and Proud" would be Brown's last Top Ten pop hit until 1985's "Living in America." Conversely, this was the beginning of his greatest success on the R&B charts. Between 1968 and 1974 Brown had forty-one R&B hits, thirty-two of which went to the Top Ten. This is extraordinary testimony to the meaning he held for the black community in the United States at the time. It would appear that as Brown's music became understood as more African, it was encoded or at least decoded by blacks and whites as having a value and aesthetic system that was largely outside the experience of most white Americans. Consequently, most white Americans found little they could relate to while, in direct contrast, black Americans embraced funk as one of the most meaningful expressive forms of the time. Brown's music also found a huge audience in Africa in the late 1960s and early 1970s, influencing the Nigerian star Fela Kuti, among other exponents of Afrobeat.

At the same time that Brown was personally dominating the R&B charts in the United States, he built up a stable of artists in his revue whom he recorded for King, Polydor, and his own People label. Among the most successful of these side projects were Vicki Anderson, Lyn Collins, Bobby Byrd, and his backing group, the JBs. Brown seemed to be an endless source of funky grooves, writing hits for himself and his stable of artists while developing legendary bands that included such luminaries as Bootsy Collins, Fred Wesley, Maceo Parker, Pee Wee Ellis, and the drummers Melvin Parker, Jabo Starks, and Clyde Stubblefield.

In the 1980s Brown and funk music fell out of fashion, only to be resurrected and revered by decade's end, owing to the inordinate number of times his earlier hits were sampled by many prominent rap artists. Despite a troubled personal life, Brown endured. He was married three times and rumors of spousal abuse were frequent. So too were his run-ins with the law, for drugs or gun possession, tax evasion, and assault. In one incident, in September 1988, police pursued Brown through South Carolina and Georgia and arrested him on a count of arrest and battery with intent to kill and a series of traffic offenses. Sentenced to six years in prison, Brown was released on probation in February 1991. In 1998 Brown was convicted of another drug-related offense and arrested for domestic violence in 2004.

Brown continued to tour, record, and earn the numerous accolades that might be expected of an elder statesman. He received the Grammy Lifetime Achievement Award in 1992 and was inducted into the Rock and Roll Hall of Fame in 1996. In 2003 he received a Kennedy Center Honor for his achievements and influence in popular music. He was even, in March 1997, recognized by the State Legislature of Georgia, a body not hitherto known for its funkiness. A joint House and Senate resolution declared him "the minister of the new super heavy funk," and credited James Brown with bringing "a spark of energy and excitement to an otherwise listless U.S. music scene." He died of congestive heart failure after being hospitalized for pneumonia, in Atlanta, on 25 December 2006.

FURTHER READING

Brown, James, and Bruce Tucker. *James Brown: The Godfather of Soul* (1986).

Brown, Geoff. *James Brown: A Biography* (1996).

Rose, Cynthia. *Living in America: The Soul Saga of James Brown* (1990).

ROB BOWMAN

Brown, Jeannette Elizabeth (13 May 1934–), organic chemist and educator, was born in the Bronx, New York, the only child of Ada May Fox, a homemaker, and Freddie Brown, a maintenance worker who later became a postal worker. Brown's education was obtained in various schools of New York, and she received her high school diploma from New Dorp High School, Staten Island, NewYork, in 1952. Upon completing high school, she continued her educational pursuits by enrolling at Hunter College of the City University of New York, which was free to eligible high school graduates. In 1956 she graduated with a B.A. in Chemistry and two years later earned her M.S. at the University of Minnesota, where she was the first African American woman to receive any degree in chemistry. In her two years at the university, she conducted research titled "A Study of Dye and Ylide Formation in Salts of 9-(p-Dimethylaminophenyl) Fluorene." Her research resulted in a compound that was white at room temperature and pink when heated above room temperature; this compound was possibly one of the very few compounds synthesized that appeared to be both a liquid and a solid and changed appearance at different temperatures. These types of compounds are called liquid crystals. This synthesis by Brown is important because this strange "stuff" called liquid crystals could be produced in large amounts for scientific research and other uses.

By the time she completed her M.S., industry in general was just opening up to African Americans. Prior to that period, most African Americans who became chemists worked for the federal government or at historically black colleges and universities since industry was not an option for many. She was hired at CIBA Pharmaceutical Company in 1958 where she worked for several years as a junior chemist. She was the second woman and the third African American hired by the company. After leaving CIBA, she accepted a position as an organic medicinal chemist at Merck Sharp and Dohme Research Laboratories, where she worked from 1969 to 1995 and was fortunate to serve as a member of a team that was very productive and appreciative of her talent and skills. When this team synthesized the Cilastatin sodium component of Primaxin, an antibiotic, Brown shared in the success in many ways. For example, her name was included as one of the authors of the publication about the synthesis, and she was invited to a dinner held for the team by the head of the laboratory to celebrate the success of the team. In addition to the article that she coauthored on this synthesis, she was author or coauthor of fourteen other scientific articles and five patents. One of the patents is in her name only. Her suggestions of new targets for development were respected as she conducted research on other drug candidates for human and animal health. Her tenure at Merck lasted twenty-five years.

In addition to conducting research and publishing her work in scientific journals, Brown served as a member of Merck's Black University Liaison Committee in 1978. This committee was charged with identifying African Americans for employment at Merck and encouraging black students to major in chemistry or biology and to earn graduate degrees. Brown was awarded the Merck Management Award for directing the carrying out of the charge of this committee, especially for her work in improving the chemistry department at Grambling University in Louisiana. From 1993 until 1995, while still employed at Merck, she went on a detail assignment to serve as a visiting professor at the New Jersey Institute of Technology (NJIT), where she helped write the NJIT Alliance for Minority Participation in Science proposal. Additionally, she served as the science adviser to the NJIT Urban Elementary Outreach Program, and she designed, developed, and coordinated the NJIT Trust K–8 Professor Development Program.

She also worked in a number of other educational capacities. Brown's appointment at NJIT was on a year-to-year basis as a visiting faculty member. Later, from 1998 to 2002, she served as the director of the Regional Center for the National Science Foundation–funded New Jersey Statewide Systemic Initiative. At this center the staff worked with minority students and their science teachers to increase their knowledge of science so that more students would choose to study science and engineering in college and work in those fields once they completed their studies. The teaching abilities of the teachers were made stronger so that they could help more students and appreciate science better. Also, Brown was responsible for improving mathematics and science education in Essex and Hudson counties, New Jersey, by implementing the programs of the statewide systemic initiative, which were designed to improve the teaching and learning of math and science, and she introduced these programs to teachers and administrators. She did this in her role as the New Jersey regional director of the Statewide Systemic Initiative in Science and Mathematics Education.

Brown became an active member of several professional societies: American Chemical Society (ACS), National Organization for the Professional Advancement of Black Chemists and Chemical Engineers (NOBCChE), Association for Women in Science (AWIS), American Association for the Advancement of Science (AAAS), New York Academy of Sciences, National Science Teachers Association (NSTA), New Jersey Science Teachers Association, New Jersey Science Leadership Association, and National Association of Science Writers. She was also a fellow of the WestEd National Academy for Science and Mathematics Leadership and a 2004 Société de Chimie Industrielle (American Section) fellow of the Chemical Heritage Foundation. As a fellow of the Chemical Heritage Foundation, Brown studied the history of African American women chemists.

Committed to broadening black participation in science and mathematics in the private sector, Brown has visited high schools to talk about the importance of science and mathematics, acting as a role model to students and as a career adviser to teachers and university students. She also has lectured at career-day programs and at special scientific outreach programs, and she has served as an ambassador to the Grambling University department of chemistry. As councilor for the North

Jersey Section of ACS for more than twenty-five years beginning in 1982, she has also served as a member of the Women Chemists Committee and a coordinator for the North Jersey Section Metro Women Chemists Committee. Nationally, she was chair of Project SEED from 1986 to 1988—an ACS educational program for disadvantaged high school students—and has worked as a member of the Local Section Activities Committees of ACS starting in 1989. From 2002 to 2006 she served as a member of the PERCY JULIAN Task Force of ACS, and beginning in 2005 she became a member of the Speakers Bureau. She served as a career counselor starting in 1995 and as a reviewer for proposals submitted to the National Science Foundation (NSF). From 1991 to 1998 she also served two terms as a member of the congressionally mandated NSF Committee on Equal Opportunities in Science and Engineering.

In 2001 Brown was among the few chosen to participate in the Iowa State University Women in Chemistry Project—an oral history project for the university's Archives of Women in Science and Engineering. In May 2002, while serving as regional coordinator for the New Jersey Statewide Systemic Initiative (a National Science Foundation–sponsored partnership to improve science and math education in Essex and Hudson counties; the partnership was among schools, colleges and universities, science centers and museums, businesses, and industry) at NJIT, she was presented with the Women Chemists Committee Regional Award for contributions to diversity. In 2004 she was named a scholar of the Chemical Heritage Foundation, where she completed a multimedia project focused on the development of a history of African American women chemists.

In 2005 her alma mater, University of Minnesota, placed her name on the Alumni Wall of Honor. That same year she received the ACS Award for encouraging disadvantaged students into careers in the chemical sciences, sponsored by the Camille and Henry Dreyfus Foundation—she was the second African American woman to receive an ACS award. She generously used the funds from the ACS national award to establish the Freddie and Ada Brown Award for African American and Native American middle and high school students. In 2006 she was presented the North Jersey ACS Harvey Russell Award for support to chemistry teachers. On 18 February 2007 she was one of ten persons honored as an AWIS fellow at the AAAS annual meeting in San Francisco, California.

FURTHER READING

"ACS 2005 National Award Winners," *Chemical & Engineering News*, 3 Jan. 2005.

"Association for Women in Science Announces Its 2007 Fellows," *AWIS Newsletter*, 18 Feb. 2007.

"Jeannette Brown Receives University of Minnesota Outstanding Achievement Award," *NOBCChE News* (Spring/May 2005).

"Preserving History of African-American Women Chemists," *Women Chemists* (Fall–Winter 2004).

Sweeney, L. (Tanya Zanish-Belcher, curator), "An Interview: Jeannette E. Brown," Women in Chemistry Oral History Project, Archives of Women in Science and Engineering Special Collections Department, Iowa State University (2001).

This article was written by Dr. Margaret E. M. Tolbert in her personal capacity. The views expressed in this article do not necessarily represent the views of the National Science Foundation or the United States.

MARGARET E. M. TOLBERT

Brown, Jesse (27 Mar. 1944–15 Aug. 2002), disability advocate and cabinet secretary, was born in Detroit, Michigan, but grew up in Chicago. He attended Catholic University in Washington, D.C., and Roosevelt College in Chicago. He graduated from Chicago City College and subsequently enlisted in the U.S. Marine Corps in 1963, serving in the Vietnam War. There he was seriously wounded when an enemy bullet shattered his right arm while he was on patrol in Da Nang, leaving him partially paralyzed. In a real sense, that injury defined the rest of Brown's career.

Upon leaving the Marine Corps in 1966 Brown joined the Disabled American Veterans (DAV), an advocacy group supporting the cause of veterans injured while in military service. The organization had been founded in 1920 and given a congressional charter in 1932 and was the official voice of America's service-connected disabled veterans, representing all of America's disabled veterans, their families, and survivors. Brown worked for the DAV from 1967 until 1988, moving to the organization's national headquarters in Washington, D.C., in 1973. He became the first African American executive director of the DAV and served in that capacity from 1989 until 1993. As executive director he earned the reputation of being the nation's keenest mind regarding veterans' benefits and services.

Because of that reputation, he was tapped by President Bill Clinton to serve as the secretary of veterans affairs in Clinton's first cabinet. During confirmation hearings Brown testified that his background in veterans' advocacy gave him "an intimacy with veterans' issues that can only come from hard work, every day, year in, year out, in a single field" (*Congressional Quarterly Almanac* [1993], 427). While some senators expressed concern that Brown was too close to veterans, warning that he could never please them, Brown was confirmed by voice vote, indicating no real opposition to his nomination. Representative Sonny Montgomery, Democrat of Mississippi, praised the appointment, saying it was the "best possible appointment in these crucial times" (*Washington Post*, 17 Aug. 2002). Brown became the second secretary of the department, which had been created during President George H. W. Bush's administration, and the first African American in the post. His military record made him a perfect choice for Clinton, who had been criticized during the 1992 campaign for avoiding military service during the Vietnam War.

Once in office, Brown became a tireless advocate for American veterans. He was fond of referring to himself as the secretary "for" Veterans and often said that he would win battles with Congress because "we hold the high moral ground" (*Washington Post*, 17 Aug. 2002). During the time that he was secretary, he opposed cuts that the Office of Management and Budget (OMB) had recommended to the president and for four consecutive years increased the budget of the Veteran's Administration (VA) as a percentage of the federal budget. He helped expand benefits for Vietnam and Persian Gulf War veterans who had been prisoners of war, exposed to Agent Orange or mustard gas, or who had suffered posttraumatic stress syndrome. He also increased benefits for women veterans and for children with ailments linked to their parents' service. Brown increased the efficiency of the VA, and even convinced veterans' groups to accept the closure of veterans' medical facilities, something that VA observers had thought nearly impossible. In exchange, however, Brown expanded VA coverage so that physicians were allowed to treat veterans for all of their ailments, not just injuries received in the line of duty.

After leaving office Brown founded Brown and Associates, a planning and marketing consulting firm. His expertise figured prominently in planning and marketing initiatives at a broad variety of companies, both domestic and international. He died in Warrenton, Virginia, following a long battle with amyotrophic lateral sclerosis (ALS), commonly known as Lou Gehrig's disease. More than one thousand mourners, including former president Clinton, then-current and former cabinet officials, lawmakers, and other dignitaries joined friends and family at a service held at Washington National Cathedral. "When we lost Jesse Brown, we lost one of the greatest veterans' advocates I have ever known, and I am deeply saddened by the loss of this great American," said the Senate Veterans' Affairs Committee chairman John D. Rockefeller IV. Brown himself said that he wanted to be remembered as "someone who made a difference in the quality of veterans' lives" (*Washington Post*, 17 Aug. 2002). He left behind a wife, Sylvia, his mother, his two children, and a granddaughter. To honor his service, the DAV established the Jesse Brown Memorial Youth Scholarship program to encourage young volunteers to play active roles in the Department of Veterans Affairs Voluntary Service programs.

FURTHER READING

Congressional Quarterly Almanac (1993).

Obituary: *Washington Post*, 17 Aug. 2002.

JAMES W. RIDDLESPERGER JR.

Brown, Jesse Leroy (13 Oct. 1926–4 Dec. 1950), the first black U.S. Navy pilot, was born in Hattiesburg, Mississippi, the son of John Brown, a sharecropper, and Julia Lindsey, a schoolteacher. The family worked from sunup to sundown and lived in a typical, unpainted, pine-board house with one story and a tin roof. Behind the house were a well, an outhouse, chicken and hog pens, and a vegetable garden. John Brown was a deacon in the Baptist church, where the family worshiped each Sunday.

Young Jesse fell in love with flying at age six, when his father took him to an air show, and he marveled at the white wing walkers, parachute jumpers, and acrobatic tricks performed by the pilots of the biwinged aircraft. His father didn't have the two dollars to let his son ride in a cockpit that day, but by the time he was seven Jesse was reading *Popular Aviation* magazine by kerosene lamp late into the night. Jesse was also fascinated by movies of World War I dogfights between American and German planes and decided that he wanted to be a fighter pilot. Whenever a plane from the dirt strip at nearby Palmer's Crossing flew overhead, the youngster would wave at it with his straw hat and yell, "That's where I'm going to be someday."

On Saturday afternoons Jesse could usually be found hiding near the dusty forty-foot-wide, five-hundred-yard runway at Palmer's Crossing. Though he was repeatedly chased away by Corley Yates, the field manager and mechanic, nothing could stop Jesse from watching the biplanes rush down the runway. This war between Corley Yates and Jesse Brown went on for years. Brown's school in Lux, Mississippi, consisted of only one room with eight rows of benches. Students from first grade to eighth grade assembled each day, batting bugs in summer and shivering in winter. The powerful influence of their mother ensured that all five Brown boys were excellent students. In 1938, when Jesse was one bench from finishing Lux, he began to deliver the *Pittsburgh Courier*, a black newspaper that one day ran a long article about the black man's struggle to enter military aviation. Reading it, twelve-year-old Jesse was furious at General Hap Arnold, chief of the U.S. Army Air Corps, who said, "Negro pilots cannot be used in our present Air Corps since this would result in having Negro officers in command of white enlisted men." When the *Courier* editorialized that there was a white belief that black men did not have "the brains or fortitude or aptitude to fly military planes," Jesse cut the article out, nailed it to the wall over his bed, and then wrote a letter to President Franklin Roosevelt asking why black pilots were excluded from the air corps.

Brown attended Eureka High School, making "A" grades, playing football and basketball, and starring in track. Graduating in 1944, he chose to enroll that September at Ohio State University, against the advice of his principal and friends, who wanted him to enroll in a black college in Mississippi. Brown wanted to test his abilities, however, and was prepared to withstand prejudice at the predominantly white university. He majored in engineering and joined the track team, but as always his great interest was flying. There was a navy V-5 program at the university, and Brown took the entrance exam after being told that no African American had ever entered Selective Flight Training. Three years later, having passed all tests, he prepared for entry into the Naval Air Training Command in Glenview, Illinois, by looking into a mirror and yelling at himself, "Nigger! Nigger! Nigger!" After two weeks of training, Brown made his solo flight in a dual cockpit "Yellow Peril" Stearman, a navy training biplane, executing three perfect landings.

Although his officer instructors often derided him, and though he almost flunked out of the arduous Pre-Flight School at Ottumwa, Iowa, because he couldn't swim, Brown persisted. Though

Glenview had been tough, it was easy compared to Pre-Flight, where Brown confronted every possible physical and mental test, the final being in a Dilbert Dunker to simulate an open ocean crash. His pre-flight instruction then continued at the Pensacola, Florida, Naval Air Station, where he flew a single-wing SNJ trainer to prepare for carrier landings. As the only African American among six-hundred-odd white midshipmen, Brown felt enormous pressure and often faced outright hostility from his instructors. One vowed, "No nigger is going to sit his ass in the cockpit of a Navy fighter." Each day was a struggle, and twice he had to appear before a special board to save his existence at Pensacola because of aerial mistakes.

Brown got some relief from the strain and loneliness when he married nineteen-year-old Daisy Pearl Nix in October 1947, even though that was forbidden by training regulation. If the union were discovered, he would be headed back to Lux within twenty-four hours. He found a home for Daisy in Pensacola through the church. He could talk to her, and they could discreetly meet. Brown struggled on the ground and in the air but finally made his first carrier landing on the USS *Wright* in the Gulf of Mexico on 17 June 1948, flying an SNJ trainer. After five landings, the *Wright's* loudspeaker rasped, "Midshipman Brown qualified." On 21 October, Brown, flying a Hellcat fighter, a super aircraft of its day, won his gold wings at Jacksonville Naval Air Station. The public information office put out a press release: First Negro Naval Aviator, along with a photo. *Life* magazine published his picture. But Daisy Brown, still hidden from the navy, and in her fourth month of pregnancy, couldn't perform the traditional pinning on of his wings.

In mid-January 1949, less than a month after the birth of his daughter, Pamela, Brown left for Quonset Point, Rhode Island, for his first assignment as a fighter pilot with Squadron 32 on the USS *Leyte*. On 26 April he was sworn into the navy as an ensign, and he began flying a Bearcat three to five hours a day. Later that year he began flying a Corsair, the navy's "killer" aircraft of World War II. Since they no longer needed to hide their marriage, the Browns also rented a house in Quonset Point and entered the social life of the air station. It was the happiest time in Brown's life. In June 1950, however, North Korea invaded South Korea, and President Harry Truman decided to take America into the Korean War.

On 4 December 1950 the carriers *Leyte* and *Philippine Sea* were stationed off the northeast coast of North Korea. For three desperate days Brown and his fellow pilots had been ordered to provide maximum air support, day and night, to fifteen thousand U.S. Marines fighting their way along the bloody, body-strewn, ice-bound road to Hungnam, North Korea. More than one hundred thousand Chinese troops surrounded the marines. That morning Brown dressed quickly in long johns, coveralls, a sweater, a rubber antiexposure suit, and fleece-lined boots and gloves and proceeded to his Corsair. He headed for the infamous Chosin Reservoir and the bloody road where marines were dying around the clock. Arriving over land, Brown and his flying partners dropped to five hundred feet to search for targets. As Brown and his comrades passed overhead, Chinese troops lying on their backs unseen in the snow fired upward. When a bullet hit Brown's fuel line, his wingman, Thomas Rudner, flying close by, walked him through the safety procedures they had learned in flight school. Meanwhile, U.S. planes began circling the area, ready to use every single bit of firepower to keep the communists at bay. It did not matter to Brown's fellow pilots that his skin was black. He was simply a gallant shipmate and friend.

Brown crashed uphill, out of control. With his plane skidding over the frozen ground, only his harness kept him from being a punching bag, as the huge engine and four-bladed propeller broke off and careened away, leaving a tangle of steel and wires in the cockpit. His fellow pilots kept circling, watching for a sign of life. Finally, Brown opened the canopy, which had jammed on impact, and waved, but he could not climb out. A piece of steel had jammed his knee in that narrow space, and escape was impossible.

Tom Rudner then made a decision against all combat regulations, one that could have earned him a court-martial for destroying a navy aircraft. He decided to risk his own life and crash land, hoping he could help before Brown's two-hundred-gallon gas tank exploded. Rudner put his Corsair down as close as possible to Brown's plane, knowing that the enemy troops on the rise might shoot both of them. Talking to Brown continually, Rudner packed snow into the area of the smoke and used his own radio to call in a helicopter. Rudner kept talking to Brown while the injured pilot drifted in and out of consciousness. At one point Brown said to Rudner, "Cut my leg off," but Rudner could not. Nor could Charlie Ward, the pilot of a Sikorsky rescue helicopter, because night had fallen, making it impossible for him to see.

A few minutes later, Brown told Rudner, "Tell Daisy how much I love her." He then took a shallow breath, and as his head slumped down on his chest, Rudner and Ward wept.

Aboard the *Leyte* there was shock and disbelief. The African American stewards on board ship had carefully made Brown's bunk each morning and made sure he got the best meals. They wept bitterly as a bugle played taps and marines fired volleys off the stern. Hudner persuaded Captain Sisson, his commanding officer, that Brown would not have approved a mission to recover his dead body if it meant risking the lives of others. Sisson therefore ordered two divisions to give Jesse Brown a "warrior's funeral." Within an hour seven Corsairs (six loaded with napalm), piloted by Brown's friends, took off for Somong-ni. Arriving there, one fighter dropped down to make a run over the two aircraft. The sun was out, and the sky was blue. Brown sat in his cockpit, snow dusting his hair. Then six aircraft loaded with napalm rose to ten thousand feet while the seventh continued to climb, almost straight up, and the radios connecting them heard, "Our Father who art in heaven, hallowed be Thy name." In roaring dives, the Corsairs released their napalm pods, and Brown vanished in sheets of fiery red.

FURTHER READING

Taylor, Theodore. *The Flight of Jesse Leroy Brown* (1998).

THEODORE TAYLOR

Brown, Jill (1949–), pilot, who made aviation history when she became the first African American woman to fly for a major passenger airline in the United States, the first to be admitted to the U.S. Navy's flight school, and the first in U.S. military history to qualify as a pilot.

Brown was born in Millersville, Maryland. Her family had taken up aviation as a hobby, and she learned to fly small planes with her parents—Gilbert Brown, who was a former U.S. Air Force instrument mechanic and also owned a building construction business, and Elaine Brown, an art resource teacher in the Baltimore public schools—when she was seventeen years old. For her eighteenth birthday, she received a Cherokee 180D airplane. In 1967 Brown flew her first solo flight in a Piper J-3 Cub. She had always dreamed of becoming a commercial pilot, but her mother advised her otherwise, and on her mother's advice, she majored in home economics at the University of Maryland. After graduation, in 1973, she took

a teaching job at Oakmont Regional High School outside Boston, Massachusetts, and kept in touch with a navy recruiter, as the dream of flying still weighed heavily on her mind. She soon realized that it would take more than a degree in home economics to fulfill an urge to be somebody.

Of the 49,694 airplane pilots in the nation in 1970, only 162 were black, and only five of these were women. In 1974 the U.S. Naval Air Force began accepting women for officer's training, and Brown was finally called to try out for naval officer's training school in Newport, Rhode Island. She knew that the military would provide extensive pilot training, so she signed up, but she soon discovered that the military was not yet ready for minorities. According to Brown, she and the navy were not compatible, and she dropped out of the program after six months. She was honorably discharged, but because the military experience had left a sour taste in her mouth, she decided that she would have to find a way to fund her future pilot training herself.

Brown returned to a teaching post in Baltimore, instructing inner-city youngsters in home economics through the spring of 1976. During a July 1978 interview with *Ebony* magazine, Brown noted that the magazine had played an important part in her success. She said that while reading the April 1976 issue of *Ebony*, she came across a story on Wheeler Airlines in Raleigh, North Carolina. The story in the magazine described how Captain Warren H. Wheeler, a pilot for Piedmont Airlines, was operating the nation's first scheduled, black-owned-and-operated airline during his off-duty hours.

Brown wrote to Captain Wheeler and asked for a job—she even offered to work without pay—then followed up with a telephone call. Wheeler called her back and invited her down to take a check ride with him on a B-737 jet the next day so that they could talk. Brown said that she knew Wheeler didn't need a copilot, but he wanted to help her, because he knew that she wanted to fly for a major airline. She started out working for him as a reservationist and was paid a $300 a-month salary to write tickets, but she flew for free when there was space available. Later she was made resident copilot, and she flew extra time in order to earn more hours in the air. While doing this job she logged 1,200 flying hours—the requirement for most major airlines at the time. In May 1978 she became a pilot, flying a Beechcraft 99 for Wheeler. Brown soon realized, however, that she was being assigned to more publicity shots as the first African American female airline pilot than she was to planes, so she resigned and on 2 October 1978 took a job in Detroit flying cargo for Zantop International Airlines.

In an earlier issue of *Ebony*, Brown had read about Evans McKay, an African American who was a vice president of Texas International Airlines. She figured that if Texas International was liberal enough to hire a black vice president, they would be liberal enough to hire a black woman pilot, and they were. When she left Wheeler Airlines, she had been as well qualified as any of the other applicants seeking to enroll in flight-training programs with major airlines, so she began sending out applications. She received an immediate response from Texas International Airlines and was invited for an interview, and she subsequently enrolled in the company's training program. At that time, Brown was one of six women in a class of thirty-eight to graduate as pilots from the Texas International Airlines training program, and her status caught the eyes of the national media. In 1978, still with Texas International, she also became the first African American woman to serve as a captain on a major commercial airline. There were only 110 black pilots flying for the airlines, including the five other women.

When asked about her tenacity during an *Ebony* magazine interview in 1978, Brown responded: "Someone once said that to be a success you must find a need, then fill that need. I felt women would someday have a chance in aviation, and I was determined to be ready for it."

FURTHER READING

Burgen, Michele. "Backstage," *Ebony* (July 1978).
Burgen, Michele. "Winging It at 25,000 Feet," *Ebony* (Aug. 1978).
Smith, Elizabeth Simpson. *Breakthrough: Women in Aviation* (1981).
Smith, Jessie Carney. *Black Firsts: 2,000 Years of Extraordinary Achievement* (1944).

CLARE J. WASHINGTON

Brown, Jim (17 Feb. 1936–), athlete, actor, and activist, was born James Nathaniel Brown on Saint Simons Island, Georgia, to Theresa and Swinton Brown, a onetime boxer, who abandoned Theresa and their son two weeks after his birth. A couple of years later Theresa departed for Long Island, New York, to take a domestic job, leaving Jim to be raised by his great-grandmother and grandmother, the latter an alcoholic. By 1944 Theresa

Jim Brown, on the field in an undated handout photo. (AP Images.)

had saved enough money to send for Jim, and they were reunited in Manhasset, Long Island, for the first time in six years. Despite the usual friction of being the new kid—he was once accused by his peers of fighting dirty—Brown eventually distinguished himself athletically. He gained the attention of a local policeman, who lent Brown keys to the high school gym so that the youth could organize Police Boys' Club games whenever he and his friends wanted to play. At Manhasset High School, Jim became a starter on the football team at the age of fourteen; he also played basketball, track, and baseball. By the end of his senior year he had tallied thirteen varsity letters, earning All-State honors in all but baseball; he averaged thirty-eight points per game in basketball (including a high game score of fifty-five) and 14.9 yards per carry in football. A self-proclaimed "gang warlord" in high school, Brown managed to keep himself on the academic honor roll and graduated in 1953 with more than forty athletic scholarships from which to choose.

Brown decided instead upon Syracuse University in upstate New York. Syracuse had not offered him a scholarship, but a family friend secured enough support from Manhasset businessmen to bankroll his freshman year, confident that he would quickly play his way into a scholarship. He did not accomplish this until his sophomore year, when a teammate's injury opened up a spot for him on the football team. It was a breakout year, as he also scored fifteen points per game in basketball, ran track, and played lacrosse for the first time. In track he competed in the decathlon, placing fifth nationally. Though this was good enough to qualify for the 1956 Olympics, Brown declined, because he felt it was dishonest to devote too much time to anything other than his scholarship sport, football. Altogether he would earn ten letters in three years across four sports; he was named All-American once in football and twice in lacrosse. In the latter sport, he became the first African American to play in the storied North-South game, though he only needed to play part of it to account for half of the North's output, scoring five goals and assisting on two, in a 14–10 victory.

Graduating with a degree in physical education, Brown planned to pursue coaching when his athletic career was over. In the meantime, he ignored repeated advances from major league baseball teams, as well as the Syracuse Nationals in basketball, and he declined a three-year, $150,000 deal offered by a Syracuse promoter to become a professional boxer. He finally decided on a $15,000 deal with the Cleveland Browns of the National Football League (NFL).

As a fullback in 1957 Brown led the league in rushing, totaling 942 yards and leading Cleveland to the Eastern Division Championship while picking up Rookie of the Year honors. The following year he increased his yardage per carry by 1.2 yards to 5.9, scored eighteen touchdowns, and was named Player of the Year. He never missed a game due to injury, and he became such a dominating presence in his sport that he headed a players' revolt against Cleveland's coach, Paul Brown, in 1962. Paul Brown was subsequently fired, and the team's new coach for 1963, Blanton Collier, better utilized his star by designing plays that granted Brown more running room along the line of scrimmage. Brown responded with his best season by collecting more than a mile in total yards (1,863 at 6.5 yards per carry) and scoring fifteen touchdowns; he performed similarly the next year, and Cleveland won the NFL Championship. In 1965, Brown's final season, he averaged more than five yards per carry for the third consecutive year, scored twenty-one touchdowns, and took home his second Most Valuable Player award. He played in the Pro Bowl every single year and led the league in rushing for eight of his nine seasons.

The following autumn, however, saw Brown in Europe, filming a lead role in *The Dirty Dozen* (1967), a big-budget Hollywood picture about American convicts who become highly trained World War II soldiers. He had already appeared two years earlier in *Rio Concho* (1964), and when the Cleveland Browns owner Art Modell threatened to cut him if he did not report to training camp immediately, Brown retired to devote his full energies to a movie career. For *100 Rifles* in 1969 Brown was paid $200,000 and starred opposite Raquel Welch, with whom he filmed the first love scene between a black man and a white woman ever captured in a Hollywood picture. These three movies, along with *Ice Station Zebra* (1968), were his most successful mainstream projects.

As Brown made the transition from football star to movie star, the press became increasingly concerned with his personal life, particularly after his marriage to Sue Jones ended in the late 1960s. The couple, who had married in 1958, had three children. Brown, a regular on the Hollywood social scene, had numerous encounters with the L.A. Police Department—almost all of them involving questionable behavior by both parties—culminating in Brown's arrest when his girlfriend fell from a second-floor balcony during a domestic dispute, though she never pressed charges. A year later Brown was arrested for felonious assault in a hit-and-run traffic incident; the case was dismissed during trial. In 1978 he was found guilty of misdemeanor battery for punching a player on a golf course, and in 1986 he was again arrested in a domestic dispute, though again the charges were dropped.

In the 1960s and 1970s Brown commenced a number of charitable endeavors, most of which centered around the Black Economic Union, a collective of African American business owners dedicated to pooling and recommitting their wealth to projects such as teenage education, job training, and rehabilitation. In 1971 he was inducted into the NFL Hall of Fame, though nearly twenty years later he would threaten to withdraw on behalf of historically neglected black players. (Brown would eventually be inducted into the College Football Hall of Fame and the Lacrosse Hall of Fame, as well.) He continued making movies such as the "blaxploitation" films *Slaughter* (1972) and *Slaughter's Big Rip-Off* (1973) and the all-black western *Take a Hard Ride* (1975), but they failed to match his earlier commercial successes. In the early 1980s Brown started a movie production company, Ocean Productions, with his friend RICHARD PRYOR, but Pryor soon fired him.

In 1973 the Buffalo Bills' O. J. SIMPSON broke Brown's rushing record for a single season, and in 1984 Brown's career rushing record fell to the Chicago Bears' WALTER PAYTON. But Brown's athletic legacy was already established, and four years later he founded the Amer-I-Can Program Inc., a nonprofit organization dedicated to reaching gang members and prisoners; in 1992 Amer-I-Can played an essential role in securing a truce between L.A.'s rival gangs, the Bloods and the Crips. By 2000 Amer-I-Can had spread to twelve cities and built a reputation for developing innovative strategies to rehabilitate prisoners and troubled youths. Brown's own troubles with the authorities continued, however. He was sentenced to three years probation in October 1999 for smashing the car of his second wife, Monique Brown, and in 2002 he served four months in prison for refusing to undergo court-ordered domestic violence counseling. Brown appeared in a few more Hollywood productions, most notably as a defensive coordinator in Oliver Stone's football epic, *Any Given Sunday* (1999). It was an ironic turn for an offensive player of whom one opponent had said, "the best way to tackle Brown is to hold on and wait for help."

FURTHER READING

Brown, Jim, with Myron Cope. *Off My Chest* (1964).
Brown, Jim, with Steve Delsohn. *Out of Bounds* (1969).
Toback, James. *Jim: The Author's Self-Centered Memoir on the Great Jim Brown* (1971).

DAVID F. SMYDRA JR.

Brown, Joan Myers (25 Dec. 1931–), dancer, teacher, choreographer, and community activist, was born in Philadelphia, Pennsylvania, the only child of Nellie W. Lewis, a research and chemical engineer during World War II, and Julius T. Myers, a chef. Lewis's determination to pursue her interest in chemistry provided a model of high expectations and self-confidence for Brown that enabled her to venture into a world closed to African Americans in the 1940s and 1950s.

Brown was encouraged by a high school teacher to join an after-school classical ballet dance club and later took lessons in a private studio. Because of de facto desegregation and racism, Brown could not enroll in any of the local dance schools for white students, but this did not stop her from pursuing her dream. Instead she studied a variety of dance forms at the Sydney School of Dance in Philadelphia, a school for black dancers. Upon her graduation from high school Brown pursued a career in dance rather than a more formal education. In 1949 she won a scholarship through her Cotillion performances (formal dance productions). The scholarship allowed Brown to move to New York City in 1950 and to enroll in the KATHERINE DUNHAM School of Dance, where she remained for two years.

Brown then joined the Anjoel Dancers and performed in clubs such as the Latin Casino and others located in Atlantic City, New Jersey. In 1951 Brown married Fred Johnson, but the marriage was short-lived, and the couple divorced shortly after the Korean War. In 1955 Brown joined the Savar Dancers, an American dance troupe begun in Montreal, Canada, and patterned in the style of the *Creole Follies*, a traveling revue show. In 1958 CAB CALLOWAY recruited the dance troupe to work in his Miami Beach *Cotton Club Revue*. Brown danced with the revue for three years, after which she performed in different revues with Larry Steele and PEARL BAILEY. Brown married Max G. Brown in 1960, and the couple had two daughters, Marlisa and Dannielle, before divorcing in 1981.

Since opportunities for a talented African American classical ballet dancer in the 1950s were few, Brown decided to teach dance to African American children. While continuing to dance and choreograph with the *Club Harlem Revue* in Atlantic City, she founded her first school in 1960. Ten years later she founded the Philadelphia Dance Company, also known as Philadanco, and the accompanying Philadelphia School of Dance Arts.

Philadanco, a pilot for Pennsylvania's Comprehensive Education Training Act (CETA) Program, established an instruction and training model that incorporated successful work ethic and discipline and enabled Brown to pay her dancers. In 1973 Philadanco was one of the first companies to receive a National Endowment for the Arts Expansion Arts grant. One of only six dance companies nationally to pay its dancers fifty-two weeks of the year, Philadanco was also the first African American dance company to do so. Drawing from the work of Katherine Dunham and Lester Horton, the company and school incorporated jazz and African-influenced techniques as well as classical and modern ballet into its dancing.

As the company grew, Brown turned over the choreographic responsibilities to other guest artists, providing opportunities for choreographers who had worked in the business for many years to showcase their talent. Gene Hill Sagan was a favorite choreographer with the company, and his works are considered classics within the company repertoire. Other choreographers included CARMEN DE LAVALLADE, GEOFFREY HOLDER, TALLEY BEATTY, BEBE MILLER, and Ron Brown. *My Science*, a dance set expressly for Philadanco by Miller, examines how the imagination and science act as catalysts for each other. *Mother*, created by Ron Brown, is a celebration of women.

In 1981 the company was the first in Philadelphia to purchase its own corporate headquarters and studio facilities, with funding provided by the NEA, the William Penn Foundation, and through a private donation from the Philadelphia-based music producer Kenny Gamble. In the same year the company was one of only fifteen organizations awarded the National Choreography Planning Grant, and in 1986 the company created the first artist-housing program in the city for its principal dancers. A newly renovated studio housed Philadanco and the Dance Arts School. Further, the renovation of three houses for dancer residencies set into motion the eventual total rehabilitation of the houses located on the street.

In 1988 Brown organized the International Conference on Blacks in Dance, the first such organization of its kind. Brown saw the need for black dance companies to align with each other for creative and financial support. In 1991 the conference became the International Association of Blacks in Dance (IABD), designed to preserve and promote dance by persons of African ancestry or origin through worldwide membership. It was responsible for establishing important dance archives with the National African American Historical and Cultural Museum in Wilberforce, Ohio, and the African American Museum in Philadelphia and Howard University. The IABD continues to serve as a support system for African American dance companies in the United States and abroad.

Brown was responsible for influencing and training hundreds of artists. The Philadelphia Dance Arts School and the performing company were considered safe havens to youths and helped to provide adults with a sense of community. Philadanco performed throughout the United States, Europe, Asia, and the Caribbean as well as at the Kennedy Center and Lincoln Center and the American Dance Festival. It has been involved in collaborations with well-known organizations and performers both inside and outside Philadelphia, including the Philadelphia Orchestra, the DUKE ELLINGTON Orchestra, LOU RAWLS, and TEDDY PENDERGRASS. Individual Philadanco members went on to perform with the ALVIN AILEY Dance Company and in numerous Broadway shows. In 2000 Philadanco was invited to establish permanent residency at the Kimmel Performing Arts Center in Philadelphia.

Brown was recognized by a number of organizations for her artistic accomplishments, community activism, and leadership. Over the years she was honored with a Kennedy Center award, the Theodore L. Hazlett Memorial Award from the Pennsylvania Council on the Arts, and a Philip Morris New Work Fund Award. She also received an honorary doctorate from the University of the Arts in 1994. In addition to her roles at Philadanco, Brown held faculty positions at the University of the Arts, Howard University, and Temple University. Brown's faculty positions provided Philadanco dancers with free or reduced tuition. Reciprocally, students who interned with the company received academic credit. Brown served as a consultant for the Rockefeller Foundation's Arts and Humanities Program along with other foundations and performing arts centers. She was honored as a Dance Living Legend by New York-area presenters in tribute to five nationwide African American pioneer women founders of modern dance companies rooted in black communities. Throughout her career Brown made it her mission to bring the culture, music, history, and heritage of Africans and African Americans to the world.

FURTHER READING

Clark, Veve, and Sara Johnson. *Kaiso!: Writings by and about Katherine Dunham* (2006).

Defrantz, Thomas F. *Dancing Many Drums: Excavations in African American Dance* (2001).

Emery, Lynne Fauley. *Black Dance in the United States from 1619 to 1970* (1972).

BARBARA TOOMER DAVIS

Brown, Joe (18 May 1925–21 Nov. 1997), boxer, was born in Baton Rouge, Louisiana. Little is known about his early life or his parents, except that the family lived on the brink of poverty.

Brown worked a number of different jobs—carpentry among them—before beginning his boxing career in 1943 in New Orleans, winning a four-round decision. Almost immediately, however, his participation in the professional sport was cut short when he was drafted to fight in World War II. Brown spent nearly two years in the U.S. Navy—most of it in the Pacific Theater—during which time he continued to box, finally winning the All-Service Lightweight Championship before his discharge in 1945. Following his return to civilian life, in 1946 Brown threw himself back into professional prizefighting, averaging from seven to twelve fights a year, sometimes with only a week's rest between bouts. Despite his enthusiasm and seemingly limitless energy his career did not get off to a particularly auspicious start. From 1946 through 1948 his record was a lackluster fifteen wins (only three by knockout), eight losses, and four draws. Most of his opponents were local New Orleans fighters, but he did manage to land two big fights in 1947. In April of that year he fought and defeated Jimmy Carter, who would go on to win the lightweight championship four years later. One month later he fought the legendary Sandy Saddler, who was less than a year away from winning the featherweight crown. The hard-punching Saddler knocked Brown out in three rounds.

After this slow start, and as he began to fight more of his bouts away from New Orleans, Brown's career began to take off in 1949. Indeed Brown became a well-traveled fighter, boxing in Chicago, St. Paul, Cincinnati, and Philadelphia. He even traveled to Australia for four bouts in 1950. Again maintaining a furious pace Brown won forty-five bouts and lost only eight from 1949 through late 1956. On 2 May 1956 he fought the lightweight champion Wallace "Bud" Smith in a non-title contest held in Houston, Texas, and took a ten-round decision. The performance earned Brown a title shot, and he took full advantage of the opportunity, winning a lopsided decision over Smith in a fifteen-round rematch in August of that year. After nearly eleven years of continuous boxing, and nearly seventy fights, the thirty-year-old Brown—who had by this time acquired the nickname "Old Bones"—was lightweight champion of the world.

Over the course of the next five and a half years Brown successfully defended his title eleven times—a record for consecutive defenses of the lightweight crown that stood for seventeen years. He also fought eleven nontitle bouts to maintain his always busy boxing schedule. In spite of his record of success Brown did not achieve the fame and fortune enjoyed by many other champion boxers, in some large part due to the relative quality of Brown's opposition during his years as lightweight king. In his nearly six years as champion Brown mostly fought unknown challengers. Only two of the men he faced were themselves champion boxers: Smith, who Brown knocked out in a 1957 rematch, and Ralph Dupas, who was knocked out in six rounds and very briefly held the junior middleweight champion in 1963. Such lackluster opponents meant that Brown fought most of his championship fights in second- and third-rate venues. For example, Brown never fought in the mecca of boxing, Madison Square Garden. And during a time when boxing was a television staple, Brown's fights in places such as Houston, Denver, or Albuquerque attracted little media attention. In addition Brown's style, while celebrated by boxing purists, lacked the power that sparked fan excitement. He won by knockout in less than 50 percent of his victories. Tall and lanky, Brown frustrated his opponents with odd angles and a tight defense. Those able to penetrate that defense, however, often found Brown susceptible to being floored, as when the unheralded Ray Portilla knocked Brown out in six rounds in a 1960 non-title fight.

In April 1962 the nearly thirty-seven-year-old Brown ran up against the tough former junior welterweight champion, Carlos Ortiz. A decade younger than Brown, Ortiz dominated the fight, winning a fifteen-round decision and ending Brown's run as lightweight champion. Brown never again fought in a world championship fight. Nevertheless he kept fighting for eight more years. A heavily traveled fighter before his loss to Ortiz, he now became an absolute globetrotter. From 1963 through his last fight in 1970 Brown fought in England, Mexico, Argentina, Brazil, Venezuela, Panama, South Africa, Colombia, Puerto Rico, Italy, Finland, and France. As a former champion, Brown still held some appeal to fight promoters, but it was clear that he was now simply an opponent for younger fighters or local favorites. Brown fought forty-six times after the loss to Ortiz, winning just twenty bouts, losing twenty-four, and twice fighting to a draw. Finally in 1970, at the age of forty-five, "Old Bones" stepped away from the ring and announced his retirement.

The International Boxing Hall of Fame opened its doors in 1989, but Brown had to wait another seven years before being inducted in 1996. Just a year after joining the boxing elite, Brown passed away in New Orleans at the age of seventy-two.

FURTHER READING

Ashe, Arthur R., Jr. *A Hard Road to Glory: A History of the African American Athlete since 1946* (1988).

"Joe 'Old Bones' Brown," in *Encyclopedia of African-American Culture and History*, vol. 1 (1996).

MICHAEL L. KRENN

Brown, John (1810?–1876), fugitive slave and slave narrative author, was born in Southampton County, Virginia, the son of slaves Joe and Nancy. For most of his life as a slave he was called Fed or Benford. When he was about ten years old he and his mother were moved to nearby Northampton County, North Carolina. Eighteen months later he was sold alone and sent to Georgia, never again to see any of his kinfolk.

Bought by the ambitious and quick-tempered Thomas Stevens, Fed grew to maturity on a farm in central Georgia near the state capital at Milledgeville. Stevens drove his slaves hard, often employing whippings and other brutal punishments. Gradually Stevens accumulated much land and more than twenty slaves, becoming a "planter" by federal census standards. In the 1820s Stevens expanded his family enterprises into DeKalb County, near Cherokee territory in northwestern Georgia, and when these Indians were driven west in the late 1830s, he settled in Cass (later Bartow) County, northwest of modern Atlanta. Fed went with his master, and when Stevens died in 1840 his considerable estate, now including more than forty slaves, was divided among his heirs. Fed became the property of twenty-two-year-old Decature Stevens, an even harsher and more erratic master. Fed determined to escape slavery.

The most influential person in Fed's life, the man who taught him to love freedom, was a slave named John Glasgow. Born a free black in British Guiana, Glasgow became a sailor in the British merchant marine and married an Englishwoman from Liverpool. On a voyage to Savannah, Glasgow made the mistake of going ashore, where Georgia law took effect. As a foreign free black he was interned in the city jail. Several weeks later, when his ship sailed without him, he was sold as a slave. Glasgow became the property of Thomas Stevens. Free all his life, he could not adjust to slavery, and brutal beatings left him crippled. But he planted the image of freedom in England in the mind of the provincial, uneducated young Fed.

Fed finally ran away from Decature Stevens. Caught in Tennessee when his white accomplice betrayed him, he was brought home to face harsh punishment. But in the mid-1840s he ran away again. He had no idea how to reach England, and he ended up in a slave pen in New Orleans with the new name Benford. There he was sold to Theodoric J. "Jepsey" James, who owned rich cotton land in Washington County, Mississippi, and ninety-five slave laborers. The environment was primitive and the work exhausting on the James plantation, and after only three months Benford ran for freedom again.

This time he understood that he could reach free country by heading north up the nearby Mississippi River. Traveling by night and hiding by day, Benford reached St. Louis, Missouri, in three months. Then he crossed over into Illinois, got directions from a free black, and headed for Vandalia. A few days later another black man gave him a free pass made out to John Brown, the name that Benford carried for the rest of his life. After spending two weeks in a black community near Terre Haute, Indiana, Brown walked toward Indianapolis and got help from Quakers involved in the Underground Railroad. They sent him on to Marshall, Michigan, where he worked as a carpenter in the black community for a year. Then Brown moved to Detroit, where he joined Cornish miners and worked as a carpenter for eighteen months until his English friends returned home. Brown planned to follow them, but first he went to Canada and worked for almost six months in a sawmill at the Dawn Institute, a vocational training school for runaway slaves from the United States.

In August 1850 Brown sailed on a ship bound for Liverpool and soon rejoined his miner friends in Redruth, Cornwall. After two months he moved to Bristol and then to Heywood in Lancashire, still working as a carpenter. But he encountered strong racism, and in the spring of 1851 he went to London, where he lived for the remainder of his life. There he contacted the British and Foreign Anti-Slavery Society, whose secretary, Louis Alexis Chamerovzow, was particularly impressed with Brown's plain, direct description of American slavery.

The society carefully checked Brown's story for authenticity and then sent him on a speaking tour. British audiences responded well to Brown's story, especially to the sad story of John Glasgow. For a while Brown's speaking fees supplemented his carpentry wages, allowing him to live frugally in a boardinghouse in a working-class area of London. The British and Foreign Anti-Slavery Society's *Anti-Slavery Reporter* ran an account of Glasgow's tragedy on 1 July 1853, and other British journals repeated it. The *Leeds Anti-Slavery Series* covered it in tract 89, and *Frederick Douglass' Paper* and a few other American journals also repeated the story. In 1854 Brown and his abolitionist friends took a notarized account of Glasgow's life to the British Foreign Office, but inquiries by consuls in Charleston and Savannah led nowhere.

A year later the British and Foreign Anti-Slavery Society published *Slave Life in Georgia: A Narrative of the Life, Sufferings, and Escape of John Brown, a Fugitive Slave, Now in England.* This small, 250-page volume included the Glasgow material and also covered Fed–Benford–John Brown's entire life. Brown himself was illiterate, and so Chamerovzow wrote the book in standard middle-class English. However, the story is Brown's, the authentic autobiography of a real man and a real slave.

A second limited edition was soon published, and it was also translated into German. Americans were already familiar with fugitive slave narratives, so *Slave Life* drew little attention in the United States even though it was one of the few narratives that focused on the Deep South. Its limited royalties augmented Brown's income for a while. Soon he married an Englishwoman and became an herbalist in London, where he died. An ordinary man, Brown told an extraordinary story of black bondage in white America.

FURTHER READING

Brown, John. *Slave Life in Georgia: A Narrative of the Life, Sufferings, and Escape of John Brown, a Fugitive Slave* (1855, repr. 1972, 1991).

Boney, F. N. "The Blue Lizard: Another View of Nat Turner's Country on the Eve of Rebellion," *Phylon* 31 (1970).

Boney, F. N. "Doctor Thomas Hamilton: Two Views of a Gentleman of the Old South," *Phylon* 28 (1967).

Boney, F. N. "Slaves as Guinea Pigs: Georgia and Alabama Episodes," *Alabama Review* 37 (1984).

Boney, F. N. "Thomas Stevens: Antebellum Georgian," *South Atlantic Quarterly* 72 (1973).

This entry is taken from the *American National Biography* and is published here with the permission of the American Council of Learned Societies.

F. N. BONEY

Brown, John Mifflin (8 Sept. 1817–16 Mar. 1893), African Methodist Episcopal (AME) bishop, was born in Cantwell's Bridge, New Castle County, Delaware. Little is known of his family or early childhood. He lived in Cantwell's Bridge until he was ten. He then moved to Wilmington, Delaware, where he lived for two years with the family of William A. Seals, a Quaker. At Cantwell's Bridge, he attended a predominantly white private school. His older sister encouraged him to move to Philadelphia, Pennsylvania, where he lived with and worked for the attorney Henry Chester, who tutored him and provided him with limited religious training. Brown attended St. Thomas Colored Protestant Episcopal Church in Philadelphia.

In January 1836 Brown became a member of Bethel AME Church in Philadelphia and began private studies under the Reverend John M. Gloucester to prepare for the ministry. He also studied barbering and worked as a barber in Poughkeepsie, New York, and New York City between 1836 and 1838. In 1838 he studied at Wesleyan Academy in Wilbraham, Massachusetts. In 1841–1842 he studied at Oberlin College in Ohio but did not complete a degree. He moved to Detroit in 1844 and opened the first school for African American children in that city. After the death of a local AME pastor, Brown was appointed acting minister, serving from 1844 to 1847. His success in the pastorate led to rapid advancement in denominational affairs. He joined the AME Ohio Conference, was ordained a deacon, was assigned to the AME church in Columbus, Ohio, and was appointed principal of Union Seminary, which was the first school owned and operated by the AME Church.

In 1852 Brown became pastor at Allen Station AME Church in Pittsburgh, Pennsylvania, and joined the Indiana Conference. In February of that year he married Mary Louise Lewis; they had eight children. Bishop DANIEL A. PAYNE commissioned Brown to participate in a mission to New Orleans, Louisiana, where, over a five-year period, Brown took responsibility for building the Morris Brown Chapel. He purchased Trinity Chapel and started congregations in Algiers and Covington, serving as pastor of St. James AME Church. During his mission to New Orleans, he was imprisoned five times for allowing slaves to attend religious services. In April 1857 he requested a transfer and was reassigned to Asbury Chapel in Louisville, Kentucky. In May 1858 he was transferred to Bethel AME Church in Baltimore, Maryland. He added seven hundred members to the Baltimore congregation. He also served pastorates at the Ebenezer AME Church and at the Brite Street AME Church in Baltimore.

Brown accompanied Bishops Payne and Wayman on their mission to Virginia and established St. John's AME Church in Norfolk. He was elected corresponding secretary of the Parent Home and Foreign Missionary Society in 1864 and successfully raised over $10,000 to establish AME churches and schools in the southern United States.

In recognition of his exceptional organizational abilities, Brown was elected an AME bishop at the General Conference in Washington, D.C., and was consecrated on 25 May 1868. His first assignment (1868–1872) was to the Seventh Episcopal District (South Carolina, Georgia, Florida, and Alabama). In 1871 he was instrumental in establishing Payne Institute (later Allen University) in south Carolina. He was assigned to the Sixth District (Tennessee, Arkansas, Louisiana, and Texas) from 1872 to 1876, and he organized the west Texas, south Arkansas, west Tennessee, Denver (Colorado), Columbia (South Carolina), and north Georgia conferences and set the groundwork for an AME college in Waco, Texas (later Paul Quinn College). From 1876 to 1880 he served the Third Episcopal District (Baltimore, Virginia, North Carolina, and South Carolina); from 1880 to 1884 he served the First Episcopal District (Philadelphia, New York, New Jersey, and New England); and from 1884 to 1888 he served the Fourth Episcopal District (Missouri, Kansas, Illinois, Iowa, and California). His last assignment (1888–1892) was to the Fourth Episcopal District, which had been restructured to include Indiana, Illinois, Michigan, and Iowa.

In 1878 Brown organized and raised funds for the Liberian Mission Church. He was a supporter of the Back to Africa movement and a strong advocate for the ordination of women. He was a delegate to the World Methodist Ecumenical Conference held in London, England, in 1881 and again in Washington, D.C., in 1891. He died in Washington, D.C.

Brown's nearly twenty-five years as a bishop had a profound impact on his denomination. Bishop Henry Tanner described him as "more of an Episcopal than a Methodist by temperament." Brown's keen organizational skills and abilities as a fund-raiser did much to foster the dynamic growth of AME churches throughout the United States, Africa, and the Caribbean.

FURTHER READING

Campbell, James T. *Songs of Zion: The African Methodist Episcopal Church in the United States and South Africa* (1995).

Dvorak, Katherine L. *An African-American Exodus: The Segregation of the Southern Churches* (1991).

Wright, Richard R. *The Bishops of the African Methodist Episcopal Church* (1963).

Wright, Richard R., ed. *The Centennial Encyclopedia of the African Methodist Episcopal Church, Philadelphia, Pa.* (1916).

This entry is taken from the *American National Biography* and is published here with the permission of the American Council of Learned Societies.

STEPHEN D. GLAZIER

Brown, Josephine (1839–?), author and educator, was born in Buffalo, New York, to abolitionist and author WILLIAM WELLS BROWN and Elizabeth Schooner. The small family moved to Farmington, New York, in 1845. Her father, soon to be famous as the author of a successful slave narrative and an abolitionist lecturer, separated from her mother soon after, and moved to Boston with Josephine and her older sister Clarissa. Elizabeth Brown reportedly died in January 1851. During the years surrounding the 1847 publication of Brown's *Narrative* and his 1849 journey to Europe (after refusing to have his freedom purchased), the sisters stayed in New Bedford with the family of local activist NATHAN JOHNSON (a friend of FREDERICK DOUGLASS) and attended school.

Josephine and Clarissa went to London to join their father in June 1851 aboard the steamer *America* under the care of Reverend Charles Spear—a journey they shared with British abolitionist George Thompson. Soon after, on 13 August, they were relocated to a boarding school in Calais, France. Their father visited the sisters in January of 1852, but much of his time was consumed with lecturing and writing. After close to a year in Calais, Josephine and Clarissa returned to England, attended celebrations commemorating the anniversary of West Indian emancipation with their father, and were admitted to the elite and innovative Home and Colonial School in London, which was dedicated to teacher training.

Both Clarissa and Josephine passed the Home and Colonial School's examinations in December 1853. Clarissa took a job at a school in the small village of Berden, Essex, and little is known of her later life. Josephine, not yet fifteen, was given a post at the East Plumstead School in the London suburb of Plumstead-Woolwich. In a 27 April 1854 letter published in the 26 May 1854 *Liberator*, Brown reported that she had over a hundred pupils (including some older than she) as well as an older assistant. Further, she said she was "fond of teaching." Nonetheless, later in 1854, she decided to return to France to further her education; there, she began work on her *Biography of an American Bondman*, the story of her father's life. With characteristic humility, she asserted in her preface that she started the volume to "satisfy" the "curiosity" of her "fellow students" and decided to finish it only on finding that Brown's *Narrative* was out of print.

William Wells Brown had already returned to the United States in the interim—having finally agreed to have his freedom purchased and thus remove himself from the dangers of the Fugitive Slave Law—and Josephine Brown followed. She arrived at Boston on 10 August 1855, and, while she did not see her father much during the next months, at the end of the year, she began an unprecedented period of working with him. Advertisements in the *Liberator* in December of 1855 and January of 1856 noted, in listing an eighteen-town lecturer tour, that "Mr. Brown's daughter will accompany him, and speak in some of the above places." The 25 January 1856 *Liberator* said that she "already promises to be an effective pleader for those in bondage" and cited "The Bards of Freedom" as one of her lecture titles.

That same issue of the *Liberator* noted the December 1855 publication of her *Biography* of her father by respected Boston publisher Robert F. Wallcutt. The 104-page volume was one of the earliest biographies written by an African American woman and remains a key source for understanding Brown's life. Undoubtedly, the lecture tour was designed in part to promote sales of the book. However, Brown biographer William Edward Farrison reports that "apparently Josephine ceased traveling with her father after February" when his tour expanded outside of Massachusetts "and returned to England soon afterwards" (275). Scholars have found little about Josephine Brown after this point.

FURTHER READING

Andrews, William L., ed. *Two Biographies by African American Women* (1988).

Farrison, William Edward. *William Wells Brown, Author and Reformer* (1969).

ERIC GARDNER

Brown, Kate (1840–Mar. 1883), retiring room attendant, activist, most renowned for winning the 1873 Supreme Court Case *Railroad Company v. Brown*, was born Katherine Brown in Virginia. There are many variations of her name; in some documents, she is referred to as "Catherine Brown," "Katherine Brown," "Kate Brown," or "Kate Dodson." In the *New York Times* article "Washington, Affairs at the National Capital," her name appears as "Kate Dostie." Very few records of Brown's life survive today; as a result, much of her childhood and personal life remains unknown.

Kate Brown's recorded personal life begins with her marriage to Jacob Dodson. Jacob Dodson had a colorful past. Born in 1825, Dodson was a freeman. He spent most of his early life as a servant for the Missouri senator Thomas Hart Benton, but in 1843 Dodson began to accompany John C. Fremont, son-in-law of Senator Benton and a military officer, on expeditions to the west. In the late 1850s, Dodson was given a job at the Senate and settled down in Washington, D.C. Not long after, Dodson met Brown, and the two were married. Jacob Dodson brought two children into the family from a previous marriage, but Kate Brown never had children. Although Jacob was quite responsible in the early years of the marriage, the relationship quickly deteriorated. By 1866, Jacob became an alcoholic, had frequent affairs with other women and even went as far as threatening to shoot Kate. In the summer of 1867, Kate filed for divorce and changed her name from Kate Brown Dodson to her maiden name, Kate Brown.

Brown was hired as a Senate laundress in 1861. In regard to her work, Kate Brown was extremely diligent. In Betty Koed's narrative on the Kate Brown incident, *A Dastardly Outrage*, several senators were reported to have expressed their positive impressions of this "educated, intelligent, respectable, and to all appearance refined woman" (Koed, 2008).

Perhaps due to such approving praise, the then twenty-one-year-old Kate Brown was quickly promoted to supervise the ladies retiring room less than one year after her hiring. In this new position, Brown attended to white ladies as they took a break during their Senate visits. This contact with white women was especially unusual, as most colored employees worked out of public view.

On Saturday, 8 February 1868, Kate Brown was waiting for the train from Alexandria, Virginia, en route to Washington, D.C. She had just visited a sick relative and was returning to her home for the evening. When the train pulled into the station, it was nearly 3:00 P.M. About to step onto the train, Brown turned to see who was shouting at her and there, on the platform, stood a police officer. He motioned for her to step down and use the other car but, as Brown recalled during her testimony in a congressional hearing (*Report*, 17 June 1868, p. 12), she replied, "This car will do." The officer quickly approached her, explaining that this car was a ladies only car; moreover, it was a car reserved only for white women. Refusing to succumb to this blatant show of discrimination, Brown defied the order and boarded. Just as steadfastly as she stepped aboard, the officer attempted to physically force her off the car. The two continued their fracas which lasted nearly eleven minutes. Not until the intervention of B. H. Hinds, the secretary to Senator Morrill, did the scuffle end; but by then, Brown had already suffered severe injuries, including a bruised face and twisted limbs. Months later, Brown was still confined to the bed, suffering a lung hemorrhage and coughing up blood.

The weekend incident garnered much attention from the national media. The *Hartford Daily Courant* called it an "outrage," while many others expressed disbelief for such mistreatment. Alarmed by the offense toward a Senate colleague, Senators Charles Sumner and Justin Morrill called for an investigation into the event. Empowered by such support, Brown sued the railroad company for $20,000. The case was heard by a District of Columbia court, which awarded Kate Brown $1,500 in compensation. The Washington, Georgetown, and Alexandria Railroad Company appealed. In 1873 the case was brought before the Supreme Court. In its defense, the company argued that it had provided separate but equal facilities; however, a close scrutiny of the company's charter revealed that segregation was expressly prohibited in any form on the train in question. In the Court majority opinion, Justice Davis declared that the condition "no person shall be excluded from the cars on account of color" would be interpreted as all races must be able to use the same car at the same time. Ultimately, the Supreme Court upheld the previous court's ruling, closing the *Railroad Company v. Brown* case.

This case was among the first clashes on the segregation issue, an issue that would have a great impact in the coming century. Just twenty-three years after *Railroad Company v. Brown*, the landmark 1896 *Plessy v. Ferguson* case officially instated the Supreme Court's support for segregation. However, the verdict did not pass without opposition. Justice John Harlan, later known as the "Great Dissenter," provided the single vote against the decision. In his *Plessy v. Ferguson* dissent he called arbitrary segregation a "badge of servitude" and warned that such state enactments supporting segregation would no doubt "arouse race hate… and perpetuate a feeling of distrust between these races." Harlan's prognosis proved correct; the deteriorating race relations

inspired a call for reform, catalyzing the African American civil rights movement of the mid-twentieth century. The institution of segregation, brought to the national scene by Kate Brown's *Railroad Company v. Brown*, would change with time and soon become the cynosure of domestic politics.

While the incident left Kate Brown permanently debilitated, she was able to develop a close relationship with Senators Sumner and Morrill. Throughout her recovery period, both senators worked tirelessly to ensure she was properly compensated. Brown returned to her post just months later and continued to work in the Senate until 1881. Two years later, Brown passed away at age forty-three.

FURTHER READING

Masur, Kate. *An Example for All the Land: Emancipation and the Struggle over Equality in Washington D.C.* (2010).

The Congressional Globe, Senate, 40th Congress, 2nd Session, (10 Feb.1868), pp. 1071, 1121–1125.

Report of the Senate Committee on the District of Columbia No. 131, 40th Congress, 2nd Session (1868).

Obituary: "Washington Letter." *New York Globe*, 17 Mar. 1883.

BRIAN TONG
THEODORE LIN

Brown, Larry (5 Sept. 1905–7 Apr. 1972), baseball player-manager, was the youngest of two children born to Charlie Brown and Viola Brannon in Pratt City, Alabama. Little is known about Larry's father, a man of mixed race with whom he had little to no relationship. His mother, a domestic worker, was his rock. Upon her death in 1918 thirteen-year-old Brown was left to raise himself and found employment with a local meat-packing company. The youngster began playing with the company's all-black team and soon found the baseball diamond to be his refuge.

At age seventeen Brown began barnstorming with the Knoxville Giants and later with the Pittsburgh Keystones. His official rookie season in the Negro Leagues was in 1923 when he joined the Indianapolis ABCs. On 28 May 1923, after only nine games, he was released because of poor performance. A few weeks later, Brown found himself in a Memphis Red Sox uniform, and although he would play with several other teams throughout his career, so began his three-decade-long association with that franchise.

Nicknamed baseball's "Iron Man," decades before Lou Gehrig and Cal Ripken Jr. could lay claim to the moniker, Brown is regarded as one of the Negro Leagues' best defensive catchers. Despite getting spiked and run over and fracturing every finger on his throwing hand, he rarely missed a game behind the plate. On the contrary, he frequently played three games in one day. In 1930 alone he reportedly caught over 230 games for the New York Lincoln Giants.

Brown's on-field trademarks were his rifle arm and quick release and never removing his facemask when catching pop-ups. Some claim that Brown coached Hall of Fame great Roy Campanella on the proper techniques of catching.

Although he was known as a defensive lion, Brown was rarely regarded as an offensive threat. After becoming the regular receiver for Memphis in 1924, he batted a meager .209. Jumping to the Chicago American Giants halfway through the 1926 season, he hit a career high of .316. A personal high that year was his marriage to Anna Mae Bransford. The following year Brown celebrated the birth of his son Larry, Jr., as well as a showing by the Giants in the in the Negro World Series. Although he made a critical error in game eight, Brown redeemed himself by blasting a home run in the decisive ninth game. He also gunned down four of eight base runners. After the series Negro National League president William Hueston ruled that Brown was the property of the Red Sox and was obligated to return to Memphis. Statistics do show an impressive plate showing for Brown in 1928 when he batted .294 and led the Red Sox in games, at-bats, hits, and doubles. Overall, he sustained adequate batting averages throughout his career and ended up with a modest lifetime average of .260.

What he lacked in the hitting department the husky backstopper made up for with dynamic defensive skills. He was adept at calling plays, catching pop-ups, mowing down base runners, and smothering would-be wild pitches. Reports contend that Brown went five consecutive years without allowing a passed ball and that he missed a play at the plate only three times during a fifteen-year stretch.

Other tales tell of Brown throwing out quick-footed Ty Cobb on five consecutive attempts at stealing second base while playing winter ball in Cuba in 1924. Legend has it that Cobb was so impressed that he tried to encourage the light-skinned Brown to pass himself off as Cuban in the States to bypass the major league ban on blacks. Distrusting of the notoriously racist Cobb, Brown declined, stating that he would only go to the Majors as himself or not at all. Like Cobb, others tried to persuade Brown to pass as a Latino because he had learned to speak Spanish fluently while on the islands. Again Brown refused, convinced that he would be instantly recognized because he was already well known throughout the Negro Leagues. While with the Santa Clara and Almendares teams of 1927 and 1928, he hit .250 and .280.

A fan favorite, the handsome squatter was voted an All Star six times (1933–1934 and 1938–1941). In 1934, he was the top vote getter among catchers by nearly twenty thousand votes. In 1935, although Brown did not play, he beat out JOSH GIBSON by a few hundred votes.

Hitting may have been his weakness on the field, but off it was the bottle. Brown's penchant for alcohol caused Anna Mae to divorce him in 1939. The fact that he was a heavy drinker may also be a reason for his frequent bouncing from team to team. His journey through the Negro Leagues includes stops with the Pittsburgh Keystones (1922), Indianapolis ABCs (1923), Memphis Red Sox (1923–1925, 1927–1929, 1931, 1938–1949), Detroit Stars (1926), Chicago American Giants (1927, 1929, 1940), New York Lincoln Giants (1930), Harlem Stars (1931), New York Black Yankees (1932), Cole's American Giants (1932–1935), and Philadelphia Stars (1936–1938).

In the 1944–1945 seasons Brown acted as player-manager with the Red Sox organization. Replaced by Olan "Jelly" Taylor in 1946 and seeing limited action as a player, Brown returned as skipper in 1947, squeaking out a winning season of twenty-one wins and twenty losses. After managing the 1949 season he bowed out of baseball and married Sarah Woods. Their son Wendell was born in 1950.

Brown had a hard time accepting the failure of the Negro Leagues and struggled to find his footing in baseball after his playing days. At one point he was approached by the St. Louis Browns to become a scout, but the offer never came to fruition. Eventually he became head waiter and sometimes cook at the William Len Hotel in Memphis.

Unable to kick his drinking habit, he died of sclerosis of the liver at the age of sixty-seven in Memphis, Tennessee.

FURTHER READING

Lester, Larry. *Black Baseball's National Showcase* (2001).
Loverro, Thom. *The Encyclopedia of Negro League Baseball* (2003).
Riley, James A. *The Biographical Encyclopedia of The Negro Baseball Leagues* (1994).

BYRON MOTLEY

Brown, Lawrence (3 Aug. 1907–5 Sept. 1988), jazz trombonist, was born in Lawrence, Kansas, the son of John M. Brown, a minister in the African Methodist Episcopal Church, and Maggie (maiden name unknown), who played pump organ for the church. When Brown was six the family moved to Oakland, California, where he learned how to play piano, tuba—which he began to play in the Oakland public school system—and violin. He also briefly experimented with alto saxophone before taking up trombone, to which he became intensely devoted after the Browns relocated across the bay to San Francisco.

The family moved to Pasadena, and around 1924 Brown enrolled at Pasadena Junior College for music and premedical studies. Risking his father's disapproval, Brown dropped out of school, moved to north Pasadena on his own, and around 1927 went into jazz as a member of Charlie Echols's seven-piece band at a dime-a-dance venue, the 401 Ballroom. From 1928 to 1931 he worked with the bands of Paul Howard, Curtis Mosby, and LES HITE. The affiliation with Mosby included acting in and recording the soundtrack for the director King Vidor's movie *Hallelujah!* (1929) and performing at Mosby's Apex clubs in Los Angeles (later renamed the Club Alabam) and San Francisco. These affiliations were not continuous, however, because Brown and the drummer (soon to be vibraphonist) LIONEL HAMPTON were also contracted individually to Frank Sebastian's Cotton Club in Los Angeles, where they played under Mosby, Howard, and others, most notably LOUIS ARMSTRONG with Hite's big band in 1931.

In the spring of 1932 Brown joined DUKE ELLINGTON's big band, with which he remained for two decades, except for a brief absence in 1943. His career followed the leader's grueling schedule of far-ranging touring. In 1933 (some sources say 1934 or 1935) Brown married FREDI WASHINGTON, an actress. They divorced some years later, and at an unknown date he married Dorothea Bundrant, whom he also subsequently divorced. Obituaries do not mention any children.

Brown became one of Ellington's principal soloists, featured on recordings of "The Sheik of Araby," "Ducky Wucky" (both 1932), "Slippery Horn" (1933), "Stompy Jones" (1934), "Braggin' in Brass," "Rose of the Rio Grande" (both 1938), "Across the Track Blues" (1940), "Come Sunday" on the *Black, Brown, and Beige* suite (as premiered at Carnegie Hall in January 1943), and his own compositions "Golden Cress" and "On a Turquoise Cloud" (both

1947). Brown may be seen and heard as a soloist in the film short *Salute to Duke Ellington* (1950).

In March 1951 Brown left Ellington to work in the small band of the saxophonist JOHNNY HODGES, with which he recorded the album *Used to Be Duke* (1954). In the spring of 1955 Brown began to work as a freelancer in New York City, but a year later, when the trombonist Warren Covington resigned as a studio musician for CBS, Brown took his place. He rejoined Ellington in May 1960. Notable recordings include "The Mooche" on *Duke Ellington's Greatest Hits*, from a concert in Paris in 1963, and the album *Popular Duke Ellington* (1966). Brown also was featured again in a film short, *Playback: Duke Ellington* (1963).

Brown left Ellington and retired from music in 1970. Moving to Washington, D.C., he was appointed by President Richard Nixon to the advisory committee of the Kennedy Center. In 1974 he settled in the Los Angeles area and worked as a recording agent for Local 47 of the musicians' union. He had a stroke and not long afterward died in Los Angeles.

Brown explained on several occasions that he wanted to play trombone in a pretty manner, as if it were a cello, not in the blustery sliding fashion popular in early New Orleans jazz. Hence in his first tenure with Ellington, he was featured on romantic melodies, and he also favored clear-toned, nimble lines, as heard in "The Sheik of Araby." From 1961 to the end of his career he supplied a third type of solo for Ellington's orchestra, playing emotive, vocalized, plunger-muted melodies in the manner created by his predecessors BUBBER MILEY and Tricky Sam Nanton.

FURTHER READING

Dietrich, Kurt. *Duke's 'Bones: Ellington's Great Trombonists* (1995).
Ellington, Duke. *Music Is My Mistress* (1973).
Obituaries: *New York Times*, 9 Sept. 1988; *Jazz Journal International* (Nov. 1988): 16–17.
This entry is taken from the *American National Biography* and is published here with the permission of the American Council of Learned Societies.

BARRY KERNFELD

Brown, Lawrence, Jr. (19 Sept. 1947–), professional football player and businessman, was born in Clairton, Pennsylvania, the first of three sons of Lawrence Brown, a baggage handler for the

Pennsylvania Railroad, and Rosa Lee, a housemaid. The family moved to Pittsburgh, Pennsylvania, when Brown was only two years old. He began playing football in his junior year at Schenley High School in Pittsburgh. He chose football over baseball because he thought he had a better chance to attain a college scholarship in football. Prior to his junior year, Brown played baseball. He said that his father encouraged him to play baseball because it was a game one could play as an organized sport at a young age. His dad loved baseball and was an excellent player in his own right, though he did not play professionally but rather with neighborhood friends.

Brown played fullback in high school primarily because he had good blocking skills. He received honorable mention to the all-city football team. He graduated from high school in 1965. He was offered a scholarship to play football at Kent State University. Instead, his high school football coach suggested that Brown talk to a former Schenley High School football player who had attended Dodge City Junior College in Dodge City, Kansas. Brown did and was convinced to go to Dodge. He was named honorable mention All-American his sophomore year at Dodge and was invited to try out for the varsity football team at Kansas State University; Brown made the team and was given a scholarship. He played his junior and senior years for the Kansas State University football team, serving as a blocking back, and became the featured tailback later in his senior year.

In 1969 Brown was selected by the Washington Redskins in the eighth round of the NFL draft. Soon after Brown was drafted, Vince Lombardi was hired to replace Otto Graham as head coach of the Redskins. One day while reviewing practice and game films in slow motion, Lombardi noticed that Brown was seconds late getting off the snap. Lombardi arranged to give Brown a hearing test, and it was discovered that he was completely deaf in his right ear. Lombardi petitioned the league office for permission to install a hearing aide in Brown's helmet. The request was granted, and soon Brown was the starting running back for the team. The Redskins finished with a 7–5–2 record—their first winning season in thirteen years. That year Brown also made a Pro Bowl appearance. He was chosen for that honor three out of the following four years.

Before the start of the 1970 season, Lombardi died of cancer. Bill Austin, an assistant coach under Lombardi, was named interim coach for the 1970 season. The Redskins finished 6–8, and Austin was fired. Nevertheless, Brown gained 1,125 yards and rushed for 100 yards or more in six different games that year. George Allen was hired as head coach and general manager of the team before the start of the 1971 season.

The remedy was immediate and swift. The Redskins started the 1971 season with five wins in a row. The team made the playoffs for the first time in twenty-six years, compiling a record of 9–4–1. In 1972 Brown led the team to a 11–3 record, gained 1,216 yards (rushing for 100 yards in six different games), and led the Redskins to Super Bowl VII, which they lost 14–7 to the Miami Dolphins in the Los Angeles Coliseum. Brown was also the NFL's most valuable player (MVP) that year. The next season he scored four rushing touchdowns in a game against the Eagles on 16 December 1973. Brown was not afraid to play with injuries, and he got hurt often because of his running style. He literally threw caution to the wind when he ran the ball, often hurdling himself to gain that extra yard.

In an eight-year career Brown was MVP in 1972 and selected to play in the Pro Bowl in 1969, 1970, 1971, and 1972. He carried the ball 1,530 times in his career, gaining 5,875 yards. His best seasons were in 1972, when he gained 1,216 yards, and in 1970, when he gained 1,125 yards. He rushed for 100 yards or more twenty-one times and rushed for 100 yards or more in six games in 1970 and six games in 1972. He also scored four rushing touchdowns in a game against the Eagles on 16 December 1973. It should be noted that the season consisted of fourteen games during Brown's career.

Brown's jersey number 43 was unofficially retired, and he was selected by a special panel as one of the seventy greatest Redskins of all time. The blue-ribbon panel consisted of the former CNN news anchor Bernard Shaw; the Redskins alum Bobby Mitchell; the U.S. senator George Allen of Virginia, son of the Redskins Hall of Fame coach George Allen; the Washington broadcasting legend Ken Beatrice; Noel Epstein, editor of several *Washington Post* histories of the team; the former undersecretary of state Joseph J. Sisco; Phil Hochberg, who retired in 2001 after thirty-eight years as team stadium announcer; the Pro Football Hall of Fame historian Joe Horrigan; the WRC-TV sports director George Michael; the WTEM sports director Andy Pollin; the NFL Films president Steve Sabol; and the WRC-TV news anchor Jim Vance.

Team records held by Brown include second for most yards gained in a career (5,875 yards); fourth for most yards gained in a season (1,216 yards in 1972); most 100-yard games in a season (6 in 1970 and 6 in 1972); second for most touchdown rushes in a career (35); most touchdown rushes in a single game (4 versus the Philadelphia Eagles on 16 Feb. 1973).

After he retired in 1976, Brown worked for E.F. Hutton as a personal financial management adviser. He also worked for twelve years with Xerox and was responsible for business and community relations. He then became vice president of the Michael Companies, Inc., a commercial real estate firm based in Lanham, Maryland, leasing and selling commercial properties.

Influenced by the fact that he was hearing impaired, Brown participated on many committees for the deaf, including the board of directors of the Deafness Research Foundation (1980–1992) and the board of directors of the National Institute on Deafness and Other Communication Disorders (1989–1991). He also served on the board of associates of Galludet University, a school for the deaf in Washington, D.C. (1991–1993).

Brown married Janet, a Washington native, in 1997. The couple had two daughters, Tonya and Lauren.

FURTHER READING

Brown, Larry, and William Gilde. *I'll Always Get Up* (1973).

Attner, Paul, and Ken Denlinger. *Redskins Country: From Baugh to the Super Bowl* (1983).

Denlinger, Ken. *Washington's Redskins: The Allen Triumph* (1973).

Whittingham, Richard. *Hail Redskins: A Celebration of the Greatest Players, Teams, and Coaches* (2001).

ROBERT JANIS

Brown, Lawrence Benjamin (29 Aug. 1893–25 Dec. 1972), pianist and composer, was born in Jacksonville, Florida, the son of Clark Benjamin Brown, himself the son of a former slave. Little is known of Brown's natural mother, who died when Lawrence was three; from then on, he was raised by his stepmother, Cenia Brown.

During his youth Brown took music instruction from the well-respected William Riddick. Exhibiting incredible promise, Brown was sent to Boston to receive further instruction in his primary instrument, piano. In addition to scholarships, Brown financed his education in Boston by working as an elevator operator. In 1916 he made his professional music debut as accompanist for the tenor Sydney Woodward. With this exposure Brown caught the eye of other musicians, including the famed tenor ROLAND HAYES. Brown and Hayes toured abroad from 1918 to 1923 and received great popular acclaim. They had many important engagements, including a performance for the king and queen of England at Buckingham Palace in 1921.

While in England, Brown also took advantage of advanced training at Trinity College in London. There he had composition instruction from Amanda Aldridge, daughter of the great African American actor IRA ALDRIDGE. Brown's interest and talent in composition went beyond piano and vocal arrangements. In 1923 he performed some string arrangements with the famed cellist Beatrice Harrison at Wigmore Hall in England. Brown's profound talent at musical composition and arrangement as well as at singing and piano playing quickly proved him to be one of the most important new figures in the musical world.

Brown used his educational instruction to pursue research into folk songs, paying particular attention to the music of African Americans. His work took him to the southern United States, where he began to absorb the traditional work songs of field workers and laborers. From this research he developed his popular arrangements of hundreds of Negro spirituals, more than thirty of which were published during his lifetime in collections such as JAMES WELDON JOHNSON's *Book of American Negro Spirituals* (1925) and Brown's own *Negro Folk Songs* (1930). Brown is distinguished among arrangers of the spirituals for his attention to detail and investment in preserving the original elements of the songs. Arrangements authored by Brown include "Swing Low, Sweet Chariot," "Joshua Fit de Battle of Jericho," "Ezekiel Saw de Wheel," and "Steal Away." Many of his compositions went on to become very popular.

In 1925 the baritone PAUL ROBESON became the first major singer to perform Brown's spiritual arrangements in concert. Robeson was also the first solo singer to offer an entire concert of spirituals. This practice was continued by other African American singers such as the contralto MARIAN ANDERSON. Robeson's performance of Brown's arrangements at the Greenwich Village Theatre was the spark that generated a forty-year relationship between the two men, professionally and personally. During the 1930s they toured Europe together while Robeson reprised his role as Joe in the Jerome Kern and Oscar Hammerstein II musical *Show*

Boat. Their camaraderie on and off the stage was legendary: Robeson's bass-baritone vocal lines were often harmonized by Brown's tenor, and their political work for issues ranging from worker rights to antiapartheid organizing solidified their standing as a powerful artistic force. They performed internationally, including in New York, Paris, London, and Ireland. The pair appeared before European royalty on numerous occasions, including before the Prince of Wales and the king of Spain.

Part of the pair's popularity stemmed from their many recordings. They recorded classics such as "Nobody Knows de Trouble I've Seen," "Sometimes I Feel Like a Motherless Child," and "Joe Hill" for RCA Victor records. In 1939 Brown led the orchestra and chorus for Robeson's CBS recording of "Ballad for Americans," which garnered them international attention. The two men often offered their support and art in service of armed struggles around the globe, including a United Service Organizations (USO) camp tour during World War II. Beyond Negro spirituals and work songs Brown was also a champion of world folk music. In addition to Robeson's detailed and incisive study of the music, it was Brown who investigated this music for inclusion in their repertoire. Brown was often contacted by musicians and conductors for music of obscure folk songs.

Brown had many important relationships with artists and leaders during the course of his lifetime, including with the scholar and writer LLOYD LOUIS BROWN and with the poet and writer LANGSTON HUGHES. Brown was also a confidant for Robeson's wife, ESLANDA CARDOZA GOODE ROBESON, who often traveled with the pair. His close relationship with the Robeson family was put to the test after World War II when Robeson came under intense scrutiny for his ties to the Soviet Union. Opportunities to perform abroad were denied after the United States government revoked Robeson's passport in 1950. Despite the passport's later reinstatement, the careers and reputations of both men suffered. Brown retired in 1963 after illness ended Robeson's career. Brown never married and lived the last forty-seven years of his life as a resident of Harlem. In February 1973 he was honored by friends and family with a concert of his works at Saint Martin's Episcopal Church in Harlem.

FURTHER READING

The Lawrence Benjamin Brown Papers are in New York City at the Schomburg Center for Research in Black Culture.

Green, Jeffrey P. "Roland Hayes in London, 1921," *Black Perspective in Music* (1982).

SHANA L. REDMOND

Brown, Letitia Christine Woods (24 Oct. 1915– 3 Aug. 1976), historian, was born in Tuskegee, Alabama, the daughter of Matthew Woods and Evadne Adams, professors. Her maternal grandfather, Lewis Adams, was born a slave and after the Civil War was instrumental in establishing the Tuskegee Normal School in 1881. Her parents both taught at Tuskegee Institute, continuing the family's commitment to education. Letitia attended Tuskegee Institute High School and graduated with a B.S. from Tuskegee Institute in 1935. In 1937 she completed her M.A. at Ohio State University. While working on an advanced degree at Radcliffe College, Letitia married Theodore E. Brown, a labor economist who later worked for the Agency for International Development in the U.S. Department of State. After raising two children and becoming involved in community projects in Mount Vernon, New York, she attended Harvard University, which awarded her a Ph.D. in 1966.

As a historian, Letitia Woods Brown sought to educate people, in a variety of forums, about the African American experience and about race relations. Her career as a teacher began in 1935 when she taught in the segregated Macon County school system in Alabama. She then returned to Tuskegee, where she taught from 1937 to 1940. From 1940 to 1945 she was an instructor at another black college, LeMoyne College in Memphis, and from 1961 to 1970 she taught at Howard University, where she served on several committees, including the committee to establish the Department of Afro-American Studies. In 1968 Brown became a Fulbright professor in Australia at Monash University and at Australia National University. After brief teaching stints at Georgetown University and Goucher College, in 1971 she became the only full-time black faculty member in the College of Arts and Sciences at George Washington University.

Throughout her career, Brown taught courses in U.S. history and African American history. At George Washington University, she promoted interracial educational experiences by encouraging graduate students from George Washington and Howard universities to take courses at both institutions. While at George Washington, Brown also helped develop a course on the history of the District of Columbia. Emphasizing local rather than federal history, the course was a model for other interdisciplinary classes within the university.

Brown also taught outside the traditional classroom setting. In 1961 she instructed the first group of Peace Corps volunteers, who were eventually assigned to Ghana. For teacher in-service projects in Maryland and Virginia, she helped develop educational materials on blacks and other minorities. In 1972–1973 she served as the only historian on the panel of the National Assessment of Educational Progress, which set objectives for congressionally mandated tests for precollege students in social studies. Brown also was a professor at the Federal Executive Institute (1970–1973), after which she conducted training programs for the institute, including at the Department of Agriculture.

Brown's writing reflected broad interests that reached beyond academia to include the local history of the District of Columbia. With Elsie M. Lewis, Brown wrote *Washington from Banneker to Douglass, 1791–1870* and *Washington in the New Era, 1870–1970*, which accompanied a two-part exhibition in 1971–1972 on African Americans at the National Portrait Gallery, Smithsonian Institution. Brown's major work, *Free Negroes in the District of Columbia, 1790–1846*, was published in 1972. The historian BENJAMIN QUARLES said of the work, "In language as concise and conclusive as the court records she has searched, Professor Brown traces the ways—many of them novel—in which blacks in the District moved from slavery to freedom." Brown's other writing included an essay on residential patterns of African Americans in the District of Columbia and an article entitled "Why and How the Negro in History," published in the fall 1969 issue of the *Journal of Negro Education.*

Brown also promoted awareness of African American history and of racial issues through her work in the local community, both on public history projects and at international history conferences. As vice chair of the Joint Committee on Landmarks of the National Capital, Brown broadened the committee's criteria for designating landmarks by promoting sites important to the history of African American residents, a criterion that had been ignored by previous committees. As consultant to the Capitol Historical Society, she advocated the inclusion of the contributions of many groups, including the slaves who built the structure, in the historical narrative of the Capitol. She served on the Advisory Board of the Schlesinger Library on the History of Women in America at Radcliffe College and helped the library initiate the Black Women Oral History Project, which eventually interviewed seventy-two African American women and

published the transcripts in ten volumes in 1990. Brown's work with the Bicentennial Committee on International Conferences of Americanists led to the African Regional American Studies Conference in Lagos, Nigeria, in 1976. She served on the Advisory Committee on Historical Research for the Columbia Historical Society, helping it become more knowledgeable about local African American history, and was a cofounder of the annual conference on Washington, D.C., Historic Studies. Brown's other professional affiliations included membership on the executive board of the National Humanities Institute at Yale University, on the National Archives Advisory Council, and on the review board of the American Historical Association that oversaw the restructuring of that organization in the early 1970s.

Brown died of cancer at her home in Washington, D.C. Throughout her life she used her expertise as a historian in both academic and public arenas to increase awareness of the history of African Americans in the United States. She encouraged the reinterpretation of U.S. history both locally and nationally to include the historical experience of blacks, and she helped redefine the ways in which that history was conceptualized. Brown saw herself as "both historian and futurist. I suppose I shall continue to grapple with it—with a growing awareness that the way we organize and present data helps shape the way people think, that how we teach is as important as what we teach."

FURTHER READING

Some of Brown's papers are in the Special Collections at the Melvin Gelman Library, George Washington University, Washington, D.C., and at the Radcliffe College Archives at Harvard University.

French, Roderick. "Letitia Woods Brown, 1915–1976," *Records of the Columbia Historical Society of Washington, D.C.* 50 (1980): 522–524.

Obituaries: *New York Times* and *Washington Post,* 5 Aug. 1976.

This entry is taken from the *American National Biography* and is published here with the permission of the American Council of Learned Societies.

NORALEE FRANKEL

Brown, Linda Carol (1943–), activist, educator, and daughter of the first named plaintiff in the landmark 1954 U.S. Supreme Court school integration case, *Brown v. Board of Education*, was born in Topeka, Kansas, to Leola Brown (later Montgomery) and

Linda Brown, Ethel Louise Belton Brown, Harry Briggs Jr., and Spottswood Bolling Jr. during press conference at Hotel Americana on 9 June 1964. (Library of Congress, New York World-Telegram and the *Sun Newspaper* Photograph Collection/Al Ravenna, photographer.)

the Reverend Oliver Leon Brown. Oliver Brown, the lead plaintiff of twelve African American parents in *Brown* was an African Methodist Episcopal pastor and boxcar welder for the Santa Fe Railroad. The couple had two younger daughters, Cheryl (married surname: Henderson) and Terry (married surname: Tyler). Although the Browns lived in a multiracial, working-class neighborhood, Linda soon encountered segregation. Her white friends attended Sumner Grade School, seven blocks away. She was forced to attend Monroe, over a mile away. She had to walk through a dangerous railway yard, then catch a bus with a long, wandering itinerary. If the bus arrived too early, it left the students outside, even in bad weather.

In the 1930s the NAACP Legal Defense Fund (LDF), led by THURGOOD MARSHALL, began to challenge the Supreme Court's then-prevailing legal doctrine, which since the 1896 *Plessy v. Ferguson* case had held that "separate but equal" institutions were legal across a range of institutions, including educational institutions. By 1950, however, Marshall and the LDF won several Supreme Court cases, notably *Sweatt v. Painter* (1950), in which the Court agreed with the LDF's evidence that separate education facilities generally meant unequal. In 1950, after

Oliver Brown tried unsuccessfully to register Linda at Sumner, the NAACP invited him to join a group of lawsuits challenging elementary school segregation. The other plaintiffs came from Delaware, the District of Columbia, South Carolina, and Virginia. The NAACP regarded segregation as a nationwide, not only a Southern problem. Many studies suggest that Oliver Brown was the lead plaintiff because his surname came first in the alphabet, but another plaintiff was named Darlene Brown and thus should have been first in that case. Most likely, Oliver Brown became the lead plaintiff because he was the only male parent named among the plaintiffs. Yet this group of cases became famous as *Brown v. Board of Education*. Marshall successfully argued it before the U.S. Supreme Court. Oliver Brown testified there on Linda's behalf. On 17 May 1954, when a unanimous Court ruled that "separate but equal" school segregation was unconstitutional, the Brown family rejoiced, like many African Americans and their allies. The ruling came too late for Linda, but not for her sister Cheryl, to register at Sumner. Linda attended an already integrated junior high and high school. She developed her musical talents at her father's church. She attended Washburn University in Kansas until she started her own family and no longer had money or time for college. She married a man named Smith and gave birth to her son Charles and daughter Kimberly during the early 1960s. Her father died in 1961. She tried to guard her privacy against people who called her for interviews "at all hours of the night, not taking into consideration that I was working or that I had a family… to the point where I wasn't a person, I was a symbol… who owed them this" (Burgen).

By the mid-1970s Linda Brown Smith divorced her children's father. In 1978, anticipating renewed attention to *Brown v. Board* on its twenty-fifth anniversary, she quit her job as a data processor for Goodyear and made her living as a speaker on the case and its legacy. She decided to continue her interrupted studies at Washburn and become an education professional herself. She also continued to lead her church's choir. In 1979, with help from the American Civil Liberties Union, she moved to reopen *Brown v. Board* on behalf of her own children, who attended schools that were segregated because of housing demographics, not law.

The case did not gain a hearing until 1986. By then, she was seeking desegregation on behalf of her grandson rather than her children. She was by then married to Leonard Buckner, who had chronic heart disease and could not work. Linda Brown Buckner taught piano and ran an educational consulting firm with her sister Cheryl. In 1987 the reopened *Brown* case was thrown out of court, but by 1989 the Tenth Circuit Court of Appeals reversed that ruling, citing evidence of the Topeka school system's failure to desegregate. Eventually a desegregation plan was enforced, but it was not until 1998 the Topeka school system was found to be in racial balance.

In 1988 Linda Brown Buckner, her family, and other community leaders launched the Brown Foundation for Educational Equity, Excellence, and Research. The foundation offered "scholarships to minority students entering teacher education, sponsor[ed] programs with emphasis on racial/ethnic diversity, and support[ed] historic research" (Brown Foundation Story, http://brown-vboard.org/content/brown-foundation-story). The foundation was decisive in establishing the *Brown v. Board* National Historic Site.

By 1993 Linda Brown Buckner was a Head Start teacher. By 2004, fifty years after the Brown ruling, she had remarried, apparently after being widowed. Known as Linda Brown Thompson, she was employed as a program associate at the Brown Foundation. She sometimes appeared in public with her sister Cheryl to talk about *Brown* and its repercussions. Yet she downplayed her unsought role as the "poster child" for desegregation and credited the many other ordinary people who, along with the *Brown* plaintiffs furthered this civil rights advance.

FURTHER READING

Brown v. Topeka Board of Education Oral History Collection. Kansas State Historical Society, Topeka, Kansas.

Burgen, Michele. "Linda Brown Smith: Integration's Unwitting Pioneer." *Ebony* (May 1979).

Chappell, Kevin. "Topeka 50 Years Later: The Real Story Behind the Brown in Brown v. Board of Education." *Ebony* (May 2004).

Cushman, Clare, and Melvin I. Urofsky, eds. *Black, White, and Brown: The Landmark School Desegregation Case in Retrospect* (2004).

Hays, Bradley D. "Linda Brown." In *One Hundred Americans Making Constitutional History: A Biographical History*, ed. Melvin J. Urofsky (2004).

MARY KRANE DERR

Brown, Lloyd Louis (3 Apr. 1913–1 Apr. 2003), writer, editor, and activist, was born Lloyd Louis Dight in St. Paul, Minnesota, the son of Ralph Dight and Magdalena (Paul) Dight. His mother, the German-American daughter of a Union army veteran, died when Brown was four. After his wife's death, Brown's father, a Louisiana-born African American Pullman porter, placed Brown and his three siblings in St. Paul's Crispus Attucks Home. During his upbringing at the residence, which served as both an old folks' home and an orphanage for the city's poor blacks, Brown experienced the desolate conditions of poverty, but he also received nurturing and affirming care from members of the black community. Raised largely by older members of the home, many of them former slaves, he gained an enduring respect and appreciation for the black folk stories and traditions shared with him by the home's elders. Influenced by this early experience, Brown's literary works often reflect the liberating power of black folk traditions in the face of oppression and injustice. Lloyd dropped out of St. Paul's Cretin High School after one year and embarked on a rigorous course of self-education. He studied the works of H. L. Mencken, Omar Khayyám, Toussaint L'Ouverture, and other writings on radical social thought. It was during this time that the sixteen-year-old Brown changed his name from Lloyd Dight to Lloyd Brown in homage to the nineteenth-century abolitionist John Brown.

In 1929 Brown joined the Young Communist League (YCL) and began his career as a labor organizer and political activist. While the threat of repercussions for involvement with the Communist Party under McCarthyism has obscured the relationship between the Communist Party and the African American community, there were many African Americans, from the late 1920s through the 1950s, who believed that Communism would be the best way to secure social, political, and economic equality. In the wake of the stock market crash of 1929 and the ensuing Depression, Brown traveled to Youngstown, Ohio, where he continued working as an organizer during the most turbulent years of the labor union movement. During this time he also traveled to Europe as a freelance journalist to report on the antifascist movement, and in 1933 he went to the Soviet Union to seek international support for the SCOTTSBORO BOYS, the nine young black men who were arrested in the 1930s for allegedly raping two white women. In 1937, Brown married Lily Kashin, a YCL member of Polish-Jewish descent, to whom he remained married until her death in 1996. They had two daughters, Linda and Bonnie.

In October 1940 Brown, along with several others, was convicted of "fraudulent circulation of Communist election petitions" (Pittsburgh *Sun Telegraph*, 21 Apr. 1941). While serving a seven-month sentence in Pittsburgh's Alleghany County

Jail, Brown met William Jones, a young African American man unjustly imprisoned on charges of murder and sentenced to death. From within the prison, Brown and his fellow detainees formed a defense committee and with the help of an elaborate community network outside the jail, fought to get Jones a new trial. While their efforts resulted in several stays of the execution, it was ultimately to no avail, and Jones was executed on 24 November 1941. Brown based his 1951 novel, *Iron City*, on this experience. According to literary scholar Alan Wald, *Iron City* is "possibly the first black prison novel, and certainly the first depicting the activities of political prisoners in the United States" (*Iron City*, xviii). Unlike the grim portrayals offered in popular protest fiction and epitomized in RICHARD WRIGHT's *Native Son*, *Iron City* celebrated black folk culture and affirmed individual dignity even in the face of the most severe forms of repression.

Brown served in the U.S. Army Air Force from 1942 to 1945, was stationed in Salina, Kansas, and rose to the rank of sergeant. From 1945 to 1952, Brown was managing editor of *New Masses* (later *Masses and Mainstream*), a leftist literary journal that published works by figures such as Wright, LANGSTON HUGHES, JAMES BALDWIN, and RALPH ELLISON. During this time Brown published several short stories, articles and reviews. "God's Chosen People," a fictionalized account of his experiences in the St. Paul orphanage, was listed in the O'Brien collection of *Best Short Stories of 1948*. Brown was especially well known for his scathing review of Ellison's *Invisible Man*. He charged that the novel was "profoundly anti-Negro," and that Ellison was "cut off from the surging mainstream of Negro life" ("The Deep Pit," *Masses and Mainstream*, June 1962). Throughout his career, Brown continued to observe and critique the direction of African American literature and culture. In "Which Way for the Negro Writer," Brown sharply criticized the integration-era tendency for African Americans to abandon black themes, and he insisted on the need for African American writers to render black experiences in black literature (*Masses and Mainstream*, Mar. 1951).

In the 1950s Brown left his editorship at *Masses and Mainstream* to work as a literary collaborator with the radical actor, singer, cultural scholar, and political activist PAUL ROBESON, a position Brown held until Robeson's death in 1976 Brown wrote columns for Robeson's Harlem newspaper *Freedom*, and the two collaborated on Robeson's 1958 autobiography, *Here I Stand*. Brown also published the 1976 pamphlet *Paul Robeson Rediscovered* and in 1997 a full-length biography, *The Young Paul Robeson: On My Journey Now*. The biography won the 1998 Carey McWilliams Award for Outstanding Scholarly Work in Cultural Diversity. In later years, Brown remained a tireless cultural and social critic. His articles covered topics ranging from politics and police brutality to literature and popular entertainment and appeared in numerous journals including the *New York Amsterdam News*, *Negro Digest*, the *Nation*, and the *New York Times*.

During the repressive cold war era, Brown remained an unwavering voice of the black pro-Communist left. He challenged African American writers not to abandon black themes in the promise of integration, but to insist on equality while affirming black culture and black identity. At the time of his death in 2003 Brown was working on publishing *Jubilee*, a novel he had begun writing in 1953, exploring the relationship between Communism and the civil rights movements of the 1950s and 1960s

FURTHER READING

Nelson, Paul, "Orphans and Old Folks," *Minnesota History* (Fall 2001).

Wald, Alan. "Foreword" in Lloyd Brown, *Iron City* (1994).

Washington, Mary Helen. "'Lighting a Match to Kerosene': Lloyd Brown's *Iron City*," in *The Other Blacklist: African American Writing and Activism in the Cold War* (forthcoming 2008).

Obituaries: *New York Times*, 14 Apr. 2003; *New York Amsterdam News*, 17 Apr. 2003.

SHIRLEY C. MOODY

Brown, Lucy Manetta Hughes (Apr. 1863–26 June 1911), physician and educator, was born in Mebanesville, North Carolina, one of eight children. Her parents' names are not known. There are no records of Brown's earlier education, but in 1881 she enrolled at Scotia Seminary in Concord, North Carolina, and graduated in 1885. Four years later she married David Brown, a minister, and the following year entered Woman's Medical College of Pennsylvania, founded in 1850 and the first medical school for women in America. When Brown matriculated at the school in 1891, it was one of the best medical colleges in the country.

After graduating from Woman's Medical College of Pennsylvania in 1894 Brown returned to North

Carolina and practiced medicine in her home state for two years before going to Charleston, South Carolina, where she became the first female physician of African ancestry in South Carolina. A year later, a fellow alumna from Woman's Medical College, MATILDA ARABELLA EVANS, began a practice in Columbia, South Carolina, and became the second black female physician in the state.

In 1897 Brown and ALONZO CLIFTON MCCLENNAN founded the Cannon Hospital and Training School for Nurses in Charleston, with McClennan as surgeon-in-charge and instructor of surgical nursing and hygiene and Brown as instructor of obstetric and pediatric nursing and head of gynecology and the nursing staff. This partnership not only provided health care for black patients but also, through the leadership of Brown and McClennan, provided clinical experience for aspiring black nurses. The institution was initially intended to be a training school for nurses, but there were no facilities in Charleston where black nurses could get practical training in a hospital ward, so Brown and McClennan added the hospital.

Cannon Hospital and Training School for Nurses was one of many black hospitals that were established by blacks between 1890 and 1920. In Chicago, a city of fifteen thousand blacks in the 1890s, unless blacks were patients of white doctors, there were no hospitals that would admit them until Provident Hospital was built in 1891. Hospitals for blacks were desperately needed, not only because mortality rates were significantly higher for blacks than for whites but also because white medical professionals were using these statistics as another indication of the racial inferiority of people of African descent. Leaders in the American Public Health Association declared blacks a health threat to society and devoted an entire issue of their official publication, the *American Journal of Public Health*, to the "Negro health problem," featuring articles that portrayed blacks as a medical menace. Frederick Hoffman, chief statistician for Prudential Life Insurance, contributed to the discussion of health status and race by referring to blacks as members of a "dying race" in his book *Race Traits and the Tendencies of the American Negro*, published in 1896. DANIEL HALE WILLIAMS, head of Provident Hospital, aggressively challenged these assumptions, arguing that discrimination, which forced blacks to live in unsanitary and unsafe conditions without access to medical care, was directly responsible for the discrepancy between black and white life expectancies. At a symposium around

that time, Williams and eleven other black physicians refuted the "dying race" concept and contended that speculation about the survival of blacks was meaningless and premature without a record of every birth and death in the black race for a period of at least ten years. They questioned the validity of statistics based on the observations and memories of doctors in states like North Carolina, with large black populations, but no board of health in many counties.

A few years after its founding, the Cannon Hospital and Training School began the *Hospital Herald*, which described itself as "a journal devoted to hospital work, nurse training and domestic and public hygiene," with McClennan as editor-in-chief and Brown as one of two associate editors. The journal not only served as a source of professional and personal information for those who were associated with the school, but it was also an effective promotional tool for procuring much-needed financial support. Within a short time, the work of the institution was known not only in South Carolina but also throughout the South.

Brown was a member of an elite group of nineteenth-century black women who became physicians in spite of prevailing prejudices, so pervasive in the medical profession, against race and gender. Her career had an auspicious beginning, and there were indications that she would have a long and productive professional life as a physician and nursing instructor. But illness forced her into an early retirement in 1904, and she died seven years later.

FURTHER READING

Papers on file for Lucy Hughes Brown are in the Archives and Special Collections/Black Women Physicians at Drexel University College of Medicine.

DuBois, W. E. B. *Efforts for Social Betterment among Negro Americans* (1909).

Hine, Darlene Clark. "Co-laborers in the Work of the Lord," in *"Send Us a Lady Physician": Women Doctors in America*, ed. Ruth Abrams (1985).

Morais, Herbert M. *The History of the Negro in Medicine* (1967).

GERALDINE RHOADES BECKFORD

Brown, Morris (12 Feb. 1770–9 May 1849), African Methodist Episcopal minister and bishop, was born of mixed parentage in Charleston, South Carolina, where he spent his early and middle years. Apparently self-educated, he worked as a boot maker and shoe repairman; he married Maria (maiden name unknown), with whom he had six children. Associated with the city's community of free people of color, Brown earned a reputation for assisting slaves in purchasing their freedom and for teaching and advising both free and enslaved African Americans in the region.

Soon after his religious conversion and his joining of the Methodist Episcopal (ME) Church, Brown was licensed to preach. In that role he had greater access to the slave population as well as to groups of free African Americans. As the number of blacks grew, both generally and within the African church in Charleston, Brown emerged as their leader. As a result of an 1816 dispute over a burial ground, many African church members withdrew from the ME Church. When the opportunity came later that year, Brown's congregation of about 1,400 members transferred to the new African Methodist Episcopal (AME) denomination, centered in Philadelphia and headed by Bishop RICHARD ALLEN. Brown was ordained deacon of the AME Church in 1817 and elder the following year.

The Charleston African Church, by meeting independently of white authorities and supervision, ran afoul of local and state laws intended to control religious gatherings of slaves and free blacks. Consequently, Brown and other ministers of the church served prison sentences in 1818 while protesting the repression of the free exercise of religion. Brown also attended early AME annual and general conferences, where he reported both the difficulties of being harassed by the police and the spectacular growth of the Charleston congregation; it had more than two thousand members by 1822. That year, 1822, civil authorities uncovered a conspiracy to overthrow slavery associated with the initiative of DENMARK VESEY, a lay class leader in the African church. Betrayed by slaves loyal to their masters, the conspiracy involved six other class leaders from Brown's AME community; the conspiracy ended with 131 arrests and 35 executions. Suspected of knowing about Vesey's plan (though there was no direct evidence), Brown, aided by some local white clergy who advised him to leave, saw his church forced to close. Before the year ended he went north; early in 1823 his family joined him in Philadelphia, where he served as an assistant at the Mother Bethel AME Church and as aide to the aging Bishop Allen. Occasionally he traveled as an itinerant preacher, also organizing new AME congregations. On 25 May 1828 the AME General Conference selected Brown as its second bishop. When Allen died in 1831, Brown

became the sole bishop of the denomination, and he became its senior bishop in 1836. Never forgetting his southern experience, Brown was active in the Vigilance Committee of Philadelphia, a public arm of the Underground Railroad for fugitives from slavery.

During Brown's thirteen active years in the episcopacy, the AME Church expanded westward. Brown organized the Pittsburgh Conference in Ohio in 1830 and the Indiana Conference ten years later. By the time of his death the church had congregations in fourteen states and in Canada, organized into six annual conferences, and had more than seventeen thousand members. In 1841 the denomination launched its first periodical, the *A.M.E. Church Magazine*, published until 1848; in it the initial debate was held about the right of women to preach. The AME Church also sent a representative to the 1846 international meeting of the Evangelical Alliance in London.

While in Toronto, Ontario, in 1844, Brown suffered a paralytic stroke, from which he never regained mobility. He even lost his voice in his last months, though it returned briefly just before his death in Philadelphia. By that time his son, Morris Jr., had become a well-known musician in Philadelphia, and the senior Brown had accumulated enough property to support his widow and their five other children.

Not known for literary productions or great preaching, Brown was a practical administrator and effective speaker who kept his message plain and pointed. A portrait shows him to have been a tall man with a large frame, a light complexion, and piercing eyes. His admirers named local churches after him in Philadelphia and Charleston, as well as a denominational college—Morris Brown College—that was founded in Atlanta after the Civil War.

FURTHER READING

George, Carol V. R. *Segregated Sabbaths: Richard Allen and the Emergence of Independent Black Churches, 1760–1840* (1973).

Wright, Richard R. *The Bishops of the African Methodist Episcopal Church* (1963).

Wright, Richard R., ed. *The Centennial Encyclopedia of the African Methodist Episcopal Church* (1916).

This entry is taken from the *American National Biography* and is published here with the permission of the American Council of Learned Societies.

WILL GRAVELY

Brown, Oscar, Jr. (10 Oct. 1926–29 May 2005), singer, songwriter, actor, activist, playwright, was born Oscar Cicero Brown Jr., the son of Oscar Brown Sr., a lawyer and real estate broker, and Helen Lawrence, a schoolteacher, in Chicago.

Growing up, Brown demonstrated an early attraction to and flair for language. He won elocution contests in school and was drawn to the poetry of LANGSTON HUGHES and COUNTÉE CULLEN as well as to the music of Cole Porter and Oscar Hammerstein. He wrote songs as a teenager and by age fifteen had made his show business debut in the children's radio drama *Secret City*. A year later, having skipped two grades, he enrolled at the University of Wisconsin, only to find that academia was not for him; he was drawn to creative writing but fell short in other subjects and as a consequence drifted from school to school, never graduating. Throughout this period his political sensibilities were also evolving. In 1946 he joined the Communist Party. In 1948 he ran on the Progressive Party ticket for a seat in the Illinois legislature. During this same period he became host of *Negro Newsfront*, a radio presentation that was also the nation's first issue-oriented news program focusing on the black community.

Brown left the show in 1952, the same year he ran for U.S. Congress as a Republican, although he was still a communist and would be for four more years. In 1955 he was drafted into the army and served two years. During that time he began to write songs in earnest. After his discharge he joined his father in the real estate business but never sold a single property; instead he concentrated all of his efforts on songwriting and playwriting. It would be three years before Brown's career was officially launched, then with the assistance of Robert Nemiroff, husband of the playwright LORRAINE HANSBERRY. Nemiroff passed Brown's demonstration tape to an executive at Columbia Records, and Brown signed with the company. His debut album, *Sin and Soul ... And Then Some*, was released in 1960.

Now considered a classic because of songs like "Signifying Monkey," "Bid 'Em In"—the harrowing tale of a black woman slave sold at an auction—and the trenchant lyrics of his own "Brown Baby," a lullaby written for his newborn son, the album brought Brown immediate recognition. His newfound fame also earned him the attention of Dave Garroway, host of the *Today Show*, who, in an unprecedented move, turned over an entire program to Brown's musical *Kicks and Company*, in what was essentially a backer's audition. While the play never made it to Broadway, Brown went on to share billing with such jazz greats as DIZZY GILLESPIE and JOHN COLTRANE. Moreover, his jazz connections made him the perfect choice to host the short-lived *Jazz Scene USA* in 1962. That same year, he met Jean Pace, a costume designer, who would later become his wife.

The year 1963 found Brown on tour in Europe and wowing the crowds in London with his one-man show. Critics there hailed him a "genius," and "the high priest of hip." But his London success did not follow him back to the United States. His work was too political for some in the recording industry and too angry for others. Refusing to compromise, he bore witness to the struggle against racism and the indomitable spirit of African American life with humor and deep feeling. He also set the stage for the politically conscious artists who came later and is regarded as a progenitor of Afrocentrism. By 1967, however, frustrated by his lack of commercial acceptance, Brown had found an additional outlet for his talents. Working with gang members from Chicago's infamous Blackstone Rangers street gang, he, along with his wife, wrote and produced the theatrical production *Opportunity, Please Knock* that featured over sixty gang members. The following year Richard Hatcher, mayor of Gary, Indiana, invited him to work with youngsters in a talent showcase. The Jackson 5 was one of the acts to emerge from that undertaking.

In 1969 Brown finally reached Broadway with his musical adaptation of Joseph Dolan Tuotti's play *Big Time Buck White*, starring MUHAMMAD ALI. The play enjoyed a brief run, and Brown, disheartened by a theater industry that refused to take risks, turned his attention once again to writing, producing, and performing. In 1972 he returned to the studio and subsequently released three more albums. In 1974, however, he found himself without a recording contract, a circumstance that persisted for twenty years. Still he continued to work. In 1975 he won two local Emmy Awards for a Chicago television special entitled *Oscar Brown Is Back in Town*. During this period he was also artist-in-residence at Howard University, Hunter College, and Malcolm X College in Chicago. Finally in 1980 he was tapped to host the PBS special *From Jumpstreet: The Story of Black Music*.

Brown worked throughout the 1990s also, making regular appearances on the television drama *Brewster Place* and the sitcom *Roc*. In 1995 he returned to the recording studio and released *Then and Now*, which included old and new material. But his life was not without its tragedies; in 1996 his son

Oscar Brown III, who often played nightclub dates with his father, died in an automobile accident.

Steadfast in his commitment to justice, Brown carried on. He delivered his message to the viewers of the HBO program *Russell Simmons Presents Def Poetry*. Just before his death he also received the Pan African Film Festival Lifetime Achievement Award in tandem with the presentation of a documentary about his life, *Music Is My Life, Politics Is My Mistress*. At the time of his death, Brown's body of work included a dozen operas and plays and more than 1,000 songs, only a fraction of which could be heard on ten albums. He died from complications due to a blood infection.

FURTHER READING

Brown, Oscar., Jr. *What It Is: Poems and Opinions of Oscar Brown Jr.* (2005).

Harrington, Richard. "The Many Moods of Oscar Brown Jr.: The Singer-Songwriter-Actor Melding Music and Message," *Washington Post*, 8 Mar. 1992.

Saul, Scott. *Freedom Is, Freedom Ain't: Jazz in the Making of the Sixties* (2005).

Wilson, John S. "Oscar Brown Jr. Seeking Audience For His Songs," *New York Times*, 19 Sept. 1980.

Obituary: *Black Issues Book Review*, Nov.–Dec. 2005.

DISCOGRAPHY

Kicks!: The Best of Oscar Brown Jr. (BGP Records 2004).

ELEANOR D. BRANCH

Brown, Richard Lonsdale (1893?–1915), landscape painter, was born in Indiana but was raised by his grandparents in Parkersburg, West Virginia. His parents and grandparents sent him to Charlestown Institute where he was trained in house painting. In 1904 he began studying art at West Virginia Colored Institute in Institute, West Virginia. He graduated in 1910 from the academic department, where he was trained in watercolor and where he took painting as an industrial course.

Brown then moved to Pittsburgh, Pennsylvania, where he studied pictures to compare various styles of landscape paintings, after which the Charlestown Institute invited him to teach house painting as a vocational art. Instead, Brown traveled to New York, where he lived on two dollars a week, without lodging. Brown could not afford to both sleep at a hotel and eat. He decided that he should eat, and chose to sleep on the railway cars for brief snatches of time. During the days he would try to sell his artwork to dealers, though with little success, and every evening he would stare at the work in the Metropolitan Museum of Art in New York City. He was especially influenced by Rousseau and Corot.

When art dealers refused to take him seriously because of his color, Brown became discouraged and eventually sought the opinion of his idol, George DeForest Brush, a legendary painter in Greenwich Village, New York. Brown visited Brush in 1911 for a critique of his artwork. Brush hailed Richard Brown an artistic genius and became his mentor. He helped Brown receive a grant from the newly established NAACP, and with it Brown was able to become Brush's student in New York and also to study with him at the Cornish, New Hampshire, Art Colony, during the summer of 1911.

In March 1912 Brown exhibited his impressionist paintings at the Ovington Gallery, owned by the Ovington Brothers Company, in New York. Around this time his paintings were featured on the covers of the *Crisis*, the NAACP's magazine. Brown was featured in both the December 1911 and April 1912 editions. The *Crisis* called its Easter edition the best ever issued because of Brown's cover illustration, which featured an early-spring image dominated by a central tree and with mountains in the distance. The tree is in heavy shadow but with the impression of leaves artistically rendered. "Winter Landscape," on the cover of the Christmas edition of the *Crisis*, featured a snowy scene with a sunset. Dark storm clouds taper to a fading of pink, and snowy hills are in the foreground; the picture is dominated by the sparse grass covered in snow and a few shadowed trees. Both covers show an artist interested in lighting and the isolation of landscapes. Richard Brown went on to work at the Robert Gould Shaw House, where he designed posters for W. E. B. DuBois's lectures.

Brown died at the age of twenty-four, without reaching his full potential. While no original works have been located, reproductions can be found at Harvard University, Cambridge, Massachusetts. The art historian John Cuthbert describes Brown's paintings as sharing common features with Frederick Maxfield Parrish and Willard Metcalf, whom Brown may have encountered in Pennsylvania or in Cornish, New Hampshire. Parrish shares the same love for large trees and plays similarly with light and shadow. Metcalf's paintings of winter scenes also use large expanses of snowy ground and large shadowy trees that dominate the painting and give it a feel of loneliness.

FURTHER READING

"Becomes Famous: Colored Boy of This City Is Ranked as One of the Leading Artists," *Parkersburg Sentinel*, 11 Mar. 1912.

Cuthbert, John A. *Early Art and Artists in West Virginia* (2000).

"Negro Youth Amazes Artists by His Talent," *New York Times*, 17 Mar. 1912.

KIMBERLY L. MALINOWSKI

Brown, Robert (c.1786–18 Jan. 1865), a soldier and sailor during the War of 1812, was born in Pennsylvania. At the beginning of the war he likely served in a Pennsylvania militia regiment, but sometime after March 1813 he was sent for duty at sea aboard the Lake Erie squadron under the command of Oliver Hazard Perry. Short on manpower during the outfitting of his fleet at Erie, Pennsylvania, including the twenty-gun brigs *Lawrence* and *Niagara*, Perry was forced to plead with his superior, Commodore Isaac Chauncey, to send him more men. After much wrangling, Chauncey finally sent Perry 150 men in two separate drafts, including African Americans Robert Brown, JESSE WALLS, and JAMES BROWN. Unfortunately, Perry was unhappy with the caliber of the men he received, complaining to Chauncey that "The men that came … are a motley set, blacks, Soldiers, and boys, I cannot think that you saw them after they were selected" (Altoff, 36). Although there has been debate about whether Chauncey sent Perry the dregs from his own fleet on Lake Ontario, there is no doubt that he appreciated the black sailors under his command. In answer to Perry's complaining letter, he quickly responded that "I regret you are not pleased with the men sent you … for to my knowledge a part of them are not surpassed by any seamen we have on the fleet, and I have yet to learn that the colour of the skin, or cut and trimmings of the coat, can effect a man's qualifications or usefulness. I have nearly 50 Blacks on board of this ship [the *General Pike*], and many of them are amongst my best men" (Altoff, 37). An ungrateful Perry would further complain to navy officials that if the men sent to him were representative of the men of the Great Lakes fleet, then "that squadron must be poorly manned indeed" (ibid.).

These exchanges between Oliver Hazard Perry and Chauncey serve to highlight the dichotomy of perception that exists to this day regarding the service of African American soldiers and sailors during the War of 1812 on the Great Lakes. Although Chauncey's words have gained notice, the disparaging descriptions of his men by Perry have all too often overshadowed them, and the truth probably lies somewhere in between. Subsequent events would soon leave no doubt as to the bravery and fighting skills of the black soldiers and sailors of Perry's Lake Erie squadron. The Battle of Lake Erie was fought on 10 September 1813 and was a smashing victory for the Americans over the much vaunted British Royal Navy. In a hard fought battle that lasted nearly three hours, Perry and his men defeated an experienced enemy fleet and by doing so effectively swept the British from control of Lake Erie. Robert Brown was wounded in the battle and was subsequently discharged from military service. However, the details of his service are lacking because of missing records; perhaps he served in Perry's flagship *Lawrence*, which fought the British single handedly for two hours, or maybe the *Niagara*, to which vessel Perry transferred his command to finish the fight.

After his discharge from the service, Robert Brown lived in Bedford, Pennsylvania, with his wife, Mary, and son, John, earning a living as a laborer. After his death, Mary Brown applied for and was granted a pension based on her husband's military service, which she received monthly until her death in Bedford on 4 December 1895.

FURTHER READING

Altoff, Gerard T. *Amongst My Best Men: African-Americans and the War of 1812* (1996).

GLENN ALLEN KNOBLOCK

Brown, Ron (1 Aug. 1941–3 Apr. 1996), Democratic Party activist and cabinet secretary, was born Ronald Harmon Brown at Freedmen's Hospital in Washington, D.C., the son of William Brown, who worked for the Federal Housing and Home Finance Agency, and Gloria Elexine Carter. The Browns moved to Harlem, New York, in 1947, and Ron grew up in the famed Theresa Hotel, where his father was manager. JOE LOUIS was a frequent guest, and gave young Ron the nickname "Little Brown." Ron showed his entrepreneurial skills at an early age by getting autographs of Louis, SUGAR RAY ROBINSON, and other celebrity guests at the Theresa and selling them for five dollars each to his friends. His parents, both graduates of Howard University, set Ron on a solid path to join the black middle class, which became, in many ways, the social network that would make possible many of his achievements. As a child, he met various politicians, including

Ron Brown, with president-elect Bill Clinton, at the announcement of his appointment as Commerce Secretary at a news conference in Little Rock, Arkansas, 12 December 1992. (AP Images.)

DAVID DINKINS, Congressman CHARLES RANGEL, and other notables, many of whom became his supporters in his adult life. He was the only black student at the Hunter College elementary school, and he graduated from the Rhodes School, a private preparatory school, in 1958.

Brown attended Middlebury College in Vermont and was the first African American inducted into Sigma Phi Epsilon fraternity—an action which cost the Middlebury chapter its charter in the national organization. After graduating with a B.A. in Political Science in 1962, he married Alma Arrington, a recent graduate of Fisk University from New York. The couple had two children. Brown entered the U.S. Army as a second lieutenant, serving abroad in Germany and Korea, where he was promoted to captain. But rather than continuing a military career, he left the service in early 1967 and began working for the National Urban League (NUL) while pursuing a law degree in the evenings at the St. John's University Law School in New York, graduating in 1970. Motivated in part by the feeling that he had missed being involved in the civil rights movement that was the focus of so much of the African American community in the 1960s, Brown chose to work with the NUL because it was a leading social service and civil rights organization. Brown began at the NUL as an assistant to Malcolm Puryear, deputy director to executive director WHITNEY YOUNG. Brown's talent was noticed and he rose quickly within the organization. When VERNON JORDAN assumed the role of president and CEO of the NUL after Young's death in 1971, Brown was promoted to general

counsel. In October 1973 he was appointed director of the NUL's Washington bureau, which was responsible for maintaining relations with politicians on Capitol Hill and members of the business community in the task of managing the League's agenda. Because of his effectiveness in this role, the League appointed him as liaison for its Commerce and Industry Council.

In 1980, Brown, who had been a district leader of the Democratic party in Westchester County, New York, in 1971, became increasingly interested in national politics and left the National Urban League to join Senator Edward Kennedy's presidential campaign as deputy manager. After Kennedy's unsuccessful presidential bid, the Senate Judiciary Committee hired Brown as its chief counsel, making him the first African American staff director of a major congressional committee. After the Senate passed to Republican control in 1981, Brown took a position at Patton, Boggs and Blow, a prestigious Washington lobbying and law firm. Brown's clients at the firm included Japanese electronics firms, the government of the autocratic Haitian leader Jean-Claude "Baby Doc" Duvalier, and a number of major domestic companies. In 1987 the firm made him a partner.

Brown continued to combine party political work with his lobbying activities, and in 1981 he became general counsel to the Democratic National Committee (DNC). He also was a prominent supporter of JESSE JACKSON's historic presidential bid in 1988, and Jackson invited Brown to serve as director of convention affairs for his presidential campaign. Increasingly, Jackson relied on Brown, rather than on his official campaign manager, as his key strategist in the run up to the Democratic National Convention in Atlanta. After Michael Dukakis became the Democratic presidential nominee at that convention in July 1988, Brown played a key role in cementing a relationship between Dukakis and Jackson, winning the respect of both the establishment and insurgent wings of the Democratic Party. At the convention, Brown also secured for himself a seat on the Party's national executive.

The experience and contacts he made in unifying the often fractious Democratic Party gave Brown the confidence to run for the post of DNC chairman in January 1989. Upon his election in February, he became the first African American to serve in that position. Brown and his staff, especially his political director, Paul Tully, prepared the Democrats to compete in the 1992 election by creating a "coordinated campaign" in which the national party worked closely with state party campaigns. This approach worked to the advantage of the Democratic presidential nominee, Bill Clinton, who campaigned without a strong national organization. Brown's direction of the DNC was also central in building national support for Clinton after his nomination. His choice of New York City as the party's convention site proved controversial, however, because Brown also served on the board and held stock in a company that had just won a $210 million dollar waste treatment contract from the city. Despite such negative publicity, Brown's political and business contacts in New York proved invaluable in helping the Clinton campaign gain access to one of the largest media and financial markets in the country.

Clinton, who often acknowledged that he would not have become president of the United States without Brown's help, appointed Brown as secretary of commerce in 1993. Again, Brown was the first African American to hold that position. Although he had hoped to become secretary of state, Brown settled enthusiastically into his new role, becoming one of the most vigorous secretaries of commerce in history. Believing that he could "really realize something for the American people," he traveled extensively throughout the country and around the globe to boost the standing of American business, securing numerous lucrative agreements for U.S. businesses abroad. During his tenure, a time of rapid economic growth, U.S. exports increased by over 25 percent.

Brown was not without his critics. He came under considerable attack from congressional Republicans who claimed that his trade missions favored Democratic Party supporters. In response, he stressed the bipartisan makeup of his delegations and their success in winning contracts for American firms and jobs for American citizens. Brown was particularly sensitive to the historical exclusion of minority firms and vigorously promoted expanded opportunities for minority businesses. But liberal groups like Common Cause were also critical of Brown's close ties to large corporations. The *New York Times*—hardly part of any vast right-wing conspiracy—ran a series of editorials in 1993 criticizing Brown's lack of full disclosure of his business interests.

Brown was cleared of the bribery charges leveled against him in 1993, but in 1995 Attorney General Janet Reno initiated an investigation into claims that he had submitted misleading financial disclosures and that his son Michael had been paid by an Oklahoma company in order to gain influence with his father. However, while on a trade mission to Dubrovnik, Croatia, in April 1996, a plane carrying Brown and his delegation of twelve executives of major corporations and fourteen U.S. government employees crashed during a storm in the mountains of Bosnia. At the time of his death, Ron Brown was considered by many to be the most powerful African American in the country.

FURTHER READING

Brown, Tracey L. *The Life and Times of Ron Brown* (1998).

Holms, Steven A. *Ron Brown: An Uncommon Life* (2001).

Obituary: *New York Times*, 4 April 1996.

RONALD WALTERS

Brown, Roosevelt "Rosey" (20 Oct. 1932–9 June 2004), Hall of Fame football player, was born in Charlottesville, Virginia, to Roosevelt Brown, a railroad worker, and Catherine Jackson Brown. He attended Jefferson High School, where he played trombone in the school band because his father forbade him from playing football. The football coach saw Brown and decided that a 180-pound thirteen-year-old should be playing football, not trombone. Rosey's father, who was worried because Rosey's uncle had died from a football injury, finally relented after Rosey played a full season injury free in 1945. Brown played four years of high school football, graduating in 1948.

After high school, Brown attended Morgan State University in Baltimore, Maryland, mainly because his high school coach was an alumnus. Brown was a standout lineman on the football team and was named to the 1952 Negro All-America team selected by the Pittsburgh *Courier*. He also wrestled while in college and served as the wrestling team captain for two years. He graduated in 1952 with a B.S. in Business. During the 1952 National Football League (NFL) draft, the New York Giants selected Brown in the twenty-seventh round, and he became only the second football player from Morgan State to turn pro. The Giants had not scouted Brown, and in fact no one in the organization had ever seen him play, but they took a chance after someone on the draft team saw his name on the Negro All-America list. After his college graduation, his mother put him on a train to the Giants' training camp with only ten dollars in his pocket—five from her and five from the Giants. When Brown arrived at the training

Roosevelt Brown, during a New York Giants workout at Bear Mountain in New York, 11 September 1958. (AP Images.)

camp at Gustavus Adolphus College in St. Paul, Minnesota, his 6'3", 245-pound frame tucked into a neat dark suit, fedora, and horn-rimmed glasses, team management was not sure if he was a football player. When camp opened, the offensive line coach played Brown against Arnie Weinmeister, arguably one of the best defensive tackles in football, to see what Brown could do. Brown was pounded continuously by Weinmeister, but he kept getting up and even ran laps after practice. His grit, combined with his size and speed, convinced the Giants of his potential. Brown, having never seen a professional football game before, was pretty green and had no idea how the business side of professional football worked. Unlike other rookies at the training camp who were in constant fear of being cut, Brown assumed it was similar to college and that everyone had made the team already. His first coach, Ed Kolman, the former all-league lineman for the Chicago Bears, taught Brown the basics of being a pro lineman, because everything about professional football was new to Brown, even down to the stance the coaches wanted him to use. Kolman also taught Brown that he could not try to play the opponent's game by letting the opponent dictate how he played, but Brown had to play his position his way. The Giants' coaches liked what they saw in Brown and in 1953 named him a starter on their offensive line.

Brown started as the left tackle, one of the hardest and least respected jobs in pro football. He was responsible for protecting the quarterback's blindside, usually toiling away in anonymity while the quarterback received the glory for the team's success. Not only was he a great pass blocker but he also had the speed and agility to run outside and block on running plays. Brown loved to hit people and was a punishing blocker, even taking out multiple defenders on some plays. The Giants used him occasionally on defense, when they needed a big body on goal line stands. Brown also played when he was hurt, missing only a few games over his career despite suffering concussions, broken bones, and torn ligaments.

Brown lived in Teaneck, New Jersey, and was easily recognized around town, mainly because of his affinity for expensive cars. During the off-season, he worked as a salesman for a local brewery, a job he hoped would become full-time after his football days. He was married to Linda Lock and helped raise her two children.

Brown played for the Giants for thirteen seasons before retiring in 1966 because of phlebitis. Over his career he became one of the greatest offensive lineman in the history of pro football. Brown and his contemporary Ron Mix of the San Diego Chargers were the last pulling tackles in the NFL, a job usually reserved for guards. Brown appeared in nine Pro Bowls and was named All-Pro for eight consecutive years (1956–1963). He became the first black captain for the Giants and helped them win six Eastern Conference titles. In 1956 Brown was named the Associated Press Lineman of the Year because he helped lead the Giants to the NFL Championship.

Following his retirement, Brown became one of few linemen and even fewer black football players to successfully transition into coaching. He served as an assistant line coach for the Giants from 1967 to 1968. In 1969 Brown replaced Joe Trible as the head line coach, and he became a scout for the Giants in 1971, a position he held until his death. In 1975 he was inducted into the Pro Football Hall of Fame, a feat rarely accomplished by an offensive lineman. The NFL named him to its 75-year All-Pro team in 1994 and to its All-Time team in 2000. The noted sports broadcaster John Madden named Brown to the All-Madden Millennium team in 1999.

Brown died of a heart attack while gardening outside his home in Columbus, New Jersey. Many former Giants attended his funeral to pay their respects, including the Giants owner Wellington Mara, who called Brown a "great Giant" (*Hackensack Record*, 11 June 2004). Teammate and fellow Hall of Fame member Frank Gifford said he owed his career to Brown's ability. Gifford, a running back, recalled the longest run of his career in which Brown made a tremendous block at the line of scrimmage to open a hole for Gifford. When Gifford looked up again, there was Brown out in front making another block. That play was the epitome of the abilities that made Brown a Hall of Fame football player and a respected member of the New York Giants organization.

FURTHER READING

Bechtel, Mark. "A Nimble Giant," *Sports Illustrated* 100 (21 June 2004): 29.

Silverman, Al, ed. *The Specialist in Pro Football* (1965).

Obituaries: *New York Times*, 11 June 2004; *Hackensack (New Jersey) Record*, 11 June 2004.

MICHAEL C. MILLER

Brown, Roscoe Conkling, Jr. (9 Mar. 1922–), military pilot and educator, was born in Washington, D.C., the elder of two children born to Vivian Brown, a public school teacher, and Dr. Roscoe C. Brown Sr., a dentist and newspaper editor who served in President Franklin D. Roosevelt's "black cabinet." As a young boy Brown lived with his family in Depression-era Washington, D.C., where economic troubles were as harsh as racial segregation in the city's social spheres. Public education was no exception. But Brown did not allow racial bigotry to stifle his academic interests.

Brown began his formal education at Blanche K. Bruce School, a segregated public institution named after a black U.S. senator from Mississippi elected during Reconstruction. He was fortunate to receive a first-rate education at the academically prestigious Paul Laurence Dunbar High School (formerly the M Street High School), a black public school named after the eminent black poet, and alma mater of famous Washingtonians such as CHARLES RICHARD DREW and CHARLES HAMILTON HOUSTON. Brown excelled in his studies, enjoying Latin, history, and chemistry. After graduation Brown, like many high school graduates of his generation, traveled to the North for his undergraduate studies. Brown became a scholar-athlete at Springfield College, a mostly white liberal arts school located in Massachusetts. He earned letters in football and lacrosse, making him one of the first black athletes to do so, and he graduated as class valedictorian in 1943 with a bachelor of arts in Health, Physical Education, and Chemistry.

With degree in hand, Brown heeded the call of Uncle Sam to fight the Nazi Luftwaffe by enlisting in the U.S. Army Air Corps. Three years before Brown's enlistment, blacks had been unable to join the air corps. All of that changed on 16 September 1940, when President Franklin D. Roosevelt signed the Selective Service and Training Act. This law opened the U.S. Army Air Corps to black enlistees, but on a segregated basis only. So in October 1940 an all-black aviation school was established at Tuskegee Institute, a private historically black college located in central Alabama and founded in 1881 by BOOKER T. WASHINGTON. The aviation group was called the Ninety-ninth Pursuit Squadron. A year before Brown's arrival at Tuskegee, the U.S. Army Air Corps created the One Hundredth Fighter Squadron as part of the 332d Fighter Group. The latter group was known as the "Black Red-tail Angels" by white American pilots. German opponents called them the "*Schwartze Voglemenschen*," the "Black Birdmen." Brown became a member of the One Hundredth Fighter Squadron of the 332d Fighter Group, where he later assumed the position as commander. On 4 July 1944 the all-black 332d Fighter Group was created through a merger of the existing 99th, 100th, 301st, and 302d squadrons.

From 1943 to 1944 Brown trained at the Tuskegee Army Base in Alabama, at Selfridge Field in Michigan, and Waterboro Air Base in South Carolina. During his training Brown met General BENJAMIN O. DAVIS JR., another black Washingtonian as well as a West Point graduate who became the leader of the Tuskegee Airmen. At Davis's 2002 funeral Brown referred to him as "My hero." Brown flew in sixty-eight combat missions, flying the P-51 Mustang over Germany, Austria, and the Balkans. As a result of the role black soldiers such as Brown played in World War II, President Harry S. Truman signed Executive Order 9981 to integrate the U.S. Armed Services on 26 July 1948. And because of Brown's gallantry to the American cause for freedom, he was one of 150 recipients of the Distinguished Flying Cross and a recipient of the Air Medal with eight Oak Leaf Clusters. He returned to civilian life in 1946, retiring three years later from the military with the rank of captain. Having helped make the world safe for democracy, Brown relocated to New York City, energized and focused on achieving the same ideals in his own country. Higher education was his weapon of choice.

Brown worked as a social investigator in the New York City Department of Welfare, then as a physical education teacher at West Virginia State, a historically black public college. Eager to become a college professor, Brown earned a masters of arts degree in 1949 and a Ph.D. in 1951 from New York University (NYU), specializing in exercise physiology. Brown later used this training to become a founding member of the American College of Sports Medicine in 1954. In 1988 Brown was inducted into the National Sports and Physical Education Hall of Fame. During his tenure as a professor of education at NYU from 1950 to 1977, Brown attained the rank of full professor in 1960 and in 1969 became the director of the Institute of Afro-American Affairs. In addition to his work inside the academy, Brown's film and television projects won him an Emmy Award for Distinguished Program in 1973 for his *Black Arts* series shown on CBS television. After a long and successful career at NYU, Brown accepted a position as president of the Bronx Community College in 1977 and stayed for sixteen years. In 1993 Brown created the Center for Urban Education Policy at the City University of New York to provide support to systemic school reform. Brown has been the director of the center since 1993.

To honor the service of Dr. Brown and his fellow Tuskegee Airmen during World War II, President George W. Bush awarded the airmen a Congressional Medal of Honor on 29 July 2007. Brown and five other Tuskegee Airmen accepted the medal on behalf of their friends. "We are so overjoyed," said Roscoe Brown Jr. "We are so proud today, and I think America is proud today." The Democratic senator Carl Levin from Michigan and the Democratic congressman CHARLES RANGEL from New York sponsored the legislation to honor the Tuskegee Airmen.

Brown published more than fifty articles during his academic career and received honorary degrees from the College of New Rochelle, Springfield College, the University of the State of New York, and the Regents of the State of New York. An avid believer in strengthening the mind and body, Brown completed nine New York City marathons.

FURTHER READING

Brown, Roscoe, Jr., and Bryant J. Cratty. *New Perspectives of Man in Action* (1969).

Brown, Roscoe, Jr., and Gerald S. Kenyon, eds. *Classical Studies on Physical Activity* (1968).

Ploski, Harry A., and Roscoe Brown, eds. *The Negro Almanac* (1967).

Superville, Darlene. "Tuskegee Airmen Get Congressional Medal," *USA Today*, 29 Mar. 2007.

GERARD ROBINSON

Brown, Ruth (12 Jan. 1928–17 Nov. 2006), rhythm and blues performer and actress, was born Ruth Alston Weston in Portsmouth, Virginia, the eldest of Leonard and Martha Jane (Alston) Weston's seven children. Her father, a skillful athlete who had hoped to become a professional baseball player, found work as a laborer on the Portsmouth docks and worked odd jobs at nights. His weekly wages rarely exceeded $35 per week and barely covered the needs of his growing family. Ruth's mother worked as a domestic. In 1934, when she was six years old, Ruth entered Portsmouth's George Peabody Elementary School and later attended I.C. Norcom High School. Her early years were decidedly urban. She was a weekend regular at Portsmouth's Capitol movie theater, where she cheered on the black action heroes Herb Jeffries and Ralph Cooper, and idolized the young LENA HORNE.

Ruth Weston belonged, however, to that generation of urban African Americans who were born after the Great Migration but who maintained close links to the rural South. During the long summer months of her early school years, the Westons shipped Ruth and her siblings a few miles south to their mother's childhood home in Macon, North Carolina. There the rural blues rhythms of her uncles, who whooped, hollered, shrieked, and shouted across the fields "was soaking in just as surely as the sweat was pouring out," she later recalled (Brown, 30). Her vocal style was also shaped by singing spirituals in Portsmouth's Emmanuel AME church choir, which her father directed, and by performing from age seven onward at weddings and other family functions. In her early teens, she listened to Bing Crosby, Hank Williams, and other white pop and country singers on the radio; Crosby's croon and Williams's yodel and moan would also become part of her vocal repertoire. Jazz and blues performers were rare on most southern radio stations at that time, but in 1942 a visit to some relatives in Harlem, New York, introduced her to recordings by BILLIE HOLIDAY, who along with DINAH WASHINGTON and SARAH VAUGHN greatly influenced her early preference for soulful, jazz-inflected ballads. Around this time Brown began frequenting black nightclubs in nearby Norfolk, Virginia, and was soon performing "The Chattanooga Choo Choo," among other pop standards at United Services Organizations (USO) events in and around Norfolk. She did so in secret, knowing that her father was opposed to his teenage daughter performing secular music, particularly in

Ruth Brown, singing in the Salute to the Blues concert at Radio City Music Hall, 7 February 2003. (AP Images.)

venues crowded with hundreds of young men who had flocked to the Virginia Tidewater's docks, factories, and military bases in the wake of America's entry into World War II. Despite her father's warnings and occasional beatings, Ruth persisted, even traveling to New York City in 1944, where she won first prize on Amateur Night at Harlem's famed Apollo Theater for her performance of Bing Crosby's "It Could Happen to You." She declined the offer of a week's engagement at the Apollo, but returned to Virginia considerably emboldened about her prospects as a professional performer. In 1945, after a fight between two of her suitors left one of them dead, Brown, still only seventeen, left Portsmouth to pursue a full-time musical career. At first she performed mainly on southern military bases, and in her new hometown of Norfolk, where in late 1945 she met and fell in love with Jimmy Earle Brown, a midshipman, singer, and trumpeter. At eighteen, Jimmy was only one year her senior. The couple began performing together as Brown and Brown, even before they married in Elizabeth City, North Carolina, in 1946, but Ruth later found out that

Jimmy already had a wife. Although their marriage was annulled, Ruth continued to sing with Brown and his Band of Atomic Swing throughout 1947, retaining her stage name when the couple separated a year later. In early 1948 Ruth Brown performed briefly with the LUCKY MILLINDER band, but was sacked by Millinder for delivering drinks to the band after finishing her spot. Following a brief stint at BLANCHE CALLOWAY's nightclub in Washington, D.C., Brown signed with Ahmet Ertegun and Herb Abramson's fledgling Atlantic Records in January 1949.

In May 1949 Atlantic released Brown's first single, "So Long," a blues-tinged ballad that displayed the singer's extraordinary vocal range, her moans, shouts, dips, and yelps. For this performance Abramson did not have to ask Brown to sing "like you've got tears in your eyes," as he often did. She was still on crutches and wearing painful leg braces, the consequence of a serious car crash that had left her hospitalized for nine months with two broken legs. By June 1949 "So Long" had climbed to number six on *Billboard*'s rhythm and blues chart, making it one of Atlantic's first major hits. After four unsuccessful follow-up singles, Brown released "Teardrops from My Eyes," a more up-tempo, swinging number that reached the top of the chart in October 1950 and stayed there for the next eleven weeks. Over the next decade "Miss Rhythm," as she came to be known, recorded eleven top ten singles and five number one hits for Atlantic, the most popular being the raunchy "5-10-15 Hours (of Your Love)" (1952), "(Mama) He Treats Your Daughter Mean" (1953), "Oh What a Dream!" (1954), and "Mambo Baby," Atlantic's contribution to 1954's mambo craze.

"(Mama) He Treats Your Daughter Mean" proved to be Brown's signature recording for Atlantic. It included what Abramson called her "million dollar squeal" and a shouted "-uh!" at the end of "Mama" that LITTLE RICHARD later copied for his classic, "Lucille" (Brown, 123). The song was also to some extent autobiographical, given Brown's continued troubled relationships with men, among them the tenor saxophonist Willis "Gator Tail" Jackson, a serial philanderer; Drew Brown, a heavy drinker, with whom she had a brief affair and a son, Ronald, born in 1955; and Earl Swanson, another tenor sax player, whom she married that year, and with whom she had a son, Earl Jr., in 1956. Swanson also drank heavily, beat Brown several times, and tried to control her career. The couple separated and divorced in the late 1950s.

Although some of Brown's singles crossed over into the lower reaches of the white pop charts, they were more often covered—in a less raunchy and supposedly more palatable fashion—by white singers like Georgia Gibbs and Patti Page. Brown resented that these artists got to perform her hits on *The Ed Sullivan Show* and other nationally syndicated programs, which rarely booked black artists in the early 1950s. The general crossover of rhythm and blues to the white consumer-driven *Billboard* pop chart and radio play began in mid-1954, a few weeks after the Supreme Court's decision in *Brown v. Board of Education*. In some sense, this seismic cultural shift in white musical preferences proved as significant to American race relations as the Court's school integration ruling. It certainly proved profitable for Atlantic, the "House that Ruth [Brown] Built," which was by the mid-1950s in prime position to exploit this new market, with a roster of artists that came to include the Drifters, the Coasters, and ARETHA FRANKLIN.

By the time Ahmet Ertegun sold Atlantic Records to Warner Brothers for $17 million in 1967, Ruth Brown was living on Long Island, New York. She had recently divorced her third husband, Bill Blunt, a policeman, whom she had married in 1963, and who had tried unsuccessfully to stop her from performing. Her successful recording career apparently behind her, she worked briefly as a bus driver, a teacher's aide at a Head Start program, and as a maid, and depended on federal assistance to help raise her children. As was the case with many performers during the early days of the music recording industry, the fruits of Brown's success and popularity had gone largely to her label. Brown had received no royalties—and sometimes as little as sixty-nine dollars per side—for her many hit singles on Atlantic. In need of money she wrote to Ertegun for help, receiving in return a check for $1,000 and a warning that *she* owed money to Atlantic.

In the 1970s Brown's career revived when the comedian REDD FOXX, a friend from her days touring the South with the Band of Atomic Swing, offered her a role on his hit television show, *Sanford and Son* (1972–1977). Foxx later invited her to play the role of MAHALIA JACKSON in his musical about the civil rights movement, *Selma* (1977). She also began to tour again, in Europe, as part of a package put together by Scandinavian rhythm and blues aficionados, before returning to New York in the 1980s, where she appeared Off-Broadway in an adaptation of JAMES BALDWIN's *Amen Corner*

(1982) and in the musical *Staggerlee* (1986), based on the life of outlaw STAGOLEE. It was, however, her star turn in *Black and Blue*, a musical about Harlem's famed Cotton Club in the 1920s, that brought Brown back into the national spotlight. She received rave notices for the show's premiere in Paris in 1985 and in 1989 won a Tony Award when the production moved to Broadway. Her popularity was also enhanced by her role as Motormouth Maybelle in John Waters's *Hairspray* (1987) and for her contribution to *That Rhythm Those Blues* (1988), an award-winning documentary. She also won a Grammy in 1990 for her album, *Blues on Broadway*. The standout song on both *Black and Blue* and *Blues on Broadway*, "If I Can't Sell it, I'll Keep Sitting On It," assured her fans that Miss Rhythm had lost none of her earlier sass and spice. In 1993 Brown was inducted into the Rock and Roll Hall of Fame and sang at Bill Clinton's presidential inaugural. In 1996 Brown published her autobiography, *Miss Rhythm*. Despite suffering a stroke in 2000, she continued to tour and perform regularly.

In addition to a career spanning more than six decades, Brown took a leading role in the Rhythm and Blues Foundation, a cooperative she established with the Washington attorney Howell Begle and the singer Bonnie Raitt to educate the public about the pioneering work of early rhythm and blues and rock and roll performers. The Foundation also helped hundreds of performers receive some of the monies owed to them by record companies like Atlantic, whose guiding principle in those days was summed up by its comptroller, Miriam Beinstock: "That's the whole principle of capitalism. You take advantage of people!" (Brown, 261). Atlantic Records eventually promised to endow the Foundation with $1,500,000. The Foundation also persuaded Atlantic and other record companies to recalculate the royalties paid to some of their artists in the 1950s and 1960s. Brown eventually received a check for $27,000 and 4.5 percent of the royalties on her old recordings, considerably less than today's rock, pop, and hip-hop performers who receive 10 percent. Many of her fans, however, viewed her settlement as considerably less than a pioneer like Brown deserved. As STEVIE WONDER stated, Ruth Brown "started it all. Wasn't for Ruth there wouldn't be no Aretha [Franklin], wouldn't be *nobody!*" (Brown, 184).

Brown died in Henderson, Nevada, from complications related to a heart attack and stroke she suffered in 2006.

FURTHER READING

Brown, Ruth, and Andrew Yule. *Miss Rhythm: The Autobiography of Ruth Brown, Rhythm and Blues Legend* (1996).

Ward, Brian. *Just My Soul Responding: Rhythm and Blues, Black Consciousness, and Race Relations* (1999).

Obituary: *New York Times*, 18 Nov. 2006.

STEVEN J. NIVEN

Brown, Solomon G. (14 Feb. 1829–24 June 1906), the first African American to work at the Smithsonian Institute, naturalist, and poet, was born free in what is now the Anacostia section of Washington, D.C. He was the fourth of six children born to Isaac and Rachel Brown. Little is known about Brown's family, except that his father died in 1833 and consequently the family struggled financially and lost their home in 1834. Brown received no formal education as a youngster. Because of prejudice and slavery in the 1800s, public education was not provided to free blacks living in Washington, D.C., until after the Emancipation Act in 1862. Brown was a self-educated man.

Accounts of Brown's early life indicate that there was an arrangement for him to live in the care of the assistant postmaster of Washington, D.C., Lambert Tree. Whether Brown was a household servant or an apprentice in Tree's work at the post office is unknown. This arrangement served Brown well, however, and provided him opportunities as Tree became his benefactor and in 1844 obtained a job for Brown at the post office. More importantly, in 1858, four years before the Emancipation Act, in a District of Columbia Court, Tree swore under oath that Brown was a free black. This legal declaration of Brown's freedom lessened the chances that Brown would be apprehended or detained as a slave, something that was always a concern of free blacks before slavery was abolished.

At the post office Brown worked with Joseph Henry, Samuel F. B. Morse, and Alfred Vail in the building of the first magnetic telegraph system between Washington, D.C., and Baltimore, Maryland. The first telegraph message was transmitted on 14 May 1844 from Baltimore. Later in life Brown wrote that he carried the first telegraphed message to the White House. His interest in scientific matters grew and he went on to work as a battery tender with the Morse Telegraph Company. When Joseph Henry was appointed secretary of the Smithsonian Institute, he hired Brown in 1852, and

so Brown became the first African American to work at the Smithsonian.

Brown worked for fifty-four years in various capacities at the Institute, which had been founded (after much debate) by Congress in 1846; after twelve years he served as a museum assistant with a salary of sixty dollars a month. He worked closely with the first three secretaries of the Smithsonian: Joseph Henry, Spencer F. Baird, and Samuel P. Langley. Correspondence between Brown and all three secretaries suggest that Brown made significant contributions to the operation of the national museum. According to WILLIAM J. SIMMONS's 1887 *Men of Mark*, he prepared all the illustrations for the scientific lectures given at the Smithsonian until 1887 and delivered his first public lecture in January 1855 to the Young Peoples' Literary Society and Lyceum.

Working at the Smithsonian, Brown was exposed to much information about natural history, and he became a popular lecturer to adult groups and scientific societies in the Washington area. Some of his illustrated lectures were on subjects such as geology, minerals, and embryo plants. Brown was also a political activist and served on a committee that encouraged the Freedmen's Bureau to buy land in Washington, D.C., for homesteads for newly freed blacks. Under the Territorial Government of the District of-Columbia he served three consecutive terms, from 1871 until 1874, as a member of the House of Delegates. In 1871 Washington lost its charter as a city and a territorial government was established. The territory had a governor and a council appointed by-the president, a popularly elected House of Delegates, and one non-voting delegate to the U.S. Congress. Brown was elected to the House of Delegates. This territorial government of Washington-lasted only three years, but Brown served all from 1871 through 1874.

Brown and his wife, Lucinda, whom he married in 1864, lived in the Anacostia section, later called East Hillsdale, of Washington, where they were prominent members of the community. Though they were childless, they had an extended community family. The Browns founded the Pioneer Sabbath School, which records indicate was an active organization in the community. It is reported that FREDERICK DOUGLASS and his sons were associated with the school and donated an organ to the institution. Brown was a member of the Freedman's Relief Association and trustee of the 15th Street Presbyterian Church and Wilberforce University.

In addition to his lecturing Brown also wrote and published poetry. In a poem titled "Fifty Years To-Day" to mark the fiftieth anniversary of the Smithsonian Institute in 1896, Brown spoke his mind forthrightly about the role Henry played in the development and implementation of the telegraph, which he felt that Morse had unfairly garnered all the glory for creating. Brown retired from the Smithsonian on 14 February 1906 and died the next June at his home in East Hillsdale at the age of seventy-seven.

FURTHER READING

Documents concerning Brown and his work at the Smithsonian Institute are available online at http://siarchives.si.edu/history/exhibits/documents/brown2.htm.

Hutchinson, Louise Daniel, and Gail Sylvia Lowe, compilers. "Kind Regards of S.G. Brown": Selected Poems of Solomon G. Brown (1983).

Logan, Rayford W., and Michael R. Winston, eds. Dictionary of American Negro Biography (1982).

Simmons, William J. Men of Mark (1887).

Trescott, Jacqueline. "Smithsonian Honors a Black Pioneer," Washington Post, 16 June 2004.

LINDA SPENCER

Brown, Sterling Allen (1 May 1901–13 Jan. 1989), professor of English, poet, and essayist, was born in Washington, D.C., the son of Sterling Nelson Brown, a minister and divinity school professor, and Adelaide Allen. After graduating as valedictorian from Dunbar High School in 1918, Brown matriculated at Williams College, where he studied French and English literature and won the Graves Prize for an essay on Molière and Shakespeare. He graduated from Williams in 1922 with Phi Beta Kappa honors and a Clark fellowship for graduate studies in English at Harvard University. Once at Harvard, Brown studied with Bliss Perry and, most notably, with George Lyman Kittredge, the distinguished scholar of Shakespeare and the ballad. Kittredge's example as a scholar of both formal and vernacular forms of literature doubtlessly encouraged Brown to contemplate a similar professorial career, though for Brown the focus would be less on the British Isles than on the United States and on African American culture, in particular. Brown received his M.A. in English from Harvard in 1923 and went south to his first teaching job at Virginia Seminary and College at Lynchburg.

Brown's three years at Virginia Seminary represent much more than the beginning of his teaching career, for it was there that he began to immerse himself in the folkways of rural black people, absorbing their stories, music, and idioms. In this regard, Brown is usefully likened to two of his most famous contemporaries, ZORA NEALE HURSTON and JEAN TOOMER (with whom Brown attended high school). Like Hurston, Brown conducted a kind of iconoclastic ethnographic fieldwork among southern black people in the 1920s (she in Florida, he in Virginia) and subsequently produced a series of important essays on black folkways. Like Hurston and Toomer, Brown drew on his observations to produce a written vernacular literature that venerated black people of the rural South instead of championing the new order of black life being created in cities in the North. And like Toomer, in particular, Brown's wanderings in the South represented not just a quest for literary material but also an odyssey in search of roots more meaningful than what seemed to be provided by college in the North and black bourgeois culture in Washington. After Virginia Seminary, Brown taught briefly at Lincoln University in Missouri and Fisk University before beginning his forty-year career at Howard University in 1929.

Brown's first published poems, many of them "portraitures" of Virginia rural black folk, such as Sister Lou and Big Boy Davis, appeared in the 1920s in Opportunity magazine and in celebrated anthologies, including COUNTÉE CULLEN's Caroling Dusk (1927) and JAMES WELDON JOHNSON's Book of American Negro Poetry (1922; 2d ed., 1931). When Brown's first book of poems, Southern Road, was published in 1932, Johnson's introduction praised Brown for having, in effect, discovered how to write a black vernacular poetry that was not fraught with the limitations of the "dialect verse" of the PAUL LAURENCE DUNBAR era thirty years earlier. Johnson wrote that Brown "has made more than mere transcriptions of folk poetry, and he has done more than bring to it mere artistry; he has deepened its meanings and multiplied its implications." Johnson also showed his respect for Brown by inviting him to write the Outline for the Study of the Poetry of American Negroes (1931), a teacher's guide to accompany Johnson's poetry anthology.

The 1930s were productive and exciting years for Brown. In addition to settling into teaching at Howard and publishing Southern Road, he wrote a regular column for Opportunity ("The Literary Scene: Chronicle and Comment"), reviewing plays and films as well as novels, biographies, and scholarship by black and white Americans alike. From

1936 to 1939 Brown was the Editor on Negro Affairs for the Federal Writers' Project. In that capacity he oversaw virtually everything written about African Americans and wrote large sections of *The Negro in Virginia* (1940). The latter work led to his being named a researcher on the Carnegie-Myrdal Study of the Negro, which generated the data for Gunnar Myrdal's classic study, *An American Dilemma: The Negro Problem and Modern Democracy* (1944). In 1937 Brown was awarded a Guggenheim Fellowship, which afforded him the opportunity to complete *The Negro in American Fiction* and *Negro Poetry and Drama*, both published in 1937. *The Negro Caravan: Writings by American Negroes* (1941), a massive anthology of African American writing, edited by Brown with ULYSSES GRANT LEE and ARTHUR P. DAVIS, continues to be the model for bringing song, folktale, mother wit, and written literature together in a comprehensive collection.

From the 1940s into the 1960s Brown was no longer an active poet, in part because his second collection, "No Hidin' Place," was rejected by his publisher. Even though many of his poems were published in the *Crisis*, the *New Republic*, and the *Nation*, Brown found little solace and turned instead to teaching and writing essays. In the 1950s Brown published such major essays as "Negro Folk Expression," "The Blues," and "Negro Folk Expression: Spirituals, Seculars, Ballads and Work Songs," all in the Atlanta journal *Phylon*. Also in this period Brown wrote "The New Negro in Literature (1925–1955)" (1955). In this essay he argued that the Harlem Renaissance was, in fact, a New Negro Renaissance, not a Harlem Renaissance, because few of the significant participants, including him, lived in Harlem or wrote about it. He concluded that the Harlem Renaissance was the publishing industry's hype, an idea that gained renewed attention when publishers once again hyped the Harlem Renaissance in the 1970s.

The 1970s and 1980s were a period of recognition and perhaps of subtle vindication for Sterling Brown. While enduring what was for him the melancholy of retirement from Howard in 1969, he found himself suddenly in the limelight as a rediscovered poet and as a pioneering teacher and founder of the new field of African American studies. Numerous invitations followed for poetry readings, lectures, and tributes, and fourteen honorary degrees were bestowed on him. In 1974 *Southern Road* was reissued. In 1975 Brown's ballad poems were collected and published under the title *The Last Ride of Wild Bill and Eleven Narrative Poems*. In 1980 Brown's *Collected Poems*, a volume edited by MICHAEL S. HARPER, was published in the National Poetry Series. Brown was named poet laureate of the District of Columbia in 1984.

Brown had married Daisy Turnbull in 1927, possibly in Lynchburg, where they had met. They had one child. Brown was very close to his two sisters, who lived next door in Washington. They cared for him after his wife's death in 1979 until Brown entered a health center in Takoma Park, Maryland, where he died.

Brown returned to Williams College for the first time in fifty-one years on 22 September 1973 to give an autobiographical address and again in June 1974 to receive an honorary degree. The address, "A Son's Return: 'Oh Didn't He Ramble'" (*Berkshire Review* 10 [Summer 1974], 9–30; reprinted in Harper and Stepto, eds., *Chant of Saints* [1979]), offers much of Brown's philosophy for living a productive American life. At one point he declares, "I am an integrationist …because I know what segregation really was. And by integration, I do not mean assimilation. I believe what the word means—an integer is a whole number. I want to be in the best American traditions. I want to be accepted as a whole man. My standards are not white. My standards are not black. My standards are human." Brown largely achieved these goals and standards. His poetry, for example, along with that of LANGSTON HUGHES, forever put to rest the question of whether a written art based on black vernacular could be resilient and substantial and read through the generations. Despite his various careers, Brown saw himself primarily as a teacher, and it was as a professor at Howard that he felt he had made his mark, training hundreds of students and pioneering those changes in the curriculum that would lead to increasing appreciation and scrutiny of vernacular American and African American art forms. In short, Brown was one of the scholar-teachers whose work before 1950 enabled the creation and development of American studies and African American studies programs in colleges and universities in the decades to follow.

FURTHER READING
Brown's papers are housed at Howard University, chiefly in the Moorland-Spingarn Collection.
Gates, Henry Louis, Jr. *Figures in Black: Words, Signs, and the "Racial" Self* (1987).
Gabbin, Joanne. *Sterling A. Brown: Building the Black Aesthetic Tradition* (1985).
Jones, Gayl. *Liberating Voices: Oral Tradition in African American Literature* (1991).

Stepto, Robert. "'When de Saints go Ma'chin' Home':
    Sterling Brown's Blueprint for a New Negro Poetry."
    Kunapipi 4, no. 1 (1982): 94–105.
Stepto, Robert. "Sterling Brown: Outsider in the
    Renaissance," in *Harlem Renaissance Revaluations*
    (1989).
Obituary: *New York Times*, 17 Jan. 1989.
This entry is taken from the *American National
Biography* and is published here with the
permission of the American Council of Learned
Societies.

ROBERT STEPTO

Brown, Sue M. Wilson (8 Sept. 1877–29 Nov. 1941),
clubwoman, civil rights activist, and editor, was
born Sue M. Wilson in Staunton, Virginia, the eldest
child of Marian Harris, a homemaker, and Jacob
Wilson, a recruiting agent for the mining industry. When Wilson was young, the family moved to
Muchakinock, Iowa, where she received her early
education. They eventually relocated to Oskaloosa,
Iowa, where Wilson graduated from high school.
A lifelong member of the African Methodist
Episcopal (AME) Church, Wilson became superintendent of the Muchakinock Sunday School at
the age of twenty-three. This position led to her
election as district superintendent of the church
schools, where she gained valuable organizational
experience.

On 31 December 1902 Wilson married S. Joe
Brown, an attorney in Muchakinock, who had just
opened an office in Des Moines, Iowa, where the
couple settled into a life of activism. Sue Wilson
Brown immediately became involved in the club
movement, beginning a lifetime of religious, political, sororal, and federated club work. The absence
of children made it possible for both of the Browns
to devote their attention to the black community,
locally and nationally. Just three years after her
arrival in Des Moines, Brown organized her first
group, the Intellectual Improvement Club, which
sent her as a delegate to the State Federation of
Colored Women's Clubs in Keokuk, Iowa, in 1906.
There she was appointed to a publicity post for the
federation. After three years of serving as a state
delegate for the Intellectual Improvement Club to
the State Federation of Colored Women's Clubs,
Brown represented the State Federation of Colored
Women's Clubs at the National Association of
Colored Women, where she was given a national
appointment in 1909. Brown held a national office
in the NACW the rest of her life. It was during the

early years of her marriage and club involvement
that Brown also founded and edited a monthly
magazine, the *Iowa Colored Woman*.

In 1912 Brown organized the Des Moines League
of Colored Women Voters, followed by the Mary
B. Talbert Club in 1914. She served as president
of the Iowa State Federation of Colored Women's
Clubs from 1915 to 1917, and during her tenure she
oversaw the establishment of the University Girls
Student Home in Iowa City, the first home in the
United States maintained by African American
women at a state university. The home provided
living quarters to African American women who
were ineligible to live in the State University of
Iowa's segregated dormitories. Brown and her
husband vigorously promoted the idea of interracial communication and cooperation through
the founding of the First Interracial Commission
on Civil Rights in Des Moines. Sue Wilson Brown
served as the group's first president. The Browns
also helped found the Des Moines Branch of the
NAACP in 1912, just three years after the formation of the national organization, and Brown
served as president from 1924 to 1931. From the
beginning, the charter members of the Des Moines
Branch directed their efforts toward young African
Americans, and Brown established an NAACP
Junior Chapter in 1922.

With the advent of World War I, Brown became
active in the American Red Cross and organized
the Colonel Charles Young Auxiliary for African
Americans. Since the Red Cross would not accept
blood from African Americans, members of the
Colonel Charles Young Auxiliary rolled bandages,
held fund-raisers, and provided other services to
the war effort. Brown was able to tap into local
African American's patriotism and build a successful Red Cross unit. During the 1920s Brown jug-
gled the presidencies of the Des Moines branches
of the NAACP and the Church Women's Interracial
Commission, oversaw the Junior NAACP, managed
the Protection Home for Girls, was a delegate to
the International Council of Women of the World,
served as International Matron of the Order of
the Eastern Star for Colored Women, the women's
group for Prince Hall Freemasons, was a charter
member of the Central Association of Colored
Women, and served as a steward and Sunday
school teacher at her church. She was one of the first
women to sit on the Board of Trustees of St. Paul
AME Church in Des Moines. Additionally, as a
lifelong Republican, Brown served as chair of the
Precinct Board of Registration in Polk County. She

also served as the first vice president of the National League of Republican Colored Women, ward chair of the Polk County Republican Committee, and as a delegate to Republican county and state conventions. From 1938 to 1940 she served as one of only two African American women appointed to Dr. Glen Frank's National Republican Committee on Program.

Brown and her husband were influential in bringing prominent national African American figures to Des Moines, including Joel Spingarn, JAMES WELDON JOHNSON, W. E. B. DuBois, MARY McLEOD BETHUNE, MARGARET MURRAY WASHINGTON, CHARLES YOUNG, MADAME C. J. WALKER, ROLAND HAYES, and the poets COUNTÉE CULLEN and LANGSTON HUGHES. The Browns were also friends with GERTRUDE ELZORA DURDEN RUSH and her husband, James B. Rush, and the four sat on many committees and boards together and were all charter members of the Des Moines Branch of the NAACP. Gertrude Durden Rush and Sue Wilson Brown often-followed one another as presidents of various women's clubs and organizations. Brown's organizational and leadership skills made the Sixth Biennial Conference of the Central Association of Colored Women (1938) a great success. The four-day conference was held in the Senate Chambers of the Iowa State Capitol in Des Moines and included several instructional workshops given by prominent African American women and men. The *Chicago Defender* covered the conference on 13 August 1938, praising Brown and calling the event the organization's "greatest meet."

Brown wrote *Social Ethics* (1911), *The Order of the International Grand Chapter of Eastern Star Among Colored People* (1925), and *The Central Region of the National Association of Colored Women* (1940), which provide invaluable insight into the history of black women's activism in Iowa at the beginning of the twentieth century. At the time of her death, she was a steward and superintendent of the Sunday school at St. Paul AME Church, chair of the interracial department of the Des Moines Interdenominational Council, director of the Smalls Medical Aid Fund, Inc., chair of the trustee board of the Iowa Association of Colored Women, president of the Central Association of Colored Women, director of Young People of the Northwestern Conference of the AME Church, a trustee of Monrovia College in Liberia, co-chair of the Negro Division of the Republican Party of Iowa, and a committee member on the program of the National Republican Committee.

Sue Wilson Brown is an example of the black clubwoman at the turn of the twentieth century. Active in multiple organizations, Wilson strove fro the betterment of African Americans and women. Alone, with her husband, S. Joe Brown, and with other concerned friends and allies, Wilson founded numerous associations. She was instrumental in organizing both black and white citizens, women and men, and getting them involved in various projects that served the local, state and national communities. Brown's drive, determination, and apparent ability to organize, enabled her to be involved in multiple associations simultaneously, often serving as an officer. Though Wilson was well-known during her lifetime, she has been left out of our known history and is missing from our collective memory.

FURTHER READING

Iowa Women's Hall of Fame records are housed in the Louise Noun–Mary Louise Smith Iowa Women's Archives, University of Iowa, Iowa City, Iowa.

Cash, Floris Barnett. *African American Women and Social Action: The Clubwomen and Volunteerism from Jim Crow to the New Deal, 1896–1850* (2001).

Iowa Bystander, 4 Dec. 1941.

Knupfer, Anne Meis. *The Chicago Black Renaissance and Women's Activism* (2006).

Knupfer, Anne Meis. *Toward a Tender Humanity and a Nobler Womanhood: African American Women's Clubs in Turn-of-the-Century Chicago* (1996).

"Pay Final Tribute to Mrs. S. Joe Brown," *Iowa Bystander*, 4 December 1941.

Weisenfeld, Judith. *African American Women and Christian Activism: New York's Black YWCA, 1904–1945* (1997).

LISA MOTT

Brown, Wesley A. (3 Apr. 1927–), the first African American U.S. Naval Academy graduate, was born John-Wesley Anthony Brown in Baltimore, Maryland, to William Brown, a truck driver, and Rosetta Shepherd, a seamstress. He was named after John Wesley, the eighteenth-century founder of Methodism from which the African Methodist Episcopal Zion (AMEZ) denomination was established. Owing to his parents' demanding work schedules, Brown was raised in large part by his maternal grandmother, Katie Shepherd, sometimes called "Mother Shepherd," a fierce disciplinarian with whom Brown and his parents lived. Through her, Brown developed a high regard for education, a respect for honesty, a quiet assertiveness, and a great work ethic. "You were always wrong if there was a complaint about your behavior," Brown told the biographer Robert J. Schneller Jr. during a 19 December 1995 interview for the book *Breaking the Color Barrier* (2005), in referring to his grandmother's no-nonsense attitude.

Brown was taught to read by his godmother, Marie Smith, who used the Bible as her principal text. He attended William Lloyd Garrison Elementary and Robert Gould Shaw Junior High, but he learned important lessons about perseverance, politeness, and the sense of duty outside of the classroom, too, even when working at Elite Cleaners with his mother and father, who after long hauls as a truck driver would allow Brown to help distribute the family's leftover food to needy neighbors. He loved visiting D.C.'s historic area and studying its buildings, including the White House, and was thrilled when Eleanor Roosevelt visited him and other children during an Easter egg hunt on the White House lawn.

When Brown entered Dunbar High School he had not yet decided on a naval career, but by 1942, at about age fifteen, he "arranged [his] high school studies so as to get as much math and science as possible," he told the *Washington Post* for a 1989 article, and joined the military cadet corps. He rose to the rank of colonel and worked the graveyard shift as a junior clerk for the navy, feeling a kinship with officers and noting the navy's emphasis on engineering.

Brown graduated from Dunbar in 1944 at age seventeen, and it was only shortly thereafter that his burgeoning military prowess came to the attention of the legendary New York congressman ADAM CLAYTON POWELL JR. For Powell, the prospect of finding a black to apply and graduate from the U.S. Naval Academy had become a serious concern because the five previously admitted blacks had failed to graduate, in no small part because of the academy's racist atmosphere. Brown, who had been taking technical courses at Howard University to prepare for army service, was startled by a phone call in spring 1945 from Powell, who offered Brown the Naval Academy nomination. Brown accepted and, stepping up his studies for the entrance testing, was soon briefed by George Trivers, a black plebe who had attended the academy in 1936. His preparations were successful and, despite the attempts of a pre-qualifying dentist to disqualify him because his upper and lower teeth didn't quite touch, Brown matriculated into the academy following testing.

Brown's first year, 1945, at the academy was the roughest. He accrued some 103 demerits, many of them unfairly assessed, for the likes of bogus dress-code infractions, marching out of sync, and chewing gum. Yet Brown was not easily riled by the false charges and avoided the trap of overreacting or retaliating. "I developed a feeling that maybe they were trying to run me out of the place," Brown recounted in the *Saturday Evening Post*. Powell was so disturbed that he reportedly investigated Brown's treatment. Despite all this, Brown, who roomed by himself the entire four years at the academy, persevered. His affable but determined attitude won over most of his peers at the academy, as did his keen wit and athleticism. In addition to his engineering studies Brown participated in chess, fencing, and cross-country, something that future U.S. president Jimmy Carter, then an academy upperclassman, would later recall in his autobiography, noting that the indefatigable Brown would "always" outrun him (54).

Brown graduated with a bachelor's degree on 3 June 1949 as the first black academy graduate and 20,299th midshipman. In April 1950 he married Jean Beverly Alston of Philadelphia. The couple, who divorced in July 1962, had four children, Willetta, Carol, Wesley Jr., and Gary. Requests for interviews and related matters, following a barrage of worldwide publicity about Brown's graduation, were coordinated by Navy Lieutenant Dennis Nelson, a member of the "Golden 13," which became in February 1944 the first group of black commissioned naval officers. During a speaking trip to Chicago with Nelson, Brown encountered the black athlete JESSE OWENS, who requested Brown's autograph.

During his twenty years in the Civil Engineer Corps, Brown rose to the rank of lieutenant commander, serving as managing officer for huge engineering projects in the United States and around the world, including the Philippines, Hawaii, and the Antarctic, before his retirement in 1969. Brown, who acquired postgraduate credits at Rensselaer Polytechnic Institute in New York and other colleges, remarried on 24 July 1964 to Crystal Malone, the first black to integrate a U.S. college sorority (at the University of Vermont). They returned to Washington, with Brown taking on the position of facilities master planner for Howard University from 1976 to 1988. Active in community and history affairs that included lecturing to historical groups and at schools (including the Naval Academy), Brown received many awards. A $50 million field house bearing Brown's name at the Naval Academy, recognizes a warrior who faced down a century of institutional racism at one of the nation's most important military academies.

FURTHER READING
Wesley Anthony Brown's papers are at the Howard University Moreland-Spingarn Research Center in Washington, D.C.

Brown, Wesley. "The First Negro Graduate of Annapolis Tells His Story," *Saturday Evening Post*, June 1949.

"First Navy Grad Makes Good," *Ebony* (Apr. 1960).

Hill, Shaun L. "Road to Naval Academy All Uphill for NW Man," *Washington Post*, 24 Aug. 1989.

Schneller, Robert J., Jr. *Breaking the Color Barrier: The U.S. Naval Academy's First Black Midshipmen and the Struggle for Racial Equality* (2005).

DONALD SCOTT SR.

Brown, Willa (22 Jan. 1906–18 July 1992), pilot and aviation educator, was born Willa Beatrice Brown in Glasgow, Kentucky, the only daughter of Hallie Mae Carpenter and Eric B. Brown, a farm owner. After 1910 the family, as part of the migration of African Americans from the rural South to northern cities, moved to Terre Haute, Indiana, hoping for greater opportunities in employment and education. There her father worked in a creosote factory. He was also pastor of the Holy Triumphant Church in 1920 and of the Free Church of God in 1929.

At Wiley High School, Brown was one of only seven black students in the hundred-member chorus. During her high school years she also did part-time domestic work. Brown graduated in 1923 and entered Indiana State Normal School, a teacher training school that later became part of Indiana University. She majored in business, minored in French, and joined the Alpha Kappa Alpha sorority. In September 1927, ready to begin her teaching career, Brown headed for Gary, Indiana. The home of U.S. Steel, Gary was known for its innovative school system (with swimming pools, laboratories, and adult education) and served as a model for other American cities. Called the "City of the Century," it experienced a building boom and a population surge of eastern Europeans and African Americans who came for jobs in the steel mills.

The number of African American children in Gary rose from 267 in 1916 to 1,125 in 1920 and to more than 4,000 in 1930. The influx of African Americans generated resentments among whites. When eighteen blacks were admitted to Emerson High School, more than six hundred white students walked out. This led to the opening in April 1931 of Roosevelt School, a state-of-the-art high school for black students. There Brown chaired the commercial department, which taught typewriting and stenography; she also taught those subjects at the evening school for adults. She introduced a typewriting club, which produced the *Annex News*, perhaps the only student newspaper in Gary's schools.

On 24 November 1929 Brown married Wilbur J. Hardaway. A graduate of Tuskegee Institute and the newly elected alderman of the Fifth Ward, he was one of Gary's first black firemen when its "colored" fire station was created two years earlier. Brown continued to teach, using four summer vacations to complete her bachelor's degree, which she received in August 1931. The Hardaways' stormy marriage ended a few months later, but Brown remained in Gary and taught through the end of the school year.

Brown then moved to Chicago and chose positions where she could put her skills to good use during the Depression. From 1932 to 1939 she worked for the federal government as well as in private venues. Her employers included Dr. Julius H. Lewis, the first African American faculty member of the University of Chicago's medical school (1937–1938); Dr. THEODORE K. LAWLESS, a renowned African American dermatologist and philanthropist (1938–1939); and HORACE CAYTON, coauthor of *Black Metropolis* (1939). While working as a drugstore cashier in 1934, Brown met JOHN C. ROBINSON, a pilot. She joined the Challenger Aero Club, created by Robinson in 1931, and found herself in a circle of African American aviation enthusiasts. Being at Chicago's Harlem Airport was exhilarating for Brown, who "was always an outdoor person." She began preparatory courses at the Aeronautical University, established in 1929 by the Curtiss-Wright Flying Service. That there were classes for African Americans at all was thanks to the outstanding efforts of Robinson and CORNELIUS R. COFFEY, who had had to threaten legal action before they were admitted some years earlier. They then were hired to teach other African Americans.

On 13 May 1934 Brown was seriously injured in a car accident while returning from a Mother's Day visit. She was hospitalized with a broken arm, several broken ribs, and a fractured vertebra. After recovering from the accident she continued flying, earning a student license in 1937 and a private pilot license in 1938. Brown's charisma, energy, and talent for attracting attention were evident when she arrived at the *Chicago Defender* to request coverage of an air show that a group of thirty flyers planned to stage. An editor, Enoch P. Waters, reported that the older reporters "polished their eyeglasses to get an undistorted view …[Brown] made such a stunning appearance in white jodhpurs, white jacket, white boots, that all the typewriters suddenly went silent." The flyers got their publicity.

Waters suggested forming a national organization as a clearinghouse for information about African Americans' aviation activities. On 16 August 1937 the National Airmen's Association of America (NAAA) received its charter, with the *Chicago Defender* providing the mailing address. Some other charter members included Cornelius Coffey, CHAUNCEY SPENCER, a pioneer pilot and civil rights activist, and JANET BRAGG, also a pioneer pilot. Brown, as secretary, assumed public relations duties. Her letters, flying visits to black colleges, and radio addresses helped the group grow and establish chapters in other cities. For the next decade, her life became one of ceaseless and aggressive effort for the inclusion of blacks into the aviation mainstream and the country's war mobilization. Chauncey Spencer said, "Willa was persistent and dedicated. She was the foundation, framework, and the builder of people's souls. She did it not for herself, but for all of us" (author interview, 3 June 1995). Brown and Coffey founded the Coffey School of Aeronautics in 1938, with Coffey as president and chief flight instructor and with Brown as director.

In 1939 Brown became the first African American woman to receive a commercial pilot license with a ground instructor rating and a radio license. That same year, as war approached, the Civilian Pilot Training Program (CPTP) was launched to provide a source of trained manpower. Although the CPTP was working through colleges only, the Coffey school wanted certification as a training center. Brown successfully conducted separate demonstrations for government officials of college and non-college students' flying, to prove that Negroes could absorb technical education, a point in doubt since a 1925 War Department report. An article in *Time* magazine (25 Sept. 1939) reported that Brown "has labored mightily to whip up interest in flying among Negroes, get them a share in the …training program." About two hundred pilots were trained, and many went on to secondary training at the segregated Tuskegee (Alabama) Army Air Field, which produced America's black air corps, the Tuskegee Airmen.

Brown was appointed federal coordinator for the Chicago unit of the CPTP in February 1940 and remained there until 1943. In 1942 she became the first African American member of the Civilian Air Patrol (CAP) in Illinois, one of 400 pilots accepted of the 1,560 who had applied in Illinois. As lieutenant of the segregated squadron, she had charge of 25 pilots, several light planes, and four army training biplanes. The Coffey school closed at war's end, and on 7 February 1947 Coffey and Brown married. This marriage also was short-lived, ending in divorce. Brown was married for the third time in 1955, to the Reverend J. H. Chapell, whom she met while they were both employed at the Great Lakes Naval Training Base in Waukegan. In 1962 Brown returned to teaching high school–level aeronautics and commercial subjects; she continued teaching until her retirement in 1971. That year she became the first black woman appointed to the Federal Aviation Administration's Women's Advisory Committee on Aviation, serving until 1974.

In recognition of her leadership, Brown was invited to speak at the Tuskegee Airmen's fourth annual convention in August 1974. She was unable to attend, but in remarks read at the meeting, she wrote, "We desperately wanted blacks to fly and we desperately wanted them to be accepted into the Army Air Corps as cadets …we threw the word 'I' out of our vocabulary altogether. We needed everybody's help…. The YMCA, the Chicago Urban League, the Chicago Board of Education, NAACP, the Eighth Regiment Armory, civic-minded individuals in all walks of life, other flying schools in the area, and, of course, churches of all denominations supported the effort." Brown was the first black woman to make aviation her career, and she tirelessly promoted opportunities for other African Americans in the field. She was honored as a pioneer in the "Black Wings" exhibition at the National Air and Space Museum in 1982. She died in Chicago.

FURTHER READING

Gubert, Betty Kaplan, Miriam Sawyer, and Caroline Fannin. *Distinguished African Americans in Aviation and Space Science* (2001).

Johnson, Jesse J. *Black Women in the Armed Forces, 1942–1974: A Pictorial History* (1974).

Waters, Enoch P. *American Diary: A Personal History of the Black Press* (1987).

Obituary: *Chicago Sun Times*, 20 July 1992.
This entry is taken from the *American National
Biography* and is published here with the
permission of the American Council of Learned
Societies.

BETTY KAPLAN GUBERT

Brown, William Alexander (fl. 1817–1823), theater manager and playwright, was born in the
West Indies, probably on Saint Vincent, before
1780. Little is known about Brown's early life. He
worked for some years as a steward on passenger
ships, then left the sea and settled in New York
City, where he worked as a tailor. The 1820 census
shows him as middle-aged and free, living with his
wife and daughter. At about this time he opened
a public garden in the grounds behind his house
on Thomas Street, between West Broadway and
Hudson Street. An open-air cabaret offering light
refreshments and music, the African Grove, as he
called it, served the city's African American population, which was excluded from the other larger
public gardens in the city.

The African Grove presumably opened in the
spring of 1821, but the only knowledge of it comes
from a story in the *National Advocate* of August of
that year. A few weeks later another story reported
that the Grove had been forced to close because of
complaints from its neighbors. Brown moved his
entertainment indoors—the season for an open-air
resort was coming to an end anyway—and formed
a company of actors to present an abridged production of Shakespeare's *Richard III* in an upper floor
of his house. The first performance was given on 17
September. The complaints presumably continued,
because a week later the company's second performance of *Richard III* was in a house on Mercer
Street at Bleecker, then an undeveloped part of
town. By the end of the year Brown attempted
to move his theater back to the center of the city,
arranging to present plays in Hampton's Hotel,
a porterhouse next door to the Park Theatre, the
only other theater in New York. Unfortunately, the
Park's manager, Stephen Price, was intolerant of
competition and entirely unscrupulous. He caused
a performance on 7 January 1822 to be raided by the
police, who hauled the actors from the stage and
arrested them.

Brown issued a defiant handbill, excerpts from
which appeared in the *Commercial Advertiser*,
and returned to finish the season at Mercer Street.
Early in 1822 Brown leased a lot on the east side
of Mercer Street above Houston and had a theater

built on the property. The theater opened in early
August with productions of *The Poor Soldier*
and *Don Juan*. A few days later a band of white
hooligans broke up a performance and assaulted
Brown and the actors, destroying costumes, scen-
ery, and props. The police responded promptly,
and the ringleaders were arrested, but damage was
done that affected subsequent performances. It is
unknown whether the vandals were working on
behalf of Price.

The repertoire of the African Company included
Shakespeare's *Richard III*, *Othello*, and *Macbeth*,
other standards like John Home's *Douglas* and
August von Kotzebue's *Pizarro*, and contemporary
hits like *Tom and Jerry* and Mordecai Noah's *The
Fortress of Sorrento*. In addition Brown wrote a play
called *The Drama of King Shotaway*, which the company presented in January 1822 and again in June
1823. The play, which Brown described as "written
from experience," dealt with a 1795 insurrection
on Saint Vincent led by Chatoyer, the paramount
chief of the Caribs, against the British. The play was
never printed, and its text has been lost. Indeed, the
play may never have been written down; there is
evidence that suggests that Brown was illiterate. He
may have dictated the play in detail or he may have
simply outlined the plot and the content of each
scene and allowed his actors to improvise the dialogue. His company seems to have relied on improvisation to a great extent even when presenting
published plays, Shakespeare excepted. The playbill
of their production of *Tom and Jerry* shows only
a general similarity with the then-popular play by
W. T. Moncrieff, and a notice of their production of
The Poor Soldier praised the company for presenting "this familiar play … so artfully, that … I found
it impossible to tell what would come next."

Brown had intended the African Company,
like the African Grove, to serve New York's black
community, which was limited to the upper balcony at the Park Theatre. Playbills from September
and October of 1821 were addressed to "Ladies and
Gentlemen of Colour." But before long, reports in
the *National Advocate* drew the attention of white
New Yorkers, and whites eventually outnumbered
the blacks in the audience. Brown began addressing
his bills to "The Public." In late October 1821 he had
announced that a section at the back of his theater
would be reserved for whites; by autumn 1822, it was
the black members of the audience for whom a section of the house was being set aside. Nonetheless,
Brown and his company presented plays dealing
with controversial issues. *Pizarro*, a standard play

from the Anglo-American repertoire, and Brown's own *Shotaway* both concerned armed resistance to colonial domination. The theater's interpretation of *Tom and Jerry* included a scene set in a southern slave market, and the company also offered a short play based on the exploits of the Jamaican antislavery folk hero Three-Finger'd Jack.

In July 1823 a man named William Brown filed for bankruptcy. This is likely to have been Brown, although records of the bankruptcy proceeding have been lost. Tax records also show that he remained responsible for the taxes on the land on which his theater stood. The theater must have represented a heavy investment, and its demise was probably hastened by the vandalism spree and by a citywide epidemic of yellow fever that forced Brown to close the theater in early October 1822 and take his company on a tour. In any event, during the 1823–1824 season the African Company was under the direction of JAMES HEWLETT, its leading actor. This was to be the company's last season. In March 1825 the land on which the building stood was sold, and its new owner assumed responsibility for the taxes.

Nothing more is known of Brown's life, his commonplace name making him impossible to trace. A notice published in 1880 says that on 19 December 1823 a man named Brown presented an African theatrical company in Albany, but this has not been confirmed to be William Brown and his company.

The African Company was the first successful theater company in the United States to be managed and staffed by African Americans; Brown's *Shotaway* was the first play to have been written by an African American; its Mercer Street theater was the first building to have been erected for use by an African American theater company. In addition to James Hewlett, IRA ALDRIDGE began his career with the African Company, though the only reference during the years when the African Company was active that connects Aldridge to the company is a criminal complaint that he filed for assault against one of the louts involved in the vandalism spree of 1822.

FURTHER READING

McAllister, Marvin. *White People Do Not Know How to Behave at Entertainments Designed for Ladies and Gentlemen of Colour: William Brown's African and American Theater* (2003).

Richards, Jeffrey H. *Drama, Theatre, and Identity in the American New Republic* (2006).

Thompson, George A., Jr. *A Documentary History of the African Theatre* (1998).

White, Shane. *Stories of Freedom in Black New York* (2002).

This entry is taken from the *American National Biography* and is published here with the permission of the American Council of Learned Societies.

GEORGE A. THOMPSON

Brown, William H. (c. 1836–5 Nov. 1896), Civil War sailor and Medal of Honor winner, was born a slave in Baltimore, Maryland. Almost nothing is known of Brown's early life. However, based on the location of his residence after the Civil War, he probably worked as a slave on one of the many plantations in St. Mary's County between the Pautuxent and Potomac rivers in Maryland's Tidewater region. Brown probably fled from his master during Union army operations in Maryland and Virginia and was one of the thousands of slaves who made their way northward to Union lines. Brown and others were looking to gain their freedom as word of President Abraham Lincoln's Emancipation Proclamation quickly spread. The proclamation was issued on 1 January 1863 after the Union victory at the Battle of Antietam in northern Maryland and granted freedom to the vast majority of slaves in the South. By early 1864 William Brown had escaped slavery and made his way to New York City.

According to Civil War military records, William H. Brown enlisted for one year in the U.S. Navy on 23 March 1864. His height is listed as five feet nine inches, and his age recorded as twenty-eight. Brown's activities in the navy for his first two weeks are unknown. Rated a landsman, a position similar to that of an entry-level seaman with no prior sea experience, Brown may have received some brief training as a seaman at the Brooklyn Navy Yard. However, it is also possible that he was employed as a servant to yard officers or as a common yard laborer, perhaps even before he officially joined the navy. Indeed, the vast majority of former slaves (both men and women) who attained freedom in the safe confines behind Union lines were often employed in this manner. Although there was no indication that William Brown would be an outstanding sailor when he joined the navy, future events would soon prove that he would indeed merit recognition of the highest order.

On 10 May 1864 William H. Brown was assigned to USS *Brooklyn*, a newly recommissioned warship being sent to take part in the operations of Admiral David Farragut's Western Gulf Squadron off the coast of Mobile, Alabama. Along with Engineer's

Cook JAMES MIFFLIN, Brown was one of a number of African American sailors who served on the wooden-hulled, 2,500-ton sloop of war. Much like Mifflin, Brown joined the ship's crew on the day she sailed for southern waters, perhaps as a last-minute replacement. The *Brooklyn* and the other ships in Farragut's squadron were employed to stop Confederate blockade runners in the Gulf Coast area. The use of black sailors by the Union navy was by no means unusual; whether freeborn or "contraband" slave, approximately eighteen thousand African Americans were employed by the navy during the Civil War, comprising 20 percent of its manpower. No matter what rating these black sailors may have held, the service they performed was vital and, in many cases, of heroic proportions. Among those men cited for valor during the war were AARON ANDERSON, JOACHIM PEASE, JOHN LAWSON, and ROBERT SMALLS.

Commanded by Captain James Alden, the *Brooklyn* and its crew arrived off Mobile Bay on 31 May 1864. The ship would spend the next two months plying the waters of the Gulf Coast, but it saw limited action. This may have been a period in which William Brown gained his "sea legs" and learned the ways of a sailor, performing simple maintenance chores and basic sail-handling duties. Perhaps even more importantly, Brown was also trained in his battle-station duties as an ammunition passer, charged with supplying the ship's cannons with shot and powder in the heat-of battle. Soon, he would fully employ the ammunition-related skills he had begun learning.

By August 1864 Admiral Farragut had all the ships—as well as coordinated ground forces—needed to attack the last port on the Gulf Coast that remained in Confederate hands: Mobile, Alabama. On a morning in August 1864 Farragut and his forces moved in for the attack. The *Brooklyn* had to pass close by the Confederate-manned Fort Morgan, which guarded the approaches to the bay. And with William Brown and James Mifflin aboard serving as ammunition passers, the *Brooklyn* steamed alongside the Union monitor *Tecumseh* under the guns of the fort. Suddenly, disaster struck. While engaging the Confederate ram *Tennessee*, the *Tecumseh* struck a mine (in those days called "torpedoes") and veered out of control. Badly damaged, the *Tecumseh* quickly sank, going down with ninety-four of its crew. From the flagship USS *Hartford* Admiral Farragut led his force on, issuing his immortal battle cry of "Damn the torpedoes, full speed ahead!"

Meanwhile, in grave danger from the mines that sank the *Tecumseh*, the *Brooklyn* was forced to stop and reverse itself, steering clear of the danger. The ship, in range of Fort Morgan's guns, took a terrific pounding and suffered fifty-four killed and forty-three wounded. Landsman William Brown and Engineer's Cook James Mifflin's battle station was hit twice by enemy fire, but Brown remained at his post and continued to carry powder throughout the battle.

By 10:00 A.M. a major Union victory was won, and the last Confederate blockade-running port on the Gulf Coast was now in Union hands. Indicative of the overall contribution of black sailors to this victory were the efforts of the four men awarded the Medal of Honor for heroism and devotion to duty under fire at Mobile Bay: William H. Brown and James Mifflin on the *Brooklyn* and WILSON BROWN and John Lawson on the *Hartford*.

Following the battle, William Brown continued his service on the *Brooklyn*, and it is likely that it was here, in front of the entire ship's company, that he was awarded the Medal of Honor on 31 December 1864. The day after receiving his medal, he was transferred to the old frigate USS *Potomac*, serving as a receiving ship at the navy yard in Pensacola, Florida. Brown served until 1 April 1865, when he received his discharge and began a new life as a freeman and civilian, returning to Maryland and settling in St. Mary's County. According to 1870 federal census records, William H. Brown lived with his wife, Caroline (b. c. 1840), and children Susan (b. 1856) and Jane (b. 1868) in Chaptico and worked as a farm laborer. By 1880 the Browns moved to Milestown, living with their children Jane (called "Jinnie"), Frances (b. 1873), and Josephine (b. 1876). William H. Brown, perhaps beleaguered from his years as a slave and rigorous naval duty, died at the relatively young age of fifty-nine and was buried in Arlington National Cemetery.

FURTHER READING

Quarles, Benjamin Arthur. *The Negro in the Civil War* (1953).

Reidy, Joseph P. "Black Men in Navy Blue during the Civil War," *Prologue* (Fall 2001).

U.S. Navy. *Medal of Honor, 1861–1949: The Navy* (1950).

GLENN ALLEN KNOBLOCK

Brown, William Wells (Mar. 1815–6 Nov. 1884), slave narrator, novelist, playwright, historian, and abolitionist leader, was born in Lexington, Kentucky, the son of a slave mother, Elizabeth, and

William Wells Brown gained recognition for his autobiographical slave narrative published in 1847, the account of his travels in Europe published in 1852, and his novel *Clotel; or, the President's Daughter: A Narrative of Slave Life in the United States* (1853). (Courtesy of Documenting the American South, University of North Carolina at Chapel Hill Libraries.)

George Higgins, the white half-brother of Brown's first master, Dr. John Young. As a slave, William was spared the hard labor of his master's plantation, unlike his mother and half-siblings, because of his close blood relation to the slave-holding family, but as a house servant he was constantly abused by Mrs. Young. When the family removed to a farm outside St. Louis, Missouri, William was hired out in various capacities, including physician's assistant, servant in a public house, and waiter on a steamship. William's "best master" in slavery was Elijah P. Lovejoy, publisher of the *St. Louis Times*, where he was hired out in the printing office in 1830. (Lovejoy was an antislavery editor who would be murdered seven years later for refusing to close his abolitionist newspaper.) There William acquired some education, though not literacy.

William's work on the steamship opened his eyes to the idea of freedom, since he observed the comings and goings of free people every day. His abuses at the hands of a drunken master, Major Freeland, who amused himself by tying his slaves in the smokehouse and burning tobacco at their feet in a game he called "Virginia play," persuaded William to seek freedom for himself and his family as soon as an opportunity arose. Perhaps William's most formative year in slavery was 1832, when he was hired out to James Walker, who ran boatloads of slaves down the Mississippi River to the lucrative New Orleans slave markets. During this year William observed firsthand the deepest degradations and cruelties of the slave trade, detailed in his later writings, as families were separated and unruly slaves were tortured and killed. William himself took part in preparing slaves for auction by darkening the gray hair of older slaves and arranging the slaves in happy scenes of dancing and card playing.

On his return to St. Louis in 1833, at the urging of a sister, William made his first attempt at escape, crossing the river into Illinois with his mother in a stolen skiff. After ten days of traveling at night and sleeping during the day, William and his mother continued their journey in daylight, only to be retrieved by slave catchers within a few hours. Once again William's near relation to his master saved him from being sent to the New Orleans slave market, unlike his mother, and he was ultimately sold to a steamship owner. Within a few months William escaped again, walking off the ship into the city of Cincinnati, choosing the date of 1 January 1834, as his first day of freedom. During his walk north William added "Wells Brown" to his name, in honor of the Quaker who helped further his escape and nursed him through illness brought on by exposure. As a free man based in Cleveland, Brown quickly got work as a steamship steward on Lake Erie, helping as many as sixty-nine slaves escape to Canada during one seven-month period. Brown also married Elizabeth Schooner in the summer of 1834; their first child, a daughter, was born in the late spring of 1835 but died several months later. Two more daughters, Clarissa and Josephine, were born to the couple in 1836 and 1839, respectively. In 1836 the Browns moved to Buffalo, New

York, where Brown continued his participation in the Underground Railroad and became a leader of the local black community's temperance organization. During this busy period Brown devoted himself to the cause of abolition and quickly acquired literacy.

In the mid-1840s Brown moved to Boston without Elizabeth, taking their daughters with him to be educated at a boarding school in New Bedford while he traveled as an antislavery lecturer. In 1847 he published the *Narrative of William Wells Brown, a Fugitive Slave, Written by Himself*, which went through numerous editions in both the United States and England, surpassed in popularity only by one other slave narrative, that of FREDERICK DOUGLASS, published two years earlier. Brown also published *The Anti-Slavery Harp: A Collection of Songs for Anti-Slavery Meetings* (1848). That same year, his last master in slavery, Enoch Price, offered to buy Brown's freedom for $325, an offer that Brown widely publicized, along with his refusal. He wrote, "God made me as free as he did Enoch Price, and Mr. Price shall never receive a dollar from me or my friends with my consent" (Heermance, 15). This refusal necessitated Brown's removal to Europe, which he arranged in 1849 as a delegate to the International Peace Congress in Paris. At the congress, Brown was warmly received by Alexis de Tocqueville and Victor Hugo, among other European luminaries. Brown achieved great renown as an antislavery lecturer throughout Great Britain, and he was also a frequent contributor to several British newspapers. In 1851, after his wife's death, his two daughters joined him in England, and in 1853 he published the first travel memoir by an African American, *Three Years in Europe*.

In 1854 he added to his list of firsts by publishing the first novel by an African American, *Clotel; or, The President's Daughter*. In this novel Brown fictionalizes the relationship between Thomas Jefferson and the slave SALLY HEMINGS through the story of their daughter and draws on his experiences as a firsthand observer of the slave trade in his detailed accounts of slaves being "sold down the river" and in auction scenes. Elegantly written and sentimental in the style of the day, *Clotel* is a sprawling, heavily plotted novel that sold relatively well and established Brown as the first African American man of letters. Brown was clearly entranced with its themes, for he continued working on the novel for years, publishing new versions in 1860, 1864, and 1867.

Also in 1854 Brown was persuaded to let friends buy his freedom so he could return to the United States and continue his work in the abolition movement. He maintained his literary output during this period, updating his *Narrative* and *The Anti-Slavery Harp* and expanding his travel narrative under the title *The American Fugitive in Europe* (1855). In 1856 he wrote his first play, *The Doughface Baked; or, How to Give a Northern Man a Backbone*, another first for African American writers in a new genre. The play satirized the Reverend Nehemiah Adams of Boston, who defended slavery; the written text for this play is lost. Brown's play *The Escape; or, A Leap for Freedom* (1848) achieved more renown through public readings, though no record exists of either play being staged fully. In 1860 Brown married Anna Elizabeth Gray, with whom he had one daughter, Clotelle, in 1862.

Brown's lifelong interest in medicine, begun under slavery, led him to study on his own in England and the United States, and in 1864 he treated the wife of the abolitionist William Lloyd Garrison. Around this time he began writing "M.D." after his name to indicate that he was actively practicing medicine, medical school not being a requirement during this period. He maintained an office for the purpose for over a decade in the 1860s and 1870s, though he clearly divided his time among many other endeavors, chiefly his writing and a renewed dedication to the temperance cause. During the Reconstruction period, Brown advocated temperance for free African Americans as essential for elevating their condition. While lecturing in the South for the temperance cause in 1871, Brown narrowly escaped death at the hands of the Ku Klux Klan.

In the 1860s Brown turned to yet another genre of writing, publishing his first work of history in 1863, *The Black Man, His Antecedents, His Genius, and His Achievements*, which consisted of fifty-four biographical sketches of African Americans "designed to reduce white 'colorphobia'" (Ellison and Metcalf Jr., 4). He also published a detailed account of black soldiers in the Civil War, *The Negro in the American Rebellion* (1867). He continued his output of historical works with *The Rising Son* (1873), a wide-ranging study of blacks in the United States, Africa, and the Caribbean. His last publication was an expanded autobiography titled *My Southern Home; or, The South and Its People* (1880). He died in Boston.

William Wells Brown remains an enduring figure in African American history and literature for his writing, his activism, and his remarkable story of survival and triumph over slavery, illiteracy, and systemic racism. He was well regarded in his own time in the United States and Europe, and his writing, particularly his depiction of the slave trade in the various versions of his novel *Clotel*, retains a sharpness of wit and pointed observation for twenty-first-century readers.

FURTHER READING

Brown, William Wells. *My Southern Home; or, The South and Its People* (1880).

Brown, William Wells. *Narrative of William Wells Brown, a Fugitive Slave, Written by Himself* (1847) in *From Fugitive Slave to Free Man: The Autobiographies of William Wells Brown*, ed. William L. Andrews (1993).

Ellison, Curtis W., and E. W. Metcalf Jr. *William Wells Brown and Martin Delany: A Reference Guide* (1978).

Farrison, William Edward. *William Wells Brown: Author and Reformer* (1969).

Heermance, J. Noel. *William Wells Brown and Clotelle: A Portrait of the Artist in the First Negro Novel* (1969).

Whelchel, Love Henry. *My Chains Fell Off: William Wells Brown, Fugitive Abolitionist* (1985).

ALICE KNOX EATON

Brown, Willie (20 Mar. 1934–), politician, was born Willie Lewis Brown Jr. in Mineola, Texas, to Lewis Brown, a part-time waiter, and Minnie Collins, a maid. From the age of four he was raised by his mother and his grandmother, Anna Lee Collins, after his father abandoned the family. What Brown lacked in wealth was more than made up for by the caring and love given to him by these two women and his three siblings. Driven by his desire to make his mother and grandmother proud, he tackled any task given to him with determination. Later in life he said of his family, "They believed in me, taught me the value of hard work and the importance of education, and nurtured my sense of dignity of self worth."

Willie Brown's childhood was plagued by segregation, racism, and hatred. In a society where Jim Crow laws were the norm, Brown excelled in school. A strong and reliable community, which had grown close in the face of prejudice, provided a stable and inspiring influence in Brown's early life. Upon graduating second in his class from Mineola Colored High School in 1951, he accurately assessed that the opportunities available to

him in Mineola were limited and therefore set his sights on San Francisco. Prompted by her son's promise to go to college, Minnie Collins gave her consent.

Once in San Francisco, Brown found that his segregated high school had not prepared him for higher education. Unable to meet entrance qualifications for even the most lenient of schools, Brown faced an uncertain future. In what Brown would later recall as the first of many San Francisco miracles, Duncan Gillis, a member of the administration of San Francisco State College, took a chance and accepted him into the school. Proving true to his character as a determined and hard worker, Brown soon matched his fellow students.

San Francisco State also provided Brown with his first taste of politics. Soon after starting classes he found a peer group and became involved in campus politics, becoming a member of the NAACP and working for Adlai Stevenson's presidential campaign in 1952. Brown earned his degree in political science in 1955 and then went on to Hastings Law School, where he was elected president of his class and received his doctor of law degree in 1958. During that same year he married former classmate Blanche Vitero; they had three children.

Although San Francisco was not as hostile to African Americans as Brown's hometown was, he still found his opportunities to practice law limited by the color of his skin. Understanding that few big law firms were willing to hire black lawyers, he established his own firm dedicated to helping the people of his neighborhood. Although this work was far less glamorous than working for a prestigious law firm, Brown was proud and felt blessed for what he was able to do. In addition to practicing law, he was active in the civil rights movement. Just like everything else in his life, he worked hard and without reservation to procure rights and opportunities for African Americans and other minorities. As a lawyer and civil rights activist, the next logical step for Brown was to enter politics. In 1962 he ran for a position in the state assembly and was defeated. Undeterred, he ran for the same seat in 1964 and this time won. Brown became only the fourth African American assembly member at a time when the state senate was devoid of all minorities. In spite of this obstacle, Brown became an instrumental figure in and the public face of the Democratic Party throughout the 1960s and 1970s. In 1972 Brown delivered a powerful speech in front of a national audience at

Willie Brown Jr., chairman of California's Assembly Ways and Means Committee, 31 May 1971. (AP Images.)

the Democratic National Convention, which sent his popularity skyward.

Jesse "Big Daddy" Unruh stepped down as speaker of the assembly in 1969, and Brown saw the opportunity to attempt to fill the vacancy. Unfortunately this was not meant to be, and he lost the election to become speaker. In 1980, after six years of political recuperation, Brown was finally elected to the position of speaker of the assembly with the support of twenty-eight Republicans and twenty-three Democrats, out of the eighty total assembly members. Brown served as speaker of the assembly until 1995, when term limits forced him to step down.

Although Willie Brown's political achievements were greatly influenced by his intelligence and ability, his personality gained him not only fame and notoriety but also respect. While a member of the state assembly his loyalty to his party and allies gained him the appreciation of both Republicans and Democrats. He was described as a brash, confident, and intelligent man who could get things done by the exertion of his considerable will. Notorious for his expensive suits and for driving around San Francisco in expensive cars, Brown captured the

heart of the city. Fashion magazines praised him, *Playgirl* named him one of its ten sexiest men, and he even played a part in the movie *The Godfather: Part III.*

Upon leaving the position as speaker of the assembly, Brown's political career was far from over. On 8 January 1996 Brown was elected mayor of San Francisco. As mayor, Brown was dogged by accusations of corruption, as his straight talking and flashy lifestyle led to both controversy and increased fame. He left office in 2004. James Richardson famously quotes President Bill Clinton after meeting Brown in San Francisco as saying, "Now I've met the real Slick Willie."

FURTHER READING

Brown, Willie. *First among Equals: California Legislative Leadership 1964–1992* (1999).
Clucas, Richard. *The Speaker's Electoral Connection: Willie Brown and the California Assembly* (1995).
Green, Robert. *Willie L. Brown, Jr: Daring Black Leader* (1974).
Richardson, James. *Willie Brown: A Biography* (1997).

ARTHUR MATTHEW HOLST

Brown, Willie (2 Dec. 1940–), professional football player, was born William Ferdie Brown in Yazoo City, Mississippi. One of eleven children, Brown showed an enthusiasm for athletics at an early age, and in high school he signed up for the track, basketball, and football squads. Football was Brown's passion, however, and in 1959 he entered Grambling State, a well-known historically black university in Grambling, Louisiana. Brown became a football star at Grambling but did not play the position he would later make his own in the pros.

In 1962 Brown left Grambling, but being largely unknown outside the university, he was not drafted by a professional team. Instead, he signed as a free agent with the American Football League (AFL) Houston Oilers, only to be cut during training camp. The time in training camp was instructive, however, for it was there that Brown began to play defensive back for the first time and to experiment with the bump-and-run coverage that he later perfected to an art. Rejected by the Oilers, Brown in 1963 signed with the Denver Broncos and became a starter midway through his first season with the team. As a defensive back, Brown's assignment was to shut down wide receivers and running backs, and his four years with the Broncos were good ones. He snagged fifteen interceptions and began to build a reputation as a reliable shut-down corner. In his second year with the team, during a game against the New York Jets, Brown pulled down four interceptions, tying a league record. He also earned a place in the 1964 AFL All-Pro Game, and his performance in that contest won him honors as outstanding defensive player.

Brown's reputation as a Bronco was solid, but it was his time with the Oakland Raiders that made him a professional football star. Traded to the Raiders in 1967, Brown became part of a winning team full of talented players on both the offensive and the defensive sides of the football, something the Broncos lacked during his time there. Among his teammates were the future Hall of Famers ART SHELL, Gene Upshaw, Ted Hendricks, Fred Biletnikoff, and Dave Casper. The coach was John Madden, also a future Hall of Fame inductee. A professional football powerhouse, Brown's Oakland Raiders amassed an amazing 12-year record of 125 wins and just 35 losses. From 1970 to 1978 Brown, widely recognized as one of the league's best defensive backs, picked off fifty-four passes, returning two for touchdowns. He was selected as an all-star ten years in a row, beginning in 1964. In the 1976 Super Bowl XI against the Minnesota Vikings,

Brown picked off a pass from Fran Tarkenton and returned it seventy-five yards for a touchdown, an NFL championship record that stood for nearly three decades. Brown later singled out that game as the most memorable in his storied career.

Brown retired after the 1978 season and in 1979 joined the Raiders as defensive backfield coach, a position he held for nearly a decade and during which the team piled on two more championship victories, in Super Bowl XV (1981) and Super Bowl XVIII (1983). He was inducted into pro football's Hall of Fame in 1984, his first year of eligibility.

In 1991 Brown took the position of head football coach at Long Beach State. In 1995 he returned to the Raiders in a front office position. He and his wife Yvonne have three children.

An important member of one of professional football's most successful and storied franchises, Brown was the heart of the defensive backfield in one of the league's most fearsome, physically intimidating, and effective units. Among his numerous honors, he was named to the AFL-NFL 25-Year All-Star Team, the Louisiana (1992) and Mississippi (1994) halls of fame, and the AFL All-Time Team (1969). Asked about the secret of his pro football success, Brown replied: "I attributed my success to working hard, knowing what I wanted and knowing I could do things better than the average person. The most important ingredient I had was really wanting to be good. You didn't have to tell me that I was good. I never wanted to be embarrassed on the field. I had a commitment not only to myself but also to my team. And this is what I worked towards" (Oakland Raiders).

FURTHER READING

Flores, Tom. *Tom Flores's Tales from the Oakland Raiders Sidelines* (2007).

Neft, David. *The Football Encyclopedia: The Complete History of Professional NFL Football from 1892 to the Present* (1991).

Oakland Raiders. "Willie Brown," http://raiders.com/common/article.aspx?id=1612 (n.d.).

JASON PHILIP MILLER

Brown, Willie (15 Aug. 1962–), ventriloquist, was born Willie L. Brown in New Haven, Connecticut, to Willie L. Brown Sr. and Dorothy Seay. At the age of thirteen, Brown began watching the situation comedy *Soap*, in which ventriloquist Jay Johnson played the character Chuck, with his wooden dummy Bob. This was one of Brown's early inspirations to become a ventriloquist. His other influence was the legendary African American ventriloquist Willie Tyler. Brown's mother purchased her thirteen-year-old son's first ventriloquist dummy as a Christmas present, and he practiced three to four hours a day in front of the mirror to develop his skills before he made his first public appearance. Brown felt that if he was not a good ventriloquist, he would be made fun of for playing with dolls. His rigorous practice schedule went on for several months until Brown performed in the annual talent show at Nationwide Insurance, his-mother's employer. He came in first place, and, as his confidence grew, he wanted to become a better ventriloquist.

Brown attended Hamden High School, in Hamden, Connecticut. Immediately after high school, Brown attended Hampton University in Virginia, where he gained widespread popularity by staging shows for the fraternity and sorority functions, as well as off campus at the local military bases. In 1980, he-was named the "Most Promising" ventriloquist at-the Vent Haven Ventriloquist Convention in Fort Mitchell, Kentucky. He graduated from Hampton in 1984 with a bachelor's degree in Media Arts and moved to Prince George's County, Maryland, a suburb of Washington, D.C. He soon went to work for Xerox Corporation as a marketing representative. He moonlighted as a ventriloquist and comedian in bars and comedy clubs in the Washington, D.C., and Maryland area, and he also performed for private birthday parties and entered talent shows. In 1980, while in Washington, D.C., Brown married his college sweetheart, Wanda Shaw, and the couple had two children, Willie Brown III and Lajan Nicole Brown.

In the late 1980s, Brown began working with comedian Chris Thomas, and on many nights Brown would perform with Thomas at the Oak Tree Night Club on Saint Barnabas Road in Oxon Hill, Maryland. It was there that he honed his skills as a ventriloquist, becoming sharper with his delivery and his technique. Brown eventually left Xerox and took the stage full time in 1992. In 1992, he and his sidekick, Woody, helped the city of Winchester bring in the new year with a performance at the city's fifth annual music and performing arts celebration. That same year, he made his first appearance on Black Entertainment Television, with D. L. Hughley hosting the *BET Comic View*. In 1994, Brown received a grant form the District of Columbia to design a stand-up comedy show on WHMM-TV Channel 32. *Comedy Jam*, cowritten and produced by Brown, became one of the highest rated programs in the station's history and earned Brown a Corporate Public Broadcasting award. In May 1995, he became the first African American ventriloquist to appear on HBO's *Russell Simmons' Def Comedy Jam*.

In 1999 Brown moved from Washington, D.C., to Los Angeles to pursue his career, and he became a paid regular at the Comedy Store on Sunset Boulevard. He has appeared in television commercials for American Airlines, Kellogg's, Skittles, and McDonald's, and in two episodes, of Showtime's television series *Barbershop*.

In 2005 Brown relocated to Atlanta, Georgia, to be closer to his seventeen-year-old son. His daughter was in college at the University of Maryland, and his wife in Atlanta. Following his move, Brown toured many states working with people such as Cedrict the Entertainer, Martin Lawrence, D. L. Hughley, and Steve Harvey. He has released a comedy album, called *Willie Brown & Woody, On the Up and Up* (1997), and a video, *How to Be a Ventriloquist* (2004).

FURTHER READING

Honoree, Clovis. "Willie Brown and Woody: Seeking God's Will and Fame and Fortune," *Man2Man* (March–May 2006).

Scott, Amber. "It's All Wood: Willie and Woody Show What They're Made Of," *About Time* (December 1995).

CHARLIE TOMLINSON

Brown, Wilson (1841–24 Jan. 1900), escaped slave, navy landsman, and U.S. Medal of Honor recipient, was born in Natchez, Mississippi, in 1841 of unknown parentage. Brown was a slave in Mississippi on a cotton plantation, and nothing is known of his childhood or to whom he belonged. In the early 1860s, at the start of the Civil War, Brown ran away from his master on a skiff that eventually managed to reach a Union ship stationed on the Mississippi River. This encounter with the navy probably accounts for his subsequent enlistment. The navy was a likely choice for an escaped slave; many escaped slaves, as well as free blacks from the North, were often drawn to the service because of its better pay and purported fairer treatment of blacks. Brown enlisted in the Union navy on 18 March 1863 under the title "1st Class Boy" and was officially described as a "Contraband Negro ... five feet, eight inches. He gave his age as twenty-two (22) years" (Katz, 77).

Because of the spatial limitations of a vessel at sea, blacks and whites in the navy were usually not segregated as they were in the U.S. Army. This meant that men of both races ate, slept, and worked together. In fact, according to U.S. Navy Civil War records, there were not many, if any, crews that were completely white, and African Americans often made up more than a quarter of the crews on most ships. Some historians report that as a consequence of these closer relations, Medals of Honor awarded to blacks who served in the navy were often seen as less politically motivated, and thus as more substantial and deserved honors, than those that were awarded to blacks who served in the army. Yet although blacks and whites usually served side by side in the U.S. Navy during the Civil War, African Americans were not allowed to rise above the rank of ordinary seaman and were usually employed as gunners, landsmen, and occasionally as pilots. In one extraordinary case, that of ROBERT SMALLS, an African American commanded a vessel in service to the navy (one that he had stolen from the Confederates during his escape from slavery), but he did not hold a rank in the chain of command.

Brown's Medal of Honor was earned for his participation in the Battle of Mobile Bay on 5 August 1864, a part of the U.S. attack on Fort Morgan and the seizure of an important rebel port city. That day, Brown was aboard USS *Hartford*, Admiral David Farragut's vessel. Brown, along with another former slave, JOHN LAWSON, was operating the "shell-whip," the mechanism below deck that delivered ammunition to the cannons, when Admiral Farragut ordered his men to fire at CSS *Tennessee*, an ironclad ram. Both Lawson and Brown, along with the four other crew members who were operating the shell-whip, were knocked unconscious by the *Tennessee's* initial volley. The lower deck was reportedly covered in the blood of the crew, and when Brown and Lawson returned to consciousness, they noted that the other four members of his crew had been killed or grievously wounded. Nevertheless, Brown and Lawson, who were gravely wounded, refused to leave their post and continued to operate the shell-whip to supply ammunition to the guns above. Both Lawson and Brown received the Medal of Honor for their valiant actions on that day.

Little is known of Brown's activities following the Battle of Mobile Bay. He did have a wife, but her name is not known. However, what is known is that he died in Natchez, Mississippi, in 1900 as the owner of a home on at least one acre of land. Interestingly, Brown was not recognized by historians as African American until at least the middle of the twentieth century, in part because he was nominated for the Medal of Honor without any mention of his race. As opposed to those African Americans who served in the army, recommendations for medals and other awards for black navy men were often submitted without any mention of race, adding credence to the notion that the navy often presented a more equitable situation for African Americans than did the army. Although Brown's service was indeed exceptional in its own right, it remains historically significant precisely because it underscores the often shifting boundaries and contradictions of racial segregation in the U.S. military.

FURTHER READING

Bennett, Michael J. *Union Jacks: Yankee Sailors in the Civil War* (2004).

Katz, William Loren. "Six 'New' Medal of Honor Men: William H. Brown, Wilson Brown, William Loren Katz, Adam Paine," *Journal of Negro History* (Jan. 1968).

Mikaelian, Allen, and Mike Wallace. *Medal of Honor: Profiles of America's Military Heroes from the Civil War to the Present* (2002).

Ramold, Steven J. *Slaves, Sailors, Citizens: African Americans in the Union Navy* (2002).

MARLENE L. DAUT

Browne, Marjorie Lee (9 Sept. 1914–19 Oct. 1979), educator, author, and one of the first black women in the United States to obtain a Ph.D. degree in Mathematics, was one of two children born to Lawrence Johnson Lee and Mary (Taylor) Lee in Memphis, Tennessee. Before she was two years old her mother died and her father remarried. Her father, a railway postal clerk, and her stepmother, Lottie Lee, a school teacher, instilled in her the value of hard work and gave her a love for mathematics. Lawrence Lee had attended college for approximately two years and was regarded as a talented student of mental arithmetic.

In a 1979 interview Browne remarked, "I always, always, always liked mathematics! As far back as I can remember, I liked mathematics because it was a lonely subject. I do have plenty of friends, and I talk with them for hours at a time. But I also like to be alone, and mathematics is something I can do completely alone" (Kenschaft, 186). She was encouraged to pursue her studies with passion.

After attending the local public schools in Memphis, Marjorie Lee was sent to LeMoyne High

School, a private institution organized by Methodists and Congregationalists after the Civil War. By the time she had completed her high school studies she had earned a reputation as a gifted mathematician, and also as a competitive athlete who won the Memphis city women's tennis singles championship. Matriculating at Howard University in Washington, D.C., she continued to develop mind and body; she excelled in academics, shined in tennis, and stood out in the university choir. With the onset of the Depression she was able to attend school uninterrupted through a series of jobs, loans, and scholarship. She went on to graduate cum laude in 1935.

After graduation she accepted a position at Gilbert Academy, a private secondary school in New Orleans, where she taught mathematics and physics. Shortly thereafter she enrolled at the University of Michigan in Ann Arbor, where she went on to earn an M.S. degree in Mathematics in 1939; this placed her in a select category among the first women to receive an advanced mathematics degree in the United States.

Between 1942 and 1945 Browne became an instructor at Wiley College in Marshall, Texas, and during the summers worked towards her doctorate at the University of Michigan, where in 1947 she accepted a teaching fellowship. Browne's doctoral dissertation topic, "On One Parameter Subgroups in Certain Topological and Matrix Groups," was written under the supervision of Professor G. Y. Rainich. In 1948 she became an elected member of Sigma Xi, and in 1949 completed all her requirements for her degree and graduated with a Ph.D. in Mathematics, only the second black woman in the United States to do so. She shares this position with EVELYN BOYD GLANVILLE, who also received the Ph.D. degree in Mathematics in 1949 from Yale University. EUPHEMIA LOFTON HAYNES, who received a Ph.D. in Mathematics from Catholic University in 1943, appears to be the first black women to hold this distinction.

Because of her outstanding scholarly accomplishments and teaching record Dr. ALFONSO ELDER, president of North Carolina College at Durham (later North Carolina Central University) recruited Browne as a faculty member in 1949. She remained a member of the faculty until her retirement in 1979. For twenty-five years she was the only person in the department to hold a Ph.D. and in 1951 was named the chair of the mathematics department. She held this position until 1970.

Between 1952 and 1953 Browne studied at Cambridge University in England on a fellowship from the Ford Foundation. The grant allowed Browne to study combinatorial topology and to travel throughout Western Europe. Browne also was a National Science Foundation Faculty Fellow studying computing and numerical analysis at the University of California at Los Angeles. From 1965 to 1966 she was successful in securing another fellowship while studying differential topology at Columbia University, in New-York.

Under Browne's able leadership she helped North Carolina Central University to become the first predominately black institution in the United States to be awarded a National Science Foundation Institute for secondary teachers of mathematics. For over thirteen years she served as the director of the Institute. In 1955 she published a scholarly article called "A Note on the Classical Group" in the American Mathematics Monthly but most of her career was devoted to teaching and leading.

Besides maintaining a full schedule of teaching, administrative duties, and research Browne also found time to write grants to support the meager budget of her department. In 1960 she was the principal author of a successful proposal that won a grant of sixty thousand dollars from IBM, a grant that allowed her university to obtain its first computer for use in academic computations. This landmark achievement set the university apart from all other historically black colleges and universities in the United States.

In 1969 Browne's department received the first Shell Grant for awards to outstanding students, the importance of which brought great prestige to North Carolina Central University, among the first black schools to receive such an honor.

In 1975 the North Carolina Council of Teachers recognized Browne's contribution to the continuance of education for secondary teachers by awarding her the first W.W. Rankin Memorial Award for Excellence in Mathematics Education.

Marjorie Lee Browne died of a heart attack at the age of sixty-five and is buried in her adopted home of Durham, North Carolina. North Carolina Central University named a scholarship in her honor.

FURTHER READING
A clipping file related to Browne is held in the Reference Section of the James E. Shepard Memorial Library, Durham, North Carolina.
Kenschaft, Patricia. "Marjorie Lee Browne," in *Black Women in America: An Historical Encyclopedia* (1993).

Newell, Virginia K. *Black Mathematicians and Their Works* (1980)

ANDRE D. VANN

Browne, Robert Span (17 Aug. 1924–5 Aug. 2004), economist, philanthropist, and educator was born to William H. Brown, a government employee, and Julia Brown (maiden name unknown), a homemaker, in Chicago, Illinois. He was the youngest of three children. William's employment with the City of Chicago afforded Browne a middle-class upbringing on the city's Southside, which was home to a large African American community. His family lived just a few blocks south of Washington Park, an area where the well-off, but not the most elite, residents lived.

Browne became fascinated with economics while attending the University of Illinois at Champaign-Urbana in the early 1940s. He was the only African American economics major at that university to graduate with honors in 1944. Despite his own relatively comfortable middle-class background, his research focused on those less privileged than himself, particularly on the lack of economic opportunity among African Americans during the Great Depression. After graduating from college, Browne was drafted in the U.S. Army, receiving an honorable discharge in 1946. In 1947, he returned to graduate studies, receiving a master's in business administration from the University of Chicago. He continued his studies at the London School of Economics and later completed the course work toward his doctorate at the City University of New York.

Browne's life and politics steeped in Black Nationalism and economics suggest a different trajectory than those explored by earlier scholars. Browne's expansive political networks also highlight three relatively understudied characteristics of black activism, specifically the multiracial, transnational, and interfaith connections that he and others established. The earlier scholarship on the early 1960s tends to focus on either the black-white and Jewish–Christian coalitions of the civil rights era or the black separatist politics of groups such as the Nation of Islam. Browne, however, worked with Vietnamese nationalists in the United States, Southeast Asia, and France.

Browne started his teaching career at Dillard University in New Orleans in 1947 and was industrial field secretary for the Chicago Urban League from 1950 to 1952. Browne had a strong desire to travel the world. He took his life savings and traveled to twenty-four countries in Europe, the Middle East and North Africa. Thereafter, Browne joined the U.S. Agency for International Development (USAID) and worked as an International Trade Advisor, spending six years, from 1955 to 1961, in Cambodia and Vietnam. While on the South Asian peninsula, Browne protested the U.S. involvement in the Vietnam Conflict. In 1956, Browne married Huoi Nguyen, a woman of mixed Vietnamese and Chinese ancestry, an action that ultimately led to his removal from his government post. Browne and Nguyen raised their four children, Hoa, Mai, Alexi, and Marshall, in the United States.

Browne returned to academia following his tenure at USAID to teach economics and international affairs. He split his time between two New Jersey universities, Fairleigh Dickinson and Rutgers, where he developed a course on the economics of the ghetto. Browne continued protesting the Vietnam Conflict by organizing demonstrations against it and through the launch of the teach-in movement in 1966.

He also ran as an independent for the U.S. Senate representing New Jersey on an anti-Vietnam platform with the position that African Americans should not participate in combat against other people of color. Browne ultimately withdrew six weeks before the election, disappointed that his candidacy had not led the state to participate in a major teach-in about the war.

Paradoxically, Browne, while participating in the National Conference on Black Power in 1967, supported a resolution that called for the separation of the United States into sovereign entities—one country for whites and the other for blacks.

After his failed candidacy, Browne shifted his focus to the economic development of African Americans by founding three African American self-help organizations during the late 1960s to early 1970s. The Black Economic Research Center (BERC) is an applied research center for African American economists working on black economic development projects. BERC was an institutional expression of the black power movement of the late 1960s. The Emergency Land Fund sought to reverse the decline in black land ownership in the South. The 21st-Century Foundation, an endowed public foundation based in New York, advances strategic African American philanthropy. Browne, the consummate economist, also founded *The Review of Black Political Economy*. The Review was conceived and born at a time of heightened consciousness among black economists who wished to address serious issues related to the economic status of the black community.

In 1980, Browne relocated from New York to Washington, D.C., where he was appointed by the U.S. Department of Treasury as the first executive director to the African Development Bank, based in Ivory Coast for a two-year stint. After his tenure, Browne transitioned back to academia as a senior research fellow of African studies at Howard University. He also served as staff director of the subcommittee on international finance of the House Committee on Banking, Finance and Urban Affairs from 1986 to 1991. While on the Hill, Browne worked on issues related to the World Bank, the International Monetary Fund, and Third World debt. He also served as JESSE JACKSON's economic policy advisor during his 1984 presidential campaign.

Browne left government service in 1992 when he earned the prestigious Ford Foundation research fellowship. He entered semiretirement in 1993, becoming an economic consultant for Washington-based organizations, including Africare, the Congressional Black Caucus, and the Institute for Policy Studies. Moreover, Browne consulted for the Clinton presidential transition team on U.S.–Africa trade policy. Browne relocated to Teaneck, New Jersey, in 2004. He died of heart disease Aug. 5 at the Helen Hayes Hospital in West Haverstraw, New York, at the age of seventy-nine.

FURTHER READING

Sullivan, Patricia. *Activist Economist Robert S. Browne* (2004).

Wu, Judy Tzu-Chun. *An African-Vietnamese American: Robert S. Browne, the Antiwar Movement, and the Personal/Political Dimensions of Black Internationalism* (2007).

Obituary: New York Times, 15 August 2004.

JAMAL DONALDSON BRIGGS

Browne, Robert Tecumtha (16 July 1882–15 Oct. 1978), writer, was born in La Grange, Texas, the son of James Browne, a farmer and carpenter, and Mary Elizabeth Dowell Browne. He attended public schools and entered the first class at Samuel Huston College in Austin, Texas, in 1900. Established by the Freedmen's Aid Society of the Methodist Episcopal Church, this all-black college was where Browne developed an early interest in teaching, civil and human rights, and religion.

As a student leader, Browne served as Texas representative to the Young People's Religious and Educational Congress in Atlanta in 1902 and campaigned to repeal the poll tax amendment to the Texas state constitution in 1903. After graduation he was elected vice president of the Texas State Teachers Association and taught at schools in Austin and Fort Worth over the next decade.

In 1904 Browne married Mylie De Pre Adams of Corsicana, Texas, with whom he had one child, Robert T. Jr. In 1908 he entered service in the U.S. Army as a record clerk in San Antonio, Texas. Two years later Browne's wife died, and he transferred to work at an army post in New York City, leaving his son to be raised by family members in Texas. Browne settled in Harlem and commuted daily downtown to U.S. Army Quartermasters Headquarters near Battery Park. Off-duty, Browne devoted many hours to the YMCA (Colored), the Negro Civic League of Greater New York, Equity Congress, and St. Mark's Church, where he founded the Methodist Brotherhood and the Brooks Library of Negro Literature (named for the church's pastor). As founder of the Negro Library Association, he and his love for books connected with a like-minded bibliophile, ARTHUR ALFONSO SCHOMBURG. Browne enrolled at City College in New York to pursue his master's in Experimental Chemistry and Literature.

Browne also pursued his interest in Hindu and Buddhism and theosophy—a blend of science and religion, as taught by the Russian emigrant Helena Blavatsky, and earlier by Paschal Beverly Randolph, a founder of the nineteenth-century Hermetic Brotherhood of Luxor. Browne put his own ideas down in an unpublished manuscript, titled "Hyperspace and Evolution of New Psychic Faculties." In 1915 Browne's hyperactive career and pursuits gained him a place in *Who's Who in the Colored Race*.

In 1918 Browne confided to Schomburg and other black scholars that he did not believe his manuscript would get a fair reception from white editors and publishers. White Americans, Browne believed, would-not be inclined to accept complex mathematical theorems and profound philosophical concepts knowing they came from the mind of a black person. His strategy to win publication was simple: he would keep his race secret. Browne chose a major publisher, E.P. Dutton & Co., to which he sent his four-hundred-page manuscript. Dutton's executives were sufficiently impressed and, without ever meeting their future author, offered Browne a contract. Communicating with his publisher and editor for more than a year only by mail, he finished the book. Dutton retitled Browne's work *The Mystery of Space: A Study of the Hyperspace Movement and an Inquiry into the Genesis and Essential Nature of Space.*

The Mystery of Space received immediate acclaim. In 1920 a *New York Times* reviewer gushed, pronouncing Browne's opus as the "greatest of all latter-day books on space." Impressed by Browne's juxtaposition of science and spiritualism, the literary critic Benjamin De Casseres lauded the author: "It is written by a mathematician, a mystic, and a thinker, one who, endowed with a tremendous metaphysical imagination, never lets go any point of the threads of reality.... He knows all the weapons of the astronomers, the mathematicians, the atomists, and the lesser-act mystagogues. He knows them all and laughs at them." The British physicist E. N. Andrade wrote that Browne's work was filled with "profoundly original thoughts," and the critic Lilian Whiting described Browne's work as "one of the most fascinating books imaginable."

But Browne's sudden acceptance by major media critics was outdone only by the speed of its disappearance. His race became known to his editor and publisher and, presumably, to the critics who were the early champions of his work. Browne's momentary rise to fame, or simply recognition, ended quickly. Curiously, Browne's reputation among African Americans did not survive much beyond the summer of 1921 either. His book was ignored or rejected by black clergy, if perhaps understandably, for Browne had seemingly ignored Christianity in his thesis about the nature of God. As he attempted to embrace all religions to achieve a universal brotherhood, he had consciously avoided placing Jesus, Muhammad, Buddha, or any others as a supreme savior.

In response to the turnaround, Browne then embarked on a lifestyle that made it increasingly difficult to follow his life path through the 1920s, and consequently the rest of his life. Shut out of the mainstream, he developed a new strategy for advancing his ideas: he would change his race and his name. Browne moved from Harlem to an all-white neighborhood in Bedford-Stuyvesant, Brooklyn. He told both his landlord and neighbors that he was a scholar from India. Sporting a turban, Browne began to receive mail under two names: his own and as a new persona, Mulla Hanaranda. Unexpected visitors were not welcome.

Browne's book had put him in mail contact with scientists and theologians throughout the world.

Among them was Arvid Reuterdahl, the dean of engineering at St. Thomas University in St. Paul, Minnesota. With Reuterdahl, Browne cofounded the Academy of Nations, an international organization of scholars sharing an interest in the potential symbiosis of religion and science. Browne wrote most of its hundred-page constitution. Though the academy's purpose was world peace, Browne was clearly aware that its thrust was American, European, and Asian in design. In correspondence with its members, none of whom were aware that he was an African American, Browne deftly made certain that the organization was open "to all people, races, and nations." Reuterdahl, meanwhile, held out the belief that the industrialist Henry Ford would back the idea to the hilt, but the academy never attracted more than about fifty members.

In 1925 Browne's second book, *Cabriba: The Garden of the Gods*, was published under his alias, Mulla Hanaranda. In the novel, Browne's protagonist declares America, despite its imperfections, to be the world's greatest hope for peace: "For it is not a single, highly specialized race of men that live upon its soil; but a great composite people.... And in them play the mysterious forces of a dominant life which, like the raging flood of primordial energy, are shaping, molding, creating, the race that is to be."

In August 1928 another incarnation of Browne seems to have appeared, this time as editor of the *Negro World*. Listed on the paper's masthead as "Rev. R. T. Brown" and writing numerous articles in every issue, Brown (sans *e*) wrote eloquently about MARCUS GARVEY's philosophy, "Africa for the Africans at home and abroad," as a necessary stage in the development of world peace. He reminded *Negro World* readers that "Emerson, Confucius, Buddha, Lincoln, Christ, passed through the same experiences through which you must now prepare to stand, in your onward, upward climb up the ladder of lasting success." Working two separate spans of time as editor between 1928 and 1933, Browne resigned shortly before the *Negro World* published its last issue. At age fifty-one, he transferred his civilian job with the U.S. Army to a military post in the Philippines.

Stationed in Manila, Browne's quartermaster unit purchased and imported supplies for the American military presence in the western Pacific; it was considered a plum tropical assignment by American officers, like Lieutenant Colonel Dwight D. Eisenhower, who enjoyed the local golf courses, and General Douglas MacArthur, whose family occupied several rooms at the Hotel Manila. For his part, Browne enjoyed the absence of racial hostilities in the Philippines.

In January 1942 the Japanese army invaded Manila. Browne and some 3,800 other foreigners—Americans, Australians, Britons, Canadians, Dutch, French, Poles, and Norwegians—were classified as "enemy nationals" and imprisoned at the Santo Tomas Internment Camp. During his incarceration Browne taught courses in religion and philosophy. As the enemy induced food shortages and starvation of camp inmates, he taught mind power and food visualization techniques that helped provide some relief, though many internees died from hunger and malnutrition. "I weighed 212 pounds at the outbreak of the war with Japan and when released I had seen myself disappear to a mere 120 pounds," Browne told the *Amsterdam News* upon his return to the United States in June 1945.

Returning to New York City Browne remarried and adopted a Philippine girl. For a time he traveled across country, trying unsuccessfully to find his son, with whom he had lost contact. In the 1950s he founded the Hermetic Society for World Service, a theosophic religion. His weekly lectures were frequently advertised in the *New York Times* throughout the next two decades. At the time of his death, Browne had published nineteen books.

FURTHER READING

Robert T. Browne's personal papers are located at the Hermetic Society for World Service in New York City and the Dominican Republic. Personal correspondence can also be found among the Arvid Reuterdahl Papers at the University of St. Thomas in St. Paul, Minnesota.

Fikes, Robert, Jr. *Negro Educational Review* (Jan.–Apr. 1998).

Mather, Frank L., ed. *Who's Who of the Colored Race: A General Biographical Dictionary of Men and Women of African Descent* (1915).

Moore, Christopher Paul. *Fighting for America: Black Soldiers, the Unsung Heroes of World War II* (2005).

Sinnette, Elinor D.V. *Arthur Alfonso Schomburg: Black Bibliophile and Collector* (1989).

CHRISTOPHER PAUL MOORE

Browne, Roscoe Lee (2 May 1925–11 Apr. 2007), actor, voiceover artist, director, and writer, was born to Sylvanus, a Baptist minister, and Lovie (Lee) in Woodbury, New Jersey. Browne attended Lincoln University of Pennsylvania, graduating with a literature degree in 1946, and went on to do graduate work at Middlebury College and Columbia University. He also studied in Italy. He competed in college track and was the Amateur Athletic Union indoor track champion of the one-thousand-yard run. While attending college, Browne was named an All-American athlete.

In 1946 Browne embarked upon two careers, teaching English, French, and literature at his alma mater, Lincoln University, while also holding a sales position at the Schenley Import Corporation. He left teaching in 1952 but kept his sales job until 1956; meanwhile, another profession had caught his attention. He joined the acting company at the Long Wharf Theater in New Haven, Connecticut, and then he won his first acting job on Broadway in 1952. Browne became well known for his Shakespearian roles. He made many appearances with the New York Shakespeare Festival. He had roles in *The Taming of the Shrew* and *Julius Caesar* in 1956, as Balthazar in *Romeo and Juliet* and as Aaron in *Titus Andronicus* in 1957. He was an understudy for the role of Othello in 1958 and for the Fool in *King Lear* in 1962 at the Delacorte Theatre in New York's Central Park. Browne appeared as a guest artist at the Spoleto Festival in Italy and performed Shakespeare in Toronto for the Canadian Broadcasting Corporation (CBC). He was also an artist in residence at London's Old Globe Theater.

Browne appeared on Broadway in *The Cool World* (1960), *General Seeger* (1962), and *Tiger, Tiger Burning Bright* (1962). Browne's first television appearance was on an episode of *The Defenders* in 1962. Browne's first appearance in films was in Shirley Clarke's 1962 film *The Connection*. Browne received critical notice in the *New York Times* for his Broadway stage role as the "Narrator" in *The Ballad of the Sad Café* in 1963. Around this time, Browne made a concerted effort to bring black-oriented dramas to life on the stage and screen as seen in his portrayal of Christopher in the film *Black Like Me* in 1964. He appeared in *The Cool World* also in 1964. Browne earned a Best Actor Obic Award for an Off-Broadway adaptation of Melville's *Benito Cereno* in 1965. He played in *Danton's Death* (1965) and directed *Hand Is on the Gate* (1966). He took part in *An Evening of Negro Poetry and Folk Music* at the Delacorte Theater in 1966. Browne's spoken word recordings include *Enjoyment of Poetry: Memorial Program for Claude McKay* (1967). He worked at the Pittsburgh Playhouse in 1966–1967 and then joined Playhouse in the Park in Cincinnati, Ohio, the following year. He appeared in the films *The Comedians* in 1967, *Up Tight!* (with RUBY DEE and Raymond St. Jacques) in 1968, and Alfred Hitchcock's *Topaz* in 1969. During the 1969–1970 season, he was a member of the acting company at the New Theatre for Now in Los Angeles; he then joined the American Conservatory Theater in San Francisco. In addition to his work on Broadway, Browne appeared onstage in *The Dream on Monkey Mountain,* which opened in 1970 and earned him a Best Actor award from the Los Angeles Drama Critics Circle Award.

He was featured opposite actors John Wayne and Bruce Dern in *The Cowboys* (1972) as the sage cook for a young cattle-drive crew. He also appeared in a number of "blaxploitation" films, including *Superfly* (1972) and *Superfly TNT* (1973). He also had a role in the film *Uptown Saturday Night* (1974). Also, beginning in the early 1970s, in between film, stage, and television work, Browne performed at colleges and universities throughout the United States along with fellow actor Anthony Zerbe. The program, *Behind the Broken Words*, featured the actors on an empty stage, interpreting passages from literature and drama.

Browne went on to make a number of guest appearances on other TV shows such as *Magnum P.I.*, *Soap*, *Will and Grace*, and *ER*. He was inducted into the Black Filmmakers' Hall of Fame in 1977. Browne was cast as a regular in NBC series *McCoy* (with Tony Curtis in 1975–76), played the role of Philip Harrison on the NBC series *King* (1978), was also a regular on the CBS show *Miss Winslow and Son* (1979), and, perhaps most memorably, as the butler on *Soap* (1980–81). His appearance on *Barney Miller* garnered an Emmy Award nomination for Outstanding Single Performance by a Supporting Actor for his role in the episode "The Escape Artist," while his guest role in the episode "The Card Game" on *The Cosby Show* in 1986 earned Browne an Emmy Award and another Los Angeles Drama Circle nod. That year, he also appeared in the film *Jumping Jack Flash*. He also had recurring acting roles on *Falcon Crest* (1988).

Browne's voiceover work for animated features began in 1989 when he supplied the voice of Max Miles in the syndicated *Ring Raider*. Also that year he once again won the Los Angeles Drama Critics Circle Award for his role in the play *Joe Turner's Come and Gone* in 1989. Browne frequently appeared in television drama specials, including *Stuck with Each Other* (1989), *Columbo Saturday Mystery* (1990), and movies in the 1990s for Showtime and Cinemax. He returned to Broadway in the role of Holloway in *Two Trains Running* (1992) that earned a Tony nomination for best performance by the lead actor in a play and the Circle Award for the third time. This performance contributed to the Helen Hayes award for his theater work. Also in 1992 he had a role in *The Mambo Kings* and provided recorded voice tracks for *The Autobiography of Malcolm X* with Joe Morton (1992).

His voiceover work includes *Oliver & Company* (1988), *Babe* (1995), and *Babe: Pig in the City* (1998). He was the voice of "Wilson Fisk, the Kingpin," for *Spider-Man*, running on Fox/UPN from 1995 to 1999. In the 2000s he appeared as himself in "The Papp Project" for *American Masters* on PBS in 2001 and also wrote his own poetry and short stories. He also appeared in *Hamlet* (2000), *Treasure Planet* (2002), *Behind the Broken Words* (2003), *The Fly on the Wall* (2004), *The Batman* (2005), and *Garfield: A Tail of Two Kitties* (2006).

Browne had served on the board of numerous organizations, including KPFK/Pacifica Radio, Los Angeles Free Public Theatre, and The Millay Colony for the Arts. He gave spoken word performances with the Boston Pops and Hollywood Bowl Orchestras, the Los Angeles Philharmonic, and the orchestras of New Orleans, St. Louis, and Pittsburgh. Browne's spoken-word recordings won several Audie Awards. Browne died of cancer at the age of eighty-one.

FURTHER READING
Troupe, Quincy. "Roscoe Lee Browne," *Essence* (Dec. 1976).
Obituary: *New York Times*, 12 Apr. 2007.

PAMELA LEE GRAY

Browne, Rose Butler (19 Mar. 1897–1 Dec. 1986), educator and author, was born in Boston, Massachusetts, the daughter of John R. Butler, a brickmason, and Hannah F. McClenney. She grew up in a close-knit family that espoused the tenets of family, church, and service to others.

Browne lived in a poor community in Boston and completed her earliest training in Malden through the fifth grade, at which time her family moved to Newport, Rhode Island. After graduating from Rogers High School she entered Rhode Island State College, receiving the EdB degree before matriculating at the University of Rhode Island, where she earned the master of education degree. She began her teaching career in the fall of 1921. Nine years later she resumed her studies, this time at Harvard University. In June 1937 she received the Ed.D degree and became the first African American woman and only the second African American to receive this distinction from the nation's oldest university.

Rose Butler married the Reverend Doctor Emmett T. Browne, a Baptist minister noted for his work in Virginia and West Virginia. They were the parents of one son. Browne taught at Virginia State College, where she served as chair of the psychology department. She also held the post of chair of the department of education at Bluefield State College. In 1948 Browne accepted the post of professor and chair of the department of education at North Carolina College at Durham (later North Carolina Central University). She made numerous improvements to the curricula, including the addition of a special education program. Also, her faculty helped to develop, plan, and equip the first permanent home for the school of education, which became the James Taylor Education Building.

Browne led the school to full accreditation by the National Council of the Accreditation of Teacher Education. In the 1950s, under her leadership, the institution graduated its first Ph.D.. During the turbulent 1960s she championed the cause of civil rights and supported students who participated in the civil rights movement. While her husband pastored the Mount Vernon Baptist Church of Durham, she assisted him in the affairs of the church and the local Durham community. She also operated a summer school for sixty black children between the ages of two and six years old. Browne served on the Human Relations Commission, Women in Action for the Prevention of Violence, Bright Leaf Council, the Harriet Tubman Branch of the Young Women's Christian Association (YWCA), and was a leader of Troop 23 Girl Scouts of America.

As a scholar Dr. Browne published widely in local, regional, and national publications. Upon her retirement from the college in 1963 she was presented the Hamilton Watch Award for outstanding service as a teacher, leader, and scholar. Among her many memberships and associations she belonged to the American Association for the Advancement of Sciences, American Association of University Professors, Pi Lambda Theta Honor Society for Women in Education, North Carolina State Teachers Association, Palmer Memorial Institute, National Association of College Women, North Carolina Federation of Negro Women's Clubs, American Childhood Education International, Association of Student-Teachers, and National Society for the Study of Education. Of special importance was her affiliation with the Alpha Kappa Alpha Sorority, Inc., the oldest black sorority in the United States.

Dr. Brown was the recipient of various honors, which included the honorary doctor of education from Rhode Island College of Education, 1950; the dedication of the Rose Butler Browne Residence Hall at Rhode Island College, 1968; the honorary doctor of humane letters from Roger Williams College, 1977; and the Proclamation of Rose Butler Browne Day in Providence, Rhode Island, 1977.

In 1969 she coauthored with James W. English her acclaimed autobiography, *Love My Children—The Education of a Teacher*. In it she argued that the education of young people was the responsibility of all Americans. She was opposed to programs that "called for new appropriations to relieve conditions" and instead fought for "changes in attitudes that would be a foundation for harmony between black and white America."

In 1975, having retired from teaching at North Carolina College in 1963, Browne moved to Providence, Rhode Island. She died there following an extended illness and was interred in Durham, North Carolina.

FURTHER READING

The papers of Dr. Rose Butler Browne from her tenure at North Carolina College at Durham are housed in the James E. Shepard Library, North Carolina Central University.

Browne, Rose Butler, and James W. English. *Love My Children—The Education of a Teacher* (1969).

Center for Urban Affairs, North Carolina State University. "Rose Butler Browne," in *Paths toward Freedom* (1976).

Sanders, Arthrell D. "Rose Butler Browne—A Bouquet for Her Children, for Their Children, for Theirs, and for Theirs," *NCCU Now* (Summer–Fall 2001).

ANDRE D. VANN

Browne, Theodore (1910?–1 Jan. 1979), playwright and actor, was born in Suffolk, Virginia, and raised in New York City. There is no documented record of Browne's early childhood and family life. While living in New York he completed high school in the Bronx at DeWitt Clinton High School, graduated soon thereafter from City College of New York, and gained his first stage experience as a young actor.

In 1935 Browne moved to Seattle, Washington, where he became active with the Seattle Repertory Playhouse, a progressive local theater led by the University of Washington professors Burton and

Florence James. The following year the Jameses helped establish the Negro Repertory Company (NRC), Seattle's African American unit of the Federal Theatre Project (FTP), a nationwide Depression-era initiative under the New Deal's Works Progress Administration that provided employment and artistic opportunities for theater artists, including many African Americans, across the country. Browne was an active presence within the NRC as an actor, resident playwright, and acting coach for the ensemble's mostly amateur casts. He received favorable critical notices for portraying the title character in *Noah* (1936), a musical comedy by Andrey Obey that was the NRC's inaugural production. Browne also performed in other NRC productions, including the Seattle staging of Paul Peters and George Sklar's leftist agitprop drama *Stevedore* (1936). But his biggest splash came within the NRC came as a dramatist. Browne's adaptation of Aristophanes's *Lysistrata* (1936)—which recast Aristophanes's ancient comedy in the fictional modern African kingdom of Ebonia—enjoyed widespread advance praise from local reviewers and sold thousands of tickets prior to its August 1936 opening. But the production closed after a single performance, in response to complaints about its risqué content.

The following year the NRC staged Browne's original drama *Natural Man* (1937), a retelling of the legend of the black folk hero JOHN HENRY and his fabled contest against a steam-powered drill during America's nineteenth-century railroad boom. The play portrayed John Henry both as a working-class hero triumphing over the forces of modern industrial mechanization and as a black hero who overcomes racist exploitation and oppression. Critics and historians regard *Natural Man* as Browne's finest work and among the best plays written and staged under the auspices of the FTP. Browne also assembled for the NRC a revue of swing music, dancing, and comic sketches entitled *Swing, Gates, Swing* (1937).

In the late 1930s Browne returned to the East Coast, relocating in Boston but remaining active in New York City. Preparations began in 1939 for two New York productions of his plays. The New York Negro Unit of the FTP (located at the Lafayette Theatre in Harlem) announced a spring 1939 staging of *Go Down, Moses* (later renamed *A Black Woman Called Moses*), Browne's biographical drama about HARRIET TUBMAN. The production started rehearsals but was soon abandoned. Around the same time, the renowned actor Rex

Ingram expressed interest in headlining a commercial production of *Natural Man*, but this project failed to secure financing. Browne also worked on several writing projects with the FTP's Boston Negro Unit in the late 1930s, none of which reached the stage before the demise of the Federal Theatre in 1939.

In 1940 Browne joined THEODORE WARD, LANGSTON HUGHES, and other leading African American dramatists as a founding member of the new Harlem-based ensemble called the Negro Playwrights Company. It is unlikely that Browne, still primarily a Boston resident, was actively involved in launching the company, which folded after its first production, a revival of Ward's political drama *Big White Fog*. In April 1941 Browne was awarded the Rockefeller Foundation's prestigious Playwriting Fellowship, becoming the first African American to receive this prize. With the stipend he wrote a new play (never produced) about African American minstrel performers. Soon after winning the Rockefeller grant, another Harlem neighborhood theater company—the American Negro Theater (ANT)—mounted a well-received revival of *Natural Man*. The production advanced Browne's public stature as a playwright, though he later claimed that the ANT had mishandled his work by focusing too heavily on the drama's sociopolitical message at the expense of its folkloristic qualities.

Sometime during World War II Browne entered the army as a private and was stationed at Fort Huachuca, Arizona. A September 1944 article in the *Chicago Defender* tells of Browne writing a "radio-style ... script telling the story of the Negro in American wars," which was performed at the dedication of a new mural titled *The Negro Soldier*. Following his service in the military, Browne returned to the Boston area, where he held jobs as a teacher and as a proofreader for a commercial printing company. His creative activities during the decades following World War II were sporadic and varied. He penned a "novel of suspense" titled *The Band Will Not Play Dixie*, which was published in 1955. He returned to the stage at least once, in the cast of the 1956 Broadway musical *The Ponder Heart* (based on Eudora Welty's novel). In a 1975 interview Browne spoke of a new historical drama he had composed titled *The Day of the Midnight Ride of Paul Revere*, which he had hoped might be staged in connection with America's Bicentennial celebrations. On 6 May 1977 Massachusetts's governor Michael Dukakis and Boston's mayor Kevin H.

White honored Browne and his achievements by officially dedicating that day as Theodore Browne Day. Less than two years later, Browne died of a heart attack in Boston at age sixty-eight. He was survived by his wife, Alberta.

Theodore Browne was an influential pioneer in the historical evolution of the African American stage. He stood at the forefront of efforts by black theater artists in the early and mid-twentieth century to combat the falsifications of the minstrel stage and the commercial American theater industry and to establish a tradition of serious and politically ambitious spoken drama that would counteract the long tradition of racial stereotype within American culture.

FURTHER READING

A recording and transcript of an 22 October 1975 interview with Theodore Browne are housed at the Fenwick Library, George Mason University, Fairfax, Virginia.

Abramson, Doris. *Negro Playwrights in the American Theatre, 1925–1959* (1969).

Alexander Street Press. *Black Drama, 1850–Present,* available online at http://www.alexanderstreet2.com/BLDRLive.

"Browne, Theodore," in *Early Black American Playwrights and Dramatic Writers: A Biographical Directory and Catalog of Plays, Films, and Broadcasting Scripts,* ed. Bernard L. Peterson (1990).

Obituary: *Washington Post,* 6 Jan. 1979.

JONATHAN SHANDELL

Browne, William Washington (20 Oct. 1849– 21 Dec. 1897), fraternal society leader and banker, was born in Habersham County, Georgia, the son of Joseph Browne and Mariah (maiden name unknown), field slaves. As a young child he was called Ben Browne and was chosen to be the companion of his owner's son. A subsequent owner who lived near Memphis trained Browne as a jockey for race circuits in Tennessee and Mississippi. During the Civil War he plotted an escape with fellow slaves. When his owner learned of the conspiracy, he transferred Browne to a plantation in Mississippi. Despite the difficulties of tramping fifty miles without a compass, Browne persuaded three other young slaves to join him in a successful escape to the Union army at Memphis. After learning that his owner could demand his return, Browne fled upriver as a stowaway.

Browne later worked as a saloon servant in Illinois, where his barroom experiences made him a teetotaler, and as a farm laborer in Wisconsin, where he attended school for the first time. He also was a servant aboard a navy gunboat on the Mississippi and was a paid substitute in an infantry regiment. In 1869 he left Wisconsin to return to Georgia, where he taught school and studied for the ministry in Atlanta at what later became the Gammon Seminary. In 1871 he moved to Alabama to teach in the public schools. Two years later he married Mary A. "Molly" Graham. Childless, they adopted two children. In 1876 Browne was ordained a minister in the Colored (later Christian) Methodist Church at Piedmont, Alabama.

Browne believed that alcoholic drink stood in the way of the uplift of his race. Blacks convicted of the crime of public intoxication were disenfranchised. More important to Browne, money used to buy alcohol was money unavailable to buy land. To promote temperance among their people, Browne and two other black reformers asked the Good Templars in Alabama, a white fraternal temperance society, to let blacks organize Templar lodges. Refusing, the Good Templars offered instead to help Browne and company organize the United Order of True Reformers in Alabama, a fraternal temperance society for blacks that had been created by the Good Templars of Kentucky in 1873. In 1874 Browne became a full-time worker for the True Reformers; presumably the Good Templars paid his salary. In 1875 the True Reformers of Alabama organized the Grand Fountain, a statewide lodge, and became independent of the Good Templars. Browne was the first Grand Worthy Secretary, and in 1877–1880 he served as Grand Worthy Master. Browne cared little about ritual and regalia but cared a great deal about black people saving money, buying land, and helping one another. He wanted his organization to acquire the power to issue life insurance and operate a bank. Rivals in the African American community, fearing that Browne would overshadow them, persuaded the Alabama legislature to reject his request for the charter he needed.

At the end of 1880, disillusioned with Alabama, Browne moved to Virginia, the birthplace of his parents. The True Reformers there had invited him to take charge of their organization, which had lost most of its members to a rival society. From 1881 to his death he served as Grand Worthy Master of this Grand Fountain, with headquarters at Richmond, Virginia. Overcoming internal dissension, Browne made the True Reformers the dominant black fraternal society in Virginia and also established fountains in other states. In perhaps as early as 1881, members of the True Reformer society ceased to be pledged to abstinence. Although Browne briefly served as pastor of a Colored Methodist church at Richmond, he resigned when the local bishop insisted that he abandon his True Reformer work. The African Methodist Episcopal Church recognized Browne as a minister, but he never had his own church again.

Emphasizing economic progress, the True Reformers became a mutual insurance organization with many auxiliary businesses. To supplement the modest life insurance that all members of the lodge paid for, the True Reformers offered larger policies that Browne called the Classes. In addition, Browne's order pioneered for black insurance enterprises the practice of charging older members more because of the greater likelihood of their imminent death. In 1888 the Virginia legislature chartered a True Reformer savings bank, which opened for business in 1889 with Browne as its president. Although another black bank in Washington, D.C., was the first one to conduct business, the True Reformer bank was the first black-controlled financial institution to receive a charter. The order constructed a large headquarters building at Richmond in 1891 and later operated general stores, a hotel, a weekly newspaper, and a printing plant, and it also acquired farms and other real estate. Browne raised money and purchased land for an old-age home that was established after his death.

W. E. B. DuBois, ordinarily critical of African Americans who made economic improvement their priority, characterized the True Reformers as "probably the most remarkable Negro organization in the country." This tribute, in *Economic Co-Operation among Negro Americans* (1907), no doubt owed much to DuBois's belief in the African origins of the True Reformer strategy of economic cooperation.

Unlike many large black fraternal societies, the True Reformers accepted women as members. Women had special responsibility for a juvenile auxiliary, the Rosebuds. Like the adult order, the children's society stressed the importance of saving, investment, and mutual assistance, all grounded in self-respect.

Always a controversial figure whose domineering personality occasioned many quarrels, Browne acquired new enemies in the mid-1890s. In 1894 he asked the True Reformers to pay him for what he called his "plans," the conception that he had brought to Virginia from Alabama of a business-oriented fraternal society. In 1895 they promised him fifty thousand dollars, and they turned over more than half that amount to his widow before a court order—meant to prevent the loss of money meant for insurance purposes—stopped further payments.

In the same year two black men—JOHN R. MITCHELL JR., editor of the *Richmond Planet*, and the Massachusetts legislator Robert Teamoh—visited the Virginia governor's mansion in the company of the white members of a Massachusetts delegation. Worried that blacks in general would suffer the consequences of this violation of social segregation, Browne denounced Mitchell and Teamoh in a letter to a white newspaper. In response, most black newspapers accused Browne of being subservient to white supremacists. (In fact Browne possessed great racial pride, boasting that he, unlike most black leaders, was of pure African descent.) Browne also quarreled with members of his True Reformer inner circle during his last years. In 1897 he denounced his protégé, W. P. Burrell, the Grand Worthy Secretary, and passed over his best-known lieutenants in designating an Acting Grand Worthy Master to serve while he battled cancer. After wandering from physician to physician in search of a cure, he died in Washington, D.C.

Browne's Grand Fountain prospered for a decade or so after his death, eventually attaining an adult membership of around sixty thousand. After the bank collapsed in 1910 the order lost most of its members, and it disappeared altogether during the depression of the 1930s. Browne's renown faded with those of the Grand Fountain and other African American fraternal societies.

FURTHER READING

Burrell, W. P., and D. E. Johnson Sr. *Twenty-Five Years History of the Grand Fountain of the United Order of True Reformers, 1881–1905* (1909).

Davis, Daniel Webster. "The Life and Public Services of Rev. Wm. Washington Browne" (1910), in *The Black Lodge in White America: "True Reformer" Browne and His Economic Strategy*, by David M. Fahey (1994).

Watkinson, James D. "William Washington Browne and the True Reformers of Richmond, Virginia," *Virginia Magazine of History* 97 (July 1989).

This entry is taken from the *American National Biography* and is published here with the permission of the American Council of Learned Societies.

DAVID M. FAHEY

Bruce, Blanche Kelso (1 Mar. 1841–17 Mar. 1898), black political leader and U.S. senator during the Reconstruction era, was born in Farmville, Virginia, the son of Polly (surname unknown), a slave. The identity of his father is unknown, but he took the surname of the man who owned his mother before he was born. His childhood as a slave on a small plantation, first in Virginia, then briefly in Mississippi, and finally in Missouri did not significantly differ, as he later recalled, from that of the sons of whites. This relatively benign experience in slavery perhaps owed a great deal to the fact that he was the light-skinned favorite of a benevolent master and mistress. He shared a tutor with his master's son and thus obtained the education that prepared him for later success. During the Civil War, despite the benevolence of his owner, he fled to freedom in Kansas, but after slavery was abolished he returned to Missouri, where he reportedly established the first school in the state for blacks, at Hannibal.

After the war Bruce briefly attended Oberlin College in Ohio, but following the passage of the Reconstruction Acts of 1867, which provided for black political equality in the former Confederate states, he moved to Bolivar County in the Mississippi Delta. Soon after his arrival, the district commander appointed him a voter registrar in neighboring Tallahatchie County. He also organized plantation blacks into the new Republican Party and soon attracted the attention of state party leaders.

When the first Mississippi legislature under the new order met, Bruce was elected sergeant at arms of the state senate. A man of magnificent physique and handsome countenance and possessed of impeccable manners, Bruce won the support of white Republicans like Governor James Lusk Alcorn as well as blacks. In 1871 he won election to the joint office of sheriff and tax collector of Bolivar County. The Republican state board of education also appointed him county superintendent of education. He virtually created the biracial but segregated system of education in the county and secured the support of whites for it. In all of these positions he gained a reputation for financial integrity.

Bruce also invested in land and within a decade had attained the status of planter. In 1872 he was named to the board of levee commissioners for a three-county district—a group with the power to raise revenue and build embankments in the Delta region. Bruce's political and financial success

Blanche Kelso Bruce, the first African American senator from Mississippi, c. 1870. (Library of Congress, Brady-Handy Photograph Collection.)

and his promotion of labor stability among black workers had the effect of moderating the opposition of conservative planters to Republican control in Bolivar County. By 1874 Bruce's fame had spread beyond the Delta. His political skill and his moderation had won him support from all factions of the Mississippi Republican Party. In February the legislature elected him to the U.S. Senate by a nearly unanimous vote, which included the support of a few conservative Democrats. In March 1875 Bruce took his seat in the Senate, becoming the nation's second black senator and the first black to be elected to a full term. In the Senate he served on four committees, including the important select committees on Mississippi River improvements and on the Freedmen's Bank. As chairman of the latter committee, he led the effort to reform the management of the institution and provide relief for depositors. But a Bruce-sponsored Senate bill to obtain congressional reimbursement for black victims of the bank's failure did not pass. He also spoke out against a Chinese exclusion bill and for a more humane Indian policy. Bruce took these positions primarily because of the harsh implications that such a racist, exclusionist policy had for blacks.

Bruce's main interest in the Senate was the defense of black rights in the South at a time when state and local Republican governments were replaced by hostile conservative ones. Although he was usually unobtrusive in attempting to persuade Congress, and specifically its Republican members, to enforce the Reconstruction amendments to the Constitution, he became passionate in denouncing the violence and intimidation that characterized the Mississippi election of 1875, overthrowing Republican rule.

Despite bitter setbacks for blacks during this period, Bruce remained committed to the Reconstruction goal of black assimilation into American society with all of the rights of whites. He opposed both of the organized efforts at black migration of the late 1870s, the Kansas Exodus and the Back-to-Africa movement. He did so on the grounds that neither destination had much to offer blacks and that the rights of the race could yet be achieved in white America. His prestige among blacks suffered considerably because of his opposition to emigration. In 1878 he married JOSEPHINE BEALL WILLSON [BRUCE], the daughter of a prominent black dentist of Cleveland, Ohio; they had one son. After their marriage and the couple's acceptance into white Washingtonian society, Bruce became largely insulated from the black masses.

During his last years in the Senate he devoted much of his time to Republican Party affairs and black education. In Mississippi he joined with two other black leaders, JOHN R. LYNCH and James Hill, to dominate the state Republican organization, gaining important federal patronage for his supporters. In promoting black education, he advanced the self-help doctrine, which ultimately became associated with BOOKER T. WASHINGTON.

With the Democrats in control of the state legislature, Bruce made no effort to obtain reelection to the U.S. Senate. After the expiration of his term in 1881, he continued to live in Washington but retained his plantation in Mississippi. He also continued to participate in national Republican politics and was a popular speaker on behalf of black education. In 1881 President James Garfield appointed Bruce register of the U.S. Treasury, and he continued to hold the office during Chester A. Arthur's administration. In 1884–1885 he served as director of the black exhibits in the Industrial Cotton Centennial Exposition held in New Orleans. These exhibits focused on the material progress that blacks had made since Emancipation. In 1896 he received strong support for a seat in William McKinley's cabinet, but he had to settle for his previous position of register of the Treasury. Bruce died of diabetes in Washington, D.C.

FURTHER READING

The Blanche K. Bruce Papers are held at the Rutherford B. Hayes Presidential Center Library, Fremont, Ohio. Howard University Library, Washington, D.C., also has a collection of Bruce papers, including letters.

Gatewood, Willard B. *Aristocrats of Color: The Black Elite, 1880–1920* (1990).

Harris, William C. "Blanche K. Bruce of Mississippi: Conservative Assimilationist," in *Southern Black Leaders of the Reconstruction Era* (1982).

This entry is taken from the *American National Biography* and is published here with the permission of the American Council of Learned Societies.

WILLIAM C. HARRIS

Bruce, Henry Clay (3 Mar. 1836–1 Sept. 1902), author of a slave narrative, was born to slave parents in Prince Edward County, Virginia. The Lemuel Bruce family, including Pettis and Rebecca (Bruce) Perkinson, owned Henry Bruce and his mother and siblings. Bruce's many siblings included his younger brother, BLANCHE KELSO BRUCE, the senator from Mississippi from 1875 to 1881.

Bruce spent most of his early childhood years on plantations and farms in Virginia, Missouri, and—briefly—Mississippi. Pettis Perkinson brought Bruce, his mother, and siblings back to Chariton County, Missouri, where he permanently settled in 1850. From the age of nine, Bruce was frequently hired out to other employers in the community and worked at a variety of occupations, including brick making, tobacco manufacturing, and general farm labor. Bruce had a self-described "desire to learn" and was taught to read by his young owner and playmate, William Perkinson. The older Bruce children taught their younger siblings, and all were literate before emancipation.

In March 1864, in the midst of the Civil War, Bruce ran away with his future wife, Pauline Brown, a young woman belonging to a neighboring slaveholder. The couple headed for Leavenworth, Kansas, where they married on 31 March 1864. The Bruces had at least four children: Alonzo, Eliza, Samuel, and Nora. For the next decade, Bruce made the transition to freedom while working at a variety of jobs, including running his own mercantile business. He also became involved in Kansas Republican Party politics and, eventually, was elected as the doorkeeper of the Kansas State Senate in 1881. After Pauline Bruce died in 1880, Bruce married a Missouri-born woman named Nannie and lived with her until his death in 1902.

Starting in 1881 Blanche K. Bruce, who served as the register of the U.S. Treasury after his time in the Senate, secured his brother a number of federal government positions, including work in the Post Office Department and the Federal Pension Office. Bruce was employed for two decades as a federal pension examiner, receiving a number of promotions and keeping his job through both Republican and Democratic administrations.

In 1895 Henry Bruce published his memoirs, which were titled *The New Man. Twenty-Nine Years a Slave. Twenty-Nine Years a Free Man.* The book is autobiographical, but also serves as a platform for Bruce to reflect on the experiences of African Americans in both slavery and freedom. Bruce provided his readers with a detailed description of life in antebellum Virginia and Missouri. He described the work slaves did, the treatment they received, and their association with others in the community. Bruce also commented on race relations during the antebellum years, placing the blame for problems on uneducated, poor, white people, whom he believed were "the natural enemies of the slaves" (Bruce, iv). Bruce argued that quality of "[b]lood and education" determined the character of both white and black people (Bruce, 127). He was intolerant of any individual who lacked self-respect and motivation or who engaged in what he considered to be superstitious practices. Bruce described his experience of slavery as mild, but attributed his favorable treatment to his own superior work ethic and morality. He implied that slaves brought many of their own problems on themselves, although he acknowledged that slaves worked harder for slave owners who treated them well.

Bruce wrote of life after emancipation, placing the blame for racism on the shoulders of the "poor white" people, suggesting that the southern upper classes were inclined toward kindness to their former slaves. Bruce believed that white Americans should not discriminate against Americans of African decent and should refer to them as "Colored Americans" because they were trustworthy, hardworking, loyal, and patriotic citizens of the United States. They deserved respect because they did not

have divided national loyalties, embrace socialism, or foment labor unrest like recent immigrants to the country.

Equally critical of elite African Americans, Bruce argued that many placed more emphasis on a person's freed status prior to the Civil War than on an individual's intellect or character. Bruce may have resented the fact that some members of the black aristocracy of Washington, D.C., may not have accepted him, a former slave, into their social circles. He also encouraged African Americans to take pride in the progress made since slavery and to support one another in business ventures rather than continue to patronize white businesses. He argued that economic success was the key to improving the position of African Americans in the future and devoted an entire chapter of his book to Washington's work at the Tuskegee Institute.

In recent years scholars have been troubled by many of Bruce's views, painting him as an assimilationist and dismissing much of what he wrote about slavery and emancipation. Yet Bruce's ideas were similar to those held by many educated and affluent African Americans in the late nineteenth century. In addition, his memories of slavery and southern culture show the diverse ways in which African Americans experienced slavery. Bruce acknowledged that he had no authority with which to state his views, but he believed that as a common man he offered "an impartial and unprejudiced view" of both slavery and freedom. Bruce died in Washington, D.C., after a two-week illness.

FURTHER READING

Bruce, Henry C. *The New Man. Twenty-Nine Years a Slave. Twenty-Nine Years a Free Man* (1895).

Gatewood, Willard B. *Aristocrats of Color: The Black Elite, 1880–1920* (1990).

Obituary: *Washington Post*, 2 Sept. 1902.

DIANE MUTTI BURKE

Bruce, John Edward (22 Feb. 1856–7 Aug. 1924), journalist and historian, was born in Piscataway, Maryland, the son of Martha Allen Clark and Robert Bruce, who were both enslaved Africans. In 1859 Major Harvey Griffin, Robert Bruce's owner, sold Robert to a Georgia slaveholder. Raised by his mother, John lived in Maryland until 1861, when Union troops marching through Maryland freed him and his mother, taking them to Washington, D.C., where John lived until 1892. In 1865 John's mother worked as a domestic in Stratford,

Connecticut, where her son received his early education in an integrated school. One year later they returned to Washington, D.C., where John continued his education. Although he did not complete high school, he enrolled in a course at Howard University in 1872. John married Lucy Pinkwood, an opera singer from Washington, D.C. In 1895 he married Florence Adelaide Bishop, with whom he had one child.

Bruce began his journalistic career at eighteen as a general helper to the Washington correspondent of the *New York Times*. He was also employed as a correspondent in New York for John Freeman's *Progressive American*, which published Bruce's first article, "The Distillation of Coal Tar." Between 1879 and 1884 Bruce, under the pen name "Rising Sun," started three newspapers: the *Argus* (1879), the *Sunday Item* (1880), which was the first African American daily, and the *Washington Grit* (1884). Following the publication of the *Grit*, which was known for its frank style, T. THOMAS FORTUNE, editor of the *New York Freeman*, referred to Bruce as "Bruce Grit." In order to maintain financial stability as a journalist, Bruce worked the majority of his life as a messenger in the federal customhouse in Westchester, New York, retiring in 1922.

Throughout his life Bruce was an active proponent of African American civil rights. In 1890 Fortune founded the Afro American League (AAL), a pioneer civil rights organization that supported African American suffrage. Recognized as a talented speaker, Bruce addressed delegates at the AAL inaugural convention in Washington, D.C. Citing the Constitution, he examined the legal justification of African American citizenship. He contended that the federal government had failed to protect African American civil rights, and as long as white violence and African American disfranchisement continued, "a blot will remain on the escutcheon."

Between 1896 and 1901 Bruce served as an associate editor of *Howard's American Magazine*, for which he published an influential pamphlet, *The Blood Red Record*. The pamphlet, which was advertised in a number of African American newspapers, was a condemnation of lynching and racism in the American justice system. Bruce listed the names and "alleged" crimes of more than a hundred African American men who were killed by white mobs. According to Bruce, whites denied African Americans an opportunity to receive a fair trial. Whites, he argued, receive a trial by jury even if they "assassinate the President of the United States." Bruce's scathing remarks on American justice revealed its historical legacy of racism.

Leaving *Howard's American Magazine*, Bruce moved to Albany, New York, and worked as a journalist for the *Albany Evening Journal* and the *Times Union*. He also contributed articles to the *New York Age*, the *Cleveland Gazette*, and the *Washington Colored American*, three prominent African American newspapers. In Albany, Bruce continued to work for African American civil rights. In 1898 he joined the Afro American Council, founded by Bishop ALEXANDER WALTERS of the African Methodist Episcopal Church. In "Concentration of Energy," Bruce insisted that the only way for African Americans to obtain political and economic power is "with intelligent organization." He urged African Americans to invest in banks owned by blacks, and he encouraged African American cooperative economics. In July 1905 W. E. B. DuBois organized the Niagara Conference to protest BOOKER T. WASHINGTON's accommodationist philosophy and segregation in the South. Bruce, a proponent of African American civil rights, was invited by DuBois to attend the conference, but he did not have the money to travel to the historic meeting.

Bruce was an active member in a number of African American literary societies, such as the American Negro Academy founded by ALEXANDER CRUMMELL, an intellectual and scholar. Bruce believed that African Americans must engage in the realm of ideas because, as he said on the occasion of becoming president of the literary Phalanx Club, "The battle of this race is an intellectual one" and "anybody of earnest and clear-thinking, clear headed men is a potent and powerful force." Moreover he said that the "secret of power is knowledge," and whites aspire to "repress black men who are seeking this power."

Another major interest for Bruce was history. On 18 April 1911 Bruce, along with ARTHUR SCHOMBURG, a renowned bibliophile, founded the Negro Society for Historical Research (NSHR), which was a precursor of CARTER G. WOODSON's Association for the Study of African American Life and History. The NSHR sought to "teach, enlighten, and instruct our people in Negro history and achievement." Bruce viewed history as a medium to combat intellectual racism and promote racial pride. Before the founding of the NSHR, Bruce published *Short Biographical Sketches of Eminent Negro Men and Women in Europe and the United States* (1910). Designed for children, the text contained short biographies of prominent African American leaders in order to "awaken race pride."

In addition to his historical and political tracts, Bruce wrote short stories, poems, plays, and one novel, *The Awakening of Hezekiah Jones* (1916). The novel describes the life of Jones, an African American official elected in a southern city. At the end of the novel Jones experiences an "awakening" and recognizes the political necessity of racial unity. Because Bruce's literary activities mirrored his ideology, his art served a political function.

After World War I, Bruce became increasingly disenchanted with the pace of African American progress. Following the war, race riots, lynchings, and racial inequality intensified throughout the nation, and in 1919 Bruce became a major figure in the largest black nationalist organization for people of African descent, MARCUS GARVEY's Universal Negro Improvement Association (UNIA). Between 1921 and 1923 Bruce served as a contributing editor of Garvey's *Negro World*, his opinions appearing as "Bruce Grit's Column." Five years after joining UNIA in 1919, Bruce died in Bellevue Hospital in New York City.

Unlike Washington, DuBois, and Garvey, Bruce has not received a great deal of scholarly attention despite the fact that he was so well known that five thousand people attended his funeral. As a distinguished African American journalist, Bruce's articles were read not only in the United States but also throughout the African diaspora. His tenacity and political participation became a model for African American journalists, historians, and political activists.

FURTHER READING

Bruce's papers are in the Schomburg Center for Research and Black Culture, New York Public Library.

Crowder, Ralph L. *John Edward Bruce: Politician, Journalist, and Self-Trained Historian of the African Diaspora* (2004).

Gilbert, Peter, comp. and ed. *The Selected Writings of John Edward Bruce: Militant Black Journalist* (1971).

Seraile, William. *Bruce Grit: The Black Nationalist Writings of John Edward Bruce* (2003).

Obituary: *New York Times*, 11 Aug. 1924.

This entry is taken from the *American National Biography* and is published here with the permission of the American Council of Learned Societies.

DAVID ALVIN CANTON

Bruce, Josephine Beall Willson (29 Oct. 1853–15 Feb. 1923), educator and clubwoman, was born in Philadelphia, Pennsylvania, just before her parents, Elizabeth Hartnett and Joseph Willson, moved their young family to Cleveland, Ohio. Her father, who had been born free in Georgia, was a dentist and the author of *Sketches of the Higher Classes among Colored Society in Philadelphia* (1841). Willson, her brother, and her three sisters grew up among the black elite. Her parents emphasized education and accomplishment—her mother was both a skilled musician and a music teacher—and Willson trained to be a teacher after graduating from Cleveland's Central High School in 1871. She then served as one of the first black teachers in Cleveland's integrated elementary schools.

She met her future husband, the U.S. senator BLANCHE KELSO BRUCE, in June 1876, when he traveled to Ohio for the Republican National Convention. The two corresponded and became friends, though the family biographer Lawrence Otis Graham suggests that the Willson family had reservations about Bruce's slave background and color. (The Willsons were quite light skinned; the 15 March 1883 *Christian Recorder*—echoing much of the press of the day—said, for example, that Josephine was "so light in complexion that no one would suspect her race.") Nonetheless, the pair was married in a small but expensive ceremony in the Willson home on 24 June 1878. Both the ceremony and the couple's subsequent four-month honeymoon in Europe garnered some national press attention, as did white Washington's hand-wringing over how to welcome (or not welcome) a black senator's bride. Still, the most liberal among Washington's whites, as well as a small group of prominent African Americans, formed a circle that aided Josephine Bruce's Washington "debut"—a New Year's Day gathering she hosted on 1 January 1879.

The Bruces had one son, ROSCOE CONKLING BRUCE SR. (named for the New York senator who had escorted Blanche at his swearing-in), in April 1879 and amassed significant real estate, including homes in Washington, as well as a plantation in Bruce's home state Mississippi. By the time Bruce left the Senate in 1880, the young family was firmly established among the tiny black aristocracy in Washington. Though Bruce was appointed register of the U.S. Treasury in 1881, the 1880s and early 1890s were complex times for the Bruces. Blanche jockeyed to keep both a Mississippi power base and a national role in the face of Reconstruction's fall, and Josephine split her time between serving as the senator's wife and living with her family, who had moved to Indianapolis. After Blanche Bruce lost his appointment as register of the U.S. Treasury in 1885, he, too, moved to Indiana, but the Bruces moved back to Washington in March 1888. He was appointed Washington's recorder of deeds in 1890.

Josephine Bruce began selectively working with African American and women's groups while her husband was still in the Senate. She worked, for example, with the Washington African American exhibit at the World's Industrial and Cotton States Centennial Exposition in New Orleans in 1884 and 1885 and served as convention president at the meeting of the National Federation of Afro-American Women in Boston in 1895. She became much more active in the black clubwoman's movement in the later 1890s—especially after her son, Roscoe, moved north to attend Phillips Exeter in late 1896. She helped found the Booklover's Club, and her initial work with the Colored Women's League (with MARY ELIZA CHURCH TERRELL and Helen Appo Cook), as well as her ties to JOSEPHINE ST. PIERRE RUFFIN, led to a lifelong association with the National Association of Colored Women (NACW). Blanche, twelve years Josephine's senior, died 17 March 1898. The next year BOOKER T. WASHINGTON offered Bruce the role of lady principal (in essence, dean of women) at Tuskegee University in Tuskegee, Alabama, and she was named one of two national vice presidents of the NACW.

Though she worked at Tuskegee until 1902—and though her son also took a job there after he graduated from Harvard—some evidence suggests that she found the students and surroundings at the rural southern school foreign and uncomfortable. She was never admitted to Washington's inner circle, and tensions between the two likely grew when she ran against Washington's wife, MARGARET MURRAY WASHINGTON, for the national presidency of the NACW in 1901. (Both lost to JOSEPHINE SILONE YATES. Some members of the NACW perceived both as too tied to whites, especially after both attended a white women's club meeting just before the election instead of one held by Buffalo's black PHILLIS WHEATLEY Club.)

After leaving Tuskegee, she split much of her time for the next two decades among her family's home in Indianapolis, where her mother died in 1907 and her two younger sisters had established teaching careers; Kelso Farm, the Bruce residence in Maryland; Josephine, Mississippi, a town named for her and close to her substantial Mississippi plantation; and Washington, D.C., where she added a large home at 1327 Columbia N.W. to her already substantial real estate holdings. She continued to be active in the club movement—organizing, lecturing, and publishing brief essays in journals like the *Voice of the Negro*—and devoted significant time to managing her properties and aiding her son.

All proved frustrating. Bruce again stood for the national presidency of the NACW in 1906, but withdrew her name from consideration when concerns over her light skin and her ties to whites entered the debate. While she continued to be active in the NACW, as well as the Woman's Christian Temperance Union, the World Purity Federation, and the fledgling NAACP, she became less and less of a national presence among clubwomen. The Mississippi plantation became a continual drain on her finances and her time, in part because of her status as a black woman absentee landlord in an increasingly Jim Crow South. Roscoe Bruce left Tuskegee in 1906 to begin a troubled tenure in Washington's black schools. Though he served several years as assistant superintendent (in essence, head of the African American schools), he was forced out in 1921 after years of criticism from Washington's black community and a series of scandals. His subsequent positions offered neither the prestige both mother and son craved nor the funding to make him self-sufficient. He took a position as a principal of black schools in Kimball, West Virginia, and Bruce sold her Washington home and joined him there in early 1923. She died soon after.

Smart, savvy, and privileged in ways available to few nineteenth-century African Americans, Josephine Bruce made important marks among Washington's black elite, and, more broadly, within the clubwoman's movement and the drive for black women's education.

FURTHER READING

Some of Josephine Bruce's papers are in the Blanche K. Bruce collections at the Library of Congress and Howard University and the Roscoe C. Bruce Collection at Howard.

Gatewood, Willard B. "Josephine Beall Willson Bruce," in *Black Women in America*, ed. Darlene Clark Hine (1993).

Smith, Jessie Carney. "Josephine Beall Bruce," in *Notable Black American Women*, ed. Jessie Carney Smith (1992).

Winch, Julie, ed. *The Elite of Our People: Joseph Wilson's Sketches of Black Upper-Class Life in Antebellum Philadelphia* (2000).

Obituary: *Cleveland Gazette*, 26 May 1923.

ERIC GARDNER

Bruce, Roscoe Conkling, Sr. (21 Apr. 1879–16 Aug. 1950), educator, journalist, and lecturer, was born in Washington, D.C., the only child of JOSEPHINE BEALL WILLSON BRUCE and the U.S. senator BLANCHE KELSO BRUCE, a Republican of Mississippi. When Senator Bruce was to take his oath of office, Mississippi's senior senator James Alcorn refused to escort him to the front of the Senate chamber. An embarrassing silence fell over the chamber until Senator Roscoe Conkling of New York extended his arm to Senator Bruce and escorted him forward. Senator Bruce was so grateful for the courtesy that he named his son for the gentleman from the Empire State.

Roscoe Conkling Bruce Sr. attended the M Street High School in Washington, D.C., and subsequently spent two years (1896–1898) at the prestigious Phillips Exeter Academy in Exeter, New Hampshire. He won distinction in scholarship and journalism, was a member of the Golden Branch, the oldest debating society in country, and was also one of the editors of the academy's *Exonian*, Phillips Exeter's student newspaper and supposedly the oldest continuously running secondary school newspaper in the country. Bruce entered Harvard College in 1898 and graduated with an AB degree in 1902, magna cum laude. He won a reputation by winning the Pasteur Medal for debating in 1898, offered by Baron Pierre de Coubertin of Paris, to stimulate interest in the problems of French politics. Out of a field of fifty men Bruce was one of the three men chosen to represent Harvard in a debate against Princeton in 1899. In 1900 Bruce was selected to represent Harvard in the Harvard-Yale oratorical contest, and he was awarded the Coolidge Debating Prize. According to the *Washington Post*, on 17 December 1901 Bruce was elected class orator by the Harvard senior class, defeating his white opponent by a vote of 2 to 1. Upon graduation from Harvard he became a member of the Phi Beta Kappa Society.

The Tuskegee Normal and Industrial Institute offered Bruce the position of academic director, and for the next four years (1902–1906) he not only directed the academic department but also taught various subjects. During his tenure at Tuskegee he married Clara Washington Burrill of Washington,

ROSCOE CONKLING BRUCE.

Roscoe Conkling Bruce Sr., pictured in an undated newspaper article describing his participation in the Twelfth Annual Negro Conference at the Tuskegee Institute. (Library of Congress.)

D.C., on 3 June 1903. The Reverend FRANCIS JAMES GRIMKÉ of the Fifteenth Street Presbyterian Church in Washington, D.C., performed the ceremony.

In the fall of 1906 Bruce accepted a position with the District of Columbia Public Schools as a supervising principal in the Tenth Division. In 1907 Superintendent William E. Chancellor appointed him as assistant superintendent of the African American schools, a position Bruce held for fourteen years. The influence and experience at Tuskegee Institute helped to shape the characteristic of Bruce's progressive educational policy in Washington, D.C. Bruce emphasized industrial and business instruction and sought to convert the Armstrong Manual Training School into a technical high school. He was insistent that at least one industrial course be required of every student at the distinguished Dunbar High School, the first African American high school in the United States. Two vocational schools, one for boys and another for girls, were established on the basis of his recommendation with the approval of the superintendent of schools and the board of education. Perhaps his most notable contribution to Washington, D.C.'s public schools was to allow the school system to be reorganized under the Congressional Organic Act of 1906. This act vested control of the public schools in a board of education consisting of nine members, all of whom had five years' residence in Washington, D.C., immediately preceding their appointments, and three of whom had to be women. The members of the board, who served without compensation, were appointed by the District of Columbia Supreme Court judges for three-year terms of office.

In July 1921 Bruce resigned from the district's public school system and accepted a position in Kimball, West Virginia, to organize modern high school facilities for African American youth living in more than a dozen communities. In the fall of 1921 Bruce was appointed principal of the Browns Creek District High School in Kimball, West Virginia.

In 1927 Bruce became the resident manager of the recently opened Dunbar Apartments located on Seventh Avenue in Harlem. The Dunbar Apartments were created to provide decent housing and services for low-income African American residents. Initiated and financed by John D. Rockefeller Jr., the Dunbar complex, designed by the architect Andrew J. Thomas, was the first cooperative housing enterprise for African Americans.

In the early 1930s Bruce became the editor in chief of the HARRIET TUBMAN Publishing Company. Associate editors of the publishing house included not only his wife, Clara, but also other notables, GEORGIA DOUGLAS JOHNSON, KELLY MILLER, ARTHUR ALFONSO SCHOMBURG, and MARY ELIZA CHURCH TERRELL among them. In addition to his work as editor, Bruce prepared the manuscript for a supplementary reader for use by eighth and ninth graders in public school titled *Just Women*, a history of notable African American women.

At the age of seventy-one Roscoe Conkling Bruce Sr. died in New York City and was interred in the historic Woodlawn Cemetery in Washington, D.C. He was survived by his three children, Clara Josephine, Roscoe Conkling Jr., and Burrill Kelso Bruce. His wife, Clara W. Burrill Bruce, died on 22 January 1947 at the age of sixty-five.

FURTHER READING

Bruce's papers are housed in the Moorland-Spingarn Research Center, Manuscript Division, Howard University, Washington, D.C., and in the District of Columbia Public Schools, Charles Sumner School Museum and Archives, Washington, D.C.

Lewis, David Levering. *W. E. B. DuBois: Biography of a Race* (1993).

Sollars, Werner, Titcomb Caldwell, and Thomas A. Underwood, eds. *African Americans at Harvard* (1993).

E. RENÉE INGRAM

Bruner, Peter (1845–1938), memoirist and soldier, was born in Clark County, Kentucky, twenty miles southeast of Lexington (where, in the decades leading to the Civil War, slaves accounted for approximately half of the population), to an enslaved mother and her white owner, John Bell Bruner. He had two siblings, also presumably the children of his master.

Bruner ran away many times as a young man—on one occasion he even made it all the way to the Ohio River—but each time was recaptured and returned to increasingly brutal treatment. Frustrated by Bruner's repeated escape attempts, his master had a set of leg shackles specially made to tie his slave to the wall each night to keep him from running. Bruner's owner also forced him to march through the town wearing the shackles as a warning to other slaves who might consider running away.

Soon after Peter Bruner's last unsuccessful escape attempt—this one during the Civil War—John Bell Bruner was apprehended by the so-called Union Home Guard, a group sympathetic to the Union that acted as a sort of reserve for local emergencies, for sympathizing with the Confederate cause. The Guard ordered the Bruner family to unchain Peter-Bruner. When his master returned Bruner was treated better but was suspicious of his changed situation. Bruner ran away one final time in 1864 following this incident.

On his way North Bruner sought out Union soldiers at Camp Nelson in Kentucky, widely known as a refuge for runaway slaves, where he informed them of his desire to fight the rebels. Although the Union army did not recruit black men in that region at that time, the Twelfth U.S. Heavy Artillery regiment was created for black soldiers two weeks later and Bruner enlisted immediately. In the army Bruner suffered many of the typical hardships of a Civil War soldier: frostbite, hunger, exhaustion, illness, and fear. After a long illness he was made a nurse in a hospital ward, a job he could not stand to keep because of all the death that surrounded him. He quit that job and returned to the field.

Following the completion of his service, in 1866, Bruner moved to Oxford, Ohio, and went to school there, but soon became bored and left. He married Frances Procton in Oxford in March 1868 and had five children. For many years Bruner struggled to find steady employment and was stuck in a cycle of debt common to many freed slaves in the decades after the Civil War. He borrowed money to buy land, but a number of problems on the farm forced Bruner to borrow even more. On several occasions unscrupulous landowners unilaterally revoked land contracts that Bruner had entered into. It was not until he was hired as a construction worker and night watchman by the Western Female Seminary in Oxford that he managed to find steady work and a guaranteed paycheck. After the election of Ulysses Grant, the women at the seminary asked Bruner to give a speech, which was later published in *Harper's Weekly* and other papers, thus beginning his life as a speaker and writer. Following yet another attempt to start a successful farm Bruner went on to work for Oxford University and Miami University of Ohio as a maintenance worker and as a doorman.

At some point in the late nineteenth century Bruner began work on his memoir, the only written record of his life, *A Slave's Adventures toward Freedom, Not a Fiction, but the True Story of a Struggle*. Originally written down by his young daughter Carrie before her death in 1900 and then forgotten, Bruner rediscovered the manuscript when his house caught fire in August 1913 and decided to have it published in 1918. Despite all of the hardships Bruner faced, his biography nonetheless opens with a dedication remarking on his belief in an America in which anyone, "by industry and saving, can reach a position of independence and be of service to mankind"(7).

FURTHER READING

Bruner, Peter. *A Slave's Adventures toward Freedom, Not a Fiction, but the True Story of a Struggle* (1918).

LAURA MURPHY

Bryan, Andrew (1737–6 Oct. 1812), clergyman, was born at Goose Creek, South Carolina, about sixteen miles from Charleston. His slave parents' names are unknown. GEORGE LIELE, the itinerant African American Baptist minister from Savannah, Georgia, baptized Bryan in 1782. Bryan married Hannah (maiden name unknown) about nine years after his conversion. Jonathan Bryan, Andrew's master and a New Light Presbyterian sympathetic to the evangelical movement in the South, allowed him to exhort both blacks and whites. About 1790 a white landowner allowed Bryan to build a wooden shed on the outskirts of Savannah at Yamacraw.

There Bryan held religious meetings for African Americans, both slave and free, between sunrise and sunset. When white opposition arose, Bryan and his hearers retreated to the nearby swamp to conduct their religious activities.

The evangelical revivals fostered by the Second Great Awakening drew blacks and whites together into common religious circles. In 1788 Abraham Marshall, a white Baptist clergyman, ordained Bryan, baptized about fifty of his followers, and organized them into a congregation known as the Ethiopian Church of Jesus Christ. By strict Baptist rules, the constitution of the church was an irregular act, since a council of Baptist clergy was not involved. Nevertheless, the Ethiopian Church of Jesus Christ became a center of Baptist activity among African Americans in the Savannah region.

During the British occupation of Savannah, whites, fearful of slave insurrection, imprisoned Andrew and his brother Sampson. While defending himself before the city magistrates, Andrew Bryan, according to a report in the *Baptist Annual Register*, "told his persecutors that he rejoiced not only to be whipped, but *would freely suffer death for the cause of Jesus Christ.*" Jonathan Bryan arranged for the release of Andrew and Sampson and allowed Andrew to resume worship services in a barn on his estate at Brampton. A Savannah court ruled that the congregation could hold meetings between sunrise and sunset, which it did without significant opposition during the next two years. By 1790 Bryan's church had 225 full communicants and about 350 converts. Renamed the First African Baptist Church, it became a member of the predominantly white Georgia Baptist Association, which had decided that Marshall's irregular action in organizing the congregation was justifiable, given the circumstances.

In 1794, with financial assistance from influential whites, Bryan purchased a plot of land in Savannah for a permanent church building. In 1795 Jonathan Bryan died, and his heirs allowed Andrew to purchase his freedom for fifty pounds sterling. Bryan's congregation prospered, growing to over seven hundred members by 1800. In that year Bryan wrote the English Baptist John Rippon, publisher of the *Baptist Annual Register*.

With much pleasure, I inform you, dear Sir, that I enjoy good health, and am strong in body, at the age of sixty-three years, and am blessed with a pious wife, whose freedom I have obtained and an only daughter and child who is married to a free man, tho' she, and consequently under our laws, her seven children, five sons and two daughters, are slaves. By a kind Providence I am well provided for, as to worldly comforts, (tho' I have had very little given me as a minister) having a house and lot in this city, besides the land on which several buildings stand, for which I receive a small rent, and a fifty-six acre tract of land, with all necessary buildings, four miles in the country, and eight slaves; for whose education and happiness, I am enabled thro' mercy to provide.

The First African Baptist Church sponsored the formation of a daughter congregation, the Second African Baptist Church, in 1799. Second African eventually sponsored the organization of the Ogeechee or Third African Baptist Church. At the time of Bryan's death, First African Baptist had 1,458 members. ANDREW COX MARSHALL, Bryan's nephew, succeeded him as pastor. The First African Baptist Church, with its roots in the work of Liele and Bryan in the Savannah region and the preaching of DAVID GEORGE on the Galphin plantation at Silver Bluff, Georgia, has been called the first independent African American Baptist church in North America. Recent research has uncovered earlier Baptist slave congregations, but Bryan and First African remain important in early black Baptist history. When Bryan died in Savannah, the white Savannah Baptist Association eulogized him, declaring, "This son of Africa, after suffering inexpressible persecutions in the cause of his divine Master, was at length permitted to discharge the duties of the ministry among his colored friends in peace and quiet, hundreds of whom, through his instrumentality, were brought to a knowledge of the truth as 'it is in Jesus.'"

Andrew Bryan pioneered in efforts to plant the Christian faith under the Baptist banner among fellow blacks in the post–Revolutionary War era. Though not without opposition, he enjoyed a surprising degree of religious freedom during the evangelical renaissance in the South. After the insurrections led by DENMARK VESEY in 1822 and NAT TURNER, a fellow Baptist, in 1831, the white South severely restricted black preaching. Nevertheless, the seeds sown by Bryan and others during the earlier decades matured. Historically, more African Americans, slave and free, have belonged to Baptist churches in the South than to any other denomination.

FURTHER READING

The principal sources of information on Bryan are the occasional Baptist almanacs, known as the *Baptist Annual Register*, edited and published by John Rippon, the English Baptist, in the early 1790s and republished in "Letters Showing the Rise and Progress of the Early Negro Churches of Georgia and the West Indies," *Journal of Negro History* 1 (Jan. 1916): 69–92.

Davis, John W. "George Liele and Andrew Bryan, Pioneer Negro Baptist Preachers," *Journal of Negro History* 3 (Apr. 1918): 119–127.

Sobel, Mechal. *Trabelin' On: The Slave Journey to an Afro-Baptist Faith* (1979).

Washington, James M., Jr. *Frustrated Fellowship: The Black Baptist Quest for Social Power* (1986).

This entry is taken from the *American National Biography* and is published here with the permission of the American Council of Learned Societies.

MILTON C. SERNETT

Bryant, Hazel Joan (8 Sept. 1939–7 Nov. 1983), theatrical producer, director, actress, playwright, and singer, was born in Zanesville, Ohio, one of five children (three girls and two boys) of Harrison James Bryant, a bishop in the African Methodist Episcopal (AME) Church, and Edith Holland Bryant, a social worker. The family lived in Ohio, Kentucky, and Baltimore, Maryland. Bryant acknowledged her parents, sisters, and religion as the main influences in her life. Her talent as a singer was evident when she performed in church choirs. After graduating from Peabody Preparatory School of Music in Baltimore in 1958, Bryant attended Oberlin Conservatory in Ohio. She continued her music training at the Mozarteum in Salzburg, Austria, and studied opera in Vienna and Venice. She toured Eastern Europe with the Robert Shaw Chorale.

With her European training and singing experience, Bryant returned to the United States in the early 1960s to pursue a career as an opera singer but found few opportunities for African Americans in opera. Her unsatisfactory experience in the opera world influenced her decision to study theater. She studied acting with Stella Adler and Harold Clurman and later worked in New York and Canada. Bryant's theater roles in New York included Off-Broadway performances, as well as Broadway roles in *Funny Girl* in 1967 and *Hair* (Trescott). However, her experiences in theater mirrored her opera experience, and she found few challenging opportunities or roles that were not stereotypical for black actresses.

Undaunted by the open-heart surgery she underwent the previous year, Bryant decided in 1968 to start a theater project that would provide an outlet for African Americans who were dissatisfied with the lack of options for black performers on Broadway. She envisioned bringing together black directors, designers, performers, filmmakers, composers, and others to create new works. Bryant founded the Afro-American Total Theatre in New York City in June 1969. The company focused on black musical theater and aimed to reflect the black community in its projects. Bryant served as the troupe's producer, director, writer, administrator, and casting director.

In preparation for running Afro-American Total Theatre, Bryant and others involved in the organization initiated the Origins project, in which they interviewed African Americans involved in theater to learn from and document their experiences. In addition to producing works by new theater artists, the Afro-American Total Theatre ran a training program for photography, film, television, and radio. The Afro-American Total Theatre received funding from national, state, and local grants, private donations, corporations, and churches.

The first original Afro-American Total Theatre production was a one-act musical, *Mae's Amees*, which Bryant wrote with Hope Clarke and Hank Johnson. She went on to write or cowrite at least ten plays at the theater and produce more than two hundred musicals and plays in her lifetime. Afro-American Total Theatre included street theater in its early years partly because the spaces the artists used had no air-conditioning, requiring the company to perform in the streets during the summer. This developed into the Lincoln Center Street Theater (summer performances at Lincoln Center Plaza) and later into the Lincoln Center Street Theater Festival.

Under Bryant's leadership, the Afro-American Total Theatre joined six other black theater groups in the New York area in 1970 to form the Black Theater Alliance. Its members sought to overcome obstacles that were insurmountable individually. The four priorities of the cooperative were "fund raising, technical expertise, advocacy, large public showcase" (Jones, 59). Bryant was the alliance's first secretary. The Black Theater Alliance, which lasted almost ten years, formed workshops to help its members gain proper training in theater management, administration, and technology.

Bryant's Afro-American Total Theatre became the Richard Allen Center of Culture and Art in 1976, named after RICHARD ALLEN, a founder of the AME Church. The newly expanded theater received donations from the AME Church and moved to a location near Lincoln Center in New York City. In 1979 Bryant and the Richard Allen Center produced *Black Nativity*, a LANGSTON HUGHES musical play based on the Gospel of Luke, with words and music from the African American tradition. The venture was a success and was eventually produced for television with performances at Ford's Theatre in Washington, D.C., and in 1981 in Rome and the Vatican, including an excerpt done for the Pope. The Afro-American Total Theatre also toured twenty-seven countries in six months performing *Black Nativity*. Bryant produced another celebrated adaptation with an all-black cast of Eugene O'Neill's *Long Day's Journey into Night* in 1981. The production was part of the New York Shakespeare Festival.

Bryant's influence extended throughout the African American theater world and beyond. She was a member of the Theater Panel of the New York State Council on the Arts and the New York City Board of Cultural Affairs. On the day of her death, Bryant delivered a speech on theater arts studies to the Third World Institute at the United Nations. She died of heart disease, which had afflicted her throughout her life.

In a 1982 interview Bryant shared: "It makes me unhappy when I go into a city and I don't see a play from the Black American culture being produced. In England you see Chekov [sic] and you see French and Spanish and Canadian writers being produced all over the world, and I think our writers ought to be" (Jones, 74). Hazel Joan Bryant devoted her life to providing outlets for African American theater artists to share their culture and community with the world.

FURTHER READING

Unpublished manuscripts of selected plays written by Hazel Bryant are housed in the Schomburg Center for Research in Black Culture in New York, New York. Interviews with Bryant are available in the Hatch-Billops Collection in New York.

Jones, Duane. "An Interview with Hazel Bryant," in *Artists and Influences* (1982).

Peterson, Bernard L., Jr. *Contemporary Black American Playwrights and Their Plays: A Biographical Directory and Dramatic Index* (1988).

Trescott, Jacqueline. "Whirlwind of the Arts," *Washington Post*, 29 Oct. 1981.

Wilson, Robert J. *The Black Theater Alliance: A History of Its Founding Members* (1974).

Obituary: *New York Times*, 10 Nov. 1983.

HEATHER MARTIN

Bryant, Ray (24 Dec. 1931–2 June 2011), jazz pianist, was born Raphael Homer Bryant in Philadelphia, Pennsylvania, one of eight siblings. His mother, Eleanor Coates, was an accomplished pianist and led the local church choir at Tenth Memorial Baptist Church; his father, Thomas Bryant Sr., sang in the church choir and was a supervisor at the Nicholson File Company, an industrial file manufacturer. Two other brothers were also Philadelphia jazz musicians, the bassist Tommy Bryant and the drummer and singer Len Bryant.

Ray Bryant began playing piano at age six and also played bass in Central High School. He began playing professionally at age twelve and at fourteen joined what would be the last of the independently chartered black musicians' unions affiliated with the American Federation of Musicians—Local 274. Bryant and his brothers played around Philadelphia, which was a hotbed of jazz after World War II and throughout the 1950s, while working and studying with ELMER SNOWDEN, a guitarist and banjo player who was the original bandleader of the Washingtonians, which was later led by DUKE ELLINGTON. Bryant learned the new style of bebop by listening to the pianist RED GARLAND, who was in the city at the time. Bryant toured with the guitarist TINY GRIMES from 1948 to 1949 and then freelanced the next few years in Philadelphia by working in the house band at the Jam Session, a nightclub owned by the New Orleans–style clarinetist Billy Krechmer at 627 Ranstead Street. During his tenure there Bryant backed the Dixieland musicians Jack Teagarden and Johnny Smith.

From 1953 to 1956 Bryant was the house pianist at one of the most famous modern jazz clubs in the country, the Blue Note, located at Fifteenth Street and Ridge Avenue in Philadelphia. Called the House that Progressive Jazz Built, it was the nightclub where all the major jazz stars and future legends would be booked. Ray Bryant played with CHARLIE PARKER, MILES DAVIS, LESTER YOUNG, J. J. JOHNSON, Kai Winding, SONNY STITT, and a host of others. The gig became an on-the-job university for Bryant, and he quickly made a name for himself. At this time the style of bebop was acquiring new characteristics, becoming blusier with darker and rougher tone colors and gaining a hard-driving pulse with consistent swinging. It was called hard bop, and the musicians who specialized in this new style hailed from Philadelphia and Detroit. Bryant was right in the middle of it.

From 1956 to 1957 Bryant accompanied the singer CARMEN MCRAE, and in 1957 they recorded two albums with the drummer Specs Wright and the bassist Ike Isaacs: *Mad about the Man* and *Afterglow*, both for Decca. This was the year that Bryant also made his first record as a leader with his *Ray Bryant Trio*, for Prestige. Bryant also appeared and recorded with COLEMAN HAWKINS, ROY ELDRIDGE, and JO JONES at the 1957 Newport Jazz Festival, playing a solo on "I Can't Believe You're in Love with Me."

Ray Bryant moved to New York City in 1958 and played in various musical lineups featuring SONNY ROLLINS, Curtis Fuller, and CHARLIE SHAVERS, among others. In 1960 Bryant's composition "Little Susie" became a hit (later "Changes," recorded by MILES DAVIS, which also became a hit), and ART BLAKEY recorded another of Bryant's songs, "Cubano Chant." As can be heard on his tune "Slow Freight," Ray Bryant was a powerful blues pianist as well. Working mostly in a trio format or as a single, Bryant conveys an assuredness of musicality that evidences a unique and comprehensive approach to jazz piano. He was in consistent demand as an accompanist and as a soloist for more than four decades, working and recording with Zoot Sims, Benny Carter, Benny Golson, DIZZY GILLESPIE, and LEE MORGAN.

In 1960 Bryant accompanied ARETHA FRANKLIN on her first album for Columbia Records. That same year he won the *Down Beat* poll for best new star. Over the years Bryant appeared and recorded at festivals around the world, including the Montreux Jazz Festival, the Montreal Jazz Fest, the JVC festival, and a *Solo Live in Tokyo* date in 1995. In 1999 the former radio personality Joel Dorn, an old friend from Philadelphia, asked Bryant if he had any old tapes lying around the house from any past concerts. One tape was from a long-forgotten solo concert in France; a sound engineer gave Bryant a tape of the performance after the gig. In 2000 Dorn's new reissue label, Label M, released the highly acclaimed CD *Somewhere in France*.

Bryant played in New York at the Ninety-second Street Y's Kaufmann Concert Hall in July 2005 for a presentation of jazz pianos styles with Bill Charlap, Hank Jones, Mulgrew Miller, and Renee Rosnes. Bryant was inducted into the American Jazz Hall of Fame in 1999. The *New York Times* jazz writer

Stephen Holden said of Bryant, "A Gibraltar-like emotional solidity and a style directly connected to the wellsprings of black musical tradition are the hallmarks of Ray Bryant's solo piano work" (*New York Times,* 29 June 1986). He died in New York City at the age of seventy-nine.

FURTHER READING

Feather, Leonard, and Ira Gitler. *The Biographical Encyclopedia of Jazz* (1999).

Gioia, Ted. *The History of Jazz* (1997)

Hamilton, A. "The Art of Improvisation and the Aesthetics of Improvisation," *British Journal of Aesthetics* 40 (2000).

Holden, Stephen. "Ray Bryant, the Pianist, in Recital," *New York Times,* 29 June 1986.

SUZANNE CLOUD

Bryant, Richard Renard (27 Sept. 1966–), U.S. Navy submarine commander, was born in St. Louis, Missouri, the son of John and Audrey (Crouch) Bryant, and "one generation removed from poor southern sharecroppers." His parents divorced while he was young, and Bryant spent his earliest years living in Kinloch, a black suburb of St. Louis. Among the biggest influences in his early life were his grandparents Julius and Ruby Crouch. He later moved to Indianapolis to live with his father and attended a combination of Catholic and public schools until enrolling in Cathedral High School. A 1984 graduate of the school, Bryant related that "it was here that I got a strong foundation," excelled academically, and was a drum major in the band and captain of the Brain Game team, the school's version of a debate team. While Bryant was a sports enthusiast and was first coached by his father, he also had an interest in the military that was fueled by "those great black and white World War II movies." Thus, Bryant decided to join the military because he favored "the concept of the camaraderie of military service and also had the sense that it was a good way to go." Though Bryant was interested in both the navy and the air force, the traditions in the navy and the greater options that service offered helped make up his mind. He was nominated by Indiana Senator Dan Quayle for the U.S. Naval Academy at Annapolis and subsequently accepted, beginning his naval career as part of the class of 1988.

Midshipman Bryant's time at the Academy was academically rigorous and exciting. Originally "hell-bent on being an aerospace engineer and flight officer, I ended up just the opposite, graduating with a degree in marine engineering and being a submarine officer." His decision to join the submarine force occurred in part by chance; taking a midshipman's cruise from May to August 1985, Bryant joined the crew of the submarine *Nathaniel Greene* operating out of Scotland. The only midshipman aboard, Bryant was well trained and began the qualified enlistment process while aboard. The result was that Bryant was "sold on the camaraderie," decided that "that's what I wanted to do," and became a submariner.

Bryant's decision to become a submarine officer, with the goal to gain his own command, came at an interesting time in the submarine force. By the late 1980s and through the 1990s, there were only a small number of African Americans who had risen to command, the first being the legendary C. A. "PETE" TZOMES in 1983. Following Tzomes were six other men who gained command from 1983 to 1998: TONY WATSON, WILLIAM BUNDY, JOSEPH P. PETERSON, MELVIN WILLIAMS JR., CECIL D. HANEY, and BRUCE E. GROOMS. Collectively known in navy circles as the Centennial 7 (the first seven black commanders in the submarine force's first one hundred years), this group of submarine commanders helped to pave the way for future generations of black naval officers. Even so, the obstacles that remained for Bryant and other future prospective black commanders were both varied and daunting; because such men were well trained in the nuclear field and opportunities in the private sector abounded, the navy's retention rate for these individuals was abysmal. Then, too, very subtle racial issues could also be a factor. Because the number of African Americans serving in the force was quite small, the development of a personal chemistry between wardroom personnel with both generational and cultural differences was sometimes difficult to establish. For those blacks on the road to command as prospective executive officers, the line between success and failure was often a thin one. Although Bryant experienced no such racial issues, it is telling that during his early years as a submarine officer he never served shipboard with another black officer.

Following his graduation from the Naval Academy, Bryant underwent training in nuclear power for two years, taking courses he frankly describes as "very hard work," and attributing his success to fellow trainees and roommates who lent their support. His first shipboard assignment as an officer was on the *Daniel Boone* from 1990 to 1992. Serving under Captain Bruce Cavey, a man whom he describes as one who "believed and invested a lot in me," Bryant excelled and was named COMSUBRON (Commander Submarine Squadron) Sixteen Junior Officer of the Year in 1992, an honor that "broke me out among my contemporaries" and gave him a strong career start. Cavey furthered Bryant's career by sending him back to the Naval Academy as a company officer to further hone his leadership abilities. It was in this role from 1992 to 1995 that Bryant was active in promoting the ideals of leadership and began his own personal mission of mentoring those who followed him, as well as developing "a passion to increase opportunities for minorities in the Navy's officer corps." Bryant's future duties would prove to be equally successful. He was the flag aide to Rear Admiral Tony Watson, a Centennial 7 pioneer whom Bryant describes as "the bedrock" for all future black submariners, at COMNAVCRUITCOM (Commander Navy Recruiting Command) in Washington, D.C., from 1995 to 1996. During this time, Bryant also earned his master's degree in Engineering Management at George Washington University. Subsequent duty included deployment as navigation and operations officer aboard the *Montpelier* in the Mediterranean Sea and Arabian Gulf under Captain Dave Eyler, who "laid the groundwork for my professional knowledge and competence," and later under Captain Ron LaSalvia, "a very competent navigator," from 1996 to 1998. Bryant also served as executive officer on the *Hyman G. Rickover* from 2000 to 2002 under Captain Peter Young ("a great tour"). After a stint of shore duty, Bryant attended the National War College in 2005 and graduated with a master of science in National Security Affairs. The following year he became just the eighth African American to gain command of a submarine when he was assigned to the Fast Attack submarine *Miami*. For the success in his navy career, Bryant credited not only those men of the Centennial 7 who served as role models and mentors, but also the many white officers who contributed to his development.

In the mid-2000s Bryant was a frequent speaker to student groups, helping to "contribute the culmination of my experiences and work back to our society." As commander of the *Miami*, he continued as a leader in promoting submarine force diversity—two of his department heads on the *Miami* were also African Americans, a first-time occurrence in the force. In 1992 Commander Richard Bryant married Stephanie Gaines-Bryant, a well-known radio personality and newscaster in the Washington, D.C., area, and together they had four children, Richard Jr., twins Christian and Kendall, and Gabriel.

FURTHER READING

The quotations in this entry are based on the author's phone interviews and e-mail exchanges with Commander Bryant, as well as other career-related data provided by him, 26–28 February 2007.

U.S. Navy. "Commander Submarine Group Two, USS *Miami*, CMDR Rich Bryant" (2006).

GLENN ALLEN KNOBLOCK

Bryant, William Maud (16 Feb. 1933–24 Mar. 1969), U.S. Army Special Forces soldier and Medal of Honor recipient, was born in Cochran, Georgia, the son of Sebron Bryant. His mother's name is not known. Bryant's parents were divorced when he was a child, and he subsequently went to Detroit to live with an uncle. During his high school years he lived in Newark, New Jersey, and graduated from the Newark Vocational and Technical High School in 1951. Bryant then returned to Detroit, where he enlisted in the army on 16 March 1953, at the end of the Korean War.

The time period in which William Bryant joined the army was a transitional one indeed; the idea of segregating black soldiers in their own units, as had been the army's practice since the Civil War, had only been recently abolished by an executive order from President Harry Truman in October 1951, resulting in the disbanding of the 24th Infantry Regiment and the dispersal of its black personnel among the other regiments fighting in Korea. Now, prior to America's next war in Vietnam, a new crop of professional soldiers would emerge, men like Bryant, EUGENE ASHLEY JR., and MATTHEW LEONARD, who were trained and served in an integrated and more racially enlightened atmosphere. While it is true that racial issues would arise during the Vietnam War and never completely disappeared, they no longer centered on the old debate about the fighting or leadership abilities of African Americans. It was these prewar black enlistees, many of whom had risen to the rank of noncommissioned officers (NCO), who would set the example through their leadership both on and off the field of battle for the many young black men that came to fight in Vietnam, both enlistees and draftees. The importance of this leadership role, cannot be overstated when it is remembered that African Americans served in the

Vietnam War in disproportionately higher numbers than white soldiers, a controversial situation that would itself heighten racial tensions at home as the war progressed.

Prior to his service in Vietnam, William Bryant gained valuable experience and training, both stateside and in Europe. Serving as a sergeant in Company A of the 5th Special Forces Group, 1st Special Forces (Green Berets), he went to Vietnam in the fall of 1968 with prior training in the areas of heavy weapons handling, long-range reconnaissance, counterinsurgency tactics, explosive ordnance, parachute jumping, and special forces airborne intelligence analysis, as well as having taken an advanced noncommissioned officer's course. Bryant would soon have a chance to put all of these skills to use in heavy combat. In March 1969 he was in command of Civilian Irregular Defense Group (CIDG) Company 321, 2nd Battalion, 3rd Mobile Strike Force, in Long Khanh Province in the Republic of Vietnam. As the name of Bryant's command suggests, the CIDG units consisted of local Vietnamese nonprofessional soldiers who worked closely with American Special Forces units, often in remote areas behind enemy lines, in a program established by the army in 1961. Bryant was leading his CIDG company during combat operations on 23–24 March when it became surrounded and took heavy fire from three North Vietnamese regiments. In the thirty-four-hour fight that ensued, Bryant was a dynamo, establishing a perimeter for his unit, directing fire, and caring for the wounded, showing "extraordinary heroism" and "providing the leadership and inspirational example of courage to his men" (Hanna, 153) in the face of enemy fire. When ammunition ran low, Bryant retrieved the ammunition boxes his men needed, and when there was a slowdown in the fighting, he led a patrol outside the perimeter to gain intelligence. When the patrol subsequently came under attack and was pinned down, Bryant fought off one attack on his own, and encouraged his men to repel subsequent attacks that enabled them to return to their position. As the fighting continued, William Bryant led a patrol in an effort to break through the enemy positions, but was pinned down by heavy fire coming from reinforced bunker positions. Severely wounded in this part of the fighting, Bryant nonetheless stayed in command and was able to radio for air support and direct their fire on the enemy positions. Once the air strikes were completed, Bryant led the charge against an enemy position and single-handedly wiped it out. While regrouping for one final assault on the enemy position, Sergeant First Class William Bryant was killed instantly by an enemy rocket attack.

William Bryant was subsequently recommended for the Medal of Honor, which award was approved, and the medal was presented to his parents by President Richard Nixon during a White House ceremony on 16 February 1971. Bryant has the distinction of being the last African American to date (2011) to earn the Medal of Honor. He is buried in the Raleigh National Cemetery in Raleigh, North Carolina, and was survived by a wife and four children.

FURTHER READING

Hanna, Charles W. *African American Recipients of the Medal of Honor* (2002).

Shaw, Henry Jr., and Ralph Donnelly. *Blacks in the Marine Corps* (2002).

GLENN ALLEN KNOBLOCK

Brymn, Tim (5 Oct. 1881–3 Oct. 1946), dance-orchestra leader, military bandleader, and songwriter, was born James Timothy Brymn in Kinston, North Carolina, to Peter and Eliza. He attended Shaw University in his home state and continued his education at the National Conservatory of Music in New York, which had once boasted Antonin Dvořák among its teachers and WILL MARION COOK among its pupils. In New York, Brymn teamed up with the lyricist CECIL MACK (Richard McPherson), and together they wrote some songs for the publishing firm of Joseph Stern. In 1901 they had their first song hit, "Josephine, My Jo," which was interpolated into the Williams and Walker show *Sons of Ham*. Brymn and Mack followed up the next year with "Please Go 'Way and Let Me Sleep." By this time Brymn was also writing with others besides Mack. His "My Little Zulu Babe" was recorded by Williams and Walker near the end of 1901; in this case Brymn's co-composer was the now forgotten W. S. Estren.

In 1904 Brymn accompanied the Williams and Walker company to England, where he served as music director for the successful London run of their musical *In Dahomey*. In 1906, once more in the United States, Brymn became music director for the Smart Set traveling shows, which enjoyed a long and prominent run on the African American touring circuit. Brymn interrupted his Smart Set work at least once, settling in as bandleader at the Pekin Theater in Chicago during 1907–1908.

However, with the Smart Set he wrote the scores for a number of shows featuring their star SHERMAN H. DUDLEY; among these productions were *The Black Politician* (1908) and *His Honor, the Barber* (1909). In the latter Brymn worked with many of the greatest black talents in the theater of the day, including Mack, CHRIS SMITH, FORD DABNEY, and Jim Burris. Among Brymn's contributions (again with Mack) was "Porto Rico," which capitalized on a new craze for Latin American themes. Brymn continued his associations with some of these men and showed a quick eye for new trends throughout the era before World War I. In 1912 he and Smith penned the remarkable "I've Got the Blues but I'm Too Blamed Mean to Cry," one of the earliest known blues songs. Brymn was helping set new musical trends during this period. It was also around this time that he moved permanently to New York.

Early in 1914 Brymn became the conductor of New York's Clef Club Orchestra, following the schism that climaxed with the departure of its founding director, JAMES REESE EUROPE. Brymn was soon a leading New York bandleader, his ascendancy confirmed by conducting duties at some of the Times Square roof garden theatrical "midnight frolics." He also provided ragtime and other syncopated dance music for the fast crowd that frequented New York's after-hours nightspots. At the first of these, the Shelburne Hotel and Restaurant, his band included the young New Orleans clarinet virtuoso SIDNEY BECHET, who had not yet switched to soprano saxophone, the instrument with which he later became associated. By the time Brymn ended this run of engagements at the fashionable Times Square roof gardens and enlisted in the American Expeditionary Forces, he was fronting an orchestra of twenty men.

Brymn's career reached its climax in World War I. He organized and led the band of the 350th Field Artillery Regiment, the most prominent African American marching band in France aside from Jim Europe's. This band, known as the Black Devils, was featured in the parades commemorating the end of the war. Reportedly Brymn's band played with such vigor in a victory parade on their return that President Woodrow Wilson was moved to step out of his car in the procession, telling his aides "I simply *must* march to this music!" Brymn's Black Devils band toured the United States successfully following demobilization in 1919 and also made recordings. At this time they were sponsored by the renowned opera singer Ernestine Schumann-Heink. Their recordings for the Okeh label were all issued in the spring of 1921 and included both the standard pop fare of the day and more blues- or ragtime-oriented songs by African American songwriters. Among the latter were "Arkansas Blues" (Spencer Williams and Anton Lada), "It's Right Here for You" (PERRY BRADFORD), "The Jazz Me Blues" (Tom Delaney), and "The Memphis Blues" (W. C. HANDY).

This choice of repertoire reflects Brymn's connections with the leading African American songwriters in Tin Pan Alley during this period, especially those also active as publishers in the Gaiety Theater Building in Times Square. The association with Handy seems to have been the closest. Brymn penned the lyrics for Handy's instrumental "Aunt Hagar's Children Blues" in 1921, words that went on to be as famous as the music itself. This is probably Brymn's best-known song, and he himself directed an early vocal ensemble recording of it in 1923, leading a group known as Tim Brymn's Black Devil Four (a vocal quartet with piano and bells) for the Okeh label. Brymn also worked with white Tin Pan Alley songwriters. The song "Stop! Rest a While" was used in the 1921 black show *Put and Take*; in this case both music and lyrics were jointly attributed to Brymn and L. Wolfe Gilbert. By this time Brymn's best songwriting years were coming to an end. In 1921 he became manager of the New York office of the publishing house run by CLARENCE WILLIAMS and ARMAND PIRON, then in the process of relocating from Chicago.

Brymn passed the last half-century his life in relative obscurity, mostly working as a coach to other entertainers. His connection with W. C. Handy remained strong, and through the connection Brymn was occasionally able to issue a new song; as late as 1930 Handy Brothers Music Company published his "Toot Toot, Dixie Bound in the Morning." Again Brymn penned the lyrics, working with the composer Chris Smith; by this time their connection went back at least two decades. However, the prominence they had enjoyed in the first decade of the twentieth century was behind them, and it was only their friendships with more-current show business figures such as Handy that kept them on the fringes of show business.

Though Brymn was not responsible for the creation of many blues or jazz standards, he was an important talent in black Broadway shows and in the early years of the blues craze. In addition to the songs noted above, his known works include "La Rumba," "Shout, Sister, Shout," "Moonlight," "Camel Walk," "I Take Things Easy," "Those Tantalizing

Eyes," "Look into Your Baby's Face and Say Goo Goo," "Valse Angelique," "Cocoanut Grove Jazz," "After Tea," "This Is the Judgment Day," " 'Round My Heart," "If You Don't I Know Who Will," and "My Pillow and Me." A complete catalog of his works has not yet been assembled. Brymn was probably of more importance as a bandleader than as a creative artist, both as a Clef Club colleague of James Reese Europe and as Europe's only real rival among military bandleaders with the American Expeditionary Forces in France during 1918–1919.

FURTHER READING

ASCAP Biographical Dictionary of Composers, Authors, and Publishers (1952).

Peterson, Bernard L. *Profiles of African American Stage Performers and Theatre People, 1816–1960* (2001).

Obituaries: *New York Times*, 4 Oct. 1946; *Variety*, 9 Oct. 1946.

ELLIOTT S. HURWITT

Bubbles, John (19 Feb. 1902–18 May 1986), dancer, singer, entertainer, and actor, was born John William Sublett in Louisville, Kentucky. His parents' names are not known. His early childhood was spent in Indianapolis, Indiana, where his family was part of a touring carnival; by the age of seven, John was performing on the stage, participating in amateur contests as a singer. Accounts differ as to when he returned to Louisville and when he met his vaudeville team partner, Ford Lee "Buck" Washington. Some sources list their ages as ten and six, respectively, while others list them as thirteen and nine. The team began working professionally by 1915 as "Buck and Bubbles," an act combining music and comedy.

They would remain together for nearly forty years, originally combining Washington's talents as a pianist with Sublett's as a singer; when his voice changed, Sublett turned to tap dancing as his primary talent. As they developed their act, the two took odd jobs to help support themselves and their families. While employed as ushers in the gallery at the Mary Anderson Theater in Louisville, they worked on their act after hours and were seen by the theater's manager. When an opening in the program arose, Buck and Bubbles were hired to perform, but they had to appear in blackface, posing as white minstrels, since the theater did not allow African American acts on the stage. An audition for a touring show, *The Kiss Me Company*, ensued and Sublett

John Bubbles, often described as "the father of rhythm tap," changed the face of tap dance, c. 1964. (Library of Congress, New York World-Telegram and the *Sun Newspaper* Photograph Collection.)

became Washington's legal guardian so that Buck would be allowed to tour at such a young age. In September 1919 the duo reached New York and played without blackface at the Columbia Theater on Forty-seventh Street, across from the mecca of vaudeville, the Palace. The act was an immediate success, becoming one of the few black acts to tour on the Keith, Orpheum, and other white vaudeville circuits. African American acts were primarily relegated to the Theater Owners' Booking Association (TOBA or "Toby"), which circulated acts to theaters in African American communities. According to Bubbles, "We were easy to book because we didn't conflict with most acts. Nobody wrote for us or gave us lines. We thought funny and that's the way it came out onstage" (Smith, 59). Buck and Bubbles became the first African American act to be held over at the Palace, the first to play Radio City Music Hall, and only the second to be featured in the Ziegfeld Follies in 1931, after headlining in Lew Leslie's *Blackbirds of 1930*.

In 1927 RCA Victor made test recordings of Buck and Bubbles that were not released. From nine sides recorded for Columbia between 1930 and 1934, only two were released: "He's Long Gone from Bowling Green" and "Lady Be Good." The duo made recordings in London in 1936, and there is reportedly a solo album released by Bubbles, *From Rags to Riches*. In 1935 George Gershwin cast Bubbles as the original Sportin' Life in *Porgy and Bess*. Washington was also in the cast, as "neither took a job without the other being hired" (*Variety* Obituary, 110). Later, Buck and Bubbles became the first African Americans to perform on television, in New York in 1939. The team became popular in Europe as well, touring extensively.

Buck and Bubbles' performances on film began in 1929 with a series of Pathé comedy shorts: *Black Narcissus, Fowl Play, In and Out, Darktown Follies, High Toned*, and *Honest Crooks*. These were followed by *Night in a Niteclub* (1934), *Calling All Stars* (1937), *Varsity Show* (1937), and *Atlantic City* (1944). In 1943, billed as John W. Sublett, rather than John Bubbles, as he was more popularly known, he performed the featured role of Domino Johnson in MGM's *Cabin in the Sky*, the all-black cast musical starring ETHEL WATERS, LENA HORNE, and EDDIE "ROCHESTER" ANDERSON. Sublett won critical acclaim for his solo number, "Shine," a song written by DUKE ELLINGTON, which some critics perceive as a subtle, incisive protest against racism. Other film appearances include *I Dood It* (also known as *By Hook or by Crook*, 1943), *Laff Jamboree* (1945), *Mantan Messes Up* (1946), and *A Song Is Born* (1948).

After Washington's death in 1955, Bubbles continued as a solo performer until 1967, when a stroke left him partially paralyzed and sent him into semi-retirement. In 1955 he appeared in the German film *Solang' es hübsche Mädchen gibt*, released in the United States as *Beautiful Girls* (1958). Bubbles is among the legendary tap dancers featured in the film documentary *No Maps on My Taps* (1979). He was also the first African American entertainer to appear on *The Tonight Show Starring Johnny Carson*. Some of his other major television appearances include *The DuPont Show of the Week* (1961), *The Lucille Ball Show* (1962), and *The Belle of 14th Street* (1967), a vaudeville re-creation conceived for Barbra Streisand. As a solo act, he appeared regularly with Danny Kaye, Judy Garland, and Anna Maria Alberghetti. During the 1960s he toured Vietnam with Bob Hope and earned the Award of Merit from the U.S. government. There was little work after 1967, but in 1979 George Wein called upon Bubbles to sing at the Newport Jazz Festival. In 1980 Bubbles returned to the New York stage in *Black Broadway*, a musical revue, and was honored by the American Guild of Variety Artists (AGVA) with a lifetime achievement award. That same year a recording of excerpts from *Porgy and Bess*, by LEONTYNE PRICE and WILLIAM WARFIELD, featuring Bubbles as Sportin' Life, was released by RCA Victor.

Bubbles, often described as "the father of rhythm tap," which was also known as "jazz tap," changed the face of tap dance. When he was eighteen years old, he was laughed out of the Hoofers Club, a Harlem gathering place where the foremost tap dancers in the nation openly challenged and competed against each other. This event served to heighten his drive to be acknowledged as a dancer and sent him into intensive practice. At that time, tap dancers stayed on their toes and included a great deal of "flash," or gymnastic virtuosity, in their acts. Bubbles pared down his body movement and added his heels to his tap combinations, creating more syncopated rhythms while exhibiting mastery in the speed and complexity of the steps he improvised.

Soon, dancers came to his shows to try to copy his style. Bubbles frustrated them by changing his steps with each performance. "Double over-the-tops," a difficult figure-eight pattern, and "cramp rolls," a complex sequence of heel-toe combinations, were among his signature innovations. His style is said to have prepared the way for the rhythms of bebop jazz. Hollywood called upon Bubbles to tutor Fred Astaire, Eleanor Powell, and Ann Miller, among other renowned dancers. In the words of FAYARD NICHOLAS, of the famed Nicholas Brothers dance team, "What you used to see Fred Astaire do in the movies, Bubbles had done long before." Bubbles's last appearance as a performer occurred in 1980 at a tribute to George and Ira Gershwin at the Kennedy Center Library. A cerebral hemorrhage took his life at his home in Baldwin Hills, near Los Angeles, California.

FURTHER READING

Goldberg, Jane. "John Bubbles: A Hoofer's Homage," *Village Voice*, 4 Dec. 1978.
Smith, Bill. *The Vaudevillians* (1976).
Obituaries: *New York Times*, 20 May 1986; *Variety*, 21 May 1986; *Annual Obituary*, 1986.

FREDA SCOTT GILES

Buccau, Quamino (Feb. 1762–c. 1850), a devout Methodist, was born near New Brunswick, New Jersey, one of five children of slave parents. Buccau's life would have been lost forever if not for *Memoir* of *Quamino Buccau, a Pious Methodist* (1851), published by William J. Allinson, an abolitionist member of a prestigious Burlington, New Jersey, Quaker family and a member of the Burlington County Antislavery Society. The two men, both Burlington residents from different races and backgrounds, shared a profound commitment to the doctrine of Christian love and charity. In an era of racial discord, the force of their mutual esteem is clearly evidenced throughout the pages of Allinson's tract about the humble, old black man whom he characterized as "lowly in heart" (Allinson, 8).

Buccau was someone with keen insight, never complaining about his predicament. For instance, he knew that his name was of African origin, that to retain it was a privilege, and thus wore it with pride. There were many slaveholders who upon possession immediately stripped the enslaved of African names as a means of asserting authority.

According to John C. Inscoe, "A wide variety of names like Quamino, Musso, Cush, ... appear on early slave lists, but none of these survived for long" (532). In 1772 at age nine, Buccau leased Quamino to Abraham and Elcie Schenk "for a term of years" (4). In the eyes of a child, the difference between "leased" or "sold" was of no importance; all that mattered was the confusion of being taken from home by strangers. Later, as a house servant, Quamino was transported out of state, moving with the Schenk family to the northern part of New York. Not until nine years later, in 1781, did his owner send someone to bring the eighteen-year-old Quamino back to New Jersey. Slave parents protected their children by coaching them on how to survive adverse conditions through obedience. As a result Quamino was dutiful with a "kindly heart" and took pride in being a "good boy" (6). Still, the conditions under which he lived were better than most, and there were no physical, emotional, nor psychological mistreatment. However, "Whilst in this situation, he was compelled to witness every public execution, with the idea that a salutary lesson would thus be impressed, and, unhappily, the opportunities were by no means rare" (5). The message was clear—stay in line or suffer the consequences. Quamino could not hide the compassion he felt for what he witnessed firsthand.

Christianity came to Quamino forcefully in a spiritual experience one day during a walk home through the woods. His religious experience was intense and set in motion a lifelong commitment to Christianity and serving others. One Sabbath when returning home, a road appeared before him that led up into the mountains with horses following.

Quamino was so overwhelmed that he considered the strange happening a message from God, and thereafter he became a devout believer. In 1788, at age twenty-six, he married Sarah, a slave woman with a small son working in another household. Secure in the doctrine of Christian love, the couple survived the hardships of separations and infrequent visits that often challenged the longevity of slave unions. Together they had one son. His old slave master Buccau died, but not before stipulating in his will that Quamino and his siblings could select another slaveholder from the Buccau family or neighboring households. During slavery, it was rare for last wills and testaments to give victims of oppression a voice in ownership after the master's death; rare, too, that the heirs would adhere to the departed's wishes so obediently. Quamino chose the eldest son of Buccau's offspring to be his owner, but the arrangement was short-lived and troubled. After a short time his master beat him without cause, and it so offended Quamino that he refused to work for him. Subsequently, in 1792, shortly after his marriage, Quamino was sold away from the Buccau household for the first time, to the Smock family. Now married but living apart from his wife, Quamino learned that she had been sold to slaveholders who mistreated her. The distraught husband immediately sought help from his new master, and soon after, arrangements were made for Sarah to join the Smock household. The couple would live together for the next fifty years. Quamino and Sarah were later sold to Dr. John Griffith of Boundbrook, New Jersey, a long-time member of the New Jersey Abolition Society. Upon Griffith's death his estate was administered by his son, William J. Griffith, a lawyer of some prominence and respectability. In the disposition of his father's last will and testament, the young Griffith made the decision to free Quamino and Sarah. On 25 September 1806 William J. Griffith processed documents that freed the couple. For many years, devout in their Christian beliefs, Quamino and Sarah worshiped at the African Methodist Episcopal (AME) Church but also regularly attended Society of Friends religious services. This was understandable, as the two religions were closely aligned in principle, and Burlington County had a large Society of Friends population. William J. Allinson was a pharmacist in Burlington, New Jersey, interested in the preservation of history and a close friend of abolitionist poet John Greenleaf Whittier. Allinson met Quamino when he visited his shop and also at the meeting house.

Sarah died in 1842 after fifty-four years of marriage. Before Quamino's death eight years later, the generosity of many Quaker neighbors and friends was clearly evidenced in the attention paid to him as a lonely widower. There were visits from many religious men of distinction, both Quaker and Methodist, who came by to visit the elderly, blind, and humble old man to share scriptures and words of comfort. Quamino died at the age of eighty-eight.

Quamino Buccau lived as a devout Methodist with principles that William J. Allinson, a noted abolitionist, deemed worthy of record. He once remarked to friends that, "I don't know much about freedom, but I wouldn't be a slave ag'in, not if you'd give me the best farm in the Jarsies." As a kind and sensitive gentleman, Quamino had a strong sense of humility with Christian beliefs that neutralized the hostility of being enslaved.

FURTHER READING

Allinson, William J. *Memoir of Quamino Buccau, a Pious Methodist* (1851).

Inscoe, John C. "Carolina Slave Names: An Index to Acculturation," *Journal of Southern History* (Nov. 1983).

Pomfret, John E. "West New Jersey: A Quaker Society, 1675–1775," *William and Mary Quarterly* (Oct. 1951).

GLORIA GRANT ROBERSON

Buchanan, Beverly (8 Oct. 1940–), artist, was born in Fuquay, North Carolina, and adopted as Beverly Buchanan by Marion and Walter Buchanan. Her father worked as the dean of the School of Agriculture at South Carolina State College, the only state school for African Americans in that state. Buchanan was raised in Orangeburg, where South Carolina State is located, and often traveled the state with her father as he met with farmers. At an early age she was captivated by the landscape of the rural South and the simple architecture of the dwellings there. Buchanan enjoyed drawing the people she encountered on these outings with her father. Despite her early inclination toward art, in 1958, upon graduating from high school, she enrolled at Bennett College, a historically black women's college in Greensboro, North Carolina. In 1962, Buchanan earned a bachelor of science degree in Medical Technology from Bennett and moved to New York, where she worked as a medical technologist for the Veteran's Administration in the Bronx and attended the prestigious Columbia University in Manhattan. In 1968, she was awarded a master

of science in Parasitology from Columbia and a master's in Public Health in 1969. Buchanan was working as a health educator for the East Orange Health Department and had been accepted to medical school when in 1971 she decided to revisit her passion for art and enrolled in a class at the Art Students League taught by Norman Lewis, an award-winning painter. Only a year later, in 1972, her work was the sole focus of an exhibition in New York at the Cinque Gallery. During this period she met ROMARE BEARDEN, the eminent artist and writer, who became her close friend and counsel. Buchanan was rapidly evolving in the art world. Her work, in paintings and sculpture, depicting first urban ruins and then the poetic beauty of the impoverished rural South, for which she is best known, was swiftly being included in group exhibitions. In 1977, abandoning her degrees and career in New York, Buchanan followed her heart and moved to Macon, Georgia, in order to devote her full time and attention to her zest for art. She worked diligently, and her craft evolved into a style belonging to none other, particularly as she began to incorporate raw materials. In 1980, she was awarded both the John Simon Guggenheim Memorial Foundation Fellowship and the National Endowment for the Arts Fellowship. Buchanan used photographs of her subjects to recall the images as she created. Oftentimes these photos would be positioned next to her original work of art. In 1984, she became the artist-in-residence at the Museum of Arts and Sciences in Macon, Georgia, and the following year she relocated to Atlanta, Georgia. Three years later, Buchanan moved to Athens, Georgia, where she continued to develop sculptures that to her reflected the simplistic techniques of the people who created the objects of her inspiration.

In 1990, Buchanan received the National Endowment for the Arts Fellowship in Sculpture and the Pollock-Krasner Foundation Award. Buchanan was nominated by her alma mater, Bennett College, in 1997 and won the Georgia Women in the Visual Arts Honoree Distinguished Alumni Citation Award, and the same year she was recognized by the National Association for Equal Opportunity in Higher Education. She was awarded the Anonymous Was A Woman Award in 2002, and the 2003 visiting artist at Spring Island, South Carolina, designation; and in 2005 was a distinguished honoree of the College Art Association Committee for Women in the Arts.

Buchanan's work has been exhibited extensively throughout the United States. Her paintings and sculptures are a part of collections at the Metropolitan Museum of Art and the Whitney Museum of Art in New York City; the Carnegie Museum of Art in Pennsylvania; the High Museum of Art in Atlanta, Georgia; the Asheville Art Museum in North Carolina; the Columbia Museum of Art in South Carolina; the Morris Museum of Art in Augusta, Georgia; the Addison Gallery of American Art at Phillips Academy in Andover, Massachusetts; and the Tubman African American Museum in Macon, Georgia. She has environmental sculpture installations throughout Georgia; in Miami, Florida; and Winston-Salem, North Carolina.

FURTHER READING

Iverem, Esther. "Sculpture Shaped from Time, Trouble and Triumph," *Washington Post*, 7 July 1998.

Leonard, Pamela Bloom. "Buchanan's Shacks Becoming Hospitable," *Atlanta Journal Constitution*, 12 Dec. 1997.

Reynolds, Jock. *House and Home: Spirits of the South: Max Belcher, Beverly Buchanan, and William Christenberry* (1994).

SAFIYA DALILAH HOSKINS

Buchanan, Junious "Buck" (10 Sept. 1940–16 July 1992), football player and businessman, was born in Gainesville, Alabama, one of four children of Wallace Buchanan, a steelworker, and Fannie Mae Buchanan, a bank employee.

At Birmingham's prestigious Arthur Harold (A.H.) Parker Industrial High School, known as the "largest Negro school in the world," (Carolyn McKinstry interview). Buchanan worked diligently to master his growing physical stature and athletic ability. Reaching six feet five inches in his senior year, Buchanan became a star athlete and was voted captain of both basketball and football teams. For Buchanan, as well as others who attended A. H. Parker from the late 1940s to the mid-1960s, the instructors were responsible for providing the students with a sense of race pride and inspired them to achieve beyond the expectations of the outside world.

In addition to the teachers at A. H. Parker High School, Buchanan had several coaches and mentors who influenced his development as both individual and athlete. From the strict discipline of head football coach Major Brown to the modeling of proper behavior and character by coach, teacher, and uncle Glennon Threat, Buchanan blossomed. However, in his senior year, Buchanan went unnoticed by

colleges at a time when scholarships for African American athletes were few and far between. Writing a letter on behalf of his nephew and pupil, Threat contacted legendary Grambling State University head football coach EDDIE ROBINSON, who offered Buchanan a full scholarship.

Buchanan began attending Grambling, located in Grambling, Louisiana, in 1959. Playing on the Tigers' basketball team as a freshman, he befriended and played second team to future National Basketball Association Hall of Famer Willis Reed. It was during Buchanan's basketball career at Grambling that he learned to block shots, which produced the coordination and confidence to knock down passes on the football field, a skill that opposing offenses would later fear. A phenomenal athlete, the six-foot, seven-inch, 275-pound Buchanan was clocked running the 40-yard dash in 4.9 seconds and the 100-yard dash in 10.2 seconds. He would eventually play both offense and defense for the Tigers. With the ability to run from sideline to sideline, Buchanan, along with college teammate Ernie Ladd, dominated the Southwestern Athletic Conference (SWAC). He earned All-American, All National Athletic Intercollegiate Association (NAIA), and the Most Valuable Player (MVP) Award from his Grambling teammates and coaches. In 1963, in a preseason exhibition game Buchanan, along with future teammate and NFL Hall of Famer BOBBY LEE BELL, anchored the collegiate All-Star team that beat the Green Bay Packers, the champions of the 1962 National Football League (NFL) season. Buchanan was a top draft choice for the NFL, as well as the upstart American Football League (AFL). Buchanan would leave college his senior year to pursue a professional football career, but over a six-year period he would return to the university to finish his degree. In May 1969, he would graduate from Grambling State University with a bachelor's degree.

Drafted by both the NFL and AFL in 1963, Buchanan chose to sign with Lamar Hunt's AFL Dallas Texans, which became the Kansas City Chiefs in the fall of 1963. He had felt compelled to sign with the Texans because his selection marked the first time that any professional football team had drafted a player from a black college in the first round. After two seasons Buchanan established himself as an all-star defensive tackle, single-handedly changing the game of pro-football with his size, quickness, and overall athletic ability. As a result, Al Davis, managing partner of the division rival Oakland Raiders, drafted the six-foot-seven-inch, 265-pound

Gene Upshaw to neutralize the effective Buchanan. During thirteen seasons with the Chiefs (1963–75), Buchanan was all-pro six times, served as the team's co-captain, was the team MVP twice, played on the AFL championship team in 1966, played in Super Bowl I in 1967, and won the Super Bowl in 1970, defeating the Minnesota Vikings 23-7. Following his retirement from the Chiefs in 1975, Buchanan served from 1976 to 1978 as an assistant coach for the NFL's New Orleans Saints and the Cleveland Browns. He left football all together in 1979 to start up All Pro Construction Company and All Pro Advertising in Kansas City, Missouri. Buchanan and his first wife Billie had two sons, Eric and Dwayne, and a daughter, Nicole. He remarried in 1984, to the former Georgia Thomas, a school teacher in the Kansas City School District.

In 1986 Buchanan founded the Black Chamber of Commerce of Greater Kansas City; he served as its first president from 1986–1989. In 1989, John Ashcroft, then governor of the state of Missouri, elected Buchanan to the Kansas City Board of Election Commissioners. The following year, in 1990 Buchanan was inducted into the Pro Football Hall of Fame in Canton, Ohio. From 1990 to 1992, Buchanan received numerous awards for his civic activities, including the Golden Torch Award given by the University of Missouri–Kansas City. After battling lung cancer for more than two years, he died in 1992. He was fifty-one years old.

FURTHER READING

Birmingham Civil Rights Institute Oral History Project transcript. Dr. Horace Huntley interview with Carolyn McKinstry, 23 April 1998.
"Hungry Man Helped Chiefs Rout Denver," *Washington Post, Times Herald*, 30 October 1966.
McKenzie, Michael. *Home of the Chiefs* (1997).
Parker, Arthur Harold. *A Dream That Came True* (1933).
Porter, David L. *African American Sport Greats* (1995).
"Remembering Buck," *Kansas City Star*, 17 July, 1992.

PELLOM MCDANIELS III

Buckner, Milt (10 July 1915–27 July 1977), jazz pianist, organist, and arranger, was born Milton Brent Buckner in St. Louis, Missouri. Details of his parents are unknown. His brother Ted was a jazz saxophonist who became a member of JIMMIE LUNCEFORD's big band; the brothers were not related to jazz trumpeter Teddy Buckner.

The boys' mother died when Milt Buckner was eight years old, and their father died the following year. Milt went to live with a foster father, the trombonist John Tobias, in Detroit, Michigan; Ted also moved and lived in the home of Fred Kewley, a saxophonist who worked with Tobias in Earl Walton's Orchestra. Milt took up piano at age ten, and he reported that Tobias made him practice six hours a day. After Tobias and his wife separated, Milt was raised by the drummer George Robinson, also a member of Walton's band. Ted's foster father Kewley owned a record shop and music studio where Milt heard the latest jazz and played with Ted in a rehearsal band.

By his mid-teens, Milt Buckner was playing professionally. He dropped out of high school before graduating. After hearing CAB CALLOWAY's ensemble, he was inspired to teach himself to write scores for big bands. Impressed by the effort, Walton's band members sent him to the Detroit Institute of Arts, where he studied arranging, composition, and harmony for two years while continuing to perform locally.

Around 1932, while with the drummer Don Cox, Buckner developed the "locked-hands" or "block-chord" style later popularized by the pianist George Shearing. Derived from an effort to evoke in Cox's five-piece band a sound reminiscent of a big band with massed brass and reed sections, the locked-hands technique involved moving about the keyboard with the hands striking in rhythmic unison. In this manner Buckner played a melody in octaves and harmonized that melody with the other fingers in an essentially fixed position, allowing for small adjustments to make the harmonies work the right way.

Cox's band played at Wood's Dancing School and was broadcast nightly on WXYZ. Buckner left in 1934 to serve briefly as a staff arranger for McKinney's Cotton Pickers, but he was back in Cox's band after a few months, resuming the dance and broadcasting work. In 1935 he toured with Jimmy Raschell's band, in which he once again played alongside his brother Ted. That year he met Gladys (maiden name unknown), whom he married in 1936.

Buckner left Raschell in January 1937 to settle in Detroit before the birth of his daughter. After working with Cox once again, Buckner rejoined Raschell in 1940, at which point he resumed touring with his family. He returned to Detroit, where he remained until November 1941, when he sat in with the vibraphonist LIONEL HAMPTON's big band and was immediately asked to join.

Through much of the 1940s, Buckner toured nationally with Hampton. He explained to the interviewer Max Jones, "I was known as an arranger with Hamp more than as a pianist." Among Buckner's recorded arrangements were "Nola" (1941), "Hamp's Boogie Woogie," "The Lamplighter," and "Overtime" (all 1944), "Slide, Hamp, Slide" (1945)—the last four titles were also composed or co-composed by Buckner—"He-ba-ba-re-bop" (1945), "Rockin' in Rhythm" (1946), and "Goldwyn Stomp" and "Hawk's Nest" (both 1947). Additionally, although the original arrangement of the band's biggest hit, "Flying Home" (1942), was credited to Hampton, Buckner told Jones, "I guess I made about 15 arrangements of that tune."

After leaving Hampton in September 1948, Buckner attempted to establish a big band. In March and June 1949, before the endeavor failed completely, the big band made a few recordings, including "M. B. Blues." He rejoined Hampton from July 1950 to August 1952, during which time he gradually switched from piano to organ, initially playing a theater instrument at an engagement in Los Angeles before purchasing a Hammond electronic organ. Buckner participated in a number of Hampton's "soundies" (film shorts for video jukeboxes), including those for the songs "Air Mail Special" (1950) and "Slide, Hamp, Slide" (1951). He also appeared with Hampton in the movie *Harlem Jazz Festival* (1955).

Apart from recordings—including a session under his own name in 1953—nothing is known of Buckner's activities from 1952 to 1955, when he formed an organ trio with the drummer Sam Woodyard and the saxophonist Danny Turner, both heard on the quintet album *Rockin' with Milt* from that same year. Woodyard soon left to join DUKE ELLINGTON, but Turner remained with Buckner for four years, during which time Buckner had modest hits with "Count's Basement" and "Mighty Low" from the album *Rockin' Hammond* (1956). After further changes in membership, the trio split up in 1964. Buckner then performed as a soloist at Playboy clubs and worked thereafter as a freelance musician.

Buckner performed at Lennie's-on-the-Turnpike in Boston, Massachusetts, with the tenor saxophonist ILLINOIS JACQUET and the drummer Alan Dawson, and from 1966 onward he played in Europe once or twice annually, often with Jacquet and the drummer Jo JONES. On the first of these tours he played piano, but otherwise he continued to focus mainly on the Hammond organ. Buckner and Jones performed in the film *L'Adventure de jazz* (1969–1970), and the two men accompanied the reunited duo of Slim and Slam—the guitarist and singer SLIM GAILLARD and the vocalizing bassist SLAM STEWART—at the 1970 Monterey Jazz Festival. Buckner also took part from time to time in reunions with Hampton, including performances at the Newport–New York Jazz Festival in 1973 and an engagement at the Rainbow Grill in New York City.

Buckner's recordings in Europe included the albums *Buddy Tate Featuring Milt Buckner* (1967) and *Crazy Rhythm* (1967–1968), both under tenor saxophonist Tate's co-leadership; Buckner's own *More Chords* (1969); Jacquet's *Genius at Work* (1971) and *Jacquet's Street* (1976); and Hampton's *Blues in Toulouse* (1977). Buckner also played in the documentary movie *Swingmen in Europe* (1977). Hampton's session in Toulouse was recorded shortly before Buckner's death of heart failure, which occurred while he was setting up his instrument for a job with Jacquet at a nightclub in Chicago.

Buckner was among a number of leading keyboard players and arrangers who carried on the swing style from the late swing era into the 1970s. His delightfully unpretentious personality was epitomized by his reaction to questions about his principal contribution to jazz. Asked repeatedly about this, he expressed no bitterness over Shearing's having popularized the locked-hands style. He asserted that everyone copied: he had taken ideas from EARL HINES and would have imitated ART TATUM had Tatum's style not been so impossibly difficult, and he saw no reason why Shearing should not have also benefited in this way.

FURTHER READING
Fulford, Bob. "Milt Buckner," *Down Beat* 22 (15 June 1955): 13.
Pease, Sharon. "Hamp's Pianist Reared by Band," *Down Beat* 10 (1 Oct. 1943): 14.
Vacher, Peter. "The Milt Buckner Story," *Jazz and Blues* 2 (Dec. 1972): 15–18.
Obituary: *New York Times*, 30 July 1977.
This entry is taken from the *American National Biography* and is published here with the permission of the American Council of Learned Societies.

BARRY KERNFELD

Buhaina, Abdullah Ibn. *See* Blakey, Art.

Bulah, Sarah (also spelled Sarah Beulah) (fl. 1950), civil rights activist, was a plaintiff on behalf of her daughter Shirley Bulah in *Bulah v. Gebhart* (1952) a companion case to *Brown v. Board of Education* (1954). Nothing is known of Sarah Bulah's early life or parentage, or even the date of her marriage to Fred Bulah. She was a longtime resident of Hockessin, Delaware, located west of Wilmington and along the Pennsylvania border, where the family maintained a farm and sold produce. Sarah and Fred adopted a daughter, Shirley, when she was fourteen months old after her biological parents abandoned her in April 1945.

Sarah Bulah's role in legal history began in the fall of 1950, when Fred complained to her about the lack of transportation services for black students in their community. He also criticized the arbitrary nature of the state's policy. She agreed and, in her husband's name, began a letter-writing campaign requesting transportation for her daughter. Unbowed by repeated denials from school officials, Bulah offered her own counterproposal to the supervisor of transportation: since the bus for the white students passed her home twice on its daily rounds, it could pick up Shirley at the house and drop her off at the post office, which was only two blocks from the black school, Hockessin School No. 107. "To take my child to school would not reroute the bus at all," she asserted. "Put her off at the post office and pick her up at the post office and bring her right back to my door. The bus is not full. So that isn't an excuse" (Fred Bulah to Governor Carvel, 12 Oct. 1950, Governor's Papers, Delaware Public Archives). Still, school officials would not relent, citing the state constitution, which mandated segregation in education. Undaunted by the negative responses, Bulah then approached LOUIS REDDING, the local attorney for the NAACP, and they discussed the matter. "He said he wouldn't help me get a Jim Crow bus to take my girl to any Jim Crow School," reporter CARL ROWAN recorded Bulah saying, "but if I was interested in sendin' her to an integrated school, why, then maybe he'd help" (Rowan, chap. 3). She agreed to his terms and the letter writing continued, addressing the board of trustees for Hockessin School No. 29 and the state board of education. But this time, with Redding's support, Bulah broadened her appeal, seeking admission to the white school and a bus for Shirley. Her request denied once again, she filed suit on behalf of Shirley against the state board of education with the support of her counsel.

Sarah's protests were not always well received. She received hate mail. And while many in the black community supported her efforts, she was,

according to Rowan, "something less than a hero to the other Negro parents in the area," a testament to a running debate within black communities about the relative merits of desegregation (Rowan, chap. 4). Sarah's own history was significant to some. She was Fred's second wife and considered a relative newcomer to town—in spite of almost a decade in residence. Shirley's physical appearance was also grounds for concern. Some in the community were suspicious of Sarah's motives because Shirley was light-skinned, and they considered Sarah's desire to send her daughter to an integrated school as an aspiration to distance and distinguish her daughter from other black children. More specifically, Reverend Martin Luther Kilson, pastor of the Chippey African Union Methodist Church in Hockessin, tried to talk Bulah out of the lawsuit. In his opinion, the effort to integrate Hockessin schools had been instigated by outsiders to the community: "All we wanted was a bus for the colored. Redding …and some members of the National Association for the Advancement of Colored People [introduced] this issue of segregation" (Rowan, chap. 4). Kilson was concerned about upsetting what he believed were the good relations between blacks and whites in the community. He also thought many in the community would rather have black teachers for their children. "They didn't want to be mixed up with no white folks," he concluded (Rowan, chap. 4). And the possible closing of School No. 107, should desegregation plans come to fruition, was also a matter of deep concern. As well as a center of learning, this black school—like many others—served as a community center where local people could meet and hold gatherings. The black teachers in School No. 107 also expressed ambivalence about Sarah's efforts. Integration, for many educators, represented the potential loss of a job, the end of a hard-earned career, and a loss of security and status not widely enjoyed in the black community. After Sarah's initial request for a bus, Constancia Beaujohn, one of two teachers at School No. 107, only reluctantly helped Sarah fill out a transportation request form, thinking it a waste of time. After the Bulahs had won their case before the state courts, Shirley failed third grade despite strong performances in the previous two grades, an act that Bulah believed was retribution for her lawsuit.

Redding, along with co-counsel Jack Greenberg, successfully argued her case, along with *Belton v. Gebhart* (1952), in which ETHEL BELTON was the lead plaintiff, in the Delaware Chancery Court. The state appealed the decision to the Supreme Court of Delaware, lost, and applied for a writ of certiorari from the U.S. Supreme Court, which then agreed to hear the case along with four others from South Carolina, Virginia, Kansas, and the District of Columbia in what came to be known as *Brown v. Board of Education*. Here, the High Court ruled that racially segregated education was in violation of the Equal Protection Clause of the Fourteenth Amendment. Bulah's challenge to Jim Crow segregation and her subsequent relationship with Redding were significant in that they represented a channeling of popular sentiment, amid a growing post–World War II assertiveness against Jim Crow, through rather circumscribed ideological and institutional means—in this case by the integrationist politics of the NAACP.

FURTHER READING

Copies of Bulah's correspondences to the governor and officials at the Department of Public Instruction are located in the Papers of the Governor and the Papers of the State Board of Education-Department of Public Instruction at the Delaware State Archive in Dover, Delaware, and the Papers of the National Association for the Advancement of Colored People at the Library of Congress in Washington, D.C.

Kluger, Richard. *Simple Justice: The History of* Brown v. Board of Education *and Black America's Struggle for Equality* (1975).

Peters, William. "The Schools That Broke the Color Line," *Redbook: The Magazine for Young Adults*, reprinted from October 1954, NAACP Papers, Library of Congress.

Rowan, Carl T. "Delaware Wants Its Schools to Be 'Separate, Equal,'" in "Jim Crow Schools on Trial: The Persons, the Places, the Issues," *Minneapolis Morning Tribune*, reprinted from December 1953, Kenneth Clark Papers, Library of Congress.

With All Deliberate Speed: The Legacy of Brown v. Board of Education (2003). Film.

BRETT GADSDEN

Bullard, Eugène (9 Oct. 1895–12 Oct. 1961), combat pilot, was born Eugene James Bullard in Columbus, Georgia, the son of William Octave Bullard, a laborer and former slave, and Josephine Thomas. Both parents were of African American and Creek Indian descent. In 1906 Bullard, the seventh of ten children, ran away from home, ending his formal education. He lived for a time with a band of gypsies, who taught him to ride racehorses. He then worked as a horse handler, jockey, and laborer in several southern states. Bullard gained the respect of several employers by his quiet insistence on treatment with dignity and equality, an ethos instilled in him by his father and strengthened by his sojourn with the tolerant, English-born gypsies.

Early in 1912, Bullard made his way to Norfolk, Virginia, where he stowed away on a freighter bound for Europe. Set ashore in Aberdeen, Scotland, Bullard worked his way south, joining a traveling vaudeville troupe, Freedman's Pickaninnies, in Liverpool later that year. There he also trained as a prizefighter and won his first fight, on points, in early 1913. A good but not exceptional fighter, Bullard fought under the auspices of African American welterweight champion Aaron Lester Brown, "the Dixie Kid." On 28 November 1913, Bullard first fought in Paris, achieving a twenty-round win not reported in local boxing papers. Bullard discovered in Paris his ideal milieu, where people of all races and nationalities found acceptance and equal opportunity. The following spring, after touring the Continent with Freedman's Pickaninnies, Bullard settled in Paris. Adept at languages, he earned his living both as a fighter and as an interpreter for other fighters. At about this time he began to use the Francophone version of his name, Eugène Jacques Bullard (pronounced Bull-*ar*).

In August 1914 war broke out in Europe. On 19 October 1914, shortly after his nineteenth birthday, Bullard enlisted in the French Foreign Legion. He saw action as a machine gunner in some of the bitterest fighting on the Western Front. Following crippling losses along the Somme in April 1915, three Foreign Legion regiments were consolidated into one.

Late that summer, Bullard's father wrote to the U.S. secretary of state, pleading that his son, not yet twenty, be "freed at once and sent home" from the war. "He must have made a mistake when he enlist [*sic*]," William Bullard wrote, and enclosed a document certifying that his son's birth date as recorded in their family Bible was 9 October 1895. (In his autobiography, Bullard himself several times gave his birth year as 1894, from which has stemmed ongoing confusion.) The American ambassador in Paris was notified of the elder Bullard's request, but since under French law a nineteen-year-old was not underage, neither the American nor the French government took further action (Lloyd, 41–42).

After heavy fighting in the Champagne region in autumn 1915, Bullard and other surviving Legionnaires were transferred to regular French regiments, Bullard to the 170th Infantry, a crack unit known to the Germans as the "swallows of death." Early in 1916, the 170th was sent to Verdun, a sector notorious for its savage fighting, and in March of that year Bullard sustained a crippling thigh wound, for which he received the Croix de Guerre.

Unable to continue ground fighting, Bullard transferred to aviation gunnery. His recuperation complete, he began training in October 1916, soon transferred to fighter pilot training, and on 5 May 1917 received pilot's license number 6950 from the Aéro Club de France. Moving on to advanced pilot training, in August Bullard was assigned to squadron 93 of the Lafayette Flying Corps, a group of American fighters under French command. With squadrons 93 and 85, Bullard flew at least twenty missions over the Verdun sector. He reported shooting down at least two enemy planes; as happened to other flyers, however, there was no corroborating evidence, so these were not scored as official "kills."

A competent pilot appreciated by his comrades, Bullard nevertheless was abruptly removed from aviation and returned to the 170th Infantry as a noncombatant. Circumstantial evidence suggested that, while other pilots of the Lafayette Flying Corps were transferred to the American Army Air Corps, Bullard was remanded because of his race. The United States would not commission an African American aviator until 1942.

Bullard was discharged from the military on 24 October 1919, nearly a year after the armistice. Since his war wounds prevented serious resumption of his boxing career, he instead became a jazz drummer and later was central to the management of Le Grand Duc, one of the most noted Parisian jazz clubs between the wars. Ada Louise Smith, known as BRICKTOP, first headlined there before opening her own Montmartre club. The roll call of musicians and guests at Le Grand Duc included the most celebrated names in Paris in the 1920s. Bullard also became the proprietor of Gene Bullard's Athletic Club and owner of another celebrated jazz club, L'Escadrille, in the 1930s.

In 1923 Bullard married Marcelle Straumann, daughter of a socially prominent family. The couple had two daughters and also a son, who died in infancy. Bullard's deep commitment to his businesses was incompatible with his wife's society interests. They separated after eight years and divorced in 1935; Bullard retained custody of his two daughters.

At the outset of World War II, Bullard assisted French counterintelligence by reporting information gleaned from the conversations of Nazi visitors to his establishments. When Germany invaded France in May 1940, Bullard, with many others, left Paris to fight. Unable to reach the 170th Infantry to the east, Bullard volunteered with the 51st Infantry at Orléans. After he was severely wounded in June, his French commanding officer, who had also been his superior at Verdun, ordered him to flee south, fearing that Bullard would be executed if captured. Making his way overland to Spain, Bullard eventually reached New York, medical treatment, and involvement with Charles de Gaulle's Free French movement. During and after the war, Bullard lived in Harlem and was active with New York's French community. He returned briefly to France in 1950–1951, while unsuccessfully seeking compensation for the loss of his Parisian businesses. At the invitation of the French government, he assisted at the relighting of the eternal flame at the Arc de Triomphe in 1954. In 1959 he was made a chevalier of the Legion of Honor, France's highest award; he received fifteen medals in all from the French government. Bullard died in New York and is buried in the French War Veterans' plot, Flushing Cemetery, Queens, New York.

For many years after World War I, the conventional stance of American authorities was that blacks did not have the mettle or the intellect to fly. In France, Bullard was widely recognized as an athlete, war veteran, and leader in Parisian expatriate society. However, his achievement in daring to train and fly as a combat pilot was given little recognition in the United States until well after his death. In 1989, Bullard was inducted into the Georgia Aviation Hall of Fame. He is depicted on the noteworthy *Black Americans in Flight* mural at the St. Louis International Airport, dedicated in 1990. A memorial bust at the Smithsonian Institution's National Air and Space Museum was unveiled in 1991, and on 14 September 1994, Bullard was posthumously commissioned as a second lieutenant in the U.S. Air Force.

FURTHER READING

Correspondence and manuscript relating to the writing of Bullard's unpublished autobiography are part of the Louise Fox Connell Papers, Schlesinger Library, Radcliffe College, Cambridge, Massachusetts. The text of Bullard's autobiography, *All Blood Runs Red: My Adventurous Life in Search of Freedom* (completed 1961) is in the possession of Bullard's daughter and grandson.

Carisella, P. J., and James W. Ryan. *The Black Swallow of Death* (1972).

Cockfield, Jamie H. "All Blood Runs Red," *Legacy: A Supplement to American Heritage* (Feb.–Mar. 1995): 7–15.

Lloyd, Craig. *Eugene Bullard: Black Expatriate in Jazz-Age Paris* (2000)

Stovall, Tyler. *Paris Noir: African Americans in the City of Light* (1996)

Obituaries: *New York Times*, 14 Oct. 1961; *New York Amsterdam News*, 21 Oct. 1961.

This entry is taken from the *American National Biography* and is published here with the permission of the American Council of Learned Societies.

CAROLINE M. FANNIN

Bullins, Ed (2 July 1935–), playwright, editor, educator, activist, and leader of the Black Arts Movement, was born Edward Artie Bullins in Philadelphia, Pennsylvania, to Edward Dawson Bullins, whose occupation is unknown, and Bertha Marie (Queen) Bullins, a civil service employee. Raised by his mother, Bullins attended a largely white elementary school, where he excelled in academics. He spent summers vacationing in Maryland farming country. His world changed in middle school when he was transferred to Ferguson Junior High School in inner-city Philadelphia and joined the Jet Cobras, a street gang. His adolescence was spent in "the Jungle," a tough Philadelphia neighborhood, where he sold bootleg whiskey, lost his front teeth in one street fight, and nearly died from a stab wound in another.

In 1952 Bullins dropped out of Franklin High School and enlisted in the U.S. Navy, where he became a lightweight boxing champion and educated himself by reading voraciously. Discharged in 1955, he enrolled in the William Penn Business Institute and took courses for three years before relocating to Los Angeles. He earned his GED and then enrolled at Los Angeles City College, where he founded *Citadel*, the campus black literary magazine, and met Pat Cooks, whom he married in June 1962 (the couple divorced in January 1966).

In 1964 Bullins moved to San Francisco, attending San Francisco State University and eventually launching a career as a playwright. He found theater to be the most accessible medium for his intended audience, explaining in a 1973 interview, "I found that the people I was interested in writing about or writing to—my people—didn't read much fiction, essays, or poetry" (*The New Yorker*, 16 June 1973). He wrote his first play, *How Do You Do? A Nonsense Drama* (1965), when he was drunk one night and, pleased with the outcome, decided to keep writing. *Clara's Ole Man* (1968), his first major work, was a powerful portrayal of African American class conflict. Both plays were produced at the Firehouse Repertory Theatre in San Francisco.

Bullins's early works met with cool critical reception because of their incorporation of obscene language and their unconventional dramatic format. Nevertheless, Bullins found both inspiration and encouragement in LeRoi Jones (AMIRI BARAKA), having seen Jones's *Dutchman* and *The Slave* in 1965. With Baraka, HUEY NEWTON, BOBBY SEALE, and ELDRIDGE CLEAVER, Bullins established Black House, which later developed into the San Francisco headquarters of one of the most influential black political organizations of the time, the Black Panther Party, for which Bullins briefly served as the minister of culture.

He left Black House in late 1966 following an ideological clash between revolutionary and aesthetic cultures; other House members, led by Cleaver, saw no role for theater in their vision for social change. Inspired by Baraka's Black Arts Repertory Theatre in Harlem, Bullins helped found Black Arts/West in San Francisco with the playwright MARVIN X and others.

Shortly thereafter a New York agent introduced Bullins to Robert Macbeth, the founder and artistic director of the New Lafayette Theatre in Harlem. The New Lafayette was established to serve the black community by producing plays by black writers who lived in and wrote for and about the black community. In 1968 Bullins became its resident playwright and would later serve as associate director (he would keep both positions until the theater closed in 1973 because of lack of funds). The New Lafayette followed principles Bullins laid out in an informal manifesto printed in the 1968 issue of *The Drama Review*, which he himself edited. Productions of the Black Theatre Workshop fell into two classes: "Black Revolutionary Theatre," or agitprop art and activities, and "Theatre of Black Experience," which explored black American life. Writing plays of both kinds, Bullins confronted his black audience with negative depictions, challenging them to change their situations and personal choices for improved prospects. Playwrights such as Richard Wesley and Martie Charles got their start under the auspices of the Black Theatre Workshop.

His editorial success established, Bullins founded the magazine *Black Theatre* and edited six issues between 1968 and 1972. While visiting

London in 1968, he met his second wife, Tracy ("Trixie") Warner. Before their marriage ended in 1981, the couple had children, including a son who died tragically in a car accident in 1978. Bullins created the Bullins Memorial Theatre in Oakland, California, in his memory in 1988.

From 1973 to 1983 Bullins taught playwriting at colleges and universities nationwide, worked as playwright-in-residence at numerous theaters, and served as writers' unit coordinator for the playwright's workshop at the New York Shakespeare Festival from 1975 to 1982. He earned a B.A. in English and Playwriting from Antioch University in 1989 and an MFA in Playwriting from San Francisco State University in 1994. In 1995 Bullins was appointed Distinguished Artist-in-Residence at Northeastern University, where he also served as acting director of the Center for the Arts.

Representative plays from Bullins's extensive career include *It Has No Choice* (1966); *Goin' a Buffalo* (1967); *A Son Come Home; The Electronic Nigger;* and *Clara's Ole Man* (1968, American Place Theatre), for which Bullins was awarded the Vernon Rice Drama Desk Award; *In New England Winter*, which earned him his first Obie Award (1971); and *The Taking of Miss Janie*, for which he received both an Obie Award and the New York Drama Critics Circle Award (1975). Some of Bullins's many honors include Guggenheim Fellowships (1971, 1976), Rockefeller Foundation playwriting grants, an AUDELCO (Audience Development Committee, Incorporated) Award, an honorary doctorate of letters from Columbia College Chicago (1976), two National Endowment for the Arts grants (1974 and 1989), and recognition as a "Living Legend" at the National Black Theatre Festival in Winston-Salem, North Carolina, in 1997.

Ed Bullins acknowledged the literary influence of Amiri Baraka, Eugene O'Neill, and Samuel Beckett while citing political inspiration from MALCOLM X and ELIJAH MUHAMMAD, clearly connecting his aesthetic aspirations to his political goals. Through his marked impact on continuing generations of university students, practitioners, and audiences, Bullins left a significant influence on American theater.

FURTHER READING

Anderson, Jervis. "Profiles-Dramatist," *New Yorker* (16 June 1973).

Hay, Samuel A. *Ed Bullins: A Literary Biography* (1997).

VIRGINIA ANDERSON

Bullock, Barbara (24 Nov. 1938–), painter and mixed-media artist, was born in Philadelphia, Pennsylvania, to James and Janey Bullock, of whom little else is known. She was the youngest of three children. An inquisitive child who was always making things, Bullock's creativity blossomed under the watchful eye of her mother and, later, her stepmother. When Bullock was twelve years old, her mother died, marking the beginning of a spiritual quest that eventually led her to becoming an artist.

Bullock's formal art education began in 1958 at the Samuel Fleisher Art Memorial, a Philadelphia institution that provided free instruction to adults and children. The 109-year-old school had a reputation for fostering the growth and development of artists, and Bullock stayed there for a year. Later she attended the Hussian School of Art in Philadelphia, from 1965 to 1966. Bullock arrived there at a time when the school still followed the traditional academic approach to art, using plaster casts of Greek sculptures to teach the fundamentals of anatomy and drawing. Bullock often found she could not relate to these all-white classical figures and rebelled by painting her own black figures. She met like-minded African American artists such as sculptor John Simpson, who became a pivotal influence on her. Simpson introduced Bullock to his Philadelphia art circle, including his friends Charlie Pridgen, Joe Bailey, Ellen Powell Tiberino, Moe Brooker, Charles Searles, Richard Watson, and Cranston Walker. Bullock would associate with this nucleus of creative people for decades afterward.

Many of Simpson's friends maintained studios on Market Street near City Hall, and there they often expounded upon their commitment to documenting reality, definitions of black art, and the importance of other disciplines to the plastic arts. While visiting these studios, Bullock valued the spirited discussions about contemporary American art and the role of the black artist. They also discussed the use of color and form in painting and sculpture as it compared with music composition, especially jazz. Important Pan-African themes also emerged in these encounters. The group valued the work of Nigerian-born artist Twins Seven-Seven, who straddled the divide between traditional African art and contemporary art. The group also came under the influence of Ile Ife, an Afrocentric cultural center in North Philadelphia. Named after the holy Yoruba city in modern-day Nigeria, the Ile Ife center fostered intercontinental exchanges between African American artists and their African counterparts. During this creative ferment,

Bullock's mature work would evolve as she questioned her Western art school training and began to look for an alternative informed by a black aesthetic. Beginning in the 1970s Bullock began taking numerous trips to Africa to explore her identity as an African American woman. She also studied African cultural practices and rituals and the varied concepts of beauty found in Africa and the African diaspora. She researched information on the slave trade to uncover the truth about the roles both Africans and Europeans played in it. She became interested in ancestral worship and the retention of African practices, religion, and culture in the New World experience. In 1986 she became committed to the idea of exploring the entire African continent. She made votive sculptures, altars, and works that expressed her spirituality and interpreted her memories, reflecting information she gleaned firsthand from her travels to Mali, Niger, Ghana, Côte d'Ivoire (Ivory Coast), Ethiopia, Egypt, Senegal, and South Africa. She discovered the complexity of Africa and wanted her experiences to be shaped by the sights, sounds, and smells of the various regions she traversed.

Bullock was a colorist whose work burst with energetic movement and rhythmic undulations. Most of her pieces are somewhat abstract and allude to anthropomorphic and animal forms and foliage. Her language of color was designed to create moods and bring a life force to her work. In 2006, however, she moved away from African references and dedicated a body of work to the Hurricane Katrina tragedy in New Orleans. Inspired by the blues recordings of the African American guitarist KEVIN MOORE (KEB' MO'), Bullock constructed huge assembled paper-relief theatres. In the piece *Come on in My Kitchen Cause it's Going To Be Raining Outside*, the kitchen floor is composed of reddish orange, yellow, and black tiles with a black fork, knife, and spoon falling off the right-hand corner of the composition. Shapes and forms that reference foliage and debris make up the chaotic center panel of the piece. This work captured the destructive properties of Hurricane Katrina while alluding to the life that went on beforehand.

Bullock had an illustrious career as a visual artist. From 1971 to 2007 she supported herself partly by conducting mixed-media workshops on collage, bookmaking, games, and explorations in color. She exhibited in a diverse array of venues including established and alternative galleries, colleges throughout the Mid-Atlantic region, and museums in New Jersey and Philadelphia. Like many African American artists, Bullock struggled throughout her career to gain recognition in the American arts mainstream. She received a number of prestigious awards, including the Pew Fellowship in the Arts, the Pennsylvania Council on the Arts Fellowship, the New Jersey Governor's Award in Arts Education, a Master Artist Award from the American Fine Art Society, and a commission in 1990 for public art at the Philadelphia International Airport.

FURTHER READING

Algotsson, Sharne, and Denys Davis. *Spirit of African Design* (1996).

Myers, Kay Z. *Art and Religion: The Many Faces of Religion* (1997).

Sayjet, Kim. *The Chemistry of Color: African American Artists in Philadelphia 1970–1990* (2005).

A. M. WEAVER

Bullock, Dick (c. 1802–1 Jan. 1854), slave craftsman, bateau man, and business agent for John Jordan and the Jordan and Irvine Company of Lexington, Virginia, was born in Amherst County in western Virginia. He grew up along the James River where he apprenticed in blacksmithing, carpentry, and navigation and earned the sobriquet "Dick the Boatman." Bullock was likely a descendant of the Igbo, who were the predominant cultural group of the region. Many of these people and their descendants became skilled craftsmen. From 1740 to 1790 many Igbo people were brought directly to Virginia from Igboland by William and Thomas Randolph, who were slave traders and plantation merchants. By 1744 Nicholas Davies, the former bookkeeper for the Randolphs, brought vast slave holdings to Amherst County derived from the same source. Upon his death in 1794 Davies manumitted many of his blacks, bequeathing each family one hundred acres of land. The mobility with which these blacks, free and enslaved, navigated the social and rural landscape differed considerably from those in other portions of the state. Other Igbo were floated up the James River, and even sold as couples at entrepôts and then left to work land where owners needed to comply with land grant requirements. Gender balance in the area was almost equal and promoted the quick propagation of families with Igbo lineage.

When Dick was eighteen, his then owner Mrs. Bullock of Amherst County, Virginia, leased him to John Jordan as a boatman and blacksmith for an annual fee of one hundred dollars. The lease continued for nine years until Jordan purchased Bullock in 1829. Annual leases had very specific stipulations that were followed by the lessor on varying levels. The standard agreement was that the lessor provided a blanket, a new set of clothing, shoes, and a hat along with housing and food. Obviously not all lessors provided equally well for their leased slaves. John Jordan fulfilled his contract to the slave owner and slave in an exemplary manner. The Jordan operations supplied a new pair of shoes, a new coat, new socks, two shirts, two pairs of pants, a blanket, and a weekly pint of whiskey to each worker. The Jordan and Irvine dry goods store served as the point of distribution for personal needs, and this is where boatmen could make purchases against their pay, which was 10 percent of their annual lease. As requirements for performing their jobs, skilled workers carried guns, tools, and rode horses with unsupervised mobility—extraordinary liberties for slaves. Bullock became well known as Jordan's head boatman and business agent on the James River, making deliveries and accepting cash payments for merchandise. Vessels carried hogsheads of tobacco, iron furnace products, and items ordered from the Jordan and Irvine store to businesses along the river. Boatmen, who were primarily black, were integral to this development. Bullock was the most notable one from Balcony Falls and oversaw ten other men. During the height of the bateau era, from 1775 to 1850, there were 300 to 400 boats on the river with three men floating each canoe.

By 1824 Bullock had been floating the Blue Ridge Gorge for three years and knew it well when the James River Company decided to focus on taming specific areas of this body of water. Balcony Falls was the most treacherous set of rapids and responsible for the death of many and the loss of much tobacco and merchandise. In 1823 John Jordan and his work crew of one hundred men, of whom 60 percent were black, began construction of the Balcony Falls canals. As the main commercial highway, the James River linked eastern and western Virginia, supplying goods to the western side of the Blue Ridge Mountains and the opportunity for commercial development. The Balcony area is on the western side of the Blue Ridge and at the intersection of Rockbridge, Amherst, and Bedford counties. Bullock was listed as a worker and partially responsible for designing the canals.

As a blacksmith and carpenter, Bullock also worked in iron furnaces and foundries owned by Jordan and on other contracted projects. Because of his carpentry skills he was also able to build bateaux that strongly resembled Igbo canoes. The original bateaux and canals were phased out and replaced by pack boats after the James River and Kanawha canals were built in the 1840s. During his later years he continued to live in the black workers' community, established during the canal construction, on Big Piney Mountain overlooking the James River.

On 1 January 1854, Bullock was injured and eventually died after attempting to rescue fellow workers. A flash flood had sent a boatload of thirty-four slave railroad workers down the Balcony Falls Gorge. The old bateau men Frank Padgett and Bullock had been asked to lead the rescue efforts and saved most of the men. But on the third trip down the gorge, the rescue boat crashed on a rock and killed Padgett. Bullock's legs were crushed, and he died shortly afterward. He is probably buried overlooking the James River in Seventeen Stones Cemetery, where Igbo-inscribed stones mark the graves of revered ancestors.

FURTHER READING

Chambers, Douglas Brent. "He Gwine Sing He Country: Africans, Afro-Virginians, and the Development of Slave Culture in Virginia, 1690–1810," Ph.D. diss., University of Virginia (1996).

Gomez, Michael. *Exchanging Our Country Marks: The Transformation of African Identities in the Colonial Antebellum South* (1998)

Hall, Gwendolyn Midlo. *African Ethnicities in the Americas: Restoring the Links* (1989).

Malcolm-Woods, Rachel. "Igbo Talking Signs in Antebellum Virginia: Religion, Ancestors and the Aesthetics of Freedom," Ph.D. diss., University of Missouri–Kansas City (2005).

Pinchbeck, Raymond W. *The Virginia Negro Artisan and Tradesman* (1926)

Walsh, Lorena. *From Calabar to Carter's Grove: The History of a Virginia Slave Community* (1997)

RACHEL MALCOLM-WOODS

Bullock, Matthew Washington (11 Sept. 1881–17 Dec. 1972), athlete, football coach, college administrator, lawyer, and public servant, was born in Dabney, North Carolina, to former slaves Jesse Bullock and Amanda Sneed Bullock. Looking for better educational prospects for their seven children and perhaps seeking to escape Ku Klux Klan harassment, his parents moved the family north when Bullock was eight years old. After a brief stay in Boston, the family settled in Everett, Massachusetts, in about

1894, where Bullock first made a name for himself as an athlete. At Everett High School he excelled at football, baseball, and ice hockey, and his teammates elected him to serve as the captain of each of these teams his senior season.

After graduating in 1900 Bullock entered Dartmouth College, which, like many schools outside of the South, admitted black students and encouraged them to participate in the life of the school. Bullock took advantage of the wide range of extracurricular activities at Dartmouth, performing in the glee club for four years, serving on several class committees, and earning election to the senior class honor society. Bullock also continued his athletic career, winning three varsity letters in football and four letters in track-and-field.

Playing end on the football team from 1901 to 1903 Bullock helped Dartmouth to a 24-4-1 record, and he received considerable acclaim for his skills. His collegiate career ended prematurely, however, during a game against Princeton University near the end of his senior season. The trip to New Jersey got off to a bad start for Bullock when the Princeton Inn, a non-school affiliated establishment, refused to serve him, forcing the black athlete to find accommodations away from his teammates. Things only got worse during the game when several Princeton players ganged up on him and knocked him out of the contest with a separated shoulder.

Unlike many contemporary northern schools, Princeton did not admit African Americans, and because of this prejudicial attitude some commentators accused the Tigers of intentionally injuring Bullock. The Princeton faithful, however, denied any racial motivations. One player explained: "We didn't put him out because he is a black man.... We're coached to pick out the most dangerous man on the opposing team and put him out" (*McClure's*, July 1905, 271–272).

Bullock graduated from Dartmouth in 1904, but his career in college football was not finished. As a testament to the seriousness with which they took integrated athletics in the early twentieth century, some northern colleges elevated African Americans to leadership positions. One such school, the Massachusetts Agricultural College (later the University of Massachusetts) hired Bullock to coach its football team. In the fall of 1904 he became one of the first salaried black football coaches at an integrated college when he manned the sidelines for the Aggies.

The following year he entered Harvard Law School and was unable to return to his coaching job

in Amherst. To help fund his legal studies, though, Bullock coached the nearby Malden (Massachusetts) High School football team for two seasons.

Bullock earned his law degree from Harvard in 1907, and the Mass Aggies immediately reengaged him. While plotting his professional career he directed the MAC football team for two more seasons, compiling an overall three-year record of 13–9–4.

After his final season as the Aggies' coach, Bullock briefly moved to Chicago, where he passed the Illinois bar exam, but he soon left for Georgia and a position at Atlanta Baptist College (later Morehouse College). At Atlanta Baptist he taught Latin, history, and social studies and served as the football coach and athletic director. In 1910 he married Katherine Wright; the couple would have two children. Following the 1911 season, Bullock, along with the famed African American sportswriter and administrator Edwin B. Henderson, inaugurated the practice of choosing annual all-star football teams from the rosters of historically black colleges.

Bullock passed the Georgia bar exam in 1912 and left Atlanta Baptist to work as a lawyer in private practice, but the peripatetic Bullock accepted a dean's position at Alabama Agricultural and Mechanical College in 1915. He stayed at Alabama A&M for only two years, when he was drafted to serve in World War I. Using his athletic training and leadership skills, Bullock worked as the YMCA educational secretary at Maryland's Camp Meade and then as the physical director to the 369th U.S. Infantry in France, a segregated unit serving in France.

After the war Bullock returned to New England, passed the Massachusetts bar exam, and settled in the Boston metropolitan area. For two years he served as the executive secretary of the Boston Urban League and in 1921 ran unsuccessfully as the Republican candidate for the Massachusetts State House from the Roxbury district. He received an appointment as a Special Assistant Attorney General of Massachusetts in 1925, and two years later he became the first African American to serve on the state parole board, a position he held for many years, becoming the board's chairman in 1944.

Throughout these years Bullock continued his career as a racial activist. In 1922 he authored a piece of legislation for the state Republican Party making membership in the Ku Klux Klan illegal in Massachusetts. The bill failed to pass but

Bullock helped publicize the effort and told of his grandfather's death at the hands of the original KKK years earlier. Twelve years later he unsuccessfully urged the American Bar Association to pass a resolution in support of federal antilynching legislation.

Bullock retired from public service in 1949 and worked as a lawyer until the mid-1960s. During his later life, he spent much time evangelizing for the Baha'i faith, his adopted religion. He traveled the country in support of his spiritual mission and served on several national Baha'i committees. In recognition of his varied accomplishments, Dartmouth awarded him an honorary doctorate in 1971. A year later he died at his daughter's house in Detroit, Michigan.

FURTHER READING

Berryman, Jack. "Early Black Leadership in Collegiate Football: Massachusetts as a Pioneer," *Historical Journal of Massachusetts* (June 1981).

Berryman, Jack W., and John W. Loy. "Historically Speaking: Matthew Bullock," *Black Sports* 2 (Feb. 1973).

"Bullock, Matthew Washington," in *Who's Who in Colored America*, ed. Joseph J. Boris (1927).

"Bullock, Matthew Washington," in *Who's Who in Colored America*, ed. G. James Fleming and Christian E. Burckel (1950).

"Matthew W. Bullock," in *In Spite of Handicaps*, ed. Ralph W. Bullock (1927).

GREGORY BOND

Bumbry, Grace (4 Jan. 1937–), soprano and mezzo-soprano, opera and concert singer, was born Grace Melzia Ann Bumbry in St. Louis, Missouri, the youngest child of Melzia Walker and James Bumbry. Her mother, originally from the Mississippi Delta, was a teacher, and her father was employed by the Cotton Belt Route Railroad as a freight worker.

Grace Bumbry came from a musical background. Her parents sang in the choir of Union Memorial Methodist Church, and her oldest siblings, Charles and Benjamin, sang in the Young People's Choir, which she joined by age eleven. At age seven Grace began piano lessons with her mother, an aspiring singer. Although she was not excited about the piano, Grace acquired the basic rudiments of music, such as sight-reading. Bumbry's home was always abuzz with singing and other musical activities, and she often provided the piano accompaniment for songs she sang and for the youngsters visiting her home.

Displaying an immense talent and deep passion for singing, Bumbry attended Sumner High School in St. Louis. There she came into contact with an important and influential teacher and mentor, Kenneth Billups. Prominent nationally as a choral director, he saw great potential in Bumbry and taught her the fundamentals of singing. Under his watchful eye, Billups developed Bumbry's vocal talent.

While still in high school, Bumbry sang "O don fatale" from Verdi's *Don Carlos* for MARIAN ANDERSON, who became another mentor. Anderson was so impressed with Bumbry's extraordinary voice that she introduced her manager Sol Hurok to Bumbry. Through the advocacy and support of Billups and Sarah Hopes, the choir director of her church, Bumbry competed in a KMOX radio station teenage talent contest in 1954 while in high school. She won a trip to New York, a $1,000 scholarship to study at the St. Louis Institute of Music, and a U.S. war bond of one thousand dollars. Since blacks were not allowed to attend the institute, she was offered substitute private lessons by the board of trustees. Bumbry, her parents, and teachers despised this form of segregation and declined the offer.

Shortly afterward, in 1954, she competed on the television program *Arthur Godfrey Talent Scouts*. Singing "O don fatale," she won and received several college scholarships. After graduation in 1954 from Sumner High School, she selected Boston University. But after a-year in Boston she transferred to Northwestern University in Evanston, Illinois, in 1955. There she was coached by the noted German American soprano and great opera diva Lotte Lehmann and also studied voice lessons from the leading Metropolitan Opera tenor Armand Tokatyan.

One of the most sought-after vocal coaches, Lehmann became director of the Music Academy of the West in Santa Barbara, California, where she taught voice. Bumbry, one of her protégés, perfected various lieder and operatic works, which Lehmann critiqued. Very impressed by Bumbry's talent, Lehmann invited her to study during the summer at the academy and offered her a scholarship. Lehmann's teaching helped establish her career.

It was at this period when the confusion and dispute about the classification of Bumbry's voice began. Lehmann categorized her voice as a mezzo-soprano, whereas Tokatyan classified it as a soprano. The operatic roles and literature for the two voice types were also different. This was a dilemma as she was coached by Lehmann in operatic mezzo-soprano roles, but Tokatyan trained her as a soprano. Although Lehmann envisioned a big operatic career for Bumbry, her young, bashful, and quiet student only saw a profession as a concert singer. Eventually Lehmann persuaded her to focus on an operatic career and coached her with more dramatic operatic roles.

Three of the earliest operatic awards Bumbry won were the Marian Anderson Scholarship (1957), the John Hay Whitney Award (1957), and the Metropolitan Opera Auditions of the Air (March 1958). With the award of one thousand dollars from the latter, Bumbry traveled to Europe during the summer to study French repertoire with the famous French baritone Pierre Bernac. She graduated from the Music Academy of the West in 1959.

Like many other black singers before her, Bumbry turned to Europe for better opportunities as an operatic and lieder singer. She made her European debut in June 1959 at Wigmore Hall in London. Her Paris Opéra debut occurred in March 1960 in Verdi's *Aida*. She also signed a contract for a lead mezzo-soprano with the Basel Opera in Switzerland for four seasons.

Bumbry received her biggest opportunity when Wieland Wagner selected her to sing the lead role of Venus in his grandfather Richard Wagner's opera *Tannhäuser* at the Bayreuth Festival in Bayreuth, Germany. Wieland Wagner was attempting a very avant-garde production of the original 1845 Dresden version of *Tannhäuser*. The thought of a black singer performing a role that was customarily sung by a white, Nordic-type singer caused much controversy prior to the performance. Bumbry made a highly successful debut as Venus at the Bayreuth Festival on 31 July 1961, receiving a thirty-minute ovation, forty-two curtain calls, and international recognition and acclaim.

One result of Bumbry's success was a $250,000 contract with Sol Hurok, who arranged her concert at a state dinner at the White House on 20 February 1962 at the request of John and Jacqueline Kennedy. On 6 July 1963 Bumbry married the twenty-seven-year-old Polish-German tenor Erwin Andreas-Jaeckel, whom she met in Basel. Her husband later relinquished his job and became manager of her busy career. During the 1970s Bumbry decided to switch from mezzo-soprano to exclusive soprano repertoire. She and her husband-manager squabbled over this decision, of which he disapproved. Combining the roles of manager and husband proved to be too much, and the couple divorced in 1972. They had no children.

Bumbry performed in concert and opera halls throughout the world, including several appearances at the Metropolitan Opera, Alice Tully Hall, Carnegie Hall, La Scala, the Salzburg Festival's Grand Festival House, Covent Garden, and Newark's Symphony Hall. She also sang with the Bolshoi, the Vienna State, and the New York City operas. She performed extensively and recorded major operas, oratorios, and lieder, including Bellini's *Norma*, Bizet's *Carmen*, Dukas's *Ariane et Barbe-bleu*, Gershwin's *Porgy and Bess*, Gluck's *Orfeo ed Euridice*, Handel's *Messiah*, Janáček's *Jenufa*, Mascagni's *Cavalleria Rusticana*, Massenet's *Le Cid*, Puccini's *Tosca*, Saint-Saëns's *Samson et Dalila*, Strauss's *Salomé*, Verdi's *Aida, Attila, Don Carlos, Judas Maccabaeus, Requiem, Macbeth*, and *Nabucco*.

In 1994 she organized the Grace Bumbry Black Musical Heritage Ensemble, consisting of singers, drummers, and dancers to perform traditional black spirituals and gospel music. On 2 September 1997 Bumbry sang her farewell to the opera world as Klytemnästra in Richard Strauss's *Elektra* in Lyons, France. In the decade following her farewell, she returned to the concert and opera stage on numerous occasions.

After her retirement, she served as the special adviser for UNESCO. She conducted several voice master classes in the United States and Europe, including at the Summer Academy of the Mozarteum in Salzburg, the Juilliard School of Music in New York, and Northwestern University. She was also artist-in-residence at the University of Michigan.

A member of Zeta Phi Beta Society, Bumbry received the Lawrence Tibbett Award from the American Guild of Musical Artists Emergency Relief Fund, with a scholarship fund established in her name. She also received the honor of *Kammersanger* of the Vienna State Opera in July 2003 for her outstanding contributions to opera. She is the recipient of three honorary doctorate degrees from St. Louis University, Rockhurst College in Kansas City, and the University of Missouri.

Throughout her career, Bumbry was a favorite with audiences around the world, who often rewarded her with thunderous ovations and curtain calls. Critics praised her stunningly beautiful, dramatic, and brilliant voice, with its excellent flexibility and wide vocal range.

FURTHER READING

Bailey, Ben E. "Grace Ann Bumbry," in *Notable Black American Women*, ed. Jessie Carney Smith (1991).

Kasow, Joel. "Interview with Grace Bumbry," *Opranet* (2 Feb. 1997).

Klein, Howard. "She's Come a Long Way from St. Louis," *New York Times*, 10 Dec. 1967.

Movshon, George. "Grace Melzia Bumbry—From Playgirl to Soprano," *New York Times*, 2 Jan. 1977.

Noh, David. "Sieglinde in Santa Barbara," *Opera News* (Apr. 2004).

Wolf, Gillian. "Grace Bumbry," in *Contemporary Black Biography: Profiles from the International Black Community*, ed. Barbara Carlisle Bigelow (1994).

BARBARA BONOUS-SMIT

Bunche, Ralph (7 Aug. 1904–9 Dec. 1971), scholar and diplomat, was born Ralph Johnson Bunche in Detroit, Michigan, the son of Fred Bunch, a barber, and Olive Agnes Johnson. His grandmother added an "e" to the family's last name following a move to Los Angeles, California. Because his family moved frequently, Bunche attended a number of public schools before graduating first in his class from Jefferson High School in Los Angeles in 1922. He majored in Political Science at the University of California, Southern Branch (now University of California, Los Angeles [UCLA]), graduating summa cum laude and serving as class valedictorian in 1927. He continued his studies in political science at Harvard, receiving his M.A. in 1928, and then taught at Howard University in Washington, D.C., while working toward his Ph.D. at Harvard. In 1930 he married Ruth Ethel Harris; they had three children. Bunche traveled to Europe and Africa researching his dissertation and received his Ph.D. from Harvard in February 1934.

Concerned with the problems facing African Americans in the United States, Bunche published numerous articles on racial issues and the monograph *A World View of Race* (1936). He and his colleague John P. Davis organized a 1935 conference called "The Status of the Negro under the New Deal," at which Bunche criticized the Franklin D. Roosevelt administration and the New Deal. He was also involved in the creation of the National Negro Congress, an attempt to bring white Americans and African Americans of different social and economic backgrounds together to discuss race matters. In the final years of the decade Bunche contributed research and reports to a Carnegie study on American race relations headed by the sociologist Gunnar Myrdal. The resulting

Ralph Bunche, diplomat and political scientist who won the 1950 Nobel Peace Prize, 16 May 1951. (Library of Congress, Photo by Carl Van Vechten.)

work, *An American Dilemma: The Negro Problem and Modern Democracy*, published in 1944, was a landmark study of racial conflicts in the United States. The rise of totalitarianism in Europe and the outbreak of war in 1939 worried Bunche, who feared that a Nazi victory in Europe would spur the growth of fascism in the United States, with disastrous consequences for African Americans. In 1941 he entered public service, accepting a position as a senior analyst in the Office of the Coordinator of Information (later the Office of Strategic Services). As head of the Africa Section, Bunche urged his superiors to approach the problem of postwar decolonization of European holdings in Africa. His proposal was rejected, and he transferred to the Department of State in 1944.

Bunche served as an adviser to the American delegations at the conferences in Dumbarton Oaks and San Francisco concerning the creation of the United Nations (U.N.). Recognized for his contributions on colonial and trusteeship policies, he was appointed a member of the U.S. delegation to the

1945 meeting of the Preparatory Commission of the U.N. and the first session of the U.N. General Assembly in 1946. In April 1946 Bunche took a temporary position on the U.N. Secretariat as director of the trusteeship position. The temporary position became permanent, and he served on the U.N. Secretariat for the remainder of his life.

In 1947 Bunche was appointed to the U.N. Special Committee on Palestine. He drafted both the majority report, which recommended a partition of the territory between Palestinians and Jews, and the minority report, which called for the creation of a federal state. The U.N. General Assembly accepted the partition plan, and Bunche was named the principal secretary for a commission designed to oversee its implementation. With the outbreak of war in 1948, Bunche was appointed as an assistant to the U.N. mediator, Count Folke Bernadotte. Following Bernadotte's assassination in September of that year, Bunche became the acting mediator. He successfully negotiated armistice agreements between Israel and several Arab states and was awarded the 1950 Nobel Peace Prize for his efforts.

Bunche's commitment to the U.N. did not prevent him from speaking out against racial discrimination in the United States. In 1949 he turned down a position as assistant secretary of state, noting that he did not want to experience the blatant discrimination against African Americans that existed in the nation's capital. Bunche was appointed an undersecretary general for special political affairs in 1954. With the outbreak of the Suez crisis in 1956, he was again called upon to use his diplomatic skills in a Middle Eastern conflict, and he organized the U.N. Emergency Force that was responsible for peacekeeping activities in the region. His Middle East experience prepared him for the difficulties he faced in 1960, when he organized and commanded both the military and civilian branches of the U.N. peacekeeping force sent to the Congo. He again directed a peacekeeping force when conflicts erupted on the island of Cyprus in 1964.

Bunche continued to press for the civil rights of African Americans. Although he still hoped for a society free from racial division, the civil rights conflicts of the late 1960s troubled him greatly. He participated in the 1965 march from Selma to Montgomery with MARTIN LUTHER KING JR. However, Bunche found himself under attack from leaders such as STOKELY CARMICHAEL and MALCOLM X, who argued that he had served white society and abandoned his African heritage. In turn, Bunche denounced the separatist agenda of the Black Power movement. Health problems, many related to diabetes, slowed him in the final years of his life. He died in New York City.

During his lifetime Bunche garnered international recognition and numerous awards for his U.N. service, including the U.S. Medal of Freedom in 1963. Although his position earned him the derision of many civil rights leaders in the 1960s, he was dedicated to the cause of African American civil rights throughout his career. By using his diplomatic skills in the service of the U.N., he promoted the cause of peace in a world that sorely needed men of dedication and ability in this area.

FURTHER READING

Bunche's papers are at the Library of the University of California, Los Angeles, and the United Nations Archives in New York City. A smaller collection is at the Schomburg Center for Research in Black Culture of the New York Public Library.

Keppel, Ben. *The Work of Democracy: Ralph Bunche, Kenneth B. Clark, Lorraine Hansberry, and the Cultural Politics of Race* (1995).

Rivlin, Benjamin, ed. *Ralph Bunche: The Man and His Times* (1990).

Urquhart, Brian. *Ralph Bunche: An American Life* (1993)

This entry is taken from the *American National Biography* and is published here with the permission of the American Council of Learned Societies.

THOMAS CLARKIN

Bundy, William F. (12 Aug. 1946–), U.S. naval officer and submarine commander, was born in Baltimore, Maryland, the son of William and Paulyne Bundy. His father was a World War II army veteran and construction worker, and his mother was a homemaker. Bundy attended high school at Baltimore City College, a premier all-boys school that was integrated—"a pretty big deal in those days." Bundy experienced few problems and received "a very good foundation; … the integrated environment prepared me for competition later in life." In 1963, at the age of seventeen, Bundy became interested in joining the naval reserves after watching them in action as a sea cadet at Fort McHenry. However, his true inspiration to join the navy came from his aunt, Joan Johnson, who served in the WAVES during World War II. Once in the reserves, Bundy gained valuable sea experience aboard the destroyer-escort *Darby*. Among those who served as a mentor to Bundy was Steward First Class Raymond

Pye, a Purple Heart recipient in World War II, who "looked out for me and made sure I had an opportunity to advance."

Graduating from high school in June 1964, Bundy enlisted in the navy, making the transition from the reserves. After serving in an oceanographic unit, Bundy volunteered for submarine duty, making the transition as a sonar technician first class with just over three years on active duty. His first submarine duty was aboard the Fast Attack boat USS *Sturgeon*, where he was the only minority member of the ship's crew during a deployment where the ship earned a Meritorious Unit Citation. Bundy qualified to earn his Silver Dolphins, an insignia specific to the submarine force that signifies an enlisted man has fully qualified as a submarine crewman. In 1970 Bundy advanced to chief sonar technician while assigned to the Submarine Training Center Pacific at Pearl Harbor in Hawaii. Serving as an instructor, he began to question his future: "I was thinking of getting out of the Navy.... I had put in for the Warrant Officer Program, but had been turned down because I 'lacked experience as a chief.'" However, Bundy persevered, and while running a sonar analysis training program, he completed his undergraduate studies at the University of Hawaii. His abilities, fortunately, were fully recognized by his bosses, including Captain Lyons and Lieutenant Commander Wade Taylor, and in 1974 Bundy was selected for Officer's Candidate School (OCS).

Bundy's selection for OCS came at a turbulent time in the navy's history in regard to race relations; in late 1972 racial conflicts arose aboard the carriers *Kitty Hawk* and *Constellation* at the same time that the navy was campaigning diligently to enlist black recruits. Further problems arose in 1974 with increasing media focus on the navy's Steward's Branch and the lack of fair treatment accorded its minority enlisted men. To his credit, Chief of Naval Operations Admiral Elmo Zumwalt recognized the navy's need to implement vast changes and began to issue his famed "Z-grams," Zumwalt's directives on racial matters by 1970. While such changes would take time, the movement of such proven men as Bundy and others into positions of leadership was a step in the right direction. Bundy would later recall that "the sub force needed more officers, and it sounded like a good deal to me." Working under the ideal that "opportunities are generated by people who can open doors," Bundy's OCS experience was extremely positive, and he graduated in 1975, first in a class of approximately two hundred candidates, of whom few were minorities.

From OCS, Bundy attended Basic Officer Submarine School and Polaris Missile Officer training before his assignment to the *Sam Houston* (Blue crew) as missile, torpedo, fire control, and sonar officer. It was there, during two deterrent patrols from 1976 to 1977, that Ensign Bundy earned his Gold Dolphins and gained valuable experience under Commander John P. Weikert, "a terrific CO who really took an interest in my development." Bundy's performance was, in fact, so outstanding, that he was "handpicked" for service on the commissioning crew of the *Ohio*, the navy's first Trident submarine, and he was further trained in strategic navigation systems. However, Bundy's service on *Ohio* was not to be. In 1978 he was sent to the Fast Attack boat *Richard B. Russell* "to augment her wardroom during an independent deployment"—*Russell* earned a Navy Unit Commendation during that deployment in the Atlantic Ocean. After further training, Lieutenant Bundy was assigned to the Fast Attack boat *Memphis* in 1979 as combat systems officer, serving in two major deployments, including one that took the crew around the world and earned them a Navy Unit Commendation. William Bundy would subsequently serve on the Nuclear Operations Staff, Atlantic Command, where he was responsible for nuclear targeting and strategic weapons system. This important duty earned Bundy a Defense Meritorious Service Medal for his achievements.

Bundy returned to sea aboard the missile boat *Lafayette* (Gold crew) as navigator and operations officer, completing two deterrent patrols from 1984 to 1985 and subsequently served as executive officer aboard the diesel boat *Blueback*. From there, Lieutenant Commander Bundy served on the staff of Submarine Group Five before being selected to command the *Barbel* in June 1988, one of three diesel boats remaining in the submarine force. In gaining his command, Bundy was just the third African American, after C. A. "PETE" TZOMES and TONY WATSON, ever to do so, thereby becoming an early member of a group later known as the Centennial 7, the navy's first seven black submarine commanders in the force's first one hundred years. Even more telling was the fact that Bundy was the only former enlisted man ever to achieve that feat. As Bundy related: "I understood two things.... I was one of the few guys to come from the enlisted ranks.... [T]hat was the bigger achievement. The second, being African American, didn't play as much for me at the time because opportunities were opening up."

Despite the age of his boat, Bundy and the crew of *Barbel* were forward deployed and excelled under extremely difficult conditions. *Barbel* under Bundy's command earned the Battle Efficiency E, Damage Control DC, and Communications C prior to being decommissioned in 1989.

Commander Bundy's subsequent naval service was equally impressive; from *Barbel* he served as chief staff officer in Submarine Squadron Three and in 1993 he became director of the Naval Officers Candidate School in Newport, Rhode Island, until his retirement in 1994.

Through all his years of service, Bundy held true to several connected ideals: "Each generation of African Americans has opened the door to opportunity for the next generation.... I have lived that story. As I look back, at every juncture there were always people that had an interest in me and moved me along in my career, as long as I was willing to do the work. Just as people have done for me, I've done the same for others." In that effort Bundy was successful, serving as friend and sponsor to those men, black and white, who came after him, as well as offering sound and practical advice to those black submarine officers and commanders that followed in his footsteps. ROGER G. ISOM, the skipper of the *Cheyenne*, recalled that after experiencing his first shipboard casualty, "Will just told me to be myself ... simple advice, but it was what I needed to hear, and it helped me" (personal interview, 4 Mar. 2007). After his retirement Bundy earned a doctorate of philosophy at Salve Regina University, completing a dissertation on technology leadership and governance, and became a research professor at the U.S. Naval War College. He married Jeanne Pacheco in 1979, a homemaker, and they had two sons and a daughter: William Bundy Jr., a Naval Academy graduate and submarine officer; Raymond; and Andrena Seawood, the wife of a minister.

FURTHER READING

The quotations in this entry come from the author's phone interviews with Dr. Bundy, 11–16 March 2007, and follow-up conversations and e-mail exchanges.

Knoblock, Glenn. *Black Submariners in the United States Navy, 1940–1975* (2005).

GLENN ALLEN KNOBLOCK

Burch, Charles Eaton (14 July 1891–23 Mar. 1948), educator, literary scholar, and biographer of the English novelist Daniel Defoe, was one of five sons born to Helena Burch in Saint George's, Bermuda.

Nothing is known of his father. Charles Burch was educated in the elementary and secondary schools of Bermuda. Burch met and married Willa Carter Mayer, who at one time served as a professor of education at Miner Teacher's College in Washington, D.C. She also served as a supervisory official of the public schools of the District of Columbia and authored *Clinical Practices in Public School Education* (1944). Whether or not they had children is not known.

Burch attended Wilberforce University in Wilberforce, Ohio, from which he was awarded a B.A. in 1914. Four years later, he earned a M.A. from Columbia University. Fifteen years later in 1933 he was awarded a Ph.D. in English from Ohio State University. He taught at several institutes of higher education, one of which was Tuskegee Institute during 1916–1917. From 1918 to 1921 he served as an instructor of English at Wilberforce University in Ohio. He also served on the faculty of Howard University in Washington, D.C., from 1921 to 1948 as a professor of English, eventually becoming head of the English department.

Burch made many scholarly contributions to Howard University, one of which was the development of an African American literature course titled "Poetry and Prose of Negro Life." As head of the English department during his fifteen-year tenure at Howard University, Burch recruited scholars and teachers who helped strengthen the department and the African American literature course that he had previously developed. Burch wrote essays on the lives of a variety of subjects, including PAUL LAWRENCE DUNBAR. "A Survey of the Life and Poetry of Paul Lawrence Dunbar" was the subject of Burch's master's thesis at Columbia University.

Burch published numerous scholarly articles and became well known as he developed into an influential expert in eighteenth-century English literature. He emerged as an authority on the life and works of the English novelist and journalist Daniel Defoe. Burch wrote essays on Defoe's life and writings of the era of 1706–1731 and journeyed to Scotland, where Defoe had been politically active in the eighteenth century, several times to do extensive research. His intense study produced many publications on various related topics. The *Howard University Record* published Burch's essay "Daniel Defoe's Views on Education" in 1922. The essay was revised for the *London Quarterly Review* in 1930, and remained in progress for a more intense study, which led Burch to spend time at Edinburgh University in Scotland, researching Defoe's life and studying with H. J. C. Grierson during 1927–1928.

Burch's research at the National Library of Scotland from 1927–1928 produced a series of articles concerning Defoe's life and activities connected to the political union of Scotland and England in 1707. Burch established Defoe's authorship of pamphlets and writings that were not previously attributed to Defoe. Burch wrote four essays during this time: "An Equivalent of Daniel Defoe" (*Modern Language Notes* 37844 [June 1929], 378), an article in which Burch addressed an excerpt from *Equivalent*, a poem written anonymously in 1706 about Defoe (Burch stated that the poem is a "Scotch satire" of Defoe and his views in favor of the union of England and Scotland, and suspected the author to be Dugald Campbell, who had expressed similar attitudes against both the union and Defoe); "Defoe's Connections with the *Edinburgh Courant*" (*Review of English Studies* 5 [Oct. 1929], 437–440); "Attacks on Defoe in Union Pamphlets," (*Review of English Studies* 6 [July 1930], 318–319); and "Wodrow's List of Defoe's Pamphlets on the Union" (*Modern Philology* 28 [Aug. 1930], 99–100), an article in which Burch described his examination of a collection of pamphlets ascribed to Defoe. Burch stated how likely it is that five pro-union pamphlets included in the librarian Robert Wodrow's list are accepted as genuine pamphlets written by Defoe. Burch said they were written by Defoe because it is likely that Defoe assisted Wodrow in compiling union notes and documents and that the style of writing is that of Defoe's. (Wodrow was a Scottish clergyman who served as a librarian at Glasgow University after he received his M.A. degree.) Two of Burch's essays on Defoe's literary relationship contributed to Burch's doctoral dissertation while he studied at Ohio State University. Those essays were "The English Reputation of Daniel Defoe: British Criticism of Defoe as a Novelist 1719–1860" and "Defoe's British Reputation 1869–1894" (*Englische Studien* 67 [1932], 18–98 and 68 [1934], 410–423).

In April 1937 an article by Burch was published in *Philological Quarterly* titled "Notes on the Contemporary Popularity of Defoe's Review." This article produced support of Defoe's reputation with the people of London concerning Defoe's periodical. In April of that same year the *London Quarterly and Holborn Review* published Burch's essay "The Moral Elements in Defoe's Fiction." This article focused on Defoe's character and personality and greatly influenced Defoe's biographical writers.

Burch again traveled to Scotland to do further research at the National Library and the archives of Edinburgh University in 1938. He spent six months during this visit doing more biographical research that produced more articles over the next ten years. Burch's research on the life of Defoe during this study abroad produced "Defoe and the Edinburgh Society for the Reformation of Manners" (*Review of English Studies* 16 [July 1940], 306–312), an article in which Burch explained his notes pertaining to the minutes of an organization called the Edinburgh Society for the Reformation of Manners, of which Defoe was a member. Defoe desired to be a member of a different branch, called the Societies in London for Reformation. Defoe was admitted on 3 April 1707 and later agreed to correspond with the former branch and requested reformation manuals for the branch that he had recently joined. Burch explained in his footnotes that the manuscript, dated 7 March 1707, was brought to his attention by Dr. H. L. Sharp of the Edinburgh University Library. Burch also produced "Benjamin Defoe at Edinburgh University, 1710–1711" (*Philological Quarterly* 19 [Oct. 1940], 343–348); and "Defoe and His Northern Printers" (*Publications of the Modern Language Association of America* 60 [Mar. 1945]: 121–128), this latter being an article in which Burch described a controversy that Defoe encountered between his Scottish printer, Mrs. Agnes Campbell Anderson, and a rival of hers named James Watson. Watson wanted to discredit Defoe and Mrs. Anderson because she printed Defoe's controversial articles about the union of England and Scotland. Mrs. Anderson owned the largest printing shop in Scotland and continued to print Defoe's articles, and on 12 May 1712, as her printing license was about to expire, she called on Defoe for his influence and help.

Burch contributed other writings pertaining to Defoe, including "The Authorship of a Scots Poem (1707)" (*Philological Quarterly* 22 [Jan. 1943], 51–57); "An Unassigned Defoe Pamphlet in the Defoe-Clark Controversy" and "A Discourse Concerning the Union: An unrecorded Defoe Pamphlet?" (*Notes and Queries* 188 [5 May, 16 June 1945], 185–187, 244–246); and "Defoe's First *Seasonable Warning or the Pope and the King of France Unmasked* (1706)" (*Review of English Studies* 21 [Oct. 1945], 322–326), an article in which Defoe attempted to persuade "the inhabitants of Edinburgh … to wish for a union"; and "Defoe's 'Some Reply to Mr. Hodges and Some Other Authors'" and "The Authorship of 'A Letter Concerning Trade from Several Scots Gentlemen that are Merchants in London,' etc. (1706)" (*Notes and Queries* 193 [21 Feb., 6 Mar. 1948], 72–74,

101–103). In 1948 the *American PeoplesEncyclopedia* published articles by Burch about Defoe and the Scottish novelist Tobias Smollett.

Burch suffered and died of a heart attack in Stamford, Connecticut. At the time of his death, several writing projects were in progress. One was an essay first published in 1922 in which Burch intended to do an expanded study. In progress also were two unfinished book-length projects. One was about the life of Defoe and the other was about Defoe's pamphlets on the union. Mordecai W. Johnson, then president of Howard University, delivered the eulogy at Burch's funeral, which was held in Andrew Rankin Memorial Chapel, located on the main campus of Howard University.

As a literary authority on the life and writings of Daniel Defoe, Charles Eaton Burch ranks high as a scholar and a specialist of eighteenth-century English literature. One year after his death the English department at Howard University established the Charles Eaton Burch Memorial Lectures, an annual series of lectures that features outstanding scholars.

FURTHER READING

Burch's essays and other writings are in the Moorland-Spingarn Research Center of Howard University. His writings are also listed in the *CambridgeBibliography of English Literature* and the *New Cambridge Bibliography of English Literature*, and in Velma McLin Mitchell's "Charles Eaton Burch: A Scholar and His Library" (*College Language Association Journal*, 16 [1973]: 369–376). A portion of Mitchell's work titled "The Charles Eaton Burch Collection in Founder's Library" was catalogued at Howard University before the writings were dispersed.

Arvey, Verna. "Charles Eaton Burch, Who Treads an Unbeaten Path," *Opportunity* (1942).

Mitchell, Velma McLin. "Charles Eaton Burch: A Scholar and His Library," *College Language Association Journal* (1973).

Obituaries: *Washington Star*, 25 Mar. 1948; *Washington Post*, 27 Mar. 1948.

FLORENCE M. COLEMAN

Burch, J. Henri (1836–1883), journalist, musician, and politician, was born James Henri Burch in New Haven, Connecticut, to Charles Burch, a wealthy black minister, and his wife. Burch was the sole black student at Oswego Academy in New York, where he was trained in journalism and music.

He lived in Buffalo, New York, before the Civil War, where he became involved in the antislavery movement and taught music. Burch became an active member in the Garnet League, which championed the rights of former slaves. Upon moving to Baton Rouge, Louisiana, Burch quickly worked his way in the political circles of Louisiana, serving in the Louisiana House of Representatives and the Louisiana Senate.

At age thirty-two, with his father's encouragement, Burch left the North for Louisiana to aid and educate free blacks during Reconstruction. Soon thereafter Burch began directing the local school for blacks and began his rise through the Louisiana state government. In 1868 Burch was elected to the Louisiana House of Representatives, representing East Baton Rouge. Burch was one of thirty-five blacks elected to the Louisiana House in 1868. In 1870, along with P. B. S. PINCHBACK, the first African American governor and the grandfather of the Harlem Renaissance writer JEAN TOOMER, Burch began publishing the *Louisianian*, a local newspaper. One year later Burch purchased the *Baton Rouge Courier*, renaming it the *Grand Era*, which he published and edited until 1878.

During the 1871 Louisiana congressional session, partisan politics saw both Democrats and Republicans vying for control of the house. During this time Burch was nominated as Speaker of the House. However, Burch lost to Mortimer Carr by a vote of 7 to 85. Burch was nominated again during the middle of the congressional session as a result of dissatisfaction with Mortimer Carr as speaker, but again Burch lost the election, this time to Colonel George W. Carter by twenty-five votes.

Also in 1871 Burch became a well-known opponent of Governor Henry Clay Warmoth, the first Reconstruction governor of Louisiana. Burch led the movement to remove Warmoth from office that resulted in Warmoth's impeachment on 9 December 1871. The death of Lieutenant Governor OSCAR JAMES DUNN, a close friend of Burch's, in 1871, as well as the election of 1872, saw Burch's influence and participation grow. Dunn's death and Pinchback's nomination to replace Dunn as lieutenant governor sparked a debate in the Louisiana House of Representatives. Many in Louisiana, including the U.S. senator William P. Kellogg, believed that Burch represented the black population of Louisiana more accurately than did Pinchback. During this time and as a result of Pinchback's nomination to replace Dunn as lieutenant governor, Burch came to be at odds with

Pinchback. Under the suspicion that Dunn was poisoned, Burch, along with his political allies CAESAR CARPETIER ANTOINE, William P. Kellogg, and Stephen B. Packard, fought for supremacy of the Louisiana state government.

After the Republican convention of 1872 in New Orleans, all divisions within the party were healed. With rallies organized by Burch, the Republican Party nominated Kellogg for governor, Antoine for lieutenant governor, Pierre G. Deslonde for secretary of state, Charles Clinton for auditor, William G. Brown for superintendent of education, and Pinchback as congressman-at-large. Burch himself was elected to the Louisiana Senate in 1872. In 1872 Burch was one of twelve black senators of the thirty-six in Louisiana.

In 1873 Burch was appointed head of the seven-man Committee on Enrollment and Engrossment in Louisiana. Burch was also a part of the two-member committee that investigated securities deposited by banks and banking companies. In 1874 Burch was appointed leader of the Penitentiary Committee. Burch, an opponent of the penitentiary, proposed legislation that called for reforms in the prison system. Burch's bill, which called for the separation of inmates according to crimes, as well as for the improvement of inmates' food, lodging, and clothing, failed to win the support of the Louisiana congress. While Burch was in the state senate, he was an advocate of higher education and sought to allocate money to repair and maintain buildings at Louisiana State University. Also, reflecting his desire to promote civil rights, Burch urged a joint resolution, asking the U.S. Congress to aid in the elimination of slavery in Cuba. As a result of Burch's support of Cuba, he was given the title of General Representative of the Republique of Cuba Abroad. Burch went on to serve in the state senate from 1872 to 1878. Also in 1878 he was forced to leave Baton Rouge by armed whites seeking to end African American influence in Louisiana politics.

Apart from politics Burch was well known throughout Louisiana social circles as a popular singer and performer. Burch hosted well-attended parties at his home, often entertaining other black politicians. Burch married the Dunn's widow. A journalist, Burch wrote for the Republican *Standard* based out of Carrollton, Louisiana, in 1869, and was one of the founders of the New Orleans *Louisianan* in 1870.

An independent thinker who aligned himself with the Republican Party, Burch was a controversial figure in Louisiana politics throughout his years in the state legislature. As a member of the Louisiana state government, he worked tirelessly to promote and advocate for the black population of Baton Rouge and Louisiana at large. He died of cancer in 1878.

FURTHER READING

Perkins, A. E. "James Henri Burch and Oscar James Dunn in Louisiana," *Journal of Negro History* (1937).

Vincent, Charles. *Black Legislators in Louisiana during Reconstruction* (1976).

MICHAEL J. RISTICH

Burdett, Samuel (1846?–?), businessman, antilynching advocate, and pioneering member of Seattle, Washington's black middle class, was born in Kentucky, but exactly when or where has not been established. Some indications of Burdett's background, however, emerge from the 1850 census of Bullitt, Kentucky. One "Sam'l Burdett" is listed as a four-year-old black child living in the household of a white Burdette family headed by a fifty-year-old man named Pyton Burdett, who had a wife and seven children. A black woman named Louisa Burdett is also included in the household along with three black children, among them, "Sam'l." The status of Louisa and her three children as either slaves or free persons is not indicated. Whatever her background in 1850, it is clear that ten years later Louisa had prospered. In 1860 the Bullitt, Kentucky, census listed Louisa Burdett, thirty-six, with three children including a fourteen-year-old Samuel living in their own dwelling house and listed as a separate family. Additionally, their real estate was valued at $300 and their personal estate at $100. This data strongly suggests that Samuel Burdett had an ambitious and resourceful mother.

Samuel Burdett participated in the Civil War between 1864 and 1865, and was reportedly present at Lee's surrender to Grant. After the war he joined the Ninth Cavalry, where he became a veterinary surgeon and served for eighteen years. Like many other African American men, Burdett's military service widened his horizons, rejuvenated his connection to the nation, and provided him with skills he parlayed into a career. Sometime in 1872 he married a woman named Belle. Not much is known about her origins, except that she and her parents were also from Kentucky.

In 1891 the couple moved to Seattle, Washington, where Samuel worked as a veterinarian until 1900 and then headed a mining and loan company. While in Seattle, the Burdetts helped create the foundations of middle-class society for African Americans in the Northwest. The same year he moved to Seattle, Burdett founded the Cornerstone Grand Lodge of the York Masons, a group that organized entertainment, social activities, and financial loans. In 1893 Burdett organized a life insurance group called the "Supreme Altar of the Ancient Order of the Sons and Daughters of Ham." Its ambitious purpose was not only to provide financial protection from disasters, but apparently also to elevate the mind and morals of his fellow African Americans. A historian of Seattle's black middle class, Esther Hall Mumford, noted that the Burdetts were considered a leading family and owned a grand piano.

Like many other African Americans who left slavery and the South behind, Burdett's migration north and west was marked by increasing political radicalism and a growing claim on the right of full participation in American citizenship. In Seattle Burdett was active in the Afro-American League, helped organize Juneteenth festivities, and worked for the state Republican Party. In 1898 he volunteered to recruit and organize a regiment of "Aframerican Infantry" to serve in the Spanish-American War. His offer was ultimately rejected but displayed the willingness of black veteran patriots to risk their lives and break down racial barriers through military service.

Increasingly, Burdett used his high social standing to tackle the controversial topic of lynching. Although IDA B. WELLS-BARNETT, a prominent journalist, had been writing and giving speeches denouncing mob violence, no progress had been made in ending the plague that infected the entire nation. In 1900 Burdett published *A Test of Lynch Law, an Expose of Mob Violence, and the Courts of Hell* that passionately attacked lynching and connected such mob violence to the larger problem of black oppression. Burdett described coming across a crowd in Seattle listening to a phonographic exhibit of the Paris, Texas, lynching in which a white mob burned a black man named Henry Smith to death. For a few cents people could listen to Smith's dying screams. This episode was a remarkable example of how the terrors of lynching were not limited to the South, but reached almost every corner of the United States and inspired activists such as Burdett to work for racial justice. Burdett also revealed in his book that he was a founding member of the International Council of the World. According to Burdett this group, organized in 1901, was dedicated to ending racial violence. The group offered a $500 reward for the apprehension and conviction of any person involved in the death of a lynching victim. Burdett also claimed that the council hired detectives to investigate lynchings in the South. These methods demonstrate the wide variety of approaches activists took in the early years of the antilynching campaign. Later in the second and third decade of the twentieth century, the NAACP would dominate antilynching work with its famous journalistic exposés and efforts to make lynching a federal crime. Burdett's group did not have the same kind of financial resources or national exposure, and yet their pioneering efforts show the valiant and determined roots of this struggle. The exact year of Burdett's death is unknown, although it may be telling that the 1910 Seattle census does not list either Samuel or Belle Burdett.

FURTHER READING

Dray, Philip. *At the Hands of Persons Unknown, the Lynching of Black America* (2002).

Mumford, Esther Hall. *Seattle's Black Victorians, 1852–1901* (1980).

Trudeau, Noah A. *Like Men of War: Black Troops in the Civil War, 1862–1865* (1998).

MICHELLE KUHL

Burgaw, Israel (c. 1738–c. 1811), activist, listed in some records and Philadelphia city directories by the names of Burgoe, Berge, or Burgu, was evidently a free African American by the time his name appears in public records, when he was already over fifty years of age. No information about his precise date or place of birth, status at birth, parentage, marriage or children, or date of death has come to light. The 1790 census records show that he shared a house at 19 Cresson Alley, Philadelphia, Pennsylvania, with three other free African Americans, possibly his family. Over a decade later he is listed in the St. Thomas African Episcopal Church Birth and Baptismal Register as an adult of sixty-five years, who was baptized on 23 January 1803. No other persons named Burgaw appear in the records spanning the years 1796–1837, which suggests that his immediate family had already dispersed by this time, or, alternatively, that he had no family members requiring religious rites.

Apart from his involvement as a founding congregant of St. Thomas African Episcopal Church in 1794, records have revealed no active participation in church business, whether in the form of construction work, collecting donations, or holding office. Little more is known about Burgaw beyond his place of residence in Philadelphia and his occupation. During the period in which he lived on Cresson Alley, he made a living as a wood sawyer, a job far less skilled than carpentry, involving the simple sawing of building materials such as planks, beams, and posts, or firewood. No matter how robust or industrious he might have been in the trade that he followed for several decades at least, city officers, who fixed the price of a cord of wood, would have limited his earning potential. Throughout the 1790s, the nation's temporary capital, Philadelphia, experienced a building boom to house government officers, congressmen, and incoming tradesmen. Although carpenters and other artisans had the opportunity to prosper as they helped erect new houses and tenements, the city imposed significant restraints on workmen's autonomy in those occupations heavily populated by African Americans. Indeed, Burgaw remained during this period in a modest dwelling—a simple earthfast (or post-in-ground) structure—located in the rear of a house on Cherry Street, which was owned and occupied by Benjamin Cathrall (or Catherill), a Quaker school teacher, and his family.

The reasons for Burgaw's residence on Cathrall's lot are not clear, but proximity hints at a personal connection. Benjamin Cathrall, born in 1737, was the son of Edward Cathrall of Burlington, New Jersey, who was probably one of the founding members of the New Jersey Association for Helping the Indians (1757). Benjamin married Sarah Parker at a Quaker monthly meeting (date unknown) in Burlington, and, at some point thereafter, they relocated to Philadelphia where he earned his living as a schoolteacher. Dedicated to the eradication of the slave trade, he was one of the signers of the Quaker Anti-Slavery Petition to the Continental Congress (1783). Motivated by religious and family precepts he may have accepted responsibility for housing Burgaw because the sawyer had been a slave belonging to him or another family member before Quakers mandated the repudiation of slavery in 1780, or he may have helped release him from bondage, or he may simply have taken to heart the moral injunction to foster the African American community's development in a postslavery society. The relatively high number of African American households in the neighborhood, along with the specific examples of JAMES ORONOCO DEXTER, a free African American who occupied a house owned by the Quaker Ebenezer Robinson, and Robert Venable, a free man who occupied a house owned by the Quaker Nicholas Rash, indicate that the local Quakers, many of them linked by marriage, encouraged each other to offer proximate housing or jobs to free African Americans. The similar age of Cathrall and Burgaw points to the possibility of a lifelong connection, yet when he died in 1805 Cathrall willed no legacy to his neighbor. However, it seems that Cathrall's widow or another family member continued to provide for Burgaw during his lifetime, for he remained in his residence at least until 1811, when his name last appears in the public record, in a city directory listing people of color.

Archaeologists excavated Cathrall's property during the years 2000–2001 pending the construction of Philadelphia's Constitution Center. Besides exposing the dimensions and structure of Burgaw's dwelling, they turned up items such as glass beads and ceramic fragments that may well have belonged to household members. These items can help modern Americans comprehend details about Burgaw's daily life at the turn of the nineteenth century as well as the nature and comparative value of African American material possessions during the early republic. Burgaw's most important known contribution to American culture was his involvement, with some 245 other individuals of African descent, in establishing the St. Thomas African Episcopal Church, an outgrowth of the Free African Society. The church, under the leadership of the first African American priest to be ordained in the Episcopal Church, ABSALOM JONES, opened for worship on 17 July 1794 and was incorporated as an institution for the sole use of African Americans in 1796.

FURTHER READING

"Chapter 3: The Revolution, Nationhood and Rapid Development, 1775–1801." *Independence: Historic Resource Study.* Available from http://www.cr.nps. gov/ history/online_books/inde/hrs/hrs.htm.

SUSAN B. IWANISZIW

Burgess, John (11 Mar. 1909–24 Aug. 2003), Episcopal bishop, was born John Melville Burgess in Grand Rapids, Michigan, the second son of Theodore Thomas Burgess, a train porter, and Ethel Inez Beverly, a kindergarten schoolteacher. He attended the public elementary school and Central High School in Grand Rapids, Michigan. In his boyhood he worked as a newsboy, took piano lessons, and was an acolyte at St. Phillip's Episcopal Church. In his teenage years he worked for a construction company, and while attending the University of Michigan he supported himself as a waiter and dishwasher. He graduated with a degree in Sociology in 1930.

Bishop Burgess was one of the first black graduates of the Episcopal Theological School in Cambridge, Massachusetts, where, in 1934, he received his Master of Divinity degree. In 1938 he was called to St. Simon Cyrene Episcopal Church, in Lincoln Heights, Ohio. At an Episcopal Church Conference for Colored Church Workers in 1944 he met his wife, Esther Taylor, and they married the next year in her home parish in 1945 in Fredericton, New Brunswick, Canada. They subsequently had two daughters, Julia and Margaret. Burgess served as chaplain at Howard University from 1946 to 1956. In 1951 he became the first black canon at Washington Cathedral in Washington, D.C., while retaining his position at Howard. He reached other milestones in the Episcopal Diocese of Massachusetts, as when he became archdeacon of Boston and superintendent of the Episcopal City Mission in Boston, assuming both roles in 1956. In 1962, he became the first black Episcopal priest to be popularly elected as suffragan bishop of the Diocese of Massachusetts within the regular order of the Episcopal Church. EDWARD T. DEMBY was the first African American Episcopal bishop, but before Burgess black bishops had been elected to serve only black people or had been elected and appointed to Haiti or Liberia by the House of Bishops. In 1969 Burgess again made history as the first black elected as a diocesan bishop in the Episcopal Church, serving in that capacity from 1970 until his first retirement in 1975. During his tenure in Boston, Burgess was at the forefront of revitalizing urban ministry, confronting racism in public education, supporting efforts toward prison reform, and fighting the restoration of the death penalty. He provided significant leadership as an ecumenical leader in a coordinated effort to maintain peace in the early stages of the rancorous Boston school desegregation crisis. Burgess successfully built bridges between the black and white communities. He played a significant role as the president of the Black Ecumenical Commission, an organization formed by black clergy and laity of predominantly white denominations. Inspired in part by the national effort spearheaded by JAMES FORMAN and the Black Economic Development Committee, the commission secured, in 1971, more than $3 million from their denominations in response to a demand for reparations on the local level. This was one of the few positive responses to the so-called Black Manifesto for Reparations for Slavery.

Bishop Burgess also remained a very popular figure in his diocese, with reforms designed to increase lay participation in the decision-making structure of the church. He also modeled shared leadership with the Right Reverend Ben Arnold, who was elected suffragan bishop of Massachusetts in 1972. Together they reformulated the urban mission strategy of the diocese and pioneered efforts to establish links with community-based social activists. The latter initiative became institutionalized as the Burgess Urban Fund by the Episcopal City Mission, which was created in honor of Burgess's retirement. This grant program was influential in swaying the philanthropic community in Boston to redirect their giving to grassroots organizations committed to economic development, housing, and racial reconciliation.

Bishop Burgess also drew attention to the importance of supporting community-based programs in the other twenty-one cities in the Diocese of Massachusetts. A strong supporter of lay ministry, he expanded the diocesan staff to include competent laymen and laywomen in the areas of Christian education, finance, and children's ministries. He also instituted many reforms in the diocesan structure to increase its efficiency. For example, he restructured the moribund archdeaconry system into a much more representative district system, thereby increasing the size of the Diocesan Council. At the end of his tenure the Diocese of Massachusetts was a much more inclusive diocese.

In 1976 Burgess and his wife moved to New Haven, Connecticut, where he served as bishop in residence and then as interim dean of the Berkeley Divinity School at Yale University. Using New Haven as his base, he continued an active ministry for many years, serving as assistant bishop in several dioceses and as a missionary presence in the Netherlands Antilles (Curaçao). In 1990 he and Esther retired to their summer home in West Tisbury, Massachusetts, on Martha's Vineyard.

These highlights of his career hardly do justice to the breadth and depth of his influence within the national Episcopal Church and the Anglican Communion. While he will be remembered for these achievements, Burgess gained his keen sense of social justice and his zeal to combat racism and violence during his early ministry at St. Phillips and St. Simon Cyrene at the height of the Depression. The brutal tactics used by the automobile industry to disrupt the formation of an integrated United Auto Workers Union and the struggles of the poor families in his congregations in coping with discrimination, the Depression, and the advent of World War II engendered in him the necessary sensitivity to be an effective chaplain at Howard University and a strong advocate for social justice from the pulpit of the National Cathedral in Washington, D.C.

While the bulk of his career was focused on institutional leadership and social policy, Burgess remained a deeply spiritual man. Before his marriage he had taken vows with the Order of the Holy Cross. This deep spiritual well, coupled with his practical experience, made him a powerful preacher and advocate in every cause that he undertook. Even in his retirement he brought those skills to bear in helping stabilize the fledgling black caucus within the Episcopal Church, the Union of Black Episcopalians. As a result of his leadership, both local and national church positions, lay and clerical, have been opened to black Episcopalians across the board.

Burgess also wrote many articles on social justice, urban ministry, and black preaching. In his *Black Gospel/White Church* (1982), he places in context some of the great sermons preached by black clergy during 192 years of black history in the Episcopal Church, melding a sharp critique of racism in the church with a keen social analysis of the role that black Episcopalians have played in the church and in society.

By opening the doors to the highest level of decision making in the Episcopal Church, Burgess paved the way for such African American notables as Bishop John Walker of Washington, D.C.; BARBARA HARRIS, the first woman elected bishop in the Anglican Communion; and some fourteen other black diocesan and suffragan bishops in the Episcopal Church. All of these people and countless others owe much to his courage, foresight, and perseverance. The length of his career is itself a testimony to the strength of his call and the inspirational leadership that he provided for all people of goodwill in the church.

Burgess's career spanned a period of considerable social change in the United States. Clearly, he understood the priorities of economic and social justice and was able to articulate and exemplify practical ways in which the church could be an effective instrument in the struggle for justice on many fronts. His leadership lent credibility and momentum to the ecumenical movement that was attempting to find its way in the mid-twentieth century, and undoubtedly he helped realize the dreams of those early black priests and laypeople whose faithfulness to a church that scorned them laid the foundation for future change. He was much sought after as a mentor to aspiring clergy of all colors and seen as a role model for black clergy and laity who sought careers at higher levels of institutional management in the life of the church. This has left a lasting legacy in the church and the world including over twenty bishops of color and many laypeople in significant management positions at both the national and diocesan levels of the church. And, finally, his ministry became the model for effective leadership for blacks in society and helped encourage the aspirations and contributions of people like Senator EDWARD BROOKE, Justice THURGOOD MARSHALL, and MARGARET BUSH WILSON of the NAACP. These and countless other black Episcopalians looked up to and admired Burgess as a trailblazer for blacks in the Episcopal Church and as a champion of social justice and world peace.

FURTHER READING
Obituaries: *Boston Globe* and *New York Times*, 27 Aug. 2003.

EDWARD W. RODMAN

Burgos, Julia de (17 Feb. 1914–4 Aug. 1953), poet and activist, was born in Carolina, Puerto Rico, the daughter of Francisco Burgos Hans, a member of the National Guard, and Paula García. The family was extremely poor, which may explain the deaths of six of Julia's twelve siblings. Despite their poverty, for Julia, a bright and studious child, the Burgos family found the means for an education. In 1933 she received a teaching degree from the University of Puerto Rico.

It was during Burgos's college years that she became a member of the Nationalist Party, a leftist group that proposed the independence of Puerto Rico gained by guerrilla force. She befriended Pedro Albizu Campos, a Harvard-educated lawyer and president of the party, who on several occasions invited Burgos to join him in addressing crowds during political rallies. Eventually she fully accepted nationalism and became an effective political speaker and activist. During the Spanish civil war she sided with the Republican faction. It has been suggested that her first poems were inspired by that fratricidal war, but none of her work from those years survived.

Burgos's commitment to social causes led to her first job in 1934, when she worked briefly for the Puerto Rico Emergency Relief Administration

(PRERA). That same year she married Ruben Rodriguez Beauchamp, a journalist. In 1935 she served as a teacher in an isolated country town. In 1936 and 1937 Burgos took part in educational radio programs organized by the Department of Education for the Universidad del Aire, but because of her political involvement she was dismissed and marked as a "revolutionary." During this period she wrote several plays for children, and in 1937 she published a collection of poetry titled *Poemas exactos a mí misma* (Poems like Myself). A second collection, *Poemas en veinte surcos* (Poems in Twenty Furrows), followed the next year. These early collections establish her favorite literary motifs: nature and love as sources of the poetic inspiration.

Economic hard times persisted, and the young poet was forced to hand sell her privately printed work to help pay her mother's medical bills. Burgos's efforts to make her poetry known paid off, and in 1939 the Instituto de Literatura Puertorriqueña awarded her a prize for her next poetry collection, *Canción de la verdad sencilla* (A Song of Simple Truth). This collection develops a strong feminist self and includes love poems with a highly erotic discourse. Recognition of her literary talent came fast as she was introduced to important local figures like the poets Luis Palés Matos and Luis Lloréns Torres.

Burgos's marriage ended in divorce in 1937 because of her inability to bear children. Her infertility left a feeling of emptiness that haunted her entire life and shaped her feminist and erotic poetry. In 1939 Burgos met a wealthy Dominican, Dr. Juan Isidoro Jiménez Grullón, who took her as his mistress. She made a short trip to New York City in 1940; there she was well received by the Hispanic intelligentsia but also experienced racial and sexual discrimination by the elitist intellectual community of New York.

In 1940 her lover's career took Burgos to Cuba. During her two-year stay she furthered her college education at the University of Havana. There she met experimental surrealist poets and political activists. She produced another poetry collection, *El mar y tú* (The Sea and You), published posthumously in 1954. Politically Burgos continued her involvement in the cause for Puerto Rican independence by organizing public rallies.

Burgos's personal life was in trouble, however. Her relationship with Grullón was rapidly deteriorating. Reluctant to acknowledge his relationship with a beautiful woman of mixed race and humble upbringing, he refused to get married. In her later poetry there is a clear tendency toward feminism marked by eroticism as a weapon against male chauvinism.

Burgos left Cuba for New York City in 1942. The 1940s marked the beginning of heavy Puerto Rican migration to industrial American cities, as thousands of unemployed laborers tried to escape harsh poverty in Puerto Rico. Burgos hoped to find work as a journalist or a teacher. Instead, she found herself trapped in several odd or low-paying jobs, such as office clerk or saleswoman.

In 1943 Burgos married Armando Marín, and the next year she and her husband moved to Washington, D.C. Back in New York in 1945, she continued writing, and in 1946 she received a prize from the Instituto de Cultura Puertorriqueña. Burgos's continued involvement with the cause for Puerto Rican independence became more painful with the defeat of a nationalist revolt in 1950. Deeply distressed and socially isolated by her inability to become part of American society, Burgos resorted to alcohol to cope with acute depression. In March 1949 she began treatment for alcoholism at Loeb Memorial Home for Convalescents, a process that was to continue in various institutions. During the early months of 1953 she was hospitalized in Goldwater Memorial Hospital, where she produced two poems in English, "Farewell in Welfare Island" and "The Sun in Welfare Island." These poems reflect her loneliness in a foreign land and her inability to cope with feelings of isolation.

Suffering from pneumonia, Burgos collapsed on a New York City street corner and was dead on arrival at Harlem Hospital. Her identity was unknown, and she was buried in Potter's Field, a cemetery for the indigent. A month later relatives identified her from a photograph taken at the morgue, exhumed her body, and buried her in her beloved Puerto Rico.

Burgos has become a major figure of the Hispanic American movement. Along with other women activists, such as the Puerto Rican nationalist Lolita Lebrón, Burgos adds a feminist dimension to the Hispanic cause for social and ethnic equality. Above all her poetry and her feminist voice, challenging traditional sexual taboos, act as a connecting force between Hispanic women and women everywhere fighting for equal rights.

FURTHER READING

De Báez, Yvette Jiménez. *Julia de Burgos: Vida y poesía* (1966).

Marting, Diane E., ed. *Spanish American Women Writers* (1990).

This entry is taken from the *American National Biography* and is published here with the permission of the American Council of Learned Societies.

RAFAEL OCASIO

Burke, Selma Hortense (31 Dec. 1900–29 Aug. 1995), sculptor, art educator, and mentor, was born in Mooreseville, North Carolina, one of eight children of Mary L. Elizabeth Jackson Cofield Burke, a homemaker and a teacher, and Neal Burke, a Methodist minister. Burke's artistic experiences began in childhood, when she played in the pliable soil around her North Carolina home: "I shaped my destiny early with the clay of North Carolina rivers. I loved to make the whitewash for my mother, and was excited at the imprints of the clay and the malleability of the material" (Krantz and Koslow). She was further inspired by the art objects that her father and uncles brought back with them from their travels in Africa, the Caribbean, and Europe. As a chef aboard ships, her father had the chance to both preach and explore in other countries, bringing back artwork. Her uncles were missionaries who traveled extensively, returning with mementos that inspired Burke.

Despite her family's support of her art, Burke pursued a more practical career as well, and she became a registered nurse in 1924. She was briefly married in 1928 to Durant Woodward, who died a year after their wedding. She continued her medical education at the Woman's Medical College in Philadelphia, acquiring a nursing post with a wealthy woman. During the next four years she was introduced to a range of people and experiences. After the death of her patient, she decided to quit nursing and pursue her art career.

She moved to New York in 1935 and became an artist's model and student at Sarah Lawrence College in Bronxville, New York. Though she did not get a degree, she received a Boehler Foundation Fellowship in 1938, with which she was able to spend a year in Europe, studying with the sculptor Aristide Maillol, the painter Henri Matisse, and the ceramist Michael Povolney. Returning to the United States in 1939, she attended Columbia University and taught sculpture at the Harlem Community Art Center, then directed by AUGUSTA SAVAGE, a New York artist. The HCAC was part of the Works Progress Administration started during the Depression to keep Americans working. Savage's

artistic contemporaries included HORACE PIPPIN, William Scott, JACOB ARMSTEAD LAWRENCE, and ROMARE BEARDEN. Burke bravely accepted the challenges of sculpture, a medium with substantial material costs and considered too physically demanding for women to undertake. Inspired by the Modernism of the Harlem Renaissance and the School of Paris, Burke worked with a variety of sculptural mediums and methods, including marble, brass, directly carved wood, and lost-wax, bronze casts.

During the 1930s Burke met the writer CLAUDE MCKAY. They married, divorced, married a second time, and divorced finally in 1940. This same year, she started the Selma Burke School of Sculpture in New York City. Burke continued her studies and graduated from Columbia University with a master's degree in Fine Art in 1941, assisted by a Rosenwald Fellowship. At the beginning of World War II, she briefly worked as a navy truck driver, but an injury forced her to stop.

In 1943 Burke entered a competition to create a portrait of President Franklin Delano Roosevelt and won the Fine Arts Commission prize to sculpt the president in a relief plaque. Upon seeing the finished work, Eleanor Roosevelt reportedly told Burke, "It's very well done, but you've made him too young." Burke's reply was quoted in the *New York Times*: "I've not done it for today, but for tomorrow and tomorrow." The bust was said to have influenced John R. Sinnock, chief engraver at the U.S. mint, in designing the Roosevelt dime, in circulation since 1945.

After the war, Burke maintained a studio in Greenwich Village, producing many stone pieces. In 1949 she married the architect Hermann Kobbe. Together they moved to Bucks County, Pennsylvania. Burke sculpted there for the next six years, until Kobbe died. She maintained this home even when she started the Selma Burke Art Center in Pittsburgh in 1968, and it remained in operation until 1981. During this time, she also worked for the Pennsylvania Council on the Arts, serving under three governors. She taught at Haverford, Livingston, and Swarthmore colleges until the 1970s.

She continued to work on her own sculptures, completing *Mother and Child* in 1968 and *Big Mama* in 1972—works that focused on black culture and a woman's experience. In 1979 President Jimmy Carter presented Burke with the Award for Outstanding Achievement in the Visual Arts, and in 1989 she was awarded an *Essence* magazine award in honor of her achievements in the arts. Retiring from her academic and administrative duties in 1981, Burke worked from her Bucks County studio, producing one of her most well-known works, a brass bust of MARY MCLEOD BETHUNE. She continued to work on her art until her death, leaving unfinished a sculpture of ROSA PARKS. Burke donated her large collection of European and African art, as well as her own work, to Winston-Salem University in North Carolina.

FURTHER READING

Fax, Elton. *Black Artists of the New Generation* (1977).
Gale Research. *Notable Black American Women* (1992).
Hine, Darlene Clark, Elsa Barkley Brown, and Rosalyn Terborg-Penn, eds. *Black Women in America: An Historical Encyclopedia* (1993).
Kranz, Rachel, and Philip J. Koslow. *The Biographical Dictionary of Black Americans* (1999).

ROBIN JONES

Burke, Solomon (21 Mar. 1940–10 Oct. 2010), soul singer, was born in Philadelphia, Pennsylvania, in 1940 (sometimes cited as 1936) to Vince and Josephine Burke. Vince, a Jamaican immigrant, worked as a chicken plucker in a kosher market, while Josephine was an ordained preacher. Burke followed in his mother's footsteps; by age seven he had begun delivering sermons at the church founded by his grandmother, Eleanora A. Moore, and soon became known as the "Wonder Boy Preacher." At twelve Burke was delivering sermons on the radio and leading tent revivals in Maryland, Virginia, and the Carolinas.

In 1955 Burke proposed that his vocal group, the Gospel Cavaliers, enter a talent show at the local Liberty Baptist Church. His bandmates had other plans, however, so Burke went as a solo act. His performance so impressed the wife of a Philadelphia DJ that she helped Burke secure a recording contract with the New York label Apollo. He proceeded to record with Apollo for the next two years, making gospel-influenced records that echoed Roy Hamilton. Burke scored a minor hit in 1956 with "You Can Run (but You Can't Hide)," a song based around the slogan of the former heavyweight champion JOE LOUIS (who received a writer's credit in exchange for some half-hearted promotional efforts). By 1957 Burke had become suspicious that the label was not paying him properly; disillusioned, he left the music business and became a licensed mortician in Philadelphia. Burke was running his own funeral home when a friend convinced him to return to the studio. After recording briefly for Singular, he was signed by Atlantic's Jerry Wexler, who was urgently searching for a flagship artist to replace RAY CHARLES. Atlantic initially tried Burke on a lush, overproduced ballad, but Wexler then made the novel decision to have Burke interpret "Just out of Reach," an otherwise undistinguished country song once recorded by Patsy Cline, among others. Burke had been given "Just out of Reach" because of his versatility, but in the process, he succeeded in staking out the gospel/country hybrid that would become the basis of southern soul. The song also proved commercially successful, reaching the top ten of the R&B charts and cracking the national top thirty in 1961—quite a feat for such an unlikely fusion. Burke himself offered some possibly apocryphal anecdotes about the confusion surrounding his race at the time, including his astounding claim that he was once booked to perform in front of an audience of Klansmen.

From 1961 to 1964 Burke carried Atlantic. His hits included "Cry to Me," his first collaboration with the producer Bert Berns and a favorite of the Rolling Stones during their cover-band days, "Down in the Valley," "Got to Get You off of My Mind," and "The Price," on which Burke perfected the spoken, sermonlike interlude that became a staple of the genre. During this period he crowned himself the "King of Rock 'n' Soul," adding a crown and throne to his already larger-than-life persona and highly theatrical stage show.

Following the murder of SAM COOKE in 1964, Burke and his fellow Atlantic artists OTIS REDDING, WILSON PICKETT, JOE TEX, and Don Covay began discussing a strategy to carry on Cooke's legacy of activism through business independence in the recording industry. The five came up with the concept of a loosely defined collective called the "Soul Clan," an R&B Rat Pack whose name intentionally played off of the name of the forces they sought to counteract. They planned to tour together, advocate for themselves and other artists in the industry, and help out the less fortunate. Unfortunately, this dream remained largely abstract until Redding's 1967 death prompted the Soul Clan to enter the studio, or at least all commit their voices to the same track. The resulting single, "Soul Meeting" and its flip side "That's How It Feels" had little to do with their initial lofty goals and was without Pickett, who backed out.

While Burke's fellow Clansmen had achieved new heights of crossover success, the King himself had not quite managed to change with the times. Compared to the raw emotion of Redding or Pickett, he could sound almost mannered; for all his country influence, it was more Grand Ole Opry than the backwoods funk so vital to the Stax sound. *King Solomon* (1967) and *I Wish I Knew* (1968), his two final Atlantic efforts, however, proved he was capable of updating his sound. In 1969 he cut a memorably impassioned version of Credence Clearwater Revival's "Proud Mary" for Bell. He was then to bounce from label to label throughout the 1970s, flirting with funk and disco as on the oddly named *Back to My Roots* (1976).

In the 1980s the ever-shrewd Burke made a near brilliant career move, deciding to return to his classic sixties crowd and court the soul purists and roots music crowd. He toured regularly and recorded for specialty labels like Rounder, offering his trademark rollicking rock and soul without any concessions to current trends or attempts at toning down its eternally youthful fervor. He may have had a limited audience, but it allowed Burke to bolster his reputation and virtually guaranteed stability.

The new century saw Burke make yet another bold, canny statement with the striking *Don't Give Up on Me* (2002). Teaming up with the rock producer Joe Henry to present himself as a national treasure accessible to all tastes and still relevant, Burke both reinforced his niche appeal and made himself into an American icon. High-profile fans like Brian Wilson, Bob Dylan, Tom Waits, Van Morrison, Elvis Costello, and Nick Lowe all contributed originals to the album, all motivated by their respect for Burke. Henry wisely eschewed replicating Burke's signature sound, instead opting for a spare approach that placed all the attention on Burke's formidable vocal abilities. He followed this album in 2005 with the Don Was–produced *Make Do with What You Got*, a return to his familiar sound with the added perspective of *Don't Give Up on Me*.

Burke had twenty-one children, seventy-five grandchildren, and thirteen great-grandchildren, several of whom were a part of his touring act. He died in Amsterdam in the Netherlands at the age of 70.

FURTHER READING

Guralnik, Peter. *Sweet Soul Music* (1986).

DISCOGRAPHY

Don't Give Up on Me (ANTI-80358).
If You Need Me (Atlantic 8085).
King Solomon (Atlantic 8158).
Soul Alive! (Rounder 611521).

NATHANIEL FRIEDMAN

Burke, Yvonne Brathwaite (5 Oct. 1932–), politician and attorney, was born Perle Yvonne Watson, the only child to James Watson, a janitor, and Lola (maiden name unknown), a real estate broker, in Los Angeles, California. Her parents migrated to Los Angeles in 1921 from Paris, Texas, where her father had been a farmer and her mother worked as a teacher. Difficulties in Texas caused her parents to move west. Upon arrival in California her father took up work as a janitor for Metro Goldwyn Mayer (MGM) Studios and later became a labor organizer. Her mother left her teaching career to become a real estate broker.

Throughout her life Burke was exposed to art, drama, and music, developing a deep appreciation for culture. It was her father's work as a labor organizer, however, that helped to politicize her. James Watson was a charter member of the Building Service Employees International Union (later the Service Employees International Union—one of the largest, most active unions in the country). Burke remembered her father as one who believed in the struggle for workers' rights, a belief and a passion he passed along to his daughter. Burke was just fourteen years old when she marched on her first picket line. Such early involvement in the labor movement would help her to understand labor issues, foster a commitment to workers' rights, and win the support of labor unions in her runs for public office.

Burke developed a passion for public speaking while attending Manual Arts High School (a public high school in Los Angeles), a talent that would be useful to her as both an attorney and a politician. At age seventeen Burke enrolled at the University of California, Berkeley, then transferred in her junior year to the University of California, Los Angeles (UCLA), where she majored in political science. She earned her bachelor's degree from UCLA in 1953. While in college she also worked as a fashion model, often appearing in leading black magazines, including *Ebony*, *Tan*, and *Our World*. As a student at UCLA she attended a party for a nephew of the noted civil rights attorney Loren Miller; while there she was encouraged to think about law as an avenue through which she could push for the rights of African Americans. This early encounter with Miller helped convince Burke to pursue a law degree. She became the first black woman since 1928 to be admitted to the University of Southern California's School of Law, from which she earned her juris doctor in 1956.

Despite graduating in the top one-third of her law school class, no law firm would grant Burke an interview. Committed to her career in law and left with few options, Burke opened her own law office. In 1957 she married Louis Brathwaite, a mathematician. The marriage ended in divorce several years later.

As an attorney Burke practiced real estate law, integrating the realty board in the early 1960s. She also served as a deputy corporation commissioner and hearing officer on the Los Angeles Police Commission during the 1965 Watts Riots. She was then hired as a staff attorney for the McCone Commission, the body charged with investigating the root causes of the unrest. Her work with the commission contributed greatly to her political development.

She became determined to run for public office. Influenced by the leadership of AUGUSTUS "GUS" HAWKINS (the first African American from the West to win a seat in Congress), in 1967 she was elected to the California State Assembly to represent the 63rd Assembly District, and so became the first African American woman in the California state legislature. She served three terms. At the top of her legislative agenda were the issues that particularly challenged African Americans, including education, economic development, and environmental justice. During her time as a member of the state legislature she met her second husband, Dr. William Burke, who went on to found the Los Angeles City Marathon. They married in 1972. In that same year she served as vice chair of the Democratic National Convention—a position that won her national recognition, and from which she launched her bid for the United States Congress. Elected in 1972 she was the first African American woman member of congress from California. Pregnant with her daughter Autumn in 1973, Burke was also the first representative to serve while pregnant. As such she was instrumental in defining federal maternity leave policy.

Burke served in Congress for six years but chose not to seek reelection in 1978. Instead she ran unsuccessfully for the Democratic nomination for attorney general of California. Burke returned to her private legal practice in 1979. In 1992 she reemerged in the political world as a candidate for the Los Angeles County Board of Supervisors. She won her seat as supervisor for the 2nd District. In 1993 she was named chair of the Board of Supervisors, the first African American to hold this post. She was also a chair of the Los Angeles Federal Reserve Bank, was vice chair of the 1984 United States Olympics Organizing Committee, and served on boards of numerous noteworthy organizations and corporations.

FURTHER READING

Gill, LaVerne McCain. *African American Women in Congress: Forming and Transforming History* (1997).

Gray, Pamela Lee. "Yvonne Brathwaite Burke: The Congressional Career of California's First Black Congresswoman, 1972–1978," Ph.D. diss., University of Southern California (1987).

MELINA ABDULLAH

Burks, Mary Fair (c. 1920–21 July 1991), English professor, civil rights activist, and scholar of African American literature, was born Mary Fair and raised in Montgomery, Alabama. Little information is available about her family. Burks bucked the Jim Crow system of segregation even as a child in the 1930s, using whites-only elevators, restrooms, and other facilities in what she later called "my own private guerilla warfare" (Bolden, 241). At age eighteen she earned a bachelor's degree in English Literature from Alabama State College, and a year later earned her master's degree from the University of Michigan. She returned to Montgomery to teach English at the Alabama State Laboratory High School and, later, at Alabama State College. Burks married the principal of Alabama State Laboratory High School, Nathaniel Burks. The couple would have one son, Nathaniel W. Burks Jr.

She became head of the Alabama State College English department, and later earned her doctorate from Columbia University in Education.

In 1949 Burks, with fellow Alabama State College English professor JoAnn Robinson, founded the Women's Political Council (WPC), a grass-roots organization of local professional black women, to address issues of importance to Montgomery's black population, such as voter registration and education programs. "The WPC was formed for the purpose of inspiring Negroes to live above mediocrity, to elevate their thinking, to fight juvenile and adult delinquency, to register and vote, and in general to improve their status as a group. We were 'woman power,' organized to cope with any injustice, no matter what" (Robinson, 23). Burks was the group's first president, and although Robinson took over presidency of the group in 1950 Burks remained involved with the organization. Burks and Robinson made inroads with the

Montgomery mayor's office and the Montgomery City Commission. They informed the commissioners of their goals of getting involved with the city to resolve nuisance issues of special interest to the African American community, and WPC members were invited to attend city meetings that involved minorities. The WPC worked to find solutions to the city's troubles that were in the interest of the black community. The partnership between city officials and the WPC effectively ended in 1955 when the struggle for integration on buses began.

In the segregated South, public buses were open to blacks, but seating was limited to a small area at the back of each vehicle, while whites sat in the front. Even in those instances in which the black section was completely full and the white section entirely empty, no African American rider was allowed to take a white seat. In March 1955 the WPC took issue with the arrest of fifteen-year-old Claudette Colvin for taking a seat in the whites-only section of a bus. Nine months later ROSA PARKS was arrested and fined for the same offense, and her seemingly simple actions launched a movement. The WPC had long considered the notion of a boycott against the Montgomery bus system. There were frequent reports of blacks being mistreated and sometimes beaten by white drivers. The outrage over the Rosa Parks incident fueled their idea. Burks and her group wasted no time in organizing the boycott. Word spread quickly, and ministers of every black church in Montgomery announced the boycott in church on Sunday, so that there was almost complete compliance on the morning of Monday, 5 December 1955. For the next 381 days blacks walked miles to work, church, and school, as well as to shop and socialize. They walked in the sweltering summer heat and the winter cold. As news of the boycott spread, black Montgomery churches received donations from all over the world.

The relatively humble publicly stated goals of the Montgomery bus boycott were for "better seating arrangements" for blacks—which was seen as a difficult enough task—and to get some black drivers behind the wheel. While the full desegregation of public buses seemed an implausible goal, the women of the WPC were bent on achieving it, but knew that saying so publicly would only elevate the tension and violence of the struggle. Desegregation was, however, the ultimate result of the boycott. On 5 June 1956, a three-judge federal court ruled segregation on buses violated the fourteenth amendment

to the Constitution that guarantees equal government treatment of all citizens. Blacks and whites gradually began using the buses again. Men like Dr. MARTIN LUTHER KING JR., EDGAR D. NIXON, Rufus Lewis, and others were credited for the achievements of the boycott, but it was Burks and her group who did the daily work of maintaining and organizing thousands of blacks through a long and difficult protest. Burks was "very vocal and articulate, especially in committee meetings," according to Montgomery Improvement Association secretary Erna Dungee (Burns, 16). Dungee recalled that in the meetings, the women "let the men have the ideas and carry the ball. [The women] were kind of like the power behind the throne."

The boycott represented a triumph for civil rights, but the aftermath proved bitter for Burks and the other organizers. Between 1958 and 1960 news spread that the Alabama State College faculty members who had been supporters of the boycott were under investigation by a special state committee. The first professor investigated was tried in absentia, without a hearing, and was not only terminated from his position at the college but also ordered by state officials to leave the city of Montgomery. As political pressures grew Burks resigned from her position and took a job teaching literature at the University of Maryland, Eastern Shore. She remained a professor there until her retirement in 1986.

FURTHER READING

Burks, Mary Fair. "Trailblazers: Women in the Montgomery Bus Boycott," in *Women in the Civil Rights Movement: Trailblazers and Torchbearers, 1941–1965*, ed. Vicki L. Crawford, Jacqueline Anne Rouse, and Barbara Woods (1990).

Bolden, Tanya. *The Book of African-American Women: 150 Crusaders, Creators, and Uplifters* (1997).

Burns, Stewart. *Daybreak of Freedom: The Montgomery Bus Boycott* (1997).

Levanthal, Willy S. *The Children Coming On … A Retrospective of the Montgomery Bus Boycott* (1998).

Robinson, JoAnn. *The Montgomery Bus Boycott and the Women Who Started It* (1987).

Obituary: Salisbury, Md., *Daily Times*, 25 July 1991.

BRENNA SANCHEZ

Burleigh, Angus Augustus (1848–1939), Civil War veteran, preacher, and teacher, was born free to an English sea captain and an African American mother on a ship sailing on the Atlantic Ocean. When Angus was two years old, his father died, and Angus and his mother were sold into slavery in Virginia, and later taken to Kentucky. He spent a majority of his early years in Virginia and learned how to read prior to the outbreak of the Civil War, an illegal pursuit for slaves. In 1864, now enslaved in Kentucky, at the age of sixteen Burleigh ran away from his master and enlisted in the Union Army at Frankfort, Kentucky. Upon enlisting Burleigh was trained at Camp Nelson in Kentucky, which was one of the largest areas for gathering African American soldiers during the Civil War. Burleigh became a sergeant with Company G 12th United States Colored Troops (U.S.C.T.). Once the Civil War ended Burleigh planned to head north to pursue an education. As he was making the trip he met John Fee, who was passionate about making his college, Berea College in Kentucky, a mixed-race school, so he invited Burleigh to attend there, and Burleigh became the first African American enrolled at that institution. Upon arriving at Berea College, he was already literate and inspired many other African Americans to follow his footsteps to better their lives and economic prospects by getting an education. Determined to get an education, Burleigh had to work in a brickyard to pay his way through school.

In 1869 Burleigh taught for one semester in Garrard County Kentucky, which instilled his passion for education and promoting desegregated schools. He believed that education was the key to African American success in the United States. "The colored man's success in every avocation will depend, not so much at being 'at par' with the white man, but the circumstances force it, and the future demands, that he should be par-excellent to the average white man ... his standard must be higher" (Peck, 452).

While at Berea College, Burleigh had a huge drive to be successful. Many of his colleagues and mentors described him as being driven to succeed and persistent in academic work. After nine years at Berea, he graduated in 1875 as the only black student in his graduating class of four and Berea's first African American graduate. Also in 1875, at age twenty-six, Burleigh married his college love, Louisa, his lifelong wife; they later had three children: Cornelius, Otto, and Olive. They then moved to the North, where Burleigh was ordained as a Methodist Episcopal minister and began preaching and teaching.

As a minister, Burleigh traveled the country holding pastorates in different states including New York, Illinois, Wisconsin, Indiana, Virginia, Iowa, Michigan, and Minnesota. His most important job title was serving as chaplain to the Illinois State Senate. In the *Saint Paul Globe* of St. Paul, Minnesota, 19 October 1896, it is recorded that Burleigh took over St. Mark's Church, one of the largest African American churches, and the people were thrilled and hoping he would lead them into a successful year. By 1910 Burleigh had left the Midwest, moving to the Los Angeles area of California. Even there, he was in demand as a speaker and, according to the newspaper announcements, kept a very busy schedule of engagements even into his seventies. Through his own example, he pursued an education after experiencing slavery and became a respected African American clergyman and speaker. His passion and love for preaching reached many people as they looked to him as a role model of what education can provide for the African American society. His legacy no doubt inspired African Americans after him to pursue education to create a better life for themselves and their families. Before passing away on 24 May 1938, Burleigh lived to be one of Berea College's oldest graduates, for which he was recognized in 1934.

FURTHER READING

Bureau of the Census. Census of the United States: 1910—Population for the State of California. 0601 Sheet number 1 B.

Peck, Elisabeth. *Berea's First Century, 1855–1955* (1955).

Sears, Richard D. *A Utopian Experiment in Kentucky: Integration and Social Equality at Berea, 1866–1904* (1996).

Wilson, Shannon H. *Berea College: An Illustrated History* (2006).

GENEVIEVE SKINNER

Burleigh, Henry Thacker (2 Dec. 1866–12 Sept. 1949), composer and spiritual singer, was born in Erie, Pennsylvania. Little is known about his parentage. When he was a boy, his excellent singing voice made Harry, as he was known, a sought-after performer in churches and synagogues in and around his hometown. In 1892, having decided on a career in music, Burleigh won a scholarship to the National Conservatory of Music in New York City. His matriculation coincided with the arrival of the Czech composer Antonín Dvořák, who taught there for four years. Dvořák, who was intensely interested in indigenous American music, found a valuable resource in the young Burleigh, who sang for him various African American spirituals. From Burleigh, Dvořák first heard "Go Down, Moses," "Roll, Jordan, Roll," "Were You There," "Swing Low," and "Deep River." When Dvořák set an arrangement of Stephen Foster's "Old Folks at Home," he dedicated it to Burleigh.

Buoyed by Dvořák's interest, Burleigh was further encouraged by what he interpreted to be fragments of these spirituals in Dvořák's famous New World Symphony. Some analysts agreed, but others took exception to this interpretation. An aesthetic dispute quickly took on political overtones. "Nothing could be more ridiculous than the attempts that have been made to find anything black … in the glorious soulful melody which opens the symphony," opined one New York critic. "Nothing could be more white. … Only a genius could have written it." While a few figures in the outwardly refined world of concert music had expressed some appreciation of African American traditions, Burleigh saw how readily this attitude could yield to prejudices that were ultimately no different from the racism he had encountered throughout his life. Burleigh never forgot the lesson. Indeed, when his own compositions first came before New York critics in the late 1890s, the composer encountered the same perverse efforts to reduce art to racial categories. One critic, admitting Burleigh's quality, proclaimed that "in his excellent songs [Burleigh was] more white than black."

Despite the sincere appreciation he received from such a luminary as Dvořák, Burleigh was wary of the white-dominated music world because of its bigotry and its tendency to place music into racial categories. He was also uncomfortable with the growing popularity of minstrelsy and jazz in the early twentieth century, for he feared that African American musical traditions could too easily be caricatured and mocked. Minstrel songs, he declared, "are gay and attractive. They have a certain rhythm, but they are not really music. The mistake [in capitalizing on their appeal] was partly the fault of the Negroes, partly the result of economic pressure."

Burleigh would never compromise his art, as he was sensitive to how easily it could be miscast and distorted. At the same time, though, he never abandoned the ideal that the cultural store he could bring forth in his singing and songwriting had a universality and hence a potential to transcend identities and labels. The spiritual, he felt, provided "the accent that is needed, a warm personal feeling which goes directly to the heart of the people." It had meaning as an articulation not only of African American culture but of the general human experience, particularly of the great human yearnings for freedom and universality, illustrated by what Burleigh believed to be the two most profound stories in scripture—those of Moses and of the Resurrection. To Burleigh, the spirituals embodied these profound sentiments. Dvořák's response to them revealed how they could resonate in the soul of another musically sensitive person who was as yet unacquainted with any component of American culture. During World War I Burleigh found this point further underscored when a song he wrote called "The Young Warrior" became a popular marching tune among troops in the Italian army.

While working as a notator and editor in a New York publishing house, Burleigh continued to compose, almost exclusively as a songwriter, and throughout his life he sang. He became a celebrated performer of spirituals in several New York churches and compiled and published the first full anthology of African American religious music. He died in New York City in relative obscurity, but his music has been posthumously rediscovered and appreciated.

FURTHER READING
Simpson, Anne K. *Hard Trials: The Life and Music of Henry T. Burleigh* (1990).
Southern, Eileen. *The Music of Black Americans: A History* (1971).
This entry is taken from the *American National Biography* and is published here with the permission of the American Council of Learned Societies.

ALAN LEVY

Burley, Dan (7 Nov. 1907–30 Oct. 1962), journalist and jazz musician, was born Daniel Gardner Burley in Lexington, Kentucky, the son of James Burley, a former slave and Baptist minister, and Anna Seymour Burley, an educator who served under BOOKER T. WASHINGTON at the Tuskegee Institute. His father died when he was five years old, and in 1917 his mother, then remarried, moved the family to Chicago. Accounts differ as to whether Burley graduated from Wendell Phillips High School, but he attended, and his experience there cultivated a talent for writing, and his extracurricular activity taught him the jazz piano.

Burley began writing for the *Chicago Defender* between 1925 and 1928, according to some accounts while he was still attending high school. After leaving the weekly newspaper, Burley traveled the country, making his living through odd jobs and piano playing before returning to write for the *Chicago Bee* in 1932. He acted as sports and theater editor and columnist for the *Bee*, while simultaneously working as a correspondent for the Associated Negro Press, but a contractual dispute in 1937 convinced him to move to New York. At the *New York Amsterdam News*, Burley edited the city, sports, and theater pages. He was also a columnist for the *Amsterdam News* and the *New York Age*, and his growing renown allowed him to meet and marry Gustava McCurdy, a concert singer and the first black woman to sing the "Star-Spangled Banner" in Madison Square Garden.

His "Back Door Stuff," a social gossip column in the *Amsterdam News*, often featured jive writing, developing a style imitative of the inner-city speech Burley heard in Chicago and Harlem. In 1945 he published *Dan Burley's Original Handbook of Harlem Jive*, a dual representation and linguistic analysis of that speech, including short stories, poems, and translations of classical and Shakespearean literature into jive. He located the origins of jive in early 1920s Chicago, and used the created language to emphasize the social and economic plight of those in the inner city. The *Handbook*'s combination of cultural critique and language manipulation drew the admiration of a wide range of readers, from ELIJAH MUHAMMED to H. L. Mencken to LANGSTON HUGHES.

After completing the *Handbook*, Burley began a relatively brief period of jazz recording, a sound he referred to as "skiffle." He had used the term since childhood, describing an upbeat, tinkling piano style popular in party scenes of Chicago and Harlem. After recording with LIONEL HAMPTON in 1946, Dan's Circle Session produced an album featuring songs such as "South Side Shake" and "Lake Front Blues." A later session for Arkay Records produced "Chicken Shack Shuffle" and "Skiffle Blues."

Prior to the end of World War II, he traveled with a performing group to India and Burma, appearing as master of ceremonies in shows for black troops. Burley's obsession with music led him to disc jockey for New York radio stations WLIB and WWRL during his time with the *Amsterdam News* and *Age*. He also appeared in the DIZZY GILLESPIE film *Jivin' in Be-Bop* and acted as master of ceremonies for many of the variety shows at Harlem's Apollo Theater. He created the annual *Amsterdam News* midnight benefit at the theater, known as the Welfare Fund Program.

Burley's sports writing for the papers was far more intense and direct than was his experimentation with jive. His accounts often lauded the athletes who impressed him, but his pen turned critical at perceived injustices. Burley argued vehemently for baseball's integration throughout the early 1940s and used sports as an example of the need for desegregation in all facets of American life. During the war, he criticized the boxer Joe Louis for fighting for the segregated U.S. Navy and denounced the 1942 detention of Joe DiMaggio's Italian immigrant father. After baseball integrated in 1947, Burley vigorously denounced the racist epithets hurled at JACKIE ROBINSON, LARRY DOBY, and others. Burley's sports writing led him to become the first African American member of the New York Boxing Writers Association.

In 1951 Burley returned to Chicago to serve as associate editor of the Johnson Publishing Company's *Jet* and *Ebony* magazines. A spinoff from the popular *Ebony*, *Jet* appeared the same year Burley arrived in Chicago, and he is sometimes credited with the idea for the popular entertainment periodical. He stayed at the Johnson publications until 1957 then briefly acted as the managing editor for the *Chicago Crusader*. After his return to Chicago, Burley's financial situation became more and more tenuous. He never again earned the salary he received in New York. In the last years of his life, Burley worked for the *Defender* again and created his own weekly paper, the *Owl*, along with freelancing for a variety of white mainstream publications.

Gustava McCurdy died before Burley left New York, and upon his return, he met and married his second wife, Gladys, the manager of a Chicago school bus company, who entered the marriage with two children from a previous marriage. In 1952 Dan Burley's only child, D'Anne, was born. Declining salaries and a growing family prompted him to write a sequel to his *Handbook*, *Diggeth Thou?*, in 1959. He self-published the book and even sold the manuscript on the streets of Chicago.

The toll of editing and writing had given Burley a heart attack in the late 1950s, and doctors and friends encouraged him to lighten his workload. He ignored the advice, and not long after died of a second heart attack.

The text of *Diggeth Thou?* demonstrates that though the circulation did not match that of the *Handbook*, Burley was still able to enunciate the jive language that made his name. In pieces like "Diggeth Thou? (Mose on the Lam from Egypt, Alabam)," he also demonstrated his concern with the necessity of civil rights in all facets of American life. Fewer were listening, but the message remained strong and competent. Each entry had an almost musical rhythm. Whether Burley was engaged in music or sports, his use of those disciplines as vehicles for social commentary was constant.

FURTHER READING

Burley, Dan. *Dan Burley's Original Handbook of Harlem Jive* (1944).

Burley, Dan. *Diggeth Thou?* (1959).

Frank, Stanley. "Now I Stash Me Down to Nod," *Esquire* 21 (June 1944).

Nowakowski, Konrad. "Dan Burley—His Career as a Pianist and Writer," in *South Side Shake: 1945–1951*, by Dan Burley. Compact Disc, Wolf Records. WBJ 008 CD.

Reisler, Jim. "Dan Burley: The Most Versatile Black Journalist of His Generation," in *Black Writers/ Black Baseball: An Anthology of Articles from Black Sportswriters Who Covered the Negro Leagues* (1994).

Obituaries: *Jet*, 8 Nov. 1962; *New York Amsterdam News*, 3 Nov. 1962.

THOMAS AIELLO

Burnett, Calvin Waller (18 July 1921–12 Oct. 2007), painter and printmaker, was born in Cambridge, Massachusetts, to Nathan Burnett Sr., a physician and surgeon, and Adelaide Waller, a homemaker. Though his parents, especially his father, hoped he would pursue a medical or legal career, Burnett instead evinced an interest in art, one perhaps originating with his parents' own. Calvin appreciated his father's drawings and a painting of an apple done by his mother that was displayed at their home.

As a young boy Burnett routinely copied Mickey Mouse and other characters from the comics in the Sunday paper with such skill that his parents reserved a small section of the kitchen counter for his use. They also took him to area museums, where he was particularly impressed with Greek sculpture and engaged in prolonged discussions with both parents about the objects on view. He was further encouraged by visits to his grandparents' home, where some of his cartoon drawings were displayed on the walls.

During his junior year at Cambridge High and Latin School, he took art classes at a nearby Works Project Administration (WPA) program, where he learned to paint in oils. In 1939 he received a scholarship to study watercolor techniques at an adult education center across town.

Burnett entered the Massachusetts College of Art in 1938 to study drawing, painting, printmaking, and design under faculty who impressed him with their unorthodox instructional styles, in contrast to the otherwise highly traditional curricula. Graduating in 1942 he received a BFA in Painting, just a few weeks before his father's death. Vision problems prevented Burnett from being drafted into the military, yet he was involved in the wartime effort. He went directly from art school to work in the area's navy yards, preferring manual labor to a job as a draftsman or in the commercial art trade because he believed it would compromise his fine arts training. Moving between Charlestown and South Boston for the duration of the war, he continued to produce art in his free time, often getting ideas from themes and scenes around the shipyards and making drawings of servicemen he observed at hospitals and the USO (United Service Organizations) center near Dudley Station in Boston. The dedicated Modernist and former teacher Lawrence Kupferman was instrumental in facilitating two important exhibitions for Burnett at the Institute of Modern Art in 1943 and 1944 from this and an earlier body of work. At the conclusion of the war in 1945, Burnett was released from the shipyards at the end of August and within a few weeks enrolled in evening classes at the School of the Museum of Fine Arts Boston. During the day he worked at a number of part-time and freelance jobs, including sign painter, illustrator, and silkscreen artist.

At the Boris Mirski Gallery in Boston in 1946, he had his first solo exhibition, comprising oil paintings and drawings created while he worked at the shipyards. The art critic Frederick White featured his work in an *ARTnews* article that included a reproduction of one of his pieces. Another show that year, this one featuring early drawings from his sketchbook, was mounted at Harvard's Germanic Museum, later renamed the Busch-Reisinger Museum, arranged through his long association with the Cambridge Art Association, a professional organization in which he held membership for a number of years.

The year 1947 was one of tremendous acclaim and activity for Burnett. He was selected by Massachusetts College of Art president Gordon Reynolds to represent the institution in an exhibition highlighting the artistic achievement of a single recent graduate from six art schools organized by Bartlett Hayes at the Addison Gallery of Art in Andover, Massachusetts. More of his earlier work, including a few watercolors, oil paintings, and drawings with social protest themes, were shown at the Barnett-Aden Gallery in Washington, D.C. He successfully submitted to the Atlanta University Annual Art Competition and Exhibition for the first of many such accomplishments over the next twenty years, winning numerous purchase prize awards.

Burnett returned to the Massachusetts College of Art in 1949, still interested in Modernist concepts and taking painting and printmaking classes, though he graduated in 1951 with the B.S. in Art Education. While enrolled in a watercolor class with the Abstractionist Arthur Corsini, he met classmate and future wife Torrey Milligan. Burnett taught briefly, in 1949–1950, in the Boston public schools before returning to commercial work. In fall 1951 he became the first art teacher at Boston's Elma Lewis School of Fine Art, a unique institution founded for black youth in 1950 by the arts advocate and leader Elma Ina Lewis and structured around a teaching program that emphasized character-building and multidisciplinary arts instruction incorporating performance and exhibitions. When Lewis founded, in 1968, the National Center of Afro-American Artists (later the Museum of the National Center of Afro American Arts) in Roxbury, Massachusetts, Burnett continued his involvement, as an artist member, in her work. He then taught at the DeCordova Museum, and took a part-time position teaching required art courses for Concord Academy, including evening adult classes as well as Saturday student sessions as needed. In 1954 he ran the museum's summer art camp in Haystack Mountain, Deer Isle, Maine, where he taught printmaking. He left DeCordova in 1956 to become a professor at the Massachusetts College of Art, a position he would hold until his retirement in 1986.

During the 1950s Burnett participated in two shows at the Institute of Contemporary Art in Boston. He began studying painting again at Boston University in 1957 with Reed Kay, a distinguished teacher of painting techniques, and Lithuanian-born David Aronson, an acclaimed sculptor and Expressionist painter who founded the fine art department at the university. Still employed at the Massachusetts College of Art, Burnett had his second solo exhibition at the Massachusetts Institute of Technology in Cambridge. The next year he had a third one-artist show at Marlboro College in Vermont. He won second prize in the twenty-fifth anniversary National Fine Print Competition in 1959 for a woodcut of Milligan, receiving the largest amount of money given at that point for a relief print. He was awarded an additional $1,000 to produce an edition of the image. In 1960 he completed his MFA, and he and Milligan were married. They had one daughter, Elizabeth Tobey Burnett, born 31 October 1962.

Burnett began doctoral work at Boston University in 1961, completing the necessary coursework in 1970. In 1962 he published his first portfolio of prints, titled *Maidenhood*. The following year, a second group of prints, *Six Serigraphs*, was produced, and in 1964 Impressions Graphic Workshop in Boston published his *Portents and Omens*. In 1963 he cofounded the Boston Negro Artists Association. Still teaching at the art college while matriculating at the university, he also had solo shows at Lowell State College in 1965, West Virginia State College in 1966, and Framingham State College in 1970. His instructional book on drawing and perspective, titled *Objective Drawing Techniques*, was released in 1966, and he was later promoted to head the printmaking department. In 1970 the Brooklyn Museum showed a major Burnett piece, an untitled four-panel mixed media painting inspired by work for his MFA, depicting from left to right a female figure dancing, an angel reminiscent of Giotto (in a broader commentary on religion), a self portrait, and slogans related to women's rights. The piece resulted from a decade of work. He went on to have retrospectives at the Massachusetts College of Art in 1982 and the National Center of Afro American Artists in 1995, with exhibitions at Pennsylvania State University and Studio Museum in Harlem. In 1986 Burnett became professor emeritus at the Massachusetts College of Art.

Over the course of his career Burnett won six purchase prize awards at Atlanta University Annuals, in 1953, 1955, 1960, 1963, 1966, and 1968. He received additional awards from Boston Printmakers in 1959, 1962, and 1964; the Cambridge Art Association in 1946, 1949, and 1961; the New England Print Competition in Marion, Massachusetts, and in Connecticut in 1960; the Jordan Marsh New England Artist Annual Purchase Prize in 1967; the

Cambridge Centennial Exhibition; the Wharton Settlement; and the Busch-Reisinger Museum. At one time a board director of the Boston Printmakers Association, he also held memberships with the Institute of Contemporary Art in Boston and the National Conference of Artists. Burnett died in Massachusetts in 2005.

FURTHER READING

Driskell, David. *Two Centuries of Black American Art* (1976).

Schomburg Center for Research in Black Culture, and Thomas Riggs. *St. James Guide to Black Artists* (1997).

Smithsonian Archives of American Art. Oral History Interview with Calvin Burnett. Available at http://www.aaa.si.edu/oralhist/burnet80.htm/.

Obituary: *Boston Globe,* 12 Oct. 2007.

AMALIA K. AMAKI

Burnett, Carol E. (11 Mar. 1935–), pediatrician and pioneer in medical studies for African Americans, was born in New York City, the second daughter of Lionel and Hilda Burnett, who immigrated to the United States from Barbados in the 1920s. Her father obtained a position in the post office, and her mother was a seamstress. Her parents valued education for their children, so they moved from Manhattan to the Bronx, seeking neighborhoods that had the best schools for their girls. Carol was very bookish and spent much of her time in the public library. Because of her good academic record—she skipped a grade in elementary school—she was accepted into Hunter High School, a selective high school for girls. She was only one of four black girls in a class of thirty; this was the only time she had been in a predominantly white school, but her classmates all accepted her without discrimination.

When she graduated she went on to attend Hunter College, at the time the only women's college run by the City of New York. Hunter was a tuition-free school for New York City residents who met the high educational requirements. Although Burnett had an excellent academic record, many tuition scholarships were not available to African American students in 1952. Burnett's love of science was nurtured at Hunter, and she enrolled in the chemistry field major, which combined a chemistry-intensive major and a math/science minor. She was also inspired by Paul DeKruif's *Microbe Hunters,* where DeKruif dramatizes the pioneering bacteriological

work of such scientists as Leeuwenhoek, Spallanzani, Koch, Pasteur, Reed, and Ehrlich, and by her paternal uncle, who was a physician in Barbados. She met another mentor in her junior year at Hunter, the associate physics professor Gertrude Buggein Wertenbacher. Dr. Wertenbacher inspired Burnett to consider medicine as a career and suggested she apply to one of the historically black southern medical schools, which were the few medical schools that accepted black students. Burnett did not want to leave New York City because she was afraid of the racism in the South. Dr. Wertenbacher suggested she apply to all the medical schools in New York, and she offered to pay the application fee. Fortunately for Burnett, the Albert Einstein College of Medicine was opening and accepted its first class of medical students in 1955.

When Burnett graduated from Hunter College in 1956, cum laude and Pi Beta Kappa, with a B.S. in Chemistry, she applied to the Albert Einstein College of Medicine and was accepted as a member of its second class. She was also accepted at the State University of New York Downstate Medical School, but she felt the climate at Albert Einstein Medical School was warmer toward her as a black student. She turned down a full-tuition scholarship, saying that she needed to pay her way—a decision she later regretted because she had to work her way through medical school in faculty members' laboratories as a laboratory technician. But because the medical school was in the Bronx where she lived, she was able to commute to school and do most of her studying in her medical school lab. She received her M.D. degree in 1960, becoming the first African American to graduate from the Albert Einstein College of Medicine and a member of the second graduating class. She interned at Mount Zion Hospital in San Francisco and began her pediatric residency at Los Angeles Children's Hospital. There she encountered racism from staff and patients, so she returned to the Bronx to finish her residency at Lincoln Hospital, which was affiliated with the Albert Einstein College of Medicine. She became board certified in pediatrics in 1970.

Her career began with the health department in Staten Island. Then she obtained a position in pediatrics at Elmhurst Hospital in Queens. Later when Elmhurst Hospital was acquired by Mount Sinai Hospital, she entered academic medicine by becoming the assistant dean for admissions and student affairs at Mount Sinai School of Medicine. As a member of the admissions committee, she sought to diversify the entering class of medical students. In addition she had a pediatric practice at Jewish Child Care. In 2000 she retired from active medical practice but remained on the admission committee until her health caused her to retire completely. She never married, choosing rather to focus on her career.

FURTHER READING

Goldstone, Stephen E. "Carol Burnett: A Class Act, Einstein Alumna Remembers Her Debut," in *E=MD2, The Magazine for the Alumni of Albert Einstein College of Medicine Alumni Magazine* (Summer 2003).

                    JEANNETTE ELIZABETH BROWN

Burnett, Charles (13 Apr. 1944–), writer, director, producer, was born in Vicksburg, Mississippi. His parents' names are unknown, but his father is believed to have been in military service at the time, while his mother worked as a nurse's aide. At the age of three, his family moved to the Watts section of Los Angeles, seeking jobs in California's postwar economy. Unfortunately, the end of World War II also meant the end of well-paid wartime jobs, and the Burnetts struggled to find work. Soon after the move, his parents parted, leaving Burnett to be raised by his grandmother.

Burnett's teenage years from 1957 to 1963 overlapped with the civil rights era, which by the early 1970s had profoundly transformed the United States. In Watts and other inner-city ghettos, the struggle to overturn *de jure* segregation and discrimination promised to address the institutional racism that cut off Watts from the prosperity and progress evident elsewhere. The reality fell far short of that dream, and expanding opportunities for the black middle class meant that those who could afford to move out of Watts did, leaving, in Burnett's words, "a big vacuum in the community" (Reynaud, 326). Railroaded through an educational system that encouraged high dropout rates, Burnett graduated from high school and enrolled in college in 1964 to avoid the draft.

A year after Burnett entered Los Angeles Community College (LACC), Watts became a national symbol for poverty and black defiance. In August 1965 a police stop sparked the six-day Watts riot, involving forty thousand people and sixteen thousand members of the National Guard and local police. When the smoke cleared, thirty-four people had been killed, over one thousand had been injured, and four thousand had been arrested. The Watts riot resonated strongly with Burnett and the general

public because it demonstrated that racial inequality went well beyond the reach of civil rights legislative reform. In the years that followed, hundreds of riots broke out across the country, and in 1968 voters responded by electing President Richard Nixon and his "law and order" platform, ushering in a rightward move in U.S. politics and culture. While at LACC, Burnett majored in electronics, but he found himself drawn to creative writing and filmmaking so he matriculated in the fall of 1968 at the University of California, Los Angeles (UCLA), which was internationally known for its film program. He received a B.A. in 1971 and a MFA in 1973.

Burnett's arrival at UCLA coincided with the arrival of a number of other black students. In 1969 students and assistant professor Eliseo Taylor established the Ethnocommunications Program, an affirmative action program that brought the first group of nonwhite film students to UCLA and recruited people who later became well-known filmmakers. Together, future filmmakers like Burnett, Haile Gerima, Larry Clark, Alile Sharon Larkin, Billie Woodberry, Masilela Ntongela, and others formed a loose filmmaking collaborative later known as the L.A. Rebellion. Comprised of Africans and African Americans, the group aimed to represent black people in ways absent from both mainstream Hollywood film and the blaxploitation genre, which during its heyday (1969–1974) was dominated by crime and action plots. Between 1970 and 1982 members crewed on each other's films, organized study groups, lectures, and exhibits, and brought filmmakers from Cuba and elsewhere to campus, making UCLA a hub of African diasporic activity. The group facilitated Burnett's desire to make films about Watts and the complexities of the black working class.

While at UCLA, Burnett directed two short films *Several Friends* (1969) and *The Horse* (1973) before embarking upon his masterpiece, *Killer of Sheep*, his MFA thesis project completed in 1973 but not released until 1977. This drama starred people from Watts and Burnett's friends and family instead of professional actors, juxtaposing scenes in the life of Stan, a slaughterhouse worker, and neighborhood children who find adventure and joy despite their grim environment. The film reflected the influence of famed British documentarian Basil Wright, with whom Burnett studied at UCLA. Burnett has also cited James Agee and Walker Evans's *Let Us Now Praise Famous Men* (1939) as an important model. A collection of photographs, reportage, and stream-of-consciousness writing, the book depicted the lives of three white sharecropping families in rural Alabama. "The whole idea," Burnett once said, "is to observe something without manipulating it. At the same time, you're trying to find this area to hang on to and tell a story, while trying to keep that distance" (Kim, xx). *Killer of Sheep* won awards at the Houston and Berlin film festivals and in 1991 was one of the first films to be included in the Library of Congress's National Film Registry. Sometime during the 1970s Burnett married the actor, producer, and costume designer Gaye Shannon-Burnett, with whom he subsequently had two sons.

Burnett followed up *Killer of Sheep* with the comedy *My Brother's Wedding* (1983), which was financed by British and German television. In 1988 Burnett won a coveted John D. and Catherine T. MacArthur "genius grant," a five-year, $500,000 award given to a select few for their exceptional creativity and likely future success. In the 1980s and 1990s he also won grants from the Guggenheim Foundation, the Rockefeller Foundation, the National Endowment for the Arts, and the J. P. Getty Foundation. The MacArthur "genius grant" enabled Burnett to finance and direct *To Sleep with Anger* (1990), his first feature-length film with professional actors, such as DANNY GLOVER and Mary Alice. The film wove together southern folklore and contemporary L.A. life in its story of generational and cultural conflict. *To Sleep with Anger* ushered in a period of incredible productivity for Burnett, with the director releasing several film and television projects in the 1990s and 2000s, including *The Glass Shield* (1994); *Nightjohn* (1996); *The Wedding* (1998); *Selma, Lord Selma* (1999); *Finding Buck McHenry* (2000); *Nat Turner: A Troublesome Property* (2003); and "Warming by the Devil's Fire" (2003), an episode in director Martin Scorsese's PBS series on the blues. A consistent theme of each of these projects is Burnett's interest in history and memory, black creativity and resilience, and southern folk culture's impact on urban life.

FURTHER READING

Kim, Nelson. "A Conversation with Charles Burnett," *Senses of Cinema* (March 2003). Available at http://www.sensesofcinema.com/contents/directors/03/burnett.html.

MacDonald, Scott. *A Critical Cinema 3: Interviews with Independent Filmmakers* (1998)

Massood, Paula J. "'An Aesthetic Appropriate to Conditions': *Killer of Sheep*, (Neo)Realism, and the Documentary Impulse," *Wide Angle* (Oct. 1999).

Reynaud, Berenice. "An Interview with Charles Burnett," *Black American Literature Forum* (1991).

Young, Cynthia. *Soul Power: Culture, Radicalism and the Making of a U.S. Third World Left* (2006)

CYNTHIA A. YOUNG

Burns, Anthony (31 May 1834–27 July 1862), fugitive slave, born in Stafford County, Virginia, was the youngest of thirteen children. His mother, whose name is not recorded, served as cook for John and Catherine Suttle of Stafford Court House. His father, third husband of Anthony's mother and another of the Suttle slaves, quarried sandstone for the construction of federal buildings in Washington, D.C. Financial reversals following the death of John Suttle impelled Catherine to move the family to Aquia Creek and to sell off a number of slaves, including five of Anthony's siblings. When Catherine died, her son Charles Francis Suttle, by then a dry-goods merchant in Falmouth, mortgaged the remaining slaves and began hiring them out. For two years, 1847–1848, Anthony worked for William Brent, a Falmouth grocer and close friend of Suttle's. In 1849, refusing a third year with Brent (and threatening to escape unless his refusal was honored), he was hired by Ariel Foote to assist in the construction of his house at Hartwood; however, during the work Burns's right hand was badly mangled in an accident with a steam-powered saw with the result that ever afterward nearly an inch of bone stuck through the skin of his wrist. The following year Burns was engaged in Falmouth by a man who turned out not to have enough work for him, so his services were sublet to a local wholesale merchant. In 1851 he was hired to a Fredericksburg tavernkeeper, and the next year, in the same town, to an apothecary. When in 1853 Suttle required that Burns work for Brent's brother-in-law in Richmond, the slave again refused and found employment for himself in a Richmond flour mill where one of his own brothers worked. Since Suttle was now living in Alexandria, the supervision of Burns fell to Brent as Suttle's agent, and it was Brent who in 1854 placed Burns with Charles Millspaugh, a Richmond druggist.

Burns's escape was unwittingly facilitated when Millspaugh hit upon the plan of having Anthony find his own work as a day laborer, turning over his wages at stipulated intervals. Working at the docks Burns soon found a sympathetic northern sailor who agreed to help him stow away. Some time in February, after a long, cold, and cramped voyage, Burns arrived in Boston, found work and joined the Twelfth Baptist Church, which was led by the Reverend Leonard Grimes. Incautiously, Burns wrote a letter to a brother in Virginia, which, though sent through Canada to disguise its origin, contained information that betrayed his whereabouts. Suttle, learning of this, traveled to Boston with his friend Brent to claim Burns under the 1850 Fugitive Slave Law.

On the evening of 24 May 1854 Burns was arrested by the U.S. marshall Watson Freeman and Deputy Asa Butman on a warrant issued by the Fugitive Slave Law commissioner Edward G. Loring and jailed at the Massachusetts Court House in one of several rooms rented by the federal government. When word of the arrest leaked out, the Boston Vigilance Committee, a biracial group of local activists committed to the defense of fugitive slaves, swung into action. At the hearing before Commissioner Loring on the morning of 25 May, Richard Henry Dana appeared as lead counsel for the defense, advised by two other prominent committee members, the Boston minister Theodore Parker and the antislavery orator Wendell Phillips. Reverend Grimes set out to raise funds to purchase Burns's freedom, while the Committee, nearly two hundred strong, gathered to plan its strategy. The first decision was to call a public protest meeting at Faneuil Hall for Friday night, the 26th, while various schemes were discussed to liberate Burns by force.

Between four and five thousand people attended the Faneuil Hall meeting, at which the principal speakers were Parker and Phillips. Indignation ran especially high because the Burns case exactly coincided with the adoption of the Kansas-Nebraska Act, which repealed the Missouri Compromise of 1820 and opened the western territories to slavery. Suggestions from the podium that Burns ought to be forcibly removed from custody prepared the audience to act when the startling announcement was made that a group of mostly black Bostonians was even then mounting an assault on the court house. In the ensuing riot, led by the radical abolitionist and Unitarian minister Thomas Wentworth Higginson of Worcester, one of the marshall's guards, James Batchelder, was killed. The effort to free Burns was repulsed. Leonard Grimes succeeded in raising the $1,200 asking price, but Suttle, under political pressure, now refused to sell before the hearing concluded and Burns was returned to Virginia. Despite the serious legal objections that Dana was able to raise and the alibi witnesses he presented over the next several days, Burns was finally remanded to slavery by the commissioner's decision on 2 June. On that day, with Boston under martial law, an overwhelming military escort conducted Burns from the court house down State Street to the docks before an outraged crowd estimated at fifty thousand.

This most important and publicized fugitive slave case helped to precipitate a radical change in northern attitudes, generated support for the free-state movement in Kansas, and was especially influential among the Massachusetts abolitionists who would support John Brown over the next five years. The political repercussions of the case were profound. That fall Whig and Democratic incumbents were ousted by Know-Nothing candidates who, in 1855, passed a Personal Liberty Law that made slave recapture all but impossible. No fugitives were thereafter returned from New England. The case was the immediate occasion for Henry David Thoreau's 1854 lecture "Slavery in Massachusetts" and Ralph Waldo Emerson's 1855 lecture on "American Slavery." It elicited important poems from Walt Whitman and John Greenleaf Whittier.

Back in Virginia, Burns was incarcerated in a Richmond slave pen for four months before being sold to a North Carolina planter for $905. News of Burns's altered situation having reached his friends in Boston, Leonard Grimes managed to renew the pledges of the previous year and to make arrangements for the purchase of the slave's freedom. Released to Grimes in Baltimore, Burns revisited Boston and went on to attend Oberlin College on a donated scholarship. There and at Fairmont Theological Seminary in Cincinnati he prepared for the ministry. A brief pastorate in Indianapolis preceded his move to the fugitive slave community at St. Catherines, Ontario, where he presided over Zion Baptist Church and where he died of tuberculosis at the age of twenty-eight.

FURTHER READING

The Boston Slave Riot, and Trial of Anthony Burns, Containing the Report of the Faneuil Hall Meeting; the Murder of Batchelder; Theodore Parker's Lesson for the Day; Speeches of Counsel on Both Sides, Corrected by Themselves; Verbatim Report of Judge Loring's Decision; and, a Detailed Account of the Embarkation (1854).

Stevens, Charles Emery. *Anthony Burns: A History* (1856).

von Frank, Albert J. *The Trials of Anthony Burns: Freedom and Slavery in Emerson's Boston* (1998).

ALBERT J. VON FRANK

Burns, Ursula M. (20 Sept. 1958–), CEO and entrepreneur, was born in the Baruch housing project on the Lower East Side of Manhattan, New York, and raised by a single mother who took in ironing and ran a daycare center to make ends meet. Education was important to the family, and her mother set money aside money to send Burns and her two siblings to Catholic school, from which she graduated in 1976. She matriculated to the Polytechnic Institute of New York, taking a Bachelor's of Science degree in Engineering in 1980. The following year, she went on to take a master's in Mechanical Engineering from Columbia University. Between degrees, she worked as an intern at the Xerox Corporation (which, in part, funded her tuition) and was subsequently offered a job by that company.

Burns's initial work at Xerox centered mainly around product development, where she made a name for herself as a member and leader of various project teams. During her first decade with the company, she held a number of such assignments and played a variety of roles before coming to the attention of one of Xerox's chief executives, Wayland Hicks, during a number of thoughtful confrontations over the corporation's diversity hiring standards. In early 1990 Hicks offered her a job as his executive assistant. Burns was, at first, reluctant. She misunderstood the importance of the position, believing it to be secretarial in nature and without the possibility of advancement. Eventually, however, she accepted and found that the position of executive assistant was a major lift to her career. In 1998 she married Lloyd Bean, a fellow Xerox employee. The couple would go on to have two children. In 1991 she openly (if tactfully) challenged Xerox's CEO Paul Allaire during a monthly managerial meeting, again over the issue of the company's hiring practices. When Allaire later called her into his office, Burns believed that she would be fired, or at least reprimanded. Instead, she was offered a position as Allaire's executive assistant.

Having served with Allaire, Burns returned to project development work, and in 1999 she was named corporate vice president for global manufacturing. A year later however, seeing the corporation engaged in various kinds of trouble—including falling under the scrutiny of the Securities and Exchange Commission (SEC)—Burns decided it was time to leave Xerox. She'd come to the attention of various other companies and had a number of job offers. She was convinced

Ursula Burns, Xerox CEO, answers a question at a 2010 symposium on energy reinvestment at the Newseum in Washington, D.C. (AP Images.)

to stay, however, and in 2000 was named senior vice president of strategic services. By this time Anne Mulcahy had taken over Allaire's role as CEO and the challenge of saving Xerox from ruin. She named Burns the president of Xerox's Business Group Operations, which took an important role in turning the company around and was responsible for bringing in an enormous part of Xerox's profits. The move was enough to get her noticed by *Fortune Magazine*, which in 2006 named her one of its "50 Most Powerful Women." In 2007 Burns was named the president of Xerox, then still under Mulcahy, and was elected to its board of directors. Two years later, in July 2009, Burns took over Mulcahy's spot as CEO. She did not realize to what extent her rise at the company had been watched outside the business community. When word of her promotion made the news, she began receiving phone calls from well-wishing strangers, including the basketball legend MAGIC JOHNSON and the political and community leader JESSE JACKSON.

As CEO of Xerox, Burns has faced a number of challenges: continuing the financial rehabilitation of the company, limiting the outsourcing of Xerox jobs oversees, and riding out the worst national economic crisis in many decades. She has led efforts to increase the environmental sustainability of Xerox and to build the array of services that the company offers its clients.

Among her many roles and activities outside Xerox, President BARACK OBAMA in 2009 named Burns to shepherd the White House program on science, technology, engineering, and math (STEM). A year later, President Obama asked her to act as vice chair on the President's Export Council, a committee tasked with communicating the needs and views of the larger business community to the White House. She was appointed to the boards of directors of American Express, For Inspiration and Recognition of Science and Technology (FIRST), and Columbia University's National Center on Addiction and Substance Abuse, among numerous others, and has served as an advisor to the U.S. Olympic Committee. In 2009 *Forbes Magazine* ranked Burns as the 14th Most Powerful Woman in the World, ahead of First Lady MICHELLE OBAMA (40th), media mogul OPRAH WINFREY (41st), U.S. Secretary of State Hilary Clinton (36th), and Britain's Queen Elizabeth II (42nd).

FURTHER READING

Bryant, Adam. "Xerox's New Chief Tries to Redefine Its Culture." *New York Times*, 20 Feb. 2010.

Byrnes, Nanette, and Roger Crockett. "An Historic Succession at Xerox." *Business Week*, 8 June 2009.

JASON PHILIP MILLER

Burnside, R. L. (23 Nov. 1926–1 Sept. 2005), blues musician, was born Robert Lee Burnside in Harmontown, Lafayette County, Mississippi, and lived most of his life near Holly Springs, Mississippi. As a teenager, he worked as a sharecropper on several Mississippi Delta cotton plantations. During those years he learned to play the guitar from his neighbor, the legendary blues performer MISSISSIPPI FRED McDOWELL, having been inspired to play after hearing the song "Boogie Chillen" by his fellow Mississippian JOHN LEE HOOKER. Burnside later played with McDowell on Saturday nights at juke joints and house parties in the area.

In the late 1940s Burnside moved to Chicago, joining a wave of Mississippi migrants who had been displaced by the mechanization of cotton picking and moved in search of wartime manufacturing jobs. There he worked in a foundry and lived with family members who had also made the journey north. Burnside's time in the northern metropolis was brief and painful. Though he met his future wife Alice Mae and began performing with MUDDY WATERS, his father, brother, and uncle were all murdered while he was there, an experience he later reflected on in the songs "Hard Time Killing Floor" and "R. L.'s Story."

In 1959 he moved back to Mississippi and resumed work on a plantation. Sometime shortly after moving back, Burnside shot a man who attempted to run him out of his home. He spent six months in prison, released after a white plantation foreman in need of his labor during cotton-picking season convinced the judge to release him. Burnside said of the murder: "It was between him and the Lord, him dyin'. I just shot him in the head" (*New Yorker*, 4 Feb. 2002).

In the late 1960s Burnside attracted the attention of the folklorist George Mitchell, who recorded him for the Arhoolie label in 1967. During these years he also recorded songs on the Vogue, Swingmaster, and Highwater labels, but supported himself and his family through farming and commercial fishing. Through the 1970s and 1980s Burnside's band the Sound Machine (with his sons Joseph and Daniel Burnside, and his son-in-law Calvin Jackson) were a staple at rural Mississippi juke joints and house parties, and his recordings earned him invitations to perform at festivals and tours in the United States and Europe. Until the early 1990s, though, Burnside was little known outside rural Mississippi (one of the few places in the United States where the blues still thrived and continued to produce talented, young artists), and among a small circle of middle-aged, mostly white blues aficionados.

Burnside began to acquire wider notoriety after being featured in the documentary *Deep Blues* (1991), a film accompaniment to the acclaimed book by Robert Palmer. The book and the film are largely credited with introducing to a broad audience the blues not as a historical artifact but as a living tradition. In 1992 the Fat Possum recording label, which specialized in releasing material of relatively unknown rural blues artists and in rejuvenating dormant recording careers such as Burnside's, released the live album *Bad Luck City*. In 1994 Palmer produced Burnside's first full-length album, *Too Bad Jim*, which earned critical praise. Two years later Burnside recorded *A Ass Pocket of Whiskey* with the Jon Spencer Blues Explosion for the indie rock label Matador Records. Critics, already suspicious of Spencer for his supposed satirization of the blues in his own recordings, panned the album, and purists derided it as a mutilation of Burnside's style. Yet Burnside said he enjoyed his recording sessions with Spencer and relished his sudden fame among the growing number of young blues fans. And he certainly did not shun the financial windfall. Having lived most of his life in dire poverty, Burnside, by the late 1990s, annually earned more than one hundred thousand dollars through record sales and tours. Despite his success, Burnside remained close to his Mississippi roots. He continued to perform with his extended family and the noted blues artist Junior Kimbrough at Kimbrough's juke joint in Chulahoma, Mississippi. Junior's Place, also immortalized in the film *Deep Blues*, became a favorite haunt for blues devotees, who traversed Mississippi's desolate back roads for a chance to hear these living legends ply their craft.

Burnside's later years were marked by more commercial success and personal loss. In 1998 his dear friend and collaborator Kimbrough passed away following a stroke. That same year Fat Possum released *Come On In*. On it, two noted rock and rap producers injected samples and looping techniques into Burnside's driving blues. One of the album's tracks, "It's Bad You Know," garnered modest radio airplay and was featured in the HBO television series *The Sopranos*. In 2000 Junior's Place burned to the ground and was not rebuilt, robbing Burnside, his extended family, and the surrounding community of their main performing and gathering space. In 2001 Burnside suffered a heart attack and ceased performing. He died in Memphis, Tennessee, on 1 September 2005.

Burnside's recordings for Fat Possum only hint at the power of his performances. His droning, single-chord progressions stretched out sometimes more than thirty minutes, with an oft-repeated line punctuated by falsetto affectations. His jam sessions at Junior's Place often induced a hypnotic trance in his listeners in a manner comparable to the musical traditions of West Africa. Burnside's music captured the hardscrabble lives, deep-rooted cultural traditions, and resilient spirit of his fellow rural black Mississippians. His rhythmic style bore the marks of the fife and drum band tradition. His songs spoke of work life, Saturday night tangos with "white lightning" and women, domestic disputes, and violent encounters along darkened roads. His

narrated toasts and use of characters was reminiscent of the work songs sung on sharecropping plantations. It was this sense of authenticity, this notion that Burnside embodied the experiences of rural black southerners and their culture that proved so appealing to the predominantly middle-class, white audience who fueled his latter-day commercial success.

FURTHER READING

McInerney, Jay. "'White Man at the Door': One Man's Mission to Record the 'Dirty Blues'—before Everyone Dies," *New Yorker* (4 Feb. 2002).

Obituary: "R. L. Burnside, 78, Master of Raw Mississippi Blues," *New York Times*, 2 Sept. 2005.

DISCOGRAPHY

Burnside on Burnside [Live] (Fat Possum).
Sound Machine Groove (HMG).
Too Bad Jim (Fat Possum).

ANDREW W. KAHRL

Burrell, Berkeley Graham (12 June 1919–30 Aug. 1979), business executive and civic leader, was born in Washington, D.C., the son of Hayward G. Burrell and Fannie Miles. Although his parents' occupations are unknown, both his father and his mother were natives of the District of Columbia, and Burrell's roots in the area ran deep. After graduating from Dunbar High School at the age of fifteen, he worked as a driver for a local pharmacy and apparently also drove a cab for a while. He married at age sixteen (his wife's name is unknown), and the marriage produced a son before ending in divorce seven years later.

In 1941 Burrell gained a position at the federal Bureau of Standards, where he worked in the glass section producing prisms and bombsights. He also attended nearby Howard University between 1941 and 1943 but did not graduate. He entered the U.S. Army in 1945 and rose to the rank of first sergeant before receiving his discharge from active duty in 1946. Determined to go into business for himself, he returned to his hometown and with a hundred dollars in capital opened a dry cleaning store. Having chosen his first location wisely, he was soon able to open three additional stores, only to struggle to meet payments when the other locations proved less successful. Burrell's early struggles to achieve success in business shaped his later views on minority-owned businesses. He also took an interest in local civil rights activities, becoming a member of both the Urban League and the National Association for the Advancement of Colored People (NAACP).

By 1951 Burrell's resources were sufficient enough for him to consider expansion, and with thirty thousand dollars in borrowed funds he purchased a large dry cleaning facility that came with nineteen retail outlets. Although he was soon recalled to active duty in the army with the advent of the Korean War, he managed to maintain the business with the help of a new partner, A. Parthenia "Pat" Robinson, the daughter of a North Carolina barber. Burrell married her in 1951; the marriage produced no children, but it provided Burrell with a strong partner in all of his business affairs.

As Burrell's Superb Cleaners continued to grow, Burrell sought to communicate his hard-earned business experience to other African American entrepreneurs. Long active in the National Business League (NBL)—an organization founded by BOOKER T. WASHINGTON in 1900 with the goal of empowering African American businessmen—Burrell became the organization's president in 1962. By this time a prominent figure in local business circles (he served on three occasions as president of the District of Columbia's Chamber of Commerce), Burrell admired the philosophy of the NBL's founder and deplored the NBL's then-moribund condition. Possessing a "burning desire to rebuild it," according to his oral history, he initially ran the organization's affairs out of the back of his own office. He succeeded in his goal; by 1970 the organization had grown from thirteen chapters to seventy-six, with a staff of sixteen (from none when Burrell took over) and more than ten thousand members nationwide. Ironically, this revitalization occurred at a time when Washington's reputation was coming under increasing criticism from the younger, more militant members of the growing civil rights movement, many of whom viewed him as an Uncle Tom.

Much of the growth enjoyed by the NBL was thanks to Burrell's success in involving the federal government in its operations. He sought funding for minority businessmen as early as 1963 from the Small Business Administration (SBA), and in 1967 he achieved his greatest success with Project Outreach, a program funded by the Department of Commerce and meant to promote African American businesses in selected cities. By 1972 NBL-sponsored projects in sixteen cities were receiving one million dollars annually, and although overall results proved disappointing—owing in large part to the inexperience of some program beneficiaries—Burrell retained both his guarded optimism and his pragmatism. Anticipating that large-scale federal promotion of minority business startups might be a thing of the past, he shifted the NBL's focus in the later years of his presidency toward assisting existing business.

Although honored for his work—he received the SBA's Small Businessman of the Year Award in 1965 and was listed as one of *Ebony* magazine's "100 Most Influential Blacks in America" during the 1970s—Burrell often felt frustrated by what he saw as a lack of understanding of basic business principles and practices on the part of many African Americans. In an effort to educate African Americans about the business achievements of their predecessors, he coauthored with John Seder *Getting It Together: Black Businessmen in America* (1971), which contained inspiring success stories. During the 1970s he also wrote a nationally syndicated column, "Down to Business," which ran in several African American newspapers. A longtime Republican, he advised several presidents on business matters and was particularly close to Richard Nixon, serving as vice president on his Advisory Council for Minority Enterprises.

In addition to his dry cleaning enterprise, Burrell also operated the Merchant Prince Corporation, which produced African American greeting cards. He lectured on business topics at a number of universities, including Morgan State, Vanderbilt, Fisk, and Howard, and he served as a board member of the Joint Council on Economic Education and the Corporation for Blacks in Public Broadcasting. Burrell was also a longtime civic booster of his hometown, serving on its Citizens Traffic Board, the D.C. Apprenticeship Council, and the Police Chief's Advisory Committee on Community Relations; he was also a senior warden of Saint Mary's Episcopal Church. Burrell died in Washington after having a heart attack at a church meeting.

FURTHER READING

Though there is no known collection of Burrell's papers, he was the subject of a 1970 oral history interview held as part of the Ralph J. Bunche Oral History Collection at the Moorland-Spingarn Research Center at Howard University, Washington, D.C.

Obituaries: *Washington Post*, 31 Aug. 1979; *New York Times*, 2 Sept. 1979; *New York Amsterdam News*, 8 Sept. 1979.

This entry is taken from the *American National Biography* and is published here with the permission of the American Council of Learned Societies.

EDWARD L. LACH JR.

Burrell, Kenny (31 July 1931–), Grammy Award–winning guitarist, composer, and jazz educator, was born Kenneth Earl Burrell in Detroit, Michigan, during the Depression to parents about whom little information is available. It is known that he was the youngest of three sons, and that his family enjoyed music as part of their daily lives. His mother played piano and sang in the choir at Second Baptist Church, Detroit's oldest black congregation. Burrell's father played banjo and ukulele, which may account for Burrell's and his brother's mastery of stringed instruments.

Because there was a piano in the home, it became the first instrument Burrell played as a child. He performed once before an audience in a school auditorium. Listening to saxophonists like LESTER YOUNG and COLEMAN HAWKINS, saxophone was his first love, but his family could not afford to buy him one. Burrell began playing guitar and, at age twelve, settled for the inexpensive instrument—strings and a bit of wood—because his family could afford it. He learned guitar technique by watching his older brother Billy play guitar at small clubs around Detroit and by listening to records by DUKE ELLINGTON, COUNT BASIE, Benny Goodman, and the Mills Brothers that his older brothers brought home.

By 1946, when Burrell was fifteen, Billy had switched to electric bass and played with the Willie Anderson Trio at Club Sudan. Influenced by his brother's electric bass and CHARLIE CHRISTIAN's electric guitar on Benny Goodman, LIONEL HAMPTON, and Harry James records in the early 1940s, Burrell liked the ability to solo due to the volume control that amplification gave the formerly acoustic instruments. Following Billy to gigs, Burrell began sitting in with professional musicians at Club Sudan and other nightspots.

At Wayne State University, Burrell studied theory and composition, took private jazz and classical guitar lessons, and spent evenings in clubs listening to saxophonist CHARLIE PARKER and trumpeters MILES DAVIS and DIZZY GILLESPIE. Burrell's style in his first group with Tommy Flanagan and MILT JACKSON's brother Alvin was inspired by the NAT KING COLE Trio but changed as Kenny became interested in hard bop. In 1951, at age nineteen and still in college, Burrell played with hard-bop trumpeter Dizzy Gillespie and made his debut recording with Gillespie, bassist Percy Heath, vibraphonist Milt Jackson, and alto saxophonist JOHN COLTRANE. Gillespie wanted Burrell to go on tour but Burrell wanted to finish school.

After earning a bachelor of arts in Music in 1955 Burrell went on a six-month tour with OSCAR PETERSON. Moving to New York in 1956 he performed in clubs, in Broadway pit bands, and on stage or in the studio with such artists as Benny Goodman, JAMES BROWN, BILLIE HOLIDAY, LENA HORNE, Tony Bennett, Nat King Cole, GENE AMMONS, Stan Getz, YUSEF LATEEF, Coleman Hawkins, and Jimmy Smith.

In 1956 he recorded *Introducing Kenny Burrell, All Night Long and All Day Long* with trumpeter Donald Byrd, a fellow Detroit native and Wayne State University graduate. This session was followed by sessions with John Coltrane, PAUL CHAMBERS, and Kenny Clark. In 1957 he recorded under the name "Kenny Burrell and His Four Sharps" for JVB. In 1960 Burrell signed with Columbia Records and released *Weaver of Dreams*, featuring Burrell's vocals and guitar, but the record did not attract much attention. In 1961 Burrell recorded four instrumental sessions that ended up staying on the shelf until nine of the tracks were released in 1983 on the LP *Bluesin' Around*. Complete sessions were released in 2002 by Euphoria as part of *Moten Swing*, its jazz guitar reissues. In 1963 he recorded *Midnight Blue* and in 1964 began a series of orchestral recordings, *Guitar Forms*, for Verve, which included a tribute to Benny Goodman and Charlie Christian, *A Generation Ago Today*.

Burrell moved to California in 1971 and recorded *'Round Midnight* and *Stormy Monday* for the Fantasy record label. In 1975 he recorded *Ellington Is Forever*, a tribute to the great composer and bandleader. In the mid-1970s he led jazz workshops at the University of California, Los Angeles (UCLA), and in 1978 taught "Ellingtonia," the first university course on Duke Ellington. Known as Ellington's favorite guitarist, although he never played with him, Burrell played banjo on *Hot and Bothered* by Ellington's son Mercer in 1984. In 1985 and 1986 Burrell toured with the Phillip Morris Superband. In 1996 Burrell accepted the position of director of the UCLA jazz studies program.

Beginning as a hard bopper, Burrell released more than ninety-six recordings, was a featured guitarist on more than two hundred, including sessions with ART BLAKEY, HERBIE HANCOCK, and QUINCY JONES, and played on hundreds more as sideman. His compositions have been recorded by artists such as Ray Brown, Jimmy Smith, GROVER WASHINGTON JR., John Coltrane, June Christy, Frank Wes, and Stevie Ray Vaughn. As his career continued his style achieved a mellow richness. In 1997 he wrote and recorded a composition that the Boys Choir of Harlem premiered at Lincoln Center. In 1998 a DEE DEE BRIDGEWATER performance of his composition "Dear Ella" won a Grammy Award for Best Vocal Performance. He continued his prolific recording career into the 2000s, releasing *Lucky So and So* in 2001 and *Blue Muse* in 2003. He received the 2004 Down Beat Jazz Educator of the Year Award and was named a Jazz Master by the National Endowment for the Arts in 2005.

FURTHER READING

Boyd, Herb. *Detroit Jazz Who's Who* (1984).
Gallert, Jim, and Bjorn Lars. *Before Motown: A History of Jazz in Detroit, 1920–60* (2002).
Gillespie, Dizzy, with Al Fraser. *Dizzy: To Be or Not to Bop: The Autobiography of Dizzy Gillespie* (1982).
Jové, Josep Ramon. *Vidas de jazz: Joe Newman, Clark Terry, Jeff Jerolamon, Kenny Burrell, Herb Ellis, Hank Jones, Jimmy Cobb, George Cables, Stéphane Grappelli, Randy Weston, ... Danilo Pérez, Antonio Hart (Serie música)* (1995).

SUNNY NASH

Burrell, William Patrick (25 Nov. 1865–18 Mar. 1952), civic and organization leader, was born in Richmond, Virginia, to William P. Burrell, a butler and hotel waiter, and Mildred Burrell, a washerwoman. His parents had been slaves, most likely in Richmond, and his uncle James B. Burrell was prominent among African American entrepreneurs in the early years after Emancipation. Burrell was one of fourteen children, but his intelligence and energy made him stand out.

Reportedly Burrell was selling ice water to thirsty Richmonders at the age of five, and he soon became his mother's assistant, gathering and returning the clothes she washed. Burrell experienced conversion in 1877 and formally joined the Moore Street Baptist Church, having served the church's Sunday school as librarian and secretary from the age of nine. He was successively elected church clerk, janitor, deacon, treasurer, and trustee. Elected assistant secretary of the Richmond Baptist Sunday School Union at eleven, he became its secretary, chaplain, and longtime president. In that role Burrell delivered a protest in April 1904 against the local transit company's decision to segregate street cars, which helped to inspire a lengthy, albeit unsuccessful, black boycott of the Jim Crow cars.

In January 1881, when he was fifteen, Burrell was presented to William Washington Browne, who wanted to hire a secretary. Browne had come to Richmond from Alabama, where in 1874 he had chartered the United Order of True Reformers, a racially separate offshoot of the Grand Lodge of Good Templars, a white temperance society. Browne was a Methodist and pastor of the Leigh Street Methodist Episcopal Church until his congregation asked him to choose between the church and the True Reformers. He was a successful organizer of local chapters, including a branch in Richmond, but his ambitions went beyond operating a financially strapped temperance society, technically subordinate to racist whites. He envisioned the order as the basis for an African American insurance and business enterprise. When Richmond members of the faltering local fountains, or chapters, of the True Reformers called Browne, he saw the opportunity to institute his plan.

Browne's plan at first required that each member of the True Reformers purchase for $1.50 a death-benefit certificate that would pay a fixed sum to the member's heirs. Neither continued expansion of the membership nor reductions in the promised death benefit could make this scheme workable, and in 1885 the True Reformers, with fifty-one fountains, abandoned the onetime assessment for a system of fees based on the ages of members and prospective members. As it took on the outlines of a life-insurance company, the True Reformers also remained a fraternal order, with local fountains subordinate to the Grand Fountain, where Browne, the Grand Worthy Master, was in charge.

At his right hand was William Patrick Burrell, who was elected the order's Grand Worthy Secretary in 1884, the year he graduated with honors from the Richmond Normal and High School. He was an advocate for the adoption in 1885 of the actuarial system based on members' ages for the death benefit. That year he and Browne thoroughly revised the ritual and constitution of the True Reformers to fit better the focus on the insurance feature. That year also, on Burrell's recommendation, the order opened its first business office in Richmond.

William P. Burrell was hired to teach in the Richmond public schools in 1885 and taught until 1889, at which time the True Reformers boasted 254 chapters and 6,500 members. On 24 December 1885 Burrell married Mary E. Cary, a native of Richmond and a school teacher. They had four children, and, of them, two sons lived to adulthood.

The insurance system proved profitable, and the True Reformers began purchasing real estate in Richmond and other cities as the order spread.

On 3 April 1889 the Savings Bank of the Grand Fountain United Order of True Reformers opened in Richmond, the first chartered bank in the United States owned by African Americans. Mary Burrell served as the bank's first clerk. In 1891 the order dedicated a new hall that housed the bank, business offices, and meeting rooms. It was the largest building in Richmond owned by blacks, and the order continued to expand, adding a hotel, a weekly newspaper, general merchandise stores in several Virginia cities, and a home for aged members west of Richmond.

As the True Reformers became the largest black-owned fraternal society and business in the nation, the Burrells became community and state leaders. He was president of the Richmond Baptist Sunday School Union, and she helped found the Women's Baptist Missionary and Educational Association of Virginia and served as secretary of the Virginia State Federation of Colored Women's Clubs. Both were among the leaders who founded the Richmond Hospital in 1902, and in 1909 he organized Richmond's branch of the Virginia Colored Anti-Tuberculosis League.

Burrell's most important concern was to improve business practices for black-owned insurance companies, many of them inspired by the True Reformers. In 1901 Governor James Hoge Tyler named him one of the state curators for Hampton Normal and Agricultural Institute, and he served through 1912. Burrell was a strong supporter of the annual Hampton Negro Conference and addressed it several times on business topics. His call at the 1904 conference for insurance companies operated by African Americans to cooperate in scientific compilation of actuarial tables inspired the formation of the Federated Insurance League, a business association of which he became the first president. With D. E. Johnson Sr., Burrell wrote the celebratory *Twenty-Five Years History of the Grand Foundation of the United Order of True Reformers, 1881–1905* (1909).

Meanwhile the True Reformers headed toward disaster. Despite boasting some sixty thousand members and real estate valued at nearly $400,000, the order had borrowed heavily from the Reformers' Savings Bank to finance its properties and its unprofitable retail stores. In early 1910 the board of directors closed the stores, vainly hoping that the action might improve the order's finances. By October, with $50,000 in death benefits unpaid, the state sent a bank examiner to scrutinize the books. He told Burrell on 21 October that the bank

was insolvent. Burrell was stunned. The board of directors met and closed the bank on 26 October. That night the bank's cashier disappeared, as did the $50,000 he had embezzled.

Burrell promised to give his all to make matters right, but as the receivers worked through the bank's chaotic books it gradually became clear that the depositors had lost everything. The order's real estate was overvalued and heavily mortgaged to the now defunct bank. The bank's largest debtor was the order itself, with the also defunct Reformers Mercantile and Industrial Association alone owing nearly $300,000, a sum greater than the bank's deposits.

Following Browne's death in 1897, Burrell became the figure most closely associated with the True Reformers, although his province was the insurance feature, and he apparently had little clout with his fellow directors. He declared his innocence and maintained that he had unsuccessfully protested the board's failed ventures, but the audience at one public meeting refused to hear him when he rose to speak. The Sunday school union denied him reelection as its president.

Burrell and the five other directors were finally indicted in August 1911 on twenty counts, including that they permitted an insolvent bank to continue to receive deposits. Two weeks later Burrell resigned as Grand Worthy Secretary. He was the first tried, in late April 1912. The jury deadlocked, and the judge dismissed the case, but he was indicted and tried again on 28 May 1912. That jury acquitted him, and the prosecutor then dropped charges against the others. The outcome produced widespread dissatisfaction, as was reported by the *Richmond Planet*.

The Burrells departed for Brooklyn, New York, where Burrell sold insurance. They had moved to New Jersey by 1914, when Burrell was one of the organizers of BOOKER T. WASHINGTON's tour of the state. In 1915 Burrell helped to organize the Federation of Colored Organizations of New Jersey, which he and his wife both served as officers. Mary Burrell also became a leader of the Federation of Colored Women's Clubs of New Jersey, and the family was active in the Republican Party. Burrell served terms as a doorkeeper and a file clerk for the state legislature, and his younger son, John Mercer Burrell, an attorney, represented Essex County in the legislature from 1933 to 1936.

William Patrick Burrell became a social worker during the 1930s, and in 1942, at the age of seventy-seven, was ordained a Baptist minister. Although apparently never the pastor of his own church, Burrell taught a school for ministers at a church in Newark, New Jersey. He died in a hospital in that city.

FURTHER READING

Burrell, W. P., and D. E. Johnson Sr. *Twenty-Five Years History of the Grand Fountain of the United Order of True Reformers, 1881–1905* (1909).

Fahey, David M. *The Black Lodge in White America: 'True Reformer' Browne and His Economic Strategy* (1994).

"William Patrick Burrell," *Dictionary of Virginia Biography* (2001).

JOHN T. KNEEBONE

Burrill, Mary P. (Mamie Burrill) (c. 1884–1946), playwright, teacher, and activist, was born in Washington, D.C., the daughter of Clara and John Burrill. She attended the M Street School, originally named the Preparatory High School for Colored Youth, and there developed an interest in literature and theatrics. Upon graduating high school in 1901, she moved with her family to Boston, where she enrolled at Emerson College and became one of the first African Americans to graduate from the school in 1904.

In 1905 Burrill moved back to Washington, D.C., and began a career in teaching that would last almost forty years. She alternated between Armstrong Technical High School and her alma mater, renamed Dunbar High School after the African American poet PAUL LAURENCE DUNBAR. Burrill taught English and drama, eventually accepting a permanent position at Dunbar, one of the leading schools for African Americans in the Washington, D.C., area in the early twentieth century. The majority of her students were underprivileged teens from working-class families. Through her lessons on theatrical performance and interpretative reading, Burrill stressed the importance of speech and diction. Her dedication to drama and teaching inspired many of her students, some of whom went on to become prominent figures in theater. WILLIS RICHARDSON, for example, became the first black dramatist on Broadway with his 1923 play *The Chip Woman's Fortune.*

While teaching at Dunbar, Burrill also served as director of the School of Expression, a division of the Washington, D.C., Conservatory of Music, from 1907 to 1911. In that post she instructed students on elocution, public speaking, and dramatics. She also gained prominence as an eloquent orator. Beginning in the 1920s, Burrill narrated the Christmas production of *The Other Wise Men* with the Howard University Choir for a period of fifteen years. One of her closest companions during this time was LUCY DIGGS SLOWE, Howard University's first dean of women, with whom she shared a house.

In the early 1910s Burrill began to write plays, although only two are known to have survived. She published her first play, *Aftermath*, in 1919. The one-act play centers on the return of an African American soldier to South Carolina after World War I. When his family informs him that his father was lynched, his sadness turns to anger and frustration as he cannot comprehend how he can serve and defend a country still tarnished by racism. The play proceeded the period of escalated racial violence known as the "Red Summer." Numerous race riots occurred throughout the United States in cities such as Washington, D.C., Chicago, Charleston, Knoxville, and Omaha. As the lynchings escalated, a number of women campaigned to end the racial violence, which was directed primarily at African American men. Female playwrights used the theater to dramatize the injustices of lynching, and *Aftermath* represents one of the first such attempts by female playwrights to openly discuss and criticize racial violence. Burrill weaves together aspects of social protest and folk drama to bring the issues of lynching and racism to the forefront of her piece.

The play appeared in the April 1919 issue of the socialist Max Eastman's left-wing periodical *Liberator*. The only known production of the piece occurred on 7 May 1928 during the sixth annual David Belasco Little Theatre tournament at the Frolic Theatre in New York City. Produced by the Kigwa Players and Workers' Drama League, the play received negative reviews after the production company altered the ending without Burrill's consent, something the playwright considered "a serious artistic blunder" (Perkins, 79). It is believed that the white producers revised the original ending, which they deemed too controversial.

They That Sit in Darkness was Burrill's second play. The piece chronicles the life of a young black woman forced to abandon her aspirations of attending college after the death of her mother. Among its concerns the play criticizes the denial of contraceptives and birth control education to the African American community. The political significance of this play led to its publication in a special September 1919 edition of the *Birth Control*

Review, "The Negroes' Need for Birth Control as Seen by Themselves." Burrill joined numerous other authors at the time, including Djuna Barnes and F. Scott Fitzgerald, who employed their fiction to call attention to the birth control movement.

In 1929 Burrill returned to Emerson. She received a bachelor's degree in Literary Interpretation in 1930. That same year she received Emerson's Best Junior Play Award for her piece *Unto the Third and Fourth Generations*, a reworking of *They That Sit in Darkness*. The school's yearbook published the work that same year.

Burrill's maintained friendships with several prominent literary figures, among them ANGELINA WELD GRIMKÉ, GEORGIA DOUGLAS JOHNSON, and ALICE DUNBAR-NELSON. Burrill retired from teaching in 1944 and moved to New York City. Through her plays the pioneering Burrill sought to confront issues of great importance to African Americans. After she died she was buried in Woodlawn Cemetery in Washington, D.C.

FURTHER READING

Beal, Suzanne Elaine. "'Mama Teach Me French': Mothers and Daughters in Twentieth Century Plays by American Women Playwrights," Ph.D. diss., University of Maryland, College Park (1994).

Cole, Carole L. "The Search for Power: Drama by American Women, 1909–1929," Ph.D. diss., Purdue University (1991).

Perkins, Kathy A., and Judith L. Stephens. *Strange Fruit: Plays on Lynching by American Women* (1998).

Young, Patricia Alzatia. "Female Pioneers in Afro-American Drama: Angelina Weld Grimké, Georgia Douglas Johnson, Alice Dunbar-Nelson and Mary Powell Burrill," Ph.D. diss., Bowling Green State University (1986).

FRANK CHA

Burris, Roland (3 Aug. 1937–), politician and the first African American statewide elected office-holder in Illinois, was born in Centralia, Illinois, the son of Earl, a worker with the Illinois Central Railroad, and Emma Burris. His family also ran a store to supplement his father's railroad wages. Because both of his parents were busy during the day, when Burris was four years old he would often accompany his older siblings to school, where he would sit on the platform outside the door, listening to the class being conducted inside.

While he attended Centralia Township High School, he was active in sports, becoming an All-State defensive safety in football, in spite of being only five feet six inches inches tall. He also became increasingly aware of racial discrimination in his community during high school, and at sixteen he helped to integrate the Centralia public pool. When the city unofficially designated the pool for whites only, his father determined that this situation was unacceptable and arranged for a lawyer to meet them at the pool gates. Although the lawyer did not show up, young Burris's Memorial Day dive proved a powerful symbolic message that the municipal pool was for all Centralia's residents, regardless of race. Sufficiently embarrassed, the city fathers, those who used their power to emphasize that African Americans were unwelcome at the pool, never filed a formal declaration. That experience left him with a burning determination to become a lawyer and attain public office, so that he would have the power to make changes on a much larger scale than he could affect as a private person.

Burris attended Southern Illinois University at Carbondale, where he and his Alpha Phi Alpha fraternity brothers documented racial discrimination on the part of local merchants. Their work spurred the university to mandate reforms in racial policy, such as policies that encouraged African Americans to enroll, various programs to help them succeed, and pressure on discriminatory merchants to treat African American customers with the same respect they gave white ones. Burris obtained his B.A. in Political Science in 1959 and subsequently spent a year as an exchange student in Hamburg, Germany, before pursuing a law degree at Howard University, where he was senior class president. While at Howard, he met and married Berlean Miller, with whom he had two children, Roland II and Rolanda. He obtained his law degree in 1963 and spent the next year working for the U.S. Treasury Department as a bank examiner, an officer who reviews bank operations, including lending policies, guidelines, and practices, in Chicago.

Burris was the first African American to examine banks and faced significant hurdles in having his authority recognized. After finishing his training as a bank examiner, he arrived at the Livestock National Bank in Chicago to examine it, only to have the door guard refuse to admit him, unable to believe that a black man could hold such a responsible position. Burris passed his credentials through the door, but the guard would not budge. Someone called an officer, who was sufficiently impressed by the title of "comptroller of the currency" on Burris's badge to permit him to come inside and sit down, but would not allow him to go further until his boss arrived and vouched for him.

When his first child was born in 1964, Burris decided he needed a job that would not require him to travel as his work as a bank examiner did. He took a position at Continental Bank, the biggest bank in Illinois, working in the trust and tax division, and later in commercial lending. By the time he left Commercial Bank in 1973, he had worked his way up to vice president in spite of systemic racism in the banking industry. During that period he made his first foray into politics, running for the state legislature in 1968, and finishing last in a field of five.

Burris left the bank to join the Illinois governor Dan Walker's cabinet as director of the Department of General Services. In 1976 Burris made a run for state comptroller but lost. He briefly became national executive director and chief operating officer of Operation PUSH, People United to Save Humanity, the Reverend JESSE L. JACKSON SR.'s organization. However, Burris had philosophical and practical differences with Jackson, which ultimately led to Burris's decision to return to Illinois politics and attempt another run for state comptroller.

The 1978 election was a success, making Burris the first African American elected to statewide office in Illinois. On the day he took office, Burris visited Abraham Lincoln's Tomb in Springfield and gave a brief speech in which he spoke of a sense of connection with Lincoln, of the martyred president's approval of his achievement.

During his term as comptroller, Burris recognized the severity of the economic downturn of the 1980s more quickly than did Governor James R. Thompson, who remained optimistic even after things became problematic. However, Burris took severe criticism from black legislators for opposing a tax increase and was even accused of being an "Uncle Tom."

While comptroller, Burris ran for the U.S. Senate in 1984 but lost in a four-way primary. In 1989 he announced a bid for governor, but the state Democratic organization preferred state Attorney General Neil F. Hartigan, and Burris ended up settling for running for attorney general. Although Hartigan was defeated by the Republican contender, Jim Edgar, the long-serving Illinois secretary of state who had been instrumental in implementing tougher drunk-driving statutes, Burris won his race for attorney general. Once again he was a Democrat serving under a Republican governor and found himself in frequent conflicts with Edgar over the proper scope of the attorney general's office.

As attorney general, Burris established legal divisions for civil rights and for the interests of women and children. However, these divisions were under-funded and had such minimal staffing that they were not able to carry out their mandates. Burris also came into conflict with the Chicago Council of Lawyers, refusing to cooperate with this reform group's investigation of the state's legal office. He was accused of allowing politics to dominate his office and of doling out patronage appointments to unqualified persons and thus creating a mediocre staff that could not accomplish its duties. His response to the investigation revealed a serious weakness in his character, namely a tendency to be thin-skinned and to respond poorly to criticism.

In 1994 Burris again decided to run for governor. However, although he carried Chicago with a 46 percent plurality, he lost the primary to Dawn Clark Netsch, who held his old post of comptroller. He then left the office of attorney general to return to Jones, Ware & Grenard, a law firm with which he had worked for a time after stepping down as comptroller and before becoming attorney general. His intention was to step back and rest for a while, but no sooner had he resumed his law practice than he was running for mayor of Chicago against Richard M. Daley, who had previously beaten all rivals for the office, including such prominent black politicians as Eugene Sawyer, Timothy C. Evans, Danny K. Davis, and R. Eugene Pincham. Burris ran as an Independent rather than a Democrat in order to face Daley in the general election rather than the primary but was still soundly beaten. However, Burris found consolation in the relatively higher return on his campaign investment—while Dailey spent more than $3 million to win 340,000 votes, Burris had spent only $250,000 to win 220,000 votes.

In 1998 Burris's plans for a second gubernatorial campaign were nearly derailed when his campaign manager, Ron Greer, suffered a fatal stroke. Suddenly Burris had to rebuild his campaign team. Burris concentrated his campaign on improving education and on combating incivility in public life, including the growing problem of road rage. He ultimately lost the Democratic primary to Glen Poshard of Marion, a longtime southern Illinois teacher. Poshard would lose the general election to the Republican candidate George Ryan.

In 2002 Burris again ran for governor, this time concentrating on education and on reassuring the state's high-performing public schools that their budgets would not be reduced in order to bring the weaker schools, particularly the inner-city schools of Chicago and East St. Louis—long recognized as centers of egregious inequality—up to par. However, Burris failed to secure the Democratic nomination and again returned to his law practice.

On 30 December 2008 Roland Burris was appointed by Illinois Governor Rod Blagojevich to fill the U.S. Senate seat vacated by president-elect BARACK OBAMA. Burris's appointment was somewhat tainted as Blagojevich was concurrently under investigation for trying to sell the seat for personal gain. While many called for the appointment to be thrown out, Burris took the oath of office on 15 January 2009. Burris's tenure in the Senate was short lived. Much of his time in that body was devoted to fighting ethics charges arising from his appointment by Blagojevich, who was under federal indictment for allegedly seeking to "sell" Obama's vacant seat to possible candidates, including Burris. Burris denied the charges, and was later cleared—though admonished—by a Senate Ethics panel in 2010, the year he stepped down from the Senate.

Burris received numerous awards for his work against racial discrimination, domestically and internationally, such as *Ebony*'s 100 Most Influential Black Americans, (1979–1995); Southern Illinois University Carbondale's Ten Most Distinguished Alumni in the History of the University (1997); National Bar Association's Distinguished Accomplishments in the Field of Law (1993); *City and State*'s One of the Top Three Government Financial Officers in the Nation, (1989); and National Football League Players Association's Mackey Award (1989). He also held a part-time adjunct professorship at his alma mater, Southern Illinois University at Carbondale.

FURTHER READING

Roland Burris has not placed his personal papers on deposit with any archives. However, official documents from his terms as Illinois comptroller and Illinois attorney general may be found in those offices or in the Illinois State Archives.

Dudley, Karen. *Great African Americans in Government* (1997).

Merriner, James L. "What Makes Roland Run?," *Illinois Issues* (Jan. 1998).

Weatherford, Carole. *Great African-American Lawyers: Raising the Bar of Freedom* (2003).

LEIGH KIMMEL

Burris, Samuel D. (1808–c. 1869), antislavery activist and Underground Railroad conductor, was born in Kent County, Delaware. Nothing is known of his father. Little is known of his early years except that his mother was a free woman of color, and that as a young adult he moved to the Philadelphia, Pennsylvania, area, became a farmer, married, and started a family. No information about his wife and children is available. In the mid-1840s he became involved in the antislavery movement and began assisting slaves who were attempting to make it to freedom. Burris welcomed fugitives into his home, hid them for a day or two, supplied them with food and water, and sent them on their way. He became friends with leading abolitionists, including CHARLES PURVIS, one of the founders of-the American Anti-Slavery Society (1833), and WILLIAM STILL, best known for his post–Civil War book titled *The Underground Railroad, a Record of Facts, Authentic Narratives, Letters, &c.*, which detailed the loosely knit group of antislavery activists—black and white—who devoted their time, energy, and money to helping slaves escape from bondage.

In 1847 Burris expressed his fear about the dangers of helping runaways. If caught, especially in certain states, black conductors might themselves be sold into slavery. In Delaware, for example, helping slaves escape "was a crime next to murder if committed by a colored man." Burris not only welcomed fugitives into his home but also, during the late 1840s, ventured into Kent County, Delaware, to guide blacks out of slavery. In June 1847, while attempting to lead Maria Mathews across the border into Pennsylvania, he was arrested, jailed, tried, and convicted of helping slaves to escape. He was fined five hundred dollars. Unable to pay, he was kept in jail for ten months. Later he was sentenced to be sold into slavery for fourteen years. "When the hour arrived, the doomed man was placed on the auction-block," William Still explained, "two traders from Baltimore were known to be present; how many others the friends of Burris knew not." The usual opportunity was given to traders and speculators to examine the human property, and Burris's head, arms, legs, and extremities were all closely scrutinized. When the bidding began Burris expected to be sold. The final bidder, however, was Isaac Flint, a Quaker who had learned about Burris's plight, raised five hundred dollars to purchase him, and disguised himself at the auction. In fact Flint represented a group of Burris's friends, abolitionists from Pennsylvania and northern

Delaware. Burris did not know until after he was "knocked down" that Flint was a friend. The two men promptly returned to Pennsylvania.

In the Burris family's effort to raise funds to help Flint purchase Burris, they had gone deeply into debt and lost their farm, becoming nearly destitute. They tried to regain some of their economic well-being but were unable to do so. In 1851 the Burris family immigrated to California, where gold had been recently discovered. Settling in the San Francisco area, Burris took an active role in abolitionist and civil rights issues. In 1862 he led a drive to raise relief funds for "contraband"—as slaves fleeing into Union lines were called—in Philadelphia. In the same year he signed, along with ten others, a petition to improve schools for African American youngsters in the San Francisco area. There were three hundred black children in the city, but their school accommodated only sixty pupils. "We need another, better and larger place," he and the others said, "a building convenient, healthful and capable of holding" 150 pupils. He also pointed out that the black children needed "a school of a higher grade" and "additional teachers." It is not known where Burris died.

FURTHER READING

Lapp, Rudolph M. *Blacks in Gold Rush California* (1977).

Still, William. *The Underground Railroad, a Record of Facts, Authentic Narratives, Letters, &c.* (1872; repr. 2005).

Williams, William H. *Slavery and Freedom in Delaware, 1639–1865* (1996).

This entry is taken from the *American National Biography* and is published here with the permission of the American Council of Learned Societies.

LOREN SCHWENINGER

Burroughs, Margaret Taylor Goss (1 Nov. 1917–21 Nov. 2010), artist, educator, and museum founder, was born Margaret Victoria Taylor in St. Rose, Louisiana, the youngest of three daughters of Christopher Alexander Taylor, a farmer, and Octavia Pierre Taylor, a domestic worker and schoolteacher. As a small child Margaret Taylor learned that her great-grandmother had been enslaved. Taylor and her two sisters were enamored by the stories told to them about their Creole, white, and African heritage by their French-speaking Creole grandmother. When the five-year-old Taylor moved to Chicago with her family and many other North-migrating African Americans, she took with her an appreciation for the enriched oral tradition common to her beloved St. Rose community.

In Chicago the young Taylor adjusted to life in a northern city. While in the South, Taylor's mother had taught in a one-room schoolhouse with little or no classroom supplies; in Chicago, Taylor attended a school that had many classrooms. While in the South she would have been applauded for speeding up on her alphabet lesson in class; in Chicago she was punished and told to wear a dunce cap for going too far in her alphabet lesson. That experience ignited her desire to help students realize their fullest potential, rather than have it stifled through embarrassing and demeaning punishments in the classroom. Taylor excelled academically and cultivated an interest in art. After attending James A. Doolittle School she went on to attend St. Elizabeth's Catholic School, Carter Elementary, and Englewood High School.

In her high school years she became disillusioned by the promise of the American dream. It was as if she entered a stage of personal revolution and evolution. She took note of the economic, social, and cultural discriminations against people of color. She questioned more than she accepted, and she was critical of the systems of segregation and inequalities. In her autobiography Taylor states that during this time in her development "the 'whys' began to mean something" (55).

It was during this time that she also nurtured a growing interest in African and African American history and culture. At age sixteen Taylor joined the National Association for the Advancement of Colored People Youth Council, with which she marched and spoke out against the injustices of the day. During her senior year of high school, Taylor sought admission to Howard University in Washington, D.C. Although she received a tuition scholarship to Howard, her parents, who were struggling through the Depression, could not afford room-and-board fees. Taylor instead attended school closer to home. With the help of her Carter School art teacher Mary Ryan, Taylor obtained an elementary and secondary teaching certificate from the Chicago Normal School (now Chicago State University) in 1939. She then entered the profession in which she could turn those questioning "whys" that she posed during high school into exclamatory "whats!" During her teaching days Taylor had her outspokenness challenged, but she remained true to her beliefs.

In 1939 Taylor married Bernard Goss, a serviceman who fought in World War II and a fellow artist. Their union produced a daughter, Gayle. Soon after Goss's return from the war, he and Taylor divorced. With a daughter to raise and a generation to educate, she filled the role of mother and schoolteacher set by her own mother. The stories of her great-grandmother's strength kept her going during this difficult time. While substitute teaching in the Chicago public school system, she earned her bachelor of fine arts degree from the School of the Art Institute of Chicago. During this time, she constructed the egg tempera painting *I've Been in Some Big Towns*. She began teaching at DuSable High School in 1946, where she remained an art educator for the next twenty-two years. Taylor's career as a teacher in public schools allowed Taylor to work against the injustices she experienced as a student. In 1947 her first children's book, *Jasper, the Drummin' Boy*, was published. While teaching she returned to the School of the Art Institute to earn a master of fine arts degree in 1948. In 1949 Taylor married Charles Burroughs, a New York-born, Russian-speaking artist who was as fond of travel as Margaret was. They were married until Charles Burroughs died in 1994 at the age of seventy-four.

Her published children's books include *Did You Feed My Cow?: Rhymes and Games from City Streets and Country Lanes* (1955) and *Whip Me Whop Me Pudding and Other Stories of Riley Rabbit and His Fabulous Friends* (1966). Her visual artworks include a watercolor, *Ribbon Man, Mexico City Market*, inspired by her experience at the Institute of Printing and Sculpture in New Mexico; an oil painting, *Insect* (1963); two bronze sculptures, *Black Queen* and *Head* (1963); and a marble sculpture, *Head* (1965). *For Malcolm: Poems on the Life and the Death of Malcolm X*, an anthology edited by Burroughs and DUDLEY FELKER RANDALL in 1967, showcased African American writers and leaders. The following year, *What Shall I Tell My Children Who Are Black?* was published.

After a career as a high school art teacher, Burroughs became a college professor at Wilson Junior College (now Kennedy King College) in Chicago, where she taught for ten years until her retirement in 1978. During her years of teaching, Burroughs, her husband, and their close friends cultivated the idea of establishing a museum devoted to the preservation of African and African American art, history, and culture. It was during their talks in the Burroughs home that the idea for America's first independent African American museum was born.

First called the Ebony Museum of Negro History, the museum opened on 21 October 1961 in the Burroughses' home and consisted of their personal collection of African American art and artifacts. Later renamed the Museum of Negro History, it offered Chicago residents and visitors an opportunity to learn from and reflect upon the beauty and richness of African American and African history and culture. Finally adopting the name the DuSable Museum of African American History and Culture in 1993 in honor of the black explorer JEAN BAPTISTE POINTE DU SABLE, the museum is a reflection of the tireless efforts of Burroughs, its founder and first CEO and president, who during the early growing years of the museum continually sought opportunities to hone her skills as a museologist.

While producing award-winning art and masterly poetry, Burroughs continued to speak out against injustice as she did during her early teaching days. In the midst of the civil rights movement, she and Charles H. Wright, the namesake of Detroit's Charles H. Wright Museum of African American History, founded the Association of African American Museums in 1967, a national organization dedicated to the promotion of African American museums. She continued to further publish books of poetry; in 1970 *Africa, My Africa* was published, speaking to African cultural pride and heritage. Burroughs received several honorary degrees and honorary memberships, accompanied by many accolades. In 1981 she was appointed by President Jimmy Carter to serve on the National Commission on Negro History and Culture and also served on the Chicago Public Schools Board of Education. Chicago Mayor HAROLD WASHINGTON declared 1 February 1986 as Dr. Margaret Goss Taylor Burroughs Day.

Burroughs died in Chicago at the age of 95.

FURTHER READING

Burroughs, Margaret T. G. *Life with Margaret: The Official Autobiography* (2003).

Obituary: *New York Times*, 27 Nov. 2010.

LANESHA DEBARDELABEN

Burroughs, Nannie (2 May 1879–20 May 1961), school founder, was born Nannie Helen Burroughs in Orange, Virginia, the daughter of John Burroughs, a farmer and itinerant Baptist preacher, and Jennie Poindexter, a cook and former slave. After moving to Washington, D.C., with her mother in 1883, Burroughs graduated in 1896 with honors in had spoken eloquently on "Women's Part in the World's Work" to the First Baptist World Alliance in London in 1905, also edited the *Worker*, a quarterly missionary magazine, which she began in 1912 and then revived in 1934, with the support of the white Woman's Missionary Union of the Southern Baptist Convention. Burroughs also convinced the Woman's Convention to found the National Training School for Women and Girls, Incorporated (NTS), which opened on 19 October 1909 in Lincoln Heights, Washington, D.C. Serving as school president until her death, Burroughs raised money, primarily among black women, to pay off the $6,000 purchase price. NTS also received some support from the white Woman's American Baptist Home Mission Society. The school's title did not include the word "Baptist," since it admitted young women and girls of all religious denominations. Enrollment rose to between 100 and 150 students, who could choose either the trade school or the seminary; the latter offered four divisions: seventh and eighth grades, a four-year high school, a two-year normal school, and a two-year junior college. By 1934 more than two thousand girls and women from the United States, the Caribbean, and Africa had taken academic, domestic science, trade, social service, and missionary training courses. To pay for their education, some students worked on campus, while others were domestic servants during the summer. By 1960 the school's physical plant had expanded from one to nine buildings and from six to thirteen acres.

Keenly aware of the limited employment opportunities for black women, Burroughs emphasized preparing students for employment as ladies' maids and laundresses. Domestic work, she believed, should be considered professional and even unionized. Burroughs inculcated a creed of racial self-help through her "three Bs—the Bible, the bath, and the broom: clean life, clean body, clean house." Students were trained to become respectable workers by being pious, pure, and domestic. But instead of being submissive, they were to become proud black women, inspired by a required course in African American history and culture. In 1927 Burroughs presented a paper to the Association for the Study of Negro Life and History on "The Social Value of Negro History." Under her leadership, NTS served as a center for African American community organizations and hosted the 1923 convention of the International Council of Women of the Darker Races. Burroughs, who participated with

Nannie Burroughs helped found the National Training School for Women and Girls in Washington, D.C., in 1909 and served as its president until 1961. (Library of Congress.)

business and domestic science from the Colored High School on M Street. When racial discrimination barred her from obtaining a position either in the Washington, D.C., public schools or the federal civil service, Burroughs worked as a secretary, first for the Baptist *Christian Banner* in Philadelphia and then for the National Baptist Convention's Foreign Mission Board. She moved to Louisville, Kentucky, in 1900, when the Board's headquarters relocated there, and she stayed in Louisville until 1909. Studying business education, she organized a Women's Industrial Club for black women, which evolved into a vocational school.

In 1900 Burroughs helped found the separate Woman's Convention, an auxiliary to the National Baptist Convention, and she served for forty-eight years as its corresponding secretary. Recruiting about 1.5 million black women—more than 60 percent of the entire convention's membership—the Woman's Convention was a congress of delegates from local churches, district associations, and states. It promoted charity work and home and foreign missions. Burroughs, who black clubwomen in memorializing the Anacostia home of FREDERICK DOUGLASS, was active in the NAACP and served in the 1940s, along with MARY MCLEOD BETHUNE, as one of two black women vice presidents on its national board.

Burroughs fought for thirty years for NTS's independence. When the National Baptist Convention of the United States of America Inc., its new name after an internal division in 1915, charged that the school lacked a valid charter, Burroughs proclaimed, "This is God's hill," entrusted to her "and to the Negro Baptist women of America" for the black women of the world. The National Baptist Convention withdrew support from the school in June 1938 and urged that the Woman's Convention also sever its connections. Although the National Baptist Convention voted in 1939 to dismiss Burroughs from the Woman's Convention, the women rallied behind her. She continued to serve as corresponding secretary during the years when the school had no official financial support. In 1939 its charter legally incorporated several changes adopted earlier: the self-perpetuating board of trustees changed its name to the National Trade and Professional School for Girls, the board was streamlined, and the property was conferred to the Woman's Convention. The school began a fund-raising campaign, since insufficient funds had caused it to close from 1935 to 1938. In 1947 new leaders of the National Baptist Convention formally endorsed the school, and in 1948 the Woman's Convention elected Burroughs president. Renamed in her honor in 1964, the school was designated a National Historic Landmark in 1991.

Burroughs spoke out on many contemporary political and social issues, for which she was put under surveillance by the federal government in 1917. She argued that until black men and women freely exercised their Fifteenth Amendment voting rights, they could not stop lynching and racial discrimination. Forming networks with other activist women such as Mary McLeod Bethune and MAGGIE LENA WALKER, Burroughs chaired the National Association of Colored Women's (NACW) Anti-Lynching Committee, was a charter member of the Anti-Lynching Crusaders, and belonged to the Commission on Interracial Cooperation's Women's Division. A regional president of the NACW, Burroughs chaired its Citizenship Department, which encouraged women to organize citizenship groups. She founded and became president of the short-lived National Association of Wage Earners, whose purpose was to affiliate working women

with the NACW clubwomen. Burroughs, president of the National League of Republican Colored Women, was appointed in 1932 by President Herbert Hoover to chair a committee reporting on African American housing at the President's Conference on Home Building and Home Ownership. During the Depression she assisted families in the nation's capital by helping to set up a medical clinic, convenience store, and the farming, canning, and hairdressing operations of the self-help Cooperative Industries Inc.

In 1944 Shaw University in Raleigh, North Carolina, conferred on Burroughs an LLD, and in 1958 the Washington chapter of the Lincoln University Alumni Association honored her at its annual Founders Day Banquet. She never married. Burroughs died in Washington, D.C. The District of Columbia honored her by naming 10 May 1975 the first Nannie Helen Burroughs Day.

Although contemporaries compared her to BOOKER T. WASHINGTON because of her advocacy of industrial education, she accepted neither black subservience to whites nor female subordination to male authority. Indeed, she told African American men to "glorify" black women for their many family and community contributions and not treat them as "slaves and servants" (*Pittsburgh Courier*, 23 Dec. 1933). Fighting brilliantly and stubbornly for the Woman's Convention, the National Training School, and for racial pride, Burroughs became a powerful role model for future generations.

FURTHER READING

Burroughs's papers are in the Library of Congress.

Barnett, Evelyn Brooks. "Nannie Burroughs and the Education of Black Women," in *The Afro-American Woman: Struggles and Images*, ed. Sharon Harley and Rosalyn Terborg-Penn (1978).

Easter, Opal V. *Nannie Helen Burroughs* (1995).

Harrison, Earl L. *The Dream and the Dreamer* (1956; repr. 1972).

Obituary: *Washington Post*, 21 May 1961.

This entry is taken from the *American National Biography* and is published here with the permission of the American Council of Learned Societies.

MARCIA G. SYNNOTT

Burruss, King Hezekiah (31 Oct. 1881–26 Aug. 1963), bishop, founder, and overseer of the National Convention of the Churches of God,

Holiness, and civil rights leader, was born in East Baton Rouge, Louisiana, to Mr. and Mrs. Senior and Lottie Burruss. The 1880 U.S. Census for Louisiana in East Baton Rouge listed his parents' household as follows (young King had not been born yet): Senior Burris (spelling of surname) 34, father; Lottie, 28, mother; William, 9, brother; Senior, 7, brother; Emma, 4, sister; and Benjamin, 1, brother. Living beside them were other close Burris relatives. According to *King Hezekiah Burruss: And 25 Years of Progress*, King H. Burruss was born three miles from Baton Rouge into a deeply religious family. His father was a farmer and was able to afford to hire private teachers for his children, as Negro children had no school to attend in that part of the state at that time. However, King's world changed when his father died and his mother suddenly became head of the household and had to work as a field hand. Because of her meager wages, it was necessary for the children to go out and search for work. King wanted to do his part and he found work at a local box factory.Before leaving Louisiana, he met and married Miss Minerva Coleman. Four children were born to this union: Titus Paul, Adell V., Joseph T., and Gideon A. Early in his ministry, King Burruss began to work with the Reverend Charles Price Jones, a former Baptist minister, who had come to the Churches of Christ, Holiness. In 1894 Reverend Jones and Reverend Charles Harrison Mason formed the Church of God in Christ as a holiness body, following their exclusion from fellowship with black Baptists in Arkansas. Mason took most of the body into a Pentecostal expression of worship in 1907. Others followed Jones and became part of the Church of Christ (Holiness) U.S.A. Jones and Burruss together founded many churches is Mississippi and Texas that were part of the Churches of Christ (Holiness) U.S.A. By 1920 Burruss had migrated to Georgia, where the Census shows he was living with his wife Minerva and their children in Atlanta on Ashby Street. He began a church in Atlanta in 1914 that belonged to the Church of Christ (Holiness) U.S.A., and by 1920 the Atlanta congregation was large enough that it was able to host the National Convention of the Church of Christ (Holiness) U.S.A. Shortly after this convention, however, Burruss formed the Churches of God, Holiness. He became the first bishop and president. Just prior to this, in 1917, Burruss had to complete a World War I draft registration.Bishop Burruss believed that his mission in life was to fulfill the Great Commission found in the New Testament book of Mark 16:15: "And he said unto them, Go ye into all the world, and preach the gospel to every creature" (KJV Bible). A few years later, after applying for and receiving a passport, Bishop Burruss set sail in 1924 aboard the S.S. *Parks* to visit England, France, Switzerland, Italy, Egypt, and Palestine. He stated on his passport application that his occupation was a "Minister of the Gospel" and that his purpose for traveling for the next three months was for observation and biblical study. Also on his application, his eldest brother William attested to his being born in the United States and that he became his legal guardian after the passing of their father in their youth. After his multicountry tour and pilgrimage to the Holy Land, he returned to the United States, leaving Liverpool, England, on the S.S. *Baltic* and arriving in New York on 21 February 1925.Throughout his ministry, not only did he continue to establish churches mainly throughout the east coast and southeast, but he also started churches in Cuba and in Panama. During the national conventions, he would invite various guest speakers, including members of the American Bible Society.He used the media available to him at the time to spread the Gospel of Jesus, the "Good News," by producing a weekly radio broadcast that aired on Sunday nights. His church purchased property onHunter Street, SW. He was committed to outreach in the community and participated during the civil rights era as a leader in the local NAACP. He also invited civil rights groups to have meetings at the church and served as chair on an important NAACP committee. He met with and joined other local ministers of the gospel, including the Reverend Dr. MARTIN LUTHER KING JR. Following his death on 26 August 1963, at the age of eighty-one, his mantle was passed on to his eldest son Titus Paul Burruss. His other children also served in the ministry, his son Gideon became an elder, and his son Joseph pastored several churches and became a presiding elder. He left a rich legacy to follow and cherish.

FURTHER READING

Cobbins, Ortho B. *History of the Church of Christ (Holiness) U.S.A., 1895–1965* (1966).

Cornelius, Ruth L., and Fenuel P. Jones. *King Hezekiah Burruss: And 25 Years of Progress* (n.d.).

Jones, C. P. *His Fullness* (1901).

TINA C. JONES

Burton, Annie Louise (c. 1858–c. 1910), domestic and restaurateur, was born on the Farrin plantation near Clayton, Alabama. She was the daughter of the Farrins' female cook and the male owner of a plantation located approximately two miles away from the Farrin plantation. Burton's mistress was persistent in her attempts to get Burton's father, who was from Liverpool, England, to acknowledge his daughter, but he ignored Burton whenever she was in his presence. During the Civil War, Burton's mother left the Farrin plantation and her children after an argument with her mistress led to her being whipped. Several years later, Burton and her siblings were reunited with their mother when she returned to the plantation after the war had ended and took her children to their new home. The Farrins demanded that Burton's mother return her children to them until she threatened to go to the Yankee headquarters. In 1866 the family moved to Clayton, and Burton was hired as a nanny. During this period, Burton learned how to read, write, cook, and perform household chores. She worked as a domestic for other families in the immediate area, elsewhere in the South, as well as in the North. In the mid- or late 1870s, Burton, after an illness, joined a black church in Macon, Georgia, and was baptized. When she moved to Boston in 1879, she was unable to find an African American church, and she attended the Warren Avenue Baptist Church before she joined Tremont Temple.

Death claimed Burton's fiancée, mother, brother, and older sister. After her mother's death, Burton assumed responsibility for her younger siblings; and after her older sister Caroline's death in 1884, Burton returned to the South in order to take care of Caroline's young son, Lawrence. A man who was not related to the boy and who showed little interest in him acted as Lawrence's guardian until Burton sued for custody of her nephew and won.

Also in 1884, Burton opened a restaurant in Jacksonville, Florida. After the eatery became profitable, Burton moved from a two-room residence to a four-room house; she placed three cots in two of the rooms and rented each cot for one dollar a week to hotel workers. Burton moved to Boston and established a restaurant there. In 1888, she married Samuel H. Burton; the couple rented a boarding house, but the venture proved unsuccessful. According to scholar Yolanda Pierce, Burton's decision to become an entrepreneur indicates her refusal to accept the prevalent postbellum belief that employment opportunities for recently freed

Annie Louise Burton, c. 1890.

slave women were limited to working as domestics in white households.

Education was important to Burton. Lawrence, with his aunt's financial assistance, attended Hampton Institute (now University). Burton, who attended Lewis High School in Macon, Georgia, for six months after her mother's death, continued her education in Boston in 1900 by attending the Franklin Evening School for five or six years. Burton wrote an autobiographical essay, and after the headmaster read it, he encouraged Burton to expand it into a book. *Memories of Childhood's Slavery Days* was published in 1909.

FURTHER READING

Burton, Annie L. *Memories of Childhood's Slavery Days.* 1909. In *Six Women's Slave Narratives* (1988).

Pierce, Yolanda. "Her Refusal to Be Recast(e): Annie Burton's Narrative of Resistance." *Southern Literary Journal* 36, no. 2 (2004): 1–12.

LINDA M. CARTER

Burton, LeVar (16 Feb. 1957–), actor and director, was born Levardis Robert Martyn Burton Jr. in Landstuhl, Germany, to Levardis Robert

Levar Burton, delivering the keynote speech to Public Broadcasting Service annual meeting in San Francisco, 9 June 1999. PBS announced its continued drive to provide quality, nonviolent, educational television programming for children ages 2–11. (AP Images.)

Burton Sr., a career army photographer, and Erma Christian. The couple separated when their son was three. Erma returned to the United States with her son and his two elder sisters and settled in Sacramento, California. The family were devout Roman Catholics, and Burton decided at thirteen to enter a Catholic seminary to become a priest. While there, he changed his mind and decided to become an actor instead.

Burton's big break came while he was a drama student at the University of Southern California's School of Theatre. While playing Ali Hakeem, the Persian rug dealer in the musical *Oklahoma!*, he tried out for the miniseries *Roots*, based on ALEX HALEY's landmark book, tracing the generations of his family through America and back to Africa. Burton landed the part and dazzled the nation as Kunta Kinte, a Mandinka man captured in Gambia in 1767, brought to America on a slave ship, and sold into slavery in Maryland.

More than 100 million Americans watched *Roots* when it aired in 1977, and 85 percent of all homes with televisions viewed some part of the twelve hours. It was the third most-watched show in television history, behind the last episode of *M*A*S*H* and the "Who Shot J.R.?" episode of *Dallas.* "For African Americans … the story had the effect of providing an anchor for pride and reaffirming yourself. For white Americans, the reaction was, 'I had no idea. I had no idea it was like that,'" Burton remembered in a 2002 interview with the *Sacramento Bee.* "'Roots' pushed everyone's button" (Alim).

Burton won an Emmy for his performance in *Roots.* Afterward he was a celebrity. He indulged in the perks of his fame, buying his first car and a large apartment in the hip neighborhood of Marina del Rey, California. His career did not take off quite as expected, however. He found a small role in the film *Looking for Mr. Goodbar* in 1977 and a part in the Steve McQueen film *The Hunter* in 1980, hoping that larger feature film roles would be forthcoming. They were not—at least, not immediately.

Burton found more success in television, appearing with Powers Boothe and JAMES EARL JONES in the 1980 television movie *Guyana Tragedy: The Story of Jim Jones.* He worked steadily throughout the 1980s, acting in a variety of TV movies and appearing in guest roles on popular television shows such as *Fantasy Island* and *Murder, She Wrote*, and made-for-television movies like *Emergency Room, Booker,* and *The Jesse Owens Story.*

Burton found his niche as an advocate for literacy in children. In 1983 he began appearing as the host of a PBS children's show called *Reading Rainbow.* In it, he gave a short introduction to the day's theme, after which he or a guest read a children's book aloud and suggested books for further reading. The show quickly found a wide audience among children and parents, with 6.5 million viewers in its first season. "LeVar is someone kids relate to," executive producer Tony Buttino told Carol Mauro in a 1984 interview. "He instills in children a total feeling of trust" (Mauro, 21). Burton remained with the show until 2007. Over the years he won a number of Emmy awards for his work as both host and executive producer for the show. He was also honored with a number of NAACP Image awards for his involvement in the show. In addition to his roles in *Roots* and *Reading Rainbow*, Burton is best remembered for his starring role as Lieutenant Commander Geordi La Forge on the long-aired series *Star Trek: The Next Generation*, which began in 1987. The show, a sequel to the 1960s series *Star Trek*, followed the space adventures of a new cast of Starfleet officers aboard USS *Enterprise*. Burton's character, the chief engineer on the starship, was born blind but wore a specially constructed visor that allowed him to see. Like the original on which it was based, the show developed a dedicated and quirky fan base among sci-fi aficionados, inspiring the 1997 documentary *Trekkies* (in which Burton appears). Two *Roots* costars appeared in several episodes of *Star Trek: The Next Generation* with Burton: his character's parents, played by Ben Vereen and Madge Sinclair. Burton also began directing episodes of *Next Generation* in 1993; his directorial debut, "Second Chances," guest-starred the first African American female astronaut, MAE JEMISON.

The cast was close. When Burton married the actor and makeup artist Stephanie Cozart in 1992, his best man was his costar Brent Spiner, who played an android on the series. Groomsmen included Patrick Stewart, who played Captain Picard, Geordi La Forge's commanding officer; Jonathan Frakes, who played Lieutenant Commander William Riker, second in command aboard the *Enterprise;* and Michael Dorn, who played La Forge's Klingon colleague, Lieutenant Worf.

After the series ended in 1994, the *Star Trek: The Next Generation* franchise began producing movies, and Burton had a chance to realize his big-screen dreams. He starred as Geordi La Forge in all five movies, including *Star Trek Generations* in 1994; *Star Trek: First Contact* in 1996; *Star Trek: Insurrection* in 1998; and *Star Trek: Nemesis* in 2002. Of the films, *First Contact* was the most successful, earning more than $90 million at the box office and finding an audience outside of the many *Star Trek* fans.

Burton was busy with other projects throughout the *Star Trek* era. In 1993 he became the voice of a character named Kwame in the animated series *Captain Planet and the Planeteers* and *The New Adventures of Captain Planet*. President Bill Clinton nominated him to the National Commission on Libraries & Information Science in 1996. In 1997 Burton published a science fiction novel *Aftermath*, about the aftereffects of an enormous earthquake and race war in the United States. He and his wife had a daughter, Michaela, born in 1994 as a result of in vitro fertilization. The couple was candid about their struggle with infertility and was honored by the nonprofit group Resolve: The National Infertility Association for their efforts. Burton also has a son, Ian, born in 1980.

Burton continued to act and direct in a variety of television projects after *Star Trek*. He directed a Showtime original movie called *The Tiger Woods Story*, as well as episodes of two other *Star Trek* spin-offs: *Star Trek: Voyager* and *Star Trek: Deep Space Nine*. He acted in a short-lived 1995 series called *Christy*, about a young teacher in a rural mountain community in 1912. In 2002, in honor of the twenty-five-year anniversary of *Roots*, Burton hosted a television special called *Roots—Celebrating 25 Years: The Saga of an American Classic*. Original cast members LESLIE UGGAMS, Ben Vereen, and MAYA ANGELOU joined Burton to reflect on the series's cultural impact.

"The genius that Alex gave us was the courage to be introspective," Burton said in a 2002 interview with the *Columbus Dispatch* (Feran). "You couldn't be part of that viewing audience and not be introspective…. In my own universe, there was a real reorientation around the whole idea of having descended from slaves who were something before they were slaves—an organized people with a history, a culture, a richness of culture…. For me, a lot of the power in the documentary is the voices of other Americans, not just the famous but the non-famous, reminding us how deeply personal a journey all Americans went on as a result of watching *Roots*."

Burton's *Reading Rainbow* and *Star Trek* experiences speak to an important part of his childhood experiences. He "found in science-fiction books a world where he was comfortable," Adam Smeltz reported for the *Centre Daily Times* in 2007. In a speech to the fiftieth annual William Allen White Children's Book Awards in 2002, Burton said that watching television as a kid inspired him to pursue his dreams. As a boy, he found it difficult to identify with characters in books he read because they were not black. Watching NICHELLE NICHOLS, who played the communications officer Lieutenant Uhura on the original *Star Trek* series, was an inspiration for him. "What it said to me was when the future comes, there'll be a place for you," Burton told the crowd. "Dreams really do come true" (Jordan).

FURTHER READING

Alim, Fahizah. "For a Nation of Viewers *Roots* Still Resonates," *Sacramento Bee*, 18 Jan. 2002.

Brown, Jeremy K. *Current Biography* (Mar. 2000).

Feran, Tim. "*Roots* Had Dramatic Effect on Actor, TV, Nation," *Columbus Dispatch*, 17 Jan. 2002.

Jordan, Ray. "People," *St. Louis Post-Dispatch*, 19 Jan. 2002.

Mauro, Carol. *Dial* (July 1984).

Smeltz, Adam. "Burton Reflects on Life in Books," *Centre Daily Times*, 30 Jan. 2007.

MEREDITH BROUSSARD

Burton, Thomas (4 May 1860–23 Mar. 1939), physician, businessman, and writer, was born in Madison County, Kentucky, the youngest of fifteen children of Eliza and Edwin, who were slaves. Burton and his mother remained on the plantation after Emancipation as paid laborers, and he continued working at the "old homestead" after her death in 1869 until he was sixteen, at which time he left following an altercation with the owner.

In 1880 Burton was "converted to God" and subsequently experienced an insatiable desire for learning. Despite discouraging comments from those who thought that twenty was too old to start school, Burton was not dissuaded and determined that nothing was going to prevent him from getting an education except sickness or death. Burton worked for one more year as a farmhand in Richmond, Kentucky. One January morning in 1881, he put a few items in a carpetbag and $9.75 in his pocket and walked fifteen miles to the school that the older slaves on the plantation had talked about.

When Burton arrived at Berea College, there was no evidence of the violence that had been associated with its founding more than twenty-five years earlier. John G. Fee, an ardent abolitionist and devout Christian, had founded the school in 1855 for anyone, regardless of race, who wanted an education, a noble but a dangerous aim in the slave state of Kentucky in the mid-nineteenth century. But in spite of vehement opposition, which included beatings and, ultimately, threats on his life, Fee refused to close the school. Burton was an excellent student and made rapid progress. To his delight, within months he could read and write well enough to send letters.

After graduating from Berea, Burton taught school in Waco, Kentucky, but thoughts of medicine kept "haunting" him and he went to Indianapolis to obtain a medical education, which at that time consisted of a year's apprenticeship with a local physician and at least two years of a proprietary medical school. During his first year in Indianapolis, Burton was an apprentice with a Dr. Chavis. Then, working as a waiter, lumberjack, and general handyman to support himself, Burton continued his studies at the Medical College of Indiana and the Eclectic College of Physicians and Surgeons for two years, graduating from the latter in 1892.

In 1892 Burton established a practice in Springfield and became one of four black physicians in the state of Ohio. That same year, former president William McKinley, who was at that time governor of Ohio, commissioned him as assistant surgeon of the ninth Infantry of the Ohio National Guard, a position that carried the rank of captain. In 1893 Burton married Hattie B. Taylor from Cythiana, Kentucky, with whom he would have two children, Gladys and Thomas William Jr.

Early in his career Burton established himself as a leader in his profession. Not only did he practice in Springfield but he also maintained offices in Zanesville and Xenia, near Wilberforce University. In 1896 Burton and Dr. H. R. Hawkins of Xenia founded the Ohio Mutual Medical Association, the first black medical society in Ohio. But, at that time, many black health professionals in Ohio belonged to white organizations and saw no need for a separate association for blacks, and within two years the Ohio Mutual Medical Association was declared defunct.

When the attempt to form a local organization failed, Burton became active in the National Medical Association, which was founded in 1895 by MILES VANDAHURST LYNK, Robert F. Boyd, DANIEL HALE WILLIAMS, Henry S. Butler, and eight other physicians. Lynk, publisher of the first black medical journal, *the Medical and Surgical Observer*, and a longtime advocate for a national organization of black health professionals, decided to hold the inaugural meeting in Atlanta while the physicians were attending the Cotton States and International Exposition. IRVINE GARLAND PENN chaired the first session, which was held at the First Congregational Church of Atlanta. In March 1909 the association began issuing its official publication, the *Journal of the National Medical Association*, which under the editorship of CHARLES VICTOR ROMAN became a vehicle for vigorous protests against racism in American medicine.

After Burton became the NMA. vice president for Ohio, he made another effort to establish a black medical society in Ohio. This time the response was more favorable because blacks were increasingly barred from membership in white professional groups, following the legal codification of racial separatism by the U.S. Supreme Court ruling in *Plessy v. Ferguson*. For two years, Burton was president of the revitalized association, which served black health professionals in Ohio for many years.

Burton was also an astute businessman. In 1894 he opened up the first drug store owned and operated by a black man in Springfield. He later led a movement to establish the first black hospital in Springfield, but the project failed and the equipment and supplies that had been purchased for the proposed health-care facility were sold to an Indiana hospital. Later Burton purchased a resort and became head of a sanatorium in Mt. Clemens, Michigan. But not all of Burton's business interests were related to health care. The same year that he opened the drugstore, he bought a shoe store, and in 1985 Burton organized and successfully operated *The Loyal Legion of Honor*, the first Springfield newspaper committed to African American news. In 1901 Burton represented Springfield's Business League at the annual meeting of the National Negro Business League in Chicago. His detailed account of each event, from an opening session that included remarks from an Illinois elected official and the welcoming words of BOOKER T. WASHINGTON to the closing events, gave unique insights into the scope of black business at the turn of the century.

As a black physician in Springfield, Ohio, Burton was a leader in his African American community and active in many organizations. He was a member of the free masons, the Order of the Elks, and several other lodges, and Trinity AME church, serving as trustee and superintendent of the Sunday school for thirty years. He died just one day before the forty-seventh anniversary of his arrival in Springfield.

FURTHER READING

Burton, Thomas William. *What Experience Has Taught Me: An Autobiography of Thomas William Burton* (1910).

Morais, Herbert M. *The History of the Negro in Medicine* (1967).

Obituary: *Springfield Daily News*, 24 Mar. 1939.

GERALDINE RHOADES BECKFORD

Burton, Walter Moses (9 Aug. 1840–4 June 1913), politician and activist, was born into slavery in North Carolina. Both he and his mother, Susan, were owned by the wealthy Thomas Burke Burton, who moved to Fort Bend County, Texas, from Halifax County, North Carolina, in the 1850s. Most accounts claim that the slaveholder favored Burton, taught him to read and write, and, after the Civil War, sold land to him; some accounts claim that Burton supported his former owner's wife when she was widowed during Reconstruction.

On 28 September 1868 Burton married Abba Jones (sometimes listed as Abby and sometimes as Hattie). The couple had three children: Horace J., Hattie M., and an unnamed child who died in infancy. Susan Burton lived with the young family until her death c. 1890.

Propertied, literate, and articulate, Burton quickly became active in the local Republican Party, the local Union League, and larger Reconstruction efforts. In 1869 he was elected sheriff of Fort Bend County and held that position for at least two years. During the early 1870s he bought and sold several pieces of land in Fort Bend County and grew fairly wealthy; a story in the 12 May 1881 *Christian Recorder* estimated that his property was worth more than $50,000.

In 1873 Burton was appointed to the Republican Party's State Executive Committee and won a seat in the state senate. Though his election was initially certified, the Democratic challenger objected to the fact that three variations of Burton's name appeared on some ballots, and Burton was not allowed to take his seat until February 1874. Burton came in as a member of a Republican minority in a state that had shifted to favor white Democrats' calls to dismantle Reconstruction efforts. Events tied to this shift, which culminated in the 1875 Texas Constitutional Convention and in many ways marked the end of Reconstruction in Texas, interrupted most of the rest of his first term.

Burton, though, was not dissuaded. Fort Bend County had a significant black population, and Burton was also generally supported by a number of whites. He was reelected to the state senate in 1876 and held his seat until 1882. When he left the senate, several members presented him with a gold-mounted ebony walking stick as a token of respect. While in the senate, he worked actively for black education and was involved in the 1876 creation of Texas's Agricultural and Mechanical College for Colored Youth, which was initially planned to occupy a former plantation called Alta Vista. The school opened in March of 1878 but was under constant financial strain and legislative attack. It grew into a pair of normal schools, though; one of these, Prairie View Normal School, later became Prairie View A&M University. Though some sources note that his wife was once thrown off of a train for refusing to leave a whites-only coach, Burton's work in more general civil rights battles was more limited.

Throughout his time in the state senate, Burton was active in Republican Party politics at the state level. He served as one of the vice presidents at both the 1878 and 1880 state conventions. After leaving state government, he remained a force in

Fort Bend County, where he farmed and continued to engage in real estate dealings, even when racial tensions intensified in Fort Bend in the late 1880s. However, the growth of Jim Crow in Texas kept him out of office and gradually lessened his role in the party. He was a member of the Republican Platform Committee at the 1892 state convention, but eventually retired to Fort Bend, where he died. Burton was a pioneer among black politicians in Texas and a key force in the beginnings of black higher education in the state.

FURTHER READING

Brewer, John Mason. *Negro Legislators of Texas and Their Descendants* (1970).

Pitre, Merline. *Through Many Dangers, Toils, and Snares: The Black Leadership of Texas, 1868–1900* (1985).

Wharton, Clarence. *Wharton's History of Fort Bend County* (1939).

ERIC GARDNER

Bush, Anita (1 Aug. 1883–16 Feb. 1974), an actress, and theatrical producer, was born in Washington, DC. The names of her father, a tailor, and her mother are unknown.

Known as "The Little Mother of Colored Drama," Anita Bush was an unlikely, though enormously influential, pioneer of African American dramatic theater. Bush was born in Washington, D.C., and moved with her family to Brooklyn, New York, when she was two. Her father was a tailor with many show business customers. Bush and her sister helped to deliver costumes, and both became captivated by the theater. While still a child, Bush landed bit parts in plays at the Bijou and Columbia theaters in Brooklyn and the Park Theatre in Manhattan. She later told an interviewer she "fell in love with grease paint, costumes, backstage drama," (Thompson, 1987, p. 60) and that she was determined to make a career in show business.

Among the show business customers of Bush's father was the famous [BERT] WILLIAMS & [GEORGE] WALKER troupe. Williams & Walker's groundbreaking musical play, *In Dahomey*, debuted in 1902 and moved in 1903 to New York, where it became the first black musical to open on Broadway. Bush prevailed on George Walker to give her a part and, with the reluctant blessing of her father, she joined the company as a dancer. She subsequently toured England and Scotland with the production. She remained with Williams & Walker until 1909, performing in the chorus of four other shows.

In 1910, Bush formed her own dance troupe, "Anita Bush and Her 8 Shimmy Babies," to tour the East Coast. In 1913, she fell backstage and seriously injured her back, ending her career as a dancer. While recuperating she developed the idea of forming a troupe of black actors to perform dramatic material. Both black and white audiences enjoyed African American performers in musical comedies, but the conventional wisdom of the day was that audiences were not ready for dramas featuring black actors.

In 1915, Bush convinced the manager of Harlem's Lincoln Theater, Eugene Elmore, that dramas staged by a black repertory company could fill the struggling theater. The Lincoln had recently remodeled, adding hundreds of seats, but it was not drawing large audiences with a combination of vaudeville and motion pictures. She told Elmore that she had assembled a company (she hadn't), and that she could have a play ready to open in two weeks.

The first, hastily assembled incarnation of the Anita Bush Stock Company, remarkably, was comprised of A-list performers: CHARLES GILPIN, who later would be acclaimed as one of America's finest actors for his performances in Eugene O'Neill's *The Emperor Jones*; Carlotta Freeman, a star of Ernest Hogan's Musical Comedy Company; Arthur "Dooley" Wilson, who later would achieve lasting fame as the piano player Sam in the film *Casablanca* (1942); and Andrew Bishop, who would go on to win praise for both stage and film roles. The company gave its first performance at the Lincoln on 15 November 1915 in the comedy *The Girl at the Fort*. It indeed succeeded in drawing large audiences, and the troupe introduced a new play every two weeks for six weeks. On 27 December, following a dispute with Maria C. Downs, the Lincoln's owner, Bush moved the company to the larger Lafayette Theatre on 7th Avenue between 131st and 132nd Streets. The troupe subsequently became known as the Lafayette Players Stock Company, with a repertoire comprised largely of truncated Broadway melodramas and comedies. Bush later launched touring companies, also called Lafayette Players, based in Chicago and Baltimore.

Bush left the Lafayette Players in 1920. The company relocated to Los Angeles in 1928 and dissolved in 1932—a victim of the Great Depression. During its nearly seventeen-year history, the Lafayette Players performed more than 250 plays, with more than 360 actors passing through its ranks, including many of the most successful black actors of the age.

In 1921, Bush appeared in an all-black western film, *The Crimson Skull*, billed as a "Baffling Western Mystery Photo Play." Bush costarred with Lawrence Chenault and the rodeo legend BILL PICKETT. What apparently was a reedited version of the film that more prominently featured Pickett's dazzling riding and roping skills was released as *The Bull-Dogger* the following year. Subsequently, Bush largely disappeared from acting, although she served as the executive secretary of the Negro Actors Guild in the 1920s and taught at the Harlem YMCA, which was at that time an important theatrical venue. She briefly resurfaced in 1937 in Swing It, a Works Progress Administration production, but then faded into obscurity.

After being all-but-forgotten for decades, Bush enjoyed a brief period of recognition for her contributions in the final years of her long life, with articles appearing in *Jet* and other magazines targeting black readers.

FURTHER READING

Thompson, Cordell S. "Black History: Anita Bush Called 'Mother,'" *Jet* (18 Feb. 1971).

Thompson, Francesca. "The Lafayette Players," in Errol Hill, ed. *The Theater of Black Americans: A Collection of Critical Essays* (1987).

Obituary: Thompson, Francesca. "Final Curtain for Anita Bush," *Black World* (July 1974).

DAVID K. BRADFORD

Bush, George Washington (1790?–5 Apr. 1863), pioneer, farmer, and cattleman, was born probably in Pennsylvania or Louisiana. His mother was Scotch-Irish, his father perhaps West Indian. He may have been born as early as 1770, but that would have made him seventy-four years old by the time that he came to Oregon in 1844. Oral tradition among the family gives his birth year as 1779.

Bush was a successful cattle trader in Missouri beginning around 1820, and he became quite wealthy. In 1831 he married Isabella James, a German woman; they had five children. Because Missouri was not well disposed toward people of color, Bush took the opportunity to travel west in a wagon train led by Michael T. Simmons of Kentucky.

Bush found Oregon only a little more tolerant than Missouri. The provisional government voted to exclude blacks and to whip those who would not leave, but the legislation was apparently never enforced. The land north of the Columbia River, which, it was thought, would become British, beckoned the Simmons party. On high open ground

south of what is now Olympia, Washington, Bush staked a claim that has since been known as Bush Prairie. It was the first-American settlement on Puget Sound. Bush is thought to have brought a considerable sum of money with him. With the food and supplies that this money afforded, the little colony was able to survive the first cold winter. The Bush home soon became a haven for the exhausted pioneers who came into the area.

When the treaty of 1846 set the boundary between British and American claims at the forty-ninth parallel, Bush found himself in American territory. He continued to raise wheat and cattle. Although he pioneered his settlement on Puget Sound, his property was at risk because the census of 1850 had listed him as "Negro," and, as such, he could not own property. By the time that Washington Territory was formed in 1853, the Bush claim was one of its most valuable properties. It consisted of 640 acres, which under the Donation Land Law every married man could claim.

Bush had made many friends by this time because of his willingness to share what he had with those less fortunate than himself. It is thus not surprising that these friends banded together under the leadership of Simmons and put through the Washington territorial legislature in 1853 an act specifically exempting Bush from the prohibition of ownership.

In 1854 Congress was memorialized to help Bush perfect his claim, under the Donation Land Law. The memorial stated that Bush:

> Has resided upon and cultivated said tract of land continuously from said year 1845 to the present time, and that his habits of life during said time have been exemplary and industrious; and that by a constant and laborious cultivation of his said claim, and by an accommodating and charitable disposal of his produce to emigrants, he has contributed much towards the settlement of this Territory.

Although he was allowed to keep his land, Bush was denied citizenship. One of the leading men of his community, he never had the right to vote.

Bush lived just long enough to hear of the Emancipation Proclamation being issued in January 1863. After his death at his home, residents of the area continued to speak of him with respect as one who overcame the difficulties of pioneer life, not only for his family but for many other settlers as well. Ezra Meeker, a pioneer of 1852 who later went on to prominence, spoke of Bush's generosity when the large number of immigrants in 1852–1853 caused a food shortage:

> The man divided out nearly his whole crop to new settlers who came with or without money.... "Pay me in kind next year," he would say to those in need; and to those who had money he would say, "don't take too much … just enough to do you"; and in this wise divided his large crop and became a benefactor to the community.

If success can be measured by material possessions, financial security, and the love and respect of one's family and friends, Bush was a very successful man.

FURTHER READING

The Afro-American Collection at the Washington State Historical Society contains many short items on Bush.

Morgan, Murray. *Puget's Sound: A Narrative of Early Tacoma and the Southern Sound* (1979).

Reese, Gary Fuller. *The George Washington Bush Reader: A Compilation of Writings about the Life and Times of the First African American Settler in Washington* (1992).

This entry is taken from the *American National Biography* and is published here with the permission of the American Council of Learned Societies.

FRANK L. GREEN

Bush, John (1725–c. 1757–58), provincial soldier during the French and Indian Wars of the mid-eighteenth century, prisoner of war, and originator of the Lake George School of powder-horn engraving, was born in the north parish of Shrewsbury (later Boylston), Massachusetts, one of eight children of George Bush, a free black landowner, and his wife, whose name is unknown but who is believed to have been from South America. Nothing is known of John Bush's early life or whether he ever married or had children.

In 1747, during the final years of King George's War, Bush enlisted as a provincial soldier of Massachusetts, and served sporadically for the next eight years as part of the modest garrisons of twenty to one hundred men manning the forts that protected settlements in the Connecticut River Valley. He was on recurring and often extended duty (with deployments ranging from three to sixty-four weeks at a stretch) at remote Forts Massachusetts, Shirley, No. 4, and Dummer. Bush spent his twenties during that eight-year stretch, on frontier duty almost half of the time.

When war between France and Great Britain broke out again in North America in 1754, Bush and his brothers enlisted in the Massachusetts provincial service. Bush served again at Fort Massachusetts for almost a year until his brother Joseph replaced him.

In September 1755 full-blown warfare resumed on the Lake George frontier of northern New York. John Bush's brother, George Jr., served with General William Johnson's forces at Lake George during the 8 September 1755 battle and died of his wounds three weeks later. The remaining two brothers served together as part of the winter garrison of some 400 men living in newly roofed but still windowless barracks, holding Fort William Henry against the French from 27 November 1755 to 14 March 1756. Joseph Bush served that winter with Captain Jeduthan Baldwin's company of Colonel Josiah Browne's Massachusetts regiment, but perished the following spring, probably the victim of one of the fevers that ran rampant. John Bush served at Fort William Henry with Captain James House's company until he mustered out in March 1756.

Bush enlisted again for the summer 1756 campaign (with Captain Joseph Ingersoll's company of Colonel Jonathan Bagley's Massachusetts regiment) and served again at Fort William Henry as company clerk—a recognized master of spelling and penmanship as well as of military form.

In the British and provincial army camps at Lake George during the opening years of the Seven Years' War (French and Indian War), soldiers sought souvenirs of their military experience. Bush became a skillful engraver of powder horns, made from the outer shells of hollowed-out cow horns and used as waterproof containers for gunpowder. The images and calligraphy engraved on the horns became one of the earliest forms of American folk art. Bush originated the Lake George School of engravers working during the early campaigns of the Seven Years' War in North America (Guthman, *Antiques*, 494). Collector and historian William H. Guthman identified key attributes of Bush's calligraphy, format, and decoration that were soon adopted by later carvers in the Lake George School

The earliest wartime souvenir horns that were confidently attributed to John Bush were dated 1755–1756. During long years of service on the western frontier, Bush had served repeatedly under Captain Ephraim Williams Jr., who was the brother of Thomas Williams and older cousin of William

Williams; two surviving horns, one signed by Bush, belonged to a "William Williams" and a "Dr. Thomas Williams."

On stylistic evidence, Guthman suggested that at least three earlier horns—all with ties to Shrewsbury, Massachusetts—may have been engraved by Bush between 1748 and 1750. These horns bear the names and dates Samuel L. Crosby, 1748; Asa Hopgood, 1749; and Levi Whitney, 1750 (Guthman, *Antiques*, 494). Guthman believed that the Crosby horn demonstrated Bush's launch of the Lake George School. Four horns (belonging to Nathan Whiting, Jesse Austin, David Baldwin, and Israel Putnam) attributed by Guthman to John Bush were made at Fort William Henry between September and November 1756 and employed the same verses and similar decorative elements Bush had used on the signed horn he carved for Dr. Thomas Williams the previous year. There has been some contention regarding these attributions by other historians.

Correspondence in 1891 between a descendant of David Baldwin (owner of one of the Fort William Henry horns) and historian Rufus Grider suggests that Grider had identified Bush a century ago as an expert engraver: "Your horn was made by a professional horn decorator—his name was John Bush. He had a certain sett of patterns—which he used partly on every horn he decorated & although he may not have subscribed himself [autographed], once acquainted with his work, one can know it" (Guthman, *Drums a'Beating*, 92–93).

Bush continued to serve during the siege of Fort William Henry a year later. He was captured when the fort fell to a French army on 10 August 1757 and was taken north to Canada as a prisoner of war. Surrender terms were not uniformly observed after this battle, and several survivors were massacred. Black British and provincial soldiers, in particular, were reportedly singled out by Indian attackers: "they Pickt out the negrows Melatows and Indiens and dragged them Away and we Know not what is Become of them" (Steele, 123). "They killd & Scalpt all the Sick & wounded before our faces, and then took out from Our troops, all the Indians and negroes and Carried them off" (Kochan, 356). By the end of 1757 more than 300 of the Fort William Henry garrison were still listed as missing.

By September 1757 the French governor-general in Canada had begun shipping home to France prisoners captured in the capitulation of Fort William Henry so that they did not become a burden on dwindling food supplies in New France (territory which included much of what is now Canada east of the Rockies and large portions of the American Midwest south to Louisiana). Bush escaped servitude in New France, the fate of many other blacks, and was shipped to France as a prisoner of war. He died "on board in the Passage to France" (*Boston Gazette*, 9 Oct. 1758).

Bush's artistry was so distinctive that key elements such as his floriated capitals and animal and fish icons were adopted by other carvers after Bush "went missing" after the 1757 siege of Fort William Henry. The Lake George School of carvers had its origin in John Bush's richly decorative work.

FURTHER READING

The Last Will and Testament of John Bush is located in the Massachusetts State Archives, Worcester County Probate Records, Cabinet 10, Case #9402.

Bush, George. Letter to Gov. Thomas Pownall, 14 Sept. 1758. Massachusetts Archives, vol. 77.

Dresslar, Jim. *Folk Art of Early America: The Engraved Powder Horn* (1996).

Guthman, William H. *Drums a'Beating, Trumpets Sounding: Artistically Carved Powder Horns in the Provincial Manner, 1746–1781* (1993).

Guthman, William H. "Powder Horns Carved in the Provincial Manner," *Magazine Antiques* (Oct. 1993).

Kochan, James L., ed. "Joseph Frye's Journal and Map of the Siege of Fort William Henry, 1757," *Bulletin of the Fort Ticonderoga Museum*, vol. 15, no. 5 (1993).

Padeni, Scott A. "Forgotten Soldiers: The Role of Blacks in New York's Northern Campaigns of the Seven Years' War," *Bulletin of the Fort Ticonderoga Museum*, vol. 16, no. 2 (1999).

Steele, Ian K. *Betrayals: Fort William Henry & the "Massacre"* (1990).

NICHOLAS WESTBROOK

Bush, John Edward (15 Nov. 1856–11 Dec. 1916), businessman and politician, was born a slave in Moscow, Tennessee. Nothing is known about his father. In 1862 his master moved him and his mother, whose name is unknown, to Arkansas to keep them from being freed when the Union army moved into western Tennessee. Bush's mother died when he was seven years old. He was educated in the freedmen's and public schools of Little Rock, Arkansas, and was considered a good student by his teachers. He paid his school tuition by molding bricks. In 1876 he graduated from high school with honors and was immediately appointed principal of Capital Hill School, a public institution for African Americans in Little Rock. In 1878 he moved to Hot

Springs, where he was named to head that city's African American high school.

In 1879 Bush returned to Little Rock, where he married Cora Winfrey, the daughter of a wealthy contractor, Solomon Winfrey. The couple had four children. Bush was a member of the Missionary Baptist church. He obtained a job as a clerk in the city post office's railway service, rising to the position of district supervisor. He held this position until 1892. Bush also invested in Little Rock real estate and dealt in city properties for the rest of his life. In 1889 he began publishing an African American newspaper, *American Guide*.

According to his own account, Bush decided in 1882 to organize an African American insurance company in response to the experiences of a local black woman who faced discrimination in trying to raise funds to bury her husband. With another postal employee, Chester W. Keatts, Bush founded the Mosaic Templars of America, an African American fraternal organization that provided burial and life insurance for its members and was also a loan association and a hospital. The association bought Bush's newspaper and renamed it *Mosaic Guide*. By 1913 the group claimed some eighty thousand members.

In the 1880s Bush became involved in Republican politics in Arkansas, an activity that may have secured him his job with the post office. His early role is obscure, although by 1883 he was busy in the party's Sixth Ward organization in Little Rock. By 1884 he won election as a delegate to the Pulaski County Republican Convention; as a delegate to the state convention, where he served as secretary; and as a member, by proxy, of the state executive committee. In the 1884 county convention he unsuccessfully pushed for more nominations for county offices to be allotted to African Americans. In subsequent years he filled a variety of jobs and positions in city and county party organizations. By 1892 he had become important enough to serve as a delegate to the Republican National Convention, a position that he held again in 1912.

In politics Bush was associated with Powell Clayton, a former governor and U.S. senator who was the state's party boss, and MIFFLIN W. GIBBS, a prominent attorney and party leader. In 1898 Bush, with the backing of Clayton, secured from President William McKinley the position of U.S. receiver of public lands. Bush survived repeated efforts to remove him over the next fourteen years. His chief opposition came from so-called lily-white Republicans in Arkansas who sought to purge

blacks from the party. Ultimately the patronage of Clayton and of white businessmen in Little Rock, along with support from BOOKER T. WASHINGTON, allowed Bush to continue in the position until the Republicans lost the White House in 1912.

Bush, a successful businessman and politician, became an early supporter of the policies of Washington. He joined Washington's National Negro Business League in 1900 and served on its national executive committee, and in 1905 he convinced Washington to visit Little Rock. Bush openly embraced Washington's policy of black self-help and nonconfrontation. Even so, he refused to accept the idea that African Americans should be second-class citizens. As early as 1891 he led protests in an unsuccessful effort to block Democratic legislative efforts to segregate railroad coaches. He continued to oppose infringements on African American civil rights thereafter, leading protests against efforts in 1903 to segregate streetcars in Arkansas and supporting black boycotts of several streetcar lines within the state. Bush died in Little Rock.

FURTHER READING
Bush, A. E., and P. L. Dorman, eds. *History of the Mosaic Templars of America: Its Founders and Officials* (1924).
Smith, C. Calvin. "John E. Bush of Arkansas, 1890–1910," *Ozark Historical Review* 2 (Spring 1973).
Obituary: *(Little Rock) Arkansas Gazette*, 15 Dec. 1916.
This entry is taken from the *American National Biography* and is published here with the permission of the American Council of Learned Societies.

CARL MONEYHON

Bush, William Owen (4 July 1832–14 Feb. 1907), noted farmer, was born to GEORGE WASHINGTON BUSH (c. 1790–1863), a pioneer in the Oregon Territory, and Isabella James (c. 1809–1866), a German American. William was the eldest of five sons born in Missouri: Joseph Tolbert, Rial Bailey, Henry Sanford, and January Jackson.

William's grandfather Mathew Bush is believed to have been the son of a sailor from the British West Indies who married an Irish American woman named Maggie. William's father, George, was born in Pennsylvania and received a Quaker education from the Stevenson family for whom Mathew worked. The Bush family moved to Cumberland County, Tennessee, with the Stevensons and, as a free black man, Mathew was later able to inherit a portion of the Stevenson estate.

George Bush left Tennessee as a young man to join the U.S. Army. He fought at the 1812 Battle of New Orleans with Andrew Jackson before traveling to the West as a fur trapper. He then settled in Clay County, Missouri, where in 1831 he married Isabella James.

William Bush moved west with his family at the age of twelve in 1844. The family chose to move to the territory because Bush's father, the son of a free black man, had traveled the area in the 1820s with the Robideaux Company and the Hudson's Bay Company and believed that the Pacific Northwest, owned jointly by the British and the United States, would be free of legal discrimination. When the family arrived in the fall of 1844, they discovered that the territory's provisional council had passed a black exclusion law in June that prohibited the Bush family from living south of the Columbia River. Other pioneers traveling with the family decided they would not settle anywhere without the Bush family, and the group moved north to Puget Sound in 1845. In 1846 the Treaty of Oregon settled the U.S.-British dispute, and the Bushes found themselves living under the Oregon Territory exclusion laws. There Bush's mother gave birth to another son, Lewis N., in December 1847.

In 1850 Congress passed the Donation Land Act, threatening the family with loss of the land they settled. The act allowed married couples to claim 640 acres of land, and some Thurston County residents argued that the exclusions laws prohibited the elder Bush from claiming the land being farmed by the family. Because the United States had based its claim to the Puget Sound area on the settlement founded by Bush and he had friends in the territorial legislature—many of whom had benefited from the family's generosity in hard times—the legislature petitioned Congress to pass a special act giving George and his wife title to the land known as Bush Prairie. Congress complied, and the family retained ownership of its land into the twentieth century.

Although William Bush learned the techniques of successful farming from his father and became one of Washington State's most noted farmers, like other young men his age he first followed the lure of gold to California. Disappointed by his failure to find gold, he returned to Oregon and purchased a farm south of Tumwater, Washington, on Mound Prairie. On 26 May 1859 he married Mandana Smith Kimsey (1 June 1826–1899), the widow of Duff Kimsey and daughter of Dr. J. Smith and Nancy Scott Wisdom Smith. Mandana had been born in Howard County, Missouri, and migrated to Oregon in 1847 with her husband and parents.

Bush and his wife returned to Bush Prairie in 1870 with their three children, George O., John Shotwell, and Mandana Isabella, known as Belle. In 1872 they and Bush's brothers helped organize the Western Washington Industrial Association, an agricultural association focused on gaining recognition for Washington Territory farm products. Bush's abilities as a farmer brought him state and national awards in the years that followed. In 1875 he won a local award that helped convince the territory to sponsor an exhibit of his wheat at the 1876 Philadelphia Centennial Exposition where he won a gold medal. In 1893 he exhibited vegetables and grains at Chicago's Columbian Exposition and again won medals and certificates, bringing Thurston County and Washington State to national prominence and earning himself an appointment to the Advisory Council of the World's Congress Auxiliary of Farm Culture and Cereal Industry. In 1899 Bush was elected to the first state legislature's house of representatives, where he served two terms. He helped draft the bill that established Washington State's agricultural college under the 1862 Morrell Act, which designated tracts of public domain to support an agricultural college in every state.

The 1900 census record shows Bush, age sixty-seven, as head of the household living in South Union Precinct of Thurston County and lists his occupation as "Farmer." A woman, possibly named Hannah Kennedy, is listed as a grandchild, age fifty-one, occupation "Housekeeper." Her age indicates that she may have been Mandana's grandchild from her first marriage. Another grandchild, age eighteen, is also listed.

Bush died in Olympia, Washington, on 14 February 1907 at age seventy-three. His obituary praised him for his contributions in bringing prominence to the state. Although still a youth at the time of his family's arrival in the Oregon Territory, Bush carried the load of a man in helping his family clear land, build, and plant fruit trees, vegetables, and wheat. The Bush family's skills produced harvests that sustained the family and numerous other pioneers. Bush's noted skills helped establish high agricultural standards for Washington State.

FURTHER READING
Blankenship, Georgiana Mitchell. *Early History of Thurston County, Washington, Together with*

Biographies and Reminiscences of Those Identified with Pioneer Days (1914).

Katz, William Loren. *The Black West: A Documentary and Pictorial History of the African American Role in the Westward Expansion of the United States*, rev. ed. (2005).

MOYA B. HANSEN

Bush-Banks, Olivia Ward (27 Feb. 1869–8 Apr. 1944), writer, was born in Sag Harbor, New York, the daughter of Abraham Ward, probably a fisherman, and Eliza Draper. Both were members of the Montauk Indian tribe of Long Island and both were also of African descent. When Olivia was just nine months old her mother's death forced the family to move to Providence, Rhode Island. Shortly after her father's remarriage, Olivia came under the guardianship of her maternal aunt Maria Draper, whom she credited with having given her an education and preparing her for life. Her aunt's determination and endurance, Olivia believed, resulted from her Native American upbringing. Olivia graduated from Providence High School, where she was trained as a nurse and developed strong interests in drama and literature.

In 1889 Olivia married Frank Bush in Providence and soon gave birth to two daughters, but the couple divorced by 1895. From the end of the century to about 1915, Olivia Bush shuttled between Boston and Providence, taking any available job to support her family. She also wrote poetry and in 1899 published her first volume of verse, *Original Poems*, which yielded some small financial rewards. The collection consisted of ten poems, including elegies extolling African American courage and virtue ("Crispus Attucks," "The Hero of San Juan Hill"), imaginative odes to faith and perseverance ("My Dream of the New Year"), and verses celebrating the ecstasies of religion ("Treasured Moments," "The Walk to Emmaus"). Several works from *Original Poems* were reprinted in the *Voice of the Negro*, one of the premier African American periodicals of the first decade of the twentieth century. Bush shared publication in the *Voice* with other notable African American poets such as JAMES DAVID CORROTHERS, GEORGIA DOUGLAS JOHNSON, and DANIEL WEBSTER DAVIS.

Caring for her children and for her Aunt Maria made writing as a full-time career difficult. In about 1900 Bush became assistant drama director of the Robert Gould Shaw Community House in Boston. From 1900 to 1904 she also contributed to the *Colored American Magazine*, and thus she had poems published in the two journals that had the largest circulation among African Americans in the decade before 1910.

Bush's second collection, *Driftwood* (1914), expanded the themes set forth in *Original Poems*. *Driftwood* included poems, short prose pieces, and several elegies addressed to Abraham Lincoln, FREDERICK DOUGLASS, William Lloyd Garrison, Wendell Phillips, and PAUL LAURENCE DUNBAR, who praised the volume in his preface. Bush soon departed from the pious sensibility shown in both volumes of poetry; her only published play, *Memories of Calvary: An Easter Sketch* (c. 1917), was also her last effort at purely religious pastoralism.

After about 1916 Olivia Bush married Anthony Banks, a Pullman porter. They lived in Chicago, where she founded the Bush-Banks School of Expression and became a drama instructor in the public schools. While at the Shaw Community House, she had decided that drama was indeed her creative strength. It was perhaps during this period (around 1920) that Bush-Banks's unpublished play, "Indian Trails; or, Trail of the Montauk," was written. This play, whose characters closely depict the society of the Algonquian, demonstrates Bush-Banks's knowledge of and facility with the nuances of the Algonquian language and material culture. Only small fragments of the play survive, but it was probably written in response to a 1918 New York State Supreme Court case, *Wyandank Pharaoh v. Jane Ann Benson et al.*, which declared that the Montauk tribe had become extinct because of intermarriage, mostly with blacks but also with whites. The play is a romantic idyll with political and cultural undertones; while it mourns a dissolving Montauk unity, it also reaffirms that unity when O-ne-ne (Wild Pigeon) brings word that whites have agreed to return land to the tribe.

The fragmentation of the Montauks as a result of the *Benson* case caused Bush-Banks to redirect her creative energies and pursue the African American experience as a principal form of expression. During the early years of the Depression she furthered her artistic interests and also began her journalistic efforts in African American culture. She championed the artists, musicians, and writers of the Harlem Renaissance and was associated with LANGSTON HUGHES, COUNTÉE CULLEN, A. PHILIP RANDOLPH, PAUL ROBESON, W. E. B. DuBois, and many other leading lights of the period. She also participated in the Federal Theater Project of the Works Progress Administration in 1936, coaching drama for three years in Harlem at the Abyssinian Community Center run by the Reverend ADAM CLAYTON POWELL

SR. The 1930s seemed also to bring about a change in the tone of Bush-Banks's works. Perhaps the class consciousness that typified the Harlem Renaissance clashed with Bush-Banks's earlier coming to terms with her African Indian heritage. Several unpublished short sketches, including "Greenwich Village Highlights" (c. 1929), "New Year Musings" (1932), and "Black Communism" (1933), as well as an unpublished one-act play, "A Shantytown Scandal" (c. 1935), indicate Bush-Banks's growing disaffection with the Harlem Renaissance, which seemed to suffer a sharp decline in spirit at the onset of the Depression.

Perhaps Bush-Banks's lasting contribution to the literature of the Harlem Renaissance is her "Aunt Viney's Sketches," a cycle of stories that themselves are folk pronouncements on the Depression and on the Harlem scene. (In 1937 Bush-Banks sent six Aunt Viney stories to the Library of Congress, but the copyright application was left unfinished.) She may have intended the title character as a contrast to the young slave woman created by Dunbar in his short story "Viney's Free Papers"; Dunbar's Viney uses her newly found freedom as a weapon against her community. Bush-Banks's Aunt Viney is a mature, lively, sagacious African American woman whose hard-won folk wisdom, conveyed through the richness and power of vernacular speech, renders both racial pride and deft cultural criticism. In this Bush-Banks strongly echoes the efforts of her predecessors, notably Dunbar and CHARLES CHESNUTT, and she precedes Langston Hughes's famous "Simple" tales, which first appeared in 1943.

Although only two volumes of poetry, a play, two poems ("A Picture," 1900, and "On the Long Island Indian," 1916), and three essays in magazines ("Undercurrents of Social Life," 1900, and "Echoes from the Cabin Song" and "Essay on John Greene," both 1932) represent Bush-Banks's published works, her total output reveals a creative life that touched other lives. Not only did she provide documentation and social criticism of the Harlem Renaissance but her literary contributions to that period and the one immediately preceding it are also considerable. Bush-Banks died in New York City.

FURTHER READING

Guillaume, Bernice F., ed. *The Collected Works of Olivia Ward Bush-Banks* (1991).

This entry is taken from the *American National Biography* and is published here with the permission of the American Council of Learned Societies.

NATHAN L. GRANT

Bussey, Charles (1919–15 June 1996), law enforcement officer, community organizer, and mayor, was born in Stamps, Lafayette County, Arkansas, but lived most of his life and built his career in the state capital, Little Rock. His mother, Annie Bussey, lived in Stamps, with his father Charlie Bussey, who worked at the local sawmill. A childhood friend of MAYA ANGELOU's, Bussey and his sister, Delvira Bussey, who became a schoolteacher, shared a deep concern for the welfare and future of children. He moved to Little Rock in the 1940s and opened an appliance shop and on 11 October 1945 married Maggie Clark. Though unsuccessful in the appliance business, by 1950 he had become the state's first black deputy sheriff and was later assigned to the prosecuting attorney's office as an investigator. As deputy sheriff he founded the Junior Deputy Baseball program, and many of those who have since worked in Little Rock city government remember wearing the honorary badges given to the young athletes. As an illustration of his commitment to the community and its children, Bussey mortgaged his home to provide lighting for ball field lights.

At a time when African Americans had first to weigh white interests before promoting the black community, Bussey adroitly positioned himself as a key agent of compromise in the city. The violent white resistance to federally mandated school desegregation tarnished Little Rock's reputation for racial fairness in the late 1950s. Television cameras captured the shocking assaults by white adults on the nine black children (LITTLE ROCK NINE) seeking to enter Little Rock High School. With Little Rock a byword for racial hatred, a group of local white leaders saw the need to change the city's image. Bussey was able to take advantage of that desire and became a bridge between the city's black and white communities. During the urban renewal programs of the late 1950s and early 1960s he served as a peacekeeper in the black community, although he was viewed by both black and white critics as merely a tool for defusing tensions. However, others suggested that Bussey was a man who understood how to exploit advantage—primarily for the good it could do to promote Little Rock. In the 1960s, his vigilance in noticing career and political opportunities for young people positioned him to connect young African Americans with the job opportunities created by the Neighborhood Youth Corps and the Community Action Program. He wielded the greatest influence over Little Rock's Model Cities Program, a political training ground for African American politicians.

As Little Rock's "unofficial black mayor," in 1969 he won election to Little Rock's city board of directors—the first African American to hold elected office in the state since the 1880s. In a career that would stretch over more than two decades he directly served his community through public office, changing the face of Little Rock city government.

His position on the city board of directors was an at-large seat, requiring broad support throughout Little Rock. At that time only about one-third of Little Rock's citizens were African American. The next generation of black leaders, such as city board member Les Hollingsworth, may have been more assertive in demanding civil rights than the pragmatic Bussey, but the black community closed ranks in support of Bussey at election time. However, as a result of the white backlash against civil rights gains for blacks Bussey, along with all other black candidates was defeated in 1976.

Bussey won reelection in the next election and served as a member of the city board from 1979 until his retirement in 1990. At that time, the mayor was not elected directly by the voters of Little Rock, but was instead elected by the other six board members. In November 1981, at the age of sixty-two and after serving the city in various capacities for more than thirty years, Charles Bussey was unanimously elected the city's first black mayor—a position he had sought since at least 1974.

At the time of Bussey's election as mayor, it was the city manager of Little Rock who served as supervisor of city government. However, the position of mayor was more than just an "honorary" position, as some critics claimed. Those who understood the board's politics recognized that while the position of mayor was primarily symbolic, it was coveted by the other council members because of its prestige and the accompanying authority to promote the agenda.

Although Bussey was actively involved in the NAACP, the *Arkansas Democrat-Gazette* noted that one white critic publicly called him an "Uncle Tom," a charge that Bussey and other black leaders dismissed. Bussey reportedly dismissed the charge saying, "I've never marched or picketed in my life, but if another man wants to do that, that's his bag. I can't do it." He is best seen as a pragmatic master at supporting the (mostly white) business community while working behind the scenes to use his extensive connections to assist the economically disenfranchised in the black community. The local press wrote that his role of "godfather [and] protector of the black community," was a self-generated image that never matched reality, but his colleague Myra Jones noted in an interview that when delegations from Little Rock attended conferences of the National League of Cities and other national meetings, Bussey—as the best connected and most skilled—was the head of Little Rock delegations.

Charles Bussey played a central role in improving Little Rock's image in regard to race relations. By the 1990s it had emerged as one of the country's most progressive cities with a model "Racial and Cultural Diversity Commission," and other symbols of having overcome its racist past.

Bussey was viewed as a mentor to emerging political leaders across the community. The white politician Jim Dailey, elected mayor of Little Rock in 1995, recalled serving with Bussey on the city board in the early 1970s, and noted that when he was first running for office the dapper Bussey was among the first to come visit him. Similarly, city board member and future state representative Myra Jones recalls that when she first came before the board on a zoning issue, Bussey approached her after the meeting and encouraged her future career with, "Ms. Jones, maybe you should run for the Board." He would continue to be one of her main political mentors even after she ran for higher office at the state level.

In the summer of 1990 Bussey announced his retirement, proudly claiming that "every day of my life, somewhere I'm helping somebody." During his career he mentored scores of people including future mayors, city managers, and state representatives. Always known for his impeccable dress, he conducted business with a style that made his the face of an era in Little Rock politics. He passed away just five years later after a lengthy illness, leaving behind his widow Maggie and two sons, both attorneys, Charles Larry Bussey and Carl William Bussey. In the fall of 2006, Carl accepted his father's posthumous induction into the Arkansas Black Hall of Fame. Perhaps the most telling tribute is that among the many streets in Little Rock memorialized with names of famous African American leaders, Charles Bussey Avenue is the only one to extend from one side of town to the other, through black and white communities.

FURTHER READING
Marquis, Don. "Bussey Looks Back, Gives Credit to Faith: Bussey Launched Many Rising Political Stars." *Arkansas Democrat-Gazette*, 21 June 1990.
Obituary: *Arkansas Democrat-Gazette*, 16 June 1996.

BRET A. WEBER

Bustill, Joseph Cassey (1822–1895), school teacher and active shipping agent on the Underground Railroad, was born in Philadelphia to a prosperous mixed-race family with roots predating the American Revolution.

His grandfather, Cyrus Bustill, was the son of a slave-owning Quaker named Samuel Bustill, by an enslaved woman in Bustill's household. Born in Burlington, New Jersey, on 2 February 1732, Cyrus arranged after his father and owner's death to be apprenticed in a bakery, owned by another Quaker. He later purchased his freedom with the proceeds of his work, and then opened his own bakery. Cyrus Bustill's wife, Elizabeth Morrey, was the daughter of an Englishman and a Lenni Lenape woman, giving to their descendants an English, African, and Native American heritage. According to a family tradition, four years after his marriage in 1773, Cyrus delivered bread to George Washington's army at Valley Forge during the winter of 1777–1778.

Joseph Bustill was a younger son of DAVID BUSTILL, Cyrus's youngest son, born in 1787, and his wife, Elizabeth Hicks Bustill of Swedesboro, New Jersey. Educated in the best schools of the day, Joseph was said by his daughter Anna to have begun work with the Underground Railroad at the age of seventeen.

Around 1843, Bustill began teaching school in Wilmington, Delaware, joining Unity Lodge 711, Grand United Order of Odd Fellows, on 6 October 1845. He remained active in the order (based in England, since the Odd Fellows in America would only charter lodges with a "white" membership) for the fifty years until his death. In 1853, he moved to Harrisburg, where he continued teaching while taking up his most active period of work on the Underground Railroad. Fugitives from enslavement routinely hid at his home on Walnut Street near 4th Street—an area known as Tanner's Alley—or at the nearby home of William Jones. A sympathetic justice of the peace would notify him of any pursuit under federal fugitive slave laws, and a network of churches, private homes, lodge halls, and other locations were available for hiding his passengers. At this time about nine hundred free African Americans lived in Harrisburg, nearly 12 percent of the population.

Bustill is frequently mentioned in William Still's memoir, *The Underground Railroad* (1872). In a letter dated 24 March 1856 he wrote to "Friend Still" that he and others had lately formed the Fugitive Aid Society, and referred to "five large and three small packages I sent by way of Reading, consisting of three men and women and children." He had dispatched them on the Reading Road to gain five hours time, because "it is expected the owners will be in town this afternoon."

A letter dated the following 28 April informs Still of an offer from Mr. Henry Fiery of Washington County, M.D., "the owner of those three men, two women and three children." He "graciously condescends to liberate the oldest in a year, and the remainder in proportional time, if they will come back; or to sell them their time for $1300." Returning a month later, according to a 26 May letter, Fiery "much to his chagrin received the information of their being in Canada." A more sophisticated and cryptic telegram, dated 31 May 1856, informs Still that "I have sent ... at two o'clock four large and two small hams." His daughter, Anna Bustill Smith, recalled him saying that he had helped over a thousand fugitives to safety.

In the late 1850s Bustill married Sarah Humphrey at Gettysburg, a lady born into the Chippewa tribe near Niagara Falls. It is family tradition that she could not return to her village after marrying a "colored" man but received gifts from her parents. In 1863, he returned to Philadelphia, teaching school for another ten years. Together with OCTAVIUS VALENTINE CATTO he led the twenty-four delegates from Philadelphia to the Pennsylvania Equal Rights League, which convened at Harrisburg 8–10 February 1865. When the Fifteenth Amendment to the federal constitution was ratified, providing that the right to vote should not be abridged on account of race, color, or previous condition of servitude, the Philadelphia Union League appointed Bustill chairman of the committee organizing a parade to celebrate the occasion, which extended for four miles. For a time, he was a trustee of the Banneker Institute, organized in 1853 to provide "discipline to the mind" and serve as "a young men's instruction society."

Bustill retired from teaching in 1873, moving from Philadelphia to Lower Oxford Township, in Chester County, Pennsylvania, in the vicinity of Lincoln University. He built a large house of twenty-two rooms, often renting rooms and providing board to Lincoln students. It is probable, but not explicitly documented, that the daughter of Bustill's older brother Charles, Maria Louisa, was visiting her uncle when she first met a Lincoln theology student, William Drew Robeson, whom she would later marry. Their youngest son, PAUL ROBESON became one of the most famous and accomplished Americans of the twentieth century.

Bustill held a number of high offices in the Odd Fellows, including Grand Treasurer and Most Venerable Patriarch. He is recorded as a speaker at the order's 29th A.M.C., (though Odd Fellows documents refer only to "the AMC," an 1874 report of the Commission on Friendly Societies to the British Parliament does make mention of the "Annual Moveable Committee") held in Chatham, Ontario, 1874. Bustill presented, at a convention in Washington, D.C., on 13 January 1869, a protest against the partial exclusion of colored people from the franchise after ratification of the Fourteenth Amendment. Like many prominent reformers of the late nineteenth century, he was a member of the American Moral Reform Society.

Bustill was a founder of the short-lived Montana Agricultural Emigrant Aid Association, organized in Philadelphia 17 January 1871. Among the seventeen officers and directors were David Bustill Bowser (experienced at steamboating on the Mississippi), William Henry Dorsey, Dr. David Rossell, and general superintendent J. Lambert Dutrieulle, stationed in Helena, Montana, to assist new arrivals sponsored by the association. Although a substantial African American presence never developed in Montana, there were thriving communities, sustained by local African Methodist Episcopal churches, in both Helena and nearby Great Falls until around 1920. Although segregated, they were reasonably well accepted by settlers of other skin colors.

It was Bustill's suggestion that led the Philadelphia city council to set aside as a park the site, at Third and Beach Streets, where William Penn signed a treaty with Native American nations granting him permission to settle Penn's Woods. The Bustill family was proud of its descent from the Lenni Lenape who signed that treaty. He died at home at the age of seventy-three.

FURTHER READING

Brown, Lloyd L. "The Proud Bustills," in *The Young Paul Robeson: On My Journey Now* (1997).

Smith, Anna Bustill. "The Bustill Family," *Journal of Negro History*, Oct. 1925.

Still, William. *The Underground Railroad* (1872).

CHARLES ROSENBERG

Butcher, Elizabeth (fl. 1825–1841), free woman of color, property holder, and slave owner, was a resident of Natchez, Mississippi. Nothing is known about her early life. Her status at the time of her birth, free or enslaved, as well as her parentage

are undetermined. Butcher lived in Natchez for at least twenty years of her life and accrued property during that time due to a relationship with a white man, John Irby. She then came close to losing it when another white man, Robert Wood, attempted to wrest it from her by exploiting her vulnerability as a free woman of color.

In 1834 John Irby wrote his last will and testament, which clearly named Butcher as the administrator of his estate, which consisted of the White House Tavern, surrounding land, buildings, two horses and buggy, household and kitchen furniture, his bank deposits, and two slaves, Alexander and Creasy. Two years later he added a codicil acknowledging that he had sold Alexander and bought another slave, Eliza, and her three children, David, Nancy, and George. Butcher was thus to inherit a total of five slaves at his death. This legacy was a result of Butcher's care as a nurse and housekeeper in Irby's household for nearly twenty years. John Irby unmistakably wished for his property to pass to her and to make arrangements for her to be provided for with this bequest.

Taken at face value, there is no indication that this was anything but a platonic association. It is possible that Irby rewarded Butcher out of gratitude for nursing and caring for him for almost two decades. He may have had no close family members or friends living to inherit his property. There is also the possibility that there may have been something not visible on the surface between the two. Regardless of the nature of the relationship by which she procured it, Butcher had to struggle through the courts to hold onto her inherited property. In 1839 Butcher was enmeshed in a legal battle with a white man, Robert Wood, for the right to administer the estate.

Wood, acting as the administrator of another estate, for the heirs of the deceased James Redman, petitioned the Adams County Probate Court to be granted the power of administration over the Irby estate as well. His primary claim was that there was a gambling debt that had been incurred by Irby in his lifetime that was due to the estate of James Redman. He charged that Butcher had not yet repaid it in her administration of the Irby estate. He was granted the powers of administration over the estate and seized four of the five slaves and was poised to sell them off. He was unable to complete this action due to some legal technicalities, but the court granted him permission instead to try to sell the White House Tavern. Shortly thereafter the court authorized him to sell the five slaves. Wood advertised their sale, but Butcher petitioned the court before they and the property were sold.

She charged that she had not been notified that her power of administration of Irby's estate was challenged, revoked from her, and reassigned to Wood. She had never formally revoked her letters of administration to the estate. Instead Wood endeavored to acquire them without her knowledge and to dispose of the five slaves, the tavern, and the remainder of the estate, all of which he claimed were worth no more than $5,000, before she was able to act and protect her holdings. He was almost successful.

The court ordered Wood to defend the retention of his power of administration over Irby's estate. Wood pulled out his last card, charging that Butcher was "a woman of color and as such is incapable of accepting or holding the office of Administratrix on Said Estate, under the Law of the Country" (*Robert W. Wood [Admins.] of John Irby vs. Elizabeth Butcher*). This point of the case is crucial. If Butcher resembled the great majority of Natchez free property-holding women of color, then almost certainly she was of mixed race. If it were not readily apparent to the court that she was of African ancestry, Wood may have felt this could have cost her the estate under the laws of Mississippi, which required that free people of color hold property under a white sponsor. But Butcher's answer exhibits her confidence in her claim to the estate as "she admits that she is a free woman of color but denied that she is thereby rendered incapable of accepting or holding the Office of Executrix upon the Estate of John Irby Deceased" (*Robert W. Wood [Admins] of John Irby vs. Elizabeth Butcher*).

The Probate Court agreed with Butcher's legitimacy as administrator and ultimately provided her relief. The judge ruled that Butcher had the right to retain her power of administration for the following reasons: no other administrator had been named in Irby's will; the amount due Redman's estate was misrepresented to the court; and, finally, Butcher had not been notified of Wood's action, as was her right. Wood went on to appeal the decision to the Mississippi High Court of Error and Appeals, but they upheld the lower court's ruling and he was ordered to pay her court costs.

Elizabeth Butcher's legal struggle was not an aberration in the lives of free people of color. Whites frequently preyed upon people of African descent, free and enslaved, by contesting the wills of their friends or relatives who bequeathed property or freedom to black men and women. Butcher was fortunate in not having her fortune reversed in Wood's appeal, but unfortunately, after this case, she was lost to the historical record and nothing is known of her life following the court battle.

FURTHER READING
Robert W. Wood (Admins.) of John Irby vs. Elizabeth Butcher, Mississippi High Court of Error and Appeals, Case #679 (1841).

NICOLE S. RIBIANSZKY

Butler, Jerry (8 Dec. 1939–), singer, songwriter, and politician, was one of four children born to J. T. and Alveria Butler, in Sunflower, Mississippi. The Butlers, a Mississippi sharecropping family, moved to Chicago in 1942, where they lived in the Cabrini-Green Housing Projects. J. T. Butler worked a variety of jobs to support his family until his death in 1953, and, following his passing, relatives and friends moved in to help the family make ends meet. Jerry, active in the Church of God in Christ (COGIC), soon became known around his community for his musical ability and rich baritone voice, and he quickly began performing as a gospel artist with friends and fellow COGIC members. One of Jerry's friends, a prodigious musician and songwriter named CURTIS MAYFIELD, would soon join Butler in a singing group called the Roosters. The group subsequently changed its name to the Impressions. Signing to Vee-Jay Records in 1957, the Impressions then began a run of success that would place them at the center of the Chicago soul scene of the 1960s.

In 1958 the group had its first major success, with the release of "For Your Precious Love." In this tender love ballad, Butler delivered a warm and quietly intense lead vocal that would become his trademark and earn him the affectionate nickname, "the Iceman." Before the single's release, and much to the chagrin of the other Impressions, Vee-Jay decided that Butler was a marketable solo persona and released the single under the name Jerry Butler and the Impressions. Butler had not approved this, but after "For Your Precious Love" became a smash, Butler split amicably from the group. Butler and Mayfield continued to work together throughout the 1960s, and their association would be as rewarding a partnership as was to be found in the era's R&B. Butler became one of the major artists in the Mayfield-driven Chicago soul empire of successful records—an empire that also included artists like Major Lance, Gene Chandler, and the post-Butler Impressions. Mayfield participated in the writing and recording of most of Butler's early hits, a string of tracks, including "He Will Break Your Heart" and "I'm A-Telling You," that were characterized by the Iceman's rich vocals and Mayfield's unique arrangements and production style. Often awash in acoustic guitars, with subtle Latin rhythms, Butler's 1960s hits are examples of the "sweet soul" that Mayfield and his collaborators produced throughout the decade. The "sweet soul" sound fell on the spectrum between the deep emotions of gospel and the sophisticated, pop-oriented music of Detroit's hugely successful Motown Records and Mayfield's hero, SAM COOKE. (Butler also took a liking to a southern singer named OTIS REDDING, whose early hits were clearly modeled after Butler's slow-burning ballad style. Later the two cowrote "I've Been Loving You Too Long," a song that became a major hit for Redding.)

In 1967 Butler signed to Mercury Records, and in association with the Philadelphia, Pennsylvania–based songwriting-production team of Kenneth Gamble and LEON HUFF, who were soon to launch their own hugely successful soul label in Philadelphia, recorded two albums of glimmering, lushly orchestrated music that serves as a sonic bridge between the "sweet soul" scenes of the 1960s and 1970s. Apart from being artistic successes, these albums also produced two number one hits for Butler, both cowritten with Gamble and Huff: "Hey Western Union Man," an exuberant love song that proved that Butler's talent was not limited to slow material, and "Only the Strong Survive," a gospel-inflected call for strength and determination that carried political resonance at the birth of the Black Power movement. (Butler and the Gamble and Huff team charted two other top ten singles, "Never Give You Up" and "Are You Happy?" in 1968 and 1969.) This phase of Butler's career was as commercially successful as his earlier alliance with Curtis Mayfield.

Butler continued to record music throughout the 1970s, charting several hits throughout the course of the decade. In 1971 he reached number eight with "If It's Real What I Feel," and later scaled the charts again with two 1972 duets with the singer Brenda Lee Eager ("Ain't Understanding Mellow" and "Close to You") and, that same year, a cover of Philadelphia soul stars the O'Jays ("One Night Affair"). His association with Mercury gave way to brief tenures with both Motown Records and a reunion with Gamble and Huff at their record label, Philly International.

By the 1980s Butler's hit-making potential had dried up, but the Iceman was just at the beginning of a second career, this time turning his attention to Chicago politics. Butler, much like his old friend and collaborator Mayfield, had long been concerned with political issues, and in the 1980s he applied that longstanding passion toward direct political involvement. He avidly supported the campaign of HAROLD WASHINGTON, Chicago's first black mayor, during the middle part of the decade. At the end of the 1980s Butler became a commissioner for Cook County, Illinois, and was an elected alderman by the close of the 1990s. Butler's commitment to public service—nurtured by his appreciation for the campaigns of the civil rights movement—led him from the center-stage spotlight to an office in the Cook County Municipal Building. In 1988 he also became the president of the Rhythm and Blues Foundation; he was reelected to a second term in that position in 1998. In 2000 Butler, with Earl Smith, published his autobiography, *Only the Strong Survive*, which is a combination of reminiscences and analysis of current musical and political issues. In the early twenty-first century, Butler, still respected and beloved among soul audiences, performed occasionally. His strong voice and his hits—from "For Your Precious Love" to "Only the Strong Survive"—retained their power and emotional impact. JERRY "THE ICEMAN" BUTLER, whose journey began as the child of Mississippi sharecroppers, emerged a king of 1960s soul music and, later in life, a player in big-city politics.

FURTHER READING

Butler, Jerry, with Earl Smith. *Only the Strong Survive* (2000).

Lytle, Craig. "Jerry Butler," in *All Music Guide to Soul*, ed. Vladimir Bogdanov (2003).

Werner, Craig. *Higher Ground: Aretha, Curtis, Stevie and the Rise and Fall of American Soul Music* (2003).

DISCOGRAPHY

The Best of Jerry Butler (Rhino Records 75881).

The Philadelphia Sessions (Mercury Records 586498).

CHARLES L. HUGHES

Butler, Mary Dell (28 Dec. 1924–14 Jan. 1986), recreation commissioner, PTA president, and community advocate, was born Mary Dell Byrd in Greenville, Texas, to Eliza Henderson and George Byrd, who worked as a porter for the railroad. Mary had a twin sister named Adele—the only children in the family—and attended grade school and high school in Greenville. After high school, Byrd married Charlie Joe Christian and had two daughters,

Georgia and Beverly. The marriage lasted only a few years, and at age twenty-one, she moved to Long Beach, California, with her two daughters. There she met Richard Butler, and the two were married in 1948. The couple had six sons: Anthony, Reginald, Douglas, Stanley, Timothy, and Eric. It was because of her children that Butler became engaged in school and civil rights activism.

The 1954 Supreme Court ruling in *Brown vs. Board of Education* declared segregation in public schools to be unconstitutional and that separate educational facilities were inherently unequal. Butler followed this ruling closely and joined various PTA boards—at a time when such boards had few black members—to do her part in *Brown vs. Board*'s implementation. When her daughter Georgia began attending Polytechnic High School, Butler became involved and was appointed the first black PTA president at Long Beach's Whittier Elementary School. According to her son Anthony, she once stated, "I want this world to be a better place for them, and if I don't do something about making it a better place, no one else will." During the 1960s Butler became employed at St. Mary's Medical Center, first as a secretary and later as an emergency room technician. She managed to hold down a full-time job, raise her children, participate on PTA boards, and work on community projects. When her children became involved in sports activities, Butler began attending their basketball, football, and baseball games. In 1970 she was appointed president of the Long Beach Recreation Commission and worked to establish new programs for the children within the community. She credited the recreation programs with saving countless children from the streets and enjoyed displaying the athletic trophies received by her sons. Butler was especially proud of an award from the city for her many years of service to youth, particularly in the fields of education and recreation.

In 1970 Butler became the first black person to head the Polytechnic High PTA—and would be a member for twenty-five years. In the 1960s and 1970s when racial problems beset Polytechnic High School, Butler proved to be a leader and peacemaker. She helped to organize the Poly Community Interracial Committee, which was founded in order to identify and address racial problems within the school and to help prevent further racial turmoil. Parents, teachers, and students would meet to talk about the problems and how best to address them. Butler also pushed for the construction of the Poly Redevelopment Project, which would provide low-cost apartments on Atlantic Avenue near Polytechnic High School. In 1980 she became a member of the Long Beach Unified School District Personnel Commission and became known for her activism with community and school groups serving the inner city. Butler also served on the Recreation Commission for ten years and became the first African American to serve as president of this commission. With her many other responsibilities, she also held memberships in the Community Planning Council, the Long Beach chapter of the NAACP, and the Neighborhood Adult League. She worked with the Interracial and Concerned Parents Committees, the Heart Association, the Community Improvement League, the Girl Scouts, the Boy Scouts, and the Cancer Society.

At the age of sixty-three, Mary Dell Butler died of cancer. Butler's oldest daughter, Georgia, remembers her mother as a true pioneer. In an interview, she said, "mother believed in making things happen for herself and her family, and she was always doing things to aid other people." Her forty years of community service prompted the City of Long Beach to establish the Mary Dell Butler Volunteer of the Year Award. This award was established to honor a volunteer who exemplifies Butler's high standards of dedication and public service. To further honor Butler, the City of Long Beach named the Mary Dell Butler Elementary School for her in 1992, the city's first school to be named for an African American.

FURTHER READING

Cohn, Carl A. "Tribute to a Community Leader," *Long Beach Press Telegram*, Sept. 1993.

Day, Aaron L. *History Lessons* (2005)

Harper, Karen S. *Mary Dell Butler: Making a Difference, Long Beach* (2005)

Ivy, Carol. "Beautiful Activists Named," *Long Beach Press Telegram*, May 1974.

Tucker, Indira Hale, and Aaron L. Day, eds. *The Heritage of African Americans in Long Beach: Over 100 Years* (2007).

Obituary: *Long Beach Press Telegram*, 16 Jan. 1986.

AARON L. DAY

Butler, Melvin Arthur (2 May 1938–14 Nov. 1973), educator and linguist, was born in Monroe, Louisiana, the son of Mr. and Mrs. James H. Butler Sr. In 1956 he graduated as the valedictorian from Monroe's Carroll High School and then graduated magna cum laude with a B.A. from Morehouse College in Atlanta, Georgia. In 1962 he earned an M.A. from the University of Texas at Austin, and in 1968 he got his Ph.D. in English from the University of Michigan, where he specialized in linguistics. His doctoral dissertation, "Lexical Usage of Negroes in Northeast Louisiana," was completed in 1968. It grew from questions addressed in his master's thesis, "The Vocabulary of Negroes in Austin, Texas." Focusing on seven counties in northeast Louisiana in his dissertation research, Butler interviewed individuals using established questionnaire techniques and demonstrated that black speakers in those communities exhibited coastal southern patterns in their lexical (vocabulary) usage. Such terms as *croker sack* (rather than *tow sack*, generally used by white speakers) and *mosquito hawk* (rather than *snake doctor*) were used by most speakers interviewed. Nonstandard verb forms were also frequently used; examples are *holp*, *seed*, and *dremp* (rather than *helped*, *saw*, and *dreamed*). Butler also studied at the University of London. He received graduate fellowships between 1961 and 1968 from the Woodrow Wilson Foundation, the Danforth Foundation, and the Southern Education Foundation.

Butler's murder in 1973, just five years after he received his doctorate from the University of Michigan, cut short a promising academic career. However, in the brief years that he was in academia Butler had many distinguished accomplishments and made critical contributions, particularly in encouraging university students and in serving as a role model as he moved into university administration. In 1969, four years after joining the faculty of Southern University in Baton Rouge, he was promoted to professor and became chair of the English department. Under his leadership, the English department at Southern, for years the largest predominantly black public university in the country, expanded its curriculum from a single course in black American literature to seven such courses and two courses on the language of black Americans. Committed to disseminating truth about the black experience in America and promoting serious study of black speech, Butler gave numerous talks in Baton Rouge, throughout Louisiana, and at universities elsewhere in the country, including Yale, where on two occasions he gave talks on "Black Language." There were no books in print on Black English in the late 1960s. Some instructors at Southern recall how helpful it was to be able to consult Butler when they

encountered local linguistic patterns with which they were unfamiliar.

Butler's doctoral dissertation was significant as part of the body of work on African American speech produced by black linguists who emerged in the 1970s. Several of his publications drew upon material from that dissertation, such as the 1969 article "African Linguistic Remnants in the Speech of Black Louisianans" and the 1971 article "The Implications of Black Dialect for Teaching English in Predominantly Black Colleges." Butler, like other early researchers, understood that unsupported assertions characterizing Black English as inferior to other dialects of American English interfered with the effective teaching of black students.

During 1972 and part of 1973, Butler chaired a committee of the Conference on College Composition and Communication (CCC) that was in charge of composing a document to support the "Students' Right to Their Own Language" resolution that had been adopted by the CCC Executive Committee in 1972 (and subsequently by the CCC membership in 1974). Adoption of the resolution by the membership was significant. The CCC is the college and university section of the National Council of Teachers of English, a sixty-thousand-member, pedagogically oriented professional organization in the United States for teachers of English at all levels. Butler was killed before the publication was completed, but he has been credited with assisting in the completion of the document by means of his skillful diplomacy—although he was not able to witness the fruits of his labor. His diplomacy was important, since the resolution was quite controversial; the careful editing the publication received throughout the committee process was crucial to its ultimate adoption. The document was published as a special issue of the CCC journal, *College Composition and Communication* (*CCC*), titled "Students' Right to Their Own Language." In the preface to that publication (still in print and also available on the Internet) special thanks were given for Butler's work; the preface also expressed the hope that this special issue would be "a lasting tribute to his efforts" (*CCC* 25, Fall 1974).

Butler was also the first editor of the Southern University journal *Black Experience*, and he established Southern's English department–sponsored Annual Black Poetry Festival (1972). The festival, very popular with students, continued for seven years after his death. In addition, Butler made himself available to work on race-relations matters within correctional institutions and law enforcement offices in Louisiana. One reason his early death was shocking to many was because it apparently occurred in connection with counseling work that Butler was involved in as a correctional institution volunteer.

Butler's activities during his brief professional life motivated many people. In an "In Memoriam" article in the *CLA Journal*, Charles H. Rowell, who was once Butler's Southern University colleague, suggested that Butler's professional life was characterized by "ardent efforts to correct myopia about the Black Experience and Black American speech" (431–433).

FURTHER READING

Butler, Melvin. "African Linguistic Remnants in the Speech of Black Louisianans," *Black Experience* (1969).

Butler, Melvin. "The Implications of Black Dialect for Teaching English in Predominantly Black Colleges," *CLA Journal* 15 (1971): 235–239.

Rowell, Charles H. "In Memoriam," *CLA Journal*.

"Students' Right to Their Own Language," *College Composition and Communication* 25 (Fall 1974).

BETHANY K. DUMAS

Butler, Nace (?–6 Aug. 1819), a fifer in the Second Maryland Regiment during the War of Independence, enlisted in 1776 and served for the duration of the war. At least two other black men served in the same regiment. A position as a musician was not an uncommon assignment for African Americans, particularly in the first years of the conflict. The army raised by the Continental Congress was initially multiracial, but soon after George Washington took command in the spring of 1775 he ordered recruiting officers not to enlist African Americans. In a council of war on 8 October 1775, Washington and other prominent officers decided unanimously to bar all slaves and—by a wide majority—all African Americans from enlisting in the Continental army. Confronted with a shortage of soldiers, Washington reversed this decision. By the end of the war African American soldiers had usually served longer terms of enlistment than their white counterparts.

Early in the war, there were few African American enlistments from Maryland, and not until October 1780 did that state allow the enlistment of slaves into its regiments. Maryland had to fill regiments demanded by the Continental Congress, but it also had to protect a long coast constantly threatened by British incursions. Slaves constituted about 25 percent of the state population, and the prospect of arming them raised whites' fears of social disorder. In addition, slaves were so valuable in the labor force that many planters were unwilling to part with them regardless of military necessity. Gradually the state legislature came to a position favoring African American participation in the armed forces. Indeed by 1781 the legislature was debating the wisdom of raising an African American regiment, but opposition to that idea proved too great.

The Second Regiment participated in many battles, including those at Guilford Courthouse and Camden. Maryland and Delaware were unusual in having troops present at almost every major battle of the war. Thus Butler saw far wider service than most soldiers because of his unit's activity and the long duration of his enlistment.

It is known that Butler married an Irish woman named Mary in 1782 while he was on furlough and that after the war he returned home. But his biography then becomes complicated by the existence of at least two Nace Butlers living in Annapolis in the 1780s. An Ignatius Butler, calling himself Nace, was a runaway slave who lived in Annapolis for a time. He had escaped from Nat Ewing of St. Mary's County, Maryland. According to an advertisement placed by Ewing, the runaway, Ignatius, was a "dark mulatto man named Nace, who calls himself Nace Butler about 22, combs his hair back, which is pretty long for one of his complexion 5'8" ... an artful designing rogue; he lately petitioned the general court for his freedom which petition still remains undetermined. His father lives with Mrs. Bradford at Bladensburg, where he has been since he ran away. He went last October to Annapolis, where he passes as a freeman" (*Maryland Gazette*, Feb. 1785).

Another Nace Butler, although described as a mulatto, of the same approximate age and from the same locale as the other, was married to a mixed-race woman named Nanny and was legally established as a freeman by 1804. A circumstantial case could be made that they were the same man, but it appears unlikely, and, therefore the status of Nace Butler the fifer, whether slave or free, remains undetermined.

Not until 1828 did the United States grant pensions to surviving soldiers; before then, pensions had been granted only to those injured during the war, and these were later restricted to cases of demonstrated need. In 1836, however, the widows of soldiers could also receive pensions. Congress, however, declined to grant pensions to those who were either still slaves or widows of slaves. Butler's widow, Mary, living in Anne Arundel County, Maryland, applied for a widow's pension soon after the passage of the 1836 law and again in 1840, as Nace himself had never received a pension. She appeared before a judge of the Orphans Court, but her claim was rejected. In 1850 Mary Butler's nephew, Charles Butler, attempted to pursue any money due to his aunt, but again the claim was rejected.

FURTHER READING

Greene, Robert Ewell. *Black Courage, 1775–1783: Documentation of Black Participation in the American Revolution* (1984).

Nash, Gary. *Race and Revolution* (1990).

National Society Daughters of the American Revolution. *Minority Revolutionary War Service, Delaware Maryland New Jersey, 1775–1783* (1998).

Stewart, Mrs. Frank Ross. *Black Soldiers of the American Revolutionary War* (1978).

M. KELLY BEAUCHAMP

Butler, Octavia E. (22 June 1947–24 Feb. 2006), science fiction writer, was born Octavia Estelle Butler in Pasadena, California, the only child of Laurice James Butler, a shoe shiner, and Octavia Margaret Guy, who sometimes found work as a domestic. Butler's father died when she was young, so she was raised by her mother. Butler's consciousness of her family's struggle for financial stability in both Louisiana and California would eventually form the basis for an important theme in her writing, which introduced an underrepresented black, female perspective into science fiction and fantasy writing.

Butler recognized early in childhood that writing was her passion. A shy and sometimes lonely child, she read voraciously at the encouragement of her mother, who brought home castoff books from her employers' families. But Butler was influenced by other forms of entertainment, too. After watching *Devil Girl from Mars*, described by Butler in an interview as a "silly" science fiction movie in which beautiful Martian women attempt to colonize Earth's men, she decided that she could write better stories herself. She also loved radio programs—which she called "theater of the mind"—and science documentaries. Such diverse sources helped to shape her lifelong fascination with the intersections of science and narrative (Rowell, 53).

At the age of ten Butler begged her mother for a typewriter and at thirteen began submitting her work for publication. After graduating from high school in 1965, she worked a variety of warehouse, factory, and secretarial jobs while attending Pasadena City College, from which in 1968 she earned an associate of arts degree. As she slowly gained confidence in her abilities, Butler took any writing classes she could, including those offered at California State University, Los Angeles; University of California, Los Angeles; and the Open Door Program of the Screenwriters Guild of America, West. These classes helped her to establish relationships with other writers, including the science fiction authors Harlan Ellison and Theodore Sturgeon. It was Ellison who encouraged her to participate in the Clarion Science Fiction and Fantasy Writers' Workshop in 1970, where she met the prominent African American science fiction writer SAMUEL R. DELANY. This six-week course immersed Butler in a science fiction community and helped launch her career. In 1971 she sold her first short story, "Crossover," to *Clarion*, the workshop's anthology, and her first novel, *Patternmaster*, was published five years later. Over the next thirty years, she went on to publish ten more novels and several short stories and nonfiction pieces.

As a young reader Butler recognized that early science fiction tended to reproduce predictable race and gender hierarchies, and her work makes tremendous progress toward rectifying this disparity. Her fiction features recognizable science fiction tropes, including interplanetary travel, futuristic settings, and individuals with powers that far surpass those of ordinary humans. Yet she complicates the genre by consistently including black women as empowered characters whose social position challenges American racial stereotypes. Her female characters demonstrate that a balance of physical and emotional strength combined with intellect and sympathy will endure long after physical power alone has expended itself. The characters and the texts are neither polemical nor one-dimensional, as even the most heroic of her characters exhibit weaknesses and flaws.

As much as Butler influenced science fiction as a genre, her work also drew upon and contributed to the African American literary tradition more generally. Her family's history and her own experience as a working-class African American coming of age during the civil rights period actively informed her depiction of race, and she rooted her fiction in African American history and literature. An early novel, *Kindred* (1979), features an African American woman living in 1976 who is drawn back in time to the antebellum South to save the life of a white ancestor and slave owner. The protagonist's interactions with the slaves she meets complicate her perception of the lived experience of slavery. This novel, Butler explains, was an attempt to answer criticism by some in her generation who considered their ancestors insufficiently rebellious in response to the slave system. Her novel implicitly warns against using a late twentieth-century standard to judge the actions of those who attempted to survive slavery. Another of Butler's novels confronts American slavery directly. *Wild Seed* (1980), her "prequel" to the Patternmaster series, is a complex allegory of the transatlantic slave trade, drawing upon the cultural history of pre-colonized Africa to trace the path of Africans kidnapped into slavery, transported across the Atlantic in the Middle Passage, and enslaved for generations in the United States.

Both of these novels qualify as neo-slave narratives, joining SHERLEY ANNE WILLIAMS's *Dessa Rose* (1986), Charles Johnson's *Middle Passage* (1990), and TONI MORRISON's *Beloved* (1987) as contemporary reworkings of the form. In returning to the slave narrative from the vantage point of the late twentieth century, Butler draws explicit attention to the enduring effect of slavery on both black and white Americans. In terms of literary production, Butler advanced a developing tradition, blending the historical past and imagined futures in a mutually informative way and making her contributions to the African American literary tradition as significant as her influence on science fiction.

While still concerned about the relationship between the past and the future, Butler, in her later novels, paid particularly close attention to the potential repercussions of America's social problems. In the Xenogenesis series, published in the 1980s, and her subsequent novels *Parable of the Sower* (1995) and *Parable of the Talents* (1998), Butler mixed an awareness of the United States' history of social inequalities with concerns about violence and environmental deterioration. Worried about the "inevitability of unintended consequences," Butler forecast the repercussions of these conditions into a troubled future (Butler, "A Few Rules," 364).

Octavia Butler's literary accomplishments were recognized not only by her peers in the science fiction community but also by larger professional organizations. Several of her short stories won the most prestigious awards in science fiction. "Speech Sounds" (1983) won a Hugo Award in 1984. Her novella *Bloodchild* (1984) won several awards, including the Hugo (1985) and Nebula (1984). Her short story "The Evening and the Morning and the Night" (1987) was nominated for a Nebula Award as was her novel *The Parable of the Sower*. Its companion novel, *Parable of the Talents*, won a Nebula Award in 1999. Perhaps the most noteworthy recognition of Butler's contribution to American culture came in 1995, when she was awarded a MacArthur Foundation "genius" grant, a cash prize recognizing the recipients' creativity and independence in their chosen fields.

In an informational note appended to her novel, *Wild Seed*, Butler describes herself as "comfortably asocial—a hermit in the middle of a large city, a pessimist if I'm not careful, a feminist, a Black, a former Baptist, an oil-and-water combination of ambition, laziness, insecurity, certainty, and drive." In this statement Butler reveals her own complexity in much the same way that she captures the interconnectedness of humanity in her fiction. She links past, present, and future, male and female, black and white, human and alien in a web that enriches readers' understanding of race, gender, and human nature. Octavia Butler's contribution to science fiction writing and contemporary African American literature cannot be underestimated.

Butler relocated to Seattle, Washington, in 1999. She died there, at the age of fifty-eight, after a fall that may have been the result of a stroke. An intensely private person, Butler lived alone at the time of her death and left no immediate survivors.

FURTHER READING

Butler, Octavia. *Bloodchild and Other Stories* (1995).
Butler, Octavia. "A Few Rules for Predicting the Future," *Essence* (May 2000).
Kenan, Randall. "An Interview with Octavia Butler," *Callaloo* 14, no. 2 (1991).
Rowell, Charles. "An Interview with Octavia E. Butler," *Callaloo* 20, no. 1 (1997).

CYNTHIA A. CALLAHAN

Butler, Selena Sloan (4 Jan. 1872?–7 Oct. 1964), community leader and child-welfare activist, was born in Thomasville, Georgia, the daughter of Winnie Williams, a woman of African and American Indian descent, and William Sloan, a white man who reportedly supported Selena and her older sister but lived apart from the family. Even after her mother died, presumably when Selena was fairly young, Selena kept quiet about her father's identity. Communication between them was minimal. At age ten, having been schooled by missionaries in Thomas County, she was admitted on scholarship to the

Atlanta Baptist Female Seminary (now Spelman College) in Atlanta and received her high school diploma in 1888 as a member of the school's second graduating class. After graduation she taught English and elocution in the public schools in Atlanta until around 1891, when she took a position at the State Normal School in Tallahassee, Florida (now Florida Agricultural and Mechanical State University).

In 1893 she married Henry Rutherford Butler, a pediatrician from North Carolina and one of the first black physicians to establish a practice in Atlanta. Later he became a partner in one of the nation's first black-owned drugstores and the first such drugstore in Georgia. The couple had one child. Throughout their marriage the Butlers traveled extensively within the United States and abroad. In 1894, while Henry took continuing medical coursework at Harvard Medical School in Cambridge, Massachusetts, Selena attended the Emerson School of Oratory in Boston to further her elocution skills. At the same time she continued her work with the Atlanta Women's Club, of which she was a charter member, and represented it at the organizational meeting of the National Federation of Colored Women's Clubs in Boston in the late 1890s.

After returning to Atlanta in 1895, the Butlers established residence in the Old Fourth Ward, a fashionable black neighborhood near the campus of Morris Brown University (now Morris Brown College). That same year the board of education asked Butler to run a pioneering night school for black adults held at the Yonge Street School. She also established, edited, and published the *Woman's Advocate*, a monthly newspaper focused on the interests of African American women. In the early 1900s, unable to find a kindergarten class that would admit her son Henry Butler Jr. because of his race, Butler established a kindergarten in the basement of her home that the neighborhood children also attended. In 1911, after these youngsters were in elementary school, Butler founded the nation's first black parent–teacher association. About eight years later it developed into the statewide Georgia Colored Parent Teacher Association (GCPTA), later named the Georgia Conference of Colored Parents and Teachers. Continuing her efforts on behalf of the education of black children, in 1926 Butler established and became founding president of the National Congress of Colored Parents and Teachers, which merged with the white national PTA in 1970. At that time she was designated as a

national founder, along with Alice McLellan Birney and Phoebe Hearst, who had founded the previously all-white national PTA.

Butler's role in black community affairs extended well beyond education. An active club woman, she served as a delegate to the founding convention of the National Association of Colored Women in Boston in 1896 and as the first president of the Georgia Federation of Colored Women's Clubs. Interested in promoting better relations between blacks and whites, she and her husband were members of the Georgia Commission on Interracial Cooperation, founded in Atlanta in 1919. At the end of World War I, Butler was honored by the American Red Cross for her help in entertaining black enlistees at Camp Gordon near Atlanta and for leading the Atlanta office's sale and distribution of war savings stamps and certificates. Butler became an organizer of the Ruth Chapter of the Order of the Eastern Star in Atlanta and was grand lecturer of the lodge in Georgia. In 1930 she joined a group of white and black southern women in forming the Southern Women for the Prevention of Lynching. In 1943 this group was absorbed into the Southern Regional Council along with the Georgia Commission on Interracial Cooperation. Butler's influence was also felt nationally. Sometime in 1930–1931 President Herbert Hoover asked her to serve on his White House Conference on Child Welfare and Protection as a representative of the National Congress of Colored Parents and Teachers. In this capacity she served on the Infant and Pre-school Child Committee, whose work contributed to the writing of the memorable "Children's Charter."

A few years after her husband's death in 1931, Butler sojourned in Europe with her son, by then a graduate of Harvard Medical School. During her stay in London, Butler worked with the Nursery School Association headed by the duke of Gloucester and also assisted Lady Astor Washead's cancer association campaign. After the United States entered World War II, Butler followed her son to Fort Huachuca in Arizona, where he underwent officer training. While there she organized a Gray Lady Corps and again worked with the American Red Cross. She returned to Atlanta in 1947 and later followed her son and daughter-in-law to Los Angeles, where Henry Butler Jr. was the first black physician on the staff of Good Samaritan Hospital. Active in the Congregational Church, Butler served on the boards of the Sojourner Truth Home and of Las Madrinas, the mothers' organization of Alpha Kappa Alpha sorority. She died in

Los Angeles and was buried next to her husband in Oakland Cemetery in Atlanta.

Butler played an important role in the development of interracial efforts on behalf of the welfare and education of children and as a leader and mentor within the black community. Her work with the Georgia Colored PTA forged a successful link with its white national counterpart, and she was unusually successful at achieving communication between the two groups at the local level. Her efforts to improve civic-mindedness within the black community made her an important figure in national as well as African American history.

FURTHER READING

Biographical material is in the Robert W. Woodruff Library, Atlanta University Center.

Read, Florence Matilda. *The Story of Spelman College* (1961).

Wesley, Charles H. *The History of the National Association of Colored Women's Clubs* (1984).

Obituaries: *Atlanta Daily World*, 8 Oct. 1964; *Atlanta Journal and Constitution*, 7–9 Oct. 1964.

This entry is taken from the *American National Biography* and is published here with the permission of the American Council of Learned Societies.

MICHELLE M. STRAZER

Butler, Susie Dart (1888?–June 1959), librarian and clubwoman, was born Susan Dart in Charleston, South Carolina, to the Reverend John Lewis Dart, pastor at Morris Street Baptist Church and Shiloh Baptist Church and editor of the *Southern Reporter*, and Julia Pierre, a former teacher. Dart was educated at the Charleston Institute, a school run by her father, and at his alma maters, Avery Institute and Atlanta University. She then traveled north to attend McDowell millinery school in Boston, a move which later led her to open the first millinery shop owned by an African American in Charleston when she returned home in 1913. She was successful, employing a number of women and girls and shipping hats to customers in the state and throughout the region. After five years Dart closed the shop and volunteered for the Red Cross during World War I. Following the war, in 1921, she shifted her work interests to education, opening one of the city's first kindergartens for black children. Working with a fellow Atlanta University graduate, she operated this school for ten years.

In 1912 Dart married Nathaniel Lowe Butler, a native of Boston and real estate agent. They had one son, Nathaniel Jr. Susie Dart Butler became active in her community through the burgeoning women's club movement. She was the first treasurer of the Phillis Wheatley Club, named for the poet PHILLIS WHEATLEY, founded in 1916, and dedicated to self-improvement and community service. The club took up the topics of African American history and literature, raised funds for local black schools, and contributed to the Fairwold Home for Delinquent Girls, the most important project sponsored by the South Carolina Federation of Colored Women's Clubs. In 1919 Butler became club president, and under her leadership the Phillis Wheatley Club maintained its affiliation with the state federation despite difficulties in raising the necessary dues. Butler was also a founding member of the Charleston City Federation, president of the Book Lovers' Club, and president of the Modern Priscilla Club, which focused on improving educational and recreational opportunities for young people and visiting and serving the Old Folks Home in Charleston. One of the most important early leaders of the South Carolina Federation of Colored Women's Clubs, she held several offices, including that of official historian, and was on the board of directors for the Fairwold Home for Delinquent Girls.

Butler also chaired the Charleston chapter of the Commission on Interracial Cooperation (CIC), an interracial organization affiliated with the local YWCA, as well as the national CIC. The Charleston chapter helped provide playgrounds for local black youth and supported educational projects.

Butler's most important contribution to African American history is as one of the most outstanding librarians in early-twentieth-century South Carolina. She acquired her love of books from her father, who had an excellent collection and who maintained a reading room for the young men of his parish until his death in 1915. As chair of the Charleston CIC, Butler convened a committee to conduct a survey of the number and kinds of books available to African Americans in Charleston. Interested in opening her father's collection to all African Americans, but especially to young people in need of education, Butler organized his books and raised money through dances, parties, and a concert to renovate the former printing office of her father's newspaper. She whitewashed the walls, built shelves, and acquired additional books, until in 1927 Butler opened the library and soon began holding story hours for young children there. Working in partnership with Clelia McGowan, a white leader in the CIC, she sought financial support from the Julius Rosenwald Foundation and the Carnegie Endowment. The Rosenwald Fund agreed to provide funding for five years to establish a free public library in Charleston, with access for African Americans guaranteed, albeit in segregated facilities. The Dart Hall Branch, the first branch of the Charleston County Library system for African Americans opened on 31 July 1931, making 3,600 books available to its patrons. The library was located in Dart Hall, a building owned by Butler and formerly used as a school by her father. She leased the building to the county for one dollar per year.

Butler worked on staff at the Dart Hall Branch as the children's librarian, along with Julia McBeth and Mary Sparks. In 1932 Butler trained in library science at Hampton University in Virginia. Because of her interest in African American history, the Dart Hall Branch became a depository for materials by and of relevance to African Americans, including newspapers, periodicals, and manuscripts, later collected in the African American Materials Project. She worked at the library until her retirement in 1957.

In 1932 the Regional Housing Authority in Atlanta asked Butler to conduct a survey of housing conditions for African Americans in Charleston. She called together eight clubwomen to survey the living conditions of Charleston's poorest black residents. The results of their survey eventually led to the development and construction of several housing projects, the first built in 1936.

Butler was an active member of Plymouth Congregational Christian Church, the American Library Association, a founding member of the librarians' section of the South Carolina State Teachers' Association, a board member of the Red Cross, and a board member of the Robert Shaw Boys' Club. She was honored as the Charleston Chapter of Links, Inc., Woman of the Year in 1957, shortly before her death.

FURTHER READING

Johnson, Joan Marie. *Southern Ladies, New Women: Race, Region, and Clubwomen in South Carolina, 1890–1930* (2004).

Josey, E. J. *Handbook of Black Librarianship* (1977).

Simms, Lois Averetta. *Profiles of African-American Females in the Low Country of South Carolina* (1992).

Walker, Lillie S. "Black Librarians in South Carolina," in *The Black Librarian in the Southeast*, ed. Annette L. Phinazee (1980).

JOAN MARIE JOHNSON

Butler, William (no birth or death dates), a sergeant in the 369th U.S. Infantry Regiment, 93rd Division (provisional), was one of the first World War I recipients of the Distinguished Service Cross, America's highest military award, second only to the Medal of Honor. Captured German dispatches reported his heroic action, commenting on his "bloodthirstiness." Little is known about Butler's life, however. He was from Salisbury, Maryland, where in the early 1900s he was known as "a slight, good-natured colored youth [who] until a few years ago was a jack of trades in a little Maryland town" (*New York Times*, 28 Apr. 1919). He moved to New York City and in 1916 enlisted in the old 15th New York Regiment, the state's first all-black National Guard regiment. In 1917 he went overseas with the 15th and, after it was renumbered the 369th Infantry, fought in all its battles on the Western Front, where he received not only the Distinguished Service Cross but also the Croix de Guerre, France's highest military decoration.

On the night of 18 August 1918, in the Masion-de-Champagne Sector, after the German army had launched its last major offensive against the Allies, Butler was crouched in a trench while nearby a squad of his own men, led by Gorman Jones, a white lieutenant from Alabama, had just been captured by a large raiding party. A late transfer into the 369th, Jones was not fond of the blacks he found himself commanding. Because it was night, the Germans failed to see Butler as he jumped out of the trench, yelling, "Look out, you bush Germans, I'm comin'!" Jones, afraid that he and his men would get killed, ordered Butler not to fire. Butler, still charging the Germans, yelled back, "Not yet sir, but soon!" (Baltimore *Afro-American*, 11 Oct. 1918). The Germans wheeled around on the charging Butler. At that moment Jones cracked one of his captors on the jaw and took off running. "Now let 'em have it, Sergeant!" he shouted. According to a war correspondent, Butler came "a-roaring and fogging through the darkness with his automatic, and nobody knows how many Germans he killed" (Baltimore *Afro-American*, 11 Oct. 1918). He tossed grenades at the fleeing enemy, chasing most of the survivors into the night. When he returned he had captured an officer and several enlisted men. His action saved the entire squad, including

Lieutenant Jones, who had been wounded in the melee. Told by a medic that he had to be evacuated to a dressing station, Jones snapped, "You go to hell. I'm going to stay with the outfit. They're fighting men" (Baltimore *Afro-American*, 11 Oct. 1918). Later, Colonel William Hayward, the 369th's commander, found a report in a captured German dugout and was amused when he read that the Americans had been rescued by a blood-thirsty "enemy group in over-whelming numbers" when, in fact, the deed had been done by a lone soldier (William Hayward Report to Assistant Chief of Staff, American Expeditionary Forces, 7 Jan. 1919). The 11 October 1918 Baltimore *Afro-American* heralded Butler as "Maryland's Greatest Hero." On 27 April 1919, in a ceremony in New York City before five thousand people, Hayward pinned the Distinguished Service Cross and Croix de Guerre on Butler's chest, making him at the time the 369th's most decorated African American soldier. (More than eighty years later the American Distinguished Service Cross was awarded posthumously to the 369th's Sgt. Henry Johnson.) There is nothing known of Butler following the war.

FURTHER READING

Butler, William. American Distinguished Service Cross citation, War Department General Orders No. 37.

Corey, Herbert. "Our Boys Are Rough on Huns," Baltimore *Afro-American*, 11 Oct. 1918.

Harris, Stephen L. *Harlem's Hell Fighters: The African-American 369th Infantry in World War I* (2003)

Hayward, Col. William. Report to Assistant Chief of Staff, American Expeditionary Forces, 7 Jan. 1919.

Little, Arthur W. *From Harlem to the Rhine* (1936).

"Maryland Negro Gets Decorations," Baltimore *Evening Star*, 28 Apr. 1919.

STEPHEN L. HARRIS

Butterfield, G. K. (27 Apr. 1947–), politician, was born George Kenneth Butterfield in Wilson, North Carolina, to Addie Davis, a schoolteacher, and George Kenneth Butterfield Sr., a dentist. The family was prominent in the local African American community, and Butterfield's father was the first African American in the twentieth century to hold a seat on the Wilson city council.

Butterfield attended local schools, including Charles H. Darden High School, from which he graduated in 1967. He matriculated to North Carolina Central University in Durham, pursuing bachelor's degrees in sociology and political science, in the meantime serving in the U.S. Army for

G. K. Butterfield, Congressman, in an official photo.

two years. Butterfield graduated from N.C. Central in 1971. He remained at that institution to earn his J.D. in 1974, after which he embarked on a career in law.

Following graduation, Butterfield returned to Wilson and there maintained a private law practice—through which he gained a reputation for taking cases of interest to the poor as well as to underrepresented minorities (including voting rights cases)—until 1988. In that year, he ran for and won a seat as resident superior court judge, a position he held for twelve years. In 2001 North Carolina Governor Mike Easely appointed him to the state's supreme court to fill an open spot, but the next year Butterfield lost in the supreme court election and was subsequently reappointed by Easely to his previous position on the superior court.

Meanwhile, Butterfield had been pondering a political career. In 2004 a seat opened in North Carolina's First District in the eastern part of the state. Butterfield sought the office, and defeated his Republican and Libertarian opponents. He was sworn into the U.S. House of Representatives on

20 July 2004. He was reelected in 2006 and 2008 by wide margins and faces reelection in the 2010 midterms.

In Congress, Butterfield proved a reliable member of his caucus. He joined the Congressional Black Caucus (CBC) and usually voted with the progressive wing of his party. In 2007 he became the first House member from his state to act as Chief Deputy Whip, the role of which is to help propel legislation through the process and into law. Among his committee appointments, Butterfield serves on the influential Energy and Commerce Committee, as well as the Committee on Standards of Official Conduct. He has likewise served on the Committee on Agriculture and the Committee on Armed Services. He also sit on a number of sub-committees, including the Subcommittee on the Environment and Hazardous Materials, and the Subcommittee on General Farm Commodities and Risk Management. He is vice chair of the Subcommittee on Energy and Environment.

Butterfield made news during the hotly contested 2008 Democratic primary when he became the first member of his state's congressional delegation to endorse freshman Senator Barack Obama (D-Illinois) in his bid for the presidency. He has since been a strong supporter of the Obama administration and its policy goals, including the landmark healthcare reform legislation signed into law on 23 March 2010. He is divorced from his wife, Jean Farmer-Butterfield, a North Carolina state representative, with whom he has two daughters.

FURTHER READING

Christopher, Maurice. *Black Americans in Congress* (1976).

Freedman, Eric, and Stephen A. Jones. *African Americans in Congress: A Documentary History* (2007).

JASON PHILIP MILLER

Butts, Calvin Otis, III (22 July 1949–), minister and activist, was born on the Lower East Side of New York. His father was a chef, and his mother was an administrator of welfare services. Both had migrated from rural Georgia to the city in hopes of making a better life for themselves and their family. As a young boy, Calvin recalled visiting the church he would one day lead, the Abyssinian Baptist Church in Harlem, where he was mesmerized by the Reverend ADAM CLAYTON POWELL JR., a figure who seemed to speak from the pulpit of that Gothic sanctuary with a voice of thunder. When

Calvin O. Butts, III, attending the 27th Annual Benefit Gala of the New York chapter of One Hundred Black Men, Inc., at the New York Hilton Hotel, 22 February 2007. (AP Images.)

Calvin was eight the family left their low-income housing development in Manhattan for a black suburb in Queens. From there Calvin was bused, over the protests of white parents, to a junior high school in the upscale Forest Hills section of Queens. Calvin adjusted well to this experiment in forced integration and graduated as president of his class in 1967.

During Butts's freshman year at Morehouse College in Atlanta, Dr. MARTIN LUTHER KING JR., the college's most famous alumnus, was assassinated. Butts was so consumed by the passion of that tragic moment that in the days of rioting that followed he participated in firebombing a business. Shortly thereafter, he vowed never to use violence again as a means of protest. Butts intended to major in industrial psychology, but the tumult of the times caused him to switch to philosophy with a concentration in religion. He received his degree in 1971 and entered Union Theological Seminary in New York City. As a divinity student, he delivered a sermon condemning homosexuality that demonstrated an early moral certitude and crusading spirit that would characterize much of his career. Later he would moderate his views on homosexuality to include an adamant defense of the rights of gays and lesbians to live free of political discrimination. In 1972 Butts was recruited by Reverend William Epps, associate minister of Abyssinian Baptist Church, who was looking for young, dynamic ministers to assist Reverend SAMUEL PROCTOR, who had just assumed leadership of the 4,000-member church. As Reverend Proctor's assistant, Butts was expected to perform weddings, funerals, hospital visitations, and to supervise many of the church's youth programs. During this period, he married his wife, Patricia, with whom he would have three children. He received his master's degree from Union Theological Seminary in 1975 and then earned a doctorate from Drew Theological School in 1982. Butts began to develop a reputation as an effective community organizer when, as chair of the Harlem branch of the YMCA, he was able to raise over $750,000 in city and private funds for renovations and services.

In 1983 his penchant for political activism became evident when he boldly took up the issue of police brutality. Strongly implying that the local congressional representative CHARLES RANGEL was not doing enough to combat this problem, Butts went directly to congressman JOHN CONYERS JR., an African American representative from Michigan who chaired the House Subcommittee on Criminal Justice, and arranged a series of high-profile public hearings on police brutality in Harlem. The charged political atmosphere of those events fueled the first speculations that Reverend Butts might be interested in running for elected office, possibly challenging Congressman Rangel for his seat. Many people believed that Butts's leadership led to the appointment of the city's first black police commissioner.

In 1985 Butts served as chairman of a campaign to elect Vernon Mason, an apprentice deacon of his church, as district attorney of New York against the incumbent Robert Morgenthau. Mason failed in this bid, but in 1987 he, Alton Maddox, and the Reverend AL SHARPTON championed the cause of Tawana Brawley, a black teenager whose claim of being raped by six white police officers created a racial crisis in the city before it was exposed as a hoax. Butts was not accused of making any of the libelous accusations for which Mason, Maddox, and Sharpton were later convicted, but his involvement caused some to suspect Butts of becoming a media hound. He responded that

a minister has an obligation to be a gadfly, calling attention to the plight of the poor and powerless. Butts became a lightning rod for criticism because of his refusal to denounce the leader of the Nation of Islam, LOUIS FARRAKHAN, for referring to Judaism as a "dirty religion." One-third of the New York Philharmonic Orchestra boycotted a concert at Abyssinian Baptist Church in protest. Butts attempted to explain that "All I'm saying to the Jewish community is, don't dictate to me. I understand your anger. I'm not a fool…. In fact, I quite respect what the Jewish people have done. But please don't make me a boy and tell me what to do" (*New York Times*, 9 Aug. 1987). Butts argued that he was willing to repudiate Farrakhan's anti-Semitic remarks, but believed that Farrakhan's message of self-help and personal responsibility needed to be heard.

During the 1980s Butts began to achieve national recognition by challenging manufacturers of alcohol and tobacco products that targeted their advertisements to increase consumption in the black community. He led a series of highly publicized marches in Harlem with supporters who painted over billboards promoting cigarettes and liquor—particularly those advertisements that seemed designed to attract young consumers. His tactics were provocative, often courting arrest, but his cause resonated around the country. Some distributors of these products agreed to stop advertisement in distressed neighborhoods within ninety days, while others agreed not to advertise within five blocks of schools, playgrounds, or churches.

When Reverend Proctor announced his retirement in 1989, the board of deacons overwhelmingly selected Butts as their new pastor. Like Adam Clayton Powell Jr., Butts had become a powerful political operator. His sermonic style could exhibit the passion of the most accomplished Baptist preachers, but it could also be thoughtful, even cerebral, when examining complex issues. As a manager, he increased membership and the church's financial endowment. Through the Abyssinian Development Corporation, Butts built over 600 housing units; the corporation constructed a senior citizens' home and acquired the historic Renaissance Ballroom and Smalls' Paradise. Like Reverend FLOYD FLAKE in Queens, Butts had gotten his church involved in the arena of public education through its Thurgood Marshall Academy, a junior and senior high school. He was instrumental in bringing over $75 million in urban renewal projects to Harlem, including a $15 million mega supermarket that offered a greater selection of food at lower prices than was typically available from the mom-and-pop stores that populated the area.

Politically, Butts remained a controversial and often unpredictable figure. He became one of the most recognizable personalities in the fight against "gangster rap." His crusade against pornography and misogyny—particularly the practice of referring to black women as "bitches" and "whores"—brought him into heated conflict with the rapper ICE-T, who believed his attention was misdirected. Nevertheless, Butts threatened to stage street rallies at which he would ride a steamroller over what he considered to be offensive music and he led a group of angry parents to the headquarters of Sony Music. Though a Democrat, Butts endorsed the Independent presidential candidate Ross Perot in 1992, claiming that the Democratic Party had taken the black vote for granted. He excoriated the conservative religious right, exclaiming at one point that "the church is more responsible for racism than any other institution in America" (*New York Amsterdam News*, 2 Nov. 1996). In 1997 he even called for the resignation of the Reverend Henry J. Lyons, the president of his own denomination, the National Baptist Convention U.S.A., for embezzling more than a million dollars from the organization and for having an affair with an employee. In 1998 Butts again crossed party lines to endorse the Republican governor of New York, George Pataki, for reelection.

Reverend Butts's influence extended from the church and political arena to numerous corporate boards, charities, and educational institutions. He served as president of the Council of Churches of the City of New York, vice chair of the board of directors of the United Way of New York City, and member of the Central Park Conservancy. In 1999 the trustees of the State University of New York elected Reverend Butts president of the College at Old Westbury, a position he occupied while continuing to lead his congregation.

FURTHER READING

Reverend Butts's papers are not yet available.
　However, the Schomburg Center for Research in Black Culture, New York City Public Library, has extensive material on the Abyssinian Baptist Church and on Harlem's cultural and political history. In addition, the Abyssinian Baptist Church makes available certain documents to researchers at it site.

Christian Century, 15 Dec. 1993.

Dreyfuss, Joel. "Harlem's Ardent Voice," *New York Times Magazine*, 20 Jan. 1991.

SHOLOMO B. LEVY

Byard, Gloria (19 Sept. 1950–), field hockey player, field hockey coach, and educator, was born Gloria Jean Howard in Salem, New Jersey, to Roosevelt and Ida Mae Howard. Her father worked on a farm, and her mother as a domestic employee; neither of her parents finished high school. Byard grew up in Woodstown, New Jersey, in an old farm house with no running water, bathrooms, or heating. She has described her adolescence as "challenging"—following her brother's death she took on additional responsibilities as the eldest sibling, playing an active role as caregiver to her five youngest sisters. As a counterbalance to her busy and demanding home life, Byard relied on her love of field hockey and her athletic ability as a source of inspiration and hope for future successes. In high school she began reading field hockey rule books and imagining someday being profiled in such a publication.

After graduating from Woodstown High School in 1969 she married Raymond Byard III, and soon afterward had her first child, a daughter, Toni. She worked for three years before both she and her husband decided to pursue a college education to provide a better future for themselves and their child. Byard enrolled in Glassboro State College in 1972 (her husband at Rutgers-Camden), where she successfully combined her educational pursuits with her love of athletics. Byard made the field hockey team at Glassboro, where she often showed up to practices and games with her young daughter in tow. As the team's senior member she took on a leadership role and was regarded by her college teammates as a motherly figure. With her husband's help and support she trained extensively, taking part in development programs held by the U.S. Field Hockey Association. She attended level B and A camps which serve as a stepping stone to gaining a coveted spot on the national team. Byard's hard work and determination paid off in 1974 during her junior year in college, when she became a member of the United States Field Hockey Team and the first African American to earn a spot on the touring team. As part of that contingent Byard got to travel outside the United States for the first time in her life, flying to places like Barbados, Trinidad, and Tobago. The process however, was not without its hardships especially in such a competitive environment, where "everyone wanted to hear their name called for the starting lineup" (interview with the author, 2011). There were many times when as the only African American on the U.S. touring team Byard felt lonely and secluded, and teammates were reluctant to room with her or go out to dinner with her.

As an elite athlete Byard was looking forward to showcasing her abilities on an international level and was well on her way to making the Olympic team for the 1980 summer games to be held in Moscow. Her plans were thwarted first in 1979 when she gave birth to her son, Raymond Jr., and then by the eventual boycott of the summer Olympics by the United States. Byard has admitted that while making the Olympic team would have been a challenge, particularly after having her second child, she was confident that her "speed, heart, and determination" (*Rowan Today*) would have given her a huge advantage in the qualification process.

With her amateur field hockey career having come to an end, Byard turned her full attention to education and coaching. Byard began teaching in 1976 at A.P. Schalick High School in Pittsgrove Township, New Jersey. She went on to establish the field hockey program at Salem Community College in 1980, and earned coaching of the year honors at SCC in 1981. Over the years Byard has accumulated an impressive number of accolades including the prestigious Golden Apple Award in 2002 and 2003 as Health and Physical Education teacher at Glassboro High School. In 1987 she was inducted into the Rowan University (Glassboro State College) Sports Hall of Fame and is also a member of the Salem and Gloucester Counties Sports Hall of Fame for her contributions to and promotion of field hockey.

With Byard as their head coach, the Glassboro High School Lady Bulldogs field hockey team won the South Jersey Group sectional championships through the 2005/6–2008/9 seasons. She was chosen as coach of the year in 2005 by the South Jersey Field Hockey Club. In 2007 the Lady Bulldogs were selected as Gloucester County Team of the year. Byard reached her 100th win as a coach in 2008.

FURTHER READING

"Olympic Achievements." *Rowan Today* (Fall 2008): 13.

Byard, Gloria. Interview by Stanley El, *American Dream Radio Show*, podcast audio, January 13, 2011, http://www.rowan.edu/today/data/cast/AD20110112.mp3.

DÁLIA LEONARDO

Byas, Don (21 Oct. 1912–24 Aug. 1972), tenor saxophonist, was born Carlos Wesley Byas in Muskogee, Oklahoma. The names and occupations of his parents are unknown, and little is known of Byas's early life or musical training. As a teenager in the late 1920s he played alto saxophone with BENNIE MOTEN and WALTER PAGE, and then in the early 1930s he played with his own group. He switched to tenor in 1933 and settled in California. Over the next few years he played with LIONEL HAMPTON in 1935; with Eddie Barefield and BUCK CLAYTON in 1936; with DON REDMAN, LUCKY MILLINDER, and ANDY KIRK from 1939 to 1940; and with Benny Carter in September 1940. He recorded with Timme Rosenkrantz in 1938, and in September 1940 he cut two tunes with BILLIE HOLIDAY and Her Orchestra.

Byas's career reached its turning point when he joined the Count Basie Band. In "Harvard Blues," made in May 1940 with the Basie group, Byas played a solo that typifies his style at the time. It has been vividly described by the musician and jazz historian Gunther Schuller:

> Perfectly constructed, it is simple and affecting, poignant and languorous. Playing softly with a sense of intimacy not often encountered in jazz, Byas places each of his notes as if they were a series of incontrovertible truths.... Listen especially ... for Byas's anguished moan, followed by a simple downward scale (255).

Already Byas had the huge tone that became his trademark. He was technically flawless even at breathtaking speeds, playing in a style influenced by ART TATUM. Harmonically, at least, he was more advanced than COLEMAN HAWKINS was.

In 1941 Byas took over the chair in Basie's band that was formerly held by LESTER YOUNG. In addition to his work with Basie and with smaller, Basie-led groups, Byas recorded prolifically throughout the 1940s with a variety of groups as a sideman and, increasingly, under his own name. In 1944 he seemed to be everywhere. In late May he recorded several tunes with Coleman Hawkins and His Sax Ensemble, appearing as a costar in this illustrious group. In early June, Byas cut three tunes on Folkways with MARY LOU WILLIAMS and Her Orchestra, contributing a particularly noteworthy collaboration with Williams for "Man o' Mine." In September he recorded four tunes with HOT LIPS PAGE and His Orchestra, showcasing his massive tone in "These Foolish Things," and in November he recorded again with Hawkins. Finally, he was a member of DIZZY GILLESPIE's first small group on Fifty-Second Street, and he briefly replaced Gillespie in CHARLIE PARKER's quintet the following year.

In addition to playing with Parker, Byas continued to perform and record prolifically in 1945, leading his own quartet and quintet in a variety of venues and sessions. In January he recorded four tunes with the Don Byas All-Stars and, in October, four more with a quartet (both sessions were for the Black and Blue label). Byas's unique mix of boppish harmonies and swing rhythms is clearly in evidence in a Town Hall concert with SLAM STEWART, TEDDY WILSON, and others, particularly in the group's rendition of the bop standard "I Got Rhythm." During that summer he often played with Parker at the Downbeat Club on Fifty-Second Street, then during intermissions he would move to an adjoining club to play duets with Hawkins.

Byas did not slow down at all in 1946. He won the Esquire Silver Award, performed in January with LEONARD FEATHER's Esquire All-Americans (the group included DUKE ELLINGTON, JOHNNY HODGES, and LOUIS ARMSTRONG), and in February recorded with Gillespie. He also waxed his second version of "Body and Soul" that year, which remains one of the few to rival the legendary Hawkins effort and has been described as "yet another ravishing tenor seduction of the melody, virtuosic and ardent" (Giddins, 50). That summer Byas traveled to Europe with Don Redman's band and, attracted by the enthusiastic reception, decided to move there permanently, first to France and subsequently to the Netherlands and then Denmark.

Despite his physical absence from the American scene, Byas continued to tour and record prolifically over the next decade. He worked frequently as a soloist throughout Europe and performed regularly at festivals such as the Paris Jazz Fair. In 1950 he toured the Continent with Ellington, and in the early 1950s he recorded some extraordinary sessions for Vogue with ROY ELDRIDGE. Byas cut a number of sides for Blue Star records between 1946 and 1952. The later 1950s were somewhat quieter, but he became more visible again beginning in 1960. He returned to the United States for the first time since his move to Europe to appear at the 1960 Newport Jazz Festival, and he shared the stage with Hawkins and Benny Carter for a 1960 Jazz at the Philharmonic tour. He appeared in a 1961 tribute to CANNONBALL ADDERLY on Columbia Records and played strongly in a January 1964 live session recorded for Black Lion records in Copenhagen. He ended the decade with a 1968 recorded meeting with BEN WEBSTER. In 1970 Byas played with the drummer ART BLAKEY in the United States and toured Japan with him. Byas recorded a 1971 session with strings and made his final recording in 1972, a quartet date in Holland that included the Spanish pianist Tete Montelieu. In the last years before his death, Byas also continued to play in jazz and dance bands throughout Europe. He died of lung cancer in Amsterdam.

Byas was the most brilliant of Hawkins's followers. Though he never varied his phrasing as much as Hawkins did, Byas's playing was almost as evocative, with its huge tone and plangent emotionalism in ballads and his technical perfection in up-tempo pieces. And though his rhythmic conception remained rooted in swing, he was a crucial transitional player between the swing and bop eras; he was a highly influential precursor of bop in his extensive use of substitute chords. In the end, his unique combination of bop harmonies, swing rhythms, and lyric intensity guarantees Byas's place in jazz history.

FURTHER READING
Giddins, Gary. *Rhythm-a-Ning: Jazz Tradition and Innovation in the 80s* (1985).
Piazza, Tom. *The Guide to Classic Recorded Jazz* (1995).
Schuller, Gunther. *The Swing Era: The Development of Jazz, 1930–1945* (1989).
Obituary: *New York Times*, 29 Aug. 1972.

DISCOGRAPHY
Wilke, D. B. *A Don Byas Discography, 1938–1972*.
This entry is taken from the *American National Biography* and is published here with the permission of the American Council of Learned Societies.

RONALD P. DUFOUR

Byrd, Bobby (15 Aug. 1934–12 Sept. 2007), vocalist, pianist, songwriter, and music producer, was born Robert Howard Byrd in Toccoa, a small town in the Appalachian country of northeastern Georgia. He was raised there by his grandmother and his mother, Zarah Byrd. She took her children, including Bobby, to shape-note singing concerts. Once popular in Appalachia, shape-note, or sacred harp, is a style of musical notation designed to aid congregational singing. Zarah Byrd taught her children how to play the piano and steeped them in the African American gospel singing tradition at Mount Zion Baptist Church in the town's Whitman Avenue.

Georgia Mae Williams, the pianist at Mount Zion and Bobby's second piano teacher, was another great contributor to his musical education.

From a young age, Bobby Byrd excelled at voice and piano. He also did well with sports and was active in school clubs. He even became the only young man in the state to join the New Homemakers Association. Bobby Byrd was elected president of his class at Whitman Street High School, and served as its valedictorian upon his graduation in 1953. Music historian Fred Hays describes Bobby Byrd as a "natural-born leader" whose "first love" and whose greatest leadership ability lay in music.

Georgia Mae Williams and her husband Nathan "Bub" Williams ran a gospel group, the New Mixed Choir, which broadcast from Mount Zion at 7:05 A.M. every Sunday over radio station WLET. They likely inspired Bobby Byrd and his older sister Sarah (born 12 May 1932 in Toccoa) to sing in a series of gospel groups that became the Gospel Starlighters. When their mother and grandmother were not present to discourage them from "the devil's music," Bobby and Sarah enjoyed singing popular songs like "Sentimental Reason." With Piano Red as their talent scout, Bobby and Sarah Byrd and their cousin Agnes Oglesby travelled to Atlanta and recorded several of Bobby's gospel compositions on NRC. The fate of these recordings is, at this writing, unknown.

In 1952 or 1953, Bobby Byrd's basketball team in Toccoa played against a prison team that included JAMES BROWN. Brown, then a nineteen-year-old inmate at the nearby Alto Reform School, was serving hard labor for a burglary conviction and impressed the other prisoners with his vocal skills. Byrd and Brown struck up a friendship and admired each other's musical talents. Aided by their churchgoing, respectable reputation, the Byrd family arranged for Brown's early release on parole and gave him a home and work. Brown joined Bobby Byrd's singing group, which by then had evolved into a secular venture called the Flames. As James Brown's first backing band, the Famous Flames rose with him to international stardom. Because of the helping hand he and his family lent James Brown at such a critical juncture, Bobby Byrd has sometimes been called the "godfather of the godfather of soul."

James Brown and the Bobby Byrd-led Famous Flames scored their first hit singles with "Please, Please, Please" in 1956 and "Try Me" in 1958. Byrd stayed with Brown through many more chart successes, including 1963's legendary album *Live at the Apollo*, recorded at Harlem's famed Apollo Theater in October 1962. Byrd also achieved several solo hits during the 1960s, including "Baby, Baby, Baby" (1964), a duet recorded with Anna King. At live performances with Brown and the Famous Flames, Byrd worked up the crowd until Brown made his dramatic entrance onto the stage. Byrd was given credit as co-author on a number of songs that the Brown enterprise made famous, including "Get Up, Get into It, and Get Involved," "Hot Pants," and "Sex Machine." Perhaps Bobby Byrd's most widely and instantly recognizable vocal track is his invigorating, shouted refrain of "Get on up!" on "Sex Machine."

Byrd was the only member of the Flames to stay on with Brown's second backing band, the JBs, which debuted in 1970. Brown did produce and receive co-author credit on one of Byrd's first and best-selling solo hits, 1971's "I Know You Got Soul." Yet the two longtime friends and musical collaborators conflicted over author and producer credits and royalties on other songs. In 1973 Bobby Byrd broke off from James Brown and spent the next three decades as a solo artist. Byrd often performed with his second wife, Vicki Anderson, a soul/R&B singer and a James Brown alumnus. His first marriage, to Gail Byrd, ended in divorce. Vicki Anderson's daughter and Byrd's stepdaughter, Carleen Anderson, is also a soul/R&B singer.

While Byrd continued to do well as a professional musician in the 1970s, he no longer enjoyed the same level of celebrity he had known as part of Brown's band. He felt for many years that his contributions were unrecognized and unappreciated. However, starting in the late 1980s and early 1990s, younger African American artists like Eric B. and Rakim, Public Enemy, A Tribe Called Quest, Ice Cube, Big Daddy Kane, and Jay-Z began to pay Bobby Byrd homage, sometimes by covering his songs, but more frequently by sampling his solo hits or his work with the Brown outfit.

This resurgence of interest in Byrd led to the release of the single "On the Move" (1994) and a "greatest hits" album (1995). Byrd and his wife toured Great Britain with the Soulpower Allstars. Byrd also reconciled with James Brown and began to perform with him again. Vicki Anderson and Bobby Byrd performed at Brown's lavish funeral in 2006, where Byrd sang solos on "I Know You Got Soul" and "Sex Machine."

At age 73, Bobby Byrd died from lung cancer at his home in Loganville, Georgia. Along with Vicki and Carleen Anderson, he was survived by his three children from his first marriage; at least three children from nonmarital relationships; and a brother and two sisters. A headline in the online music magazine *Mojo* (19 Sept. 2007) aptly announced: "Bobby Byrd Dies, World Less Funky." As true as this was, the loss of Byrd's deep, insistent, energizing voice and his other musical gifts was not total. By that time, Internet video and audio technologies not only were able to preserve his work but make it globally available to new and deeply appreciative audiences.

FURTHER READING

"Bobby Byrd," in *Funk*, ed. Dave Thompson. (2001).

Hay, Fred J. "Music Box Meets the Toccoa Band: The Godfather of Soul in Appalachia," *Black Music Research Journal*, 22 March 2003.

Rhodes, Don, and Brenda Lee. *Say It Loud!: My Memories of James Brown, Soul Brother No. 1* (2008).

Obituaries: *Augusta (GA) Chronicle*, 13 Sept. 2007; Rolling Stone com, Rock and Roll Daily, 13 Sept. 2007; *Times (UK)*, 19 Sept. 2007; *Washington Post*, 15 Sept 2007.

DISCOGRAPHY

James Brown Live at the Apollo (1963).

James Brown's Original Funky Divas (1998).

Bobby Byrd Got Soul: The Best of Bobby Byrd (1995).

MARY KRANE DERR

Byrd, Flossie Marian (8 Aug. 1927–), educator, was born in Sarasota, Florida, the eldest of seventeen children of John Byrd, a bricklayer, and Elizabeth "Lizzie" Byrd, a homemaker. The family returned to Monticello, Florida, in 1941 to establish residence on their property in a house built by a carpenter friend of the family. Times were hard, but the family was fairly self-sufficient. On their farm they raised swine, chickens, and cows, and tended a large garden for home consumption. They grew cash crops—corn, peanuts, watermelons, and cotton—on a small scale. In addition to self-sufficiency, education was important to her parents. They were determined that their surviving fourteen children would secure an education despite the hardships and discrimination that African Americans faced.

For one year, after their move to Monticello in 1940, Byrd attended Bunker Hill School, a two-room rural school located on Lake Road. She and her brother Johnny walked four miles through the woods to school and four miles back each day. In 1941 her parents enrolled her in the tenth grade at Howard Academy High School, the only high school in Jefferson County for African Americans. She and Johnny were accompanied by their sister Juanita on the daily twelve-mile, round-trip walk to high school. Byrd graduated from high school as valedictorian in 1944 and entered the then Florida A&M College that fall, earning a B.S. in Home Economics with honors in 1948.

She began her career in 1948 as a high school home economics teacher at Quinn High School in Apalachicola, Florida; taught briefly at her old high school, Howard Academy in Monticello; and later took a job at Douglas High School in Live Oak, Florida. Those experiences comprised the first five years of her professional career.

When asked why home economics was her career choice, she said, "At the time that I enrolled in college, the most that an African American female could aspire to was being a teacher, a secretary, a nurse or a social worker. Actually, teachers and secretaries were the careers that we knew most about. I learned in later years that nursing and social work, primarily professions for white women, were slowly becoming options for African American women."

Prevented by law from attending the nearby Florida State University in Tallahassee, she instead received a scholarship in 1953 to attend graduate school out of state. The following year she received an MEd in Home Economics Education from Pennsylvania State University.

After earning her master's, in 1954 she began teaching at Florida A&M University in the home economics department, where she stayed for five years. In 1962 she relocated to Prairie View A&M University in Prairie View, Texas. Beginning as an educator of teachers in home economics, she taught undergraduate and graduate courses in the home economics curriculum. The following year Byrd took a break from her work at Prairie View A&M to earn her Ph.D. in Home Economics with minors in child development and educational psychology and measurements at Cornell University in Ithaca, New York. In 1964, back at Prairie View A&M, she became professor and dean of the College of Home Economics, a position she held for twenty-three years. She was appointed associate vice president for academic affairs in 1987, a position she held for four years. Immediately following that, she was named vice president for academic affairs in 1991, and then provost for academic affairs in 1993.

Byrd served on thirty-two organizational and advisory boards and committees, was an officer in eight home economics organizations, held membership in eight professional organizations, and wrote *Education in Jefferson County, Florida, in Historical Perspective*, published in 1997. She published articles in the *Journal of Home Economics* and other scholarly journals. Her research interests included concept formation and family membership disability, and family resource management. A member of Delta Sigma Theta Sorority, four honor societies, as well as a retired certified family and consumer scientist, she completed work and research funded by the U.S. Department of Agriculture, the U.S. Public Health Service, and the U.S. Office of Education.

Byrd achieved several firsts in her lifetime. She was the first person of any race in Jefferson County, Florida, to earn a Ph.D., the first African American to be awarded the Distinguished Service Award by the American Home Economics Association in 1990, the first female to be appointed vice president for academic affairs at Prairie View A&M University, and the first person to be appointed provost and vice president for academic affairs. She retired from education in 1994 and was awarded emerita status by the Texas A&M University System.

Byrd received the Florida A&M University Distinguished Alumna Award in 1968 and was inducted into the Gallery of Distinction for Agriculture and Home Economics graduates of Florida A&M University in 1990.

FURTHER READING

Byrd, Flossie M. *Education in Jefferson County, Florida, in Historical Perspective* (1997).

CORNELIA AKINS TAYLOR

Cable, Theodore (3 Sept. 1890–12 Jan. 1963), athlete, dentist, and politician, was born in Topeka, Kansas, to Gary W. Cable, a teacher and postal worker, and Mary Ellen Montgomery Cable, a public school administrator and civil rights activist. In 1894 the family moved to Indianapolis, Indiana, where Cable attended public school and graduated from integrated Shortridge High School in 1908. He moved on to the exclusive Phillips Exeter Academy in New Hampshire for the next school year and enrolled at Harvard University in 1909.

Cable had not participated in organized athletics in high school, but he tried out for the freshman track team at Harvard and caught the eye of Coach Pat Quinn. With Quinn's guidance, Cable developed rapidly. In the annual Harvard-Yale freshman meet, he won the hammer throw and he also performed well in the 220-yard hurdles and the broad jump (now the long jump) in intramural competitions.

He easily made the varsity track-and-field team the next year and was a consistent point winner for Harvard during his last three seasons. As a sophomore he set a new school hammer-throw record and won the event in the annual Harvard-Yale meet. In the summer of 1911 he competed with a combined Harvard–Yale squad that traveled to England to challenge a team representing Oxford and Cambridge universities.

In 1912, as a junior, he saw even greater success. Against Yale, Cable completed a rare double by winning first place in both the hammer throw and the broad jump. He then established another Harvard school record in the hammer throw when he captured the national title at the Intercollegiate Amateur Athletic Association of America (IC4A) championships. Soon after, he finished second at the U.S. Olympic hammer-throw trials. The cash-strapped American Olympic Committee, though, could fund only one competitor and invited Cable to travel with the team as a self-financed "supplementary." Cable could not raise the money and was unable to go to London. In his final season at Harvard, Cable continued to excel. He won the hammer throw against Yale for the third straight year, and he repeated as the IC4A champion in the event.

Cable did not concentrate solely on track. To improve his conditioning, he tried out for varsity football as a senior and, despite never having played, worked his way up to the second team. Although he never appeared in a game, he impressed his teammates and the coaching staff. An accomplished violinist, Cable was a four-year member of the Pierian Sodality, the student orchestra, and served as its librarian in 1910. At Harvard he specialized in romance languages and spoke fluent French, Spanish, and Italian. He graduated in 1913.

He moved back to Indianapolis and taught for two years in the public schools, but he returned to his studies and received a degree from the Indiana Dental College, which became Indiana University School of Dentistry, in 1919. He soon established a successful dental practice that he ran for the next thirty years. In 1920 he married Wilhemina Morris, but the couple divorced within ten years. Cable would marry four more times, but he had no children.

In 1935 he was elected to the Indianapolis City Council. The first African American on the council, he ran as a Democrat and served until 1938. The following year he won a one-year term in the Indiana House of Representatives, the first black Democrat in that body. Cable was a member of the state housing board for eleven years, and during World War II he was a member of the Indianapolis Bi-racial Committee and the Indiana Advisory Defense Council.

An active community member, he played violin in the Indiana Theatre Orchestra and was a captain in the Civil Air Patrol and a wing commander in the Indiana National Guard. He was a member of the oral surgery staff at Indianapolis City Hospital and, from 1947 to 1949, operated the Mary E. Cable Dental Clinic, a free dental clinic named in honor of his mother. An avid sportsman and adventurer, he owned his own plane, played tennis, and learned to ski.

In 1949 he and his fifth wife, Janice Cable, moved to New York City, where he established another lucrative dental practice. He was an active member of city and state dental associations and also of the New York Harvard Club. He and his wife divorced in 1962. He remained in New York until he died in a one-car accident the following year. He was buried in his hometown of Indianapolis.

FURTHER READING

"Cable Has Come Fast and Is Now Harvard's Best Hammer Thrower," *Boston Globe*, 8 Apr. 1911.

January, Alan F., and Justin E. Walsh. *A Century of Achievement: Black Hoosiers in the Indiana General Assembly, 1881–1986* (1986).

Judd, Maurice. "Former Harvard Man with Remarkable Career," *Indianapolis Freeman*, 20 Dec. 1913.

Obituaries: *Amsterdam News* and *Indianapolis Recorder*, 19 Jan. 1963.

GREGORY BOND

Caesar, Adolph (5 Dec. 1933–6 Mar. 1986), actor, was born in Harlem, New York, in 1933, though some sources list his birth year as 1934. Little is known about his early life beyond the fact that he grew up in Harlem and attended George Washington High School in the neighborhood. After five years in the navy, Caesar entered New York University to study drama. Upon graduation in 1962, he continued to study voice on his own.

Caesar's voice was deep, penetrating, and mellifluous, and had a range from baritone to bass.

Caesar had contracted laryngitis when he was twelve years old, and the illness had the effect of maturing his voice. By the time he was in his teens, girls were calling just to hear his voice on the phone. He supported himself as a voiceover announcer for television commercials, making 97 percent of his income this way, working as a voiceover artist after he graduated from NYU. Caesar sold such products as Certs, Renault's Le Car, Kentucky Fried Chicken, and Nikon cameras. He also provided the television and radio tag-line "A Mind Is a Terrible Thing to Waste" for the United Negro College Fund. Each commercial, he felt, was a little performance.

Caesar performed with highly regarded regional theater groups, such as New York Shakespeare Festival, Lincoln Center Repertory Company, the American Shakespeare Festival in Stratford, Connecticut, the Inner City Theater and Center Theater Group at the Mark Taper Forum in Los Angeles, the Oregon Shakespeare Festival, and the Minnesota Theater Company. He also appeared on television in episodes of *General Hospital* (1969), *The Guiding Light* (1984), and *The Twilight Zone* (1986).

Beginning in 1970 Caesar worked with the Negro Ensemble Company. When the Ford Foundation helped to create regional theaters in 1966, it also supported one for black artists. The Negro Ensemble Company was only supported by the Ford Foundation for a few years and had to scale back its original plans for annual salaries and training programs for actors and development programs for playwrights. Actors were invited back for roles that played to their strengths, for example three actors, Adolph Caesar, Duane Jones, and Douglas Turner Ward playing Douglass in *Frederick Douglass*. Caesar stated he learned a lot in regional theater, but he never expected to receive a major role in the mixed-race companies. He was glad to have the Negro Ensemble Company as an outlet. Caesar performed in several productions including *The Brownsville Raid* (1976), *The River Niger* (1972), *The Great McDaddy*, *Frederick Douglass. Through His Own Word* (1972), the one-man show The *Square Root of the Soul* (1977), and *A Soldier's Play* (1981), a role that would change his career. Caesar's work in *A Soldier's Play* was photographed by Bert Andrews, the first black full-time photographer to document the black theater movement, and his performances influenced young actors.

In 1977 Caesar conceived and performed *The Square Root of Soul*, a show that attempted to portray the black experience in America through the use of forty poems. The *New York Times* critic Richard Eder thought the play did not come off well. The themes of the poems were similar, but their quality varied too much. Caesar was best when he acted out the poems rather than reading them, but this was not enough to carry the evening.

Caesar played Sergeant Walters in the Pulitzer Prize–winning, CHARLES HENRY FULLER JR. drama *A Soldier's Play* for the Negro Ensemble Company and in its film version *A Soldier's Story* (1985). As Sergeant Walker, Caesar played a complex, sad, self-loathing character who was killed at the beginning of the play. The rest of the play was an investigation of the crime that occurred on an army base in Louisiana during World War II. It was the first time Caesar had received national recognition during his long acting career. He was proud of the production though surprised at the acclaim, never expecting nine black men on stage in a drama to receive such attention. In addition to critical acclaim, Caesar won an Obie (1981) and a New York Drama Desk Award (1982). For his work in the film adaptation, he received an Academy Award nomination for Best Supporting Actor and a Los Angeles Film Critics Award.

In 1985 Caesar appeared in Steven Spielberg's film adaptation of ALICE WALKER's Pulitzer Prize–winning novel, *The Color Purple*, playing the father-in-law of the main character, an abused black woman. In 1986 Caesar acted in *Club Paradise* and the made-for-television film *Getting Even* (an ABC After School Special).

Caesar continued acting until the very end of his life and was working on a new film, *The Tough Guys* (1986), starring Kirk Douglas and Burt Lancaster, when he fell ill. Caesar was taken to the Los Angeles County USC Medical Center where he died a half hour later of a heart seizure. Caesar was fifty-two years old and a resident of New York City when he died. He was survived by his wife, Diane, his three children, Tiffani, Alexandria, and Jack, and his brother Herbie.

FURTHER READING

Elam, Harry, Jr., and David Krasner, eds. *African-American Performance and Theater History: A Critical Reader* (2001).

Lawson, Carol. "Broadway," *New York Times*, 22 Jan. 1982.

Williams, Mance. *Black Theater in the 1960s and 1970s: A Historical-Critical Analysis of the Movement* (1985).

Obituaries: *New York Times* and *Washington Post*, 7 Mar. 1986.

SHEILA BECK

Caesar, John (?–17 Jan. 1837), African Seminole (Black Seminole) leader, warrior, and interpreter, was born in the mid-eighteenth century and joined the Seminole nation in Florida, one of the many groups of African Seminole Indians who fought to maintain an autonomous and independent nation. There are few written records to reveal the early life histories of the many escaped Africans and American Indians in the maroon communities across the Americas, and Caesar's life proves no exception. By the time his exploits were recorded in U.S. military records, Caesar was well acculturated to Seminole life and politics, and thus he had probably been a longtime member of the Seminole nation. His work as an interpreter between Native Seminoles and the U.S. military, however, reveals his early upbringing among English-speaking Americans. He grew up in a time of intense conflict between the Seminoles and European colonists, and had become a seasoned war veteran by the time of the Second Seminole War (1835–1842). Like many African Seminole women and men, Caesar had a spouse living on one of the local plantations, alongside the St. Johns River.

During the First Seminole War (1817), Caesar was a prominent leader who conducted raids on neighboring plantations and sought out runaway slaves and free African Americans to join the Seminole nation. He was closely associated with the Seminole leader King Philip (Emathla), and together the two men battled the soldiers of the U.S. government during two wars. Acknowledged by U.S. military leaders and local plantation owners as a brilliant and powerful foe, Caesar followed a strategy of developing ties with enslaved African Americans on plantations in the St. Johns River area, using these relationships to acquire supplies and recruit slaves to join the African Seminole resistance.

African Seminoles like Caesar had a complex political and social relationship with Native Seminoles. The escape of slaves from plantations was encouraged by the early Spanish colonists who were in competition with English colonies over Florida territory. Although some Native Seminoles held African Seminoles as slaves, especially in the nineteenth century, African Seminoles had significant autonomy and political influence, particularly as the maroon nation grew in size and strength. There was significant intermarriage and cultural exchange among the various local communities which included African Seminoles, Native Seminoles, free and enslaved African Americans, and members of various Native American nations who joined forces with the Seminoles. Although some African Seminole slaves faced a form of slavery comparable to that practiced by European American plantation owners, others were adopted into Seminole clans, enslaved for a limited period of cultural adaptation to the new nation, and could marry and have children who would be free citizens of the nation. Caesar, like most African Seminoles, adopted the language and many of the cultural traditions of his Native Seminole counterparts, and African Seminoles brought their own African cultural traditions as well, which had a significant influence on the development of Seminole culture. Because African Seminoles were faced with the threat of enslavement on southern plantations, many served as fearless leaders in the Seminole wars against the United States in order to prevent the defeat of the Seminole nation. Many Native Seminoles also had their lives inextricably linked with those of African Seminoles because of intermarriage, and were unwilling to abandon their African Seminole family and friends to slave traders and plantation owners.

There were many other influential African Seminoles, including JOHN HORSE and ABRAHAM, the latter serving as the chief associate, adviser, and interpreter to Seminole chief Micanopy. Like his counterpart Abraham, Caesar was the head adviser and interpreter to a Seminole chief, King Philip, father of Wild Cat and leader of the St. Johns River Seminoles. Caesar and Abraham worked together to sow the seeds of discontent among plantation slaves in Florida, and to develop relationships with free blacks and slaves who would assist in re-supplying the war effort. Caesar was successful in convincing numerous African slaves to join the Seminoles in their struggle for freedom.

In December 1835, with the beginning of the Second Seminole War, Caesar and King Philip attacked and destroyed numerous St. John's sugar plantations. Slaves joined the Seminoles in further attacks, which continued into 1836. The Second Seminole War lasted for nearly seven years, and was characterized by the perspective of General Thomas Jesup, who declared: "This, you may be assured is a negro and not a Indian war" (Thomas S. Jesup Papers, University of Michigan, Box 14). African Seminoles, Native Seminoles, and escaped African slaves fought together in battles that cost the U.S. military dearly.

The incident for which Caesar is perhaps best known occurred in early March 1836. General Gaines and his troops were suffering the effects of a lengthy siege by the Seminole warriors, when Caesar unexpectedly arrived at Gaines's campsite to announce that the Seminoles wished to discuss a cease-fire agreement. Gaines agreed, and the parties met the next day in a series of discussions, with Caesar and Abraham serving as interpreters. Caesar's role in initiating the negotiations remains a matter of debate; in any case, the talks ended abruptly with the arrival of General Clinch, whose advance forces fired on the Seminole participants. Although Gaines claimed a victory after his troops' withdrawal, the Seminoles gained strategic advantages, with the cease-fire holding long enough for the Seminoles to regroup and reinforce their position.

With the arrival of General Thomas S. Jesup in late 1836, the war took on a new and disturbing dimension, with Osceola's fighters pushed back into King Philip and John Caesar's St. Johns River territory. Caesar organized runaway slaves and a number of Native Seminoles into small bands of warriors, and attacked the plantations just outside St. Augustine. Caesar's attacks were effective, and to strengthen his position he went on raiding parties to acquire horses. On 17 January 1837, he and his men were discovered attempting to steal horses from the Hanson plantation, and that evening, as they sat around their campfire, they were attacked by Captain Hanson's men, who killed three warriors, including Caesar.

Caesar's untimely death did not diminish the importance and influence of his life. His effectiveness at recruiting slaves from the plantations forced the U.S. military to negotiate over the issue of African Seminoles, and this resulted in the removal of African Seminoles alongside Native Seminoles, rather than their immediate re-enslavement on southeastern plantations. He was a major leader in a powerful maroon nation, which offered a unique opportunity for autonomy and freedom for Africans and American Indians who dared to escape plantations and European American colonial oppression. Caesar served as a potent symbol of an alternative vision for both African Americans and American Indians, that of merging cultures and political alliances. The two communities combined forces, and this new alliance proved a powerful and convincing tool in the hands of John Caesar, an African Seminole visionary, warrior, and political strategist.

FURTHER READING
Mulroy, Kevin. *Freedom on the Border* (1993).
Porter, Kenneth. *The Black Seminoles* (1996).

JONATHAN BRENNAN

Caesar, Shirley Ann (13 October 1938–), gospel singer and evangelist known as the "First Lady of Gospel," was the tenth of thirteen children born to Hannah and James Caesar in Durham, North Carolina. Her tobacco-worker father, active as a local preacher and singer with his Just Come Four Quartet, died when Caesar was about seven. Her mother, who was partially disabled, ran a small store from the back porch of the house; the children worked to support the family. Educated in the Durham public schools, she played piano and sang with two sisters, a cousin, and occasionally one of her brothers at churches, schools, and other functions. She joined the Charity Singers, her earnings supplementing the family income. Known as Baby Shirley, Caesar joined her pastor Bishop Frizelle Yelverton of Mount Calvary Holy Church when he preached at churches in the Carolinas and Virginia (he also had a weekly local radio show). In 1951 Caesar joined Thelma Bumpass and the Royalettes, touring throughout the Carolinas for about seven years. By 1954 she was also touring with LEROY JOHNSON.

After graduating high school in 1957 Caesar spent a year at North Carolina Central University. She left to join ALBERTINA WALKER's Chicago-based Gospel Caravans. Caesar had already developed her personal style of the dramatic, narrative "preaching song." She spent eight years with the

Shirley Ann Caesar, singing "Oh Happy Day" during her induction into the Gospel Music Hall of Fame, 30 October 2000. (AP Images.)

Caravans, leaving in 1966 when Walker refused to allow her to sign a solo recording contract with Hob Records.

After a brief solo stint Caesar formed the Caesar Singers. In 1969 Caesar signed with Hob and recorded her first solo album, *I'll Go*. During this time she began to expand her religious ministry. In 1970 she founded the Shirley Caesar Outreach Ministries, Inc. to provide the needy in her Durham community with a range of health and family services. Her ministry also included radio broadcasts, revivals, crusades, and gospel concerts. Caesar's career expanded and she began performing in venues such as Carnegie Hall and Lincoln Center. In 1971 she won her first Grammy award for "Put Your Hand in the Hand of the Man from Galilee." In 1974 she and JAMES CLEVELAND were featured on the album *King and Queen of Gospel*. In 1975 "No Charge" became a gospel hit and it crossed over to the country charts. Despite the song's success, Caesar briefly found herself without a recording contract. She signed with Roadshow Records in 1977. Her first release was titled *First Lady*, prompting the title the "First Lady of Gospel" (she had dismissed earlier attempts to refer to her as the "Queen of Gospel Music" after MAHALIA JACKSON's death in 1972). Label executives had pushed her to record contemporary gospel. Only two songs were well received: "Faded Rose" and "Miracle Worker." She recorded her second Roadshow album, *From the Heart* (1975); sales were mediocre. Uncomfortable with contemporary gospel, Caesar returned to traditional gospel. In 1980 she signed with Word Records and released *Rejoice*, which won a Grammy and a Dove Award. In 1982 she released the best-selling *Jesus, I Love Calling Your Name*.

Her career continued to flourish in the 1980s. In 1980 she founded the annual Shirley Caesar Crusade Convention. She increased her touring and recording with the Caesar Singers. In 1984 she recorded her fourth Word album, *Sailin' on the Sea of God's Love*, which won two Grammys. In 1985 Caesar recorded two more award-winning albums *Celebration* and *Christmasing*. In 1988 she recorded her immensely successful first live album, *Live in Chicago*, which topped the *Billboard* charts for most of 1989. Her award-winning song "Hold My Mule" was also a hit on the country charts.

Her personal life saw several major changes during the 1980s. In January 1983 she met Harold Ivory Williams, senior bishop of the Mount Calvary Holy Churches of America, at a citywide revival in Durham. She wed Williams in a lavish ceremony on

26 June 1983 at Durham High School Auditorium. In 1981 she enrolled at Shaw University in Raleigh, North Carolina, and finally received her undergraduate degree, graduating magna cum laude with a B.S. in Business Administration. In fall 1985 her mother suffered a debilitating stroke. After her mother's death on 8 November 1986 at the age of 84, Caesar recorded the tribute song and video "I Remember Mama," the first gospel music video.

Caesar became increasingly involved in Durham religious and community affairs. She served seven years as copastor of her husband's Mount Calvary Holy Church in Winston-Salem. In 1987 she successfully ran for Durham City Council, winning 68 percent of the vote. She served only one four-year term, deciding to devote time to her marriage, ministry, and career. Although she retired from public office in 1991, Caesar continued to be actively involved in community affairs in the Triangle area, comprising Raleigh-Durham and Chapel Hill.

Caesar ventured into film, television, and musical theater. She first appeared onscreen in the 1983 documentary *Gospel* (David Leivick and Frederick A. Ritzenberg, directors), which also featured the Mighty Clouds of Joy and James Cleveland. She appeared in her own concert films *Live in Memphis ... Hold My Mule* (1988) and *Shirley Caesar Live ... He Will Come* (1996), in addition to the music video "I Remember Mama" (1989). She made her feature film debut with a cameo role in Gregory Nava's *Why Do Fools Fall in Love* (1998). She also appeared in Jonathan Lynn's *The Fighting Temptations* (2003). In 2005 she played Mama Jack in Lisa France's *The Unseen* (2005). Caesar has also made several television appearances. In the late 1960s she appeared with the Caravans on Chicago's *Jubilee Showcase*. In 1998 she was cast as Aunt Shirley in an episode of the gospel-themed United Paramount Network (UPN) situation comedy "The Good News." The following year she played Grace in UPN's "The Parkers" (a spin-off of the series "Moesha").

In the 1990s Caesar ventured into musical theater. She was cast in the Broadway revival of Vy Higginsen's gospel musical *Mama I Want to Sing* (1994). She performed in the remainder of the trilogy, *Sing! Mama 2* (1995) and *Born to Sing! Mama 3* (1996). Caesar also appeared at New York's Madison Square Garden with Cissy Houston (mother of singer Whitney Houston) in *This Is My Song*.

Since the age of twelve, Caesar felt destined to become a minister. In August 1990 she became pastor of Mount Calvary Word Faith Church in Raleigh.

Under her leadership the congregation grew from two dozen to over a thousand members.

Caesar recorded more than forty albums. She won eleven Grammys, thirteen Stellar Awards, and eighteen Dove awards. In 1999 she received a National Heritage Fellowship from the National Endowment for the Arts. Caesar was inducted into the Gospel Music Association's Hall of Fame in Nashville, Tennessee, in 2000.

FURTHER READING

Caesar, Shirley. *Shirley Caesar: The Lady, the Melody, and the Word, the Inspirational Story of the First Lady of Gospel* (1998)

"First Lady of Gospel," *Ebony* (November 1977).

Harrington, Brooksie. "Personal Narrative in Gospel Performance: Shirley Caesar's 'The Four Angels,'" *Southern Folklore* (1997).

Harrington, Brooksie Eugene. "Shirley Caesar: A Woman of Words." Ph.D. diss., Ohio State University, 1992.

Holden, Stephen. "*Born to Sing! Mama 3*. (Paramount Theater, New York, New York)," *New York Times*, 9 March 1996.

Jones, Bobby, and Leslie Sussman. *Touched by God* (1998).

"Shirley Caesar: Putting the Gospel Truth into Politics," *Ebony* (December 1988).

GAYLE MURCHISON

Cahn, Jean Camper (26 May 1935–2 Jan. 1991), lawyer and social activist, was born Jean Camper, the daughter of JOHN E. T. CAMPER, civil rights activist and physician, and Florine Thompson. She grew up in Baltimore with her sister Elizabeth—she also had two stepbrothers and two stepsisters from her father's first marriage to Louise G. Nixon. The Camper household was a regular meeting place for local NAACP figures and national civil rights leaders, such as THURGOOD MARSHALL and her godfather PAUL ROBESON. Camper drew inspiration from her father's career as a doctor and a civil rights advocate, but a series of ugly personal incidents soon underscored the need to expand the struggle for racial justice.

Jean's younger brother, John Jr., suffering from a treatable ear infection, was refused treatment by Johns Hopkins University hospital because of his race. The hospital eventually admitted the boy, but only after the infection had spread, forcing doctors to remove part of his brain. The incident left Camper enraged. Other similar incidents served only to increase her fury at racial injustice. She gained entrance into the exclusive Emma Willard School for Girls in New York on the recommendation of the theologian HOWARD THURMAN, but the white girls resisted her presence, and some refused to live near her dormitory room. One girl told Jean that Jean's mother should be washing the floors of her house.

After graduation, Jean enrolled at Northwestern University in Evanston, Illinois, and integrated the freshman dormitory. At the close of her first year, she suffered from rheumatic fever and spent the next year at home. In the fall of 1953 she enrolled at Swarthmore College in Pennsylvania, where she met her future husband, Edgar S. Cahn. Swarthmore officials expressed their dismay over the relationship between Camper and Cahn. Camper further enraged the Swarthmore community by patronizing a local barbershop, a move that sparked a cross burning on her dormitory lawn. When she took Cahn home to visit her parents in Baltimore, they were stopped by Maryland police and threatened with arrest for violating state antimiscegenation laws.

Shortly after Camper graduated from Swarthmore in 1957—Cahn had completed his studies the previous year—the two were married. The same year she began her studies at Yale Law School while her husband completed a Ph.D. in English at Yale and then also enrolled at Yale Law School, finishing in 1963. Jean Cahn converted to Judaism and Jonathan, her first child, was born the day of her first law school examination. Her second child, Reuben, was born while the couple was in England on a Fulbright fellowship. Cahn earned her LLB in 1961, and the next year she and her husband were hired on a Ford Foundation grant to help run antipoverty programs in New Haven, Connecticut. She became associate general counsel for the New Haven Redevelopment Agency and staff attorney for the first neighborhood legal services program for the poor. The experience proved pivotal for Cahn herself as well as for the development of legal aid for the poor and for the course of President Lyndon Johnson's Great Society antipoverty programs.

Based on her New Haven experience, Cahn and her husband authored their famed 1964 *Yale Law Journal* essay, "The War on Poverty: A Civilian Perspective." Ultimately it lead to creation of the Legal Services Corporation, a federally funded program that remained true to Cahn's original vision to "promote equal access to justice in our Nation and to provide high quality civil legal assistance to low-income persons" (Legal Services Corporation).

With characteristic energy, passion, and vision, the Cahns argued that the government's War on Poverty was a military-like operation implemented by professionals, conducted by a monopoly power, and calculated to "minimize casualties to the military." What was missing in the well-intended war, they asserted, was the civilians' perspective, the people's power to dissent from prevailing government views and "compel responsiveness" (Cahn and Cahn, "The War on Poverty: A Civilian Perspective," *Yale Law Journal* [1964], 1329). The Cahns wisely argued that creating programs without providing a mechanism for public response and for articulating grievances was as inefficient as it was unjust. As the Cahns asserted: "Businessmen and officials alike take pause and reflect before acting to the detriment of persons who are not defenseless. The poor have no such protection" (Cahn and Cahn, "The War on Poverty: A Civilian Perspective," *Yale Law Journal* [1964], 1340). Given that the right to legal counsel in criminal cases was only established in 1963 with the famed *Gideon v. Wainwright* case, the Cahns' insistence that the poor be guaranteed legal counsel in civil cases was indeed new and radical. The piece impressed a number of figures in the Lyndon Johnson administration, especially Sargent Shriver, head of the Office of Economic Opportunity (OEO).

In 1963 the couple moved to Washington, D.C., where Jean Cahn had taken a position at the African Desk at the State Department—she had taught international law at the Yale Law School—and her husband went to work for Attorney General Robert Kennedy. Jean Cahn then was hired by Shriver, who gave her responsibility for setting up the legal services program. In a brilliant move Cahn quickly secured approval from the American Bar Association (ABA), winning over the ABA president Lewis Powell. Powell's support helped convince the conservative association of the merits of Cahn's approach. The program not only provided legal services to people who would not have had access to the nation's courts but also created critical employment opportunities for minority lawyers. By 1967 the OEO was spending over $40 million on legal services for the poor. But Shriver soon soured on Cahn, preferring to place in her position a white male attorney who would deal with a legal profession dominated by white males. Outraged by yet another act of discrimination, Cahn resigned and denounced Shriver before a meeting of the ABA. Her husband declined to tender his resignation, believing that his presence was necessary for the program's survival; this act strained their marriage almost to the breaking point. Tensions became overwhelming when Shriver compelled Edgar Cahn to draft a response to his wife's ABA attack.

In 1966 Jean Cahn helped found the federally funded Center for Community Action Education (CCAE), directed by former Congress of Racial Equality (CORE) national director JAMES FARMER. The CCAE established literacy programs in churches, schools, and community centers. While working as an adjunct professor at Howard University from 1967 to 1971, Cahn organized the Institute for Political Services to Society, which studied the District of Columbia government's response to civilian grievances, and coupled the CCAE program to a new master's of law program in law and poverty at George Washington University. Also in 1967 Cahn joined the legal team that defended Representative ADAM CLAYTON POWELL JR. against corruption charges before a congressional committee and brilliantly argued his case before the U.S. Supreme Court to reverse Congress's vote to expel him. Powell valued Cahn over the male members of his team: "The sister is the one who knows what she's talking about" (Waldman).

The next year Cahn founded the Urban Law Institute (ULI) at George Washington University on an OEO grant, hiring law school students to serve as advocates for the District of Columbia's low-income residents. The ULI intended to "make the legal system and the rule of law itself relevant and responsive to the problems of the poor" (Waldman). It filed hundreds of law suits to halt bus fare increases, compel local television stations to hire African Americans, challenge slum lords, and make the District of Columbia's government more responsive. The ULI's high visibility caused consternation in the new Richard Nixon administration and at George Washington University, which became increasingly uneasy over Cahn's troublemaking clinical law program. Even the faculty voted to end support for the institute. When Donald Rumsfeld (who as a congressman opposed creation of the OEO) took over direction of the program under President Nixon, Cahn's ULI was doomed. After nearly three years, the university decided that Cahn and ULI's provocative work should go. Angered at what she viewed as a betrayal, Cahn exclaimed, "Well, I'll just start my own damn law school" (Waldman).

The Cahns approached Antioch College in Yellow Springs, Ohio, with many branch campuses and a well-deserved reputation for innovation, to found the Antioch Law School in the District of Columbia. The new school embodied the ULI's clinical approach to instruction and its singular commitment to practicing poverty law. The *Washington Post* enthusiastically supported the school, and Baltimore's U.S. representative PARREN J. MITCHELL exclaimed that the Antioch idea "means that given the courage and commitment of black folks, racism, apathy, bigotry, deceit, hypocrisy—all of these can be beaten into the ground" (*Washington Post*, 31 July 1971). With the Cahns serving as co-deans—making Jean Cahn the first black female founder of a law school and the first black female dean of a law school—the enterprise began admitting an unprecedented number of women and minority students. Although the school embodied the Cahns' ideal of "a law school organized around a teaching law firm" (Smith, 102), it ironically proved difficult to implement in practice. A demanding schedule and a requirement that students should live with the poor to better understand their needs produced much unhappiness. Outdated facilities, low faculty pay, and accusations of chaotic rule destroyed faith in the Cahns, particularly after they hired Blackman's Volunteer Liberation Army to guard the college campus. Yet in one year students at the school filed one thousand cases on behalf of the District of Columbia's poor, making Antioch Law School "the largest public-interest law firm in the country" (Waldman). But by 1977 the school was collapsing. Black faculty members left, and after the Cahns denounced their own faculty as racists who would have preferred an all-white faculty, relations completely broke down. Faculty members publicly rebuked the "chaos, turmoil and conflict they [the Cahns] have engendered … for five years" (*Washington Post*, 25 May 1977).

Jean Cahn's health began to deteriorate, and the school faltered further, although more minority faculty members were hired. In 1976 Cahn suffered a stroke that paralyzed much of her left side for over a year while leaving the burden of running the school on her husband. The Cahns had to mortgage their own house to pay the school's bills, and after a financial dispute between the Cahns and Antioch College ended up in court, the school administration in Yellow Springs fired the couple in January 1980. Edgar Cahn then suffered a massive heart attack, and their law school limped on until it closed in 1988. It reopened as the District of Columbia Law School in 1991 and in 1998 as the University of the District of Columbia David A. Clarke School of Law. Despite its unfortunate end, the Antioch experiment had trained over 1,500 public interest lawyers and 450 paralegal workers and filed an astonishing 10,000 lawsuits for the poor.

Cahn remained in the District of Columbia, although her husband took a job at the University of Miami Law School. From 1984 to 1986 she served as a distinguished scholar at the London School of Economics and was distinguished visiting professor at Middlebury College. The couple reunited, and in 1985 Cahn moved to Miami, where she began to practice law again. In 1989 she was diagnosed with cancer but continued to practice poverty law until her death in Miami.

FURTHER READING

Cummiskey, John W. "Access to Justice: The Birth of Legal Services," *Michigan Bar Journal* (Oct. 1999).

Smith, J. Clay, Jr. *Rebels in Law: Voices in History of Black Women Lawyers* (1998).

Waldman, Steven. "A Perfect Combination of Chutzpah and Soul," *Washington Post* (18 Aug. 1991).

Obituaries: *New York Times*, 6 Jan. 1991; *Washington Post*, 17 Feb. 1991.

DONALD YACOVONE

Cailloux, André (25 Aug. 1825–27 May 1863), soldier, was born in Plaquemine Parish, Louisiana, the son of André Cailloux, a slave skilled in masonry and carpentry, and Josephine Duvernay, a slave of Joseph Duvernay. On 15 July 1827 young André was baptized in St. Louis Cathedral in New Orleans.

After the death of Joseph Duvernay in 1828, Joseph's sister, Aimée Duvernay Bailey, acquired André Cailloux and his parents and brought them all to New Orleans. There André probably learned the cigar-maker's trade from his half-brothers, Molière and Antoine Duvernay, the freed sons of his mother, Josephine, and her master Joseph Duvernay. After he was manumitted by his mistress in 1846, Cailloux married another recently freed slave, Félicie Coulon, on 22 June 1847. Cailloux adopted Félicie's son, Jean Louis, and the couple had four more children, three of whom survived into adulthood.

Cailloux and his wife moved into the ranks of the close-knit New Orleans community of approximately eleven thousand free people of color (*gens de couleur libre*, Creoles of color, or African Creoles). African or African French or Spanish in ancestry, French in culture and language, and Catholic in religion, free people of color occupied an intermediate legal and social status between whites and slaves within Louisiana's tripartite racial caste system. Denied political rights, free people of color nevertheless could own property, make contracts, and testify in court. They constituted the most prosperous and literate group of people of African descent in the United States, with a majority earning modest livings as artisans, skilled laborers, and shopkeepers, while a few enjoyed greater wealth. Some free people of color owned slaves, either for economic reasons or as a way of bringing together family members. Although most free people of color were of mixed race, they ran the gamut of phenotypes. Cailloux, for example, bragged of being the blackest man in New Orleans.

By the mid-1850s Cailloux, who had learned to read and write, had become a respectable, independent cigar maker. He resided in a Creole cottage worth about four hundred dollars, and purchased his slave mother, reuniting his family. Cailloux had his children baptized in the Catholic church, and sent his two sons to *L'Institution Catholique des Orphelins dans l'Indigence* (*Institute Catholique*), a school run by African Creole intellectuals influenced by the inclusive and egalitarian ethos of the 1848 French Revolution. Cailloux's peers elected him an officer of *Les Amis de l'Ordre* (the Friends of Order), one of the numerous mutual aid and benefit societies established by free people of color during the decade. These provided forums in which people of color could exercise leadership and engage in the democratic process.

By the late 1850s, however, the legal, social, and economic position of free people of color had deteriorated, and in 1861, Cailloux sold his cottage at auction. After the Civil War began, free people of color answered the governor's request that they raise a militia regiment by forming the Defenders of the Native Land, otherwise known as the Louisiana Native Guards Regiment. They did so out of fear of possible reprisals if they failed to respond positively, and in the hope of improving their circumstances. Mutual aid and benefit societies formed themselves into companies for service in the regiment. Cailloux, for instance, assumed the rank of first lieutenant in Order Company. Louisiana officials, however, intended the regiment more for show than for combat.

When Confederate forces abandoned the city of New Orleans to Federal forces in late April 1862, the Louisiana Native Guards disbanded. In August 1862, however, U.S. General Benjamin F. Butler, suffering from a shortage of troops and fearing a Confederate attack on the city, authorized the recruitment of three regiments of free people of color, the first units of people of African descent formally mustered into the Union Army. While the field grade officers were white, the company officers were free people of color.

Cailloux received a commission as captain in the First Regiment. He quickly raised a company of troops, the majority of whom were Catholic free men of color drawn from the city's Third District, where he worked and attended meetings of *Les Amis de l'Ordre*. But despite a formal directive that restricted enlistments to free men, Cailloux also welcomed runaway slaves, both French and English speaking. He no doubt shared the hope expressed by African Creole activists in the pages of their newspaper *L'Union*, that military service would give blacks a claim to citizenship. Gentlemanly, athletic, charismatic, and confident, the thirty-eight-year-old Cailloux cut a dashing figure, belying the stereotype of black servility and inferiority.

Cailloux and the men of the Native Guards, however, faced daunting challenges. They suffered discrimination and abuse at the hands of white civilians, soldiers, and their own national government. In the field, they found themselves consigned primarily to guard duty or to backbreaking manual labor. To make matters worse, General Nathaniel P. Banks, Butler's successor, determined to purge the Native Guard Regiments of their black officers.

Yearning to prove themselves in combat, Cailloux and two regiments of the Native Guards received their chance on 27 May 1863 at Port Hudson, Louisiana, one of two remaining Confederate strongholds on the Mississippi River. There Cailloux's company spearheaded an assault by the First and Third Regiments against a nearly impregnable Confederate position. As the Native Guards approached to within about two hundred yards of the entrenched Confederate force, they encountered withering musket and artillery fire and the attacking lines broke. Cailloux and other officers attempted to rally their men several times. Finally, in the midst of the chaos, Cailloux, holding his sword aloft in his right hand while his broken left arm dangled at his side, exhorted his troops to follow him. Advancing well in front, he led a charge. As he reached a backwater obstacle, he was struck and killed by a shell. The remaining Native Guards retreated, as did Union forces all along the battle line that day. Cailloux's body lay rotting in the broiling sun for forty days until the surrender of Port Hudson on 8 July 1863.

Cailloux's heroics encouraged those supporting the cause of using black troops in combat. *L'Union* declared that Cailloux's patriotism and valor had vindicated blacks of the charge that they lacked manliness. To memorialize Cailloux, African Creole activists orchestrated a public funeral in New Orleans presided over by the Reverend Claude Paschal Maistre, a French priest recently suspended by the archbishop of New Orleans for advocating emancipation and the Union cause. Emboldened by Cailloux's heroism, blacks, both slave and free, asserted their growing political consciousness. They packed the city's main streets in unprecedented numbers as the military cortege bearing Cailloux's casket made its way to St. Louis Cemetery Number 2. Maistre eulogized Cailloux as a martyr to the cause of Union and freedom; Northern newspapers gave extensive coverage to his death and funeral; George H. Boker, a popular poet, memorialized Cailloux in his ode, *The Black Captain*; and African Creole activists in New Orleans elevated him to almost mythic status, invoking his name in their campaign against slavery and on behalf of voting rights.

In October 1864 delegates to the National Negro Convention literally wrapped themselves in Cailloux's banner. With the First Regiment's bloodstained flag hanging in a place of honor, numerous speakers invoked Cailloux's indomitable spirit and heroism and launched a nationwide campaign for black suffrage through the creation of the National Equal Rights League. Both in life and in death, André Cailloux, whose surname means "rocks" or "stones" in French, served to unite and inspire people of color in their struggle for unity, freedom, and equality.

FURTHER READING

Edmonds, David C. *The Guns of Port Hudson: The Investment, Siege, and Reduction*, 2 vols. (1984).

Ochs, Stephen J. "American Spartacus." *American Legacy*, Fall 2001, 31–36.

Ochs, Stephen J. *A Black Patriot and a White Priest: André Cailloux and Claude Paschal Maistre in Civil War New Orleans* (2000).

Wilson, Joseph T. *The Black Phalanx* (1890).

Obituary: *New York Times*, 8 Aug. 1863.

STEPHEN J. OCHS

Cain, Lawrence (5 May 1844–29 Feb. 1884), slave, farmer, teacher, Reconstruction-era state legislator and lawyer, was born in South Carolina's famed

Edgefield District. He was literate and the favored slave of Major Thomas Carwile, the commissioner in equity of Edgefield. Cain was probably raised much like other slave children on Edgefield plantations: they would be cared for by an elderly lady while their mothers worked in the fields until the children were about six or seven years old, when they were sent to work in the fields, many serving as water carriers or weed pullers. In some instances they were sent to work by the side of an adult. Generally the children were called "quarter workers" since they produced about one-fourth as much labor as an adult. It is not known exactly how Cain learned to read and write, but it is likely that he was taught by his owner, as he was known as his owner's "pet"—meaning he was a favorite of his owner. Loyal to the Carwile family, he went to war as the valet of a member of the family whose identity remains unknown. Cain was taken as a prisoner of war and was later exchanged as a Confederate soldier.

By 1866 he was teaching approximately thirty pupils in a one-room school, using assistance he received from the Salem, Massachusetts Freedmen's Aid Society and from other blacks in the community. According to the United States census of 1870, Cain and his wife, Ella, were twenty-six years old, owned $1,500 in real estate, and had a personal estate worth $450. By 1880 Cain was the father of four children, and his wife was also a school teacher. He taught school in a building that was a crude lean-to log cabin—commonly called a church school, it did little more than protect the students from the elements. In 1868 Cain was elected a member of the lower house of the state's general assembly, representing Edgefield. The same year he and thirteen others advised Gov. Robert K. Scott that Edgefield Democrats were assassinating African Americans to keep them from power. They requested "some defense, if we cannot get this we will all be killed or beat to death" (Foner, 35). In 1869 he served as a delegate to the South Carolina Labor Convention. The convention served several purposes, addressing the economic and political problems of the state and seeking to protect black laborers by encouraging the general assembly to enact legislation that would resolve some of its ills. The convention also acted as a platform to vocalize the economic position of laborers and to recognize the freedman as a citizen. Cain remained in the state legislature until 1872 when he entered the state senate, serving there until 1876. Cain was a faithful and diligent worker for the Republican Party, serving as chairman of the county committee. Repeated death threats kept

him from campaigning. He also filled a variety of other posts, including state registrar, a census enumerator, an assistant marshal, assistant county assessor, commissioner of elections, and a member of the board of regents for the state lunatic asylum. In belated response to his 1868 warning to the governor, Cain became a colonel in the state militia in 1873 and served in that capacity until 1876, the year of the formal end of Reconstruction.

Prior to 1869 the black residents of Edgefield had worshipped at the First Baptist Church along with white parishioners. They were allowed to occupy the gallery of the church but were not permitted to sit with whites on the main floor. The church had many rules that applied to the entire congregation, such as no talking in the sanctuary and no smoking or drinking. Blacks were fined or expelled from the church for the slightest infraction. Although anyone could be expelled from the church, it appeared that the black parishioners received more punishment than their white counterparts. Whites repeatedly reported black members to the church for many untrue offences such as lying, swearing, drinking, dancing, and gambling. Eventually the black parishioners withdrew and founded the Macedonia Baptist Church under the leadership of Senator Cain. On 13 July 1869 Mrs. Rebecca Bland deeded five acres of land, for the sum of $99.27, to the church's trustees to build the church.

In 1869 Cain purchased forty-six and one-half acres of land from his former owner Thomas W. Carwile for $400. He enrolled as a student at the University of South Carolina Law School in 1873 and received his LLB in 1876, but he apparently did not open a practice. After the Reconstruction era ended, he moved to Columbia, South Carolina, where for several years he held the position of deputy collector of internal revenue. Despite repeated threats he continued to work for the Republican Party. He attended the national convention in 1876 and in 1882 served as chairman of his county Republican committee. He died in Columbia of tuberculosis in 1884.

FURTHER READING

Bryant, Laurence C. *Legislators in South Carolina, 1868–1902*.

Foner, Eric. *Freedom's Lawmakers: A Directory of Black Officer Holders During Reconstruction* (1993).

Rubin, Hyman, III. *South Carolina Scalawags* (2006).

Stone, William. *A Record of Service in the Freedmen's Bureau* (1866–1868).

Zuczek, Richard. *State of Rebellion: Reconstruction in South Carolina* (1996).

Obituary: *Edgefield (S.C.) Advertiser*, March 6, 1884.

AGNES KANE CALLUM

Cain, Richard Harvey (12 Apr. 1825–18 Jan. 1887), clergyman and politician, was born to free parents in Greenbriar County, Virginia (now West Virginia). In 1831 his family moved to Gallipolis, Ohio. Cain was educated at local schools and worked on an Ohio River steamboat before being licensed to preach in the Methodist Episcopal Church in 1844. Complaining of racial discrimination in the church, he resigned and joined the African Methodist Episcopal (AME) Church. Assigned a pulpit in Muscatine, Iowa, he was ordained a deacon in 1859. He returned to Ohio and in 1860 attended Wilberforce University. From 1861 to 1865 he served as pastor at Bridge Street Church in Brooklyn, New York, and was elevated to elder in 1862. He participated in the 1864 national black convention in Syracuse, New York, that advocated abolition, equality before the law, and universal manhood suffrage. Cain married Laura (maiden name unknown), and they adopted a daughter.

In 1865, following the Civil War, church leaders sent Cain to Charleston, South Carolina. He reorganized the Emanuel AME Church, which had been disbanded by white leaders in 1822 in the hysteria that accompanied the DENMARK VESEY slave-revolt conspiracy. Under Cain's leadership the church became South Carolina's largest AME congregation by 1871. In 1866 Cain was appointed superintendent of the southern division of the AME Conference. He successively edited two Republican newspapers, the *South Carolina Leader* from 1866 to 1868 and the *Missionary Record* from 1868 to 1878. The *Missionary Record* was sponsored by the AME Church and was influential in the state's black community. In 1865 Cain attended the Colored Peoples' Convention in Charleston, where he wrote one of the documents published by the convention, "Address to the People of South Carolina." In the address Cain called for "evenhanded justice" and the right of black men to vote, to have trials by jury, and to acquire homesteads. The address also advocated abolition of the recently adopted black code, a series of measures designed to restrict blacks to menial and agricultural labor while sanctioning corporal punishment and imposing vagrancy and curfew laws that did not apply to whites.

Cain became one of South Carolina's leading political figures after Congress enacted Reconstruction legislation in 1867 that reestablished military authority over the southern states, granted black men the right to vote and hold political office, and disenfranchised those who had supported the Confederacy. Active in the Republican Party, Cain represented Charleston in the 1868 state constitutional convention. He was elected to the state senate in 1868. Although he lost reelection in 1870, he was selected chair of the Republican Party in Charleston from 1870 to 1871, and in 1872 he was elected to Congress as South Carolina's at-large representative, serving from 1873 to 1875. He did not run for reelection immediately but was elected again in 1876, serving from 1877 to 1879. Cain also served as president of the Enterprise Railroad Company, a corporation formed by black leaders in Charleston in 1870 to operate a horse-drawn streetcar line to haul freight between the South Carolina Railroad terminal and the wharves on the Cooper River. The railway did not prosper, and white businessmen took it over by 1873.

Cain was blunt, assertive, and sometimes inconsistent on issues that affected the destiny of black people. One issue that he persistently supported was proposals to make land available to freedmen. At the 1868 constitutional convention he introduced a resolution to petition Congress for a one million dollar loan to aid in the purchase of land, but Congress failed to act on it. In 1869 he supported the establishment of a state land commission and served as one of its agents. The commission, which was authorized to purchase land and redistribute it to landless blacks and whites, proved to be corrupt and ineffective. In 1871 Cain himself purchased two thousand acres near Charleston, which were subdivided, named Lincolnville, and sold in twenty-five-acre parcels. When Cain failed to make payments on the mortgage and foreclosure proceedings were initiated, he was indicted for obtaining money under false pretenses. Because of a legal technicality his case never came to trial. Though he promised to return money that he had, little was ever repaid.

Cain's support for civil rights measures was more equivocal than his advocacy for land apportionment was. In 1868 he opposed a civil rights bill in the state senate that was designed to prohibit discrimination in public facilities, but he strongly supported a similar measure in 1874 in the U.S. House, saying, "We do not want any discrimination to be made. I do not ask for any legislation for the colored people of this country that is not applied to the white people of this country. All that we seek is equal laws, equal legislation, and equal rights throughout the length and breadth of this land."

Considered a political maverick, Cain alienated some Republicans and fellow blacks through his sharp attacks on northern white Republicans. In 1870 he joined other black leaders, including ROBERT DeLARGE, ALONZO RANSIER, and MARTIN R. DELANY, in successfully demanding that white Republicans concede to black men a greater portion of major political offices. In 1871 he shocked and enraged Republicans when he supported the Democrats in the municipal election, arguing in the *Missionary Record* that black men should cooperate with whites. He joined Martin Delany in 1871 in criticizing white Republican leaders who patronized only light-skinned black leaders; he and Delany also condemned the light-skinned black men who acquiesced in the arrangement, thereby excluding darker black men from positions of power. Cain excoriated Republicans of both races for their constant conflicts over political patronage—conflicts that were, Cain insisted, destroying the Republican Party.

In 1880 he was ordained a bishop in the AME Church and presided over a district comprising Louisiana and Texas. He helped found and served as president of Paul Quinn College, an AME institution in Waco, Texas. Later he served as bishop of a district comprising New York, New Jersey, and Pennsylvania. Cain died at his residence in Washington, D.C.

Richard H. Cain was one of South Carolina's foremost Reconstruction leaders. As an AME minister, a newspaper editor, and a Republican politician, Cain was forceful and controversial in insisting that black people have the right to participate in all levels of the political system and should have greater opportunities to acquire wealth through land ownership.

FURTHER READING

Several letters from Cain are in the Governors' Papers in the South Carolina Department of Archives and History.

Christopher, Maurine. *America's Black Congressmen* (1971).

Holt, Thomas. *Black over White: Negro Political Leadership in South Carolina during Reconstruction* (1977).

Mann, Kenneth. "Richard Harvey Cain, Congressman, Minister and Champion for Civil Rights," *Negro History Bulletin* 35 (Mar. 1972): 64–66.

Simmons, William J. *Men of Mark: Eminent, Progressive, and Rising* (1887).

Williamson, Joel. *After Slavery: The Negro in South Carolina during Reconstruction, 1861–1877* (1965).

This entry is taken from the *American National Biography* and is published here with the permission of the American Council of Learned Societies.

WILLIAM C. HINE

Caldwell, Charles (1831 or 1832–25 Dec. 1875), blacksmith and state legislator, was born to slave parents whose names have not been recorded. Nothing is known of his childhood, other than that he had one brother, Sam. By the time he reached adulthood, Charles Caldwell was working as a blacksmith in Clinton, a small village in Hinds County twelve miles from Jackson, Mississippi. Given that Mississippi's slave population expanded rapidly in the three decades after 1830, it is quite possible that Caldwell was born in another state to planters who had then brought or sold him on the lucrative Mississippi market.

Caldwell's skilled trade provided him a degree of relative autonomy in his work and may have enabled him to travel with fewer restrictions than the average plantation slave. Slave blacksmiths, carpenters, barbers, and other skilled workers often learned to read and write, as Caldwell did, and generally enjoyed a high status within the African American community. The high status of such craftsmen continued after slavery. During Reconstruction more than four hundred black artisans served as officeholders. As one of sixteen African American Republican delegates who participated in Mississippi's Constitutional Convention in 1868, Caldwell was arguably the most politically accomplished of them. Although blacks accounted for three-fifths of the Mississippi electorate, eighty-four of the convention's one hundred delegates were white. Contrary to later claims that carpetbaggers dominated this so-called black-and-tan convention, two-thirds of the delegates were native-born southerners. Caldwell took an active role in the proceedings of the convention, generally voting with the more radical Republican faction and, after much effort, helping to form a constitution that greatly expanded the powers of Mississippi's state government. It established an integrated public school system, legalized interracial marriages, and granted the vote to all adult men, regardless of property and race.

The convention also secured property rights for all citizens, regardless of race or gender, though the final constitutional provisions were less radical than Caldwell had hoped. During the convention debates he testified that, even after slavery, the freed people had no protections against whites who seized their property. The convention agreed with Caldwell's proposal that the state's new constitution recognize former slaves' right to property. Caldwell's proposal would have also secured the property rights of thousands of black women who, in the post–Civil War era and for the first time, had begun to legally purchase their own goods, crops, poultry, and livestock. A separate amendment by Caldwell's colleague, THOMAS W. STRINGER, however, subsumed women's property rights in favor of those of their husbands. In the end the convention's proposed constitution was defeated by the narrowest of margins in a statewide referendum in June 1868 that was marked by fraud and the violent intimidation of black voters.

At some time after the convention but before the referendum, Caldwell was tried before a magistrate at Clinton for having shot and killed a white man. A white attorney who aided Caldwell's defense later told a U.S. Senate investigation that this was the first recorded instance in Hinds County of a black man killing a white. In a decision that signaled a new era in race relations in Mississippi, the magistrate quickly dismissed the case for lack of a cause when it was established that the victim had attempted to shoot at Caldwell first but had missed. Although Caldwell had acted in self-defense and had been exonerated by a white magistrate, his victim was the son of a prominent judge and belonged to one of the leading families in the county. White resentment of Caldwell and depictions of him as a "notorious and turbulent negro" were probably sparked by this shooting.

After the state adopted a somewhat revised constitution in December 1869, Caldwell stepped down from his seat on the Hinds County Board of Police to serve as one of only five African Americans in the thirty-three-member Mississippi Senate. During his five years in that body, he earned a reputation as one of the more radical and defiant black Republicans, and as a loyal supporter of Mississippi's Maine-born Republican governor Adelbert Ames. Nevertheless, even whites who resented the presence of northern carpetbaggers and their own former slaves in such exalted positions had a grudging respect for Caldwell. In the senate, Caldwell voted with the Republican majority to endorse the Fourteenth and Fifteenth amendments to the U.S. Constitution and for measures to bring about an end to racial discrimination in Mississippi.

Caldwell's support for gender equality continued. He worked closely with Sarah Ann Dickey, an Ohio-born white woman who had arrived in Clinton in 1870 to teach at the town's first public school. When Ku Klux Klansmen threatened her, and native whites refused to take Dickey as a boarder, Caldwell offered her a room in his house. Dickey later relied heavily on Caldwell's political connections in the state capital when she founded the Mount Hermon Seminary, a school for black women modeled on her Massachusetts alma mater, Mount Holyoke, in Jackson in 1875. Caldwell chaired the biracial board of trustees of Dickey's seminary. Caldwell's support for women's rights is also evident in his work to secure passage of a law requiring married men to seek their wives' consent before selling their property. He and his legislative colleagues were less successful in challenging the entrenched economic power of Mississippi's white planters, in spite of mass protests in Hinds County in the early 1870s in support of rent controls and against low wages. By the time of the 1875 elections, however, Caldwell's energies, and those of his colleagues were focused increasingly on resisting a statewide wave of white violence against blacks and white Republicans. Several hundred citizens, mostly black, were killed by the Ku Klux Klan and similar racist "white line" groups between 1870 and 1875. The federal government intervened in response to only one of these attacks, when between forty and eighty African Americans were killed at Vicksburg in December 1874.

While Reconstruction's opponents were determined to secure victory in the 1875 elections by violence, if necessary, Caldwell was equally resolute in his efforts to ensure the integrity of the constitutional process. On 4 September 1875 Caldwell invited a prominent white Democrat to give the opening speech at a large Republican barbecue and rally. Though Caldwell had urged the 1,500 blacks in attendance to avoid alcohol and to leave their guns at home, his careful preparations failed to prevent what became known as the Clinton Riot. As Caldwell had hoped, the predominantly black crowd gave the white Democratic speaker a respectful hearing. Shortly after a white Republican began to speak, however, the calm was broken by several shots, followed by general pandemonium. One account of the event suggests that a black policeman had asked two whites to leave the rally when he discovered them consuming alcohol. The white men allegedly started shooting but ran away when it became apparent that African Americans outnumbered them. A group of young black men, possibly unarmed, tracked the white men down and beat them to death. Two African Americans were also killed in the melee.

Caldwell attempted to secure order but was unable to prevent four days of violence in which whites from Hinds County, aided by specially trained mercenaries from Vicksburg, known as the "Modocs," systematically hunted down and killed fifty or more African Americans in Clinton and the surrounding area. Around fifty of the Modocs— named after a tribe of fierce-fighting Californian Indians—visited Caldwell's home. The senator had not yet returned, but his wife (little is known of the union, except that the woman's name was Margaret Ann, and that the couple had a son, who was named for his father) later testified before a congressional committee that the Modocs robbed and vandalized the Caldwell home and killed several of their neighbors. She recalled that the leader of the mercenaries vowed to kill Senator Caldwell: "[I]f it is two years, or one year, or six; no difference…. We have orders to kill him, and we are going to do it" (Lemann, 115).

In response to the violence at Clinton and a similar white riot at Yazoo City, Governor Ames attempted to disarm the white paramilitary bands and clubs that had recently formed throughout the state. He assembled a state militia of two white and five black companies and appointed Caldwell as captain and commanding officer of the first of these companies to muster, Company A of the Second Regiment of the Mississippi Infantry. Although Caldwell and his men readied themselves for action, Ames was reluctant to force a confrontation with the white paramilitaries. In October 1875, however, the governor assigned Caldwell's company to deliver arms to another state militia company at Edwards Depot, thirty miles west of Jackson. The mere sight of Caldwell and his three hundred men, in uniform, armed, and in high spirits, their banners flying behind them, terrified whites, regardless of the fact that Caldwell's men were on official state business. A day after Caldwell delivered the arms to Edwards Depot, Governor Ames gave in to pressure from white Democrats and abandoned the militia experiment.

Without the protection of the militias, the elections of November 1875 were marked by fraud, violence, and intimidation. Many Republicans remained at home on election day, fearing that they would be attacked or killed. Caldwell and thousands of black Mississippians nonetheless insisted on casting their ballots for the Republicans, but they were unable to prevent the Democrats from winning both houses of the Mississippi legislature. White mob violence continued after the election, resulting in the deaths of NOAH B. PARKER and five others at Rolling Fork in early December 1875. It was expected that Caldwell would be a compelling witness at the proposed U.S. Senate investigation of the Clinton Riot and other election irregularities, but he did not live long enough to testify. On Christmas Day in 1875, Caldwell left his home to meet a white friend, Buck Cabell, for a drink. Cabell had not previously been connected to white resistance groups, but what followed suggested he was not the friend Caldwell believed him to be. The two men sat in a cellar and raised their glasses to each other. The sound of the glasses clinking was apparently a signal for a marksman waiting outside the cellar window, who shot Caldwell in the back of the head. Margaret Ann Caldwell later reported to Senate investigators her husband's dying words, told to her by a witness: "Remember when you kill me you kill a gentleman and a brave man. Never say you killed a coward" (Lemann, 158). His body was then riddled with bullets. Other blacks in the vicinity, including Caldwell's brother, were also executed.

In the 1940s the historian Herbert Aptheker suggested that it "is altogether likely that one day Mississippi school children, Negro and white, will be taught to revere the name of Charles Caldwell" (Aptheker, 187).

FURTHER READING

Extensive testimony regarding Charles Caldwell's activities as a state senator, the violence that preceded the 1875 elections, and his assassination can be found in *Mississippi in 1875. Report of the Select Committee to Inquire into the Mississippi Election of 1875*, United States Congress, 1875.

Aptheker, Herbert. *To Be Free: Studies in American Negro History* (1948, repr. 1969).

Griffith, Helen. *Dauntless in Mississippi: The Life of Sarah A. Dickey, 1838–1904* (1965, repr. 1978).

Lemann, Nicholas. *Redemption: The Last Battle of the Civil War* (2006).

STEVEN J. NIVEN

Caldwell, Wilson (27 Feb. 1841–8 July 1898), slave, janitor, magistrate, teacher, principal, and the first black elected official in Chapel Hill, North Carolina, was born Wilson Swain at the home of University of North Carolina president David Swain in Chapel Hill. His father was (Doctor) November Caldwell, a slave of the former university president Joseph Caldwell; his mother was Rosa Burgess, a slave of Swain's. Under the law and practice of slavery in North Carolina, children took on the surnames of their owners, not of their fathers. As a child Wilson Swain was a personal servant to Robert Swain, his owner's son, and then as a young teenager he was an apprentice to the University of North Carolina's chief gardener, Mr. Paxton. In violation of law and custom, but due, no doubt, to the university atmosphere, he was taught to read and write.

As an adult, Wilson Swain served the University of North Carolina in a variety of roles both as an enslaved man and as a free man. Before and during the Civil War, he performed duties as a university servant. In this capacity he tended to student needs, such as making morning fires, carrying water, and cleaning rooms as well as being a "waiter" (or attendant) in science labs and classrooms. He was able to earn money by performing extra services for the students; for example, he was paid twenty-five cents a month for shoe blacking.

Wilson Swain took the surname Caldwell at the end of the Civil War. At that time he, together with his former owner, David Swain, went in search of the Union troops who were taking control of central North Carolina in order to ask for clemency for Chapel Hill. Even though they never encountered the troops, Chapel Hill was spared harsh treatment at the hands of Union soldiers (though some supporters of the Confederacy would disagree with this assessment).

Caldwell became a paid university employee. His duties remained the same as before the war but the number of students at UNC diminished to almost none during Reconstruction. To supplement his income, Caldwell took in student boarders in his home in the western section of Chapel Hill (the "Negro quarter"). Though the exact date is unknown, Wilson Caldwell married Susan Kirby in this period, and was father to twelve children, seven of whom preceded him in death.

In 1868 Caldwell was appointed an Orange County justice of the peace by the Reconstruction governor William Holden. Caldwell served in this role for a year and presided over at least one case involving a former university professor (at issue was a supposedly stolen dog). According to Battle's sketch (1895) Caldwell's political role was viewed with suspicion by local white citizens who opposed

black enfranchisement and Republican rule and saw Holden's elevation of a black man as an offense against North Carolina. Ku Klux Klan activity in protest against the Reconstruction government increased in Orange County, and Wilson Caldwell's father was harassed.

Owing to poor wages, an increasingly hostile political climate, and the imminent closing of the university, Caldwell opened a "free school" for black children in Chapel Hill in 1869 and served as its principal for the excellent middle-class salary of $17.50 a month. He then moved to Pasquotank County near Elizabeth City to run a similar school there for $25 a month. When the university opened in 1875 Caldwell returned to his chosen profession as a university servant and was once again a popular and respected man on campus. His name appears in many reminiscences and letters written by members of the Chapel Hill community. In 1884, to increase his income and to support his large family, Caldwell moved to Durham, a new city eight miles from Chapel Hill, and one growing rich on tobacco and cotton. Caldwell became the valet for Julian Carr, an industrialist and Durham's leading citizen. Neither the work nor the town satisfied Caldwell; he returned to Chapel Hill in 1885, first to farm his own twelve acres and then to work at the university. He is reputed to have said about his return, "Durham is no place for a literary man" (Battle 1895).

In 1886 Wilson Swain Caldwell became the Curator of South Building (the main university building) and head of the university's labor corps. His appointment was accepted unanimously and enthusiastically by the faculty. Also in 1886 Wilson made history by being elected to the Chapel Hill Board of Commissioners. He won a seat reserved for university employees and defeated a candidate who was a university faculty member. Caldwell voted regularly for the Republican ticket.

Wilson Caldwell remained at UNC for the remainder of his life; he died a respected university employee. Shortly before his death, an article celebrating his accomplishments appeared in the *North Carolina University Magazine*. The author was the former president of the university and then professor of history, Kemp Battle. Upon Caldwell's death, President Battle offered the eulogy at the request of Wilson's pastor at the Congregational Church. Various political and economic leaders (including his former employer, Julian Carr) attended the funeral of this former slave, government official, and teacher. After his death, a UNC alumnus,

William Peele, published a short pamphlet celebrating Wilson Swain Caldwell's life.

In his *History of the University of North Carolina Volume 2* (1912), President Battle said, "Caldwell was in all his career in life truthful, faithful, intelligent, respectful but free from obsequiousness" (559.) Unlike Caldwell, most African Americans who labored for the university in its first one hundred years remain nameless and obscure. Caldwell is remembered on a monument in the African American section of the Old Chapel Hill cemetery on the campus of UNC, a monument under which he is buried, close to several of his children. The inscription on this monument reads:

> Members of the class of 1891 place this
> stone in the memory of Wilson Swain Caldwell,
>   who lies here
> November Caldwell
> David Barham and
> Henry Smith
> Who served the University faithfully

FURTHER READING

Archival sources relating to Wilson Swain Caldwell may be found in the Manuscripts Department and University Archives at the University of North Carolina at Chapel Hill.

Battle, Kemp P. *History of the University of North Carolina Vol. 2* (1907–1912). http://docsouth.unc.edu/nc/battle2/menu.html.

Battle, Kemp P. *Sketch of the Life and Character of Wilson Caldwell* (1895).

An excellent Web resource with more information about the history of the University of North Carolina and of many of the people mentioned in this entry can be found at http://museum.unc.edu.

TIMOTHY J. MCMILLAN

Cale, Hugh (27 Nov. 1838–22 July 1910), merchant, public official, religious leader, and longtime state legislator, was born in Perquimans County, North Carolina, the eldest son of free, mixed-race parents John Cail (Cale) and Elizabeth Mitchell, a homemaker, who were married in 1827. His father worked as a miller, later as a fisherman, and moved his large family—as many as nine children—to Edenton in nearby Chowan County in the 1850s. Little is known of Hugh Cale's early life or education, although he had learned to read and write by the end of the Civil War.

After the Union army occupied much of northeastern North Carolina in early 1862, Cale began working as a manual laborer for federal installations at Fort Hatteras and Roanoke Island. In 1867 he moved to Elizabeth City, North Carolina, where he commenced a singularly successful career as a grocer and held a number of local offices during and after Reconstruction.

Cale served four terms as a Republican in the North Carolina General Assembly, representing Pasquotank County, and is best remembered for his dedication to the cause of education. During his final term in 1891 he sponsored a bill creating the state's newest normal (teacher training) school in his adopted town, the forerunner of Elizabeth City State University, on whose campus a residence hall was later named in his honor. Beginning in 1882 he served as trustee of the private Zion Wesley Institute (later known as Livingstone College) in Salisbury, North Carolina. From 1891 to 1899 he also served as a trustee of the state's first public institution for African American students, North Carolina Agricultural and Mechanical College for the Colored Race (later known as North Carolina A&T State University).

But Cale's energies were equally devoted to local affairs. After several failed attempts to gain local office, he served eight years as a local magistrate and four years as the treasurer of Elizabeth City, after being elected to that post in 1874. He also served as a poll inspector, grand juror, city lamplighter, and provisioner of the county poorhouse, and helped the town to acquire its first fire engine. A trustee of the local cemetery for African Americans, Cale served as president of Pasquotank County's first African American fair. He was also a member of the Pasquotank County Board of Education and served two terms as a Pasquotank County commissioner.

A devout member of the African Methodist Episcopal Zion denomination, Cale was a steward in the Mount Lebanon Church. Known as a confirmed non-smoker, a converted teetotaler, and an active Mason, he was "very temperate in habits, having taken his last drink of spiritous liquor in 1865" (Tomlinson, 104). Cale was also a prudent businessman. By 1879, his prosperous grocery business had enabled him to accumulate at least 12,000 dollars in local real estate, according to that year's legislative biography. In 1885 he is recorded as owning farmland, seven lots in Elizabeth City, and more than $2,500 in personal property.

As one of eighteen African Americans, all Republicans, who were elected to the North Carolina General Assembly in 1876, Cale was the second member of his race to represent predominantly black

Pasquotank County in the house, after THOMAS A. SYKES, who served from 1868 to 1872. Later described as "a character to be reckoned with," Cale was reelected in a three-way race in 1878, outpolling both of his white opponents combined (*News and Observer*, 27 July 1910).

In 1884 he won a third term, again one of more than a dozen African American legislators elected. But as the Republican Party's relative success and overall numbers began to decline, the number of African Americans also dwindled; in the 1891 legislature, Cale was of just one of five African American GOP Republican state legislators of his race, and the last Republican of either race to represent his county for decades to come, as the county was represented only by white Democrats after 1891 until the end of the twentieth century.

Known for a characteristic streak of independence, Cale occasionally sided with the majority Democrats, but only "when convinced that his party is advocating the wrong measure" (*Assembly Sketch Book*).

He served on a number of House committees, including Fishing Interests, Insane Asylum, Penal Institutions, Corporations, and Immigration. He left office in 1891, concentrating afterward on his business and real estate investments.

After Populist-Republican "fusion" prevailed on the statewide level in the mid-1890s, Cale returned to active politics, serving as an alternate district delegate in 1896 to the Republican national convention in St. Louis, at which William McKinley was nominated for president. In 1898 Cale sought to regain his old seat in the general assembly, again running for the House as the Republican nominee, but his candidacy was derailed in the white-supremacist Democratic landslide that year. After most African Americans were disfranchised by constitutional amendments in North Carolina in 1902, Cale never sought public office again.

In June 1867 Cale was married to Alabama native Mary A. Wilson (c. 1845–?). The couple had no children, although they helped raise Cale's younger brother John and niece Elizabeth. After Mary Cale's death, Cale wed Fanny Bruce in 1896. Hugh Cale died in 1910 after a brief illness. His funeral was described by the *News and Observer* (27 July 1910) as "one of the largest that has been held in the city in some time," featuring a brass band and impressive funeral dirge and attracting a large crowd of both white and black mourners. Cale's name is inscribed in stone of the floor of the Pasquotank County courthouse he voted to build, and a state highway historical marker was erected in his honor in 1994, near his grave in Elizabeth City.

FURTHER READING

Assembly Sketch Book (1885).

Foner, Eric. *Freedom's Lawmakers: A Directory of Black Officeholders during Reconstruction* (1993)

Kenzer, Robert C. *Enterprising Southerners: Black Economic Success in North Carolina, 1865–1915* (1997).

Tomlinson, J. S. *Tar-Heel Sketch-Book, A Brief Biographical Sketch of the Life and Public Acts of the Members of the General Assembly of North Carolina, Session of 1879* (1879).

Obituary: *News and Observer*, 27 July 1910.

BENJAMIN R. JUSTESEN

Caliver, Ambrose (25 Feb. 1894–29 Jan. 1962), educator, college administrator, and civil servant, was born in Saltville, Virginia, the youngest child of Ambrose Caliver Sr. Little is known about his parents, but very early in his life he and his two siblings moved to Knoxville, Tennessee, where they were raised by an aunt, Louisa Bolden. Bolden, a widowed cook who took in boarders to make ends meet, allowed Caliver to accept a job at a very young age. According to one account, the young Caliver was working in a coal mine by the time of his eighth birthday. Early employment, however, did not prevent him from attending school regularly. After receiving an education from Knoxville's public school system, he enrolled at Knoxville College, where he obtained his B.A. in 1915. He eventually earned an M.A. from the University of Wisconsin (1920) and a Ph.D. from Columbia University (1930).

After graduating from Knoxville, Caliver immediately sought employment as an educator. In 1915 he married his childhood sweetheart, Rosalie Rucker, and they both took various teaching jobs, first in Knoxville and then in El Paso, Texas. By 1917 they had returned to Tennessee, where they received faculty positions at Fisk University in Nashville. Caliver's acceptance of the position at Fisk was significant, because he became one of the few black faculty members hired on campus. Caliver began working at Fisk during one of the most tumultuous points in the university's history. Under the leadership of Fayette A. McKenzie, Fisk gained the unwarranted reputation of being out of touch with the African American population. Caliver assisted in changing this perception. An ardent believer in the industrial and manual arts, he encouraged Fisk's students to take woodshop and other courses that would teach them how to work with their hands. Caliver believed that these skills would not only benefit the students financially but also make them assets to the local black community. According to one observer, one of Caliver's more memorable moments at Fisk was when he drove a bright red wagon that his students had made in his workshop across the platform during a university assembly.

Fisk administrators soon recognized the talent of their young faculty member and quickly gave him other responsibilities. In a continuing effort to strengthen the school's ties to the local black community, Caliver organized the Tennessee Colored Anti-Tuberculosis Society. Serving four years as the organization's director and chair of its executive committee, Caliver sought to increase awareness and prevent the spread of the disease among Tennessee's African American population. His other major administrative appointments at Fisk included a spell as university publicity director in 1925, and as dean of the Scholastic Department the following year. In 1927 Caliver was appointed Fisk's first African American dean of the university.

Fisk only briefly enjoyed Caliver's services as dean. Two years after his appointment, he took a one-year leave from his duties to complete the requirements for his doctorate at Columbia University. Caliver never returned to his position at Fisk. Shortly before his graduation, he received two job offers—one for a faculty position at Howard University and, shortly afterward, another for a position at the U.S. Office of Education. In 1930 he accepted the latter job and became the Office of Education's Specialist in Negro Education. It was in this post that Caliver made what is arguably his most lasting contribution to African American education.

During his tenure in the U.S. Office of Education, Caliver participated in numerous studies and published several articles and monographs dealing with the status of African American education. These works included the pamphlets *Bibliography on the Education of the Negro* (1931), *Background Study of Negro College Students* (1933), and *Rural Elementary Education among Negro Jeanes Supervisors* (1933). Some of his monographs during this period were *The Education of Negro Teachers in the United States* (1933), *Secondary Education for Negroes* (1933), and the *Availability of Education to Negroes in Rural Communities* (1935). Caliver

was also instrumental in creating the National Advisory Committee of the Education of Negroes. This group, consisting of many leading educators from across the United States, sought to discuss the problems and develop programs to enhance black education. Hoping to benefit the greatest number of African Americans, the organization tended to focus on issues in secondary schools, such as poor facilities and inadequate materials, rather than on inadequacies in African American institutions of higher learning.

The study of secondary schools undoubtedly contributed to what Caliver saw as the greatest problem facing black education: adult illiteracy. According to some estimates, approximately one quarter of the 12.6 million African Americans were illiterate. Caliver was determined to place this issue in the national spotlight. To accomplish this, he reached out to prominent African American organizations and leaders and encouraged them to take a more active role. Caliver also called for the preparation of instructional materials, the creation of teacher-training workshops, and the development of adult-education programs at historically black colleges and universities. He oversaw the creation of several readers to increase literacy. These readers, "A Day with the Brown Family," "Making a Good Living," and "The Browns Go to School," not only increased literacy skills but also emphasized family living, thrift, and leisure activities.

In addition to his contributions to adult education, Caliver also succeeded in utilizing radio as a tool for education and instilling racial pride. In 1941, with funding from such philanthropic groups as the Julius Rosenwald Fund, he created *Freedom's People*, a nine-part series examining African American life, history, and culture. From September 1941 through April 1942, the National Broadcasting Company broadcast the program, one of the first of its kind devoted exclusively to African Americans. *Freedom's People* taught its listeners not only about famous black historical figures but also about the contributions of blacks in the areas of science, music, and industry. The program featured guest appearances by some of the most prominent African Americans of the day, including JOE LOUIS, A. PHILIP RANDOLPH and PAUL ROBESON.

For the next two decades Caliver's efforts in adult education and literacy increased. From 1946 to 1950, he directed the Office of Education's Literacy Education Project, and in 1950 he became the assistant to the commissioner of education. By 1955

Caliver was the chief of the Office of Education's Adult Education Section. This new appointment, along with his election as the president of the Adult Education Association of the United States six years later, contributed to his reputation as one of the most ardent crusaders against illiteracy in the federal government. Ambrose Caliver died in January 1962, still working as diligently as he had in his youth. At the time of his death he was moving forward with plans to expand and increase the services of the Adult Education Association of the United States.

FURTHER READING

Daniel, Walter G., and John B. Holden. *Ambrose Caliver: Adult Educator and Civil Servant* (1966).

Wilkins, Theresa B. "Ambrose Caliver: Distinguished Civil Servant." *Journal of Negro Education* 31 (Spring 1962): 212–214.

Obituary: *Washington Post*, 2 Feb. 1962.

LEE WILLIAMS JR.

Calloway, Blanche Dorothea Jones (9 Feb. 1902–16 Dec. 1978), the first woman to lead an otherwise all-male orchestra, was the older sister of the well-known bandleader CAB CALLOWAY. Born in Rochester, New York, Blanche and her three younger siblings moved to Baltimore when she was a teenager. She grew up in a comfortably middle-class family; her father, Cabell, was a lawyer and her mother, Martha Eulalia Reed, taught music. Calloway's father died in 1910, and her mother married insurance salesman John Nelson Fortune a few years later and had two more children.

Calloway's mother likely instilled a love of music in all of her children; Calloway's brother Elmer also briefly pursued a musical career. Martha made sure that young Calloway took piano and voice lessons as a child, but Martha never imagined music as a career for a proper young woman. She expected that her daughter would pursue a "respectable" career as a nurse or teacher. Inspired by African American women cabaret and blues entertainers like FLORENCE MILLS and IDA COX, Calloway dreamed of a musical career. With the encouragement of her music teacher, Calloway auditioned for a local talent scout. Calloway's talent impressed the scout and he wanted to book her for local events, but she resisted. To her mother's dismay, Calloway dropped out of Morgan College in the early 1920s to embark on a music career, a career that would span fifty years.

She worked in local Baltimore clubs and performed in the musical *Shuffle Along* with EUBIE BLAKE and NOBLE SISSLE in 1921. Her big break came in 1923 when she joined the national tour of the all–African American musical revue *Plantation Days*, which featured her idol Florence Mills. When the show ended in Chicago in 1927, Calloway decided to stay in Chicago, the jazz music capital in the 1920s. She became a popular attraction in local Chicago clubs. She also toured extensively, performing at exclusive venues like the Crio Club in New York and to capacity crowds in Atlantic City, Boston, Kansas City, New York, Pittsburgh, and Saint Louis. In 1925 she capitalized on the public craze for "race records" and recorded two records ("Lazy Woman Blues" and "Lonesome Lovesick Blues") with her new group, Blanche Calloway and Her Joy Boys. The Joy Boys featured some of the hottest young talent in jazz like trumpeter LOUIS ARMSTRONG in some of his earliest recordings, drummer William Randolph "Cozy" Cole, and saxophonist BEN WEBSTER.

In the late 1920s she appeared with Rueben Reeves and recorded on Vocalion Records. In 1931 she appeared at the Pearl Theater in Philadelphia. She caught the attention of Kansas City bandleader ANDY KIRK who asked her to tour with him and his band, the Clouds of Joy. Calloway learned a great deal about managing a band and booking performances. She also discovered that she often overshadowed her mentor. Around 1930 or 1931 Calloway made a serious attempt to start her own orchestra. Stories vary as to how this came about. In one version, Calloway convinced several of Kirk's band members to defect. Kirk caught wind of the plot and ended his association with Calloway. In another, Pearl Theater manager Sam Steiffel noted the popularity of Calloway and considered using her to replace Kirk as bandleader. Kirk learned of Steiffel's plans and dropped Calloway from the remaining tour dates. In 1931 Calloway succeeded in forming an orchestra and revived the name Blanche Calloway and Her Joy Boys. She became the first women ever to lead an all-male orchestra, and they recorded for RCA Victor. She later changed the name to Blanche Calloway and Her Orchestra. Calloway and her orchestra were considered one of the best groups in the country. A 1933 article in the *Pittsburgh Courier* ranked Calloway and the Joy Boys among the top ten outstanding African American orchestras. A year earlier, a reviewer praised Calloway's professionalism, management, and talent.

Yet Calloway faced difficulties flourishing in a racially segregated and male-dominated music world. As an African American performer, she often suffered the indignities of racial bigotry. She had to perform for segregated audiences. While on a tour in 1936, she used the ladies' room at a filling station in Yazoo, Mississippi. As a result, police pistol-whipped an orchestra member, jailed him and Calloway for disorderly conduct, and fined them both $7.50. While in jail, another orchestra member stole all of the group's money and abandoned the band in Mississippi. The musicians scattered, and Calloway sold her yellow Cadillac for cash to leave Mississippi. Like fellow female performer trumpeter VALAIDA SNOW, Calloway earned a reputation as an exceptional musician but few opportunities outside of the roles of singer or dancer existed for women at that time. Also Calloway's flamboyant performance style and provocative lyrics challenged normative assumptions about "respectable" female performers. Though such antics contributed to her brother Cab's success, Blanche found it increasingly difficult to get bookings by the mid-1930s.

Calloway had been a strong influence in her brother Cab's career and iconic performance style. She herself was a lively performer known for her animated style, musical skill, and raucous stage presence. She taught him a great deal about performing, and the two performed together as a brother and sister act. She helped him get his first break with a stage role in the *Plantation Days* revue when a cast member fell ill. She may even have inspired his signature "Hi De Hi" chant in his song "Minnie the Moocher." Cab had said that he came up with the phrase when he forgot the words during a performance. Calloway's "Just a Crazy Song," which she had previously performed and then recorded in early 1931, opens with her wailing "Hi Hi Hi, Ho De Ho De Ho," echoed by a band member in a classic call and response. Calloway's own signature song, "Growlin' Dan," which she cowrote, recounts the tale of Minnie the Moocher and the King of Sweden and also features the phrase "Ho De Ho De Ho." The two likely collaborated with one another and borrowed frequently from each other's acts.

Calloway found it difficult to make a living in the mid-1930s as the few opportunities for women band leaders dried up. In 1938 she broke up her orchestra. In 1940 she formed a short-lived all-women orchestra since "all-girl" groups were popular during war time. She struggled to get bookings and the group soon disbanded. She worked as a solo act until the mid-1940s, when she moved to a Philadelphia suburb with her husband and became

a socialite. She pursued civic causes and served as a Democratic committeewoman. Misfortune dogged Calloway, who discovered that her husband was a bigamist in late 1943.

In the early 1950s she moved to Washington, D.C., and managed a nightclub the Crystal Caverns to support herself. When a bandleader abandoned future R&B star RUTH BROWN at a nearby club, Calloway hired her to perform at the Crystal Caverns. She became Brown's personal manager and took the young performer under her wing. Brown credits Calloway with discovering her and helping her land a deal with Atlantic Records.

Calloway continued to achieve significant firsts in the last decades of her life. In the late 1950s Calloway moved to Miami and resumed her political activism. She became the first African American precinct voting clerk, and she is reputed to be the first African American woman ever to vote in Florida when she cast a ballot for the 1958 election. She became a member of the NAACP and CORE and served on the board of the National Urban League. In 1964 she and about forty other African American women participated in a protest with the NATO Women's Peace Force in The Hague, Netherlands. In the 1960s she worked as a disc jockey and program manager for Miami radio station WMBM. She converted to Christian Science, which she credited with helping her fight a twelve-year battle with cancer. Around 1968 she formed Afram House Inc., a successful mail order company that offered cosmetics designed exclusively for African American women. In the last years of her life, she married her high school sweetheart and moved back to Baltimore. She died of breast cancer.

FURTHER READING
Arwulf, Arwulf. *All Music Guide to Jazz: The Experts' Guide to the Best Jazz Recordings* (1998).
"Blanche Calloway Jones." *Black Perspective in Music 7*, No. 2 (Autumn 1979).
Foster, Catherine. "In Cab Calloway's Family, One Intrepid Woman Inspires Another; Daughter Portrays Bandleader Aunt," *Boston Globe*, 9 Nov. 2003.
Pfeffer, Murray L. "Blanche Calloway." *Big Bands Database Plus*. Available at http://nfo.net/usa/c1.html.
Prozdowski, Ted. "Cab's Clan: Chris Calloway Celebrates Her Aunt Blanche," *Boston Phoenix*, 21–27 Nov. 2003.

SHENNETTE GARRETT

Calloway, Cab (25 Dec. 1907–18 Nov. 1994), popular singer and bandleader, was born Cabell Calloway III in Rochester, New York, the third of six children of Cabell Calloway Jr., a lawyer, and Martha Eulalia Reed, a public school teacher. In 1920, two years after the family moved to the Calloways' hometown of Baltimore, Maryland, Cab's father died. Eulalia later remarried and had two children with John Nelson Fortune, an insurance salesman who became known to the Calloway children as "Papa Jack."

Although he later enjoyed a warm relationship with his stepfather, the teenaged Cab had a rebellious streak that tried the patience of parents attempting to maintain their status as respectable Baltimoreans. He often skipped school to go to the nearby Pimlico racetrack, where he both earned money selling newspapers and shining shoes and began a lifelong passion for horse racing. After his mother caught him playing dice on the steps of the Presbyterian church, however, he was sent in 1921 to Downingtown Industrial and Agricultural School, a reform school run by his mother's uncle in Pennsylvania. When he returned to Baltimore the following year, Calloway

Cab Calloway propelled to stardom with his exuberant "Minnie the Moocher." (Library of Congress, Photo by Carl Van Vechten, 1933.)

recalls that he resumed hustling but also worked as a caterer, and that he studied harder than he had before and excelled at both baseball and basketball at the city's Frederick Douglass High School. Most significantly, he resumed the voice lessons he had begun before reform school, and he began to sing both in the church choir and at several speakeasies, where he performed with Johnny Jones's Arabian Tent Orchestra, a New Orleans–style Dixieland band. In his senior year in high school, Calloway played for the Baltimore Athenians professional basketball team, and in January 1927 he and Zelma Proctor, a fellow student, had a daughter, whom they named Camay. In the summer after graduating from high school, Calloway joined his sister Blanche, a star in the popular *Plantation Days* revue, on her company's midwestern tour, and, by his own account, "went as wild as a March hare," chasing "all the broads in the show" (Calloway and Rollins, 54). When the tour ended in Chicago, Illinois, he stayed and attended Crane College (now Malcolm X University). While at Crane he turned down an offer to play for the Harlem Globetrotters, not, as his mother had hoped, to pursue a law career, but instead to become a professional singer. He worked nights and weekends at the Dreamland Café and then won a spot as a drummer and house singer at the Sunset Club, the most popular jazz venue on Chicago's predominantly African American South Side. There he befriended LOUIS ARMSTRONG, then playing with the CARROLL DICKERSON Orchestra, who greatly influenced Calloway's use of "scat," an improvisational singing style that uses nonsense syllables rather than words.

When the Dickerson Orchestra ended its engagement at the Sunset in 1928, Calloway served as the club's master of ceremonies and, one year later, as the leader of the new house band, the Alabamians. His position as the self-described "dashing, handsome, popular, talented M.C. at one of the hippest clubs on the South Side" (Calloway and Rollins, 61) did little to help his already fitful attendance at Crane, but it introduced him to many beautiful, glamorous, and rich women. He married one of the wealthiest of them, Wenonah "Betty" Conacher, in July 1928. Although he later described the marriage as a mistake, at the time he greatly enjoyed the "damned comfortable life" that came with his fame, her money, and the small house that they shared with a South Side madam.

In the fall of 1929 Calloway and the Alabamians embarked on a tour that brought them to the mecca for jazz bands of that era, Harlem in New

York City. In November, however, a few weeks after the stock market crash downtown on Wall Street, the Alabamians also crashed uptown in their one chance for a breakout success, a battle of the bands at the famous Savoy Ballroom. The hard-to-please Savoy regulars found the Alabamians' old-time Dixieland passé and voted overwhelmingly for the stomping, more danceable music of their rivals, the Missourians. The Savoy audience did, however, vote for Calloway as the better bandleader, a tribute to his charismatic stage presence and the dapper style in which he outfitted the Alabamians.

Four months later, following a spell on Broadway and on tour with the pianist FATS WALLER in the successful *Connie's Hot Chocolate* revue, he returned to the Savoy as the new leader of the Missourians, renamed Cab Calloway and His Orchestra. In 1931 the band began alternating with DUKE ELLINGTON's orchestra as the house band at Harlem's Cotton Club, owned by the gangster Owney Madden and infamous for its white-audiences-only policy. Calloway also began a recording career. Several of his first efforts for Brunswick Records, notably "Reefer Man" and "Kicking the Gong Around," the latter about characters in an opium den, helped fuel his reputation as a jive-talking hipster who knew his way around the less salubrious parts of Manhattan. Although he denied firsthand experience of illicit drugs, Calloway did admit to certain vices—fast cars, expensive clothes, "gambling, drinking, partying [and] balling all through the night, all over the country" (Calloway and Rollins, 184).

It was 1931's "Minnie the Moocher," with its scat-driven, call and response chorus, that became Calloway's signature tune and propelled him to stardom. The most prosaic version of the chorus had Cab calling out, "Hi-de-hi-de-hi-di-hi, Ho-de-ho-de-ho-de-ho" or, when the mood took him, "Oodlee-odlyee-odlyee-oodle-doo" or "Dwaa-de-dwaa-de-dwaa-de-doo," while his orchestra—and later the audience—responded with the same phrase. Calloway recalled in his autobiography that the song came first and the chorus was later improvised when he forgot the lyrics during a radio broadcast. The song's appeal was broadened in 1932 by its appearance in the movie *The Big Broadcast* and in a Betty Boop cartoon short, *Minnie the Moocher*. Radio broadcasts from the Cotton Club and appearances on radio with Bing Crosby made Calloway one of the wealthiest entertainers during the Depression era. The Calloway Orchestra embarked on several highly successful national tours and in 1935 became one of the first major black jazz bands to tour Europe.

Although the Calloway Orchestra was arguably the most popular jazz band of the 1930s and 1940s, most jazz critics view the bands of Ellington, Armstrong, and COUNT BASIE as more musically sophisticated. ALBERT MURRAY's influential *Stomping the Blues* (1976) does not even mention Calloway, although it does list several members of his orchestra, including the tenor saxophonist CHU BERRY and the trumpeter DIZZY GILLESPIE, who joined the band in 1939 and left two years later, after he stabbed Calloway in the backside during a fight. With the drummer COZY COLE and the vibraphonist Tyree Glenn, the Calloway Orchestra showcased its rhythmic virtuosity in several instrumentals, including the sprightly "Bye Bye Blues" and the sensual "A Ghost of a Chance," both recorded in 1940.

It was, however, Calloway's exuberant personality, his cutting-edge dress style—he was a pioneer of the zoot suit—and his great rapport with his audiences that packed concert halls for nearly two decades. In the 1940s he was ubiquitous, appearing on recordings, radio broadcasts of his concerts, and in movies such as *Stormy Weather* (1943), in which he starred with LENA HORNE, BILL "BOJANGLES" ROBINSON, KATHERINE DUNHAM, and Fats Waller. In 1942, he hosted a satirical network radio quiz show, *The Cab Calloway Quizzicale*. Calloway even changed the way Americans speak, with the publication of *Professor Cab Calloway's Swingformation Bureau* and *The New Cab Calloway's Hepsters Dictionary: Language of Jive* (1944), which became the official jive language reference book of the New York Public Library. The *Oxford English Dictionary* credits Calloway's song "Jitter Bug" as the first published use of that term. The end of World War II marked dramatic changes in Calloway's professional and personal lives. In 1948 the public preference for small combos and the bebop style of jazz, pioneered by Gillespie, among others, forced Calloway to break up his swing-style big band. One year later Calloway divorced Betty Conacher, with whom he had adopted a daughter, Constance, in the late 1930s, and married Zulme "Nuffie" McNeill, with whom he would have three daughters, Chris, Lael, and Cabella. His career revived, however, in 1950, when he landed the role of Sportin' Life in the revival of George Gershwin's *Porgy and Bess* on Broadway and in London and

Paris. The casting was inspired, since Gershwin had modeled the character of Sportin' Life on Calloway in his "Hi-de-hi" heyday. From 1967 to 1970 he starred with PEARL BAILEY in an all-black Broadway production of *Hello, Dolly!*, and in 1980 he endeared himself to a new generation of fans, with his performance of "Minnie the Moocher" in the film *The Blues Brothers*, with John Belushi and Dan Aykroyd. That role led to appearances on the television shows *The Love Boat* and *Sesame Street* and on Janet Jackson's music video "Alright," which won the 1990 Soul Train award for best rhythm and blues/urban contemporary music video.

In June 1994 Calloway suffered a stroke at his home in White Plains, New York, and died five months later at a nursing home in Hockessin, Delaware. President Bill Clinton, who had awarded Calloway the National Medal of the Arts a year earlier, paid tribute to him as a "true legend among the musicians of this century, delighting generations of audiences with his boundless energy and talent" (*New York Times*, 30 Nov. 1994). Calloway, however, probably put it best when he described himself in his autobiography as "the hardest jack with the greatest jive in the joint."

FURTHER READING

Calloway's papers are held at Boston University.

Calloway, Cab, and Bryant Rollins. *Of Minnie the Moocher and Me* (1976).

Schuller, Gunther. *The Swing Era: The Development of Jazz, 1930–1945* (1989).

Obituary: *New York Times*, 20 Nov. 1994.

STEVEN J. NIVEN

Calloway, DeVerne Lee (17 June 1916–23 Jan. 1993), politician and activist, was born India DeVerne Lee in Memphis, Tennessee, the eldest of four children. Her parents were Charles Howard Lee, a railroad worker, and Sadie Mae. Growing up in a poor household, Calloway took on responsibilities such as family laundry and cooking to help make ends meet. Calloway's parents were devout Seventh-Day Adventists and required that their children attend church most Saturdays. As a student at Seventh-Day Adventist Grammar School and later at Booker T. Washington High School, Calloway began increasingly to challenge her parents' faith practice. Observing her father's frequent encounters with racial discrimination, Calloway was uncomfortable with what she perceived to be a disconnect between her family's bleak material

existence and a faith tradition that required such a deep commitment of time, energy, and resources but offered little in return. For about four years Calloway attended church on Sundays with her friends and studied Buddhist and Jewish faith traditions.

When Calloway enrolled as a freshman at the historically black LeMoyne Institute (later LeMoyne-Owen College) in Memphis, she stopped attending church altogether. Calloway reasoned that community activism would make an adequate substitute for weekly religious worship. She joined the staff of a local settlement house and for about two years taught underprivileged children crafts such as weaving and sewing. Inspired by the example of a professor, Calloway became an organizer for the Southern Tenant Farmers Union. Working with black sharecroppers awakened Calloway's political consciousness as she witnessed firsthand the extent to which economic discrimination plagued black communities of the Mississippi Delta.

Calloway earned a B.A. in Sociology and English in 1938. She would later do graduate work at Northwestern University in Evanston, Illinois; Pendle Hill, a Quaker school in Wallingford, Pennsylvania; and Atlanta University. Following graduation she moved to Atlanta to begin a teaching career. After just one year at Cedartown School, Calloway was fired because of her battles with school administrators and local store owners over the discriminatory treatment of black teachers and consumers. The budding activist later taught in Vicksburg, Mississippi, and Cordele, Georgia.

In the wake of World War II, Calloway moved to Philadelphia to work as a secretary for a Republican judge. She immersed herself in the world of formal politics by attending election campaign meetings and preparing speeches. Calloway met SADIE ALEXANDER and her husband, RAYMOND PACE ALEXANDER, pioneers in the fight for civil rights. The "guiding lights," as Calloway described the couple, fueled her interest in politics and the power of activist couples to affect meaningful social change.

After working for the USO in Pennsylvania and Arizona in 1942, Calloway joined the American Red Cross the same year. For the next three years she lived in Calcutta, India, where she joined other black women working to meet the needs of black soldiers. The women wrote letters, organized recreational activities, served meals, sewed, and organized tours. Calloway organized black soldiers who were forced by military policy to attend the celebration of a pool opening on 3 July instead of 4 July, when white soldiers were scheduled to gather. Collectively the protesters refused to attend the ceremony.

During her four years abroad, Calloway drew connections between race and class inequality in the United States and social problems in other regions of the world. In addition to organizing black workers Calloway took copious notes documenting the structure of India's caste system. Her goal was to write "the great novel" that would situate racial disparities within a global framework and in so doing bring to the public's attention the vast exploitation of the lower classes and racial minorities worldwide.

In 1946 Calloway moved to Chicago, where she began writing full time. She worked for *Our World*, a New York–based black magazine. After the publication went out of business in 1948, Calloway worked for the Fair Employment Practices Council, the Jewish Welfare Fund, and the Chicago Health Department. She joined the Congress of Racial Equality. In the summer of 1948, while working for several months as a part-time secretary for the Redcaps, a union organization in Chicago, she met ERNEST CALLOWAY, a labor organizer. The two married in 1948. They had no children.

In 1950 the couple moved to St. Louis when Ernest received and accepted a special invitation from Teamsters leader Harold Gibbons to establish a research department. Unemployed in St. Louis, DeVerne Calloway filled her time by becoming involved in local politics. She worked with the NAACP and in 1952 campaigned for two presidential primary candidates, W. Averell Harriman and Adlai Stevenson. In 1956 voters elected Ernest Calloway president of the St. Louis NAACP, in large part owing to DeVerne's supportive efforts. She helped increase the prominent civil rights organization's membership from two thousand to eight thousand. In 1961 the couple published a newspaper, the *Citizen Crusader* (later *New Citizen*), dedicated to black local politics. While engaged in a wide array of lobbying efforts, Calloway observed a need to combat black city dwellers' political apathy and wished to address it. She ran for state representative from the Thirteenth District in November 1962 and became the first black woman elected to the Missouri legislature.

While in office Calloway pushed for the expansion of rights for welfare recipients and the disabled by supporting Missouri Old Age Assistance and Aid to Dependent Children programs. She lobbied for the passage of a fair employment bill, doing much of the behind-the-scenes work required to pass a law that expanded the restriction on the number of hours women could work to include telephone operators. She supported stronger protection for women workers and their children, the extension of rights for unemployed pregnant women, a more progressive state Labor Relations Act, and the passage of a state minimum wage law. Calloway served on other supportive bodies, including the Accounts Committee responsible for Missouri House expenditures and the Insurance, Election, and State-Federal Relations committees. Calloway was one of the leading voices supporting the reproductive rights of women and an ardent supporter of the Equal Rights Amendment. As chair of the State Institutions and Properties Committee, Calloway compiled "A Report on the Human Conditions at Missouri State Penitentiary" (1974), which documented prisoner death rates, physical abuse, inadequate medical care, violations of due process of law, and racial discrimination. Portions of this pathbreaking study were later used in an American Civil Liberties Union (ACLU) lawsuit.

After ten consecutive terms in the Missouri House of Representatives, Calloway retired in 1980. She was a member of many community groups, including the Young Women's Christian Association, the Youth Brigade, the Union Sarah Economic Development Committee of St. Louis, the People's Art Center, Americans for Democratic Action, and the National Council of Negro Women, and was the recipient of numerous awards. Bedridden since 1990 because of a debilitating stroke, Calloway died of a heart attack at the age of seventy-six in Memphis, Tennessee, where she had move with her sister in December of 1992. DeVerne Lee Calloway's long legacy of activism answered a call to directly engage political systems and thereby translate civil rights protests and demonstrations into concrete social policy. The stateswoman offered a more expansive vision of social change that connected race, gender, and class issues in compelling and new ways.

FURTHER READING

Calloway's papers and two oral history interviews dated 9 Sept. 1971 and 23 Feb. 1983 are in the Western Historical Manuscript Collection, University of Missouri–St. Louis.

Christensen, Lawrence O., William F. Foley, Gary R. Kremer, and Kenneth H. Winn, eds. *Dictionary of Missouri Biography* (1999).

Dains, Mary K., ed. *Show Me Missouri Women: Selected Biographies* (1989).

Obituary: *Saint Louis Post-Dispatch*, 25 Jan. 1993.

KEONA K. ERVIN

Calloway, Ernest (1 Jan. 1909–31 Dec. 1989), labor activist, journalist, and educator, was born in Heberton, West Virginia, the son of Ernest Calloway Sr.; his mother's name is unknown. The family moved to the coalfields of Letcher County, Kentucky, in 1913, where Calloway's father, "Big Ernest," helped organize the county's first local chapter of the United Mine Workers of America. The Calloways were one of the first black families in the coal-mining communities of eastern Kentucky, and Ernest was, by his own description, "one of those unique persons … a black hillbilly." Calloway attended high school in Lynchburg, Virginia, but ran away to New York in 1925 and arrived in the middle of the Harlem Renaissance. He worked as a dishwasher in Harlem until his mother fell ill, when he returned to Kentucky at age seventeen and worked in the mines of the Consolidated Coal Company until 1930. During the early 1930s he traveled as a drifter around the United States and Mexico.

Calloway came to the end of his resources at a tent colony near the small town of Ensenada in the Baja Mountains of Mexico in 1933. There he had a frightening hallucinatory experience that changed his life. "Damnedest experience that whole night," he later recounted to an interviewer. "I think this was the first time that, the morning after getting out of those mountains and that frightening experience, the first time that I really began thinking about myself and about people and what makes the world tick." He returned to the coal mines of Kentucky determined to move beyond a drifter's existence.

Inspired by his strange experience in the mountains, Calloway submitted an article on marijuana use to *Opportunity*, the magazine of the National Urban League, in 1933. *Opportunity* rejected it, and, sadly, a copy of it did not survive. The magazine did ask him to write another article, however, on the working conditions of blacks in the Kentucky coalfields. He submitted the second article, "The Negro in the Kentucky Coal Fields," which appeared in March 1934. This article resulted in a scholarship for Calloway to Brookwood Labor College in New York, a training facility for labor organizers founded by the pacifists Helen and Henry Fink and headed by A. J. Muste. Moreover, the article began Calloway's long involvement with labor issues.

From 1935 to 1936 Calloway worked in Virginia and helped organize the Virginia Workers' Alliance, a union of unemployed Works Progress Administration workers. He helped organize a conference in 1936 to ally the labor movement with the unemployed—groups organized by socialists, communists, Trotskyists, and unemployment councils. After turning down an offer to recruit African Americans into a front group for the U.S. State Department and its intelligence services, Calloway moved to Chicago in 1937. There he helped organize the Red Caps, as railway station porters were known, and other railroad employees into the United Transport Employees Union. He also helped write the resolution creating the 1942 Committee against Discrimination in the Congress of Industrial Organizations (CIO). When the first peacetime draft law came into effect in 1939, Calloway was among the first African Americans to refuse military service as a protest against race discrimination. Although the case received national publicity, it was never officially settled, and Calloway never served in the Jim Crow U.S. Army.

Calloway's career in news journalism began when he joined the National CIO News editorial staff in 1944. Two years later he married DeVerne Lee, a teacher who had led a protest against racial segregation in the Red Cross in India during World War II. DEVERNE CALLOWAY later served as the first black woman elected to the state legislature in Missouri. She did much to increase state aid to public education, improve welfare grants, and reform the prison system in the state.

In 1947 Calloway received a scholarship from the British Trade Union Congress to attend Ruskin College in Oxford, England, where he spent a year. He then returned to the United States and began working with Operation Dixie, the CIO's southern organizing drive in North Carolina. Because of a dispute over organizing tactics in an attempt to unionize workers at R. J. Reynolds Tobacco Company, Calloway left the CIO in 1950 and returned to Chicago. Harold Gibbons of the St. Louis Teamsters union enlisted him to establish a research department for Teamsters Local 688 in St. Louis, which was at that time one of the most racially progressive union locals in the nation.

In the 1950s Calloway played a pivotal role in civil rights and labor activism in St. Louis. In 1951, three years prior to the U.S. Supreme Court's school desegregation decision in *Brown v. Board of Education*, Calloway advised Local 688 on a plan to integrate the St. Louis public schools; the St. Louis Board of Education rejected the Teamsters proposals. The St. Louis branch of the NAACP elected Calloway president in 1955. Within the first two years of his presidency, membership grew from two thousand to eight thousand members. He led successful efforts to gain substantial increases in the number of blacks employed by St. Louis taxi services, department stores, the Coca-Cola Company, and Southwestern Bell. Under his leadership, the group helped defeat a proposed city charter in 1957 that did not include support for civil rights.

Calloway's political involvement included serving in 1959 as campaign director for the Reverend John J. Hicks, who became the first black elected to the St. Louis Board of Education. Calloway also directed Theodore McNeal's 1960 senatorial campaign. McNeal won by a large margin, becoming the first black elected to the Missouri Senate. In 1961 Calloway worked as the technical adviser for James Hurt Jr. in his successful campaign as the second black to be elected to the St. Louis school board. He also helped his wife, DeVerne, win her historic spot in the Missouri legislature in her first bid for public office.

In 1961 the couple began publishing *Citizen Crusader*, later named *New Citizen*, a newspaper covering black politics and civil rights in St. Louis. It provided Calloway with a larger platform for his writing than anything had previously. During this period he developed a passion for explaining in numbers and tables the arithmetic of African American political power in St. Louis. The newspaper lasted until November 1963, but even after it stopped publishing, the Calloways continued to produce newspapers, including one entitled *Truth*, in support of their political allies. As a testament to the effectiveness of these papers, in 1964 supporters of Barry Goldwater published their own version of *Truth*, complete with an identical masthead, solely to take a stand against a local Democratic Party candidate endorsed by the Calloways' *Truth*.

Calloway worked with the Committee on Fair Representation in 1967 to develop a new plan for congressional district reapportionment. Supported by black representatives in the Missouri legislature and a coalition of white Republicans and Democrats, the plan created a First Congressional District more compatible with black interests. In 1968 Calloway filed as a candidate for U.S. Congress in the new district but was defeated in the Democratic primary by William Clay, who became the first black elected to the U.S. Congress from Missouri.

In 1969 Calloway lectured part-time for St. Louis University's Center for Urban Programs. He became an assistant professor when he retired as research director for the Teamsters in June 1973 and, later, Professor Emeritus of Urban Studies at St. Louis University. From his modest roots, Calloway pursued a multifaceted life, all the while creating a record of thoughtful reflections on public events and history over a lifetime of change. He suffered a disabling stroke in 1982 and died after a series of additional strokes. His name is still spoken with reverence in his hometown and among people familiar with his work.

FURTHER READING

Ernest Calloway's papers, as well as those of DeVerne Calloway, are in the Western Historical Manuscript Collection–St. Louis at the University of Missouri–St. Louis.

Burnside, Gordon. "Calloway at 74." *St. Louis Magazine* (March 1983).

Bussel, Robert. "A Trade Union Oriented War on the Slums: Harold Gibbons, Ernest Calloway, and the St. Louis Teamsters in the 1960s." *Labor History* 44, no. 1 (2003): 49–67.

Cawthra, Benjamin. "Ernest Calloway: Labor, Civil Rights, and Black Leadership in St. Louis." *Gateway Heritage* (Winter 2000–2001): 5–15.

KENNETH F. THOMAS

Calloway, Nathaniel Oglesby (10 Oct. 1907–3 Dec. 1979), author, chemist, physician, scientist, and civil rights activist, was born in Tuskegee, Alabama, to James Calloway and Marietta Oglesby. Nathaniel attended elementary and secondary school in Tuskegee, and in 1926 he received a fellowship to enroll at Iowa State University. While there he earned his B.S. in Chemistry in 1930 and obtained his Ph.D. in Organic Chemistry in 1933. Calloway's dissertation was titled "Condensation Reactions of Furfural and Its Derivatives." Upon graduation he returned to Tuskegee, where he led the department of chemistry at Tuskegee Institute from 1933 to 1935. Then he taught in Fisk

University's chemistry department until 1940. In 1933 Calloway married, and he and his wife eventually had four children.

In 1940 Calloway moved to Chicago and began the daunting task of being an instructor of pharmacology and a medical student at the same time. Upon learning that he would not be allowed to treat white patients when he did his clinical studies, Calloway transferred to the University of Illinois Medical School, from which he received his MD in 1944. Upon graduation he was appointed to the staff at the University of Illinois Hospital. There he was chosen to lead the research medical ward. Calloway's interests in chemistry and medicine began to merge. He applied his knowledge of chemistry to the field of endocrinology. During this time Calloway's duties included oversight of government-sponsored studies on convalescence. Calloway's research indicated that early ambulation for patients after operations was beneficial: he observed faster improvements in patients who became active than in those who remained confined to their beds.

In 1947 Calloway was appointed medical director of Provident Hospital, a historically African American institution in Chicago. There he turned his interests toward geriatrics and aging. Later, in 1964, Calloway proposed a "general theory of senescence," a theory that served as the basis of more than twenty articles that he authored and published in the *Journal of the American Geriatrics Society*. In 1949 he stepped down from his post at Provident Hospital and with a group of colleagues founded the Medical Associates of Chicago. This practice was established with the express purpose of serving inner-city Chicago.

During this time, possibly as a result of his experiences as an inner-city doctor, Calloway became a civil rights activist and from 1955 to 1960 was the president of the Chicago Urban League. In a letter published 8 October 1955 in the *Chicago Tribune*, Calloway addressed the issues surrounding growing racial tensions:

The Chicago Urban league [sic] is being completely reorganized with only one thought in mind, service to the community. The Urban league I am certain can become the most powerful organization for interracial goodwill in the city. The Urban league is not and has never been an organization that sought to disturb the peace and quiet of existence of the various groups of people in Chicago.

The league has sought on the other hand to simply help the majority to understand one of Chicago's minorities and at the same time to help this minority realize that with citizenship comes responsibilities and to teach newly displaced people who have come to an industrial community how to be good citizens.

In 1963 Calloway left Medical Associates to become chief of medical services at the Veterans Administration Hospital in Tomah, Wisconsin. In 1969 he became president of the Madison, Wisconsin, branch of the National Association for the Advancement of Colored People. But Calloway also continued his interests in medical research. In 1968 he wrote and published the *Databook on Aging and Senescence*, describing his statistical studies on aging. Combining his interests in race and in medicine, Calloway published three additional books in the 1970s.

FURTHER READING
Calloway, Nathaniel Oglesby. *Biological and Medical Aspects of Race* (1977).
Calloway, Nathaniel Oglesby. *Genes, Germs, and Slaveships* (1976).
Calloway, Nathaniel Oglesby. *Genesis! To Freedom? The Biological and Medical Aspects of the Afro American* (1972).
Greene, Harry Washington. *Holders of Doctorates among American Negroes* (1946).
Guzman, Jessie Parkhurst, ed. *Negro Year Book: A Review of Events Affecting Negro Life, 1941–1946* (1947).
KECIA BROWN

Calvin, Floyd (Joseph Calvin) (13 July 1902–1 Sept. 1939), journalist, radio broadcaster, and founder of Calvin's News Service, was born in Washington, Arkansas, to Joseph Edward and Hattie Ann (Mitchell). Calvin attended the Rural School in Clow, Arkansas, until the seventh grade. From 1916 to 1920 he attended Shover State Teacher Training College in Arkansas, and from 1920 to 1921 he was enrolled at Townsend Harris Hall, City College in New York City.

In 1922, shortly after leaving City College, Calvin was hired by the labor activist A. PHILIP RANDOLPH as the associate editor of the *Messenger* magazine. The *Messenger*—the third most popular magazine of the Harlem Renaissance, after the *Crisis* and *Opportunity*—had been founded in 1917 by Randolph and the economist CHANDLER OWEN to advance the cause of socialism to the black masses. They believed that a socialist society was the only one that would be free from racism. *The Messenger* contained poetry, stories, and essays from the finest writers of the day, including Calvin himself, PAUL ROBESON, ZORA NEALE HURSTON, WALLACE THURMAN, and DOROTHY WEST. Meanwhile in 1923 Calvin married Willa Lee Johnson, and the couple had three children. Willa Lee was born in Mineral Springs, Arkansas, and graduated from Lane College in Jackson, Tennessee, and immediately embarked on a teaching career. Willa Lee relocated north when she married Floyd Calvin and took over Calvin's News Service at Calvin's death.

While working for the *Messenger* in 1923, Calvin wrote an investigative series about conditions in the Jim Crow South called "Eight Weeks in Dixie." In the final installment of the series, an article titled "The Present South," Calvin examined the reverberations of the lynching of a young black man in Hope, Arkansas—from the immediate consequences of the killing to the ongoing flight of young people like Calvin to the industrial cities of the North to the more pernicious effect: the black community's general unease over threats to their property and their lives. Deeply moved by eyewitness testimonies, Calvin wrote: "On July 27th John West, Negro, was taken from the streets of Hope and lynched. I did not see it. I saw its effects" (Calvin, Floyd J. "The Present South," *Messenger*, 5 Jan. 1923).

In 1924 Calvin began work as the eastern district managing editor for the *Pittsburgh Courier*, based in New York, the most widely circulated African American newspaper of the time. Calvin was known for his progressive stance on social issues, and he openly disagreed with one of the *Pittsburgh Courier*'s most notable and controversial writers, GEORGE SAMUEL SCHUYLER. Whereas Schuyler believed that African Americans should reject "race consciousness" in favor of complete "Americanization," Calvin, while neither for nor against amalgamation, did not see the need and desire of the African American population to assimilate into the larger society as necessarily anathema to race consciousness. Later Calvin became the special features editor for the *Courier*, a position he held until 1935. In that position Calvin chronicled the experiences of successful African American men and women. Calvin traveled more than ten thousand miles, visiting every state in the South and Southwest, gathering information, doing extensive research, and conducting revealing interviews, material which eventually became the basis of many of his human interest and feature stories. Some of the outstanding articles were those featuring the role of African American individuals in educational institutions, as bankers, educators, social workers, and insurance agents. At a time in American journalism when blacks were largely portrayed negatively in the mainstream press, Calvin's profiles, essays, and editorials served as a balancing, more realistic representation of African American life.

On 2 October 1927 Calvin made history when he debuted as a host of the first radio show to focus on black journalism. Broadcast on New York's WGBS, it was sponsored by the *Pittsburgh Courier*. Calvin's "Some Notable Colored Men" featured Calvin reading the names of one hundred African American men of distinction. On 26 November 1927 Calvin editorialized on the radio about the role of "Negro Journalism" in the American press. He used his platform on the radio to report on the happenings and evolution within the African American arts community. In fact, when the *Pittsburgh Courier Hour* was terminated at WGBS and subsequently picked up by its competition, WCGU, Floyd's first broadcast on the new station was on the subject of "The Negro in Art" in connection with an exhibit of fine arts by black artists at the International House on Riverside Drive.

The year 1935 proved to be another pivotal year in Calvin's career. He started Calvin's News Service, used by African American weeklies, which numbered 150 by the time of Calvin's death. Calvin's News Service offered recipes, features, and opinions, in addition to news of particular interest to the African American community.

Floyd J. Calvin died at the Medical Center in New York City after a brief, undisclosed illness. He was just thirty-seven years old. At the time of his death Calvin was a member of Churches of the Living God Church, an Elk, and a registered Republican.

FURTHER READING

Boris, Joseph J. *Who's Who in Colored America, 1928–1929* (1929).

Sampson, Henry T. *Swin' on the Ether Waves: A Chronological History of African Americans in Radio and Television Programming, 1925–1955* (2005).

Smith, Jessie Carney. *Black Firsts: 4,000 Ground-Breaking and Pioneering Historical Events* (2003).

ROBYN MCGEE

Cambridge, Godfrey (26 Feb. 1933–29 Nov. 1976), actor and comedian, was born in New York City, the son of Alexander Cambridge, a bookkeeper, and Sarah (maiden name unknown), a stenographer. Godfrey's parents emigrated from British Guiana in the West Indies to Sydney, Nova Scotia, later settling in Harlem. Although his parents were trained professionals, neither could secure work in their fields. Consequently Godfrey's father became a day laborer, digging ditches, unloading coal cars, and unpacking trucks, and his mother worked in the garment district of New York City.

Critical of Harlem's schools, Cambridge's parents sent him to Sydney for grammar school, where he lived with his grandparents until he was thirteen years old; he then returned to New York to enroll at Flushing High School in Queens. He excelled academically and engaged in a variety of extracurricular activities. He was dubbed the "Unforgettable Godfrey Wonder Boy Cambridge" in his high school yearbook, which foreshadowed his penchant for comedy by adding that he always had "a laugh, a chat, a gay retort, perhaps sometimes a pun" for everyone.

Cambridge began at Hofstra College on a scholarship in 1949, but to his parents' dismay he dropped out in his junior year and turned later to a career in acting. In 1956 he won acclaim for his role as a bartender in the Off-Broadway revival of *Take a Giant Step*. Thereafter came parts in many highly rated television dramas, but as always, roles for black actors were scarce. In desperation Cambridge accepted any available performance work, including one time entering a "laughing contest," in which he was voted one of the country's four "laugh champions." He translated his experiences in menial day jobs into nighttime stand-up routines at small clubs and coffeehouses.

After appearing on Broadway in prominent dramas but in small roles, Cambridge got his big break in 1961 in the Off-Broadway production of Jean Genet's *The Blacks*. He played the character Diouf, an elderly black man who assumes the role of a white woman, wearing a blonde wig and grotesque whiteface makeup, and is raped and murdered. His performance earned him the *Village Voice*'s coveted Obie Award. The following year Cambridge was nominated for a Tony Award for his portrayal of Gitlow, the archetypal Uncle Tom in OSSIE DAVIS's satire of plantation life, *Purlie Victorious*. Later Cambridge performed the role in the film version, *Gone Are the Days!* (1963).

For the next several years Cambridge appeared in *The Living Premise*, an improvisational satirical revue. He was booked at the Blue Angel and Village Vanguard clubs, and performed on the college-campus circuit as a stand-up comic. His fame soared in 1964 as a result of three stints as a guest on the highly popular late-night television show, *The Jack Paar Program*. The success of these stints led to many bookings in nightclubs and many roles in films, and to a long-term recording contract with Epic records. His first album, *Ready or Not, Here's Godfrey Cambridge*, was among the top five best-selling albums of 1964. Cambridge recorded three other comedy albums: *Them Cotton Pickin' Days Is Over*, *Godfrey Cambridge Toys with the World*, and *The Godfrey Cambridge Show*. A talented writer who generated his own materials, Cambridge also contributed to a short-lived satirical magazine, *Monocle*. Cambridge published a book, *Put-Downs and Put-Ons*, in 1967.

After *Gone Are the Days!* Cambridge announced in the mid-1960s that he would seek roles that delineated him "as a man, rather than as a Negro." His national popularity broadened his options. He was cast as an Irishman in *The Troublemaker* (1964), as a CIA agent in *The President's Analyst* (1967), as a gangster in *The Busy Body* (1967), as a concert violinist in *The Biggest Bundle of Them All* (1968), and as a Jewish taxicab driver in *Bye, Bye Braverman* (1968). Cambridge received high praise for his performance as the lawman Gravedigger Jones in Ossie Davis's film based on the CHESTER HIMES novel *Cotton Comes to Harlem* (1970) and for his performance in the MELVIN VAN PEEBLES–directed comedy *The Watermelon Man* (1970), in which Cambridge plays a white bigot who awakens to find himself turned into a black man overnight. Onstage Cambridge was applauded by critics for his playing of the slave Pseudolus in a road production of *A Funny Thing Happened on the Way to the Forum* (1967) and for his role in the play *How to Be a Jewish Mother* (1967), in which he costarred with Molly Picon.

Cambridge married the actress BARBARA ANN TEER in 1962, but the marriage ended in divorce two and a half years later. He died in Hollywood of a heart attack while making a film.

Physically Cambridge was heavyset, sometimes overweight—his girth adding dimension to his satirical approach. His own comedy was filled with irony, and he was particularly fond of lampooning the stereotypes of both whites and blacks: "Nothing worries [a white] more than the sight of a Negro walking down his street carrying the real estate section of the *New York Times*." Cambridge insisted that his comedy transcended racial issues and reflected the travails of the little man, regardless of race. "I attack whatever is attackable. I take up the cudgels for the common man, black or white, and deal with his problems," Cambridge said. Mel Watkins noted, "Cambridge did not avoid racial issues.... he was a brilliant satirist, and although he did not concentrate on them, the contradictions and absurdities of bigotry often entered into his expansive social satire" (509).

FURTHER READING
Cambridge, Godfrey. *Put-Downs and Put-Ons* (1967).
Arnez, Nancy Levi, and Clara B. Anthony.
　"Contemporary Negro Humor as Social Satire,"
　Phylon 29 (Winter 1968).
Watkins, Mel. *On the Real Side* (1994)
This entry is taken from the *American National Biography* and is published here with the permission of the American Council of Learned Societies.

JOSEPH BOSKIN

Cameron, James Herbert (25 Feb. 1914–11 June 2006), survivor of a lynching attempt, civil rights activist, and founder of America's Black Holocaust Museum, was born in La Crosse, Wisconsin, to James Herbert Cameron, a barber, and Vera Cameron who was employed as a laundress, cook, and housekeeper. At the age of fifteen months, James was the first African American baby ever admitted as a patient to the St. Francis Hospital in La Crosse, where he underwent an emergency operation on the abdominal cavity. By the time James started school, his parents had moved to Birmingham, Alabama, and his parents separated.

When Cameron was sixteen he was living with his mother, two sisters, and grandmother in Marion, Indiana. His stepfather Hezikiah Burden hunted and fished long distances from home so was away from his family most of the time. The family lived in a segregated section of Marion, Indiana, which counted about four thousand blacks among its total population of twenty-five thousand in 1930.

Cameron had graduated from the D.A. Payne School in Marion and planned to attend McCullough High School. During the summer in 1930 he shined shoes in the interurban railway station to earn money. On an August evening of 1930 he was riding in a car with his friends Abram Smith and Thomas Shipp when Smith said he wanted to

hold up somebody and pulled out a gun. After finding a man and a woman in a parked car, Smith handed the gun to Cameron. When Cameron realized during the holdup that the white, male target was one of his shoe-shine customers, he handed the gun back to Smith. Disavowing any association with the robbery and any further association with Smith and Shipp, he ran home. Having run for four or five minutes, Cameron was some distance away when he heard the sound of gunfire, and he continued to run.

The police found him at home, took him to the police station, and proceeded to interrogate him about the incident while beating him. Cameron signed a paper under duress, later learning it was a confession admitting that Smith raped the woman and that Shipp shot the man. Cameron, who was booked on charges of bad associates, armed robbery, criminal assault, rape, and probable first-degree murder, was placed in the Grant County jail with Smith and Shipp.

On 7 August 1930 a crowd of white people gathered around the jail. Rumors of a lynch mob were reported in newspapers and radio broadcasts in the Midwest. Marion's black men moved their families for safekeeping to Weaver, Indiana (a town that had been a station on the Underground Railroad during slavery days), and planned to return with arms to combat the mobsters. Many whites as well as blacks tried unsuccessfully to call the governor to intervene. When the victim of the shooting died, an armed crowd of whites around the jail grew to ten to fifteen thousand. They ripped out the door of the jail with a sledgehammer, and the sheriff did not stop them. The mob seized Thomas Shipp, beat and hanged him, and proceeded to do the same to Abram Smith.

The mob returned to the jail from the courthouse square, where they had hanged the men from a tree, to seize Cameron. They beat him with weapons, mauled him on the way to the courthouse lawn, and placed his head into a noose. By this time a number of people in the crowd had witnessed enough violence to listen to someone who shouted that Cameron was innocent. They removed the noose and took him back to the jail.

While Cameron was transferred for safekeeping to other facilities of incarceration, some whites in Marion clamored for the state attorney general's office to investigate the lynching. The NAACP collected money for Cameron's defense and sent NAACP Executive Secretary WALTER FRANCIS WHITE to investigate the lynching.

Cameron's mother employed the prominent Indianapolis attorneys Robert L. Bailey and Robert L. Brokenburr for his defense while Cameron was in the state reformatory at Pendleton. They secured a change of venue to Anderson, Indiana, where Cameron was transferred to await trial. The sheriff in this venue protected Cameron and made him a "turnkey trusty," which meant that successful performance of Cameron's jail duties depended upon whether he proved to be trustworthy.

Bailey and Brokenburr succeeded in obtaining three postponements of the trial while having some of the charges dropped each time. Cameron's trial opened 29 June 1931 on a charge of being an accessory before the fact to first-degree murder. Court testimony of the victim's female companion exonerated Cameron. His signed confession was thrown out of court. On 7 July 1931 he was found guilty of being an accessory before the fact to voluntary manslaughter and sentenced to imprisonment at Pendleton for a term of not less than two years or more than twenty-one years. After serving four years of the sentence, he was released from prison on a five-year parole. During his term of imprisonment, Cameron enrolled in school; he eventually obtained a high school degree and completed two years of community college.

Cameron moved to Detroit. He was employed in a variety of jobs, including milk deliveryman, table waiter, laborer, janitor, salesman, small business owner, and reporter. In 1938 he married Virginia Hamilton and had five children.

In the 1940s he became president of the Madison County branch of the NAACP in Anderson, Indiana, and organized other NAACP chapters in Muncie and South Bend, Indiana. From 1942 to 1950 he served as director of Indiana's Civil Liberties Union, reporting violations of the equal accommodations laws to end segregation.

He and his family relocated to Wisconsin in 1953, where he established an air-conditioning and refrigeration business. In Milwaukee he became involved in work to end housing discrimination there. During the 1960s he joined the civil rights marches on Washington. He also wrote 240 articles and pamphlets detailing racial injustices and spoke before groups in the United States and Europe.

In 1988 he founded America's Black Holocaust Museum, Inc., in Milwaukee, Wisconsin, a nonprofit venture dedicated to preserving the history of lynching in the United States and the African American struggle for equality. He served as its director and president.

In 1991 he wrote to the then governor of Indiana, B. Evan Bayh III, asking for a pardon from the state for the indiscretion of his youth. The pardon was issued on 3 February 1993, and Cameron received it along with a key to the city of Marion, Indiana.

Cameron's story received media attention from *Ebony* and *The Oprah Winfrey Show*. In 1999 he was awarded an honorary doctor of humanities degree from the University of Wisconsin. In 2002 he received the National Education Association's CARTER G. WOODSON Memorial Award, a human rights award. James Cameron died in Milwaukee on 11 June 2006.

FURTHER READING
Cameron, James. *A Time of Terror* (1982).
Madison, James H. *A Lynching in the Heartland* (2001).
Thornbrough, Emma Lou. *Indiana Blacks in the Twentieth Century* (2000).

ROSE PELONE SISSON

Campanella, Roy (19 Nov. 1921–26 June 1993), baseball player, was born in Philadelphia, Pennsylvania, the son of John Campanella, an Italian American fruit-stand owner, and Ida Mercer, an African American. Campanella grew up in the Germantown and Nicetown neighborhoods of Philadelphia. There he played catcher briefly for the Simon Gratz High School team before joining a black semiprofessional team, the Bachrach Giants, at the age of fifteen. A year later he quit high school and joined the Baltimore Elite Giants in the Negro National League (NNL). There BIZ MACKEY, one of the greatest catchers in the Negro Leagues and player-manager for the Elite Giants, schooled Campanella in the art of catching.

Soon the Elite Giants' starting catcher, Campanella played eight years in the NNL (1937–1942 and 1944–1945), where he was an adept defensive receiver and a powerful hitter. He appeared in the Negro League all-star game, known as the East-West Classic, in 1941, 1944, and 1945. During the winter months Campanella usually played in Mexico, Venezuela, Puerto Rico, or Cuba, playing in Caguas in 1940–1941 and 1941–1942, in Santurce in 1944–1945, in San Juan in 1946–1947, and in Marianao in 1943–1944. He also played for Monterrey in the Mexican League for parts of the 1942 summer season and again in 1943. He learned Spanish and sometimes managed his winter ball clubs. In 1941 Campanella married Ruthe Willis. The couple had three sons and two daughters.

Campanella was in Venezuela in early 1946 when the Brooklyn Dodgers general manager

Branch Rickey asked him to return to the United States, where the Dodgers offered him a contract to play for their Class B farm club in Nashua, New Hampshire. Rickey had signed JACKIE ROBINSON to play for the Dodgers' Class A club in Montreal only months before. Campanella played in 1946 in Nashua and the next year in Montreal, where his manager, Paul Richards, said that "Campanella is the best catcher in the business—major or minor leagues." The 5 foot 9½ inch, 195-pound Campanella joined the Dodgers in 1948. He was sent to St. Paul, Minnesota, after three games in order to integrate the American Association, but in July, the Brooklyn manager Leo Durocher insisted that Campanella return to his club. He had nine hits, including two home runs and a triple, in his first three games after being promoted. Campanella anchored the fabled Brooklyn "boys of summer," who won the National League pennant five times between 1949 and 1956. He was catching for the Dodgers when they won the 1955 World Series over the New York Yankees.

The second black player in the majors, Campanella was one of the major leagues' first black superstars. During his ten seasons, he won three Most Valuable Player awards (1951, 1953, and 1955), and in 1953 he established single-season records for a catcher by hitting forty-one home runs, collecting 142 runs batted in, and recording 807 putouts. Campanella was selected to eight consecutive all-star teams, from 1949 to 1956. His career batting average was .276, with 1,161 hits, 242 home runs, and 856 runs batted in. Campanella also established a record for durability by becoming the first man to catch at least one hundred games for nine consecutive seasons, despite a series of injuries.

Campanella opened a liquor store in Harlem during his Brooklyn career. While driving home from the store on 28 January 1958, his car skidded into a telephone pole and turned over. Two of Campanella's vertebrae were crushed, leaving him paralyzed from the waist down. But his courageous struggle to live and regain an active life made him an inspiration for those with disabilities. Campanella told his story in *It's Good To Be Alive*. Originally published in 1959, the book was made into a television movie in 1974.

An exhibition game on 8 May 1959 between the Dodgers and the Yankees to raise funds to help pay Campanella's considerable medical expenses drew a crowd of 93,103 paying fans, setting a record for the largest game attendance in baseball history. In 1969 Campanella became the second black player voted into the National Baseball Hall of Fame.

Campanella moved to Los Angeles in 1978 to work in the Dodgers' community services department. He was also an instructor for the club during spring training, despite being confined to a wheelchair.

Campanella's first wife died in 1963. At the time of his death in Woodland Hills, California, he was survived by his second wife Roxie Doles, whom he had married in 1964, and his five children. Known for the infectious joy he had for the game as much as for his skills, Campanella said, "To play in the big leagues, you got to be a man, but you got to have a lot of little boy in you, too."

Campanella might have been the greatest catcher in major league baseball history, despite playing only ten seasons in the majors. Though baseball's color line blocked Campanella's entry at the beginning of his career and a tragic car accident prematurely brought it to an end when he was thirty-six, his fellow Hall of Famer Ty Cobb captured the opinion of many in the baseball world when he said that "Campanella will be remembered longer than any catcher in baseball history."

FURTHER READING

Campanella, Roy. *It's Good To Be Alive* (1959, rpt. 1995).
Riley, Jim. *Biographical Dictionary of the Negro Baseball Leagues* (1994).
Rogosin, Donn. *Invisible Men: Life in Baseball's Negro Leagues* (1983).
Shapiro, Milt. *The Roy Campanella Story* (1958).
Tygiel, Jules. *Baseball's Great Experiment: Jackie Robinson and His Legacy* (1983).
This entry is taken from the *American National Biography* and is published here with the permission of the American Council of Learned Societies.

ROB RUCK

Campbell, Bebe Moore (18 Feb. 1950–27 Nov. 2006), author, journalist, and playwright, was born Elizabeth Bebe Moore in Philadelphia, Pennsylvania, the daughter of George Moore, a farm agent, and Doris Moore, a social worker whose maiden name is unknown. Shortly after her birth, her parents separated, and Campbell relocated with her mother to a row house in North Philadelphia. Although both parents maintained close links with their child and fostered her early interest in weaving imaginative stories, it was Doris Moore who enrolled her daughter in an academically challenging and predominately white elementary school and later in an equally exacting high school.

Campbell attended the University of Pittsburgh, where she graduated with a B.S. in Elementary

Education in 1971. Immediately afterward she embarked on a career teaching public school in Pittsburgh, Atlanta, and Washington, D.C. Like JESSIE FAUSET, the most prolific author of the Harlem Renaissance, and the playwright and poet ANGELINA GRIMKÉ, who wrote while teaching at the illustrious all-black Dunbar High School, Campbell sought the financial security of the teaching profession. Her decision to become a public school teacher was simple. "When you're an upwardly mobile, African-American daughter you are either going to be a nurse, a teacher, or a social worker," she observed. "You want something so you can take care of yourself…. See, as a black person, your college education was not for this erudite purpose. It was to get you a job, to secure your place in middle-class America so you wouldn't have to scrub somebody's floors," she pragmatically concluded.

Although the economically tenuous position of black females in American society propelled Campbell toward the teaching profession, her greatest desire was to become a journalist. While in Washington, D.C., she successfully obtained employment at *Black Enterprise* as a correspondent. At the same time, she wrote.

Her first marriage, to Tiko Campbell, produced one daughter, Maia, but ended in divorce. In 1984 she married Ellis Gordon Jr. who had one son from a previous marriage.

Campbell's first book, *Successful Women, Angry Men: Backlash in the Two-Career Marriage* (1986), was a nonfictional account of women's and men's attitudes and coping strategies deployed in the dual-career marriage. Drawn from scores of personal interviews conducted while she was a reporter, Campbell concluded that beneath the rhetoric of joint responsibility and co-parenting espoused by many husbands, the actual burdens of child-rearing and housework remained largely the province of wives. Although Campbell offered advice for married couples, she cautioned that if left unchecked, domestic and professional tensions would take their toll on one's health, career, and marriage.

Campbell's first novel, *Your Blues Ain't Like Mine* (1992), described an intricate network of relationships that bound white to black, male to female, and rich to poor. Set in the 1950s and echoing the life and death of EMMETT TILL, a young African American who was brutally lynched in 1955, the book told the story of Armstrong Todd, who met his untimely death at the hands of an insecure, poor white male who murdered with the hopes of finally earning his father's approval. In the book, dysfunctional white male relationships spilled over into the lives of their wives, who were battered and yet convinced they were prized, as well as onto their sons, who struggled to create themselves in images unlike that of their fathers. This malaise of exploitation, manipulation, and dysfunction was a product of slavery, which was not engaged directly even though it functioned as a subtext in each of Campbell's novels. Concealed under the rhetoric of racial inferiority was the capitalist system that financially benefited wealthy whites by polarizing individuals along racial, gendered, and classed lines to interrupt potentially empowering alliances. One of the novel's central characters, Ida Pinochet, transgressed these boundaries by organizing a union of white and black female workers, and armed by history, her search for paternity ended not with the name of her white father but with the redistribution of his assets.

Your Blues Ain't Like Mine was followed by three novels that all became *New York Times* best sellers: *Brothers and Sisters* (1994), *Singing in the Comeback Choir* (1998), and *What You Owe Me* (2001). Like Campbell's first novel, *What You Owe Me* also revolved around the theft of assets from a black woman, Hosanna Clark, a maid in a Los Angeles hotel. The apparent thief was Gilda Rosenstein, Hosanna's Jewish business associate and friend. The story that emerged was one of betrayal and redemption as Hosanna's progeny recovered the missing funds and Gilda recovered monies stolen from her father by the Swiss during World War II.

Black women writers emphasize the complexity of black women's lives. Writers like ANN PETRY, through protagonists like her Lutie Smith in *The Street* (1991), illustrate how numerous forces prey upon and conspire to frustrate black women and mothers. Campbell's work stands out in its depiction of black women who share resilience and a refusal to be victimized.

While not primarily an author of historical novels, Campbell wrote with a precision and specificity born of meticulous research. Influenced by TONI MORRISON, whose work speaks the unspeakable, Campbell wrote articles and a book on mental illness in the black community that rendered it in terms that were familiar and therefore haunting. In June 2003 her play on the subject, *Even with the Madness*, debuted in New York. In 2005 she revisited the subject with the novel *72-Hour Hold*.

Campbell's insistence on reaching her primarily black female audience was seen in the diversity of magazines that printed her works and of literary genres in which she wrote. *Essence*, the *New York Times Magazine*, and *Black Enterprise* were among the publications that featured her work, while her literary repertoire included the novels for adults and for children, essays, memoirs, and plays. She died at her home in Los Angeles from complications of brain cancer.

FURTHER READING
Campbell, Jane. "An Interview with Bebe Moore Campbell," *Callaloo* (Fall 1999).
Conklin, Christine. "Novel Territory," *Pitt* (Nov. 1994).
McHenry, Susan. "This Property Is Not Condemned," *Black Issues Book Review* (Sept.–Oct. 2003).
Obituary: *New York Times*, 28 Nov. 2006.

LESLIE E. CAMPBELL

Campbell, Delois Barrett (12 Mar. 1926–2 Aug. 2011), singer, was born in Chicago, the seventh of ten children of Susie and Lonnie Barrett Sr. from Mississippi. Lonnie served as a deacon at the family's church, Morning Star Missionary Baptist, and was a longtime member of the National Bricklayers Union. Susie was a chorister at the church. Barrett sang her first church solo at the age of six. During the 1930s and 1940s three of Delois Barrett's sisters and one brother died from tuberculosis, events that had the effect of strengthening her Christian faith and commitment to sacred music.

Barrett, her younger sister Billie, and her cousin Johnnie Mae Hudson formed the Barrett and Hudson Singers in 1941, directed by an aunt, Mattie Dacus. Soon after graduating from Englewood High in Chicago at the age of sixteen, Barrett joined the ROBERTA MARTIN Singers, one of the most accomplished gospel groups in the country. Unlike her friend DINAH WASHINGTON, who was a previous member of the group, Barrett never crossed over to secular music. Instead, for a decade she traveled with the group across the country, refining her voice and stage presence in front of church audiences. Other members of the group included Bessie Folk, Norsalus McKissick, Robert Anderson, Willie Webb, and Eugene Smith.

In 1950 Barrett married Frank Campbell, who worked both as a Baptist minister and as a tailor. She stopped touring to take care of their four children, but she continued to record with the Roberta Martin Singers for another eight years and performed regularly in Chicago with her two sisters, Billie GreenBey (b. 1928) and Rodessa Porter (b. 1930). To help support her family, she also sang for a local funeral parlor. Although Campbell assisted with the music program at her husband's small church, she refused to make his church her full-time priority and give up her ambitions to travel and perform.

Singing with GreenBey and Porter, Campbell fully matured as a singer and achieved her broadest critical acclaim. Known as the Barrett Sisters, they developed a reputation for impeccable harmonization, which led some people to consider them the greatest gospel trio of all time. In 1963 their group recorded its first album with Savoy Records in Newark, New Jersey, followed by many others on various labels. This same year they debuted on the Chicago-area television show *Jubilee Showcase*, which featured studio performances of African American sacred music and was hosted by the Jewish civil rights activist Sid Ordower. Through the 1960s and 1970s their more than a dozen Sunday morning television appearances introduced them to large, interracial audiences and helped to solidify their reputation as one of the most important vocal groups from the golden age of gospel music. Attesting to their roots in early gospel tradition, they sang while standing relatively still and used gestures and facial expressions to enrich the message from their voices. One of their most popular songs from this period was the rhythmically dynamic rendition of the gospel standard "I'll Fly Away."

In spite of these early successes, stardom eluded the Barrett Sisters until the late 1970s. At this point the three embarked on the first of thirty European tours and established themselves as "the continent's favorite gospel group" (Heilbut, liner notes). In 1981 the sisters were featured in George T. Nierenberg's award-winning gospel documentary titled *Say Amen, Somebody!* This film brought the Barrett Sisters broad recognition for many years because of its continual screenings at film festivals and by educators. The sisters performed regularly into their seventies, although medical complications related to arthritis relegated Campbell to a wheelchair and decreased the frequency of her public appearances. In May 2007 Chicago Theological Seminary awarded Campbell and her sisters honorary doctorate degrees.

The venues at which the Barrett Sisters performed included Constitution Hall in Washington, D.C., Orchestra Hall in Chicago, Lincoln Center in New York, the Theatre Deville in Paris, France, and several National Baptist Conventions and many churches across the United States. They sang for the king of Sweden, for the president of Zaire, and for a 1990 public television special titled *Going Home with Patti*

LaBelle. In the twenty-first century they sang across the United States, including at two annual Jazz and Heritage Festivals in New Orleans, at a memorial for Dr. MARTIN LUTHER KING JR. in Boston, and in Chicago on Campbell's eightieth birthday.

Observers have noted that behind Campbell's success and popularity lies a long history of tragedy. Two of Campbell's children died before reaching their twenties, including her teenage daughter who contracted hepatitis. Furthermore, her musical success never translated into riches or long-term economic stability. Her close bond with her sisters and her deep Christian faith helped her to survive such adversity. Campbell took musical inspiration from a wide variety of sources. Madame Lula Mae Hurst, an early gospel soloist, instilled in Campbell an appreciation for opera. According to Porter, the Barrett Sisters admired the popular white group the Andrews Sisters, whom they heard over the radio and whose harmonies they practiced.

Other important vocal influences included Roberta Martin and MAHALIA JACKSON, whose singing Campbell emulated at one point in her career and at whose funeral she sang. Indicating mutual feelings of admiration, Jackson once said that Campbell's voice "opens up like a rose." The gospel great MARION WILLIAMS also spoke highly of Campbell's voice. According to the historian and producer Anthony Heilbut, Campbell's booming soprano voice was a larger version of GreenBey's alto and Porter's coloratura, mirroring the difference between Campbell's full frame and their more petite builds (*Gospel Sound*). Her voice moved from an operatic timbre and vibrato to a rougher and more aggressive sound associated with gospel shouting, usually within the course of a single song. Campbell thereby appealed to listeners' sense of beauty and their appreciation of technical facility through her rich and resonant tones, while also reaching them on an emotional and spiritual level through her visceral vocal approach.

Delois Barrett Campbell remained one of the finest and longest-lasting exponents of classic gospel music. Into the twenty-first century she promulgated a style of singing that bore the impress of her training in Chicago from the 1930s to the 1950s, when the city served as the hub for the development of gospel music. Her voice will be remembered as a powerful expression of faith, blending opera and gospel technique and harmonizing to perfection with the voices of her sisters. She died in Chicago at the age of eighty-five.

FURTHER READING

Calloway, Earl. "Barrett Sisters Celebrate with Concert," *Chicago Defender*, 13 Oct. 1973.

Heilbut, Anthony. *The Gospel Sound: Good News and Bad Times* (1997).

Heilbut, Anthony. Liner notes, in *The Best of Delois Barrett Campbell and the Barrett Sisters* (1995).

Reed, James. "Barrett Sisters Enjoy Singing Gospel Truth," *Boston Globe*, 17 Jan. 2004.

Reich, Howard. "Gospel Sisters," *Chicago Tribune*, 12 Mar. 2006.

"Stardom: The Barrett Sisters Celebrate in Song," *Chicago Defender*, 28 July 1975.

Young, Bob. "The Gospel Truth: Barrett Sisters Just Divine," *Boston Globe*, 16 Jan. 2004.

BRIAN HALLSTOOS

Campbell, Earl (29 Mar. 1955–), football player, was born Earl Christian Campbell in Tyler, Texas, to Bert Campbell, a laborer, and Ann Collins. The man who would eventually be known as "The Tyler Rose" was named after the obstetrician who delivered him. His mother was unable to settle on a name for her sixth child and deferred the honor to her physician, Dr. Earl Christian Kinzie. The Campbell family would eventually include eleven children before Bert died of a heart attack when Earl was only eleven. Campbell's childhood was one of hard work and poverty. His father earned little as a worker in the rose fields that dominated Tyler, and Ann struggled to maintain a subsistence income after her husband's death. The Campbell children worked as soon as they were able. Campbell followed his father into the rose fields by day and worked evenings at the local K-Mart. Despite the additional responsibilities and work Campbell inherited upon his father's death, he developed a love of football and made time to accommodate it. His size, talent, and maturity made him a "man among boys" when he competed against children his own age. He idolized the linebacker Dick Butkus and determined to play that position exclusively.

When Campbell entered John Tyler High School as part of one of its earliest segregated classes, coaches insisted that he use his rare physical skills on offense and moved him to running back. During his senior season, 1973, the obscure Tyler team won the state football championship on the broad shoulders of the Campbell family; Earl starred alongside his brothers Steve and Tim that year. He was heavily recruited by the nation's major college football programs, something that would not have happened had he entered high school just a few years earlier. Since black high

Earl Cambell, of the University of Texas Longhorns, autographs a football in Dallas, Texas. The All-American running sensation won the Heisman Trophy in 1978. (AP Images.)

schools were ignored by universities during the segregated era, two of Campbell's older brothers who excelled at football had not been recruited.

Family was at the center of Campbell's life, and it was therefore unsurprising that he chose to attend the University of Texas. He had no trouble adjusting to major college competition, running for more than 900 yards and winning the Southwest Conference Newcomer of the Year Award as a freshman. He followed with an even stronger sophomore campaign, but an injury-plagued and unproductive junior season led many to question whether the "Tyler Rose" had peaked. Texas fired Campbell's coach, mentor, and close friend Darrell Royal after that season, a move for which Campbell felt responsible because of his poor play. Rising to face his doubters, Campbell lost thirty pounds and made his senior year a memorable one, rushing for 1,744 yards and winning the Heisman Trophy in 1977. Unlike many superstar college athletes of the era Campbell remained in school to complete his bachelor's degree.

As Campbell prepared to enter the National Football League, the Houston Oilers traded up in the draft in order to select him. He stated that he felt God did not want him leaving Texas. The shy, humble country boy was an anomaly in the celebrity-driven NFL. When the Oilers purchased him a luxury Cadillac, he returned it as too extravagant for his needs. His transition to the pros was aided by his physical maturation; his combination of speed, power, and sheer size made him nearly impossible to bring down. He ran for 1,450 yards in 1978, winning both the Rookie of the Year and Most Valuable Player awards. He led Houston deep into the playoffs in 1978 and 1979 but not to the Super Bowl. In 1980 Campbell's near-record 1,934 rushing yards led to another playoff berth but again no championship. As a result the Oilers' coaching staff was sacked. The new staff oversaw a rapid descent from a perennial playoff team to mediocrity. Campbell continued to put up impressive statistics on these unsuccessful teams. Campbell married his junior high sweetheart, Reuna Smith, in 1980; the couple would have two children, Earl II and Tyler.

Having rushed for more than one thousand yards in five of his six seasons as an Oiler, Campbell was traded to the New Orleans Saints in the middle of the 1984 season. The coach who had drafted him onto the Oilers, Bum Phillips, was coaching the Saints and wanted to make Campbell his centerpiece. Unfortunately, Campbell's bruising running style took a toll on his body. Because it often took five men to bring him down, he absorbed thousands of hits during his career. After finishing the 1984 season with the Saints and returning for a full but substandard season in 1985, Campbell retired. His pro career consisted of a mere eight seasons, three of which were mediocre. But the brevity of his NFL career did not diminish its glory. In 1991 he was elected to the Pro Football Hall of Fame, despite playing for only a short time. The Tyler Rose did not turn in many great seasons in the NFL, but they were outstanding enough to ensure his place in history.

Upon his retirement Campbell worked as a mentor to incoming athletes at his alma mater, the University of Texas. He also parlayed his love of cooking into a restaurant venture in Austin, Earl Campbell's on Sixth; the restaurant closed in 2001 as a result of poor management. In addition to his work with incoming University of Texas athletes he also ran Earl Campbell Meat Products, supplying his home recipes to grocers and restaurants.

Only four men have ever been honored as "Hero of Texas" by the state legislature: Davy Crockett, Sam Houston, Stephen F. Austin, and Earl Campbell. His short but spectacular professional career belied his long-standing significance to Texans. His stardom at the University of Texas helped unify a state that had been bitterly divided throughout the segregated era. His declaration, "I am not a black man," I am a man," carried as much force as any of his hits on the football field.

FURTHER READING

Campbell, Earl, and John Ruane. *The Earl Campbell Story: A Football Great's Battle with Panic Disorder* (1999).

Blair, Sam. *Earl Campbell: The Driving Force* (1980).

Miller, Paddy Joe. *The Tyler Rose: The Earl Campbell Story* (1997).

Reid, Jan. "Earl Campbell," *Texas Monthly* 29.9 (Sept. 2001).

EDWARD M. BURMILA

Campbell, Elmer Simms (2 Jan. 1906–27 Jan. 1971), cartoonist, author, artist, and graphic illustrator, was born in St. Louis, Missouri, to Elmer Cary Campbell, a high school administrator, and Elizabeth Simms, a painter and homemaker. Campbell moved to Chicago to live with an aunt and to take advanced art classes at Elmwood High School. In 1923, while a student there, he won a national contest for an editorial cartoon about Armistice Day. After graduation, Campbell attended the Lewis Institute and the University of Chicago, where he worked at *The Phoenix*, a humor magazine. He also worked as a post office messenger and railroad car waiter. Campbell was accepted to the School of the Art Institute of Chicago and completed three years of study there before returning to St. Louis to work briefly at Triad Studios, a commercial art studio. He then moved to Harlem to live with an aunt and attend the Art Students League, where he studied printmaking with George Grosz. He took classes at the Academy of Design, did freelance gag writing in which he scripted punch lines for cartoons, and sold his own cartoons to make a modest living.

Campbell's work on *The Phoenix* led to interviews with editors associated with his Chicago coworker Ed Graham, who had since become a well-known cartoonist. E. Simms Campbell, as he was then known, entered the commercial art world in his twenties as a cartoonist and artist for the *New Yorker* and the National Association for the Advancement of Colored People's magazine *The Crisis*. He later sold cover art to *Life* and *Judge* magazines and wrote gag strips for the *Saturday Evening Post*.

Campbell rented an apartment at the prestigious Dunbar Building on Seventh Avenue in New York, where bandleader CAB CALLOWAY and musician DUKE ELLINGTON were among his fellow lodgers. Campbell and Calloway frequented the Cotton Club, one of the hot spots in Harlem, and became fast friends. Campbell's frequent socializing did not affect his work life: he worked hard, turning out three hundred to five hundred pieces of art each year at the height of his career. His watercolor illustrations of jazz musicians and nightlife, including a cultural map of Harlem, were inspired by his late nights out on the town.

Campbell authored art manuals in the 1930s and illustrated a children's book, *Popo and Fifina*, in 1932, featuring text by LANGSTON HUGHES. He illustrated a book of Haitian poetry by Binga Dismond titled *We Who Die & Other Poems* (1943). Campbell was married in 1936 to Constance; when she died in 1940, he married her younger sister Vivian. Vivian and Elmer's child, Elizabeth Ann, married noted photographer and filmmaker GORDON PARKS.

The artist Russell Patterson introduced Campbell to Arnold Gingrich, editor of *Esquire* magazine from 1933 to 1946. Patterson encouraged Campbell to incorporate women into his cartoons, and Campbell's *Cuties* cartoon for *Esquire* became his best-known work and the first syndicated feature drawn by a black artist. His work for *Esquire* also made him the first African American artist hired by a national magazine. The harem girl drawings in *Cuties* first appeared in autumn 1933 in the premiere issue of *Esquire*. Gingrich credited Campbell with the success of the publication, since each issue featured as least one piece by Campbell. When he was not submitting full-page original work, Campbell roughed out illustrations for other staff artists and submitted punch lines, or "gag lines," for cartoons for other members of the staff. The scantily clad *Cuties* were so popular that Avon books published the collected cartoons in paperbacks for sale to military troops abroad during World War II. The twenty-five-cent *Cuties* volumes featured the women making comments about men, life, fashion, and clothing. King Features Syndicate represented the *Cuties* cartoons until the late 1960s. Campbell was also credited with the creation of the *Esquire* mascot. Sculptor Sam Berman was given a Campbell sketch of Esky, a pop-eyed, mustachioed character, and

Berman constructed a three-dimensional ceramic Esky figure that would be used on every cover of the magazine.

When *Esquire* moved from watercolor illustrations to photography around 1957, Campbell was hired to create original art for the new magazine *Playboy*. *Phantom Island*, a Campbell-drawn cartoon, had a long run for King Features. Campbell's commercial artwork was used in advertisements for Springmaid, Hart Schaffner and Marx, and Barbasol. His distinctive signature appeared in the lower portion of each piece of commercial art.

The irony of Campbell making a successful living drawing white women in lingerie at a time when southern state laws mandated jail terms for blacks whistling at white women was not lost on Campbell. He wrote articles about racism (and also music) for *Esquire*.

Cartoons from the turn of the century through the 1920s typically showed black figures in what was termed "cue ball" style, because the human figures lacked shadowing or detail work. Human heads were drawn as solid-colored circles with the eyes, ears, and lips attached. This unnatural characterization was transformed by the group of cartoonists that included Campbell. Black cartoon characters depicted in illustrations were shown with shading and highlighting that depicted more natural looking facial colorings and features.

Campbell worked for more than forty years as one of the most successful illustrators and cartoonists in the industry. After returning to the United States from Switzerland following an absence of nearly 14 years, he died of cancer in 1971 (his wife, Vivian, had also died of cancer the previous year). Campbell's funeral was held in the White Plains Community Unitarian Church, in the same community where in 1938 he had lost a legal challenge to purchase a home because of segregationist legal restrictions. By 2000, more than one hundred black cartoonists worked in editorial and panel cartooning as a result of the pioneer work of artists such as E. Simms Campbell.

FURTHER READING

Calloway, Cab, with Bryant Rollins. *Of Minnie the Moocher & Me* (1976).
"Country Gentleman," *Ebony* (Aug. 1947).
Driskell, David. *Two Centuries of Black American Art* (1976)
Lewis, David Levering. *When Harlem Was in Vogue* (1982).
Porter, James A. *Modern Negro Art* (1969).
Powell, Richard J. *Impressions/Expression: Black American Graphics* (1980).
Stromberg, Fredrik. *Black Images in the Comics: A Visual History* (2003).
Obituary: *New York Times*, 29 Jan. 1971.

PAMELA LEE GRAY

Campbell, Grace (1882–8 June 1943), a pioneer member of the Socialist Party of America and the American Communist Party and a founding member of the African Blood Brotherhood, was born in Georgia to William Campbell, from the British West Indies, and Emma Dyson Campbell, from Washington, D.C. Her family moved to Texas by 1892, then to Washington, and she moved to New York City about 1905. Many sources continue to state in passing that she was born in the Caribbean and studied at Tuskegee, though this is more likely a different woman named Grace Campbell. The important role of Caribbean immigrants in New York's progressive movements may have contributed to this confusion. The historian Winston James offers a more detailed and compelling case that she was born in Georgia, which is consistent with the information Campbell apparently provided to the 1920 and 1930 census.

Campbell became active in Socialist Party politics soon after moving to New York, associating around 1917 with Harlem's "step-ladder" public agitators, including HUBERT HARRISON, RICHARD BENJAMIN MOORE, WILFRED ADOLPHUS DOMINGO, and A. PHILIP RANDOLPH. Active in the Association for the Protection of Colored Women, a forerunner of the National Urban League, she ran a home for young mothers and babies, the Empire Friendly Shelter. She also worked for the City of New York, starting in 1915 as a probation officer, then parole officer, until 1924. That year she ranked first of 164 on a competitive civil service examination, with 91.32 percent. She filled the sole vacancy to become a court attendant for Courts of Sessions, with a salary of $2,500 per year, holding onto this job through all her years of political activity, until her death in 1943.

Campbell was the socialist candidate for New York's state assembly in 1919 (receiving 7 percent of the vote) and 1920 (10.5 percent), one of the first women of any color to run for public office in the state. OWEN CHANDLER and A. Philip Randolph supported her in the pages of the *Messenger*, which described her as "the first colored woman to be named for public office on a regular party ticket in the United States of America." In 1921 she served as secretary of the Twenty-First Assembly District Socialist Club in Harlem.

She was the only woman among the founders of the African Blood Brotherhood, modeled in part on the Irish Sinn Fein, and the only woman on ABB's Supreme Council. J. Edgar Hoover's Bureau of Investigation (later the FBI) described her as "one of the prime movers in the organization." The council met at her home, 206 W. 133rd Street, and she dealt with much of the organizational correspondence. Together with CYRIL V. BRIGGS, she generated the twice-weekly Crusader News Service, directed to what was then called the Negro press.

In 1920 Campbell helped found, and served as an officer of, the Friends of Negro Freedom, an organization opposed to MARCUS GARVEY and the United Negro Improvement Association's emphasis on race-based capitalism. The same year, she was an organizer of the People's Educational Forum, a joint effort of socialists such as A. Phillip Randolph from *The Messenger* and communists such as OTTO HUISWOOD (born in Suriname, formerly in the Dutch West Indies), which met every Sunday in the Lafayette Theater. A lively black socialist discussion and debating event, the forum adopted its motto from Shakespeare's *Macbeth*: "Lay on MacDuff! And damn'd be him that first cries 'Hold, enough.'" Another public slogan was "Knowledge is Power."

Campbell was a speaker at one of three mass meetings organized by ABB in June 1921, following the invasion of the black community in Tulsa, Oklahoma, by a rioting white mob that killed 150–200 men women and children. ABB experienced an increase in membership, as it advanced self-defense and protection, while denying insinuations that it had organized or provoked the race riot in Tulsa.

Along with Briggs and ABB founder Richard B. Moore, she became disenchanted with the Socialist Party's failure to specifically address black concerns. They gravitated toward the Communist (Workers) Party, not so much the American party, but the Communist International of which it was a part. The poet CLAUDE MCKAY wrote enthusiastically to Campbell from Russia, where his warm reception without discrimination was widely acclaimed, as was Lenin's "Theses on the National and Colonial Questions" and his personal intervention in 1920 to see that African American concerns were addressed in Communist Party strategy.

Campbell joined the Communist Party around 1922, noted by a Bureau of Investigation agent, and reflected in the use of her home for meetings

of the local branch of the Workers' Party by 1923. In November of that year, the African Blood Brotherhood effectively merged with the local branch of the Workers Party. Campbell was an early influence on the decision of the Harlem attorney WILLIAM L. PATTERSON to join the party.

In 1928, Campbell, with Moore and Huiswood's wife Hermina, led the Harlem Tenants League in a popular fight to save New York's Rent Law. The league led rent strikes, protested evictions—including organizing teams to move furniture back into apartments after eviction—and lobbied for housing codes to ensure landlords maintained adequate heat.

Campbell chaired the Negro Workers Relief Committee, initially organized to aid miners who lost their jobs during a strike in Pennsylvania, then assisting victims of flooding in Mississippi in 1927 and a hurricane in Florida in 1928. The executive committee included WILLIAM PICKENS and W. E. B. DUBOIS of the NAACP, two Harlem ministers, and seven fellow communists. After a devastating hurricane struck Florida in 1928, with rising allegations that black families were getting little or no aid, the Negro Workers Relief Committee was quoted in the *Chicago Defender*, charging that relief was being delivered 80 percent for whites, 20 percent for blacks. Campbell issued a statement on 16 November, "Too long have we left our helpless brothers and sisters and their children to the tender mercies of the Red Cross with its notorious record for eviltry and the vilest sort of discrimination." Others, including MARY MCLEOD BETHUNE, sent to Florida by the NAACP, and CLAUDE BARNETT, director of the Associated Negro Press, reported that the Red Cross was making every effort to assist black as well as white families.

Campbell was estranged from the party for a time after the expulsion of its former chair, Jay Lovestone (whom she supported), in 1929 and did not return to active participation until 1932. Campbell was also disgusted with the insertion of party factional disputes into the meetings and work of the Tenants League. Through the 1930s, she continued to have conflicts with party leadership, as did many of her longtime associates, including Briggs and Moore. McKay recalled that after Campbell inspired a Harlem audience with a proposal to establish cooperative stores, to alleviate unemployment and increase community control of local commerce, the party declined to support it.

The circumstances of Campbell's life when she died at age sixty have not been documented—not even a final note from an FBI file or the infamous

House Un-American Activities Committee (HUAC). She appears to have still been working for the City of New York court system, as she had done throughout all her political life, since 1915. Winston James writes, "History has been unkind to Grace Campbell." The final unkindness appears to be that her passing was little noted.

FURTHER READING

James, Winston. *Holding Aloft the Banner of Ethiopia: Caribbean Radicalism in Early Twentieth Century America* (1998).

Kleinberg, Eliot. *Black Cloud: The Great Florida Hurricane of 1928* (2003).

Kornweibel, Theodore. *Seeing Red: Federal Campaigns against Black Militancy, 1919–1925* (1998).

Solomon, Mark. *The Cry Was Unity: Communists and African Americans, 1917–36* (1998).

Turner, Joyce Moore, and W. Burghardt Turner. *Caribbean Crusaders and the Harlem Renaissance* (2005).

Watkins-Owens, Irma. *Blood Relations: Caribbean Immigrants and the Harlem Community, 1900–1930* (1996).

CHARLES ROSENBERG

Campbell, Israel S. (1815–13 June 1898), escaped slave and minister, was born in Greenville County, Kentucky. Until Campbell was in his thirties, he worked for various masters in Kentucky, Mississippi, and Tennessee, respectively. When Campbell was approximately eighteen years old, he married a slave named Matilda. In 1837 the Campbells joined a church and were baptized. Less than two years later, Campbell began preaching. By the late 1840s, Campbell was a widower, and he was determined to not endure slavery any longer; thus, he fled to Canada, where he was reunited with Washington Campbell, one of his six siblings. The brothers were partners in several Canadian business ventures.

After passage of the Fugitive Slave Act in 1850, Campbell became an agent for HENRY BIBB's *Voice of the Fugitive*, which was the first black newspaper in Canada; Campbell was also a delegate to the Fugitive Convention of Canada, and on behalf of the organization, he collected money for fugitive slaves. In 1855 Campbell attended Oberlin College in Ohio for six months, bought his freedom from his Tennessee master, became a Canadian citizen, and was ordained by a Baptist church in Canada. Six years later, Campbell's *An Autobiography: Bond and Free; or, Yearnings for Freedom, from My Green Brier House: Being the Story of My Life in Bondage,* *and My Life in Freedom* was published; he hoped that the book would generate enough money for him to purchase freedom for his two daughters and son, who remained in Tennessee.

In addition to Campbell's slave narrative, his legacy is based on his involvement with various Baptist churches in Canada and the United States. As an associate of the Baptist Association for Colored People (now known as the Amherstburg Regular Missionary Baptist Association), Campbell helped the Canadian organization grow to ten churches during his tenure. From 1856 to 1860, Campbell was the pastor of Sandusky Baptist Church in Ohio. After serving as a missionary in Louisiana and Texas, Campbell cofounded Antioch Baptist Church (now known as Antioch Missionary Baptist Church) in Houston in 1866 and was the church's interim pastor. Campbell was appointed the pastor of the African Baptist Church in Galveston in 1867. That same year when the city's residents had to contend with an outbreak of yellow fever and a hurricane, Campbell assisted his church members in whatever ways he could. Under his leadership, African Baptist was reorganized as the First Regular Missionary Baptist Church (now known as Avenue L. Missionary Baptist Church), which was the first independent African American church in Texas, and the congregation increased from forty-seven to five hundred members. In 1868 Campbell was one of three organizers of the Regular Missionary Lincoln Baptist Association, which was the first association of African American Baptists in Texas, and he served as the organization's first moderator.

Campbell, who was hailed as "the Father of Black Texas Baptists," remained the pastor of First Regular Missionary Baptist Church until 1891. He died in La Marque, Texas, on 13 June 1898.

FURTHER READING

Beck, Rosalie. "Israel S. Campbell." *Handbook of Texas Online.* Texas State Historical Association, http://www.tshaonline.org/handbook/online/

Early, Joe, Jr. "Israel S. Campbell: The Father of Black Texas Baptists." *Baptist History and Heritage* 39, no. 3–4 (2004): 98–102.

LINDA M. CARTER

Campbell, James Edwin (28 Sept. 1867–26 Jan. 1896), poet and educator, was born in Pomeroy, Ohio, the son of James Campbell, a laborer, and Lethia Stark. He graduated from the Pomeroy Academy, having completed the course in Latin and German, in 1884. Beginning to teach, Campbell spent the next two years in schools near Gallipolis, Ohio, and also in Rutland, Ohio, where he was offered a position as principal of the white schools, an offer he declined.

In 1886 Campbell briefly left teaching to edit the *Pioneer*, a newspaper published in Charleston, West Virginia, and, subsequently, to edit the *West Virginia Enterprise*, also published in Kanawha County. Neither job was to last, however, and within a short time Campbell returned to Pomeroy, where he involved himself heavily in politics. A notable public speaker who had made his debut shortly after his graduation from high school, Campbell took to the stump in 1887 on behalf of the Ohio Republican Party, and during the 1888 election he spoke in both Ohio and West Virginia. In 1890 he served as a delegate and secretary to the Meigs County, Ohio, Republican Convention and as a delegate to the party's convention for the Twelfth Ohio Congressional District.

Campbell's early years were also notable for the beginning of his writing career. He had begun to write poetry while in school. Subsequently his work appeared in newspapers and periodicals, as well as in his first volume, *Driftings and Gleanings*, published in Charleston in 1887. Campbell's early verses were modeled on Victorian popular poetry and dealt with common themes of love and nature as well as with classical topics. Unlike most of his African American contemporaries, Campbell at first wrote little on racial themes, although he was among the first African American poets to focus on the issue of interracial love, notably in "The Pariah's Love," a lengthy poem that appeared in the April 1889 *A.M.E. Church Review*.

In 1890 Campbell returned to his work as an educator, becoming principal of the Langston School in Point Pleasant, West Virginia, on the Ohio River. A short time later, in August 1891, he married Mary E. Champ, herself a teacher at Wilberforce College. Then in 1892 he became principal of the newly founded West Virginia Colored Institute (later West Virginia State University) in Charleston. Adding to his fame as a speaker, Campbell used his position as principal to spread ideas of discipline and uplift throughout the state's black communities while attempting to attract students to the school. He also became active in the West Virginia Teachers' Association and was elected its president in 1893.

Campbell's career at the institute and as an educator came to an end in 1894 when, after some administrative controversy, he was forced to resign. Moving to Chicago the following year, he returned to journalism, joining the literary staff of the *Chicago Times-Herald* and writing for other newspapers and periodicals.

It was during this time that Campbell made his most important contribution as a poet through his innovative work in African American dialect. Dialect poetry, when Campbell came to it, was problematic, having close ties to the "plantation tradition" of writing of the late nineteenth century—a tradition developed by white writers that glorified the Old South and entrenched dominant racial stereotypes. Nevertheless, dialect poetry began to attract African American practitioners and became by the end of the century a major form among black poets. When Campbell began to write dialect poetry in the late 1880s he was one of the first African American poets to do so. He published his major collection of dialect poetry in a book entitled *Echoes from the Cabin and Elsewhere* (1895).

The significance of Campbell's poetry grew out of its faithfulness to folk sources rather than to literary sources. While most African American dialect writers avoided the excesses of the plantation tradition, they remained fairly close to that tradition's generally idyllic focus on antebellum life and, especially, to its language, using a version of dialect that suggested more than it represented black folk speech. In his language, in particular, Campbell moved further than most from the conventions of the form, his version of dialect more closely representing, grammatically and phonetically, actual speech. To be sure, like most other African American dialect poets, Campbell evoked quaint themes and took comfort in a belief that African Americans were quickly casting off the speech and customs that his poetry portrayed. Nevertheless, although his own fame was rapidly eclipsed by the phenomenal success of the most noted black writer in the form, PAUL LAURENCE DUNBAR—a man whom Campbell knew and liked—Campbell was one of the first American poets to try to capture and to give poetic shape to a vision of African American folk life and society.

Campbell's career showed great promise during the last year of his life, but on a brief visit to his parents' home in Pomeroy during the 1895 Christmas season he fell ill; he showed symptoms of pneumonia at first, followed by typhoid symptoms and peritonitis. He died a few weeks later. Though his potential was unfulfilled, Campbell remains an important figure in the creation of an African American literary tradition.

FURTHER READING

Sherman, Joan. *Invisible Poets: Afro-Americans of the Nineteenth Century*, 2d ed. (1989).

Wagner, Jean. *Black Poets of the United States: From Paul Laurence Dunbar to Langston Hughes*, translated by Kenneth Douglas (1973).

Woodson, Carter G. "James Edwin Campbell: A Forgotten Man of Letters," *Negro History Bulletin* 2, no. 2 (Nov. 1938).

Obituary: *(Pomeroy, Ohio) Tribune-Telegraph*, 29 Jan. 1896.

This entry is taken from the *American National Biography* and is published here with the permission of the American Council of Learned Societies.

DICKSON D. BRUCE

Campbell, Lucie E. (1885–3 Jan. 1963), gospel composer and teacher, was born in Duck Hill, Mississippi, the daughter of Burrell Campbell, a railroad worker, and Isabella Wilkerson. Lucy's mother was widowed several months after Lucy's birth, and the family soon moved from Carroll County to Memphis, Tennessee, the nearest major city. Lucie and her many siblings struggled to survive on their mother's meager wages, which she earned by washing and ironing clothing. Given the family's insubstantial income, it could afford a musical education for only one child, Campbell's older sister Lora. Lucie eventually learned to play piano, however, through her own persistence, a gifted ear for music, and a little help from Lora.

Lucie Campbell was a bright student who easily mastered elementary school and middle school, winning awards in both penmanship and Latin. Even before graduating from Kortrecht Senior High School (later Booker T. Washington High School) as the class valedictorian, she began teaching classes at Carnes Grammar School. Although Campbell taught full-time to support herself, she still maintained keen interests in music and in the Baptist Church, of which she remained a lifelong member. In 1904 Campbell founded the Music Club in Memphis, which was intended to promote local musical activity in the black community. By this time she was singing at First Baptist Church, as well as playing the organ for Central Baptist Church. In later years she also helped to organize the Bethesda Baptist Church. Campbell continued to teach history and English for the Memphis public school system, moving to Booker T. Washington High School in 1911. She remained there for many years and was a well-respected, devoted, and strict instructor.

In 1916 Memphis was the site for the Baptist Church's newly formed Sunday School Congress. This body had emerged the previous year as a result of a huge internal schism within the denomination, a schism in which the National Baptist Convention was rent in two during a bitter dispute over the ownership of its publishing board. The organization consequently became two entities: the National Baptist Convention, U.S.A., and the National Baptist Convention of America. Campbell remained affiliated with the National Baptist Convention, U.S.A., and was asked to join eight other people in organizing the crucial meeting of the congress. Because she was both an active church musician and a well-recognized singer, Campbell was quickly elected as the first music director of the Sunday School and National Baptist Training Union, the Baptist organization devoted to the dissemination of church doctrine and music. Publishing gospel songbooks and hymnals became an integral part of the union's mission, and eventually important works such as *Gospel Pearls* (1921), *Spirituals Triumphant Old and New* (1927), and *Inspirational Melodies #2* (n.d.) were published by a variety of allied houses—especially the Sunday School Publishing Board of Nashville, Tennessee—and then publicized through the congress. In addition to her duties as music director, Campbell also served on the committee in charge of choosing the music for *Gospel Pearls*.

Within three years Campbell herself began writing and publishing gospel songs, one of the first African American women to do so. "The Lord Is My Shepherd," written and copyrighted in 1919 but not published until 1921, was her initial offering, appearing first in *Gospel Pearls*. Campbell continued to compose and publish gospel songs during the 1920s, and two of her best-known numbers, "Just to Behold His Face" and "Heavenly Sunshine," premiered in 1923. During this period not only did Campbell remain active in her church and at Booker T. Washington High School but she became a student as well, enrolling at Rust College, a predominantly black school some fifty miles southeast of Memphis. In 1927 Campbell graduated with a liberal arts degree. Much later, in 1951, she earned an M.S. from Tennessee State.

Campbell's style added significantly to the development of African American gospel music during the seminal decades of the 1920s and 1930s. She loved the older-lined hymns and slower-paced songs, which reflected not only her affection for the older performance practices but also her respect for her own musical heritage. Campbell also composed more moderately paced hymns, such as "When I Get Home" (1947), that are generally marked by her use of light syncopation and responsorial structure. Like THOMAS A. DORSEY, Campbell was a deft lyricist who stressed self-sufficiency and introspection as important parts of the Christian life. Her compositions, with lyrics so strongly relevant to contemporary black life, helped to bridge the gap between the older hymns and the modern gospel songs. Campbell's penchant for waltz times and other triple meters proved to be another of her major contributions to the tradition.

During a remarkable thirty-two-year stretch from 1930 to 1962, Campbell managed to present one new composition at each of the annual meetings of the National Baptist Convention. At the June 1932 convention held in Memphis, Campbell wrote, produced, and directed *Ethiopia*, a grand musical pageant with dozens of participants. This production, along with *Memphis Bound*, was among several musical extravaganzas that Campbell orchestrated during her career. One of her most widely performed compositions, "He Understands; He'll Say, 'Well Done,'" debuted to great acclaim at the 1933 convention. Campbell's contributions to gospel music were not, however, limited to these conventions: Campbell also directed choruses, chorales, and other large congregational singing groups.

Gospel compositions continued to flow from Campbell's pen at a steady rate. In 1947 she published no fewer than nine compositions, including "In the Upper Room," which was often performed during the late 1940s and well into the 1950s. In 1954, just as the popularity of this song was fading, Campbell retired from the Memphis school system after more than four decades. She was widely hailed as a positive role model for her thousands of students, in whom she strove to instill a strong sense of pride. Campbell was often asked to speak at functions on the importance and virtues of Christian womanhood.

Following her retirement Campbell continued to write songs and serve as the music director of the Sunday School and National Baptist Training Union. In 1960 she married the Reverend Countee Robert Williams, a lifelong friend, and after living nearly all of her life in Memphis, she moved to Nashville, where she died shortly thereafter. Her death was most widely noted in Memphis, where she was movingly eulogized during a large funeral service. Twenty years later a group of friends placed a commemorative stone on her grave as part of a heartfelt memorial honoring her life and accomplishments.

Campbell's importance as a pioneer in twentieth-century black gospel music is difficult to overstate. She was one of a handful of women accorded first-class status in the largely male-dominated world of the National Baptist Convention. This status was especially uncommon in the 1920s when her early compositions and the national leadership that she provided helped to shape the direction taken by the organization. Furthermore, Campbell stands out as a highly respected gospel composer whose work bridged older hymns and modern gospel songs. She is remembered as an outstanding teacher, a talented singer and composer, and a pioneer in the Baptist congress.

FURTHER READING

There is material on Campbell, including interviews and photographs, at the Archive Center of the National Museum of American History, Smithsonian Institution.

Kilkenny, Niani, and Rebecca E. Curzon, eds. *The Songs of Lucie E. Campbell: Gospel Music Composer* (1984).

Lornell, Kip. *"Happy in the Service of the Lord": African-American Sacred Vocal Harmony Quartets in Memphis*, 2d ed. (1995).

Reagon, Bernice Johnson, ed. *We'll Understand It Better By and By: Pioneering African American Gospel Composers* (1992).

This entry is taken from the *American National Biography* and is published here with the permission of the American Council of Learned Societies.

KIP LORNELL

Campbell, Luther (22 Dec. 1960–), rap artist and entrepreneur, was born in Miami Beach, Florida. His father, Stanley Campbell, who emigrated from Jamaica, was a janitor, and his mother, Yvonne Campbell, worked as a beautician. Campbell grew up in the impoverished Liberty City area of Miami and had to share a bedroom with his four brothers. Although his family was relatively stable and able to send his three older brothers to college, Campbell had to learn to survive in a dangerous environment. In a gang-related incident in Campbell's neighborhood, for instance, a fourteen-year-old male shot to death his best friend in 1986. Campbell developed his entrepreneurial skills early on by selling ice cream and lemonade

Luther Campbell, photographed at his home in Miami, Florida, in 2006. (AP Images.)

from his mother's kitchen to children from the neighborhood. He went to predominantly white schools on football scholarships and started disc-jockeying for school dances.

Before Campbell became a member of the rap group 2 Live Crew in 1986 at age twenty-six, he had already opened the teen club PacJam in Liberty City and promoted concerts for rap artists like Run-DMC and the Fat Boys. The group 2 Live Crew was founded in California by Chris Wong Won (Fresh Kid Ice) and David Hobbs (DJ Mr. Mixx) but because of its success in Florida, was reconstituted as the Miami 2 Live Crew with additional members Mark Ross (Brother Marquis) and Luther Campbell, who assumed the pseudonym Luke Skyywalker both as a stage name and as the name for his newly founded independent record company. In 1986 they recorded the first in a long string of what became known as "booty raps"— "Throw the 'D'" (as in "dick"). Campbell built up his own distribution network, going from store to store to promote the record and eventually selling an impressive two hundred thousand copies of the

song. After shortening its name to 2 Live Crew, the group recorded its first full-length album, 2 *Live Is What We Are*, for Skyywalker Records in 1987, selling more than five hundred thousand copies almost exclusively in black, urban communities. The two elements of 2 Live Crew's music that distinguished it from other rap groups of the time were its emphasis on an uptempo and steady bass beat (dubbed "Miami Bass") and sexually explicit street language that bordered on the grotesque. This was also evident on the group's second release, *Move Somethin'*, in 1988. After realizing that minors were attracted to his music, Campbell invented a parental guidance sticker for the album that later became a standard in the recording industry. In addition, the album was released in a "dirty" and a "clean" version. This was also the case for the follow-up *As Nasty as They Wanna Be* from 1989, with which the 2 Live Crew crossed over into the white pop market and stirred up a major controversy over the content of rap lyrics. Without radio airplay or a large promotional campaign, the album went double platinum, selling more than 2 million copies worldwide.

As the success of the 2 Live Crew was mounting, the group became entangled in a number of legal matters over copyright and obscenity issues. The filmmaker George Lucas forced Campbell to drop his pseudonym Luke Skyywalker and almost ruined the rechristened Luke record company, which had to destroy all its merchandise. Another filmmaker, Stanley Kubrick, sued the group for using samples from his movie *Full Metal Jacket* in its 1989 hit single "Me So Horny." An additional blow was the backlash from conservative religious groups, resulting in a number of trials in Florida. In June 1990 a federal court judge in Fort Lauderdale pronounced *As Nasty as They Wanna Be* obscene, which was a first for an album in U.S. history. Shortly afterward a black record store owner was arrested for selling the album to an undercover cop, and, also in 1990, three members of the 2 Live Crew, including Campbell, were tried after performing songs from their album at a concert. As a consequence, Campbell launched a massive media offensive. In interviews, he cited the First Amendment and argued that the obscenity ruling was an impediment of free speech. HENRY LOUIS GATES JR., then a professor of English at Duke University, wrote an op-ed piece for the *New York Times*, defending what he saw as the group's continuation of black vernacular traditions and appeared in the October 1990 trial, in which the group was finally acquitted of obscenity charges.

Profiting from the media exposure, 2 Live Crew signed a million-dollar distribution deal with Atlantic Records and released *Banned in the U.S.A.*, which proved to be another commercial success for Campbell. However, his subsequent efforts with the group and as a solo artist did not reach the same commercial and critical acclaim. Campbell's autobiography *As Nasty as They Wanna Be* was rejected by large publishing houses in the United States and eventually came out with a Jamaican publisher in 1992. Although he won a Supreme Court decision that his parody of Roy Orbison's "Oh Pretty Woman" did not infringe copyright laws, Campbell had to declare bankruptcy in 1995 after being ordered to pay the Luke Records rapper MC Shy D $1.6 million in royalties. However, Campbell continued to record and work as a strip club owner and host of an X-rated, pay-per-view show on Black Entertainment Television. Campbell had four children with three different women.

The rise and fall of Luke Records was mirrored by the short-lived success of other black-owned independent rap labels like Eazy-E's Ruthless Records and Master P's No Limit Records. Furthermore, Luther Campbell's bass-heavy music with 2 Live Crew introduced the South to hip-hop music, which up to that point had been dominated by rappers from the West Coast and the Northeast. Finally, the controversies over whether Campbell's lewd lyrics were protected by the First Amendment and whether the blatant misogyny of 2 Live Crew, which drew on comedians like RICHARD PRYOR and Rudy Ray Moore, was steeped in a venerable black folk tradition reflected similar debates over sexuality in African American culture on a larger level.

FURTHER READING

Campbell, Luther, and John R. Miller. *As Nasty as They Wanna Be: The Uncensored Story of Luther Campbell of the 2 Live Crew* (1992).

George, Nelson. *Hip-Hop America* (1998).

Light, Alan, ed. *The Vibe History of Hip-Hop* (1999).

DISCOGRAPHY

As Nasty as They Wanna Be (Luke 91651).

Banned in the U.S.A. (Atlantic 91424).

ULRICH ADELT

Campbell, Sarah (Aunt Sally) (1813?–13 Apr. 1888), the first non-Indian woman to view the Black Hills. Conflicting information exists about her early years, but all sources agree that she was born in Kentucky, in 1813 or perhaps 1824. The 1813 date

appeared in one of her obituaries. In later years she told of traveling up the Missouri River on the first steamboat in 1831, perhaps as a servant, cook, or lady's maid. Employment on the riverboats plying the Missouri River trade from St. Louis north during the mid-1800s provided opportunities for many black Americans to experience a measure of freedom, save some money, and have an adventure. Often they settled in one of the many northern river ports. Sarah Campbell made the most of that opportunity. She worked many years on the river before purchasing property in the river town of Bismarck in present-day North Dakota (a territory when Campbell settled there; North Dakota became a state in 1889).

Information about her marriage has been lost. In Bismarck she was known as Mrs. Sarah Campbell, a woman of character, perhaps widowed, and apparently illiterate. She enjoyed a reputation as a fine cook, a skilled nurse and midwife, and a shrewd manager of her life. Her location in Bismarck, near the army's Fort Abraham Lincoln, positioned her to secure occasional employment at the fort, where she was recruited by the sutler (the civilian trader who provided whiskey, food, and special provisions to the soldiers) to accompany him on General Custer's Black Hills Expedition of 1874. Campbell was the only woman in the party, charged with creating treats to supplement army rations. Records suggest that she was respected and liked by the men. Although legends persist that she cooked personally for the general, official documents note the presence of Custer's own male cook.

The months-long expedition included William Curtis, the star reporter for the *Chicago Inter-Ocean* and *New York World*. Curtis enjoyed interviewing the colorful, competent, savvy Campbell. His interviews, which attempted to capture her pungent Black English, were reported in both newspapers. Curtis wrote that Campbell characterized herself as the first white woman to enter the Hills, and she was delighted to discover that the hills were not really black. She thrilled at the French Creek discovery of gold, where she joined the other expedition members to stake a claim, "No. 7, Below Discovery."

She returned to Bismarck with the expedition, but when immigration to the Hills became legal in 1876, she came back, establishing herself first at Crook City, then at Galena, as a cook and midwife. Eventually she filed a claim at Elk Creek in Lawrence County and developed a small ranch. From the streets of frontier Deadwood, she adopted a white orphan named Anthony Herr. The two built a good life together. Herr panned for gold; Campbell ranched and worked as laundress, nurse, and midwife. Well known and loved, she was noted in laudatory obituaries by the various Black Hills newspapers. She is buried in a mountain cemetery west of Galena, South Dakota.

FURTHER READING
Rezatto, Helen. *Tales of the Black Hills* (1983).
Sundstrom, Jessie. "Black Women in the Black Hills," *Sixth Annual West River History Papers* (1998).
VanEpps-Taylor, Betti Carol. *The African American Experience in Dakota Territory and South Dakota, 1800–2000* (2007).

BETTI CAROL VANEPPS-TAYLOR

Campbell, T. M. (11 Feb. 1883–1956), agricultural educator and government worker, was born Thomas Monroe Campbell in Elbert County, Georgia, the son of William A. Campbell, a Methodist minister and tenant farmer. Little is known about his mother, who died when Tom was five years old. Left to fend for themselves after their mother's death, Tom and his younger sister ate raw sweet potatoes and whatever else they could scavenge. Their father's work as an itinerant preacher caused him to spend much of his time away from home, and Tom's four elder siblings were "hired out"—three worked in the households of white families and one worked for the doctor who had cared for their mother while she was ill.

Criticized by his neighbors for neglecting his children, William Campbell remarried. His new wife, whose name is not known, was a widow with three children of her own. William Campbell stopped traveling and focused on farming in order to take care of his sizeable family. Reduced by financial troubles to tenancy, he brought home the children he had hired out and put them to work in the fields, but soon began to hire them out again. When William Campbell's second wife died, he married a woman (whose name is unknown) who encouraged him to educate his children. Under the influence of his third wife, William Campbell promised to allow Tom to join his brother Willie, who had gone on to attend Tuskegee Institute. When he reneged on his promise, however, a determined Tom followed in his brother's footsteps, running away to Tuskegee in 1899. Before Willie could help Tom to get fully settled at the school, he died in an outbreak of typhoid and malaria.

Tom Campbell told the registrar at Tuskegee that he wished to study carpentry or a similar trade—he had had his fill of farming—but the registrar signed him up for agriculture anyway. Recounting the experience in his 1936 autobiography, *The Movable School Goes to the Negro Farmer*, Campbell wrote, "Imagine my surprise when I learned that agriculture was farming" (48). While taking night classes he worked odd jobs such as whitewashing, hauling wood, and driving BOOKER T. WASHINGTON's buggy. Campbell studied agriculture with GEORGE WASHINGTON CARVER, and he graduated after seven years at the Institute.

Campbell must have impressed his instructors at Tuskegee, for in 1906 Booker T. Washington recommended that the federal Department of Agriculture hire Campbell as its first African American demonstration agent. The Department of Agriculture started hiring agricultural educators to help farmers fight the boll weevil in the early 1900s and soon expanded the role of its demonstration agents to helping farmers modernize their work. This program was institutionalized in 1914 when the Smith-Lever Act set up the Extension Service to help educate the public about new farming techniques, among other subjects. Campbell, based at Tuskegee, was to teach African American farmers living near the Institute better ways of farming as an employee of both Tuskegee and the Department of Agriculture (Campbell, 92). Campbell carried out his mission by traveling to nearby farms in order to show farmers useful agricultural techniques. His wagon loaded with tools, plants, and livestock (and the truck that replaced it years later) was called the "movable school." Through the movable school Campbell sought to show farmers how to raise crops more productively, care for livestock, and build modern homes. He believed that if farmers could grow their own food (many southern farmers grew only cash crops—such as cotton—and had to purchase their food) they would save money, which could then be used to buy their own farms. It was through land ownership, he thought, that poor farmers could escape the crop lien system, which he considered responsible for trapping many southern farmers in an endless cycle of debt. "It is simply this system of tenancy, or living hand to mouth," he wrote in his autobiography, "that has taken hold of the people to such an extent that it affects the whole life and psychology of the average Negro community as it likewise terribly retards the economic development of the entire South" (148).

Promoted to field agent, Campbell supervised agricultural education work among black farmers in several southern states. Campbell also oversaw home demonstration work, which aimed to teach farmers' wives how to prepare nutritious meals, preserve home-grown foods, and keep their homes tidy and sanitary. Because many poor southern families lived in one- or two-room shacks, often with ill family members, Campbell recruited a nurse to travel with the movable school after 1920. The nurse showed farm families how to care for infants and sick family members and avoid spreading diseases prevalent at the time, such as tuberculosis.

Campbell hoped that his lessons would help poor black Southerners lift themselves out of poverty, make rural life more satisfying and profitable, and encourage African Americans to stay on farms at a time when many black southerners were migrating to northern cities. Campbell considered it important for the future of southern agriculture that talented farmers remain in the region. It is difficult to judge how successful Campbell was in persuading farmers to adopt his agricultural methods since few farmers left records describing how they farmed. Many farmers attended his farming workshops, but not all who heard his ideas could afford to follow his suggestions; debt kept the poorest farmers—such as sharecroppers—from adopting Campbell's practices, many of which involved the purchase of new tools.

In 1930 Campbell won the Harmon Foundation award for distinguished service in the field of agriculture. He conducted a study of agriculture and education in West Africa for the Rockefellers' General Education Board in 1944–1945. In 1947 he received a Superior Service Award from the Secretary of Agriculture. Campbell retired in 1953.

Campbell was married to Anna Ayers, a graduate of Tuskegee and a trained nurse. All of their six children also graduated from Tuskegee. Campbell is remembered for his desire to help poor black farmers improve their lives and for seeking to make southern agriculture more productive and rewarding.

FURTHER READING

Campbell's papers are housed in the Tuskegee University Archives and Museums, Tuskegee, Alabama.

Campbell, Thomas Monroe. *The Movable School Goes to the Negro Farmer* (1936).

Brackeen, L. O. "From Illiteracy to Fame," *Opportunity* (1947).

Jenness, Mary. *Twelve Negro Americans* (1936).

ELIZABETH A. HERBIN

Campbell, Tunis Gulic (1 Apr. 1812–4 Dec. 1891), abolitionist and Georgia politician, was born free in Middlebrook, New Jersey, the son of John Campbell, a blacksmith, and an unknown mother. From 1817 to 1830 he attended an otherwise all-white Episcopal school in Babylon, New York, where he trained to be a missionary to Liberia under the auspices of the American Colonization Society. Rebelling against his training and calling himself "a moral reformer and temperance lecturer," Campbell moved to New Brunswick, New Jersey, converted to Methodism, joined an abolition society, and began to preach against slavery, colonization, alcohol, and prostitution. He joined FREDERICK DOUGLASS on speaking tours and participated in the Colored Convention Movement, a new nationwide organization that aimed at racial uplift and black voting rights.

From 1832 to 1845 Campbell lived and worked in New York City as a steward at the Howard Hotel. Later, for an undetermined period, he worked at the Adams House in Boston, where he wrote *Hotel Keepers, Head Waiters, and Housekeepers' Guide* (1848), the first book by an American on how to run a first-class hotel. Appended to the text was a recommendation from his New York employer calling Campbell "an unusually intelligent, dignified, attentive, and obliging man … of unblemished moral character, with a disposition to elevate the condition and character of persons of his color." While living in Boston, Campbell married Harriet (whose maiden name is unknown), with whom he had two children and adopted another. In 1861 Campbell relocated his family to New York City, where he managed a bakery.

Early in the Civil War, Campbell volunteered to join the army, but the nation accepted no black soldiers at that time. After Abraham Lincoln's Emancipation Proclamation (1863), a white friend of Campbell's persuaded Secretary of War Edwin Stanton to commission Campbell to report to General Rufus Saxton and help resettle black refugees around Port Royal, South Carolina. Campbell worked with Saxton for nearly eighteen months before Congress established the Bureau of Refugees, Freedmen, and Abandoned Lands in March 1865. Saxton appointed Campbell a bureau agent and assigned him to supervise resettlement on five Georgia islands.

Campbell transported settlers to Ossabaw, Delaware, Colonel's, Sapelo, and St. Catherine's islands, where he approved land divisions in forty-acre plots, distributed food from the bureau and from northern philanthropic groups, organized the men into militia companies, established schools, oversaw planting, and instructed the former slaves on representative government. His wife and sons joined him as teachers in the schools on St. Catherine's. By December 1865 they had helped nearly one thousand newly freed people to acquire land of their own.

In Washington, President Andrew Johnson reversed these gains by pardoning white planters and ordering their property returned to them. The bureau revoked the land deeds held by freedmen and encouraged blacks to sign labor contracts with their former masters. Campbell used his militia units to resist, but when U.S. troops confronted him, he was forced to capitulate. Removed from his position for defying presidential Reconstruction, Campbell moved to mainland Georgia and signed a rent-to-own agreement for BelleVille plantation in McIntosh County. He began his own resettlement program, offering settlers the chance to grow crops on plots of their own, using the proceeds of the harvest to buy the land. Once the mortgage was paid, the land would be theirs. Incessant rains spoiled these plans.

When Congress took charge of Reconstruction in March 1867, Campbell registered freedmen to vote in McIntosh, Liberty, and Tatnall counties in southeastern Georgia. In this capacity he strengthened his position as the most prominent black man in an area with a black majority of 2 to 1. On the state level Campbell was elected vice president of Georgia's Republican Party. In ensuing elections, voters elected him to the state constitutional convention, to the Georgia senate, and to the position of justice of the peace.

From 1868 to 1873 Senator Campbell served his constituents. He spoke personally with Senator Charles Sumner and President Ulysses S. Grant about the need for establishing and enforcing the Fifteenth Amendment, which protected the vote for black men. Campbell also testified before the congressional committee investigating the Ku Klux Klan. Within Georgia, Campbell promoted laws to establish equal educational opportunities, abolish imprisonment for debt, revise the judicial selection process to include jurors of both races, stop discrimination on public conveyances, and provide protection at polling places to ensure fair voting.

From his office as a local justice of the peace and his pulpit in the African Methodist Episcopal Church, from his new house in Darien and in his capacity as the local political boss of the black community, Campbell tried to protect freed people from physical abuse. He fined or jailed whites who assaulted them. He held frequent meetings to advise the people on labor contracts, religion, politics, and militancy. He ran a cohesive black power structure that counseled blacks to advance "without compromise" but "in harmony" with whites as far as possible.

In 1872 conservative white Georgians surged back into power and began a concerted effort to remove prominent black politicians. In a series of extraordinary moves that culminated in 1876, Campbell was stripped of his senate seat; then after his election to the state house, a fraudulent recount took that seat, too. He also was indicted and jailed for malfeasance in his position as justice of the peace, which stemmed from a year-old case in which Campbell had jailed a white man for contempt of court.

After a failed intervention by armed black supporters and by the U.S. attorney general to make the government of Georgia correct the injustice, Campbell spent nine months in a Savannah jail and a year as a convict hired out by the Georgia penitentiary to a rich farmer in middle Georgia. Afraid to return to Darien after his release in January 1877, Campbell left Georgia for Washington, D.C. He wrote a short autobiography and returned to preaching.

In 1882 Campbell traveled to McIntosh County to campaign against an old rival. Local authorities quickly put him in jail for a few days, as a warning, before releasing him. The local newspaper printed an assessment: "Do not fear … he is not boss now." But one month later, the same paper acknowledged: "The colored people of this county have the greatest confidence in Tunis G. Campbell, and are willing to let him … do just as his sweet will dictates." Campbell picked the opposition candidate for the state legislative contest, and voters overwhelmingly voted for his choice, Hercules Wilson, a black man. Campbell left the state for good on 30 December 1882. The events of his life thereafter are unknown. He died in Boston.

Campbell made a significant impact in his roles as abolitionist lecturer, Freedmen's Bureau agent, state senator, black adviser, and community organizer. During Reconstruction few African Americans had more power or accomplished as much in helping their constituents gain equal rights. Even after he was gone, his political machine controlled local elections until 1907, when the state of Georgia disenfranchised blacks. At that time the only African American in the legislature was Amos Rodgers of McIntosh County. The historical image of Campbell has shifted from that of a black carpetbagger who exploited blacks for personal gain to that of an honest reformer committed to equality.

FURTHER READING

Sufferings of the Rev. T. G. Campbell and His Family in Georgia (1877).

Drago, Edmund L. *Black Politicians and Reconstruction in Georgia: A Splendid Failure* (1982).

Duncan, Russell. *Freedom's Shore: Tunis Campbell and the Georgia Freedmen* (1986).

This entry is taken from the *American National Biography* and is published here with the permission of the American Council of Learned Societies.

RUSSELL DUNCAN

Campbell, William Craig "Bill" (25 May 1953–), politician, was born in Raleigh, North Carolina, to Ralph Campbell, a janitor, and June Campbell, a secretary. With both parents involved in activism—Ralph was a NAACP chapter president, and June organized civil rights events at schools and churches—Campbell was thrust into public service at a young age. At age six, he and his older brother, Ralph Jr., handed out leaflets for the NAACP; at age seven, when Raleigh nominally adopted integration, Campbell became the first black child to attend a white public school when he enrolled at Murphy Public School. Though thirty black families had originally registered their children, after intimidation and Ku Klux Klan threats, Campbell was the only child not to be withdrawn by the start of the school year. Though his father received a threatening phone call from the KKK, and though he himself was the subject of frequent taunts, Campbell endured and remained the only black child in his school for five years.

After finishing William G. Enloe High School in 1971, Campbell enrolled in Vanderbilt and graduated in three years with a degree in history, sociology, and political science. He then entered Duke Law School to be close to his family, and received his J in 1977. Following his graduation, Campbell took a job with the prestigious Atlanta firm of Kilpatrick and Cody, where he had clerked the previous summer.

Campbell joined the Department of Justice's antitrust division in Atlanta in 1979, but left in 1981 to join the firm where he would eventually become a partner, Ellis, Funk, Goldberg, Labovitz, and Campbell. That fall, Campbell was elected to the Atlanta City Council, where he served for three consecutive terms until 1993. As a representative

from some of the city's blossoming neighborhoods, Campbell was a part of "the changing of the guard" for black politicians, as the *New Republic* put it. Calling him a "rising, young black city councilman," the article quoted Campbell as saying that "candidates who have shown the community that they are going to pay attention to the nitty-gritty local issues—getting the garbage picked up, seeing that the police are there—will be the ones who succeed in the 1980s and 1990s" (*New Republic*, 24 Nov. 1986, 14).

The telegenic Campbell promoted legislation that highlighted civic responsibility, such as banning private clubs' discrimination and getting local constituents involved in neighborhood issues. During the 1980s, Campbell also became involved with a new Atlanta group called 100 Black Men, Inc., which linked successful black professionals with underprivileged students and communities to provide counsel and tutoring.

When the Atlanta mayor MAYNARD JACKSON decided to step down in June 1993, citing weakness from heart bypass surgery, Campbell ran for the executive office. Though he subsequently won, becoming the city's third African American mayor, the campaign was not without controversy. An election run-off between him and the former Fulton County Commissioner Michael Lomax became heated when Campbell's name emerged in a federal bribery investigation on contracts at Hartsfield International Airport, and Campbell flew to Dallas to submit to a lie detector test in order to preempt further controversy. In a press conference six days before the mayoral runoff election, Campbell revealed the results (a pass) of the test.

In his first term, Campbell focused on the city's business renaissance and policing methods (he appointed the city's first female police chief), as well as improvements to the urban infrastructure in time for the 1996 Summer Olympics. A seeming star on the rise, Campbell participated in the opening ceremony's torch lighting, and had his name bandied about for a possible cabinet post in the second Clinton administration.

By 1997, however, some of the goodwill seemed to evaporate amid continuing rumors of Campbell's cronyism. The *Atlanta-Journal Constitution*, in a 21 November editorial before the mayoral election, "reluctantly" endorsed his opponent, City Council President Marvin Arrington, saying, "Another four years of Campbell would bring the city a repeat of the past four: a mayor who hogs the spotlight and makes no tough decisions, all the while insulting friends and enemies alike. The city cannot afford more of that" (*Atlanta-Journal Constitution*, 21 Nov. 1997). After a campaign filled with both African American candidates hurling racially tinged comments at one another, Campbell was reelected.

After his second term, Campbell cohosted a daily talk show on an Atlanta radio station and ran a media-consulting firm. In January 2003, he took a job with the popular litigator Willie Gary's firm, moving to West Palm Beach with his wife, Sharon Tapscott, an education administrator whom he had married in 1978, and their two children, Billy and Christina Lynn.

In August 2004, following a five-year probe by federal investigators, Campbell was indicted on seven counts of racketeering (including charges resurrected from the Hartsfield International Airport scandal), bribery, and wire fraud dating back to 1996. The former mayor continued to proclaim his innocence throughout the proceedings in 2006, often calling the investigations "racist" and "an inquisition." Though the trial contained lurid testimony—including that of two former mistresses—the jury acquitted him of racketeering and bribery charges. Three months later, however, Campbell was convicted on three counts of tax evasion. In June 2006, U.S. District Judge Richard Story sentenced him to thirty months in prison; while praising some of Campbell's public service, Story also chastised him, "As the trial progressed, I was overcome, almost appalled, by the breadth of misconduct in your administration" (*Atlanta-Journal Constitution*, 14 June 2006).

Campbell served his sentence at the Federal Correctional Institute in Miami and a Salvation Army halfway house, before being remanded to home confinement. He was released in 2008.

FURTHER READING

"Bill Campbell Succeeds Maynard Jackson," *Ebony*, Feb. 1994.
"Prison for Ex-Mayor," *Atlanta-Journal Constitution*, 14 Jun. 2006.
Thomas, Chandra R. "Your Guide to the Bill Campbell Trial," *Atlanta Magazine*, Sept. 2005.
West, Paul. "Breaking Rules: The New Black Politics," *New Republic*, 24 Nov. 1986.

ADAM W. GREEN

Camper, John Emory Toussaint (27 Feb. 1894–21 Nov. 1977), physician, political activist, and civil rights advocate, was born in Baltimore, Maryland, to Mary J. Cromwell, one of the first black teachers in Baltimore, and John Heyward Camper, principal of an elementary school in Sparrows Point, Maryland. Camper had two brothers and several sisters. The Campers lived in Sparrows Point from about 1896 until 1900, when John's father's death forced a move to Towson and then to Baltimore. John attended eighth grade in Baltimore and graduated in 1913 from what would become the city's Douglass High School. He worked as a longshoreman and steelworker before receiving a bachelor of science degree in 1917 and a medical degree in 1920 from Howard University. A strong and gifted athlete, he was named several times to the All-American Colored Football Team, became the assistant coach for the Howard football team in 1920, and from 1921 to 1922 was the coach of the Morgan College (later Morgan State University) football squad. Even after he began his medical career in 1920, Camper remained interested in sports, serving as a member of Howard University's Board of Athletic Control in 1926 and 1927. While he was still a medical student, he was drafted by the army at the close of World War I but served only two months at Fort Des Moines, Iowa, before receiving an honorable discharge.

After completing his medical training, Camper worked at Old Provident Hospital and served on the state board that oversaw the Crownsville State Mental Hospital. He maintained a private practice for the rest of his life. On 7 September 1920 he married Louise G. Nixon; they had four children. His first marriage ended in divorce, and he later married Florine Thompson and had two more daughters.

Camper's first brush with racism occurred after he returned to Baltimore at the end of World War I. Still wearing his uniform, he was ordered by a train conductor to remove himself to the Jim Crow car. When he refused, the conductor called a policeman. He asked Camper if he had a ticket. Camper replied that he did, and the policeman then turned to the conductor and said: "Well, he's in the uniform of the U.S. Army. He'll ride where he damned please!" (Maryland Historical Society Oral History Interview). When Camper threatened to kill the conductor if he touched him, the incident ended.

In the early 1940s Camper became involved with Baltimore's branch of the NAACP, led by the legendary LILLIE MAE CARROLL JACKSON, who had staged protests against employment discrimination since the 1930s. He admired Jackson and supported her work, especially her campaign against the telephone company that refused to hire African American operators. He also helped found MeDeSo, a Baltimore club for black physicians and dentists that funded many Baltimore NAACP activities. Frustrated by the nation's failure to live up to the democratic rhetoric of World War I, Camper became incensed by the unprovoked killings of blacks—including uniformed soldiers—by white Baltimore policemen during the early years of World War II. Indeed, as Camper angrily recalled, one white policeman earned a reputation for murdering blacks "just like you'd shoot ducks" (Maryland Historical Society Oral History Interview).

On 1 February 1942 Officer Edward R. Bender shot a black soldier in the back during an argument over a taxi. The incident enraged Camper and the entire black Baltimore community. With Jackson and CARL MURPHY, owner of the newspaper the *Afro-American*, Camper organized a protest: "March on the State Capitol!" he exclaimed (Cahn, 285). To implement the plan, Camper and Murphy created the Citizens' Committee for Justice, in which he worked closely with Juanita Mitchell (CLARENCE MITCHELL's wife and Jackson's daughter) to speak for Baltimore's black community and organize the demonstration. Camper—with Jackson's tireless assistance—employed his network of MeDeSo colleagues and friends to gather a sufficient number of cars, trucks, and buses to transport protestors to Annapolis. To focus state and national attention on the march, Camper invited the firebrand New Yorker ADAM CLAYTON POWELL JR. to serve as keynote speaker. On the evening of 23 April 1942 Powell addressed an overflow crowd at a local church, inspiring them to turn out the next day for the historic march. Over two thousand angry protestors surrounded the state capitol on 24 April to demand an end to the killings, the firing of the Baltimore police chief, the hiring of black policemen, and equal opportunity in housing, employment, and education. The unprecedented action produced results.

Governor Herbert R. O'Conor created a legislative committee of black and white members to study the status of Baltimore blacks. He included the Annapolis march leaders on that committee and on other legislative committees to address black housing, employment, and health in Baltimore. O'Conor's move was designed more to placate the protestors than to produce meaningful change. But the city's police chief eventually resigned, and some African Americans were added to the police force.

Camper became an overseer of the Crownsville Mental Hospital and was appointed to the Prison Board (the first black to serve there) over the objections of its white members. Camper and the Citizens' Committee for Justice became a force in the community, initiating voter registration drives and continuing the NAACP's campaign to pressure local retailers to hire African Americans. As chairman of the Total War Employment Committee, Camper worked to desegregate state defense industries, backed by President Franklin D. Roosevelt's Executive Order No. 8802 that barred government contractors from engaging in any employment practices that discriminated on the basis of race, color, creed, or national origin.

Camper's influence continued to grow after World War II. In 1946 Governor O'Conor appointed Camper to his nine-member State Fair Rent Commission. Camper, as chairman of the Baltimore Citizens' Committee for Justice, joined with lawyers, bankers, businesspeople, and representatives of the real estate industry to recommend policies that would "keep rents, in a vast majority of cases, at a fair level" (*Washington Post*, 16 July 1946). At the urging of his fellow physician William Watts, Camper joined Henry A. Wallace's Progressive Party, becoming state co-chair in 1947 and 1948 and a candidate for the U.S. House of Representatives. Wallace attracted the support of many African Americans such as Camper who respected his bravery in campaigning against segregation in the South. Energized by Wallace's commitment to civil rights, Camper led the state party in a series of protests that employed a wide range of tactics, some that would not become common for another ten years. In March 1948 he protested the threatened defrocking of a Methodist minister, Richard H. Bready, for spending too much time working for the Progressive Party and not enough on his Cumberland, Maryland, church. Camper denounced the act as a "witch hunt," asserting that a "group of bigots in Cumberland have taken punitive action against a minister who dares to entertain independent political convictions" (*Washington Post*, 30 Mar. 1948). The next month Camper filed suit on behalf of the Progressives to compel the Baltimore Board of Supervisors of Elections to open their registration books for examination. He sought to verify the names of people who were signing petitions to get party candidates such as himself on the ballot, but the city declined to cooperate. Nevertheless, Wallace and his running mate Glen H. Taylor, Camper, and two other Progressive

Party congressional candidates did make it onto the state ballot.

In May 1948 Camper and party co-chair James Stewart Martin sent an open letter to Maryland governor William Preston Lane and Baltimore mayor Thomas D'Alesandro Jr. (father of the future House Speaker Nancy Pelosi), calling on them to enforce the Supreme Court's recent decision barring restrictive real estate covenants. "No longer," Camper insisted, "may the courts uphold racial and religious segregation." He believed that the Court had struck a blow against Jim Crow and anti-Semitism and called upon the state to extend "the spirit of the decision to the fields of education, recreation and employment. America and Maryland must be freed completely of every vestige of discrimination and segregation" (*Washington Post*, 5 May 1948).

In July 1948, as part of wider assault on segregated public facilities, Camper and a group of about twenty-three black and white (male and female) protestors staged an interracial tennis match in defiance of city ordinances that segregated such public facilities. When police ordered the group to leave, the protestors sat down—some laid down—compelling authorities to arrest the protestors and carry them off the courts. Over five hundred supporters jeered the police as they removed the group. Camper and the state director of the Progressive Party, Harold Buchman, denounced the arrests as "a flagrant violation of the constitutional rights of these well-mannered, orderly players." One member of the Young Progressives exclaimed that they would not "recognize any color line" (*New York Times*, 12 July 1948).

Newspaper reports, following national trends, expected that Republicans, led by presidential candidate Thomas E. Dewey, would carry most state races in 1948. Camper's own bid for a congressional seat in the Fourth District encountered some resistance. Although the party publicized arrangements for a rally at a firehouse in Glen Echo, Maryland, town officials, who had previously agreed to rent the facility, at the last minute revoked permission. While town officials denied that politics motivated their decision, Camper and his allies clearly saw the move as an attack on his campaign and an attempt to limit party members' "civil rights" (*Washington Post*, 25 Apr. 1948). Nevertheless, Camper attracted enormous attention and drew PAUL ROBESON, Eleanor Roosevelt, Elenore Gimble, LENA HORNE, and even JOE LOUIS to Baltimore to help him bring out the vote. Harry S. Truman's victory in 1948 stunned pollsters. The competition between the Democratic Truman, the Republican Dewey, the Socialist Norman Thomas, the Dixiecrat Strom Thurmond, and the Progressive Wallace appeared to swing the election to the Republicans, who did carry Maryland. In his district Camper garnered only 6,552 votes to the Democrat's 38,486 and the Republican's 21,084. Allegations of voter fraud, vote rigging, and intimidation proved real when Camper entered one polling station and found cronies of the city machine buying votes with money and liquor. Unintimidated, Camper rolled up his sleeves and chased the thugs from the station. It is not clear if a clean election would have seen Camper elected. He remained with the Progressive Party, hoping to gain strength in the 1950 elections. He became chairman and leader of the state Progressive Party in February 1950, but cold war politics and the onset of the Korean War put an end to the ultraliberal party. He resigned his chairmanship in August, disgusted with the party's extreme opposition to the war.

During the early 1950s Camper and his well-to-do associates in MeDeSo assisted the NAACP's Legal Defense Fund and its campaign to win the historic *Brown v. Board of Education* Supreme Court case. With the fund's war chest at low ebb, Camper and MeDeSo raised $15,000 to see the case through to victory. Camper had maintained his medical practice throughout his fight for civil rights. Locally he became known as the "NAACP Doctor," treating indigent blacks who usually could not afford to pay for his services. Additionally, beginning in 1930, he served as the medical examiner for the Household of Ruth, a women's auxiliary of the African American Odd Fellows fraternity, of which he was a member. He also belonged to the Freemasons, the Elks, the National Medical Association, and the Maryland Medical, Dental, and Pharmacy Association and was a charter member of the Gamma chapter of Phi Beta Sigma fraternity. His courageous work earned him a place on the NAACP Honor Roll, and he received a merit award from the Citizens' Committee for Justice in 1947. Camper never wavered in his struggle "for freedom for millions of human beings," as he declared in 1948, "of their black brothers in Nigeria … in Panama … [with] oppressed peoples all over the world" (Cahn, 283). "Maryland was fortunate," Robeson remarked, "that there could be a man of such character and love for his people" (*Baltimore Sun*, 22 Nov. 1977). Camper practiced medicine for fifty-seven years and died after a brief illness at Baltimore's Provident Hospital, which was founded in the year of his birth and where he began his medical career.

FURTHER READING

Of particular importance is a transcription of a 1976 oral history interview (OH.8134) with Camper in the collections of the Maryland Historical Society.

Cahn, Jonathan D. "A Doctor's Legacy: Dr. John E. T. Camper and the MeDeSo," *Journal of the National Medical Association* (1980).

Lewis, Edward S. "Profiles: Baltimore," *Journal of Educational Sociology* (Jan. 1944).

Sullivan, Patricia. *Days of Hope: Race and Democracy in the New Deal Era* (1996)

Obituary: *Baltimore Sun*, 22 Nov. 1977.

DONALD YACOVONE

Campfield, Louis Mirault (4 Sept. 1875–26 Apr. 1924), federal Weather Bureau employee, was born in Savannah, Georgia, like his parents, Cyrus and Laura Mirault Campfield, and all four of his grandparents. Laura Mirault was descended from at least two wealthy mulatto families from the French colony of St. Domingue (now Haiti), who fled to Savannah around 1800. Although this was the most stable and prosperous period of rule by Toussaint Louverture, his administration was resented by the wealthy mulatto population, many of whom had owned slaves, and resented the political triumph of "les noirs." In Savannah, they faced new legislation by a self-consciously "white" Anglo political establishment, beginning in 1808, to impose restrictions on free people of color. Nevertheless, Louis Mirault, born about 1780, established a prosperous tailor business, and Aspasia Cruvellier Mirault, born about 1790, opened an acclaimed pastry shop and acquired real estate.

Accordingly, at least half of Campfield's family had been free for a century or more, albeit under severe legal disabilities prior to the Civil War, and subjected to the new forms of legal disability uniformly imposed, beginning around the time he was born, upon both previously free and formerly enslaved people of color. In 1895, when Campfield came to adulthood, the United States in general, and the southern states in particular, were entering the most viciously unrestrained and irrational period of overt legislated racism in the nation's history. During this trying period, the family retained some degree of prosperity,

and Campfield was able to pursue a quiet career in the civil service, working his way up to a position requiring scientific acumen, which common assumptions of the day denied a man of his color could possess. The details of his formal education are unknown.

When Louis was born, Cyrus Campfield was a partner in the Campfield and Morel jewelry store. Laura Campfield remained at home, caring for a household that included older brothers James, William, and Henry, and older sister Lucy. The oldest boys, ages twenty and seventeen in 1880, both had jobs as retail clerks. The family was listed by census enumerators as "mulatto," as were some of their neighbors, while others were listed as "black," and a few listed as "white" were either born in Ireland or descended from Irish immigrants (Census, 1880). Later children included Cyrus Campfield, born 27 November 1881, and Charles Gary Campfield, born 19 September 1884. Two other children, Susan and John, may have died in childhood.

Campfield began employment with the Weather Bureau at least as early as August 1894, as a messenger in the Savannah station, working nine hours a day on weekdays. At that time, "weekday" meant every day except Sundays or holidays. The messenger was one of three or four persons assigned to the station, responsible for preparing stencils of weather maps and cotton-region bulletins, delivering or mailing maps and bulletins, and looking after signal lanterns. The station was responsible for regular observations of the local weather, preparing maps and special bulletins with information for cotton growers in the region, providing cold wave and frost warnings, tabulating data for newspapers, and in particular providing data each night for the Savannah *Morning News*.

Around 1900 Campfield married Lucy Ann Miller. Their first child, a son named for his father, was born 11 December 1901, and a daughter, Letitia, probably named for her maternal grandmother, was born in late 1909. In 1901 Campfield was earning $480 per year as a messenger, while Harry B. Boyer, the local forecast official in charge of the station was paid $1500. Boyer's assistant, Gilbert W. McDowall, titled the station's observer, earned $840. Weather stations were authorized by civil service rules to employ sixteen- and seventeen-year-olds as "messenger boys," and during World War I, the minimum age was lowered to fourteen. Persons eighteen years of age or older were hired as "messengers" (Weather Bureau Personnel and Topics, July 1918, 4).

The messenger position in Savannah was left vacant for at least six months in 1902, after Campfield transferred in July to the bureau's central office in Washington, D.C. Campfield's pay grade and job title were unchanged; his duties including folding publications, maintaining an index card file, and typewriting. In early 1903 he was promoted to a salary of $600 per year, still working as a messenger, and in May 1903 was reduced back to $480. In July he was promoted back to $600, and in August to $660. His work occasioned little other written notice, except that the Chief Clerk's office determined in September 1903 that he should do typewriting only occasionally.

In February 1905 Campfield was promoted to Clerk, Class D, with similar duties, and a raise to $900 a year. In July 1905 he returned to the Savannah weather station as one of Boyer's two assistant observers, taking a small cut in pay to $840. The only evidence that race may have played a role in his assignments is that he remained second assistant for the remaining eighteen years of his career, under a succession of first assistants. James Jones, a new first assistant the same year Campfield returned, made a smaller salary ($720 per year). A new first assistant, Edward S. Wiest, came in July 1906, also earning $720. Fred L. Disterdick, who became first assistant in July 1907, had a salary of $1000, which rose to $1200 in July 1909, while Campfield remained at $840.

In 1913, Charles M. Strong took charge of the office as local forecaster; in 1920 he became the first supervisor of the station with the title of meteorologist. Fifteen years older than Campfield, Strong had previously been an assistant at three stations, and in charge at eight others, before coming to Savannah. He remained in charge at Savannah until after Campfield's retirement. For the first eight years, they were joined by John E. Lockwood as first assistant, until he was reassigned to Milwaukee, Wisconsin. Beginning in 1921, Campfield worked with Howard J. Thompson as first assistant for five years, and in his final year, with George B. Wurtz for six months, and then William A. Mitchell.

Campfield retired 27 October 1923, on account of total disability, and died the following April. Lucy Ann Campfield moved to Cambridge Massachusetts, where she lived with the family of her sister Sarah, married to Oscar H. Fitzallen, and their mother, Letitia Miller (Census, 1930). The younger Louis M. Campfield died of pneumonia at the age of 29 on 25 February 1931 in Wilkinsburg, Pennsylvania.

He had been employed as an electrical engineer by Westinghouse Co. in East Pittsburgh, and was four months short of completing a master's degree at the Carnegie School of Technology. Married 25 June 1929 to Olga Suplit of McDonald, Pennsylvania, a daughter of Belgian immigrants, he was survived by his mother, his wife, and their nine-month-old son, also named Louis Mirault Campfield (*McDonald Record*, Obituaries, 27 Feb. 1931). In a curious irony to America's continued preoccupation with "race," the 1930 census listed all of these survivors as "white," although only Olga Campfield had been so described in previous enumerations.

FURTHER READING

There are no published biographies of Campfield.
> The most detailed information on his work for the Weather Bureau is preserved at the National Archives, RG 27, Records of the Weather Bureau, Administration and Fiscal Records, Miscellaneous Personnel Records of the Weather Bureau, 1866–1958, especially Box 6, 7, 26, and 27. A brief summary is also available at: http://www.history.noaa.gov/nwsbios/nwsbios_page8.html#l_campfield

Sumler-Edmond, Janice L. *The Secret Trust of Aspasia Cruvellier Mirault: The Life and Trials of a Free Woman of Color in Antebellum Georgia* (2008).

CHARLES ROSENBERG

Canady, Alexa I. (7 Nov. 1950–), neurosurgeon and professor of neurosurgery, was born Alexa Irene Canady in Lansing, Michigan, to Elizabeth Hortense Golden Canady and Clinton Canady Jr. Her father was a graduate of the School of Dentistry at Meharry Medical College in Nashville, Tennessee, and practiced in Lansing. Her mother graduated from Fisk University at the age of nineteen, was active in civic affairs, became the first African American elected to the Lansing Board of Education, and served as national president of the Delta Sigma Theta sorority. Canady's grandmother began to teach school at the age of sixteen and taught elementary education at Lane College in Tennessee. Canady married George Davis, a retired naval medical corpsman and recruiter, in 1988.

The Canady family lived outside Lansing on land sold to them by a man who wanted to punish the city for not rezoning his property so that he could not build a gas station. Selling to a black family was his act of revenge. Canady and her younger brother were the only blacks in the local elementary school. Her second-grade teacher was fired after altering test results on the California Reading Test: the teacher gave Canady's high score to a white boy. She nevertheless was an honor student and was named a National Achievement Scholar in 1967.

Alexa Canady entered the University of Michigan as a math major. She was passionate about the subject but received only average grades. After her brother informed her of a minority health career program, she switched her program of study. She earned a B.S. degree and entered Michigan's medical school, where she graduated cum laude. Canady interned at Yale's New Haven Hospital and was appointed to a residency in neurosurgery, making her the first black and the first women resident in neurosurgery history. On her first day as a resident an administrator referred to her as "the new equal opportunity package." Many people questioned her ability to succeed in this all-male, all-white profession, but Canady triumphed.

After spending five years at the University of Minnesota, Canady became a pediatric neurology fellow at Children's Hospital in Philadelphia. Next she took a position at Henry Ford Hospital in Detroit. Finally she was hired by Children's Hospital of Michigan (CHM) and took a position on the faculty of Wayne State University in Detroit as a clinical associate professor. In 1997 she became a full professor of neurosurgery. Her areas of expertise are cranial facial abnormalities, epilepsy, hydrocephalus, pediatric neurosurgery, and tumors of the brain and spinal cord. After being appointed director of pediatric neurosurgery at age thirty-six, she turned a marginal program into a world-class facility that gained a reputation for saving young people with gunshot wounds.

As chief of neurosurgery at CHM she handled the most difficult cases. Parents from all over the world brought their children to this hospital to be treated by Canady and her associates. She trained all four neurosurgeons on her staff and did work on the development of such projects as neuroendoscopic equipment, hydrocephalus and shunts, and pregnancy and shunt complications. Canady received many offers from various medical schools to serve as dean, but she preferred the high-stress work that she did at CHM, saving and improving the lives of children. She also was very much concerned about the community and spent as much time as possible mentoring high school students.

Canady retired from Children's Hospital of Michigan in June 2001 and moved to Pensacola, Florida, where she began practicing medicine on a limited basis. She is a consultant to the Food and Drug Administration, and she chairs the Neurological Devices Panel of the FDA's Medical Devices Advisory Committee. She has won numerous awards, including induction into the Alpha Omega Alpha honorary medical society in 1975, a Teacher of the Year award at Children's Hospital of Michigan in 1984, induction into the Michigan Women's Hall of Fame, a Woman of the Year award from the American Medical Women's Association in 1993, an honorary degree from Marygrove College in 1994, and an Athena Award from the University of Michigan Alumnae Council in 1995.

FURTHER READING

Lanker, Brian. *I Dream a World: Portraits of Black Women Who Changed America* (1989).
"Surgeon Heals with Grace, Devotion to Young Patients: Dr. Alexa Canady," *Detroit News*, 19 May 2002.

DEBORAH LOIS TAYLOR

Canady, Herman George (9 Oct. 1901–1970), social psychologist, was born Herman George Canady in Okmulgee, Oklahoma, son of Howard T. and Ana Canady. His father was a minister. Herman Canady was a student at Douglass Elementary School and Favor High School in Guthrie, Oklahoma. Upon graduating from high school he enrolled at Northwestern University Theological School in Evanston, Illinois, a suburb north of Chicago. While a student at Northwestern, Canady was awarded a Charles F. Grey Scholarship for his outstanding performance. Canady developed an interest in the behavioral sciences in Theological School and in 1927 graduated from Northwestern University with a Bachelor of Arts degree in Sociology and a minor in Psychology. The following year he earned a Master of Arts degree in Clinical Psychology from Northwestern.

In September 1928, Canady became a member of the faculty at West Virginia Collegiate Institute, later called West Virginia State College, and chair of the psychology department. In 1935 he published "Individual Differences among Freshmen at West Virginia State College," in the *Journal of Negro Education*. In April 1936, Canady published, "The Effect of "Rapport" on the I.Q.: A New Approach to the Problem of Racial Psychology," in the *Journal of Negro Education*, marking a milestone in his research and career. The findings of his study on "the effect of rapport" concluded that test results can be dramatically impacted by the nature of the relationship between a test-taker and proctor. Prior to his findings no researcher had taken into account the racial implications of psychology regarding intelligence testing and rapport. In November 1936, the *American Journal of Sociology* published a study conducted by Canady, "The Intelligence of Negro College Students and Parental Occupation." The *Journal of Negro Education* featured another Canady study in 1938, "Psychology in Negro Institutions," which revealed that of fifty historically black institutions surveyed only fourteen had psychology departments and they were primarily focused of educational psychology.

Canady was awarded a General Education Board Fellowship in 1939; he took a leave of absence from his post as chairman at West Virginia State College and returned to Northwestern University to pursue his doctorate. During his doctoral tenure at Northwestern, Canady conducted research for the completion of his dissertation, "Adapting Education to the Abilities, Needs and Interests of Negro College Students." In 1941 Canady graduated with a Ph.D. in Psychology from Northwestern; the same year he returned to position at West Virginia State College and resumed his work as a psychologist and researcher. In 1942, "A Scale for the Measurement of the Social Environment of Negro Youth," appeared in the *Journal of Negro Education*.

In 1943, Canady published *A Study of Sex Difference in Intelligence: Test Scores among 1,306 Negro College Freshmen*. In 1948, the *Journal of Negro Education* published "The Psychology of Youth," a Canady study and in another volume published his research, "Individual Differences and Their Educational Significance in the Guidance of the Gifted and Talented Child."

Canady committed the life of his career to West Virginia State College. He did however invest himself in professional pursuits that took him out side of the institution. In 1946 Canady was sponsored by the American Friends Service Committee to visit colleges and schools as a lecturer. In 1947 he was the Consultant to the Pacific Coast Council on Intercultural Education and Intercultural Projects of the San Diego City Schools. In 1947 he became a part-time clinical psychologist for the West Virginia Bureau of Mental Hygiene until 1968. From 1948 until 1953 Canady was a part-time clinical psychologist for the Mental Health Unit at the Veteran's Administration in Huntington, West Virginia. The Alpha Chapter of Omega Psi Phi Fraternity honored Canady as Man of the Year in 1949. In 1950

he was the designated diplomat of the American Board of Examiners in Professional Psychology. Kappa Alpha Psi Fraternity presented Canady with the Middle Eastern Provincial Achievement Award in 1951. Canady was appointed chairman of the department of psychology at the West Virginia Academy of Science in 1952–53 and again from 1955 until 1956. He had also been chairman of the department of psychology for the American Teacher's Association from 1938 until 1945.

Though not much is known about his personal life, Canady had two children. Herman Canady Jr. was a prominent West Virginian in his own right, having been the first black student to attend the historically white Charleston High in Charleston, West Virginia, and the second African American to graduate from the West Virginia University law school. In 1982 he was appointed circuit court judge of Kanawha County, the first African American to hold the honor, and in 2001 served as president of the West Virginia Judicial Association.

Canady died in 1970 leaving behind a rich legacy. He was responsible in part for the founding of the West Virginia Psychological Association, the West Virginia State Board of Psychological Examiners, and the Charleston West Virginia Guidance Clinic. He was a member of the Sigma Xi fraternity, Kappa Alpha Psi, and Alpha Kappa Delta. Canady was a fellow of the American Academy of the Advancement of Science and an American Psychological Association fellow. He was president of the West Virginia State Psychological Association from 1954 until 1955. Canady belonged to the American Association of University Professors and the West Virginia State Teachers Association. Canady received the Northwestern University Alumni Merit Award and he was awarded an honorary doctorate from Western Virginia State College. Canady's research on IQ has endured as a model of how to examine intellectual aptitude without disregard for any variables.

FURTHER READING

Canady, Herman G. *The Effect of "Rapport" on the I.Q.: A New Approach to the Problem of Racial Psychology*. Journal of Negro Education 5, no. 2 (Apr 1936): 209–219.

Parham, Thomas A. *The Psychology of Blacks: An African Centered Perspective*, 3rd ed. (1999).

Valencia, Richard R., and Lisa Suzuki. *Intelligence Testing and Minority Students: Foundations, Performance Factors and Assessment Issues* (2000).

SAFIYA DALILAH HOSKINS

Candy (?–1693), slave and accused witch, was one of the few blacks in colonial New England to be born in the English colony of Barbados. Candy came to Salem Village, Massachusetts, with her owner Margarett Hawke sometime in the years immediately preceding the notorious witchcraft panic of 1692. As with many of the key players in the Salem witch trials, Candy has left little in the historical record other than the accusations against her, court testimony, and the judgment against her. Still, even this small amount of information is compelling. There were strong economic and political ties between Salem and Barbados, resting on the shipping industry and trade in slave-manufactured goods, particularly sugar and cotton. In fact the Reverend Samuel Parris and his famous Amerindian slave Tituba also were from Barbados and it was in his household that the witch panic of 1692 began.

On 2 July 1692 Candy was arrested for the crime of witchcraft in a later wave of accusations made by Mary Wallcot and Ann Putnam. Ann Putnam was the twelve year old who was one of the first afflicted in Salem. Her name appears over four hundred times in the Salem Witchcraft court documents and she was famous for her violent, physical reaction to the accused; eighteen year old Mary Walcott was also a frequent accuser. It is interesting and no doubt significant that Candy was not arrested in the first round of accusation, as the slave woman Tituba had been; neither being a person of color or a slave, it appeared, was enough to automatically attract the attention of the accusing girls. Once arrested and examined, however, Candy used her position as an outsider to her advantage. Unlike the only other black woman arrested, Mary Black, Candy confessed to her activity as a witch in some detail. She did not provide the sophisticated symbolic imagery of the devil and his color-coded animal familiars—such as the black dog, the yellow bird, and the red rat—as Tituba had done, rather offering material evidence of her Satanic actions. While spectral evidence was being used to convict others, Candy turned over physical objects that she asserted were part of her witch practice, including two pieces of cloth that she used for sympathetic magic in the manner of voodoo dolls. In the trial transcript there was dramatic evidence of the efficacy of these objects—three girls (Mary Warren, Deliverance Hobbs, and Abigail Hobbs) were afflicted by the pinching of the cloth, and when "a bit of one of the rags being set on fire, the afflicted all said they were burned, and cried out dreadfully" (*Salem Witchcraft Papers*, vol. 1). Candy also displayed bits of grass and cheese that she said she used for magical purposes. All of these are evidence of sympathetic magical practices but not necessarily of Satanic power to torment through mere will and spectral projection.

While Candy's confessions show a strong understanding of European notions of witchcraft (and possibly African sorcery), her use of the court to accuse her mistress is of even greater significance. As an alien, a woman, and a slave she could be seen-as powerless, and yet she was able to use her status to resist punishment in an effective fashion—she tied her fate to that of her free white owner. Her 4-July 1692 testimony includes the following exchange:

Q. Candy, are you a witch?
A. Candy, no witch in her country. Candy's mother no witch. Candy no witch Barbados. This country, mistress give Candy witch.
Q. Did your mistress make you a witch in this country?
A. Yes, in this country mistress give Candy witch. (Salem Witchcraft Papers, vol. 1).

Understanding the power of the Essex County community's belief in witchcraft, Candy saved her own life by cleverly casting blame upon her owner, Margarett Hawkes, and by confessing to witchcraft but not to bringing Caribbean or African magic into Salem. It is significant that Candy denied her witchcraft as having roots in Barbados and, by extension, Africa. Many white colonials viewed Africans and Native Americans and their religious ceremonies as naturally connected to the demonic. In one simple statement, Candy asserted that she was bedeviled by a white Christian woman and not the other way around, an argument that might be expected to carry great weight since as a slave she by definition occupied a position of subjection. The truth of her testimony appeared to be corroborated by the spectral evidence offered by the accusing girls. All of this served to place Hawkes in jeopardy: "the black man and Mrs. Hawkes and the negro [Candy] stood by the puppets or rags and pinched them, and then they [the girls] were afflicted" (*Salem Witchcraft Papers*, vol. 1). Candy's testimony implicating Hawkes played upon Puritan expectations:

Q. What did your mistress do to make you a witch?
A. Mistress bring book and pen and ink, make Candy write in it.
Q. What did you write in it?—She took a pen and ink and upon a book or paper made a mark. (Salem Witchcraft Papers, vol. 1)

Candy was led to Satan directly by her mistress through the classical method of signing the devil's book. In the end, as were all others who confessed, Candy was found not guilty of her crimes. She had successfully survived the onslaught that took many innocent lives. With the end of the trials Candy disappeared from the historical record and from popular memory, usurped by Tituba as the famous woman of color from Salem.

FURTHER READING

Boyer, Paul, and Stephen Nissenbaum, eds. *The Salem Witchcraft Papers: Verbatim Transcripts of the Legal Documents of the Salem Witchcraft Outbreak of 1692* (1977).

Cracker, Wendel. "Spectral Evidence, Non-Spectral Acts of Witchcraft, and Confession at Salem in 1692," *Historical Journal* 40.2 (1997).

Salem Witchcraft papers. Available at http://etext. virginia.edu/salem/witchcraft/texts/transcripts.html.

TIMOTHY J. MCMILLAN

Cannady, Beatrice Morrow (9 Jan. 1889–19 Aug. 1974), editor and civil rights activist, was born Beatrice Hulon Morrow in Littig, Texas. She was one of the fourteen children of George Morrow, a farmer, and Mary Francis Carter. Little is known about Cannady's childhood, but she reputedly graduated from Wiley College in Marshall, Texas, in 1908. She taught briefly in Louisiana and Oklahoma, though her passion was voice and piano, which she studied at the University of Chicago in the summer of 1908 and 1909.

Her decision to leave Illinois in the spring of 1912 and move to Portland, Oregon—a city with just one thousand African Americans—was inspired by a long-distance relationship with Edward Cannady, a "hat-check man" at the elegant Portland Hotel and a cofounder of *The Advocate*, a newspaper founded in 1903 for African Americans. She abandoned her dream of becoming an opera singer, cashed in her return train ticket, and married Edward in June 1912. They were together for eighteen years and had two children, George and Ivan, before divorcing in 1930.

Shortly after their wedding, Beatrice Cannady began working as *The Advocate's* business manager, associate editor, and editorial and news writer. She seemed to thrive on the challenges of publishing a weekly paper, and used the publication to "boost" African American culture, businesses, and religion.

Cannady also found herself drawn to social reform. In 1914 she helped found the Portland branch of the National Association for the Advancement of Colored People (NAACP) and served as its first secretary. Two years later she sued the Portland school board for its practice of segregating African Americans at public swimming pools at two local elementary schools, but the case was dismissed. Undaunted, Cannady turned to other means to counteract stereotypes and eliminate race antipathy. She gave hundreds of lectures to civic and religious groups, as well as to Oregon high school and college students, and was on many occasions invited to fill church pulpits. Her objective was to educate white audiences about African American contributions to history, art, and literature. Cannady invited students to her home to continue the conversation about race relations and encouraged people to borrow from her extensive personal library that included copies of the *Crisis* and other publications, sheet music for spirituals, books about black history, and signed works by authors such as LANGSTON HUGHES.

Sunday afternoon teas, often attended by several hundred people of various races, ethnicities, and religions, were another way for Cannady to promote better race relations. Sometimes the teas, held at her northeast Portland home, welcomed visitors like the NAACP's WILLIAM PICKENS. Other events were held in memory of the abolitionist and civil rights activist FREDERICK DOUGLASS, to discuss the poetry of PAUL LAURENCE DUNBAR, or to celebrate Negro History Week. At each gathering the goal was to combine entertainment, culture, and history with local, national, and international politics to inform and educate guests.

Cannady also took advantage of the new medium of radio to discuss African American progress, history, and accomplishments with white audiences. She was convinced that race antipathy could be eliminated if people were sufficiently educated, and Negro History Week, suggested by the historian CARTER GODWIN WOODSON in 1926 and designed to be a national event, evolving into Black History Month, offered the perfect occasion for her broadcasts.

But Cannady did not limit her outreach to Oregonians. In August 1927 she was invited to New York City, where she served as a hostess for W. E. B. DuBois's Fourth Pan-African Congress and delivered a talk on the final day about "Negro education." Upon her return to Portland she organized a "miniature" Congress that featured reports from the previous meeting, local speakers, and addresses by individuals such as the noted clubwoman NETTIE J. ASBERRY, music, exhibits, and poetry. The event received considerable media coverage in both the white and black press. The following summer, the NAACP's JAMES WELDON JOHNSON invited Cannady to Los Angeles to speak about "Negro Womanhood as a Power in the Development of the Race and the Nation" at the NAACP's nineteenth annual conference. While in Southern California she addressed a number of white audiences on subjects such as the work of the organization.

These activities—combined with her position as editor of *The Advocate* and the novelty of being the first black woman to practice law in Oregon after graduating in 1922 from Portland's Northwestern College of Law—enhanced her standing in the city. By 1929 she was known as the unofficial ambassador of goodwill, and the Portland Council of Churches nominated her for the Harmon Foundation's annual award for Distinguished Achievement among Negroes in the field of race relations. Her role as spokesperson for the African American community was particularly important during the 1920s, when the Ku Klux Klan was active in Oregon. She challenged Governor Ben W. Olcott to prevent the Klan from holding public demonstrations and met with the Portland mayor George L. Baker several times to protest D. W. Griffith's film *The Birth of a Nation*, which was shown repeatedly in the city between 1915 and 1931. During those tumultuous years Cannady used the *Advocate* to keep readers informed about the status of race relations in Oregon, criticize the federal government for failing to take action to protect African American citizens from lynchings, and editorialize against the "vicious" film that glorified the formation of the KKK.

Cannady attracted media attention again in 1936, when she became the first African American woman in Oregon to run for elected office. Although she did not garner enough votes to advance to the general election, eight thousand people—almost all of whom were white—endorsed her bid for state representative. The defeat may have factored in to her decision later that year to move to Southern California. Cannady also may have wanted to be closer to family who had settled there, and she had recently ended a brief second marriage to the *Advocate* employee Yancy Jerome Franklin 1931.

Cannady spent the rest of her life pursuing the things she was passionate about, but in a far less public way. She wrote for the *Precinct Reporter*, a newspaper in Perris, California, and held informal interracial gatherings at the Perris ranch she shared with her third husband, Ruben Taylor. Six years after her death in Los Angeles, the African American newspaper the *Portland Observer* paid tribute to Cannady's long career, calling her a "combatant in the seemingly interminable fight for civil rights for Black Americans" (9 Oct. 1980).

FURTHER READING

Beatrice Morrow Cannady's scrapbook is housed in the Research Library of the Oregon Historical Society in Portland, Oregon.

Mangun, Kimberley. "'As Citizens of Portland We Must Protest': Beatrice Morrow Cannady and the African American Response to D. W. Griffith's 'Masterpiece,'" *Oregon Historical Quarterly* (Fall, 2006).

Mangun, Kimberley. "The (Oregon) *Advocate*: Boosting the Race and Portland, Too," *American Journalism* (Winter, 2006).

Taylor, Quintard. "Susie Revels Cayton, Beatrice Morrow Cannady, and the Campaign for Social Justice in the Pacific Northwest," in *African American Women Confront the West: 1600–2000* (2003).

KIMBERLEY MANGUN

Cannon, George Dows (16 Oct. 1902–31 Aug. 1986), physician and political activist, was born in Jersey City, New Jersey, the son of GEORGE E. CANNON and Genevieve Wilkinson. His father was a prominent and politically connected physician who graduated from Lincoln University in Pennsylvania and the New York Homeopathic Medical College. His mother, a teacher, was descended from a leading Washington, D.C., family that had been free before the Civil War. Cannon and his sister, Gladys, grew up in an eighteen-room red brick house on a main Jersey City thoroughfare where their parents regularly received a retinue of prestigious visitors, including BOOKER T. WASHINGTON, numerous doctors from the all-black National Medical Association, and several Republican Party officeholders. Cannon greatly admired his father and emulated his professional and political involvements.

At his father's alma mater, Lincoln University, a Presbyterian institution, Cannon performed acceptably but without academic distinction. He scored well enough in his premedical courses, however, to be eligible for medical school upon graduation from Lincoln in 1924. Cannon gained admission to Columbia University's College of Physicians and Surgeons through the intervention of his father, who knew the president of the university. Despite enduring racially prejudiced professors, Cannon completed his freshman year with passing grades on all of his exams. His father's accidental death in April 1925 kept him from classes for a short time. Although Cannon fulfilled all of his class and laboratory assignments, his brief absence became a pretext for the dean to fail him in all of his courses. Cannon believed that racial prejudice and the manner of his admission had stirred a dislike for him. Because the Howard and Meharry medical schools would not admit him during the following fall, he entered Howard's graduate school to study for a master's degree in Zoology with the famed ERNEST EVERETT JUST. Impressed with Cannon's proficiency and saddened by his sorrowful experience at Columbia, Just recommended him to Rush Medical College in Chicago. Though the staff at Rush was less racist than that at Columbia, Cannon and the other black student, LEONIDAS BERRY, were told that each had been admitted so that the other one would not be lonely. Nonetheless, Cannon excelled in his work and made up for the lost time resulting from his ouster at Columbia. He was diagnosed with tuberculosis, however, during the final month before graduation. Treatment at a sanatorium in Chicago for nearly two years preceded his reentry to Rush. He earned an MD on 18 December 1934 after an internship at Chicago's all-black Provident Hospital. Continued health problems put Cannon into the Waverly Hills Hospital, a Louisville, Kentucky, sanatorium from 1934 through 1936, where he received treatment and pursued a medical residency. In the meantime, he had married his college sweetheart, Lillian Mosely, on 25 December 1931. The uncertainties surrounding his health compelled the couple to forgo parenthood, and they never had children.

Despite Cannon's fragile health, he vigorously developed as a leading New York City physician. He did not want to be bound to Harlem Hospital for staff privileges, so he tried throughout the late 1930s and 1940s for admittance to other hospitals. He was accepted on the staff of the Hospital for Joint Diseases in 1944. At the Triboro Tuberculosis Hospital, a racist physician, who opposed his appointment, eventually died and thus cleared the way for Cannon's appointment in 1947. He also gained privileges to treat and admit patients at the hospital for the Daughters of Israel. Cannon still encountered racist roadblocks at other facilities. He targeted hospitals with religious affiliations to admit black physicians to their staffs. Catholic, Episcopal, and Presbyterian hospitals rebuffed him. In the latter case, his membership at St. James Presbyterian Church in Harlem did not matter. At Lutheran Hospital a sympathetic

white colleague made Cannon his substitute in the x-ray department, but hospital authorities overruled him. Jewish hospitals were more receptive. Mt. Sinai Hospital initially brought in Cannon as an assistant adjunct radiologist. Over time his radiology training at Triboro and his success at Mt. Sinai earned Cannon the respect he deserved among his black and white peers.

Cannon engaged in other struggles for black professionals and patients. He belonged to the integrated Physicians Forum, an alternative organization to the racially restrictive county medical societies and their parent group, the American Medical Association (AMA). Forum doctors focused on health care for the disadvantaged and fought racism in medical institutions. In Harlem he joined the Upper Manhattan Medical Group, a branch of the Health Insurance Plan of the City of New York, which rendered services through a prepaid health delivery system. Through the Physicians Forum, Cannon challenged the fee-for-service payment practice that most AMA doctors preferred. The improvement of conditions at Harlem Hospital also drew Cannon's attention. As president of the all-black Manhattan Central Medical Society and chairman of its Subcommittee on Health and Hospitals, Cannon exerted pressure upon city officials, who then corrected the lack of x-ray equipment, the absence of psychiatric services, and the inadequate number of surgeons to perform tonsillectomies. They also pressed city officials to open to blacks all municipal nursing schools beyond the two at Harlem and Lincoln hospitals.

Though a maverick Democrat, Cannon did not hesitate to form coalitions with radicals, including communists. As chair of the Non-Partisan Citizens' Committee in 1943 and 1945, he backed the successful candidacy of BENJAMIN JEFFERSON DAVIS JR., a Communist, as Harlem's representative to City Council. Cannon himself was asked to run for city council and the state senate, both positions that he could have easily won. Whenever his party seemed too passive on civil rights matters, he supported candidates from other political groups. In 1948, for example, Henry A. Wallace, the Progressive Party presidential candidate, in Cannon's opinion, was a stronger advocate for civil rights than either Governor Thomas E. Dewey, the Republican, or President Harry Truman, the Democrat. Hence, Cannon became the chairman of the Harlem Wallace-for-President Committee. Cannon held that it was possible to work with communists and Progressives on matters of race.

Though he eschewed radical ideologies, Cannon's involvement with the Physicians Forum and its efforts for government-guaranteed health care and his political cooperation with radicals suggested to zealous anticommunists that Cannon's political sympathies were suspect. He was an enemy of Russia, he often said. Nonetheless, anyone who wished to work with him on black advancement was always a welcome ally.

Cannon's affiliations with the NAACP and the NAACP Legal Defense Fund (LDF) complemented his political activism. He served as the chairman of the life membership campaign for the New York state NAACP, and between 1956 and 1966 he held the same position for the national organization. At a dinner that he attended with Vice President Richard M. Nixon, Cannon planned to challenge the future president to buy an NAACP life membership. Before Cannon could successfully press his point, a black Nixon supporter said that the vice president should not pursue this symbolic action. Cannon, however, never forgot Nixon's affront to the NAACP. In 1962 Cannon became the secretary of the LDF, a position he held until 1984. Hence, during the height of the civil rights movement, he sided with the integrationist thrust of the NAACP and the LDF. The Black Power movement never drew support from Cannon.

His social and political activism extended to higher education. In 1947 Cannon became an alumni trustee of Lincoln University in Pennsylvania and later chairman of the board of trustees. His Lincoln classmate HORACE MANN BOND had become in 1946 the first black president of the university, and each believed that Lincoln could become a model for racially integrated higher education. Though Cannon did not share Bond's intense zeal for African studies and forging stronger connections with emerging African nations, both understood that training leaders for various professions on both sides of the Atlantic was a crucial mission for their institution. Cannon developed positions on the role of faculty, continuation of the theological seminary, the need for greater alumni support, and the necessity of confronting the hostility of whites in neighboring Oxford, Pennsylvania. Cannon's frequent and detailed correspondence with Bond and his several successors showed a deep involvement in the affairs of Lincoln University that lasted through the 1980s. When Lincoln became the principal trustee of the Barnes Foundation, a repository of priceless modern art in suburban Philadelphia, Cannon delved into another area of educational and cultural affairs that further distinguished his alma mater.

When Cannon died in 1986, his Rush classmate Leonidas H. Berry eulogized Cannon and observed that his fragile health gave him a special empathy for his patients and motivated his extensive efforts for the uplift of African Americans. He lived to be an octogenarian despite diagnoses that belied the possibility for such a long and consequential career.

FURTHER READING

The George D. Cannon Papers are held at the Schomburg Center for Research in Black Culture of the New York Public Library. See also the George D. Cannon Files, Horace Mann Bond Papers, Lincoln University, Pennsylvania.

James, Daniel. "Cannon the Progressive." *New Republic*, 18 Oct. 1948.

DENNIS C. DICKERSON

Cannon, George Epps (7 July 1869–6 Apr. 1925), physician and social and political activist, was born one of twelve children to Barnett Glenn Cannon and Mary Tucker Cannon, a former slave. He was born in Fishdam (later Carlisle), South Carolina. Northern Presbyterians offered education for Cannon at the Brainerd Institute in South Carolina and at Lincoln University in Pennsylvania. Hearing that J. C. Price, a prominent African American educator and African Methodist Episcopal Zion (AMEZ) minister, was a Lincoln graduate convinced Cannon to attend the Presbyterian school. Work as a Pullman porter covered his expenses at Lincoln, and as an athletic and abstemious undergraduate he emerged as a leader among his peers in the class of 1893. He became one of nine classmates to enter medicine, and like another Lincoln graduate, Eugene P. Roberts, class of 1891, he entered the New York Homeopathic Medical College and Flower Hospital. Again his position as a porter helped to pay for his education; as an attendant in the private car of a successful businessman, Cannon earned enough to pay his fees. He received his MD in 1900 and settled permanently in Jersey City, New Jersey, where his oldest brother, John, already resided.

Cannon established a thriving medical practice in which most of his patients were immigrant whites, with a smaller number of African Americans. Although he belonged to the New Jersey Homeopathic Society, Cannon's main loyalties lay with the National Medical Association (NMA) and its local affiliate, the North Jersey Medical Society. Moreover, a merged group of NMA affiliates in the Northeast formed the Interstate Medical Association, and Cannon served as its president. Founded in 1895, the NMA provided African American doctors, dentists, and pharmacists with professional networks that exclusionary white groups denied them. He regularly contributed articles to the *Journal of the National Medical Association*, especially on colon and pelvic diseases. He was involved in naming three commissions (sponsored by the National Medical Association) to investigate tuberculosis, hookworm, and pellagra in the African American population. He also presented papers at NMA national meetings and at the local society. He became chairman of the NMA's executive board and at various times spoke on civic and political issues relevant to the membership.

During World War I, in an NMA article titled "The Negro Medical Profession and the United States Army," Cannon discussed his protests to the War Department about the exclusion of African American physicians from the Medical Reserve Corps; instead, these physicians had been drafted into the regular army without officer commissions. By the time Cannon navigated bureaucratic mazes within the federal government, the secretary of war had responded by saying that no vacancies existed for African American physicians and that the war had ended, thus making the matter moot. In 1925, however, Cannon and his NMA colleagues successfully lobbied to block plans to hire an all-white medical staff at the federally funded Tuskegee Veterans Hospital in Alabama. Additionally, Cannon interacted with the Rockefeller Foundation, which agreed to administer Rosenwald Fellowships for African American medical students.

Politics offered Cannon opportunities to increase his influence and benefit African Americans. Perhaps an election loss for the state legislature had persuaded him to become a political broker. While a fellow Lincoln alumnus and NMA officer, Walter G. Alexander, served in the legislature and passed important laws on public health, Cannon, through his leadership of the state's African American Republicans, forged alliances with New Jersey Republican officials. At times Cannon delved into factional fights within his own party. A senatorial primary in 1924, for example, found Cannon and Alexander supporting rival candidates and stirred bitter feelings among them and others. Though Cannon's candidate won, he organized a "harmony" conference to unify the state's African American leaders.

These state activities paralleled Cannon's national Republican Party involvements. He was head of the National Colored Republican Conference that endorsed Calvin Coolidge for president but criticized congressional incumbents for their poor records on antilynching laws, Haiti, Liberia, and other issues relevant to African Americans. Cannon also successfully vied for a delegate seat to the 1924 Republican National Convention, where he seconded Coolidge's presidential nomination. The publisher of the *Pittsburgh Courier*, ROBERT L. VANN, spoke for many when he castigated Cannon for failing to give a strong speech in favor of African American civil rights. For Cannon, however, his convention appearance confirmed his growing reputation as a broker within the Republican Party.

Cannon's innocuous comments about Coolidge's colorblind commitment to civil rights, offensive to Vann, obscured Cannon's persistent advocacy and actions for African American advancement. In Jersey City, for example, Cannon's efforts were key to the hiring of black policemen. When traveling in the south to an NMA meeting in 1914, Cannon encountered second-class accommodations on the Southern Railway and published his letter of protest to a company official in the *New York Age*. He also submitted to the newspaper the company's apology and drew a commendation from the editorial page for his public stand against segregation in interstate travel. In another meeting at the Mother AMEZ Church in Harlem, Cannon declared that African Americans must fight for "equal rights and privileges" and that the federal government should enforce the Fourteenth and Fifteenth Amendments as vigorously as the newly enacted Eighteenth Amendment, which outlawed alcohol.

As president of the Committee of One Hundred of Hudson County, New Jersey, Cannon led a protest in 1915 against a congressional bill to ban intermarriage in the District of Columbia. In 1916 the same group, in cooperation with the Federation of Colored Organizations of New Jersey, pressed the state legislature to prohibit plays and other productions that denigrated African Americans. Cannon's committee also supported state appropriations for the manual training and industrial school at Bordentown and protested against a separate Negro Welfare Bureau in the state's labor department.

In his involvement with the NAACP, Cannon's Republican ties clashed with his connections to the civil rights organization. In 1925 he resigned from the organization's national board of directors because the NAACP appeared hostile to the

Republican Party, especially to President Coolidge and Senator Walter Edge, Cannon's candidate for re-election from New Jersey. The NAACP had blamed Edge for lack of interest in antilynching legislation, a charge that Cannon strongly denied. Moreover, Cannon blamed the NAACP for lackluster support of Harlem's Republican congressional candidate, Charles H. Roberts, an African American dentist. The NAACP's anti-Republican bias, said Cannon, led it to support the Progressive Party. Despite responses from JAMES WELDON JOHNSON, the head of the NAACP, Cannon withdrew from the board of directors.

Shortly after he settled in Jersey City, Cannon helped to establish Lafayette Presbyterian Church. The few African American worshippers at the First Presbyterian Church desired their own parish, and Cannon in 1900 became a charter member and later an elder of the new church. Often he represented his congregation at meetings of the Presbytery of Jersey City and presented its requests for financial assistance to the body. Eventually he was named to the Committee of Freedmen and to the denomination's National Committee on Missions. He also joined the Afro-American Presbyterian Council, a northern network that met annually. Twice, in 1922 and 1924, he addressed the group: in Pittsburgh on "The State of the Country" and in Jersey City on "Men's Work in the Church." These activities, along with an address to the Interdenominational Ministers' Union of New York and Vicinity on "The Preacher as Viewed from the Pew," reveal Cannon as a respected churchman.

Additionally, Cannon joined the Improved Benevolent and Protective Order of Elks of the World and was an incorporator of the Grand Lodge in 1906. He was a delegate to the national convention in 1907 from Progressive Lodge 35 in Jersey City. Because he disdained how African Americans appeared subservient and stereotyped in the white-controlled cinema, Cannon in 1917–1918 founded the FREDERICK DOUGLASS Film Company. An African American theatrical company, the Lafayette Players, acted in the first film, *Winning His Suit*. The second film was a documentary, *The Negro Soldier in World War I*. When white film distributors pressured African American theater owners to drop Douglass Company productions, the company collapsed.

After a trip to Philadelphia for a Lincoln University Alumni Association dinner, Cannon took a city bus to his home. As he stepped from the bus, the vehicle accelerated and hurled him to the curb. The fall broke his ribs and gave him a concussion, and he succumbed to a pulmonary embolism a few days later. That the Coolidge Administration was considering him for a diplomatic position to either Haiti or Liberia testifies to his national importance in the medical, social, and political affairs of African Americans. His wife, Genevieve Wilkinson Cannon, and two children, George Dows and Gladys, survived him.

FURTHER READING
Dickerson, Dennis C. "George E. Cannon: Black Churchman, Physician, and Republican Politician," *Journal of Presbyterian History* 51.4 (Winter 1973): 411–432.
Obituary: *New York Times*, 7 Apr. 1925.

DENNIS C. DICKERSON

Cannon, Gus (12 Sept. 1883–15 Oct. 1979), musician, medicine show entertainer, and jug band leader, was born on the Henderson Newell plantation north of Red Banks (Marshall County), Mississippi, the son of the former slave John Cannon and Ellen (maiden name unknown), sharecroppers. Cannon, one of at least nine children, left home when he was still in his early teens and began a life as an itinerant laborer, working in agriculture as well as at a number of menial jobs, including river roustabout, plumber's assistant, ditch digger, and railroad worker. From an early age Cannon also made money playing music.

Cannon's first instrument was a banjo that he made from a tin dough pan and a discarded guitar neck. He got his next banjo from a brother who had won it gambling. Since this instrument had a raccoon-hide head that would not remain taut, Cannon carried "a gang of paper" in his pockets so that he could start a small fire to retighten the raccoon skin before playing (Cannon, Stax LP).

"Old John Booker" was Cannon's first song; he learned it from an older man, Saul Russell, who lived along Mississippi's Sunflower River. Wandering from place to place in search of work Cannon met Bud Jackson, from Alabama, from whom he learned to finger pick a jig in 6/8 time, as well as the song "Going 'Round the Mountain." He also learned to play slide guitar from Alex Lee of Clarksdale, Mississippi. Cannon later applied the slide technique to the banjo, as in his first recording, the Delta standard "Poor Boy Long Ways from Home" for Paramount Records in 1927.

Reports vary on how exactly Cannon came to play the jug. Some state that he learned to play from Chappie Dennison, who played a piece of pipe, from Jim Guffin, a jug blower, or—as Cannon himself stated in a 1972 interview—from Bob Dennison, who played a "quill pipe" on Ninth Street in Nashville, Tennessee. Regardless of the instrument Cannon was taught on, the technique is the same, the real instrument being the musician's mouth, with the jug, bottle, or pipe used only for amplification. Eventually, Cannon played a jug made from sheet metal and equipped with a neck harness, leaving his hands free to play the banjo.

Cannon first came to Memphis, Tennessee, about 1913, with his first wife Bessie. By 1920 Memphis had become Cannon's permanent home base and would remain so for the rest of his life.

Cannon played many instruments including the banjo, jug, kazoo, fiddle, guitar, piano, cornet, and trombone, and his versatility as a musician, comedian, and juggler made him a favorite with audiences of the traveling medicine shows for which he performed. Among the shows he traveled with were those of Dr. Stokey (who, unlike most of these "Doctors," was African American), Dr. E. B. Miller, Dr. W. B. Milton (these last two may have been the same), Dr. Benson, Dr. C. Hankenson, Dr. Willie Lewis, and Dr. Streak. These shows traveled and performed extensively throughout the Southern and Midwestern states. Cannon told the British blues scholar Paul Oliver, "I worked with a man out of Louisville, I worked through Mississippi, I worked through Virginia, I worked through Alabama, I worked through Mobile, Gulfport, Bay St. Louis—far as I been down, playin' my banjo on them doctor shows" (Oliver, 85).

Cannon accompanied his fellow Memphis-based medicine show performers and blues musicians FURRY LEWIS and Jim Jackson to Chicago in 1927, where the three auditioned for Vocalion Records's Mayo Williams. Lewis and Jackson recorded for Vocalion, but Williams had Cannon record for the Paramount label, six songs either solo or accompanied by the ragtime guitar master Blind Blake, and released under Cannon's medicine show stage name, Banjo Joe. At this same session Cannon accompanied Blind Blake on his classic recording of "He's in the Jail House Now." These are the earliest known recordings by Cannon, who always insisted that he had recorded for Columbia or Victor Records in Mississippi during the first decade of the twentieth century.

The following year, 1928, Cannon, accompanied by Noah Lewis and Ashley Thompson, recorded for Victor as the Cannon Jug Stompers. On later Jug Stompers recordings, Elijah Avery or Hosea Woods replaced Thompson on guitar, but the influential harmonica player Lewis and the jug and banjo rhythms provided by Cannon remained the defining features of their recordings. Using the name Beale Street Boys on Brunswick Records in 1929, Cannon also recorded as a duet with Hosea Woods. The Cannon Jug Stompers recorded twenty-six songs for Victor between January 1928 and November 1930. The Beale Street Boys's session for Brunswick Records resulted in one record being released.

After 1930 Cannon continued to play either solo or in small jug band ensembles, on the streets, and for white parties. He did not record again until 1956, when Sam Charters visited Memphis in search of blues artists who had made records prior to World War II. Charters recorded Cannon's repertoire, some of which was released by the Folkways label. Cannon recorded a limited edition LP for the fledgling Stax label (soon to play an important role in the dissemination of Memphis soul music) in 1963 and recorded his last commercial sides for Adelphi in 1969 (including his composition "Lela," named for his third wife—nothing is known of his second wife, Olyda). Cannon appeared in an early Hollywood film *Hallelujah!* (1929), as well as in several documentaries, including *The Blues* (1963), *The Devil's Music—A History of the Blues* (1976), and *Good Mornin' Blues* (1978).

One of the oldest of the first generation of black musicians to record commercially, Cannon's performance repertoire included a diverse mixture of old fiddle songs, minstrel show pieces, rags, pop songs, and blues. The music that Cannon recorded in the 1920s was typical of the music played by Southern, usually rural, black musicians in the early years of the twentieth century, before the record companies helped make blues the dominant secular musical genre in African American culture.

Scholars have remarked on the deep African roots of Cannon's music. Both the blues researcher Sam Charters and the folklorist Harold Courlander commented on the similarity of Cannon's banjo playing to that of the West African *halam*: "Gus Cannon played banjo passages that resembled in pitch, pattern, rhythm, and tempo the sounds produced on West African lutes" (Courlander, 214). Courlander thought that this was especially true of Cannon's version of the first song he had learned, "Old John Booker." The Ethnomusicologist David Evans claimed that Cannon's jug blowing was also an African cultural survival: "The jug and kazoo … were derived from African 'voice disguisers,' which were used frequently in connection with masked rituals to represent spirit voices" (Evans, 39).

Though his work was firmly based in ancient tradition, Cannon was also an important innovator. According to the folklorist Cecelia Conway, Cannon "developed an unorthodox 'picking'—not 'stroking'—style, which contributed to his becoming a famous jug band leader" (Conway, 125).

Sam and Kirk McGee and other old-time white recording artists of the 1920s and 1930s studied Cannon's early records; folk revivalists of the 1950s and early 1960s were first exposed to Cannon's music through the commercially released field recordings made by Charters in the mid-1950s. The 1963 recording of Cannon's composition "Walk Right In" by the folk revivalist group the Rooftop Singers rose to the top spot on *Billboard*'s sales chart, bringing Cannon new recognition. Other "folk" and rock and roll groups—from the Jim Kweskin Jug Band to the Lovin' Spoonful to the Grateful Dead—recorded their own renditions of Cannon's and the Jug Stompers's songs.

Following the Rooftop Singers's hit recording of his best-known song, "Walk Right In," Cannon was the subject of several stories in the national media. He made a few concert appearances outside of Memphis and continued to play locally for white functions such as private parties, riverboat excursions, and blues festivals. By 1970 Cannon's health had seriously declined and he rarely appeared in public.

As the leader of the best of Memphis's great jug bands, Cannon had a profound influence on American music. The journalist Bruce Cook observed that if there was such a thing as a distinctively "Memphis Sound" (a term used by Memphis-based record companies to promote local soul music), "it originated with the rhythmic rumbles that issued forth from those Beale Street jugs" (Cook, 121). Even more originated with these jug bands according to the jazz writer Max Harrison: "It seems plausible that such ensembles are the earliest known direct ancestors of the jazz band" (Harrison, 229).

FURTHER READING

Biographical information is based on Fred J. Hay and William Lynds's May 1972 interview with Cannon, as well as Cannon's narration on his Stax LP *Walk Right In* (1963) and Bengt Olsson's liner notes to the Herwin LP *Cannon's Jug Stompers: The Complete Works in Chronological Order, 1927–1930* (1973).

Charters, Samuel B. "Workin' on the Building: Roots and Influences," in *Nothing but the Blues: The Music and the Musicians*, ed. Lawrence Cohn (1993).

Conway, Cecilia. *African Banjo Echoes in Appalachia: A Study of Folk Traditions* (1995).

Cook, Bruce. *Listen to the Blues* (1973).

Courlander, Harold. *Negro Folk Music U.S.A.* (1970)

Evans, David. "Goin' up the Country: Blues in Texas and the Deep South," in *Nothing but the Blues: The Music and the Musicians*, ed. Lawrence Cohn (1993).

Harris, Sheldon. *Blues Who's Who: A Biographical Dictionary of Blues Singers* (1979).

Harrison, Max. "Jazz," in *The New Grove Gospel, Blues, and Jazz*, ed. Paul Oliver (1986).

Oliver, Paul. *Conservation with the Blues* (1965).

Olsson, Bengt. *Memphis Blues and Jug Bands* (1970).

Wilkins, Lane. *Walk Right In: Based upon the Life and Times of Gus Cannon* (1995).

Obituary: *Living Blues* 44 (1979): 57.

DISCOGRAPHY

Dixon, Robert M. W., John Godrich, and Howard W. Rye. *Blues and Gospel Records, 1890–1943* (1997).

Leadbitter, Mike, and Neil Slaven. *Blues Records 1943–1970: A Selective Discography* (1987).

FRED J. HAY

Cannon, Katie Geneva (3 Jan. 1950–), Presbyterian minister, educator, and womanist ethicist, was born in Concord, North Carolina, the daughter of Corine Emmanuelette Lytle, a domestic and Avon saleswoman, and Esau Cannon, a millworker, both of whom were elders in the local Presbyterian church. Cannon grew up with three sisters, three brothers, her parents, and her extended family in the Fishertown community, a part of the rural, segregated town of Kannapolis, North Carolina, the home of Cannon Mills. Her earliest work was as a domestic, cleaning the homes of nearby white mill workers. At the age of seventeen Cannon graduated from George Washington Carver High School and then enrolled at nearby Barber-Scotia College, where she graduated magna cum laude in 1971 with a B.S. in Elementary Education.

In August 1971 Cannon enrolled in Johnson C. Smith Theological Seminary at the Interdenominational Theological Center (ITC) in Atlanta, where Dean James H. Costen encouraged her to abandon her plans for a two-year Christian education degree and transfer to the three-year ministerial degree and pursue ordination as a pastor. From 1972 to 1974 Cannon held a Rockefeller Protestant Fellowship from the Fund for Theological

Education, and in 1973 she won the Isaac B. Clark Preaching Award from the ITC. Cannon graduated with an MDiv in 1974, and on 23 April 1974 the Presbytery of Catawba ordained her, making her the first African American woman to be ordained as a minister in the United Presbyterian Church in the United States of America.

Cannon enrolled the following fall in a Ph.D. program in Hebrew Bible at Union Theological Seminary in New York, where she received fellowships from the Fund for Theological Education, the Ford Foundation, and the Roothbert Fund. From 1975 to 1977 she served as pastor of East Harlem's Presbyterian Church of Ascension while she completed her doctoral course work. She then changed her focus from Hebrew Bible to theological ethics and worked with the feminist theologian Beverly Harrison. In her dissertation Cannon sought to combine feminism with theological ethics as she studied the work of ZORA NEALE HURSTON and attempted, as she later wrote in her dissertation, "to relate the Christian doctrines preached in the Black Church to the suffering, oppression and exploitation of Black people in the society" (Cannon 1983, 1). While she continued to work on her dissertation in Christian Ethics, Cannon served as instructor of Christian theological ethics at New York Theological Seminary. In 1983 she became the first African American woman to receive a Ph.D. from Union Theological Seminary.

From 1983 to 1984 Cannon served as a visiting scholar in the woman's studies in religion program at Harvard Divinity School, and she joined the faculty of the nearby Episcopal Divinity School the following year. In 1987–1988 Cannon was honored with a Conant Grant from the Episcopal Church and with the Young Scholar Award from the Association of Theological Schools. In 1992 she moved to Philadelphia to become associate professor of Christian ethics at Temple University, and in July 2001 she became the Annie Scales Rogers Professor of Christian Ethics at Union Theological Seminary–Presbyterian School of Christian Education (Union-PSCE) in Richmond, Virginia. She delivered her inaugural lecture, "The Switching of Robes and Hoods: The Ethical Praxis of Zora Neale Hurston," on 28 January 2004. Cannon has also held a number of significant visiting appointments, including visiting lecturer at Yale Divinity School in 1987, fellow at Radcliffe College's Bunting Institute from 1987 to 1988, visiting professor at Wellesley College in 1991, and Lilly Distinguished Professor of Religion at Davidson College in 2005.

Cannon served on the boards of directors for the Women's Theological Center (Boston) and the Society of Christian Ethics and served as president of the Society for the Study of Black Religion. At the 1997 All Africa Council of Churches in Addis Ababa, Ethiopia, Cannon was a delegate for the Presbyterian Church (USA), and in 1989 she represented the United States at the inaugural meeting of African Women Theologians in Accra, Ghana.

Cannon's landmark essay "The Emergence of Black Feminist Consciousness" was first published in *Feminist Interpretation of the Bible* (1985), edited by Letty M. Russell, and is widely acclaimed as the inaugural work of the womanist movement, which takes its name from a neologism by the writer ALICE WALKER and which is informed by the intersection of feminist theology and black theology. Cannon edited or coedited *God's Fierce Whimsy: Christian Feminism and Theological Education* (1985), *Inheriting Our Mothers' Gardens: Feminist Theology in Third World Perspective* (1988), and *Interpretation for Liberation* (1989). In 1988 Scholar's Press published her revised dissertation, *Black Womanist Ethics*, in the American Academy of Religion Academy series. Cannon republished her most significant articles in *Katie's Canon: Womanism and the Soul of the Black Community* (1995). She contributed to *The Black Studies Reader* (2004), edited by Jacqueline Bobo, et al., *Feminist and Womanist Essays in Reformed Dogmatics* (2006), edited by Amy Plantinga Pauw and Serene Jones, and *Deeper Shades of Purple: Womanism in Religion and Society* (2006), edited by Stacey M. Floyd-Thomas. Other significant works include a study of her former homiletics professor at the ITC, *Teaching Preaching: Isaac Rufus Clark and Black Sacred Rhetoric* (2002), and a study of Hurston's account of the Ruby J. McCollum trial.

FURTHER READING

The Resource Center for Women and Ministry in the South in Greensboro, North Carolina, and Union Theological Seminary–Presbyterian School of Christian Education (Union-PSCE) in Richmond, Virginia, contain archival material related to Cannon's career.

Cannon, Katie Geneva. "The Fruit of My Labor," in *I've Known Rivers: Lives of Loss and Liberation*, ed. Sara Lawrence-Lightfoot (1994).

Cannon, Katie Geneva. *Katie's Canon: Womanism and the Soul of the Black Community* (1995).

Cannon, Katie Geneva. "Resources for a Constructive Ethic for Black Women with Special Attention to the Life and Work of Zora Neale Hurston." Ph.D. diss., 1983.

Brown, Karen V., and Phyllis M. Felton. *African American Presbyterian Clergywomen: The First Twenty-Five Years* (2001).

Risher, Dee Dee, and Katie Cannon. "Giving Forward," *Other Side* (Mar.–Apr. 1997).

DAVID B. MCCARTHY

Canty, Marietta (30 Sept. 1905–9 July 1986), actress, was born in Hartford, Connecticut, to Henry Carl Canty, a city hall elevator operator, and Mary Ann Gamble Canty, a housewife. She was born Mary Etta Canty, but later decided to change her name to Marietta because she felt it was a more memorable name for when she went on Broadway. She was the fourth born of five children (Arnold, Henry Jr., Carl, and Emily). She attended Northeast Elementary School and Hartford Public High School, where she became well known for her excellence in elocution and singing. She was a fervent member of the Metropolitan African Methodist Episcopal Zion Church on Main Street in Hartford, where she also exhibited her exquisite singing voice.

At age eighteen, Marietta was asked to be a last minute replacement for her brother Carl in a Charles S. Gilpin Players Production in Hartford. She was given the pants that her brother was supposed to wear in the play and was then hurried rather haphazardly onto the stage. Thus began her acting career. She became one of fifteen new members of the Gilpin Players. Throughout the 1920s and 1930s, Marietta Canty, with the Gilpin Players, performed original productions as well as their renditions of various traditional, well-known plays. By 1933, Canty was performing on Broadway. While in nursing school (Lincoln Hospital School of Nursing, New York City) she auditioned for a part in *Run Lil' Chillun*, and was awarded a role. Unfortunately, her opportunity to perform on Broadway was delayed for a short time due to the fact that it *Run Lil' Chillun* was made possible only by federal work funds, and in order for Canty to participate in the play, she had to be on welfare. Since she was not in this situation, she could not continue with the production. She temporarily took a job as a governess to support herself.

When Jerry Werlin, a member of the Works Progress Administration Theater Project, saw how well Canty acted in her performances at the Harlem Public Library, he introduced her to John Houseman, who was the director of the project's African American section. It was after an audition with John Houseman that she came back to Broadway. Some of the first plays that she acted in include *Kiss the Boys Goodbye* and *Horse Fever* with Gene Tierney and Ezra Stone, respectively. By 1936, she was in *Correspondent Unknown*, playing the part of the loyal servant Bessie. In 1933, she was able to get a walk-on role in the film version of *The Emperor Jones*.

One of the biggest accomplishments during her extraordinary career came in 1940, when she performed in a stage production of *The Night of January 16th*, in Miami Beach, Florida. It was the first time in the state of Florida that African American actors performed on stage with an all-white cast for an all-white audience. The audience and various critics were highly pleased with Canty's performance. Canty and Kelsey Pharr II, another African American actor in the play, helped make it possible for African Americans to act in more plays and break down the racial barrier.

In 1941, Canty was cast in the play *No Time For Comedy* because of her remarkable performance in the *Night of January 16th*. The producer of *No Time For Comedy*, Francis Lederer, encouraged Canty to act in films. After several screen tests, Marietta Canty appeared in the movie *The Lady Is Willing* in 1942. This was her first film since her walk-on appearance in *The Emperor Jones* in 1933.

Marlene Dietrich, one of the stars of *The Lady Is Willing*, requested in 1942 that Canty have a special part in her next movie, *The Spoilers*, because Dietrich was so impressed with Canty's delightful performance in *The Lady Is Willing*.

Canty appeared in many popular and award-winning movies over the next decade, including *The Magnificent Pope* (1942), *Three Hearts of Julia* (1943), *Irish Eyes Are Smiling* (1944), *Sweet Homicide* (1946), *Johnny Comes Flying Home* (1946), *Mother Is a Freshman* (1949), *My Foolish Heart* (1949), *Father of the Bride* (1950), *A Streetcar Named Desire* (1951), *Valentino* (1951), *The Bad and the Beautiful* (1952), and *The Man Called Peter* (1955).

In 1952, though, Canty temporarily gave up acting to care for her ailing mother, Mary Canty, refusing to accept any job offers for more than a year. When her mother died in April of 1953, Canty resumed her acting career, and went on to appear in a variety of television shows and stock productions.

A talented singer and actress, Marietta Canty was kind, well liked, and trusted by the people that she met. Rachel M. Richardson, a good friend of the Canty family is quoted as saying, "She had a wonderful personality. She had loads of friends and she could make friends with someone the first time she talked to you" (*Hartford Courant*). When she was off the set of *Rebel without a Cause* (1955), she spent time counseling the troubled star of the movie, James Dean. The James Dean Club actually sent the Canty family flowers and condolences in appreciation for her help with James Dean's issues.

Canty paved the way for African Americans to appear more often in films. Although the roles she played were almost always maids and servants, she performed with remarkable dignity. Displeased with the unfortunate lack of diversity of the parts into which African Americans were cast, Canty and other African American actors formed their own professional version of the Gilpin Players to provide an alternative to the never-changing role as the loyal, wise servant to white coactors, or as a comical character, not to be taken seriously by the audience.

Rebel without a Cause was the last movie in which she appeared. She also had a brief stint with radio, performing along with Acadamy Award–winner HATTIE MCDANIEL on the *Beulah Show*, where Canty played a decorous, overly proper Northerner who was mocked and ridiculed for her prim manner of speaking. In 1956, she was offered the role of the maid on the *Danny Thomas Show*. Around this time Canty's father became ill, so she rejected this offer and permanently gave up her job as an actress to care for her father. She worked as a nurse for Hartford's Terry Steam Turbine Corporation until she retired in 1971. When she stopped acting in 1956, she was fifty-one years old.

In the years following her acting career, she was still heavily connected to her church, serving as the president of the Local Home Mission of the African Methodist Episcopal Zion Church from 1960 to 1980 and as conference director for the New England Annual Conference of the AME Zion Church from 1956 to 1980.

Canty was also very much involved with the community outside her church. She served as a justice of the peace from 1966 to 1973. She was a member of the Hartford Urban League and the board of the Hartford chapter of the Young Women's Christian Association, and president of the Hartford council of the National Council of Negro Women. Even though she was finished with professional acting, she never really let acting and theater go. She volunteered at the Union Settlement House in Hartford, giving acting lessons to youth in her community.

In 1961 and 1963, Canty ran unsuccessfully for office on the Hartford City Council. She ran as a Republican. Her proposals included the use of more streetlights along North Main Street, the implementation of more, improved day care centers, and new bus routes to accommodate the changes in population that Hartford was undergoing.

Though, like the vast majority of African American actors, Canty was never nominated for the highest awards (such as the Academy Awards or Tony Awards), she was recognized many times for her exemplary citizenship and her various community service efforts. She received the Certificate of Service and Award of Recognition from the Red Cross, the Club 51 Driver for the Blind Award of Recognition in 1960, the Humanitarian Award from the Hartford Section of the National Council of Negro Women in 1969, and the Hartford Neighborhood Centers Certificate of Appreciation.

Canty died while at home in 1986, when she was eighty years old. She was buried at Northwood Cemetery in Windsor, in the Wilson Section plot.

Her house was put on the African American Freedom Trail, which has over fifty sites of importance to the history of African Americans. The two-family house, bought by her family in 1931, and which they still own, is located on Mahl Avenue in Hartford.

With her energy and professionalism in the theater and film industries, and her dedication as a community activist, Marietta Canty spent her life breaking down barriers for generations to follow.

FURTHER READING
Hartford Courant, 29 July 1986.
Hartford Courant, 12 July 1986.
Hartford Courant, 10 July 1986.

ANGELA AISEVBONAYE
NATALY BERNARD

Capehart, Harry Jheopart (2 May 1881–1954), lawyer, state legislator, and antilynching crusader, was born in Charleston, West Virginia, one of five children born to Joseph Capehart, a merchant, and Maggie Woodyard. It is likely that both of his parents were former slaves. Capehart attended local public schools, but at some point during his early youth—when is not precisely known—his father died, and Harry had to balance his eagerness for continued schooling with the new responsibilities of helping his mother to feed and clothe the family.

Times were hard, and the fear of want a persistent problem. He later spoke of having to delay his education "for several years," though the exact time and duration remain uncertain.

What is known is that Capehart attended Howard University in Washington, D.C., intent on taking a degree in law. This he did in 1913, earning his LLB. He relocated to Keystone, West Virginia, in the southwest corner of the state and took up a law practice. In 1917 Capehart married Anna Hurley, a teacher. The couple would go on to have two children. Safely established in the legal profession, he began to dabble—and successfully— in real estate. Money and influence equaled political power. Capehart had long been interested in Republican Party politics, but in 1918 he mounted a campaign for the state legislature and won. In that year there were three African Americans in the legislature, Capeheart, T. G. [THOMAS GILLIS] NUTTER, and T. J. Coleman.

Capeheart was reelected two years later. In the state body, he served on a number of influential committees, including the Taxation and Finance Committee, among others.

It was during his time in the state legislature of West Virginia that Capehart made his lasting accomplishment, and one that signaled the beginning of the end of the period in American race relations known to historians as the "nadir," when lynching was rampant throughout the South, and Jim Crow laws were established throughout the region. By 1920 the number of lynchings had decreased somewhat, but that year the United States still witnessed five hundred instances of racially motivated mob violence. Making matters more difficult for antilynching activists were the laws passed to either frustrate or block the prosecution of those taking part in mob violence against blacks. It was into this environment that Capehart introduced what became known as the Capehart Anti-Lynch Law, widely seen at the time as a significant step forward in state action against racially motivated vigilantism and murder. The law carefully laid out the definition of what a mob is, as well as a mob participant, in an effort to foil the legal ambiguities (many of them intentionally designed) that perpetrators had frequently used to evade punishment. It established punishments for those who participated in mob action (even when they did not actively take part in a homicide) and even offered victims of lynch mobs recourse against their local governments (inasmuch as local authorities and police were often among the mob or saw to it that lynchers were not brought to justice). The bill passed the legislature sometime in 1921 and was signed into law by West Virginia's Democratic governor, John Jacob Cornwell. A 1921 edition of the *Crisis* hailed the law as one of the most promising and forward-looking of its kind.

For his part, Capehart retired from the state legislature at the end of his term in 1922. He continued to pursue his legal and real estate careers and, as the member of a number of civic-minded organizations, to advocate for the advance of African Americans through the pursuit of education and social and civic achievement.

FURTHER READING
"Anti-Lynching Bill in West Virginia," *Crisis*, May 1921.
Tolnay, Stewart E., and E. M. Beck. *A Festival of Violence: An Analysis of Southern Lynchings, 1882–1930* (1995).

JASON PHILIP MILLER

Capers, Virginia (22 Sept. 1925–9 May 2004), actress and singer, was born Eliza Virginia Capers in Sumter, South Carolina. Nothing is known of her parentage or her early education. She attended Howard College and studied voice at Julliard University before pursuing a career as a singer and actress. One of the results of her classes at Julliard was that she became proficient in several languages, a skill that would serve her well in her later career.

While barely into her twenties, Capers met Abe Lyman. Leader of the popular Lyman Orchestra, he offered Capers the opportunity to tour with his orchestra and perform on his radio program. She put her linguistic abilities to good use on Lyman's radio program, where she was sometimes called upon to sing in Yiddish; after the program left the air in 1947, she was able to find roles in Yiddish theater productions in New York City. She was also actively involved with the Lafayette Players, an African American theater company associated with the Lafayette Theatre, the first stock company in Harlem, New York.

Capers made her Broadway debut in 1957 in *Jamaica*, as an understudy for ADELAIDE HALL, the American-born singer who was returning after decades of performing in England. The musical by Harold Arlen parodied calypso music, which was then enjoying great popularity thanks to the recordings of HARRY BELAFONTE. Capers stayed with the production for more than a year, from October 1957 to April 1959. She next appeared in another Arlen musical, *Saratoga*. The play was based on Edna Ferber's best-selling novel *Saratoga Trunk*. The success of the novel did not translate to the stage, and the production ran only from December 1959 to February 1960.

In the 1960s Capers turned from theater to film and television, the media in which she made most of her appearances for the remainder of her career. Her first television appearance was in 1961 in an episode of *Have Gun—Will Travel*, a Western series known for its use of minority performers. As a full-figured African American woman whose career began in the 1950s, it is not surprising that she played maids and mothers on a few occasions, but her television and film roles were surprisingly diverse. She was cast in a number of Westerns; in addition to *Have Gun—Will Travel*, she appeared on the television series *Daniel Boone* (1966) and in the feature films *The Ride to Hangman's Tree* (1967), *Support Your Local Gunfighter* (1971), and *Big Jake* (1971).

Over the course of her career Capers worked with some of the nation's best-known African American performers. She worked with RICHARD PRYOR three times, in *Lady Sings the Blues* (1972), *The Toy* (1982), and *Jo Jo Dancer, Your Life Is Calling* (1986). She also appeared with PAUL WINFIELD and Robert Hooks in *Trouble Man* (1972), an early blaxploitation film, and with Glynn Turman and D'Urville Martin in *Five on the Black Hand Side* (1973), a family-oriented black film made in an attempt to counter the crime and sexual debauchery of blaxploition pictures. In addition, she appeared with SIDNEY POITIER in *The Lost Man* (1969); JAMES EARL JONES in *The Great White Hope* (1970), a fictionalized biopic about the life of boxer JACK JOHNSON; MORGAN FREEMAN in *Teachers* (1984); and LAURENCE FISHBURNE and ANGELA BASSETT in *What's Love Got to Do with It* (1993). Her other film appearances included *Norwood* (1970), *Ferris Bueller's Day Off* (1986), and *Howard the Duck* (1986). Her last film appearance was in the independent short *Move,* which was screened at the Jamaican Film and Music Festival in 2002.

While Capers was active in film, television provided an even more rewarding and busy career. She appeared in nearly fifty different television series and portrayed a range of characters, including doctors and judges. Most notably, she appeared in two different episodes of *Julia* (1969), the first television series to star an African American woman, DIAHANN CARROLL; Capers portrayed Julia's acquaintance, Mrs. Deering. She won an Emmy Award in 1973 for her guest appearance on the television series *Mannix*, portraying a deceptively maternal drug dealer in the episode "Out of the Night."

She was also a regular on two different television series, the short-lived crime drama *Downtown* (1986) and the highly regarded *Frank's Place* (1987–1988), on which she portrayed funeral-parlor owner Bertha Griffin-Lamour. Between 1990 and 1995 Capers had a recurring role as Grandma Hattie Banks on *The Fresh Prince of Bel-Air*, and in 1998 and 1999 she portrayed recurring character M'Dear on *The Hughleys*.

In 1973 Capers returned to Broadway in *Raisin*, the musical version of LORRAINE HANSBERRY's *A Raisin in the Sun*. The play ran from October 1973 to December 1975; Capers won the Tony Award in 1974 for Best Actress in a Musical for her portrayal of the family matriarch, Mama Lena Younger. The theater critic Clive Barnes described Capers as "tremendous in just about every sense you can use the word" (*New York Times*, 19 Oct. 1973). In 1979 she appeared in the Broadway production of *A Raisin in the Sun*.

As her career neared its end, Capers received many awards for her acting accomplishments. In the 1990s she was proclaimed a "Living Legend" by the National Black Theatre Festival and received the PAUL ROBESON Pioneer Award and the NAACP Image Award, which "recognizes "individuals whose work exemplifies talent and professionalism throughout the years and who have served as pioneers in the motion picture and television industry." Capers died in 2004 from complications resulting from pneumonia. She was survived by a son, Glenn S. Capers.

FURTHER READING

Bogle, Donald. *Brown Sugar: Eighty Years of America's Black Female Superstars* (1980).

Obituaries: *New York Times*, 12 May 2004; *Playbill*, 12 May 2004.

RANDALL CLARK

Cardozo, Francis Louis (1 Feb. 1837–22 Jul. 1903), minister, educator, and politician, was born in Charleston, South Carolina, the son of a free black woman (name unknown) and a Jewish father. It is uncertain whether Cardozo's father was Jacob N. Cardozo, the prominent economist and editor of an anti-nullification newspaper in Charleston during the 1830s, or his lesser-known brother, Isaac Cardozo, a weigher in the city's customhouse. Born free at a time when slavery dominated southern life,

Francis Louis Cardozo became the first black state official in South Carolina during Reconstruction. (Library of Congress.)

Cardozo enjoyed a childhood of relative privilege among Charleston's antebellum free black community. Between the ages of five and twelve he attended a school for free blacks, then he spent five years as a carpenter's apprentice and four more as a journeyman. In 1858 Cardozo used his savings to travel to Scotland, where he studied at the University of Glasgow, graduating with distinction in 1861. As the Civil War erupted at home, he remained in Europe to study at the London School of Theology and at a Presbyterian seminary in Edinburgh. In 1864 Cardozo returned to the United States to become pastor of the Temple Street Congregational Church in New Haven, Connecticut. That year he married Catherine Rowena Howell; they had six children, one of whom died in infancy. During his brief stay in the North, Cardozo became active in politics. In October 1864 he was among 145 black leaders who attended a national black convention in Syracuse, New York, that reflected the contagion

of rising expectations inspired by the Civil War and emancipation.

In June 1865 Cardozo became an agent of the American Missionary Association (AMA) and almost immediately returned to his native South Carolina. His brother THOMAS CARDOZO, the AMA's education director, was accused of having an affair with a student in New York, and Francis Cardozo replaced him while also assuming the directorship of the Saxton School in Charleston. Within months the school was flourishing under his leadership, with more than one thousand black students and twenty-one teachers. In 1866 Cardozo helped to found the Avery Normal Institute and became its first superintendent.

Unlike many South Carolinians of mixed race, Cardozo made no distinction between educating blacks who were born free and former slaves, nor did he draw conclusions, then common, about intellectual capacity based on skin color gradations. Instead, he was committed to universal education regardless of "race, color or previous condition," a devotion he considered "the object for which I left all the superior advantages and privileges of the North and came South, it is the object for which I have labored during the past year, and for which I am willing to *remain* here and make this place my home."

Despite the fact that he claimed to possess "no desire for the turbulent political scene," Cardozo soon found himself in the middle of Reconstruction politics. In 1865 he attended the state black convention in Charleston, where he helped draft a petition to the state legislature demanding stronger civil rights provisions. In 1868, following the passage of the Reconstruction Acts by Congress, he was elected as a delegate to the South Carolina constitutional convention. From the onset he was frank about his intentions: "As colored men we have been cheated out of our rights for two centuries and now that we have the opportunity I want to fix them in the Constitution in such a way that no lawyer, however cunning, can possibly misinterpret the meaning."

Cardozo wielded considerable influence at the convention. As chair of the Education Committee, he was instrumental in drafting a plan, which was later ratified, to establish a tax-supported system of compulsory, integrated public education, the first of its kind in the South. Despite his support for integration, however, he also understood the logic articulated by black teachers of maintaining support for separate schools for blacks who wanted to avoid the hostility and violence that often accompanied integration. Consistently egalitarian, he opposed poll taxes, literacy tests, and other forms of what he called "class legislation." Moreover, he fought proposals to suspend the collection of wartime debts, which he thought would only halt the destruction of "the infernal plantation system," a process he deemed central to Reconstruction's success. In fact, Cardozo argued, "We will never have true freedom until we abolish the system of agriculture which existed in the southern states. It is useless to have any schools while we maintain the stronghold of slavery as the agricultural system of the country." Thus, he called for a tripartite approach to enfranchisement: universal access to political participation and power, comprehensive public education, and reform initiatives that guaranteed equal opportunity for land ownership and economic independence.

After the convention, Cardozo's career accelerated. A "handsome man, almost white in color … with … tall, portly, well-groomed figure and elaborately urbane manners" (Simkins and Woody), Cardozo played a central role in the real efforts to reconstruct American society along more democratic lines. In 1868 he declined the Republican nomination for lieutenant governor in the wake of white claims of Reconstruction "black supremacy." Later that year he was elected secretary of state, making him the first black state official in South Carolina history, and he retained that position until 1872. In 1869 Cardozo was a delegate to the South Carolina labor convention and then briefly served as secretary of the advisory board of the state land commission, an agency created to redistribute confiscated land to freedmen and poor whites. In this capacity, he helped to reorganize its operations after a period of severe mismanagement and corruption. As secretary of state, he was given full responsibility for overseeing the land commission. In 1872 he successfully advocated for the immediate redistribution of land to settlers and produced the first comprehensive report on the agency's financial activities. By the fall of 1872, owing in large part to Cardozo's efforts, over 5,000 families—3,000 more than in 1871—had settled on tracts of land provided by the commission, one of the more radical achievements of the Reconstruction era.

In 1870, the same year that the federal census estimated his net worth at an impressive eight thousand dollars, Cardozo was elected president of the Grand Council of Union Leagues, an organization that worked to ensure Republican victories throughout the state. His civic activities included serving as president of the Greenville and Columbia Railroad, a charter member of the Columbia Street Railway Company, and a member of the Board of Trustees of the University of South Carolina. Some sources report that he enrolled in the university's law school in October 1874; however, no evidence exists that he ever received a degree.

From 1871 to 1872 Cardozo was professor of Latin in Washington, D.C., at Howard University, where he was considered for the presidency in 1877. In 1872 and 1874 he was elected state treasurer, vowing to restore South Carolina's credit. During his first term as treasurer he oversaw the allocation of more money than had been spent "for the education of the common people by the government of South Carolina from the Declaration of Independence to 1868, a period of ninety-two years" (Cardozo, *The Finances of the State of South Carolina* [1873], 11–12). In the words of one conservative newspaper editor, Cardozo was the "most respectable and honest of all the state officials." Despite his long-standing reputation for scrupulous financial management, he was accused in 1875 of "misconduct and irregularity in office" for allegedly mishandling state bonds. Though he claimed reelection as treasurer in 1876, he officially resigned from the office on 11 April 1877. Subsequently tried and convicted for fraud by the Court of General Sessions for Richland County in November 1877, Cardozo was eventually pardoned by the Democratic governor Wade Hampton before his sentence, two years in prison and a fine of four thousand dollars, was commuted.

Following the ascendancy of the new Democratic government and the final abandonment of Radical Reconstruction in 1877, Cardozo moved in 1878 to Washington, D.C., and secured a clerkship in the Treasury Department, which he held from 1878 to 1884. Returning to education in the last decades of his life, he served as principal of the Colored Preparatory High School from 1884 to 1891 and from 1891 to 1896 as principal of the M Street High School, where he instituted a comprehensive business curriculum. A prominent member of Washington's elite black community until his death there, Cardozo was so revered by his peers, black and white, that a business high school opened in 1928 was named in his honor.

FURTHER READING

The Francis L. Cardozo Family Papers are held at the Library of Congress. *Proceedings of the 1868 Constitutional Convention of South Carolina* (Charleston, 1868) help to locate Cardozo's ideas within the context of Reconstruction debates. The *Twentieth Annual Report on the Educational Condition in Charleston, American Missionary*

Association (1866) contains Cardozo's assessment of black education in the aftermath of the Civil War.

Foner, Eric. *Reconstruction: America's Unfinished Revolution, 1863–1877* (1988)

Holt, Thomas. *Black over White: Negro Political Leadership in South Carolina during Reconstruction* (1979).

Richardson, Joe M. "Francis L. Cardozo: Black Educator during Reconstruction." *Journal of Negro Education* 48 (1979): 73–83.

Simkins, Francis, and Robert H. Woody. *South Carolina during Reconstruction* (1932).

Sweat, Edward F. "Francis L. Cardozo—Profile of Integrity in Reconstruction Politics." *Journal of Negro History* 44 (1961): 217–232.

This entry is taken from the *American National Biography* and is published here with the permission of the American Council of Learned Societies.

TIMOTHY P. MCCARTHY

Cardozo, Thomas W. (19 Dec. 1838–1881?), educator and politician, was born in Charleston, South Carolina, the third son of Lydia Williams, a freewoman of color, and Isaac Nunez Cardozo, a prominent white Jewish businessman. Cardozo's elder brothers, the Glasgow University–educated FRANCIS LOUIS CARDOZO and Henry Cardozo, were both prominent politicians and educators in Reconstruction-era South Carolina. Like his brothers, Thomas enjoyed the privileges of Charleston's freeborn black elite in his youth, attending private schools in the city, but experienced a reversal in his family fortunes following the death of his father in 1855. Apprenticed for a time to a Charleston manufacturer of rice-threshing machines, the youngest Cardozo moved to New York City with his mother in 1857 because of growing hostility to and legislative restrictions against free blacks in South Carolina. He continued his studies at Collegiate Institute in Newburgh, New York, and beginning in 1861 taught for several years in Flushing, Queens, and married a fellow teacher, Laura Williams, of Brooklyn.

In April 1865, with the Civil War in its final stages, Cardozo returned to Charleston to direct the American Missionary Association's (AMA) educational efforts among the freedmen of his native city. Although he earned approval for finding building space and books and hiring new teachers, the brash and prickly Cardozo clashed with a number of his colleagues. In August 1865 the AMA dismissed him from his post—replacing him with his brother Francis—when it discovered that he had had an affair with one of his students in New York City. Cardozo admitted the affair but denied that he had misappropriated AMA funds and channeled money to the woman. When the AMA's leadership effectively prevented him from securing a post elsewhere, Cardozo opened a grocery store in Charleston, then served in 1866 as superintendent of a New England Freedmen's Aid Society school in Baltimore. Moving to Syracuse, New York, he began to write for the *National Antislavery Standard* and raised funds to continue his educational work among the freedmen, this time in Elizabeth City, North Carolina, where in 1869 he established a normal school for 120 students. Cardozo also immersed himself in local politics, running unsuccessfully for sheriff of Pasquotank County in 1870, a loss that he attributed to the racism of white Republicans, but which white Republicans blamed on Cardozo's excessive radicalism and ambition.

His political and educational ambitions thwarted in both Carolinas, Cardozo moved in early 1871 to teach at a newly opened normal school for blacks in Vicksburg, Mississippi, home to several of his wife's relatives. While Laura Williams Cardozo was soon promoted to principal of the school, her husband was more concerned with furthering his political ambitions, writing articles on Reconstruction Mississippi for the Washington-based *New National Era* and immersing himself in Warren County's contentious factional politics. In November 1871, just a few weeks after satisfying the state's residency requirement for seeking public office, Cardozo won election as circuit court clerk of Warren County. Both in his journalism and in his Republican Party activism, Cardozo earned a reputation as a passionate advocate for racial equality and for ending racial segregation in public accommodations. Ironically, given his own recent arrival in Vicksburg, Cardozo, writing under the pseudonym "Civitas," penned articles for *New National Era* claiming that Mississippi had reached its "full quota" of politicians and had no need of job seekers from other states (Brock, 195). While his blunt manner continued to earn Cardozo more than his share of political enemies, his aggressive work for the Republican cause also earned him valuable allies, notably the U.S. congressman JOHN ROY LYNCH and the future U.S. senator BLANCHE KELSO BRUCE. Cardozo was elected as Mississippi's delegate to the 1873 National Equal Rights Convention in Washington, and his growing profile and the political importance of his base in Warren County assured him the Mississippi

Republican Party nomination for the post of secretary of education in the 1873 elections.

In the general election Cardozo defeated his opponent with ease, becoming, along with Lieutenant Governor ALEXANDER K. DAVIS and Secretary of State James T. Hill, one of the first three African Americans elected to state office in Mississippi. Cardozo's tenure as secretary of education was initially free of controversy. His attempt to standardize textbooks and curb spending and his unwillingness to challenge segregated schooling was hardly radical and probably accounted for his cordial relations with white educational leaders. He soon became a victim, however, of the growing "white line" campaign by conservative Mississippi Democrats who sought to discredit the state's new Radical Republican government, and particularly its most prominent black members. Rumors that he had been imprisoned in both South Carolina and New York and was a fugitive from justice had circulated since the 1873 election but gathered steam in August 1874 when white-line conservatives gained control of Warren County and began an investigation into alleged corruption by their Republican predecessors. The investigation unearthed evidence that Cardozo had falsified witness statements while serving as circuit court clerk and had appropriated the expenses of these nonexistent witnesses for himself. In November 1874 a biracial grand jury indicted Cardozo on two charges of falsifying witness affidavits and five charges of embezzling two thousand dollars from the state land redemption fund. While some of Cardozo's political allies defended him against the charges, notably Blanche K. Bruce who helped to post his twenty-two-thousand-dollar bond, several of his many political enemies, black and white, willingly testified against him. Believing the charges against Cardozo to be a godsend to his Democratic opponents, Republican Governor Aldrich Ames also disassociated himself from his secretary of state for education.

After vital evidence indicating Cardozo's guilt went missing and a biracial jury failed to agree upon a verdict at Cardozo's trial in Vicksburg in May 1875, a retrial was set for the state capitol of Jackson because of increasing racial tensions in Vicksburg. Two months after his first trial, Cardozo appeared at a Fourth of July political rally in the latter city, which prompted a full-scale riot in which white mobs gunned down and killed several African Americans. His fate was sealed, however, by the defeat of the Mississippi Republican Party in the 1875 elections, a campaign marked by vote rigging and intimidation of black

and white Republicans throughout the state. Upon taking office in 1876, white conservatives launched impeachment proceedings against Cardozo, offering several new charges of malfeasance and misappropriating state funds for his personal use as secretary of education. With the evidence of his guilt strong and the political forces arrayed against him even stronger, Cardozo resigned on 22 March 1876 rather than face impeachment. He then left the state, moving to Newton, Massachusetts, where he worked for the U.S. postal service until his death in 1881.

Talented, ambitious, ruthless, and a connoisseur of "sparkling champagne ... and pure Habana [cigars]," Cardozo was in many ways a fairly typical politician of Gilded Age America. His abuse of political office for financial gain was also quite common but was a particularly dangerous indulgence for a black politician in the Reconstruction South. Cardozo's malfeasance had repercussions not only for his own reputation but also for the reputation of all southern black politicians, who were deemed guilty and corrupt by association.

FURTHER READING

Brock, Eulin W. "Thomas W. Cardozo: Fallible Black Reconstruction Leader," *Journal of Southern History* (1981).

Harris, William C. *The Day of the Carpetbagger: Republican Reconstruction in Mississippi* (1979)

Richardson, Joe Martin. *Christian Reconstruction: The American Missionary Association and Southern Blacks, 1861–1890* (1986).

STEVEN J. NIVEN

Cardozo, William Warrick (6 Apr. 1905–11 Aug. 1962) physician and medical researcher specializing in sickle-cell anemia, was born in Washington, D.C., to Francis L. Cardozo, a district school supervisor, and his wife Judy, last name unknown. Cardozo married sometime in the 1930s. He and his wife, Julia, a social worker, had one daughter named Judy. Cardozo's father and grandfather, both named Francis Lewis, were prominent educators in Washington, D.C. According to family lore, the Cardozos descended from a free mulatto woman who was part Indian (name unknown) and a Spanish Sephardic Jew named Isaac Nunez Cardozo. Issac Cardozo was a plantation owner in South Carolina whose son was an ordained Congregational minister and South Carolina's secretary of state during Reconstruction.

William Warrick Cardozo and his sisters were light in complexion, and sometimes, for business purposes, his sisters were able to pass for white. One of six children, Cardozo was his parents' only son and was educated in the district's public schools and at the Hampton Institute, graduating with an AB in 1929. He attended medical school at Ohio State University and graduated in 1933. From 1933 to 1935 he interned at City Hospital in Cleveland, Ohio, and served as a resident in pediatrics. In 1935 Cardozo was awarded a two-year fellowship in pediatrics at Children's Memorial Hospital and at Provident Hospital, both in Chicago. While at Provident Hospital, Cardozo trained under Dr. DANIEL HALE WILLIAMS, the pioneering African American surgeon.

In 1937 Cardozo established a private practice in pediatrics in Washington, D.C. He chose pediatrics at a time when few physicians (and even fewer African American physicians) specialized in it. A 1948 article in *Ebony* highlighted the depth of the problem. Of 3,500 pediatricians listed in the United States, fewer than thirty-five were African American, and no southern states registered an African American pediatrician. During this era, the death rate among black infants was more than twice that of whites. Cardozo joined the faculty of Howard University College of Medicine as a clinical professor of pediatrics. A grant from the African American fraternity Alpha Phi Alpha supplied funding for his early research into sickle-cell disease. Through his research, Cardozo determined that sickle-cell anemia was found almost exclusively in people of African descent. Additionally, he found that many patients lived for long periods with sickle-cell disease, that not all patients with sickle-cell disease are anemic, and that there was no therapy to cure the disease. In October 1937 Cardozo published the paper, "Immunological Studies in Sickle Cell Anemia," one of the first articles of its kind on sickle-cell disease, in the *Archives of Internal Medicine*. In the same year that Cardozo published his research in sickle-cell disease, he performed medical research on gastrointestinal diseases and on childhood growth and development.

In addition to his pediatrics practice and research activities, Cardozo worked as medical inspector for the Washington, D.C., Board of Health for twenty-four years. Judy Cardozo Rouse, Cardozo's only child, worked for the U.S. State Department. Cardozo died suddenly at his home in Washington, D.C.

FURTHER READING

The Francis Lewis Cardozo Family Papers, 1864–1968, are available in the Archival Manuscript Material, Library of Congress, Washington, D.C., Madison Reading Room.

Aetna Foundation. *William Warrick Cardozo, 1905–1962* (1986).

"Why Every Child Needs a Doctor: Pediatricians Prevent Illness as Well as Care for the Sick," *Ebony* (Dec. 1948).

KECIA BROWN

Carew, Jan (24 Sept. 1920–), writer and educator, was born Ian Alwyn Cuthbert Rynveld Carew in Agricola Rome, British Guiana (later Guyana), the son of Charles Alan Carew, a farmer and artist, and Kathleen Ethel Robertson, a teacher. His parents worked in New York while the family lived in Harlem from 1925 to 1927.

In 1939 Carew briefly taught at Berbice School for Girls in New Amsterdam, Guiana, and in 1940 graduated from Berbice high school in New Amsterdam, receiving an Oxford/Cambridge Senior Certificate, the equivalent of two years of college. He was called up to the British Army Coast Artillery Regiment from 1939 to 1943 and served as a customs officer from 1940 to 1943 for the British Colonial Civil Service in British Guiana. In 1943 and 1944 he worked for the government of Trinidad and Tobago as a price control officer before continuing his education abroad.

Carew came back to the United States in 1945 and attended Howard University during the 1945–1946 academic year and (Case) Western Reserve University from 1946 to 1948. After a short return to Guyana he traveled to Europe in 1949, where he received a scholarship to Charles University in Prague for 1949–1950 on the recommendations of the Guyanese politician Cheddi Jagan and PAUL ROBESON. In 1949 he lived in Paris and met Pablo Picasso, Andre Gide, and RICHARD WRIGHT, and studied at the Sorbonne under Julio Curie but did not receive a degree. After living in Paris as a writer and artist Carew briefly became editor of *De Kim* poetry magazine in Holland. Moving in 1953 to London, where he maintained a pied-a-terre (home away from home) for twenty years, he toured as an actor with the Laurence Olivier Company from 1953 to 1955. He lectured on race relations at the University of London Extra-mural Department from 1952 until 1959. A writer and broadcaster with the British Broadcasting Corporation (BBC) overseas service from 1953 to 1964, he wrote a series of television plays for Associated Television.

In 1962 Carew became director of culture for the Jagan government in British Guiana. As Latin American correspondent for the *London Observer* he reported on the October 1962 Cuban Missile Crisis from Cuba. In 1963 he toured West Germany as guest of the Ministry of Culture, and in 1963 and 1965 visited the USSR as guest of the Soviet Writer's Union. These experiences served as the basis for *Moscow Is Not My Mecca* (1964), reflecting the alarm among Third World students in Moscow when the authorities failed to deal with racism there. As editor of *Magnet*, in February 1965 he met MALCOLM X in London and described the experiences and conversations in *Ghosts in Our Blood* (1994). In 1965–1966 he was adviser to the president and editor of the *African Review*, a magazine published by the publicity secretariat of the Kwame Nkrumah government of Ghana before its overthrow. In 1966 he moved to Toronto and wrote poetry, stories, features, and television plays, and conducted interviews for the Canadian Broadcasting Corporation (CBC) until 1968.

In 1969 Carew moved to the United States and became a Council on Humanities Senior Fellow and Lecturer as novelist and poet in Third World literature and creative writing at Princeton University (and at Livingston College, Rutgers University) until 1972. He was a guest lecturer at Yale in 1969. In 1972–1973 he was a Burton Fellow at Harvard Graduate School of Education. In 1973 Carew accepted a position at Northwestern University in Evanston, Illinois, as tenured professor of African American and Third World studies, where he chaired the department from 1973 to 1976 and became professor emeritus in 1987. From 1987 until 1989 he lived in Tlaquepaque outside Guadalajara, Mexico, and wrote an unpublished manuscript, "The Butcherbird Still Lives." Carew served as visiting professor of Caribbean and Latin American literature at Hampshire College in 1986–1987, Visiting Clarence J. Robinson Professor at George Mason University from 1989 until 1991, and visiting professor of Latin American literature and history at Illinois Wesleyan University from 1991 to 1993. He was director of the Center for the Comparative Study of the Humanities at Lincoln University in Pennsylvania from 1993 until 1996. In 2000–2001 he was Visiting Distinguished Liberal Studies Professor of Pan-African Studies at University of Louisville. He was a guest lecturer at other universities, too, including Rutgers, New York University, the University of London, and Yale.

Despite all this activity, Carew was a prolific writer. His first two novels, *Black Midas* and *The Wild Coast*, both published in 1958, present "vivid Guyanese settings" (Robinson, 375). Later fiction reflects wide-ranging experiences, such as *The Last Barbarian* (1960), set in Harlem, and *Moscow Is Not My Mecca* (1964), set in the former Soviet Union. His children's books, *The Third Gift* (1975) and *Children of the Sun* (1980), are beautifully illustrated fables that, Carew told an interviewer, are "based upon a fusion of African and Amerindian folklore and use folk archetypes to carry moral messages to new generations." Carew's work, whether fiction or nonfiction, explores themes of indigenous and African presences in the Americas (Robinson, 375). In 1982 he lived in Grenada before the 1983 U.S. invasion and published *Grenada, the Hour Will Strike Again* in 1985. In 1988 he issued *Fulcrums of Change: The Origins of Racism in the Americas and Other Essays*. In 1994 he published *Ghosts in Our Blood: With Malcolm X in Africa, England and the Caribbean*, a record of the meetings and conversations between the two in London in February 1965. Also in 1994 an unauthorized version of his history of Christopher Columbus, *Rape of Paradise*, was published. A dozen editions of six of his books have appeared in foreign languages.

Carew was an adviser on Appropriate Technology to Prime Minister Michael Manley in Jamaica from 1976 until 1978, since 1978 has acted as co-founding director of Caribbean Latin American Society for Culture and Science, and was a consultant to the Cultural Division of the Organization of American States (OAS) from 1980 until 1985. In 1982 he chaired the Dennis Brutus defense committee. He was a consultant on African Art to the Field Museum of Natural History, Chicago, from 1983 until 1986; director of the Caribbean Foundation for Rural Development and Education, which had projects in Surinam and Grenada; adviser on appropriate technology to government of Jamaica, 1976–1978; member of the Caribbean Society for Culture and Science; chairman of the executive board of the Black Press Institute, 1982; adviser to the Illinois Senate Committee on Higher Education, 1984; and president of the Association of Caribbean Studies, 1982–1996. Beginning in 1987 he sat on the editorial board of *Race and Class*, which in early 2002 published a special issue, "The Gentle Revolutionary: Essays in Honour of Jan Carew," in recognition of his eightieth birthday in 2000.

Carew's fiction and TV work received several awards, including the Canada Arts Council Fellowship in 1969, and London *Daily Mirror*'s award for Best Play of 1964 for "The Big Pride."

The Afro-American studies program at Princeton University established the Jan Carew annual Lectureship Award in 1975. He received the Illinois Arts Council award for fiction in 1974; the 1979 Pushcart Prize for "Caribbean Writer and Exile" (1978); the Walter Rodney Award from the Association of Caribbean Studies, 1985; National Film Institute Award for *Black Midas* screenplay, 1985; and London HANSIB Publication Award, 1990. He received the Paul Robeson Award for "living a life of art and politics," in 1998 from the Free Library of Philadelphia. He won the Clark-Atlanta University Nkyinkyim Award in 2002 and the Caribbean-Canadian Lifetime Creative Award from the Caribbean Canadian Literary exposition in 2003.

Carew married Joan Mary Murray in London on 14 June 1952. Their daughter, Lisa St. Aubin de Teran (born in 1953), went on to become a well-known British writer. After their marriage ended, Carew again married, this time to the Jamaican writer Sylvia Winter, in 1958; they divorced in July 1971. In 1972 he married the Canadian Jamaican Pauline Aquant and they divorced in 1975. In September 1975 he married Joy Gleason, then an instructor in literature at Malcolm X College, Chicago, and later a lecturer in Pan-African studies and acting associate director of the International Center at the University of Louisville. Carew's journalism, activism, and scholarship reflect the belief that art, literature, and advocacy should be integral parts of the struggles against racism and social inequality.

FURTHER READING

The University of Louisville, Ekstrom Library, has collected some of Carew's papers.

Carew, Joy Gleason, and Hazel Waters. "The Gentle Revolutionary: Essays in Honour of Jan Carew," *Race & Class* 43.3 (Jan.–Mar. 2002).

Kwayana, Eusi. "Jan Carew: Mission within the Mission," *ChickenBones: A Journal for Literary and Artistic African-American Themes* (2002).

Robinson, Lisa. "Carew, Jan," in *Africana: The Encyclopedia of the African and African American Experience*, ed. Kwame Anthony Appiah and Henry Louis Gates Jr. (1999).

RICHARD SOBEL

Carew, Rod (1 Oct. 1945–) baseball player, was born Rodney Cline Carew in Panama to Eric Carew, a construction worker, and Olga Carew. Delivered in the rear car of a segregated train between his hometown of Gatun and Ancon, Panama, he was named for the doctor who helped his mother with the birth. Growing up in an impoverished section of town, Carew found exercise swimming in the Panama Canal. He began to play baseball with his friends, using paper bags to field tennis balls, and would listen to games broadcast from America on armed forces radio. Though very close to his mother, Carew suffered abuse from his father, who thought him weak and sickly. When Carew was fifteen, his mother, who had immigrated to New York, pooled her resources and with the help of his godmother, Margaret Allen, a nurse who assisted his birth, sent for him and his brother, Dickie.

Carew attended George Washington High in New York City but, struggling to learn English, opted not to try out for the school's baseball team. Instead he joined a competitive, integrated sandlot league in the Bronx, where he first started playing second base. Carew's quick hands and excellent hitting drew scouts to the games, and in 1964 he signed with the Minnesota Twins, following graduation.

Carew hit well in the Cocoa Rookie League in Florida that year and finished second in the league in batting in 1965 with Single-A Orlando; however, at odds with his teammates and homesick for his mother, he remained sullen off the field. He made strides both personally and professionally in Wilson, North Carolina, in the Single-A Carolina League in 1966 and the following spring broke camp with the Twins as the starting second baseman. In his first major-league game, Carew had two hits against the Baltimore Orioles, and at midseason was named to the All-Star team. Though the Twins stumbled in their postseason hunt, Carew finished sixth in the batting race and was named the American League (AL) Rookie of the Year.

While Carew was no slugger (he reached double digits in home runs just twice), he was a classic contact hitter, scattering base hits to every part of the field. After hitting .332 in 1969, Carew started a streak of fifteen consecutive seasons with a .300 or higher batting average, a mark preceded only by Hall of Famers Honus Wagner, Ty Cobb, and Stan Musial. An adroit bunter and running threat, Carew stole home seven times in 1969 and seventeen times in his career. Named to eighteen consecutive All-Star teams, Carew led the AL in batting every year from 1972 to 1978, except in 1976, when he lost to George Brett of the Kansas City Royals by two points.

A self-proclaimed loner in his first years in the majors, Carew suggested that his moodiness and reticence with the press was a by-product of his relationship with his father (Mueser, Anne

Marie, *The Picture Story of Rod Carew*, 1980). Over time he evolved into a friendly clubhouse leader and ambassador for the sport, as evinced by his acceptance of the humanitarian ROBERTO CLEMENTE Award in 1977. That season turned out to be his best: chasing the .400 mark for much of the year, he appeared on the cover of *Time*, earned more than 4 million votes for the All-Star team, hit for baseball's highest average (.388) in twenty years, and was named the American League MVP.

Eager for a shot at the World Series and a more equitable contract, Carew was traded to the California Angels before the 1979 season. Though he only played 109 games in his first year with the Angels, now as a full-time first baseman, he helped lead his new team to its first-ever division title. Carew maintained his streak of over-.300 seasons through 1983 but dropped below the mark the following year. He picked up his three thousandth hit on 4 August 1985 and retired at the end of the year, when the Angels opted not to pick up his contract. He remained a celebrity in Panama and saw his uniform number permanently retired from all sports in his home country.

Carew was elected to the National Baseball Hall of Fame in 1991, the twenty-second player to gain entry on his first try. Six months later he was inaugurated. Carew served as hitting coach with the Angels for eight years and with the Milwaukee Brewers for two; he later rejoined the Twins, who retired his number in 1987, as a member of the team's executive staff.

Carew met his wife, Marilynn Levy, at a Minnesota nightclub in 1968. Though Levy was Jewish and hesitant to tell her parents about Carew, the two eventually married after the 1970 season. Contrary to a line in comedian Adam Sandler's popular "Chanukah Song" (1994), Carew never converted to Judaism, but the couple did raise their three daughters in the faith. When his youngest, Michelle, became stricken with a rare form of leukemia, he began national pleas on her behalf. However, the ethnic mix of Panamanian and Russian backgrounds made it hard to find a donor, and she succumbed to the disease in 1996. Carew maintained his spokesman role for minority bone-marrow donor drives and his fund-raiser position for pediatric disease prevention.

Along with his dedication to charities and the underprivileged, Carew became a role model for his perseverance from a tough childhood and poverty to the heights of prosperity in sports. While other Latin players had opened the doors to American baseball before him, Carew became the first major Panamanian player. Subject to bouts of racism early in his career, he remained impassive even after receiving death threats following his inter-racial, mixed-faith marriage. Carew cemented his status as an ambassador for the game and an idol for a new generation of Latin ballplayers when he became the first athlete awarded the Panamanian Medal of Honor.

FURTHER READING
Carew, Rod, with Ira Berkow. *Carew* (1979).
Carew, Rod, with Frank Pace and Armen Keteyian. *Rod Carew's Art and Science of Hitting* (1986).
"Baseball's Best Hitter Tries for Glory," *Time* (18 July 1977).

ADAM W. GREEN

Carey, Archibald James, Jr. (29 Feb. 1908–1981), minister and activist, was born to Archibald J. Carey Sr., a Methodist minister, and Elizabeth Davis Carey in Chicago, Illinois. He attended Doolittle Elementary School and graduated from Wendell Phillips High School in 1925. As a youth Carey exhibited strong speaking skills and won the Chicago Daily News Oratorical Contest in 1924. In his adolescent years he was much influenced by his father, a staunch Republican politician, who took him to a private meeting with President Theodore Roosevelt.

After high school the young Carey pursued his education at the local Lewis Institute, where he earned a B.S. in 1928. He married Hazel Harper Carey, with whom he had one daughter, Carolyn. In 1929 he was ordained by his father, who had become a bishop in the African Methodist Episcopal (AME) Church. The following year Carey was assigned to the Woodlawn AME Church in Chicago, where he served for nineteen years. The young pastor pursued his theological studies at nearby Garrett Theological Seminary, which awarded him the BD in 1932. Because Carey pastored congregants facing a multitude of legal problems, he decided to enter law school in order to be able to help them. He graduated with the LLB from the Kent College of Law in 1935. This same year he was elected to the board of directors of the Illinois Federal Savings and Loan Association, for which he served as vice president and president.

Carey first worked as a partner in the law firm of Prescott, Carey, and Cooper. He showed interest in civil rights by hosting the first national convention of the Congress of Racial Equality (CORE) at Woodlawn AME in 1943. CORE was founded in Chicago in 1942 by a group of black and white students to challenge discrimination and segregation in restaurants and stores through sit-ins. From 1943 to 1947 Carey worked as an attorney in the state department of revenue. Carey's political work as a Republican minister was much inspired by the militant tradition of the AME Church. Carey was typical of black progressive ministers in that he viewed politics as part of his ministerial calling to help improve the lot of the black race. Soon he became interested in electoral politics and in 1947 was elected alderman for the Third Ward. Carey's victory was pathbreaking because it was the first time that a candidate won who was not a part of Chicago's political machine. Carey was able to win the aldermanic elections because of his reputation as a reformer lawyer, Woodlawn AME's contribution to the protest against racism, and the political prominence of his late father (1868–1931) who had been a political adviser to former Chicago mayor William H. Thompson.

In 1949 Carey left Woodlawn AME, which had grown from 49 to 1,500 members. His time as a pastor of a large AME congregation gave him status and secured him another transfer, this one to Quinn Chapel AME, where his father had worked as a minister from 1898 to 1904. In 1950 Carey was elected president of the AME Connectional Council. That same year he ran unsuccessfully for Congress. In 1951 he was reelected to the city council against the wishes of the local political machine. In 1952 he spoke at the Republican National Convention. Many later noted that Dr. MARTIN LUTHER KING JR.'s speech at the 1963 March on Washington was similar in several respects to Carey's 1952 speech. Both speeches end with the first verse of Samuel Francis Smith's song, "My Country 'Tis of Thee," and contain similar references to various places and mountains.

Carey campaigned for Dwight D. Eisenhower in his first presidential run in 1952. Upon his election Eisenhower appointed Carey a U.S. chief alternate delegate to the General Assembly of the United Nations (U.N.) in 1953. Carey was the third black to represent America at the U.N. There he worked on the Genocide Pact (1953) that made it an international crime to kill people because of their race, color, nationality, or religion. Carey also worked for the improvement of diplomatic relations between the United States and Liberia, which won him in 1955 the Citation and Medal of Knight Commander in the Liberian Humane Order of African Redemption from President William Tubman of Liberia.

When in 1955 Carey lost his aldermanic position to RALPH HAROLD METCALFE, Eisenhower appointed him to the President's Committee on Government Policy, which he went on to chair for three years.

Carey campaigned hard for Eisenhower's reelection in 1956. In 1960 he was nominated for a judgeship on the Superior Court of Cook County but lost the election. Two years later he ran unsuccessfully for judge on the probate court. In 1964 he made national news by switching to the Democratic Party when Republicans nominated Senator Barry Goldwater—who had voted against the 1964 Civil Rights Act—as their presidential candidate. Carey's exit from the Republican Party followed the growing disaffection of blacks who had voted en masse for presidential candidate John F. Kennedy in 1960. Carey's standing in the AME Church rose to the point that in 1961 he was granted the privilege to be a guest speaker at the Tenth World Methodist Conference in Oslo, Norway.

Carey continued to involve himself in local politics even after he had lost his seat on the city council. He worked with other ministers to fight police brutality and deter young blacks from engaging in riots. In 1965 he joined King during the Selma-to-Montgomery March. In 1966 he ran successfully for judge on the Circuit Court of Cook County. His workload having increased, he resigned from Quinn Chapel the following year. He worked as a judge until 1980. Carey continued to support theological education by working as trustee of Garrett Theological Seminary and Interdenominational Theological Center in Atlanta, Georgia, for many years. His life was devoted to making black life more respectable in Chicago.

FURTHER READING

Brooks, Deton. "Early Training Moulded Carey for Leader Role," *Chicago Defender* (National Edition), 7 Aug. 1943.

Calhoun, Lillian S. "And Carey's Political Future: Democrat or Republican?," *Chicago Defender* (National Edition), 10 Oct. 1964.

Grimshaw, William J. *Bitter Fruit: Black Politics and the Chicago Machine, 1931–1991* (1992).

Murphy, Larry G., J. Gordon Melton, and Gary L. Ward. *Encyclopedia of African American Religions* (1993).

Rather, Ernest R. *Chicago Negro Almanac and Reference Book* (1972).

Williams, Ethel L. *Biographical Directory of Negro Ministers* (1975).

DAVID MICHEL

Carey, Mutt (1891–3 Sept. 1948), jazz trumpeter, was born Thomas Carey in Hahnville, Louisiana, a small town west of New Orleans. Nothing is known of his parents, but of seventeen siblings, five of his brothers, including the legendary trombonist and bandleader Jack Carey, were also musicians. His first instruments were drums, guitar, and alto horn, but around 1912 he started playing cornet, working in his brother Jack's ragtime marching band and other similar groups. In 1914, along with the clarinetist JOHNNY DODDS and the bassist POPS FOSTER, he played in the trombonist KID ORY's band and in 1917 toured with Billy and Baby Mack's Merrymakers revue in a group that included Dodds and the pianist Steve Lewis. After leaving the Merrymakers, on the suggestion of the cornetist KING OLIVER, Carey took a job with the clarinetist Lawrence Duhé's Original Creole Band at the Pekin Café in Chicago, but not liking the northern climate, he returned to New Orleans in 1918. Subsequent local work included jobs with the trumpeter Chris Kelly's band at the Bulls' Club and with the clarinetist Wade Whaley at the Bucktown Tavern in Jefferson Parish, a tough lakeside resort area on the West End.

In November 1919 Carey went to Los Angeles to join Ory's group at the Cadillac Café on Central Avenue. In 1920 or 1921 the band played at the Creole Café in Oakland and, while on a later engagement at the Wayside Park Café, also in Oakland, participated in the first recording session by a black jazz band. Recorded in June 1922 in Los Angeles and first issued on the Nordskog label under the name of Spikes' Seven Pods of Pepper, the two instrumental sides, "Ory's Creole Trombone" and "Society Blues," were quickly rereleased with a new pasted-over label reading Ory's Sunshine Orchestra. Also recorded at the same session were four sides on which the band accompanied the blues singers Roberta Dudley and Ruth Lee. Although far less important musically than the pacesetting 1923 recordings by King Oliver's Creole Jazz Band, the Ory coupling does present Carey in a favorable light. His tone is broad, his phrasing is relaxed and rhythmic, and though he does no improvising, his lead is both confident and assertive. In addition to being the first black band to record jazz, in 1923 Ory's group was the first jazz band of any kind to play for radio broadcast.

In late 1925, when Ory left for Chicago to record with LOUIS ARMSTRONG's Hot Five and to work in King Oliver's Dixie Syncopators, he turned his band over to Carey. In his new capacity, Carey changed the name of the group to "Pop" Mutt and his Jeffersonians, enlarged the personnel, and worked fairly steadily at various venues in Los Angeles through the late 1930s. In 1927, while working at the Liberty Dance Hall under the name Papa Mutt's Liberty Syncopators, Carey's band (after the departure of the former Ory bassist Ed "Montudi" Garland) consisted of the trombonist Leon White, the reedmen Joe Darensbourg and Leonard Davidson, the pianist Elzie Cooper, the guitarist and banjoist Frank Pasley, and the drummer Minor "Ram" Hall. In addition to playing in cabarets and at taxi dance halls, during the silent film era the band was frequently hired to play on Hollywood film sets, providing atmospheric music for such stars as Greta Garbo, although there is no indication that they ever appeared on screen. Unfortunately, since Carey did no recording at all during this lengthy period, the sound of his band must be left to speculation.

With the advent of World War II, Carey stopped playing music full time and took a job as a Pullman porter with the Southern Pacific Railroad, but he also continued to play musical engagements whenever possible. Carey became active again as a full-time musician in early 1944, when Ory reformed his Creole Jazz Band for a contracted thirteen-week run of appearances on Orson Welles's *Mercury Theater* on CBS. Regulars in the band were Carey, the pianist Buster Wilson, the guitarist Bud Scott, the bassist Garland, and the drummer ZUTTY SINGLETON. The seminal New Orleans virtuoso Jimmie Noone played clarinet with the band until his death in April, succeeded by Whaley, the Ellington star BARNEY BIGARD, and finally Darensbourg.

In addition to the Welles broadcasts, the Ory band worked regularly at such Los Angeles venues as the Tip Toe Inn, the Jade Palace, and the Beverly Cavern while recording extensively for Crescent, Exner, Decca, Good Time Jazz, Columbia, and V-Disc. Between May 1944 and January 1946 the band also participated in a series of specially recorded performances for Standard Oil Company of California. With supporting educational lectures on the music's history, these shows were specifically designed for direct broadcast to elementary and secondary schools in an attempt to bolster appreciation of American folk music. Surviving discs from this series were released in 1991 on the American Music label. The only recordings the trumpeter made during this period that were not with Ory were those on Riverside accompanying the pianist-singer Hociel

Thomas in August 1946. From the spring of 1946 through February 1947 the Ory band worked at the Green Room in San Francisco, and unauthorized recordings of the band's closing night performances were released in 1992, also on the American Music label. Although technically flawed, these recordings are the only examples of how the band actually sounded on the job.

After leaving Ory in the summer of 1947, Carey went to New York and by November had recorded his first and only leader dates under the name of Mutt Carey and his New Yorkers. For these sessions Carey used the house band of the *This Is Jazz* radio series: the trombonist JIMMY ARCHEY, the clarinetist ALBERT NICHOLAS, the pianist Hank Duncan, the guitarist Danny Barker, the bassist Foster, and the drummer BABY DODDS. On the second of the two recording dates, Nicholas and Duncan were replaced by EDMOND HALL and CLIFF JACKSON, respectively. Following this session and a few concert appearances, Carey returned to Los Angeles, where he worked intermittently with his own bands. While in the process of forming a new band, he died in Elsinore, California, a vacation resort near Los Angeles.

From the Welles broadcasts of early 1944 through his last sessions in November 1947, Carey displayed a characteristically penetrating sound, with and without the use of his plunger mute. But his notes often cracked, and his range was limited. For the most part, though, his spare, rhythmically relaxed expositions of the melody, albeit phrased in a raggy rather than swinging manner and with a wide, shuddering vibrato, set a reliable lead for the ensemble. Carey appears at his best on Ory's 1944–1945 Good Time Jazz recordings with OMER SIMEON and Darnell Howard as guest clarinetists, on the 1946 Columbia album with Bigard, and on his own final sessions for Century, later reissued on Savoy. Here, on "Shim-Me-Sha-Wabble," "Slow Drivin'," "Ostrich Walk," and "Cake Walking Babies," he is the epitome of the tonally distinctive New Orleans lead trumpet player, while the band's relatively straight readings of "Joplin's Sensation," "Chrysanthemum," and "The Entertainer" are among the first and finest revivals of orchestral ragtime on record.

FURTHER READING
Bigard, Barney. *With Louis and the Duke* (1986).
Darensbourg, Joe. *Jazz Odyssey: The Autobiography of Joe Darensbourg* (1988).
Stoddard, Tom. *Jazz on the Barbary Coast* (1982).

Obituary: *Jazz Journal* 1, no. 11 (1948).
This entry is taken from the *American National Biography* and is published here with the permission of the American Council of Learned Societies.

JACK SOHMER

Carlisle, Cato (fl. 1777), Revolutionary War sailor, is a man about whom little is known. Thought to have been a slave at some time in his life, Carlisle enlisted for service in the Continental navy aboard the sloop of war *Ranger* in July 1777 at Portsmouth, New Hampshire. This 18-gun, 318-ton craft was commanded by the famed Captain John Paul Jones. Earlier writers have erroneously stated that Carlisle, as well as another black member of *Ranger*'s crew, SCIPIO AFRICANUS, were slaves owned by Captain Jones. Though Cato Carlisle was a free black from the Piscataqua region, records do not state whether he was already a freeman or used his enlistment bounty money to buy his freedom. Just who Carlisle's former master was is open to speculation. Two possibilities include the Carlisle family of Portsmouth or Captain Daniel Carlisle of Westmoreland, New Hampshire.

Despite the meagerness of details regarding Cato Carlisle's origin, his service at sea during the American Revolution is, like that of other men such as JAMES FORTEN and CAESAR TARRANT, indicative of the great contributions made by black men during the war in helping man the ships of war that operated on behalf of the rebellious colonies in the Continental navy, the state navies, and numerous privateers. Though the use of black men, both free and slave, was often a subject of debate when it came to the land forces, their service in the war at sea was without controversy because of their previous history. Blacks had already been active in the maritime trade in the colonies for more than a hundred years, serving in many capacities from lowly cabin boys all the way up to ship owners, captains, and pilots. When manpower shortages occurred early in the war, it was only natural that black sailors be accepted for sea service. Among the first black seamen in the war were Suriname and Dragon Wanton and Loushir, all owned by the commander in chief of the fledgling navy, Esek Hopkins. These men served on the brigs *Cabot* and *Andrea Doria*.

Cato Carlisle's specific actions aboard *Ranger* under Captain John Paul Jones are unknown, but his service may be followed with that of his commander. *Ranger* set sail on its maiden voyage from

Portsmouth on 1 November 1777 bound for France, and later for the waters off England. Along the way it captured two enemy brigs. Upon his arrival in France at Paimboeuf, however, Captain Jones was obsessed with gaining a more prestigious command, viewing the newly built *Ranger* as an unsuitable warship. While Jones was off in Paris meeting with the American commissioners, he left orders for the maintenance of his ship. Thus, it was that men such as Cato Carlisle, Scipio Africanus, and the rest of *Ranger's* crew were employed in a whole host of mundane naval chores, including cleaning the bottom of the ship. By the time Captain Jones returned, his crew was an unhappy lot.

Ranger finally departed Paimboeuf on 13 February 1778. The sloop stopped at Quiberon Bay where for the first time ever the stars-and-stripes flag of America, fluttering at the mast of *Ranger*, was saluted by a foreign power. However, the crew's hope for action was to be delayed, because Captain Jones wished to sail in company with a French frigate. Making for the port of Brest, Jones tarried there until finally setting sail on 10 April 1778. Four days out, *Ranger* and its crew captured a brigantine and several days later a cargo ship off the coast of Ireland, both without a fight. Operating in the Irish Sea, *Ranger* and its crew raided Whitehaven Island and St. Mary's Isle. The crowning achievement on this cruise, and one of the few victories for the Continental navy during the entire war, was the capture of the British sloop of war *Drake*.

Following this successful cruise, *Ranger* and its crew returned to France, but troubles soon broke out between John Paul Jones and his crew. The crewmen were unhappy about the extended length of their service but also with their share of the prize money from *Ranger's* captured vessels and with Jones's treatment of one his officers, Lieutenant Thomas Simpson. Of the 140 enlisted men on the ship, 77 signed a petition to the American commissioners in France, presenting their grievances, calling themselves "the Jovial Tars Now on board the Continental Sloop of war *Ranger*." Among these petitioners were Cato Carlisle and Scipio Africanus. If any proof were needed that these men were not the slaves of Captain Jones, their signature on this petition surely provides just that.

Following its actions overseas, and the subsequent departure of Captain John Paul Jones to a new command, *Ranger* left France under command of Lieutenant Simpson. The *Ranger* saw further action in the North Atlantic and to the south in the Caribbean and off Charleston, South Carolina, in late 1779 and early 1780. By this time it is uncertain whether Cato Carlisle was still a member of its crew, but this seems likely. *Ranger* saw its service in the war ended when it was captured in Charleston in May 1780 when that city fell to British forces. If Cato Carlisle was still a crewman at this time, he would have been in a perilous and uncertain situation. Though white sailors were usually paroled and eventually sent home by the British, black sailors often had a different fate in store for them; sometimes they were sold into slavery in the West Indies, or they might be pressed into continued service in the royal navy. Whether any such fate befell Cato Carlisle is unknown, but his presence is never again documented in New Hampshire.

Whatever Cato Carlisle's fate, his free and honorable naval service under the legendary John Paul Jones well illustrates the important role played by black seamen in helping to achieve American independence.

FURTHER READING

Knoblock, Glenn A. *"Strong and Brave Fellows": New Hampshire's Black Soldiers and Sailors of the American Revolution, 1775–1784* (2003).

Morison, Samuel Eliot. *John Paul Jones: A Sailor's Biography* (1959).

Quarles, Benjamin Arthur. *The Negro in the American Revolution* (1961).

Sawtelle, Joseph G., ed. *John Paul Jones and the "Ranger"* (1994).

GLENN ALLEN KNOBLOCK

Carlisle, Una Mae (26 Dec. 1915–7 Nov. 1956), jazz pianist, singer, and composer of popular songs, was born in Zanesville, Ohio, the daughter of Edward E. Carlisle and Mellie (maiden name unknown), a schoolteacher. The assertion that Una Mae was born in Xenia, Ohio—published in many references—does not conform to family records. With piano training from her mother, Una Mae sang and played in public at age three in Chillicothe, Ohio. After participating in musical activities at church and school in Jamestown and Xenia, Ohio, she began performing regularly on the radio station WHIO in Dayton while still a youngster. In 1932 she came to the notice of THOMAS "FATS" WALLER in Cincinnati and quickly became his protégée and the beneficiary of his counsel.

Until the end of 1933 Carlisle worked alongside the well-known entertainer Waller, both on tour and in his *Rhythm Club* broadcasts for the Cincinnati station WLW, which boasted the highest wattage of any radio station in the country. She soon came to emulate Waller's keyboard style as well as his witty delivery of novelty songs. In a biography of his father, Waller's son contends that Carlisle came to his father's attention as a backup singer on the Waller recording of "Mean Old Bedbug Blues," made in New York in July 1932, during Carlisle's summer vacation from high school. This special relationship with Waller, while notably tempestuous, continued on a personal level until his death in 1943; in Carlisle's professional life Waller's influence extended much longer, as she made recordings with ensembles patterned after her mentor's and with instrumentalists associated with him.

After graduating from high school in 1933, Carlisle moved to Chicago and then to New York City. She was employed for a brief period in 1934 as a showgirl at the Cotton Club. Disenchanted, she then worked for a short time as a copyist-arranger for the music publisher Irving Mills before joining a touring company of Lew Leslie's *Blackbirds* revue for a London run in 1936. (Leslie's famous *Blackbirds* series, like many others at this time, featured songs, dances, and "plantation" skits by an all-black cast for the benefit of white audiences.) Remaining in Europe between 1937 and 1939, Carlisle accepted club engagements as a soloist in as many as eighteen countries and was known to sing in seven languages; her repertoire reflected the crowd-pleasing Waller approach and included such humorous numbers as "Two Old Maids in a Folding Bed." In Paris, where she enjoyed a lengthy residency at the Boeuf sur le Toit, she reportedly studied harmony at the Sorbonne and operated her own nightclub in Montmartre.

In London in May 1938 her recording career as a leading artist was launched by Leonard Feather with a set of recordings influenced by the combo style championed by Waller. Carlisle also appeared in minor musical roles in several films in England and France; in *Crossroads* she introduced the song "Darling, je vous aime beaucoup" (1935), by Anna Sosenko, to European audiences. During her stay on the Continent she formed friendships with many celebrities in show business and high life, such as JOSEPHINE BAKER, Maurice Chevalier, and the Duke of Kent. In 1937 she was the guest of the Egyptian royal family in Cairo for three weeks during festivities surrounding the lavish nuptials of King Farouk; she performed at the royal wedding reception.

Deteriorating conditions in Europe in 1939 hastened Carlisle's return to the United States, where she established a reputation in New York City clubs, such as the Village Vanguard, Kelly's

Stables, the Plantation Club, and Hotel Dixie, and made recordings. She sang on Waller's evergreen hit "I Can't Give You Anything but Love" (1939) and, more important, led her own all-star combo on the Bluebird label during 1940 and 1941. Among her illustrious collaborators in this endeavor were the saxophonists LESTER YOUNG and Benny Carter and the bass player JOHN KIRBY. The most successful of her fifteen recordings, "Walkin' by the River" (1940) and "I See a Million People" (1941), were renditions of her own compositions—tuneful ballads with lyrics by Robert Sour—and earned BMI awards. Arrangements of both were heard nationally on *Your Hit Parade*, the radio program that identified the ten most popular songs in America each week. Carlisle was the first African American woman to achieve such a distinction as a composer of popular songs.

Subsequent recordings of these songs, in particular by such notable musicians as Benny Goodman, ELLA FITZGERALD, and CAB CALLOWAY, contributed to her growing reputation. Carlisle composed as many as five hundred songs before 1952. She appeared in three full-length musical films devoted to performances by prominent African American artists: *Stars on Parade* (1944), *This Joint Is Jumpin'* (1947), and *Boarding House Blues* (1948). Her celebrity and stature are also suggested by her inclusion in the short documentary *The Negro in Entertainment* (1950), for which she shared billing with W. C. HANDY, ETHEL WATERS, LOUIS ARMSTRONG, DUKE ELLINGTON, and Fats Waller.

In 1950 Carlisle's popularity earned her a radio series in her own name originating in New York City and syndicated coast-to-coast by the American Broadcasting Corporation; she hosted a similar radio program from 1951 until 1953. Her work in radio was of historic significance because she was the first African American musician to be featured on her own nationally syndicated radio program. In 1950 she began to record on the Columbia label with the saxophonists DON REDMAN and Bob Chester. Forced by chronic illness to retire in 1954, she returned to her family in Ohio but died in Harlem. At the time of her death she was married to John Bradford, a onetime dancer.

Carlisle, known for her striking appearance and her feisty personality, possessed a clear, vibrant, rich voice and was equally adept in performing love ballads and up-tempo dance songs. Despite her collaboration with seasoned jazz musicians of the first order, her recorded performances do not identify her as a dynamic improviser in the jazz tradition. The jazz historian Gunther Schuller assesses her work as a jazz artist as "second-rate." In his autobiography, however, the jazz critic Leonard Feather, who produced Carlisle's earliest recordings, remembered Carlisle as an "uncommonly capable" pianist and singer. Periodically there are suggestions of the poignancy of BILLIE HOLIDAY and of those inflections that characterize the African American tradition, but in general the interpretative style and the emotional content of her singing are more influenced by the commercialized mainstream of popular music of the day. Carlisle's keyboard playing is grounded in the "bouncy" stride style, while her instrumental solos demonstrate an easy command of conventional material without calling much attention to her ingenuity. Long after Carlisle's death, Feather lamented her failure to realize the full extent of her promise as a musician: "Perhaps because of a lifestyle as self-indulgent as Fats' own, Una Mae never reached the plateau of fame to which her talent and beauty might have been expected to bring her" (128). Nevertheless, in a career that stopped rather suddenly in her prime, Carlisle distinguished herself as a nightclub entertainer, a recording artist, a song composer, and a radio personality.

FURTHER READING

A folder of newspaper clippings and memorabilia compiled under the supervision of Carlisle's sister and nephew is in the Greene County Room of the Greene County Public Library in Xenia, Ohio.

Dahl, Linda. *Stormy Weather: The Music and Lives of a Century of Jazzwomen* (1984).

Feather, Leonard. *The Jazz Years: Earwitness to an Era* (1987).

Handy, D. Antoinette. *Black Women in American Bands and Orchestras* (1981).

Placksin, Sally. *American Women in Jazz, 1900 to the Present: Their Words, Lives, and Music* (1982).

Sampson, Henry T. *Blacks in Blackface: A Source Book on Early Black Musical Shows* (1980).

Smith, H. "Una Mae Carlisle Takes Final Bow," *Record Research* 11, no. 5 (1957): 24.

Vance, Joel. *Fats Waller: His Life and Times* (1977)

DISCOGRAPHY

Una Mae Carlisle, Maxine Sullivan, and Savannah Churchill, 1942–1944 (Harlequin CD 19 [1992]).

This entry is taken from the *American National Biography* and is published here with the permission of the American Council of Learned Societies.

MICHAEL J. BUDDS

Carmichael, Stokely (29 June 1941–15 Nov. 1998), civil rights leader, later known as Kwame Ture, was born Stokely Standiford Churchill Carmichael in Port-of-Spain, Trinidad, British West Indies, the son of Adolphus Carmichael, a carpenter, and Mabel (also listed as May) Charles Carmichael, a steamship line stewardess and domestic worker. When he was two, his parents immigrated to the United States with two of their daughters. He was raised by two aunts and a grandmother and attended British schools in Trinidad, where he was exposed to a colonial view of race that he was later to recall with anger. He followed his parents to Harlem at the age of eleven and the next year moved with them to a relatively prosperous neighborhood in the Bronx, where he became the only African American member of the Morris Park Dukes, a neighborhood gang. But although he participated in the street life of the gang, he had more serious interests. "They were reading funnies," he recalled in an interview in 1967, "while I was trying to dig Darwin and Marx" (Parks, 80). A good student, he was accepted in the prestigious

Stokely Carmichael in March 1971, quotes from the book *Malcolm X Speaks* during an address at the Third World Conference at the University of Houston, in Texas. (AP Images.)

Bronx High School of Science. When he graduated in 1960 he was offered scholarships to several white universities, but a growing awareness of racial injustice led him to enroll in predominantly black Howard University in Washington, D.C. Impressed by the television coverage of the protesters at segregated lunch counters in the South, he had already begun to picket in New York City with members of the Congress of Racial Equality (CORE) before he entered college in the fall of 1960. Carmichael became an activist while still in his first year at Howard, where he majored in philosophy. He answered an ad in the newsletter of the Student Nonviolent Coordinating Committee (SNCC), a student desegregation and civil rights group, and joined the first of the interracial bus trips known as Freedom Rides organized in 1961 by CORE to challenge segregated public transportation in the South. He was arrested for the first time when the bus reached Mississippi. He was jailed frequently in subsequent Freedom Rides, once serving a forty-nine-day term in Mississippi's Parchman Penitentiary.

After graduating in 1964, Carmichael joined SNCC full time and began organizing middle-class volunteers of both races to travel into the South to teach rural blacks and help them register to vote. From his headquarters in Lowndes County, Mississippi, he was credited with increasing the number of black voters of that county from 70 to 2,600. Lacking the support of either the Republican or the Democratic Party, he created the all-black Lowndes County Freedom Organization, which took as its logo a fierce black panther. Growing impatient with the willingness of black leaders to compromise, he led his organization to shift its goal from integration to black liberation. In May 1966 he was named chairman of SNCC.

In June of that year, after JAMES MEREDITH's March against Fear from Memphis to Jackson had been stopped when Meredith was shot, Carmichael was among those who continued the march. On his first day, he announced his militant stand: "The Negro is going to take what he deserves from the white man" (Sitkoff, 213). Carmichael was arrested for trespass when they set up camp in Greenwood, Mississippi, and after posting bond on 16 June he rejoined the protesters and made the speech that established him as one of the nation's most articulate spokesmen for black militancy. Employing working-class Harlem speech (he was equally fluent in formal academic English), he shouted from the back of a truck, "This is the 27th time I've been

arrested, and I ain't going to jail no more. The only way we gonna stop them white men from whuppin' us is to take over. We been saying freedom for six years and we ain't got nothing. What we gonna start sayin' now is Black Power!" (Oates, 400). The crowd took up the refrain, chanting the slogan over and over.

The term "Black Power" was not new with Carmichael—RICHARD WRIGHT had used it in reference to the anticolonialist movement in Africa, and ADAM CLAYTON POWELL JR. had used it in Harlem—but it created a sensation that day in Mississippi, and Carmichael instructed his staff that it was to be SNCC's war cry for the rest of the march. The national press reported it widely as a threat of race war and an expression of separatism and "reverse racism." ROY WILKINS, leader of the NAACP, condemned it as divisive, and MARTIN LUTHER KING JR. pleaded with Carmichael to abandon the slogan. But although King persuaded SNCC to drop the use of "Black Power" for the remainder of the march, the phrase swept the country. Carmichael always denied that the call for black power was a call to arms. "The goal of black self-determination and black self-identity— Black Power—is full participation in the decision-making processes affecting the lives of black people and the recognition of the virtues in themselves as black people," he wrote in his 1967 book, written with Charles V. Hamilton, *Black Power: The Politics of Liberation* (47).

In August 1967 Carmichael left SNCC and accepted the post of prime minister of a black militant group formed by HUEY P. NEWTON and BOBBY SEALE in 1966, the Black Panther Party, which took its name from the symbol Carmichael had used in Mississippi. As its spokesman he called for the Southern Christian Leadership Conference (SCLC), the NAACP, and the Nation of Islam to work together for black equality. That year he traveled to Hanoi to address the North Vietnamese National Assembly and assure them of the solidarity of American blacks with the Vietnamese against American imperialism. In 1968 he married the famous South African singer Miriam Makeba; the couple had one child.

Carmichael remained with the Black Panthers for little more than a year, resigning because of the organization's refusal to disavow the participation of white radicals, and in 1969 left America for Africa, where he made his home in Conakry, capital of the People's Revolutionary Republic of Guinea. By then completely devoted to the cause of socialist world revolution emanating from a unified Africa, he became affiliated with the All-African People's Revolutionary Party, a Marxist political party founded by Kwame Nkrumah, the exiled leader of Ghana then living in Guinea as a guest of its president Sekou Touré. Carmichael changed his name, in honor of his two heroes, to Kwame Ture, and toured U.S. colleges for several weeks each year speaking on behalf of the party and its mission of unifying the nations of Africa. Divorced in 1978, he married Guinean physician Marlyatou Barry; the couple had one son. His second marriage also ended in divorce.

During the 1980s Ture's message of Pan-Africanism inspired little interest in the United States, and the attendance at his public appearances fell off. As the *Washington Post* reporter Paula Span noted shortly before his death, "Back in the United States, there were those who felt Ture had marginalized himself, left the battlefield. His influence waned with his diminished visibility, and with the cultural and political changes in the country he'd left behind." He also came under criticism for anti-Semitism because of his persistent attacks on Zionism. A collection of fourteen of his speeches and essays published in 1971, *Stokely Speaks: Black Power Back to Pan-Africanism*, included such inflammatory assertions as "The only good Zionist is a dead Zionist," and was attacked in the press. The bulletin of the Anti-Defamation League of B'nai B'rith criticized his campus addresses, calling him "a disturbing, polarizing figure" who caused hostility between blacks and Jews.

In 1986, two years after the death of his patron Sekou Touré, Ture was arrested by the new military government on charges of subversive activity, but he was released three days later. Despite the continued fragmentation of Africa and the diminished influence of Marxism, he never lost his faith in the ultimate victory of the socialist revolution and the fall of American capitalism. To the last he always answered his telephone "Ready for the revolution," a greeting he had used since the 1960s. In 1996 he was diagnosed with prostate cancer, with which he believed he had been deliberately infected by the FBI. Despite radiation treatment in Cuba and at New York's Columbia-Presbyterian Medical Center during his last year, he died of that disease in Conakry.

Kwame Ture left a mixed legacy. His provocative rhetoric was widely opposed by black leadership: King decried his famous slogan as "an unfortunate choice of words," and Wilkins condemned his militant position as "the raging of race against race." But Ture's childhood friend Darcus Howe wrote of him in a column in the *New Statesman* (27 Nov. 1998), "He will be remembered by many as the figure who brought hundreds of thousands of us out of ignorance and illiteracy into the light of morning."

FURTHER READING
Carmichael, Stokely, with Ekwueme Michael Thelwell. *Ready for Revolution. The Life and Struggles of Stokely Carmichael (Kwame Ture)* (2003).
Carson, Clayborne. *In Struggle: SNCC and the Black Awakening of the 1960s* (1981).
King, Martin Luther, Jr. *Where Do We Go from Here: Chaos or Community?* (1967).
Oates, Stephen B. *Let the Trumpet Sound: The Life of Martin Luther King, Jr.* (1982).
Parks, Gordon. "Whip of Black Power." *Life* (19 May 1967), 76–82.
Sitkoff, Harvard. *The Struggle for Black Equality, 1954–1980* (1981).
Span, Paula. "The Undying Revolutionary." *Washington Post*, 8 Apr. 1998.
Van Deburg, William L. *Modern Black Nationalism: From Marcus Garvey to Louis Farrakhan* (1997).
Obituary: *New York Times*, 16 Nov. 1998.
This entry is taken from the *American National Biography* and is published here with the permission of the American Council of Learned Societies.

DENNIS WEPMAN

Carnegie, M. Elizabeth (19 Apr. 1916–20 Feb. 2008), nurse, educator, and leader, was born Mary Elizabeth Lancaster in Baltimore, Maryland, the fourth child of John Oliver Lancaster, a musician, and Adeline Beatrice Swann, a homemaker. In 1918 the Lancasters divorced and M. Elizabeth went to live with her mother's sister in Washington, D.C., where she attended public school. The family had little money and Carnegie worked part-time at a whites-only cafeteria. She graduated from Dunbar High School at age sixteen. Like many girls who were good at a science but who lacked the money to pay for college, Carnegie pursued a diploma in nursing at a hospital-affiliated school. Such schools typically gave students small stipends as well as free tuition in exchange for their labor on hospital wards. Carnegie added two years to her age to get admitted to the all-black Lincoln School of Nursing in New York City. She graduated in 1934.

The hospitals of the day that catered to black patients were often little more than shacks. Perhaps for this reason Carnegie pursued federal employment by taking the civil service examination. Only two federal hospitals accepted black nurses—the all-black Veteran's Hospital in Tuskegee, Alabama, and Freedmen's Hospital in Washington, D.C. Since assignment to Freedmen's depended on successful completion of a one-year probationary period at Veteran's, Carnegie spent a year at Tuskegee before transferring to Freedmen's Hospital.

Few nurses in the 1940s held college degrees. Yet in 1940 Carnegie enrolled at West Virginia State College to earn a bachelor's degree. She financed her education by providing nursing service to the students in exchange for tuition, room, and board, and earned additional money by working summers at Homer G. Phillips Hospital in St. Louis, as well as at a Girl Scouts' camp. In June 1942, after earning a baccalaureate from West Virginia with a major in sociology and a minor in psychology and history, Carnegie joined the faculty of the nursing program of the Medical College of Virginia as a clinical instructor and supervisor of obstetrics nursing. When World War II broke out Carnegie applied to the Navy Nurses Corps but was refused admission because the Corps did not admit black nurses.

World War II created such a nursing shortage that the federal government pushed for the training of black nurses at a time when many nursing schools refused to admit African Americans. Carnegie took advantage of this wartime opportunity. In 1943, at the encouragement of the National Nursing Council for War Services, historically-black Hampton Institute in Virginia agreed to establish a baccalaureate program in nursing. Since Carnegie lacked a master's degree that would qualify her for a position as dean, she became assistant dean of the nursing program and acting dean until a permanent hire could be made, something that occurred shortly after the school opened in February 1944, when a white dean was hired. Carnegie continued as assistant dean and is regarded as the founder of the first baccalaureate nursing program in the state of Virginia. In 1977 the college's nursing archives were named in her honor.

Near the end of her first year at Hampton, Carnegie received a fellowship from the General Education Board of the Rockefeller Foundation. She enrolled at the University of Toronto in Canada in a one-year nursing certificate program equivalent to an American master's degree. In Toronto she married Eric Carnegie in December 1944. The marriage, which officially ended in 1954, essentially fell apart in 1945 when Eric Carnegie refused to leave Canada for the segregated South when Florida A&M College in Tallahassee offered Carnegie a position as the first dean of the school of nursing.

Upon joining Florida A&M Carnegie began working to bring down racial barriers. Black nurses were unable to fully participate in the American Nurses' Association because many Southern state branches refused to accept African American members. The Florida State Nurses Association (FSNA) accepted black members in 1942 but refused to permit black nurses to participate in any manner other than paying dues, a situation Carnegie likened to taxation without representation. In 1947 Carnegie was elected president of the Florida Association of Colored Graduate Nurses, which automatically made her a courtesy member of the FSNA but limited her to attending business meetings. When Carnegie ran for election to the FSNA board in 1949 she received the highest number of votes of any candidate and was elected first to a one-year term, then to a three-year term. This groundbreaking achievement helped demolish segregation in nursing.

Carnegie returned to school in 1951. Few black women had advanced degrees, and the black nurses who blazed trails into academia constantly felt pressure to prove their worth. In 1952 Carnegie received a master's degree in Educational Administration from Syracuse University. The *American Journal of Nursing* hired her in 1953 as an assistant editor. In 1970 she became senior editor of *Nursing Outlook*, a sister publication of the *American Journal of Nursing*. Carnegie continued her education, earning a doctoral degree from New York University in 1972. The National League for Nursing, the leading educational association for nursing, published her dissertation, "Disadvantaged Students in R.N. Programs: A Comparative Study of School-Completion Records of Two Groups of Socioeconomically Disadvantaged Students in Programs Leading to Registered Nurse Licensure." In 1973 she became chief editor of *Nursing Research*, and upon her retirement in 1978 she became president of the American Academy of Nursing for a year. She also started her own business as a consultant on scientific writing and served as a visiting professor of nursing at a number of universities and in endowed chairs at Adelphi University in New York and Memphis State University in Tennessee.

The written history of American nursing was limited to white nurses until Carnegie decided to write about the unsung history of black nurses. Carnegie edited or contributed chapters to nearly twenty books. Her 1991 book, *The Path We Tread: Blacks in Nursing, 1854–1984*, immediately became a classic and earned the *American Journal of Nursing*'s book of the year award. The recipient of numerous awards and honorary degrees, Carnegie was elected in 2000 to the American Nurses' Association Hall of Fame in honor of her contributions to the development of nursing as a profession, science, and discipline. Carnegie died at the age of 91 at her home in Chevy Chase, Maryland.

FURTHER READING

Carnegie, M. Elizabeth. *The Path We Tread: Blacks in Nursing, 1854–1990* (1991).

Hine, Darlene Clark. *Black Women in White: Racial Conflict and Cooperation in the Nursing Profession, 1890–1950* (1989).

Hine Darlene Clark, ed. *Black Women in the Nursing Profession: A Documentary History* (1985).

Schorr, Thelma, and Anne Zimmerman. *Making Choices, Taking Chances: Nurse Leaders Tell Their Stories* (1988).

Obituary: *Washington Post*, 7 March 2008.

CARYN E. NEUMANN

Carney, Harry Howell (1 Apr. 1910–8 Oct. 1974), jazz baritone saxophonist, was born in Boston, Massachusetts. His mother's given name was Jenny; other details of his parents are unknown. Carney studied piano at age six, switched to clarinet, and then took up alto saxophone in the seventh grade, when he met the saxophonist JOHNNY HODGES. Soon he was working professionally in Boston.

In late June 1926 DUKE ELLINGTON heard Carney, hired him for a local job, and obtained permission from Carney's parents to take him on the road. While with Ellington, Carney took up baritone saxophone, which gradually became his principal instrument. He resumed his schooling in the fall but returned to Ellington when his schedule allowed, including a trip to New York City during Christmas vacation in 1926, when he first recorded with Ellington's band.

On 8 March 1927 Carney left Boston for New York with the saxophonist Charlie Holmes. Carney worked at the Savoy Ballroom and then with Henry Saparo's band at the Bamboo Inn while making further recordings with Ellington and occasionally joining him at the Kentucky Club. Impressed that Carney already had a car and his own instruments,

Ellington hired him permanently, commencing with a summer 1927 tour of New England. Then followed the band's famous stand at the Cotton Club from 1927 to 1931 and more than four decades of national and international touring, during which Carney's career paralleled Ellington's closely.

Among Carney's few independent or semi-independent activities were two recording sessions in 1936 and 1937 with the singer BILLIE HOLIDAY and the pianist TEDDY WILSON, participation in a jam session at Benny Goodman's Carnegie Hall concert in January 1938, and a number of recordings with bands led by musicians closely associated with Ellington, including the clarinetist BARNEY BIGARD, the cornetist REX STEWART, the trumpeter COOTIE WILLIAMS, and Hodges. None of this work approached the significance of Carney's performances for Ellington, including recorded solos in "East St. Louis Toodle-oo" (1927), "Doin' the Voom Voom" (1929), "Harlem Speaks" and "Jive Stomp" (both 1933), "Saddest Tale" (1934)—in which he played bass clarinet—"In a Sentimental Mood" (1935), "Solitude" (1938), "Perdido" (1942), "Prelude to a Kiss" (1945), and "Sophisticated Lady" (1969), on the album *Duke Ellington's 70th Birthday Concert*. Carney may be seen and heard with the band in the film shorts *Black and Tan* (1929), *Salute to Duke Ellington* (1950), *Solitude* and *Sophisticated Lady* (both 1952), and *Duke Ellington and His Orchestra* (1965), as well as in the films *Monterey Jazz* (1973) and *Memories of Duke* (1980).

Carney was widely admired as a kind, responsible gentleman. One such testimony among many came from Stewart, who wrote that Carney "is cultured, knowledgeable, and also blessed with such an abundance of good nature that he enriches most scenes by his presence" (134). He loved to drive, and from around 1949 he doubled as Ellington's chauffeur. Later in life Carney became fond of golf, which he played whenever the band held residencies in Las Vegas. Not long after Ellington's death, Carney himself died in New York City. He was survived by his wife, Dorothy; details of the marriage are unknown.

Carney was the first great jazz baritone saxophonist. Under Ellington's leadership, he took an instrument that had elsewhere been used mainly in a splatty bass role and instead made it into the gruff, full-voiced foundation of a big band saxophone section. So authoritative was his playing that he could sometimes be heard leading the section from below—even though the lead instrument in a big band section usually plays the highest-pitched melody, as Hodges or Bigard normally did with Ellington's reeds. Carney also established the baritone saxophone as a convincing solo instrument, particularly in his gorgeous interpretations of ballad melodies.

FURTHER READING

Dance, Stanley. *The World of Duke Ellington* (1970).
Ellington, Duke. *Music Is My Mistress* (1973).
Stewart, Rex. *Jazz Masters of the Thirties* (1972).
Obituary: *New York Times*, 10 Oct. 1974.
This entry is taken from the *American National Biography* and is published here with the permission of the American Council of Learned Societies.

BARRY KERNFELD

Carney, William Harvey (1840–after 1901), soldier, was born in Norfolk, Virginia, the son of William Carney and Ann, a former slave. Little is known of his parents or of his early years. As a young boy he expressed an interest in the ministry and, at the age of fourteen, attended a covertly run school under the tutelage of a local minister. Later he moved

William Harvey Carney, Union Army sergeant who won the Gilmore Medal and the Congressional Medal of Honor, c. 1900. (Library of Congress.)

to New Bedford, Massachusetts, where he took odd jobs in the hope of saving sufficient funds to acquire his religious training.

In 1862, despite strong opposition, Abraham Lincoln signed a bill authorizing the recruitment of African American troops. In January 1863 Governor John Andrew of Massachusetts was permitted to raise a black regiment. Since the black community was relatively small in that state, recruiters turned to enlisting men from other states, using such prominent abolitionists as FREDERICK DOUGLASS, William Lloyd Garrison, and Wendell Phillips as recruiting agents. Despite the availability of employment in the North for African Americans, the threat of being put to death by the Confederate army if they were captured as Union soldiers, and the fact that they would have to serve under white commissioned officers, the ranks of the Fifty-Fourth Massachusetts Regiment were filled by the end of April, and Governor Andrew began securing men to fill the Fifty-fifth Massachusetts Regiment. In February 1863 Lieutenant James W. Grace, a businessman turned recruiting agent, opened a recruiting office in New Bedford, a town considered ideal for enlisting suitable men because of the large community of educated African Americans residing there. That year, at the age of twenty-three, Carney joined the Morgan Guards, which eventually became Company C of the Fifty-Fourth Massachusetts Regiment rather than a separate regiment. Evidently Carney was viewed as having strong potential, for when the New Bedford enlistees left for camp, he was listed on the roster with the rank of sergeant. Within two months of active duty, Carney participated in one of the bloodiest battles witnessed by African American soldiers during the Civil War, the assault of 18 July 1863 on Fort Wagner on Morris Island near Charleston, South Carolina. Two days prior to the assault, the men of the Fifty-Fourth were first put to the test, seeing action on James Island, South Carolina. Under heavy fire, they came to the aid of the Tenth Connecticut Regiment, possibly saving three companies from total annihilation by the Confederate forces. The unwavering front of African Americans coupled with the shower of mortar from the Union navy forced the enemy to retreat. The performance of the African American regiment impressed General Alfred H. Terry, commander of the 4,000-man division, and as the Union troops withdrew, the Fifty-Fourth received its orders to proceed to Morris Island, which controlled the harbor entrance to Charleston.

From its inception, the Fifty-fourth Massachusetts Colored Infantry, under the command of the white colonel Robert Gould Shaw, the scion of a wealthy Boston merchant family, had to prove itself worthy of entering the battlefield in Union blues. Thus even though they had been deprived of sleep, food, and water for several days, Shaw volunteered his men to lead the charge on the bastion, a mission that exacted a terrible toll because of the lack of normal assault preparation. Although open at the rear, Fort Wagner, or Battery Wagner, was only approachable from the south and presented a formidable structure. Equipped with sixteen to twenty guns mounted on the ramparts, its bombproof interior could house an entire regiment of men. Moreover it had artillery support from other Confederate strongholds nearby, including Fort Sumter, James Island, Sullivan's Island, and Fort Gregg. To compound the difficulties of an assault, any frontal invasion would encounter unfavorable terrain, with marshland on the left, sea and then sand stretching in front, and a ditch that forced men advancing from the right flank to wade through knee-high water.

The Union orders were to take the fort by storm with the Fifty-fourth leading the way, followed closely by other units and aided by artillery support from the navy. Thus the men of the Fifty-Fourth entered the battlefield, muskets loaded but not capped, bayonets fixed, only to find later that the Ninth Maine, Tenth Connecticut, Sixty-Third Ohio, and Forty-Eighth and One Hundredth New York were not in position to lead the second wave of the assault. At 7:45 P.M. on 18 July the assault unfolded as the Fifty-Fourth Massachusetts Regiment, following the lead of Colonel Shaw, marched toward the fort. When the advancing line was within approximately two or three hundred yards of the perimeter, the Confederate troops opened up a barrage of fire, quickly bringing down the formation. Despite heavy casualties from shell and musket fire, the men of the Fifty-Fourth pressed forward.

Prior to the assault Brigadier General George C. Strong, the field commander for whom the battery was later renamed, had addressed the Fifty-Fourth, telling the recruits to do honor to the nation. When he asked who would carry the national flag in case the color bearer fell in action, Shaw replied that he would. Shaw was one of the first to reach the summit, but as he raised his sword to rally his men on, shouting, "Forward, Fifty-Fourth," he was fatally struck in the chest. At the same time the color sergeant, John Wall, who was carrying the flag, also began to fall. Carney was close enough to see both men start to topple, and he heroically commandeered the colors and prevented the flag from falling to the ground. Despite wounds in both legs, his chest, and his right arm, he forged ahead, clutching the flag, which he planted on the crest next to the regimental colors. He managed to keep it aloft even as he lay on the outer slope surrounded by a hail of bullets. The lines of the Fifty-Fourth Massachusetts were decimated by the time a second charge of reinforcements reached them. Only then was Carney able to return to friendly lines, albeit on one knee, still protecting the colors. When he eventually staggered into a hospital tent, he collapsed, reportedly uttering the words, "Boys, the old flag never touched the ground."

For his act of courage, Sergeant Carney was one of four soldiers from the Fifty-Fourth Massachusetts who received the Gilmore Medal, and he was the first African American awarded the Congressional Medal of Honor. The citation of the latter read, "For conspicuous gallantry and intrepidity at the risk of life, above and beyond the call of duty, in action involving actual conflict with an opposing armed force."

When Carney was discharged from the army in 1864, he returned to New Bedford, Massachusetts. After spending some time at home, he moved, for no known reason, to California. He returned to New Bedford in 1870. For the remainder of his years he resided in Massachusetts, where he worked as one of four African American letter carriers, retiring in 1901 after thirty-one years of service. Following his retirement from the postal service, he worked as a state employee in Boston. It is believed that he died in Boston.

Carney's home in Norfolk, Virginia, is a historic site, officially known as the Sergeant Carney Memorial House. The American flag saved by Carney resides in Memorial Hall, Boston, Massachusetts, and his face is enshrined on Boston Common in the monument sculpted by Augustus Saint-Gaudens that pays tribute to Colonel Shaw and his warriors.

FURTHER READING

Greene, Robert Ewell. *Black Defenders of America, 1775–1973: A Reference and Pictorial History* (1974).
Robinson, Wilhelmena S. *Historical Negro Biographies* (1969).
This entry is taken from the *American National Biography* and is published here with the permission of the American Council of Learned Societies.

DALYCE NEWBY

Carpenter, Rosie Lee (25 Jan. 1922–), educator and civil rights activist, was born Rosie Lee Noland in Mantua, Greene County, Alabama. Her father, Garfield Noland, who died when Rosa was two years old, and her mother, Nellie Maxwell Noland, were sharecroppers. The fourth of seven children, Carpenter experienced the hardships of the share-cropping system that left but little time in the year for school attendance. Her mother, however, encouraged the children to become educated, and her mother's brother, John Maxwell, a formally-educated minister who lived in West Virginia, urged Carpenter to work hard to find greater educational opportunities. At one point she went to live with her father's sister in Pickens County because the schools were better. Later she attended Somerville School in Pickens County, where the principal, O. J. Brooks, recruited her for the basketball team and provided room and board. She eventually enrolled at Industrial High School in Tuscaloosa, where she studied cosmetology from 1942 until 1943.

On 18 January 1943, however, Carpenter's mother was killed in a tornado that also destroyed the family's home. Carpenter and three younger siblings went to live with an older married sister, Annie Thomas, in Eutaw, Alabama, where Carpenter worked as a hair stylist and eventually earned a high school diploma in 1944. Because of the shortage of teachers in rural areas during World War II, Carpenter was encouraged to apply for the emergency teaching certification and began her career in education in the fall of 1944 when she accepted a position at Burton Hills Elementary School in Union, Alabama, another small community in Greene County. Shortly thereafter she married Willie J. Carpenter and had two children with him, Joyce Lynette Carpenter and Charles Earl Carpenter.

During the next two decades, Rosie Lee Carpenter remained dismayed at the inequities in education, the lack of employment opportunity for African Americans, and the strict Jim Crow laws still pervasive in Greene County. In 1968, with the election of the Rev. Peter J. Kirksey as the first black member of the board of education, Carpenter saw an opportunity for change. At that time Greene County was the fifth poorest county in the nation and had a population that was 82 percent black but had just elected its first black official. A number of civic leaders throughout Alabama likewise saw potential, and when John Cashin, a dentist from Huntsville, Alabama, and HOSEA L. WILLIAMS, director of voter registration and political education for the Southern Christian Leadership Conference (SCLC) came to the county, they challenged the white political machine and helped black people to redefine themselves as citizens. Carpenter, her sister, Annie Thomas, along with Inez Johnson, Florence Kirksey, and Juanita Walton were women who also redefined citizenship and local leadership in Greene County.

When the congregation at First Baptist Church in Eutaw refused to allow the church to be used for mass meetings, Carpenter, his sister, Thomas, and Johnson sought out the pastor and convinced him to allow the church to be used. The Carpenter home became a site for planning and strategizing, despite the threats, intimidation, and cross burnings by local whites. Along with SCLC's field staff, Carpenter was dispatched to farms and plantations throughout the county to register eligible voters. She helped to identity the slate of candidates for the National Democratic Party of Alabama (NDPA) and to create the ballot that enabled new voters to vote for that slate with a simple mark under the emblem of the NDPA eagle. Throughout June and July of 1969, with the help of Hosea Williams and SCLC's national staff, Carpenter organized economic boycotts of businesses in Eutaw, the county seat, as well as small stores and cafes in Boligee, Union, and other small communities throughout Greene County. Along with her voter registration and election activities, she organized committees for housing and food for SCLC field staff that had come to work in the county elections. As a consequence, in August 1969 voters elected Frenchie Burton, Harry C. Means, Vassie Knott, and Levi Morrow as the first black members of the Greene County Commissioners Court along with James Posey and Robert Hines as new black members to the board of education in Greene County.

Even as she sustained her leadership role and political activities in Greene County, Carpenter, with Thomas, began traveling throughout Alabama to help other communities with boycotts, election strategies, and citizenship education after the historic Greene County election. In Eutaw she continued sociopolitical activities as co-chairperson of the local commemorative service for the MARTIN LUTHER KING JR. national holiday and was an active participant in meetings relating to county-level issues. In December 1984 Carpenter was appointed to the Greene County racing commission after a lawsuit deposed the slate of commissioners appointed by Governor Wallace. Because of the suit, her position was not activated until

February 1985. Carpenter resigned her position as Greene County racing commissioner in the same year, citing personal reasons stemming from a conflict with her retirement income. Her sister, Annie Thomas, was appointed to the position Carpenter left. Following her 1985 retirement from the board of education and racing commission, Rosie Lee Carpenter maintained her energy, enthusiasm, and commitment to making the vision of social justice and equality a reality for her community.

FURTHER READING

"Activities Commemorate Dr. King." *Greene County Democrat*, 13 Jan. 1977.

James, Hunter. *They Didn't Put That on the Huntley-Brinkley: A Vagabond Reporter Encounters the New South* (1993)

"Thomas Named to Racing Board." *Greene County Democrat*, 6 Feb. 1985.

ALMA JEAN BILLINGSLEA BROWN

Carr, Johnnie (26 Jan. 1911–22 Feb. 2008), civic leader and civil rights activist, was born Johnnie Rebecca Daniels, the youngest of five surviving children of John Daniels and Anna Richmond Daniels, prosperous farmers from the outskirts of Montgomery, Alabama. John Daniels died when Johnnie was nine years old, but her mother, Anna Daniels, supported the family by raising bees, chickens, and cows and selling vegetables, eggs, and honey. Disciplined by the strong Christian belief of their mother, the Daniels children were raised with the values of service, self-help, and education.

Unable to manage the farm by herself, Anna Daniels moved with her younger children to the city of Montgomery a few years after her husband's death. In 1925, when Carr had advanced enough in her studies, she was sent to the Montgomery Industrial School, also known as Miss White's School because it was run by Alice White, who had come south to educate African American girls. At Miss White's School, Carr met her lifelong friend and activist coworker Rosa Louise McCauley, who would marry and become ROSA PARKS. After the closing of Miss White's School in 1927, Carr continued her education through the ninth grade, which was the highest grade possible at that time for black students in the Montgomery public school system. Because there was no black high school in the city, students wishing to earn a high school diploma were required to enroll at Alabama State College. While her schoolmate, Rosa McCauley, became a seamstress, Carr studied practical nursing, and at age seventeen she

married Jack Jordan. Two daughters, Alma Lee and Annie, were born to that marriage before it dissolved. For a time, Carr supported her children working as a nurse. On 12 February 1944 she married Arlam Carr, and one son, Arlam Carr Jr., was born to that union. Arlam Carr Sr., who remained her husband for more than sixty years until his death in July 2005, also remained a staunch supporter of her work with the Montgomery chapter of the National Association for the Advancement of Colored People (NAACP), the Montgomery Improvement Association (MIA), and the historic Montgomery bus boycott.

Carr was compelled to begin working with the NAACP in the 1950s. She had clear memories of the nine SCOTTSBORO BOYS, who in the 1930s were convicted of rape on trumped-up charges in Scottsboro, Alabama. Carr also had vivid recollections of an era in which the absence of black judges, lawyers, and law enforcement officers meant virtually no justice for black people in Alabama. As independent agents for the Atlanta Life Insurance Company, the Carrs' livelihood was not directly dependent on the white business or political establishment. Carr was therefore able to work on membership drives for the NAACP, a system by which ten women would each solicit memberships of one dollar each for the organization. Because of their success in recruiting new members, Johnnie Carr subsequently became youth council director and Rosa Parks became secretary for the Montgomery chapter of the NAACP.

Beginning in December of 1955, around the time Rosa Parks refused to give up her bus seat to a white patron, Johnnie Carr actively participated in the Montgomery bus boycott. Acting as community bridge leader, she attended mass meetings, dispensed information, arranged for the distribution of flyers, and solicited support in her neighborhood and her other circles of influence. Like Jo ANN ROBINSON, MARY FAIR BURKS, Thelma Glass, and others from Montgomery's Women's Political Council, Johnnie Carr helped to form a critical link between the community and the formal leadership of men like EDGAR DANIEL NIXON, RALPH ABERNATHY, and MARTIN LUTHER KING JR. As chair of the MIA welfare committee, she assumed responsibility for helping those who were punished for participation in the boycott by investigating evictions and other reprisals and then reporting back to the organization. She also participated in fundraising activities, such as community bake sales, and helped provide lunches and dinners for MIA mass meetings, marches, and demonstrations.

Johnnie Carr continued to be at the forefront of the Montgomery bus boycott until November 1956, when a Supreme Court ruling declared bus segregation unconstitutional. Sustaining her participation in later economic boycotts and movements for open housing and desegregation of public accommodations, she eventually became the first female elected to the presidency of the Montgomery Improvement Association. The Carrs also allowed their son, Arlam Carr Jr., to become the primary litigant in the lawsuit to integrate the public school system in Montgomery. Although the family was harassed and threatened, and the colitigant, United Methodist minister Reverend Thompson, was forced to transfer to Mississippi, the Carrs continued the lawsuit until 1964 when Judge Frank Johnson ruled in favor of desegregation. In September of 1965 Arlam Carr Jr. became one the first thirteen black students to enroll at Montgomery's all-white Lanier High School.

Encouraged by the courage and commitment of leaders like E. D. Nixon, Martin Luther King Jr., Rosa Parks, and CORETTA SCOTT KING, Johnnie Carr continued her activist work into the early twenty-first century. Active in her church and a participant in local charities and organizations like the Friendly Supper Club and Leadership Montgomery, she traveled across the nation to share her experience, skills, and abilities with others struggling for social justice and equality. In March 2004 she received the third Rosa Parks Woman of Courage Award, which is given annually by the Southern Poverty Law Center and Troy State University at Montgomery.

FURTHER READING

Carr, Johnnie, and Randall Williams. *Johnnie: The Life of Johnnie Rebecca Carr with Her Friends, Rosa Parks, E.D. Nixon, Martin Luther King Jr., and Others in the Montgomery Civil Rights Struggle* (1995).

Robnett, Belinda. *How Long? How Long? African American Women in the Struggle for Civil Rights* (1997)

Williams, Donnie, and Wayne Greenshaw. *The Thunder of Angels: The Montgomery Bus Boycott and the People Who Broke the Back of Jim Crow* (2005).

Williams, Randall. *Johnnie Carr: A Life of Quiet Activism* (2002)

ALMA JEAN BILLINGSLEA BROWN

Carr, Leroy (27 Mar. 1905–29 Apr. 1935), blues singer, pianist, and composer, was born in Nashville, Tennessee to John Carr. Little is known about Carr's family. His mother's name is unknown. His father was a native of Nashville who worked as a porter at Vanderbilt University. Carr's parents separated when he was about six years old, and he moved with his mother and sister, Marrice Delores, to Indianapolis, where he spent most of his life. A self-taught pianist, Carr traveled with a circus, worked as a bootlegger, and served time in the army before teaming up with the guitarist Francis "Scrapper" Blackwell to play at parties, tent shows, and dance halls throughout the South and Midwest. The two musicians had met in the mid-1920s when Carr, an inveterate drinker, bought some of Blackwell's bootleg corn liquor. With the exception of a few records made independently, Carr and Blackwell worked together for the whole of their careers and shared billing on most of their recordings.

An Englishman remembered only as Mr. Guernsey managed Carr. From his office in an Indianapolis music store, Guernsey arranged Carr's personal appearances and first persuaded the Vocalion label to record him.

Carr's first recording session, which took place on 19 June 1928 in Indianapolis, yielded an immediate hit, "How Long–How Long Blues." The song is generally thought to be based on "How Long, Sweet Daddy, How Long," which had been recorded by ALBERTA HUNTER in 1921 and again by IDA COX in 1925. Carr made the song his own, using different lyrics and slightly altering the melodic line. "How Long–How Long Blues" went on to become one of the best-selling blues records of all time and was covered by BLIND LEMON JEFFERSON, TAMPA RED, BIG JOE TURNER, LEAD BELLY, JOHN LEE HOOKER, RAY CHARLES, Tim Hardin, Eric Clapton, and numerous others. MUDDY WATERS said it was the first song he ever learned.

"How Long–How Long Blues" pointed toward the more urban, jazz-tinged blues of the 1930s and World War II. Singing in a relaxed, smooth vocal style and using clear diction, Carr created a polished, sophisticated sound that broadened the appeal of blues. He combined real blues sensibility with the suavity of the crooners who were beginning to make full use of the electric microphone, foremost among them Bing Crosby. Before the new microphone and recording technologies were introduced, vaudevillians like MA RAINEY or street singers like Blind Lemon Jefferson had needed huge voices to project their music.

Carr recorded more than one hundred sides in six years, making him among the era's most prolific artists. He made most of his records in Chicago and New York, issuing all kinds of material: novelty tunes ("Papa's on the House Top," 1930); sentimental ballads (Irving Berlin's "How about Me?" 1929); vaudeville-type songs ("You Got Me Grieving," 1934); and hokum material in the style of the influential piano-guitar duo Tampa Red and Georgia Tom ("Don't Start No Stuff," 1934).

Even after the onset of the Depression, Carr continued to sell a large number of records, which influenced many subsequent blues performers during the 1930s and early 1940s. The Delta blues icon ROBERT JOHNSON, who came of age when the horizons of provincial musicians were greatly broadened by the phonograph, appropriated lyrics, vocal phrasings, falsetto punctuations, and even entire melodies from Carr's 78-rpm discs. The most influential guitarist of his time, Johnson's licks sometimes imitated Blackwell's accompaniment, and Johnson's beat echoed Carr's piano shuffle groove. Most notably, Carr's "I Believe I'll Make a Change" (1934), "When the Sun Goes Down" (1935), and "Mean Mistreater Mama" (1934) served as blueprints for Johnson's "I Believe I'll Dust My Broom" (1936), "Love in Vain" (1937), and "Kind Hearted Woman Blues" (1936), respectively.

Carr also had a profound effect on the guitarist T-BONE WALKER and the pianists Champion Jack Dupree and OTIS SPANN. NAT KING COLE's first hit, "That Ain't Right" (1942), was a Carr-inflected blues, and the lonesome passion of Carr's voice on songs like "Midnight Hour Blues" (1932) set the stage for Ray Charles.

The authorship of the songs that Carr and Blackwell recorded is uncertain. Most people credit Carr with writing them, but late in life Blackwell claimed that he and his sister, Mae Malone, wrote most of them. Blues scholars such as Paul Oliver claim that many of the songs credited to Carr were in fact written by Blackwell, but they offer no proof, and there is no real way of knowing.

Whoever wrote them, the resulting texts were often very beautiful, as in "Blues before Sunrise" (1934), a haunting ballad later covered by John Lee Hooker, ELMORE JAMES, and Ray Charles. Bob Dylan borrowed its lyrics for his own "Lonesome Day Blues" on the 2001 album *Love and Theft*.

During the early 1930s Carr was one of the most popular blues musicians in the country. In spite of this success, his personal life continued to suffer as a result of his intensifying alcoholism. He alluded to excessive drinking in many of his recordings, including "Straight Alky Blues" (parts one and two, 1929), "Hard Times Done Drove

Me to Drink" (1930), and "Sloppy Drunk Blues" (1930). Two months after Carr had recorded eight sides for the Bluebird label, he died in Indianapolis of nephritis, probably linked to long years of drinking moonshine alcohol. The last song that he recorded was "Six Cold Feet in the Ground" (1935).

The *Indianapolis Recorder* noted in its obituary that "thousands thronged the Patton Funeral home … for one last look at the man whose bizarre combination of bluish notes struck a deep sympathetic response in the souls of thousands of colored people throughout the country." He was survived by his wife, Margret (maiden name unknown) and a daughter, Eva Mae Carr. The date of his marriage is unknown. Many blues were composed in Carr's memory, including Blackwell's "My Old Pal Blues" (1935), Bumble Bee Slim's "The Death of Leroy Carr" (1935), and Bill Gaither's "Life of Leroy Carr" (1940).

Carr was inducted into the Blues Hall of Fame in 1982, and his songs remained standards for every variety of blues musician.

FURTHER READING

Cohn, Lawrence. *Nothing but the Blues* (1993).

Piazza, Tom. *Whiskey Is My Habit, Good Women Is All I Crave: The Best of Leroy Carr*, CD liner notes (2004).

Wald, Elijah. *Escaping the Delta: Robert Johnson and the Invention of the Blues* (2004).

Wyman, Bill, and Richard Havers. *Bill Wyman's Blues Odyssey: A Journey to Music's Heart and Soul* (2001).

Obituary: *Indianapolis Recorder*, 4 May 1935.

MICHAEL GRAY

Carr, Sister Wynona (23 Aug. 1924–12 May 1976), gospel, R&B, and pop singer and songwriter, was born in Cleveland, Ohio. Carr began studying piano at age eight. When she was 13, she entered the Cleveland Musical College to study voice, piano, harmony, and arranging. While in her midteens, she began performing in Baptist churches across the region. At age 20, she moved to Detroit to become a choir director and formed her own group, the Carr Singers, with whom she toured the Midwest and the South. Carr, with her alto voice, also became a member of the famous Wings Over Jordan Choir, who were aired regularly on a popular family radio program in the Cleveland area; from that group sprang the Wilson Jubilee Singers, yet another group with which Carr would perform.

It was with the Carr Singers that she caught the attention of J. W. Alexander of the Pilgrim Travelers, a group she also later joined. Alexander sent a demo of her singing to Art Rupe, president of Specialty Records. Carr cut her first record with Specialty in 1949, releasing "Each Day" and "Lord Jesus" with Austin McCoy's combo. Immediately upon its release, listeners found her jazzy sound reminiscent of Sister Rosetta Tharpe, and Rupe capitalized on the similarity by dubbing her "Sister" Wynona Carr. Carr herself didn't care for the moniker because she did not like being compared to a nun.

Rupe planned Carr's new billing in time for her next release, also set for 1949, but it never materialized. The plan was to release "I'm A Pilgrim Traveler," a gospel version of the old blues song "St. James Infirmary," along with "I Heard the News (Jesus Is Coming Again)," a tune that borrowed heavily from the 1948 R&B hit "Good Rockin' Tonight." But Rupe changed his mind, deciding they were too similar to R&B and that Carr, with her lively and dynamic delivery, was too daring for gospel listeners of the day. She continued to tour, but did not record again until 1950 when she did a new, but stylistically traditional, rendition of "Our Father" with Brother Joe May, Specialty's biggest gospel star at the time. That recording also went unreleased. Carr continued her gospel cuts with Specialty, and in the summer of 1952, she gained her one big success as a gospel singer with her hit "The Ball Game," produced by Joe Von Battle, who later recorded Aretha Franklin's first tracks. The song described the struggle between Jesus and the Devil in baseball terminology and became one of Specialty's top-selling gospel tunes. In all, Carr recorded about 24 gospel sides with Specialty between 1949 and 1954, in addition to having several hits with the Sallie Martin Singers.

By 1954 Carr was back in Detroit, serving as church organist and directing the choir at the New Bethel Baptist Church, presided over by Reverend C. L. Franklin, father of Aretha Franklin, then twelve years old, who credited Carr as one of her influences. That year Carr did numerous club dates with Tharpe and Marie Knight, performing gospel with an R&B edge.

With "The Ball Game" as her only big gospel hit, Carr grew disenchanted with pure gospel and continued to push Rupe to let her record pop, jump blues, and ballads. Rupe finally relented. In late 1955 Carr dropped both the moniker "Sister" and her last name and decided to go by simply "Wynona" to mark her evolution into a true rhythm singer.

Her first Specialty recordings under her new name and new sound were "Nursery Rhyme Rock" and "Please Mister Jailer." In 1957 Carr ventured into the new rock and roll craze that was sweeping the nation, releasing the mournful "Should I Ever Love Again?" and "Till The Well Runs Dry," which reached number 15 on the *Billboard* black singles chart but fell into obscurity when Carr contracted tuberculosis and could neither tour nor promote the record.

Between 1955 and 1959 Carr recorded over 20 rock and roll and R&B sides for Specialty, most of which she wrote herself, as she had most of her gospel tunes. Despite her hits, she failed to achieve the sales or recognition that both she and Rupe had hoped for. She finally left Specialty Records in 1959 and returned to her parents' home in Cleveland to recuperate.

When she had recovered enough from her illness, Carr signed with Frank Sinatra's newly created label, Reprise Records, and released one unsuccessful pop album there. With yet another recording failure, Carr decided to play hometown clubs only occasionally over the next few years, and her career never regained the momentum she had built before she fell ill. By 1970 she had opted to retire from performing altogether because of deteriorating health, including depression over what she felt was a failed career. Ironically, Carr made more money from publishing than recordings. Many of her songs were eventually recorded and made popular by other better-known artists, including the vocal group Manhattan Transfer's use of "Operator" as their closing song on their weekly 1975 CBS television variety show. But Carr's health continued to decline until she passed away on 12 May 1976 in Cleveland.

The highly versatile and progressive Carr wasn't fully appreciated in her time. The gospel-loving crowd largely overlooked her talent, perhaps due to her throaty and sensual contralto voice and her incorporation of jazz, blues, and R&B influences, which may have been deemed inappropriate and too secular for the genre. Carr was also strikingly beautiful and stylish in her attire, and thus didn't fit the stereotypical gospel image. Her image and subsequent lack of acceptance by gospel lovers made her crossover to R&B and rock and roll a logical move, but even Carr's R&B material wasn't appreciated in its day, in spite of its similarities to other R&B and rock and roll artists on the Specialty label, including Little Richard, Larry Williams, and Lloyd Price. Carr's gospel and R&B recordings found a new audience when Ace Records released a Specialty retrospective that included all of Carr's recordings for the label, as well as previously unreleased material such as a recording with the Reverend C. L. Franklin and his Detroit New Bethel Baptist Church Choir.

Other artists that recorded Carr's gospel songs include the Edwin Hawkins Singers and Joe Liggins ("Don't Miss That Train"), the Five Blind Boys of Mississippi ("Our Father"), the Persuasions ("The Ball Game"), and the Sallie Martin Singers.

FURTHER READING

Bogdanov, Vladimir. *All Music Guide to the Blues* (2003).

MARY ANNE HANSEN

Carroll, Diahann (17 July 1935–), singer and actress, was born Carol Diahann Johnson in the Bronx, New York, the elder daughter of John Johnson, a subway conductor, and Mable, a nurse. Carroll, who had a younger sister Lydia, began performing

Diahann Carroll, March 1955. The first African American actress to win a Best Actress Tony Award. (Library of Congress, photo by Carl Van Vechten.)

at an early age in school plays and as a "tiny tot" in the Abyssinian Baptist Church Choir of Harlem. At age ten she won a scholarship for voice lessons at the Metropolitan Opera and later attended the High School of Music and Art in Manhattan alongside Billy Dee Williams.

At the age of 15, Carroll began modeling clothes for *Ebony* magazine. Although she enrolled at New York University to study sociology, her passion for vocal performance won out. In her early college years she won a weekly televised talent competition called *Chance of a Lifetime* for three consecutive weeks. This national recognition spurred her bookings in New York venues, beginning in the Latin Quarter. Despite frequent opening night jitters (often taking the form of hives), she secured performance spots at such illustrious venues as New York's Waldorf-Astoria Hotel, Miami's Fountainebleu and Eden Roc, Chicago's Black Orchid, and Paris's Olympia Theatre.

In 1954, at the age of nineteen, Carroll played her first roles on Broadway and in film. Onstage she scored accolades as Ottilie in Harold Arlen's short-lived musical adaptation of Truman Capote's *House of Flowers*. On-screen she supported DOROTHY DANDRIDGE in *Carmen Jones* (1954), a cinematic take on Georges Bizet's opera *Carmen*. Carroll quickly established herself as a talented mezzo-soprano who consistently delivered mellifluous, dramatically expressive performances. She also gained popular momentum through television appearances on numerous variety and talk shows, including *The Red Skelton Show* and *The Steve Allen Show*. Impressed with Carroll's performance in *House of Flowers*, the renowned composer Richard Rodgers tried to cast her as an Asian character in the 1958 Broadway production of *Flower Drum Song*. While this casting endeavor failed, largely due to Carroll's self-described audition appearance as "the tallest, brownest Oriental you've ever seen," Rodgers maintained a profound interest in her career. After seeing her oeuvre mature through supporting roles in various films, notably Samuel Goldwyn's adaptation of *Porgy and Bess* (1959), in which Carroll appeared with SIDNEY POITIER (with whom she reportedly had an eight-year romance), Dorothy Dandridge, SAMMY DAVIS JR., and PEARL BAILEY, Rodgers both wrote for Carroll and cast her in his Broadway musical *No Strings* (1962), for which she was the first African American woman to win a Tony Award for best actress. Even before this professional acknowledgement by her peers, she was named Entertainer of the Year in 1961 by

Cue magazine, a reputable and widely read publication that covered New York City's cultural scene.

After several successful stints on the big and small screens, Carroll stepped into the titular role in *Julia* (1968–1971), a television comedy that altered the course of racial representation in popular culture. The executive producer Hal Kantner, upon conferring with the National Association for the Advancement of Colored People about the dearth of positive or complex black representations on television, successfully pitched *Julia* to the NBC network. In this role Carroll became the first African American woman to lead a prime-time show without portraying a servant or a rube, as in the 1950 cases of *Beulah* or *Amos and Andy*. Playing a widowed nurse who lost her husband in Vietnam and moved to Los Angeles with her son Corey, Carroll gained acclaim as a positive role model for the African American community. *Julia* was hailed as a character who gracefully accepted the demands of motherhood and a solidly middle-class career. At the same time the program was criticized for portraying a virtually "white Negro" who had never experienced day-to-day racism and did not acknowledge a past fraught with the question of racial difference in America.

The show was alternately praised for presenting a strong and self-possessed black woman and critiqued for contributing to a culture where black men did not need to figure into the family structure. Additionally, the program garnered praise for successfully integrating blacks and whites into a cohesive narrative world, while it was also taken to task for placing Julia and her son in a world without interaction with other blacks. Regardless of its controversies, the program was a popular and critical success in its first season, garnering Emmy nominations for the series, Carroll, and other cast members, as well as a win for Carroll at the Golden Globes. In her role as Julia, Carroll was one of the first black women whose image was successfully merchandised as dolls, paper-doll booklets, coloring books, and trading cards, all of which became collectible and remained so in the early twenty-first century. Despite an additional Golden Globe nomination for Carroll in 1970 as best actress in a television program, *Julia* endured for only three seasons.

Carroll resurfaced in the film *Claudine* (1974), starring as a mother of six who falls in love with a garbage man, for which she earned Golden Globe and Oscar nominations as best leading actress in a motion picture. After this critical apex, she worked steadily in film and television, delivering performances in miniseries like *Roots* (1977) and adaptations like MAYA ANGELOU's *I Know Why the Caged Bird Sings* (1979). Perhaps her best-known television role of the 1980s was in the campy drama *Dynasty*, where she played Dominique Devereaux, rival to Joan Collins's Alexis Colby (1984–1987). After *Dynasty*'s cancellation, Carroll's roles ranged from an appearance on the sitcom *A Different World*, for which she earned an Emmy nomination as best guest actress, to the role of the priestess Elzora in Kasi Lemmons's film *Eve's Bayou* (1997). In the twenty-first century Carroll appeared in the television dramas *Soul Food* (2003) and *Grey's Anatomy* (2005).

Carroll married four times. In 1956 she married Monte Kay, with whom she had a daughter before they divorced in 1963. In 1973 she married Fredde Glussman; they divorced the same year. In 1975 she married Robert Deleon, who died in an auto accident in 1977. In 1987 she married Vic Damone; they divorced in 1996. In 1998 Carroll was diagnosed with breast cancer. After a successful recovery, she became an active spokesperson and advocate for the National Women's Cancer Research Alliance and the Susan G. Komen Breast Cancer Foundation.

FURTHER READING

Carroll, Diahann, with Ross Firestone. *Diahann: An Autobiography* (1986).

CASEY MCKITTRICK

Carroll, Hattie (3 Mar. 1911–9 Feb. 1963), subject of popular civil rights ballad by the renowned American folksinger Bob Dylan, lived her adult life, and possibly childhood, in Baltimore, Maryland. The sensationalist circumstances surrounding Carroll's death, which occurred eight hours after being assaulted by a wealthy white farmer at the hotel where she was working, coupled with the short sentence given to Carroll's victimizer, sparked a national outcry over the treatment of blacks in the United States. Within months of the verdict, Bob Dylan—at the time a relatively unknown twenty-two-year-old—wrote the song "The Lonesome Death of Hattie Carroll," a haunting elegy that would memorialize the incident, although with considerable inaccuracy. Little information is available on Carroll's early life, but at the time of her death she was a resident of Cherry Hill, the first planned neighborhood for African Americans in the United States and a major residence for returning black World War II veterans.

Carroll's husband, James F. Carroll, was a veteran. The Carrolls had eleven children, not ten as described by Dylan, and eight grandchildren.

On the night of her death Carroll was working as a barmaid at the Spinsters' Ball, an exclusive, annual charity event held at the Emerson Hotel in downtown Baltimore. In attendance was William Devereux Zantzinger, a twenty-four-year-old tobacco farmer from southern Maryland, and his wife Jane. Both arrived at the ballroom extremely intoxicated, and William Zantzinger began immediately harassing attendees and hotel staff with a toy cane. Perturbed that a waitress would not bring him a drink quickly enough, he approached the bar where Carroll was working and demanded to be served. Carroll, busy serving another customer, told Zantzinger "just a minute, sir." Enraged, Zantzinger replied, "I don't have to take that kind of shit off a nigger," and rapped the fifty-one-year-old on the shoulder with his cane. Carroll, who, a medical examiner's report would later determine, suffered from "hardened arteries, an enlarged heart, and high blood pressure" (*Mother Jones*, Nov. 2004), immediately became ill, and was taken to nearby Mercy hospital. She died eight hours later of a brain hemorrhage.

While Carroll was in the hospital, Zantzinger had been arrested and charged with disorderly conduct; after news of her death reached the police station where he was being held, homicide was added to the charges. In the meantime, other employees of the Emerson Hotel came forward, and Zantzinger faced two counts of assault in addition. Though a hearing the following Monday denied him bail, an appeal to Baltimore Superior Court—unopposed, notably, by the prosecutor William J. O'Donnell— overturned the judgment, and Zantzinger was set free until trial.

Given the deteriorating climate of race relations in the United States in 1963—it was only weeks later that MARTIN LUTHER KING JR. and two thousand other demonstrators were jailed in Birmingham—Zantzinger's quick release guaranteed that the story would command national attention. On 22 February *Time* magazine published a dispatch from Zantzinger's sprawling estate in West Hatton, "one of the most prosperous tobacco operations in Charles County," and newspapers including the Spokane, Washington, *Spokesman-Review* and the *St. Petersburg Times* printed coverage of the case. Additionally, in late March a reprinted article about the incident—placed alongside the poem *The Ballad of Hattie Carroll* by the socialist poet Don

West—appeared in *Broadside Magazine*, a folk music bulletin mimeographed and disseminated in New York City's West Village neighborhood. Dylan was deeply involved with the left-leaning publication, and the lyrics and notes to his song "Train a-Travelin'" were published on the front page of the same volume, just two pages ahead of West's poem and an article by Roy H. Wood headlined "Rich Brute Slays Negro Mother of 10." Although the story's original publisher is not disclosed, typesetting similarities suggest it was the *Baltimore Afro-American*, which was providing continual coverage of the saga.

Carroll's funeral was held at the Gillis Memorial Christian Community Church in Baltimore, where she sang in a choir for adults over forty-five. In contrast to the picture of despair conveyed by Dylan and West, Carroll was "president of a Negro social" club, according to *Time*, and in obituary photographs appeared fashionably dressed. Despite only a week passing since Carroll's death—and many of the incident's details, such as the court finding that Carroll was struck only once, on the shoulder, yet to emerge—Wood's report declared that the "waitress" and "mother of 10" died after "being felled by blows" from the "wooden cane" of Zantzinger, who was from a "prominent political family." Nevertheless, many of these inaccuracies made their way into *The Lonesome Death of Hattie Carroll*, first performed on the Steve Allen television show on 25 February 1964. Thus Dylan's version of events became irrevocably conjoined to the story's popular narrative.

On 15 March 1963, the assistant Baltimore medical examiner presented his findings at a pretrial hearing. After describing Carroll's preexisting medical conditions, he concluded that Carroll's death was induced by "stress caused by Zantzinger's verbal abuse, coupled with the assault" (*Mother Jones*), and a trial date was immediately set. However, Zantzinger's attorneys were able to successfully petition for a change of venue, and the trial, which began on 19 June of the same year, was moved from Baltimore to Hagerstown, a city in semirural western Maryland. Additionally, a panel of three judges would supplant a jury trial.

The trial was a maelstrom of racial discord, with the prosecution insisting that Zantzinger believed himself "lord of the plantation." The defense claimed Zantzinger gave Carroll nothing more than a "playful tap," and painted him as a naïve, harmless boor. Seven days later, the judges announced their verdict: Zantzinger was guilty of involuntary manslaughter, not murder, in addition to disorderly conduct and assault. He posted $25,000 in bail, and was released until sentencing in late August, freeing him to work on his busy summer harvest. At sentencing Zantzinger was fined $625, and given six months jail time, to begin in mid-September, again, to give him time to work on his farm. Many were outraged, and the story once again made national headlines. The head of the Baltimore chapter of the NAACP, Reverend Jentry McDonald, issued a statement condemning the "dual standard of justice and punishment." "We shudder to think of this sentence," McDonald wrote, "if this dastardly act had been committed by a colored man and his victim had been a white woman" (*Baltimore Afro-American*, 31 Aug. 1963).

Because Dylan accurately notes Zantzinger's short sentence, it's clear he was aware of the incident's latest developments—including Zantzinger's conviction on involuntary manslaughter, not murder. Nonetheless, the lyrics for *The Lonesome Death of Hattie Carroll*—recorded in October 1963 and released in 1964 on the celebrated album *The Times They Are a-Changin'*—almost exclusively references the erroneous accounts given by Wood and West. Dylan, a masterful writer who had already composed two songs about racial injustice, "The Death of Emmitt Till" (1963) and "Only a Pawn in Their Game" (1963), was considered a voice of conscience in a nation wracked by social strife, and it was hardly surprising that he would take up the case of Hattie Carroll. Wood's and West's early accounts, however, may have been too hard to resist; writing in *Broadside* in 1964, acclaimed folksinger and music critic Phil Ochs praises the almost-perfect narrative created by Dylan, asking "What more effective beginning could [Dylan] have chosen than to use the sound of the name William Zantzinger and the description of the weapon, 'with a cane that he twirled round his diamond ring finger,' to carry over to the man?" (*Broadside*, 20 July 1964). Dylan's liberties, it has been frequently suggested, could have easily brought a libel suit.

After his release from prison Zantzinger returned to Charles County, where he lived until his death in January 2009.

Hattie Carroll and her husband James (who died in 1987) are both interred at the Baltimore National Cemetery, a military cemetery under the jurisdiction of the Department of Veterans Affairs.

FURTHER READING

Clinton, Heylin. *Bob Dylan: Behind the Shades Revisited* (2003).

Frazier, Ian. "Legacy of a Lonesome Death." *Mother Jones*, Nov. 2004.

"Maryland: The Spinsters' Ball," *Time*, 22 Feb. 1963.

ADAM ROSEN

Carroll, Vinnette (11 Mar. 1922–5 Nov. 2002), director, playwright, and actress, was born in New York City, the elder of two daughters of upper-middle-class parents, Edgar E. Carroll, a dentist, and Florence Morris, a teacher, both from Jamaica, West Indies. When Carroll was three, her parents sent her and her sister Dorothy to live with their grandparents in Falmouth, Jamaica, while Carroll's father completed his dental training at Howard University. Seven years later Carroll and her sister returned to New York, where their father's dental practice was thriving. The family's town house in the Sugar Hill section of Harlem eventually became a hub of activity that included frequent gatherings of neighborhood children and black community leaders.

Raised to be an achiever, Carroll absorbed this intellectually and culturally charged atmosphere. Her mother made sure that Carroll took music lessons and attended diverse cultural events, particularly those featuring black artists. Although Carroll wanted to become an actress, her father encouraged both of his daughters to pursue medical careers. After graduating from Wadleigh High School in 1940, Carroll earned her bachelor's degree in Psychology from Long Island University in 1944 and her master's in Psychology from New York University in 1946. She interned in New York State mental institutions before working as a clinical psychologist with the New York City Bureau of Child Guidance. At the same time Carroll began studies toward a Ph.D. in Psychology at Columbia University and also took night classes at Erwin Piscator's Dramatic Workshop at the New School for Social Research. She quickly eschewed both her clinical and doctoral work in 1948, when she received a scholarship to attend the workshop full time.

Carroll also studied with the famed acting coaches Lee Strasberg and Stella Adler. In the summer of 1948 she made her professional acting debut as Addie in Lillian Helman's *The Little Foxes* at the Southold Playhouse in New York. She performed in several other plays, including a touring production of George Bernard Shaw's *Caesar and Cleopatra* produced by Richard Aldrich. Once the tour ended in late 1950, Carroll proactively addressed the lack of substantive roles for black actresses by creating a one-woman show composed of selections from the writings of notables such as LANGSTON HUGHES, T. S. Eliot, MARGARET WALKER, and others. She toured with this show throughout the United States and the West Indies from 1952 until 1957. Carroll made her Broadway acting debut in a 1957 production of Robert E. Sherwood's *Small War on Murray Hill*. The short-lived project closed after only nine days. Several other roles followed, and in 1962 she won an Obie Award for her "distinguished performance" as the matriarch Sophia Adams in *Moon on a Rainbow Shawl*.

While pursuing her stage career Carroll also taught drama at the School for the Performing Arts beginning in 1955, and it was there that she discovered her talent for directing. She staged a production of *Dark of the Moon* at New York's Lenox Hill Playhouse in 1960 and went on to a successful commercial staging in Canada. That success led the Ford Foundation to award Carroll a grant for directing. She directed several projects for the Equity Library Theater and the Forty-First Street Theater in 1961 and 1962, most notably Hughes's "song-play" *Black Nativity*. She also directed and narrated a television version of the play, which was broadcast in Great Britain and the United States during the 1962 Christmas season.

As a playwright, Carroll adapted *God's Trombone*, JAMES WELDON JOHNSON's book of religious poetry, into the musical review *Trumpets of the Lord*, which opened off Broadway in 1963 at the Astor Place Playhouse and starred CICELY TYSON, AL FREEMAN JR., and Lex Monson. A subsequent Broadway revival of *Trumpets* closed after only seven performances in 1969. In 1964 Carroll's work as an actor was given the highest honor bestowed in television when she won an Emmy Award for her poetic dramatizations in *Beyond the Blue*, which aired on WCBS-TV in February of that year.

In 1967 Carroll worked with the Inner City Repertory Company, a federally funded project in the Watts area of Los Angeles, where only two years prior, bloody and racially charged riots had caused irreparable destruction. Within a few weeks Carroll had successfully integrated Inner City's all-white staff and troupe, prompting the New York State Council on the Arts director John B. Hightower to invite Carroll to head the council's new Ghetto Arts Program. This program was proposed and designed by New York State governor Nelson A. Rockefeller in 1966 to seek out, encourage, and train talented young black and Hispanic artists. In 1967, under the umbrella of the larger program, Carroll founded the Urban Arts Corps. During the

New York City Center's Black Expo Week in April 1969, the troupe presented *But Never Jam Today*, an urban version of *Alice's Adventures in Wonderland* and *Through the Looking Glass*, which Carroll conceived and directed.

Carroll resigned as director of the Ghetto Arts Program so she could focus on keeping the Urban Arts Corps afloat. She pooled funding from the New York State Council on the Arts and private and corporate donors to secure an adequate home space for the group. Offices, rehearsal rooms, and a small theater on West Twentieth Street in New York's Chelsea neighborhood were put at Urban Arts' disposal. During their first season, the Urban Arts Corps staged several productions, most notably *Don't Bother Me, I Can't Cope*, which marked the beginning of Carroll's collaboration with the composer Micki Grant. The production won two Obie Awards, a Drama Desk Award, and the Outer Circle Award for Outstanding Musical of the 1971–1972 season. In 1972 Carroll became the first black woman to direct on Broadway when a revised and expanded version of the musical opened and ran for over one thousand performances, earning her a Tony Award nomination for Best Director. Carroll and Grant collaborated on numerous projects over the next few years, but the 1976 musical *Your Arms Too Short to Box with God* is perhaps their greatest collaboration and Carroll's penultimate achievement as a writer and director.

Commissioned by the Italian government for the 1975 Festival of Two Worlds in Spoleto, Italy, *Your Arms Too Short to Box with God* re-visioned the biblical Gospel of Saint Matthew through interpretive dance and gospel music. The musical had a six-week engagement in Spoleto, then returned to the Urban Arts Corps Theater in New York, where the theatrical producer Frankie Hewett saw it. He took the production to Washington, D.C., Chicago, and Philadelphia and then back to New York at Broadway's Lyceum Theater in 1976, where it ran for over a year. The productions won three Tony nominations, including Carroll's second for Best Director of a Musical. After a successful national tour in 1978, *Your Arms Too Short to Box with God* returned to Broadway in 1980 and again in 1982.

Carroll continued to nurture her acting career during the 1970s. She made an uncredited appearance in the 1970 film *Cotton Comes to Harlem* directed by OSSIE DAVIS, and she received critical acclaim for her portrayal of the black abolitionist and feminist SOJOURNER TRUTH in the 1974 CBS-TV special *We the Women*. In 1976 Carroll guest starred as the West Indian Dr. Thatcher Wynell in several episodes of the hit CBS-TV series *All in the Family*.

In 1985 Carroll bought a house in Lauderhill, Florida, and soon after founded the Vinnette Carroll Repertory Company in Fort Lauderdale. She continued her career-long commitment to featuring work by playwrights and actors of color. As she revealed in a 29 October 1967 interview with the *Los Angeles Times*, "I have had a great deal of hurt in the theater both as a Negro and as a woman, but I don't get immobilized by it. I tell myself that no one individual is going to make it impossible for me."

Carroll remained artistic director of the eponymous company until 2001. She passed away at her home the following year from heart disease and complications from diabetes. Never married, she was the adoptive mother of the actor Clinton Derrick-Carroll.

FURTHER READING

Greene, Marjorie. "Negro Director: A Hit with Two Strikes," *Los Angeles Times*, 29 Oct. 1967: D1.

Hine, Darlene Clark, ed. *Black Women in American: An Historical Encyclopedia*, vols. 1 and 2 (1993).

McClinton, Calvin A. *The Work of Vinnette Carroll, an African American Theatre Artist* (1999).

Mitchell, Loften. *Voices of the Black Theatre* (1975).

SHARON D. JOHNSON

Carruthers, George R. (1 Oct. 1939–), scientist and inventor, was born in Cincinnati, Ohio, but grew up on Chicago's South Side. His father, a civil engineer, encouraged young George to study the sciences. As a child he developed a passion for the stars that drove him to build his first telescope at age ten. Though he went on to garner three science fair awards as a youth and did well in physics and chemistry, his passion did not always translate into success in his math studies.

Carruthers graduated from Chicago's Englewood High School, then he earned a bachelor of science degree in aeronautical engineering from the University of Illinois in Urbana-Champaign in 1961. He earned a master's degree in nuclear engineering in 1962 and a doctorate in aeronautical and astronautical engineering in 1964 from the University of Illinois. Upon graduation, Carruthers joined the Rocket-Astronomy Program at the Naval Research Laboratories in Washington, D.C., where he later became a senior astrophysicist and head of the Ultraviolet Measurements Group in the Space Science Division.

Carruthers was in his mid-twenties when he began his work on a design for an electromagnetic imaging device. He was awarded a patent in 1969 for his invention of the "Image Converter Used for Detecting Electromagnetic Radiation Specially in Short Wave Lengths," in the words of the patent application. Carruthers is widely regarded in scientific circles as the first person to find proof of molecular hydrogen in interstellar space. He did this in 1970 with an experiment on a sounding rocket—a rocket that does not achieve orbit—that took a spectrographic image of a star.

Carruthers led a team of scientists that developed a lunar surface ultraviolet camera and spectrograph that was used on the moon by the *Apollo 16* crew in 1972. A spectrograph is an instrument that separates different wavelengths of light so they can be measured independently. Most spectrographs work by directing light of different wavelengths in different directions. Ultraviolet (UV) light is a patch of electromagnetic radiation located between visible light and x-rays on a spectrum. UV emissions give the best clues to the nature of hot celestial objects, such as stars that are twice to ten times as hot as our sun. The Earth's atmosphere absorbs most UV emissions from space, making a UV camera operating in space or on the moon a valuable source of information. The Carruthers team's spectrograph became the world's first moon-based observatory.

The moon observatory made history with its ability to take the first pictures—some two hundred images—of the airglow belts of the Earth's ionosphere, the region in the upper atmosphere where ionized gasses reflect radio waves, making shortwave communication possible over long distances. The moon camera also took ultraviolet pictures of the stars. The camera was left on the moon, but a second version was used on the 1973 *Skylab* flight to shoot images of the comet Kohoutek.

Carruthers, who likes to keep his personal life private, was married in 1973. No other information is available on the nuptials.

Carruthers acted as principal investigator or coinvestigator on numerous space science projects for the National Aeronautics and Space Administration (NASA) and the U.S. Department of Defense in the following decades. Space projects included a 1986 rocket experiment that captured a UV image of Halley's comet and an experiment on the Air Force Space Test Program's Advanced Research and Global Observation Satellite (ARGOS) unmanned mission in which an image of a Leonid shower meteor entering the earth's atmosphere was recorded. This marked the first time a meteor was captured in UV from a space-borne camera.

Carruthers also has worked with data from the Global Imaging Monitor of the Ionosphere (GIMI), one of nine space research and technology instruments aboard ARGOS in service from 1999 to 2002. The GIMI observed far-UV airglow emissions in the upper atmosphere and the obscuration of UV-bright hot stars due to absorption by oxygen in the upper atmosphere as they appear to "set" behind the satellite as it orbits Earth. Carruthers's work contributed to the study of UV emissions of meteors as they enter Earth's atmosphere and occultations of UV starlight as a means for measuring Earth's upper-atmospheric density and its variation with solar activity.

Carruthers has garnered numerous awards, including the Arthur S. Fleming Award in 1971, the Exceptional Achievement Scientific Award from NASA in 1972, and the Warner Prize from the American Astronomical Society in 1973. In 1987 Carruthers was one of the first one hundred recipients of the Black Engineer of the Year award presented by *US Black Engineer* magazine. In 2000 the National Institute of Science presented him the Outstanding Scientist Award, and in 2003 he was inducted into the National Inventors Hall of Fame in recognition of his ultraviolet electrographic camera invention. In 2004 *Science Spectrum* magazine and Career Communications Group, Inc., selected Carruthers as one of the "50 Most Important Blacks in Research Science."

FURTHER READING

Brodie, James Michael. *Created Equal: The Lives and Ideas of Black American Innovators* (1993).

Carwell, Hattie. *Blacks in Science: Astrophysicist to Zoologist* (1977).

Henderson, Susan K., ed. *African-American Inventors*, vol. 2, *Bill Becoat, George Carruthers, Meredith Gourdine, Jesse Hoagland, Wanda Sigur* (1998).

JAMES MICHAEL BRODIE

Carson, Ben (18 Sept. 1951–), pediatric neurosurgeon, was born Benjamin Solomon Carson in Detroit, Michigan, the son of Robert Carson, a minister of a small Seventh-Day Adventist church, and Sonya Carson. His mother had attended school only up to the third grade and married at the age of thirteen; she was fifteen years younger than her husband. After his father deserted the family, eight-year-old

Ben and his brother, Curtis, were left with their mother, who had no marketable skills. Sonya worked as a domestic when such jobs were available, and she struggled with bouts of depression, for which, at one point, she had herself admitted to a psychiatric hospital. Despite her disabilities, she became the biggest factor in determining Ben's later success, which she and Ben attribute to divine intervention.

Except for two years in Boston, Ben grew up in a dangerous and impoverished neighborhood in Detroit. Initially, he did so poorly in school that by the fifth grade even he classified himself as "the class dummy." In part, his difficulties resulted from a failure to detect his need for eyeglasses. Nevertheless, when Sonya noticed the poor academic performance of her two sons, she instituted insightful strategies, curtailing their play activities and television viewing and demanding that the boys read two books each week and write reports on them for her to review—despite the fact that she could barely read herself. (Later she, too, went on to college.) Her stern intervention was also accompanied by positive reinforcement. When she learned of Ben's nascent interest in medicine, she said reassuringly, "Then, Bennie, you will be a doctor" (Carson, 27). Her parenting techniques catapulted Ben from the bottom of the fifth grade to the top of his seventh grade class.

Ben then became a normal teenager, desiring both stylish clothes and acceptance from his peers. As a result of this shift in his priorities, his grades plummeted from As to Cs, and he even confronted his mother angrily because she would not buy the fashionable clothes that he craved. She devised a scheme for him to manage the household expenses with her salary, saying that the remaining money could be used to buy the things he wanted. When Ben began this exercise, he was astounded and wondered how she made ends meet, because the money was gone before he had paid all the bills. Ben learned an invaluable lesson; he appreciated his mother's tenacity, curtailed his sartorial demands, and focused once again on his studies.

As a teenager Ben had a volatile temper, and at fourteen he attempted to stab a friend with a pocketknife simply because the boy would not change the radio station. Ben believes that it was through divine providence that his knife struck only his friend's belt buckle. This experience initiated another transformation in his life. He began to pray for help controlling his anger, he avoided trouble outside school, and he ended up graduating third in his class.

During Carson's freshman year at Yale University, he writes, "I discovered I wasn't that bright" (Carson, 73), and he wondered if he had what it would take to succeed in the highly competitive pre-med program. Aubrey Tompkins, the choir director of the Mt. Zion Seventh-Day Adventist Church, encouraged him and helped him regain his confidence. In retrospect, Carson wrote that "the church provided the stabilizing force I needed" (Carson, *Think Big*, 65). After receiving his B.A. in 1973, Carson entered the University of Michigan School of Medicine, where he studied with Dr. James Taren, a neurosurgeon and dean, who advised his students, when confronted with the choice of whether or not to operate, to "look at the alternatives if we do nothing" (Carson, *Think Big*, 65). This statement has resonated throughout Carson's professional career as a neurosurgeon. Another of his teachers, Dr. George Udvarhelyi, impressed upon him the importance of understanding the patient as much as the patient's diagnosis. Through this advice, Carson developed the gentle bedside manner of a good country doctor. In 1975 Carson married Lacena "Candy" Rustin; they subsequently had three sons.

Carson received his MD in 1977 and fulfilled his residency at Johns Hopkins University School of Medicine, where he was often mistaken for an orderly—despite the fact that he wore the white lab coat that should have identified him as a doctor. Carson was not only undaunted by such prejudice, he actually thrived on debunking racial stereotypes. From 1982 to 1983 he served as chief resident in neurosurgery at Sir Charles Gairdner Hospital in Australia before Dr. Donlin Long recommended and engineered his appointment as chief of pediatric neurosurgery at Johns Hopkins. At the time of his appointment, Carson was only thirty-three years old and already considered a rising star in his field.

Carson gained international renown and made medical history in 1987, when he led a surgical team of seventy people in a twenty-two-hour operation that successfully separated the seven-month-old Binder twins, who were joined at the skull. In 1994 he performed a similar operation on conjoined South African girls, one of whom died during the operation and the other two days later; three years later he successfully separated six-month-old Zambian boys. Performing approximately four hundred operations per year in his pediatric unit, Carson has assisted surgeons all over the world.

In July of 2003 Carson was an assisting surgeon in a widely publicized attempt to separate twenty-nine-year-old Iranian sisters, joined at the backs of their heads, who themselves decided that a fifty-fifty chance that one or neither would survive the operation was better than continuing to live in a conjoined state, where they could not pursue their individual and distinct interests. Following the failure of this operation and the deaths of both sisters, Carson determined not to perform any more such operations on adults.

In August 2002, Carson successfully underwent surgery himself for prostate cancer, which had not metastasized. Carson was honored with the NAACP's Spingarn Medal in 2006 and with the Presidential Medal of Freedom in 2008.

In addition to his practice, Carson has written numerous articles for medical journals; an autobiography, *Gifted Hands: The Ben Carson Story* (1990); and two motivational books, *The Big Picture* (1999) and *Think Big* (1992). He has been an outspoken champion of such issues as racial diversity, affirmative action, and health care reform. In 1994 Carson and his wife founded the Carson Scholars Fund, which offers scholarships to encourage children to take an interest in science, math, and technology and to balance the attention given to sports and entertainment with an appreciation of academic achievement.

FURTHER READING

Carson, Ben. *The Big Picture: Getting Perspective on What's Really Important in Life* (1999)

Carson, Ben. *Gifted Hands: The Ben Carson Story* (1990)

Carson, Ben. *Think Big: Unleashing Your Potential for Excellence* (1992)

THOMAS O. EDWARDS

Carson, Julia May Porter (8 July 1938–15 Dec. 2007), U.S. congresswoman, was born Julia May Porter in Louisville, Kentucky, to Velma Porter, a maid, and Clifford McGuire. In 1939 Velma and Julia moved to Indianapolis, Indiana. In 1955 Carson graduated from Crispus Attucks High School in Indianapolis. She attended Indiana Central Business College and went on to complete three years of college over her lifetime. She attended Indiana University–Purdue University from 1970 to 1972, St. Mary of the Woods College from 1976 to 1978, and Martin University in Indianapolis from 1994 to 1995.

As a youth Carson delivered newspapers, waited tables, and did summer farm labor to earn money. After high school she was a secretary, working for the United Auto Workers Local #550 until 1965. She married Sammy Carson, a laborer, in 1956. She sought a divorce that was granted in 1963 and was given custody of her two children. Later she also reared two grandchildren.

Julia Porter Carson's experience in politics began in 1965 when she worked until 1972 as a secretary and then as a congressional aide in Indiana's Tenth District for the U.S. congressman Andrew Jacobs Jr. In 1972 she was elected to the Indiana House of Representatives, serving from 1973 to 1976, and from 1977 to 1990 she served in the Indiana Senate. As state representative and senator, Carson focused on families, sponsoring legislation to ease collection of child support, as well as legislation to foster in-home health care. In 1984 the *Indianapolis Star* newspaper named her Woman of the Year. While she was a member of the Indiana General Assembly, Carson held the position of human resources manager at Cummins Engine Company. She was also proprietor of a clothing store called J. Carson, but the store's debts necessitated its closing in the late 1990s.

In 1990 Carson was elected to the position of Center Township trustee of Marion County. The Center Township post was one of administering to low-income people in the major metropolitan area of Indianapolis. She took on the poor-relief office when it was facing an enormous deficit while the number of people on assistance was rapidly increasing. Her administrative strategy included an ambitious workfare program to remove people from welfare and provide them with jobs and educational experiences. Procedures to protect against fraud were used to reduce the astronomical debt. Serving as trustee from 1991 to 1996, Carson improved the overall financial status of the agency, reducing by half the number of aid recipients while reducing taxes. Her fiscal achievements won bipartisan admiration. In 1997 the Center Township government building was renamed the Julia M. Carson Government Center. In 1992 she was again named the *Indianapolis Star*'s Woman of the Year.

In 1996 Carson, a Democrat, ran for election to the 105th U.S. Congress and won, becoming the first African American and the first woman that Indianapolis sent to Congress. Also elected to the five succeeding congresses, she began serving in 3 January 1997.

During the 105th Congress (1997–1998), she was a member of the Veterans' Affairs Committee that included subcommittees on health care issues and veterans' benefits; she held this seat through 2002. She also served as a member of the House Committee on Financial Services that included the Subcommittee on Housing and Community Opportunity and the Subcommittee on Financial Institutions and Consumer Credit. Beginning in 1997 Representative Carson prioritized children's issues, such as support for affordable quality child care for working families and access to a comprehensive education, including programs such as Head Start, children's safety, and health care.

During the 106th Congress (1999–2000), Carson cosponsored legislation to facilitate the identification of children who would qualify for Medicaid or for the Children's Health Insurance Program. Also supporting measures for the prevention of abuse and neglect of children and of animals, she received the Humane Legislator of the Year Award in May 2000. In the same Congress, Carson introduced a bill authorizing that a Congressional Gold Medal be awarded to civil rights figure ROSA PARKS. The bill was signed into law by President Bill J. Clinton in May 1999. In 1999 Carson joined with the Congressional Caucus for Women's Issues. As cochair of the Violence against Women Team in the caucus, she announced support for legislation on needs such as women's safety, health, education, and career issues. Highlights of her term in the 106th Congress also included her work for public safety. Carson was named in April 2000 as Legislator of the Year by the Indiana Public Health Association for supporting good public health policy. In August 2000 she was named Taxpayer Hero by Taxpayers for Common Sense Action, a national budget watchdog organization.

During the 107th Congress (2001–2002), Carson introduced the Responsible Fatherhood Act to develop programs aimed toward empowering men to take an active family role. She cited a lack of economic opportunities and parenting skills as barriers that prevented fathers from rearing their children. In 2001 she established the Latino Program to offer help to the growing Latino community in Indianapolis and received a high rating in 2002 from the National Hispanic Leadership Agenda on issues important to Latinos. She also addressed the need for affordable housing, and the issue of predatory lending practices became a priority for Carson. When scandals of corporate fraud against mainstream workers and investors surfaced, Carson was at the forefront of the fight to address issues of corporate accountability.

After the 2000 census, congressional districts were realigned. As a result, the Democrat Carson was placed in the Seventh District, a more heavily Republican district than her former Tenth District. However, she won the 2002 election to the 108th

Congress (2003–2004). In January 2003 she became a member of the Committee on Transportation and Infrastructure, vacating her seat on the Veterans' Affairs Committee but continuing to support veterans' interests. Under the jurisdiction of the Transportation and Infrastructure Committee, Carson worked on civil aviation, ground transportation, and water resources management. In 2003 she sponsored the National Defense Rail Act to fund development of the nation's railroad system, citing the need for a more balanced system of transportation alternatives and the need for reducing dependence on foreign oil.

From her seat on the Financial Services Committee, Carson addressed issues such as consumer protection in credit reporting. In October 2003 she also introduced a bill amending the Consumer Credit Protection Act in order to provide consumer protection in debt management organizations. Aware of the need for financial literacy among constituents, she also hosted town forums while working with the chair of governors of the Federal Reserve System. In 2003 she sponsored the Bringing America Home Act to end homelessness and address needs such as the health and income of the 3.5 million people in the United States without adequate housing.

During 2004 Carson continued to support health care issues. As millions of children were still uninsured, she introduced the Children's Express Lane to Health Coverage Act to build on the legislation she cosponsored in 2000 to streamline provision of health insurance. She sponsored the Veteran's VOTE Act in 2004 to secure voting rights for veterans honorably discharged from military service but who were denied the right to vote after serving time in prison for a felony conviction. She cited post-traumatic stress disorder from combat as a factor contributing to convictions in the lives of veterans.

In 2004 Carson was elected to the 109th Congress for the years 2005–2006, and in 2006 to the 110th Congress for 2007–2008. During these terms she continued to serve on the Financial Services Committee and the Committee on Transportation and Infrastructure and to support veterans' issues. She died in Indianapolis, Indiana, at the age of sixty-nine,, after a battle with lung cancer.

FURTHER READING

Hawkings, David, and Brian, Nutting, eds.
  Congressional Quarterly, Politics in America 2004, the 108th Congress (2003).

Indianapolis Star, available online at http://www.indystar.com/library/factfiles.

ROSE PELONE SISSON

Carson, Robert (Sonny Carson) (22 May 1929?–20 Dec. 2002), activist and author, was the eldest of six children born to working-class parents in Orangeburg, South Carolina. When Carson was three years old, his parents moved the family to Brooklyn, New York, where they were among the first African Americans to integrate the predominantly Irish-Italian neighborhood of Bedford-Stuyvesant. This racially charged environment and the young Carson's experience as a black student in a white school helped shape his later beliefs as an activist.

In his teenage years Carson was an excellent student but showed an equal propensity for street life. He became a ranking member of a neighborhood gang the same year he entered junior high school. By the time he was sixteen years old Carson had been arrested several times for petty crimes ranging from stealing cigarettes to throwing a snowball at a teacher. He committed his first serious crime when he robbed a Western Union messenger of $100; he was sentenced to three years in a juvenile correctional facility. He was released at the age of nineteen.

Shortly after returning home to Brooklyn, Carson enlisted in the U.S. Army to escape the backlash of a street life that was fast catching up with him. Despite his reluctance to submit to the rigid authority of the military, he became a paratrooper in the Eighty-Second Airborne Division and was shipped to Seoul, Korea, to serve in the Korean War. While on guard duty, Carson was shot in the leg during an ambush and was soon honorably discharged from the service.

In 1958 Carson met Claire Wells, the woman who would become his wife. The couple had a son and settled into a quiet, suburban life in Queens, seemingly a world away from the social and political unrest in other black communities. Claire was a legal secretary and a public school teacher. Carson took a job with the U.S. Postal Service and worked nights for the New York Transit Authority. But by October 1964 Carson had grown restless with and resentful of his tidy life while so many of his people suffered under the weight of racial oppression. Inspired by the speeches of MALCOLM X and spurred by a need to be part of the solution, Carson left his wife, who was pregnant with their second son, to join in the civil rights activities mounted by the Congress of Racial Equality (CORE) and the Southern Non-Violent Coordinating Committee (SNCC), in the South.

After the death of his wife, Carson returned to New York with an agenda for the growing agitation in poor, black communities. He joined the Brooklyn chapter of CORE and was named community relations director in 1967; he was promoted to executive director a year later. His first course of action was to lead a rally on Fulton Street, the borough's main business district, to promote black entrepreneurship and encourage local business owners to invest in the community. Under the direction of Carson, nearly two thousand men and women paraded to the Fulton Street rally to hear speeches by BOBBY SEALE and FLOYD McKISSICK, then the national director of CORE.

The summer of 1967 thrust Carson into a position of real community leadership and burgeoning political power. Racial tensions were high, and rioting was a product of the frustration in Brooklyn's ghettos. Carson represented the people in a series of meetings with Mayor John Lindsay, addressing the underlying causes of anger in Brooklyn's black community. That year Robert Kennedy offered Carson a seat on the Bedford-Stuyvesant Restoration Corporation, the first community development organization in the country. Carson subsequently helped establish Medgar Evers College, a city university nestled in the heart of downtown Brooklyn.

A series of public face-offs with the United Federation of Teachers and the New York City Board of Education, however, made Carson a household name in the city and a champion for the struggle of disadvantaged people across the nation. In 1968 thirteen white teachers in the Ocean Hill–Brownsville section of Brooklyn were found inadequate and incapable of educating the black and Latino children they were charged with teaching. The governing board ousted them from their respective schools; three hundred fellow teachers walked off the job in support of them, sparking a citywide teachers' strike.

Carson, aware of the effect the strike would have on a community already struggling for equal education, led the fight to keep Ocean Hill–Brownsville schools open. He assembled a network of parent and community volunteers to lead classes in place of the picketing teachers, making it possible for students to remain in school despite the strike. Even more significant was his outspoken advocacy for community control of schools, which placed boards composed of parents, students, and teachers in cooperative charge of children's education. Carson's charismatic leadership and creative civil disobedience helped draw national attention to the ongoing community control debate.

In 1968 Carson, his Brooklyn chapter, and sixteen other local chapters severed ties with national CORE, citing the organization's conservatism and failure to stay in touch with real issues in the black community. With its moderate parent organization no longer acting as watchdog, the independent Brooklyn CORE walked the fine line between civil protest and blatant disregard for the law.

Carson published his autobiography, *The Education of Sonny Carson*, in 1972 under his adopted name, Mwlina Imiri Abubadika. The book detailed his transition from street hustler to enlightened community activist. Paramount Pictures retained the rights to make a film version of the book, and the movie was released in 1974. During filming, Carson was arrested on charges of murder, attempted murder, and kidnapping after allegedly participating in a shooting that left one Brooklyn man dead and another seriously injured. Carson was acquitted of all but the kidnapping charges and served seventeen months in a New York prison.

In the 1980s Carson invested his energy and leadership in the battle against crack cocaine, which was decimating black communities. He organized the Black Men's Movement against Crack and was instrumental in shutting down several neighborhood crack houses. Carson was also a founding member of the December 12th Movement, an organization dedicated to fighting institutionalized racism, in particular police brutality.

Carson remained involved in community activism on the local and national levels through the 1990s and the early 2000s. His Committee to Honor Black Heroes, an organization born from the discovery of an African burial ground in downtown Manhattan and the struggle to return those ancestors to their native soil, became his signature project of that era. He was also at the forefront of the movement to rename Brooklyn's Fulton Street to honor HARRIET TUBMAN. Carson died in a heart attack-induced coma in 2002, three years before the thoroughfare was officially conamed Harriet Ross Tubman Avenue.

FURTHER READING

Abubadika, Mwlina Imiri. *The Education of Sonny Carson* (1972).

Jacoby, Tamar. "Sonny Carson and the Politics of Protest," *City Journal* (1991).

Obituary: *New York Times*, 23 Dec. 2002.

JANELLE HARRIS

Carter, Alprentice "Bunchy" (12 Oct. 1947–17 Jan. 1969), founder and principal organizer of the Southern California chapter of the Black Panther Party (BPP), was born in Shreveport, Louisiana, to Evon Carter Little information is published about his early life. Evon Carter moved the family to Los Angeles, California, in the early 1950s. Carter became known to friends and relatives by the name "Bunchy" Carter would introduce himself as "Bunchy … like a bunch of greens."

During the time Carter's family moved to Los Angeles, black youth built street organizations in South Central Los Angeles to defend themselves against white supremacist youth gangs in predominately white neighborhoods adjacent to the African American community. One of those street organizations was the Slausons (named for Slauson Avenue, which runs through South Central). Bunchy rose as a leader of the Slausons in the early 1960s. The Slausons, with 5,000 members, was the largest street force in Los Angeles during the early 1960s. Carter led a 500-member contingent called "the Renegades."

Carter was convicted for armed robbery in 1963 and sentenced to a four-year sentence at Soledad Prison in central California. While incarcerated, Carter joined the Nation of Islam (NOI) in Soledad. MALCOLM X's decision to leave NOI in 1964 persuaded many incarcerated Muslims to follow his lead. Another Muslim convict, ELDRIDGE CLEAVER, was instrumental in convincing Carter to leave NOI and support Malcolm X's interpretation of Islam and black revolutionary nationalism. The two prisoners founded Soledad's African History and Culture class in 1966. Upon their release, Cleaver and Carter planned to rebuild Malcolm X's post-NOI organization, the Organization of Afro-American Unity (OAAU), as a vehicle for organizing a black revolution.

Cleaver was released on parole to San Francisco, California, in December 1966. Upon meeting and being impressed with the fledgling Black Panther Party for Self-Defense in Oakland, Cleaver abandoned the plans to rebuild OAAU and joined the BPP, under the leadership of the organization's founders HUEY NEWTON and BOBBY SEALE.

Cleaver soon emerged as the group's Minister of Information. Carter, who was released from Soledad in the summer of 1967, initially did not share Cleaver's positive impressions of the BPP. According to Cleaver, Carter implored they "not get hung up with these college boys (both Newton and Seale were college educated)." Refusing to join Cleaver's new organization, Carter returned to Los Angeles. There he found his old community more radicalized, a consequence of the confrontations between African American youths and the Los Angeles Police Department and National Guard during the August 1965 Watts uprising. After Watts, Los Angeles blacks had joined and formed several militant organizations dedicated to the concept of Black Power.

Carter found employment at a Teen Post in South Central Los Angeles. The Teen Post was an anti-poverty program launched in the wake of the Watts uprising. The program consisted of counseling, employment, job training, and recreational activity for urban youth. Teen Post provided Carter with employment—as required by his parole—and also served as a vehicle for politicizing and organizing black youth. Carter facilitated forums to politically educate South Central residents and inspire them to be part of a revolutionary and paramilitary group he was building called "the Radicals." Eventually, however, Carter changed his mind about affiliation with the Oakland-based Black Panther Party for Self-Defense. A major factor in his change of heart was the arrest of BPP Minister of Defense Huey Newton following a gun battle with Oakland police on 29 October 1967. After Newton's arrest, Carter called Cleaver and volunteered to be a part of the organization. Cleaver then came to Los Angeles at Carter's invitation to speak to "the Radicals" and to consolidate them into a BPP chapter.

The Southern California chapter of the BPP announced its existence on 18 February 1968. Carter recruited from his Teen Post "Radicals" group, close friends, and former Slausons and Renegades. He was named Deputy Minister of Defense for the Southern California chapter, serving as the de facto leader of the chapter. In this capacity, Carter also relied on his street connections to build an underground Panther cadre, often referred to as the "Wolves." According to Carter associate Geronimo ji-Jaga (aka GERONIMO PRATT), the true identities and activities of the Wolves were not revealed to rank-and-file Panthers.

Carter enrolled at the University of California at Los Angeles (UCLA) in the fall of 1968. He and other BPP members and other activists received special admissions to UCLA through the High Potential program, which utilized nontraditional criteria for college admissions. At UCLA, tensions between the BPP and Organization Us, a rival black nationalist organization led by Maulana Ron Karenga, came to a head. Both organizations vied to be the "vanguard" or central organization of the Black Power movement in Los Angeles. Counterinsurgency strategists, particularly in the Federal Bureau of Investigation, exploited the competition between the BPP and Organization Us to heighten the level of hostilities.

The rivalry between the BPP and Organization Us would lead to a gun battle on the UCLA campus on 17 January 1969. Tensions were high due on campus due to differences between members of the two groups concerning the leadership and direction of the newly formed Black Studies department on campus. A conflict between a BPP member and Organization Us member escalated from argument to a fist fight and ultimately to a shooting that resulted in the death of Carter and one of his BPP comrades, John Huggins. Carter's death was devastating to the Southern California BPP and the Black Power movement in Los Angeles.

Alprentice Bunchy Carter remains a hero who is saluted by black activists and those in solidarity with the African American Freedom Movement. Like Malcolm X and GEORGE JACKSON, Carter made the transition from black criminal and convict to a life committed to revolutionary activism.

FURTHER READING

Cleaver, Eldridge. *Target Zero: A Life in Writing*. Edited by Kathleen Cleaver (2006).

Cleaver, Kathleen, and George Katsiaficus. *Liberation, Imagination, and the Black Panther Party* (2001).

Curtis Austin. *Up Against the Wall: Violence and the Making and Unmaking of the Black Panther Party* (2006).

Jones, Charles E., ed. *The Black Panther Party Reconsidered* (1998).

AKINYELE K. UMOJA

Carter, Anson (6 June 1974–), hockey player, was born in Toronto, Ontario, the second of three children, to Horace Carter, an assessor for Revenue Canada, and Valma Carter, a Ministry of Transportation employee. Carter's parents arrived from Barbados in 1967 and settled in the neighborhood of Scarborough, an immigrant-heavy neighborhood of Toronto. Athletics were in Carter's family—his father played cricket in Barbados and his mother ran track—and Carter was playing street hockey at the age of four and ice hockey at eight.

Conquering his initial struggles with skating, Carter became a standout forward in Canada's minor hockey leagues, playing for the Agincourt Lions, the Metro Toronto Hockey League's Triple-A Don Mills Flyers, and finally, at seventeen, the elite Tier II, Junior-A Wexford Raiders. With other black teammates on his teams as a youth—his neighborhood produced another black Barbadian hockey player in the goalie Kevin Weekes—Carter rarely heard comments about his race while playing the white-dominated game. When his parents witnessed racist invective hurled at their fourteen-year-old son during a tournament in Guelph, Ontario, they bolstered his confidence in a conversation about prejudice and obstacles, which Carter would later recall when dealing with taunts by opposing players and fans.

After graduating from Agincourt Collegiate Institute in 1992, Carter was selected by the NHL's Quebec Nordiques with the 220th pick in the draft. The future star opted instead to go to Michigan State University on a baseball and hockey scholarship, with the intention of becoming a stronger player, as well as being premed to line up a career in orthopedics. At hockey-mad Michigan State, Carter stopped playing baseball and switched his major to sociology to concentrate solely on the ice. Following a thirty-goal, fifty-four-point sophomore season, he helped Canada to a gold medal in the World Junior Championships. Carter was named second team All-America, and a finalist for the NCAA Hobey-Baker Trophy following a thirty-four-goal, fifty-one-point junior season. As team captain his senior year, he led his team in scoring for the third straight time. The Washington Capitals traded for his draft rights in April 1996, and Carter soon starred for their American Hockey League affiliate, the Portland Pirates, tallying thirty-eight points in twenty-seven games. After nineteen games in a call-up to the Capitals, he was packaged in a multiplayer trade to the Boston Bruins in March 1997.

Carter became a fan favorite in Boston, earning the nickname "A.C.," and establishing himself as a goal-scoring forward on the rise. After an auspicious first complete year with the Bruins in 1997–98 in which he tallied forty-three points in seventy-eight games, Carter fell into a contract dispute during the off-season. He played briefly with the Utah Grizzlies of the International Hockey League before settling on a two-year contract. After returning from an ankle injury, Carter scored twenty-four goals, racking up forty points in just fifty-five games with the Bruins.

After a 1999–2000 season in which Carter emerged as a leader on the ice (his forty-seven points in fifty-nine games was second most on the team, drawing praise from the Bruins icon Ray Borque), the right wing once again had contractual conflict with the Bruins' front office. Boston balked at paying the hefty price tag for Carter and traded him to the Edmonton Oilers. Carter tied for the team lead with sixty points in 2001–2002, and he was leading the club the following season when the cash-strapped Oilers traded him to the New York Rangers, who were vying for a playoff spot.

When the Rangers missed in their bid for the postseason, Carter suited up for the Canadian team in the World Championships in May 2003. His heavily reviewed game-winning goal in overtime against Sweden gave his nation its first title in six years, and Carter was presented with the key to the city of Toronto that July. The following season, he was traded twice—first to the Capitals for the superstar Jaromir Jagr and then to the Los Angeles Kings, close to where he had established his off-season home some years earlier.

With an eye toward other fields, noting that the NHL had few blacks in front office and coaching jobs, Carter cultivated an interest in the music industry. Reaping the networking benefits of living in Los Angeles, Carter founded a production company and hip-hop record label called Big Up Entertainment.

In August 2005, Carter signed a one-year deal with the Vancouver Canucks, posting a career high of 33 goals; the following season, he signed with the Columbus Blue Jackets before being traded to the Carolina Hurricanes. After the Oilers released him following a brief tryout in September 2007, Carter signed with the Swiss team HC Lugano for the remainder of the season, totaling three goals and five assists in fifteen games.

Carter and his wife, Erika, had a daughter, Mikayla, born in 2006.

FURTHER READING

Gray, Jeff. "A Hockey Hero's Wobbly Start," *Globe & Mail*, 13 May 2003.

Harris, Cecil. *Breaking the Ice: The Black Experience in Professional Hockey* (2004).

ADAM W. GREEN

Carter, Betty (16 May 1929–26 Sept. 1998), jazz vocalist and record company founder, was born Lillie Mae Jones in Flint, Michigan, the daughter of James Jones, a factory worker who also led a Baptist church choir, and Bertha Cox. Carter grew up in Detroit, where she attended North Western High School. She later studied piano at the Detroit Conservatory, and it is rumored that she falsified her age to be admitted. In 1946 she began singing at local clubs and sitting in on sessions with DIZZY GILLESPIE's big band and CHARLIE PARKER's quintet.

Carter, considered a bit of an eccentric, was ahead of her time with her unique style of vocals. Unlike the comparatively smooth sounds of her predecessors SARAH VAUGHAN and ELLA FITZGERALD, Carter's husky voice was then unusual; it was often described as having a saxophone-like quality. While touring with LIONEL HAMPTON from 1948 to 1951, Carter took the stage name "Lorraine Carter," but her flavorful improvisations and distinguishing scatting style inspired Hampton to give her the nickname "Betty BeBop." She eventually dropped "Lorraine" and adopted "Betty." The years with Hampton were difficult for the young singer. On several occasions he fired her. Each time, Hampton's wife, Gladys, simply rehired

Betty Carter, known as the "Godmother of Jazz," sings at her home in Brooklyn, New York, May 1978. [AP Images.]

Carter, insisting that she acquire some solid experience before going out on her own. Carter also faced many obstacles working with various managers and recording companies. Never willing to conform to or imitate popular styles, she was labeled as troublesome and for many years went virtually unrecognized. After leaving Hampton's band in the early 1950s, she recorded the vocals on King Pleasure's *Red Top* in 1952. In 1955, with RAY BRYANT, she recorded *Meet Betty Carter and Ray Bryant*. In 1958 she worked with MILES DAVIS. In 1965 Carter married James Redding; they had two sons and would eventually divorce. During this period she toured and recorded with RAY CHARLES (*Ray Charles and Betty Carter*, 1961). Two of their most memorable duets—"Baby It's Cold Outside" and "Georgia on My Mind"—made Charles a household name. Carter remained on the tour circuit, performing in Japan in 1963, London in 1964, and France in 1968.

In 1969 Carter founded her own record label, Bet-Car Productions, and started hiring and mentoring aspiring jazz musicians. Her unselfish nurturing of young musical talent earned her the title "Godmother of Jazz." Her talented protégés included the pianists John Hicks, Marc Cary, Mulgrew Miller, Benny Green, Stephen Scott, and Cyrus Chestnut; the drummers Clarence Penn, Lewis Nash, and Jack DeJohnette; and the bassists Buster Williams, Dave Holland, Chris Thomas, Michael Bowie, and Curtis Lundy. Her 1975 appearance in Howard Moore's musical *Don't Call Me Man* as well as performances in 1977 and 1978 at the Newport Jazz Festival gave rise to several club engagements through the mid-1980s. Audiences again were becoming enthusiastic over Carter's style. Her classic 1979 recording *The Audience with Betty Carter* eventually received a Grammy nomination. But it was her 1987 release *Look What I Got!* that earned her a 1988 Grammy Award and finally provided overdue recognition for her work in jazz. *Look What I Got!* became the first independently produced jazz album to achieve this honor. Over a career of almost fifty years, she recorded thirty albums.

In 1997 Carter received the National Medal of Arts Award from President Bill Clinton. She remained as fierce a supporter of music education as she was a critic of the commercial jazz market. Accusing producers of having an inability to see beyond the available quick cash, Carter deplored the shift from original, intellectual jazz to an emphasis on producing hit records. She consistently pressured recording companies to create a larger budget for jazz and commit more marketing dollars to the production of upcoming artists instead of reissuing jazz classics from the 1930s and 1940s. She continuously reminded her students that "the Lord didn't stop giving out talent with DUKE ELLINGTON." Consistent with this philosophy was her creation in 1993 of Jazz Ahead (later adopted by the Kennedy Center), a music program that accepted twenty young students annually to develop their talent. Each year the program ended with a weekend of inspiring performances by the youthful musicians. Betty Carter died in her Brooklyn home.

Carter's vehement independence alienated some, but her originality advanced an innovative jazz, and her demand for excellence inspired a new generation of artists. While other jazz musicians enjoyed celebrity, she employed daring technique to transform her individuality into a distinctive sound.

FURTHER READING

Bauer, William R. *Open the Door: The Life and Music of Betty Carter* (2002).

Carr, Ian, Digby Fairweather, and Brian Priestley. *Jazz: The Rough Guide; The Essential Companion to Artists and Albums*, 2d ed. (2000).

Obituary: *Washington Post*, 27 Sept. 1998.

This entry is taken from the *American National Biography* and is published here with the permission of the American Council of Learned Societies.

NOLEN HARRIS

Carter, Bo (21 Mar. 1893–21 Sept. 1964), blues singer, was born Armenter Chatmon in rural Hinds County, Mississippi, about fifteen miles west of Jackson, the son of Henderson Chatmon and Eliza Jackson, both farmers. His father was also a musician whose reputation as a fiddler dated back to country dances in the days of slavery. His mother played guitar. All nine brothers and one sister in the family played various instruments. Armenter Chatmon nicknamed "Bo," played violin, guitar, bass, banjo, and clarinet, learning mainly from an older brother, Lonnie. Another brother, Sam, whose later recollections constituted the main body of information about the family, said Lonnie was born early in the 1890s and was the first to learn music, so he taught each of the younger siblings.

It was Bo Chatmon who first organized the musical siblings as a business enterprise around 1917. Working in various groupings as they came of age, brothers Bo, Lonnie, Willie, Edgar, Lamar,

Sam (whose given name was Vivian), Larry, Harry, and Charlie (a stepbrother) played parties, picnics, and resorts, relying heavily on white audiences and the square dance repertoire they had learned from their father. As their popularity grew, the brothers added blues, fox trots, and pop hits, learned mostly from Lonnie, the only sibling who could read music. To handle multiple bookings, the brothers began to divide up into two or more groups. They also began to include a musical cousin and neighbor, Walter Vincson, a guitar prodigy who worked around Jackson in the early 1920s with such accomplished blues artists as TOMMY JOHNSON, Ishmon Bracey, and Charlie McCoy.

According to Vincson, disagreements over how earnings should be divided caused the brothers to disband at some point in the mid-1920s. Bo Chatmon moved north to the Delta region of the state and got a job on a plantation near Hollandale. Lonnie, Sam, and Vincson followed, and by 1928 the four were playing in the Hollandale area.

In December 1928 Chatmon went to New Orleans and launched the family's recording career, cutting three issued sides as the vocalist and leader in a string-band format—violin, guitar, and mandolin—for the Brunswick label. It is most likely that Chatmon was the violinist, accompanied by Vincson on guitar and McCoy on mandolin. Vincson by this time was considered an adopted Chatmon, and McCoy continued to work with the family off and on until the mid-1930s.

Within a year or so after the initial Brunswick session, a talent scout for Okeh Records heard a Chatmon group playing at a white square dance in Itta Bena, Mississippi, and arranged a recording session in Shreveport, Louisiana. The session, held on 17 February 1930, was supervised by the record distributor Polk Brockman, who suggested that the musical family adopt a catchy name. They settled on the Mississippi Sheiks, "sheik" being then-current slang for a ladies' man. That session, featuring Lonnie on violin with Vincson on guitar and possibly Chatmon on second violin, was a huge success. It yielded eight issued sides, among them the hits "Stop and Listen" and "Sitting on Top of the World," the latter of which became an American standard, reprised by bluegrass, swing, rock, pop, and blues groups.

Lonnie and Vincson continued to form the core of the Sheiks over the next five years, although Sam and Harry Chatmon and McCoy often joined them at recording sessions. Bo, who by then had changed his musical persona to Bo Carter, also participated in many of the sessions and toured extensively with the Sheiks. Still, Bo maintained an identity separate from the group, recording as a featured artist or as the Mississippi Sheiks with Bo Carter. As a solo artist, Carter produced more than one hundred recorded titles between 1928 and 1940, displaying an intricate and richly textured picking style on guitar and a seemingly inexhaustible talent for risqué lyrics—"Banana in Your Fruit Basket" was a typical title.

Bo also played on a number of recordings that were issued under fanciful pseudonyms. In late 1930, for example, when he and the Sheiks recorded for Okeh in Jackson, the session included McCoy on a half-dozen instrumentals attributed to the Mississippi Mud Steppers. McCoy also backed Carter and Sam Chatmon at a January 1931 session for Brunswick in Chicago, with sides attributed to the Mississippi Blacksnakes and the Tennessee Shakers.

In 1931 alone Bo produced twenty-four issued sides for Okeh and played with the Sheiks on twelve additional sides. As the Great Depression deepened, however, recording dates dropped off. Carter and the Chatmons traveled to Grafton, Wisconsin, in 1932 to record for Paramount, a once-thriving blues label that had fallen on hard times. The session produced a dozen issued sides but failed to save Paramount, which folded that same year. In 1933 the brothers went to New York City for what turned out to be their final session for Okeh. The next year, in San Antonio, Texas, Carter and the Sheiks recorded for Bluebird, a low-budget label started by RCA Victor. It was around this time that Carter acquired a steel-bodied National guitar, an instrument well suited to his increasing output of blues-oriented material.

Although Carter and the Chatmons recorded as the Mississippi Sheiks for the last time in January 1935, they were far from finished as recording artists. Carter recorded a dozen sides for Bluebird in February 1936 and a dozen more in October. The October session at the St. Charles Hotel in New Orleans also resulted in ten sides by Lonnie and Sam Chatmon, recording as the Chatmon Brothers. Vincson was at the October session too, recording as a featured artist with piano accompaniment. When not recording, Carter and the Sheiks were on the move throughout the 1930s, touring Mississippi, Louisiana, and Texas and as far north as Illinois and New York. Even after the Sheiks no longer issued records, they continued to perform with traveling minstrel and medicine shows.

Carter recorded for Bluebird until 1940, but his eyesight was failing, and his popularity was in decline. In 1936 he settled in Glen Allan, Mississippi, about twenty-five miles south of Greenville. In the early 1940s he moved to Walls, Mississippi, just south of Memphis, and later moved into Memphis, where he faded into obscurity and poverty. When the British blues researcher Paul Oliver located him in 1960, he was blind and barely able to play guitar. He died four years later of a cerebral hemorrhage at a Memphis hospital and was buried in Sharkey County, Mississippi, in the Nitta Yuma Cemetery, between Anguilla and Hollandale.

Lonnie Chatmon moved to Anguilla in 1937. He operated a "juke joint" bar there and later opened a second near his family's original homestead in Hinds County. In failing health due to heart problems, he died around 1951.

Vincson, the adopted Chatmon, moved to Chicago in 1941. He recorded for Bluebird in August of that year, then dropped out of the music business for nearly two decades. He resurfaced during the 1960s-era blues revival, recording an album for Riverside in 1961 and playing on a Sheiks reunion album issued by Rounder in 1972. He died in a nursing home in 1975 and was buried in Holy Sepulchre Cemetery in Worth, Illinois.

McCoy, the part-time Sheik, also landed in Chicago. He worked as an accompanist with such major blues artists as MEMPHIS MINNIE and JOHN LEE "SONNY BOY" WILLIAMSON, formed a jazz-blues group known as the Harlem Hamfats, and remained active in music through the 1940s. He later entered a psychiatric hospital, where he died of a paralytic brain disease in 1950. He was buried in Restvale Cemetery, also in Worth.

The last of the original Sheiks, Sam Chatmon, remained in Mississippi for a number of years, working as a plantation supervisor in Arcola before moving back to Hollandale. He too resurfaced during the blues revival, playing in California, touring on the festival circuit, and recording for Arhoolie, Blue Goose, Rounder, and Advent. He appeared on network television in 1976 as a spokesman for Mississippi, was featured in the documentary film *Good Morning Blues*, and became the principal interpreter of his family's history for music researchers. He died in Hollandale in 1983. He was survived by a son, Sam Chatmon Jr., who recorded in Chicago in the 1960s.

Bo Carter and the Mississippi Sheiks were among the most prolific recording artists of their day and were enormously popular with African Americans.

The Sheiks put out almost one hundred sides—not counting the many sides issued under pseudonyms. Carter's record output put him in a league with Memphis Minnie and other top blues artists of his era. Bo was also a superb guitarist, adorning his vocals with sophisticated runs and chords. Along with McCoy, he ranks among the best instrumentalists ever to come from the Jackson–Hinds County area of Mississippi. Vincson, who on his own records was often identified as Walter Vinson or Walter Jacobs, was a fine guitarist too, but he always relinquished the lead to Lonnie Chatmon's fiddle when recording as a Sheik.

Early critics and record collectors, impressed by the more hard-edged blues of musicians such as Tommy Johnson and CHARLEY PATTON, tended to criticize Bo Carter and the Sheiks for their blending of black and white styles, their heavy doses of double entendre, and their repertoire of good-time dance blues. Even their huge record output was held against them, as if commercial appeal precluded historical importance. Later researchers, more attuned to the African American string band tradition and the deep cultural roots of so-called party blues, accorded the Chatmons and their colleagues a more prominent niche in musical history.

The Chatmon family's music spanned more than 120 years. It originated in a string band tradition catering to white consumption. It then evolved into a good-natured blues style that catered almost exclusively to the African American "race market" during the Depression. Later, with Sam Chatmon Jr., it melded into the big-city electric blues sound that presaged rock and roll.

FURTHER READING

Dixon, Robert M. W., and John Godrich, comps. *Blues and Gospel Records, 1902–1943* (1982).

Gart, Galen. "Sam Chatmon," *Blues Unlimited*, July 1971.

McKee, Margaret, and Fred Chisenhall. *Beale Black and Blue: Life and Music on Black America's Main Street* (1981).

DISCOGRAPHY

Leadbitter, Mike, and Neil Slaven. *Blues Records 1943–1970: A Selective Discography*, vol. 1 (1987).

This entry is taken from the *American National Biography* and is published here with the permission of the American Council of Learned Societies.

BARRY LEE PEARSON AND
BILL MCCULLOCH

Carter, Dennis Drummond (1 Jan. 1814–c. 1885), musician, educator, and activist, was born to free parents in Drummondtown, Accomack County, Virginia. His father died when Carter was about eight, and his mother, whose maiden name was probably Drummond, cared for Dennis. When one of his cousins, Henry Drummond, was bound out to an area slaveholder named Thomas R. Joynes because of his status as an orphan, Carter's mother began to fear that her son would also be enslaved should something happen to her. Determined that her son stay free, she moved with him to Philadelphia in about 1825. There Carter's musical talents flowered, in part under the tutelage of the famous black Philadelphia bandleader FRANCIS JOHNSON.

Carter toured with Johnson's band sporadically during the 1830s, 1840s, and early 1850s, reportedly joining Johnson's 1837 trip to Great Britain and an 1851 trip to Sulphur Springs, Virginia. In addition to working as a musician Carter seems to have begun giving music lessons during this time. His success is noted in the 1847 Quaker Census of African Americans in Philadelphia, which refers to him as "very industrious," notes $600 in personal property and a $600 annual income, and says that Carter was renting a house on Parker Street for $108 per year. Carter may have married in the 1840s, as both the 1847 Quaker Census and the 1850 Federal Census list a woman named Rebecca Carter living with him—though she might have simply been a paternal relative.

Between mid-1850 and early 1852, Carter, like hundreds of free blacks in the North, moved to California, drawn by the promise of the Gold Rush. While the spotty available evidence from this period suggests that he continued to work as a musician, he spent much more time mining. He chose to settle in Nevada County, California, though he seems to have had close ties to the larger black communities in Sacramento and San Francisco. During the 1850s and 1860s, he became active in civil rights efforts, including early battles for equal schools and suffrage, and was a subscriber to *Frederick Douglass's Paper*. Like many of his fellow black California activists—ranging from PHILIP BELL to PETER ANDERSON—Carter was also deeply involved in the Prince Hall Masons, and was twice chosen (in 1863 and again in 1868) as the state's Most Worshipful Grand Master.

In part because of changes to the mining industry and California's economic structure, Carter returned to music in the late 1850s; by the mid-1860s, in addition to working as a musician and music teacher, Carter was leading Nevada City's band—a group that performed at most official and many unofficial city functions. By 29 August 1866, the date of his marriage to Mary Jane "Jennie" Correll, Carter was well-respected by both area whites and California blacks. He had a steady income and owned a small home, which his new wife lovingly described in a column in the 17 January 1868 San Francisco *Elevator* as "a brown cottage with six rooms" of which "the first room is furnished with a melodeon and contra baso [sic]; the second with a trumbone [sic] and cornet; the third with a violincillo [sic] and a bugle; the fourth with a guitar and two canaries; the fifth with a violin and dog; the sixth with an old fiddle and cat."

During Reconstruction, Carter was recognized as a key leader among Nevada County African Americans. He continued to fight for equal schools and suffrage, was a leader in planning celebrations of the Fifteenth Amendment, served on a range of statewide committees set up by the reborn black convention movement, worked as an agent for Anderson's San Francisco–based *Pacific Appeal*, and maintained close ties with Bell's competing newspaper the *Elevator*. This last may have been a factor in Jennie Carter's rise to local fame as a columnist for the *Elevator*, for which she wrote over seventy pieces between 1867 and the mid-1870s.

The Carters seem to have had a strong, mutually supportive marriage but no children. Jennie Carter's growing health problems and Carter's own advancing age slowed them a bit, though they regularly traveled to Sacramento, San Francisco, and even Nevada to see friends and to aid in political activities and Emancipation celebrations in the 1870s. Jennie Carter died on 10 August 1881 in their Nevada City home, and Dennis Carter seems to drop from the public record soon after. Some sources suggest he moved to San Francisco and continued teaching.

Both as a musician and as an early black activist in the West, Dennis Carter is worthy of further study.

FURTHER READING
Beasley, Delilah. *Negro Trail Blazers of California* (1919).
Carter, Jennie. *Jennie Carter: A Black Journalist in the Early West*, ed. Eric Gardner (forthcoming 2007).

ERIC GARDNER

Carter, Edward, Jr. (26 May 1916–30 Jan. 1963), a U.S. Army soldier in World War II and Medal of Honor recipient, was born in Los Angeles, California, the son of Edward and Mary (Stuart) Carter. While Carter Sr. was a native of Colorado, his wife Mary was of Anglo-Indian heritage, a native of Calcutta, India. Both of Carter's parents were Christian missionaries, and it would be an understatement to say that his early life was anything but typical for the time. In fact, Carter Jr. at a young age gained a wide perspective of the world; he traveled with his missionary parents to Calcutta in 1925 and spent two years in that country. Sadly, it was a tumultuous time for the Carter family; not only was his father abusive to young Edward, but his mother also left his father, only to die a short time later. Carter Sr. subsequently moved his family to Shanghai in 1927, where he married again. The Carters lived here for eight years and it was in China that Carter Jr. gained his first military experience. Not only did he attend a military academy during these formative years, but he even volunteered to join the Chinese and British forces when the Japanese attacked Shanghai in 1932. When his father found out that he was serving on the frontlines, he ordered his son home. However, Carter Jr. had developed a love for adventure and the military life, and grew increasingly estranged from his missionary father. When Italy invaded Ethiopia in 1935, he went to the American consulate in Shanghai and offered to join in the fight against Italy. The consulate refused the nineteen-year-old's request, and instead offered him a career in the merchant marine. Carter subsequently sailed the Pacific on a freighter for some months before returning to Los Angeles in 1935. During the Great Depression, Carter had a tough time finding employment, but soon enough his attention was drawn elsewhere. When the Spanish Civil War broke out in 1937, Carter signed on for a merchant vessel heading to Spain. Here, he joined the Republican forces and fought in a unit known as the Abraham Lincoln Brigade, an integrated volunteer force of whites and African Americans. It was in Spain that Carter saw his first real military action. Not only was he wounded in action and captured and imprisoned for a time by the fascist army of Francisco Franco, but it was also here that he fought against German troops for the first time. It would not be the last. Carter spent over two years in Spain before returning to Los Angeles in 1940. In less than two years, he would again be at war.

On 26 September 1941, Carter Jr. enlisted in the army. He subsequently attended boot camp in Texas, and here encountered, for perhaps the first time in his life, real racial prejudice. Nonetheless, this did not deter Carter in his new career. In fact, from the start, due to his prior experience in China and Spain, he proved himself an excellent marksman, and a born leader. After completing basic training, Carter was assigned to a quartermaster truck company, and was soon promoted to sergeant. Support units, such as the one Carter served in, was where most African American soldiers were assigned duty in the early years of the war. Combat opportunities for black soldiers serving in segregated units would not become a reality until the last year of the war, and even then for only a limited number of men. Though Carter served in a support unit, he was desirous of seeing actual combat and longed to go overseas. His truck company was eventually sent for overseas duty in 1944, arriving first in England before being sent to France in November. With the army in need of men after the Battle of the Bulge in December 1944, Carter was one of several thousand African Americans who volunteered for combat, doing so in January 1945. After an initial training period, he was assigned to D Company of the 56th Armored Infantry Battalion, serving in General George Patton's 3rd Army during its drive through Germany. While Carter had to accept a reduction in rank to private in order to gain a combat posting, he soon proved his leadership and fighting skills and was promoted to sergeant, the first black soldier in his unit to be promoted. His company commander would later state that "he was the ideal soldier...he was one of the best leaders we had in that company" (Carter and Allen, p. 103). On 23 March 1945, Carter and the rifle squad he commanded were riding aboard a tank and advancing toward the German town of Speyer when they took heavy bazooka fire from a large building several hundred yards distant across open ground. Carter volunteered to lead his squad to the building, but while doing so the squad took heavy fire, killing two of Carter's men and badly wounding the third. Carter continued to the enemy building alone, being wounded by gunfire while advancing in the hand, arm, and leg. Reaching the building, Carter took cover and, when, several hours later, a group of eight German soldiers emerged in an attempt to capture him, he killed six of them in a brief firefight, and captured the other two. He then returned across the open ground to his unit, using his two prisoners as a shield. Because of his actions, the American forces were able to advance on Speyer and take the town. Carter, in the meantime, was sent to a hospital to recover from his wounds. For his actions on 23 March, Sergeant Edward Carter Jr. would receive the Distinguished Service

Cross (DSC), the army's second-highest award, the following year. It is interesting to note that Carter's commanders debated a recommendation for the Medal of Honor, but decided against it due to the army practices then in force. They instead decided that a recommendation for the DSC would be more likely to pass muster.

The heroism of black soldiers and sailors, men like Carter, VERNON BAKER, LEONARD HARMON, and CHARLES THOMAS, is indicative of the overall contribution made by African Americans in World War II. Indeed, over a million black men served in the army alone, performing their duties on par with that of white soldiers in the face of institutionalized racism. While many men were relegated to support units both stateside and overseas, a number of men, like Carter, saw combat action in segregated infantry, armored, and tank destroyer units and as pilots. Even African Americans serving in truck companies (such as the famed "Red Ball Truckers") as Carter once did, would gain a grudging respect for their skill and dedication. However, the recognition that mattered the most, the award of the Medal of Honor, was a different matter; of the 432 such awards made during the war, not one was bestowed on an African American serviceman. This kind of recognition would not be granted for another fifty years.

After being wounded in action multiple times, thereby earning the Purple Heart Medal with two oak leaf clusters, Sergeant Carter spent time recovering in a hospital, only to appear back with his unit in April 1945. It soon was discovered that Carter had left the hospital, gone AWOL, without permission to return to his unit, but no matter. His commanding officers were glad to have him back. Carter subsequently served with his unit until the end of the war in Europe before returning stateside and gaining an honorable discharge from the army on 30 September 1945. However, with so many servicemen returning home, Carter had difficulty supporting his family and subsequently reenlisted in the army in 1946 in Virginia. He was soon stationed in California and assigned the task of training segregated National Guard units there for two years before being sent to Fort Lewis, Washington, to serve in a military police unit. When he received his discharge from the army there on 21 September 1949, after his second tour of duty expired, Carter subsequently tried to enlist yet again but was prevented from doing so. The army simply did not want him back, a situation that baffled and angered Carter, who believed that he had served his country

voluntarily and with valor. Appeals by a distraught Carter fell on deaf ears, and despite enlisting the help of the ACLU and the NAACP, he never again served in uniform. Years later, his family would discover that Carter's loyalty to his country had been in question, simply due to his exotic upbringing in India and China, and his service in Spain, a precursor of the McCarthyism that would sweep the country in the not-too-distant future. Carter would subsequently work a variety of jobs and, with the help of his wife Mildred, supported his family. However, he also suffered from his war wounds and developed other health problems. After suffering a bout with cancer, he died in Los Angles. He was interred in the Veterans Cemetery there in his full dress uniform with all his medals.

Carter might have remained a forgotten hero were it not for a later generation of historians and his own family's efforts to have his name cleared. By the 1980s the subject of African American service in World War II was being evaluated more closely by historians and the public alike, as were the army's specific award policies in regard to black soldiers—why had no black soldier been awarded the Medal of Honor? Under mounting pressure, the army commissioned a study by Shaw University to study the issue in 1992, and after four years of research it was concluded that at least ten soldiers, all Distinguished Service Cross holders, would have been awarded the Medal of Honor were it not for their race. Among these men was Sergeant Edward Carter Jr. Finally, fifty-two years after the battle at Speyer, Carter's posthumous Medal of Honor was awarded to his family in a historic White House ceremony by President Bill Clinton on 14 January 1997. The very next day, Carter was reinterred in Arlington National Cemetery. Further, upon learning of the reasons for the refusal of the army to allow Carter to continue his service in 1949, President Clinton sent a formal letter of apology to the Carter family in July 1999.

FURTHER READING

Carter, Allene G., and Robert L. Allen. *Honoring Sergeant Carter: Redeeming a Black World War II Hero's Legacy* (2003).

Converse, Elliot V., Daniel K. Gibran, John A. Cash, Robert K. Griffith, and Richard H. Kohn. *The Exclusion of Black Soldiers from the Medal of Honor in World War II* (2008).

Hanna, Charles W. *African American Recipients of the Medal of Honor* (2002).

GLENN ALLEN KNOBLOCK

Carter, Elmer Anderson (1890–16 Jan. 1973), writer and editor, was born in 1890; his parents' names and his birthplace are now unknown. Little is known of his early life and education. He married Thelma Johnson, with whom he had one daughter. Carter and his wife lived in New York City at the same address, 409 Edgecombe Avenue, from the 1940s until their deaths.

A devoted New Yorker, Carter was a prolific writer and speaker for civil rights, especially concerning jobs, housing, and public office. A committed member of the National Urban League, on 23 July 1928 he delivered a speech on employment and fair housing issues during Negro Week on the Common. In September of that year he took over the editorship of *Opportunity: Journal of Negro Life*, the Urban League's in-house magazine, when CHARLES SPURGEON JOHNSON stepped down as editor. With more than 10,000 subscribers when Carter took over, the magazine published monthly until he left in 1945, when it turned quarterly; it ceased publication in the winter of 1949. Johnson and then Carter made sure the magazine contributed to black literature while also offering insightful articles on social and political issues of importance to all people but especially

Elmer Anderson Carter, 1941. Elmer Carter (left), presents the Spingarn Award to author Richard Wright, 1941. (Library of Congress.)

to African Americans. To this end, many African American artists and writers showcased their talents in the magazine. Carter's editorial influence helped bring more scholarly articles and social information that was not available or was simply overlooked in popular newspapers and magazines of the early 1900s. Carter also wrote for the magazine and other publications. In June 1932 Carter's article "Eugenics for the Negro," published in *Birth Control Review*, proved to be an important piece on a controversial subject. At the time many writers argued that it might be better for African Americans to refrain from having children in poor communities that did not provide many opportunities for the offspring.

In 1942 his article "Shadows of the Slave Tradition" for *Survey Graphic* explored the legacies of black heritage and what it meant for New York's and the country's future. For Carter, the way to expose prejudice was through sharp writing, and the best path for fighting it lay in political and legal action. Carter's later writings were more overtly political, such as "Fighting Prejudice with Law" in the *Journal of Educational Sociology* (Jan. 1946) and "Practical Considering of Anti-Discrimination Legislation: Experiences under the New York Law against Discrimination" in the *Cornell Law Quarterly* (Fall 1954). He also wrote a book about the National Urban League in New York.

Carter was not just a writer and speaker but also an important political figure in New York from the 1930s to the 1960s. Partway into Carter's career as an editor at *Opportunity*, New York governor Herbert Lehman appointed him to the three-person Unemployment Insurance Appeal Board with a term of six years. This appointment began Carter's public career as a lifelong political ally for African Americans who were unfairly treated at work and were denied proper housing. After leaving the magazine in 1945, Carter became the first director of the New York State Commission against Discrimination. When the group reorganized to become the State Division of Human Rights, he was its first director. He resigned in 1961, leaving the group to other leaders. For the next two years he served as special assistant on race relations for Governor Nelson A. Rockefeller. He died in 1973.

FURTHER READING

Johnson, Abby Arthur, and Ronald Maberry Johnson. *Propaganda and Aesthetics: The Literary Politics of Afro-American Magazines in the Twentieth Century* (1979).

Johnson, Charles S. "The Rise of the Negro Magazine," *Journal of Negro History* 13 (1928).

Nelson, Cary. *Repression and Recovery: Modern American Poetry and the Politics of Cultural Memory, 1910–1945* (1989).

Obituary: *New York Times*, 19 Jan. 1973.

CHRISTINE G. BROWN

Carter, Eunice Hunton (16 July 1899–25 Jan. 1970), attorney, was born in Atlanta, Georgia, the daughter of the Canadian-born WILLIAM ALPHAEUS HUNTON, an executive with the Young Men's Christian Association (YMCA), and ADDIE WAITES HUNTON, a field worker with the Young Women's Christian Association (YWCA) in Europe. Carter's parents had three other children, but only Carter and her younger brother lived to adulthood. After the race riots of 1906, Carter's family left Atlanta for Brooklyn, New York, where Carter attended public schools. When her mother went to Strasbourg, which was at that time in Germany, to study at Kaiser Wilhelm University from 1909 to 1910, Carter accompanied her.

Carter attended Smith College in 1917, graduating cum laude with a B.A. and an M.A. in 1921. Her master's thesis was titled "Reform of State Government with Special Attention to the State of Massachusetts." Following in her parents' footsteps, Carter went into public service. For eleven years she was employed as a social worker with family service agencies in New York and New Jersey. In 1924 she married Lisle Carter, a Barbados native and dentist who practiced in New Jersey. The couple had one child.

Eunice Carter took occasional classes at Columbia University, finally committing herself to night classes at the Fordham University School of Law, where she completed her LLB in 1932. She was admitted to the New York Bar Association in 1934. That same year she made an unsuccessful bid for a seat in the New York state assembly. Between 1935 and 1945 she belonged to the National Association of Women Lawyers, the National Lawyers Guild, the New York Women's Bar Association, and the Harlem Lawyers Association. She served as secretary of the Committee on Conditions in Harlem after the riots there in the spring of 1935. An Episcopalian and a Republican, Carter began a private practice after law school and also started her active career in social organizations. In August 1940 an *Ebony* article listed Carter as one of seventy known Negro women who had become lawyers since 1869 ("Lady

Lawyers," 18). Carter remained in private practice only briefly before William C. Dodge hired her to be a prosecutor for New York City magistrate and criminal courts. As a prosecutor, Carter tried many cases against prostitutes, most of which she did not win. Because the same bail bondsman and lawyer represented these women, Carter suspected that a larger organization was controlling prostitution. She told her boss, who dismissed her suspicions. However, Thomas Dewey, a special prosecutor investigating organized crime, took her suspicions seriously and eventually hired Carter as an assistant district attorney. She became part of a team that Dewey organized to investigate rackets and organized crime, particularly as it involved "Dutch" Schultz (Arthur Flegenheimer). She is also acknowledged for developing valuable evidence in the case against "Lucky" Luciano. Because of Carter's skills, in 1941 Dewey named her head of a Special Sessions Bureau overseeing juvenile justice. Eventually supervising more than 14,000 criminal cases per year, Carter served as a trial prosecutor until 1945.

Carter then returned to private practice and greater involvement in civic and social organizations and the movement for equal rights for women. She was a charter member, chairperson, trustee, and member of the Executive Board of the National Council of Negro Women (NCNW), founded in 1935 by MARY MCLEOD BETHUNE and twenty other women. Carter was also a member of the Roosevelt House League of Hunter College, and was active in the National Board of the YWCA (1949), the YWCA's administrative committee for its Foreign Divisions, the Panel on Women in Occupied Areas under Communism, and the Association of University Women. In 1945, as the chair of the NCNW's committee of laws, Carter, with her close associate Mary McLeod Bethune, attended a San Francisco conference that organized the United Nations. She was also very active in the local YWCAs of Harlem and Manhattan. Carter served as the secretary of the American Section of the Liaison Committee of International Organizations and the Conference on the Group of U.S. National Organizations; as a consultant to the Economic and Social Council for the International Council of Women (1947); as the chairperson of the Friends of the NAACP; as the vice president of the Eastern Division of the Pan-Pacific Women's Association and the National Council of Women of the U.S. (1964); and as the co-chair of the YWCA's Committee on

Development of Leadership in Other Countries. In 1954 Carter visited Germany to serve as an adviser to the German government on women in public life. In 1955 she was elected to chair the International Conference of Non-Governmental Organizations of the United Nations. She was also a trustee of the Museum of the City of New York and a member of the Urban League. Carter retired from law in 1952. She died in New York City.

FURTHER READING

The following collections contain information on Carter: a vertical file on Carter in the Woodruff Library of the Atlanta University Center; the National Council of Negro Women papers at the National Archives for Black Women's History in Washington, D.C.; and the Eunice Carter portrait collection in the New York Public Library Research Library.

Berger Morello, Karen. *The Invisible Bar: The Woman Lawyer in America, 1638 to the Present* (1986).

Obituaries: *New York Times*, 26 Jan. 1970; *New York Amsterdam News*, 31 Jan. 1970; *Jet*, 12 Feb. 1970.

This entry is taken from the *American National Biography* and is published here with the permission of the American Council of Learned Societies.

FAYE A. CHADWELL

Carter, Hawkins W. (23 Mar. 1843–Aug. 1920), farmer, shoemaker, and longtime state legislator, was born in Warren County, North Carolina, the third son of free, mixed-race parents Hawkins Carter and Elizabeth Wiggins, who were married in 1845. Few details are known of his early life or education, only that his father, a prosperous farmer, could afford to hire a young white teacher, W. J. Fulford, to tutor his eight children in 1861, the last year before the Civil War.

During the Civil War, the teenage Carter served as an officer's attendant for a Warrenton acquaintance, Captain Stephen W. Jones of the Forty-sixth North Carolina Regiment's Company C, raised at Warrenton in early 1862. Jones's company saw action at Antietam and other battles, and Jones was wounded at Spotsylvania Court House, where Carter presumably helped care for him. The eldest son of the Warren County sheriff and a former deputy sheriff himself before the war, Jones was the same age as Carter, whose service was officially noted in the state's Confederate pension records and who, three decades later, named his youngest son Stephen after his employer.

After the end of the war, Carter's local reputation as an industrious farmer and shoemaker helped him rise to political prominence as a five-term Republican legislator, among the county's longest serving and best known officeholders in that era. Warren County was a fertile ground for Republican political activity during and after Reconstruction, with a population nearly three-quarters African American at its 1880 peak. Under an unusual postwar power-sharing arrangement, Warren County's black Republicans were regularly allotted most legislative seats and a few local offices, while most local and county offices in other counties were generally reserved for white Democrats.

In 1874 Warren County's three-term state senator, JOHN ADAMS HYMAN, became the first African American to represent the newly redrawn "Black Second" congressional district in the U.S. House of Representatives. In that same year, newcomer Carter won the first of five consecutive elections to the state's general assembly from Warren County, compiling a commanding majority and joining another dozen African American members in the 1874–1875 North Carolina House of Representatives. Reelected to the house by a narrower margin in 1876, Carter widened his winning margin again for his third term in 1878. As a sign of his growing statewide influence, he was named by the Democratic leadership during the 1879 session to membership on three committees, including a prestigious post on the House Finance Committee, as well as those on corporations and railroads, post roads, and turnpikes.

In 1880 and 1881 Carter was chosen to be school committeeman for his Warren County township, helping oversee the county's segregated common schools. As an 1880 Republican candidate to represent the Nineteenth District (Warren County) in the state senate, he was one of just two African Americans to win election to that body. Upon his reelection in 1882, he was among four African American senators. During his senate years, he served on the Senate Committee on Agriculture, Mechanics, and Mining, as well as the Committee on Deaf, Dumb, and Blind Asylum. After serving in the 1883 legislature, Carter retired from active politics, but remained an influential voice behind the scenes.

The postwar federal census of 1870 describes Carter as comparatively prosperous, owning $140 in real estate and $360 in personal property. He was married twice. On 23 May 1866 he married Thomas

Elizabeth Toney (b. 1839), who died sometime after 1870. On 17 February 1874 he married Nannie W. Boyd (b. 1852); their family grew in time to include eleven children, ten of whom lived to adulthood. The Carter family included at least five daughters—Pattie, Elizabeth, Maria, Helen, and Maryand— four sons, Walter, Hawkins Jr., Alex, and Stephen.

In 1892 the political situation in North Carolina entered upon a tumultuous new phase, as many farmers, Republicans, and an increasing number of disgruntled Democrats endorsed the populist aims of the new People's Party. Carter emerged among a handful of African American supporters of populist candidates for local and state office, including black populist candidates in Warren County. Such action was close to political heresy, especially since Carter's preferred candidate for register of deeds, Tom Hawkins, faced the state's longest-serving African American elected official, Warrenton's Mansfield F. Thornton. Carter's candidate lost that race, Thornton held the office until 1900, and Carter never sought public office again.

Yet Hawkins Carter's political vision was soon vindicated by the unexpected success of the Republican-Populist fusion movement. Fusionists captured the general assembly in 1894 and helped elect a Republican governor, Daniel L. Russell, in 1896, inaugurating a brief but memorable new era for the state's African American officeholders.

At the time of his death, Carter continued to farm the land he had owned for more than sixty years. More than forty years after winning his final election, Carter continued to hold Warren County's record for consecutive elections—five—to the general assembly, a record not broken until the middle of the twentieth century.

FURTHER READING

Anderson, Eric. *Race and Politics in North Carolina, 1872–1901: The Black Second* (1981).

Foner, Eric. *Freedom's Lawmakers: A Directory of Black Officeholders during Reconstruction* (1993).

Kenzer, Robert C. *Enterprising Southerners: Black Economic Success in North Carolina, 1865–1915* (1997).

BENJAMIN R. JUSTESEN

Carter, James (18 Dec. 1925–26 Nov. 2003), prison musician, was born to sharecroppers in Greenwood, Mississippi. The names of his parents have not been recorded. Like most children in the Mississippi Delta at that time, Carter assisted his family in bringing in the cotton crop, which was particularly precarious during the severe agricultural depression of the 1930s that drastically reduced the price of cotton. With little or no formal education, Carter left home at age thirteen, in 1939, in search of work. Not finding any, he enlisted in the U.S. Navy during World War II—some sources suggest he served in the U.S. Marines—and served on cruisers in the Pacific theater. He returned to Greenwood when the war ended. In 1947 he married his childhood sweetheart, a sharecropper's daughter named Rosie Lee whose maiden name is unknown. The couple had three daughters.

Work was no easier to come by after the war than it had been before the war, and Carter turned to a sporadic life of crime. He served sentences in the Mississippi State Penitentiary at Lambert—the notorious Parchman Farm—on four occasions during the 1950s and 1960s. Twice he was jailed for theft, once for what he called a "fool play …. I did a little shooting," and the final time for violating the terms of his parole by carrying a loaded weapon (Grier). The *London Daily Telegraph* later noted Carter's admission that he had lived a violent life: "You been places, you fight, then you get home and you are bitter" (4 Dec. 2003). But he also believed that his weapons possession charges had been trumped up by a racist Mississippi sheriff and that his sentence of several years of hard labor at Parchman was unjustified. Carter described Parchman as "the headquarters of racial segregation. We was no better than slaves" (*Telegraph*). Indeed, the historian David Oshinsky described the inhumane working conditions, brutal beatings, whippings, sexual abuse, and murder of prisoners at Parchman as "worse than slavery."

While Carter was serving time at Parchman's Camp B in 1959, he and several other prisoners working on a chain gang chopping wood encountered the musicologist Alan Lomax, who recorded them performing the traditional work song "Po' Lazarus." Shortly before his death in 2002, Lomax, who in the 1930s and 1940s was the first person to record the blues singers LEAD BELLY and MUDDY WATERS, told National Public Radio that Carter and fifty other black men "were working under the whip and the gun and they had the soul to make the most wonderful song I'd ever heard" (*Los Angeles Times*, 9 Dec. 2003). Interviewed decades after recording "Po' Lazarus," Carter recalled that he had learned it from an older Parchman inmate, a knife man named Red Kid, and that singing it had helped him and his fellow prisoners get through the long days laboring under a blazing Mississippi sun. "In them days," he told the reporter Chris Grier in 2002, "work was work. Swinging that ax …. But you get that song goin'," and "you can get along pretty good." Although Carter later did not recollect the meaning of the song, the lyrics are quite similar to his own situation. Po' Lazarus is accused of a minor crime and hunted down by an unscrupulous sheriff. When the high deputy refused to arrest Po' Lazarus, "a dangerous man" who had stolen from a plantation commissary, the sheriff himself went in search of him, determined to bring him back "dead or alive." He found Lazarus "hidin' in the chill of a mountain with his head hung down" but still defiant that he had "never been arrested by no one man." Upon hearing this, the high sheriff shot Lazarus dead

> with a mighty big number
> With a forty five
> Lawd, Lawd
> With a forty five. (Brown, 54)

Lazarus is then laid out on the floor of the commissary, no doubt as a warning to other potential transgressors of white justice. The wounds on Lazarus's side, however, just like Jesus' wounds, identify him with the righteous. The folklorist STERLING BROWN suggests that Po' Lazarus belongs to the pantheon of African American folk heroes and real-life fugitives, such as JOHN HENRY, STAGOLEE, and RAILROAD BILL, who attempt to trick the white forces of law and order and sometimes succeed.

The same year that Carter recorded "Po' Lazarus," his wife left the Delta for Chicago, where she founded a storefront church, the Holy Temple Community of God, in 1965. She also invested in property, later purchasing the apartment building where she lived. In December 1967 she secured her husband's parole from Parchman. On arriving in Chicago, James Carter found work as a punch press for General Electric, as a shipping clerk, and as a custodian for the Chicago board of education. Much of the time though he was unemployed and in poor health, largely as a result of his confinement and hard labor at Parchman Farm.

In late 2001, while he was hospitalized with bronchitis, Carter was visited by Lomax's daughter Anna Lomax Chairetakis and Don Fleming of the Lomax Archives in New York, who informed him that his recording of "Po' Lazarus" had been included as the lead track on the soundtrack album

of the Ethan Coen and Joel Coen film *O Brother, Where Art Thou?* (2000). The album, which at that time had sold more than four million copies, had just been nominated for a Grammy Award. A photograph of Carter taken by Lomax during the recording, social security details, and the investigative efforts of Grier confirmed that he was the same James Carter. Told that the album had gone quadruple platinum and had sold more copies than that year's releases by MICHAEL JACKSON and Mariah Carey, an astonished Carter exclaimed to Grier: "I'm gonna call Michael Jackson up. Tell him I'm gonna slow down. Let him catch up to me." Chairetakis then handed Carter a royalty check for $20,000, though increased sales of the soundtrack album ultimately netted Carter and his family more than $100,000 in royalties. In addition to the efforts of the Lomax Archives to track him down, Carter undoubtedly benefited from RUTH BROWN and her Rhythm and Blues Foundation's campaign against unscrupulous recording industry practices that denied African American performers their due royalties.

Carter attended the 2002 Grammy ceremonies, where the *O Brother* soundtrack won six awards, including Best Album. He greatly enjoyed the unexpected fame and fortune that arrived late in a life that had seen little of either, and he devoted some of his royalties to helping the food bank and buying a van for his wife's church. Carter died in Chicago from a massive stroke shortly before his seventy-eighth birthday.

FURTHER READING

Brown, Sterling. "Negro Folk Expression: Spirituals, Seculars, Ballads, and Work Songs," *Phylon* 14.1 (1953): 45–61.

Grier, Chris. "'O Brother, Where Art Thou?' Chicago, It Turns Out," *Sarasota Herald-Tribune*, 26 Feb. 2002.

Oshinsky, David M. *"Worse Than Slavery": Parchman Farm and the Ordeal of Jim Crow Justice* (1996).

Obituaries: *New York Times* and *London Daily Telegraph*, 4 Dec. 2003; *Los Angeles Times*, 9 Dec. 2003.

STEVEN J. NIVEN

Carter, James Garnett (Garneth) (15 Dec. 1877– 1949), longtime U.S. consular officer in Madagascar and France, who declined appointment as U.S. Minister to Liberia, was born in Brunswick, Georgia. He was the son of Margaret Carter and an unnamed father. Around 1892, his mother married J. C. Bryan, a minister who helped raise James, his older brother William Richard Carter and younger sister Maggie, and half-sisters Vernetta and Edna. Four other siblings died in infancy.

James G. Carter was initially educated in the grammar, normal, and industrial schools of Brunswick. With the help of his brother William, a schoolteacher and graduate of Tuskegee Institute, he was then able to enter Tuskegee Institute in the mid-1890s. After graduating from Tuskegee in 1897, Carter entered the tailoring trade; he also served as a letter carrier, notary public, and editor-manager of a small newspaper in Brunswick until 1906. In August of that year, he passed the entrance exam for the U.S. consular service and was initially appointed as U.S. consul in Sivas, Asiatic Turkey, in September 1906, but never assumed duties there. Instead, he was appointed in November of that year as U.S. consul in Tamatave, Madagascar, replacing Consul WILLIAM H. HUNT, and was confirmed by the U.S. Senate.

Carter was among a small group of black consular officers recruited by the State Department during the second administration of President Theodore Roosevelt. Others included Consul WILLIAM J. YERBY, consul at Dakar, Senegal; and consuls JAMES W. JOHNSON and Herbert R. Wright, who served initially at Puerto Cabello, Venezuela.

For the next decade, Consul Carter served the small U.S. mission at Tamatave, a major seaport of the French colonial possession off the east coast of Africa. His reports from Tamatave, on market opportunities for U.S. manufacturing products, the discovery of petroleum in 1908, electrification projects, and public improvements, were widely circulated within the Department of State and reprinted in commercial publications.

When the consulate at Tamatave was closed in 1916, Carter was transferred to the island's capital of Tananarive (now known as Antananarivo), where he served as consul until 1927. In 1924, Carter was among four African Americans designated as career Foreign Service Officers under provisions of the newly enacted Rogers Act, along with colleagues Hunt and Yerby—all given the rank of FSO-7—and newcomer CLIFTON R. WHARTON SR. (Palmer, 10).

In February 1927, President Calvin Coolidge announced Carter's appointment in national newspapers as the new U.S. Minister Resident and Consul General in Liberia, a post vacant for more than a year. For reasons still unclear—but perhaps related to efforts by the Advisory Commission on Education in Liberia, a shadowy, U.S.-based multiagency group dominated by religious leaders and private philanthropists, to involve Carter in its work (Hill, 475)—Carter never assumed duties in Monrovia. By June 1927, he had withdrawn from consideration for the post, which went instead a month later to attorney William T. Francis of Minnesota.

Later that year, Carter was transferred to Calais, France, as U.S. consul, and remained in Calais until May 1940, when he and two U.S. Treasury customs attachés fled the city to escape Nazi bombardment. The account of their perilous journey to Bern, Switzerland, by automobile through German lines—including a German military escort to Luxembourg and a stopover in Stuttgart—appeared under the headline "U.S. Consul Flees War" (*New York Times*, 29 May 1940), which noted Carter's status as "one of the few Negroes ever to attain consular rank in the United States foreign service."

Carter soon returned to France, after being reassigned as U.S. consul in Bordeaux, briefly the wartime capital of France. In 1941, Carter was transferred and promoted to consul general at his earlier post in Tananarive, Madagascar, then controlled by the Vichy government of France. Carter remained there until 1942, when he retired, after thirty-six years of service. His retirement left Wharton as the last active African American foreign service officer from the 1924 group.

Carter returned to the United States in 1942. No details are available about his family or about his life in retirement. According to Department of State records, he died in 1949.

FURTHER READING

Harlan, Louis R., and Raymond W. Smock, eds. *The Booker T. Washington Papers* (1975).

Hill, George J. "Intimate Relationships: Secret Affairs of Church and State in the United States and Liberia, 1925–1947." In *Diplomatic History* (2007).

Palmer, Ronald D. "Black Pioneer State Department Foreign Service Officers, 1924–1969" (1970).

Register of the Department of State, 23 Dec. 1918 (1919).

United States Chiefs of Missions: Liberia. Available at http://history.state.gov/departmenthistory/people/carter-james-garneth.

BENJAMIN R. JUSTESEN

Carter, Jennie (c. 1830–10 Aug. 1881), writer and activist, was probably born in New Orleans or New York with the given name Mary Jane, although information surrounding her parentage and youth is limited. She seems to have spent time in Illinois, New York, and Kentucky, and worked as a teacher as well as, briefly, a governess; she also claimed some involvement aiding fugitive slaves escaping from Missouri via the Underground Railroad. She moved west with her first husband, a Mr. Correll, who is believed to have been a minister, in the early 1860s. It is only after her 29 August 1866 marriage to the musician, educator, and activist DENNIS DRUMMOND CARTER in Nevada City, California, that Carter's biography begins to come into focus.

In June of 1867, under the name "Mrs. Ann J. Trask," Carter wrote to PHILIP ALEXANDER BELL, the editor of the *San Francisco Elevator*, and suggested that he include a story designed for children in each issue of his weekly paper. She volunteered to write the column, and when Bell published her letter in the 5 July 1867 *Elevator*, he followed it with her first effort, a sentimental story of the death of a beloved dog Nino that had belonged to "Trask." Soon after, as Carter herself observed in a 16 August 1867 column, she found herself going well beyond her plan to write for children and "wound up writing for everybody." Over the next seven years Carter contributed more than seventy pieces to the *Elevator*, most simply labeled "Letter from Mud Hill"—Mud Hill being Carter's joking designation for Nevada City. She sent Bell a set of poems in late 1867, and although he published two, he asserted that he much preferred her prose, which made up the bulk of her subsequent contributions. Late in 1867 Carter took up the pen name "Semper Fidelis" (Latin for "always faithful") for her contributions. While several of her letters—especially the earliest—focus on domestic issues and lean heavily toward the sentimental, Carter, like many activist women of her time, defined the "domestic" to include both home and nation. Much of her work addressed a range of political issues with an increasingly strong tone. While her early work used the narrative voice of "Mrs. Trask," a "genial woman" of sixty years, she gradually set aside both this persona and, by the early 1870s, the use of pen names altogether.

Carter's *Elevator* columns show active thinking, quick wit, and a deep commitment to civil rights. She wrote with especial fervor about the need for the Fifteenth Amendment—and she celebrated its ratification with great joy. In part because she witnessed the antiblack rhetoric of many women's suffrage activists (especially Susan B. Anthony and Elizabeth Cady Stanton during their association with the racist Democrat George Francis Train), she did not, however, favor women's suffrage and argued instead that women should focus on aiding men (and raising boys) to vote effectively. She was firmly Republican, although she recognized and attacked those Republican politicians who attempted to use African American votes without advancing civil rights. In this vein she was especially critical of Democrats and former Confederates, and wrote with emotion and much pain about African American experiences in slavery and the racist reaction to Reconstruction. She also advocated rights for Chinese immigrants, believing that they deserved openness and fairness—a view rare among her colleagues.

Carter's columns were successful enough that, in 1869, she submitted work—again under the pen name Semper Fidelis—to the *Christian Recorder*, the official organ of the African Methodist Episcopal (AME) Church. After the paper published her first piece, the *Recorder* began running ads that promised further work from Semper Fidelis and identified the author as "Mrs. D. D. Carter." Whether the *Recorder*'s revelation of her identity surprised her or not, she published only one additional piece there. Obituaries suggest that she published work in other periodicals, though such have not yet been recovered. Her first loyalties, nonetheless, were to the *Elevator* and Bell. When the paper—always in financial trouble—seemed on the brink of collapse in January 1868, she wrote a call for contributions under her own name that was republished in several issues of the paper. Even when rheumatism and a host of other ailments slowed her pen in the early and mid-1870s, she continued to publish work in the *Elevator*, ranging from political commentary to reports of blacks in California and Nevada to Christmas stories. She may have published work in the *Elevator* well into the later 1870s, though copies of the paper from this period are not extant.

As she grew older Carter apparently turned more and more to her home life, and one day while working in her beloved garden she suffered a fatal heart attack and died in her Nevada City home. Her passing was mourned in local papers, but her work, which provides both rare documentation of blacks in the West and a voice as rich and complex as her better-known contemporaries like FRANCES ELLEN WATKINS HARPER, was all too quickly forgotten.

FURTHER READING

Carter, Jennie. *Jennie Carter and the San Francisco Elevator: "Always Faithful" in the African American West*, ed. Eric Gardner (2007).

ERIC GARDNER

Carter, Mae Bertha (13 Jan. 1923–28 Apr. 1999), civil rights activist, was born to Isaiah ("Zeke") Slaughter and Luvenia Noland, sharecroppers, on the Smith and Wiggins Plantation in rural Bolivar County, Mississippi. Mae Bertha and her four brothers and sisters were expected to join their parents in the cotton fields as soon as they were old enough to pick bolls at harvest time.

The Slaughter children attended all-black, separate and unequal schools during "split sessions" that were scheduled around the planting, chopping, and harvest seasons in the cotton calendar. After Zeke Slaughter left the family, nine-year-old Mae Bertha began working for wages in the cotton fields at thirty cents an hour to help support the family. When she was sixteen years old, in 1939, she married Matthew Carter. Their family, which would eventually include thirteen children, began sharecropping for themselves. From 1956 to 1965 they lived and worked on the Pemble plantation on the outskirts of the town of Drew, in Sunflower County, Mississippi.

Carter was baptized at Union Grove Baptist Church at the age of twelve and remained a committed Christian for the rest of her days. Her life's work in the church led her seamlessly to civil rights activity. Matthew and Mae Bertha Carter joined the Cleveland, Mississippi, chapter of the NAACP in the mid-1950s, in part because they enjoyed the weekly meetings at New Kingdom Baptist Church. "It broadens my concepts," Carter said of the NAACP (Curry, 47). AMZIE MOORE, a Cleveland businessman, U.S. postal worker, and outspoken leader of the chapter, became a close family friend.

In August 1965 the Drew school district mailed "freedom of choice" forms to the parents of the town's schoolchildren. In theory the euphemistically named policy offered African American parents the chance to send their children to any schools in the district, even those that remained all-white a decade after the U.S. Supreme Court's decision in *Brown v. Board of Education*. In reality, however, the school board hoped that the plan would satisfy the letter of the law (specifically, Titles IV and VI of the 1964 Civil Rights Act, which provided greater federal enforcement mechanisms for the desegregation of public schools) while violating its spirit. Drew whites fully expected that blacks would be too intimidated to register their children in "white" schools.

The Carters were the only African Americans in Drew to register their children in the previously all-white schools. The response from local whites was swift and brutal. A day after the Carters returned their forms on 12 August, the overseer of their plantation paid the Carters' house an early-morning visit with an offer to help them withdraw their forms. He explained that the children would undoubtedly be better off in the all-black schools (which received a small fraction of the district's funds as measured on a per-student basis when compared to "white" schools and were in session only when it was convenient for the cotton calendar). The overseer must have been flabbergasted when, as he discussed the matter with Matthew Carter in the front yard, Mae Bertha Carter appeared on the home's front porch with a portable record player and a recording of President John F. Kennedy's 11 June 1963 address to the nation. "We are confronted primarily with a moral issue. It is as old as the scriptures and is as clear as the American Constitution," Kennedy proclaimed through the speakers of Carter's record player. "The heart of the question," he said, "is whether all Americans are to be afforded equal rights and equal opportunities, whether we are going to treat our fellow Americans as we want to be treated."

A few nights later nightriders fired shots into the Carter home, and the plantation commissary rescinded the Carters' credit. Within months they were driven from the Pemble plantation, but the seven school-age Carter children remained in the Drew public schools (an eighth, their youngest, Carl, entered the first grade in 1967). According to Ruth Carter she and her brothers and sisters initially "jumped at the chance to integrate the school[s] because at least we could get away from the cotton fields, and because it would … later on, make the world a better place. We knew it was the right thing to do" (Curry, 110).

It may have been the right thing to do, but the burden of desegregating the Drew schools fell heavily on the shoulders of the eight Carter children, whose schoolmates regularly hurled invectives and much worse at them (according to the children, their teachers were generally more polite but not much more charitable toward them). Looking back on the experience, Ruth Carter admitted, "I got so depressed. It seemed like I just filled up with hatred from my toes to the top of my head…. I hated Mississippi. I hated the white man. I hated my teachers. I hated everything" (Curry, 112). Other Carter children described similar feelings. Mae Bertha Carter, who estimated that she herself had received no better than a fifth-grade education but was blessed with a bottomless pool of mother wit, organized after-school therapy sessions for the family during which the children discussed the day's events at school, cried together, prayed together, and plotted survival strategies for the future.

Representatives of the American Friends Service Committee (AFSC) and the NAACP Legal Defense and Education Fund, who traveled to the Delta regularly to assist the Carters in their federal suit against the Drew school district, found in Carter a woman of steadfast faith—an unyielding belief in the value of Christ's message to the world and deep confidence in the value of education—and intense, if disguised, worry, tormented by her desire to give her children the best possible education. She remained a pillar of strength for the children, but as she wrote the AFSC's JEAN FAIRFAX in 1965, every morning after the school bus had picked them up for school, "I went in and fell down cross the bed and prayed … praying to God. I wasn't saying a whole lot of words; just saying, 'Take care of my kids'" (Curry, 43).

The Carters' eight youngest children all graduated from the Drew public school system they integrated, and seven earned degrees from the University of Mississippi. Mae Bertha Carter was an increasingly active organizer on education issues throughout the 1970s and 1980s, working for Head Start and railing against the whites who created "segregation academies" (nominally "private" schools open only to white students) as more African Americans followed the Carters into desegregated public schools. Despite the courage of the Carters, Drew schools had fully re-segregated within a decade after the Carters children's entry—with whites remaining firmly in control of the public school system, keeping it separate and unequal. Carter never stopped opposing the politics of this arrangement; she considered this work, which stretched into the decade of the 1990s, part and parcel of her earlier civil rights efforts.

Constance Curry's 1995 book about the Carters, *Silver Rights*, introduced the family to a wider audience and established Mae Bertha Carter as an icon of the Mississippi civil rights movement. She came to personify the thousands of grassroots-level Democrats, most of them women, who sustained the movement in the South over several decades. Over the course of a wide-ranging national book tour with Curry, Carter encouraged thousands of Americans to think broadly about the civil rights movement and inspired them to become forces of positive change in their own communities. She drew connections between her struggles in the 1960s and contemporary efforts to reform the criminal justice system and maintain a social safety net during a time of "welfare reform." "It was in us to do it," she said shortly before she died from stomach cancer in Sunflower County. "You know, somebody got to do it. We are born for a purpose" (oral history interview with J. Todd Moye).

FURTHER READING

An oral history interview with Mae Bertha Carter is housed in the University of Southern Mississippi's Center for Oral History and Cultural Heritage, while Carter's decades-long correspondence with Constance Curry resides in the Constance Curry Papers at Emory University.

Curry, Constance. "School Desegregation in a Delta Town," in *Mississippi Women: Their Histories, Their Lives* (2003).

Curry, Constance. *Silver Rights* (1995).

J. TODD MOYE

Carter, Nell (13 Sept. 1948–23 Jan. 2003), singer, actor, and comedian, was born Nell Ruth Hardy in Birmingham, Alabama, one of nine children. Nell's parents were Edna Mae Humphrey, a homemaker, and her second husband, Horace Hardy, an Army sergeant. At age two, Nell witnessed his accidental electrocution death. Deeply affected by DINAH WASHINGTON, B. B. KING, and Elvis Presley records, Nell began singing in her church choir, on a local radio show called the "Y-Teens," and on the gospel circuit. She never grew taller than four feet eleven inches but had a large, commanding voice and presence. Her show business ambitions made her a "weirdo" in a social environment where "most kids wanted to be teachers or nurses" (CNN.com, *Entertainment*, 23 Jan. 2003). At age 13, the Presbyterian-raised Nell discovered that one of her grandfathers probably had Jewish ancestry. Although not converting until 1983, she started to intensively read Biblical texts and explore Judaism.

During her junior year of high school, Nell, then fifteen, began to sing in gay bars and coffee houses with a group called the Renaissance Ensemble. When she was sixteen, a male acquaintance raped her at gunpoint and impregnated her. She later recalled, "I could have had an abortion—they were around. But I had my baby, my daughter Tracey" (Gold, 36). After trying to care for her daughter herself, Nell realized she could not. Her sister Willie, who was twelve years older and had a spouse and children already, raised Tracey in the African American tradition of intrafamily adoption. Until

1994, Nell explained her daughter as the child of a failed early marriage to protect her from stigma.

In 1968, nineteen-year-old Nell Carter moved to New York City. She regularly sang at nightclubs like the Village Gate, the Rainbow Room, and Dangerfield's. She studied acting (1970–1973) at the Bill Russell School. Throughout the 1970s, she landed small musical roles in such Broadway productions as *Soon, Dude, Jesus Christ Superstar, Be Kind to People Week*, and *Don't Bother Me, I Can't Cope*. Carter also acted on the television programs *Ryan's Hope* (1975) and *The Misadventures of Sheriff Lobo* (1979). She sought further dramatic training in London, England. Her first starring role on Broadway came with the blockbuster revue of Fats Waller songs, *Ain't Misbehavin'* (1978–1982). Her arresting renditions of such songs as "Honeysuckle Rose," "Cash for Your Trash," and "Mean to Me" brought her Obie, Tony, Theatre World, and Drama Desk awards. After the show was televised (1982), Carter achieved an Emmy. During this period, she became addicted to cocaine. She had already begun to struggle with alcoholism and obesity.

Carter's *Ain't Misbehavin'* success helped her land her most well-known and best-paid role in any medium: as housekeeper for a white police officer and his family on the television program *Gimme a Break* (1981–1987). Carter won an Emmy and garnered two additional Emmy nominations and two Golden Globe nominations for this role. However, African Americans debated whether and to what extent her character, also called Nell, simply recapitulated the old, demeaning "Mammy" stereotype. On the one hand, Nell was the star, and was assertive instead of passive. On the other hand, the character worked in a historically servile job within a white household and did not have much life of her own outside their home. Carter herself said of the role, "That wasn't me; it was just a job" (Holden, p. C24).

During the series, Carter went back and forth between substance abuse and rehabilitation stays. In 1982, she wed Georg Krynicki, a businessman and son of Jewish Holocaust survivors. They initiated divorce proceedings eighteen months later. When *Gimme a Break* ended, Carter returned to New York City to sing in nightclubs, her own musical revue, and a year-long revival of *Ain't Misbehavin'*. By then she had quit cocaine. Carter was dealt a severe blow in 1988 when her beloved brother Bernard died of AIDS. Returning to Los Angeles, Carter reunited with Krynicki and tried to have children with him but experienced three miscarriages instead. In 1989 and 1990, Carter adopted two African American boys, Joshua and Daniel, whom she raised as Jews. By 1991, she stopped drinking. Yet 1992 was an especially tumultuous year for Carter. She and Krynicki finalized their divorce. She then wed Roger Larocque, a Canadian record producer, although this marriage, too, ended in divorce a short time later. Finally, Carter, who had diabetes, survived surgeries for an almost-fatal double aneurysm.

Nell Carter had additional television roles in *You Take the Kids, Ally McBeal, Reba*, and *Hanging with Mr. Cooper*. She appeared in the films *The Grass Harp* (1995) and *The Proprietor* (1996). She continued to perform onstage in such productions as *Bubbling Brown Sugar, The Vagina Monologues*, and an *Annie* revival. In a 2001 interview, Carter discussed her AIDS activism, including her volunteer work for a charity providing free meals to people with HIV/AIDS. She bluntly advised young women "to get rid of" men who refused to use condoms with them. She told young men "out there without a condom" to "think about your sister, think about your mother. Would you want someone to take a chance for them to die? It's not worth it" (Dulin).

At age 54, Nell Carter died suddenly of probable arteriosclerotic heart disease at her home in Beverly Hills, California. Still struggling with obesity, she had hoped to perform in a musical revival of *Raisin in the Sun*. Carter was survived by her three children and her domestic partner, Ann Kaser, who was awarded custody of her two adoptive sons. Carter was buried in Hillside Cemetery, Culver City, California. Susan Joseph, Carter's manager, said, "She wanted to show people her many sides" (*Jet*, 10 Feb. 2003, 49). For all her personal travails, Carter achieved just this in her multifaceted entertainment career. Carter, who once left a nine-page letter to God at Jerusalem's Wailing Wall, found comfort and sustenance in her Jewish faith throughout her many ups and downs.

FURTHER READING

Brumburgh, Gary, "Biography for Nell Carter" (n.d.), *IMDb: The Internet Movie Database*, available online at http://www.imdb.com.

Dulin, Dann, "Gimme a Break—Not! Diva Nell Carter Talks to A&U's Dann Dulin About the Loss of Her Brother and Raises Hell About AIDS," *Art & Understanding Magazine* (Sept. 2001), available online at http://www.danndulin.com/nellcarter.html.

Gold, Todd, "Oh, the Troubles She's Seen," *People*, 28 Feb. 1994.

Holden, Stephen, "The Pop Life: Nell Carter Returns," *New York Times*, 13 Apr. 1988.

"Nell Carter," in *Historical Dictionary of African American Television*, ed. Kathleen Fearn-Banks, 67–68 (2006).

Rubin, Bonnie Miller. *Fifty on Fifty: Wisdom, Inspiration, and Reflections on Women's Lives Well Lived* (1998.)

Obituaries: CNN.com Entertainment (23 Jan. 2003); *Jet* (10 Feb. 2003); *L.A. Jewish Journal* (31 Jan. 2003); *New York Times* (24 Jan. 2003); *Playbill News* (23 Jan. 2003).

MARY KRANE DERR

Carter, Robert Lee (11 Mar. 1917–3 Jan. 2012), attorney and federal judge, was born in Careyville, Florida, the youngest of eight children of Robert Carter and Annie Martin. Shortly after his birth, Robert's family joined tens of thousands of blacks migrating from the rural South to the big cities of the North, seeking a better life. Within months of settling in Newark, New Jersey, his father died, leaving his mother a widow at age thirty-nine and the sole

Robert Lee Carter, July 1955, attorney, general counsel for the NAACP, and federal judge. (Library of Congress, New York World-Telegram and *Sun Newspaper* Photograph Collection.)

support of a large family. Working as a domestic by day and taking in laundry at night, she managed to keep the family together.

Carter excelled as a student, encouraged by his mother, who hoped he would train to be a minister. In his teen years she moved the family to East Orange, New Jersey, to escape the increasing decay and desperation of Newark during the Great Depression. Graduating from East Orange High School in 1933, he entered Lincoln University in Pennsylvania on a scholarship. Upon graduating in 1937, Carter entered Howard Law School and came to the attention of its dean, WILLIAM HENRY HASTIE, and THURGOOD MARSHALL, who had preceded Carter at both Lincoln and Howard. After graduation from Howard in 1940, Carter attended Columbia University on a Rosenwald Fellowship, emerging on the eve of war with a master's degree in Law.

When America entered World War II, Carter enlisted in the racially segregated army as a private and was sent to a military base in Georgia. There he encountered pervasive racial segregation and a demeaning, dismissive racial contempt. Black soldiers were confined to menial labor rather than being trained for combat or behind-the-lines technical support. Although he was accepted to Officers' Candidate School, his career as a second lieutenant proved tumultuous. He brought charges against two white enlisted men who had made racial slurs, insisted upon entering the officer's club at his base, and refused to live off base, as other blacks did. The matter came to a head when Carter successfully defended a black soldier accused of raping a white woman by establishing that she was a prostitute who had consented to the engagement. Charges brought against him in retaliation resulted in an administrative discharge that would have made him again subject to the draft. His Howard Law School mentor, William Hastie, a civilian aide to the secretary of war, Henry Stimson, intervened, however, to secure an honorable discharge. Carter left the army in 1944 and returned to the practice of law as assistant counsel to Thurgood Marshall, then the lead attorney for the NAACP's Legal Defense Fund (LDF). At that time racial segregation remained firmly entrenched by law and custom in the South and was sustained by custom and habit in much of the rest of the country. The "separate but equal" doctrine of *Plessy v. Ferguson* (1896) still guided judicial thinking and enjoyed popular support. Few could have expected that Carter, Marshall, and a handful of young lawyers working from a small set of offices near the New York Public Library would, within a decade, persuade the U.S. Supreme Court to overturn *Plessy*.

In the postwar years the NAACP challenged segregation along a number of fronts, including housing, transportation, and schools. Carter played an increasingly prominent role in these cases. On 3 April 1950 he found himself standing before the U.S. Supreme Court engaged in oral argument in *McLaurin v. Oklahoma*. GEORGE MCLAURIN, a black man, had applied to graduate school at the University of Oklahoma. Claiming to uphold the separate but equal doctrine, the university had assigned McLaurin a separate table on the library's mezzanine, a table in a corner of the cafeteria, and a seat just outside the classrooms where his courses were taught. Carter argued that the practice effectively denied McLaurin an equal education. On 5 June 1950 the Supreme Court handed down its decisions in *McLaurin* and in *Sweatt v. Painter*, a Texas Law School case that Thurgood Marshall had argued. Both Carter and Marshall won, delivering a fatal blow to segregation at the level of graduate and professional training.

The LDF's efforts to dismantle segregation at the level of elementary and secondary education would prove more difficult. In 1950 Carter suggested gathering evidence of the damaging psychological effects of segregation on black children. Although the idea was met with skepticism by some of his colleagues, Carter found an ally in the psychologist KENNETH B. CLARK, who had developed experiments in which children selected and assigned characteristics to black and white dolls. Their results suggested that black children held negative perceptions of black dolls, the dolls that looked like them. Carter brought Clark and other social scientists into the legal struggle as it moved through the lower courts toward the Supreme Court.

In the spring of 1951, accompanied by the LDF's Jack Greenberg, Carter journeyed to Topeka, Kansas, where Oliver Brown and other black parents were suing in federal court to integrate their elementary schools. Carter called Clark and other psychologists to the stand to testify that the races did not differ in intelligence and that segregation injured black children emotionally and psychologically. When Judge Walter Huxman ruled against the parents, *Brown v. Board of Education* of Topeka, Kansas, was joined with cases from South Carolina, Virginia, and Delaware. All challenged school segregation, and all were to be decided by the Supreme Court at the same time.

In December 1952 Carter, Marshall, and other LDF attorneys stood before the Supreme Court to argue the school segregation cases. Under tough questioning from some of the justices, Carter contended that the segregation laws of Kansas denied Linda Brown her constitutional right to an equal education. With the death of Chief Justice Fred Vinson, a decision was delayed, and the cases were scheduled to be argued again before the new chief justice, Earl Warren, in December 1953. On 17 May 1954 the Supreme Court handed down its landmark decision in *Brown v. Board of Education*: it ruled unanimously that state-imposed racial segregation in the schools was unconstitutional.

The ruling provoked fierce opposition from southern whites. Alabama, for example, passed legislation requiring the NAACP to make its membership list public. Disclosure would have exposed members to intimidation or worse. To protect southern blacks' First Amendment rights, Carter, who was general counsel for the NAACP from 1956 to 1968, argued *NAACP v. Alabama* before the Supreme Court in 1958. In June of that year the Supreme Court ruled in Carter's favor, declaring that the free-speech rights of NAACP members would be violated if their names were made public and they were thereby exposed to threats from die-hard segregationists.

Over the span of his career with the NAACP, Carter won twenty-one of twenty-two cases argued before the Supreme Court. He had always had a scholarly bent and in 1968 took a one-year appointment as a Fellow with the Urban Center at Columbia University. This was followed by a period in private practice. In 1972 Richard Nixon nominated him to the federal bench as a judge with U.S. District Court, the Southern District of New York. On the bench Carter presided over a range of cases, including those involving business executives charged with white-collar crimes and cases in which members of organized crime stood accused of violent offenses. The country's continuing struggle for racial justice also engaged him, and he reflected in 1989 that the conservative public policies of the 1970s and 1980s had resulted in a racial climate that was bleaker than any he could recall. Under Chief Justice William Rehnquist, he wrote, the Supreme Court "has embarked on a studied program to return the Fourteenth Amendment's due process and equal protection clauses and the federal civil rights law to the empty formalistic readings these provisions received before 1938" (Carter, 85).

Carter recognized, however, that he and other more liberal-minded members of the federal judiciary, such as A. Leon Higginbotham, Constance Baker Motley, and Damon Keith, could still promote a form of jurisprudence based on the egalitarian principles exemplified by *Brown*. In 1998 Carter wrote an important opinion in *Prey v. New York City Ballet*, stating that lawyers hired by an employer to investigate claims of sexual harassment may have to make their findings known to the complainants. In October of 2000 he handed down a decision ordering the Sheet Metal Workers union to pay more than $2 million in back wages to minority workers against whom it had discriminated. Along the way he also held adjunct faculty positions at New York University Law School and the University of Michigan Law School and published extensively.

If Carter had merely argued *McLaurin*, his name would be in the history books. If he had simply argued for bringing the insights of psychology to the fight against discrimination, he would be remembered. If he had only argued *Brown*, he would be celebrated. And if he had merely had a thirty-year distinguished career on the federal bench, he would be honored. That he did all of these things and more speaks to Carter's extraordinary faith in using the American constitutional system to overcome the pernicious legacy of segregation and racial inequality. Robert Carter died in Manhattan in 2012. He was 94.

FURTHER READING

Information on Carter's work for the NAACP Legal Defense Fund can be found in the NAACP Papers in the Manuscript Division of the Library of Congress.

Carter, Robert L. "Thirty-Five Years Later: New Perspectives on Brown," in *Race in America: The Struggle for Equality*, ed. Herbert Hill and James E. Jones Jr. (1993), 83–96.

Greenberg, Jack. *Crusaders in the Courts* (1994).

Kluger, Richard. *Simple Justice* (1975).

Obituary: *New York Times*, 3 Jan. 2012.

JOHN R. HOWARD

Carter, Rubin "Hurricane" (6 May 1937–), boxer who was wrongfully convicted of triple homicide in two racially charged trials, was born in Delawanna, New Jersey, the son of Bertha, a homemaker, and Lloyd Carter, an entrepreneur and church deacon who stressed to his seven children the importance of family pride and unity.

The Carters moved to nearby Paterson when Rubin was six years old, and the youngster soon developed a reputation for brawling, rebelling against authority, and committing petty crimes. At seventeen he escaped from Jamesburg State Home for Boys, where he had been sentenced for cutting a man with a bottle, and joined the army. As a member of the Eleventh Airborne, he was sent to Germany, where he learned to box and won the European Light Welterweight Championship.

Discharged from the army in 1956, Carter returned to Paterson but was soon in trouble again. The following year he pled guilty to robbing and assaulting a woman and was sentenced to four years in prison. There he received various disciplinary citations for refusing to obey orders and fighting with other prisoners.

When he was released, he decided that prizefighting was his best hope for making a living. He married Mae Thelma on 15 June 1963. The couple had two children, Theodora and Raheem. With his bald head, bristling goatee, thick muscles, and whistling punches—not to mention his violent criminal record—he was given a fitting nickname: "Hurricane." The moniker also captured his flamboyant persona and strident rhetoric. As civil rights protests were gaining momentum, Carter urged blacks to use force to resist police brutality while making hyperbolic statements about how he used to shoot and stab people.

But Carter's principal renown came from his pugilistic feats. In his first two years as a professional fighter, he won eighteen and lost three fights, with thirteen knockouts. On 16 December 1964 he fought Joey Giardello for the middleweight championship. Carter lost in a close fifteen-round decision; it would be his last shot at the championship.

Carter's life soon intersected with one of the most violent crimes in the history of Paterson. Sometime after 2:00 A.M. on 17 June 1966 two black gunmen walked into the Lafayette Grill and shot four people, killing three. A police radio call announced that the two gunmen had left the crime scene in a white car. Shortly thereafter, the police picked up Carter and his young acquaintance John Artis, who were driving in Paterson in a white car. They were questioned and released, but four months later they were arrested for the murders.

The case against them centered on the testimony of two convicted felons who claimed they saw the gunmen leaving the scene while they—the witnesses—were breaking into a nearby sheet metal company. The witnesses identified Carter and Artis, who insisted on their innocence. But on 26 May 1967 an all-white jury convicted them of triple homicide and sentenced them to life imprisonment.

At a time of sweeping racial violence in cities across America, the convictions suggested that at least one city had imposed justice on lawbreakers. But Carter protested the verdict while incarcerated at Trenton State Prison; he refused to wear prison clothes or eat prison food. He was determined to fight for his freedom by appealing the results. Despite limited education, he wrote his autobiography, *The Sixteenth Round* (1974), and over the years his celebrity attracted journalists, filmmakers, athletes, advertising executives, lawyers, and civil rights activists—all committed to raising awareness of Carter's case and forcing the authorities to overturn the verdict. His most influential advocate was Bob Dylan, whose song about Carter turned him into an international cause célèbre.

On 17 March 1976 the New Jersey Supreme Court overturned the convictions of Carter and Artis on the grounds that prosecutors had failed to turn over material evidence favorable to the defendants; specifically, audiotapes revealed investigators had offered lenient treatment to the two lawbreaking witnesses in exchange for their testimony.

But Carter's freedom was short-lived. Carter, as well as Artis, was retried the following year on the same charges, though this time the prosecutors made a more direct appeal to race. They asserted that Carter and Artis killed three white strangers to avenge an earlier murder of a black man by a white man. Carter and Artis were once again convicted and returned to prison.

This time, however, most of Carter's supporters abandoned him, and his marriage ended in divorce. Instead of fighting for his freedom, he turned inward, reading books about history, philosophy, and religion, and he eventually realized that if he was going to survive in prison or out, he would have to lose his violent Hurricane persona and find a deeper meaning to his own life. But he was still stuck behind bars. (Artis would soon be paroled.) Then he received assistance from a most improbable source.

A group of young, idealistic Canadians had formed a commune in Toronto in the 1970s, and in 1979 the group essentially adopted a poor fifteen-year-old black American named Lesra Martin. As part of his education, the Canadians bought him numerous books, including *The Sixteenth Round*. Martin wrote Carter a letter in prison and soon met him in person. The commune members became convinced of Carter's innocence and dedicated themselves to helping his lawyers with the lengthy appeals process.

After the New Jersey Supreme Court had upheld Carter's second conviction, his lawyers petitioned the U.S. District Court in New Jersey, where Judge H. Lee Sarokin was assigned the case. On 7 November 1985 he overturned the conviction, concluding that the state had manipulated key witnesses, withheld material evidence, and made unconstitutional appeals to racial prejudice. At a hearing the following day, prosecutors urged Sarokin to keep Carter in prison pending the outcome of their appeals, but the judge rejected their request. After nineteen years, Carter was a free man. The prosecutors' appeals would last another three years, but Sarokin's ruling was upheld.

On 19 February 1988 the charges against Carter and Artis were officially dismissed. They were fully exonerated, though never compensated for their wrongful imprisonment.

A free man, Carter moved to Toronto, where he lived with the commune for a number of years before moving into his own home. He became the executive director of the Association in Defence of the Wrongly Convicted, which gave Carter a platform to speak out on the criminal justice system. His life story has been the subject of books and documentaries, as well as a motion picture in 1999, *The Hurricane*. DENZEL WASHINGTON played Rubin Carter.

While Carter never became a boxing champion, he will forever be known as a victor in his own journey for justice, freedom, and vindication.

FURTHER READING

Hirsch, James S. *Hurricane: The Miraculous Journey of Rubin Carter* (2000).

JAMES S. HIRSCH

Carter, Shawn Corey. *See* Jay-Z.

Carter, Stephen L. (26 Oct. 1954–), legal scholar and novelist, was born Stephen Lisle Carter in Washington, D.C., the second of five children to Lisle C. Carter Jr., a lawyer and educator, and Emily E. Carter, who worked as an assistant to the head of the National Urban Coalition. Carter attended public schools in Washington, New York City, and Ithaca, New York, before matriculating at Stanford University, from which he graduated in 1976. He then proceeded to Yale Law School, receiving his J.D. in 1979.

For the next two years Carter completed clerkships for Judge SPOTTSWOOD W. ROBINSON III of the United States Court of Appeals for the

District of Columbia (1979–1980), and Supreme Court Justice THURGOOD MARSHALL (1980–1981). He was admitted to the District of Columbia bar in 1981 and worked briefly as an associate at the Washington, D.C., law firm of Shea and Gardner before returning to Yale Law School as an assistant professor in 1982. Specializing in constitutional, contract, and intellectual property law, he rose quickly through the ranks, becoming the William Nelson Cromwell Professor of Law in 1991, the youngest person ever to hold that title. He married Enola Aird in 1981; they had two children.

Carter contributed widely to a number of law journals through the 1980s, but did not come to wide public attention until 1991, with the publication of *Reflections of an Affirmative Action Baby*. In the book Carter argued that affirmative action policies were hobbled by four fundamental flaws. First, he wrote, affirmative action implied African Americans were inferior and could not compete head-to-head against whites without special accommodations. (Carter called this the "best black syndrome," wherein an employer sought the "best black" available, assuming that he or she would not be the best candidate overall.) Second, those African Americans benefiting from affirmative action necessarily faced suspicion that they were hired because of their racial makeup, not their qualifications and accomplishments. Third, the use of racial diversity as a substitute for diversity of opinion, he wrote, fallaciously presumes all members of the same ethnic or racial group think alike. Finally, following the work of the sociologist WILLIAM JULIUS WILSON, Carter maintained that affirmative action programs seldom address the needs of the "truly disadvantaged," since benefits accrue mainly to the middle class, leaving the poor and working class behind.

Despite this devastating critique, Carter concluded that even with all its flaws, affirmative action policies are necessary, at least in the short term. Unlike many conservative critics, Carter acknowledged the persistence of racial injustices and the necessity of social and political solutions. Affirmative action should remain part of the answer, Carter asserted, only with more emphasis placed on providing opportunities for the economically disadvantaged (rather than based solely on racial background).

After this success Carter turned his attention to the theme that would dominate his writing through the 1990s: the interplay among morality, democracy, law, government, and religion. As both an evangelical Christian and political liberal, Carter felt keenly the need to explore the place of religion in a democracy and the way government and law accommodated—or failed to accommodate—devout citizens. His contemplation of these questions led to *The Culture of Disbelief: How American Law and Politics Trivialize Religious Devotion* (1993); *The Dissent of the Governed: A Meditation on Law, Religion, and Loyalty* (1998); and *God's Name in Vain: The Wrongs and Rights of Religion in Politics* (2000). While not formally a trilogy, the three books nevertheless represent an evolving examination of Carter's views of the role of religion in a democratic society.

The roots of Carter's thinking on religion and society sprang from the civil rights movement. Carter viewed the effort for desegregation and voting rights, led in large part by the clergy and with rhetoric suffused with biblical imagery, as a model for what religion's role in a democratic society ought to be. Unfortunately, he argued in *The Culture of Disbelief*, since the 1960s the significance of religion in American life had been trivialized (an odd charge when one considers that the United States, by any measure of opinion surveys and public rhetoric, is the most religious nation in the Western world). Carter dissected Supreme Court decisions dealing with issues of religious freedom and public discourse, arguing that in many cases religious concerns had been devalued. As an example Carter cited the 1990 Supreme Court decision *Employment Division, Department of Human Resources v. Smith* in which the majority ruled against Native Americans who wished to use peyote in a religious ritual.

In *Dissent of the Governed* (based on the William E. Massey Lectures delivered at Harvard University) Carter further explored religion as a necessary counterweight to the power of the state. He sharpened his critique of the American polity's devaluation of religion by attacking the "project of liberal constitutionalism," which, by consistently expanding First Amendment freedoms, offended the religious sensibilities of devout citizens. (Carter cited as an example the use of freedom of speech protection extended to pornography.) The secular state marginalizes religious dissent, Carter argued, and he questioned what allegiance the dissenters owe to a sovereign that fails to honor their beliefs. Carter's answer was two-pronged: he endorsed civil disobedience along the lines of MARTIN LUTHER KING JR.'s 1963 "Letter from a Birmingham Jail" and he urged an enhanced consideration of religious values in civil liberties jurisprudence. While in *The Culture of Disbelief* Carter described a secular civil polity that merely, though wrongheadedly, trivialized religion, in *God's Name in Vain* he adopted a more libertarian, even anti-statist position. The ever-expanding scope of liberal constitutionalism, he now argued, does not merely trivialize, but ultimately threatens religious freedom. Religion therefore becomes even more important as a countervailing force, a source of resistance against creeping secularization. Religious citizens must be politically involved, Carter argued, but warned they must not be tied too closely with particular policies or parties. Rather, religion should exercise its "prophetic voice," standing apart from narrow partisan interests, speaking truth to power.

Carter also wrote two books dealing with morality more generally. *Integrity* (1996) and *Civility* (1998) addressed those values Carter called "pre-political." Carter defined integrity as consisting of three steps: the determination of whether a particular action is right or wrong; proceeding to act on that determination; and forthrightly defending that action publicly. In *Civility* Carter defended respectful relations among individuals as the necessary "etiquette of democracy." For democracy to function properly, for all sides of political questions to be considered fully, civility must be exercised by all parties. Even while exposing these "prepolitical" virtues, Carter did not stray far from his preoccupation with religion, arguing that "religions at their best provide exactly the moral armament that is needed to resist the domination of social life by self-seeking, and thus to rescue civility in America" (*Civility*, 105).

Now well established as a major public intellectual, Carter turned his hand to fiction. Having received a multimillion-dollar advance from his publisher, he produced a novel, *The Emperor of Ocean Park*, in 2002. While Carter explicitly declared the work is not a *roman à clef*, many reviewers commented on the parallels to Carter's own life and concerns. The plot concerns the efforts of Talcott Garland, a professor at an elite law school and committed Christian, to unravel a family mystery brought to his attention following his father's death. Garland was the ideal Carter protagonist, an earnest and devout citizen dealing with the ethical and moral challenges of life in light of his religious beliefs. Shooting to the top of the bestseller lists, the book drew praise from critics for Carter's portrayal of the African American bourgeoisie, keen insights into race relations (or, in the novel's terms, the relations between the "darker" and

"paler nations"), and sly depiction of academic politics. In 2007 Carter published a second novel, *New England White*.

FURTHER READING

Nelson, Michael. "Stephen L. Carter: The Christian as Contrarian," *Virginia Quarterly Review* 79:3 (Summer 2003).

CHRISTOPHER BERKELEY

Carter, Uless (1916–), sharecropper and minister, was born in the Mississippi Delta, the tenth of twelve children of Miles Carter, a sharecropper descended from Georgia slaves owned by the forebears of President Jimmy Carter. The name of Miles Carter's wife is not recorded. The Carters lived a peripatetic existence, moving from one plantation to another, but never escaping the cycle of poverty that characterized much of black life in the Jim Crow South. Despite the hopelessness of that situation, Miles Carter was an ambitious man who occasionally advanced to the position of renter. Unlike sharecroppers who usually possessed antiquated farming tools and equipment and received only half of the value of their crop, renters often owned their own mules and implements and could expect to earn a three-quarter share of their crop, which in the Delta was inevitably cotton. Miles Carter's success as a renter required, however, that his children learn to labor hard, early, and occasionally under the discipline of his leather strap. Uless Carter attended school only to the second grade before entering the fields alongside his parents and siblings, working from before dawn until well into the night during the cotton harvest. He often went barefoot and wore clothing made from cotton bags. Despite the Carter family's sacrifices, they remained relatively powerless against unscrupulous white landowners. One of these refused to pay the family the money he owed so that he might instead pay his own son's college fees. Another confiscated their mules when Miles Carter forbade his daughters from working in his home, fearing that they would suffer from the landowner's sexual advances. When Miles Carter tried to hire a lawyer to get his mules back, a white man promptly reminded him that blacks had no recourse to justice. "You can always get another mule team," the white man said, "but you can't get another life" (Lemann, 54).

These early childhood experiences embittered Uless Carter, who in 1931, aged only seventeen, took charge of his family's affairs when most of his brothers left home and his father became an itinerant preacher. Working on the King & Anderson plantation near Clarksdale, he fought constantly with a man named Broughton, the white manager of the section the Carters farmed. Unlike some sharecroppers who fooled Broughton by pulling cotton quickly rather than picking it—pulling resulted in dirtier, less valuable bolls—Carter took pride in his work, even if this work ethic resulted in slower picking and lighter sacks at the end of the workday. His frequent confrontations with Broughton on this matter, and the latter's refusal to settle up their account, came to a head one day when Uless confronted him at the plantation office. In response Broughton broke into the Carters' barn, stole all their mules and equipment, and proceeded to plough up their land, destroying their chances of producing a crop. There was no legal recourse against such arbitrary actions, though the owner of the King & Anderson plantation did clear the family's debts because of their record as hard-working farmers. Uless Carter then began working in a restaurant in Clarksdale, but never made more than six dollars a week. In town, as on the farm, he experienced the daily indignities of second-class citizenship and witnessed frequent examples of white brutality, including the lynching of a black youth whose "crime" had been to witness the murder of a white shopkeeper by two African Americans. In 1942, fearing that he might be the next blameless victim of vigilante justice, Carter boarded the back of a bus bound for Chicago.

Upon reaching Cairo, Illinois, Carter moved to the front of that bus, something he could not do in Mississippi. Within an hour of arriving in his destination he was offered a job washing dishes that paid twenty-five dollars a week, more than four times his wage in Clarksdale. With rents low and Chicago's economy enjoying a wartime boom, Carter came to believe that he had reached the promised land. Within six months he found an even better paying job as a meat cutter at a Southside meatpacking factory, and within a year he had married, to a Kentucky migrant named Letha Mae Johnson, a factory worker and single mother of two children. Near the end of the war the couple moved from the cramped environs of the Southside to the border of Woodlawn, a once all-white neighborhood that had begun to accept black residents, thanks to the anti–restrictive covenant efforts of IRVIN MOLLISON and Carl Hansberry, and others in the Chicago NAACP. Although Carter's wife died of cancer in 1946, he married again two years later to a Kentucky-born widow named Geraldine Avery,

whom he had met at the Baptist church where he served as a deacon.

In 1949 Carter felt called by God to become a preacher. Two years later he formed his own congregation, the Full Gospel Baptist Church, and opened a storefront in the heart of Chicago's black belt, while continuing to work and earn good money as a meat cutter. When his church duties began to interfere with his factory work, his employers forced him to choose between the stockyards and his calling. Carter chose his ministry, even though his new day job, as a domestic servant for white families in suburban Chicago, paid considerably less. Still, given his experiences in the Delta, Reverend Carter appreciated that he had a choice. When his second wife left him in the early 1950s Carter dedicated his life full time to his church, and boarded in a room near the Robert Taylor Homes, a massive public housing project where many of his poor and working-class congregants lived. By the 1960s, as the hope and prosperity of the postwar years began to erode on Chicago's Southside, Carter moved his church to the now predominantly black neighborhood of Woodlawn, home to the radical antipoverty efforts of ARTHUR BRAZIER's Woodlawn Organization, and also to one of the city's most notorious armed black gangs, the Blackstone Rangers, led by JEFF FORT, an Aberdeen, Mississippi, native. The same poverty that led younger people to gravitate towards Brazier and Fort also drew older residents, many of them Mississippi migrants, to Carter's Full Gospel Baptist. In the late 1960s, however, Carter lost his congregation and his building, when a young preacher he had appointed as his assistant forced him out. Carter could have rebuilt his congregation to its former strength of three hundred had he been willing to ally with either Mayor Richard Daley's political machine or its emerging African American rivals, but he believed passionately that religion and politics should not mix. By choosing to go it alone, however, Carter saw his congregation dwindle as Full Gospel moved from one dilapidated structure to another in a Chicago Southside whose poverty was now as abject as the Clarksdale he had left three decades earlier. In 1977 he closed his church for good and moved to Flint, Michigan, two years later.

In 1985 Uless Carter turned full circle by moving from Flint back to Clarksdale, Mississippi, a pattern followed by thousands of other African Americans in the 1970s and 1980s, who returned to a South no longer segregated or plagued by racial violence. For sure, Clarksdale was no more the promised land than Chicago had been, but it was demonstrably better than it had been, particularly for the elderly. Carter retired to Federation Towers, a large, well-tended, public housing complex sponsored by the Federation of Colored Women's Clubs and subsidized by the federal government. The complex stood on the site of a plantation where he had picked cotton as a child. With Social Security—something denied his parents and grandparents—he could afford to retire in relative comfort, preach when he wanted to, and achieve the self-respect and independence he had struggled for throughout his life.

FURTHER READING

Lemann Nicholas. *The Promised Land: The Great Black Migration and How It Changed America* (1991).

STEVEN J. NIVEN

Carter, Vincent O. (14 June 1924–23 Jan. 1983), expatriate writer and artist, was born in Kansas City, Missouri, the only child of Joseph and Eola Carter. His mother worked in a laundry; his father was a hotel porter. For most of his boyhood, the Carters lived in a second-floor apartment at 618 Cottage Lane in Kansas City's ethnically diverse north end. Their street was an alley of bungalows and small houses that ran behind the dwellings of mostly Italian immigrants. Carter was shy, bookish, and smart, and developed a fine singing voice. As a schoolboy he liked to take Sunday outings on his own to the stately art museum, where he stared at Flemish paintings. Carter graduated from Lincoln High School in 1941 and entered the U.S. Army. He served three years with the 509th Port Battalion, mostly in France. On his return he worked as a railroad cook, went to college—Lincoln University in Pennsylvania, with some graduate study at Wayne State University in Detroit—and worked for a while in Michigan. For much of that time he yearned to become a writer.

In 1952 he returned briefly to Kansas City to tell his parents he was moving to France. Carter had the idea that he could do whatever he wanted there, and it seemed as if all the important black writers, and many musicians, had headed for Europe after the war. As the story goes, Carter never got comfortable in France and found reasons not to stay in Paris, then Amsterdam, then Munich. A friend invited him to Bern, Switzerland, and though he only planned to visit two days, he remained for thirty years.

Carter settled in Bern around the time JAMES BALDWIN, the African American writer, was writing his first novel, *Go Tell It on the Mountain* (1953), in a small Swiss village. There is no evidence that they ever met, though Carter must have noticed Baldwin's successes. Liselotte Haas, Carter's longtime friend in Bern, recalled talking about Baldwin with Carter. She also remembered later visits from American black activists, who tried to convince Carter to join the civil rights struggle back in the United States. Carter always said he had other things to do with his life. And for him that meant living not with anger, bitterness, and suicidal despair but for art, joy, and a credible self-image as a writer, even an unpublished one. For Carter, art transcended issues of race, although in Bern, he could never really escape his blackness.

Nonetheless, in Bern, Carter developed a charisma he never seemed to have as a young man in Kansas City. He taught English to telephone operators, bureaucrats, and their spouses. He fell in with musicians and artists and became a fixture in Bern's coffeehouse circles. A feature story which Carter submitted to a radio station got him a radio show for a while; he played music and discussed African American culture, though he resisted the programmers' desire to have him air more "Negro spirituals." He dabbled on the trumpet and flute. The shelves in his flat sagged with records—he loved Bartok and Bach as much as DUKE ELLINGTON—and with books by Shakespeare, Hesse, and Jung. And he wrote—short stories, articles, then longer works.

In 1957 he finished a memoir, or rather a collection of diary entries and anecdotes about his first few years in Bern. Like Baldwin, he recounted his experience as a rare man of black skin in the insular nation of Switzerland. And like Baldwin (whose essay "Stranger in the Village" was published in 1953), Carter encountered pointing fingers and upsetting shouts of "der Neger." He finished one novel, then in the early 1960s started on another, a sprawling thing that he considered his magnum opus. Centered on a boy's life in Kansas City, the manuscript, whose working title was "The Primary Colors," was highly autobiographical. It reflected the boy's awakenings to the world in the gritty, bustling city and the admiration he had for his hardworking, life-loving parents. It had a sense of music, not only in the story but also in the rhythm of its prose. Carter often listened to jazz or classical music when he wrote, and he once told a musician friend that while writing this novel, he treated the keyboard of his Hermes typewriter like a set of drums (Urs Frauchiger, correspondence with author, 8 May 2002).

For many years, however, he failed to interest publishers in his work. One found "The Primary Colors" to be too long and too dense; Carter had captured his characters with the real sound of thick black dialect, which early readers found to be tough going. He tried again, cutting and thinning, but the manuscript remained unsold. Herbert Lottman, an American literary critic living in Paris, once had an explanation: "He was writing, not fighting" (correspondence with author, 15 May 2002); that is, Carter was less interested in the timely political struggle that Baldwin and others were writing about than in the life of the mind and the aesthetic pursuits of fiction. If Carter's record is mostly one of failure in his lifetime, then, as Darryl Pinckney, a contemporary American writer and critic, suggests in *Out There*, "we must accept his failure, because failure is also part of the history of the black American expatriate writer in Europe" (103).

Carter increasingly turned his frustrations and creative energy toward making art. Without training, he began drawing and painting—figure studies and abstractions. A friend also introduced him to Eastern philosophy, meditation, and yoga. By the end of the 1960s he fell under the spell of an Indian mystic, the Swami Muktananda. Carter gave up drinking and smoking and adopted a body-as-temple rigor. Within a few years he and his friend Haas, a dancer and yoga teacher, made a pilgrimage to India, where he furthered his spiritual education under Muktananda. Carter became a strict vegetarian. And he gave up writing. His last-known unpublished manuscript, from about 1969, is an exploration of the layers of consciousness.

Carter returned to Kansas City twice. In 1969 he went home to bury his father, and four years later he spent more than two months with his mother as she was dying of cancer. By then, even his old neighborhood was gone, supplanted by an urban stretch of interstate highway. Yet, as he told Haas, one day he stood near the spot where he had grown up, and noticed, with the eyes of an artist, how the light remained the same (interview with author, 9 July 2002).

In 1973, the year his mother died, a publisher finally took a chance on Carter's memoir and published it as *The Bern Book: A Record of a Voyage of the Mind*. But by then Carter had no interest in promoting it. He had given up on fame. Although the book received a warm review in Kansas City, he remained virtually unknown outside Bern. His death from cancer in Bern attracted little notice except among his friends, and his remaining manuscripts gathered dust.

Twenty years later, however, a random, used-bookstore copy of *The Bern Book* triggered a series of events that led to a rediscovery of Carter and his literary potential. A Vermont publisher with roots in Kansas City had been alerted to Carter's memoir by a friend. The publisher, Chip Fleischer, found Haas in Bern, and she shared with him Carter's unpublished manuscripts. One important book stood out: the 805-page typed account of a Kansas City boyhood. Fleischer's Steerforth Press published Carter's "The Primary Colors" manuscript as *Such Sweet Thunder* in 2003 (reprinted, slightly shorter, in 2006). Fleischer, like Lottman, had seen Carter's achievement as a true work of art, an authentically voiced, meaningful portrait of a specific place and time in black America—along the racial divide of Kansas City in the 1920s and 1930s. Two decades after he died, Vincent Carter was a literary failure no more.

FURTHER READING
Pinckney, Darryl. *Out There: Mavericks of Black Literature* (2002)
Stovall, Tyler. *Paris Noir: African Americans in the City of Light* (1996)

STEVE PAUL

Carter, Walter Percival (29 Apr. 1923–31 July 1971), Baltimore area leader of the Congress On Racial Equality (CORE), and founder of Activists for Fair Housing, was born in Monroe, North Carolina, the son of Walter L. and Carrie P. Carter. Census records suggest he had at least four older sisters and an older brother, as well as a younger sister.

Carter entered North Carolina Agricultural and Technical College (NCAT) in 1941, but his studies were interrupted for military service in World War II. He enlisted as a private at Greensboro on 15 December 1942, was assigned to the Signal Corps (Natl. Archives WW II Army Enlistment Records, Record Group 64), and won five battle stars (MD House Joint Resolution 29, 26 Apr. 1972). Discharged in June 1946, Carter resumed studies at NCAT, where he worked on voter registration campaigns, participated in the campus debate team, and joined the Progressive Party. Many Americans of African descent supported Henry Wallace's 1948 campaign for president, but many thought Truman offered the best real hope for progress on civil rights, and Thomas Dewey, a firm supporter of the wartime "Double Victory" campaign, retained the loyalty of a fair number. Carter earned a bachelor's degree in 1948 and moved to Baltimore, Maryland.

He married Zerita Richardson; two daughters, Jill Priscilla and Judith Lynn, were born to the marriage.

The Baltimore chapter of CORE, which Carter joined in the 1950s, was formed in 1953. Until 1963 a majority of the local membership base were people considered "white," and after 1964, an overwhelming majority were "black." The chapter spearheaded a series of direct action campaigns, targeting downtown five-and-dime stores, the Northwood Shopping Center (particularly the movie theater), and for eight years, the Gwynn Oak Amusement Park. Much of the mass participation in these campaigns came from students at historically black Morgan State College.

Carter served as executive director of the local CORE chapter, starting around 1959. He completed a Master of Social Work degree at Howard University in the early 1960s, while organizing the 1960 Freedom Rides to the Eastern Shore of Maryland, and joining the Route 50 Freedom Riders in 1961. CORE declined to sponsor Baltimore-area civil rights volunteer William Moore's walk from Chattanooga, Tennessee, to Jackson, Mississippi, in 1963, to present Governor Ross Barnett a letter advocating that all Jim Crow laws and customs be abolished. Moore thought a southern-born "white" man might get Barnett to listen. Most of his fellow volunteers, including Carter, thought he was crazy to walk alone through the Deep South with such a message. When Moore was gunned down on an Alabama highway, many in the Student Nonviolent Coordinating Committee (SNCC) and CORE insisted on finishing the walk. Carter wired Moore's wife, Mary Moore, that the tragic killing "has struck us deeply, Bill was very close to us even though he had been with us only a short while" (Stanton, Mary. *Freedom Walk: Mississippi or Bust*, 2003, 93).

Carter was Maryland coordinator of the March on Washington in 1963, and simultaneously spearheaded the final campaign to open Baltimore's popular Gwynn Oaks Amusement Park to all residents, regardless of racial designation. CORE had targeted the privately owned park since 1952, but the policy of admitting only people recognized as "white" continued. CORE had built pressure in the previous two years, asking schools to cancel end-of-year field trips, and securing commitments from embassies in Washington, D.C., to cease participation in the amusement park's "All Nations Day."

On 4 July, Carter, Reverend Chester Wickwire from Johns Hopkins University, and clergy from a number of religious organizations launched a mass protest with over eight hundred people, responding to press inquiries, "we think everyone should celebrate the Fourth of July." Undeterred by mass arrests, as the interracial group tried to enter the park, or harassment from a band of "Fighting American Nationalists" with signs reading "Stop Rotten Red Race Mixers," picketing resumed Sunday 7 July. On 28 August, the park opened without racial restrictions, the result of a month of tense negotiations, with preparations for additional protests as necessary. To the surprise of the owners, business boomed, and the season had to be extended to accommodate overflow bookings.

The following month Carter resigned as executive director of CORE, succeeded by James Griffin. Although remaining on the executive board another two years, Carter expressed frustration at lack of support for the high-profile actions that broke racial segregation in public accommodations over the previous several years. In 1965, with Sampson Green and others, he left CORE to form Activists for Fair Housing.

"We had broken the public accommodations aspect of civil rights down" he explained, "and we knew the real civil rights battles would be fought right there where these people are whipped by everything—housing unemployment, lack of opportunities, improper schooling" (Joseph, Peniel E. *The Black Power Movement: Rethinking the Civil Rights–Black Power Era*, 2006, p. 84).

In 1968, Baltimore Mayor Thomas D'Alesandro III appointed Carter a director of the Community Action Commission, overseeing a large portion of local antipoverty programs. The city council, led by its president, William Donald Schaefer, rejected the appointment. Community Action Agency staff accused the council of a "secretive assault on the anti-poverty program and the people it serves." The *Baltimore Evening Sun* editorialized that the rejection was "capricious and wrong," calling it a "calculated rebuff to Negroes and the poor" (Williams, p. 163).

After riots in Baltimore the same year, Activists, Inc., investigated the financing practices of Morris Goldseker, who had a reputation in the 1950s as the agent who sold the best homes blacks could get. Carter and his associates documented that Goldseker made 85 percent profit turning over real estate. Carter's efforts changed the perception of blockbusting, which had been viewed as a way to get people of African descent into better housing, although many of those who signed rent to own contracts with Goldseker were bankrupted.

Carter died while giving a report at the Union Baptist Church in Baltimore, where his final words were, "I will commit the rest of my life to make this city a fit place where our kids can live" (*Archives of Maryland*, General Assembly of Maryland Joint Resolution 29, 26 April 1972). He was survived by his wife and daughters. State Senator CLARENCE M. MITCHELL eulogized, "my good friend and fellow freedom fighter, Walter Carter. I cannot forget the days when he was chairman of CORE and I was a teenager and walked many picket lines together" (Evans, Paul Fairfax. *City Life: A Perspective from Baltimore, 1968–1978*, 1981, 295).

FURTHER READING

Edelman, Lily. "The Story of the Fourth of July at Gwynn Oak." *Adult Leadership* 13, no. 2 (June 1964): 39–40, 54.

Smith, C. Fraser. *Here Lies Jim Crow: Civil Rights in Maryland* (2008).

Williams, Rhonda Y. *The Politics of Public Housing: Black Women's Struggles against Urban Inequality* (2004).

Yoes, Sean. "Gwynn Oak Park: Activists Braved Arrests, Hecklers to Integrate Amusement Park." *Afro-American Newspapers, Signature Series II: The Battle for Equal Access* (2007): 23–27.

CHARLES ROSENBERG

Carter, William Beverly, Jr. (1 Feb. 1921–9 May 1982), newspaper publisher and ambassador, was born in Coatesville, Pennsylvania, the son of William Beverly Carter and Maria Green. After a childhood spent in Philadelphia, Pennsylvania, Carter graduated in 1944 from Lincoln University, a historically black institution in Pennsylvania. As a student he was a member of Alpha Boule, Sigma Pi Phi, and Kappa Alpha Psi, and he served as executive secretary of the alumni association from 1952 to 1955. He attended Temple University Law School from 1946 to 1947 and the New School for Social Research from 1950 to 1951.

Early in his professional career, from 1943 to 1945, Carter worked as a reporter for the *Philadelphia Tribune*. He was city editor of the *Philadelphia Afro-American* from 1945 to 1948 and publisher of the *Pittsburgh Courier* newspaper group from 1955 to 1964. In 1958 he served as president of the National Newspaper Publishers Association. He made an unsuccessful run for Congress in 1954.

Carter devoted the remainder of his professional life to diplomatic service, especially in Africa, which had long held his interest. His first trip to the continent came in 1952; eventually he visited forty countries. After joining the U.S. Information Agency (USIA), his first overseas post was as press attaché at the U.S. embassy in Nairobi, Kenya, from 1965 to 1966. From 1966 to 1969 he was assigned to the embassy in Lagos, Nigeria, and from 1969 to 1972 he was a department assistant to the secretary of state for African affairs in Washington, D.C. In 1972 President Richard M. Nixon appointed him ambassador to Tanzania, a post he held until 1975, when he was recalled because of his involvement in a hostage crisis controversy.

In May 1975 the Central Committee of the People's Revolutionary Party, a Marxist group that had been waging a guerrilla war for about six years against the repressive government of General Joseph Mobutu Sese Seko of Zaire, seized three Stanford University students and a French woman from a research center. In defiance of a State Department policy against negotiating with terrorists, Carter became involved with hostage negotiations and permitted an embassy aide to take part in the ransom payment.

Secretary of State Henry Kissinger intended to dismiss Carter but was dissuaded from doing so by aides. Instead, he slated Carter for demotion to a lower-paying post with the USIA. Carter's supporters rallied behind him, and a dinner in his honor was attended by two hundred and fifty people. The Congressional Black Caucus, contending that the U.S. position on Africa was unclear, met with Kissinger and received assurances that nothing would be done to impede Carter's State Department career. In 1976, after Senate Foreign Relations Committee hearings, at which Representative CHARLES RANGEL (D-NY) testified for the caucus, Carter was appointed ambassador to Liberia, where he remained until 1979.

The appointment to Liberia was still considered a demotion; Carter had been slated to be named ambassador to Denmark until Kissinger withdrew his nomination in the wake of the hostage controversy. At that time African American senior members of the State Department represented only four percent of the department's total staff and were concentrated in African assignments. Nevertheless, in this new post Carter was honored with Liberia's highest civilian decoration, the Order of African Redemption.

Committed to civil rights both at home and abroad, Carter served from 1972 until his death as a member of the United Nations Subcommittee on Prevention of Discrimination and Protection of Minorities. In this capacity Carter was again embroiled in controversy with the U.S. government when he voted in September 1979 with the subcommittee's majority on two resolutions critical of Israeli policy. These resolutions urged Israel to negotiate with the Palestine Liberation Organization, to restore the rights of self-determination to the Palestinians, and to stop the bombardment of southern Lebanon. The U.S. State Department disassociated itself from his votes, contending that Carter was just one member of an international panel of experts who were under no instructions from their governments.

From 1979 to 1981 Carter served as ambassador at large, the first African American to hold that office, and as head of the State Department's Office for Liaison with State and Local Governments. When he retired from the State Department in 1981, he was given the agency's highest civilian citation, the Distinguished Honor Award. In April 1982 he received the Reverend James Robinson Award for Operation Crossroads, Africa, in recognition of his role in improving relations between the United States and the nations of Africa. At home his civil rights activities included involvement in the National Association for the Advancement of Colored People and the National Urban League; the Urban League of Philadelphia cited him for his work on human rights.

When Carter died in Bethesda, Maryland, he left a wife, Carlyn Brown Pogue, whom he had married in 1971, a son by a previous marriage to Rosalie A. Terry, and two stepchildren. At the time of his death he was director of development and international affairs for the Inter-Maritime Group based in Geneva, Switzerland.

FURTHER READING

Carter's oral history interview was presented to the New York Public Library's Schomburg Center for Research in Black Culture on 19 Apr. 1984.

Obituaries: *New York Times, Philadelphia Tribune,* 11 May 1982; *Washington Post,* and *Afro-American,* 15 May 1982; and *Jet,* 24 May 1982.

This entry is taken from the *American National Biography* and is published here with the permission of the American Council of Learned Societies.

ARLENE LAZAROWITZ

Cartwright, Marguerite D. (17 May 1912–5 May 1986), journalist, educator, lecturer, and actress, was born Marguerite Phillips Dorsey in Cambridge, Massachusetts, the only child of Joseph A. Dorsey,

an architect and real estate broker, and Mary Louise Ross. Marguerite Cartwright's early education was in Cambridge, Massachusetts. She later earned her B.A. and M.A. degrees from Boston University in 1932 and 1933, respectively. Her master's thesis was on the African origins of drama, contending that the Greek god Dionysus was an African. She married the chemical engineer Leonard Carl Cartwright in 1930, an interracial union that lasted over fifty years, until his death in 1982.

Cartwright combined her academic interest in theater with an application as an actress in a number of plays and films, including the play *Roll Sweet Chariot* (1934) in New York City and the film *Green Pastures* (1935). Simultaneously working as an actress and a social worker, engaging in a lifelong career as a world traveler, social critic, and civil rights activist, and continuing her education, Cartwright earned her doctorate from New York University in 1948. Her dissertation, "Legislation against Discrimination in Employment in New York State," examined legislation related to racial and religious discrimination from 1609 to 1945. Cartwright did post-doctorate studies at Columbia University in 1949 while working as an instructor at Brooklyn College. In 1948 she joined the faculty in the Hunter College sociology department, where she remained for more than ten years, teaching education, sociology, and psychology.

During this period Cartwright pursued journalistic interests that took her to all parts of the world, where she interviewed people and wrote about historic events that had a profound effect on international relations. In 1951 she covered the Zagreb Conference in Yugoslavia, where she interviewed President Josip Tito during the early years of his tenure as a world leader. She began her long association with the United Nations in 1952, first as a delegate to the U.S. Commission for UNESCO, then as a liaison officer, then as a correspondent. Between 1954 and 1956 she received a number of Ford Foundation travel grants to study human relations in six major U.S. cities and international travel funds to study the Israeli-Arab tensions in the Middle East. She also taught sociology courses at Mills College of Education from 1954 to 1955, and during the summer of 1957 she taught a course on Africa at the New School of Social Research in New York.

In 1955 Cartwright covered the historic African-Asian Conference in Bandung, Indonesia, that led to the Non Aligned movement. This conference, attended by twenty-nine African and Asian nations, was hailed as the first attempt to promote economic and cultural cooperation and to oppose colonialism. Many prominent African American journalists and politicians, such as ADAM CLAYTON POWELL JR., CARL T. ROWAN, ETHEL PAYNE, and RICHARD WRIGHT, attended. Cartwright used this opportunity to report on the daily events, speeches, and activities, regaling her readers with accounts of the various disputes, agreements, and personalities. Her profile of China's Chou En-Lai is a classic example of Cartwright's attempts to report accurately about international issues without offending U.S. sensibilities. Her last sentence sums up how she observed this dichotomy: "Instead of denying Chou's successes, we should decide what to do about it, and begin to plan our next moves." Her stories were carried in the *New York Amsterdam News*, the *Pittsburgh Courier*, and other newspapers.

Cartwright also interviewed the Gold Coast (later Ghana) prime minister Kwame Nkrumah, and at his invitation she returned for the first birthday celebration of Ghana's independence in 1957. She established a relationship with the country of Liberia, and in 1958 she received a special invitation from President William Vacanarat Shadrach Tubman to attend the 111th independence celebration of this West African country. She also began a long-term association with the country of Nigeria during this period, and in 1959 she was appointed a member of the Provisional Council, University of Nigeria, of which she became a founder-trustee. At the invitation of Nnamdi Azikiwe, the first chancellor of the University of Nigeria, Cartwright attended the celebration of Nigerian independence in 1960. As a testament to her dedication and service to the University of Nigeria, a street near the institution was named in her honor.

From the mid-1950s through the 1960s Cartwright joined the Overseas Press Club, was a charter member of the UN Correspondents Circle, wrote articles devoted to the work of the United Nations, lectured in the United States and abroad, and attended the first All-Independent African States Conference and the subsequent All African People's Conferences held in Accra, Ghana. During this time she turned her attention to Europe and the Middle East, visiting Greece, Italy, Turkey, Israel, Jordan, Lebanon, and Egypt repeatedly. On her first visit to Egypt, in 1956, she heard Colonel Gamal Abdel Nasser's historic Suez speech, during which he promoted the nationalization of the Suez Canal. She later interviewed Nasser, and she interviewed Golda Meir both when she was Israel's foreign minister and when she was Israel's prime minister.

The 1970s and 1980s brought issues dealing with women into the forefront, and Cartwright was a model of what women, if given the opportunities, could accomplish. The United Nations and other organizations took note of her leadership and recognized her activities. She was chosen to attend the United Nations Decade of Women Conference in July 1985 in Nairobi, Kenya. She received numerous awards and citations, including the highest national award from the Association of Women in Communications in 1975, the Knight Commander Order of African Redemption from the Republic of Liberia, and a key to the city of Wilmington, Delaware. Besides her work as a journalist for over three decades, Cartwright wrote numerous scholarly articles for such publications as the *Journal of Educational Sociology* and the *Journal of Negro Education*, served as editor of the *Review of Research*, and wrote extensively on race relations for *Opportunity*, *Phylon*, *The Crisis*, and the *Negro History Bulletin*.

FURTHER READING

Cartwright's papers, including all of her writings, articles, photographs, and research, are at the Amistad Research Center, Tulane University, New Orleans, Louisiana.

"Marguerite D. Cartwright." 1954 Personnel Files. Hunter College of CUNY, Wexler Library, Archives Division.

"Marguerite Dorsey Cartwright," *Directory of American Scholars*, 9th ed. (1999).

Richmond, Norman. "The Legacy of the Bandung," *Black Commentator* (9 June 2005). *Who's Who among African Americans*, 19th ed. (2006).

Obituary: *New York Times*, 9 May 1986.

REBECCA L. HANKINS

Carver, George Washington (c. 1864–5 Jan. 1943), scientist and educator, was born in Diamond (formerly Diamond Grove), Missouri, the son of Mary Carver, who was the slave of Moses and Susan Carver. His father was said to have been a slave on a neighboring farm who was accidentally killed before Carver's birth. Slave raiders allegedly kidnapped his mother and older sister while he was very young, and he and his older brother were raised by the Carvers on their small farm.

Barred from the local school because of his color, Carver was sent to nearby Neosho in the mid-1870s to enter school. Having been privately tutored earlier, he soon learned that his teacher

George Washington Carver (center, front row) seated on steps with his staff, c. 1902. (Library of Congress.)

knew little more than he did, so he caught a ride with a family moving to Fort Scott, Kansas. Until 1890 Carver roamed around Kansas, Missouri, and Iowa seeking an education while supporting himself doing laundry, cooking, and homesteading.

In 1890 Carver entered Simpson College in Indianola, Iowa, as a preparatory student and art major. Convinced by his teacher that there was little future in art for a black man, he transferred the next year to Iowa State, where he was again the only African American student. By the time he received his master's degree in Agriculture in 1896, Carver had won the respect and love of both faculty and students. He participated in many campus activities while compiling an impressive academic record. He was employed as a botany assistant and put in charge of the greenhouse. He also taught freshmen. The faculty regarded Carver as outstanding in mycology (the study of fungi) and in cross-fertilization. Had he not felt obligated to share his knowledge with other African Americans, he

probably would have remained at Iowa State and made significant contributions in one or both of those fields. Aware of deteriorating race relations in the year of *Plessy v. Ferguson* (1896), he instead accepted BOOKER T. WASHINGTON's offer in 1896 to head the agricultural department at Tuskegee Normal and Industrial Institute in Macon County, Alabama. Carver brought both his knowledge and professional contacts to Tuskegee. Two of his former teachers, James Wilson and Henry C. Wallace, became U.S. secretaries of agriculture, as did Wallace's son, Henry A. Wallace. All three granted Department of Agriculture aid to Tuskegee and provided access to such presidents as Theodore Roosevelt and Franklin D. Roosevelt.

Carver's strong will led to conflicts with the equally strong-willed Washington over Carver's incompetence at administration. His contacts and flair for teaching and research protected Carver from dismissal. In both his teaching and his research, his primary goal was to alleviate the crushing cycle of debt and poverty suffered by many black farmers who were trapped in sharecropping and cotton dependency. As director of the only all-black agricultural experiment station, he practiced what was later called "appropriate technology," seeking to exploit available and renewable resources. In the classroom, in such outreach programs as farmers' institutes, a wagon equipped as a mobile school, and in agricultural bulletins, Carver taught how to improve soil fertility without commercial fertilizer, how to make paints from native clays, and how to grow crops that would replace purchased commodities. He especially advocated peanuts as an inexpensive source of protein and published several bulletins containing peanut recipes.

Carver never married, but he came to regard the Tuskegee students as his "adopted family." He was a mentor to many, providing financial aid and personal guidance. Devoutly religious in his own way, he taught a voluntary Bible class on campus.

At the time of Washington's death in 1915, Carver was respected by agricultural researchers but was largely unknown to the general public. Long in the shadow of Washington, Carver became the heir to the principal's fame after being praised by Theodore Roosevelt at the funeral. In 1916 he was inducted into the Royal Society for the Arts in London. Then the peanut industry recognized his usefulness. In 1921 a growers' association paid his way to Washington, D.C., so that he could testify at congressional tariff hearings, where his showmanship in displaying peanut products garnered national publicity. In 1923 Atlanta businessmen founded the Carver Products Company, and Carver won the Spingarn Medal of the National Association for the Advancement of Colored People. The company failed but obtained one patent and much publicity. In 1933, for example, an Associated Press release overstated Carver's success in helping polio patients with peanut oil massages. Carver became one of the best-known African Americans of his era.

His rise from slavery and some personal eccentricities—such as wearing an old coat with a flower in the lapel and wandering the woods at dawn to commune with his "Creator"—appealed to a wide public. Advocates of racial equality, a religious approach to science, the "American dream," and even segregation appropriated Carver as a symbol of their varied causes. Carver made some quiet, personal stands against segregation, but he never made public statements on any racial or political issues. Thus his name could be used for contradictory goals. He relished the publicity and did little to correct the exaggerations of his work, aside from humble protestations regarding his "unworthiness" of the honors that came in increasing numbers.

Though some of this mythology was unfortunate, Carver served as a role model to African Americans and as a potent force promoting racial tolerance among young whites. The Commission on Interracial Cooperation and the Young Men's Christian Association sent him on lecture tours of white campuses in the 1920s and 1930s. On these occasions Carver converted many who heard his lectures to the cause of racial justice. To them Carver was no "token black" but a personal friend and confidant. Indeed, many people who met Carver, Henry Ford among them, were made to feel they were "special friends."

Carver never earned more than $1,200 a year and refused compensation from peanut producers. Nevertheless he was able to accumulate almost $60,000 because he lived in a student dormitory and spent very little money. In 1940 he used his savings to establish the George Washington Carver Foundation to support scientific research—a legacy that continues at Tuskegee University. He died three years later in Tuskegee. Although his scientific contributions were meager relative to his fame, Carver did help hundreds of landless farmers improve the quality of their lives. And his magnetic personality and capacity for friendship inspired and enriched countless individuals.

FURTHER READING

Most of Carver's papers are at the Tuskegee University Archives in Alabama.

Holt, Rackham. *George Washington Carver: An American Biography* (1943; rev. ed., 1963).

Kremer, Gary R. *George Washington Carver in His Own Words* (1987).

McMurry, Linda O. *George Washington Carver: Scientist and Symbol* (1981).

This entry is taken from the *American National Biography* and is published here with the permission of the American Council of Learned Societies.

LINDA O. MCMURRY

Cary, Lorene (29 Nov. 1956–), writer, professor, and activist, was born in Philadelphia, Pennsylvania, the daughter of John Cary, a junior high school science teacher, and Carole Hamilton, a one time hairdresser and elementary school special education teacher. Cary's mother took an active role in guiding her early education in public schools in the

Philadelphia suburbs. In 1972, in a move that had tremendous significance personally and academically for the young teenager, Cary, with her mother's encouragement, entered the prestigious St. Paul's Preparatory School in New Hampshire. Historically an all-male, all-white institution, St. Paul's in the 1970s was actively seeking to change its elitist image by admitting girls and African Americans. Although Cary had eagerly sought admission to St. Paul's, her experiences there were mixed. While she was successful academically and socially, she often felt isolated, never entirely a part of St. Paul's established world or its newer world of black students. In 1974 Cary graduated from St. Paul's, and her experiences there would one day serve as the inspiration for her first book, the highly acclaimed memoir *Black Ice*.

In 1978 Cary earned her B.A. and M.A. degrees from the University of Pennsylvania in 1978. Having won a Thuron Fellowship for student exchanges between Britain and the United States, she studied at Sussex University in England, where she earned an M.A. in Victorian Literature. After college Cary pursued a writing career, becoming a writer for *Time* magazine in 1980 and then serving as an associate editor for *TV Guide*. In 1983 she married the Reverend R. C. Smith, with whom she had two children. The couple settled in Philadelphia, and Cary continued her writing career.

Cary achieved considerable professional success in the early 1990s. In 1991 Alfred A. Knopf published *Black Ice*, which portrayed not only the ordeals faced by many high school students, for example, acquaintance rape, but also the more specific problems experienced by a black student in a basically white world, including the difficulty in dealing with tokenism and with white students who believe that they are without prejudice. Cary movingly chronicled her youthful efforts to keep her female, lower-middle-class, black identity in a hegemonic world that was still primarily white, male, and upper class. In 1992 the American Library Association named *Black Ice* one of its Notable Books. That year Cary also received an honorary doctor of letters degree from Colby College in Maine, one of several honorary degrees that she would receive. In 1993 she became a contributing editor for *Newsweek*. She also worked as a freelance writer; her articles appeared in *Essence*, *Mirabella*, *Newsweek*, the *New York Times*, *Obsidian*, *Philadelphia*, and the *Philadelphia Inquirer Sunday Magazine*.

The Price of a Child, Cary's second book and first novel, was published in 1995. Inspired by an account of a runaway slave, JANE JOHNSON, Cary's novel takes place in 1855, as did Johnson's flight. The novel centers on Ginnie Pryor, a young black woman who escapes slavery but must give up her youngest child in the process. While the time, the place, and the central characters are all far removed from the world of *Black Ice*, there are thematic similarities, particularly the emphasis on the cost to a black woman of trying to find a new life in a white world without sacrificing her black cultural identify. For Ginnie Pryor a partial solution to that riddle lies in claiming a new name, Mercer Gray, a new home in the North, and a new vocation as a speaker for the abolition of slavery. Mercer's new role is only a partial solution, however. By the conclusion of the novel, Mercer concedes that she will never truly have her own way, that "the price of freedom is vigilance" (316). And she still has not reclaimed her child, although the hope remains that she may yet do so.

The late 1990s were a productive time for Cary. In 1998 she established Art Sanctuary at the Church of the Advocate in North Philadelphia with the goal of bringing black artists and thinkers to the black community. Lecturers and performers there included TERRY MCMILLAN, SONIA SANCHEZ, and JOHN EDGAR WIDEMAN, as well as prominent black musicians, historians, and photographers. Additionally, as a senior lecturer in creative writing at the University of Pennsylvania, Cary was the 1998 recipient of the Provost's Award for Distinguished Teaching. That year she published her third book and second novel, *Pride*. With its contemporary setting and its focus on four female characters, *Pride* may seem a far step from *The Price of a Child*, and in many ways it is. *Pride* tells the story of four best friends who are about to turn forty: Aretha, an Episcopal priest; Audrey, an alcoholic; Roz, a politician's wife suffering from breast cancer; and Tam, an unlucky-in-love college professor. The women are all African American, and *Pride* shared with Cary's other works an insistence on the importance for black women of maintaining their black identity—in this particular novel through an affirmative black sisterhood.

The success of Cary's books and her numerous awards were testimonies to her worldwide influence. In 1996 she received the SHIRLEY CHISHOLM Award in the Humanities and in 1999 the American Red Cross Spectrum Rising Star Award. These honors were followed by, among others, the Women's Way Agent of Change Award in 2002 and the Philadelphia Award in 2003. Also in 2003 Cary's novel *The Price of a Child* was named the inaugural book in the One Book, One Philadelphia project sponsored by the Free Library of Philadelphia, the Mayor's Office, and a number of civic and commercial organizations seeking to encourage reading throughout the city. In support of the effort, the Free Library acquired two thousand copies of the novel, as did the public schools for use in African American studies courses, and there were 250 events throughout Philadelphia focusing on *The Price of a Child*. In 2006 Cary published *Free! Great Escapes from Slavery on the Underground Railroad*.

FURTHER READING

Cary, Lorene. *Black Ice* (1991).

Cahill, Susan. *Writing Women's Lives: An Anthology of Autobiographical Narratives by Twentieth Century American Women Writers* (1994).

Harris, Trudier. *Saints Sinners Saviors: Strong Black Women in African American Literature* (1991).

Lopate, Phillip. "An Epistle from St. Paul's," *New York Times*, 31 Mar. 1991.

ALICE DRUM

Cary, Lott (c. 1780–10 Nov. 1828), Baptist preacher and missionary to Africa, was born on a plantation in Charles City County, Virginia, thirty miles from Richmond, the son of slave parents (names unknown). His grandmother Mihala had a strong influence on Lott's early religious development. He married around 1800 and, with his first wife (name unknown), had two children. Lott's master sent him to Richmond in 1804 as a hired slave laborer. He worked in the Shockoe Tobacco Warehouse first as a laborer and then as a shipping clerk. (The spelling of Cary's name as "Carey" is probably due to confusion in some primary sources with the well-known English Baptist, the Reverend William Carey. Lott Cary, however, signed his name as "Cary.")

Cary attended the predominantly white First Baptist Church, as did other blacks in Richmond. He experienced conversion in 1807 after hearing a sermon on Jesus and Nicodemus. Allowed to earn money by selling waste tobacco, Cary purchased his freedom and that of his two children in 1813. His wife had died by this time. Anxious to study the Bible, Cary enrolled in a night school taught by William Crane. There he learned to read, write, and do elementary arithmetic. His studies allowed him to assume greater responsibilities at the tobacco warehouse and achieve more economic independence; he eventually rose to the position of foreman with a salary of $800 per year. He remarried

about 1815; with his second wife (whose name also is unknown) he had one child.

Cary felt called to the Christian ministry and began to hold meetings for Richmond's African American residents. The First Baptist Church licensed him around 1814 after a trial period. Contemporaries credited him with extraordinary abilities as an extemporary speaker. Cary's strong interest in foreign mission work began when he heard Crane report on the plans of the American Colonization Society (ACS) for establishing colonies of African Americans in West Africa and conducting Christian missions. Cary sought to arouse interest in Africa among fellow blacks in Richmond and, along with Crane, was instrumental in organizing the Richmond African Baptist Missionary Society in 1815. Because of white opposition to unregulated black organizations in the wake of the insurrection of GABRIEL in 1800, Crane, one of the white members of First Baptist, served as president of the missionary society. Cary was recording secretary.

Cary developed an even stronger interest in going to Africa as a Christian missionary after the visit of Luther Rice to Richmond in 1817. He sought support from the white Baptist General Missionary Convention. When asked why he should want to leave America for the uncertainties of Africa, Cary said: "I am an African, and in this country, however meritorious my conduct, and respectable my character, I cannot receive the credit due to either. I wish to go to a country where I shall be estimated by my merits, not by complexion; and I feel bound to labor for my suffering race" (Gurley, 148). The Baptist Board of Foreign Missions and the ACS endorsed Cary in 1819. The ACS had been organized in December 1816 by whites who were interested primarily in removing blacks (especially free blacks) to West Africa; most ACS members did not oppose slavery as an institution. Cary's reservations concerning the policies of the ACS apparently were overshadowed by his desire to see Africa and conduct mission work there. He served the ACS without pay.

Cary and a group of twenty-eight colonists, plus a number of children, departed from Norfolk, Virginia, onboard the brig *Nautilus* bound for Sierra Leone in January 1821. Before leaving America, Cary and six other colonists, including his close friend Colin Teague, organized a missionary Baptist church. As he boarded ship Cary told those who had assembled to see the *Nautilus* off, "It may be that I shall behold you no more on this side of the grave, but I feel bound to labor for my brothers, perishing as they are in the far distant land of Africa. For their sake and for Christ's sake I am happy in leaving all and venturing all" (Gurley, 149). The Richmond African Baptist Missionary Society gave seven hundred dollars to support Cary. This was the first effort by black Baptists in America to do mission work in Africa.

After a voyage of forty-four days, Cary and the other colonists arrived at Freetown, Sierra Leone, which the British government had taken over in 1808 for the settlement of "Liberated Africans" whom the British navy freed from captured slave ships. Agents of the ACS had urged the U.S. government to establish a freed-slave colony on Sherbro Island, down the coast from Freetown, but when Cary arrived in 1821 no provisions had been made for them. The new arrivals were required to cultivate farms and do other labor in Sierra Leone. Soon after their arrival, Cary's second wife died of tropical fever, leaving him to care for three children. While in Sierra Leone, Cary did missionary work among the Vai tribe at Cape Grand Mountain.

By December 1821 arrangements had been made for the purchase of land from King Peter, the principal chief around the cape, for another settlement. This later became part of the Republic of Liberia. In early 1822 Cary and his family moved to Mesurado (now Cape Monrovia). Jehudi Ashmun, a representative of the ACS, served as colonial agent of the colony of about 130 members, and Cary acted as health officer and inspector. In addition to assisting Ashmun in defense of the colony against the forces of King Peter, who was resentful of the colony's expansion, in 1822 Cary established a Baptist church in Monrovia that grew to about seventy members by 1825. Known as Providence Baptist, the church had its nucleus in the missionary congregation Cary and fellow Baptists had organized before leaving the United States. Cary also established a day school in Monrovia, which was moved to Cape Grand Mountain in 1827 but eventually closed because of insufficient funding.

In 1823 conflict developed between the earliest colonists and Ashmun, who attempted to redistribute town lots because of the arrival of additional settlers. The controversy escalated to the point where some colonists were charged with sedition and stealing rations. Although Cary initially opposed Ashmun, he mediated the dispute between the disgruntled colonists and the governing authorities. Liberia was established with a permanent government in 1825 as a colony of the United States; Ashmun became governor. Cary was elected vice agent of the colony in September 1826. When Ashmun became ill and left for the United States in March 1828, the entire administrative responsibility of the colony fell into Cary's hands. After Ashmun's death in August 1828, Cary was appointed governor of the more than twelve hundred settlers of Liberia.

In late 1828 a native group known as the Bassa, with whom the colonists had been having periodic conflict, robbed a factory at Digby, a settlement north of Monrovia. Cary called for a show of force by the settler militia. On 8 November 1828 he was making cartridges in the old agency house when a candle was accidentally upset. The ammunition exploded. Seriously injured, Cary died two days later; he was buried in Liberia. A monument was later erected that bore the inscription "Lott Cary's self-denying, self-sacrificing labors, as a self-taught Physician, as a Missionary and Pastor of a Church, and finally as Governor of the Colony, have inscribed his name indelibly on the page of history, not only as one of Nature's Noblemen, but as an eminent Philanthropist and Missionary of Jesus Christ." In 1897 black Baptists in America organized the Lott Cary Foreign Missionary Convention in honor of Cary's pioneering labors in Liberia.

FURTHER READING

Fitts, Leroy. *Lott Carey: First Black Missionary to Africa* (1978).

Gurley, Ralph Randolph. *Life of Jehudi Ashmun, Late Colonial Agent in Liberia, with an Appendix Containing Extracts from His Journal and Other Writings, with a Brief Sketch of the Life of the Rev. Lott Cary* (1835).

Taylor, James B. *The Biography of Elder Lott Cary* (1837).

This entry is taken from the *American National Biography* and is published here with the permission of the American Council of Learned Societies.

MILTON C. SERNETT

Cary, Mary Ann Shadd (9 Oct. 1823–5 June 1893), educator, journalist, editor, and lawyer, was born in Wilmington, Delaware, the daughter of Abraham Doras Shadd and Harriet Parnell. Although she was the eldest of thirteen children, Mary Ann Shadd grew up in comfortable economic circumstances. Little is known about her mother except that she was born in North Carolina in 1806 and was of mixed black and white heritage; whether she was born free or a slave is unknown. Shadd's father was also of mixed-race heritage. His paternal

Mary Ann Camberton Shadd Cary, an advocate of self-reliance, helped found the *Provincial Freeman,* a newspaper aimed at black refugees in Canada. (Austin/Thompson Collection, by permission of Moorland Spingarn Research Center.)

grandfather, Jeremiah Schad, was a German soldier who had fought in the American Revolution and later married Elizabeth Jackson, a free black woman from Pennsylvania. Abraham Shadd had amassed his wealth as a shoemaker, and his property by the 1830s was valued at $5,000. He was a respected member of the free black community in Wilmington and in West Chester, Pennsylvania, where the family had moved sometime in the 1830s, and he served as a delegate to the American Anti-Slavery Society in 1835 and 1836.

Mary Ann Shadd continued her family's activist tradition by devoting her life to the advancement of black education and the immediate abolition of slavery. As a youth she attended a private Quaker school for blacks taught by whites, in which several of her teachers were abolitionists. During the 1840s she taught in schools for blacks in Wilmington, West Chester, New York City, and Norristown, Pennsylvania. When passage of the Fugitive Slave Act of 1850 endangered the freedom of free blacks as well as fugitive slaves, Shadd joined the faction of black abolitionists who promoted the controversial cause of voluntary black emigration to Canada. This movement illustrated the depth of disillusionment

with the United States that had developed among many blacks since the 1840s. Angered and disappointed in the continued tolerance of slavery and the upsurge of violence against free blacks, a faction of black activists broke from the American abolitionist organization and from those black abolitionists who preferred to stay and fight oppression in the United States. Between 1850 and 1860 approximately forty thousand blacks fled to southern Ontario. Shadd found employment in 1851 as a teacher of blacks in Windsor, Ontario, and was later joined by several members of her family. Shadd taught school and became a fervent spokeswoman for the emigration movement. Like most teachers in the black settlements, she had to struggle to keep her schools open, facing such obstacles as inadequate supplies, ramshackle school buildings, inclement weather, and the frequent outbreak of cholera and measles.

In addition to teaching, Shadd was a talented writer. One of the most important enterprises was her participation with the Reverend SAMUEL RINGGOLD WARD in the founding in 1853 of the *Provincial Freeman,* a newspaper dedicated to promoting the interests of Canadian blacks, in Toronto, Ontario. The *Provincial Freeman* functioned as Shadd's vehicle for promoting Canada as a haven for the oppressed and for condemning the United States. In addition, she wrote extensively on the topics of temperance, antislavery, anticolonization, black education, and women's rights.

Shadd also used the podium effectively for promoting her ideas, despite the resistance she often encountered against women who engaged in the traditionally male activity of public speaking. After much debate, for example, she was given the opportunity to address the all-male delegation at the Eleventh Colored National Convention in Philadelphia in 1855. One man in the audience noted that her eyes were "small and penetrating and fairly flash when she is speaking." He described her as a "superior woman … however much we may differ with her on the subject of emigration." At another engagement, an observer praised her as "a woman of superior intellect, and the persevering energy of character." On her lecture trips, however, she often found the platform closed to women. While in Rockford, Illinois, she wrote to her brother Isaac that the citizens were "so conservative … as not to tolerate lectures from women." In both her writings and her speeches, Shadd spoke her mind, often roundly criticizing leading black men in the United States and Canada for providing inadequate support for Canadian black communities.

Her outspoken and candid manner often brought her into conflict with other black Canadian activists during the 1850s over such issues as the appropriate means for funding black schools and for raising money to help newly arrived blacks. Her most publicized feud was with HENRY BIBB and Mary Bibb, American-born free black activists who had helped in the establishment of the black settlement in Windsor the year before Shadd arrived. What began as a disagreement over policies escalated into a bitter personal feud between Shadd and the Bibbs that was well publicized in their rival newspapers and in Shadd's lengthy correspondence with George Whipple, secretary of the American Missionary Association. In his *Voice of the Fugitive*, Bibb chastised her for criticizing him, calling her unladylike, while Shadd described him as "a dishonest man."

The Bibbs favored all-black schools sponsored by the Canadian government, but Shadd sought to break down all racial barriers, favoring privately funded schools that made no distinctions about color. Although she encouraged black parents to make concerted efforts to sustain the schools, finding the necessary funds was a formidable barrier. Shadd finally was forced to appeal to the American Missionary Association for assistance.

Shadd also criticized the activities of the Refugee Home Society, an organization that Henry Bibb had started in 1850 to distribute land, clothing, and money to black refugees. Shadd accused Bibb of corruption and of perpetuating a "begging scheme." According to Shadd, who charged that corrupt agents pocketed the money, few such resources actually went to the refugees. She argued further that too much assistance would prevent black settlers from becoming self-reliant.

Her marriage in 1856 to the widower Thomas F. Cary, a barber and bathhouse proprietor from Toronto, did not prevent her from continuing to write, lecture, and teach. When at home in Chatham, she worked on the newspaper and cared for Thomas Cary's three children. They had two children of their own, one in 1857 and another in 1860. Shadd Cary continued to lecture and write for the *Provincial Freeman*. She also operated her school until 1864. During the Civil War she traveled to the United States to help recruit soldiers for the Union army. In 1869 Mary Ann Shadd Cary, by then a widow, moved to Washington, D.C., with her two children. Later, she lived with her older daughter, Sarah E. Cary Evans, a schoolteacher. Between 1869 and 1871 she began her studies in law

at Howard University but stopped for unknown reasons. She resumed her studies in 1881 and received her degree in 1883, the only black woman in a class of five, although there is no evidence that she actually practiced law. She also continued her support for women's rights. In 1878 she delivered a lecture at the annual National Woman Suffrage Association Conference. She died at home in Washington.

Mary Ann Shadd Cary stands as one of the most significant, yet least recognized abolitionists who worked on behalf of black emigration and the sustenance of black settlements in Canada. At the same time, her lifelong challenge of racism and sexism made Cary an important figure in the struggle for racial and sexual equality during the nineteenth century.

FURTHER READING

Manuscript collections on the life of Mary Shadd Cary are in the Moorland-Spingarn Library at Howard University in Washington, D.C., and the Ontario Black History Society in Toronto.

Bearden, Jim, and Linda Jean Butler. *Shadd: The Life and Times of Mary Ann Shadd Cary* (1977).

Ripley, C. P., and M. A. Herrle. *The Black Abolitionist Papers, Vol. II: Canada, 1830–1860* (1987).

Sterling, Dorothy, ed. *We Are Your Sisters: Black Women in the Nineteenth Century* (1984).

This entry is taken from the *American National Biography* and is published here with the permission of the American Council of Learned Societies.

SHIRLEY J. YEE

Cass, Melnea (16 June 1896–16 Dec. 1978), civic leader and civil rights activist, was born Melnea Agnes Jones in Richmond, Virginia, the daughter of Albert Jones, a janitor, and Mary Drew, a domestic worker. Seeking broader employment and educational opportunities, the Jones family moved to Boston, Massachusetts, when Melnea was five years old. Her mother died when she was eight, and she and her two sisters were entrusted to the care of an aunt, Ella Drew. After one year at Girls' High School in Boston, she was sent to St. Francis de Sales Convent School, a Roman Catholic school for black and Indian girls in Rock Castle, Virginia. There household management was taught in addition to the academic curriculum; she graduated as valedictorian of her class in 1914.

When she returned to Boston, she was unable to find work as a salesgirl because of her race. Instead, she was employed as a domestic worker until her marriage to Marshall Cass in December 1917; she resumed domestic work during the Depression, when her husband lost his job as a dental laboratory technician. The marriage lasted until his death in 1958. The couple had three children.

While her husband was serving in World War I, Cass moved in with her mother-in-law, Rosa Cass Brown, who introduced her to community and church activities and persuaded her of the importance of the vote for women. At Brown's urging, Cass became a leader in the local suffrage movement and also joined the NAACP.

In the 1920s Cass joined the Kindergarten Mothers, later renamed the Friendship Club, of the Robert Gould Shaw House, in the heart of the black community in Boston's South End. With other neighborhood mothers, she raised money for Shaw House. Cass served twice as president and also as secretary of the Friendship Club. The group established the first nursery school in the black community, which became a model for later day care centers. The motto she selected for the Friendship Club, "If we cannot do great things, we can do small things in a great way," exemplified Cass's personal philosophy.

Her work at Shaw House started Cass on a lifetime of community service. She served as secretary, vice president, president, and chairman of the board for the Northeastern Region of the National Association of Colored Women's Clubs and in the 1960s was vice president of the national organization. During World War II, she was one of the organizers of Women in Community Services; in the 1960s she was community resources chairman and was active in recruiting girls for the Job Corps. In 1949 she was a founder and charter member of Freedom House, a private social service and advocacy agency, initiated by Muriel S. Snowden and Otto Snowden to aid and develop the black community. In the 1950s she joined the Women's Service Club and was its sixth president, serving for seventeen years, during which time she oversaw the development of the Migrant Service Program and the initiation, in 1968, of a federally funded homemaker training program. It was said of Cass that "it would be difficult to find a single successful black individual in Boston who hadn't been given a boost by her"; indeed, she was available to lend a helping hand to every individual in need, whatever his or her station in life.

The city of Boston began to call upon Cass's talents in the 1950s when she was appointed the only female charter member of Action for Boston Community Development, an agency that was established to help people displaced by urban renewal and that later administered the city's poverty program; she served as its vice president for eight years, retiring in 1970. For ten years she was a member of the Board of Overseers of Public Welfare for the city of Boston, an advisory group to the mayor and the Welfare Department.

Throughout her adult life, Cass was a leader in the struggle against racial discrimination. She participated in A. PHILIP RANDOLPH's drive to organize the sleeping car porters. In 1933, nearly twenty years after she was denied employment as a salesgirl, she joined demonstrations led by WILLIAM MONROE TROTTER to get Boston department stores to hire blacks. The next year she demonstrated in favor of the hiring of black doctors and nurses at Boston City Hospital. For many years she was on the board of the Boston YWCA but left the organization in 1951 because of its discriminatory practices; she rejoined years later only after many policy changes had been made. A life member of the NAACP, she served in many capacities in the Boston branch and held the presidency from 1962 to 1964, when the NAACP organized demonstrations against the Boston School Committee and held sit-ins to support desegregation and protest inequality in the curriculum for black children. She continued the tradition started by William Monroe Trotter of annually laying a wreath in honor of CRISPUS ATTUCKS, and she successfully lobbied for Boston to observe the birthday of FREDERICK DOUGLASS.

In her seventies, Cass became a spokesperson for the elderly, serving as president of the Roxbury Council of Elders, chairperson of the Mayor's Advisory Committee for Affairs of the Elderly (1975), and chairperson of the Massachusetts Advisory Committee for the Elderly (1975–1976). National recognition came in 1973 when Elliott Richardson appointed her to represent consumers' Medicare interests on the National Health Insurance Benefits Advisory Council.

Patriotic and church organizations also benefited from her participation. Among other affiliations and offices, as state president of the United War Mothers of America, she was the first black woman to hold that office in a national patriotic organization. She was also the first woman, black or white, elected state president of the Gold Star and War Parents of America. At St. Mark Congregational Church in Roxbury she was a charter member of the Mothers' Club and chaired the Social Action Committee. In 1967 she was the first woman to deliver a sermon for Woman's Day from the pulpit of the Ebenezer Baptist Church in Boston.

On many occasions, the community expressed its appreciation for her contributions. As early as 1949 the Friendship Club of Shaw House gave a banquet in tribute to her "efficient leadership, wise counsel, dependability, and fair judgment." In 1966 Mayor John Collins proclaimed 22 May "Melnea Cass Day," and more than 1,000 people attended a salute to the "First Lady of Roxbury." In 1974, at the recommendation of the Massachusetts State Federation of Women's Clubs, she was named Massachusetts Mother of the Year, and in 1977 she was designated one of seven "Grand Bostonians." Several facilities were named in her honor: the Melnea A. Cass Metropolitan District Commission Swimming Pool and Skating Rink (1968), the Melnea A. Cass Clarendon Street Branch of the YWCA (1976), and Cass House, a mixed-income apartment development (1989). Malnea A. Cass Boulevard opened in Boston in 1981.

At age seventy-nine Cass expressed the philosophy that had guided her life of service: "I am convinced that my life belongs to the whole community, and as long as I live, it is my privilege to do for it whatever I can, for the harder I work the more I live" (funeral program, St. Mark Congregational Church). She died in Boston. "By doing many small things in a great way" she had improved life for Boston's black community and won the respect and admiration of Bostonians of all races.

FURTHER READING

Melnea Cass's papers are kept at the Northeastern University Libraries in Boston, Massachusetts. Her oral history recorded with Tahi L. Mottl in 1977 is published in *The Black Women Oral History Project*, ed. Ruth Edmonds Hill, vol. 2 (1991). The original tapes and two folders of newspaper clippings and memorabilia are in the files of the Black Women Oral History Project, Schlesinger Library, Radcliffe College, Cambridge, Massachusetts.

Hill, Ruth Edmonds. "Melnea Cass "First Lady of Roxbury," in *Notable Black American Women*, ed. Jessie Carney Smith (1992).

Obituaries: *Boston Globe*, 20 Dec. 1978; *Bay State Banner*, 21 Dec. 1978.

This entry is taken from the *American National Biography* and is published here with the permission of the American Council of Learned Societies.

PATRICIA MILLER KING

Cassell, Albert Irvin (5 June 1895–30 November 1969), architect, planner, and developer, was born in Towson, Maryland, and grew up in Baltimore, the third child of Albert Truman and Charlotte Cassell. His father drove a coal truck and played trumpet for the Salvation Army Band; his mother brought in extra income doing washing. As a fourteen-year-old, Cassell expressed an ambition to build at Douglass High, a segregated public vocational school. While studying carpentry he enrolled in a drafting course with Ralph Victor Cook. Cook became a mentor to Cassell and encouraged him to pursue a college education in architecture at Cornell University, where Cook had been an early African American graduate of engineering.

Cassell entered Cornell in 1915, but two years into the program, World War I interrupted his studies. Cassell enlisted in the U.S. Army. In 1919, he returned to the United States from France with an honorable discharge. Because Cornell granted "war degrees" to students whose studies were interrupted by military service, Cassell received the professional Bachelor of Arts in Architecture degree in 1919. That year William Augustus Hazel, an established black architect and teacher at the Tuskegee Institute, hired Cassell. Hazel and Cassell worked together on the design of five "Boys Trade" buildings. Like other campus structures they were envisioned and realized by faculty and students from architecture, construction, and other trade schools. Cassell thus participated in BOOKER T. WASHINGTON's vision for the college—trade education as a route to self-sufficient black economic communities. Later in 1919, Hazel left Tuskegee to start a School of Architecture at Howard University, and by 1920, he turned again to Cassell, bringing him to Washington, D.C., to teach and work on the design of a new Home Economics building.

In 1922, Hazel abruptly left Howard, and Cassell took over his positions. As director of the architecture department, Cassell maintained Hazel's direction for the new program: "professional" architectural studies that emphasized artistic elements and history. Cassell was more focused on the multidimensional challenges of his role as university architect. After 1924, physical planning of the campus became Cassell's sole focus, after he turned over leadership of the school to HILYARD ROBINSON, a black professor and architect who had once worked for Cassell's firm.

Cassell ultimately created a twenty-year master plan for Howard, giving shape to the university's ambitious intentions. He was involved in a variety of roles to realize the plans, including the selection, planning and acquisition of sites for an expansion project that brought the school large grants from sources including a Rockefeller family foundation and federal New Deal funds. To make these plans concrete, individual buildings at Howard were designed by the architectural firm that Cassell maintained in an on-campus office. The most important of these, completed between 1934 and 1939, was Founder's Library, which became the home of the important Moorland-Springarn collection of black history.

While Louis E. Fry Sr., an African American architect in Cassell's office, is credited with significant design details (Ethridge, 3), the library demonstrates key aspects of Cassell's campus-wide vision. The building is finished in the "Georgian Revival Style," referencing early American architecture, Independence Hall in Philadelphia, and buildings at Harvard University. To visually unify Howard's campus, Cassell used this same style for all the building designs. The library became a landmark on the Washington, D.C., skyline. The significance of the library and expansion to the black community and nation were underscored in the building dedication speech by Harold Ickes, a cabinet secretary serving Franklin Delano Roosevelt, whose Interior department helped fund the library.

Before the library opened, a conflict between Cassell and Howard's president Mordecai Johnson boiled over. Johnson was known for volatility, having clashed with faculty members including biologist ERNEST EVERETT JUST and philosopher ALAIN LOCKE. The complicated disagreement over issues related to land acquisition for the expansion escalated, leading to Cassell's termination in 1938. In 1941 a Washington, D.C., Superior Court lawsuit was settled in Cassell's favor.

In 1938, Cassell entered into a real estate development partnership with Washington radio evangelist Elder Lightfoot Michaux to create Mayfair Mansions, a large housing development in northeast Washington, D.C. He also did the site planning and architectural design required to secure about four million dollars in federally subsidized loans to finance construction. Between 1942 and 1946, 595 units were completed on 28 acres of land. Mayfair was unusual in that it was a development for middle-class black homeowners built privately with federal dollars—funds typically targeted to finance white suburban developments. But in 1951, Mayfair's financing came under investigation by the Senate. A Mayfair partner, George Allan, was accused of accepting bribes from Michaux in exchange for approving loans when Allan was a Federal Housing Administration official. As the scandal unfolded Cassell was subpoenaed by the Senate, and had his membership suspended by the American Institute of Architects. In the end, Cassell was swindled by Michaux and lost his ownership stake in Mayfair.

Cassell and his architecture firm, Cassell, Gray & Sulton, were responsible for diverse projects, including campus buildings at Morgan State University (Baltimore), as well as churches, schools and public housing for black war veterans in the greater Washington, D.C., area. From the 1930s until the 1960s, Cassell worked entrepreneurially on a real estate and town planning scheme called "Chesapeake Heights." He envisioned an all black town and resort on 520 acres along Maryland's Chesapeake Bay. Although the project was retrogressive in its dependence on segregated housing patterns, it presaged development trends. Cassell started buying property for Chesapeake three decades before Columbia, Maryland, a comparable planned town, was completed in the late 1960s.

Of Cassell's six children from two marriages (to Martha Ann Mason and Flora B. McClarty), three became architects: Charles Irvin Cassell, Martha Ann Cassell Thompson and Alberta Jeanette Cassell Butler. Cassell hired Alberta for two years, and worked on the Chesapeake project with his son. Although Chesapeake Heights failed to receive hoped for federal loans for construction, Cassell continued to pursue the plan until his death in Washington, D.C. in 1969. Cassell's works were not necessarily pioneering, but innovative buildings are rare achievements that mobilize and synthesize technical, economic, social, political, and creative resources. Cassell was remarkably successful at overcoming adversity, collaborating with powerful individuals and entities to build at a large scale, and to realize buildings of enduring symbolic value.

FURTHER READING

Albert I. Cassell's papers are at Moorland-Springarn Research Center, Founder's Library, Howard University.

Ethridge, Harrison M. "Howard University Founder's Library," *Historic American Buildings Survey* (1979) Library of Congress: HABS Document No. D.C.-364 (available online).

Mitchell, Melvin. *The Crisis of the African-American Architect* (2001).

Obituary: *Washington Evening Star*, 2 December 1969.

TODD PALMER

Cassey, Peter (1 Oct. 1831–16 Apr. 1917), minister and educator, was born in Philadelphia, Pennsylvania, one of the six surviving children of Joseph and Amy Matilda (Williams) Cassey. The Casseys were both part of Philadelphia's black elite and politically active. Joseph Cassey, a barber, wig manufacturer, and moneylender who sometimes partnered with the black abolitionist and reformer ROBERT PURVIS, had come to Philadelphia from the West Indies in the first decade of the nineteenth century, built a successful business, bought real estate, retired as a gentleman in 1840, and left an estate worth perhaps $75,000 when he died in 1848. Amy Cassey was the daughter of New York Episcopal priest PETER WILLIAMS JR., for whom Peter Cassey was named; she married CHARLES LENOX REMOND two years after Joseph Cassey's death. Joseph served as an agent for William Lloyd Garrison's abolitionist paper *Liberator*, and Amy was active in the Philadelphia Female Anti-Slavery Society. Much of their activism addressed education: both were active in the Gilbert Lyceum (a Philadelphia black literary society), and Joseph supported interracial education efforts like Prudence Crandall's school at Canterbury, Connecticut, and the quasi-collegiate New York Oneida Institute.

Growing up in this environment shaped Peter Cassey's sense of duty and commitment deeply. In addition to an education in the Cassey home and some of Philadelphia's early black schools, he learned barbering and plied his trade—along with dentistry and bleeding (a popular practice of treating patients by removing quantities of their blood)—in Philadelphia before going west in 1853. Cassey settled in San Francisco, where he worked as a barber; he and Charles H. Mercier ran a barbershop in the Union Hotel for a time. San Francisco quickly became a center of black Californian activism, and Cassey, though not a delegate, engaged with the state-level black conventions of 1855, 1856, and 1857 which led, among other actions, to the creation of San Francisco's first black newspaper, the *Mirror of the Times*, in 1856.

In 1860 he moved to San Jose, where he became active in Trinity Episcopal Church. Confirmed at Trinity Church on 26 April 1863, Cassey was ordained as a deacon by Reverend William Ingraham Kip on 13 September 1866—the first African American in the West so recognized—though by then he was already serving as minister to San Jose's black Episcopalians. By the late 1860s and especially the 1870s, in addition to his congregation in San Jose, Cassey was traveling at least monthly to San Francisco, where he aided in the founding of Christ Mission and other Episcopalian efforts focused on African Americans.

He also founded the Phoenixonian Institute (also sometimes listed as the St. Phillip's Mission School for Negroes) in San Jose in the early 1860s. A combination residential and day school, the Phoenixonian was California's first secondary school for African Americans. The curriculum included courses in mathematics, the sciences, literature, and music. Blacks across the state supported the school, in part through resolutions passed at the 1863 and 1865 Colored Citizens Conventions (the former had been organized by Cassey); funding was also provided by students who could pay tuition, fund-raisers like student concerts, occasional support from California's Episcopal churches, and, between 1865 and 1874, funding from the San Jose School Board. During this period the institute operated, in essence, as San Jose's "separate but equal" attempt at providing a secondary school for African Americans; when San Jose finally set up a separate public high school, it was the death knell for the institute.

At some point, Cassey married Annie (her last name is unknown), and the couple had at least one daughter, Amy; census data suggests that they also adopted at least two children, the Nicaraguan-born Ada White and Henry Cassey. Annie both taught and aided Cassey in fund-raising for the school. Her death on 3 September 1875—so close to the demise of the Phoenixonian Institute—seemed to push Cassey from San Jose. He was listed in the 1880 federal census of Oakland. Most biographers have noted that Cassey accepted a call to preach in New Bern, North Carolina, in 1881. Until recently, though, the facts surrounding the rest of his life were absent from the scholarly record.

In North Carolina and later in Florida, though, Cassey built a new life, a new family, and a new ministry. He stayed in New Bern until about 1895. There, he built St. Cyprian's Church into a small but thriving community and married Ella N. (her full last name is unknown), a local woman who helped him establish a small school and occasionally taught. The couple had twelve children, eight of whom survived into adulthood: Peter, Alfred, Frank, Joseph, Ruth, Philip, Bertram, and Edward. By 1896 the family had moved to Florida. Though they were living in South Jacksonville in 1900, they spent most of the two decades prior to Peter Cassey's death in St. Augustine. There, Cassey again helped build an Episcopal church—also called St. Cyprian's—and worked with his wife in community education efforts. Cassey, a key figure in black Episcopal history on both coasts and an important early educator, died in St. Augustine in 1917, and most of his large family moved to Detroit soon after.

FURTHER READING
Beasley, Delilah. *Negro Trail Blazers of California* (1919).
Nolan, David. "A Moment in Black History: St. Cyprian's Episcopal Church," *St. Augustine Record,* 24 Feb. 2003.
Parker, Elizabeth L., and James Abijian. *Walking Tour of the Black Presence in San Francisco* (1974).
Ridout, Lionel. "The Church, the Chinese, and the Negroes in California, 1849–1893," *Historical Magazine of the Protestant Episcopal Church* 28 (1959).

ERIC GARDNER

Cassius, Samuel Robert (8 May 1853–10 Aug. 1931), evangelist, farmer, educator, postmaster, justice of the peace, and "race man," was born Samuel in Prince William County, Virginia. Even though an oral tradition among Cassius's descendants insists that Robert E. Lee was his biological father, circumstantial evidence suggests that James W. F. Macrae, a white physician and politician and relative of Robert E. Lee, was probably his father and Jane, an enslaved African, was his mother (Robinson). After emancipation Cassius probably added the names "Robert" to commemorate Robert E. Lee's kindness of purchasing him and his mother to prevent them from being sold to the Deep South, and he may have attached "Cassius" to honor the ancient Roman general, as many slaves adopted names of famous people from classical antiquity (Robinson). Little is known about Samuel's mother, a slave who served in the Macrae household. While working for the Macrae family as a "house servant," Jane became literate and she in turn taught young Samuel to read from a *John Comly Speller*. The opportunity to achieve literacy placed Cassius ahead of his class when he entered the public school system of the nation's capital.

After President Abraham Lincoln issued the Emancipation Proclamation, Cassius and his mother relocated from Virginia to Washington, D.C.

There Cassius attended the first public school for African Americans which opened on 1 March 1864. In this school, Cassius encountered a white female instructor, Miss Frances W. Perkins, who whetted his appetite for knowledge and literature, steered him toward a ministerial career, and "molded my mind into what it is today" (Robinson).

While living in the nation's capital, Cassius married his first wife, Effie Festus-Basil from Columbus, Ohio. This union produced eleven children. Cassius also met President Abraham Lincoln, whom he called the "negroes' Moses" (Robinson). From this experience Cassius developed a penchant for politics and eventually named one of his sons Amos Lincoln Cassius (1889–1982). This son became a reputable preacher in Churches of Christ. Cassius met four other United States presidents: Andrew Johnson, Ulysses S. Grant, Rutherford B. Hayes, and James A. Garfield. These brief encounters with chief executives probably during their inaugurations profoundly affected Cassius's mind, as he learned to look to the federal government for protection of fellow African Americans. In addition, while in the District of Columbia, Cassius was on "intimate terms" with black politicians such as FREDERICK DOUGLASS, JOHN MERCER LANGSTON, BLANCHE KELSO BRUCE, and HIRAM RHOADES REVELS, all of whom envisioned an "optimistic future" for American blacks (Robinson).

In the early 1880s Cassius left Washington, D.C. and relocated to Brazil, Indiana, where he worked as a coal miner and where he converted to the Stone-Campbell movement (Disciples of Christ and/or Churches of Christ), a religious group committed to restoring New Testament Christianity. In 1885 Cassius began preaching in Terre Haute, Indiana, and Danville, Illinois. By 1889 Cassius had moved to Sigourney, Iowa, where he had a short preaching career.

Two years later Cassius, like countless other African Americans in search of better evangelistic, economic, and social opportunities, took up residence in the Oklahoma Territory. Like other fellow black Americans, Cassius initially viewed Oklahoma as a "black man's paradise." In 1895, Cassius's first wife, Effie, died, and three years later he married his second wife, Selina Daisy Flenoid, with whom he fathered twelve children.

Cassius altogether lived in Oklahoma for thirty-one years, working as an educator, farmer, postmaster, justice of the peace, and politician-preacher. An earnest disciple of BOOKER T. WASHINGTON, Cassius sought to duplicate the Tuskegee educator's efforts in Oklahoma by establishing the Tohee Industrial School in the Oklahoma Territory. Cassius, like Washington in Alabama, sought to educate the hands and heart. Because of insufficient monetary support and because of the rise of the Colored Agricultural and Normal University (now Langston University), Cassius's school fizzled out. Cassius also occupied the postmastership of Tohee, and he served as justice of the peace "because the white merchants here were robbing them out of everything in the name of the law" (Robinson). Cassius was a member of the Negro Protective League in Oklahoma, a political organization designed to prevent Oklahoma from becoming the forty-sixth state in the Union. Black Oklahomans feared that if Oklahoma gained admission into the Union, its legislators would enact Jim Crow legislation, which is exactly what happened. Therefore Cassius in 1908 penned an illuminating article in the *Western Age*, describing travel accommodations for white Oklahomans as "heaven" and facilities for blacks as "hell." Burdened with legal woes, saddled with financial difficulties, and stalked by racial discrimination, Cassius departed Oklahoma for the Ohio Valley in 1922, disillusioned, with dashed hopes and aborted dreams and convinced that white leaders in the Stone-Campbell fellowship plotted to destroy his preaching ministry.

In 1925, Cassius reissued his book, *The Third Birth of a Nation*. The first edition, published in 1920, consisted of fifteen chapters and seventy-six pages. The second edition, issued five years later, comprised twenty-six chapters and 120 pages and contained a social commentary on Genesis 1–11. For Cassius the first book in the Bible authenticated the humanity and dignity of all black people who were made in God's image. Cassius appropriated the Tower of Babel story to insist that God wanted whites and blacks to be separate but equal. Cassius added the new chapters in light of the famous 1925 Scopes trial, in which William Jennings Bryan argued for the veracity of the Bible. In Cassius's mind, an assault on the Book of Genesis was an attack on the black man. Cassius wrote *The Third Birth of a Nation* to address white racism and to excoriate African Americans for their moral and religious "shortcomings." The book was in part a response to Thomas Dixon's incendiary novel, *The Clansman*, and D. W. Griffith's inflammatory movie, *The Birth of a Nation*, and it was in part a rebuke of fellow blacks for their excessive emotionalism and fanaticism in worship. Cassius also exposed the heart of America's race problem as economic

competition between whites and blacks. More importantly Cassius's answer to the race question in America was separation.

But Cassius's primary passion was to advance what he believed was the "pure Gospel" among African Americans. Therefore he used proceeds from his book to proclaim the word of the Lord to "my people." Calling himself a "globetrotter" (Robinson), Cassius became the first black national evangelist among Churches of Christ by traveling throughout the United States and by planting approximately fifty congregations. Even though most of the churches Cassius established fizzled out, he blazed the trail for countless other African American preachers in Churches of Christ who succeeded him. Cassius died in 1931 in Colorado Springs, Colorado.

FURTHER READING

Some of Samuel Robert Cassius's writings are housed in the Disciples of Christ Historical Society, Nashville, Tennessee.

Robinson, Edward J. "'Like Rats in a Trap': Samuel Robert Cassius and the 'Race Problem' in Churches of Christ," Ph.D. diss., Mississippi State University (2003).

Robinson, Edward J. *To Lift Up My Race: The Essential Writings of Samuel Robert Cassius* (2008).

Robinson, Edward J. *To Save My Race from Abuse: The Life of Samuel Robert Cassius* (2007).

EDWARD J. ROBINSON

Catlett, Big Sid (17 Jan. 1910–25 Mar. 1951), drummer, was born Sidney Catlett in Evansville, Indiana, the son of John B. Catlett, a chauffeur. His mother (name unknown) was a cook. Catlett briefly studied piano before playing drums in school, an activity that he continued at Tilden Technical High School after the family moved to Chicago. There he studied under the theater orchestra drummer Joe Russek.

Catlett worked with lesser-known bands and on occasion substituted for ZUTTY SINGLETON in CARROLL DICKERSON's band, which included LOUIS ARMSTRONG, at the Savoy in 1928. Later that year Catlett joined Sammy Stewart's orchestra at the Michigan Theater. In 1930 the band toured from Chicago to New York, picking up the tenor saxophonist LEON "CHU" BERRY along the way. Catlett left Stewart in New York and began working with the banjoist ELMER SNOWDEN at Smalls' Paradise. He joined Benny Carter's big band, recording in June 1932 and then playing in New York. Carter, moving from the leader's position into the saxophone section, allowed FLETCHER

HENDERSON to lead the band from December 1932 to January 1933. Catlett remained associated with Carter in 1933, including recordings under Spike Hughes's leadership in an eight-piece group known as the Chocolate Dandies, and under Carter's name ("Symphony in Riffs").

Catlett played in REX STEWART's big band at the Empire Ballroom from summer 1933 to autumn 1934, during which time he recorded four titles with Eddie Condon, including "The Eel." He joined SAM WOODING's dance orchestra briefly and then McKinney's Cotton Pickers (1934–1935). In Chicago he again played with lesser-known groups and led his own sextet at the Stables in 1935. Catlett joined the big bands of Jeter-Pillars in St. Louis (1935?–1936), of Henderson at the Grand Terrace Ballroom in Chicago (Mar.–mid-July 1936), of DON REDMAN (fall 1936–late 1938), and of Armstrong (late 1938–spring 1941). In November 1938 Catlett recorded with ROY ELDRIDGE in Berry's quartet, contributing a solo on "Forty-Six West Fifty-Two." Around 1939 he also played on Sundays with JELLY ROLL MORTON's band at Nick's in New York. He made recordings intermittently with SIDNEY BECHET from 1939 to 1941, including "Old Man Blues," in which Catlett played a passage on tom-tom drums, paying homage to DUKE ELLINGTON (1940). He participated in Carter's reincarnation of the Chocolate Dandies—this time as a sextet with Eldridge and COLEMAN HAWKINS—for their finest session on 25 May 1940, including "I Can't Believe That You're in Love with Me" (the master take). According to Stewart, Catlett at some point, perhaps during this period in New York, became the favorite drummer for chorus girls at the Apollo Theater, owing to his sensitivity in accompanying dancing.

After a short stay with Eldridge's big band, Catlett joined Benny Goodman (mid-1941–Oct. 1941); among his recordings with Goodman is "The Count." Catlett returned to Armstrong's big band (Nov. 1941–summer 1942) and then played in New York with TEDDY WILSON's small group (c. Aug. 1942–early 1944). Except for a brief attempt to establish a big band late in 1946, Catlett led small swing groups from 1944 into 1947 at jazz clubs on Fifty-second Street in New York, at the Streets of Paris in Hollywood, and in Chicago, Detroit, and other cities. BEN WEBSTER often worked as his sideman, and from this association came an acclaimed recording session in March 1944, with Catlett soloing for "Sleep." According to MARY LOU WILLIAMS, Catlett, while leading at the Three Deuces in New York, probably in the mid-1940s,

got into an argument with the band and temporarily fired them all, then successfully played the night as a soloist—an unusual feat for a drummer of that era and a testimony to his musicality.

As a freelance musician Catlett recorded "Afternoon of a Basie-ite" with LESTER YOUNG at the end of 1943. He was featured in the film *Jammin' the Blues* (1944). He participated in one of the first studio sessions in the new bebop style, recording "Salt Peanuts" and "Shaw Nuff" with CHARLIE PARKER under DIZZY GILLESPIE's leadership (May 1945); his usual deft cymbal work and penetrating, irregular snare and bass drum accents fit in perfectly. In August 1946 another reincarnation of Carter's Chocolate Dandies, in a group including Webster and BUCK CLAYTON, found Catlett drumming forcefully in "Cadillac Slim" and revealing a hidden talent by singing the ballad "Out of My Way" in a clear-toned, full, handsome baritone.

Catlett starred in a concert with Armstrong in February 1947 at Carnegie Hall in which he was particularly showcased in "Tiger Rag." The success of the concert was one factor that led to the formation of Armstrong's All Stars, with Catlett as one of its founding members, in August of that year. The group performed at the jazz festival in Nice, France, in 1948, and—unusually for Catlett, who was widely regarded as one of the most tasteful accompanists in jazz—he was publicly criticized by Armstrong for drumming overexuberantly.

Catlett had to retire from the group because of heart and kidney ailments in April 1949, returning to his father's home in Chicago. One month later he was working with Eddie Condon in New York on NBC television and in the recording studio. Back in Chicago he became the house drummer at Jazz, Ltd., playing traditional jazz and Dixieland with Bechet, Miff Mole, Georg Brunis, and Muggsy Spanier. During this period Catlett and his wife, Gladys (maiden name and marriage date unknown), had their son, Sid Catlett Jr. (later a basketball star at the University of Notre Dame). Early in 1951 Catlett contracted pneumonia. He was apparently recovering when he suffered a fatal heart attack while attending a jazz concert at Chicago's Opera House.

Catlett was a superb showman who twirled, threw, and caught the drumsticks, and who walked around playing from odd angles or keeping the beat on objects other than the drum set—including fellow musicians—without disrupting the rhythm. More significantly, he was one of the most precise and musical drummers of his era, comfortable playing in any of the prevailing styles or with any size of ensemble. The clarinetist BARNEY BIGARD, who played with Catlett in Armstrong's All Stars, reports, "He was just lovable .... He knew all the musicians and was real popular with them all .... When he took a solo it was like you could hear that melody line right through it all .... He was good for a soloist because he'd push you. He would never get in your way .... Sid ... was one of the best time keepers. Just fantastic" (Bigard, 106–107).

FURTHER READING

Balliett, Whitney. "Big Sid," in *The Sound of Surprise: 46 Pieces on Jazz* (1959).

Hoefer, George. "Big Sid," *Down Beat* (24 Mar. 1966): 26–29.

Stewart, Rex. "My Man, Big Sid (Sidney Catlett)," in *Jazz Masters of the Thirties* (1972).

Obituary: *New York Times*, 27 Mar. 1951.

This entry is taken from the *American National Biography* and is published here with the permission of the American Council of Learned Societies.

BARRY KERNFELD

Catlett, Elizabeth (15 Apr. 1915–2 Apr. 2012), sculptor, printmaker, and teacher, was born Alice Elizabeth Catlett to Mary Carson, a truant officer, and John Catlett, a math teacher and amateur musician who died shortly before Elizabeth's birth. Elizabeth and her two older siblings were raised by their mother and paternal grandmother in a middle-class neighborhood of Washington, D.C. Encouraged by her mother and her teachers at Dunbar High School to pursue a career as an artist, she entered Howard University in 1931, where she studied with the African American artists JAMES LESESNE WELLS, LOÏS MAILOU JONES, and JAMES A. PORTER. After graduating cum laude with a B.S. in Art in 1935, Catlett taught art in the Durham, North Carolina, public schools before beginning graduate training at the University of Iowa in 1938. Under the tutelage of the artist Grant Wood, Catlett switched her concentration from painting to sculpture and undertook the study of African and pre-Columbian art. From Wood, Catlett gained a respect for disciplined technique, and when he encouraged her to depict subjects derived from her own experience, she focused on African American women and the bond between mother and child, themes that would occupy her for a lifetime. Catlett received the University of Iowa's first MFA in 1940, and the following year *Mother and Child* (1940, limestone),

Elizabeth Catlett, May 2003, poses in front of her "Invisible Man" sculpture in New York City. (AP Images.)

a component of her thesis project, won first prize in sculpture at the American Negro Exposition in Chicago. After a summer teaching at Prairie View College in Texas, Catlett was hired as head of the art department at Dillard University in New Orleans in 1940. The following summer, while in Chicago studying ceramics at the Art Institute of Chicago and lithography at the Southside Community Art Center, Catlett met the artist CHARLES WHITE. The couple married later that year and eventually settled in Harlem, New York, in 1942, where they thrived as part of the area's African American creative community. Catlett continued her studies at the Art Students League and with sculptor Ossip Zadkine. She taught at the Marxist-based Jefferson School, and sat on the arts committee of one of the largest Popular Front organizations in Harlem. Catlett's job as promotional director of the George Washington Carver School, a community school for working people, brought her into contact with working-class and poor people for the first time.

As her politics crystallized, so too did her commitment to depicting the reality and courage of working Americans and to producing work for African American audiences. In 1945 she was awarded a grant from the Rosenwald Fund to produce a series depicting black women. The renewal of the grant for the next year allowed for the completion of the innovative series *The Negro Woman*, fifteen linoleum cuts documenting the epic history of African American women's oppression, resistance, and survival. An integrated narrative of text and prints, the series depicts the historic figures SOJOURNER TRUTH, HARRIET TUBMAN, and PHILLIS WHEATLEY along with images of field hands, washerwomen, segregation, and lynching.

Fellowship funds also brought Catlett and White to Mexico in 1946, where in addition to finishing *The Negro Woman* series, Catlett hoped to resuscitate her failing marriage. Although the couple returned to New York and filed for divorce several months later, this first trip to Mexico proved pivotal for Catlett both professionally and personally. In early 1947 she returned to Mexico City, where she had befriended a circle of Mexican artists that included Diego Rivera, Frida Kahlo, and David Alfaro Siqueiros. Soon after, she made Mexico her permanent residence and joined the printmaking collective, Taller de Grafica Popular (TGP), or the People's Graphic Art Workshop, through which she had produced *The Negro Woman* series. The TGP supported progressive and nationalist causes through graphic materials that communicated directly with the primarily illiterate public. Attracted to the workshop's creatively collaborative environment and its engagement with audiences, Catlett made the TGP her artistic home for the next decade and remained a member until 1966. It was in 1947, as well, that Catlett met and married the Mexican artist Francisco Mora. Between 1947 and 1951, the couple had three children, Francisco, Juan, and David.

In Mexico Catlett found a vital environment for politically committed art, which had become less permissible in the United States by the late 1940s, especially after the establishment of the House Un-American Activities Committee in 1947. From her arrival in Mexico until the mid 1950s, Catlett focused on printmaking, primarily lithography and linoleum prints, inexpensive mediums that are easily reproduced. Topical and populated with both Mexican and African American families and workers, Catlett's print work during this period is graphically bold, combining elements of expressionism and Soviet social realism with a visual vocabulary drawn from Mexican and African sources.

When her youngest child entered kindergarten in 1956, Catlett returned to sculpture, although she continued to make prints. Shortly after her arrival in Mexico, Catlett had studied ceramic sculpture and pre Columbian art with Francisco Zuniga and in the mid-1950s she studied woodcarving with Jose L. Ruiz. In 1958, Catlett became the first woman professor of sculpture at Mexico's National School of Fine Arts, and a year later she became head of the department, a position she held until her retirement in 1976.

Catlett had arrived in Mexico a highly educated and technically sophisticated artist with a developed style. In Mexico, her sculptures continued to feature simple and fluid forms with few embellishments and a reverence for materials. Whether in marble, onyx, bronze, terra cotta, or woods, her sculptures are concerned with volume and space. They convey a sense of monumentality even in small and medium-size pieces. The influence of Henry Moore, Jan Arp, and Constantin Brancusi can be seen in her smooth and highly polished surfaces and organic forms. But while they flirt with abstraction, her sculptures remain figurative. Representations of ethnicity and the female body, specifically images of motherhood and the body of the black woman, Catlett's pieces continually revisit themes and compositions of earlier works.

At the National Conference of Negro Artists in 1961, Catlett delivered a keynote address that called for politically engaged art: "We must search to find our place, as Negro artists, in the advance toward a richer fulfillment of life on a global basis. Neither the Negro artist nor American art can afford to take an isolated position" (*Fifty-Year Retrospective*, 20). The speech raised her profile within the art community but also increased pressure from the U.S. State Department, which identified her as an "undesirable alien." Catlett became a Mexican citizen in 1962 and found herself barred from the United States until 1971, when she was finally granted a visa to attend her first solo exhibition in the United States, held at the Studio Museum in Harlem. Beginning with her initial Mexican exhibition in 1962, there was steady demand for her work in both Mexican and American exhibitions, and after the Studio Museum exhibition, she regularly received solo shows, seventeen in the 1970s alone, mostly in the United States.

Through the Black Arts Movement and the women's movements of the 1960s and 1970s, Catlett renewed her interest in American politics and themes and, in turn, her work drew attention from intellectuals and curators in the United States. Her sculptural and print works from this period comment directly on topical issues, including the imprisonment of ANGELA DAVIS in *Freedom for Angela Davis* (1969, serigraph) and race riots in *Watts/ Detroit/Washington/Harlem/Newark* (1970, hand colored linocut). Catlett's support of black nationalism can be seen in such works as *Homage to My Young Black Sisters* (1968, cedar), *Malcolm X Speaks for Us* (1969, color linocut), *The Torture of Mothers* (1970, color lithograph), *Negro es Bello* (1968, lithograph), which includes renderings of Black Panther buttons, *Homage to Black Women Poets* (1984, mahogany), *Black Unity* (1968, mahogany), represented by a clenched fist on one side and a pair of faces on the other, and *Target* (1970, bronze), a bust of a black man as seen through the cross-hairs of a gun sight. Catlett's commitment to the Black Arts Movement included exhibiting at black institutions where her work would be seen by African American audiences.

Upon her retirement from teaching in 1976, Catlett and Mora, who died in February 2002, moved to Cuernavaca, Mexico. In 1982 she took a second apartment in New York and began spending more time teaching and lecturing in the United States. Catlett continued to produce work through the 1980s, 1990s, and into the new century. Her work has been included in every major exhibition of black artists from the 1960s to the present, and she has received numerous exhibitions, awards, and commissions in Mexico, the United States, and Europe. Called the "dean of black American female artists" by the *New York Times*, Catlett has received six honorary doctorates and honors from a host of institutions, including the cities of Atlanta, Cleveland, Little Rock, Philadelphia, Dallas, and Washington, D.C., the Philadelphia Museum of Art, and the National Council of Negro Women. In September 2002, the Cleveland Museum of Art mounted *Elizabeth Catlett: Prints and Sculpture*, a major exhibition spanning the artist's sixty-year career.

In 2003 Catlett received the International Sculpture Center's Lifetime Achievement in Contemporary Sculpture Award, but showed no intention of retiring. That same year, aged eighty-eight, she was commissioned to create a monumental bronze relief of "Invisible Man: A Memorial to RALPH ELLISON," in Riverside Park in New York City. In 2010, aged 95, she was awarded an honorary Doctorate in Fine Arts from Syracuse University, and completed a 10-foot sculpture of MAHALIA JACKSON, which was inaugurated in New Orleans' Treme neighborhood. Catlett

died in April 2012 at her home in Cuernavaca, Mexico.

FURTHER READING
Catlett's papers are held at the Amistad Research Center, Tulane University, New Orleans.
Hampton University Museum. *Elizabeth Catlett, Works on Paper, 1944–1992* (1993).
Herzog, Melanie. *Elizabeth Catlett: An American Artist in Mexico* (2000).
Lewis, Samella. *The Art of Elizabeth Catlett* (1984).
Neuberger Museum of Art. *Elizabeth Catlett Sculpture: A Fifty-Year Retrospective* (1998).

LISA E. RIVO

Cato, Minto (23 Aug. 1900–26 Oct. 1979), mezzo-soprano, was born La Minto Cato in Little Rock, Arkansas. She attributed her unusual first name to a grandmother of French extraction. Her father, Roy Cato, was the son of a Native American father. There appears to be no connection between this Minto Cato and the English actor (1887–1960) who went by the same name. Although her immediate family included no professional musicians, an aunt sang and played piano. Cato attended the Washington Conservatory of Music following her studies at Armstrong High School. While still in her teens, she taught piano in the public schools of Monticello, Arkansas, and Athens, Georgia. In 1919 she established a music studio in Detroit, where her parents settled permanently in 1930.

Cato entered show business at Detroit's Temple Theater in 1922 with the B. F. Keith vaudeville circuit. For most of the 1920s she worked steadily with impresario Joe Sheftell, whom she married around 1923. Their daughter, Minto Cato Sheftell, was born around 1924. In 1922 Sheftell's shows were called the *Creole Bronze Revue* and played primarily in the northeastern United States. Later in the 1920s Sheftell's tours as "Joe Sheftell and His Black Dots," then as the *Southland Revue*, took the couple all over the world. In one tour ending in 1927 Cato and Sheftell were in Hawaii, Samoa, Fiji, Australia, and New Zealand, returning home by way of Alaska, Canada, and Mexico. Their work also took them throughout Europe, and to Palestine. Cato appeared in New York throughout the 1920s, including at the Cotton Club in 1924 and later in the show *Hot Chocolates* at Connie's Inn. When Cato appeared with the Whitman Sisters traveling show in Pittsburgh in October 1927, she and Sheftell had apparently separated. As of late January 1929 she had left the Whitmans and returned to her home in Harlem. In the spring of that year she worked as a solo act at Chicago's Regal Theater, accompanying herself at the piano. Cato was also an impresario in this period, with such shows as the *Frivolities of 1928*. At her peak as a vaudeville producer, she had a sixteen-person "flash act," working the Keith's, Loew's, Fox, and Pantages theater circuits, and also the Tivoli circuit in Australia, New Zealand, and Hawaii.

A trained classical singer, Cato found her greatest success performing show music. The high point of her work in this area came in 1929–1930, with producer Lew Leslie's *Blackbirds* shows. In the first edition, in the fall of 1929, her costars included LOUIS ARMSTRONG; she would appear with him again in 1931. In *Blackbirds of 1930* she premiered EUBIE BLAKE and ANDY RAZAF's "Memories of You," one of the great ballads of the jazz age. Her roles in such productions (as Mammy Jones and Aunt Jemima) perpetuated stereotypes of African Americans, holdovers from the minstrelsy still typical at the time. Cato's personal life was deeply affected by her work in *Blackbirds*. She took as a lover the show's lyricist, Razaf, one of the great writers of the Harlem Renaissance and a prolific hit-maker. The two cohabited for several years in the early 1930s, although Razaf was married to someone else. A number of Razaf's associates assumed that he and Cato were married.

In 1930 Cato appeared at the San Jose, a Spanish-language club in East Harlem, performing the song "The Peanut Vendor" in a West Indian version. Her career in show business took her to summer resorts as well, including the Paradise in Atlantic City during 1930 and 1931. Among the songs that she used successfully, both in the United States and abroad, were W. C. HANDY's "St. Louis Blues," FATS WALLER's "Honeysuckle Rose," and Jack Yellen and Lew Pollack's "My Yiddishe Momme," which was used by a great many non-Jewish entertainers. Her talents ranged beyond music as well, and in the summer of 1937 she managed a resort kitchen in Saratoga Springs, New York.

Cato's breakthrough in opera came in May 1936, when she sang the role of Azucena in a production of *Il Trovatore* sponsored by the Federal Music Project. Cato also staged and directed this performance, which featured her students from the Harlem Music Center, and the Knickerbocker Little Symphony. The singers, aged sixteen to thirty, included high school and college students, and also laborers, office workers, and domestics. Many of the sixty-one singers could not read music, and Cato taught them their parts by singing them and also wrote their Italian lyrics out on paper. Her conductor for *Trovatore* was Luigi Lovreglio.

Cato sang *Aida* with New York's Hippodrome Opera Company in April 1937 under the baton of Alfredo Salmaggi. The following summer she sang Queenie in *Show Boat* and Liza in *Gentlemen Unafraid*, both with music by Jerome Kern, with the Municipal Opera Society of St. Louis. In 1944 she was featured in a fundraiser for the National Negro Opera Company at New York's Town Hall. She performed *Aida* again in July 1944, this time in a summer season, put on by the National Negro Opera Company in Washington, D.C., that also included *Faust* and *La Traviata*. In July 1945 she appeared in a Washington fundraiser for the National Council of Negro Women. Among her last major operatic roles was in *La Traviata* with the National Negro Opera Company in 1947.

In the fall of 1944 the African American press announced that Cato was abandoning opera for show business. In the summer of 1945 she again won acclaim as Queenie in *Show Boat*, this time in Detroit. While there she performed for wounded war veterans, thus beginning a new phase in her career. Beginning late in 1945 Cato worked the American Red Cross circuit in Europe with a vocal trio. Following the breakup of this group, Cato continued as a solo act, accompanying herself on the piano. These tours took her to England, Belgium, France, and Germany, and she spent much of her time in Europe into the early 1950s. In England she appeared on BBC radio and early television, on such shows as *Starlight* and the *Variety Band Box Programme*. Her French tours took her to the resort towns of Cherbourg, Nice, and Cannes as well as the major cities. In Paris she appeared on radio, at the world-famous Hot Club, and at such top venues as the Salle Pleyel and the Théâtre du Chatelet. While there she gave the Paris premiere of the new Irving Berlin musical *Annie Get Your Gun* (under the title *Annie du Far West*). She continued to find success in Belgium, the Netherlands, and Germany.

By the late 1940s Cato's American career had fallen dormant. The mainstream opera world remained closed to African Americans, only opening up later to younger singers such as LEONTYNE PRICE. And with the numerous changes in show business styles in the mid-twentieth century, Cato was out of fashion at home. There was possibly also a less innocent explanation for her career's decline. In 1953 Cato told the *Chicago Defender* that she was blacklisted for her past connections to left-wing causes. She had performed at such events as a 1938 fundraiser to buy milk for Spanish Civil War refugee children on the Republican side. Although this antifascist cause was aligned with a democratically elected government, participation in such activities would come back to haunt American entertainers during the McCarthy era of the 1950s. Cato was a target of the House Un-American Activities Committee during this period.

Cato was honored with an award by the Manhattan-Bronx Friends of the Symphony of the New World in 1972. In her later years she was primarily active with the National Association of Negro Musicians, and they held a memorial program in Cato's honor after her death in 1979. A Catholic, she was buried at the Gate of Heaven Cemetery in Hawthorne, New York. In addition to her daughter, her survivors included a brother, Marion Cato of Atlanta, Georgia.

FURTHER READING

Minto Cato's papers are in the Schomburg Center for Research in Black Culture at the New York Public Library.

Singer, Barry. *Black and Blue: the Life of Andy Razaf* (1992).

Southern, Eileen. *Biographical Dictionary of Afro-American and African Musicians* (1981).

ELLIOTT HURWITT

Cato, Willmer Reed (19 June 1924–30 Oct. 2006), World War II sailor and Silver Star Medal recipient, was born in Hanna, Oklahoma, the son of Mary Cato. Little recorded information exists on his father. He later graduated from Lincoln High School in Vernon, Oklahoma, where he was a three sport athlete. Upon graduating from school in 1942, Cato worked as a mechanic for a local construction company. His brothers Sachan and Smith were already serving in the army and training as paratroopers when he was drafted for military service in 1943.

After receiving his draft notice, Willmer Cato was inducted into the U.S. Navy in June 1943 at Oklahoma City, Oklahoma, and subsequently completed his initial recruit training, likely at Bainbridge, Maryland. Like the vast majority of African American men that served in the navy under combat conditions during World War II, Cato was assigned to serve in the Steward's Branch. This segregated part of the navy, which was established by 1910, was manned largely by African Americans, as well as men from the Philippines and the island of Guam. Their job as stewards (early on called "mess attendants") was to serve the officer cadre aboard the ship in which they were serving.

The duties of a steward, which included cooking and/or preparing the officer's meals, manning the officer's galley and mess, and tending to the officer's quarters, was largely reflective of the domestic jobs held by many African Americans in the South during the Jim Crow era. However, despite their lowly status in the navy's hierarchy, the service of men like Cato, LEONARD HARMON, and MARION PORTER was significant and more important to the navy than most in the general public realize, even to this day. The men of the Steward's Branch were not just servants, but they were also fighting sailors; all had important battle-station duties when their ship was operating under combat conditions, whether it was manning a gun position, serving as part of a damage control party, performing lookout duties, or helping to tend the wounded in the heat of battle. Indeed, it was in these trying situations that African American sailors did serve, if only for a short periods of time, with some measure of equality, compared with their white shipmates. While recognition for the valorous actions of the men of the Steward's Branch was often biased (no black sailor was ever awarded the Medal of Honor) and has received little public attention, a number of black men were awarded other prestigious awards and combat decorations, such as the Navy Cross, the Navy and Marine Corps Medal, and the Silver and Bronze Star medals.

Upon completing his initial training, Willmer Cato first saw duty in the European theater, serving aboard the battleship *Texas* during the D-Day invasion of Normandy on 6 June 1944. By 1945 he was transferred to service in the Pacific, assigned to LCS (L)-86, a landing craft support ship, on which he was the only African American member of the crew. On 27 May 1945, Cato and the crew of LCS (L)-86 were operating off Okinawa, performing radar picket duty, when they came under heavy Japanese kamikaze attack. Among the ships stricken in the attack was another radar picket ship, the destroyer *Braine*; with the ship on fire and its ammunition magazine in danger of exploding, the men of LCS (L)-86 came alongside to render assistance. Four men of the crew, including Steward's Mate First Class Willmer Cato and three other sailors, one of them the ship's executive officer, volunteered to go aboard the destroyer to help put out the fires. Going below through a jagged hole in the destroyer's deck, Cato and his shipmates fought the fires close by the ammunition magazine and, at great peril to their own lives, helped to save the damaged destroyer. Cato and his shipmates were subsequently awarded the Silver Star Medal. This high level award was bestowed on relatively few African American stewards during the war; only eight men have thus far been identified as recipients, though more may have been awarded after the end of World War II.

After earning the Silver Star, Willmer Cato continued aboard his ship until after the war's end on 16 November 1945, and received his final discharge on 15 December 1945 at Norman, Oklahoma. He later moved to Kansas City, Missouri, and attended trade school. It was here, too, that he met his future wife, Margaret Henderson.

Wilmer and Margaret, a school teacher, were married in 1955 and had two children, Alesa and Wayne. Education was a priority for the Cato family: not only did Willmer and Margaret earn college degrees, so too did both their children. Willmer Cato earned a living as a postal worker for a time and later owned his own business before retiring in 1988. Though proud of his naval service, the unassuming Cato never considered himself a hero and had frequent nightmares for many years, reliving the harrowing events that earned him the Silver Star. A popular member of the crew, Willmer Cato maintained a friendship with some members of the LSC (L)-86 for the rest of his life and attended many ship reunions over the years.

FURTHER READING

The author kindly acknowledges the help of Margaret Cato, Willmer Cato's wife, in providing personal details for this article.

Knoblock, Glenn A. *African American World War II Casualties and Decorations in the Navy, Coast Guard, and Merchant Marine; A Comprehensive Record* (2009).

GLENN ALLEN KNOBLOCK

Catto, Octavius Valentine (22 Feb. 1839–10 Oct. 1871), educator, activist, and baseball pioneer, was born in Charleston, South Carolina, to Sara Isabella Cain, a woman from a prosperous mixed-race family, and William T. Catto, a Presbyterian minister. When Catto was about five years old, his father relocated the family to Philadelphia, Pennsylvania, after being "called" to the city by the Presbytery and after some time to the ministry of the First African Presbyterian Church, a historic black church formed by the Reverend JOHN GLOUCESTER, a former slave, in 1807.

As a youngster Catto attended a number of Philadelphia-area public schools, including the Vaux Primary School. By 1854, though, he was enrolled in the newly opened Institute for Colored Youth, the forerunner of historically black Cheyney University, just south of Philadelphia.

William Catto and other black ministers convinced the Quaker administration to focus on classical topics, including Latin, Greek, and mathematics, and not just trade and agricultural subjects. Catto and other black students flourished in this environment, impressed with the political and social fervor of the school's Haitian-born principal, CHARLES L. REASON, who spoke of Haiti's successful revolt from France. Through his participation in the school's Banneker Debating Society, Catto developed a seasoned oratorical style, indicative of his confidence, forcefulness, and audacity. After traveling to Washington, D.C., and becoming the fourth graduate of the institute and delivering a rousing valedictorian speech in 1858, Catto sought and received additional coaching in Latin and Greek before returning to his alma mater, by then an influential local black institution, and becoming a teacher at age twenty in September 1859. He was described as having a light-brown complexion, perhaps slightly plump, and of average height with a love for fine clothes and the like. A highly sought after bachelor, he developed a relationship with a neighbor, Caroline Le Count. His speaking ability, as described by the legendary principal and educator of the Institute for Colored Youth FANNY JACKSON COPPIN, was exceptional.

By the early 1860s Catto had become outspoken about the evil of slavery and the need for black rights. He threw himself into the task of recruiting black soldiers for Camp William Penn, the first and largest federal facility to recruit black soldiers during the Civil War. Catto even established the black Union League Association, patterned after the primarily Republican and white Union League of Philadelphia, from which he garnered tremendous financial and political support.

When the Confederate army invaded Pennsylvania in early 1863 Catto raised a black unit, primarily consisting of his students, but was rebuffed by a white commander who claimed that black troops were not authorized to fight. In fact Catto soon became one of the only black officers in the army, a major in the First Division of the state's National Guard.

Catto also broke down barriers in organized sports when he founded and played starting shortstop for the Camden, New Jersey, Pythians, a black baseball team that on 18 September 1869 became the first all African American squad to play and beat a white team, the City Items. Catto's dream of an integrated professional baseball league was squashed, however, when the powerful National Association of Base Ball Players banned teams with African Americans on their rosters.

Meanwhile Catto continued his fight for the protection of African American voting rights through the Fifteenth Amendment to the United States Constitution, reaching at least something of a culmination of his life's mission when the amendment was ratified in Pennsylvania in October 1870. He attended conventions that supported black men's right to vote while also successfully combating segregation on Philadelphia's public transportation system, including its trains and horse-drawn trolleys. Such a staunch advocate of civil rights—a loyal Republican due to his associations with the Union League and his approval of President Abraham Lincoln's ideals—was bound to come to the attention of local white Democrats, who considered Catto to be an immense threat.

On his way to the institute on 10 October 1871, and despite the violence and intimidation by whites that had overtaken the city on election day, Catto cast his ballot at the fourth ward. Having dismissed class at the institute owing to the continued threat of white rioting, Catto was making his way down Ninth Street when he was approached by Frank Kelly, a Democratic Party operative. An account published later in the *Philadelphia Tribune*, and quoted in W. E. B. DuBois's *The Philadelphia Negro*, described what happened next: Kelly "pulled out a pistol and pointed it at Catto. The aim of the man was sure, and Catto barely got around a street car before he fell …. This occurred directly in front of a police station, into which he was carried," the *Tribune* reported, upon which "The wildest excitement prevailed" (41).

Though shocked and despite indications of police involvement in the murder, the black community generally remained agonizingly calm as the news of Catto's death spread around the city and nation. Catto's 16 October funeral procession attracted five thousand blacks and whites, "the most imposing ever given to an American Negro," DuBois wrote (40).

After a trial, Kelly was freed, having been defended by a lawyer who headed the then crooked and racist City Democratic Committee. In 1877 Catto's brother William said that his father died of the heartache caused by his son's death. Catto's lover, Caroline Le Count, never married, although she became principal of a Philadelphia public school in 1878 that was renamed for her fiancé. Despite his sad end, Catto's trailblazing accomplishments in struggling to cripple institutional racial segregation, as well as enhancing blacks' education and voting rights, made him an early example of the quintessential advocate of black empowerment.

FURTHER READING

Archival data and artifacts regarding Catto are at his former Philadelphia church, the African Episcopal Church of Saint Thomas, founded by the former slave Rev. Absalom Jones in 1792, as well as at the Library Company of Philadelphia.

Ballard, Allen B. *One More Day's Journey: The Story of a Family and a People* (2004).

Biddle, Daniel R., and Murray Dubin. "The Forgotten Hero," *Philadelphia Inquirer*, 5 July 2003.

DuBois, W. E. B. *The Philadelphia Negro: A Social Study* (1899).

Lane, Roger. *William Dorsey's Philadelphia and Ours: On the Past and Future of the Black City in America* (1991).

Silcox, Harry C. "Nineteenth-Century Philadelphia Black Militant: Octavius V. Catto (1839–1871)," in *African Americans in Pennsylvania: Shifting Historical Perspectives*, ed. Joe William Trotter Jr. and Eric Ledell Smith (1997).

Waskie, Andy. "Biography of Octavius V. Catto: 'Forgotten Black Hero of Philadelphia.'" Afrolumens Project. Available at http://www.afrolumens.org/rising_free/waskie1.html.

DONALD SCOTT SR.

Cayton, Horace Roscoe (12 Apr. 1903–22 Jan. 1970), sociologist and writer, was born in Seattle, Washington, the son of HORACE ROSCOE CAYTON SR., a newspaper publisher, and SUSIE SUMNER REVELS, a former college instructor and sometime writer. Horace's maternal grandfather, HIRAM R. REVELS [CAYTON], was elected senator from Mississippi at the height of Reconstruction. At the time of Horace's birth, the Cayton family was prosperous, middle class, and living in the heart of white Seattle. Soon after Horace's birth, however, the family experienced financial distress accentuated by the racism of Seattle. Growing up, Horace had various scrapes with the law, culminating in his arrest for driving a getaway car in a gas station robbery. As a teenager he attended, and soon dropped out of, reform school. He traveled widely, supporting himself as a manual laborer.

Eventually Cayton returned to Seattle, where he finished high school at a Young Men's Christian Association preparatory school, and entered the

University of Washington in 1925. Supporting himself with a job as a sheriff's deputy, Cayton received a B.A. in Sociology from Washington in 1931. That year Cayton won a fellowship to study sociology at the University of Chicago.

Cayton never completed his doctoral degree. He worked for two years in the sociology program at the University of Chicago and then as an editor for a Tuskegee Institute newsletter. In 1934 he worked as a special assistant to Secretary of the Interior Harold Ickes, attempting to discover how the New Deal affected African American labor. After a brief stay in Europe, Cayton taught economics at Fisk University until returning to Chicago in 1936.

From 1936 to 1939 Cayton led a Works Projects Administration (WPA) project that studied the social structure of the African American family. He was joined in this project by ST. CLAIR DRAKE, an African American anthropologist from the University of Chicago. In 1941 a grant from the Julius Rosenwald Fund allowed Cayton and Drake to organize the materials from the WPA project and supplement them with information from the 1940s. Their efforts resulted in a volume coauthored by Drake and Cayton: *Black Metropolis* (1945).

Black Metropolis blended the two dominant social-scientific methodologies used during the interwar years for the study of race relations: the Chicago school of sociology, which saw race relations as a dynamic process of assimilation, and the relatively static model of anthropological studies, which focused on caste and class. The book examined the effects of the rapid migration of African Americans into Chicago. Drake and Cayton argued that racism prevented African Americans from assimilating into the dominant culture, which made them unique among ethnic groups in the United States. Drake and Cayton included a series of participant-observer interviews with black Chicagoans, which revealed that Chicago's race relations closely resembled the caste system of the American South. Drake and Cayton closed their volume with a call for the government to do more to help African Americans achieve equality in American culture.

This call in *Black Metropolis* reflected Cayton's ongoing concern for racial equality and civil rights. Since 1934 he had been a regular columnist for the *Pittsburgh Courier*, often arguing forcefully for civil rights for African Americans. In 1940 he became the director of Chicago's Parkway House, which soon became a focus of African American cultural

life and was frequently visited by such luminaries as LANGSTON HUGHES, ARNA BONTEMPS, PAUL ROBESON, and RICHARD WRIGHT. Wright and Cayton became particularly close friends during the 1940s.

Although his time in Chicago was successful professionally, Cayton's personal unhappiness was evident in a series of failed marriages. He first married Bonnie Branch, a white social worker, in 1931; they divorced in 1936. In the two decades following World War II, Cayton and Irma Jackson were twice married and twice divorced. He last married and divorced Ruby Wright. He had no children.

Cayton was in psychoanalysis from 1943 to 1949, grappling with his profound feelings of loneliness and hostility toward white America. In 1945, just as *Black Metropolis* was about to bring some measure of national recognition to his professional life, Cayton's personal life began to disintegrate. He began seeing his work at the Parkway House as nothing more than a sop thrown to the African American community by the white power structure. In 1949 he left Chicago and moved to New York City.

During the 1950s Cayton was in and out of various New York treatment centers for alcoholism and drug addiction, conditions that he had battled throughout his adult life. Although he kept up his regular column for the *Pittsburgh Courier*, he was unable to maintain steady employment in New York. He worked a series of jobs: researcher for the American Jewish Committee from 1950 to 1951, correspondent to the United Nations for the *Pittsburgh Courier* from 1952 to 1954, researcher for the National Council of Churches from 1954 to 1958, and instructor for the City College of New York from 1957 to 1958.

In 1960 Cayton moved to California, for a time depending on his brother Revels for financial support. Again he was in and out of treatment centers for alcoholism. In 1961 he ended his regular column with the *Pittsburgh Courier* and began working in various capacities for the University of California at Berkeley. During this time Cayton began writing his autobiography, *Long Old Road* (1965), which he saw as a form of therapy, a way to grapple with the demons of racism and loneliness that had plagued him for most of his adult life. In it, frankly and openly, he discussed his alcoholism, failed marriages, and stormy relationship with the rest of the Cayton family as well as his stark feelings on American racism.

In 1968 Cayton received a grant from the National Foundation for the Arts and Humanities to write a biography of Richard Wright, his estranged friend. He traveled to Paris in connection with the Wright biography, and there he died of natural causes.

FURTHER READING

Many of Cayton's papers are lost. The largest single collection of his papers is at the Vivian G. Harsh Research Collection of Afro-American History and Literature in Chicago.

Cayton, Horace Roscoe. *Long Old Road* (1965).

Hobbs, Richard Stanley. "The Cayton Legacy: Two Generations of a Black Family, 1859–1976," Ph.D. diss., University of Washington, 1989.

Obituary: *New York Times*, 25 Jan. 1970.

This entry is taken from the *American National Biography* and is published here with the permission of the American Council of Learned Societies.

JOHN P. JACKSON

Cayton, Horace Roscoe, Sr. (3 Feb. 1859–16 Aug. 1940), newspaper publisher and editor, and political activist, was born a slave in the Port Gibson area of Mississippi. An intelligent person, he managed to get an extensive formal education, an uncommon feat for a former slave during the post-Civil War period. He furthered his education when he attended Alcorn University, whose president was former U.S. Senator HIRAM REVELS (the first U.S. senator of African descent). Among the subjects he studied was Latin, which, later as a newspaperman, he would periodically interject in his articles, especially when he was riled.

Cayton was outspoken throughout his life and had several serious scrapes because of it. Indeed, when Cayton left Mississippi after Reconstruction ended, he may have left in a dress disguised as a woman, according to Seattle resident Georgia Spencer, a distant relative. Cayton had been warned that some whites had intentions of lynching him. An older relative of Spencer, Jefferson Thomas Cayton, told her that when he was a very young boy he "remembered Uncle Horace dressed in grandma's clothes wearing a big hat and going across the field away from the house" (Georgia Spencer, interview with author, 10 Feb. 2002, Seattle, Washington). After a sojourn through several states, Cayton settled in Seattle, Washington, in 1890, the year after the Great Fire. For a while he edited the *Seattle Standard* (1892–1893), the state's first black-run newspaper, but after a disagreement

with the paper's owner, Britain Oxendine, Cayton started his own newspaper, the *Seattle Republican*, in 1894.

In 1896 Susie Sumner Revels, a daughter of Hiram Revels, traveled to Seattle from Mississippi to marry Horace Cayton. The marriage took place in July of that year. SUSIE SUMNER REVELS CAYTON became an associate editor of the *Republican*. The couple would have five children who lived to adulthood: Ruth Cayton; Madge Cayton, who earned a degree in business from the University of Washington; HORACE ROSCOE CAYTON JR., a well-respected sociologist; REVELS CAYTON, an influential and important labor leader and human rights advocate; and Lillie Cayton, a social activist in Seattle and San Diego, California.

As a hard-hitting journalist, Cayton did not take long to get the attention of Seattle's politicians and businesses. By 1901 his newspaper was already popular and read by both white and black members of the community.

His intrepid writing also caused serious trouble for Cayton with the Seattle police chief William L. Meredith. Crime and corruption were rampant. Mayor Thomas Humes's administration, including the police department, was under fire. Church groups and others were demanding change. In the midst of this fight was Horace Cayton, whose weekly *Republican* had been criticizing the city powers and alleged police corruption. On Friday, 22 March 1901, Cayton, responding to a statement by William Meredith, wrote a short editorial suggesting that if grafting policemen were run out of town, Seattle would also be rid of Meredith.

Chief Meredith, furious, had Cayton arrested on a criminal libel charge. Cayton was taken to jail like an ordinary criminal. Many Seattle residents and newspapers viewed the arrest as another example of police misconduct and were convinced that Meredith was trying to punish, humiliate and, most of all, threaten the editor for his criticism of the police. Cayton was unfazed. He struck back the following Friday with a scathing front-page rebuke, in which he excoriated Meredith, Mayor Humes, and city officials mercilessly. Two months later the Cayton libel trial began. After four days of testimony and thirteen hours of deliberation, no verdict was reached and the jury was dismissed. Cayton was therefore considered the clear-cut winner, according to the *Seattle Post-Intelligencer* report (*Post-Intelligencer*, 25 May 1901). Meredith's action against Cayton had two unexpected results: evidence presented at the libel trial, along with other factors, led to a corruption investigation resulting in Meredith being stripped of his job; and Cayton and the *Seattle Republican* became even more popular.

Cayton used the *Seattle Republican*, and, from 1916 until 1920, *Cayton's Weekly* as potent weapons to fight ferociously for the rights of African Americans and other minorities, including Chinese and Japanese. Cayton faced various threats on numerous occasions because of his newspaper articles. In 1917 during World War I he was visited by a self-proclaimed "minute man" named Blackwood along with three hoodlum friends who questioned Cayton's loyalty to the United States because of supposedly seditious editorials (*Cayton's Weekly*, 24 Nov. 1917). The next year another not-so-veiled threat was delivered by U.S. Special Prosecutor Reames who warned that newspapers such as *Cayton's Weekly* should not be allowed to be published. Evidently he was upset at Cayton's reports of lynchings and other violence against black citizens occurring throughout the country (*Cayton's Weekly*, 24 Aug. 1918, 1). Cayton, however, seemed to grow more defiant with each perceived threat, as could be seen by his subsequent articles and editorials.

Cayton provided active leadership in numerous organizations including the King County Colored Republican Club, the (Seattle) Negro Business Men's League, and the Seattle branch of the NAACP. Cayton also served as a Republican County Convention delegate on numerous occasions between 1900 and 1920. Perhaps Cayton's most important legacy is his record of the activities of Washington State's early black residents. Through his newspapers and yearbooks, Cayton left a written record of Seattle's black past that is not readily available elsewhere. Whether he realized it at the time or not, Horace Roscoe Cayton Sr. became the keeper of Washington State's black history. After a lifetime of work, Horace Roscoe Cayton died at his Seattle home at the age of eighty-one.

FURTHER READING

Cayton, Horace Roscoe. "Better Late than Never," *Cayton's Monthly* (1921).

Diaz, Ed, ed. *Horace Roscoe Cayton: Selected Writings*, 2 vols. (2003).

Diaz, Ed, ed. "Reexamining the Past: A Different Perspective of Black Strikebreakers in King County's Coal Mining Industry," *More Voices, New Stories: King County, Washington's First 150 Years* (2002).

Hobbs, Richard S. *The Cayton Legacy: An African American Family* (2002).

Taylor, Quintard. *The Forging of a Black Community: Seattle's Central District, from 1870 through the Civil Rights Era* (1994).

ED DIAZ

Cayton, Revels Hiram (5 June 1907–4 Nov. 1995), labor leader and human rights activist, was the fourth of five children born in Seattle, Washington, to SUSIE SUMNER REVELS CAYTON, a newspaper editor and community activist, and HORACE ROSCOE CAYTON SR., a journalist and publisher of the *Seattle Republican*. He was named after his grandfather, HIRAM REVELS (1827–1901), the first U.S. senator of African descent (1870–1871). Revels's brother HORACE CAYTON JR. became a prominent sociologist.

Unlike his father, who detested and distrusted labor unions because of their record of racially discriminatory practices, Revels became involved with the labor movement early in his life in the belief that unions offered all workers the best chance to better their condition. He rose through the union ranks and was at one time secretary-treasurer of the Bay Area District Council of the Maritime Union of the Pacific. He also joined the Communist Party and wrote extensively for the *Voice of Action*, a party-funded newspaper.

Cayton had no illusions about the difficult task he faced in combating the racism and racial antipathy that characterized relations between black and white workers. He once described how he left home as a teenager to work on a passenger liner, and how blacks were despised and looked down upon by white seamen: "white sailor would spit into the ocean if he had to speak to one of us" (*Chicago Defender*, 18 Nov. 1939). On several occasions, he urged direct action against discrimination. In 1934 he was involved in demonstrations against "whites only" businesses in Seattle and was arrested by local authorities the same year when he tried to speak to striking coal miners. He was taken to jail in the Washington town of Cle Elum and was subsequently released without charges—but ordered to leave the area. In 1939 he led a committee protesting the discrimination policy of a San Francisco café. Failing to make management change its policy, the Maritime Federation District Council, of which Cayton was secretary, urged all affiliated unions to boycott the establishment. In 1940 Cayton, singer PAUL ROBESON, and eight others were denied service at Vanessi's, another San Francisco establishment. They, in turn, filed a discrimination suit against the restaurant.

In the 1940s Cayton became increasingly active in efforts to end racism in the U.S. military. During the years before World War II, African Americans could enlist in the U.S. Navy, but only as messmen and stewards (who acted as servants and butlers for officers). In 1940 with a world war approaching, the navy encouraged black men to join the Naval Reserve as mess attendants. Revels Cayton lambasted the navy, pointing out that its policy was nothing more than military Jim-Crowism, and that black sailors were not only barred from ratings available to white sailors but were paid less. When the Japanese attacked Pearl Harbor on 7 December 1941, Cayton was serving as a merchant seaman in the Pacific somewhere between Japan and the Philippines. The onset of war did not stifle Cayton's criticism of racial injustice—indeed it made him more willing to speak out. As a crewmember on a ship returning wounded servicemen to the United States, he claimed in a *Chicago Defender* article that when their ship docked in Australia, the Australians treated the black seamen decently, and the only problems came from the white American soldiers who carried their racial attitudes overseas.

Cayton also condemned his fellow African Americans when, in his view, they were hindering the cause of equality. For instance, in 1944 he warned against what he described as "black self-designated race experts," whom he charged were putting the entire black race in harm's way in order to "perpetuate their soft jobs" (*Chicago Defender*, 23 Sept. 1944).

Cayton's radicalism did not go unnoticed. As a member of the Communist Party, he gained the attention of FBI director J. Edgar Hoover. A secret report reaching Hoover's desk that included surveillance information on Seattle's black population had a notation that read in part, "At one time Revels Cayton, Negro Communist Party Member … was an organizer in the Northwest" (Hill, 298).

Beginning in the 1940s Cayton took a leading role in the National Negro Congress (NNC), serving as executive secretary of the left-wing organization that had close ties to organized labor and the Communist Party. He moved to New York City and, along with the Reverend Sheldon Hale of St. Philip's Church, and others in the NNC, he lobbied in 1946 to secure passage of the stalled Wagner-Murray-Dingell bill, an effort to enact compulsory national health insurance introduced in Congress in 1943.

In 1946, in a bold and controversial action, the NNC submitted a petition to the newly formed United Nations arguing that African Americans were denied the constitutional rights afforded to other American citizens. In conjunction with the petition Cayton notified President Truman of the NNC's demand for "full freedom and absolute equality" for black Americans (*Chicago Defender*, 8 June 1946). The petition marked the NNC's zenith, for shortly thereafter the congress started falling apart amid the general anticommunist atmosphere of the era and internal divisions. Cayton blamed the collapse of the NNC on a growing reactionary trend within white trade unions. Ironically, his views of unions were slowly becoming closer to that of his father's.

Returning to San Francisco, Cayton remained active in community affairs by serving as a member of the San Francisco Human Rights Commission, as deputy director of the San Francisco Housing Authority, and as deputy mayor for social programs. He retired in 1987 at the age of 80 and died in San Francisco.

FURTHER READING

Hill, Robert A. *The FBI's Racon: Racial Conditions in the United States during World War II* (1995).

Hobbs, Richard S. *The Cayton Legacy: An African American Family* (2002).

Preece, Harold. "Grandson of Hiram R. Revels, First Race Senator From Mississippi, In Labor Ranks Helping Black Seamen," *Chicago Defender*, 18 Nov. 1939.

Taylor, Quintard. *The Forging of a Black Community: Seattle's Central District from 1870 through the Civil Rights Era* (1994).

Obituary: *San Francisco Chronicle*, 6 Nov. 1995; *San Francisco Examiner*, 7 Nov. 1995.

ED DIAZ

Cayton, Susie Sumner Revels (1870–1943), editor, writer, and community leader, was born Susie Sumner Revels in Natchez, Mississippi, the daughter of Senator HIRAM RHODES REVELS of Mississippi, the first African American to serve in the U.S. Senate, and Phoebe Revels. The name Sumner was in honor of her father's friend Senator Charles Sumner, a Massachusetts radical Republican and vehement opponent of slavery. Susie's formal education started at the school later known as Alcorn University where her father was president. When the family moved to Holly Springs, Mississippi, she completed her education at Rust College and then started teaching there at the young age of sixteen.

Revels probably started corresponding with Seattle newspaper publisher HORACE ROSCOE CAYTON SR. after he sent copies of the *Seattle Republican* to her father, whom he had known as a student at Alcorn. She then sent her own articles and short stories to Cayton, which he agreed to publish. In January 1896 Cayton published an extensive report submitted by Revels about the 1895 Atlanta Exposition. Although BOOKER T. WASHINGTON's controversial speech at the Atlanta Exposition was often reported, Revels passionately reported not this famed speech but her feelings about the Dahomey Village and the activities and exhibits in the Negro Building, which she found quite encouraging. Readers of the *Seattle Republican* no doubt got a view of the Atlanta Exposition unlikely to be found elsewhere.

Evidently what started as professional correspondence between the two evolved into a personal relationship. In 1896 Revels traveled to Seattle to marry Cayton, and the two eventually had five children: Ruth, Madge, HORACE ROSCOE CAYTON JR., REVELS CAYTON, and Lillie. Ruth died when only twenty-three, so her daughter Susan was brought up by the Caytons. A 1936 Washington's Pioneer Project interview, a Works Progress Administration (WPA) project, gave insight into Susie Cayton's personal life. In her interview, she described traveling alone from Mississippi to Seattle, Washington— quite a trek for any woman in 1896, let alone a black woman. She stated that the move was specifically to marry Horace Cayton, that she considered herself a Methodist, and that she believed Seattle was a thoroughly modern city when she arrived: "I cooked on a gas plate two years after I married," she told interviewer Jessie E. Crouch (Diaz, 11).

Cayton became the associate editor of the *Seattle Republican* and contributing editor to *Cayton's Weekly*, which operated from 1916 to 1920 after the *Republican* folded. She was an active and important participant in the publication of both newspapers. In 1909 the *Seattle Times* pointed out that the *Republican* had not missed an issue since its inception in 1894 and commented that "perhaps this is partially due to the fact that Susie Revels Cayton has been associate editor and publisher" (quoted in *Seattle Republican*, 23 July 1919). Horace Cayton long recognized his wife's importance to the paper's success and responded to the *Times*'s observation with "guilty as charged" (*Seattle Republican*, 23 July 1919).

Cayton's writing ability, already established, came to the attention of the *Seattle Post-Intelligencer*'s readers when one of her stories,

"Sally the Egg-Woman," was published in its 5 June 1900 issue. During that era, it was almost unheard of for a black woman to have her work published by a major daily newspaper; this was likely a first for Seattle. Horace Cayton thought so much of her writing that he wrote in 1917 that his wife would be among the best short-story writers in the country if only she could devote more time to writing. Not only did she help her husband edit and publish the newspaper, run a home, and raise her children but she also was deeply involved in community affairs including "uplift" organizations formed by Seattle's leading black citizens that worked to improve the lives of African Americans.

In 1906 an abandoned set of twins with rickets was turned over to an institution for the mentally ill by King County Hospital because no one could be found to adopt the black babies. Cayton was already well known for her work in the black community and was contacted for help. The historian Quintard Taylor pointed out that this event resulted in the formation of the Dorcus Charity Club. Cayton not only found a suitable temporary home for the babies, but for years the club continued its support to the children with the goal of finding them adoptive parents. The club grew into a long-lasting organization in Seattle's black community that assisted widows, provided toys to orphaned children, and even paid the medical expenses of a destitute person during her almost two-year hospital stay (Taylor, 140). Somehow Cayton managed to squeeze into her busy schedule time to participate in musical and literary programs for Seattle's black community. She also frequently contributed to the "Sunday Forum," a platform where matters of concern to the black community, such as the planned boycott of a local establishment, were presented and discussed.

The Great Depression disrupted the lives of many families including the Caytons. Yet Cayton assisted jobless workers at Seattle's version of a "Hooverville," a rundown area inhabited by many of Seattle's homeless. She became secretary of the Skid Row Unemployment Council (SRUC), an advocacy group, and she was so well thought that she was called Mother Cayton (Taylor, 100).

Even as she approached seventy years of age, Cayton continued her many community activities. After her husband died in 1940, she moved to Chicago to be close to her two oldest living children, Madge and Horace Jr. She died there in 1943, and her remains were cremated and returned to Puget Sound, according to a *Chicago Defender* obituary (7 Aug. 1943). To paraphrase the *Defender*, "It would be well for black America to review this woman's life, for she is an inspiration for the youth of today."

FURTHER READING

Diaz, Ed, ed. *Stories by Cayton: Short Stories by Susie Revels Cayton, A Seattle Pioneer* (2002).

Hobbs, Richard S. *The Cayton Legacy: An African American Family* (2002).

Taylor, Quintard. *The Forging of a Black Community: Seattle's Central District from 1870 through the Civil Rights Era* (1994).

ED DIAZ

Celestin, Papa (1 Jan. 1884–15 Dec. 1954), bandleader and trumpeter, was born Oscar Philip Celestin in Lafourche Parish, Louisiana, the son of Joseph Celestin, a sugarcane cutter, and Lucy (maiden name unknown). About 1900 Celestin got his first cornet, and for a few years he worked as a cook for a railroad. In 1902 he moved to Saint Charles Parish, where he got his first job as a musician with J. C. Trist's band. In 1906 he moved to New Orleans and worked first as a longshoreman and, in 1909, as a musician at Josie Arlinton's saloon in the local red-light district. The first New Orleans band of which he was a regular member was the Indiana Brass Band. Then he joined Jack Carey's band, where he began to play jazz. Celestin also worked with other New Orleans bands, including RED ALLEN's Brass Band, the Silver Leaf Band, and ARMAND PIRON's band. Originally called "Sonny," Celestin gradually developed a paternal bearing and became known among musicians as "Papa."

In 1910 Celestin joined the Tuxedo Band at the Tuxedo Dance Hall in the Storyville district. A year later he was joined by future musicians such as Johnny Lindsay and POPS FOSTER to form the Original Tuxedo Brass Band. Appearing with them were LOUIS ARMSTRONG, Roy Palmer, Lee Collins, and KING OLIVER; Armstrong called it the best brass band in town. The band donned black tuxedos, derby hats, and white shirts, and their attire and good manners helped develop their reputation. The band became the prototypical New Orleans jazz band.

During and after World War I the band played at debutante parties, carnival balls, country clubs, fraternity and sorority dances, yacht clubs, fine hotels, and, on every Sunday of the baseball season, Heinemann Park. In July 1924 two members of the band squeezed into an airplane with the Gates Flying Circus and gave a concert of sorts, becoming the first musicians, ostensibly, to play from an airplane. By 1922 Celestin had married Ophelia Jackson.

Celestin served as musical director and William "Baba" Ridgley as booking agent and business manager, a division of duties and talents that precipitated a split following an angry recording session in January 1925. Some of the musicians went with Ridgley, forming Ridgley's Original Tuxedo Jazz Orchestra, and others joined Celestin's Original Tuxedo Jazz Orchestra. Both bands were successful, but Ridgley abandoned his project after six years.

In his own band Celestin's sweet, melodic style was contrasted by a second cornetist who played a hotter, more modern style. Some members read music, and others did not; they generally played from memory, but they also counted measures and beats.

During the 1930s Celestin worked at college dances, carnival parties, and similar society jobs. Although he toured neighboring states, he refused many offers to leave New Orleans permanently. The Depression and the proliferation of bands with white musicians forced Celestin to work under the Works Progress Administration as a laborer.

Though Celestin played occasionally during World War II, he also had to work as a longshoreman, drive a truck, and work as a chauffeur. In 1944 he was hit by a car when leaving his job at a defense plant and was kept in bed for two years while his broken legs mended. His wife nursed him back to health and encouraged his return to the horn.

During the 1946–1947 tourist season Celestin began work at the Paddock Lounge on Bourbon Street. Soon the New Orleans jazz revival was under way, and crowds flocked into the nightclub. Although the band used Celestin's name, he was not the actual leader. He did lead another band that played private engagements, especially the departure of luxury ships. In 1951 he left the Paddock to concentrate on these other engagements, but he still worked an occasional Bourbon Street nightclub job. He also appeared on radio and television, and his band appeared in the 1953 film *Cinerama Holiday*. In May 1953 Celestin played for the White House Correspondents' Association, receiving a certificate of appreciation signed by President Dwight D. Eisenhower. When Celestin died in New Orleans, the trombonist Eddie Pierson became the band's new manager, but Celestin's widow was considered the band's leader and received a share of its pay.

Celestin was a showstopper. When his band rendered "Tiger Rag," Celestin would claw, then roar and shake. He excelled at entertaining as well as at band leading, and his showmanship was a major reason for his popularity and success. Armstrong and Sweet Emma Barrett praised Celestin's fairness and courtesy, and he was known for developing young musicians. Critics sometimes complained that his work was too melodic and predictable, but Celestin simply knew what the audience wanted. Sid Davilla, a clarinetist and Bourbon Street nightclub owner, told David Brinkley that when Celestin put a tight mute in his trumpet and played "Just Telephone Me," the cash register fell silent and no one ordered a drink. Celestin's popularity with New Orleanians was so great that his records and his legend have been passed down to younger generations, both in the United States and around the world.

FURTHER READING

Materials related to Celestin's career are available at the William Ransom Hogan Jazz Archive, Howard-Tilton Memorial Library, Tulane University, New Orleans, Louisiana.

Curren, John G. "Oscar 'Papa' Celestin," *Second Line* (Jan.–Feb. 1955).

Haby, Peter R. "Oscar 'Papa' Celestin 1884–1954," *Footnote* (June–July 1981).

Obituaries: *New York Times* and *New Orleans Times-Picayune,* 16 Dec. 1954.

This entry is taken from the *American National Biography* and is published here with the permission of the American Council of Learned Societies.

RICHARD B. ALLEN

Celia (c. 1818–22 Sept. 1848), the first woman executed by the state of Florida, was born a slave in Georgia, the eldest of six children of Jacob Bryan, a white planter, and Susan (maiden name unknown), who was Bryan's slave and also his common-law wife. Legal documents indicate that in January 1830 Bryan brought Susan and his children to a plantation in Duval County, Florida.

In November 1842 Jacob Bryan executed a legal deed of manumission to emancipate Susan and several of his children, though the historical record is unclear as to whether Celia was one of those freed. Manumission of slaves had been possible in Florida under Spanish law, though usually for male slaves who had fought for the Spanish Empire, and for the common-law slave wives and slave children of white planters. As a result a sizeable free black population developed in eastern Florida, making it possible for interracial couples like Sarah and Jacob Bryan to live together openly. Spanish law had also allowed some slaves to own property, and even to file lawsuits against their owners. But after Florida became a U.S. territory in 1821 this relatively flexible system of race relations gave way to the more stringent legal code familiar to the other Southern slave states. By the time Jacob Bryan manumitted his slaves in 1842 Florida had enacted laws that severely restricted the rights of free blacks. These included a highly discriminatory poll tax, which required free blacks to pay an annual sum of eight dollars once they reached the age of fifteen, even though whites, beginning at the age of twenty-one, paid only one dollar each year. Free blacks could no longer vote, serve on juries, or testify against whites in court. They could not carry firearms, assemble in large groups, or sell liquor. The children of interracial couples could not inherit their parents' property. An 1829 law also placed severe restrictions on the laws of manumission, requiring a fee of two hundred dollars per slave. Bryan, it appears, did not pay this fee when he freed his slave wife and children in 1842, perhaps because he could not afford it. Sarah and Bryan's children also did not conform to the law's requirement that freed slaves emigrate permanently from the state of Florida within thirty days of their manumission. Instead, they continued to live and work in Duval County, believing that they were free.

There is little in the historical record about Celia or her family until December 1847, at which time Celia was arrested on suspicion of having killed Jacob Bryan. At Celia's trial the following June, it emerged that she had been working in a field when Bryan approached her, perhaps to chastise or discipline her. Celia then attacked Bryan with her hoe, which had a knife attached to the handle. The blow "cut open his skull so as to produce instant death" (Schafer, 598). Some sources indicate that Celia had been aided in her attack by two male slaves, but it seems most likely that she acted alone. The six-man, all-white jury found Celia guilty only of manslaughter, probably in recognition that she had acted in self-defense and not with malice aforethought. That the jury also recommended clemency or mercy for Celia further suggests that they believed her actions were in some sense justified. It emerged during the trial that Bryan was not only Celia's father but may have also been the father of Celia's four children, which may have earned her the sympathy of the jurors. Judge Thomas Douglas nevertheless sentenced her to death.

Doubts about the severity of the sentence and the impropriety of executing a woman prompted Governor William D. Mosely to commute Celia's sentence for three months to review what was called her "great hardship" (Schafer, 606). Some prominent white landowners also petitioned for clemency for Celia, but on 22 September 1848 she became the first woman executed by the state of Florida. The newspapers declared that Celia was "without the least remorse for the crime that she had committed" and "up to the last moment blamed her mother as the cause of her death" (Schafer, 598). Her body hung on the gallows for one hour before it was taken down and buried.

Celia's trial and execution for killing Jacob Bryan also had severe repercussions for her mother and siblings. Susan Bryan and her children, including Dennis, Mary, and Sarah, were arrested and jailed as slaves; an inventory of Jacob Bryan's estate had classified them all as slaves with a combined value of $3,800. A seventeen-month investigation by a Florida judge found that Bryan had not fully complied with the state's manumission laws, but also recognized that it had been Bryan's intention to free his wife and children. Susan Bryan and her children were granted their freedom in March 1849, but the ruling was appealed by Jacob Bryan's brother, John, and his sister, Amaziah Archer, who claimed to be the rightful heirs to his property, including his slaves. In November 1851 Judge Thomas Douglas of Florida's Eastern Circuit Court ruled that Dennis, Mary, and their mother should be freed, but that Sarah, who had not been born in Florida, should be sold back into slavery. Three months later she was put up at a public auction in Jacksonville. In 1853 the Florida Supreme Court ruled that Dennis, Mary, and Jacob Bryan's other children, including Celia, had never been emancipated. Mary was probably returned to slavery; Dennis, who had been released from jail after wealthy whites guaranteed a $4,000 bond, escaped. The court later awarded Amaziah Archer $900 to reimburse her for the loss of Dennis.

The case of the Florida slave Celia is in some respects similar to that of another slave named CELIA, who was executed in Missouri in 1855 for killing her master who had repeatedly raped her from the moment he had purchased her as a fourteen year old in 1850. In both cases there appears to have been some sympathy for the accused, probably because both women had killed men who had abused them. In earlier times both women might have received clemency, but the growing sectional divisions over slavery probably sealed their fates. States like Missouri and Florida had become increasingly intolerant of any challenge to those who owned slaves, and so slaves who killed their masters could expect no mercy. The Florida Supreme Court's 1853 ruling returning the children of Jacob Bryan to slavery also reveals the dramatic erosion of the rights that free blacks had once enjoyed.

Celia was the first woman executed by the state of Florida, and she was also the last woman executed in that state until 1998, when Judy Buenoano, a white woman who had poisoned her husband, died in the electric chair.

FURTHER READING

Rozsa, Lori. "Woman on Death Row: Echoes of a Slave's Hanging in 1848," *Miami Herald*, 29 Mar. 1998.

Schafer, Daniel L. "A Class of People neither Freemen nor Slaves: From Spanish to American Race Relations in Florida, 1821–1861," *Journal of Social History* 26.3 (1993).

STEVEN J. NIVEN

Celia (c. 1836–21 Dec. 1855), a slave executed for killing her master, was probably born in central Missouri. The names of her parents are unknown. Practically all the information that is known about Celia is taken from court records and newspaper accounts of her trial for the murder in 1855 of Robert Newsom, a farmer and slave owner in Calloway County, Missouri. Newsom had purchased Celia in neighboring Audrain County, Missouri, some five years earlier. Celia was the only female slave in the Newsom household; the five others included a young boy and four young adult males who herded the livestock and harvested the eight hundred acres of prime land that had helped elevate Robert Newsom to a position "solidly among the ranks of Calloway's residents who were comfortably well-off" (McLaurin, 8). Newsom's wife had died in 1849, and it may have been that he purchased Celia, a cook, to assist his thirty-six-year-old daughter, Virginia, in the management of the household.

It immediately became apparent to Celia, however, that Robert Newsom had purchased her primarily to serve as his concubine. At some point on the forty-mile return journey from Audrain County, Newsom, then seventy years old, raped Celia, who was at that time around only fourteen. Court records indicate that over the next four years Newsom repeatedly forced Celia to have sex with him against her will, and fathered at least one, and possibly both, of the children born to Celia between 1851 and 1854.

Perhaps to keep his liaison secret from his daughters Virginia and Mary, but certainly to provide easy access to his concubine, Newsom provided Celia with her own cabin, a relatively spacious and solid brick structure located a mere sixty paces from his own home. Newsom may have also deliberately separated Celia, the only black woman on the Newsom farm, from her fellow slaves to prevent her from forming friendships or alliances with them. Sometime after the birth of Celia's second child in 1854, however, she began a sexual relationship with one of Newsom's slaves, a man named George. When Celia became pregnant again, in early March of 1855, she did not know whether George or Newsom was the father. George then demanded that Celia abandon Newsom. Such a request may well have appealed to Celia in an ideal world, but, as George must have known, the reality of slavery gave her no such control over her master, or over her own body.

Recognizing that a direct approach to Newsom might jeopardize the lives of her children and George, as well as her own, Celia at first approached Virginia and Mary Newsom in the hope that they could persuade their father to end his sexual advances, at least while she was pregnant and sickly. That undertaking was itself dangerous, since it is unlikely that the sisters would challenge their father, the sole breadwinner in the family. The historical record also suggests that women in slaveholding families were are no less proslavery than men, and that there was little gender solidarity between slave-owning and slave women, particularly when slave women were engaged in sexual relationships with white men. The Newsom sisters do not appear to have come to Celia's defense, or if they did they failed to persuade their father to leave his female slave alone.

Sometime around 23 June 1855 Celia, who had been poorly throughout her pregnancy, confronted Newsom, begging him to leave her alone. When Newsom refused and promised to return to her cabin later that night, Celia warned him that she would resist his advances, and later found a large stick, "about as large as the upper part of a Windsor chair, but not as long," with which to defend herself (McLaurin, 30). Ignoring her imprecations Newsom duly returned to her cabin later that evening, again demanding that Celia submit to his wishes. When she resisted he advanced toward her, prompting Celia to grab the stick and bring it down heavily

on his head. Although the blow knocked Newsom to the ground, he raised himself and attempted to lunge at Celia, who again struck him on his head, this time fatally. Upon discovering that Newsom was dead Celia attempted to cover up the crime, fearing that the courts would show her little mercy, even in her pregnant state. She burned Newsom's body, and kept the fire burning throughout the night, until only his skeleton remained. She then crushed his smaller bones and hid the larger ones under the hearth. The following day Celia offered Newsom's twelve-year-old grandson two dozen walnuts to dispose of the ashes from her fire.

When Robert Newsom did not arrive home, his daughters roused their neighbors to search for him. They also informed William Powell, the leader of the search party, of their suspicion that the slave George was involved in their father's disappearance. It is unknown whether Celia had informed George of her actions, but he probably deduced that she had followed through on her threat to kill Newsom. Fearing for his own life George told Powell that he had last seen Newsom heading toward Celia's cabin. A cursory search of the cabin uncovered no body, however, and Celia flatly denied knowledge of Newsom's whereabouts. Powell then threatened to take Celia's children away from her if she did not confess, and also threatened to lynch her if she remained silent. After intensive questioning, and aware that George had abandoned her, Celia finally confessed that she, alone, had killed Newsom to defend herself from his sexual advances, and that she had burned his body and hidden the remains. The Newsome family and the Callaway County authorities continued to believe that a sickly pregnant woman must have had an accomplice, at least in destroying Newsom's body, but Celia insisted even under extensive questioning that she had acted alone.

Celia was indicted for Newsom's murder on 25 June 1855 and remained in the Callaway County jail until her trial, which began on 9 October 1855. The hearings took place during a period of growing national divisions about slavery, and about whether the institution should be expanded into the western territories acquired during the Mexican War of the 1840s. Tensions were especially high in 1855 in the borderlands between Missouri, a slave state, and Kansas, originally a free state but which at that time had two state governments, one supported by pro-slavery forces, the other by slavery opponents. As Celia's trial began, armed pro- and antislavery forces were engaged in daily skirmishes on either side of the Missouri–Kansas border, a portent of the full scale Civil War that would begin six years later.

As was the case in many other slave states Missouri law did not allow slaves to testify on their own behalf, but the court did provide Celia with counsel for her defense. The man chosen was John Jameson, a former speaker of the Missouri House of Representatives and a respected trial lawyer with more than thirty years experience in the courts. Jameson may have been selected to deflect any charge that Celia had been provided with inadequate counsel, a decision that reflected the growing legal challenge to slavery in the border states. Most courtrooms in the Deep South would have been less inclined to observe such legal niceties. Jameson did not deny that Newsom had died at Celia's hand, but he argued that the killing was "necessary to protect herself against a forced sexual intercourse" and that Newsom's actions had placed her in "imminent danger" (Higginbotham, 682). The criminal laws of Missouri, Jameson argued, made no explicit distinctions between the races, when it came to victims of rape. Section Four of the Missouri Criminal Statutes of 1845 stated simply that "homicide shall be deemed justifiable when committed by any person resisting" a felony such as rape (Higginbotham, 682). Jameson also hoped to earn sympathy for his client by informing the court of Newsom's history of forced sexual assaults on Celia. At some point during Celia's incarceration and trial, she gave birth to a child, which was stillborn.

In spite of Jameson's efforts, the trial judge, William Hall, advised the jury that they could not acquit Celia on the grounds of self-defense, and all but instructed them to find her guilty of murder in the first degree. The all-white jury duly found Celia guilty on 10 October 1855; three days later Judge Hall sentenced her to be hanged on 16 November of that year. Five days before Celia was due to be executed, however, she and another slave on death row, named Matt, escaped from the Callaway County jail, but she was subsequently recaptured. The historian Melton McLaurin has speculated that Celia's attorneys may have aided her escape in order to force the Missouri Supreme Court to hear her appeal. On 14 December 1855 the court unanimously rejected the defense appeal for a stay of execution.

Interrogated on the eve of her execution Celia continued to insist that she had acted alone and that she had not intended to kill Newsom that night. Pregnant, ill, and having suffered from Newsom's abuse for more than five years, something inside her had simply snapped. "As soon as I struck him," she confessed, "the Devil got into me, and I struck [Newsom] with the stick until he was dead, and then rolled him in the fire and burnt him up" (McLaurin, 114). Celia, still only nineteen years of age, was executed by hanging on 21 December 1855. Her case, according to the legal historian and federal judge A. LEON HIGGINBOTHAM, was even more "venal and racist" than the more famous Missouri slave case, *Dred Scott v. Sanford* (1857). Unlike Scott, who was ultimately freed and who died of natural causes, Higginbotham argues, Celia was executed because the Missouri courts held that "a slave woman had no virtue that the law would protect against a master's lust" (Higginbotham, 694).

FURTHER READING

Higginbotham, A. Leon, Jr. "Race, Sex, Education and Missouri Jurisprudence: *Shelley v. Kraemer* in a Historical Perspective," *Washington University Law Quarterly* 67 (1989).

McLaurin, Melton A. *Celia: A Slave* (2002).

STEVEN J. NIVEN

Cepeda, Orlando (17 Sept. 1937–), baseball player, was born Manuel Orlando Cepeda y Pennes in Ponce, Puerto Rico, to Pedro Anibal, a baseball player and water department worker, and Carmen Cepeda. Orlando's father, nicknamed "Perucho" (which means "bull"), was a beloved Puerto Rican athlete who suited up alongside SATCHEL PAIGE, JOSH GIBSON, and other Negro League greats in Winter League ball. Cepeda grew up poor, attributable in part to his father's meager salary and gambling debts. His father's profession attracted Cepeda at a young age; after he starred in an amateur game against a Dominican All-Star team in 1953, he drew the attention of Pedro Zorilla, a scout for the New York Giants and owner of the Winter League's Santurce Cangrejeros. Zorilla hired Cepeda as a batboy, and he was soon working out with stars such as WILLIE MAYS and ROBERTO CLEMENTE. What education he received in Puerto Rico, if any, is unknown.

Cepeda signed a minor-league contract with the Giants in March 1955 and joined the Salem, Virginia, team in the rookie Appalachian League. His life outside Puerto Rico began harshly. Coping with the death of his father from malaria, the dark-skinned Latino Cepeda endured segregation and racial epithets shouted at him on the streets. Sent to a lower affiliate in Kokomo, Indiana, Cepeda's personal and professional life improved, and he led the league with a .393 batting average. Cepeda ascended gradually through the minor-league ranks and by 1957 had caught the eye of Giants management. With the *Sporting News* touting him as the National League's best prospect in 1958, Cepeda won the starting first baseman job in spring training for the Giants' inaugural season in San Francisco.

Hitting a home run in his second major-league at-bat, Cepeda instantly became a fan favorite. Over the course of his rookie season, the city took to the newly ordained "Baby Bull" for his enthusiasm, and he took to the city for its Latin and jazz music. Despite the presence of legendary centerfielder Willie Mays, Cepeda was named the team MVP by Bay Area fans at the end of the year. His twenty-five home runs, ninety-six RBIs, and .312 batting average earned him a unanimous Rookie of the Year award.

Cepeda married Ana Hilda Piño in 1960 and had a child, Orlando Jr. Six years later he fathered a child, Carl, out of wedlock (and whom he finally met in 1995).

Cepeda continued to pace the Giants on the field. In 1961 he finished second in MVP voting; with Mays and Dominican pitcher JUAN MARICHAL, he became one of the cornerstones of a powerful franchise. In 1962 he helped San Francisco to 103 wins and a World Series appearance. Despite Cepeda's six consecutive All-Star appearances with the Giants, his relationship with manager Alvin Dark deteriorated. The manager accused the star of apathetic play and banned Spanish in the clubhouse despite the team's strong Latin contingent. Even Spanish music was banned (management insisted that enforcing one language was intended to improve clubhouse and teammate unity). After a knee injury forced Cepeda to sit out most of 1965, he was traded to the St. Louis Cardinals the following spring.

Cepeda brought his enthusiasm to the Cardinals, and by mid-season "Cha-Cha" (so nicknamed for his penchant for dancing to Latin music in the clubhouse) won the adulation of St. Louis fans and the *Sporting News's* 1966 Comeback Player of the Year award. In 1967, Cepeda led "El Birdos" to a World Series and was the first unanimous MVP winner since Carl Hubbell in 1936.

Traded after the 1968 season, Cepeda enjoyed productive seasons with the Atlanta Braves, but a knee injury and remnants of southern racism both in the city and the clubhouse left Cepeda at odds with the franchise. The Braves traded him in 1972 to the Oakland Athletics. He enjoyed a brief resurgence with the Boston Red Sox the next year under the new designated hitter rule, which allowed a player to bat for the pitcher in the American League. After a stint between the Mexican League and the Kansas City Royals in 1974, Cepeda retired with 379 home runs, a then-record for home runs by a Latin player. In 1973 Cepeda's wife, Ana, divorced him, citing his excessive infidelities. In December of the following year he was arrested by federal marshals when he picked up cartons containing marijuana at San Juan's airport. He soon became an outcast in Puerto Rico and was sentenced to five years in prison at Florida's Eglin Air Force Base. Thanks to good behavior and support from friends in Major League Baseball, Cepeda was paroled after ten months and began working at a Philadelphia halfway house. He temporarily held minor-league coaching jobs but was still a pariah at home. He moved his family to Los Angeles in 1984, but his second wife, Nydia Fernandez, whom he had married in 1975, left him, taking their two sons, Malcolm and Ali.

Formerly a devout Catholic, Cepeda embraced Buddhism in the mid-1980s and credited it for turning his life around. After meeting his third wife, Mirian Ortiz, whom he married in 1985, Cepeda attended a Giants fantasy camp and was given a job as special assistant for player development. As a liaison for the Giants, Cepeda visited hospitals, schools, and youth camps. Cepeda had long been socially active not only in Puerto Rico but also in America, where he gave inspirational talks to Spanish-speaking students in New York. As his community service was resurrected, so was his stature with the Giants and his home country. He lectured on the dangers of narcotics and became nationally recognized as one of baseball's goodwill ambassadors.

In 1993 Cepeda was elected to the Puerto Rican Hall of Fame, two years after his father's induction. Though support grew for his inclusion into the National Baseball Hall of Fame, it was the Veterans' Committee, not the writers, which elected him to the Hall in 1999.

Just the sixth Latin player and second Puerto Rican after Roberto Clemente elected to the Hall of Fame, Cepeda became one of the foremost proponents for the recognition of Latin influence in baseball. Though Latin players were still emerging in the 1960s when Cepeda had first come on the scene, they comprised almost a quarter of the 2005 opening-day rosters.

FURTHER READING
Cepeda, Orlando, with Bob Markus. *High and Inside: Orlando Cepeda's Story* (1983).

Cepeda, Orlando, with Herb Fagen. *Baby Bull: From Hardball to Hard Times and Back* (1998).

Markusen, Bruce. *The Orlando Cepeda Story* (2001).

Newman, Mark. "One More Chance," *Sporting News* (10 Jan 1994).

ADAM W. GREEN

Cesar (c. 1682–?), slave and medical practitioner who developed primitive pharmaceuticals, is thought to have been born in Africa or the Caribbean and transported to the southern colonies as a slave. He might instead have been born into slavery in South Carolina. (His name is often spelled Caesar.) The names of his parents are unknown. He may have been the descendant of skilled medicine men, who transferred medical knowledge from their native cultures to the colonies, sharing drug recipes and folk remedies that used herbs and roots, or of slave midwives, who had performed cesarean sections in Africa and taught other slaves that procedure.

Cesar might also have had Native American ancestors, because many Carolina slaves had intermarried with native tribes. Southern Native Americans were known for their potent herbal remedies. Slave physicians either were self-taught or acquired some training from fellow slaves or masters, and they became celebrities within their communities for their healing powers. Their reputations boosted their social rank, and whites became aware of their "curative knowledge."

Cesar was well known in his community for his use of roots and herbs as an antidote to poison. His pharmaceutical prowess attracted the attention of colonial leaders, and his successes were preserved in colonial records. The 24 November 1749 journal of the South Carolina Commons House of Assembly in Charleston noted that a "Member acquainted the House that there is a Negro Man named Caesar belonging to Mr. John Norman of Beach Hill, who had cured several of the Inhabitants of this Province who had been poisoned by Slaves." The legislator stated that Cesar "was willing to make a Discovery of the Remedy which he makes Use of in such Cases for a reasonable Reward." The following day the assembly appointed a committee to investigate the claim and "report what Reward the said Negro Man Caesar shall merit for his Services." By Wednesday, 29 November, the assembly "Ordered that Doctor Glen and Doctor Brisband be added to the Committee who were appointed to … examine into the Services lately done by a Negro Man called Caesar … who have it in charge to desire the Aid and Observations of any skilful Physicians they shall think fit."

Committee member Mr. Austin delivered a report to the clerk, which was read to the legislators. William Miles had informed the committee that his sister and brother had been poisoned and that Cesar had saved their lives. Miles's son had recently been poisoned and "wants Caesar to his Relief." Other testimonials included "Henry Middleton, Esq., [who] believed he was poisoned and after two doses was cured. His overseer had also been cured." A Mr. Sacheverell "informed the Committee that Caesar had undertaken to cure a Man who was violently afflicted with Fits, and, in Appearance, will effect it."

Cesar's master, John Norman, told the committee that "to his Knowledge, Caesar had done many Services in a physical Way, and in particular had frequently cured the Bite of Rattle Snakes, and never knew him to fail in any one Attempt." Norman elaborated that "Caesar had been frequently called upon as a Doctor in many Cases by the Neighbours," mentioning an "Instance to the Committee of a Negro Man that had been cured of the Yaws by Caesar when he had been twice salivated, and was covered with an intire [*sic*] Scab from Top to Toe." The committee noted that "another Point Caesar is very famous in is the Cure of Pleurisies many of which he had undertaken to the Knowledge of Mr. Norman which had had very deadly symptoms."

Cesar was then asked "on what Conditions he would discover his Antidotes, and such other useful Simples as he was acquainted with," and he replied "that he expected his Freedom, and a moderate Competence for Life, which he hoped the Committee would be of Opinion deserved one hundred Pounds Currency per Annum." Cesar told the Assembly that "he proposed to give the Committee any satisfactory Experiment of his ability they please, as soon as he should be able to provide himself with the necessary ingredients."

The committee supported Cesar's request, suggesting that "he shall have his Freedom, and an annual Allowance of one hundred pounds for Life with such a further Allowance for any other useful Discovery he may make to the Public as this House shall think fit." The house approved the committee's recommendation and "Resolved that this House will make Provision for Payment to the said John Norman of the appraised Value of the said Negro Caesar." Cesar was appraised by four people, two nominated by the house and two by Norman. On 7 December 1749 the house issued a statement "that upon due Consideration of all the Advantages the said Negro Slave Caesar (aged near sixty-seven Years) might be of to the Owner by his knowledge and Skill may be worth the Sum of five hundred Pounds Current Money of South Carolina," which the public treasurer was ordered to pay "immediately" and also "advance the Sum of fifty Pounds to be paid to the Negro Man named Caesar."

The house also requested that the *South Carolina Gazette* print Cesar's prescription for public use, which appeared in the 14 May 1750 issue. Most historians consider this the first publication of a medical cure developed by an African American; the person who actually wrote the instructions is unknown but probably was Cesar's master, an assemblyman, a local doctor, or the printer. One year later, issue number 877 of the *South Carolina Gazette*, dated 25 February to 4 March 1751, stated, "There having been so great a Demand for our Gazette of the 14th of May 1750 (wherein was published, by Order of the Commons House of Assembly, the Negro Caesar's Cure for Poison) that none were left in a short time, 'tis hoped the Re-publication of that Cure, may not be unacceptable at this Time."

Cesar described the symptoms of poisoning and revealed how he prepared his cure for poison, which called for boiling the "roots of Plantane and wild Hoar-hound, fresh or dried," and straining it. "Of this decoction let the patient take one third part three mornings fasting successively, from which if he finds any relief, it must be continued, 'till he is perfectly recovered," Cesar prescribed. "During the cure, the patient must live on spare diet, and abstain from eating mutton, pork, butter, or any other fat or oily food." He advised that they boil goldenrod roots with sassafras and "to this decoction, after it is strain'd, add a glass of rum or brandy, and sweeten it with sugar, for ordinary drink." For fevers that accompany poisoning, he suggested a wood–ash mash.

For rattlesnake bites, Cesar told physicians to "take of the roots of Plantane or Hoarhound, (in summer roots and branches together) a sufficient quantity, bruise them in a mortar, and squeeze out the juice, of which give as soon as possible, one large spoonful: if he is swell'd you must force it down his throat." He noted that "this generally will cure; but if the patient finds no relief in an hour after, you may give another spoonful which never fails." He also recommended that "to the wound may be applied, a leaf of good tobacco, moisten'd with rum."

Cesar's cures became well-known and were also published, probably near the time of his death, in 1789 at Philadelphia, and in the 1792 *Massachusetts Magazine*. They were also mentioned in William Buchan's *Domestic Medicine* (1797), which noted that Cesar's detailed description "was in the grand tradition of Sydenham, the great English clinician of the seventeenth century." Cesar's work provided a foundation for future black physicians, including JAMES DURHAM, considered the first African American doctor, who practiced in New Orleans after the American Revolution, and an unknown man described as "a Doctor among people of his color" in the 22 June 1797 issue of the Charleston, South Carolina, *City Gazette and Daily Advertiser*. Cesar's career preceded by a century and a half the acceptance of African Americans into U.S. medical schools.

FURTHER READING

Primary source material on Cesar can be found in *The Colonial Records of South Carolina: The Journal of the Commons House of Assembly March 28, 1749–March 19, 1750*, ed. J. H. Easterby, vol. 9 (1962).

Curtis, James L. *Blacks, Medical Schools, and Society* (1971).

Morais, Herbert M. *The History of the Afro-American in Medicine* (1976).

Numbers, Ronald L., and Todd L. Savitt. *Science and Medicine in the Old South* (1989).

Savitt, Todd. *Medicine and Slavery: The Diseases and Health Care of Blacks in Antebellum Virginia* (1978).

This entry is taken from the *American National Biography* and is published here with the permission of the American Council of Learned Societies.

ELIZABETH D. SCHAFER

Chamberlain, Wilt (21 Aug. 1936–12 Oct. 1999), basketball player, was born Wilton Norman Chamberlain in Philadelphia, Pennsylvania, the sixth of nine surviving children born to William Chamberlain, a janitor and handyman, and Olivia Ruth Chamberlain, a domestic maid and cook. Although Chamberlain claimed in his 1973 autobiography that he was born measuring twenty-nine inches in length, much above average, he later stated that at birth "there was absolutely nothing special about me. I was a little over twenty-two inches long" (Chamberlain, 1991, 25). At any rate, young Wilton was always the tallest in his grade school classes and became known as the "Big Dipper" or "Dip," both of which he preferred to "Wilt the Stilt," a nickname later coined by a journalist. He was also among the most athletic students, participating as a nine-year-old in 1946 in the famed Penn Relays near his West Philadelphia

Wilt Chamberlain in 1959, during his days with the Harlem Globetrotters. (AP Images.)

home. When he entered Overbrook High School in 1951, Chamberlain, by then six feet seven inches tall, continued his interest in track-and-field, excelling at sprints, the high jump, and the shot put. Although he dreamed of participating in the Olympics as a decathlete, Chamberlain increasingly focused on basketball, a sport that had just begun to allow blacks in its professional ranks and which offered greater financial rewards for his talents. Overbrook won fifty-eight of the sixty-one games in which he played, one of those rare losses coming when West Catholic High School assigned four defenders to guard him. Chamberlain's height and strength certainly gave him an advantage over most opponents, but it was his ball-handling skills and athleticism that enabled him to dominate the highly competitive Philadelphia high school leagues. He developed into an excellent dribbler and passer and, contrary to his later reputation, a highly reliable free-throw shooter. In one game, he scored a remarkable ninety points,

a figure that he would surely have repeated in other games had his coach not benched the star center to prevent embarrassing opponents. Nonetheless, in his three seasons at Overbrook, Chamberlain set a statewide scoring record of 2,252 points.

Chamberlain also excelled at the University of Kansas, though his performance did not quite match the unrealistic expectations that national journalists had raised about his prospects. In 1957 he led Kansas to the National Collegiate Athletic Association (NCAA) championship game and was selected as Most Valuable Player (MVP) of the tournament, even though his side lost in triple overtime to North Carolina. That loss devastated Chamberlain, who showed much less intensity in his junior season. He found life in segregated Lawrence, Kansas, uncomfortable, suffered racial abuse from opposing fans, and missed crucial games after an opponent kneed him in the groin. He especially resented an NCAA rule change that prohibited offensive goaltending and thus prevented the seven foot one inch player from guiding his teammates' shots into the basket. A scandal involving improper payments of at least twenty thousand dollars further clouded his college career. Although Chamberlain received no official censure, the NCAA later placed Kansas on probation for buying him a Cadillac.

Forgoing his senior year at Kansas, Chamberlain joined the Harlem Globetrotters in New York City in 1958. He loved the showmanship of players like MEADOWLARK LEMON and claimed that he learned more from his one year on tour with the Trotters than from three years at Kansas. In that year—the happiest in his life, he stated in 1974—he improved his outside shooting, a consequence of being switched from his normal position of center to guard. He also gained a love of foreign travel when the Globetrotters undertook a tour of Europe, including the first visit to the Soviet bloc by an American sports team, and were granted audiences with the Soviet leader Nikita Khrushchev and Pope John XXIII.

In 1959 Chamberlain joined his hometown Philadelphia Warriors and transformed the team's fortunes within a season. He established nine National Basketball Association (NBA) scoring records that season, including the highest average for both points and rebounds, and was voted Rookie of the Year, All-Star MVP, and the league's MVP. In that season's playoffs, however, the Boston Celtics defeated the Warriors, even though Chamberlain outscored and outplayed the Celtic's BILL RUSSELL, the dominant defensive player of that era.

The Russell-Chamberlain rivalry endured throughout the 1960s. Chamberlain usually edged Russell in terms of individual scoring, but Russell's Celtics invariably defeated Chamberlain's teams. Chamberlain followed his amazing rookie season by breaking his own scoring and rebounding records in 1960–1961, averaging 50.4 points a game. Increasingly, Chamberlain stood out as a scoring phenomenon on an otherwise lackluster Warriors team, most famously amassing one hundred points against the New York Knickerbockers in 1962, a record unlikely to be broken. Most teams found that the only way to stop him was to foul him, a particularly useful tactic, given his relatively poor (.511) performance at the foul line; Chamberlain's 5,805 missed free throws will almost certainly remain an NBA record. More impressively, given his powerful physical presence and aggressive reputation on and off the court, Chamberlain never fouled out from a game.

Although Chamberlain's scoring feats declined in his final years in the NBA, his efforts for the Philadelphia 76ers in 1966–1967 and the Los Angeles Lakers in 1971–1972 finally earned him accolades as a great team player and his only NBA championship rings. In 1966–1967, he ranked third in the league in assists, a rejoinder to those critics and fellow players who viewed him as selfish. Indeed, Chamberlain had a highly driven ego and an even higher conceit regarding his considerable abilities, qualities that did not endear him to fellow players with equally large egos but somewhat lesser talents. He also believed that because of his greater size and strength, fans and fellow players did not credit his achievements as much as they should have. "Nobody roots for Goliath," he famously complained. On the Lakers team in the 1971–1972 season, Chamberlain adopted an uncharacteristic defensive role and, playing with a broken hand in the finals, again won the NBA's MVP award. He retired one season later and in 1978, his first year of eligibility, was elected to the NBA Hall of Fame.

Unlike many professional athletes, Chamberlain enjoyed his retirement more than his playing career. He pursued several other sports—most successfully, volleyball—although his former professional status prohibited his dream of appearing in the Olympics. Chamberlain also sponsored a women's track team, Wilt's Wonder Women. His second autobiography, *A View from Above* (1991), gained him notoriety for his claim to have slept with twenty thousand women, but it also depicts a man with a lively intelligence, a fierce competitive edge, and rather traditionalist tastes. He reminisces about home cooking and NAT KING COLE and regrets the arrival of vast sports arenas and shopping malls. This memoir, albeit somewhat rambling, deals humorously with his celebrity and with shorter people's reactions to his height. Although he remained physically active throughout the 1990s, he also began to suffer from heart disease and died, apparently of a heart attack, in his Los Angeles home.

In the 1960s Chamberlain's notoriety and his scoring records helped build the national audience for what had been a minor sport. Later basketball stars, such as MAGIC JOHNSON and MICHAEL JORDAN, may have been better liked, but none matched Chamberlain's dominance in both scoring and rebounding.

FURTHER READING

Chamberlain, Wilt. *A View from Above* (1991).
Chamberlain, Wilt, with David Shaw. *Wilt: Just Like Any Other 7-Foot Black Millionaire Who Lives Next Door* (1973).

Deford, Frank. "Doing Just Fine, My Man." *Sports Illustrated* (18 August 1986).

Libby, Bill. *Goliath: The Wilt Chamberlain Story* (1977)

Obituary: *New York Times*, 13 Oct. 1999.

STEVEN J. NIVEN

Chambers, Julius LeVonne (6 Oct. 1936–), attorney, educator, and author, was born and raised in Mt. Gilead, North Carolina, the third of four children of William, an automobile mechanic, and Matilda Chambers. Growing up in a family that placed a high value on education, the twelve-year-old Chambers set his sights upon becoming a lawyer to address many of the racial inequities and injustices that he experienced coming of age in a segregated black community. Particularly formative was his experience of seeing his father unable to retain a lawyer to represent him to collect a debt owed by a white customer who had received service only to refuse to make payment.

Chambers traveled close to twelve miles to Troy, North Carolina, to attend Peabody High School, where he excelled in athletics, playing football and baseball, and was president of the student government association during his junior and senior years. He graduated from high school in May 1954, the very month of the U.S. Supreme Court's landmark ruling in *Brown v. Board of Education*. In the fall of 1954 he entered North Carolina College in Durham (later North Carolina Central University). That same year he was forced off an interstate bus because he refused to move to the back of the bus and give his seat to a white passenger.

Chambers graduated summa cum laude in 1958 with a B.A. in History, where he was again president of the student body. In 1959 he received an M.A. in History as a Woodrow Wilson Fellow at the University of Michigan. He studied law as a John Hay Whitney Fellow at the University of North Carolina at Chapel Hill, where he received the LLB degree with high honors in 1962 and was admitted to the North Carolina bar. He was a gifted student, rising to become the first in his class of one hundred and editor in chief of the *North Carolina Law Review*. Julius Chambers was not only the first African American to edit the law review but also was the first at any historically white school in the South. He was the first to be inducted into the Order of the Golden Fleece, the university's oldest and most prestigious honorary society. He spent the next year studying and teaching at Columbia University, where he received an LLM degree in 1963 from Columbia University Law

School. Also in 1963 he was selected by THURGOOD MARSHALL, counsel for the Legal Defense and Education Fund (LDF) of the NAACP and later U.S. Supreme Court Justice, to be his first legal intern. Chambers worked on civil rights cases in Virginia, North Carolina, Georgia, and Alabama.

In 1964 he began his private law practice in Charlotte, North Carolina, with Chambers, Stein, Ferguson, and Atkins, the first integrated law firm in North Carolina. Involved mostly in civil rights cases Chambers lived under the constant threat of racially motivated violence. In January 1965 he represented forty-one black plaintiffs in a suit to integrate the Shrine Bowl, a high school all-star football game played every year in Charlotte. Five days later, while he met with African Americans in a nearby church, his car exploded. Crowds of angry whites sometimes demonstrated in front of his house, which arsonists later firebombed. In November 1965, after he filed the *Swann v. Charlotte-Mecklenburg Board of Education* suit on behalf of ten black families whose children had been denied admission to all-white schools, his law offices were burned to the ground. But even all this did not quiet his resolve to fight for full equality for black children and all citizens.

On 22 April 1971 he successfully argued the *Swann* case before the U.S. Supreme Court, which upheld the use of busing to achieve desegregation. He also mounted successful arguments in *Griggs v. Duke Power Co.* and *Moody v. Albemarle Paper Company*. Both cases dealt were the Supreme Court's most significant Title VII employment discrimination decisions.

Chambers was appointed to the first board of governors of the state university system in 1972, representing North Carolina Central University. He served from 1972 to 1977 and resigned two years before his term ended owing to the board's delay in implementing integration initiatives at the universities and in improving opportunities for black students. In 1984 Chambers left the law firm to become the third director-council of the NAACP Legal Defense and Educational Fund in New York City, following in the footsteps of Thurgood Marshall and Jack Greenberg. At the LDF he became the field marshal for twenty-four attorneys and approximately four hundred cooperating attorneys around the nation. With offices in New York, Los Angeles, and Washington, D.C., the Legal Defense Fund's staff was the main litigator of more than one thousand cases that involved such issues as education, voting rights, capital punishment, employment, housing, and prisons. Under Chambers's leadership the LDF became the first line of defense against the political assault on civil rights legislation and affirmative action programs that arose during the 1970s and 1980s.

Chambers also served as president of the Southern Regional Council, an interracial organization dedicated to improving race relations and tackling regional issues, such as those involving poverty and integration. Chambers sat on the steering committees for the 1972, 1976, and 1980 Democratic Party presidential campaigns.

Chambers served as adjunct professor at the University of Virginia Law School, 1975 to 1978; University of Pennsylvania, 1978 to 1986; Columbia University, 1984 to 1992; and University of Michigan, 1985 to 1992. He was the author of numerous articles in various publications and law journals.

In 1992 Chambers accepted an urgent call from North Carolina Central to return to his alma mater and serve as chancellor. During his nine-year tenure he doubled the institution's research funding and increased the number of endowed chairs from one to fourteen, including the $1 million Charles Hamilton Houston Chair in the School of Law. He also persuaded the general assembly to fund a new building for the School of Education, and oversaw the creation of a biotechnology research institute for the study of diseases that affect minorities. That institute was later named in his honor.

Although, in 1994, he was recommended by a number of legal, educational, and political leaders for consideration as a justice on the Supreme Court, he withdrew his name from consideration, citing the wrangling partisan politics with North Carolina's U.S. Senate delegation. In 1995 Chambers was one of three lawyers who argued *Shaw v. Hunt*, the landmark legislative redistricting case before the Supreme Court. This case forced the court to decide the constitutionality of two key North Carolina congressional districts that were drawn after the 1990 census according to provisions in the 1965 Voting Rights Act to ensure equitable minority representation. In the latest ruling in this case *(Hunt v. Cromatie)*, the Supreme Court sustained two congressional districts that enabled North Carolina to elect its first black congressional representatives since Reconstruction. The end result of this legislation was the election of Representatives Mel Watt and Eva Clayton.

Chambers retired from his position as chancellor of North Carolina Central University on 30 June 2001 and reentered private practice with the firm he started in 1967. The firm—Ferguson, Stein, Chambers, Wallas, Adkins, Gresham and Sumter, P.A.—specialized in such areas as business matters, employment discrimination, education, and civil rights. In 2002 Chambers became director of the University of North Carolina Center for Civil Rights in the University of North Carolina School of Law. He was a member of Alpha Phi Alpha, Sigma Pi Phi, and the Prince Hall Masons.

Chambers was married to the former Vivian Giles, and they were the parents of two children. Upon his retirement he was viewed as one of the nation's leading civil rights attorneys and as a dedicated educational leader. His record of leadership and service intersected with those of Thurgood Marshall, Jack Greenberg, and John Hope Franklin and stands as an enduring testament to his dedication to the law and public service.

FURTHER READING

Chambers's papers are housed in the Archives and Historical Collections of the University of North Carolina at Charlotte and in the James E. Shepard Memorial Library at North Carolina Central University.

Armstrong, Robin. "Julius Chambers," in *Contemporary Black Biography* (1993).

Douglas, Davison M. *Reading, Writing, and Race—The Desegregation of the Charlotte Schools* (1995).

North Carolina Association of Black Lawyers. "Julius Chambers," in *Chronicle of Black Lawyers in North Carolina* (1984).

Vick, Marsha Cook. "Julius L. Chambers," in *the North Carolina Century—Tar Heels Who Made a Difference, 1900–2000* (2002).

ANDRE D. VANN

Chambers, Paul (22 Apr. 1935–4 Jan. 1969), bassist known as "Mr. P. C.," was born Paul Laurence Dunbar Chambers Jr. in Pittsburgh, Pennsylvania. Little is known of his parents and early life. After his mother died when he was thirteen, Chambers moved to Detroit, Michigan, with his family. In high school he played the baritone saxophone and then the tuba, but sometime in 1949 he began to play the string bass. He was soon working professionally with the guitarist Kenny Burrell, the trumpeter Thad Jones, the pianist Hank Jones, and other musicians in the Detroit area. In 1952 he began taking lessons with a bassist in the Detroit Symphony and played with a classical group called the Detroit String Band. Between 1952 and 1955 he also studied, off and on, at Cass Tech and played in the school's symphony orchestra and other student groups.

By this time Chambers had fully absorbed the bop lessons of CHARLIE PARKER and BUD POWELL, his first influences, as well as the innovations in bass playing pioneered by JIMMY BLANTON when Blanton was with the DUKE ELLINGTON Band a decade earlier. In 1955 he toured with the tenor saxophonist PAUL QUINICHETTE and also traveled through the South with the trombonist Bennie Green. Chambers moved to New York City the same year and immediately attracted attention, playing with noted musicians such as SONNY STITT, J. J. JOHNSON, and George Wallington. In October, Chambers joined the MILES DAVIS Quintet, a legendary association that lasted eight years. He appeared on all of Davis's well-known albums of the period, including *Cookin'*, *Relaxin'*, *Workin'*, and *Steamin'* (all 1956), *Porgy and Bess* and *Milestones* (both 1958), and *Kind of Blue* (1959). On *Milestones*, Chambers's seven-chorus, beautifully melodic bowed solo in "Dr. Jekyll" is particularly notable. But he is best remembered for his six-note solo at the beginning of "So What" on *Kind of Blue*. Few phrases in music immediately evoke the feeling of an entire tune as this one does.

In addition to his work with Davis, Chambers appeared as a sideman on numerous other recordings and led several sessions of his own. His first session as a leader was for Blue Note in 1955 and included an appearance by JOHN COLTRANE. After a 1956 recording for Jazz West titled *A Delegation from the East*, Chambers returned to Blue Note for a series of outstanding sessions: *Whims of Chambers* (1956), *The East-West Controversy* (1957), and *The Paul Chambers Quintet*, *Chambers Music*, and *Bass on Top* (all 1957). The personnel on all of these sessions featured the best modern jazz musicians of the day, including at various times Coltrane, the guitarist Kenny Burrell, the pianist Hank Jones, the drummers Art Taylor, PHILLY JOE JONES, and Elvin Jones, the pianist HORACE SILVER, and the trumpeter DONALD BYRD. Chambers signed with Vee Jay records in 1959 and recorded three albums that year—*Ease It*, *Just Friends*, and *Go*, all with superior performers, including his partners in the Davis rhythm section, the pianist WYNTON KELLY and the drummer Philly Joe Jones. In 1960 he waxed one final session for Vee Jay: *1st Bassman*.

As a sideman, Chambers was the most recorded bassist of his era. His sessions included the following albums: with SONNY ROLLINS, *Tenor Madness* (1956) and *Volume Two* (1957); with Coltrane, *Blue Train* (1957) and *Giant Steps* (1959); with SONNY CLARK, *Sonny's Crib* (1957) and *Cool Struttin'* (1958); with Kelly, *Kelly Blue* (1959); with HANK MOBLEY, *Roll Call* and *Soul Station* (1960–1961); with Art Pepper, *Art Pepper Meets the Rhythm Section* (1960)—notable for Chambers's walking-bass solo in "Softly, as in a Morning Sunrise"—and for Blue Note, albums by Bud Powell, Jackie McClean, DEXTER GORDON, IKE QUEBEC, Benny Golson, Kenny Dorham, LEE MORGAN, and Johnny Griffin. Appreciative of his talents, the leaders of all these sessions afforded Chambers far more solo space than was the norm for bassists.

In 1963 Chambers left Davis and formed a trio with Kelly and drummer Jimmy Cobb, known as the Wynton Kelly Trio. The group recorded several outstanding albums, particularly the classic *Someday My Prince Will Come* (1965). They also recorded as a backup rhythm section for the guitarists Kenny Burrell and WES MONTGOMERY. Suffering from tuberculosis and plagued by the ravages of heroin and alcoholism, Chambers curtailed his activity during the second half of the 1960s. He died in New York City.

Paul Chambers was one of the most important post-bop bassists. He contributed a solid harmonic/melodic foundation to any group that he played with and also helped popularize the use of the bow among jazz bassists. Though not as innovative as his contemporary Scott LaFaro, nor as fiery as such bassists as CHARLES MINGUS and RAY BROWN, Chambers helped bring hornlike, bop phrasing to the bass; he often began his phrases between the first and second beats, or on the second and fourth beats, instead of on the first and third. Such versatility made Chambers a crucial figure in the Miles Davis groups, and Chambers's presence energized the Davis recordings and many other influential sessions of the late 1950s and early 1960s.

FURTHER READING

Hentoff, Nat. "Detroit Producing Stars: Paul Chambers Big One," *Down Beat* 23, no. 1 (1956).

Owens, Thomas. *Bebop: The Music and Its Players* (1995)

Obituary: *Jazz Journal* 22, no. 4 (1969).

This entry is taken from the *American National Biography* and is published here with the permission of the American Council of Learned Societies.

RONALD P. DUFOUR